BRAND-NEW FRO~~M~~

W9-DCZ-646

Over 3000 Good-Housekeeping-Institute-tested recipes, including 1000 new ones—Enlarged chapters on pressure cookery, home freezing, quantity cookery, and leftovers—new emphasis on quick-and-easy dishes—Six new chapters on barbecues, foreign dishes, treats for children, chafing-dish, casserole and dieting dinners—New features include the popular "Susan" step-by-step recipes and many recipes from the Famous Cook Book series—Complete information on every step in food preparation from intelligent buying to attractive serving.

Good Housekeeping
Cook Book

USE NORTH CAROLINA
UN CAP
AGRICULTURAL PRODUCTS

Good Housekeeping

Cook Book

Edited by DOROTHY B. MARSH

Director of Foods and Cookery
Good Housekeeping Institute

GOOD HOUSEKEEPING BOOK DIVISION
250 WEST 55TH STREET, NEW YORK 19, N. Y.

Second Printing, May 1955

Copyright, 1942, 1944, 1949, by Hearst Magazines, Inc.
Copyright © 1955 by The Hearst Corporation
Publishers of Good Housekeeping Magazine
Printed in the United States of America
All Rights Reserved
Library of Congress Catalog Card Number: 54–10951

How to Use Our Index

If you would get the greatest use and inspiration from this cook book, and save yourself many precious minutes, you should use our Index freely.

When planning the Index, we tried to think of every way in which you might look for recipes or food information. Then we arranged the listings so you can locate what you need as speedily as possible. Here's how it works!

If You're Looking Up a Recipe by Name: All the recipes in this book (there are more than 3,000) are listed by name, alphabetically. You'll find Three-Layer Coconut Cake under Three in the Ts, Pizza in the Ps, Susan's Brownies under Susan's in the Ss, etc.

Many of our recipes are also listed under other pertinent headings. For example, Three-Layer Coconut Cake appears under Cake(s) and Coconut. Pizza appears under Bread(s). Susan's Brownies is listed under Cookies as well as under Brownies.

If You're Hunting for a New Way to Serve an Old Favorite: For example, if you're serving turkey, just look for the main heading Turkey (all main headings stand out very clearly). Under it are listed alphabetically all recipes starting with the word turkey or having turkey in their names. By running through these recipe names you'll get many fresh ideas.

If You Feel That You Just Can't Plan Another Menu: By checking the references listed under the headings Menus and Meal Planning in our Index, you'll find that our book includes well over 250 menus for all kinds of occasion, including everyday family meals for one, two, or more. (Incidentally, many of the menus have how-to-manage notes too.)

If You're a Beginner Cook: To save hunting through the book for our Susan's recipes and many other step-by-step basic dishes, turn to the headings Susan's and Step-by-Step in the Index. Under these are listed over 100 wonderful, basic, everyday dishes, all in easy-to-understand, step-by-step form.

If Any Cookery Term or Method Used in Our Recipes Is New to You: Don't take a chance. Our Index will tell you where to find what the term means. For example, if the term "emulsifier-type shortening" puzzles you, just turn to Emulsifier in the Es, or Shortening in the Ss, for the two pages on which its explanation will be found.

If You've Had One of Those Extra-Busy Days or You're an After-Five Cook: Look under our Index headings Quick and Quick-and-Easy. These were planned just for you. Here we list, or refer you to, the special sections where speedy dishes and quick-and-easy menus are grouped, as well as the helpful sections on pressure cooking, frozen foods, mixes, etc. These headings will also refer you to the chapter Quick-and-Easy Meals, where we give tips for short-cut menus, marketing, and cooking, plus a list of the many time-saving recipes in this book.

If Company's Coming: You'll find all the answers by looking under Entertaining, where almost every kind of company occasion has a page reference. (Over 100 of our favorite guest menus are in the book.)

If You Have a New Home Freezer or Want to Know Up-to-the-Moment Techniques of Freezing: The listing under Freezing will answer some of your questions. It tells you where you'll find how-tos on freezing cooked foods, meats, vegetables, etc., plus information on storing frozen foods, refreezing thawed foods, etc.

If You Want to Brush Up on Our Time Periods for Broiling, Roasting, etc.: Under the heading Charts or Timetables, we list the pages on which our many cooking timetables appear, as well as charts on freezing, on wine, on cheese, on storage periods for fresh meats, etc. (There are more than two dozen of these indispensable charts.)

If the Day Calls for an Oven Dinner: Look for the listing Dinners under Casserole in the Index. Under that listing you'll learn where to find vegetables, breads, relishes, and desserts that can bake along with your casserole (or other) main dish. Many of the simply wonderful casserole dishes in this book are listed, alphabetically by name, under Casserole.

If You're Interested in Foreign Recipes: Don't travel any farther than Foreign Flavor in the Index. Under that heading, find the country you'd like to "visit"; take note of the pages on which you'll find the dishes that are adaptations of that land's favorite fare.

If You Want a Refresher Course on Table-Setting or Serving Etiquette: See the listing under Serving, and discover where to turn for help with such details as seating guests at dinner, serving buffet style, how to be both cook and hostess, giving a large tea, setting the table, etc. The listing Centerpieces refers you to our newest ideas.

If the Man of the House Likes to Cook Out of Doors: Let *him* check the Index heading Barbe-

cues. There he'll find listed all the superb recipes in this book specially tailored for cooking outdoors, as well as pages where he can find menus, and learn about precautions and equipment for barbecuing, etc.

If You Long to Be a Better Shopper: Don't fail to turn to Marketing in the Index. There we've indexed the many chapter sections in which we discuss all the buying pointers you should know. (In the sections on meats, poultry, vegetables, fruits, etc., shopping tips are covered most thoroughly and helpfully. You will also find many diagrams of meat cuts—a big boost to beginner shoppers especially.)

If You're Never Sure Just How Much to Buy: Turn to Amounts to Buy in the Index, and let the listings under it direct you to the answers. (In Meats, Poultry, Fish, Shellfish, Vegetables, and other chapters, we tell you just how much to buy per serving.)

If You Must Spend Less on Food: To cut corners safely, check the listing under Thrifty for sections where you'll find delicious economical dishes, plus safe ways to make food pennies go farther in shopping, cooking, and meal planning.

If You're Chairman of the Food Committee and Need Help in Buying and Cooking for Large Groups: Under the heading Crowd are listed recipes, plus page references for the many helpful pointers in our chapter Cooking for a Crowd (includes amounts to buy for 25, 50, or 100 persons; marketing in quantity; figuring what to charge, etc.)

If Reducing or Gaining Weight is a Pressing Problem in Your Family: Let our Index headings Diet, Meal Planning, and Weight direct you to information tailored to your needs. (For example, if you must lose weight, see the Five-Meal-a-Day Reducing Plan. Our calorie chart will lend a hand too.)

If There Are Little Folks to Please: Look up the heading Children, under which we list the many dishes with appeal for the youngsters.

Contents

Good Housekeeping
Cook Book

How to Use Our Recipes

This cook book brings you the cream of GOOD HOUSEKEEPING's many years of experience in the kitchen. Its recipes offer you more cooking fun, help you prepare meals more quickly and easily.

You'll find more than 3,000 recipes. We've tested, revised, and tested each one again and again, to be sure it is as good and as easy as modern products and equipment can make it.

For the beginner, just discovering her way in the kitchen, we've written the directions as clearly and carefully as we can. And for the experienced cook, we've added many gourmet touches, devised new variations on old dishes, suggested menus. You'll also find:

Recipes from Our Famous Cook-Book Series. We couldn't include them all, but hundreds of your favorites are here—all taken from GOOD HOUSEKEEPING's famous monthly cook-book series. Check the Index for the recipes you liked best.

Susan's Step-by-Step Recipes. For years, young marrieds, teen-agers, and old hands in the kitchen have acclaimed Susan's famous recipes in GOOD HOUSEKEEPING. So we have included over 60 of her most popular dishes, written in her typical step-by-step, easy-to-follow style.

Quick-and-Easy Recipes. In several chapters, we've grouped together the quickest and easiest of the recipes. Look for them in such chapters as Desserts, Nibblers, Sauces, Salad Dressings, Frostings, Cakes, Poultry, etc.

Recipes for Leftovers. To help make second-day meals a delight, we've grouped recipes for using

The Last of the Bird (see Poultry) and The Last of the Meat (see Meats). And in our chapter on Leftovers, we've listed many of the fine leftover dishes to be found in other chapters.

Recipes for 2. Brides and others who cook for two will welcome the For 2 directions at the end of many of our recipes and the chapter on Cooking for Two. In dividing ingredients, our Chart of Equivalent Measures saves arithmetic.

To Assure Success

No recipe, no matter how superb, will give successful results if you do not follow it with reasonable care. So keep in mind the following points:

Read Every Word of the Recipe First. Don't start to prepare a dish until you have read through the recipe from beginning to end and are completely familiar with it.

Make Sure Utensils are the Right Size. Our recipes give the pan and/or casserole size that produces the best results. If yours are bigger, smaller, or shallower than the recipe specifies, you are flirting with failure. A too-small pan will cause the mixture to run over and you'll have a dish that's below par. A too-large one will produce an underbrowned, skimpy, or flat dish. Always use the utensil called for, and you'll have no regrets. Read Measuring Pan Sizes, p. 13.

Be Fussy about Measuring. In perfecting the recipes in this book, we used standard measuring cups and measuring spoons; we leveled off every ingredient. To duplicate our results, you must do likewise.

Brush up on measuring how-tos by reading How We Measure, p. 11.

Never Alter Essential Ingredients. In our recipes, the amounts of such key ingredients as flour, sugar, liquid, and shortening have been carefully balanced to insure just the right consistency, lightness, and tenderness.

To be equally successful in following our recipes, you must *never* alter the amounts of these ingredients. For example, if the recipe calls for ½ cup milk, use no more, no less. *Never* substitute ingredients either. For example, if a recipe calls for sifted cake flour, make very sure you're using cake flour, not another kind. It does make a difference!

Alter Seasonings If You Like. When adding seasonings, extracts, spices, onion, garlic, etc., we've tried to keep average tastes in mind. However, such ingredients may be increased, reduced, left out entirely (as with garlic), or others substituted to please your family. But be sure to taste and retaste the dish until it is just right for you.

Follow Directions Exactly. If you don't follow every step in our recipes carefully, you won't get the same fine results. For example, if, in spite of our warnings, you beat rather than stir a muffin batter, don't be surprised if the muffins have tunnels. If, contrary to directions, you let the water boil under a custard sauce, more than likely it will curdle.

Don't Increase Our Recipes. The recipes in this book have been perfected with the amounts of ingredients called for. We cannot guarantee success if you attempt to multiply ingredients and cook or bake the dish in a larger utensil. It is far safer to make up the recipe, as is, as many times as needed.

Mind the Minutes. Whenever our recipes suggest a preparation, cooking, or baking time period, follow it carefully, using whatever test the recipe indicates to determine when the food is ready for the next step or is done. For example, if a cake recipe calls for 4 min. beating in your mixer, stop when the 4 min. are up; over-beating causes failure. Incidentally, a minute minder is a good investment.

When Dish is to be Baked. Note that, in recipes for baked dishes, we not only give the baking temperature to be used but tell you when to start heating the oven so it's ready in time. Never let a dish wait while you heat the oven.

By the way, if you haven't a heat-controlled oven, buy yourself a portable oven thermometer, p. 7. It's lots better than guessing.

Number of Servings. Most recipes in this book indicate the number of servings. Remember, however, that number of servings is not necessarily the same as number of persons actually served. Recipes that make 4 servings serve only 2 if each person has a second helping. Likewise, recipes that make 6 servings serve only 3 if everyone has a full-sized second serving.

Always consider the heartiness of the rest of the meal before you estimate the number of servings you'll get from a dish.

To Serve It, to Vary It. At the end of many of our recipes, you'll find a special To Serve paragraph, which tells you just how to serve the dish and what foods combine with it well—invaluable tips when you're planning menus.

The To Vary hints suggest optional or alternate ingredients to make a dish seem brand-new when you make it again. In short, several recipes are combined in one.

To Do Ahead. We know how busy you are and how helpful it is to get some cooking done early in the day or the night before. So many of our recipes carry a To Do Ahead paragraph, which tells you just what part of the dish can be made ahead and how. Casserole dishes especially take to doing ahead.

We are indebted to Swift & Company for the diagrams of meat cuts in the chapter on Meats.

Cook's Vocabulary

COOKERY METHODS

If any of the cookery methods and terms used in our recipes are new to you, read below and you'll find directions telling you what to do.

Bake: Cook in heated oven. Called roasting when applied to meat.

Baste: Moisten food, while it is cooking, by spooning on liquid or fat.

Beat: With electric mixer, egg beater, or spoon, make mixture smooth.

Beat with Spoon: With mixing spoon (or wire whip), lift mixture rapidly, over and over, bringing underpart to surface and mixing ingredients evenly. Tilt bowl while beating.

Blanch: See To Blanch Almonds, p. 521.

Blend: Combine two or more ingredients well—usually with spoon.

Boil: Cook food in boiling liquid, in which bubbles constantly rise to surface and break. At sea level, water boils at 212°F. Once liquid boils, lower heat till just high enough to keep liquid boiling. *Slow boiling is just as effective as rapid boiling.*

Braise: In a little hot fat, brown meat slowly and *well* on all sides—about 15 to 20 min. Season; add a little water or other liquid. Cover; simmer over *low* heat till tender. (Use this method for less tender meat.)

Broil: Cook under the heat of a broiler, or over hot coals, or between 2 heated surfaces.

Brush with: With pastry brush or crumpled waxed paper, cover lightly with fat, salad oil, cream, beaten egg white, etc.

Caramelize: In skillet over medium heat, melt granulated sugar, stirring constantly, until it forms a golden-brown syrup.

Chill: Place in refrigerator or other cold place until cold.

Chop: Using knife, chopper, or chopping bowl with knife, cut up food as recipe directs.

Chop Nuts: See p. 521.

Coat: Using shaker-top can or sifter, sprinkle with flour, sugar, etc. until coated. Or roll in flour, sugar, etc. until coated. Or shake with flour, etc. in paper bag until coated.

Cool: Let stand at room temperature until it's no longer warm to touch.

Cream: With spoon, rub or work soft shortening, or soft shortening and sugar, against sides of bowl until creamy. Or use electric mixer.

Cut in Shortening: Using 2 knives, scissor-fashion, or pastry blender, cut soft shortening into flour or flour mixture until flour-coated fat particles are of desired size.

Cube: Cut into small (about ½″) cubes.

Deep-Fry: See p. 7.

5

Dice: Cut into very small (about ¼″) cubes.

Dissolve: Mix dry substance with liquid until in solution.

Dot: Scatter small bits, as of butter or margarine, over surface of food.

Double Boiler, Cook in: Fill bottom of double boiler with about 2″ water. Set double-boiler top, containing food, in place; cover. Bring water to boil; then cook as directed.

Dredge: Coat or sprinkle lightly with flour, sugar, etc.

Fold in (beaten egg whites, whipped cream, etc.): Heap on top of mixture. Pass wire whip, rubber spatula, or spoon down through mixture and across bottom; bring up some of mixture; place on top of egg whites (or cream). Repeat until egg whites (or cream) are evenly combined with mixture.

Grate: Rub on grater to produce fine, medium, or coarse particles. When grating lemon rind, remove only colored part of rind.

Grease: Rub lightly with butter, margarine, shortening, or salad oil.

Grind: Put through food chopper.

Knead: See Kneading, p. 345, steps 1 through 4.

Lard: Lay strips of salt pork or bacon on top of, or in gashes in, fish or meat. Prevents dryness.

Marinate: Let stand in a mixture, usually French dressing, for indicated time.

Melt Chocolate: Place in small bowl or custard cup; melt over *hot, not boiling,* water. Or melt, stirring, in saucepan over lowest heat. Or melt, in original wrapping, on piece of aluminum foil placed in oven while oven is heating or cooling off. Remove chocolate as soon as it's melted.

Mince: Chop fine with chopper. Or, with onion, try this: Cut in half; cut surface of half into tiny squares as deep as you like. Holding onion firmly on cutting surface, slice off ⅛″ slices.

Minced onion drops off as you slice. Repeat till all is used.

Pan-broil: Cook, uncovered, in ungreased or *lightly* greased hot skillet, pouring off fat as it accumulates.

Pan-fry: Cook in small amount of hot fat in skillet.

Parboil: Boil in water or other liquid until partially cooked, preliminary to another form of cooking.

Pare: With knife, remove outer covering, as of apples.

Peel: Pull off outer covering, as of bananas or oranges.

Pit: Remove pit or seed, as from prunes.

Preheat: Turn on oven; heat to desired baking temperature before putting in food.

Purée: Press through fine sieve or food mill.

Sauté: Cook in small amount of hot fat or salad oil in skillet.

Scald: Heat to just under boiling point (e.g., heat milk in double boiler until tiny bubbles gather at sides).

Scallop: Bake in layers with sauce. If desired, top with crumbs.

Score: With knife or fork, make shallow slits or gashes.

Sear: Brown surface quickly over high heat, as in hot skillet.

Season: Add or sprinkle with salt (or onion, celery, or garlic salt; or seasoned salt), monosodium glutamate, and pepper to taste.

Shallow-Fry: See p. 8.

Sift: Put through flour sifter or fine sieve.

Simmer: Cook just below the boiling point—about 185°F. at sea level.

Singe (poultry): Hold over flame to burn off all hairs.

Skewer: Hold in place by means of metal or wooden skewers.

Sliver: Cut or split into long, thin pieces.

Snip: With kitchen shears, cut into small pieces.

Steam: Cook in steam.

Steep: Let stand in hot liquid.

Stir: With the spoon, blend with circular motion, widening circles until all ingredients are well mixed.

Thicken: Measure liquid to be thickened. For each cupful, mix 1½ tablesp. flour with 3 tablesp. water till smooth. Stir into hot liquid; cook until thickened.

Toast: Brown in broiler, oven, toaster, or over hot coals.

Toss: Mix lightly with 2 forks or with fork and spoon.

Try Out: Fry bits of solid fat or fat meat in skillet until fat separates from membrane.

Whip: Beat rapidly, usually with electric mixer or egg beater, to incorporate air and increase volume.

When You Bake and Roast

In Heat-Controlled Oven: Modern ranges are equipped with an oven heat control, which automatically maintains the desired baking temperature.

To make sure the oven is heated to the proper temperature, set dial of heat control and turn on heat *10 to 20 min. before oven is to be used.*

With Automatic Clock Control: Some ranges have an automatic clock control for the oven. Such a control makes it possible to turn the oven on and off automatically at desired times.

When using this automatic feature, remember, an oven is *not* a refrigerator. Don't put foods —particularly those that spoil quickly without refrigeration, such as fish, chopped meats, fresh pork sausage, etc.—in the oven for an undue length of time before it is set to go on. It is good practice to limit this waiting period to 2 hours whenever possible. When you must increase it an hour or two, be sure the foods have been well chilled in the refrigerator beforehand.

With Portable Oven Thermometer: An oven heat control cannot be installed in a range that does not have one. However, a portable oven thermometer will register the temperature of the oven, and you can adjust the heat to maintain the desired temperature.

Place oven thermometer toward front and at one side of rack on which baking is to be done. Turn oven heat on full. At end of 10 min., read thermometer; adjust heat to desired temperature. When this temperature is reached, place food in oven. Adjust heat again, to maintain desired temperature.

When You Deep-Fry

Fried foods will be delicious and nutritious prepared this way:

What You Need:

Fryer: You can buy deep-fat fryers, which are light and easily handled, with a removable wire basket for lowering food into fat and draining. Such fryers can also be used as saucepans.

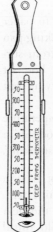

Deep-Fat Frying Thermometer: With a deep-fat fryer like that described above, you should use a deep-fat frying thermometer or combination deep-fat-frying-and-candy thermometer (a candy thermometer alone will not do) to determine the exact temperature of fat or salad oil. (See line drawing.) No other method of checking the temperature is as reliable.

Automatic Deep-Fat Fryer: An electric fryer simplifies frying because it automatically maintains the temperature you select and insures perfectly fried food. These fryers also do a fine job of cooking casserole dishes, soups, stews, pot roasts, etc. In using them, be sure to follow manufacturer's directions and timetable closely.

Fat or Salad Oil: Use any shortening or salad oil except butter, margarine, or olive oil.

Paper Towels or Brown Paper: Arrange on baking pan or in colander, to drain fried foods as soon as they are removed from fat.

How to Deep-Fry:

1. Use enough fat or salad oil to cover food completely. There should be at least 3″ between surface of fat and top of kettle, so fat will not bubble over during frying.
2. Gradually heat fat or salad oil to desired temperature, following Deep-Fat Frying Chart, below, and using deep-fat frying thermometer or Bread Test for Frying, below.
3. When fat reaches desired temperature (keep thermometer in fat during frying), promptly lower food *gently* into heated fat, using wire basket, spoon, or tongs. Do not try to fry too much at a time; too much cold food reduces temperature of fat so that food may become grease soaked before it browns.
4. Watch fat thermometer and, if necessary, adjust heat to maintain desired temperature as nearly as possible. Don't let fat overheat. Turn food as recipe directs.

When fried food is done, remove to paper towels or brown paper arranged on baking pan or in colander, to absorb excess fat from surface. If fried food should be kept hot, set baking pan in 300°F. oven while frying rest of food.
5. Always bring fat back to desired temperature before putting in second batch of food. Skim off loose food particles to prevent smoking.

Bread Test for Frying: If you do not have a deep-fat frying thermometer to determine temperature of fat or oil, the bread test is the next best thing. Drop 1″ square of day-old bread into hot fat or oil; then count time it takes to brown it.

At 370°F., a 1″ square of bread will brown in 60 sec.; at 375°F., in 40 sec.; at 390°F., in 20 sec.

DEEP-FAT FRYING CHART

Kind of Food	Fat-Thermometer Reading	Approximate Frying Time
Croquettes, and other cooked foods	390°F.	2 min.
Doughnuts, fritters	370°F.	2 to 5 min.
French fries (p. 269)	370°F.; then drain and fry at 390°F.	5 to 7 min. Until crisp and brown
Fish: Small whole fish	370°F.	3 min.
Fillets	370°F.	4 min.
Oysters, clams	370°F.	2 min.

Care of Fat or Salad Oil after Use: After each use, cool fat a little; then ladle into strainer, lined with cheesecloth, over container kept for the purpose. (Or use one of the new fat filters.) Cool; cover; store in refrigerator. (Some automatic deep-fat fryers have drain spouts to make emptying easier.)

After frying strong-flavored foods, partially cool fat; then clarify it: Add a few slices of raw potato; reheat slowly, stirring occasionally. Discard potato; strain as above.

A certain amount of fat or oil is absorbed by the food fried in it. So, every so often, add fresh fat or oil to fat saved for deep frying.

Shallow Frying

Shallow frying is an easy substitute for deep frying croquettes, French fries, doughnuts, fish, etc.

Into *deep* saucepan, put only enough fat or salad oil (see Fat or Salad Oil, above) to make 1½″ when heated. Heat to same temperatures on deep-fat frying thermometer as in Deep-Fat Frying Chart, above. Then fry food and drain as in How to Deep-Fry, above. There will be less fat left over for reuse than in deep frying, but this fat will generally be of higher quality.

To Remove Fat from Broth or Stock

1. Skim off fat with metal spoon gently lowered to surface of liquid.
2. Or lay piece of blotting paper or paper towel on surface of fat. When saturated, remove and replace with fresh piece.
3. Or wrap piece of ice in piece of paper towel, and draw lightly across surface of fat. Change paper as needed.
4. Or refrigerate broth overnight. Next day remove congealed fat with spoon.

COOKERY TERMS

Batter: A mixture, of pouring consistency, of flour, liquid, and other ingredients.

Bottled Thick Meat Sauce: Any bottled meat or steak sauce, such as A.1., Heinz Beefsteak Sauce, etc., of rather thick consistency.

Bottled Sauce for Gravy: A sauce, such as Gravy Master, Kitchen Bouquet, etc., that gives rich brown color and flavor to gravies and sauces.

Bread Crumbs, Buttered: Fresh bread crumbs prepared as follows: To each ½ cup fresh bread crumbs, add 1 tablesp. melted butter, margarine, or shortening, or salad oil; toss with fork. Nice too with a little grated cheese added.

Bread Crumbs, Dried: Bread crumbs prepared as follows: Dry out bread slices in 250°F. oven until crisp but not brown. Or let stand at room temperature until thoroughly dry.

Then place in clean, strong paper bag; roll with rolling pin to make fine crumbs. Or put through food chopper, using fine blade. (Tie paper bag to blade end of chopper to receive crumbs.) Refrigerate crumbs. Use to coat croquettes, etc.

Bread Crumbs, Fresh: Fresh bread slices crumbled between fingers. If you're using unsliced loaf, cut off end crust; pull out small crumbs with fork. Use crusts or not, as you like.

Butter Balls: Butter prepared as follows: Scald, then chill in ice water, pair of wooden butter paddles. Into ice water, drop ¼" pats of butter or margarine. When each piece is cold, roll between paddles to form ball, dipping paddles often into ice water to chill.

To make cylinders, flatten and roll balls between paddles.

Drop balls or cylinders onto chilled plate or into ice water. You may make several days' supply ahead and refrigerate it in cold water, covered.

Butter Molds: Butter prepared as follows: Scald, then chill in ice water, fancy butter molds. Pack well with butter; level off with knife; press out; chill.

Croutons: Bread prepared as follows: Butter bread slices (add bit of garlic if desired). Toast in a little hot fat in skillet or in 300°F. oven. Trim; then cut into small squares.

Or cut bread slices in ½" squares; toss in melted butter or margarine. Toast under broiler. Serve as garnish for soups or salads.

Drippings: Fat and juices that cook out of roast or poultry into shallow open pan.

Dry Ingredients: Flour, baking powder, baking soda, salt, spices, etc.

Egg Whites, Beaten Stiff: Egg whites beaten until they stand in peaks when beater is lifted from surface, with points of peaks drooping over a bit and surface still moist and glossy.

Egg Whites, Beaten Very Stiff: Egg whites beaten until points of peaks stand upright, without drooping, when beater is lifted from surface. Surface should look dry.

Egg Yolks, Well Beaten: Egg yolks beaten until thick and lemon-colored.

Eggs, Slightly Beaten: Eggs beaten just enough to blend yolks and whites.

Eggs, Well Beaten: Eggs beaten until light and frothy.

Filet or Fillet: Strip of lean, boneless meat or fish.

Clove Garlic: One of 10 to 15 bulblets, or cloves, found in a root of garlic.

A peeled clove may be added to a dish whole or halved (if pierced with toothpick, it is easy to remove after cooking). Or it may be sprinkled with a little salt; then crushed to a paste with back of spoon. Or it may be crushed in a garlic press. Or you may rub a garlic clove on inside of salad bowl or other bowl used for mixing ingredients.

Heavy or Whipping Cream: Cream containing not less than 30 per cent butter fat.

Light, Coffee, or Table Cream: Cream containing not less than 18 per cent butter fat.

Half-and-Half Cream: Mixture of half milk and half cream containing 11.5 per cent butter fat.

Meat-Extract Paste: Extract of meat, concentrated to a paste, with seasoning added.

Melted Fat: Fat heated in small saucepan over low heat until melted. Salad oil may be used in recipes that call for melted fat.

Mound: Spoonful of mixture dropped onto remaining mixture. A "mound" forms a definite heap and does not blend into the original mixture.

Nonfat Dry Milk: See p. 520.

Onion Juice: Juice scraped with teaspoon from center of halved onion.

Packaged Dried Bread Crumbs: Dried bread crumbs of uniform size, packaged in airtight containers.

Salad Oil: See p. 521.

Scallions (spring or green onions): A member of the lily family, with characteristic onion flavor. The entire scallion can be eaten. May be served cooked or as raw relish. (See Scallions, p. 291.)

Seasoned Flour: Flour mixed with seasonings in the proportions of ¼ cup flour to ¾ teasp. salt, plus ¼ teasp. each pepper and paprika.

Shortenings: See p. 524.

Skim Milk: Milk from which butter fat has been removed.

Commercial Sour Cream: Light pasteurized cream of custardlike consistency with characteristic tangy flavor produced by addition of a culture or starter. Comes in ½-pt. and 1-pt. containers.

Silver Dragées: Tiny edible, ball-shaped, silver-colored candies.

Stock or Broth: Liquid in which meat, poultry, etc. has simmered till tender.

Tender or Fork-Tender: Softened by cooking until fork pierces easily.

Tinted Coconut: Shredded coconut delicately colored as follows: Blend 1 teasp. milk or water with drop or so of desired food color. Add 1½ cups shredded coconut, also a little peppermint, almond, or vanilla extract if desired. Toss with fork until blended.

Toast Points: Toast slices, cut diagonally from one corner to opposite corner.

Top Milk: Top cream layer removed from bottle of whole, nonhomogenized milk.

Whole Milk: Milk from which butter fat has not been removed.

How We Measure

MEASURING SECRETS

Correct measuring of ingredients is essential if you would follow our recipes with consistent success. *All measurements should be level.*

In following the recipes in this cook book, remember that "cup" means cupful, "teasp." means teaspoonful, and "tablesp." means tablespoonful.

Choosing Measuring Cups: When buying measuring cups, choose one type for dry ingredients, another for liquids, as suggested below.

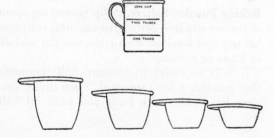

◄ **For Dry Ingredients:** Buy 2 1-cup measuring cups, each with the 1-cup line at the rim. Or for one of these cups, buy a nest of 4 graduated measuring cups consisting of a ¼-cup, ⅓-cup, ½-cup, and 1-cup measure. Such a nest of cups makes accurate measuring easy.

►

For Liquid Ingredients: Buy a 1-cup measuring cup whose rim is above the 1-cup line to avoid spilling. The 2-cup and 1-quart measuring cups are also very convenient.

◄

Choosing Measuring Spoons: When buying measuring spoons, choose one or more of the sets that come attached to a ring (see illustration), including ¼ teasp., ½ teasp., 1 teasp., and 1 tablesp. In a good set, 16 tablesp., or 48 teasp., should equal 1 cup.

MEASURING LIQUIDS

◄ **Vanilla, etc.:** Pour extract into measuring spoon until full. If thick like molasses or syrup, level off with edge, not flat surface, of spatula or knife, taking care none coats outside of spoon.

Milk, Syrups, etc.: Use a measuring cup with the rim above the 1-cup line. Set it on a level surface. Lower head, so measuring line will be at eye level, and fill cup to desired mark.

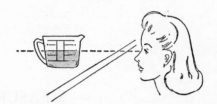

MEASURING DRY INGREDIENTS

Use a measuring cup with the 1-cup line even with the top. Or use a nest of graduated measuring cups. Use a set of measuring spoons.

◄ **Baking Powder, Salt, etc.:** Dip measuring spoon of correct size into dry ingredient until full; then lift out and level off with edge, not flat surface, of knife or spatula.

If it is necessary to measure half spoonfuls, first measure a level spoonful. Then divide contents lengthwise with knife and push off half.

Brown Sugar: If brown sugar is lumpy, roll out lumps with a rolling pin; then sift. Then spoon the brown sugar into measuring cup, packing it down with back of spoon just enough so it holds when turned out.

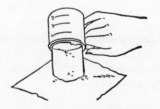

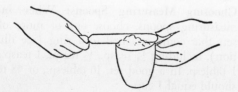

◄ **Granulated or Confectioners' Sugar:** If sugar is at all lumpy, sift first. Then spoon lightly into graduated measuring cup, leveling off with edge, not flat surface, of spatula or knife.

Flour: 1. *Just before measuring flour*, sift it once through sifter onto a square of waxed paper or into a bowl. Do not sift directly into measuring cup.

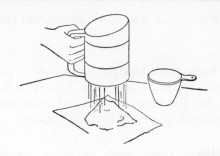

2. Then spoon sifted flour lightly into graduated measuring cup until cup is full.

3. Level off flour with edge, not flat surface, of spatula or knife, *without packing it down.*

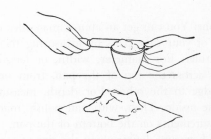

MEASURING SHORTENINGS

Shortening: Scoop shortening from can or package, and pack it firmly into a graduated measuring cup up to the top. Then level off with edge, not flat surface, of knife or spatula; remove from cup.

Butter or Margarine: Measure as for shortening, above. Or if you're using a 1-lb. print of butter or margarine, remember that each ¼-lb. stick equals ½ cup, or 8 tablesp. Half a ¼-lb. stick

equals ¼ cup, or 4 tablesp. To measure 2 tablesp., cut off one fourth of a ¼-lb. stick.

Melted Fat: If a recipe calls for melted fat, it doesn't matter whether you measure it before or after melting—the amount will be the same. However, if the fat is hard, it's simpler to measure it after melting.

Salad oil, often used as melted fat, is easily measured in a measuring cup or spoon.

MEASURING PAN SIZES

Recipes in this book suggest the size and type of cake pan, pie plate, casserole, or baking dish we have found best for each particular dish. If you would duplicate our results, it is most important that you use a pan of identical or as nearly identical size as possible.

Fortunately, more and more manufacturers of

cooking utensils are stamping the inch size or cup capacity of their baking utensils either on the utensil itself or on a sticker attached to it. So if your pans are hand-me-downs—bigger, smaller, or shallower than our recipes specify— buy yourself some modern pans.

If your pans carry no markings and you are

in doubt as to their size, these pointers will help you:

Spring-Form Pan: This pan consists of a rim (with or without a clamp) and 2 insets—a flat bottom inset for cheesecake, etc., and a tube inset for angel-food cake, etc. It is 9″ x 3″ in size.

Ring Molds: These molds range in capacity from 3½ to 11 cups, or 1¼ qt. to 3 qt., as marked on mold, and are fine for baking cakes.

Muffin or Cupcake Pans: The cups in most commonly used muffin and cupcake pans measure either 2½″ x 1¼″ or 3″ x 1½″.

Cake Pans: You can get an approximate idea of the size of your cake pans by measuring them with a ruler. For diameter, width, or length, measure across the top of the pan, from one inside edge to the other. For depth, measure down the inside. Then, with nail polish, mark the measurements on the bottom of the pan.

If you have any doubts about the size of your cake pans, it's always a safe rule to fill them only half full with batter (bake any extra batter in cupcake pans). Then the cakes can rise fully without going over the tops of the pans.

Here are cake-pan sizes used frequently in the recipes in this book. (For layer and tube pans, dimensions given are diameter by depth; for square or oblong pans, length by width by depth.)

CAKE-PAN SIZES

Layer	Square	Oblong or Loaf	Tube
8″x1¼″ 8″x1½″ 9″x1½″	8″x8″x2″ 9″x9″x2″	9″x5″x3″ 10″x5″x3″ 10″x6″x2″ 11″x7″x1½″ 12″x8″x2″ 13″x9″x2″ 15½″x10½″x1″ (called "jelly-roll pan")	9″x3½″ 10″x4″

Pie Plates: Pie plates range in size from 4″ to 10″. Our recipes call for 8″, 9″, or 10″ pie plates. Also nice to have is a deep 9″ pie plate, 2″ deep, with a fluted edge.

Casseroles and Baking Dishes: Casseroles range from 1-qt. to 3-qt. capacity and even larger; if they're of oven glass, the capacity is very plainly marked.

To check the capacity of your casseroles, fill them to the brim with water, measuring the water as you add it.

Baking dishes called for in many of our recipes are the same size as the oblong cake pans listed above.

EQUIVALENT AMOUNTS

Many foods are sold primarily by weight, but most recipes designate amounts to be used in terms of measuring cups and spoons. This table will help you buy the approximate amounts you need.

Food	Weight	Approximate Measure
Apples	1 lb.	3 medium (3 cups sliced)
Bananas	1 lb.	3 medium (2½ cups sliced)
Berries	1 qt.	3½ cups
Bread crumbs, fresh	1-lb. 1-oz. loaf	11 cups fresh bread crumbs (with crusts)
Butter or margarine	¼-lb. bar	½ cup
	1 lb.	2 cups
Cheese, American	½ lb.	2 cups grated

Cheese, cream	3-oz. pkg.	6 tablesp.
Cheese, cottage	½ lb.	1 cup
Coffee, ground	1 lb.	80 tablesp.

Makes about 50 serving cups beverage (2 tablesp. ground coffee per cup)
or " about 36 serving " " (3 " " " " ")

Cream, heavy	½ pt.	2 cups whipped
Dates, pitted	7¼-oz. pkg.	1¼ cups cut up
Egg whites, fresh	About 8 to 11 whites	1 cup
Egg yolks, fresh	About 12 to 14 yolks	1 cup
Flour:		
All-purpose	1 lb.	4 cups sifted
Cake	1 lb.	4¾ to 5 cups sifted
Whole-wheat	1 lb.	About 3½ cups unsifted
Lemon juice	1 medium lemon	3 tablesp. lemon juice
Lemon rind	1 medium lemon	1 tablesp. grated rind
Milk:		
Evaporated	14½-oz. can	1⅔ cups
	6-oz. can	¾ cup
Sweetened condensed	14-oz. can	1¼ cups
	15½-oz. can	1⅓ cups
Nuts in shell:		
Almonds	1¼ lb.	1 to 1¾ cups nut meats
Brazil nuts	1 lb.	1½ cups nut meats
Peanuts	1 lb.	2 cups nut meats
Pecans	1 lb.	2¼ cups nut meats
Walnuts	1 lb.	1⅔ cups chopped
Nuts, shelled:		
Almonds	1 lb. 2 oz.	4 cups
Pecan meats	1 lb.	4 cups
Walnut meats	1 lb.	4 cups
Brazil nut meats	1 lb.	3 cups
Orange juice	1 medium orange	⅓ cup juice
Orange rind	1 medium orange	2 tablesp. grated rind
Potatoes:		
White	1 lb.	3 medium (2⅓ cups sliced)
Sweet	1 lb.	3 medium (3 cups sliced)
Raisins	15-oz. pkg.	3 cups (not packed)
Sugar:		
Brown	1 lb.	2⅓ to 3 cups (firmly packed)
Confectioners'	{ 1 lb.	4 cups sifted
	{ 1 lb.	3⅓ cups unsifted
Granulated	1 lb.	2⅓ cups
Tomatoes	1 lb.	3 medium

EQUIVALENT MEASURES

This table is designed to help you translate amounts stated in terms of one measuring device into those of another, perhaps more convenient one, and to do the mathematics for you when you want to divide a recipe.

Speck	Less than ⅛ teasp.
⅓ of ¼ teasp.	Pinch*
⅓ of ½ teasp.	Pinch*
½ of ¼ teasp.	⅛ teasp.
3 teasp.	1 tablesp.
⅓ of 1 tablesp.	1 teasp.
⅓ of 2 tablesp.	2 teasp.
⅓ of 5 tablesp.	1 tablesp. + 2 teasp.
⅓ of 7 tablesp.	2 tablesp. + 1 teasp.
½ of 1 tablesp.	1½ teasp.
½ of 3 tablesp.	1 tablesp. + 1½ teasp.
½ of 5 tablesp.	2 tablesp. + 1½ teasp.
½ of 7 tablesp.	3 tablesp. + 1½ teasp.
2 tablesp.	⅛ cup
4 tablesp.	¼ cup
5 tablesp. + 1 teasp.	⅓ cup
8 tablesp.	½ cup
10 tablesp. + 2 teasp.	⅔ cup
12 tablesp.	¾ cup
16 tablesp.	1 cup
⅓ of ¼ cup	1 tablesp. + 1 teasp.
⅓ of ⅓ cup	1 tablesp. + 2⅓ teasp.
⅓ of ½ cup	2 tablesp. + 2 teasp.
⅓ of ⅔ cup	3 tablesp. + 1⅔ teasp.
⅓ of ¾ cup	¼ cup
½ of ¼ cup	2 tablesp.
½ of ⅓ cup	2 tablesp. + 2 teasp.
½ of ½ cup	¼ cup
½ of ⅔ cup	⅓ cup
½ of ¾ cup	6 tablesp.
2 cups	1 pt.
2 pt.	1 qt.
1 qt.	4 cups
4 qt.	1 gal.
8 qt.	1 peck
4 pecks	1 bushel
16 oz. (dry measure)	1 lb.

**Pinch is as much as can be taken between tip of finger and thumb.*

Cocktails

Once upon a time these first courses were strictly at-table fare. Today's busy hostess-cook, however, serves many of them from a tray in the living room. This allows her time to handle the last-minute details of dinner in leisurely fashion.

Not too many and not too much, that's the rule. The appetizer course, prelude ,to good things to come, should whet, not dull, appetites.

Before using these recipes, refer to How to Use Our Recipes, p. 3, and Pots and Pans, p. 692. Always use standard measuring cups and measuring spoons; measure level.

FRUIT BEGINNINGS

FINGER FRUITS

When it's fruit first in the living room, these are ideal.

Choose one or more of the following for a fruit hors-d'oeuvre platter. They can pinch-hit for first or salad course at table. Serve alone or with crackers to nibble on.

1. Pineapple chunks on toothpicks. Guests dip them into mace-sprinkled sour cream or deviled ham-and-cheese spread
2. Apple or pear wedges (dipped into lemon juice), topped with sharp-cheese spread or mixture of Roquefort and cream cheese
3. Pineapple chunks, topped with Camembert cheese
4. Pear wedges (dipped into lemon juice), to dunk into cream cheese whipped with orange juice until fluffy
5. Banana spears (dipped into lemon juice), rolled in finely chopped nuts
6. Prunes, stuffed with crunchy peanut butter
7. Avocado cubes on toothpicks (dipped into lemon juice or Spicy Dunk Sauce, p. 377). Guests dunk them in grated process American cheese

FRUIT CUPS

Fruit cups are ideal for at-table service. For fun, serve them in sherbet glasses whose rims are frosted as on p. 498. Or heap fruit in avocado quarters or halves, or in orange or grapefruit shells. Or for frosty touch, top fruit with small ball of sherbet—cranberry, pineapple, orange, lime, lemon, or raspberry. Garnish cups with fresh mint, strawberries, raspberries, fresh or maraschino cherries, or lemon or lime wedges. Or substitute grenadine or crème de menthe for some of fruit syrup. Try these fruit-cup go-togethers. They should suggest others.

1. Orange sections, seedless grapes, just-thawed frozen strawberries, sprinkling of lemon or lime juice
2. Pineapple chunks, apple slices, cubes of mint jelly
3. Canned peach slices and pineapple tidbits, sliced celery, chopped nuts
4. Pear chunks, apricot quarters, sliced bananas, canned whole-cranberry sauce, grated lemon rind
5. Any fresh, canned, or thawed frozen fruit, alone or combined with sprinkling of lemon or lime juice. Or top with chilled ginger ale; ginger ale, frozen to mush; grenadine; crème

de menthe; or wine. Or top with small amount of any of frozen juice concentrates, thawed just enough to spoon out of can

6. Drained canned fruit cocktail, chopped apple, ginger ale, grated orange rind

7. Syrup drained from any canned fruit. Boil about 5 min. with stick cinnamon, several whole cloves, and about 2 lemon slices; pour over drained fruit, plus any other fruits desired; serve chilled

MELON BALLS IN GRAPEFRUIT JUICE

½ small watermelon; or   2 cups grapefruit juice
2 honeydew or   Mint sprigs
casaba melons

If using honeydew or casaba melons, cut in halves; remove seeds. From melon meat, scoop out balls, using fruit-ball cutter or the ½ teasp. of your measuring-spoon set. Fill 6 sherbet glasses two thirds full with melon balls; add ⅓ cup grapefruit juice to each. Chill; garnish with mint. Makes 6 servings.

Melon-Ball-Lemon-Ice Cocktail: Top melon balls or cubes in each sherbet glass with small spoonful of lemon, raspberry, or mint ice.

RED-RASPBERRY-AND-PINEAPPLE
COCKTAIL

1 cup chilled fresh   pineapple
   raspberries   ¾ cup chilled orange
2 cups diced, drained   juice
   canned or fresh   Mint sprigs

Arrange fruit in layers in 6 sherbet glasses. Pour some of orange juice over each; garnish with mint. Makes 6 servings.

GRAPEFRUIT STARTER

Prepare Chilled Grapefruit, p. 389, or any of its variations. Or tuck thin avocado slices between grapefruit sections, pin-wheel-fashion; sprinkle with French dressing.

AVOCADO COCKTAIL

1 large ripe avocado   or canned lemon
¼ cup chili sauce   juice
1 teasp. horse-radish   1 tablesp. mayonnaise
½ teasp. Worcestershire   ¼ teasp. salt
1 tablesp. fresh, frozen,

Chill avocado. Blend remaining ingredients; refrigerate. Just before serving, pare avocado and cut into cubes or wedge-shaped pieces. Arrange in 3 or 4 sherbet glasses; top with sauce. Makes 3 or 4 servings.

GRAPEFRUIT-AND-AVOCADO COCKTAIL

24 fresh or canned   1 ripe avocado
   grapefruit sections   ¼ cup French dressing
¼ cup French dressing   Parsley

Combine grapefruit sections with ¼ cup French dressing. Pare avocado; halve; remove pit; cut into crosswise slices ¼″ thick. Pour ¼ cup French dressing over slices. Arrange 4 grapefruit segments and 4 avocado slices in each of 6 sherbet glasses; garnish with parsley. Makes 6 servings.

Orange-Avocado: Substitute orange sections, or part orange and part grapefruit sections, for grapefruit.

TOMATO COCKTAILS

FROSTED TOMATOES

1 small white onion   3 tablesp. mayonnaise
4 peeled, ripe large   1 tablesp. snipped
   tomatoes   parsley
1¼ teasp. salt   ½ teasp. curry powder
Speck pepper

In wooden bowl, finely chop onion and tomatoes. Add salt, pepper. Turn into ice-cube tray of refrigerator; freeze until ice crystals start to form.

     Meanwhile, combine mayonnaise, parsley, curry. Arrange frosty tomato mixture in chilled soup cups; top each with mound of curry mayonnaise. Makes 3 or 4 servings.

OLD-FASHIONED TOMATO COCKTAIL

Drain juice from 1 No. 2½ can solid-pack tomatoes (3½ cups). Season tomatoes with salt, pepper, bit of onion salt, celery seeds, snipped parsley, etc., as desired. Chill well. Serve in sherbet glasses, with lemon wedges. Makes 4 servings.

JUICE COCKTAILS

Juice cocktails are a happy choice whether for living-room or at-table service.

Living-Room Style: Arrange filled glasses on a tray along with small cocktail napkins and small plates to place under glasses if desired. Pass simple hors d'oeuvres if you wish.

At-Table Style: For a separate first course, place each filled glass on small plate (on service plate if desired). Or, simpler still, place each filled glass to right of water glass, to be sipped during main course.

FRUIT JUICE

Lime-Pineapple: Float small ball of lime ice on pineapple juice.

Cranberry-Pineapple: Combine two thirds cranberry-juice cocktail with one third pineapple juice. Or float small ball of cranberry sherbet on pineapple juice.

Sparklers: Reconstitute frozen juice concentrates (orange, grapefruit, grape, pineapple, lemonade, limeade, etc.) with chilled ginger ale instead of water. Serve at once, garnished with twist of lemon peel.

Or combine equal parts canned fruit juice (apple, whole-fruit nectar, or cranberry-juice cocktail) and chilled ginger ale.

Fruit Combos: Combine reconstituted frozen fruit juices such as these: pineapple and limeade; lemonade and orange; grape and lemonade; orange and grapefruit; orange and pineapple.

FOAMY FRUIT-JUICE COCKTAIL

⅓ cup cold water	1 tablesp. bottled or
⅓ cup granulated sugar	fresh lime juice
⅓ cup fresh, frozen, or	1 egg white
canned lemon juice	2 cups finely crushed ice
⅓ cup orange juice	

Combine all ingredients in jar or shaker. Cover; shake until light and frothy. Pour into cocktail glasses. Makes 4 servings.

HOT SPICED PINEAPPLE JUICE

Simmer 1 No. 2 can pineapple juice with 2″ stick cinnamon 10 min. Add 2 tablesp. granulated sugar and 2 tablesp. fresh, frozen, or canned lemon juice. Remove cinnamon. Serve hot. Makes 2½ cups.

PINEAPPLE-LEMON FOAM COCKTAIL

1 No. 2 can pineapple juice	⅓ cup granulated sugar
	½ cup water
⅔ cup fresh, frozen, or canned lemon juice	2 egg whites
	1 cup finely crushed ice

Combine all ingredients in jar or shaker. Cover; shake until frothy. Pour into cocktail glasses. Makes 6 servings.

TOMATO JUICE

Tomato-Sauerkraut: Combine equal parts tomato juice and sauerkraut juice; add Worcestershire to taste.

Tomato-Clam: Combine equal parts tomato juice or vegetable-juice cocktail and clam juice; season with minced onion, salt, pepper.

Peppy Tomato: To each cup tomato juice, add lemon juice, pinch dried basil, and celery salt to taste. Or add some grated cucumber and onion, plus dash tabasco and Worcestershire.

Hot Tomato: Heat 1 No. 2 can tomato juice with 1 bouillon cube. Serve hot.

P.S. Canned tomato juice and vegetable-juice cocktail, served straight from the can, are delightful.

FRUIT AND FRUIT JUICE

Arrange several pieces of fruit in each fruit-juice glass; then add juice to fill. Have a few toothpicks ready too, for those who wish to spear their fruit. Try any of these:

1. Ginger ale over seedless grapes
2. Grape juice over grapefruit sections
3. Cranberry-juice cocktail over canned apricot chunks
4. Lemonade or limeade (use frozen concentrate) over orange sections and pineapple chunks
5. Orange juice over pineapple chunks and diced fresh pears or banana slices
6. Cider over apple slices or canned pineapple tidbits
7. Pineapple juice over frozen strawberries (cut frozen block into cubes)
8. Cranberry-juice cocktail over orange sections, canned sliced peaches, or pineapple chunks

SEA-FOOD COCKTAILS

At-Table Style: Chilled, cooked, cleaned shrimp, chunks of fresh or canned lobster or crab meat, or canned tuna, etc., plus a zippy cocktail sauce, are traditionally served in lettuce-lined sherbet glasses. However, you might like one of these ways better:

1. Place sea food that has been dipped into sauce in hollowed-out small tomatoes. Set on beds of water cress on small plates.
2. Or heap sea food in green-pepper rings set on plates; spoon on sauce.
3. Or arrange sea food on small plates; place lettuce cup or romaine leaf filled with sauce in center.

Living-Room Style: Just arrange the sea food on a tray or platter, with the sauce in a custard cup, scooped-out tomato, grapefruit shell, scallop or lobster-tail shell, half an avocado shell, or seeded green-pepper half. Garnish with something green. Place toothpicks nearby, for dunking and finger eating.

SHRIMP, CRAB, OR LOBSTER

Shrimp: Allow about 6 cooked, cleaned shrimp per serving. Serve with Tangy Cocktail Sauce, p. 21.

Curried Shrimp: Allow about 6 cooked, cleaned shrimp, or 3 shrimp and 3 canned or frozen pineapple chunks, per serving. Serve with Curry Cocktail Sauce, p. 21.

Crunchy Crab and Shrimp: Allow about 2 tablesp. fresh or canned crab-meat chunks; 4 cooked, cleaned shrimp; and 2 tablesp. minced celery per serving. Serve with Superb Cocktail Sauce, p. 21.

Crab: Allow about ¼ to ⅓ cup flaked fresh or canned crab meat per serving. Serve with Tangy Cocktail Sauce, p. 21.

Lobster: Allow about ¼ to ⅓ cup cooked or canned lobster meat, in chunks, per serving. Serve with Easy Cocktail Sauce, p. 21.

Fruited Sea Food: Allow about ¼ to ⅓ cup fresh or canned crab-meat chunks, or 4 cooked,

cleaned shrimp, and 3 or 4 grapefruit sections per serving. Serve with Tangy or Easy Cocktail Sauce, p. 21.

CRAB-STUFFED AVOCADO

½ cup mayonnaise or cooked salad dressing	shire Dash tabasco 2 ripe avocados
½ cup minced celery	Lemon juice
¼ cup minced pimento	Salt
2 teasp. fresh, frozen, or canned lemon juice	1½ cups chilled, cooked or canned crab or lobster meat
⅛ teasp. Worcester-	

Combine mayonnaise, celery, pimento, 2 teasp. lemon juice, Worcestershire, tabasco. Halve avocados lengthwise; remove pits; peel; sprinkle with lemon juice and salt. Arrange each avocado half on bed of crisp greens; fill with some of crab meat; then top with some of dressing. Makes 4 servings.

MARINATED CRAB MEAT

⅓ cup salad oil	2 cups thinly sliced celery
⅓ cup dry white wine	
¼ teasp. tabasco	1 lb. flaked fresh crab meat; cooked, cut-up scallops; or any flaked white fish
¼ teasp. salt	
¼ teasp. dried thyme	
½ cup mayonnaise or cooked salad dressing	Salad greens

In bowl, combine salad oil, wine, tabasco, salt, thyme, mayonnaise. Toss with celery and crab meat. Refrigerate ½ hr. Serve on salad greens. Makes 6 servings.

OTHERS

Tuna: Allow about ¼ to ⅓ cup canned tuna, in chunks, per serving. Serve with any of Cocktail Sauces, p. 21.

Clams, Oysters, or Scallops: Allow about 6 shucked raw littleneck or cherry-stone clams or raw oysters, or 6 small cooked scallops, per serving. Serve with Tangy Cocktail Sauce, p. 21.

To Cook Scallops: Place scallops in saucepan. Add 1 cup boiling salted water for each 1 cup scallops. Boil, covered, 8 to 10 min. Drain; refrigerate until well chilled; then use in scallop cocktail.

CALIFORNIA COCKTAIL

2 grapefruit	3 tablesp. orange juice
1 cup cooked or canned lobster meat or crab meat; or ½ cup each	¼ cup catchup
	¼ cup mayonnaise

Halve grapefruit; remove pulp; cut fruit into small pieces. With scissors, snip out membrane; then notch edges of shells. Snip lobster or crab meat into bite-size pieces. (Toss lobster and crab together if using both.) Blend orange juice, catchup, mayonnaise; mix with sea food and grapefruit; use to fill shells. Makes 4 servings.

OYSTERS OR CLAMS ON THE HALF SHELL

Allow 6 to 8 oysters or clams per serving. Have shells opened at market. Serve each oyster or clam on deeper half of shell; arrange on bed of crushed ice, tucking sprigs of water cress or parsley between shells if desired. In center of each plate, place small glass or lettuce cup filled with Tangy Cocktail Sauce, p. 21; add lemon wedge.

If desired, pass horse-radish, tabasco, or Worcestershire, as well as tiny oyster crackers.

COCKTAIL SAUCES

Tangy: Combine ⅔ cup catchup; 3 tablesp. chili sauce; 2 tablesp. horse-radish; 3 tablesp. fresh, frozen, or canned lemon juice; dash cayenne pepper; dash tabasco. If desired, add minced onion or celery, grated cucumber, or pickle relish. Refrigerate. Makes 6 to 8 servings.

Superb: Combine 1 cup catchup, ½ cup Worcestershire, ½ cup grated Parmesan cheese, 1 tablesp. butter or margarine, 1 minced small onion, ⅛ teasp. pepper, and ¼ cup water. Bring to boil; turn heat very low, and simmer 30 min. Refrigerate until 2 hr. before serving. Makes 6 to 8 servings.

Curry: Combine 1 cup mayonnaise; ½ teasp. curry powder; 1 tablesp. minced onion; 1 tablesp. fresh, frozen, or canned lemon juice; and 2 tablesp. chutney. Refrigerate. Makes 6 to 8 servings.

Easy: Combine ¼ cup mayonnaise, ½ cup chili sauce or catchup, 2 tablesp. prepared mustard, 1 tablesp. Worcestershire, 1 tablesp. horse-radish, and ½ teasp. monosodium glutamate. Refrigerate. Makes 6 to 8 servings.

Quickest: Delicious cocktail sauce comes bottled.

Lemon Cocktail: Combine ⅔ cup mayonnaise; 2 teasp. horse-radish; 2 teasp. snipped chives; 2 teasp. prepared mustard; 2 to 4 tablesp. fresh, frozen, or canned lemon juice. Makes ⅔ cup.

P.S. Also see Cucumber, Louis, Red, and Sherry sauces, p. 373.

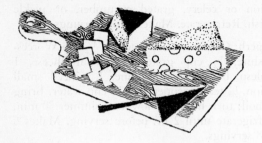

Nibblers

Whether you call them canapés, hors d'oeuvres, nibblers, or snacks, you'll be serving these tasty bites not only as a dinner prelude but as round-the-clock party fare. Probably you'll set them out on the coffee table so guests can help themselves. Guests love making their own—and you're left free to see to last-minute details in the kitchen.

Two tips to remember: Plenty of one or two kinds of nibbler is easier to prepare and more appealing than an overwhelming variety. And these tasty tidbits should be paired with a drink of some kind for greatest enjoyment.

Before using these recipes, refer to How to Use Our Recipes, p. 3, and Pots and Pans, p. 692. Always use standard measuring cups and measuring spoons; measure level.

DO-AHEAD NIBBLERS—COLD

COCKTAIL HASH

1½ cups packaged bite-size shredded wheat	1 cup pecan halves
1½ cups packaged bite-size shredded rice	¾ cup salted peanuts
	¾ teasp. garlic salt
2 cups pretzel sticks	2 tablesp. melted butter or margarine

Start heating oven to 350°F. Place all ingredients in baking pan; toss together well. Bake 15 min. Serve cold or warm. Even better if stored in tightly covered can to mellow a day or so. Makes about 25 ¼-cup servings.

SHRIMP DIP

Arrange chilled, cooked, cleaned shrimp (whole, or split if shrimp are plump) on plate or tray. In center, place bowl of Spicy Dunk Sauce, p. 377; Sharp Sauce, p. 377; or mayonnaise with prepared mustard, horse-radish, chili sauce, chives, or curry powder added. Have tiny bowl of toothpicks handy.

Shrimp-Avocado: Insert cube of avocado in center of each cooked, cleaned shrimp; secure with toothpick. Serve with bowl of sauce for dunking, as above.

SUSAN'S STUFFED RAW MUSHROOMS, see p. 291

ROQUEFORT OLIVES

Dry well-drained large stuffed olives on paper towels; roll in Roquefort-cheese spread, using knife to coat well, then chopped walnuts mixed with bit of salt; shape into balls. Refrigerate.

BOLOGNA TRIANGLES

1 3-oz. pkg. soft cream cheese	⅛ teasp. cayenne pepper
2 tablesp. milk	½ lb. thinly sliced bologna, salami, or canned luncheon meat
1 tablesp. horse-radish	
2 teasp. grated onion	
¼ teasp. tabasco	

Combine all ingredients except bologna. Spread mixture on 5 slices bologna; stack these slices; top with unspread slice. Make second stack. Wrap each stack in waxed paper. Chill well. Then cut each stack into 8 wedges. Makes 16.

SALAD PUFFETTES

Make Petite Cream Puffs, p. 395. Just before serving, split part way and fill with chicken, tuna, salmon, turkey, shrimp, or crab-meat salad (see Index). Makes 30 to 35.

COCKTAIL PRUNES

Remove pits from canned or cooked prunes; fill with one of the following; chill. Nice with coffee as late-evening nibbler.

Sharp-cheese spread
Peanut butter, mixed with crisp bacon bits
Deviled ham, mixed

with cream cheese
Cream cheese, mixed with chopped nuts

CUCUMBER RINGS

1 3-oz. pkg. soft cream cheese
1 tablesp. minced chives or onion
1 tablesp. snipped parsley
1 teasp. mayonnaise

¼ teasp. paprika
½ teasp. fresh, frozen, or canned lemon juice
1 pared medium cucumber

Combine all ingredients except cucumber. With apple corer, scoop out inside of cucumber; fill with cheese mixture. Refrigerate until served. Slice ¼″ thick.

ROLL-UPS

The Meat: Use thin slices of salami, bologna, dried beef, boiled ham, or canned spiced ham.

The Filling: Use soft cream cheese seasoned with one or more of these: grated onion, Worcestershire, prepared mustard, horse-radish.
Or use one of cheese spreads in jars (see Cheese Dictionary, p. 218).
Or use one of cheese foods (in rolls)—smoky, garlic, sharp, onion, wine, etc.
Or use wedge of chive or pimento cream cheese. These also come in jars.

To Assemble: Spread filling on meat slices; roll up each slice tightly. Chill well. Serve as is, or cut into bite-size pieces.

ONE-TWO-THREE BALLS

Use soft cream cheese, mixture of cream cheese and blue cheese (or deviled ham), or sharp-cheese spread. Add grated onion, curry, tabasco, Worcestershire, or horse-radish to taste. Shape into small balls or little logs; roll in any of the following, coating all sides. Chill well.

Snipped parsley or chives
Grated carrots or radishes
Finely chopped, hard-cooked eggs, mixed with paprika
Minced pecans, walnuts, or toasted almonds

Chopped ripe, green, or stuffed olives
Shredded coconut
Crushed corn flakes, potato chips, or pretzels
Short, thin slivers salami, bologna, or other ready-to-serve meat

CLAM BALLS

6 chopped, hard-cooked eggs
1 tablesp. minced chives or onion
½ cup drained canned

minced clams
½ teasp. salt
Speck pepper
¼ cup mayonnaise
⅔ cup chopped walnuts

Combine all ingredients except nuts. Shape into small balls. Roll balls in nuts. Refrigerate. Makes about 40.

Ham Balls: Substitute ½ cup ground, cooked ham for clams. Roll balls in crushed corn flakes instead of nuts.

CORNUCOPIAS

For each cornucopia, roll ½ thin slice bologna or salami around 1 stuffed olive or pickled onion, making cornucopia shape; secure with toothpick.
Or roll salami or bologna into cornucopia; then, into center, insert thin sliver of carrot or celery, securing with toothpick. Or fill with dab of cream cheese seasoned with horse-radish. Or fill with any spread in Spread-Your-Owns, p. 29. Refrigerate.

BRAUNSCHWEIGER OLIVES

Cut braunschweiger into thin slices. Press each slice around 1 stuffed olive. Roll in snipped parsley, coating lightly. Refrigerate.

SHRIMP ROUNDS

With 1½″ biscuit cutter, cut rounds from thin bread slices. Mix equal parts bottled tartar sauce and bottled cocktail sauce (if too "hot," add mayonnaise to taste); spread on bread. Split cooked, cleaned shrimp in halves lengthwise;

top each bread round with split shrimp half. (You may prepare and refrigerate makings early, then put them together at last minute.)

OLIVE-CHEESE SLICES

Blend 1 8-oz. pkg. soft cream cheese with 2 tablesp. fresh, frozen, or canned lemon juice; ½ teasp. grated onion; dash tabasco; and ¼ cup chopped ripe olives. Cut ends from 2 hard French rolls; hollow out. Pack cheese mixture into rolls. Wrap in waxed paper, saran, or foil. Refrigerate until well chilled. To serve, unwrap; slice.

SUPER STUFFED CELERY

We like to serve stuffed celery, living-room style. Stuff celery in one of ways below; then arrange on tray, alone or with a favorite juice. Let guests help themselves.

1. Fill crisp celery stalks, 2″ to 3″ long, with any of fillings below; refrigerate.
2. Or stuff long, wide celery stalks; chill well. Then serve, cut into bite-size pieces.
3. Or stuff crisp large stalks; put together in pairs, with fillings touching; roll tightly in waxed paper; chill well. Serve, cut into ½″ slices.

Fillings:

Olive-Nut: Into 1 3-oz. pkg. soft cream cheese, stir 4 chopped stuffed olives; 10 minced, blanched almonds; 1 tablesp. mayonnaise.

Ham and Cheese: Mash 2 tablesp. blue cheese with 1 3-oz. pkg. soft cream cheese, 1 2¼-oz. can deviled ham, some minced green pepper.

Sardine-Pickle: Mix ½ cup mashed canned sardines (without oil) with 1 grated tiny onion; 1 tablesp. lemon juice; 2 tablesp. chopped pickle; pinch salt; 2 tablesp. mayonnaise.

Sharp Pineapple: Mix 1 3-oz. pkg. soft cream cheese with ¼ cup drained canned crushed pineapple and 1 teasp. horse-radish.

Red and White: Mix 1 cup cottage cheese with 1 tablesp. minced onion, 5 minced radishes, ½ teasp. salt, ⅛ teasp. pepper.

Avocado Cream-Cheese Dunk: See p. 28.

RAW RELISH DUNK

Arrange group of Susan's Raw Relishes, p. 291, on plate or tray with bowl of Guacamole, p. 303, in center.

MELON ROLLS

Wrap chunks of honeydew melon in thin strips of Italian *prosciutto* ham; fasten with toothpicks.

TANGY OLIVES

Drain liquid from jar of olives; fill jar with French dressing. Let stand 24 hr.

Or several days ahead, add garlic clove to liquid in bottle or can of ripe olives.

KABOBS

Choose Picks: Use toothpicks, or try some of vegetable picks below. (To string food on vegetable picks, first make holes in food with skewer.)

Carrot, beet, or turnip sticks	Cucumber or green-pepper strips
Thin scallions (green onions)	Celery or white-radish sticks

String Picks With:

Ham and cheese chunks	Chicken chunks, pickled beets
Ham and canned pineapple tidbits	Thuringer-sausage cubes, pickled onions, olives, or dill-pickle chunks
Salami chunks, pickle slices	
Swiss-cheese and salami chunks	Ripe olives, raw carrot rounds
Sweet pickles, anchovy fillets	Rolled anchovies, chicken chunks
Cooked, cleaned shrimp; halved orange sections	Stuffed olives, cheese cubes
Herring cubes in wine sauce, pickled onions	Frank chunks, mustard pickles
Tuna chunks, pickled onions	Salami cubes, apple cubes dipped into lemon juice

Refrigerate until served. Arrange on tray.

LOBSTER DIPS

2 12-oz. frozen rock-lobster tails	eggs
1 cup mayonnaise	3 tablesp. minced stuffed olives
1 tablesp. anchovy paste	3 tablesp. minced sweet pickle
½ teasp. dry mustard	
½ teasp. tabasco	1 tablesp. snipped parsley
¼ teasp. garlic salt	
2 tablesp. vinegar	1 teasp. minced onion
3 chopped, hard-cooked	

Boil rock-lobster tails as on p. 188; remove meat; chill; then cut into 24 cubes. (Save 1 rock-lobster-tail shell.) Combine rest of ingredients. Turn into reserved shell; place on tray or platter. Insert toothpick into each cube of lobster meat; arrange around shell.

BLUE-CHEDDAR ROLLS

2 cups grated natural American cheese (½ lb.)	walnuts
	¼ cup snipped parsley
½ lb. blue cheese	1 teasp. grated onion
2 3-oz. pkg. soft cream cheese	Dash cayenne pepper
	½ cup finely chopped walnuts
¼ cup port wine	¼ cup snipped parsley
½ cup finely chopped	

Day before: Thoroughly combine cheeses. Add wine, ½ cup chopped walnuts, ¼ cup snipped parsley, onion, cayenne. Refrigerate till firm enough to shape into 2 or 3 rolls, about 1¼" in diameter each. Wrap rolls in waxed paper or saran. Refrigerate overnight.

Just before serving: Unwrap rolls; roll in mixture of ½ cup chopped walnuts and ¼ cup snipped parsley. Arrange on tray, with crackers and sharp knife to slice rolls thinly (or slice ahead). Makes about 22" roll—enough for a large party.

Christmas Balls: Shape mixture into 1 or 2 large balls. Wrap and refrigerate as above. Unwrap and roll in snipped parsley.

FROSTED BRAUNSCHWEIGER ROLL

1 lb. braunschweiger	cheese
½ cup catchup	
1 teasp. Worcestershire	Snipped parsley and paprika
1 3-oz. pkg. soft cream	

Skin braunschweiger; mash with fork; beat in catchup and Worcestershire. Place on waxed

paper; shape into 9" roll. Refrigerate till firm.

Remove paper from roll; place roll on tray; frost entire surface with cream cheese (if necessary, thin cheese with a little milk). Sprinkle top with parsley and paprika.

EVER-READY CHEESE LOG

½ lb. grated process sharp American cheese	pickle
	1 tablesp. chopped pimento
1 to 2 tablesp. minced onion	1 chopped, hard-cooked egg
3 tablesp. minced green pepper	½ cup finely crushed saltines
3 chopped stuffed olives	¼ cup mayonnaise
2 tablesp. chopped	½ teasp. salt

Combine cheese with rest of ingredients; form into long roll; wrap in waxed paper. Refrigerate till firm.

Serve on tray, surrounded by crackers and olives. Guests slice log as they eat.

POTPOURRI CHEESE

1 12-oz. can or bottle beer	½ teasp. salt
	1 teasp. dry mustard
6 cups grated natural American cheese (1½ lb.)	2 tablesp. soft butter or margarine
	1 teasp. Worcestershire
¼ lb. grated blue cheese	⅛ teasp. tabasco

Open beer; let stand. Mix cheeses, salt, mustard; blend in butter, Worcestershire, tabasco. Add beer gradually, beating with electric mixer until creamy.

Refrigerate mixture in covered jars. Or use to fill small covered pottery jars, as gifts. Keeps several weeks. Makes 5 cups.

VIENNESE SPREAD

4 1⅓-oz. wedges Camembert cheese	margarine
	2 tablesp. flour
1 4-oz. pkg. liederkranz cheese	2 cups heavy cream
	1½ cups chopped stuffed olives
¼ lb. crumbled blue cheese	Pinch cayenne pepper
½ lb. butter or	

Scrape off outside skins from Camembert and liederkranz cheeses. Place all cheeses, butter, and flour in saucepan; stir in cream. Cook over low heat, stirring occasionally, until cheeses are melted and mixture thickens. Bring to boil; remove from heat at once; let drip through cheesecloth into large pitcher or bowl.

Meanwhile, drain olives on paper towels. Add, with cayenne, to strained cheese mixture. Pour into small earthenware crocks or custard cups. Cover with aluminum foil or saran. Refrigerate 2 or 3 days, to mellow.

Serve as spread. Nice with pumpernickel or rye strips. Keeps 2 weeks in refrigerator. Makes about 5 cups.

DO-AHEAD NIBBLERS—HOT

BACON BITES

Early in day: With toothpicks, secure halved bacon slices around any of the following. Refrigerate.

At serving time: Broil till bacon is crisp; serve hot.

Pineapple chunks	Cooked, cleaned
Stuffed olives	shrimp
Canned peach chunks	Raw oysters
Pitted prunes	Watermelon pickles
Cooked chicken livers	Luncheon-meat cubes
Pickle chunks	Frank chunks
Brazil nuts	Vienna sausages
Pickled onions	Canned mushrooms
Raw scallops	Splits, p. 31

TOASTED CHUTNEY BITES

½ lb. braunschweiger	bread (must be soft
⅓ cup chutney	and easy to roll)
12 slices fresh white	Soft butter or margarine

Day or so ahead: Skin braunschweiger; mash well with fork; stir in chutney. Trim crusts from bread; spread bread with butter, then with braunschweiger mixture. Roll up, jelly-roll-fashion; wrap in waxed paper or saran. Refrigerate.

At serving time: Cut each roll crosswise into thick slices; toast under broiler. Makes 36.

DEVILED HAMBURGER TOAST, FINGER STYLE, see p. 358

SWISS CHEESE PIE (Quiche Lorraine), see p. 211

TOASTED CHEESE SQUARES

12 1″ cubes day-old	margarine
bread (from unsliced	1 cup grated American
loaf)	cheese (¼ lb.)
¼ cup soft butter or	

Early in day: Butter bread cubes on all sides but one. Roll cubes in cheese; arrange, with unbuttered sides down, on cake rack.

Just before serving: Set rack on baking sheet; broil squares about 2 min., or until cheese melts and browns. Serve at once. Makes 1 doz.

CHEESE PUFFS

1 cup grated natural	¼ cup butter or
American cheese	margarine
(¼ lb.)	½ cup sifted all-purpose
⅛ teasp. salt	flour

Early in day: Place all ingredients in bowl; with fingers, blend together till smooth. Refrigerate ½ hr. Form into ½″ balls; place on cookie sheet. Refrigerate.

To serve: Bake balls at 350°F. 10 to 15 min. Makes 2½ doz.

SPICY MEAT BALLS

½ lb. chuck, ground	¼ teasp. horse-radish
1 egg	⅛ teasp. nutmeg
½ cup day-old bread	Dash tabasco
crumbs	2 tablesp. salad oil
1½ teasp. minced onion	Grated American or
½ teasp. salt	Parmesan cheese
¼ teasp. pepper	

Combine beef with rest of ingredients except salad oil and cheese; shape into tiny balls. In hot oil in large skillet, sauté balls until golden on all sides.

Serve on toothpicks, with bowl of grated cheese for dunking. Makes 30 to 36.

CURRIED-TUNA TOASTIES

1 can chunk-style tuna	14 slices fresh white
(1 cup)	bread (must be soft
½ cup mayonnaise	and easy to roll)
½ teasp. onion salt	Soft butter or margarine
½ teasp. curry powder	Paprika

Day before: Combine tuna, mayonnaise, onion salt, and curry powder until creamy. Trim crusts from bread. Butter each bread slice lightly.

Then spread with about 1 tablesp. tuna mixture; sprinkle with paprika. Roll up, jelly-roll-fashion; wrap in waxed paper. Refrigerate.

Just before serving: Slice each roll crosswise into 6 or 7 slices; toast under broiler on each side. Makes 7 to 8 doz.

Chicken Toasties: Make as above, using, for filling, 1 6-oz. can boned chicken, chopped; 1 tablesp. mayonnaise; 1 tablesp. minced celery; and ¼ teasp. curry powder. You'll need 8 to 10 slices fresh white bread.

HOT BAKED-HAM MIDGETS

Bake and glaze a whole or half ham, or a cooked smoked boneless shoulder butt. (Or roast a chicken or turkey—regular, smoked, or boned-and-rolled type.) Place hot ham on platter; garnish with water cress. Set on small side table. Flank with carving fork and knife.

Nearby place napkin-lined basket containing thin slices of French, rye, raisin, or whole-wheat bread, or tiny hot biscuits. Set out bowls of relishes (pickle relish, prepared mustard, horseradish, barbecue sauce, etc.), with serving spoon in each. Cut tidbits of hot ham same size as bread slices. Guests make own midget sandwiches.

COCKTAIL PIZZAS

Make Pizza Dough:

Of Baking-Powder Biscuits: Make dough as on p. 323, or from packaged biscuit mix as label directs. Roll ½" thick; cut into 2" rounds; place on cookie sheet.

Or of Refrigerated Pan-Ready Biscuits: Unwrap biscuits; place on cookie sheet.

Or of Brown-and-Serve Rolls or English Muffins: Split each roll or muffin; place, with cut side up, on cookie sheet.

Cheese Treatment: Press ½" cubes of Mozzarella, natural or process sharp American cheese into center of each pizza round; or, if muffins, top with slices of cheese. Next top rounds with 1 teasp. chili sauce; top muffins with 1 tablesp. chili sauce. Sprinkle generously with grated Parmesan cheese, garlic salt, and dried thyme

or orégano, then with a dash salt and pepper. Drizzle on a little salad oil.

Extra Touches: Now, if desired, also top with one of these: cut-up bits of uncooked bacon; grated canned luncheon meat; dabs of deviled ham, anchovy paste, or regular or Italian sausage meat; chopped, drained canned mushrooms; flaked canned tuna; drained canned minced clams; or sliced stuffed or ripe olives.

Bake and Serve: Bake at 550°F. 5 to 8 min., or until done. Serve piping hot, in paper napkins for easy out-of-hand eating. Good too with a salad meal, with coffee, or with a soft or long, cool drink.

P.S. Packaged pizza mix is fine too.

SHORT-ORDER NIBBLERS— COLD

All these nibblers may be made up on short notice. Or if there's time, you may fix most of them ahead and refrigerate them until guests arrive.

NUTS

Brazil-Nut Chips: Start heating oven to 350°F. Cover 1½ cups shelled Brazil nuts with cold water; simmer 2 to 3 min.; drain. Cut into thin lengthwise slices; spread in shallow pan; dot with 2 tablesp. butter or margarine; sprinkle with 1 teasp. salt. Bake, stirring occasionally, 15 min., or until toasted.

Oven-Salted Nuts: Start heating oven to 350°F. Rinse shelled walnuts, pecans, or Brazil nuts, or blanched almonds, in water; dry well. Arrange in thin layer in shallow pan with butter (1 teasp. butter per 1 cup shelled nuts); sprinkle with salt*. Bake, turning often, 20 min., or until golden. For mixed nuts, bake separately; then mix.

Hot Peanuts: Open can of salted peanuts; heat in 350°F. oven. Toss with raisins if desired. Or heat unshelled peanuts.

Roasted Walnuts: Start heating oven to 350°F. Spread cracked unshelled nuts in large shallow pan. Bake 30 min. Serve hot; guests do the shelling.

Skillet-Toasted Nuts: In 2 tablesp. butter or margarine in skillet, sauté 1 cup shelled walnuts, almonds, or pecans until crunchy—5 min. Drain on paper; sprinkle with salt*, plus a little curry or chili powder if desired.

Celery, onion, garlic, or seasoned salt, or mono-sodium glutamate, may replace salt.

Dunks

Heap one or more dunks (recipes follow) in attractive bowls. Garnish with paprika, snipped chives or parsley, or a few carrot, celery, or green-pepper strips.

Serve dunks on tray, surrounded by 2 or more of these dippers. Guests dunk their own.

Melba toast	Avocado chunks
Pumpernickel strips	(dipped into
Hard-roll chunks	lemon juice,
Toast fingers	heaped in avo-
Crisp crackers	cado shell)
Pickle sticks	French fries
Corn chips	Cucumber fingers
Tuna chunks	Fresh, frozen, or
Raw cauliflowerets	canned pineapple
Pretzel sticks	chunks
Potato chips	Radishes
Raw carrot sticks or	Scallions
slices	Lobster chunks
Celery chunks,	Chicken chunks
hearts, or sticks	Salty-rye slices
Cleaned, cooked or	
canned shrimp	

ANCHOVY-CELERY COCKTAIL DUNK

1 8-oz. pkg. cream cheese	1 tablesp. fresh, frozen, or canned lemon juice
Dash paprika	
½ teasp. celery seeds	2 teasp. anchovy paste
2 teasp. minced onion	2 tablesp. cream

Cream cream cheese until smooth. Add remaining ingredients; blend until fluffy.

DRESSING FOR GREEN GODDESS SALAD, see p. 300

BLUE-CHEESE DUNK

Mix 2½ oz. blue cheese with ½ lb. cottage cheese, a little grated onion, ⅓ cup commercial sour cream. Makes 1½ cups.

AVOCADO-CREAM-CHEESE DUNK

1 medium avocado	or canned lemon juice
2 3-oz. pkg. soft cream cheese	
	⅛ teasp. salt
½ teasp. minced onion	2 tablesp. milk
1 tablesp. fresh, frozen,	

Halve avocado lengthwise; remove pit. Scoop out pulp, saving 1 shell. Mash pulp; add cheese and rest of ingredients. Serve in avocado shell. Makes 1⅓ cups.

CHEESY EGG DUNK

1 6-oz. pkg. soft chive cream cheese	¼ teasp. salt
	⅛ teasp. pepper
2 tablesp. mayonnaise	2 chopped, hard-cooked eggs
1 teasp. prepared mustard	
½ teasp. Worcestershire	3 tablesp. milk

Combine all ingredients. Makes 1 cup.

GARLIC-CHEESE DUNK

Combine 1 6-oz. pkg. soft garlic cheese with ⅔ cup commercial sour cream. Makes 1½ cups.

CLAM-AND-CHEESE DUNK

1 clove garlic	1½ teasp. Worcestershire
2 teasp. fresh, frozen, or canned lemon juice	
	Dash pepper
1 8-oz. pkg. cream cheese	1 7½-oz. can minced clams, drained
½ teasp. salt	¼ cup clam broth

Rub small mixing bowl well with garlic that has been cut in half. In bowl, blend well remaining ingredients. If thinner dunk is desired, add more clam broth. Makes about 2 cups.

CHILI-CHEESE DUNK

In electric blender, blend 2 cups cottage cheese with 2 tablesp. chili sauce and dash onion salt 10 to 15 min., or until cheese is very smooth, turning off blender often and scraping down sides. Makes 2 cups.

TANGY SALMON DUNK

1 cup flaked canned salmon or tuna	4 crumbled crisp bacon slices
½ lb. cottage cheese	⅓ cup commercial sour cream
¼ cup pickle relish	

Combine all ingredients. Makes 2 cups.

TUNA-CHEESE DUNK

1 can grated tuna (1 cup)	sweet pickle relish
3 3-oz. pkg. cream cheese	2 tablesp. snipped parsley
¼ cup dry white wine	1 teasp. grated onion
1 tablesp. mayonnaise	Dash tabasco
¼ cup well-drained	¼ teasp. salt
	¼ teasp. garlic salt

Drain tuna; blend with cream cheese, then with remaining ingredients. Makes 2 cups.

Spread-Your-Owns

Fill bowl, several small bowls, small mold, hollowed-out fresh pineapple or green-pepper half, or avocado or lobster shell with your choice of spreads (recipes follow). Arrange on attractive tray or chop plate; surround with one or more of these foundations:

Bread: rounds, squares, triangles, or fingers of white, pumpernickel, salty-rye, whole-wheat, French, cheese, nut, or raisin bread

Crisp Crackers: round scalloped, cheese, or oyster crackers; saltines; or shredded-wheat or rye wafers, etc.

Others: Melba toast; bread sticks; toast strips; tiny baking-powder biscuits, etc.

DELICIOUS CHICKEN SPREAD

1 cup minced, cooked or canned chicken	apple
2 crumbled crisp bacon slices	¼ teasp. salt
	Speck pepper
2 tablesp. diced, pared	¼ cup mayonnaise

Combine minced chicken, crumbled bacon, and diced apple with salt, pepper and mayonnaise. Makes 1 cup.

PARSLEY-CRAB SPREAD

Combine 1 cup finely flaked fresh or canned crab meat with 2 tablesp. snipped parsley; 1 tablesp. minced onion; 3 tablesp. mayonnaise; ¼ teasp. curry powder; 1 teasp. fresh, frozen, or canned lemon juice. Makes 1¼ cups.

DEVILED-HAM-CHEESE SPREAD

Combine 1 2¼-oz. can deviled ham with 1 3-oz. pkg. soft cream cheese, ½ teasp. each lemon juice and horse-radish. Makes ¾ cup.

CHEESE-AND-ANCHOVY SPREAD

3 3-oz. pkg. soft cream cheese	1 tablesp. anchovy paste
6 tablesp. light cream	½ cup chopped stuffed olives
1 teasp. Worcestershire	

Combine all ingredients. Makes 1¾ cups. For dunk, thin with a little more cream.

NIPPY SALMON SPREAD

Combine 1 cup flaked canned salmon with 1 tablesp. horse-radish; 2 teasp. bottled capers (some juice too); 3 tablesp. mayonnaise; and 2 teasp. fresh, frozen, or canned lemon juice. Makes 1¼ cups.

SHRIMP-TREAT SPREAD

Combine 1 cup minced, cooked, cleaned shrimp with ¼ cup soft butter or margarine; 1 tablesp. fresh, frozen, or canned lemon juice; ½ teasp. salt; ¼ teasp. paprika; 1 teasp. prepared mustard; and 1 teasp. Worcestershire. Makes about 1¼ cups.

SMOKY COCKTAIL SPREAD

1 can solid-pack tuna (1 cup)	pimento
½ teasp. smoke salt	1 3-oz. pkg. soft cream cheese; or 2 tablesp. mayonnaise
⅛ teasp. pepper	
2 tablesp. chopped	

Combine all ingredients. Taste; add salt if desired. Makes 1 cup.

TASTY TUNA SPREAD

1 can chunk-style tuna (1 cup)	½ teasp. soy sauce
1 3-oz. pkg. soft cream cheese	1 teasp. horse-radish
1 tablesp. mayonnaise	¼ teasp. each garlic, celery, and onion salts
1 tablesp. chopped bottled capers	¼ teasp. monosodium glutamate

Combine all ingredients. Makes 1½ cups.

TUNA WALDORF SPREAD

1 can chunk-style tuna (1 cup)	2 teasp. fresh, frozen, or canned lemon juice
1 cup finely chopped unpared apple	1 cup minced celery
¼ cup chopped nuts	⅔ cup mayonnaise or salad dressing
¾ teasp. salt	

Combine all ingredients. Makes about 3 cups.

SHORT-ORDER NIBBLERS—HOT

CORNED-BEEF ROUNDS

Toast slices of salty-rye bread on one side. With fork, break up canned corned-beef hash. Spread untoasted sides of bread with pickle relish, prepared mustard, or catchup, then with hash. Sprinkle with grated process Swiss cheese. Broil 5″ from heat till bubbly.

FRENCH-FRIE DUNK

Prepare frozen French fries as label directs, sprinkling with Parmesan cheese while they heat. Or omit Parmesan; provide bowl of catchup or chili sauce for dunking.

ENGLISH MUFFINETTES

Seeded: Spread split English muffins with butter or margarine. Sprinkle with poppy, caraway, or celery seeds. Broil till bubbly. Cut into wedges.

Blue Cheese: Spread split English muffins with butter or margarine. Sprinkle with crumbled blue cheese; or spread with blue-cheese spread. Broil till bubbly. Cut into wedges.

SNACK KABOBS

1 can luncheon meat	2 tablesp. soy sauce
24 canned pineapple chunks or tidbits, or peach chunks	1 tablesp. brown sugar
	1 tablesp. vinegar

Cut meat into 24 cubes. String meat cubes and pineapple chunks on each toothpick. Place on broil-and-serve platter or broiler pan; brush with mixture of soy sauce, sugar, vinegar. Broil, turning, until golden. Makes 24.

OFF-THE-SHELF NIBBLERS

Scan your grocer's shelves for nibbler makings you can serve on the spur of the moment. So many come in cans or packages—handy to keep on the pantry shelf, in the refrigerator or in the freezer. You serve them as is, or dressed up; the guests do the rest. We suggest:

Potato chips or sticks	Shrimp
Pretzels	Herring in wine
Popcorn—plain or cheese	Anchovy paste
Corn chips	Tuna or salmon
Crisp round crackers	Cooked tongue
Cheese crackers	Minced clams
Shredded-wheat wafers	Cocktail franks or sausages
Melba-toast rounds	Deviled ham or tongue
Salted nuts	Liver, chicken, or ham *pâté*
Coconut chips	Corned beef or corned-beef hash
Ripe, green, stuffed, or garlic olives	Luncheon meat, spiced ham, or chopped ham
French-fried onions	
Smithfield ham (serve in thin slivers)	Boned chicken or turkey
Flavored cream cheese	Nuts
Mushrooms	Cheese wedges or slices
Cheese spreads (in a variety of flavors)	Sardines

QUICKIES—MEAT

Corned-Beef Hash: Heat; season to taste with pickle relish, mustard, horse-radish, or lemon juice. Serve in bowl, with crisp crackers.

Deviled Ham or Tongue: Use as is. Or mix with pickle relish, horse-radish, grated onion or scallions, cheese, sour cream, or chopped hard-cooked eggs, etc. Guests spread mixture on bread fingers or crisp crackers.

Smithfield Spread or Deviled Ham: Halve ripe avocado; remove pit; fill with canned ham spread. Guests scoop up spread, along with some avocado, to top crackers.

Splits: Split franks (canned or regular) or Vienna sausage. Spread with pimento- or smoky-cheese spread, or cream cheese mixed with blue cheese or minced ripe olives. Put franks back together. Cut into 1″ pieces.

Chunks: On toothpicks, serve cubes of liverwurst or salami, or canned luncheon meat, spiced ham, chopped ham, or corned beef (or cheese). Use French dressing or other tangy sauce for dunking.

QUICKIES—CHEESE

Twin Cheese Rolls: Cut ½ lb. packaged process sharp cheese in half, lengthwise, to form 2 bars. Roll one bar in snipped parsley, one in caraway or poppy seeds. Set on tray. Each guest slices his own.

Cheese Spread: Place 2 or 3 glasses of cheese spread on tray. Circle each glass with parsley; arrange crackers between glasses.

Cheese-Food Rolls: Serve 1 or 2 kinds on small wooden board; provide knife. Each guest slices his own, to top assorted crisp crackers.

Cheese Wedges: Arrange individual wedges of assorted cheeses on tray, with every other wedge unwrapped. Heap crackers in center.

Orange-Chive Cheese: Mix chive cream cheese with a few orange-section bits. Serve with whole-wheat crackers.

QUICKIES—FISH

Sardines: Serve with buttered rye-bread fingers. Place a few lemon or lime wedges nearby to squeeze over sardines; or set out tiny bowl of hot chili sauce.

Sardine-Cheese: Blend 1 drained can sardines with 1 3-oz. pkg. cream cheese and grated onion, horse-radish, salt, pepper, and paprika to taste. Serve as spread for pumpernickel. Makes ⅔ cup. Serve with lemon wedge.

Caviar Fingers: Mix ¼ cup caviar; 1 teasp. fresh, frozen, or canned lemon juice; and ¼ teasp. minced onion. Spread on toast fingers. Garnish with sieved, hard-cooked egg yolks and whites, and with tiny pearl onions.

QUICKIES—OTHERS

Stuffed Nuts: Put walnut or pecan halves together in pairs, with generous filling of sharp-cheese spread.

Onion Toasties: Combine minced onion with an equal amount of mayonnaise; season with paprika, salt, pepper, Worcestershire. Spread over entire surface of cracker. Broil till bubbly.

Marinated Mushrooms: Drain juice from canned mushrooms; add French dressing to mushrooms; chill well. Drain. Serve on toothpicks.

Oyster Crackers: Heat in butter or margarine in skillet with sliced clove garlic.

Caesar Style: Drain juice from canned whole mushrooms, or green, ripe, or stuffed olives. Add bottled Caesar dressing to cover. Chill 2 hr. or so. Drain (you can reuse dressing). Serve mushrooms on toothpicks.

Chutney: Spread shredded-wheat wafers with chutney.

Deviled Crackers: Spread crisp crackers with butter or margarine seasoned with grated onion, dry mustard, Worcestershire, and dash salt and pepper. Broil till hot.

Potato Chips: Heat in oven; serve in basket. Or spread chips in shallow pan; sprinkle with grated American or Parmesan cheese; then broil lightly.

Peanut-Butter Toasties: Top each cracker with thin onion slice, dab of peanut butter, then dab of catchup. Toast under broiler.

POPCORN TRICKS

Garlicky: In skillet, heat packaged popcorn with butter or margarine and sliced clove garlic. Remove garlic before serving.

Cheese, Home Style: In skillet, heat packaged popcorn with butter or margarine; then toss with grated Parmesan or American cheese.

Seasoned Popcorn: Pop a big bowlful of popcorn; sprinkle with seasoned salt.

FROM A CHAFING DISH

See Nibblers—Off The Pantry Shelf, p. 623.

SLIMMERS

These are special nibblers for the weight watchers.

PICK-ME-UPS

Carrot Slices: Top thin carrot slices with dabs of cottage cheese.

Ham Rolls: Roll thin slices of boiled ham around cooked asparagus spears or apple, melon, celery, cucumber, or chicken fingers.

Filled Mushrooms: Wash 1 doz. medium mushrooms (about ¼ lb.); dry; remove stems. Mix ¼ cup cottage cheese with 1 tablesp. deviled ham and seasoned salt to taste. Use to stuff mushrooms.

Radish Halves: Split radishes lengthwise; top halves with cottage cheese or deviled ham.

Relish Sandwiches: Put together thin carrot, cucumber, or apple slices with cottage cheese, or with deviled ham seasoned with peanut butter.

FIX-YOUR-OWNS

Arrange one or more of the following dippers or foundations around bowl of dunk or spread; guests fix their own.

Dippers:

Tomato wedges	Chinese-cabbage
Fresh pineapple	chunks
sticks	Cucumber strips
Radishes	Carrot or celery
Green-pepper strips	sticks or fans
Scallions	Apple chunks dipped
Crisp endive leaves	into lemon juice
Raw cauliflower	
buds	

Foundations:

Cucumber slices	Fresh apple or pear
Celery chunks (cut	slices, dipped into
into 1″ lengths)	lemon juice
Carrot slices	

Dunks or Spreads:

Herb Cheese: Combine 1 cup cottage cheese with ½ teasp. grated onion; 3 tablesp. milk; dash pepper; ½ teasp. each dried sage and celery salt; and 1 tablesp. fresh, frozen, or canned lemon juice.

Rainbow Cheese: Combine cottage cheese with one or more of these: snipped chives or scallions, sliced or diced radishes, grated carrot, minced green pepper, raisins.

Anchovy-Celery Dip: Mince 2 cloves garlic. Drain oil from 1 2-oz. can flat fillet anchovies, reserving 2 teasp. oil. Mash anchovies with garlic till smooth. Stir in 2 teasp. vinegar, then reserved 2 teasp. oil. Serve in small bowl on plate; surround with raw celery sticks, radishes, or scallions that have been slit several times. Guests dunk vegetables in sauce. Makes 4 servings.

Low-Calorie French Dressing: See p. 321.

STICK-AND-PICK

Hot Kabobs: On toothpicks, string pineapple chunks or pickled onions and one of the following. Then broil till done.

Ham cubes	livers
Cooked, cleaned	Scallops
shrimp	Franks in 1″ pieces
Halved chicken	

Cold Kabobs: On toothpicks or carrot or celery sticks, string 2 or more of these:

Melon balls	cubes
Apple chunks	Chicken chunks
Orange chunks	Cooked, cleaned
Pineapple chunks	shrimp
Celery chunks	Radishes
Cherry tomatoes	Ham cubes
Luncheon-meat	

Fruits: Serve bowl of pineapple chunks with toothpicks, cherries on stems, unhulled strawberries, etc.

Soups
and Chowders

Soup may be the bright beginning of a good dinner. Or soup may be the meal's mainstay, served alone or teamed with a salad and/or sandwich, plus dessert. The recipes that follow give you soups packed with flavor, rich in good-for-you eating. Just be sure to serve the hot ones *hot,* the cold ones *cold.* Better be prepared for encores too!

Before using these recipes, refer to How to Use Our Recipes, p. 3, and Pots and Pans, p. 692. Always use standard measuring cups and measuring spoons; measure level.

A Bit of Garnish

For that finishing touch, top soup with one of these:

Slivered almonds	Snipped chives
Croutons, p. 9	Crumbled blue
Crisp ready-to-eat ce-	cheese
real	Snipped water cress
Whipped cream plus	Cut-up olives
horse-radish	Thin lemon slices
Snipped parsley	Salted whipped
Fresh herbs	cream
Popcorn	Sour cream and nut-
Browned onion rings	meg
Frank slices	Paper-thin carrot or
Crisp bacon bits	radish slices
Grated cheese	Thin celery rings
Crumbled potato	
chips	

Serve Them Simply

These days, many hot soups can be sipped in the living room, from cups or mugs, with crisp crackers or a Nibbler, p. 22, to munch on.

If you prefer to serve at-table style, don't forget those attractive pottery bowls and individual casseroles, which can make a meal-in-a-dish soup an occasion.

Go-Alongs

With soup, serve something crisp and perhaps salty: packaged crisp crackers, corn chips, potato chips, Melba toast, or buttered toast strips, etc. Or try one of our easy Nibblers, p. 22.

WITH A CAN OF SOUP

Keep a supply of cook-saving canned condensed soups on your pantry shelf. They can mean good eating at the turn of a can opener, good hospitality in a hurry. They may be served singly or in combination. Ready-to-serve soups are fine too! Choose from these; heat as label directs:

Chicken-Stock Base: chicken with rice, chicken gumbo, chicken-noodle, cream of chicken, chicken consommé, chicken broth etc.

Beef-Stock Base: beef, beef-noodle, vegetable-beef, oxtail, vegetable, bouillon, consommé etc.

Principally Vegetable: tomato, onion, green pea, black bean, cream of asparagus, cream of celery, cream of mushroom, vegetarian vegetable etc.

Thick and Hearty: bean with smoked pork or bacon, clam chowder, pepper pot, Scotch broth, gumbo creole, split pea etc.

Icy-Cold for Warm Weather: black bean, cream of celery, tomato, or cream of tomato etc. Blend with liquid as label directs; refrigerate; serve in chilled bowls. Consommé and consommé madrilene can be jellied right in can as label directs

Lighter Soups

LAST-MINUTE CHICKEN SOUP

2 tablesp. butter or margarine	1 soup can milk
1 sliced medium onion	2 chicken-bouillon cubes
⅛ teasp. mace	½ teasp. grated lemon rind (optional)
1 can undiluted condensed cream-of-chicken soup	2 tablesp. snipped parsley
1 soup can water	

In hot butter in saucepan, sauté onion until tender. Stir in mace, chicken soup, water, milk, bouillon cubes. Heat until bouillon cubes dissolve. Add lemon rind, parsley. Makes 4 or 5 servings.

TOMATO-CHICKEN BROTH

In saucepan, combine 1 can undiluted condensed chicken broth or chicken-with-rice soup; 1 soup can tomato juice; 2 slices lemon, halved; dash celery salt. Heat, covered, till boiling; reduce heat and simmer, uncovered, 5 min. Makes 4 servings.

MUSHROOM CONSOMME

3 tablesp. butter or margarine	1 can condensed bouillon plus enough water to make 3 cups*
⅓ cup thinly sliced onions	
¼ lb. mushrooms, cut into thick slices	Salt to taste
	Pepper
1 tablesp. fresh, frozen, or canned lemon juice	2 tablesp. sherry or cooking sherry (optional)

In hot butter in saucepan, sauté onions until just golden. Add mushrooms, lemon juice; cook until mushrooms are tender but not dark—about 5 min. Add bouillon, salt, pepper. Heat, but do not boil. Just before serving, add sherry. Makes 5 servings.

Or use meat-extract paste, or beef-bouillon cubes dissolved in hot water, as label directs.

ONION-AND-TOMATO SOUP

2 tablesp. butter or margarine	1 soup can water
	1 can undiluted condensed tomato soup
2 cups thinly sliced onions	1 soup can milk
1 can undiluted condensed consommé	½ teasp. Worcestershire
	¼ teasp. salt

In hot butter in saucepan, cook onions till light brown. Add consommé, water; simmer, covered, 15 min. Add rest of ingredients. Heat, but do not boil. Makes 5 servings.

DOWN-EAST BROTH

In saucepan, combine 1 8-oz. can or bottle clam juice, 1 No. 2 can tomato juice (2½ cups), 1 teasp. Worcestershire, and 2 tablesp. butter or margarine. Bring to boil. Sprinkle with parsley sprigs. Makes 4 servings.

CHICKEN-CURRY SOUP

¼ cup butter or margarine	1 cup milk
1 cup minced onions	1 can undiluted condensed tomato soup
1½ cups diced celery	2 cans undiluted condensed chicken-with-rice soup
½ teasp. curry powder	
Speck pepper	
¼ teasp. salt	

In hot butter in saucepan, sauté onions and celery 5 min. Stir in curry and rest of ingredients. Simmer, covered, 10 min., stirring once. Makes 4 generous servings.

Heartier Soups

CREAMY POTATO SOUP

6 bacon slices	chicken soup
1 cup chopped onions	2 soup cans milk
2 cups cubed potatoes	1 teasp. salt
1 cup water	2 tablesp. snipped parsley
2 cans undiluted condensed cream-of-	

In large saucepan, cook bacon till crisp; set bacon aside. Pour off all but 3 tablesp. bacon fat from saucepan; add onions; brown a bit. Add potatoes, water. Cook, covered, 15 min., or until potatoes are tender. Blend in soup, milk, salt. Heat, but do not boil. Serve garnished with bacon, parsley. Makes 4 servings.

CAN-OPENER MINESTRONE

Heat 1 can undiluted condensed vegetable soup, with 1 can undiluted condensed chicken-noodle soup; 1 soup can water; 1 No. 2 can kidney beans, undrained; 1 minced clove garlic; ⅓ cup snipped parsley.

Serve in casserole, Dutch oven, or tureen. Pass grated Parmesan cheese. Makes 4 servings.

TOMATO-CRAB BISQUE

1 can undiluted con-	densed bouillon
densed tomato soup	1 soup can light cream
1 can undiluted con-	1 cup flaked fresh or
densed cream-of-	canned crab or
mushroom soup	lobster meat
1 can undiluted con-	

Combine ingredients in order, stirring constantly. Heat over low heat until hot; *do not boil*. Serve at once. Makes 4 servings.

LOBSTER CREAM

1 frozen rock-lobster	2 minced small onions
tail	2 cans undiluted con-
Few celery tops	densed cream-of-
1 bay leaf (optional)	chicken soup
4 whole black peppers	¼ teasp. pepper
¼ cup butter or	1 teasp. paprika
margarine	

Place lobster in boiling salted water to cover, with celery, bay leaf, whole black peppers. Cook, covered, 3 min. longer than ounce weight of tail. Remove lobster; strain broth; reserve both.

In hot butter, sauté onions until golden; stir in soup, 2 soup cans strained lobster broth, pepper, paprika; heat. Meanwhile, cut lobster meat into small pieces; add to soup; simmer slowly about 10 min. Makes 8 servings.

PANTRY-SHELF PEA SOUP

½ lb. link sausages	densed vegetable
1 thinly sliced onion	soup
1 can undiluted con-	1 soup can water
densed green-pea	¼ cup sliced stuffed
soup	olives
1 can undiluted con-	

In saucepan, brown sausages and onion; drain off fat; set onion aside. Cut sausages into ½" slices; stir in soups, water. Simmer a few minutes to blend.

Serve garnished with onion rings and olive slices. Makes 4 servings.

ITALIAN FISH STEW

2 tablesp. salad or	1 soup can water
olive oil	¼ teasp. salt
1 cup chopped onions	Dash pepper
⅓ cup chopped green	2 whole cloves
peppers	1 bay leaf
2 minced cloves garlic	1 1-lb. pkg. frozen fish
1 can undiluted con-	fillets, thawed
densed tomato soup	enough to separate
1 can undiluted con-	1 lb. deveined, shelled
densed clam chow-	raw shrimp
der	¼ cup white wine

In hot oil in saucepan, cook onions, green peppers, garlic, until tender. Add soups, water, salt, pepper, cloves, bay leaf, fish. Simmer, covered, 10 min. Add shrimp, wine; simmer, covered, 15 min. Makes 6 servings.

CREAM MONGOLE WITH SHERRY

1 can undiluted con-	1 teasp. sugar
densed tomato soup	1 cup light cream*
1 can undiluted con-	2 teasp. Worcestershire
densed green-pea	5 tablesp. sherry or
soup	cooking sherry
¾ cup water	(optional)

Combine soups and water; heat over very low heat, stirring, until smooth. Slowly stir in sugar, cream, Worcestershire. Remove from heat; slowly add sherry. Makes 5 or 6 servings.

* *Half-and-half cream and milk may be used.*

TOMATO-CHEESE SOUP

In double boiler, heat 1 can condensed tomato soup, diluted as label directs. Spoon in 1 8-oz. jar pasteurized process cheese spread (cheese sauce), stirring until well blended. Heat again, adding 3 tablesp. sherry or cooking sherry if desired. Garnish with snipped scallions if desired. Makes 3 or 4 servings.

IN NO TIME AT ALL

Sherry-Black Bean: Prepare canned black-bean soup as label directs. Add sherry or cooking sherry to taste.

Cream of Avocado: Add 1 pared, pitted firm ripe, avocado, coarsely grated, and ¼ teasp. nutmeg to 1 can condensed cream-of-chicken soup. Then prepare as label directs.

Cheese: Add 1 cup grated process American cheese (¼ lb.) to 1 can condensed cream-of-mushroom soup. Then prepare as label directs.

Corn: Add 1 can cream-style corn and dash nutmeg to 1 can condensed cream-of-chicken soup. Then prepare as label directs. Nice with floats of Melba toast or crackers topped with deviled ham.

Creamy Ham: Stir 1 2¼-oz. can deviled ham into 1 can of any condensed cream soup. Then prepare as label directs.

PACKAGED SOUP MIXES

With such packaged soup mixes as chicken-noodle, onion, consommé, tomato, pea, tomato-vegetable, etc., that steaming bowl of soup for lunch or supper is ready in no time. Just try them and see how delicious they are.

SOUPS OF YOUR OWN MAKING

Hot, Cold, or Jellied First Courses

FRENCH ONION SOUP

5 tablesp. butter or margarine	5⅓ cups water
4 cups thinly sliced large onions	1 teasp. salt
	5 2″ toast rounds
¼ teasp. pepper	2 tablesp. grated
5 beef-bouillon cubes	Parmesan cheese

In hot butter in saucepan, sauté onions until deep golden brown; sprinkle with pepper. Bring bouillon cubes and water to boil; stir well. Add onions, salt; simmer, covered, 1 hr. Place 1 toast round in each soup dish; pour soup over it. Sprinkle with cheese. Makes 5 servings.

P.S. Delicious onion soups come canned or as packaged mix.

DE LUXE TOMATO SOUP

6 cups tomato juice	⅛ teasp. pepper
1 sliced medium onion	¼ teasp. sugar
2 bay leaves	⅓ cup mayonnaise
1 teasp. seasoned salt	Snipped chives

Simmer all ingredients except mayonnaise and chives, uncovered, 10 min. Lift out onion, bay leaves. Slowly stir a little tomato mixture into mayonnaise; return to rest of tomato mixture. Serve at once, topped with chives. Makes 6 servings.

QUICK TOMATO BOUILLON

Serve Hot Tomato-Juice Cocktail, p. 19.

SOUP FROM LEFTOVER BONES

Bones left over from poultry, roast, steak, etc.	1 sliced onion
	1 sliced stalk celery
	2 sprigs parsley
Any leftover stuffing (optional)	1 bay leaf
	3 whole black peppers
2 qt. cold water	2 teasp. salt
1 sliced, pared carrot	⅛ teasp. pepper

In large kettle, combine all ingredients; simmer, covered, 2 hr. Strain; season to taste. If made in advance, cool quickly as on p. 48; refrigerate. Reheat to serve. Makes 1½ qt.

To Vary: To completed soup, add some canned tomatoes, or 1 or 2 cut-up fresh tomatoes; any diced leftover meat; a little cooked rice; some curry; dried or fresh herbs; frozen mixed vegetables, etc. Simmer, covered, 10 to 15 min.

HOME-STYLE CHICKEN BROTH

1 4-lb. ready-to-cook stewing chicken, cut up	¼ teasp. pepper
	2 diced stalks celery
	1 sliced medium onion
2 qt. boiling water	2 sprigs parsley
2 teasp. salt	1 bay leaf

In kettle, combine all ingredients. Simmer, covered, until chicken is tender—3 to 4 hr. Strain; season. Cool quickly as on p. 138. Refrigerate at once until fat solidifies on surface.

To serve: Lift off fat; reheat broth. Makes about 7 cups broth. Use chicken meat in any recipe in The Last of the Bird, p. 156.

Chicken Soup: To hot chicken broth, add 1 cup diced celery; 2 sliced medium onions; ¼ cup washed raw regular or processed white rice; 1

cup cut-up, cooked chicken. Simmer, covered, 20 min., or until rice and celery are tender. Add salt and pepper to taste. Serve topped with snipped parsley or lemon slices. Makes 6 servings.

To vary: Add 1 teasp. sherry or cooking sherry to each serving. Or, just before serving, to soup add ¼ teasp. curry powder per serving.

Jellied Chicken Bouillon: Sprinkle 1 env. unflavored gelatine over ½ cup cold water to soften. Add gelatine to 3¾ cups hot chicken broth; stir until dissolved. Add ½ teasp. each salt and celery salt. Refrigerate until set. Beat slightly with fork. Top with snipped parsley. Makes 4 servings.

BLENDER VICHYSSOISE

1 cup coarsely diced raw potatoes	1 cup raw green peas
¼ cup snipped scallions	⅛ teasp. celery salt
1½ cups chicken broth	⅛ teasp. curry powder
	1 cup heavy cream

Day before: Cook potatoes with scallions, chicken broth, and peas, covered, 10 min., or until vegetables are barely tender. Place undrained vegetables in glass container of electric blender; add celery salt, curry powder. Cover; blend until smooth—30 sec. Remove; stir in cream. Refrigerate.

Serve cold, sprinkled with snipped parsley. Makes 4 servings.

CREME VICHYSSOISE

4 leeks; or 1½ cups minced onions	1 cup light or heavy cream
3 cups sliced, pared potatoes	1 cup milk
3 cups boiling water	1 teasp. salt
4 chicken-bouillon cubes	¼ teasp. pepper
3 tablesp. butter or margarine	2 tablesp. snipped chives
	¼ teasp. paprika

Cut into fine pieces leeks and 3″ of green tops. Cook with potatoes in boiling water, covered, until very tender—about 40 min. Press, without draining, through fine sieve into double boiler.

Add bouillon cubes, butter, cream, milk, salt, pepper; mix well. Reheat.

Serve hot or very cold, topped with chives and paprika. Makes 6 servings.

To Vary: Add ¼ teasp. curry powder.

FRUIT SOUP

1½ cups water	1 No. 2 can pineapple juice (2½ cups)
½ cup granulated sugar	1½ teasp. grated lemon rind
1 stick cinnamon	
2 cups grape juice	2 cups seedless grapes
3 tablesp. quick-cooking tapioca	½ cup Burgundy

Bring water, sugar, cinnamon, and grape juice to boil. Add tapioca; cook, stirring occasionally, 5 min. Remove from heat; add pineapple juice, lemon rind. Refrigerate.

To serve: Stir; add grapes, Burgundy. Makes 8 servings.

CONSOMME MADRILENE

2 cups chicken broth, p. 36 *	½ cup sliced, pared carrots
2 cups canned bouillon †	1 diced stalk celery
2 cups canned tomatoes	3 whole black peppers
1 sliced medium onion	1 teasp. salt
2 whole cloves	1 teasp. sugar

Combine all ingredients; simmer, covered, 1 hr. Strain. Serve hot or cold. Makes 4 cups.

* Or use canned chicken broth, or chicken-bouillon cubes dissolved in hot water as label directs.

† Or use meat-extract paste, or beef-bouillon cubes dissolved in hot water as label directs.

Jellied Consommé Madrilene: Sprinkle 1 env. unflavored gelatine over ½ cup cold broth or water to soften; stir into hot strained soup until dissolved. Refrigerate until set. Then beat with fork. Serve in bouillon cups, topped with lemon slices. Makes 4 servings.

P.S. Tasty consommé madrilene also comes in cans.

JELLIED TOMATO SOUP

2 env. unflavored gelatine	2¼ cups water
	2 tablesp. lemon juice
1 No. 2 can tomatoes (2½ cups)	2½ tablesp. grated lemon rind
2 beef-bouillon cubes; or 2 teasp. meat-extract paste	2 teasp. minced onion
	1 teasp. salt

Sprinkle gelatine over 1 cup tomatoes to soften. Heat remaining tomatoes with bouillon cubes and rest of ingredients. Add gelatine; stir till dissolved. Cool slightly; strain into bouillon cups. Refrigerate until set. Just before serving, beat lightly with fork. Makes 5 servings.

Creamy Soups

CREAM-OF-MUSHROOM SOUP

¼ lb. whole mush-rooms; or 1⅛ cups minced mushroom stems	cubes
	2 cups boiling water
	1 tablesp. butter or margarine
1 tablesp. butter or margarine	3 tablesp. flour
1 tablesp. minced onion	2 cups milk
¼ teasp. celery seeds	1 teasp. salt
2 chicken-bouillon	⅛ teasp. pepper

Wash whole mushrooms; chop fine. Add 1 tablesp. butter, onion, celery seeds. Simmer, covered, 5 min. Add bouillon cubes, boiling water; simmer, uncovered, 10 min.

In double-boiler top over direct heat, melt 1 tablesp. butter. Add flour; stir till smooth. Add milk, salt, pepper. Cook over boiling water, stirring, till thickened. Add mushroom mixture; heat. Makes 6 servings.

SWISS CREAM-OF-POTATO SOUP

4 pared, medium potatoes	½ teasp. nutmeg
2 diced bacon slices	Dash cayenne pepper
¼ cup minced onion	¼ teasp. dry mustard
2 tablesp. butter or margarine	1 teasp. Worcestershire
1 tablesp. snipped parsley	3 cups milk
2 teasp. salt	½ cup grated natural Swiss or process American cheese

Cook potatoes till tender as on p. 284; drain. Meanwhile, sauté bacon and onion over low heat, stirring, until brown and tender. Mash potatoes; add bacon, onion, butter, parsley, salt, nutmeg, cayenne, mustard, Worcestershire. Stir in milk. Heat over low heat, stirring. Sprinkle with cheese. Serve at once. Makes 4 servings.

CREAM-OF-CHICKEN SOUP

2 tablesp. butter or margarine	½ cup shredded, cooked or canned chicken
¼ cup flour	
3 cups chicken broth, p. 36	Salt
	Pepper
1 cup light cream	Cut-up chives or apples

In double-boiler top over direct heat, melt butter; stir in flour. Slowly stir in broth, cream; cook, stirring, over boiling water until thickened. Add chicken, salt and pepper to taste. Serve topped with chives or apples. Makes 5 or 6 servings.

Chicken Curry: Add ½ teasp. curry powder.

CREAM-OF-VEGETABLE SOUP

¼ cup minced onion	leftover cooked or canned vegetable
3 tablesp. butter or margarine	About 2 teasp. salt
3 tablesp. flour	Speck pepper
3 cups milk	½ teasp. bottled thick meat sauce, p. 9
1 cup vegetable liquid *	
About 1½ cups finely chopped or sieved,	Speck paprika

1. In double-boiler top over direct heat, cook onion in butter till tender. Stir in flour.
2. Place double-boiler top over boiling water; slowly stir in milk, then vegetable liquid. Cook, stirring, until smooth and thickened.
3. Add vegetables, salt to taste, pepper, meat sauce, paprika; heat. Makes 6 servings.

Use liquid left from cooking vegetables, or part vegetable liquid and part milk, or all milk.

To Vary: You may substitute 1 bouillon cube, dissolved in 1 cup boiling water, for 1 cup milk. Adjust salt to taste.

Cream of Broccoli: Use 2 cups finely chopped or sieved, cooked broccoli as vegetable.

Cream of Celery: Use 1½ cups sieved or diced, cooked celery as vegetable.

Cream of Corn: Increase milk to 4 cups; omit vegetable water. As vegetable, use 1⅔ cups canned vacuum-packed whole-kernel corn or 1 No. 2 can cream-style corn.

Cream of Pea: Use liquid drained from 1 No. 303 can peas as part of vegetable liquid. Use peas, sieved or partially mashed, as vegetable.

Cream of Spinach: Use 1½ cups sieved, cooked spinach as vegetable. Add pinch dried basil.

P.S. You can make wonderful vegetable soup in your blender, as manufacturer directs.

CREAM-OF-TOMATO SOUP

2 tablesp. butter or margarine	tomatoes*
3 tablesp. flour	1 tablesp. minced onion
1½ teasp. salt	¼ teasp. celery seeds
⅛ teasp. pepper	½ teasp. salt
2 cups milk	½ teasp. sugar
1 No. 2 can tomatoes (2½ cups); or 2½ cups stewed fresh	½ bay leaf; or pinch dried basil
	1 whole clove
	⅛ teasp. baking soda

1. In double boiler, melt butter. Stir in flour, 1½ teasp. salt, pepper, then milk. Cook, stirring, until smooth and thickened.
2. In saucepan, combine tomatoes, onion, celery seeds, salt, sugar, bay leaf, clove. Simmer, uncovered, 5 min. With spoon, press through strainer. Stir in soda.
3. *Just before serving,* stir tomato mixture into milk mixture. Heat, stirring. If soup curdles, beat smooth with egg beater.

Serve as is, or top with snipped parsley or chives, grated cheese, salted whipped cream, or sour cream. Makes 4 to 6 servings.

* For stewed fresh tomatoes, simmer 3½ cups cut-up tomatoes 10 min.

CREAM-OF-ONION-AND-CHEESE SOUP

3 tablesp. butter or margarine	1 teasp. salt
1½ cups thinly sliced onions	Speck pepper
	¾ cup grated process American cheese
1½ tablesp. flour	Snipped parsley
3 cups milk	

In double-boiler top over direct heat, melt butter; add onions; cook over low heat, stirring occasionally, until almost tender—about 5 min. Place over boiling water; gradually stir in flour, then milk; cook, stirring, until thickened. Add salt, pepper, cheese; stir until cheese melts. Serve topped with parsley. Makes 4 or 5 servings.

OYSTER BISQUE

1 doz. shucked large raw oysters, drained and chopped	1 small bay leaf
	⅓ cup melted butter or margarine
4 cups milk	⅓ cup flour
1 slice onion	1¾ teasp. salt
2 stalks celery	⅛ teasp. pepper
1 sprig parsley	

In small saucepan, slowly bring oysters to boiling point; remove. Scald milk with onion, celery, parsley, bay leaf; remove seasonings from milk. In large saucepan, blend butter with flour, salt, pepper; slowly stir in milk; stir over low heat until thickened. Add oysters. Nice with croutons or toast sticks. Makes 4 supper servings.

Crab or Lobster: Substitute 1⅓ cups finely chopped, flaked fresh or canned crab or lobster meat for oysters.

Meal-in-a-Dish Soups

These are hearty soups. A big steaming bowlful can make a wonderful meal. A cupful can be a good beginning to lunch or dinner.

KNIFE-AND-FORK VEGETABLE SOUP

2 tablesp. salad oil	2 outer stalks celery, cut into 1" pieces
1 large, or 2 small, fairly lean, meaty short ribs, cut into 2" squares (about 2 lb.)	4 pared carrots, cut into 1" pieces
	4 zucchini, trimmed and cut into ½" pieces
2 minced cloves garlic	
2½ teasp. salt	1 ear corn, broken into 4 pieces; or ½ cup cooked or canned whole-kernel corn
1 coarsely chopped large onion (about 1 cup)	
2 qt. hot water	
2 bouillon cubes	Pepper and salt

Early in day: Heat salad oil in Dutch oven, large kettle, or deep-well cooker; add meat and brown on all sides—about 15 min.

Sprinkle garlic with 1 teasp. salt; mash well with side of knife; add with onions to meat. Cook, stirring, 2 to 3 min. Add hot water, bouillon cubes; simmer, covered, 1½ hr., or till meat is just tender.

Add 1½ teasp. salt, celery, carrots. Cook, covered, 15 min. Then add zucchini; simmer, covered, 10 min. Lastly add corn; simmer, covered, 5 min. longer. Season to taste. Refrigerate till needed.

To serve: Reheat soup; ladle into soup plates, with big piece of meat and some of each vegetable in each serving. Serve with knife, fork, and soupspoon. Makes 6 to 8 large servings.

OLD-COUNTRY BORSCH

6 cups water	**1 bay leaf**
1 lb. beef brisket, cut into 6 pieces	**1 tablesp. salt**
2 sliced onions	**2 coarsely grated beets (about 1 cup)**
2 stalks celery, cut into 1″ lengths	**1 6-oz. can tomato paste (2/3 cup)**
4 sliced, pared medium beets (about 2 cups)	**2 tablesp. vinegar**
	1 tablesp. sugar
4 thinly sliced, pared carrots (1 1/2 cups)	**2 teasp. salt**
	1/2 pt. commercial sour cream
1 small head cabbage, cut into wedges	

Day before or early in day: In large kettle, place water, beef, onions, celery, sliced beets, carrots, cabbage, bay leaf, 1 tablesp. salt; simmer, covered, about 2 hr. Add grated beets and rest of ingredients except cream. Simmer, covered, 15 to 20 min. Cool; refrigerate.

To serve: Skim any fat from soup. Bring soup to boil over medium heat; lower heat; simmer, covered, 10 min. Serve topped with sour cream. Makes 4 to 6 servings.

DAD'S DINNER-IN-A-SOUP

2 lb. shin beef, plus split large soupbone	**green beans**
	1/2 pkg. frozen limas
4 qt. water	**1/2 pkg. frozen peas**
1 tablesp. salt	**1 12-oz. can vacuum-packed whole-kernel corn**
1/2 sliced medium cabbage	
2 chopped medium onions	**1 cubed, pared potato**
	2 tablesp. snipped parsley
6 pared carrots, cut into 3″ pieces	**3/4 cup catchup**
2 coarsely cut-up stalks celery	**1/2 teasp. ground cloves**
	1 teasp. sugar
1/4 cut-up medium green pepper	**1 teasp. salt**
	1/4 teasp. pepper
1 No. 2 1/2 can tomatoes (3 1/2 cups)	**4 whole ears corn (optional)**
1/2 pkg. frozen cut	

Day before: In large kettle, place meat, bone, water, salt. Bring to boil; skim. Add cabbage, onions, carrots, celery, green pepper, tomatoes. Cook, covered, 30 min. Add green beans and rest of ingredients except ears of corn; simmer, covered, 3 1/2 hr. Taste; season if needed.

Remove meat and bone from soup. Cut up meat; return to soup. Cool; refrigerate.

To serve: Skim any fat from soup. Bring soup to boil over medium heat. Break corn into 2″ pieces; add to soup; simmer, covered, about 10 min., or until tender. Makes 12 servings.

MINESTRONE

1 lb. shin beef with bone	**2 cups finely shredded cabbage**
5 qt. cold water	**1 1/2 cups diced, pared carrots**
3 tablesp. salt	
1 cup dried red kidney beans	**1 No. 2 1/2 can tomatoes (3 1/2 cups)**
2 tablesp. salad or olive oil	**1 1/2 cups broken-up spaghetti**
2 cloves garlic	**1 cup thinly sliced zucchini or small yellow squash**
1 minced medium onion	
1/2 cup snipped parsley	**1 pkg. frozen peas**
1/2 lb. chuck, ground	**Grated Parmesan or Romano cheese**
1/4 teasp. pepper	
1 cup diced celery	

Day before: In large kettle, place shin beef with bone, water, salt, beans. Bring to boil; skim. Cover; simmer 3 hr. In oil, sauté garlic, onion, parsley, chuck, and pepper until onion is tender; discard garlic. Remove bone from soup; cut off meat. Add meat to soup, along with onion mixture, celery, cabbage, carrots, tomatoes. Simmer, covered, 20 min., or until vegetables are tender. Refrigerate.

About 30 min. before serving: Skim fat from soup. Bring soup slowly to boil; add spaghetti, zucchini, peas; cook, covered, about 10 min. Add salt and pepper to taste.

Serve from soup tureen, large casserole, or mixing bowl, letting guests top soup with cheese. Makes 8 servings.

OLD-FASHIONED SPLIT-PEA SOUP

In kettle, place ham bone (such as that left over from cooked shank), 3 qt. water, 2 cups split green peas, 2 teasp. salt, 1/4 teasp. pepper, 1 sliced medium onion. Simmer, covered, over low heat 2 1/2 to 3 hr.

Remove bone from soup; cut off any bits of ham; add to soup, along with 1 1/2 cups slivered, cooked ham if you have it. Heat. Makes 8 generous servings.

FRANK-AND-VEGETABLE SOUP

1 qt. cold water	2 sliced stalks celery
1 cup rinsed large California dry limas	3 sliced medium onions Speck pepper
1 teasp. salt	2 teasp. celery salt
5 beef-bouillon cubes	½ teasp. dried marjoram
5 cups boiling water	
5 quartered, peeled tomatoes	1 teasp. dried sage 1½ teasp. salt
6 pared carrots	¼ teasp. seasoned salt
¼ lb. green beans	½ lb. franks

Bring 1 qt. water to full, rolling boil; slowly stir in limas so that boiling doesn't stop. Reduce heat; boil gently, covered, 1 hr., adding 1 teasp. salt last half hour (add water if needed).

Add bouillon cubes; boiling water; tomatoes; carrots, quartered lengthwise; beans, sliced lengthwise; celery; onions; pepper; celery salt. Simmer, uncovered, until vegetables are just tender—about 30 min., stirring once. Add marjoram; sage; 1½ teasp. salt; seasoned salt; franks, split lengthwise. Heat. Makes 4 to 6 servings.

LENTIL-BURGER SOUP

1 lb. lentils	3 or 4 minced cloves garlic
2½ qt. cold water	
2 tablesp. salt	2 bay leaves
¼ teasp. pepper	1 lb. lamb shoulder, ground
½ cup butter or margarine	
	1½ teasp. salt
1 No. 2 can tomatoes (2½ cups)	¼ teasp. pepper
	1 egg, slightly beaten
1 minced large onion	Flour
2 tablesp. snipped fresh dill	1 tablesp. salad oil
	¼ cup elbow macaroni

Day before or early in day: Wash lentils. Place in large kettle, with water, 2 tablesp. salt, ¼ teasp. pepper, butter, tomatoes, onion, dill, garlic, bay leaves. Cook, covered, over low heat 1 hr. 45 min.

Meanwhile, combine ground lamb with 1½ teasp. salt, ¼ teasp. pepper, and egg; form into 24 balls. Roll balls in flour; brown in hot salad oil; add, with macaroni, to soup; cook 20 min. longer. Cool; refrigerate.

To serve: Bring soup to boil over medium heat; simmer, covered, about 10 min. If desired, float tomato slices on top. Makes 6 servings.

TANGY CHICKEN SPECIAL

1 3-lb. ready-to-cook roasting chicken	¾ cup packaged precooked rice
2½ qt. cold water	2 eggs
1 tablesp. salt	¼ cup lemon juice
½ teasp. monosodium glutamate	½ thinly sliced lemon
	2 tablesp. snipped parsley
2 tablesp. butter or margarine	

Day before or early in day: In large kettle, place chicken, water, salt, monosodium glutamate, butter. Simmer, covered, about 1½ hr., or until chicken is tender. Remove chicken from soup; cut meat from bones into nice-sized pieces; return to soup. Cool; refrigerate.

To serve: Bring chicken mixture to boil. Add rice; simmer, covered, 10 min., or until rice is tender; remove from heat. Beat eggs well; slowly stir in lemon juice, then about 2 cups broth without chicken meat. Now stir this mixture into rest of soup. Garnish with lemon slices, parsley. Makes 8 servings.

ELLEN'S SHRIMP GUMBO

¼ cup butter or margarine	or 1 tablesp. meat-extract paste
2 tablesp. flour	4 teasp. Worcestershire
2 minced cloves garlic	⅛ teasp. ground cloves
2 sliced onions	½ teasp. chili powder
½ thinly sliced green pepper	Pinch dried basil
	1 bay leaf
1 No. 2 can tomatoes (2½ cups)	1½ tablesp. salt
	¼ teasp. pepper
1 No. 2 can okra, drained; or 1 pkg. frozen whole okra	3 cups water
	1½ lb. deveined, shelled raw shrimp
1 6-oz. can tomato paste (⅔ cup)	3 cups hot cooked rice
	¼ cup snipped parsley
3 beef-bouillon cubes;	

Early in day: In Dutch oven or heavy kettle, melt butter. Stir in flour; then cook over low heat until brown. Add garlic, onions, green pepper; cook slowly until tender. Add tomatoes and rest of ingredients except shrimp, rice, parsley. Simmer, uncovered, 45 min. Cool; refrigerate.

To serve: Heat tomato mixture over medium heat till just boiling. Add shrimp; simmer, covered, 5 min., or until shrimp are pink and tender. Toss hot rice with parsley. Serve gumbo in shallow plates; add "island" of parsley and rice at side of each plate. Makes 8 servings.

BOUILLABAISSE, BUFFET STYLE

2 cups olive oil	4 whole fish, boned and
3 cubed large onions	cleaned (bonito,
2 cubed large green	mackerel, bluefish,
peppers	sea bass)
3 cubed, pared large	About 5 cups water
carrots	2 tablesp. salt
50 small hard clams in	½ to 1 teasp. pepper
shell, scrubbed	1″ slices French bread
1 lb. unshelled large	Melted butter
raw shrimp	Garlic salt or minced
3 live lobsters, split	garlic

1. In very large kettle (at least 3½ gal. capacity), heat olive oil. Add onions, green peppers, carrots; brown lightly.
2. In same kettle, arrange fish in this order: clams; then shrimp; then lobster; and lastly, on top of all, whole fish.
3. Add water (enough to half fill kettle), salt, pepper. Cover kettle tightly; bring mixture to boil; reduce heat and cook 15 to 20 min., or until clams open, lobsters are pink and tender, and the whole fish flake easily.
4. While fish cook, toast bread in 425°F. oven; brush with combined butter and garlic salt. When all is done, carefully arrange each kind of shellfish and fish on separate heated platter.
5. Place 1 or 2 slices toasted bread in each soup dish. After stirring broth well, pour some over bread in each dish; arrange dishes on table, along with platters of fish.
6. Each person helps himself to different kinds of fish, placing them in soup bowl. Makes 8 to 10 servings.

Gourmet Style: Substitute dry white wine for 1 cup water. Add ½ teasp. each dried thyme and sage.

OYSTER STEW

2 doz. shucked raw	1 teasp. celery salt
oysters with liquid	¾ teasp. salt
¼ cup butter or	⅛ teasp. pepper
margarine	¼ teasp. paprika
1 tablesp. Worcester-	1 qt. milk
shire	

Carefully pick over oysters to remove bits of shell. In deep skillet or kettle, heat butter until sizzling. Add oysters with liquid, Worcestershire, celery salt, salt, pepper, paprika. Heat

until edges of oysters curl *slightly;* add milk. Heat quickly, *but do not boil.*

Serve in bowls, topped with paprika and lumps of butter. Pass oyster crackers if desired. Makes 4 servings.

De Luxe: Use part milk and part cream.

Clam: Substitute 2 doz. shucked raw soft-shell clams with liquid for oysters.

Lobster: Substitute 1 to 1½ cups cooked lobster meat for oysters with liquid.

BARNEGAT CHICKEN CHOWDER

1 6-lb. ready-to-cook	potatoes
roasting chicken	About ¼ lb. salt pork,
1 tablesp. salt	in small strips
1 bay leaf	¼ teasp. pepper
4 sliced medium onions	1 teasp. salt
4 diced, pared medium	8 cups milk

Place chicken in deep kettle; cover halfway with hot water. Add 1 tablesp. salt, bay leaf, and half of onions; simmer, covered, 2 hr., or until tender. Remove chicken; cool quickly as on p. 138; remove skin; cut meat into large cubes; refrigerate. Remove bay leaf from broth; add potatoes; simmer, covered, 15 min.

In small skillet, sauté salt pork till crisp; add remaining onions; sauté 2 to 3 min. Add to broth, with chicken, pepper, 1 teasp. salt, and milk. Heat. Makes 8 to 10 generous servings.

DANDY BEAN CHOWDER

¾ cup diced, pared	2 tablesp. flour
carrots	1½ teasp. salt
2 tablesp. butter or	⅛ teasp. pepper
margarine	1 cup milk
2 tablesp. minced onion	1 1-lb. can baked beans
2 tablesp. minced green	in tomato sauce
pepper	1 cup grated franks (3)

Cook carrots in 1″ boiling salted water, covered, till tender; drain, reserving liquid and carrots. In hot butter in saucepan, sauté onion and green pepper until golden. Add flour, salt, pepper.

To carrot liquid, add enough water to make 1 cup; combine with milk; stir into flour mixture. Heat until thickened, stirring constantly. Add carrots, beans, franks. Heat well. Makes 4 servings.

TURKEY-CORN CHOWDER

¼ cup butter or margarine	packed whole-kernel corn
4 sliced medium onions	¼ teasp. dried thyme
5 sliced, pared medium potatoes	1 cup light cream
2 sliced stalks celery	1 No. 303 can cream-style corn
4 teasp. salt	1½ teasp. paprika
½ teasp. pepper	3 cups cut-up roast turkey or chicken
2 cups water	
1 chicken-bouillon cube	2 tablesp. butter or margarine
5 cups milk	Parsley
2 12-oz. cans vacuum-	

In ¼ cup butter in large kettle or electric combination casserole-fryer, sauté onions till golden, stirring often. Add potatoes, celery, salt, pepper, water, bouillon cube. Cook, covered, 15 min., or until vegetables are tender. Add milk and rest of ingredients except 2 tablesp. butter and parsley. Heat; dot with butter; snip parsley over top. Makes 8 to 10 servings.

DINNER CHOWDER

1 pkg. frozen Fordhook limas	1 No. 2 or No. 303 can stewed tomatoes*
1 can undiluted condensed cream-of-chicken soup	2 cups grated process sharp American cheese (½ lb.)
1 can solid-pack tuna, undrained (1 cup)	¼ teasp. garlic salt
	⅛ teasp. pepper

Cook limas as label directs; drain. To limas, add chicken soup and rest of ingredients. Cook over low heat until cheese melts and soup is very hot. Makes 4 to 6 servings.

* *New-style canned tomatoes with onions, green peppers, and celery added.*

CORN CHOWDER

⅛ lb. salt pork, in ½" cubes; or 2 tablesp. butter or margarine	1 12-oz. can vacuum-packed whole-kernel corn
1 sliced large onion	About 2 teasp. salt
3 to 4 cups diced, pared potatoes	⅛ teasp. pepper
2 cups boiling water	1 qt. milk
	¼ teasp. paprika

In kettle, cook salt pork, stirring occasionally, until brown and crisp. Remove pork bits; keep warm. To pork fat, add onion; cook till tender; stirring occasionally. Add potatoes, boiling water; cover; simmer about 10 min., or until

potatoes are fork-tender. Add corn, salt, pepper, milk, pork bits. Heat well over low heat. Serve sprinkled with paprika. Pass crackers. Makes 6 servings.

To Vary: Add ¾ teasp. curry powder.

SUSAN'S FISH CHOWDER

¼ lb. salt pork	frozen haddock or cod fillets
3 sliced medium onions	
5 sliced or diced, pared medium potatoes	1 qt. milk, scalded
	1 cup undiluted evaporated milk
4 teasp. salt	
¼ teasp. pepper	3 tablesp. butter or margarine
3 cups boiling water	
1½ lb. fresh or thawed	Common crackers*

1. Cut pork into ½" cubes; cook in large kettle till brown; remove bits; reserve.
2. Add onions to pork fat; cook till tender. Add potatoes, salt, pepper, water.
3. Place fish, cut into medium-sized pieces, on top; cover; simmer 25 min., or until potatoes are tender. Remove any skin from fish.
4. Add milk, evaporated milk, butter, pork bits; heat. Arrange split crackers on top. Makes 6 servings.

* *Round crackers, especially for chowders.*

To Vary: Sprinkle a little nutmeg over chowder. Or substitute 3 tablesp. butter or margarine for salt pork.

SHRIMP CHOWDER

3 tablesp. fat	shrimp
3 sliced medium onions	1 qt. milk
1 cup boiling water	1 cup grated process American cheese (¼ lb.)
5 sliced, pared medium potatoes	
1 tablesp. salt	2 tablesp. snipped parsley
¼ teasp. pepper	
1 lb. cooked, cleaned	

In hot fat in kettle, sauté onions until tender; add water, potatoes, salt, pepper. Simmer, covered, 15 min., or until potatoes are tender. Add shrimp. Heat milk with cheese, stirring, until melted; add with parsley, to shrimp. Serve at once. Makes 4 hearty servings.

Shrimp-and-Fish Chowder: Substitute ½ lb. any white fish fillets, in large pieces, for part of shrimp. Add to onions with water, potatoes, and seasonings.

TUNA-CORN CHOWDER

2 cans solid-pack tuna (2 cups)	3 cups water
4 sliced medium onions	1 qt. milk
5 sliced, pared medium potatoes	1 pkg. thawed frozen whole-kernel corn
3½ teasp. salt	2 tablesp. butter or
⅛ teasp. pepper	margarine
	Fresh dill sprigs

Into Dutch oven or large kettle, drain oil from tuna. In oil, sauté onions till golden, stirring often. Add potatoes, salt, pepper, water; cook, covered, 15 min., or until tender. Add milk, corn, and tuna in large pieces. Heat. Float butter and dill on top. Makes 6 to 8 servings.

SPEEDY NEW ENGLAND CLAM CHOWDER

2 tablesp. diced salt pork	1 teasp. salt
3 tablesp. butter or margarine	⅛ teasp. pepper
¼ cup chopped onion	2 10½-oz. cans minced clams
1 cup boiling water	2½ cups scalded milk, or milk and cream
2 cups ¾" potato cubes	

Sauté salt pork in butter until golden and crisp. Add onion; cook until golden. Add water, potatoes, salt, pepper; cover; boil, stirring occasionally, 15 min., or until potatoes are soft.

Add clams with liquid; heat. Add milk; season to taste; then serve at once. Makes 6 servings.

BOSTON CLAM CHOWDER

3 doz. shucked raw soft-shell clams, with strained liquid	¼ teasp. celery salt
	¼ teasp. pepper
	2 teasp. salt
2 cups cold water	3 cups diced, pared potatoes
¼ lb. diced salt pork; or 2 tablesp. butter or margarine	3 cups scalded milk
	1½ teasp. salt
2 sliced medium onions	1 tablesp. butter or margarine
2 tablesp. flour	

1. Snip off necks of clams; cut fine with scissors; leave soft parts whole.
2. In saucepan, place clams (necks and soft parts) with liquid. Add water; bring to boil. Drain, reserving liquid and clams.
3. In large kettle, sauté salt pork until golden. Add onions; cook until tender.

4. Into onions, stir flour, celery salt, pepper, 2 teasp. salt, clam liquid, potatoes.
5. Cook, covered, 8 min., or until potatoes are tender. Add milk, clams, 1½ teasp. salt, butter.
6. Ladle into big soup bowls, or into mugs if you're serving out of doors. Makes 8 servings.

MANHATTAN CLAM CHOWDER

3 diced bacon slices	(3½ cups)
1 teasp. dried thyme	1½ cups diced, pared carrots
1 cup sliced onions	
3 cups cubed, pared potatoes	3 cups clam liquid
	2 doz. shucked raw hard-shell clams
½ cup diced celery	
5 cups hot water	1 tablesp. snipped parsley
2 teasp. salt	
⅛ teasp. pepper	½ teasp. dried thyme
1 No. 2½ can tomatoes	

1. In deep kettle, sauté bacon until crisp. Stir in 1 teasp. thyme and onions; cook, stirring occasionally, until tender.
2. Add potatoes, celery, water, salt, pepper. Simmer, covered, 5 min.
3. Add tomatoes, carrots, clam liquid (if you do not have 3 cups, add water to make up difference). Simmer, uncovered, over very low heat 1 hr.
4. Meanwhile, pick over clams to remove any shells. Cut clams into small pieces. Add to soup mixture, with parsley, ½ teasp. thyme.
5. Simmer, uncovered, 10 min. Add salt to taste. Makes 6 servings.

To Do Ahead: Make night before; refrigerate; heat next day.

PACIFIC-COAST CLAM CHOWDER

½ cup diced bacon, salt pork, or ham	style corn (optional)
	1 cup canned minced clams with liquid
1 minced small onion	
1 cup boiling water	½ teasp. salt
2 cups diced, pared potatoes	¼ teasp. pepper
	¼ teasp. celery salt
2 to 3 cups milk	Pinch dried thyme
½ cup canned cream-	(optional)

In large saucepan, lightly brown bacon. Add onion; cook until tender. Add water and potatoes; cook, covered, about 10 min., or until potatoes are fork-tender. Add milk, corn, clams, and rest of ingredients; heat. Makes 4 to 6 servings.

CLAM CHOWDER A LA HENRY

4 bacon slices, cut into bits	1 8-oz. can tomato sauce
2 minced medium onions	2 cups water
	2 10½-oz. cans minced clams
2 diced, pared medium potatoes	2 tablesp. flour
	3 tablesp. water

Fry bacon till crisp; pour off most of fat. Add onions; sauté till golden. Meanwhile, boil potatoes with tomato sauce, 2 cups water, and liquid from clams, covered, till tender; add bacon, onions.

Mix flour with 3 tablesp. water till smooth; stir into potato mixture. Cook till smooth and thickened—2 to 3 min. Add clams. Makes 4 servings.

PENNSYLVANIA CORN SOUP

1 3-lb. ready-to-cook roasting chicken, cut up	1 pkg. frozen green limas
1 qt. boiling water	1 pkg. frozen whole-kernel corn; or 2 cups corn off the cob, uncooked
1 chopped medium onion	
1 tablesp. salt	1 cup packaged biscuit mix
½ teasp. pepper	
1 No. 2 can tomatoes, drained	6 tablesp. cold water
	¼ cup snipped parsley

Place chicken in deep kettle. Add boiling water, onion, salt, pepper; simmer, covered, until chicken is tender—about 1½ hr. Remove chicken. To chicken broth, add drained tomatoes; simmer, covered. Meanwhile, remove chicken meat from bones; cut meat into small pieces; measure 1½ cups meat; add to chicken broth. Add limas, corn; simmer, covered, 20 min. Combine biscuit mix and cold water; drop by teaspoonfuls into hot soup; simmer, covered, 15 min. Garnish with parsley. Makes 4 generous servings.

To Do Ahead: After adding limas and corn and simmering soup 20 min., cool soup quickly; then refrigerate. To serve, bring to boil; then finish as above.

FROZEN SOUPS

Several delicious frozen condensed soups, including cream-of-potato soup, oyster stew, cream-of-shrimp soup, and fish chowder, are now available. To serve, just put can in warm water for 2 or 3 min.; then open; slide contents into saucepan; and add 1 can water or milk. Heat slowly to boiling point; then serve. Makes 2 or 3 hearty servings.

SWEDISH CABBAGE SOUP

1 tablesp. whole allspice	parsnips
2 lamb shanks (3 lb.)	1 cup sliced, pared carrots
2 beef-bouillon cubes	¼ cup snipped parsley
½ teasp. pepper	½ cup sliced celery
2 tablesp. salt	8 cups medium-shredded cabbage (2 qt.)
2 qt. water	
1 cup chopped leeks or onions	2 cups diced, pared potatoes
½ cup diced, pared	

Day before: Tie allspice in cheesecloth; place in kettle with shanks, bouillon cubes, pepper, salt, water. Simmer, covered, 2 hr. Refrigerate overnight.

About ½ hr. before dinner: Skim most of fat from top of soup. Remove meat from bones; cube. Bring broth to boil; remove allspice; add leeks, parsnips, carrots, parsley, celery. Simmer, covered, 10 min. Add cabbage, potatoes, meat; cook, covered, 20 min. Makes 6 hearty servings.

FISH MULLIGAN

3 diced bacon strips	cut into ¾″ cubes
3 sliced medium onions	¼ cup diced green pepper
1½ lb. fresh or thawed frozen cod or haddock fillets, cut into 2½″ pieces	4 teasp. salt
	¼ teasp. pepper
	3 cups boiling water
1½ lb. pared potatoes, cut into ¾″ cubes	1 No. 2½ can tomatoes (3½ cups)
½ teasp. celery seeds	2 tablesp. snipped parsley
3 pared large carrots,	

In deep kettle or Dutch oven, sauté bacon until lightly browned; remove bacon; set aside. In same kettle, sauté onions until tender. Add fish, potatoes, celery seeds, carrots, green pepper, salt, pepper, boiling water.

Simmer, covered, until vegetables are tender—about 25 min. Add tomatoes; heat. Garnish with parsley and bacon bits. Makes 6 servings.

Meats

The old American custom of serving lots of meat is a fine one. Few foods are a richer source of important food values, with fine flavor and good appetite satisfaction at the same time. These things are true of any meat if it's properly prepared, regardless of cut and grade—or whether it's cut to order, prepackaged fresh, quick-frozen, or canned. Use the recipes that follow and you can be sure of delectable meat and still make every meat penny count.

Before using these recipes, see How to Use Our Recipes, p. 3, and Pots and Pans, p. 692. Always use standard measuring cups and measuring spoons; measure level.

Busy-Day Meats

Busy-day dinners need be no problem if you make use of some of the speedy meat dishes included in these pages. Just check the lists in Quick-and-Easy Meals, p. 569.

Thrifty Meat Dishes

Many of the most delectable meat dishes in this chapter make use of less expensive meat cuts. So don't fail to review the list of some of these in Thrifty Meals, p. 560.

To Buy Meat

It takes an expert to judge the quality of meat just by looking at the color of the meat, the fat,

and the bone. So for most of us, it's safer to rely on a meat packer's brand or a Federal grade, to be sure of getting the quality we pay for.

First Check for Wholesomeness. All meat shipped in interstate commerce is Federally inspected. The round purple U.S. Inspected and Passed stamp on a cut of meat guarantees that the meat came from an animal judged wholesome by a Federal inspector and that the plant where it was processed passed sanitary regulations (Fig. A, p. 47). The stamp's purple dye is not harmful and need not be cut off the meat before cooking; usually, however, for the sake of appearance, you'll want to trim it off.

Then Look for the Packer's Brand Name. Several well-known meat packers stamp or burn on their own brands on better-quality beef, veal, lamb, and cured meats (Fig. C, p. 47). Fresh pork is seldom branded because there is less variation in the tenderness of this meat. Once you find the brand you like, stick to it.

The packer's brand on packaged and canned meats (bacon, ham, sausage, franks, etc.) indicates quality too.

Or Look for a Federal Grade. Some beef, veal, and lamb cuts carry a U.S.D.A. grade stamp to indicate quality. This shield-shaped stamp runs like a purple ribbon along the entire length of the carcass (Fig. B, p. 47).

Take beef as one example. The U.S.D.A. grades of beef are:

46

U.S.D.A. Prime: Highest grade. The supply is relatively limited.

U.S.D.A. Choice: Highest grade of beef commonly found and sold in volume in retail stores. The lean is usually bright red, firm, and velvety to the touch. It is well streaked (marbled) with little veins of fat, and has a thick, white or creamy white, firm fat covering. The meat is especially flavorsome and tender. (If the meat is aged or ripened by hanging in cold storage, the exterior lean turns a darker red and the meat becomes even juicier and more tender.)

U.S.D.A. Good: Still of excellent quality. Meat is a slightly darker red, has less fat and marbling, and somewhat thinner fat covering than U.S.D.A. Choice.

U.S.D.A. Commercial and U.S.D.A. Utility: Lower grades, with thin or very thin fat covering. These meats are lower priced and are usually better for pot-roasting and braising than for roasting.

To Store Meat

Fresh Meats:

1. If meat is wrapped in market paper, unwrap. Separate different kinds.
2. Do not wash meat; it keeps better if surface is not damp.
3. See that steaks, chops, cold cuts, and large pieces lie flat, not curled.
4. Then, with saran, waxed paper, foil, or the inner wrapping paper used by the meat dealer, *loosely* rewrap each kind, leaving ends open.
5. Keep prepackaged fresh meat in original wrapper, but loosen to allow circulation of air. Or follow label directions.
6. Store all fresh meats at once in coldest part of food compartment of refrigerator.

   Or if your refrigerator has a special meat compartment, you may store the meat unwrapped.
7. If you are unable to cook meat for the meal for which it was planned and you have a home freezer or refrigerator-freezer combination, freezer-wrap and freeze meat; then use any time up to one year. (See p. 533.)

   If you have no freezer, only the frozen-food compartment of a conventional refrigerator, you can keep freezer-wrapped meat in it 1 or 2 weeks.
8. If you lack freezing facilities, refer to the storage time guide on p. 48 for the maximum time meat may be kept in the food compartment of the refrigerator *for maximum flavor and eating pleasure.* However, this chart is only a general guide; many factors influence the length of time a meat can be kept satisfactorily. So use the meat you buy *as promptly as possible;* or freeze it as in step 7.

Cured and Smoked Meats: Today's prepackaged ham, bacon, and sausage should be refrigerated at once in their original wrapper. When removing some of the meat from the refrigerator, return the unused portion to the refrigerator at once, to retain freshness and maximum flavor.

  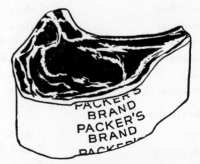

A U.S. Inspected and Passed Stamp **B** U.S.D.A. Grade Stamp **C** Packer's Brand Name

Canned Full-size Hams: These must be refrigerated as label very prominently directs.

Canned Small 1½-lb. Ham Pieces: These may be stored on pantry shelf.

Other Canned Meats: If they're not labeled "Keep in Refrigerator," they may be kept on pantry shelf.

Frozen Meats: These must be kept frozen at 0°F. or lower until ready to use.

Cooked Meats: Don't make the mistake of letting hot cooked, roasted, or leftover cooked meats stand out until cold before refrigerating them. This is a risky practice, which only invites food poisoning.

Either refrigerate the meat at once (this does not impair its flavor, despite old wives' tales), or cool meat quickly, then refrigerate at once. To hasten cooling of meat in broth, lift meat from broth to wire rack to cool; then cool kettle of broth in cold water in sink, changing water and stirring broth often. At end of ½ hr., no longer, refrigerate meat and broth at once.

In any case, *never* let cooked meat stand out of the refrigerator longer than 2 hr. And plan to use it up within 4 days.

STORAGE TIME GUIDE FOR MEATS

Kept in cold refrigerator at 36° to 40°F.

Meat (loosely covered)	Storage Limit for Maximum Quality
Uncooked Meats	
BEEF	
Corned beef	7 days
Hamburger	2 days
Pot roast	5 to 6 days
Standing rib roast	5 to 8 days
Steak	3 to 5 days
Stew meat	2 days
PORK (fresh)	
Chops	3 days
Pork sausage	2 to 3 days
Roast	5 to 6 days
Spareribs	3 days

HAM, BACON (cured pork)

Bacon	6 to 7 days
Half ham	7 days
Whole ham	2 weeks
Sliced ham	3 days
Picnic	2 weeks

LAMB

Chops	3 days
Roast	5 days
Shank	2 days
Stew meat	2 days

VEAL

Chops and steak	4 days
Roast	5 to 6 days
Stew meat	2 days

VARIETY MEATS

Brains	1 day
Heart	2 days
Kidney	1 day
Liver, sliced	2 days
Sweetbreads, cooked	2 days
Tongue, fresh	2 days
Tongue, smoked	7 days

Cooked Meats

FRANKS	4 to 5 days
HAM OR PICNIC	7 days
MEAT COOKED AT HOME	4 days

SLICED READY-COOKED MEATS

Dry sausage	1 to 2 weeks
Liver sausage	2 to 3 days
Luncheon meat	3 days
Meat loaves	3 to 4 days
Semidry sausage	7 to 8 days

UNSLICED READY-COOKED MEATS

Bologna	4 to 6 days
Dry and semidry sausage	2 to 3 weeks
Liver sausage	4 to 6 days
Meat loaves	4 to 6 days

LET'S HAVE BEEF

When you buy beef, look for the Federal U.S. Inspected and Passed stamp; then check for the packer's brand name or U.S.D.A. grade stamp, described in To Buy Meat, p. 46. Top-quality beef is bright red, with white, firm fat; in lower grades, the red deepens and the fat takes on a yellowish cast.

In the following pages, we suggest and describe favorite uses for many of the retail cuts of beef. Our diagram of the beef animal below will help you to identify these cuts better.

Rib Roast of Beef

Susan's way of roasting ribs of beef at a low temperature gives a tender, juicy, flavorful oven roast. There's little work involved, no spattering of fat, and a minimum amount of shrinkage. Yours can be just as good.

TO BUY AND STORE RIB ROAST

Rib oven roasts are among the finest, most tender, and highest-priced cuts of beef.

Select a Cut: There are usually 7 ribs in the rib section of beef from which the meat dealer cuts the 3 rib roasts below.

First-Rib Roast: This is the choicest and most tender rib roast. It comes from the short loin end of the rib section; the "rib eye" of solid tender meat predominates. In a few markets, it is known as eleventh-and-twelfth rib roast.

Center-Rib Roast: This roast, cut from the center of the rib section, is often priced lower than the first-rib roast and higher than the sixth-and-seventh rib roast. The "rib eye" of solid tender meat is somewhat less predominant in this cut than in the first-rib roast.

Sixth-and-Seventh Rib Roast: This roast, cut from the chuck (shoulder) end of the rib section, is likely to be the least tender and lowest priced of the 3 rib roasts. Its "rib eye" of solid, tender meat is the smallest of the 3 rib roasts.

Choose a Style: You can buy the rib roasts above in any of the 3 styles below:

Standing 10″ Rib Roast (Fig. A, p. 50) has 10″-long ribs, with backbone and small bones still on. A 2-rib standing rib roast, as pictured, weighs about 7 lb. If desired, the meatman can cut about 3″, or 1½ lb., from the rib ends to cook as short ribs or use in soup.

Standing 7″ Rib Roast (Fig. B, p. 50) has only 7″ ribs, because 3″ of the short ribs, plus backbone and small bones, have been cut off. A 2-rib standing rib roast, as pictured, weighs about 5 lb.

Rolled Rib Roast (Fig. C, p. 50) looked like the standing rib roast in Fig. A before it was boned, rolled, and tied, with the boned short

BEEF

ribs wrapped around the roast. It weighs about 6 lb.

Amount to Buy:

Standing Rib Roast: Buy at least a 2-rib roast. Allow ⅓ to ½ lb. bone-in roast per serving. Plan on leftovers. For easier carving, ask meat-man to cut along backbone so it can be removed easily after roasting.

Rolled Rib Roast: Buy at least a 4-lb. roast. Allow ¼ lb. boned roast per serving. Plan on leftovers.

Be sure to have the meat dealer mark the weight of the oven-ready roast on the bill to guide you in computing the roasting time.

To Store: Store as in To Store Meat, p. 47. Use within 5 to 8 days.

SUSAN'S RIB ROAST OF BEEF

1. Check roasting timetable, p. 51, to see about how long roasting will take. Plan so roast is done 20 min. before serving; it will slice more easily, and you will have time to make gravy.
2. Start heating oven to 325°F.
3. Do not wash roast. If necessary, wipe with damp cloth or paper towel.
4. If it's a standing rib roast, stand it on rib bones (Fig. A, p. 51) in shallow open pan. If it's a rolled rib roast, place on rack, with fat side up (Fig. B, p. 51). Fine roasts should never be covered; a cover holds in the steam and the meat acquires a steam-cooked, not true roast, flavor.

5. Never flour the roast; never add water. If desired, season with salt, pepper, and monosodium glutamate, or seasoned salt. But actually the salt will not penetrate the roast more than ¼″.
6. *Caution:* Roasts vary so in size, shape, amount of lean, bone, and fat, etc., that a roasting timetable can only be approximate at best. So use a roast-meat thermometer if you want to be sure that every roast is done just right. Such a thermometer indicates the interior temperature of the meat, and you can count on it to indicate when the roast is done to your liking.
7. Insert roast-meat thermometer carefully. To determine how deep meat thermometer should be inserted, place it against cut side of roast, with its point at center of roast. Note part of thermometer that is just even with top of roast. Make a hole for thermometer with skewer; then insert thermometer into center of roast up to that point. *Make sure* pointed end of thermometer does not rest on bone, fat, or gristle (Fig. A and B, p. 51).
8. Roast meat, using timetable, p. 51, as an approximate guide. Don't baste or turn. Let the roast-meat thermometer be your guide as to when the roast is rare, medium, or well done; but be sure to read the thermometer in the oven.
9. Sometimes during roasting, the meat thermometer moves out of its original position. Before removing roast from oven, you can check this by gently pressing top of thermometer; if it drops in temperature, you know the tip was not in the center of the roast. If this happens, continue to roast meat until right temperature is reached.

A   **Standing 10″ Rib Roast**   B   **Standing 7″ Rib Roast (with Short Ribs)**   C   **Rolled Rib Roast**

TIMETABLE FOR ROASTING
RIBS OF BEEF

Beef refrigerated till roasted at 325°F. Use shallow open pan. Add no water. Do not baste.

Oven-Ready Weight	Approximate Roasting Time	Meat Thermometer Reading
Standing Rib Roast		
4 lb.	1¾ hr.	140°F. (rare)
	2 hr.	160°F. (medium)
	2⅓ hr.	170°F. (well done)
6 lb.	2¼ hr.	140°F. (rare)
	2½ hr.	160°F. (medium)
	3⅓ hr.	170°F. (well done)
8 lb.	3 hr.	140°F. (rare)
	3½ hr.	160°F. (medium)
	4½ hr.	170°F. (well done)
Rolled Rib Roast		
4 lb.	2¼ hr.	140°F. (rare)
	2½ hr.	160°F. (medium)
	2¾ hr.	170°F. (well done)
6 lb.	3 hr.	140°F. (rare)
	3⅓ hr.	160°F. (medium)
	4 hr.	170°F. (well done)

For larger roasts, see p. 645.

10. When roast is done, remove to large heated platter, with broader cut surface resting on

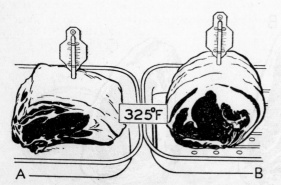

A—B Rib Roasts, Meat Thermometer in Place, Ready for Oven

platter; keep warm while making Susan's Velvety Meat Gravy, below, from drippings in pan.

To Serve: From roast, remove skewers, if any, but not string. If space permits, place one of vegetables around meat (don't crowd; let carver have plenty of room!). If it's a standing rib roast, set before host, with rib bones to his left and smaller rib ends pointing toward him, as on p. 163.

Pass gravy; Horse-radish Sauce I or II, p. 375; Worcestershire; or bottled thick meat sauce, p. 9. Pan-roasted Sweet Potatoes, p. 266, or Yorkshire Pudding, p. 329, are especially nice with rib roast.

If you're serving a rib roast cold, don't slice it hot. Refrigerate until serving time; then slice.

To Carve Rib Roast: See p. 163.

To Use Leftover Roast Beef: See p. 127 and Soup from Leftover Bones, p. 36.

SUSAN'S VELVETY MEAT GRAVY

¼ **cup fat drippings** **from roast**	¼ **cup flour** **Bottled sauce for**
2 **cups warm water** **(or cooking liquid** **from vegetables)**	**gravy, p. 9** **Salt and pepper**

1. When roast is done, keep warm on heated platter. Pour clear fat from roasting pan into bowl, leaving brown bits in pan. Measure ¼ cup of this clear fat; pour into skillet or saucepan.
2. *Pour 1 cup warm water into roasting pan; scrape and stir until all flavorful brown bits are loosened, heating mixture if necessary.
3. In skillet over medium heat, heat fat. Gradually add flour, stirring with broad spatula or spoon, until smooth and light brown. Then, stirring and scraping constantly, slowly add brown liquid in roasting pan plus 1 cup warm water.
4. Bring mixture in skillet to boiling point over medium heat; cook, stirring well, until as thick as heavy cream. Add enough bottled sauce for gravy to get just the rich color you want. Season to taste as on p. 6. If, in spite of all your care, gravy has lumps, strain.

5. If gravy must stand before serving, you may have to stir in a little water to bring it back to its right consistency. Makes about 2 cups.

If you're making gravy for meat cooked in a skillet, omit step 1 and 2; in step 3 use ¼ cup fat, and 2 cups warm water as liquid.

To Vary: Add 2 tablesp. minced chutney; ½ cup canned cranberry sauce, beaten smooth with fork; a few herbs; 2 tablesp. light cream; or a little sherry or Burgundy.

In-a-Pinch Gravy: If roast has no fat drippings, substitute butter or margarine. Use diluted canned condensed bouillon, or 2 beef-bouillon cubes dissolved in 2 cups water, as liquid; or use water plus meat-extract paste.

Pantry-Shelf Gravy: Use canned beef gravy; it's delicious. Or dilute canned condensed cream-of-mushroom soup with canned condensed consommé or bouillon. Add minced onion or chives if you wish. Nice for meat dishes.

Beef Tenderloin
(filet of beef)

Because it's always tender, cooks quickly, and is so easy to carve, beef tenderloin, the long muscle that lies just inside the rib bones, is excellent company fare.

TO BUY BEEF TENDERLOIN

For roasting, order a lower-quality grade of beef tenderloin so it will have less fat covering and, therefore, will brown well. Trim away most of fat from a top-quality tenderloin, as it prevents that luscious browning.

Amount to Buy: A whole beef tenderloin, stripped of fat and connective tissue, weighs about 4 to 6 lb. and makes 8 to 12 1″-thick servings. A half tenderloin (2 to 3 lb.) makes 4 to 6 1″-thick servings.

To Store: Store as in To Store Meat, p. 47. Use within 3 to 5 days.

ROAST BEEF TENDERLOIN

1. Start heating oven to 450°F. Remove surface fat and connective tissue from tenderloin. If desired, rub well all over with garlic. Or make several gashes in top surface of tenderloin; then insert piece of garlic in each gash (remove before serving).
2. Place tenderloin on rack in shallow open pan, tucking narrow end under to make roast uniformly thick. Brush with salad oil or bacon fat. Insert roast-meat thermometer into center of thickest part.
3. *Roast 4- to 6-lb. whole tenderloin* (with fat and tissue removed) about 45 to 60 min., or to 140°F. on roast-meat thermometer.

   Roast 2- to 3-lb. half tenderloin (with fat and tissue removed) about 45 to 50 min., or to 140°F. on meat thermometer. Meat should be crusty brown outside, pink to red inside.
4. Place tenderloin on heated platter. Keep warm while making Susan's Velvety Meat Gravy, p. 51, from drippings in pan. To

  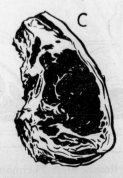

A   Filet Mignon   **B   Porterhouse Steak**   **C   Club Steak**

gravy, add ¼ lb. sautéed mushrooms and a little sherry. Pour some gravy over tenderloin; pass rest.

Or pass Quick Mushroom Sauce, p. 372, or Horse-radish Sauce I or II, p. 375. Fried onions are nice with tenderloin too.

All-American Steaks to Broil

TO BUY AND STORE STEAK TO BROIL

Because you want the most tender, top-quality steaks for broiling, ask for a packer's top brand or a top grade of beef (see To Buy Meat, p. 46). Choose one of steaks below, cut 1″ to 2″ thick.

Select a Cut:

Filet Mignon (Fig. A, p. 52): This boneless very tender, little steak is cut from the beef tenderloin (see p. 52). It is an expensive steak. A 1″-thick steak weighs 4 to 6 oz. Serve 1 thick, or 2 thin, steaks per person.

Porterhouse Steak (Fig. B, p. 52) (also called T-bone by some meatmen): This steak, from the loin end of the short loin, has a T-shaped bone and the largest portion of tenderloin. A 1½″-thick steak may weigh about 3 lb. and make 3 or 4 servings.

T-Bone Steak: This steak, from the center section of the short loin, looks like a Porterhouse but is smaller. It has a T-shaped bone and some tenderloin. A 1½″-thick steak may weigh about 1½ to 2 lb. and make 2 or 3 servings.

Club Steak (Fig. C, p. 52): This triangular steak, from the rib end of the short loin, is the smallest in the short loin and has no tenderloin. A 1″-thick steak may weigh about ½ to ¾ lb. and make 1 or 2 servings.

Boneless Loin Steak (Strip Steak) (Fig. D, below): This is a most desirable boneless loin steak with no tenderloin. However, it is not widely available. A 1″-thick steak weighs 8 to 10 oz. and makes 1 serving.

Rib Steak (sometimes called club): Sliced from the rib section, the best rib steaks are those from the loin end. A 1″-thick steak may weigh 12 to 14 oz. and makes 1 generous serving.

Sirloin Steak: A sirloin steak (full cut) is a nice buy for a family meal and is less expensive than the steaks above.

A steak from the round end of the sirloin section is the largest and is sometimes called a wedge bone (Fig. F, below). The steaks get

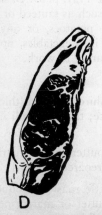

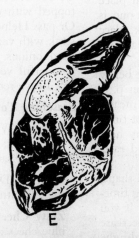

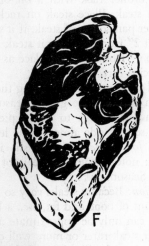

D Boneless Loin Steak (Strip Steak)	**E Sirloin Steak (Pinbone)**	**F Sirloin Steak (Wedge Bone)**

smaller as they near the short loin end; the smallest is sometimes called a pinbone (Fig. E, p. 53). A 1½″-thick sirloin steak, full cut, may weigh 3 to 4½ lb. and make 4 or 5 generous servings.

Amount to Buy: For each serving, order about ⅓ to ½ lb. boned steak, or ⅓ to ¾ lb. bone-in steak.

To Store: Store steak as in To Store Meat, p. 47. Use within 3 to 5 days. Keep frozen steaks frozen until time to cook, as label directs.

BROILED STEAK

1. Turn oven regulator to broil. If you have no oven regulator, turn broiler on full. Preheat broiler, with broiler pan in place, 10 min., or as manufacturer directs. Then, if you can, line broiler pan under rack with aluminum foil, with corners turned under, to catch drippings and save dishwashing.
2. Trim surplus fat from steak. If it's a very lean steak, like beef tenderloin, brush with salad oil.
3. With scissors or sharp knife, slash edge of fat at 2″ intervals, to keep steak from curling during broiling. If desired, rub steak with cut clove garlic; or spread lightly with prepared mustard or bottled sauce for gravy, p. 9.
4. Rub broiler rack with a bit of fat trimmed from steak. Place steak on rack. Then place broiler pan so top of steak, if it's a thin one, is about 2″ from heat. Or if steak is thick, place 3″ to 4″ from heat. Or place as manufacturer or recipe directs.
5. Broil steak on one side, using timetable below as an approximate guide. Season as on p. 6. Turn (use tongs to avoid piercing meat); broil second side almost same length of time.
6. *Test for Doneness:* Cut slit in meat near bone; note if color inside is of desired rareness. Season.
7. *Caution:* Because steaks vary so in size, shape, amount of bone and fat, etc., a broiling timetable can only be approximate at best. If you prefer steak rarer or more well done, decrease or increase broiling time below accordingly. Remember too that steak may continue to cook after you remove it from broiler.

TIMETABLE FOR BROILING STEAKS

Steaks refrigerated until broiled in preheated broiler

Thickness	Approximate Minutes per Side
Filet Mignon, Porterhouse, T-bone, Club, Rib, Pinbone Sirloin	
1″	5 min. (rare)
	6 min. (medium)
	7 to 8 min. (well done)
1½″	9 min. (rare)
	10 min. (medium)
	12 to 13 min. (well done)
2″	16 min. (rare)
	18 min. (medium)
	20 to 21 min. (well done)
Wedge-Bone and Other Large Sirloins	
1″	10 min. (rare)
	12 min. (medium)
	14 min. (well done)
1½″	12 min. (rare)
	14 min. (medium)
	16 min. (well done)

To Serve: Serve steak at once on heated platter, topped with one of Seasoning Touches, below. Or pass Help-Yourself Tray, p. 55. Or surround steak with vegetables such as sautéed or French-fried onions, mashed potatoes, or any of the wonderful vegetables in Vegetables, pp. 244 to 285. Leave room for carver to work.

Seasoning Touches:

Simple: Worcestershire; bottled thick meat sauce, p. 9; hot sauce; tabasco; chili sauce; or barbecue sauce

Buttery: Dab of butter or margarine. Or melted butter plus prepared mustard

Zesty Cheese: A little mashed Roquefort or blue cheese, some butter or margarine, and a few drops Worcestershire

Mushroom: Lots of sautéed mushrooms

Scallion Butter: Sliced scallions or snipped parsley in melted butter or margarine, with Worcestershire if you like

Lemon: Squeeze or two of lemon or lime juice

Smoky: Bit of powdered or liquid smoke

Wine Butter: Half-and-half Burgundy and melted butter or margarine

Help-Yourself Tray: Serve small bowls and pitchers filled with butter or margarine creamed with lemon juice; snipped chives; blue or Roquefort cheese; bottled thick meat sauce, p. 9; and barbecue sauce.

PLANKED BROILED STEAK

Use a special hardwood plank about 10″ x 15″ (available in housewares departments).

Cook 2 vegetables such as hot mashed potatoes, hot buttered peas, green beans, Brussels sprouts, slivered carrots, cauliflower. Broil steak (usually a T-bone) as on p. 54.

Meanwhile, heat plank in 400°F. oven. Arrange 2 hot buttered vegetables around edge of heated plank; place broiled steak in center. Spread steak with butter or Lemon Butter, p. 377; sprinkle with salt, pepper, and snipped parsley. Serve. (Plank may be set on platter or tray, or into special holder.)

MIXED GRILL

A mixed grill is a combination of meat, fish, or poultry with vegetables and maybe a fruit or two, broiled and served together. You'll find it a quick, easy, dishsaving main course. Check page references for broiling times.

1. *Choose 1 or 2 of these to broil:* steak, p. 54; hamburgers, p. 64; franks, p. 120; ham, p. 90; bacon, p. 93; kidneys, p. 116; lamb chops, p. 100; liver, p. 112; sweetbreads, p. 114; broiled fish, p. 172; broiled lobster, p. 187; broiled chicken, p. 138.
2. *Choose a vegetable or two, or a fruit, to broil:* mushrooms, p. 262; sweet potatoes, p. 265; tomatoes, p. 274; apple rings, p. 289; fresh peaches, p. 289; canned peaches, pears, or pineapple, p. 289; bananas, p. 289.

3. Preheat broiler 10 min., or as manufacturer directs. Grease broiler rack; then start broiling food that takes longest; add rest of food so that all will be done at same time, ready to be arranged and served on heated platter.

PAN-BROILED STEAK

T-bone, Club, Sirloin, or Rib Steak: Order steak cut ½″ to ¾″ thick. Rub skillet with just enough fat to keep meat from sticking; heat skillet. Rub steak with cut clove garlic if desired; place in skillet (do not cover or add water). Brown one side; turn; brown other side. Reduce heat; cook about 10 min. on each side, or till of desired doneness, turning steak to cook it evenly. Season as on p. 6.

Serve hot, with butter or margarine; Lemon Butter, p. 377; bottled thick meat sauce, p. 9; or barbecue sauce.

Minute or Cube Steaks: Minute steaks are thin steaks, ¼″ to ½″ thick, cut from the short loin or rib section.

Cube steaks are little, thin, not-so-tender steaks, such as round or chuck, that have been scored, "cubed," or "Frenched" by a special machine to cut the fibers and make the meat more tender.

Pan-broil either minute or cube steaks as above, cooking 2 to 3 min. on each side, or until done as you prefer them.

Season as on p. 6, and serve as above. Or to drippings left in skillet, add 2 tablesp. water for each steak. Heat, stirring, until rich in color. Pour over steaks. Nice between toasted, split rolls or toast slices, with or without thin sweet-onion slices.

CUBE STEAKS WITH HASTY-TASTY SAUCE

Buy 4 small cube steaks (about 1 lb.); see Minute or Cube Steaks, above. Sprinkle with 1 teasp. salt, ⅛ teasp. pepper, 3 tablesp. flour. In 3 tablesp. hot fat in skillet, brown steaks quickly on both sides. Remove.

To fat left in skillet, add 1 teasp. dry mustard; 1 teasp. Worcestershire; 3 tablesp. chili sauce or catchup; 2 tablesp. fresh, frozen, or canned lemon juice. Heat till boiling, stirring. Spoon over steaks. Serve at once. Makes 4 servings.

BEEF STROGANOFF

3 tablesp. flour
1½ teasp. salt
¼ teasp. pepper
1 lb. beef tenderloin,
   ¼″ thick
1 cut clove garlic
¼ cup butter or
   margarine
½ cup minced onions

¼ cup water
1 can undiluted con-
   densed chicken soup
1 lb. sliced mushrooms
1 cup commercial sour
   cream
Snipped parsley, chives,
   or dill

Combine flour, salt, pepper. Trim fat from meat. Rub both sides of meat with garlic. With rim of saucer, pound flour mixture into both sides of meat. Cut meat into 1½″ x 1″ strips.

In hot butter in Dutch oven or deep skillet, brown meat strips, turning them often. Add onions; sauté till golden. Add water; stir to dissolve brown bits in bottom of Dutch oven. Add soup, mushrooms; cook, uncovered, over low heat, stirring occasionally, until mixture is thick and meat is fork-tender—about 20 min.

Just before serving, stir in sour cream; heat, but do not boil. Sprinkle with parsley.

Serve with hot fluffy rice or wild rice, boiled noodles, or mashed potatoes. Makes 4 to 6 servings.

Steaks to Braise

Browning, then long slow simmering in a little water (braising), develops tenderness in less-tender beef steaks and other small or thin cuts of beef just as it does in pot roasts.

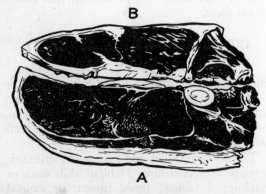

A   **Top Round Steak**
B   **Bottom Round Steak**

TO BUY AND STORE STEAK TO BRAISE

Select a Cut:

Round Steak: This popular, oval-shaped steak with its small, round bone is usually sold as one cut; but sometimes it is cut into top round and bottom round.

   Top Round (Fig. A, below) is the more tender part of round steak. (If it's of top quality, it may even be pan-broiled.) A good layer of fat, and streaks of fat in the lean, indicate better-quality meat. A 1″-thick steak weighs 2 to 3 lb.

   Bottom Round (Fig. B, below) is the less tender part of round steak. It's usually cut ½″ thick, though it may be cut thicker for Swiss steak. It may also be cut into smaller steaks, or cubed. A ½″-thick steak weighs about 12 oz.

Rump Steak: This steak, from a rump pot roast, p. 58, is usually boned. A ½″-thick steak weighs 5 to 6 oz.

Flank Steak: See Flank Steak, p. 57.

Sirloin-Tip Steak: This steak, from a sirloin-tip roast, is lean and boneless. A ½″-thick steak weighs 5 to 6 oz.

Chuck Steak: This steak is cut from a chuck pot roast, p. 58, and may have a round bone or be boned. A ½″-thick steak weighs 8 to 12 oz.

Amount to Buy: Allow ¼ to ⅓ lb. boned steak per serving.

To Store: Store as in To Store Meat, p. 47. Use within 3 to 5 days.

BRAISED STEAK

Season one of steaks above as on p. 6; dip into flour to coat lightly. In 1 or 2 tablesp. hot fat or meat drippings in skillet, brown steak *well* on both sides, turning with tongs—about 15 to 20 min.

Then add ½ to 1 cup water, tomato juice, or seasoned diluted vinegar, amount depending on

size of steak. Cook slowly on top of range or in 350°F. oven, covered, until steak is fork-tender —45 min. to 2 or 3 hr., depending on thickness of steak. Replenish water if necessary. When done, remove steak to heated platter.

Serve with gravy from pan. Or make more gravy by adding water and beef-bouillon cube (or canned bouillon) to gravy in pan. Thicken as on p. 7; season if needed. Nice with boiled or mashed potatoes and colorful vegetables.

To Vary: With water, add sliced onion or celery, diced fresh or canned tomatoes, chili sauce, chili powder, or horse-radish. Or during last half hour of cooking, add a few sliced carrots, potatoes, turnips, etc.

SWISS STEAK

1½ lb. round or rump steak, 1½" thick	3 thinly sliced large onions
2 tablesp. flour	1 diced stalk celery
1 teasp. salt	1 minced clove garlic
⅛ teasp. pepper	1 tablesp. bottled thick meat sauce, p. 9
2 tablesp. salad oil or fat	¼ cup light or dark raisins (optional)
1½ cups canned tomatoes	

1. Trim excess fat from meat. Combine flour, salt, pepper. Lay meat on board; sprinkle with half of flour mixture; with rim of saucer, pound in mixture. Turn meat; repeat until all flour is used.
2. In hot oil in heavy skillet or Dutch oven over medium heat, brown meat *well* on both sides —about 15 to 20 min.
3. Add rest of ingredients. Stir well. Simmer, covered, about 2 to 2½ hr., or until meat is fork-tender. Skim off fat if necessary.

Serve on heated platter, with sauce over and around meat. Nice with mashed potatoes, boiled noodles, or hot fluffy rice, etc. Makes 4 servings.

To Vary: Substitute canned tomato sauce or vegetable-juice cocktail for tomatoes; thicken sauce as desired; season to taste.

Or substitute 1½ cups boiling water, 2 tablesp. catchup, and ½ teasp. prepared mustard for tomatoes; thicken sauce as desired.

Or during last half hour of cooking, add diced carrots or celery, or canned peas or corn.

P.S. Swiss steak is nice reheated next day.

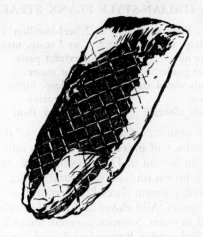

Flank Steak

Flank Steak

This thin, boneless, less tender steak from the beef flank (Fig. above) is about 12" to 14" long, 4" to 6" wide, and 1" thick; it weighs 1 to 2 lb.

Top-quality flank steak has a good portion of fat and is fine for London Broil, below. Braise leaner, low-quality flank steak as in Braised Steak, p. 56.

LONDON BROIL

Order 2½-lb. aged, top-quality flank steak; it *must* be tender. Have excess fat and membrane trimmed, and surface scored on both sides.

Preheat broiler 10 min., or as manufacturer directs. Arrange scored flank steak on greased broiler rack. If desired, rub with cut clove garlic. Brush with salad oil.

Place steak 1½" to 2" below heat; broil just 5 min. on each side. Then place on heated platter. Season as on p. 6; top with butter or margarine. Cut, diagonally across grain, into *very thin* slices. Pass mushroom sauce. Nice too for hot grilled beef sandwiches.

Blue-Cheese Topped: Refrigerate flank steak 8 to 24 hr. in mixture of 1 cup salad oil, 2 tablesp. vinegar, 1 mashed clove garlic, turning steak 2 or 3 times. Remove from oil; then broil as above. During last few minutes, spread with some blue-cheese spread.

ITALIAN-STYLE FLANK STEAK

1 2-lb. flank steak	2 beef-bouillon cubes;
2 tablesp. salad or	or 2 teasp. meat-
olive oil	extract paste
1 clove garlic	1 cup water
1 thinly sliced small	1 tablesp. butter or
lemon	margarine
4 whole cloves	1 tablesp. flour

Order steak scored at ¼″ intervals, ⅛″ deep, on
both sides. Cut into 2 pieces so it fits into Dutch
oven. In hot oil in Dutch oven, sauté steak till
golden brown on both sides; add garlic.

Arrange lemon slices between and on top of
steak pieces. Add cloves and bouillon cubes dissolved in water. Simmer, covered, about 2 hr., or
until fork-tender. Remove steak and lemon slices
to platter. Drain off pan juices—about 1 cup.
Melt butter in Dutch oven; stir in flour till
smooth. Slowly stir in pan juices. Simmer, stirring, till thickened; serve with steak. Nice with
buttered broad noodles. Makes 6 servings.

BRAISED, STUFFED FLANK STEAK

1 1½-lb. flank steak	1 tablesp. fat or salad
2 cups fresh bread	oil
crumbs	1 cup hot water
¼ cup minced onion	½ teasp. whole black
1 tablesp. snipped	peppers
parsley	1 teasp. garlic wine
½ teasp. salt	vinegar (optional)
⅛ teasp. pepper	1 cup hot water
½ teasp. celery salt	1 beef-bouillon cube
½ teasp. dried sage	¼ cup flour
1 tablesp. butter or	6 tablesp. cold water
margarine	

Have meatman score one side of steak in diamond pattern. Combine crumbs, onion, parsley,
salt, pepper, celery salt, sage; arrange on un-
scored side of steak, patting it till it nearly
reaches edges. Dot with butter. Roll up, jelly-
roll-fashion; secure with skewers or string.

In hot fat in Dutch oven, brown steak *well* on
both sides—about 15 to 20 min. Add 1 cup hot
water, whole peppers; sprinkle with vinegar.
Simmer, covered, 2 hr., or until fork-tender. Remove peppers; arrange steak on heated platter;
remove skewers.

Into liquid in Dutch oven, stir 1 cup hot water
and bouillon cube, then flour mixed with cold
water to form smooth paste. Cook until thickened. Season if needed. Makes 6 servings.

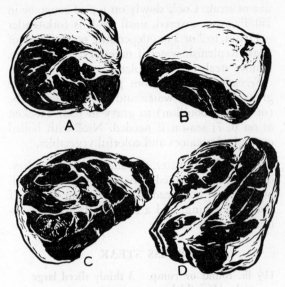

A   Boned Rump Pot Roast
B   Sirloin-Tip Pot Roast
C   Chuck (Arm or Round-
     Bone) Pot Roast
D   Chuck (Blade-
     bone) Pot Roast

Pot Roasts of Beef

Browning, then long, slow simmering in a little
water (braising), with or without vegetables,
turns less tender cuts of beef into fork-tender pot
roasts of wonderful flavor.

TO BUY AND STORE POT ROAST

You don't need to buy top-quality beef, but a
piece with a good fat covering and streaks of fat
through the lean will be juicier than a lean roast.
Here are 4 fine cuts to choose from:

Select a Cut:

Boned Rump Pot Roast (Fig. A, above): An
excellent meaty pot roast cut from the hip. (If
bone is left in, roast is too difficult to carve.)
Weighs 4 to 5 lb.

Sirloin-Tip Pot Roast (Fig. B, above): A good
meaty pot roast from side of the round; it may
lack fat covering. Have it boned, rolled, and
tied. Weighs 3 to 4 lb.

Chuck (Arm or Round-Bone) Pot Roast (Fig. C, p. 58): A fine meaty pot roast from the shoulder, with small round bone and 2 or 3 patches of fat. A 1½″-thick piece weighs 4 to 5 lb.

Chuck (Bladebone) Pot Roast (Fig. D, p. 58): A moderate-priced pot roast from the shoulder. Has 1 long bone and 2 or 3 smaller bones, plus 3 or 4 patches of fat. A 1½″-thick piece weighs 5 to 6 lb. May be boned and sold as boned pot roast.

Amount to Buy: Allow ⅓ lb. bone-in pot roast per serving, ¼ lb. boned roast per serving. Plan on leftovers.

To Store: Store as in To Store Meat, p. 47. Use within 5 or 6 days.

TO COOK POT ROAST

3 tablesp. fat or salad oil	¼ teasp. pepper
4- to 5-lb. boned rump pot roast *	1 tablesp. water
2 teasp. salt	1 sliced small onion
	Pinch dill seeds

1. In hot fat in Dutch oven or heavy kettle over medium heat, brown meat *well* on all sides, turning it as it browns and sprinkling it with some of salt and pepper. This may take 15 to 20 min.
2. Add water, onion, dill seeds. Cover tightly; simmer, *don't boil,* over low heat, turning it occasionally to cook it evenly throughout, about 4 to 4½ hr.,* or until fork-tender. If needed, add a few tablespoonfuls of hot water during cooking.
3. When meat is done, remove it to heated platter; keep warm.
4. Make gravy as follows: Skim fat from broth in Dutch oven. To broth, add water to make 2 or 3 cups liquid. Heat; thicken as on p. 7; season if needed.

To serve: Let host carve pot roast; or serve it sliced. Pass gravy in bowl. Mashed or boiled potatoes; Potato Pancakes, p. 270; or Poppy or Caraway Noodles, p. 238, are especially nice with pot roast. Pass Worcestershire, horse-radish, mustard, or chili sauce. Serves a family of 4 for 2 meals.

* *If you use a 3-lb. bone-in pot roast, 2″ thick, simmer about 2½ to 3 hr. If you use a 5-lb. bone-in pot roast, 3″ thick, simmer about 3½ to 4 hr.*

Oven Style: Use Dutch oven. Increase water to 1 cup. Bake, covered, at 350°F., adding water, if needed, to keep about ½″ liquid in Dutch oven.

With Chili Sauce: About 45 min. before pot roast is done, add 3 sliced medium onions, 1¼ cups chili sauce, and ½ cup chopped dill pickles. Don't thicken broth in kettle; just skim off fat; thin broth with a little water if it seems too thick. Season.

Curry: Add 3½ teasp. curry powder and ½ teasp. sugar with salt and pepper in step 1.

With Vegetables: About 50 min. before meat is done, add 2 cups white onions, 8 pared small carrots, and 6 to 8 pared small potatoes. Sprinkle with 1 teasp. salt; cook, covered, until vegetables are tender-crisp. Or substitute 1 lb. green beans for onions, adding them ½ hr. before vegetables are done. Serve vegetables around pot roast.

Spicy: About 45 min. before meat is done, add 1 minced clove garlic; 1 sliced, pared carrot; a few sprigs parsley; 8 whole black peppers; ¼ teasp. ginger; 1 bay leaf; 3 whole cloves; ⅛ teasp. allspice; ¼ cup vinegar. Simmer, covered, 45 min., or until tender. Remove meat; strain liquid; make gravy.

With Wine: After browning meat in step 1, add 1 minced clove garlic, pinch dried thyme, 1 bay leaf, ¼ cup red wine. When making gravy, substitute ½ cup red wine for ½ cup water.

To Use Leftover Pot Roast: See p. 127.

SAUERBRATEN

1½ cups vinegar	1½ teasp. salt
½ cup red wine	Speck pepper
1 cup water	¼ cup fat
2 tablesp. sugar	1 sliced onion
½ teasp. whole black peppers	½ teasp. mustard seeds
4 bay leaves	6 whole cloves
3 sliced onions	½ teasp. whole black peppers
12 whole cloves	⅓ cup gingersnap crumbs
1 teasp. mustard seeds	½ cup commercial sour cream *
2 teasp. salt	Salt and pepper
4 lb. boned rump or chuck pot roast	
2 tablesp. flour	

Two to four days before serving: In large bowl, make this marinade: Combine first 10 ingredients. Set meat in marinade; refrigerate, covered, 2 to 4 days, turning meat each day. (If you like a sour sauerbraten, let meat stand 4 days.)

The day: Remove meat, reserving marinade; dry meat *well* on paper towels. Combine flour, 1½ teasp. salt, speck pepper; use to coat meat on all sides. In hot fat in Dutch oven, brown meat well on all sides—about 15 to 20 min. Add ¾ cup reserved marinade, 1 sliced onion, ½ teasp. mustard seeds, 6 cloves, ½ teasp. whole peppers. Simmer, covered, about 3½ to 4 hr., or until meat is fork-tender, adding ¼ cup marinade if needed.

Remove meat to hot platter, slicing it first if desired; keep warm. Strain drippings from Dutch oven into glass measuring cup; let stand 2 min. to settle. Pour off all except bottom ⅓ cup drippings; return these to Dutch oven. Stir in crumbs. Slowly stir in 2 cups strained, reserved marinade (add water if necessary). Cook, stirring, until thickened.

Stir in sour cream; heat, *but do not boil*. Season if necessary. Spoon some gravy over meat; pass rest. Makes 8 to 10 servings.

* *Or use ½ 3-oz. pkg. cream cheese, beaten smooth with ⅓ cup milk.*

MORAVIAN BEEF WITH GRAVY

1 teasp. dried sage or poultry seasoning	3 tablesp. lemon juice
½ teasp. dried thyme	4 lb. boned chuck pot roast
1 teasp. salt	2 tablesp. fat or salad oil
½ teasp. pepper	
2 teasp. whole cloves	7 quartered, pared medium carrots
1 teasp. ground allspice	1 sliced medium onion
2 crumbled bay leaves	6 medium white onions
2 cans undiluted condensed beef bouillon	6 halved, pared medium potatoes
2 tablesp. grated lemon rind	⅓ cup commercial sour cream

Day before: In saucepan, make this marinade: Combine sage, thyme, salt, pepper, cloves, allspice, bay leaves, bouillon, lemon rind and juice. Heat, but do not boil; pour over meat in bowl. Cool. Refrigerate 24 hr., turning beef several times.

The day: Remove meat from marinade. To hot fat in Dutch oven or heavy kettle, add meat, 1 carrot, sliced onion; brown meat well on all sides—about 15 to 20 min. Add marinade; simmer, covered, 2 hr. Add rest of carrots, 6 onions, potatoes; simmer, covered, 1 hr., or until all are fork-tender.

Remove meat and vegetables to serving platter; keep warm. Strain liquid in Dutch oven; then measure. Thicken as on p. 7. Then stir in sour cream gradually; *do not boil*. Serve immediately. Makes 6 servings.

Beef Short Ribs

TO BUY BEEF SHORT RIBS

Beef short ribs (Fig. B, p. 50) are like baby pot roasts. They are cut off the ends of standing rib roasts, then into 2″ squares. Each square is streaked with lean meat and fat, and has a piece of rib bone on one side; each piece weighs 4 to 6 oz.

Amount to Buy: Allow 1 or 2 pieces per serving.

To Store: Store as in To Store Meat, p. 47. Use within 2 days.

SWEDISH BRAISED SHORT RIBS

1 tablesp. butter or margarine	½ teasp. whole allspice
3 lb. beef short ribs (cut into 4 serving pieces)	2 bay leaves
	1 cup hot water
	¼ cup cold water
1 sliced medium onion	1 tablesp. flour
1 teasp. salt	2 tablesp. heavy cream
¼ teasp. white pepper	1 teasp. sugar
1 teasp. sugar	

Heat Dutch oven until very hot; add butter, then meat. Cook over high heat until meat is very well browned on all sides. Add onion; with fork, push down into fat around meat; cook a minute or so, or until browned. Now add salt, pepper, 1 teasp. sugar, allspice, bay leaves, hot water. Simmer, covered, 1½ to 2 hr., or until fork-tender.

Remove meat to heated platter and keep hot. Skim about ¼ cup fat from liquid in Dutch oven. Stir cold water into flour; slowly add, stirring, to liquid; cook until thickened. Stir in cream and 1 teasp. sugar; bring to boil once; pour over meat; serve at once.

Especially nice with buttered carrots, green beans, and dill potatoes (make parsley potatoes, adding snipped fresh dill instead of parsley). Makes 4 servings.

BARBECUED SHORT RIBS

Order 3 lb. beef short ribs, cut into 2″ squares. Brush with 1 tablesp. bottled sauce for gravy, p. 9. Brown well in 2 tablesp. fat in Dutch oven; remove.

In same fat, sauté 2 min. 1 minced clove garlic and ½ cup each minced onions and celery. Stir in 2 tablesp. cornstarch, 1 8-oz. can tomato sauce, ½ cup water, 1 teasp. salt, ⅛ teasp. each pepper and ground allspice, 1 tablesp. each prepared mustard and vinegar; then add meat. Simmer, covered, 1½ to 2 hr., or until fork-tender. Makes 4 servings.

Pressure-Cooked: See p. 195.

Grilled: See Barbecued Short Ribs, p. 595.

Beef Stews, Curries, Meat Pies, etc.

If you would win a reputation as a cook, serve Susan's Brown Beef Stew, below. Slow, thorough browning, plus unhurried simmering with savory seasonings and colorful vegetables, bring out the meat's flavor and succulent tenderness. And the stew is almost nicer the second day!

TO BUY AND STORE BEEF FOR STEWS, etc.

Select a Cut: You may be able to buy "stew beef" in 1″ to 2″ pieces of boned meat, cut from less tender, but flavorful, cuts of beef. But be sure the beef is bright red, with white fat.

Or you may prefer to buy a piece of beef you can identify, such as one of those below, and cut it up yourself.

Chuck: This cut from the shoulder, p. 56, makes a fine stew. Costs more than some other cuts.

Bottom Round: This less tender part of the round is boneless, lean, and fine-flavored.

Neck Meat: This may be sold as boned or bone-in stew meat. It needs long cooking to become tender.

Shank Meat: This lean, flavorful meat has considerable connective tissue. It requires long cooking for tenderness. Some cuts may contain too much bone for a good stew.

Flank, Plate, Fresh Brisket: Order these low-priced cuts boned. Avoid pieces that are too fatty.

Amount to Buy: Allow 1 lb. boned beef for 4 to 6 servings.

To Store: Store as in To Store Meat, p. 47. Use within 2 days.

SUSAN'S BROWN BEEF STEW

⅓ cup flour	bouillon cubes
¼ teasp. pepper	½ teasp. salt
½ teasp. celery salt	½ teasp. Worcester-
1¾ lb. boned chuck	shire
or bottom round,	1 doz. small white
cut into 1½″ cubes	onions
¼ cup fat or salad oil	1 doz. pared small
¼ cup minced onion	carrots, whole or
1 minced clove garlic	halved lengthwise
(optional)	½ pkg. frozen peas
3¾ cups boiling water	5 hot boiled potatoes
4 teasp. meat-extract	Snipped parsley
paste; or 4 beef-	

1. In bowl, combine flour, pepper, celery salt. Drop in meat, a few pieces at a time; toss until well coated. Reserve leftover flour.
2. In hot fat in Dutch oven or deep kettle, slowly brown floured meat, a few pieces at a time, on all sides—15 to 20 min. Remove pieces as they brown.
3. To fat in Dutch oven, add minced onion, garlic; simmer until just tender. Stir in reserved flour until blended.
4. Slowly stir in boiling water, meat-extract paste, salt, Worcestershire. Add meat. Simmer, covered, over low heat about 2 hr., or until meat is fork-tender.
5. Add whole onions, carrots; simmer, covered, about 15 min. Add peas; simmer, covered, about 5 min., or until vegetables are tender.
6. Meanwhile, mash and season potatoes as on p. 6.

Serve stew right in Dutch oven or turn into casserole. Heap potatoes in ring on top of stew. Or serve stew on heated platter with vegetables heaped around it. Sprinkle with parsley. Makes 4 to 6 luscious servings.

To Vary: Substitute canned tomato sauce for part of water. Corn may replace peas.

Or in place of potatoes, make Dumplings for Stew, p. 151. Or serve stew in ring of boiled noodles.

Or make Rice Ring, p. 234. Fill center with meat from stew; group vegetables from stew around it.

Or substitute ½ to 1 cup Burgundy wine for equal amount of water.

Or substitute ½ lb. sliced mushrooms for carrots.

▶ **For 2:** Serve Susan's Brown Beef Stew one day. Use leftovers to make this meat pie: Place heated leftovers in greased 1-qt. casserole; top with ½ recipe Susan's Hot Baking-Powder Biscuits, p. 323. Bake at 450°F. 20 to 25 min., or until biscuits are done.

Irish Stew: Make stew, omitting flouring and browning of meat.

Quick: Try canned beef stew. It's delicious!

Beef Pie: Turn Susan's Brown Beef Stew, or any heated leftover stew, into casserole; top with any Flaky Pastry, pp. 407 to 410, or Susan's Hot Baking-Powder Biscuit dough, p. 323, rolled ⅛" to ¼" thick. Bake at 450°F. 20 to 25 min., or until done.

OVEN BEEF STEW

2 lb. boned chuck or bottom round, in 2" cubes	2½ cups tomato juice or water
¼ cup flour	12 small white onions
3 tablesp. salad oil	12 pared small carrots, quartered lengthwise
1 teasp. monosodium glutamate	
1 teasp. salt	1 pkg. frozen whole-kernel corn, thawed just enough to separate
3 tablesp. prepared mustard	

Start heating oven to 350°F. Sprinkle meat with flour. Reserve leftover flour. In hot oil in skillet, brown meat well on all sides—15 to 20 min. Remove meat to 3-qt. casserole.

Into oil, stir monosodium glutamate, salt, mustard, any remaining flour. Slowly add tomato juice, stirring constantly; then pour over meat. Bake, covered, 1 hr. Add onions and carrots. Bake, covered, 45 min. Add corn. Bake, covered, 15 min., or until vegetables are tender. Before serving, stir stew with fork to bring meat chunks to top. Makes 6 servings.

To Vary: Add 12 pared small potatoes with carrots; substitute peas for corn.

Lamb Stew: For beef, substitute 2 lb. boned lamb shoulder, with as much fat trimmed off as possible. Increase flour to 5 tablesp. Before stirring stew to serve it, spoon off any fat that may have risen to surface during cooking.

Veal Stew: Substitute 2 lb. boned veal shoulder for beef, 1 to 1½ cups white wine for 1 to 1½ cups tomato juice, ½ lb. mushrooms for corn. Use 5 tablesp. flour.

BEEF CURRY DELICIOUS

1 tablesp. flour	2 cups sliced onions
1⅛ teasp. salt	½ minced clove garlic
⅛ teasp. pepper	1 teasp. curry powder
1 lb. round, cut into ¾" cubes	1 beef-bouillon cube
	1 cup boiling water
¼ cup fat or salad oil	½ cup tomato juice

Combine flour, salt, pepper; roll meat in flour mixture. In 2 tablesp. hot fat in skillet or Dutch oven, brown meat well on all sides. Add rest of fat, onions, garlic; sauté until light brown. Sprinkle with curry powder; add bouillon cube, water.

Simmer, covered, 1¼ hr., or till meat is fork-tender. Add tomato juice; reheat.

Serve on hot fluffy rice, or with mashed or boiled potatoes. Pass Curry Accompaniments, p. 193. Makes 4 servings.

To Do Ahead: Day before or early in day, prepare and cook curry till tender as above. Refrigerate. At serving time, add tomato juice; reheat; serve as above.

Lamb Curry II or Veal Curry II: For beef, substitute boned lamb or veal shoulder or breast.

DANISH GOULASH

1 lb. round, ¼" thick	2½ cups cold water
3 tablesp. salad oil	1 tablesp. brown sugar
Speck pepper	3 small bay leaves
¾ cup very thinly sliced onions	3 tablesp. flour
2 teasp. salt	5 tablesp. cold water

Cut meat into ¼″ cubes; brown well in hot oil with pepper. Add onions; stir until light brown. Add salt, 2½ cups water, sugar, bay leaves. Simmer, covered, 1¼ hr., or until fork-tender. Remove bay leaves. Then stir in flour mixed with 5 tablesp. water till smooth. Cook until smooth and thickened.

Serve over Mashed Potatoes à la Phyfe, p. 268, or boiled noodles or rice. Makes 4 servings.

HUNGARIAN GOULASH

3 tablesp. butter or margarine	1½ lb. boned chuck, rump, or round, cut into 1″ cubes
3 cups thinly sliced onions	
	4½ teasp. paprika
2¼ teasp. salt	About 3 cups water
1½ teasp. paprika	

In hot butter in Dutch oven or deep kettle, sauté onions with salt until golden. Stir in well 1½ teasp. paprika, meat; simmer, covered, 1 hr. Add 4½ teasp. paprika and enough water to just cover meat. Simmer, covered, 1 hr., or until meat is fork-tender, adding more water toward end of cooking time if you want extra gravy.

Serve with boiled noodles; Poppy or Caraway Noodles, p. 238; mashed potatoes; or hot fluffy rice. Makes 4 or 5 servings.

To Vary: During last half hour of cooking, add 4 quartered, pared medium potatoes, with a little water if needed. Omit noodles.

SAVORY MEAT PIE

1¼ lb. boned chuck, rump, or round, cut into 1½″ cubes	salad oil
	½ teasp. bottled thick meat sauce, p. 9
¼ cup flour	12 small white onions
¾ teasp. salt	5 pared medium carrots, cut into large pieces
⅛ teasp. pepper	
¼ teasp. celery salt	
2 beef-bouillon cubes	Susan's Hot Baking-Powder Biscuit dough, p. 323
2¼ cups boiling water	
¼ cup bacon fat or	

1. Trim fat and gristle from meat. On waxed paper, mix flour, salt, pepper, celery salt; roll meat in flour mixture until well coated on all sides. Reserve leftover flour mixture.
2. Dissolve bouillon cubes in boiling water.
3. In hot bacon fat in deep kettle or Dutch oven, brown meat well on all sides—15 to 20 min.
4. Add leftover flour mixture, bouillon, meat sauce; stir until blended. Simmer, covered, 2 hr. Add onions; cook, covered, 10 min. Add carrots; cook, covered, 15 min., or until tender.
5. Meanwhile, start heating oven to 450°F. Make Susan's Hot Baking-Powder Biscuit dough, increasing shortening to ½ cup. Roll ½″ thick. With doughnut cutter, cut into rounds.
6. Turn stew into greased 2-qt. casserole. Arrange biscuit rounds on top; brush with milk or light cream.
7. Bake, uncovered, 20 to 25 min., or until biscuits are done. Makes 4 servings.

▶ **For 2:** Halve ingredients; use greased 1-qt. casserole. If needed, add ½ to ¾ cup water with vegetables.

To Vary: Just before arranging biscuit rounds, sprinkle meat mixture with ⅓ cup uncooked frozen peas. Or with onions, add ¼ lb. quartered mushrooms. Or for part of boiling water, substitute tomato juice or tomato sauce with a little dry mustard, a few cut-up tomatoes, or a little garlic added.

P.S. There are fine quick-frozen meat pies too.

BOILED BEEF WITH HORSE-RADISH SAUCE

3 qt. boiling water	2 tablesp. sugar
1 bay leaf	2 teasp. salt
6 whole cloves	4 lb. fresh beef brisket
2 cloves garlic	Horse-radish Sauce I or II, p. 375; or Caper Sauce, p. 372
1 small onion	
2 stalks celery	
2 tablesp. vinegar	

In large kettle or Dutch oven, combine all ingredients except meat, sauce; simmer, covered, 30 min. Add meat; simmer, covered, 3½ to 4 hr., or until fork-tender, replenishing water if needed. When meat is done, remove; slice; arrange on heated platter. Pass sauce.

Serve with boiled new potatoes. Makes 6 servings, with leftovers.

Hamburger
(ground beef)

TO BUY AND STORE HAMBURGER

Ready-Ground Hamburger: Buy it from a reliable meat dealer so you are sure of getting freshly ground beef, bright red in color. It comes in 2 styles; both are ground twice.

Regular Ground Beef should contain not more than 25 per cent fat and is likely to be the cheaper style.

Lean Ground Beef should contain not more than 12 per cent fat.

Ground-to-Order Hamburger: Buy boned chuck (it makes more economical, flavorsome, juicier hamburger than lean round); then have it ground. If you buy round, be sure to have 2 oz. suet ground with each 1 lb. round. When any of our recipes call for 1 lb. chuck (or any other meat), ground, we mean for you to buy 1 lb. boned meat, then have it ground.

Number of Grindings: Hamburger becomes more compact the more grindings it gets. This is fine for meat loaves, meat balls, etc. But if you are ordering hamburger for extra-nice, juicy, tender patties, ask meatman to grind meat coarsely—and only once.

Amount to Buy: A pound of hamburger makes 4 good servings. When other ingredients such as rice, spaghetti, or vegetables are added, it may make 5 servings. A meat loaf made with 2 lb. hamburger as the base will probably serve 4 persons for 2 meals.

To Store:

To Use Same or Next Day: Wrap loosely in waxed paper, with ends open; refrigerate at once. Be sure to use within 2 days.

To Use Within a Week: Shape into patties; stack between squares of waxed paper; wrap tightly in 2 thicknesses of waxed paper or aluminum foil. Store in frozen-food compartment or ice-cube tray of conventional refrigerator. Be sure to use within 7 days.

If You Have a Home Freezer or Refrigerator-Freezer Combination: Wrap patties in freezer-wrapping material; store in freezer. Use within 2 or 3 months.

OUR BEST-EVER HAMBURGERS

1 lb. chuck, ground once	2 tablesp. minced onion
1 teasp. salt	¼ teasp. monosodium glutamate
¼ teasp. pepper	

Toss meat lightly with salt, pepper, onion, monosodium glutamate. (Some cooks prefer to shape unseasoned chuck into patties, then to sprinkle seasonings onto both sides of patties before cooking. This eliminates too much handling.)

With help of kitchen fork, and using as little pressure as possible, divide meat; gently shape and flatten *loosely* into 4 thick patties, 3½″ x ¾″, or 8 thin patties, 3″ x ¼″. Cook in one of these 3 ways:

Skillet-Cooked: Heat 2 tablesp. fat or salad oil in skillet or on griddle. Cook patties until done as your family likes.

If patties are *thick*, we allow about 4 to 8 min. over medium heat, turning once.

If patties are *thin*, we allow about 2 to 6 min., turning once. Don't flatten or "spank" patties with spatula—it presses out juices.

Pan-broiled: Heat heavy skillet or griddle till sizzling hot. If you're afraid meat will stick, rub skillet *lightly* with fat or salad oil; or sprinkle with salt. Brown patties on both sides; then cook over medium heat for about same time periods as in Skillet-Cooked.

Oven-Broiled: Preheat broiler 10 min., or as manufacturer directs. Arrange thick patties on cold broiler rack. (If you can, line broiler pan under grid with aluminum foil, with corners turned under, to catch drippings and save dishwashing.)

Broil patties about 3″ from heat, turning once, until done as your family likes. We allow about 8 to 12 min., turning once.

After turning patties, you may top them with one of the following; then complete broiling.

1. Cheese slice, a little prepared mustard
2. Catchup or chili, soy, or barbecue sauce
3. Grated sharp cheese or ¼ cup crumbled blue cheese, mashed with ¼ cup soft butter or margarine, ½ teasp. dry mustard, 1 teasp. salt, 2 teasp. Worcestershire.

Quick: Well-known brands of frozen hamburgers come as 2-oz. or 3-oz. packaged patties.

Cook as label directs; vary as above. Especially nice for outdoor cooking.

Double-quick: Canned hamburgers make good eating in a hurry. Just heat; serve.

HAMBURGER SPREAD-ONS

Cook Our Best-Ever Hamburgers, p. 64, your favorite way. Whisk them to heated platter; spread with one of these wonderful butter spreads, made while patties cook:

To 2 tablesp. melted butter or margarine, add one of these:

2 tablesp. minced stuffed or ripe olives

2 tablesp. catchup or prepared mustard

2 tablesp. crumbled blue cheese or grated sharp cheese. Add chili sauce if you wish

2 tablesp. snipped chives, scallions, or onions

2 tablesp. chili sauce, 1 teasp. prepared mustard, pinch chili powder

¼ teasp. salt, pinch dried thyme

1 tablesp. horse-radish, pinch garlic salt

2 tablesp. chopped dill pickle or pickle relish, plus a little minced onion or garlic

2 tablesp. prepared mustard, snipped parsley

Soy or barbecue sauce, or French dressing

¼ cup canned crushed pineapple or applesauce, or apple jelly, plus pinch nutmeg

1 teasp. snipped parsley, 1 teasp. minced onion, bit of Worcestershire, salt

3 tablesp. fresh, frozen, or canned lemon juice or orange juice; pinch nutmeg

HAMBURGER GO-BETWEENS

There's a surprise inside these hamburgers! Shape Our Best-Ever Hamburger mixture, p. 64, into 8 thin patties. Place one of fillings below on half of patties; top with remaining patties. Press edges together; cook till of desired doneness.

Blue Cheese: Combine ¼ cup crumbled blue cheese, 2 tablesp. mayonnaise, 1 tablesp. Worcestershire, ½ teasp. dry mustard.

Chili-Cheese: Mix 1 cup grated process American cheese, 1 tablesp. Worcestershire, ¼ cup chili sauce.

Chili-Onion: Use Sautéed Onions, p. 263.

Relish: Top thin onion slices with prepared mustard, then with pickle relish or chili sauce.

Stuffing: Mix 2 tablesp. melted butter or margarine with 1¼ cups fine fresh bread crumbs; ½ teasp. dried thyme; a little minced onion; 1 teasp. fresh, frozen, or canned lemon juice.

Tomato-Cheese: Top thin tomato slices with onion salt, then with grated cheese.

HAMBURGER SPOON-ONS

While Our Best-Ever Hamburgers, p. 64, cook, make one of these quick sauces to top, or serve with, them:

Avery Butter, p. 372

Chive Cheese, p. 372

Curry, p. 372

Mustard, p. 375

Onion, p. 372

Quick Mushroom, p. 372

Sautéed Mushrooms, p. 262

Sautéed Onions, p. 263

Sour Cream, p. 373

Tomato-Horse-radish, p. 373

HAMBURGER TOSS-INS

Vary Our Best-Ever Hamburger mixture, p. 64, in one of these ways:

Bacon-Wrapped: Wrap thick patties in bacon slices, securing each with toothpicks; broil.

Bean Burgers: Use ¾ lb. chuck, ground. Toss in 1 cup mashed, drained canned kidney beans. Skillet-cook patties in bacon fat.

Bohemian Burgers: Increase minced onion to 3 tablesp. Toss in 3 tablesp. minced dill pickle; ½ cup minced pickled beets; and 1 cup finely chopped, cooked potatoes. Skillet-cook patties.

Cheeseburgers: Toss in 1 cup grated process American cheese (¼ lb.); add ¼ cup water.

Chip Burgers: Toss in 1 cup crushed potato chips.

Deviled Burgers: Increase minced onion to 3 tablesp. Add 1½ teasp. prepared mustard, ¼ cup catchup or chili sauce, 2 teasp. horse-radish, 1½ teasp. Worcestershire.

Extra-Juicy: Add ¼ cup undiluted evaporated milk or water.

Jumbo Burgers: Increase onion to ¼ cup. Add 1¾ cups fresh bread crumbs, 1 beaten egg, ¼ cup milk.

Herb Burgers: Add ¼ teasp. each dried marjoram and thyme. Increase onion to ¼ cup; add ¼ cup minced celery, 1 teasp. snipped parsley, ½ teasp. garlic salt. After cooking, top with 2 tablesp. melted butter or margarine, mixed with 3 tablesp. lemon or orange juice, pinch nutmeg.

Moreburgers: Add 1 cup wheat flakes, cracker crumbs, or cooked rice; or ½ cup uncooked rolled oats. Also add ½ cup milk or tomato juice, plus a little prepared mustard, horse-radish, or catchup.

Mushroom Burgers: Add ½ cup chopped mushrooms.

Nut Burgers: Toss in ½ cup chopped walnuts.

BARBECUED HAMBURGERS

Shape Our Best-Ever Hamburger mixture, p. 64, into 4 large patties. In 1 tablesp. hot fat or salad oil in skillet, brown patties on both sides.

Combine 1 cup catchup, 1 sliced onion, ¼ cup vinegar, 1 tablesp. sugar, ½ teasp. dry mustard. Pour over patties; simmer, covered, 20 min. Makes 4 servings.

Grilled: See Barbecued Hamburgers, p. 594.

PINEAPPLE BURGERS

Make sauce for Veal Inverness on Green Rice, p. 108, decreasing salad oil to 3 tablesp. Shape Our Best-Ever Hamburger mixture, p. 64, into 4 large patties; let stand in sauce 30 min., turning often; broil on one side.

Meanwhile, let 4 drained canned pineapple slices stand in same sauce. When turning patties, top with pineapple; complete broiling.

Serve patties on pineapple. Makes 4 servings.

BIG BURGER

Cook 4 sliced medium onions in boiling salted water to cover 3 to 4 min. Shape Our Best-Ever Hamburger mixture, p. 64, into 1 large patty, 6½" x ¾". Spread patty with 2 tablesp. soft butter or margarine; place, with butter side down, in hot skillet. Brown; turn. Drain onions; put in skillet around patty; sprinkle both with ¼ cup soy sauce and ⅛ teasp. pepper. Stir onions with fork. Cook till medium rare—about 6 min. Makes 4 servings.

POTATO BURGERS

½ lb. chuck, ground	3 tablesp. fat or salad
1 cup grated raw potatoes	oil
	½ teasp. dry mustard
2 tablesp. minced onion	1 tablesp. snipped
⅛ teasp. pepper	parsley
1 teasp. salt	

Mix meat, potatoes, onion, pepper, salt. Shape into 8 patties. In hot fat in skillet, sauté patties until crisp and brown; then remove from skillet; keep warm. Add mustard and parsley to drippings in skillet; heat; pour over patties. Makes 4 servings.

SUPERB BIFF A LA LUNDSTROM

1¼ lb. chuck, ground	1 minced small onion
1 cup mashed potatoes (2 medium)	2 tablesp. chopped bottled capers
2 egg yolks	1 teasp. salt
½ cup heavy cream	¼ teasp. pepper
½ cup diced pickled beets	2 or 3 tablesp. butter or margarine

With fork, mix meat, potatoes, egg yolks; gradually add cream, stirring constantly. Mix in beets, onion, capers, salt, pepper; shape into 12 thin patties, 3" in diameter. In hot butter in skillet, brown patties on both sides.

Serve on heated platter, garnished with parsley. Makes 6 servings.

HAMBURGER MIXED GRILL

See Mixed Grill, p. 55. Try these combinations:
1. Hamburgers; tomato halves; mushroom caps; French-bread slices, topped with grated cheese and sprinkling of orégano.
2. Hamburgers; scored, cooked potato halves; canned peach or pear halves, or pineapple chunks or slices.
3. Hamburgers, bacon, banana halves, franks.

BURGUNDY MEAT BALLS

¾ lb. chuck, ground	¾ cup light cream
¾ cup packaged dried bread crumbs or finely crushed corn chips	¾ teasp. salt
	¼ cup fat or salad oil
	3 tablesp. flour
	2 cups water
1 minced small onion	1 cup Burgundy wine
¾ teasp. cornstarch	2 beef-bouillon cubes
Dash allspice	½ teasp. salt
1 egg, beaten	⅛ teasp. pepper

Combine meat, crumbs, onion, cornstarch, all-spice, egg, cream, ¾ teasp. salt; shape into 30 to 32 small balls. Into hot fat in skillet, drop balls, a few at a time; brown well on all sides. Transfer balls to warm plate.

Blend flour with remaining fat in skillet; stir in water, wine, bouillon cubes, ½ teasp. salt, pepper. Cook, stirring, until smooth. Then arrange meat balls in sauce; simmer, covered, 30 min.

Serve on hot mashed potatoes, fluffy rice, or buttered noodles. Makes 6 servings.

To Do Ahead: Prepare and refrigerate the entire dish day ahead. To serve, reheat. Or shape balls ahead; refrigerate. About ¾ hr. before serving, start cooking.

MEAT-BALL STEW EN CASSEROLE

2 lb. quartered, pared potatoes	¾ teasp. Worcestershire
1½ lb. small white onions	⅔ cup milk
1 bunch small carrots, halved lengthwise	⅓ cup salad oil
1 pkg. thawed frozen peas	1½ lb. small mushrooms
2 lb. chuck, ground	1 can undiluted condensed cream-of-mushroom soup
1 egg	
1 cup day-old bread crumbs	¾ teasp. nutmeg
¾ teasp. dried marjoram	¾ teasp. bottled sauce for gravy, p. 9
2½ teasp. salt	¾ teasp. onion salt or monosodium glutamate

In large saucepan, place potatoes in layer, then onions, then carrots. Cook in 1″ boiling salted water, covered, 20 min., or until barely tender-crisp; top with peas; cover; turn off heat.

Meanwhile, with fork, lightly mix meat with egg, crumbs, marjoram, salt, Worcestershire, milk. Drop by teaspoonfuls into hot oil in skillet; brown quickly on both sides; remove. In same skillet, sauté mushrooms until tender; remove. Then, in skillet, heat soup with nutmeg, bottled sauce for gravy, onion salt.

Start heating oven to 400°F. Arrange drained peas, carrots, onions, mushrooms, and meat balls in 3-qt. casserole. Near edge of casserole, pour in sauce. Mash and season potatoes as on p. 268; arrange in mounds around edge; brush with milk. Bake, uncovered, 35 min., or till browned and bubbly. Makes 8 servings.

E. I.'S SWEDISH MEAT BALLS

2 tablesp. butter or margarine	1 lb. chuck, ground
⅓ cup minced onion	¼ lb. shoulder pork, ground
1 egg	2 tablesp. butter or margarine
½ cup milk	3 tablesp. flour
½ cup fresh bread crumbs	1 teasp. sugar
1¼ teasp. salt	1¼ teasp. salt
2 teasp. sugar	⅛ teasp. pepper
½ teasp. allspice	1 cup water
¼ teasp. nutmeg	¾ cup light cream

In 2 tablesp. hot butter in large skillet, sauté onion until golden. Meanwhile, in large mixing bowl, beat egg; add milk, crumbs. Let stand 5 min. Add 1¼ teasp. salt, 2 teasp. sugar, allspice, nutmeg, meats, onion. Blend well with fork. In same skillet, heat 2 tablesp. butter. Using 2 teaspoons, shape meat mixture into small balls, about ½″ to ¾″ in diameter. Drop some balls into skillet; brown well on all sides; remove to warm casserole; repeat until all meat balls are browned.

Into fat left in skillet, stir flour, 1 teasp. sugar, 1¼ teasp. salt, pepper; slowly add water, cream; stir until thickened. If desired, return meat balls to gravy; heat well. Or serve balls in covered casserole; pass gravy. Makes 6 servings.

To Do Ahead: Make day ahead; refrigerate. Reheat just before serving.

INGA'S MEAT BALLS

1 lb. round, ground twice	¼ cup salad oil
½ lb. pork tenderloin or boned shoulder, ground	2 tablesp. flour
	1 can undiluted condensed consommé
3 eggs, beaten	2 teasp. bottled sauce for gravy, p. 9
1 teasp. salt	½ cup sherry or cooking sherry
⅛ teasp. pepper	Buttered noodles
2 tablesp. flour	

Toss meats, eggs, salt, pepper, and 2 tablesp. flour until blended; shape very lightly into about 50 tiny balls. In hot oil in skillet, brown balls well, a few at a time; remove. Into oil left in skillet, stir 2 tablesp. flour until smooth; add consommé, bottled sauce for gravy. Return balls to skillet; simmer, covered, 5 min. Add sherry. Serve on buttered noodles. Makes 6 servings.

SUSAN'S MEAT LOAF

2 cups fresh bread crumbs	2 tablesp. horse-radish
¾ cup minced onions	2½ teasp. salt
¼ cup minced green pepper	1 teasp. dry mustard
2 eggs	¼ cup milk
2 lb. chuck, ground	¼ cup catchup
	½ cup catchup

1. When it's convenient, prepare bread crumbs, minced onions, green pepper.
2. *About 1 hour before serving:* Start heating oven to 400°F.
3. With fork, beat eggs slightly. *Lightly* mix in meat, then crumbs, onions, pepper. (Meat will be juicier and more tender if you handle it as little as possible.) Add horse-radish, salt, mustard, milk, ¼ cup catchup; combine lightly but well.
4. In bowl, shape meat into oval loaf; transfer to shallow baking dish or broil-and-serve platter; smooth into shapely loaf. Spread top with ½ cup catchup. Bake 50 min.

Serve from baking dish or broil-and-serve platter, pouring off excess juices. Or with 2 broad spatulas, lift loaf out of baking dish onto heated platter. Spoon some of juices over meat. (Nice chilled, then served sliced, too.) Makes 8 servings.

P.S. If you prefer a soft, moist exterior, bake meat loaf as directed in 9″ x 5″ x 3″ loaf pan. Pour juices from pan after baking. Unmold meat loaf onto cake rack; then place, right side up, on heated platter. Use juices for making gravy if desired.

Meat-Loaf Ring: Place the ½ cup catchup in bottom of 1½-qt. ring mold. Turn meat mixture into ring mold. Bake at 400°F. 45 min. Unmold, pouring off excess juice. Fill center with hot buttered or creamed vegetables.

One-Apiece Loaves: Form meat mixture into 6 oval-shaped loaves; arrange in greased baking pan. Bake at 400°F. ½ hr.

Last-Minute Meat Cups: Halve ingredients. Bake in 8 3″ cupcake cups at 400°F. 25 min.

Old-fashioned Meat Loaf: For 2 lb. chuck, substitute ½ lb. pork shoulder, ground; ½ lb. round or veal shoulder, ground; and 1 lb. chuck, rump, or round, ground. Make as directed, omitting ½ cup catchup for topping. Bake at 400°F. 1 hr. 10 min. Makes 6 servings.

Veal Loaf: For chuck, substitute 2 lb. veal breast, shoulder, or round, ground. Omit ½ cup catchup for topping. Bake at 350°F. 1½ hr. Makes 6 servings.

Cheeseburger Loaf: Use ½ lb. packaged process-American-cheese slices. Into 10″ x 5″ x 3″ loaf pan, lightly press enough meat-loaf mixture to cover bottom; on top, place 2 cheese slices. Repeat until both are used, ending with 2 cheese slices on top. Omit ½ cup catchup on top. Best served hot.

Frosted Meat Loaf: Omit ½ cup catchup for topping. When loaf is baked, pour off all juices. Thickly frost top with well-seasoned, creamy mashed potatoes (add some grated cheese or snipped chives if you like). Sprinkle with paprika. Broil till golden.

Italian-Style Loaf: To seasonings for meat loaf, add ¼ teasp. each dried rosemary, orégano, and basil. Substitute ½ cup canned tomato sauce, tomato juice, or diluted canned condensed tomato soup for both milk and ¼ cup catchup.

Mushroom Meat Loaf: Substitute ½ cup well-drained, chopped canned mushrooms for green pepper. Add 1 tablesp. grated lemon rind. Omit ½ cup catchup for topping.

Bacon-Dill Loaf: Substitute ¼ cup chopped dill pickle and 6 slices chopped crisp bacon for green peppers.

Rainbow Loaf: For ½ cup onions, substitute ¼ cup minced celery; ½ cup grated, pared carrots; and ¼ cup snipped parsley. Substitute 1 cup canned tomatoes for both milk and ¼ cup catchup. Omit ½ cup catchup for topping. Bake in and serve from shallow baking dish.

SPICY PEACH LOAF

1 egg	½ cup fresh bread crumbs
1 lb. chuck, ground	1 minced small onion
½ lb. fresh-pork-sausage meat	6 canned peach halves, well drained
½ cup milk	6 teasp. catchup
1¼ teasp. salt	
¼ teasp. dried thyme	

Start heating oven to 350°F. With fork, beat egg well; add chuck, sausage, milk, salt, thyme, crumbs, onion; combine lightly but thoroughly. Place in 8" x 8" x 2" pan.

Press peaches, with hollow sides up, into meat; place 1 teasp. catchup in each hollow. Bake 30 min. Pour off excess fat; bake 20 min. Cut meat, around each peach, into square. Makes 6 servings.

MUSHROOM-STUFFED MEAT LOAF

¼ cup butter or margarine	packed
1 lb. mushrooms, sliced (leave 7 whole)	1 teasp. salt
	⅛ teasp. pepper
	¼ teasp. dried thyme
	¼ cup snipped parsley
1 teasp. fresh, frozen, or canned lemon juice	2 eggs
	3 lb. chuck, ground
	1 tablesp. salt
1 minced medium onion	⅛ teasp. pepper
	¼ cup milk
4 cups fresh bread crumbs, lightly	⅓ cup catchup
	1½ teasp. dry mustard

Early in day: For stuffing, in hot butter in skillet, sauté all but 7 small whole mushrooms with lemon juice and onion 3 min. Toss in crumbs, 1 teasp. salt, ⅛ teasp. pepper, thyme, parsley. Beat eggs; with fork, lightly mix in meat, then 1 tablesp. salt, ⅛ teasp. pepper, milk, catchup, mustard. Pack half of meat mixture into 10" x 5" x 3" loaf pan; pack stuffing on top, then rest of meat. Press 7 mushrooms into top. Refrigerate.

About 1 hr. 25 min. before serving: Start heating oven to 400°F. Bake meat loaf 1 hr. 10 min. If desired, brush top with heated currant jelly. With 2 broad spatulas, lift onto heated platter.

Serve, cut into thick slices. Makes 8 servings.

LITTLE SHERRY-BARBECUED LOAVES

1 egg	2 tablesp. brown sugar
1½ lb. chuck, ground	¾ cup sherry
2 tablesp. minced onion	1 tablesp. vinegar
1½ teasp. salt	1 teasp. prepared mustard
¼ teasp. pepper	
1 8-oz. can tomato sauce	1 bouillon cube; or 1 teasp. meat-extract paste
1 cup fresh bread crumbs	¾ cup hot water
1 tablesp. cornstarch	

Start heating oven to 350°F. With fork, slightly beat egg; add meat, onion, salt, pepper, ½ can tomato sauce, crumbs; combine lightly but well. Shape into 4 oval loaves; place in shallow baking dish. Bake 40 min. Pour off most of juices.

Meanwhile, stir cornstarch with brown sugar; stir in rest of tomato sauce, sherry, vinegar, mustard, bouillon cube, hot water. Cook, stirring, until thickened. Pour over meat loaves. Bake, basting often, 30 min. Makes 4 servings.

TWO-IN-ONE RICE RING

1 egg	2 lb. chuck, ground
2 cups leftover cooked rice	1 lb. pork shoulder, ground
1 minced small onion	2 teasp. salt
½ cup grated, pared carrots	⅛ teasp. pepper
	1 cup milk

Start heating oven to 350°F. With fork, slightly beat egg; add rice, rest of ingredients. Combine lightly but thoroughly. Pack mixture into 1½-qt. ring mold. Bake 45 min. Let stand in warm place 15 min. Pour off excess juices. Loosen edges. Turn onto platter. Fill center with creamed mushrooms or other creamed or buttered vegetable. Makes 8 servings.

SUPERB SKILLET BURGER LOAF

1 egg, beaten	3 packaged process-American-cheese slices
¾ lb. chuck, ground	
¾ teasp. salt	
¼ cup minced onion	¼ teasp. pepper

About 25 min. before supper: Mix egg, meat, salt, onion. Grease 8" skillet with metal handle; lightly pat half of meat over bottom of skillet. Arrange cheese slices on top of meat; cover with rest of meat, patting smooth. Sprinkle with pepper. Cut into 4 pie-shaped wedges. Cook on top of range, over fairly high heat, until well-browned on bottom. Turn; brown other side; or slide the skillet under broiler until top of meat is nicely browned. Makes 4 servings.

MINUTE MEAT LOAVES

1 lb. chuck, ground	½ cup fresh bread crumbs
½ minced small onion	
1 teasp. salt	1 can undiluted condensed vegetable soup
½ teasp. monosodium glutamate	

Start heating oven to 450°F. With fork, mix meat lightly but thoroughly with rest of ingredients. Spoon into 12 2″ cupcake cups. Bake 15 min. Makes 12 little loaves.

HAMBURGER STROGANOFF

¼ cup butter or margarine	¼ teasp. paprika
½ cup minced onions	1 lb. sliced mushrooms
1 lb. chuck, ground	1 can undiluted condensed cream-of-chicken soup
1 minced clove garlic	
2 tablesp. flour	
2 teasp. salt	1 cup commercial sour cream
¼ teasp. monosodium glutamate	Snipped parsley, chives, or fresh dill
¼ teasp. pepper	

In hot butter in skillet, sauté onions till golden. Stir in meat, garlic, flour, salt, monosodium glutamate, pepper, paprika, mushrooms; sauté 5 min. Add soup; simmer, uncovered, 10 min. Stir in sour cream; sprinkle with parsley.

Serve on hot mashed potatoes, fluffy rice, buttered noodles, or toast. Makes 4 to 6 servings.

Hamburger Czarina: Reduce salt to 1½ teaspoon. Omit mushrooms. Substitute 1 can undiluted condensed cream-of-mushroom soup for chicken soup.

NOODLE STROGANOFF

¼ cup butter or margarine	3 tablesp. fresh, frozen, or canned lemon juice
¼ cup sliced scallions or chopped onion	
1 minced clove garlic	1 can undiluted condensed consommé
½ lb. sliced mushrooms; or 2 3-oz. cans sliced mushrooms, drained	1 teasp. salt
	¼ teasp. pepper
	¼ lb. medium noodles (2 cups)
1 lb. chuck, ground	1 cup commercial sour cream
3 tablesp. Burgundy or other red wine	Snipped parsley

In hot butter in skillet, sauté scallions, garlic, and mushrooms until lightly browned. Add meat; cook, stirring, until red color disappears. Stir in Burgundy, lemon juice, consommé, salt, pepper. Simmer, uncovered, 15 min. Stir in uncooked noodles. Cook, covered, 5 min., or until noodles are tender. Mix in sour cream; heat quickly, but do not boil.

Serve at once, sprinkled with parsley. Makes 6 servings.

HAMBURGER ON CRISP EGGPLANT SLICES

Bacon fat, or olive or salad oil	1 can undiluted condensed vegetable soup
¼ cup minced onion	
1 lb. chuck, ground	1 large eggplant
Salt and pepper	Flour

In 1 tablesp. hot bacon fat in skillet, cook onion and meat 10 min., stirring often. Sprinkle with ¾ teasp. salt, ⅛ teasp. pepper. Add soup; heat 5 to 10 min.

Meanwhile, pare eggplant and cut into ¼″ slices. Sprinkle with salt, pepper, and a little flour. Sauté in hot bacon fat, turning once, 6 to 8 min., or until golden brown. Serve topped with meat mixture. Makes 6 servings.

To Vary: Substitute hot biscuits, waffles, or toast triangles for eggplant.

CHILI CON CARNE

2 tablesp. fat or salad oil	1½ tablesp. chili powder
	2 tablesp. cold water
½ cup thinly sliced onions	¼ teasp. salt
2 tablesp. diced green pepper	1 teasp. sugar
	1½ minced small cloves garlic
½ lb. round, rump, or chuck, ground	2 cups cooked or canned kidney beans, undrained
½ cup boiling water	
1 cup canned tomatoes	

In hot fat in skillet, cook onions and green pepper until tender. Add meat; cook, uncovered, until meat starts to sizzle and brown. Add boiling water, tomatoes, chili powder mixed with cold water till smooth, salt, sugar, garlic. Simmer, covered, 1 hr. Uncover; simmer ½ hr. Add a little hot water if mixture thickens too much. Add beans; heat.

Serve in soup bowls, with rolls or crackers and a salad. Or serve over hot or toasted, split corn bread, buttered spaghetti, or fried mush.

To Vary: If you prefer a slightly thinner chili con carne, stir in about ¼ cup hot water just before serving. Or replace canned tomatoes with 1⅓ cups diced fresh tomatoes.

CREOLE-STUFFED GREEN PEPPERS

4 large green peppers	undiluted evap-
1 cup boiling water	orated milk
1¼ teasp. salt	1 No. 2 can tomatoes
1 lb. chuck, ground	(2½ cups)
¼ cup minced onion	¼ cup minced onion
½ cup minced celery	½ teasp. salt
1 teasp. salt	1 tablesp. sugar
¼ cup minced green	¼ teasp. cinnamon
pepper (optional)	6 whole cloves
1 egg, unbeaten	1 tablesp. flour
½ cup light cream or	¼ cup cold water

Wash 4 green peppers; cut thin slice from stem end of each; remove seeds. Boil peppers in boiling water with 1¼ teasp. salt, tightly covered, 5 min.

Meanwhile, combine meat, ¼ cup onion, celery, 1 teasp. salt, ¼ cup minced green pepper, egg, cream. Drain boiled peppers; stuff with meat mixture. Place in 8″ x 8″ x 2″ baking dish.

Start heating oven to 350°F. In saucepan, combine tomatoes, ¼ cup onion, ½ teasp. salt, sugar, cinnamon, cloves; simmer, uncovered, 10 min.; then strain, reserving liquid. Stir flour and cold water till smooth; add to strained liquid; cook, stirring, until slightly thickened; pour over peppers. Bake 45 to 50 min. Makes 4 servings.

STUFFED CABBAGE

Large head cabbage	2 8-oz. cans tomato
1 lb. chuck, ground	sauce
½ cup raw regular or	2 No. 2½ cans toma-
processed white rice	toes (7 cups)
1 grated small onion	Juice of 2 lemons
2 eggs	1 teasp. salt
1 teasp. salt	¼ teasp. pepper
¼ teasp. pepper	½ to 1 cup brown sugar
1 sliced large onion	

Remove 12 large leaves from cabbage. Trim off thick part of each leaf. Let boiling water stand on leaves a few minutes, so they become easy to roll.

Start heating oven to 375°F. Combine meat, rice, grated onion, eggs, 1 teasp. salt, ¼ teasp. pepper. Place mound of meat mixture in cup part of each leaf. Loosely fold over sides of each leaf; roll up.

In bottom of Dutch oven, place a few of remaining cabbage leaves. Arrange layers of stuffed cabbage, with seam sides down, and sliced onion in Dutch oven. Pour on tomato sauce, tomatoes, lemon juice. Add 1 teasp. salt, ¼ teasp. pepper. Bring to boil on top of range. Sprinkle with sugar to taste. Bake, covered, 1 hr.; uncover; bake 2 hr. Makes 8 servings.

KALDOLMAR

¼ cup raw regular or	1½ teasp. salt
processed white rice	¼ teasp. white pepper
1 cup boiling water	2 tablesp. butter or
1 cup milk	margarine
1 medium head cabbage	1 tablesp. brown sugar
⅓ lb. chuck, ground	2 beef-bouillon cubes
¼ lb. pork shoulder,	2 cups boiling water
ground	1½ tablesp. flour
1 egg	½ cup light cream
⅓ cup light cream	

Add rice to 1 cup boiling water; simmer, uncovered, 10 min., or until rice has absorbed all water. Add milk; cook over low heat, uncovered, stirring occasionally, 30 min., or until rice is tender; cool.

Meanwhile, discard wilted leaves from cabbage; cut out core. Cook cabbage in boiling salted water until leaves separate easily; drain. Separate leaves, reserving about 1 doz. of largest leaves; trim off thick center vein of each. (Use rest of cabbage for creamed cabbage another day.)

Mix rice with meats, egg, ⅓ cup cream, salt, pepper. Place about 2 tablesp. of this filling on each of reserved cabbage leaves; fold up; fasten with toothpicks. In hot butter in Dutch oven, brown cabbage rolls on all sides. Sprinkle with brown sugar; pour on bouillon cubes dissolved in 2 cups boiling water. Cook over low heat, covered, 1 to 1¼ hr., or until tender, basting occasionally. Arrange rolls in deep serving dish, removing toothpicks. Mix flour with ½ cup cream; add to pan juices, stirring. Simmer 10 min. Season if needed. Pour over rolls. Nice with boiled potatoes. Makes 4 servings.

BEEF-AND-RICE CASSEROLE

1⅓ cups packaged pre-	1 lb. chuck, ground
cooked rice	1 teasp. salt
2 tablesp. butter or	Dash pepper
margarine	1 can undiluted con-
1½ cups diced celery	densed tomato soup
3 tablesp. minced onion	¼ cup water

Start heating oven to 375°F. Start cooking rice as label directs. Meanwhile, in hot butter in skillet, sauté celery and onion until tender. Place cooked rice in greased 1½-qt. casserole; top with celery mixture.

Combine meat with salt, pepper; brown in butter remaining in skillet; arrange on top of celery. Combine soup with water; pour over meat. Bake, uncovered, 35 min. Makes 6 servings.

BEEF-AND-EGGPLANT CASSEROLE

2 teasp. butter or margarine	plants, cut into 1" cubes (about 6 cups)
½ cup fresh bread crumbs	1½ teasp. salt
3 tablesp. butter or margarine	Dash pepper
1 mashed clove garlic	Dash dried thyme
¼ cup minced onion	1 can undiluted condensed tomato soup
1 lb. chuck, ground	1 cup undiluted evaporated milk
2 pared medium egg-	

Start heating oven to 375°F. In skillet, melt 2 teasp. butter; toss with crumbs; set crumbs aside on waxed paper. In same skillet, in 3 tablesp. hot butter, lightly brown garlic, onion, meat. Add eggplant, salt, pepper, thyme; cook over low heat 10 min. Stir in soup, milk. Pour mixture into 2-qt. casserole; top with buttered crumbs. Bake, uncovered, 25 to 30 min., or until crumbs are golden. Makes 6 servings.

HAMBURGER UPSIDE-DOWN PIE

2 tablesp. salad oil	2 tablesp. catchup
¼ cup minced onion	1 teasp. chili powder
½ cup chopped green peppers	1 teasp. salt
	¼ teasp. pepper
1 lb. chuck, ground	One of toppings below
1 8-oz. can tomato sauce	

Start heating oven to 400°F. In hot oil in skillet, sauté onion, green peppers, and meat until brown. Add tomato sauce, rest of ingredients except topping; turn into 2-qt. casserole. Cover with one of toppings below. Bake, uncovered, 25 min. Turn onto serving plate, with topping side down. Makes 6 servings.

Biscuit Topping: Make ½ recipe baking-powder biscuits; or use 1 cup packaged biscuit mix. Roll dough to fit casserole.

Corn-Bread Topping:

½ cup sifted all-purpose flour	1 tablesp. sugar
¾ cup yellow corn meal	1 egg, beaten
2 teasp. baking powder	½ cup milk
1 teasp. salt	2 tablesp. salad oil

Sift flour, corn meal, baking powder, salt, sugar. Combine egg, milk; add to flour mixture, stirring until mixed. Stir in oil.

Or use ½ pkg. corn-muffin mix, made as label directs.

QUADRETTINI SPINACH

¼ cup olive oil	(2½ cups)
⅓ cup minced onion	1 tablesp. salt
3 crushed cloves garlic	½ teasp. pepper
½ cup diced, pared carrots	¼ lb. medium noodles (2 cups)
3 diced celery stalks	1 pkg. frozen chopped spinach
1 lb. round, ground	
½ cup sherry or cooking sherry	½ cup buttered fresh bread squares
1 6-oz. can tomato paste (⅔ cup)	½ cup grated process American cheese
1 No. 2 can tomatoes	Grated Parmesan cheese

Several hours ahead: In hot oil in large skillet, sauté onion, garlic, carrots, and celery until lightly browned. Add meat; cook until red color disappears. Add sherry; simmer a few minutes. Add tomato paste, tomatoes, salt, pepper. Simmer, uncovered, 2 to 2½ hr. Season if necessary.

Start heating oven to 350°F. Cook noodles and spinach as labels direct; drain very well; add to sauce. Turn into 1½-qt. casserole. Sprinkle with bread squares and ½ cup cheese. Bake, uncovered, 30 min., or until browned. Serve with Parmesan. Makes 6 to 8 servings.

PIZZA HAMBURGER

1 lb. chuck, ground	sauce
1½ teasp. salt	2 tablesp. minced onion
¼ teasp. pepper	1 cup grated process American or Mozzarella cheese (¼ lb.)
1 teasp. horse-radish	
1 teasp. Worcestershire	
1 teasp. prepared mustard	2 tablesp. snipped parsley
1 No. 2 can tomatoes, well drained; or 1 8-oz. can tomato	½ teasp. dried basil
	¼ teasp. orégano

Start heating oven to 375°F. Lightly toss meat with salt, pepper, horse-radish, Worcestershire, mustard; press against sides and bottom of 9″ pie plate. Spread tomatoes over meat; then sprinkle with rest of ingredients. Bake 20 min.

Serve cut into wedges. Makes 4 servings.

SPOON-BREAD TAMALE BAKE

¼ cup olive oil	¼ teasp. pepper
1½ lb. chuck, ground	½ cup corn meal
1 cup chopped onions	1 cup water
1 minced clove garlic	1 cup pitted ripe olives
½ cup chopped green peppers	1½ cups milk
	1 teasp. salt
1 No. 2 can tomatoes (2½ cups)	2 tablesp. butter or margarine
1 12-oz. can vacuum-packed whole-kernel corn	½ cup corn meal
	1 cup grated process American cheese (¼ lb.)
1 tablesp. salt	
1½ tablesp. chili powder	2 eggs, slightly beaten

Start heating oven to 375°F. In hot oil in skillet, brown meat; add onions, garlic, green peppers; cook, stirring, until onions are golden. Stir in tomatoes, corn, 1 tablesp. salt, chili powder, pepper; simmer 5 min. Stir in ½ cup corn meal, mixed with water; simmer, covered, 10 min. Add olives; turn into 3-qt. casserole.

Now heat milk with 1 teasp. salt and butter. Slowly stir in ½ cup corn meal; cook, stirring, until thickened. Remove from heat. Stir in cheese, eggs; pour over meat mixture. Bake, uncovered, 30 to 40 min. Makes 6 to 8 servings.

To Do Ahead: Make casserole dish early in day; refrigerate. At mealtime, bake at 375°F. 1 hr. 10 min., or until bubbling hot.

BARBARA'S TAMALE PIE

3 cups water	1 tablesp. chili powder
1 teasp. salt	2 dashes cayenne pepper
1 cup yellow corn meal	
1 tablesp. flour	½ teasp. garlic salt
1 cup cold milk	1 No. 2 can (2½ cups) tomatoes, drained
6 diced bacon slices	
1 diced medium green pepper	1 8-oz. can tomato sauce
1 minced large onion	1 cup pitted large ripe olives
1½ lb. chuck or round, ground	
	¾ cup grated sharp American cheese
2½ teasp. salt	
⅛ teasp. pepper	

Early in day: In double-boiler top over direct heat, bring water to boil. Combine 1 teasp. salt,

corn meal, flour, and milk, stirring; pour into boiling water. Cook, stirring, till mixture boils. Place over simmering water in double-boiler bottom; cook, covered, 1 hr.

In large saucepan, sauté bacon till crisp; drain off all but 1 tablesp. fat. Add green pepper, onion; sauté till tender. Add meat; brown. Add 2½ teasp. salt, pepper, chili, cayenne, garlic salt. (For a very hot chili flavor, add 1 extra teasp. chili.) Add tomatoes, tomato sauce; simmer, uncovered, 45 min. Add olives.

In greased 12″ x 8″ x 2″ baking dish, place one third of mush mixture; with spoon, press against bottom and sides of dish; fill with meat mixture. Top with remaining mush, spreading it over as much of meat as possible. Refrigerate.

About 2 hr. before serving: Start heating oven to 325°F. Sprinkle top of pie with cheese. Bake 1½ hr. to 2 hr. Makes 8 servings.

Corned Beef

TO BUY AND STORE CORNED BEEF

Today meat packers are packaging a branded fine-quality corned-beef brisket (whole or half) with a special mild cure, which is truly delicious. Rump, plate, and navel are also corned and sold in bulk or in barrel.

Look for corned beef with about a fourth as much fat as lean.

With one method of corning, the corned beef retains its red color after cooking. With the other method, only sugar and salt are used and the corned beef, when cooked, has a grayish-brown color; this type is popular in New England.

Amount to Buy: A 4-lb. piece of corned beef makes about 8 servings.

To Store: Store as in To Store Meat, p. 47. Use within 7 days.

SUSAN'S CORNED BEEF AND CABBAGE

Corned-beef brisket	1 clove garlic
3 onion slices	2 green-pepper rings
4 cloves	1 stalk celery
6 whole black peppers	1 pared carrot
1 bay leaf	Few sprigs parsley
½ teasp. dried rosemary	1 head green cabbage

1. Buy a packaged half brisket (4 to 5 lb.) or whole brisket (9 to 10 lb.). Place in large deep kettle; cover with cold water.
2. Add onion slices, studded with cloves; whole peppers; bay leaf; rosemary; garlic; pepper rings; and celery, carrot, and parsley, tied with string. Bring to boil, covered; reduce heat. Simmer half brisket 4 to 5 hr., whole brisket 5 to 6 hr., or until fork-tender.
3. Wash cabbage; cut into quarters; trim off core, leaving enough to hold cabbage intact.
4. About ½ hr. before meat is done, skim excess fat from top of liquid; arrange cabbage on meat; simmer, covered, 25 to 30 min., or until cabbage is tender-crisp.

To serve: Slice meat; put on platter, with cabbage around it. If desired, pour Quick Mustard Sauce, p. 372, over cabbage and meat. A 4- to 5-lb. half brisket makes 4 servings for at least 2 meals.

Simmered Corned Beef: Omit cabbage. When meat is tender, remove from liquid; serve hot, sliced, with Horse-radish Sauce I or II, p. 375.

Or remove meat from liquid; cool meat and water quickly; return meat to liquid; refrigerate. Serve cold, thinly sliced, with Old-fashioned Potato Salad, p. 304.

Or remove meat from liquid to plate. Cover meat with second plate; weigh down with heavy object, so meat will be well pressed. Cool. Then refrigerate 24 hr. Meat will slice nicely.

Barbecued Corned Beef: Omit cabbage. About 30 min. before meat is done, remove it to shallow open pan. Dot with whole cloves. Heat, until blended, 2 tablesp. butter or margarine; 1 tablesp. prepared mustard; ⅓ cup brown sugar, packed; 5 tablesp. catchup; and 3 tablesp. vinegar. Pour over corned beef. Bake at 350°F., basting occasionally, 30 min., or until brown.

New England Boiled Dinner: Use half brisket. About 45 min. before meat is done, skim excess fat from top of liquid. To liquid, add 6 pared medium potatoes, 6 pared carrots, 6 pared white turnips. Simmer, covered, 15 min. Add cabbage as above. Simmer until all vegetables are just tender-crisp. (You may cook beets separately to serve with corned beef.) Serve sliced meat on platter, with vegetables. Pass chili sauce, mustard pickles, or horse-radish.

Beef-Bacon Slices

Now you can enjoy a beef product that looks very much like packaged sliced bacon but has a wonderful flavor all its own. The meat, which has been sugar-cured and smoked, comes sliced and wrapped in cellophane. It may be pan-fried or broiled, and cooks in the same time as bacon.

To cook, just follow label directions; cook until crisp but not brittle. Serve with fried or scrambled eggs, waffles, pancakes, etc. Nice too in sandwiches.

LET'S HAVE FRESH PORK

Pork, with its consistent tenderness and superb flavor, is good eating the year round. But it's likely to be a better buy between November and March, when the supply is greatest.

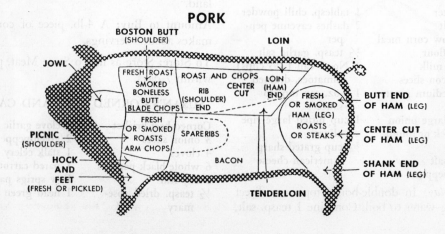

PORK

Because there is little difference in its tenderness, pork does not carry a packer's brand name or Federal grade stamp. However, be sure to look for the round purple U.S. Inspected and Passed stamp. See To Buy Meat, p. 46.

The lean of quality pork should be firm and tender, with a pinkish cast and some marbling. The fat on the outside should be firm and snowy white.

In the following pages, we suggest and describe favorite uses for many of the retail cuts of pork. Our diagram of the pork animal on p. 74 will help you to identify these cuts better.

The All-Important Rule

Always Serve Fresh Pork Well Done. All fresh pork must be thoroughly cooked. When pork reaches the well-done stage, all the pink color disappears, the meat itself becomes gray, and the meat juice is clear.

Fresh-Pork Roasts

TO BUY AND STORE PORK ROASTS

Select a Cut:

Loin Roasts: A loin of pork extends from the shoulder to the fresh ham. A loin weighing 10 to 14 lb. may be cut into chops, cut into the 3 loin roasts below, or cut to order.

For easy carving, have meatman free backbone from rib of pork roast by sawing close and parallel to backbone.

Loin (Ham) End Roast (Fig. A, below) contains tenderloin and some bone, and is difficult to carve. Weighs 3 to 4 lb.

Center-Cut Roast (Fig. B, below) is the choicest of all the loin roasts and usually the highest priced. It contains the tip end of the tenderloin and a T-shaped bone. It is often cut into center-cut chops. Weighs 6 to 7 lb.

Rib (Shoulder) End Roast (Fig. C, below) contains even more bone than the loin end. It is difficult to carve. May be cut into chops. Weighs 3 to 5 lb.

Shoulder Roasts: A whole pork shoulder is usually cut into the following cuts:

Boston-Butt (Shoulder) Roast weighs 3 to 8 lb. It may be sold boned or with bone in.

Picnic (Shoulder) Roast weighs 4 to 10 lb. It may be sold with bone in or boned, rolled, and tied.

PORK LOIN ROASTS

A Loin (Ham) End Roast   B Center-Cut Roast   C Rib (Shoulder) End Roast

Shoulder-Cushion Roast is a boned, but not rolled, picnic shoulder. It weighs 3 to 8 lb.

Leg (Fresh Ham): This cut is a fine choice for a large family, because it has a high percentage of lean meat to bone. It may also be boned, rolled, and tied. Can weigh 5 lb. and up.

Crown Roast: This is a party roast, made from the rib end of the loin. It is shaped and tied to form a circle, with the ends of the rib bones exposed. The rib ends are usually Frenched, i.e., the meat is cut from the ends of the bones. Be sure backbone has been completely removed to make carving easier.

Do not fill center with ground meat—this increases roasting time. Cover rib ends with bread squares, pieces of bacon, salt pork, or aluminum foil during roasting.

Amount to Buy: Buy at least a 3-lb. roast. Allow 2 or 3 servings per lb. bone-in pork roast, 3 or 4 servings boned roast. If you're buying a crown roast, allow 2 ribs per serving.

Be sure to have meatman note on the bill the weight of the oven-ready roast to guide you in computing the roasting time.

To Store: Store as in To Store Meat, p. 47. Use within 4 or 5 days.

ROAST PORK

1. Check roasting timetable, below, to see about how long roasting will take. Plan so pork is done 20 min. before serving; it will slice more easily, and you will have time to make gravy.
2. Start heating oven to 325°F. Do not wash pork; wipe with damp cloth if desired. Place pork, with fat side up, on rack in shallow open pan.
3. If desired, rub surface of pork lightly with:
    Seasoned salt; or salt, pepper, and monosodium glutamate
    Or dried sage, thyme, or rosemary
    Or mixture of 1 tablesp. salt, 1 tablesp. paprika, and 1 teasp. dry mustard
    Or cut clove garlic
4. Insert roast-meat thermometer through fat side into center of roast. Don't let it touch bone. If you're roasting a crown roast, insert thermometer into center of meaty part of one of chops. Don't add water; don't cover.
5. Roast pork to 185°F. on roast-meat thermometer, using timetable below as an approximate guide. Pork must be *well done* with no tinge of pink. Don't baste or turn pork during roasting.
6. *Caution:* Roasts vary so in size, shape, amount of bone and fat, etc. that a roasting timetable can only be approximate at best. So rely on a roast-meat thermometer if you want to be sure.

TIMETABLE FOR ROASTING FRESH PORK

Pork refrigerated till roasted at 325°F. Use shallow open pan. Add no water. Do not baste.

Oven-Ready Weight (lb.)	Approximate Roasting Time (hr.)	Meat-Thermometer Reading (well done)
Loin		
2 to 3	1½ to 2	185°F.
5 to 7	3 to 4	185°F.
Boston Butt (Shoulder)		
4	3½	185°F.
Bone-in Fresh Picnic (Shoulder)		
5	3⅓	185°F.
Rolled, Boned Fresh Picnic (Shoulder)		
4	3⅔	185°F.
Shoulder Cushion		
5	4	185°F.
Leg (Fresh Ham)		
5	4½	185°F.
Crown Roast (No Filling in Center)		
6 to 7	3½ to 4	185°F.

7. When pork is done, remove to heated platter; keep warm while making Susan's Velvety Meat Gravy, p. 51, from drippings in pan.

To Serve: Serve with Saucepan Applesauce, p. 400; Baked Apples, p. 400; Speedy Whole-Cranberry Sauce, p. 287; Fried Apple Rings,

p. 289; Sautéed Pineapple, p. 286; Sautéed Bananas, p. 289; pickled peaches; currant jelly; or canned cranberry sauce.

If it's a crown roast, serve as in Crown Roast of Lamb, p. 96. Or place on heated platter or chop plate; alternate mounds of mashed potatoes and baked small apples or Rosy Cinnamon Apples, p. 289, around base.

To Carve a Loin of Pork: See p. 165.

To Use Leftover Roast Pork: See p. 127 and Soup from Leftover Bones, p. 36.

PORK-CHOP ROAST

2- to 2½-lb. center-cut pork loin, cut into 4 thick uniform chops	Salt Pepper

Start heating oven to 350°F. Trim off part of fat from chops. Sprinkle all surfaces of chops generously with salt and pepper. Then put chops together in original shape; tie snugly with white cord. Stand chops on flat, bony side in shallow open pan.

Insert roast-meat thermometer into edge of one of chops; don't let it touch bone or fat. Roast 2-lb. loin 1½ hr., 2½-lb. loin 1¾ hr., or to 185°F. on roast-meat thermometer. After first hour, spoon off fat as it accumulates in pan; save for gravy.

When meat is done, remove to heated platter. Remove cord, and it's ready to serve, without carving! Make Susan's Velvety Meat Gravy, p. 51, from drippings.

Serve with quick-frozen cranberry-orange relish. Makes 4 servings.

ITALIAN PORK-AND-RICE CASSEROLE

2 tablesp. salad oil	loin, cut from bone into ¼″ slices
2 sliced medium onions	¾ teasp. salt
1 clove garlic	¼ teasp. pepper
1 10¾-oz. can beef gravy	2 tablesp. salad oil
3 8-oz. cans tomato sauce	2 cups raw regular or processed white rice
1 3-oz. can whole mushrooms, undrained	3 or 4 sliced onions
2 tablesp. snipped parsley	3 seeded green peppers, cut into eighths
1 3-lb. center-cut pork	½ teasp. salt

Day before: In 2 tablesp. hot oil in skillet, sauté 2 onions and garlic until golden; discard garlic.

Add gravy, tomato sauce, mushrooms, parsley. Simmer, uncovered, 1 hr.

Meanwhile, sprinkle meat with ¾ teasp. salt, pepper; sauté in 2 tablesp. hot oil in another skillet until well browned on both sides. Remove meat.

To drippings in skillet, add a little mushroom sauce; stir till brown bits dissolve; add to rest of sauce. In 3-qt. casserole, arrange half of meat slices; top with rice combined with half of sauce. Add half of 3 or 4 sliced onions, rest of meat. Cover with rest of onions, then with peppers. Sprinkle with ½ teasp. salt. Pour on rest of sauce. Refrigerate.

About 1¾ hr. before serving: Start heating oven to 350°F. Bake casserole, covered, 1½ hr., or until hot. Makes 8 servings.

SWEET-SOUR PORK

2 tablesp. bacon fat	packed
1½ lb. boned lean pork shoulder, cut into thin strips	2 tablesp. cornstarch
	½ teasp. salt
	1 tablesp. soy sauce
1 No. 2 can pineapple chunks	¾ cup thinly sliced green peppers
½ cup water	½ cup thinly sliced onions
⅓ cup vinegar	
¼ cup brown sugar,	

Night before: In hot bacon fat in large skillet, cook meat until golden brown on all sides. Drain pineapple, reserving syrup. Combine water, vinegar, brown sugar, cornstarch, salt, soy sauce, ¾ to 1 cup pineapple syrup. Cook until clear and slightly thickened—about 2 min. Add meat; cook, covered, over low heat 1 hr., or till meat is fork-tender. Refrigerate.

About 30 min. before serving: Heat meat mixture over low heat until steaming hot. Add green peppers, onions, pineapple chunks; cook 2 min.

Serve with hot fluffy rice. Makes 4 generous servings.

SPICY MEAT BALLS EN BROCHETTE

¾ lb. boned pork shoulder, ground	1 No. 2 can pineapple chunks, drained
1 12-oz. can luncheon meat, ground	½ cup brown sugar, packed
1 cup fresh bread crumbs	½ teasp. dry mustard
1 egg, beaten	¼ cup vinegar
¼ cup milk	¼ cup water

Start heating oven to 350°F. Combine meats, crumbs, egg, milk; shape into 18 small balls. On each 8″ skewer, place 3 meat balls, alternating each ball with 2 pineapple chunks; place in shallow open pan about 13½″ x 10″ x 2″.

Combine brown sugar, mustard, vinegar, water; stir until sugar dissolves. Pour over meat balls, along with any leftover pineapple chunks. Bake 1 hr., basting frequently.

Serve on skewers with baked pineapple chunks. Makes 6 servings.

To Do Ahead: Early in day, shape balls; refrigerate. About 1 hr. 10 min. before serving, start baking.

CALIFORNIA CHOP SUEY

½ lb. boned lean pork shoulder, cut into thin strips	1 cup celery, cut lengthwise into thin strips, then into 1″ lengths
½ teasp. salt	1 No. 2 can mixed Chinese vegetables or bean sprouts, drained
⅛ teasp. pepper	
2 tablesp. salad or olive oil	
¼ cup coarsely chopped onion	2 teasp. cornstarch
1½ cups hot water	1 teasp. sugar
2 bouillon cubes; or 2 teasp. meat-extract paste	3 tablesp. warm water
	1 tablesp. soy sauce
	Canned chow-mein noodles

Early in day: Sprinkle meat with salt, pepper. In hot oil in large skillet, cook meat about 10 min.; do not brown. Add onion; cook 5 min. Add hot water, bouillon cubes; simmer, covered, 15 to 20 min., or until meat is fork-tender. Refrigerate.

About 20 min. before dinner: To meat mixture, add celery; bring to boil, covered; cook 5 min. Add Chinese vegetables; mix lightly; heat till boiling. Combine cornstarch, sugar, warm water, soy sauce; stir into hot mixture; cook 1 or 2 min., or until slightly thickened. Taste; season if necessary.

Serve on heated chow-mein noodles, shoestring potatoes, or hot rice. Makes 4 servings.

Pork Chops

Pork chops are favorites when braised to rich-brown, tender, juicy perfection. Broiling is not as satisfactory or as safe.

TO BUY AND STORE PORK CHOPS AND STEAKS

Select a Cut:

Loin Chops:

Rib Chop (Fig. A, below) usually has 1 rib; may be boneless. A 1″-thick chop weighs 4 to 5 oz.

Center-Cut T-Bone Chop (Fig. B, below) is the most popular pork chop because it has tenderloin. A 1″-thick chop weighs 5 to 6 oz.

Boned Loin Chop is a special loin chop, with bones removed.

Shoulder End Chop (also called first cut) has considerable bone. A ½″-thick chop weighs 4 to 5 oz.

Loin End Chop is similar to the shoulder end chop but contains tenderloin. A ½″-thick chop weighs 4 to 6 oz.

PORK CHOPS

 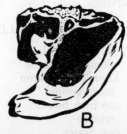  

A Rib Chop   B Center-Cut T-Bone Chop   C Bladebone Chop   D Arm (Round) Bone Chop

Shoulder Chops:

Bladebone Chop (Fig. C, p. 78) has considerable bone. A ⅓″-thick chop weighs 5 to 6 oz.

Arm (Round) Bone Chop (Fig. D, p. 78) has small bone and is a thrifty buy. A ⅓″-thick chop weighs 5 to 6 oz.

Pork Steaks: These are cut from the fresh ham (leg), and have only a small round bone. When boned, they are called pork cutlets.

Amount to Buy: Allow ½ to ¾ lb. bone-in chops per serving, ⅓ to ½ lb. boned chops per serving. One-inch thick chops take longer to cook, but make a finer appearance than thin chops.

To Store: Store as in To Store Meat, p. 47. Use within 3 days.

BRAISED PORK CHOPS OR STEAKS

Because all pork must be thoroughly cooked until there is no trace of pink, it is better and safer to braise or bake pork chops than to broil them. If broiled, chops become hard and dry before they are thoroughly cooked.

1. Choose loin or shoulder pork chops or pork steaks that are 1″ thick*; when done, they're more attractive than thinner ones. Allow 1 per person. Trim piece of fat from chops or steaks. Lightly sprinkle both sides of chops with salt and pepper or monosodium glutamate; rub with cut clove garlic if desired.
2. In skillet over low heat, heat the piece of fat; then remove. Brown chops slowly in melted fat till rich golden brown on both sides—15 to 20 min. (Spoon off excess fat as it accumulates.)
3. Add ⅓ to ½ cup boiling water; canned tomatoes; commercial sour cream; or pineapple, orange, or tomato juice. (The thinner the chops or the smaller the skillet, the less liquid is needed.) Also add a little minced onion.
4. Cover skillet. Simmer chops or steaks slowly about 45 to 60 min.,* or until fork-tender and *well done,* turning them several times during cooking. Season to taste. Remove to heated platter. Keep warm while making Susan's

Velvety Meat Gravy, p. 51, from drippings in skillet.

* If you're braising ½″ loin or shoulder pork chops, braise 30 min. after browning.

With Glazed Apples: After browning chops or steaks, add 2 tablesp. minced onion and ½ cup tomato juice. Serve with Glazed Apple Quarters, p. 289.

With Apple: Serve chops or steaks with Fried Apple Rings, p. 289, or with applesauce.

Breaded: Before browning chops or steaks, dip into flour or beaten egg, then into packaged dried bread crumbs.

Barbecued: Use ⅓ to ½ cup barbecue sauce instead of boiling water.

With Herbs: Mix each ¼ cup flour with ¼ teasp. dried marjoram, sage, or thyme. Sprinkle over chops or steaks before browning.

With Pineapple: Use ¼ to ⅓ cup syrup from canned sliced pineapple instead of boiling water. Serve chops or steaks with Sautéed Pineapple, p. 286.

SUSAN'S ORANGE PORK CHOPS

4 center-cut T-bone pork chops, 1″ thick	¼ teasp. salt
	¼ teasp. cinnamon
Salt and pepper	10 whole cloves
Paprika	2 teasp. grated orange rind
2 to 4 tablesp. water	
5 tablesp. granulated sugar	½ cup orange juice
	4 halved orange slices
1½ teasp. cornstarch	

1. Trim piece of fat from chops. In skillet over low heat, heat the piece of fat; then remove.
2. Generously sprinkle both sides of chops with salt, pepper, paprika.
3. With tongs, arrange chops in skillet. Cook till rich golden brown on both sides—15 to 20 min. (As fat accumulates, tilt pan and spoon off fat.)
4. When chops are well browned, turn heat low. Add water. Cover skillet tightly. Cook chops 45 min. to 1 hr., or until fork-tender and *well done,* turning them several times during cooking.
5. About 20 min. before chops are done, make *Orange Glaze:* In saucepan, cook sugar, corn-

starch, ¼ teasp. salt, cinnamon, cloves, and orange rind and juice, stirring, until thickened and clear. Add orange slices; cover pan; remove from heat.

Serve spoonful of Orange Glaze on each chop; garnish with orange slices. Makes 4 servings.

BAKED, STUFFED PORK CHOPS

1 cup finely diced, cored, pared cooking apples	2 tablesp. butter or margarine
¼ cup light or dark raisins	1 tablesp. minced onion
¾ cup fresh bread crumbs	3 tablesp. hot water
¾ teasp. salt	4 rib or loin pork chops, 1″ thick
1½ tablesp. sugar	Salt and pepper
	½ cup water

Mix apples, raisins, crumbs, ¾ teasp. salt, sugar. In hot butter in skillet, cook onion until tender; add to apple mixture. Sprinkle with hot water; mix well.

Trim piece of fat from chops. Slit each chop from bone side almost to fat, making a pocket. Sprinkle with salt and pepper, or monosodium glutamate, inside and out. Stuff loosely with apple mixture. In same skillet over low heat, heat the piece of fat trimmed from chops; then remove. Brown chops in melted fat till rich golden brown on both sides—15 to 20 min. Place chops in greased 2-qt. casserole. Meanwhile, start heating oven to 350°F.

Add ½ cup water to drippings in skillet; stir to loosen brown bits; pour over chops. Bake, covered, 45 min. Uncover; bake 15 min., or until fork-tender. Makes 4 servings.

BAKED FRUIT PORK CHOPS

1 lb. dried prunes	packed
4 rib pork chops, 1″ thick	2 tablesp. water
1 teasp. cinnamon	1 tablesp. salad oil
¼ teasp. ground cloves	1 teasp. salt
2 tablesp. fresh, frozen, or canned lemon juice	¼ cup hot water
¼ cup brown sugar,	4 halved, pared medium sweet potatoes

Early in day: Soak prunes in hot water to cover 5 min. Meanwhile, trim as much fat from chops as possible; then slit each chop from bone side almost to fat, making a pocket. Pit prunes; with

scissors, snip prunes fine. Add cinnamon, cloves, lemon juice, brown sugar, 2 tablesp. water; cook 2 or 3 min. Use to stuff chops, saving any leftover prune mixture.

In hot oil in skillet, brown chops till rich golden brown on both sides—15 to 20 min. Place chops in 3-qt. casserole; sprinkle with salt. Add ¼ cup hot water to drippings in skillet; stir to loosen brown bits; pour over chops. Spoon leftover prune mixture around chops. Refrigerate.

About 1½ hr. before serving: Start heating oven to 350°F. Bake chops, covered, 30 min. Add potatoes. Bake, covered, 45 min., or until chops and potatoes are fork-tender. Makes 4 servings.

BAKED PORK CHOPS WITH MIXED BEANS

4 loin or shoulder pork chops, ½″ thick	1 No. 2 can kidney beans, drained
Salt and pepper	1 No. 2 can green limas, drained
¼ cup minced onion	¼ cup catchup
1 minced clove garlic	2 tablesp. vinegar
1 teasp. brown sugar	
½ teasp. dry mustard	

Start heating oven to 350°F. Trim piece of fat from chops; in skillet over low heat, heat the piece of fat; then remove. Brown chops slowly in melted fat till rich golden brown on both sides—15 to 20 min. (Spoon off excess fat as it accumulates.) Sprinkle chops with salt, pepper; set aside.

In drippings in skillet, sauté onion and garlic 5 min., or until tender. Stir in brown sugar, mustard, beans, catchup, vinegar; mix well; season if necessary. Pour into 2-qt. casserole. Arrange chops over beans. Bake, covered, 45 min., or until chops are fork-tender. Makes 4 servings.

ZESTY PORK-CHOP BAKE

¼ lb. elbow macaroni (1 cup)	2 tablesp. flour
4 loin pork chops, ½″ thick	1 tablesp. brown sugar
2 teasp. salt	½ teasp. salt
¼ teasp. pepper	½ cup water
2 tablesp. minced onion	½ cup chili sauce
¼ cup minced green pepper	1 tablesp. vinegar
	1 No. 2 can cream-style corn

Cook macaroni as label directs; drain. Trim piece of fat from chops. Season pork chops with

2 teasp. salt, pepper. In skillet over low heat, heat the piece of fat; then remove. Brown chops in melted fat till rich golden brown on both sides—15 to 20 min.; set chops aside. Start heating oven to 350°F.

In drippings in skillet, sauté onion and green pepper 5 min., or until lightly browned. Stir in flour, then sugar, ½ teasp. salt, water, chili sauce, vinegar. Cook, stirring, until thickened. Mix in macaroni, corn. Pour into 2-qt. casserole. Arrange chops on top. Bake, covered, 1 hr., or until chops are fork-tender. Makes 4 servings.

To Do Ahead: Early in day, prepare pork-chop dish in casserole so it's all ready for baking; refrigerate. To serve, bake at 350°F. 1 hr. 20 min., or until chops are fork-tender.

Pork and Rice: Season, then brown, chops as above. Top each with onion slice. Substitute 4 15-oz. cans (or 7 cups homemade) Spanish rice for macaroni-and-corn mixture. Bake as above (or bake 40 min. in 5 individual casseroles, using 5 chops).

SKILLET PORK-CHOP DINNER

1 pkg. frozen peas	½ teasp. dried
4 loin pork chops,	rosemary
1″ thick	1¼ cups hot water
Salt	2 to 3 tablesp. fresh,
Pepper	frozen, or canned
1 tablesp. fat, salad oil,	lemon juice
or bacon fat	¼ cup orange juice
1 split clove garlic	4 ¼″-thick orange
2 tablesp. sugar	slices
2 tablesp. cornstarch	1 1-lb. can small whole
½ teasp. salt	potatoes, drained

Let peas thaw while preparing rest of dish. Sprinkle pork chops with salt, pepper. In hot fat in skillet, brown chops with garlic till rich golden brown on both sides—15 to 20 min. Set chops aside; discard garlic.

To drippings in skillet, add sugar, cornstarch, ½ teasp. salt, rosemary. Gradually stir in hot water; cook, stirring, until thick and glossy. Stir in lemon juice, orange juice.

Set 1 orange slice on each pork chop; arrange in sauce in skillet. Cook over low heat, covered, 30 min. Add broken-up block of peas, potatoes; cook, covered, basting occasionally with sauce, 20 min. Then uncover and cook 10 min., or until fork-tender. Makes 4 servings.

Pork Tenderloin

TO BUY AND STORE PORK TENDERLOIN

Pork tenderloin is a 9″- to 12″-long, tapering, tender piece of lean meat from the underside of the pork loin. It weighs ¾ to 1½ lb. It's sold whole, thickly sliced, or flattened into fillets, and is the most tender and usually the highest priced pork cut.

Frozen pork-tenderloin patties packaged by well-known meat packers are excellent; cook as label directs.

Amount to Buy: Allow 2 or 3 servings per lb.

To Store: Store as in To Store Meat, p. 47. Use within 3 days. Keep frozen tenderloin patties frozen until time to use.

BREADED PORK TENDERLOIN

3 pork tenderloins	1 egg, slightly beaten
(¾ lb. each)	2 tablesp. water
Cut clove garlic	Packaged dried bread
(optional)	crumbs
Seasoned Flour,	¼ cup fat or salad oil
p. 10	

Cut meat into 2″-thick slices. Rub lightly with garlic. Dip into Seasoned Flour, then into egg mixed with water, then into crumbs. In hot fat in skillet, cook meat until golden brown on all sides; then cook over low heat, covered, 30 min., or until tender.

Serve with Tomato Sauce, p. 376. Makes 6 servings.

BAKED, STUFFED PORK TENDERLOIN

3 pork tenderloins	(optional)
(¾ lb. each)	½ recipe Buttery Bread
Salt	Stuffing, p. 208
Cut clove garlic	

Start heating oven to 350°F. Split each tenderloin lengthwise almost all the way through. Lay flat; sprinkle with salt; rub with garlic. Spread half of each tenderloin with stuffing. Fold halves together; tie with string. Set on rack in shallow open pan. Bake 1¼ hr., or until tender; remove string. Makes 6 servings.

Pigs' Knuckles

PIGS' KNUCKLES WITH CABBAGE

4 pigs' knuckles	1 minced clove garlic
1 tablesp. salt	1 medium head green
1 cup celery tops	cabbage, cut into
1 bay leaf	2″-wide wedges
8 to 10 whole black	2 teasp. salt
peppers	

Wash knuckles; place in Dutch oven; cover with boiling water. Add 1 tablesp. salt, celery tops, bay leaf, black peppers, garlic. Simmer, covered, 2 hr., or until tender. Then add cabbage, 2 teasp. salt; cook, covered, 10 min., or until cabbage is tender. Lift cabbage and meat to heated platter. Makes 4 servings.

With Lima Beans: Omit cabbage. Soak 2 cups large California dried limas in 1 qt. cold water overnight. In morning, drain, reserving liquid. Add liquid to pigs' knuckles in Dutch oven; add enough boiling water to cover. Add 1 tablesp. salt, celery tops, bay leaf, black peppers, garlic. Simmer, covered, 2 hr., or until knuckles are tender. Add lima beans, 2 teasp. salt; cook, covered, 40 min., or until beans are tender. Makes 4 servings.

Spareribs

Spareribs are a rich, wonderfully flavored meat from the lower part of the rib bones of a pork loin. See p. 83.

TO BUY AND STORE SPARERIBS

Most spareribs are fresh pork and are pink in color. Sometimes in the South, cured ribs, grayish in color, are sold; before you use them, these must be soaked in water to remove excess salt. So know what you are buying.

There are 2 sheets, or sides, of spareribs to each pork animal. Top-quality ones have a good portion of meat between the rib bones and a thin covering over the bones. They weigh 1½ to 3 lb. Ask meatman to chop through ribs at large end.

Amount to Buy: Allow about ¾ to 1 lb. spareribs per serving.

To Store: Store as in To Store Meat, p. 47. Use within 2 days.

BARBECUED SPARERIBS

2 lb. spareribs	½ teasp. prepared
½ cup light molasses	mustard
½ cup catchup	¼ teasp. salt
½ cup chopped onions	¼ teasp. pepper
1 minced clove garlic	1 tablesp. bottled thick
3 whole cloves	meat sauce, p. 9
4 diced narrow strips	½ teasp. Worcestershire
of orange rind	¼ teasp. tabasco
Juice of ½ orange	1 tablesp. butter or
1 tablesp. vinegar	margarine
1 tablesp. salad oil	

Start heating oven to 325°F. Place spareribs in shallow open pan; cover with waxed paper or aluminum foil; roast ½ hr. Pour off fat; roast ½ hr. longer.

Meanwhile, make sauce: Combine molasses and rest of ingredients; boil 5 min. Pour off excess fat from ribs; cover ribs with sauce. Increase oven heat to 400°F. Roast spareribs, uncovered, basting often, 45 min., or until they are fork-tender, very brown, and glazed.

To serve: With scissors, cut spareribs into pieces. Makes 2 or 3 servings.

PINEAPPLE-SPARERIB BARBECUE

3 lb. spareribs	pepper
Salt	1 tablesp. cornstarch
2 tablesp. butter or	1 No. 2 can pineapple
margarine	chunks
¼ cup chopped onion	¼ cup wine vinegar
¼ cup chopped celery	1 tablesp. soy sauce
¼ cup chopped green	Dash pepper

Start heating oven to 450°F. Lightly sprinkle spareribs with salt; place in shallow open pan. Roast ½ hr.; pour off fat. Reduce oven heat to 350°F.

Meanwhile, in hot butter in saucepan, cook onion, celery, and green pepper 5 min. Stir in cornstarch, 1 cup syrup drained from pineapple chunks; cook, stirring, till transparent. Add vinegar, soy sauce, pepper, pineapple chunks; pour over ribs. Bake, uncovered, basting occasionally, 1 hr., or till fork-tender.

To serve: With scissors, cut spareribs into pieces. Makes 3 or 4 servings.

SPARERIBS

Spareribs are a wonderfully flavored meat from lower part of rib bones of a pork loin

RIB-AND-BEAN BARBECUE

4 lb. spareribs, cut into 2-rib pieces	2 tablesp. salad oil
⅓ cup soy sauce	2 dashes tabasco
3 tablesp. honey	½ teasp. dried thyme
½ teasp. salt	¼ teasp. salt
4 sliced medium onions	¼ teasp. pepper
1 cup cut-up celery leaves	2 1-lb. cans Boston-style baked beans

Start heating oven to 350°F. Place spareribs in 3-qt. casserole. Mix soy sauce, honey, ½ teasp. salt; brush some of this sauce over spareribs. Bake, covered, 2 hr.

Meanwhile, sauté onions and celery leaves in oil 5 min. Add tabasco, thyme, ¼ teasp. salt, pepper, beans. At end of 2 hr., remove spareribs from casserole; skim surface fat from drippings. To drippings, add bean mixture; top with spareribs. Brush surface of spareribs with rest of sauce. Bake, uncovered, 30 min. Makes 6 to 8 servings.

SPARERIBS, SWEDISH STYLE

About 2 lb. spareribs	¼ cup butter or margarine
¼ teasp. pepper	
1 teasp. sugar	1 tablesp. meat-extract paste; or 1 bouillon cube
1 tablesp. salt	
1 tablesp. crushed whole allspice	1 cup hot water

Day before if desired: Cut spareribs into 2- or 3-rib pieces. Sprinkle with combined pepper, sugar, salt, allspice. In hot butter in skillet, sauté spareribs, a few pieces at a time, until brown on both sides. (Be careful butter doesn't burn.) Stir in rest of ingredients. Simmer, covered, until fork-tender—about 1½ hr.

Serve hot, as main dish with gravy, made from drippings and milk or cream as in Susan's Velvety Meat Gravy, p. 51. Nice with mashed potatoes.

Or serve spareribs warm or cold, as hors d'oeuvre, omitting gravy. Makes about 3-main dish, or 8-hors d'oeuvre, servings.

SPARERIBS AND SAUERKRAUT

2 to 4 tablesp. fat or salad oil	1 No. 2½ can sauerkraut
3 lb. spareribs	¼ to ½ teasp. caraway seeds
2 sliced large onions	
¼ teasp. salt	1 grated, pared, cored cooking apple
⅛ teasp. pepper	
½ cup boiling water	

In hot fat (amount depends on fat on meat) in Dutch oven, sauté spareribs until brown on all sides. Add onions; sauté until tender. Sprinkle with salt, pepper. Add water; simmer, covered, 1 hr. Move spareribs to one side of Dutch oven; place sauerkraut, caraway seeds, and apple on other side; cook, covered, 20 to 30 min. Season to taste.

To serve: Lift sauerkraut from liquid; arrange on one end of platter. With scissors, cut spareribs into pieces; place on other end of platter. Makes 3 or 4 servings.

Fresh-Pork Sausage

TO BUY AND STORE UNCOOKED FRESH-PORK SAUSAGE

Fresh pure-pork sausage comes as links, patties, or sausage meat in rolls and packages.

Because of great differences in the quality and flavor of pork sausage, your safest guide is to buy a trusted brand. Be sure too that the sausage has been kept refrigerated at market and has a fresh pink color and odor.

Amount to Buy: Allow 1 lb. sausage links, patties, or meat for 4 servings.

To Store: Store at once as in To Store Meat, p. 47. Don't keep longer than 3 days at the most.

TO COOK FRESH-PORK SAUSAGE

Pork sausage must be cooked well done, or till it loses all its pink color and is nicely browned. But it should not be dry and crisp.

Pan-Fried Sausage Patties: Shape packaged sausage meat into ½"-thick patties. Cook slowly over low heat, turning occasionally, 12 to 15 min., or until meat is brown outside and gray inside, with no trace of pink. Pour off fat as it collects (refrigerate fat; use as in Leftover Bacon Fat, p. 93).

Pan-Fried Sausage Links: Place links in cold skillet with ¼ cup water. Simmer, covered, 5 min. (Don't boil; don't prick with fork.) Drain off water; then pan-fry slowly, turning with tongs, until evenly browned and crisp—8 to 10 min.

Baked Sausage Links: This is a nice way to cook a pound of sausage at a time. Arrange links in shallow baking pan (don't pile). Bake at 400°F., turning with tongs, until evenly browned—20 to 30 min.

To Serve: Serve sausage with eggs cooked your favorite way. Or serve on canned pineapple slices, sautéed in sausage fat. Or serve with applesauce, chili sauce, or Fried Apple Rings, p. 289.

Fully Cooked Brown-and-Serve Pork Sausage

TO BUY, STORE, AND HEAT BROWN-AND-SERVE SAUSAGE

Good news! You can now buy packaged, fully cooked sausage links with a fine fresh-pork-sausage flavor.

Amount to Buy: Allow ½ lb. fully cooked brown-and-serve sausage for 4 or 5 servings.

To Store: Keep refrigerated. Use within 10 days.

To Cook: Because brown-and-serve sausages are fully cooked, they need only a quick 3 min. browning and heating in a skillet or broiler—and there will be almost no drippings—a real timesaver. So they are excellent in mixed grills and quick-grilled sandwiches as well as fine for breakfast. Try them too in casserole and combination dishes, and in poultry stuffings.

Smoked Country and Polish Sausage

TO BUY, STORE, AND COOK SMOKED SAUSAGE

These 2 types of smoked link sausage come 4" to 5" long, or as large rings of 1 lb. or more. (Polish sausage contains garlic.) Top-quality ones are branded.

Amount to Buy: Allow about 1 lb. sausage for 6 servings.

To Store: Keep refrigerated. Use within 6 days.

To Cook: Simmer sausages in water to cover about 20 min.; drain; serve. Or simmer about 10 min.; drain; then in skillet, brown slowly on all sides.

SUNDAY-SUPPER CASSEROLE

3 cups medium noodles	or canned applesauce
1 lb. fresh-pork-sausage links	2 teasp. fresh, frozen, or canned lemon juice
¼ cup sausage drippings	⅛ teasp. nutmeg
1 cup sweetened fresh	½ cup grated process American cheese

Start heating oven to 400°F. Cook noodles as label directs; drain. Meanwhile, place sausage links in shallow baking pan; bake 25 min., turning once. Then lower heat to 350°F.

Pour off drippings from sausages; combine drippings with noodles. Arrange half of noodles in 1½-qt. casserole. Top with combined applesauce, lemon juice, nutmeg. Cover with rest of noodles; top with sausages. Sprinkle with cheese. Bake, uncovered, 20 min. Makes 4 or 5 servings.

TWELVE-O'CLOCK LENTIL-SAUSAGES

1 cup dried lentils	⅛ teasp. pepper
1 qt. cold water	1 tablesp. fat or salad oil
⅔ cup minced onions	1 tablesp. flour
1 tablesp. snipped parsley	½ lb. fresh-pork- sausage links
½ minced clove garlic	2 sliced, peeled medium tomatoes
3 tablesp. minced celery	
2 teasp. salt	

Day before: Wash and pick over lentils; soak overnight in cold water.

The day: Drain lentils, reserving liquid; heat 2 cups liquid. Add lentils, onions, parsley, garlic, celery, salt, pepper; simmer, covered, 12 to 15 min., or until nearly tender.

Drain lentil mixture; measure liquid. Place lentil mixture in greased 10″ x 6″ x 2″ baking dish. Melt fat in saucepan; stir in flour; add 1¼ cups lentil liquid; cook until thickened; pour over lentils.

Start heating oven to 350°F. Pan-fry sausage links as on p. 84. Sprinkle tomato slices with salt. Place sausages and tomatoes on top of lentils. Bake 20 min. Makes 4 or 5 servings.

LET'S HAVE CURED PORK

Hams and Picnics

Today well-known meat packers proudly brand and clearly identify each style of ham and smoked picnic on the wrapper, tag, and often the meat itself. These markings, together with the information on the wrapper, can guide you in buying just the style you want. The purple U.S. Inspected and Passed stamp on the meat itself assures its wholesomeness. If the wrapper is missing, use the buying guides below.

TO BUY HAMS AND PICNICS

If you have ample time in which to bake a ham, or smoked picnic, you will probably choose one of the uncooked, or so-called cook-before-eating, styles below.

If time is precious, however, consider a ham or smoked picnic labeled "fully cooked" or "ready to eat." Or buy a trusted canned brand.

Don't be misled by such terms as "tenderized," "tendered," etc. These are advertising slogans and must never be construed to mean that the ham is cooked.

Uncooked (Cook-before-Eating) Hams and Picnics:

Whole Ham: Today's fine, wrapped, mild-cure ham (8 to 24 lb.), labeled "Cook before eating," has a mild, rich flavor and extra

tenderness. It needs no soaking or parboiling and cooks in less time than the old-fashioned kind. However, it must be *thoroughly* cooked.

Three-in-One Ham: Instead of baking a whole ham, you may wish to have the meatman cut a whole ham (8 to 24 lb.) into a shank end, center cut, and butt end. Then you can bake the shank and butt ends and broil, pan-broil, or bake the center slices.

Half a Ham: If half a ham (4 to 12 lb.) seems the best buy for you, ask for a *full butt half* (Fig. A, below) or *full shank half* (Fig. B, below). If you want sliceable meat, don't buy an end piece of ham; the end piece is what's left *after* the center slices have been sold.

Full Shank Half of Ham: This is a real economy buy, and if you cut it in two as below, you get a choice boneless piece, which you can slice and then pan-fry, broil, or bake. The bone-in piece that's left can be simmered (allow about 25 min. per lb.).

To Cut Shank in Two: Place shank, with cut side down, on board. Then, starting at top and hugging bone closely with sharp knife, split shank lengthwise into 2 pieces—one meaty piece, the other with the bone.

Skinless, Shankless Ham: This uncooked (cook-before-eating) ham has had the bony shank end, tough skin, and excess fat removed. The meaty, round roast that is left comes wrapped and branded with detailed baking directions on the label. It carves easily and

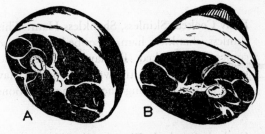

HAM

A Full Butt Half of Ham
B Full Shank Half of Ham

beautifully into big horseshoe slices, starting right at the end of the ham. It comes in sizes from 6 lb. on up; or you can buy a half ham or center slices.

Rolled, Boned Whole Ham: Here you have the advantage of easily carved, handsome slices and little waste. Completely boned and rolled, this ham (6 to 14 lb.) comes tied or wrapped in transparent casing. You can buy the whole ham, a piece, or slices by the pound, all ready to cook.

By the way, that casing on a boned ham is removed more easily before cooking than after. Just slit the casing lengthwise with the tip of a knife; then slip it off.

Smoked Picnic (Shoulder): No meat could be nicer for a small family than a smoked picnic (4 to 10 lb.). Cut from the leg end next to the pork shoulder, it not only looks like ham but has a true ham flavor when baked and glazed.

Smithfield or Tennessee-Style Ham: This ham (9 to 16 lb.) has had a long cure, or cure and smoke, and so needs special handling. See p. 89.

Cooked Hams and Picnics:

Fully Cooked or Ready-to-Eat Ham: This wrapped, cooked ham comes with bone in (8 to 22 lb.) or rolled, boned (11 to 12 lb.). You can buy it whole, by the piece, or in slices. It may be served as is, or baked, pan-fried, or broiled. Check wrapper information carefully.

Fully Cooked, Skinless, Shankless Ham: This skinless, shankless ham, described, p. 85, also comes fully cooked. It may be served cold just as it comes from the wrapper; or you may serve it hot, following the heating directions on the label.

Cooked Smoked Picnic (Shoulder): This wrapped, bone-in, cooked picnic (3 to 9 lb.)

comes all ready to serve sliced cold, quickly heated, or glazed.

Cooked Smithfield-Style Ham: This cooked bone-in ham (8 to 12 lb.), with its distinctive flavor, is sold at specialty shops only.

Boiled Ham: This is cooked, boned ham, which is sold sliced.

Prosciutto (Italian-Style Ham): This lean whole ham (12 to 20 lb.) has been pressed and aged in spices to achieve a concentrated, rich, mellow flavor. It is ready to serve, without cooking, and should be sliced paper-thin.

Canned Boned Hams and Picnics: See p. 125.

AMOUNT OF HAM OR PICNIC TO BUY PER SERVING

Uncooked, bone in	½ to ¾ lb.
Uncooked, boned	⅓ lb.
Cooked, bone in	⅓ lb.
Cooked, boned	⅛ to ¼ lb.

TO STORE HAMS AND PICNICS

Uncooked Ham or Smoked Picnic: Today's mild-cure meats must be handled like any fresh meat. Refrigerate an uncooked whole ham or picnic at once; plan to use up within 2 weeks. Use up half a ham in 7 days.

Home-Cooked, Fully Cooked, or Ready-to-Eat Ham or Smoked Picnic: Don't hold cooked ham or picnic longer than 7 days, in refrigerator.

Don't Freeze Uncooked Mild-Cure Hams or Smoked Picnics Longer than 1 Month. The fat of salted meat tends to become rancid when frozen. You may freeze leftover cooked-ham pieces, removed from bone, up to 4 to 6 weeks.

Smithfield or Tennessee-Style Hams: Because of their heavy cure, these may be stored, uncooked, in a cool place for several months. Store cooked ones in refrigerator.

BAKED HAM

1. Check wrapper directions on an uncooked (cook-before-eating) ham and follow them to

the letter. However, if the ham has no directions, check baking timetable, below, to decide about how long baking will take. Plan so ham is done 20 min. before serving; this gives ham time to firm up, and it will slice more easily. And don't forget to allow yourself 15 to 20 min. to skin and score the ham.

2. Start heating oven to 325°F. Place whole ham, with fat side up, or half ham, with cut side down, on rack in shallow open pan. (If desired, first wrap ham loosely in waxed paper or aluminum foil.)

3. Insert roast-meat thermometer through fat side into center of thickest part of ham; don't let it touch bone. Don't add water; don't cover. Then bake, using timetable below as an approximate guide.

4. *Caution:* Hams vary so in size, shape, amount of bone and fat, etc. that a baking timetable can only be approximate at best. So rely on a roast-meat thermometer if you want to be sure.

5. About ½ hr. before ham is done, remove from oven; remove wrapper. Spoon drippings from pan into small dish; save for pan-frying, etc. Cut away any rind left on ham.

6. Then quickly score ham as follows: With sharp knife, make diagonal cuts, ⅛″ deep and about ¾″ apart, across entire fat surface of ham. Repeat, at an angle, to make squares or diamonds. Then stud top of ham, in pattern, with whole cloves.

7. Drizzle on molasses, honey, or maple or maple-blended syrup. Then pat on brown sugar. Or substitute one of glazes, below.

8. Return ham to 325°F. oven for ½ hr., or until nicely glazed (internal temperature will be about 150°F.).

9. Or complete baking at 325°F. as timetable directs. Then score, stud, glaze, and bake at 450°F. until brown.

To Carve Baked Ham: See p. 166.

Baked Smoked Picnic: Follow wrapper directions; or bake as above, using timetable below as an approximate guide for baking time.

To Use Leftover Ham or Smoked Picnic: See p. 127, and Old-fashioned Split-Pea Soup, p. 40.

TIMETABLE FOR BAKING UNCOOKED (Cook-before-Eating) HAMS AND PICNICS

Refrigerated till baked at 325°F. Use shallow open pan. Add no water. Do not baste.

Weight (lb.)	*Approximate Total Baking time (hr.)	†Meat-Thermometer Reading
Bone-in Whole Ham		
8 to 10	3½	150°–155°F.
10 to 12	3½ to 3¾	150°–155°F.
12 to 15	3¾ to 4¼	150°–155°F.
15 to 18	4¼ to 4¾	150°–155°F.
18 to 22	4¾ to 5¾	150°–155°F.
Bone-in Full Butt or Shank Half Ham		
5 to 8	3¼ to 3½	150°–155°F.
Boned Whole Ham		
10 to 12	3¼ to 4	150°–155°F.
12 to 14	4 to 4½	150°–155°F.
Boned Half Ham		
5 to 8	2½ to 3½	150°–155°F.
Bone-in Smoked Picnic		
4 to 6	2½ to 3	170°F.
6 to 8	3 to 4	170°F.
8 to 10	4 to 4½	170°F.

* *Glaze, below, may be applied ½ hr. before baking time is up. Or complete baking at 325°F.; then put on glaze and brown at 450°F.*

† *Indicates internal temperature at end of total baking period. Thermometer may be removed to glaze ham.*

GLAZES FOR BAKED HAMS AND PICNICS

Spread baked ham, scored as in Step 6, above, with one of glazes below. Complete as in Step 8 and 9, above, adding rest of glaze in 2 or 3 applications (about every 10 min.) during rest of baking. Don't baste ham with glaze that has run down into drippings; it dulls luster of glaze.

Honey-Orange: Mix ½ cup honey or corn syrup with 1 cup brown sugar and ½ cup orange juice.

Marmalade: Mix 1 cup honey with ½ cup orange marmalade and dash tabasco.

Jelly: With fork, stir ½ teasp. dry mustard and 1 to 4 tablesp. horse-radish into 1 cup red jelly.

Apricot-Pineapple: Combine 1 cup brown sugar, ½ cup canned whole-fruit apricot nectar, ½ cup pineapple juice. Cook until thickened.

Cranberry: Mix ½ cup white corn syrup with 1 cup canned whole or jellied cranberry sauce.

P.S. Halve above recipes to glaze a baked half ham or smoked picnic, a simmered smoked boneless shoulder butt, or 2 cans luncheon meat or chopped ham.

TO HEAT FULLY COOKED OR READY-TO-EAT HAMS AND PICNICS

Check wrapper directions on a fully cooked or ready-to-eat ham (whole or half) or smoked picnic, and follow them to the letter.

However, if the ham or picnic has no directions, place it on a rack in shallow open pan. Heat, using timetable below as an approximate guide; score as in Step 6, p. 87; glaze as on p. 87; then bake at 450°F. until golden.

PARTY TOPPINGS FOR BAKED HAMS AND PICNICS

Bake or heat a whole or half ham or smoked picnic for complete time period as on p. 87 or above. Score as in Step 6, p. 87. Then glaze and decorate as below.

Studded: Spread scored ham or picnic with some of Jelly Glaze, above. Bake at 450°F. about 15 min., basting with more glaze. Set pecan or walnut halves or drained canned pineapple chunks, or orange cubes, in center of diamonds. Brush with more glaze; bake about 5 min.

Almondette: Spread scored ham or picnic with some of Honey-Orange Glaze, p. 87. Bake at 450°F. about 15 min., basting with more glaze. On meat, arrange sliced, slivered almonds and maraschino-cherry dots, placing 2 almonds together, fan-fashion, with cherry at base. Brush lightly with more glaze. Bake about 5 min.

Peach: *Day before:* Combine syrup from 1 No. 2½ can peach slices with ¼ cup vinegar; ½ cup brown sugar, packed; 1 teasp. whole cloves; 1 stick cinnamon. Simmer 10 min. Add peaches; bring to boil. Refrigerate. When baking ham or picnic, use 1 cup of this syrup mixed with 1 teasp. cornstarch to baste it. Garnish top of baked ham or picnic with peach slices; or arrange slices in groups around meat.

TIMETABLE FOR HEATING FULLY COOKED OR READY-TO-EAT HAMS AND PICNICS

Refrigerated till heated at 325°F. Use shallow open pan. Add no water. Do not baste.

Weight (lb.)	*Approximate Total Heating Time (hr.)	†Meat-Thermometer Reading
Bone-in Whole Ham		
8 to 10	2 to 2¼	130°F.
10 to 12	2¼ to 2½	130°F.
12 to 15	2½ to 3	130°F.
15 to 18	3 to 3½	130°F.
18 to 22	3½ to 4¼	130°F.
Bone-in Full Butt or Shank Half Ham		
5 to 8	1¾ to 2	130°F.
Boned Whole Ham		
10 to 12	1½ to 1¾	130°F.
12 to 14	2	130°F.
Boned Half Ham		
5 to 8	1½ to 2	130°F.
Bone-in Smoked Picnic		
4 to 6	2	130°F.
6 to 8	2½	130°F.
8 to 10	3	130°F.

* *Glaze, p. 87, may be applied ½ hr. before heating time is up. Or complete heating at 325°F.; then put on glaze and brown at 450°F.*

† *Indicates internal temperature at end of total heating period. Thermometer may be removed to glaze meat.*

OLD-FASHIONED COUNTRY-CURED HAMS

Smithfield and Tennessee-style hams, with their special cure and firm texture, need presoaking and boiling. Unwrap ham; soak 24 to 30 hr. in cold water to cover; drain. Then place ham in large pot or old-fashioned wash boiler (cut off tip end of ham if necessary). Cover with water; simmer, covered, until tender (allow about 25 to 30 min. per lb.), or until large bone in heavy end of ham becomes loose and protrudes. Remove ham; remove skin. If desired, score fat as in Step 6, p. 87. Top with one of Glazes for Baked Hams and Picnics, p. 87. Then bake at 450°F. 15 min.

Serve hot or cold, sliced paper-thin.

Smoked Boneless Shoulder Butt

TO BUY AND STORE SMOKED BONELESS SHOULDER BUTT

National meat packers are now marketing packaged cured, smoked boneless shoulder butts with the packer's name on the label. These have a delightfully mild, sweet cure, and taste and can be used like ham.

Amount to Buy: Smoked boneless butt weighs from 1 to 4 lb. The 2-lb. size is a fine buy for a small family.

To Store: Refrigerate as in To Store Hams and Picnics, p. 86.

SIMMERED SMOKED BONELESS SHOULDER BUTT

Place 2- to 2½-lb. smoked boneless shoulder butt in deep kettle; add boiling water to cover. Simmer, covered, allowing about 50 min. per lb., or until fork-tender. Drain.

Serve hot or cold, as is. Or serve with barbecue sauce; Horse-radish Sauce I or II, p. 375; Mustard Sauce, p. 375, Curried Pineapple Sauce, p. 373; or Savory Jelly Sauce, p. 372. Makes 4 servings, plus leftovers (use leftovers as suggested for ham on p. 127).

Savory: To boiling water in which smoked butt cooks, add 1 clove garlic, 6 whole cloves, 1 bay leaf, 4 whole black peppers. (Or omit peppers; add 1 teasp. celery seeds, ½ cup vinegar.)

Glazed: Place hot simmered butt in shallow baking pan. Spoon on ½ recipe for one of Glazes for Baked Hams and Picnics, p. 87. Bake at 450°F. 15 min.

Baked: Place hot simmered butt in shallow baking pan. Cover with honey, brown sugar, or marmalade. Bake at 400°F. about 15 min.

Pan-Fried: Cut cold simmered butt into ¼″ slices; pan-fry until brown on both sides.

PEANUT-BUTTER HAM ROUNDS

Preheat broiler 10 min., or as manufacturer directs. Cut 2- to 2½-lb. smoked boneless shoulder butt into crosswise slices, ½″ to ¾″ thick. Broil till golden on both sides.

Start heating oven to 375°F. Spread each meat slice with 1 tablesp. peanut butter. Arrange in shallow baking pan, side by side, with peanut-butter side up; add enough milk to almost cover slices. Bake about 2 hr., or until fork-tender. As milk evaporates, add more milk—enough to keep tops of slices barely covered.

When meat is fork-tender, cut around slices, being careful not to disturb browned surface; lift out onto heated platter. Makes 4 to 6 servings.

A Slice of Ham or Picnic

BAKED HAM OR PICNIC SLICE

Uncooked (Cook-before-Eating) Ham or Smoked-Picnic Slice:

1. Use ham or smoked picnic slice, 1½″ to 2″ thick. Start heating oven to 325°F.
2. With scissors or knife, snip fat edge of slice in several places to keep it from curling; stud with whole cloves.
3. Place slice in 2- or 3-qt. casserole (or use baking dish, with aluminum foil as cover). Then, if desired:
   a. Cover with ¼ recipe for one of Glazes for Baked Hams and Picnics, p. 87.
   b. Or spread with a little prepared mustard; then top with 2 tablesp. crushed corn flakes (optional).
   c. Or sprinkle with 2 tablesp. brown sugar

mixed with ⅛ teasp. ground cloves or a little mustard. Then top with drained canned apricots, peach halves, or pineapple slices if desired.

4. Now cover casserole. Bake 1½"-thick ham or picnic slice about 1 to 1¼ hr.; 2"-thick slice, 1¾ to 2 hr., or until fork-tender. Uncover last 15 to 20 min. to brown.

Fully Cooked or Ready-to-Eat Ham or Smoked-Picnic Slice: Prepare slice, 1½" to 2" thick (or thinner), as above. Bake, covered, at 325°F. 25 to 30 min.; then uncover to brown. Or bake in baking dish, uncovered, at 325°F. 30 to 40 min., or until well browned.

ORANGE HAM AND SWEETS

Start heating oven to 325°F. Snip fat edge of 1 1½"-thick slice uncooked (cook-before-eating) ham. Bake in casserole, covered, 1 hr.

Meanwhile, cook 6 to 8 medium sweet potatoes until tender, then place around ham with 4 ½"-thick orange slices. Pour on mixture of 1 cup brown sugar, packed; grated rind of 1 orange; ½ cup orange juice. Bake, uncovered, 20 min., or until brown. Makes 6 servings.

BROILED HAM OR PICNIC SLICE

1. Use ham or smoked picnic slice, ½" to 1½" thick. (See timetable below.)
2. With scissors or knife, snip fat edge of slice in several places to keep it from curling.
3. Preheat broiler with broiler pan in place 10 min., or as manufacturer directs.
4. Arrange slice on broiler rack, with top of meat about 3" below heat. Broil, using timetable below for approximate minutes per side.
5. After broiling one side of slice, you may turn it and spread lightly with one of these:
   1 tablesp. prepared mustard plus ¼ cup brown sugar
   ¼ cup tart jelly plus 1 tablesp. horse-radish
   Orange, peach, or apricot marmalade; or honey
   Melted butter or margarine, mixed with sliced scallions
   Or prepare any Broiled Fruit, p. 289; arrange on broiler pan in time to finish broiling with ham.
   Or arrange halved, cooked white or sweet potatoes; mushroom caps; tomato halves; or cooked onions, brushed with melted butter or margarine, on broiler pan in time to finish broiling with ham.

TIMETABLE FOR BROILING HAM OR PICNIC SLICE

Refrigerated till broiled in preheated broiler

Thickness of Slice	Approximate Minutes per Side
Uncooked (Cook-before-Eating) Ham or Smoked Picnic	
1½"	12 to 15 min.
1"	10 min.
¾"	7 min.
½"	5 min.
Fully Cooked or Ready-to-Eat Ham or Smoked Picnic	
1"	5 min.
¾"	3 min.
½"	5 to 8 min. (don't turn)

PAN-BROILED HAM OR PICNIC SLICE

1. Use ham or smoked picnic slices ¼" to ¾" thick. (See timetable below.)
2. Trim piece of fat from edge of slice; rub over heated skillet. With scissors or knife, snip fat edge of slices in several places to keep from curling.
3. Place slices in skillet. Pan-broil slowly, using timetable, p. 91, as an approximate guide. When slices are done, they should be nicely browned on both sides.
4. Just before slices are done, sprinkle lightly with granulated or brown sugar. Also, on top and around ham, place canned pineapple slices or chunks, peach halves, or apricot halves if desired.
5. Or after pan-broiling, remove slices to heated platter. To fat in pan, add 3 tablesp. vinegar, 1½ teasp. prepared mustard, ½ teasp. sugar, ⅛ teasp. paprika, 1 tablesp. currant jelly. Stir well; heat; pour over slices.

Or pass one of these sauces: Savory Jelly, p. 372; Quick Mustard, p. 372; Curried Pineapple, p. 373; Currant Mint, p. 372; Creamy Mustard Sauce, p. 375; Horse-radish Sauce I or II, p. 375.

TIMETABLE FOR PAN-BROILING HAM OR PICNIC SLICES

Thickness of Slices	Approximate Minutes per Side
Uncooked (Cook-before-Eating) Ham or Smoked Picnic	
¾″	6 min.
½″	4 to 5 min.
¼″	2 to 3 min.
Fully Cooked or Ready-to-Eat Ham or Smoked Picnic	
¾″	3 min.
½″	2 min.
¼″	1½ min.

BRUNCH HAM AND EGGS FOR 2

In hot butter or margarine in skillet, sauté 2 peeled firm all-yellow or slightly green-tipped bananas and 2 drained canned pineapple slices until golden. Remove to heated platter; keep warm. In same skillet, fry 2 or 4 eggs as on p. 224, adding more butter or margarine if needed.

Meanwhile, in another skillet, pan-broil 2 ¼″-thick slices fully-cooked or ready-to-eat ham 1½ min. on each side.

Serve eggs to one side of ham, bananas to other, pineapple on top of ham.

HAM A LA STUFFING

3 tablesp. melted butter or margarine	⅛ teasp. poultry seasoning
¼ cup minced onion	¼ cup cooked or canned vacuum-packed whole-kernel corn
3 tablesp. minced celery	
2 cups day-old bread crumbs	
1 tablesp. minced green pepper	1 slice fully cooked or ready-to-eat ham, 1″ thick (about 1¼ lb.)
⅛ teasp. salt	
Speck pepper	

Start heating oven to 350°F. In hot butter in large skillet, sauté onion until tender. Add celery, crumbs, green pepper, salt, pepper, poultry seasoning, corn. Heat well, stirring. Place ham in baking dish; top with stuffing. Bake, uncovered, 30 min. Makes 4 to 6 servings.

Pineapple-Stuffed Ham: For stuffing, decrease bread crumbs to 1½ cups; substitute ¾ cup drained canned crushed pineapple for corn. Bake as above. Makes 4 to 6 servings.

SCALLOPED HAM, POTATOES AND CARROTS

1 thin center slice uncooked (cook-before-eating) ham (¾ lb.)	1 cup milk
	3 cups thinly sliced, pared potatoes
2¼ teasp. flour	1 cup thinly sliced, pared carrots
1 can undiluted condensed cream-of-mushroom soup	¼ cup minced onion
	¾ teasp. salt
	¼ teasp. pepper

Start heating oven to 375°F. In skillet, brown ham lightly on both sides; remove; cut into serving pieces. Stir flour into drippings left in skillet. Add soup; then slowly stir in milk. Heat, stirring, until boiling.

In 2-qt. casserole, arrange layers of ham, potatoes, carrots, and onions until all are used, sprinkling vegetables with combined salt, pepper. Pour on soup mixture. Bake, covered, 1 hr. Uncover; bake 15 min., or until potatoes and carrots are tender. Makes 3 or 4 servings.

Party Style: Double each ingredient. Use a 4-qt. casserole; bake, covered, 1 hr.; uncover, and bake ½ hr. or until potatoes and carrots are tender. (Or bake in 2 2-qt. casseroles as above.) Makes 8 servings.

OLD-FASHIONED HAM LOAF

2 eggs	1 lb. chuck, ground
1 cup milk, liquefied nonfat dry milk, or diluted evaporated milk	1 lb. pork shoulder, ground
	½ lb. uncooked (cook-before-eating) ham, ground
2 cups fresh bread crumbs	1 No. 2 can tomatoes (2½ cups)
2 teasp. salt	
½ teasp. pepper	

Early in day: With fork, beat eggs; stir in milk, crumbs, salt, pepper; let stand until crumbs are soft. Mix in rest of ingredients. Pack into greased 10″ x 5″ x 3″ loaf pan. Refrigerate.

About 1¾ hr. before serving: Start heating oven to 350°F. Score top of loaf. Bake 1¼ hr. Pour off liquid around loaf. Bake 15 min. longer.

To serve: Let meat loaf stand a few minutes; loosen around edges. With 2 broad spatulas, lift onto platter. Garnish with parsley. Cut into thick slices; then halve lengthwise. Makes 8 servings.

TWO-DAY CARAMEL HAM LOAF

3 cups fine fresh bread crumbs	¾ lb. uncooked (cook-before-eating) ham, ground; or 1 can luncheon meat, coarsely grated
2 cups milk	
2 eggs	
½ teasp. salt	
¼ cup nonfat dry milk	
½ teasp. dry mustard	1 cup brown sugar, packed
1½ lb. round, ground	2 teasp. whole cloves

Start heating oven to 350°F. Soak crumbs in 2 cups milk 5 min. With fork, beat eggs; add salt, nonfat dry milk, mustard, meats. Toss; then, with 2-tined fork, stir in crumb mixture, tossing well. Sprinkle bottoms of 2 9″ x 5″ x 3″ loaf pans with ½ cup brown sugar and 1 teasp. whole cloves; firmly pack meat into pans. (Or sprinkle bottom of shallow open pan with ½ cup brown sugar and 1 teasp. whole cloves; place meat on top; shape into 2 flat loaves.) Sprinkle top of loaves with remaining sugar and cloves. Bake 1 hr. Remove from pans.

Serve 1 loaf hot, with drippings. Refrigerate other loaf for next day. Each loaf makes 4 servings.

One-Loaf Style: Sprinkle bottom of greased 10″ x 5″ x 3″ loaf pan with ½ cup brown sugar, packed, and 1 teasp. whole cloves. Firmly pack meat mixture into pan. Bake at 350°F. 1 hr. 15 min. Makes 8 servings.

CRANBERRY-HAM LOAF

2 eggs	before-eating) ham, ground
¾ cup milk	
1 teasp. salt	1 lb. boned pork shoulder, ground
⅛ teasp. pepper	
1 cup fresh bread crumbs	1 cup canned whole-cranberry sauce
1 lb. uncooked (cook-	¼ teasp. ground cloves

Start heating oven to 400°F. With fork, slightly beat eggs; add milk, salt, pepper, crumbs; let stand a few minutes. Add ham, pork; combine well.

In shallow baking dish, shape meat into oval loaf. Mash cranberry sauce with cloves; spread on top of loaf. Bake 1 hr.

To serve: With 2 broad spatulas, lift onto heated platter. Makes 8 servings.

Apple-Stuffed Ham Loaf: Omit cranberry sauce and cloves. Make this apple stuffing: Sauté 1 minced small onion in ¼ cup butter or margarine until tender. Add 1 diced, pared, cored large cooking apple; 3 cups ½″ fresh bread squares; ½ cup dark or light raisins, rinsed in hot water; 1 teasp. salt; ⅛ teasp. pepper; ¼ teasp. dried sage; 1 tablesp. sugar.

Press half of meat mixture into 10″ x 5″ x 3″ loaf pan; pack stuffing on top, then rest of meat. Bake at 400°F. 1 hr. Place platter on top of loaf; then turn loaf out, upside down.

Susan's Pineapple Ham Loaf: See p. 132.

Bacon

TO BUY AND STORE BACON

Different brands of bacon vary in quality, flavor, uniformity, and size of slices, and in proportion of lean to fat. Once you know the brand you like, stick to it to be sure you get exactly what you pay for.

Packaged Sliced Bacon: Sliced bacon comes in ½- and 1-lb. packages. Some is packaged in jars. See also Beef-Bacon Slices, p. 74.

Slab Bacon: Slab bacon comes in pieces with the rind on. Slice it as you need it, using a sharp knife. Or have the meatman slice it to your order.

Amount to Buy: Buy only enough bacon for 1 week, as it begins to lose its fine flavor if it's held longer. There are about 8 to 10 slices in ½ lb. Allow about 2 slices per serving.

To Store: Keep bacon in refrigerator, well wrapped and away from strong-flavored foods. Keep up to 1 week, *no longer*.

Remove bacon from protective wrapping only when ready to use it; remove only as much as you plan to cook.

Don't freeze bacon. The fat may become rancid within a month.

TO COOK BACON

Susan's Pan-Fried Bacon: In large cold skillet or on griddle over low heat, place overlapping slices of bacon, just as they come from the package. While they heat, separate them with 2 forks so they lie flat. Cook slowly over low heat, turning with 2 forks or tongs, until crisp but not brittle, spooning off fat as it accumulates.

Allow 5 to 8 min. cooking time. Don't let fat smoke or bacon flavor will be affected. Remove each slice as it browns; drain on paper towels or brown paper; keep hot.

Broiled Bacon: Preheat broiler with broiler pan in place 10 min., or as manufacturer directs. Separate bacon slices carefully, to avoid tearing; place on broiler rack. Place 3″ from heat; broil 3 to 4 min. per side, or until crisp but not brittle, turning only once. Don't let bacon burn.

Baked Bacon (ideal for cooking a large quantity of bacon): Start heating oven to 400°F. Separate bacon slices. Place, with fat edge of each slice overlapping lean of next slice, on a rack in shallow pan. Bake 12 to 15 min., or until crisp but not brittle. No turning or draining is needed; bacon browns evenly.

Bacon Curls: Slowly pan-fry or broil bacon slices until light brown but still limp. Insert tip of fork in end of each slice; turn fork to wrap bacon around it. Carefully slip bacon curl off fork; finish frying. Makes attractive garnish for omelets, chops, vegetables, cheese soufflé, etc.

Leftover Bacon: Use leftover crisp bacon bits in vegetable salads, cream soups, creamed vegetables, eggs, or sandwiches.

Leftover Bacon Fat: Refrigerate in covered jar. Plan to use within 2 weeks. Nice for seasoning green beans, green limas, greens, macaroni, scalloped potatoes, etc. Nice too for making sauces and soups, for frying eggs, potatoes, meats, etc.

BACON CHOP SUEY

1 cup raw regular or processed white rice	1½ tablesp. cornstarch
½ lb. sliced bacon	1 teasp. salt
1 cup sliced onions	⅛ teasp. pepper
1½ cups sliced celery	1½ teasp. soy sauce
1 cup sliced mushrooms	2 cups shredded cabbage
2 cups water	1 cup sliced green peppers

Cook rice as label directs; keep hot. Fry half of bacon until crisp but not brittle; remove bacon.

In bacon fat, brown onions, celery, mushrooms. Blend water with cornstarch; stir into onions; simmer, covered, 10 min. Add salt, pepper, soy sauce, cabbage, green peppers, and crisp bacon, in pieces. Cook, covered, until just tender. Meanwhile, fry rest of bacon.

To serve: Make ring of cooked rice on platter; pour suey in center; garnish with bacon slices, halved. Makes 4 servings.

Canadian-Style Bacon

TO BUY AND STORE CANADIAN-STYLE BACON

Canadian-style bacon is a cured, smoked boneless strip of pork loin, much leaner than bacon. It comes by the pound in a casing, or sliced, prepackaged, and branded by well-known meat packers. Most of it today is ready to eat, but be sure to check on this when you are buying. Cook as wrapper directs, or by any of methods below.

Amount to Buy: Buy by the pound, in one piece, to simmer or bake. Or buy sliced to pan-fry or broil. Allow about 2 to 4 oz., or 2 to 4 thin slices per serving.

To Store: Refrigerate as in To Store Hams and Picnics, p. 86.

TO COOK CANADIAN-STYLE BACON

Pan-Fried: In skillet, pan-fry ⅛″- to ¼″-thick slices of Canadian-style bacon very slowly as in Susan's Pan-Fried Bacon, p. 92, allowing about 5 min. on each side.

Broiled: Broil ¼″-thick slices of Canadian-style bacon about 3″ from heat as in Broiled Bacon, above, allowing about 5 min. for each side.

Simmered: Simmer 1- to 3-lb. piece of Canadian-style bacon in water to cover 1 to 1½ hr., or until fork-tender. Serve, sliced hot, with barbecue sauce, or sliced cold, on meat platter or in sandwiches.

BAKED CANADIAN-STYLE BACON

Start heating oven to 325°F. Slip off casing from a piece of Canadian-style bacon while holding bacon under cold running water. Place bacon, with fat side up, on rack in shallow open pan; insert roast-meat thermometer into center of bacon. Bake to 170°F. on roast meat thermometer or approximately as follows:

2-lb. piece: about 1½ hr.
4-lb. piece: about 2 hr. 20 min.
6-lb. piece: about 3 hr.

Then score surface of bacon; stud with whole cloves; spread with brown sugar, orange or peach marmalade, canned crushed pineapple, or jelly. Bake at 400°F. 15 min., or until browned. *Serve* sliced, hot or cold.

GOLDEN-TOPPED BAKED BEANS

2 1-lb. cans baked beans in tomato sauce	style bacon slices, ¼″ thick
1 tablesp. minced onion	4 ¼″-thick halved orange slices
1 teasp. prepared mustard	¼ cup brown sugar, packed
1 teasp. horse-radish	1 tablesp. butter or margarine
Prepared mustard	
8 uncooked Canadian-	Whole cloves

Start heating oven to 400°F. In deep fluted 9″ pie plate or shallow casserole (5-cup capacity), combine beans, onion, 1 teasp. mustard, horse-radish. Spread bit of mustard on each Canadian-style-bacon slice; arrange with orange slices, pin-wheel-fashion, on top of beans. Sprinkle all with brown sugar; dot with butter; stud with cloves. Bake 25 min. Makes 4 servings.

Pineapple-Style Baked Beans: Make as above, substituting 4 halved, well-drained canned pineapple slices for oranges. Substitute 1 12-oz. can luncheon meat, cut into 6 slices, for Canadian-style bacon.

LET'S HAVE LAMB

Spring lamb (lamb under 1 year of age) can be found in many markets the year round; in others, it's sold during the seasons of greatest demand—early fall and spring. Use the many different cuts to add pleasing variety to your family and company meals.

The lean of quality lamb should be pinkish to deep red in color, firm and fine-textured, with an even covering of clear, white brittle fat and a great deal of marbling.

Your guides to buying quality lamb are the round purple U.S. Inspected and Passed stamp for wholesomeness, plus the packer's trusty brand name or Federal grade stamps (they're the same as for beef, with the exception of Commercial). See To Buy Meat, p. 46.

On the following pages, we suggest and de-

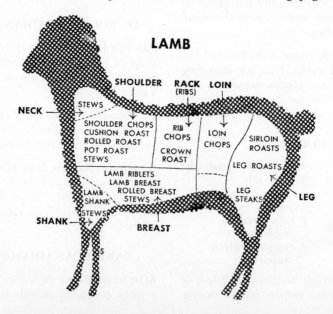

LAMB

NECK

SHOULDER   RACK   LOIN
            (RIBS)

STEWS
SHOULDER CHOPS   RIB   LOIN   SIRLOIN
CUSHION ROAST   CHOPS   CHOPS   ROASTS
ROLLED ROAST
POT ROAST   CROWN
STEWS   ROAST
                        LEG ROASTS
LAMB RIBLETS
LAMB BREAST
LAMB   ROLLED BREAST   LEG   LEG
SHANK   STEWS   STEAKS
SHANK   LEG
STEWS
SHANK   BREAST

scribe favorite uses for many of the retail cuts of lamb. Our diagram of the lamb animal on p. 94 will help you to identify these cuts better.

Lamb Roasts

TO BUY AND STORE LAMB ROASTS

Select a Cut:

Full Leg of Lamb: This roast, containing sirloin and short leg, weighs 8 to 9 lb. It's a good buy for a large family as it has little waste. It may be cut into 2 roasts, as below.

Sirloin Roast (Fig. A, below) is the broad upper end of a full leg of lamb. When cut off, it makes a good small roast of 2 to 2½ lb. It's especially nice boned and rolled.

Short Leg (Round) Roast (Fig. B, below) is the full leg of lamb *after* the sirloin roast has been cut off; it weighs 5 to 6 lb. If the meat has been trimmed from the end of the leg bone, it is called "French style."

Sometimes the end of the leg bone is cut short, and the meat is wrapped over the end. This compact roast fits nicely into a small pan for roasting. It is called an "American leg."

Half Leg: When a full leg of lamb is cut in half, either half of the leg—shank end or sirloin end—is a good buy for 2 or 3 persons. It can weigh 4 to 5 lb.

Rolled, Boned Leg: This is the full leg with bone removed; meat is rolled and tied. Roast weighs 3 to 6 lb.

LEG OF LAMB

Full Leg of Lamb cut into Sirloin Roast (A), and Short Leg (Round) Roast (B), French Style

Two-in-One Roast: Buy a full leg of lamb. Have meatman cut off 3 or 4 steaks, ½" thick, from sirloin end to pan-broil at once as on p. 100 or store in freezer for later use. Roast rest of leg.

Cushion Shoulder Roast: This square, flat roast from the lamb shoulder resembles a pillow. Bones are removed to form a pocket for stuffing. After stuffing, the open sides should be sewed or skewered. It weighs 2½ to 4 lb.

Rolled, Boned Shoulder Roast: For this cut, the shoulder of lamb is boned, rolled, and tied. It weighs 2½ to 4 lb., is tender, juicy, easy to carve.

Crown Roast: This makes a nice company dish. A small crown of lamb contains 7 ribs tied in a circle and weighs about 3 to 4 lb. A larger crown of 4 to 6 lb. may contain 2 sections of ribs sewed together. The meat is trimmed from the end of the rib bones, French style. Be sure the backbone is cut off; otherwise, crown will be difficult to carve.

Amount to Buy: Allow ¼ to ½ lb. bone-in lamb roast per serving, ¼ to ⅓ lb. boned lamb roast per serving. Allow 2 or 3 ribs per serving if it's a crown roast.

Be sure to have the meatman note on the bill the weight of the oven-ready roast, to guide you in computing the roasting time.

To Store: Store as in To Store Meat, p. 47. Use within 5 days.

ROAST LAMB

1. Use one of leg cuts, or a rolled shoulder of lamb.
2. Check roasting timetable, p. 97, to see about how long roasting will take. Plan so lamb is done 20 min. before serving; it will slice more easily, and you will have time to make gravy.
3. Start heating oven to 325°F.
4. Remove the "fell," the thin paper-like covering on the lamb, if you wish. Removing it will make the job of carving easier. Do not

wash meat; wipe with damp cloth if desired.

5. Sprinkle lamb with salt and pepper. Or add one of the following seasonings:

Chili-Mustard: Omit salt and pepper. Rub lamb with cut clove garlic; sprinkle with 1½ teasp. salt, ½ teasp. pepper, ½ teasp. dry mustard, ¼ teasp. chili powder, and 1 tablesp. caraway seeds. Add a little chili sauce to gravy.

Garlic: Rub lamb with cut clove garlic; or tuck small pieces of garlic in small gashes in surface of meat.

Herbs: Rub lamb with 1 teasp. dried marjoram, rosemary, or thyme.

Marinade: To 1 cup French dressing, add 2 sliced small onions, 2 cut cloves garlic, ½ teasp. dried thyme. Pour over lamb in deep dish. Refrigerate 6 hr. or longer, turning once. Drain; then roast.

Mint or Parsley: Make a few gashes in top of roast. Insert a few leaves or some snipped mint or parsley.

Spice: Rub 2 teasp. curry powder or ground ginger into lamb.

6. Place roast, with fat side up, on rack in shallow open pan.

7. Insert roast-meat thermometer through fat side into center of roast. Don't let it touch bone. Don't add water; don't cover.

8. Roast lamb to 175°F. on roast-meat thermometer for medium-done meat, to 182°F. for well-done meat; use timetable, p. 97, as an approximate guide. Don't baste or turn lamb during roasting.

9. *Caution:* Roasts vary so in size, shape, amount of bone and fat, etc. that a roasting timetable can only be approximate at best. So rely on a roast-meat thermometer if you want to be sure.

10. If desired, glaze roast as follows: Omit seasonings in step 5. About 20 min. before lamb is done, spread with this mixture: Combine 2 tablesp. each currant jelly and brown sugar, 1 tablesp. vinegar, and ¼ teasp. ground cloves.

11. When lamb is done, remove to heated platter. Keep warm while making Susan's Vel-

vety Meat Gravy, p. 51, from drippings in pan.

To Serve: Serve hot roast lamb with gravy or Currant-Mint Sauce, p. 372; barbecue sauce; or mint or currant jelly.

Or garnish with Broiled Peach Halves, p. 289; Broiled Pear Halves, p. 289; Sautéed Bananas, p. 289; or sprigs of fresh herbs, water cress, or parsley.

Or spread hot roast lamb with mint jelly. Or garnish roast with canned pear or peach halves set on orange or canned pineapple slices, then filled or topped with mint jelly.

To Carve a Leg of Lamb: See p. 164.

To Use Leftover Roast Lamb: See p. 127 and Soup from Leftover Bones, p. 36.

Cold Roast Lamb de Luxe: Roast lamb day before; refrigerate, unsliced, until served; then slice. Lamb will have nice color, will slice easily.

CUSHION SHOULDER OF LAMB

1. Check roasting timetable, p. 97, to see about how long roasting will take. Start heating oven to 325°F.

2. Fasten 3 sides of roast together with skewers. Season inside of pocket with salt or monosodium glutamate, allowing 1 teasp. per 1 lb. meat. Fill pocket with about 2 cups any moist bread stuffing, packing loosely. Close opening with skewers, or sew.

3. Place roast, with fat side up, on rack in shallow open pan. Don't add water; don't cover. Roast as in roasting timetable, p. 97. Complete as in step 11, above. Serve as in To Serve, above.

CROWN ROAST OF LAMB

1. Check roasting timetable, p. 97, to see about how long roasting will take. Start heating oven to 325°F.

2. Do not leave ground meat in center of crown —this increases roasting time.

3. Cover rib ends with bread squares, pieces of bacon, salt pork, or aluminum foil.

4. Sprinkle crown with salt, pepper; place with rib bones up, on rack in shallow open pan. Don't add water; don't cover. Insert roast-meat thermometer into center of meaty part of one of ribs.

5. Roast as in roasting timetable, below.

6. When crown roast is done, remove covering on ends of bones. Remove roast to heated platter. Keep warm while making Susan's Velvety Meat Gravy, p. 51, from drippings in pan.

To Serve: Serve as is. Or fill center with mashed white or sweet potatoes, buttered peas or onions, mashed squash, buttered cauliflower, sautéed mushrooms, or Spanish Rice, p. 235. Garnish with water cress; Broiled Peaches, p. 289; or Broiled Pears, p. 289.

TIMETABLE FOR ROASTING LAMB

Lamb refrigerated till roasted at 325°F. Use shallow open pan. Add no water. Do not baste.

Oven-Ready Weight (lb.)	Approximate Roasting Time (hr.)	Meat-Thermometer Reading
Sirloin Roast		
2 to 3	2 to 3	182°F. (well done)
Full, Short or Half Leg		
4 to 6	2½ to 3	175°F. (medium)
	3½ to 4	182°F. (well done)
6	3	175°F. (medium)
	3½	182°F. (well done)
8	4	175°F. (medium)
	4⅔	182°F. (well done)
Rolled, Boned Leg		
3 to 5	2¼ to 3¾	182°F. (well done)
5 to 6	3¾ to 4½	182°F. (well done)
Cushion Shoulder		
4	2½	182°F. (well done)
Rolled, Boned Shoulder		
3	2	182°F. (well done)
4	2½	182°F. (well done)
Crown Roast (No Filling in Center)		
4	3	182°F. (well done)
5	3¾	182°F. (well done)

LEG OF LAMB WITH HONEY-SOY SAUCE

6- to 7-lb. leg of lamb	½ teasp. pepper
1 teasp. salt	⅓ cup honey
	6 tablesp. soy sauce

Start heating oven to 450°F. Trim as much fat as possible from lamb. Place lamb on rack in shallow open pan. Rub with salt and pepper; brush with honey.

Pour about 1 qt. water into pan, or just enough to make water ¾″ deep. Bake lamb ½ hr. Reduce heat to 350°F. Pour half of soy sauce over lamb; roast 3 to 3½ hr. longer (about 35 min. per lb.), basting lamb every ½ hr. (at second basting, pour rest of soy sauce over lamb).

When lamb is done, remove to heated platter. Pour juices into bowl; let stand 1 min.; skim off as much fat from surface as possible. Serve juice as is over sliced lamb. Or thicken part of juice as on p. 7, save rest, unthickened, to serve next day on pancakes or rice.

SUREN'S SHISH KABOB

1 5- to 7-lb. boned leg of lamb	ground black pepper
1 minced clove garlic (optional)	½ teasp. orégano
3 chopped medium onions	1¼ teasp. salt
2 tablesp. olive oil	¼ teasp. dried thyme
⅓ cup sherry or cooking sherry	6 whole green peppers
½ to ¾ teasp. freshly	6 not-too-ripe tomatoes
	Melted butter or margarine

Night before: Cut lamb into 1½″ chunks; trim off gristle and most of fat. Put into large bowl, with marinade of garlic, onions, oil, sherry, pepper, orégano, salt, thyme. Toss well. Refrigerate 24 hr.

Shortly before serving: Start preheating broiler 10 min., or as manufacturer directs. String peppers, tomatoes, and lamb on separate 6″ skewers. Brush vegetables with butter.

Broil all, 2 to 3″ from heat, till tender, turning to cook evenly. Meanwhile, pour marinade from bowl into Dutch oven or kettle; heat. Slip tender peppers and tomatoes into Dutch oven; cut into quarters; cover. Add lamb when tender. Serve with Pilaff, p. 235. Makes 5 servings.

Kitchen Kabobs: You'll find kabobs to grill outdoors on p. 595. If you want to kitchen-broil them, preheat broiler 10 min., or as manufacturer directs. Use 6″ skewers; broil kabobs 2″ to 3″ from heat, turning with broad spatula.

POT ROAST OF LAMB SHOULDER

3 tablesp. fat	1 minced clove garlic
3- to 4-lb. rolled, boned lamb shoulder	½ teasp. celery seeds
	½ cup water
1 sliced medium onion	1 tablesp. flour
1 teasp. salt	1½ tablesp. water
⅛ teasp. pepper	

In hot fat in Dutch oven, brown lamb well on all sides—15 to 20 min. Add onion, salt, pepper, garlic, celery seeds, ½ cup water; simmer, covered, 2 hr.,* or until fork-tender. Remove meat.

Pour off juices and fat left in Dutch oven; measure. Add enough water to make 1 cup liquid; return to Dutch oven. Mix flour and 1½ tablesp. water to form smooth paste; stir into liquid; simmer, stirring, until smooth and thickened. Add bit of chili sauce or canned tomato sauce if desired. Serve with lamb. Serves a family of 4 for 2 meals.

If you use a 2- to 3-lb. lamb shoulder, allow 1½ to 2 hr., or until fork-tender. If you use a 4- to 5-lb. shoulder, allow 2¼ to 2½ hr.

Herb: Add pinch dried basil, thyme, or marjoram to other seasonings.

With Vegetables: About 30 min. before lamb is done, add 8 pared small carrots, 2 cups small white onions, and 8 scraped small new potatoes. Sprinkle with 1 teasp. salt; simmer, covered, 30 min., or until tender, adding a little boiling water if needed. Remove meat to heated platter; place vegetables around it. Make gravy as above.

Tomato: Substitute tomato juice for ½ cup water.

LAMB SUEY

2 tablesp. flour	1 cup thinly sliced celery
1 teasp. salt	
⅛ teasp. pepper	2 cups green beans, cut into 1″ pieces
1 lb. boned lamb shoulder, cut into thin strips	
	2 teasp. cornstarch
2 tablesp. salad oil	2 tablesp. cold water
1 minced clove garlic	1 tablesp. soy sauce
1 bouillon cube	3 tablesp. butter or margarine
3 cups hot water	4 cups crisp rice cereal

Combine flour, salt, pepper; use to coat lamb strips. In hot salad oil in large skillet or Dutch oven, sauté garlic and lamb until well browned on all sides. Add bouillon cube, hot water; simmer, covered, 15 min.

Add celery, beans; cook, covered, until tender-crisp—about 15 min. Stir cornstarch with cold water until smooth; add to lamb with soy sauce; simmer 5 min. Melt butter in saucepan; add rice cereal; heat thoroughly over low heat, stirring often. Arrange cereal on serving plate; spoon lamb mixture over it. Makes 5 servings.

LAMB STEW

2 lb. boned lamb shoulder	2 teasp. salt
	3 cups boiling water
3 tablesp. fat	2 teasp. celery seeds
¼ cup minced onion	8 pared medium carrots
2 or 3 minced cloves garlic	1 doz. halved small white onions
¼ cup flour	2 teasp. Worcestershire
1 teasp. salt	2 tablesp. snipped parsley
Speck pepper	

1. Remove excess fat, skin, and gristle from lamb. Cut meat into 2″ cubes.
2. In hot fat in Dutch oven or deep kettle, sauté minced onion and garlic until golden and tender; remove; set aside.
3. Meanwhile, combine flour, 1 teasp. salt, pepper; use to coat lamb lightly. Save leftover flour.
4. In hot fat left in Dutch oven, brown lamb *well* on all sides. Then add leftover flour, 2 teasp. salt, browned onion and garlic, boiling water, celery seeds.
5. Simmer gently, covered, 1½ hr., or until lamb is fork-tender. Remove any excess fat on surface.
6. Add carrots, cut lengthwise into quarters, and onions; continue to simmer, covered, until tender—about 20 to 30 min. Stir in Worcestershire; sprinkle with parsley.

Serve piping hot, as is or with Dumplings for Stew, p. 151, Golden Noodles, p. 238; or ring of Mashed Potatoes, p. 268. Or add 2 or 3 quartered, pared potatoes in step 6. Makes 4 to 6 servings.

▶ **For 2:** Make and serve as directed. Place heated leftovers in greased 1-qt. casserole; top with ½ recipe Hot Baking-Powder Biscuits, p. 324. Bake at 450°F. 20 to 25 min., or until biscuits are done.

Piquant Lamb Stew: To gravy, add a few capers or chopped pickle.

LAMB CHOPS

 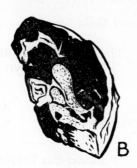  

A Center-Cut
Loin Chop

B Sirloin Chop

C Shoulder Arm
(Round) Bone Chop

D Shoulder
Bladebone Chop

Irish Stew: Omit browning of lamb in step 4. If desired, substitute 1 cup white wine for 1 cup water.

Lamb Pie: Pour Lamb Stew into 2-qt. casserole. Top with Mashed Potatoes, p. 268; Susan's Hot Baking-Powder Biscuits, p. 323, cut with doughnut cutter; or any Flaky Pastry, pp. 407 to 410, with gashes cut in it. Bake at 450°F. 20 to 25 min., or until golden and done. Makes 4 servings.

Lamb Chops or Steaks

The fat covering of lamb chops may carry a packer's brand name or Federal grade stamp to indicate quality. A good covering of firm white fat and streaks of fat in the pinkish to deep-red lean signify quality lamb chops or steaks.

TO BUY LAMB CHOPS AND STEAKS

Select a Cut:

Center-Cut Loin Chop (Fig. A, above) is a meaty chop with T-shaped bone, and is the most desirable and usually highest-priced chop. A 1″-thick chop weighs 4 to 6 oz.

Rib Chop is smaller than a loin chop. It contains rib bone and an "eye" of tender meat. A 1″-thick chop weighs 3 to 4 oz.

Double-Rib Chop has 2 rib bones and tender meat. About 2″ thick, it weighs 5 to 7 oz. Allow 1 chop per person.

French Chop has the meat scraped from the end of the rib bone; a paper frill is used to cover the bone end.

Sirloin Chop (Fig. B, above) is a good-sized and meaty chop cut from a heavy leg. A 1″-thick chop weighs about 4 to 6 oz.

English Chop is cut from unsplit ribs, is 2″ thick, weighs 8 or 9 oz. Usually the bone is removed and the flank ends wrapped around a lamb kidney, when it is called "English kidney chop." (You may cook kidney separately; serve it on top of broiled chop.)

Shoulder Arm (Round) Bone (Fig. C, above), with small round bone, and **Shoulder Bladebone Chop** (Fig. D, above), with much bone, are large, less tender, lower-priced chops. A ¾″-thick chop weighs 5 to 8 oz.

Leg Steak is cut from across the large leg of lamb, is meaty, has small round bone. A ½″-thick steak weighs 6 to 8 oz.

Lamb Riblets are 1″-thick strips of breast meat; the lean is streaked with fat and attached to a rib bone. Usually 5″ to 6″ long.

Mutton Chops (see p. 102) include rib and T-bone chops. They are larger than lamb chops. A 1″-thick chop weighs 6 to 12 oz.

Amount to Buy: Have chops and steaks that are to be broiled cut 1″ to 2″ thick. Thinner chops, ½″ to ¾″ thick, may be pan-broiled or braised. Allow about ⅓ to ½ lb. per serving.

To Store: Store as in To Store Meat, p. 47. Use within 3 days.

BROILED LAMB CHOPS AND STEAKS

1. Turn oven regulator to "broil." If you have no oven regulator, turn broiler heat on full. Preheat broiler with broiler pan in place 10 min., or as manufacturer directs. Then if you can, line broiler pan under rack with aluminum foil, with corners turned under, to catch drippings and save dishwashing.

   If your family is small and you want to broil only enough for 2, there are available small aluminum broiling pans with rack, which save washing the larger broiler pan.
2. Remove the thin "fell" covering on fat of meat. With scissors or knife, slash fat edge at 1″ intervals on a slant so meat won't curl.
3. If desired, rub meat with cut clove garlic. Rub hot broiler rack with bit of fat trimmed from meat. Arrange meat on rack; place so top of meat is about 3″ from heat. Or place as manufacturer directs.
4. Broil meat on one side, using timetable below as an approximate guide. Season as on p. 6. Turn with tongs; broil second side almost same length of time.
5. *Test for Doneness:* Make slit in meat near bone; note if color inside is of desired rareness. If meat is not quite done, continue broiling. When done, season.
6. *Caution:* Because meats vary so in size, shape, amount of bone and fat, etc., a broiling timetable can only be approximate at best. If you prefer your meat rarer or more well done, decrease or increase broiling time below accordingly. Remember, too, that meat may continue to cook after you remove it from broiler.

To Serve: Serve chops or steak piping hot, with butter; Lemon Butter, p. 377; barbecue sauce; Currant-Mint Sauce, p. 372; Quick Mushroom Sauce, p. 372; or Spanish Sauce, p. 376. Or place meat around mound of mashed potatoes; sprinkle with snipped parsley.

Mixed Grill: See p. 55.

TIMETABLE FOR BROILING LAMB CHOPS AND STEAKS

Thickness	Approximate Minutes per Side
Center-Cut Loin or Rib Chops	
1″	6 min. (medium)
	7 min. (well done)
1½″	9 min. (medium)
	11 min. (well done)
Double Rib Chops	
2″	12 min. (medium)
	15 min. (well done)
Sirloin Chops	
1″	6 min. (medium)
	7 min. (well done)
English Chops	
2″	12 to 15 min. (medium)
Shoulder (Arm or Bladebone) Chops	
1″	8 min. (well done)
Leg Steaks	
1″	8 min. (well done)
Lamb Riblets	
1″	10 min. (well done)
Mutton Chops	
1″	10 min. (well done)

PAN-BROILED LAMB CHOPS AND STEAKS

1. Buy loin, sirloin, rib, or shoulder chops, or leg steaks, cut about ½″ to ¾″ thick.
2. If desired, rub meat with cut clove garlic or piece of lemon rind. Trim piece of fat from meat. Heat skillet over low heat; rub the piece of fat over surface of skillet; then remove.
3. Arrange meat in skillet. Cook over moderate heat until well browned, turning with tongs;

pour off excess fat. Continue cooking, turning occasionally, until of desired doneness.

4. *Test for Doneness:* Make slit along bone, and note whether inside color is as rare, medium, or well done as desired.

To Serve: Season as on p. 6. Then serve hot with butter; Lemon Butter, p. 377; or Avery Butter Sauce, p. 372. Or garnish with parsley or mint. Nice with Creamed Potatoes, p. 267.

Or make this flavorful pan gravy: To drippings in pan, add 1 tablesp. water for each chop. Simmer until hot, stirring well with fork to mix in all rich drippings; season; pour over chops.

SPECIAL LAMB STEAKS

Dip 4 1"-thick leg steaks into one of mixtures below; let stand in refrigerator at least 3 hr., preferably overnight. Then broil, 3" from heat, till brown on one side—about 8 min.; turn and broil same time on other side. Makes 4 servings.

Soy Special: Combine 1 or 2 mashed cloves garlic, ⅓ cup salad oil, 3 tablesp. soy sauce, 2 tablesp. catchup, 1 tablesp. vinegar, ¼ teasp. black pepper.

Barbecue: Combine 2 tablesp. Worcestershire; 1 tablesp. vinegar; 1 tablesp. bottled thick meat sauce, p. 9; 1 tablesp. sugar; ¼ cup catchup; dash tabasco.

SPANISH LAMB-CHOP CASSEROLE

3 thin lean lamb shoulder chops	into strips
1 teasp. salt	1 cup raw regular white rice
⅛ teasp. pepper	4 beef-bouillon cubes
1 minced medium onion	1½ cups water
1 green pepper, cut	2 cups canned tomatoes

Start heating oven to 350°F. Trim piece of fat from chops. In skillet over low heat, heat the piece of fat; then remove. (Add a little oil or bacon fat if necessary.) Sauté chops in melted fat, sprinkling them with salt, pepper. When chops are brown but not done, cut each into 3 or 4 pieces. Place in 2-qt. casserole.

Pour off all but ¼ cup fat from skillet. Add onion, green pepper; cook, stirring, 5 min. Stir in rice; then pour over chops. In skillet, dissolve bouillon cubes in water; pour over chops. Pour

tomatoes over chops. Bake, covered, 1 hr., or until chops are fork-tender. Makes 4 servings.

YORKSHIRE HOT POT

4 shoulder lamb chops	cloves
1 minced clove garlic	2 teasp. salt
4 small whole onions	⅛ teasp. pepper
4 halved, pared medium potatoes	1 can undiluted condensed cream-of-mushroom soup
1 pkg. frozen cut green beans	½ soup can water
¼ to ½ teasp. ground	Paprika

Trim piece of fat from chops. In Dutch oven or chicken fryer over low heat, heat the piece of fat; then remove. Add chops, garlic to melted fat; brown chops till rich golden brown on both sides. Tuck onions and potatoes around and under chops as much as possible. Add beans, cloves, salt, pepper, soup, water. Cook slowly, covered, about 1 hr., or until all is fork-tender. If desired, thicken gravy a bit. Sprinkle with paprika. Makes 4 servings.

Lamb Shanks

Lamb shanks, which are cut from the foreleg of the lamb, yield a generous portion of lean sweet meat. One shank, weighing 1 to 2 lb., makes 1 generous serving.

To Store: Store as in To Store Meat, p. 47; use within 2 days.

INDIVIDUAL LAMB-SHANK ROASTS

4 lamb shanks, well trimmed of fat	lemon rind
1 quartered clove garlic	2 bay leaves
¼ cup flour	4 whole black peppers
2 teasp. salt	4 halved, pared medium sweet potatoes
1 teasp. paprika	
2 tablesp. salad oil	1 pkg. frozen cut green beans, thawed just enough to separate
½ cup lemon juice	
2 tablesp. grated	

Start heating oven to 350°F. Make slit in each lamb shank; insert piece of garlic in each slit. Combine flour, salt, paprika; use to coat shanks.

In hot oil in skillet, brown shanks well on all sides—15 to 20 min.; place in 3-qt. casserole. Add lemon juice to skillet; stir to loosen brown bits; pour over shanks. Add lemon rind, bay leaves, whole peppers.

Bake, covered, 1 hr. Add potatoes, beans; bake, covered, 45 min. to 1 hr. or until fork-tender. Makes 4 servings.

BRAISED LAMB SHANKS DE LUXE

4 lamb shanks, well	2 teasp. salt
trimmed of fat	¼ teasp. pepper
1 cut clove garlic	¼ cup salad oil
¼ cup flour	3 cups hot water
1 tablesp. paprika	1 clove garlic

Rub shanks well with 1 cut clove garlic. Combine flour, paprika, salt, pepper; use to coat shanks.

In hot oil in Dutch oven or heavy kettle, brown shanks well on all sides—15 to 20 min. Add water, 1 clove garlic; simmer, covered, 1½ hr., or until fork-tender. Remove shanks to platter. Skim excess fat from liquid in Dutch oven; thicken liquid as on p. 7, using any leftover flour mixture as part of flour.

Serve gravy over shanks. Makes 4 servings.

Curried: To gravy, add curry powder to taste.

Barbecued: Instead of gravy, serve with barbecue sauce or canned tomato sauce.

With Wine: For 1 cup water, substitute 1 cup Chablis, sauterne, or other white wine.

Breast of Lamb

Lamb breast is a flat piece of meat that weighs about 2 lb., is 1″ to 2″ thick and quite fatty. It can be boned and rolled for a pot roast, or stuffed, then braised. Or it can be cut into riblets and broiled as on p. 100, or simmered in a sauce.

BARBECUED LAMB BREAST

2 lb. boned lamb breast	1 sliced medium onion
1 teasp. salt	¼ teasp. paprika
⅛ teasp. pepper	1 tablesp. vinegar
½ cup chili sauce	1 cup water

Cut lamb into 4 pieces. Sprinkle with salt, pepper. Arrange in skillet with rest of ingredients. Simmer, covered, 1½ hr. Uncover; skim off fat; simmer 20 min., or until sauce is almost absorbed. Makes 4 servings.

LET'S HAVE MUTTON

Mutton, the flesh of sheep over 1 year of age, while usually considerably cheaper than lamb, is not widely sold in this country. Its flesh varies in color from dark pink to dark red. The fat has a deeper, creamier color than that of lamb and is somewhat flaky. It has a stronger flavor than lamb.

Mutton chops can be broiled like lamb chops; see timetable, p. 100.

Mutton roasts can be roasted just as lamb is roasted. However, such cuts as the leg and shoulder are usually best when pot-roasted as below.

POT ROAST OF MUTTON

Make several slits in shoulder or leg roast of mutton; insert garlic slivers. In kettle or Dutch oven, brown meat well on all sides. Slip trivet under meat. Add 1 cup water and 1 tablesp. vinegar; or use 1 cup tomato juice and ½ teasp. curry powder. Simmer, covered, allowing about 45 min. per lb. or until meat is fork-tender, adding more water if needed.

Serve hot or cold, with tomato or mustard sauce.

LET'S HAVE VEAL

Veal is young beef 4 to 14 weeks of age. It has a delicately flavored, grayish pink flesh, which resembles chicken in flavor. It is most abundant in late winter and spring. The rest of the year, most of the veal sold is *calf,* which is an animal 14 weeks to 1 year of age with a deeper-pink flesh. Veal has very little exterior fat and what it has is firm and creamy white. It has no marbling.

Your guides to buying quality veal are the round purple U.S. Inspected and Passed stamp for wholesomeness, plus the packer's trusty brand name or Federal grade stamps (they're the same as for beef). See To Buy Meat, p. 46.

Since it has so little fat, veal is at its best roasted, braised, or stewed to the well-done stage.

On the following pages, we suggest and describe favorite uses for many of the retail cuts of veal. Our diagram of the veal animal below will help you to identify these cuts better.

Veal Roasts

TO BUY AND STORE VEAL ROASTS

Select a Cut:

Loin or Rib Roast: Loin (T-bone) and rib veal roasts are fine buys. Usually, however, these sections are cut into chops.

Leg Roast: This fine meaty roast has only a small round bone; its cut surface resembles a round steak. It may be cut as a 4-lb., 6-lb., or larger roast (the center cut is especially choice). It is often cut into steaks and cutlets.

Rump Roast: This wedge-shaped piece of meat from the upper part of the leg is nice boned, rolled, then roasted or pot-roasted. It weighs 3 to 5 lb., and is fine for a small family.

Shoulder Roast: This roast is best when boned and rolled, to make carving easier. It may be roasted or pot-roasted. It weighs 7 to 8 lb. Or a smaller roast may be cut from it.

Amount to Buy: Buy at least a 3- to 4-lb. roast. Allow ⅓ to ½ lb. bone-in veal per serving; ¼ to ⅓ lb. boned veal per serving.

Be sure to have the meatman note on the bill the weight of the oven-ready roast to guide you in computing the roasting time.

To Store: Store as in To Store Meat, p. 47. Use within 5 to 6 days.

ROAST VEAL

1. Check roasting timetable, p. 104, to see about how long roasting will take. Plan so veal roast is done 20 min. before serving; it will slice more easily and you will have time to make gravy.
2. Start heating oven to 325°F.
3. If desired, rub cut surface of veal roast with cut clove garlic.
    Or make several slits in roast and insert slivers of garlic or a little dried marjoram.
    Or brush roast with soy or barbecue sauce.
    Or rub roast with dried thyme or crumbled bay leaf.
4. If roast has little fat covering, lay several thin strips of salt pork or fat bacon on top. Sprinkle with salt and pepper if desired.
5. Place roast, with fat side up, on rack in shallow open pan. Don't add water; don't cover.
6. Insert roast-meat thermometer into center of roast. *Don't let it touch bone.*
7. Roast veal to 180°F. on roast-meat thermometer, using timetable, p. 104, as an approximate guide. Don't baste; don't turn roast.
8. *Caution:* Roasts vary so in size, shape, amount of bone and fat, etc. that a roasting timetable can only be approximate at best. So rely on a roast-meat thermometer if you want to be sure.
9. When veal is done, remove to heated platter.

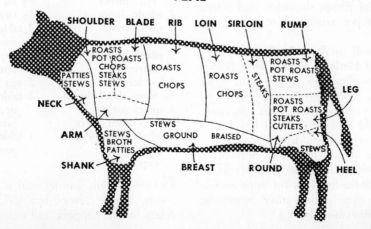

VEAL

TIMETABLE FOR ROASTING VEAL

Veal refrigerated till roasted at 325°F. Use shallow open pan. Add no water. Do not baste.

Oven-Ready Weight	Approximate Roasting Time	Meat-Thermometer Reading (well done)
Loin or Rib Roast		
5 lb.	3⅓ hr.	180°F.
Leg Roast		
3 lb.	2 hr.	180°F.
6 lb.	3⅓ hr.	180°F.
8 lb.	4 hr.	180°F.
Rump Roast		
4 lb.	2⅔ hr.	180°F.
Rolled, Boned Shoulder Roast		
3 lb.	2 hr.	180°F.
4 lb.	2⅔ hr.	180°F.
5 lb.	3 hr.	180°F.

Keep warm while making Susan's Velvety Meat Gravy, p. 51, from drippings in pan. Add sautéed mushrooms to gravy if desired.

To Serve: Serve with gravy; Quick Mushroom Sauce, p. 372; or tomato sauce. Nice with canned whole-cranberry sauce; one of Fresh Cranberry Relishes, p. 287; Glazed Pineapple Chunks, p. 287; or Sautéed Bananas, p. 289.

To Use Leftover Roast Veal: See p. 127.

POT ROAST OF VEAL

Rolled, boned veal rump, shoulder, and round roasts are nice for pot roasting. Use at least a 3- to 4-lb. roast.

Season meat; roll in flour. In 2 tablesp. hot fat or salad oil in kettle or Dutch oven, brown meat *thoroughly*—about 15 to 20 min. Place rack under meat. Add about 1 cup water or tomato juice plus ½ teasp. salt for each 1 lb. meat. If desired also add 1 clove garlic, 1 bay leaf, 1 teasp. celery salt, or ½ teasp. dried thyme.

Cover; simmer slowly over low heat or in 350°F. oven, allowing about 40 min. per lb. or until meat is fork-tender. (Or for approximate total simmering time period after browning, follow roasting timetable, above.)

About 45 min. before meat is done, if desired, cover pared potatoes and carrots, and onions, with boiling water; bring to boil; drain. Then place around meat 30 min. before it is done. Add extra salt to season vegetables.

When meat is done, remove it and vegetables to hot platter. Measure broth, adding water if needed; thicken as on p. 7. Serve with veal.

VEAL SCALOPPINE

2½ lb. boned veal shoulder	mushrooms
½ cup flour	1 No. 2 can tomatoes, strained; or 1¾ cups canned tomato juice
½ teasp. salt	
⅛ teasp. pepper	1 teasp. sugar
½ cup salad oil or fat	1½ teasp. salt
½ cup minced onions	⅛ teasp. pepper
¾ cup canned whole or sliced fresh	Hot fluffy rice

Start heating oven to 350°F. Cut veal into 1¼" cubes; roll lightly in flour combined with ½ teasp. salt, ⅛ teasp. pepper. In hot salad oil in skillet, sauté onions until tender; remove onions to greased 2-qt. casserole.

Sauté veal in oil left in skillet until brown on all sides. Place veal in casserole, along with mushrooms, tomatoes, sugar, 1½ teasp. salt, ⅛ teasp. pepper. Bake, covered, 1½ hr., or until fork-tender.

Serve with rice. Makes 5 or 6 servings.

BLANQUETTE DE VEAU
(de luxe veal stew)

2 lb. boned veal shoulder, cut into 1¼" pieces	margarine
	15 small white onions
4 whole cloves	½ lb. small mushrooms
1 small onion	½ cup veal broth
1 qt. boiling water	2 tablesp. butter or margarine
5 pared, quartered carrots	
	¼ cup all-purpose flour
1 bay leaf	3 cups veal broth
⅛ teasp. dried thyme	2 egg yolks
2 sprigs parsley	2 tablesp. fresh, frozen, or canned lemon juice
½ cup diced celery	
4 whole black peppers	1 tablesp. snipped parsley
1 tablesp. salt	
¼ cup butter or	

In Dutch oven, simmer veal with clove-studded onion, water, carrots, bay leaf, thyme, parsley, celery, whole peppers, and salt, covered, 1 hr., or until tender. Drain and reserve broth (there should be 3½ cups). Discard clove-studded onion, bay leaf, peppers.

Meanwhile, melt ¼ cup butter in saucepan; add onions; simmer, tightly covered, over low heat 25 min., or until tender. Add to cooked veal. In same saucepan, cook mushrooms in ½ cup broth, uncovered, 15 min.; add with their broth to veal.

In saucepan, melt 2 tablesp. butter; stir in flour. Slowly stir in 3 cups broth; cook until thickened. Beat yolks slightly with lemon juice. Slowly stir some of hot sauce into yolks; add to rest of sauce. Add to veal with parsley. Heat, but do not boil.

Serve in ring of fluffy hot rice, buttered noodles, or mashed or boiled potatoes on deep platter. Makes 6 servings.

P.S. This stew is delicious made the day before, refrigerated, then reheated over *very low heat* for serving.

Blanquette D'Agneau (de luxe lamb stew): Substitute 2 lb. boned lamb shoulder for veal.

VEAL PAPRIKA

2 tablesp. bacon fat or shortening	onion
	1 teasp. salt
2 lb. boned veal shoulder, cut into 1″ cubes	¼ teasp. pepper
	2 teasp. paprika
1 teasp. monosodium glutamate	1⅓ cups raw regular or processed white rice*
2 teasp. meat-extract paste; or 2 beef-bouillon cubes	1 3-oz. can sliced mushrooms
3½ cups boiling water	1 pt. commercial sour cream
1 thinly sliced medium	

To hot bacon fat in large heavy skillet or Dutch oven, add veal. Sprinkle with monosodium glutamate; sauté till browned on both sides. Dissolve meat paste in boiling water; add to veal, along with onion, salt, pepper, paprika. Simmer, covered, 45 min. Add rice, mushrooms with liquid; stir well; simmer, covered, 25 min., or until rice is done. Stir in sour cream. Add salt if needed. Makes 8 servings.

* *To use packaged precooked rice, use 2¼ cups rice, 2½ cups boiling water; reduce simmering time with veal and mushrooms to 10 min.*

VEAL STEW

Make Lamb Stew, p. 98, substituting 2 lb. boned veal shoulder for lamb.

BAKED VEAL STEW

1 tablesp. olive or salad oil	⅛ teasp. pepper
1 tablesp. butter or margarine	1 cup chicken bouillon; or 1 cup water plus 1 chicken-bouillon cube
2 lb. boned veal shoulder, cut into 1″ pieces	1 lb. small white onions
½ lb. mushrooms	1 cup white wine
2 tablesp. flour	1 bay leaf
¾ teasp. salt	1 or 2 sprigs parsley

In hot oil and butter in skillet, brown veal well. Meanwhile, pour some hot water over mushrooms 2 or 3 times (if mushrooms are small, leave on stems); drain. When veal has browned, place in 3-qt. casserole.

Start heating oven to 325°F. Into fat left in skillet, stir flour, salt, pepper; gradually stir in bouillon; cook, stirring, until thickened. Pour over veal. Add onions, wine, bay leaf, and stems snipped from parsley.

Bake, covered, 1½ hr. Add mushrooms; bake, covered, ½ hr., or till mushrooms are tender. Finely snip parsley over all. Makes 4 servings.

Breast of Veal

This flat cut, which weighs about 3 lb., comes boned or bone in and is fine for stews or for braising. It can be stuffed before braising.

BROWNED VEAL BREAST WITH NOODLES

2 lb. breast of veal, cut into 4″ squares	½ teasp. dry mustard
4 cups hot water	2 teasp. Worcestershire
1 minced small onion	¼ lb. uncooked medium-fine noodles (2 cups)
1 minced outer celery stalk	¼ cup flour
2 teasp. salt	3 tablesp. fat
¼ teasp. pepper	½ cup light cream
1 teasp. seasoned salt	

Day before: In saucepan, place veal, hot water, onion, celery, salt, pepper; simmer, covered, 1½ to 2 hr., or till meat is tender and bones loosened. Cool quickly as on p. 48. Refrigerate meat in broth at once.

About ½ hr. before serving: Remove meat from broth; slip out bones; set meat aside. Measure broth; add water, if necessary, to make 3 cups; return to saucepan. Add seasoned salt, mustard, Worcestershire; heat till boiling; add noodles. Cook, uncovered, 15 to 20 min., or until noodles are tender; do not drain.

Meanwhile, roll meat in flour; then brown well in hot fat in skillet. When noodles are tender, add cream; heat till boiling. Arrange browned meat on platter; pour noodles and sauce over all. Makes 4 large servings.

Veal Chops, Steaks, and Cutlets

Veal chops, steaks and cutlets should not be broiled. Braising is best and makes them the fork-tender, superbly flavored meat that everyone in the family enjoys.

TO BUY AND STORE VEAL CHOPS, STEAKS, AND CUTLETS

Select a Cut:

Rib Chop (Fig. A, below) has rib bone and tender meat. You may shape it by wrapping the thin end around the thicker portion and securing it with a toothpick. A ½"-thick chop weighs about 4 oz.

Center Loin Chop (Fig. B, below) has T-bone and very tender meat, and is the most desirable and most expensive veal chop. A large portion of the fat may be trimmed before cooking. A ¾"-thick chop weighs 7 to 8 oz.

Shoulder Bladebone Steak (Fig. C, below) has considerable bone, is less tender and usually less expensive than rib, loin, or leg cuts. It may be held in shape with toothpicks. A ½"-thick piece weighs 8 to 9 oz.

Shoulder Arm (Round) Bone Steak (Fig. D, below) is meaty, with round bone and little fat. It is less tender and usually less expensive than rib, loin, or leg cuts. Leave it whole or cut into serving pieces before cooking. A ½"-thick steak weighs 7 to 8 oz.

Leg (Round) Steak, cut from leg, resembles a shoulder arm-bone steak but is larger. Leave whole or cut into serving-size pieces before cooking. A ½"-thick steak weighs 1 to 1½-lb.

Cutlets are individual boned round steaks, cut about ¼" thick; sometimes they are flattened by pounding. A ¼"-thick piece weighs 3 to 4 oz. Frozen veal cutlets, packaged by well-known meat packers, are excellent; cook as label directs.

VEAL CHOPS AND STEAKS

  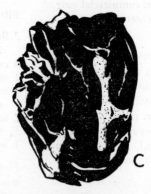 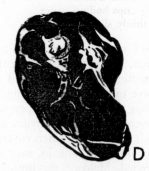

A   A Rib Chop   B Center Loin Chop   C Shoulder Bladebone Steak   D Shoulder Arm (Round) Bone Steak

Amount to Buy: Allow ⅓ to ½ lb. bone-in veal per serving, ¼ to ⅓ lb. boned veal per serving.

To Store: Store as in To Store Meat, p. 47. Use within 4 days. Keep frozen veal frozen until ready to use.

BRAISED VEAL CHOPS, STEAKS, AND CUTLETS

1. Loin veal chops are usually cut about 1″ thick. Other veal chops and steaks are cut ½″ to ¾″ thick. Season veal as on p. 6.
2. Roll veal in flour, corn meal, or fine cracker crumbs to coat all sides. Or dip into 1 beaten egg mixed with 2 tablesp. milk, then into fine cracker or packaged dried bread crumbs.
3. In 2 to 4 tablesp. hot fat or bacon fat in skillet, brown veal slowly until golden on both sides; do not burn.
4. Add ½ cup water, milk, or tomato or fruit juice. Simmer, covered, over low heat (or bake in 350°F. oven), turning once, until fork-tender as follows:

Chops, ½″ to ¾″ thick: about 45 min.
Steaks or cutlets, ½″ to ¾″ thick: about 1 hr.
Cutlets (Frenched), ¼″ to ½″ thick: about 25 min.

5. When veal is done, remove to heated platter. For gravy, to broth in pan, add enough milk to make desired amount of gravy. Thicken as on p. 7. Serve over veal.

To Vary:
1. Before coating veal, rub surface with cut clove garlic or hickory smoked salt; or brush with soy sauce; or let stand 15 min. in French dressing seasoned with herbs or chili sauce.
2. Or instead of ½ cup water in step 4, add ½ cup sweet or sour cream; diluted canned cream-of-mushroom, -celery, -chicken, or tomato soup; cooked dried prunes or apricots with syrup; or add ¼ cup tart jelly or marmalade diluted with ¼ cup water.
3. Or to water, add one or more vegetables, such as sliced onion, diced celery, green beans, or peas.
4. Or if veal is baked in oven, top each piece with grated cheese, or with slice of bacon, onion, tomato, green pepper, or lemon.

SHERRY VEAL SLICES

¼ cup flour	bread crumbs
1 teasp. salt	¼ cup fat
⅛ teasp. pepper	1¼ cups hot water
¼ teasp. celery salt	1 teasp. fresh, frozen,
¾ lb. veal-shoulder	or canned lemon
slices, ¼″ thick	juice
1 egg, slightly beaten	1 tablesp. sherry or
1 tablesp. cold water	cooking sherry
⅔ cup packaged dried	

Combine flour, salt, pepper, celery salt; use to coat veal slices well; save leftover flour mixture. Combine egg with cold water; dip veal into egg mixture, then into bread crumbs. In hot fat in skillet, sauté veal, a few slices at a time, until golden brown on both sides.

Arrange all veal slices in skillet; add hot water, lemon juice. Simmer, covered, 15 min. on each side, or until fork-tender. Remove veal to heated platter.

Thicken liquid left in skillet with leftover flour as in To Thicken, p. 7. Add sherry; season to taste. Serve over meat. Makes 4 servings.

BREADED VEAL CUTLET

1 lb. veal steak,	bread crumbs
½″ thick	¼ cup salad oil or fat
1 egg	1 can undiluted con-
2 tablesp. milk	densed cream-of-
1 teasp. salt	mushroom soup
1 tablesp. paprika	1 cup milk
½ cup packaged dried	

Cut veal into 4 pieces (cut around and discard bone). Dip into egg beaten with 2 tablesp. milk, then into combined salt, paprika, and crumbs, to coat thoroughly.

In hot salad oil in skillet, sauté veal until well browned on both sides. Mix half of mushroom soup with 1 cup milk; pour over veal; simmer, covered, 45 to 50 min. Remove veal to heated platter; pour rest of soup into pan; heat, stirring; serve over veal. Makes 2 or 3 servings.

To Vary: Brush veal with French dressing before dipping into egg and milk.

Or omit egg-crumb coating; dip veal into ¼ cup Seasoned Flour, p. 10, before browning.

Or substitute canned undiluted condensed cream-of-celery or -chicken, or tomato soup for cream-of-mushroom soup.

Crusty Style: Roll veal in flour; then coat with egg and dried bread crumbs as above; refrigerate ½ hr. Sauté in salad oil until well browned and fork-tender—about 15 min. on each side. Omit soup and milk. Serve with lemon wedges and boiled noodles, or with Tomato Sauce, p. 376.

Wiener Schnitzel: Make Crusty Style, above. Serve with lemon wedges and parsley and, if desired, with beet salad or pickled beets and skillet-fried potatoes.

Curried: Make Crusty Style, above, omitting paprika and adding 2 tablesp. curry powder to crumbs. After sautéing veal, make Susan's Velvety Meat Gravy, p. 51, from drippings in skillet.

CUTLET OF VEAL A LA SUISSE

6 thin veal cutlets (about 1½ lb.)	margarine
6 thin slices natural Swiss cheese	1 cup sauterne or Rhine wine
6 paper-thin slices cooked ham	1 cup leftover or canned beef gravy
2 tablesp. flour	½ cup light cream
½ teasp. paprika	Dash salt
⅓ cup butter or	4 to 6 drops lemon juice

Using edge of heavy saucer, pound cutlets well; halve each. On each of 6 cutlet halves, place ½ slice cheese; 1 slice ham, folded over; then another ½ slice cheese. Cover each with second cutlet half. Fasten securely with toothpicks. Coat lightly with flour mixed with paprika.

In hot butter in skillet, brown cutlets on both sides. Add ½ cup wine; simmer, uncovered, until liquid is almost completely absorbed. Add remaining wine, gravy, cream; simmer, covered, 10 min., or until fork-tender. Just before serving, add salt, lemon juice; remove toothpicks. Makes 6 servings.

BAKED VEAL CUTLETS WITH MUSHROOM SAUCE

6 bacon slices	bread crumbs
½ cup minced onions	1 tablesp. bottled thick meat sauce, p. 9
2 lb. veal steak, ½" thick	2 cans undiluted condensed cream-of-mushroom soup
1 egg	
2 tablesp. water	
½ cup packaged dried	

Start heating oven to 350°F. In skillet, fry bacon till crisp; remove. In hot bacon fat, cook onions until tender; remove. Cut veal into 8 serving pieces. Combine egg, water; beat lightly. Dip veal first into egg mixture, then into crumbs. In hot bacon fat, brown veal on both sides.

Place veal in 12" x 8" x 2" baking dish. Top with onions, bacon, meat sauce, then soup. Bake, uncovered, 30 min., or until veal is fork-tender. Makes 8 servings.

VEAL INVERNESS ON GREEN RICE

1 or 2 mashed cloves garlic (optional)	thick; or 4 veal loin chops, ¾" thick
⅓ cup salad oil	1 cup raw regular or processed white rice; or 2 cups packaged precooked rice
3 tablesp. soy sauce	
2 tablesp. catchup	
1 tablesp. vinegar	
¼ teasp. black pepper	2 tablesp. salad oil
2 lb. veal steak, ¼"	Snipped parsley

Night before: For marinade, in shallow pan, combine garlic, ⅓ cup salad oil, soy sauce, catchup, vinegar, pepper. Cut veal into serving pieces. Place in marinade; turn to coat well. Refrigerate.

About 35 min. before serving: Start cooking rice. In 2 tablesp. hot salad oil in skillet, sauté veal over medium heat about 15 min. on each side, or until nicely browned and fork-tender.

Serve on hot seasoned rice, tossed with a little snipped parsley. Makes 4 servings.

FRENCH VEAL CUTLETS

2 lb. veal steak, ½" thick	2 teasp. prepared mustard
1 tablesp. flour	1 bouillon cube
½ teasp. salt	1 cup boiling water
3 tablesp. fat or salad oil	1 cup commercial sour cream
1⅓ cups minced onions	¼ teasp. salt
2 tablesp. snipped parsley	1 tablesp. flour
1 teasp. paprika	1½ tablesp. cold water

Have meatman flatten veal ¼" thick. Cut into 5 or 6 pieces. Sprinkle with 1 tablesp. flour combined with ½ teasp. salt.

In 2 tablesp. hot fat in skillet, sauté onions until tender; remove. Add 1 tablesp. fat to skillet; brown veal until golden on both sides. Add onions, parsley, paprika, mustard, and bouillon cube dissolved in boiling water. Simmer, covered, over low heat 45 min., or until veal is very tender.

Remove veal to heated platter. To liquid in skillet, add sour cream; heat thoroughly. Stir in combined ¼ teasp. salt, 1 tablesp. flour, cold water. Cook, stirring, until thickened; pour over veal. Makes 5 or 6 servings.

VEAL PARMIGIANO

1 lb. thin veal steak	¼ teasp. dried thyme
3 tablesp. olive or salad oil	1 egg
3 finely minced cloves garlic	¼ cup packaged dried bread crumbs
1 minced onion	¼ cup grated Parmesan cheese
1 No. 2 can tomatoes (2½ cups)	3 tablesp. olive or salad oil
1¼ teasp. salt	½ lb. Mozzarella or
¼ teasp. pepper	Münster cheese
1 8-oz. can tomato sauce	¼ to ⅓ cup grated Parmesan cheese

Ask meatman to cut veal into 8 pieces, about 4½" x 2".

In 3 tablesp. hot olive oil in saucepan, sauté garlic and onion until golden. Add tomatoes, salt, pepper; break up tomatoes with spoon; simmer, uncovered, 10 min. Add tomato sauce, thyme; simmer, uncovered, 20 min.

Beat egg well with fork. Combine crumbs, ¼ cup Parmesan cheese. Dip each veal piece into egg, then into crumbs; sauté 3 pieces in 1 tablesp. hot olive oil in skillet, turning once, until golden brown on both sides. Repeat until all are done. Set slices, side by side, in 12" x 8" x 2" baking dish.

Start heating oven to 350°F. Thinly slice Mozzarella. Pour two thirds of tomato mixture over veal, straining it if desired. Arrange Mozzarella on top; spoon on rest of tomato mixture. Sprinkle with ¼ to ⅓ cup Parmesan. Bake, uncovered, 30 min. Makes 4 generous servings.

SCALOPPINE OF VEAL MARSALA

1 lb. thin veal steak	mushrooms
⅓ cup grated Parmesan cheese	Dash cayenne pepper
¼ cup butter or margarine	¼ bouillon cube; or 1 teasp. meat-extract paste
1 clove garlic	¼ cup hot water
4 or 5 thinly sliced	¼ cup Marsala wine

Have meatman flatten veal ¼" thick. Cut into 2" pieces; coat *well* with Parmesan.

In some of hot butter in skillet over medium heat, sauté garlic and veal, a few pieces at a time, until golden brown on both sides. Add rest of butter as needed and set veal pieces aside as they brown. Discard garlic.

In same butter, sauté mushrooms 5 min.; remove and set aside. To butter in skillet, add cayenne, bouillon cube, hot water; stir until brown bits clinging to pan dissolve. Add veal, mushrooms. Cook 1 min. over high heat. Add wine. Serve at once. Makes 3 or 4 servings.

Baked: Start heating oven to 400°F. After sautéing meat and mushrooms, remove to 1½-qt. casserole. In skillet, combine rest of ingredients except wine; stir until brown bits clinging to pan dissolve; pour over meat. Bake, covered, 15 min. Add wine; bake, covered, 5 min.

VEAL ITALIAN WITH CARROTS

¾ lb. veal steak, ¼" thick	(optional) 2 tablesp. salad oil
2 tablesp. flour	or fat
½ teasp. salt	1 small clove garlic
⅛ teasp. pepper	3 halved, pared
⅛ teasp. dried marjoram or thyme	medium carrots ½ cup white wine

Cut veal into 2" pieces; roll in flour mixed with salt, pepper, marjoram. In hot salad oil in skillet, brown veal well with garlic; discard garlic. Add carrots, wine; simmer, covered, 30 min., or until meat is fork-tender.

Serve on hot plates, spooning pan gravy over meat and carrots. Makes 2 servings.

THIN VEAL FORESTIER

1½ lb. thin veal steak	½ teasp. salt
Cut clove garlic	Dash pepper
Flour	⅓ cup dry vermouth
¼ cup butter or margarine	1 teasp. fresh, frozen, or canned lemon
½ lb. thinly sliced mushrooms	juice Snipped parsley

Have meatman flatten veal ¼" thick. Cut into 2" pieces. Rub both sides of each piece with garlic; sprinkle with flour. In hot butter in skillet, sauté veal, several pieces at a time, until golden brown on both sides. Heap mushrooms on top of all pieces in skillet. Sprinkle with salt, pepper, vermouth.

Cook, covered, over low heat 20 min., or until veal is fork-tender, checking occasionally to make sure it's moist and adding 1 tablesp. or so of water if necessary.

To serve: Sprinkle with lemon juice and parsley. Makes 6 servings.

VEAL CASSEROLE CHOW MEIN

½ cup butter or margarine	1 cup boiling water
2 lb. veal steak, cut into ¾" cubes	½ teasp. salt
	½ cup all-purpose flour
½ teasp. salt	1 teasp. monosodium glutamate
⅛ teasp. pepper	
½ cup chopped onions	1 teasp. celery salt
½ cup coarsely chopped green peppers	1 qt. milk, heated
	1 3-oz. can (or 3-oz. jar) chow-mein noodles
2 cups celery, cut into 1" pieces	

Early in day: In hot butter in Dutch oven, sauté veal till golden brown on both sides. Sprinkle with ½ teasp. salt, pepper; add onions, green peppers. Cook, covered, over low heat 20 to 30 min., or until fork-tender.

Cook celery with boiling water and ½ teasp. salt, covered, till tender; don't drain. Sprinkle veal mixture with flour, monosodium glutamate, celery salt; stir well. Add milk; cook, stirring, until thickened. Add undrained celery. Taste; then season if necessary. Pour into 2-qt. casserole. Refrigerate.

About 40 min. before serving: Start heating oven to 425°F. Bake casserole, uncovered, 15 to 20 min., or until bubbling. Scatter noodles on top. Bake 10 min. longer. Makes 8 servings.

SWISS VEAL WITH LIMAS

¼ cup flour	2 sliced medium onions
1 teasp. salt	½ slivered medium green pepper
⅛ teasp. pepper	
½ teasp. monosodium glutamate	1 cup tomato juice
	1 pkg. frozen green limas, thawed just enough to separate
2 lb. veal steak, 1" thick	
2 tablesp. salad oil	1 teasp. salt

Early in day: Mix flour, 1 teasp. salt, pepper, monosodium glutamate; with edge of heavy saucer, pound mixture into veal. In hot salad oil

in skillet, sauté veal until well browned on both sides; remove to 10" x 6" x 2" baking dish. In skillet, place onions, green pepper; stir, coating them with drippings; stir in tomato juice; then pour over veal. Refrigerate.

About 1¾ hr. before serving: Start heating oven to 350°F. Cover top of baking dish containing veal with aluminum foil. Bake veal 40 min. Arrange limas around veal; sprinkle with 1 teasp. salt. Bake, covered, 45 min., or until veal is fork-tender. Makes 4 servings.

DOUBLE ROLL UPS

1¼ lb. veal steak, ½" thick	1 bouillon cube
	1½ cups boiling water
1 clove garlic	1 cup grated raw carrots (medium fine)
4 thin slices cooked ham	
	½ teasp. salt
2 tablesp. flour	⅛ teasp. pepper
3 tablesp. fat	Snipped parsley
2 tablesp. minced onion	

Have meatman flatten veal ¼" thick. Cut into 4 pieces; rub each piece with garlic. Place ham slice on top of each veal piece; roll up veal and ham together, jelly-roll-fashion. Tie with string. Dip rolls into flour, coating all sides; reserve any leftover flour.

In hot fat in skillet, brown meat rolls well on all sides. Add onion and bouillon cube dissolved in boiling water; simmer, covered tightly, 30 min., or until fork-tender.

Remove rolls to heated platter. Toss grated carrots with reserved flour; add salt, pepper. Add to liquid in skillet. Heat, stirring, until liquid is thickened and smooth, and carrots are tender-crisp. Remove strings from rolls; pour gravy over rolls; top with parsley. Makes 4 servings.

COLD STUFFED VEAL-ROLL SLICES

1 qt. fresh bread crumbs	6 tablesp. butter or margarine
¾ teasp. salt	3 tablesp. minced onion
2 teasp. dried sage	1¼ lb. veal steak, ¼" thick
2 tablesp. chopped celery	
	Seasoned Flour, p. 10
2 teasp. snipped parsley	1 cup hot water
Speck pepper	

Day before: Combine crumbs, salt, sage, celery, parsley, pepper. In ¼ cup hot butter in skillet, cook onion until tender; add crumb mixture;

heat. Spread crumb mixture on veal; then roll up veal tightly and tie with string.

Start heating oven to 350°F. Roll veal in Seasoned Flour; then sauté in 2 tablesp. butter until golden on all sides. Place in 1½-qt. casserole. Add water. Bake, covered, 1 hr., or until fork-tender. Refrigerate.

To serve: Arrange veal roll, sliced, on platter, with mold of currant or grape jelly. Makes 6 servings.

LET'S HAVE VARIETY MEATS

Liver, kidney, tripe, heart, brains, sweetbreads, tongue, oxtails—these are the variety meats, the edible parts of animal meat that are not classified as flesh.

Liver

Liver—veal, calf, lamb, beef, or pork—is our richest food source of iron, so necessary to prevent nutritional anemia. It is especially rich in vitamin A, iron, copper, and B vitamins.

TO BUY AND STORE LIVER

Veal, calf, lamb, beef, and pork liver are usually sold sliced and labeled to indicate the kind of liver. All have about the same nutritional value. Veal, calf, lamb, and *young* beef liver may be pan-fried. Pork and most beef liver are best when braised.

Select One of These:

Veal Liver, the most popular and highest-priced liver, comes from milk-fed animals. Slightly more tender than calf liver, it is mild in flavor and light-colored. It is often called calf liver. Pan-fry it.

Calf Liver comes from animals fed on milk and grass and is not as light-colored as veal liver. Mild in flavor and tender, it tastes like veal liver. Pan-fry it.

Lamb Liver is also a mild-flavored, tender liver. Pan-fry it.

Beef Liver is tender to less tender, more pronounced in flavor, and lower priced. Lighter-colored beef liver is usually more tender than that which is darker red. Pan-fry or braise it.

Pork Liver is less tender, more pronounced in flavor, and usually the lowest priced. Braise it.

Frozen Sliced Liver packaged by well-known meat packers is excellent. Cook as label directs.

Amount to Buy: Allow about 1 lb. liver for 4 servings.

To Store: Keep fresh liver, loosely wrapped, in coldest part of refrigerator. Use within 24 hr. if possible. Keep frozen liver frozen until time to use.

SUSAN'S PAN-FRIED LIVER AND BACON

1. For 4 servings, buy ¾ lb. veal or calf liver, sliced ¼" thick, and ½ lb. bacon slices. Place liver slices on waxed paper; sprinkle both sides with Seasoned Flour, p. 10. Never soak or scald liver.
2. In 10" skillet over low heat, pan-fry bacon as on p. 92. Remove to pie plate lined with paper towels; keep warm.
3. In skillet, heat ¼ cup bacon fat (enough to cover bottom). Using tongs, place liver in skillet; cook quickly, turning once, till crisp brown on both sides and delicate pink inside (medium done)—about 4 min. in all. *Overcooking* makes liver tough and hard.
4. When liver is done, remove to heated platter. Pour all fat from skillet. Place skillet over low heat and add 2 tablesp. butter or margarine; heat slowly until butter is golden brown.
5. Squeeze a few drops of lemon juice onto each liver slice; then pour browned butter onto liver. Top with about 2 tablesp. snipped parsley. *Serve* on heated platter with bacon.

P.S. You may sauté a few thin onion slices with liver; or rub skillet with cut clove garlic before sautéing liver.

With a French Touch: After cooking liver and pouring off fat from skillet, sauté ¼ cup minced onion in 2 tablesp. butter or margarine about 1 min. Add ⅓ cup white wine; bring to boil; cook about 2 min., or until half original volume. Pour sauce over liver; garnish with snipped parsley.

Liver and Onions: Serve liver and bacon with Sautéed Onions, p. 263, prepared in another skillet. (Curried version is especially nice.)

Lamb or Beef Liver and Bacon: For calf liver, substitute either lamb, or high-quality young-beef liver, cut ¼" thick.

Liverwurst and Bacon: For calf liver, substitute 1 lb. liverwurst, sliced about ½" thick; do not sprinkle with salt. Use 1 tablesp. butter or margarine.

BROILED LIVER

Preheat broiler 10 min., or as manufacturer directs. Place veal, calf, or lamb liver, cut ½" thick, on broiler rack or in shallow baking pan. Brush with melted butter or margarine. Broil, about 3" or 4" from heat, turning once, until delicate pink or well done inside—about 4 to 8 min. in all. You may broil bacon at same time. Or serve as in one of variations of Susan's Pan-Fried Liver and Bacon, p. 111.

BRAISED BEEF OR PORK LIVER

Slice beef or pork liver ½" thick. Sprinkle with Seasoned Flour, p. 10. In 1 or 2 tablesp. hot bacon or other fat in skillet, brown liver on both sides. Add ⅓ cup water or tomato juice; simmer, covered, 30 min., or until fork-tender.

CREOLE BEEF LIVER

4 diced bacon slices	1 No. 2 can tomatoes
1 lb. beef or pork liver,	(2½ cups)
sliced ¼" thick	⅛ teasp. cayenne pepper
About 3 tablesp. flour	per
⅓ cup diced green	1½ teasp. salt
pepper	⅛ teasp. chili powder

In skillet, sauté bacon until nearly crisp; remove; set aside. Sprinkle both sides of liver with flour; brown in bacon fat. Add bacon, rest of ingredients. Simmer, covered, 45 min. Makes 4 or 5 servings.

EASYGOING SUPPER

¼ cup salad oil	1 cup boiling water
2 sliced onions	1 pkg. frozen peas
½ green pepper, cut	1½ teasp. salt
into strips	¼ teasp. pepper
1 lb. calf, veal, lamb,	¼ lb. medium noodles
or tender beef liver,	(2 cups)
cut into ½" strips	

In hot oil in large skillet, sauté onions, green pepper, and liver 5 min., or until tender. Stir in boiling water; frozen peas, broken into chunks; salt; pepper; uncooked noodles. Cook, covered, stirring occasionally to prevent sticking, 10 min., or until noodles are tender. Makes 4 to 6 servings.

COLUMBUS CASSEROLE

¼ lb. elbow macaroni	densed cream-of-
(1 cup)	mushroom soup
4 bacon slices	¾ cup milk
2 tablesp. bacon fat	1½ tablesp. bottled
½ lb. beef or pork liver,	thick meat sauce,
cubed	p. 9
2 tablesp. flour	1 cup canned vacuum-
1 teasp. salt	packed whole-kernel
½ cup sliced onions	corn
1 can undiluted con-	Snipped parsley

Early in day: Cook macaroni as label directs; drain. Meanwhile, sauté bacon until lightly browned; remove; drain. Pour off all but 2 tablesp. fat. Sprinkle liver with flour, salt; sauté quickly in fat until well browned; add onions and cook until they are just tender. Pour soup into 1½-qt. casserole; slowly stir in milk and meat sauce; fold in macaroni, liver and onions, corn. Top with bacon. Refrigerate.

About 1 hr. before serving: Start heating oven to 350°F. Bake casserole, uncovered, about 50 min., or until bubbling.

To serve: Sprinkle generously with parsley, especially around bacon. Makes 4 servings.

TASTY BAKED BEEF LIVER

¾ to 1 lb. tender beef	cut into 1" slices
liver, sliced ¼" thick	2 tablesp. flour
3 tablesp. butter or	½ teasp. salt
margarine	Dash pepper
⅓ cup minced onion	½ teasp. Worcester-
½ cup canned sliced	shire
mushrooms	1 cup milk
½ cup green peppers,	

Start heating oven to 350°F. Place liver in 10" x 6" x 2" baking dish. In hot butter in skillet, sauté onion, mushrooms, and green pepper about 10 min., or until light brown. Remove from heat. Slowly stir in flour, then salt, pepper, Worcestershire. Gradually add milk, stirring. Return to heat; cook until thickened. Pour over liver. Bake, uncovered, 25 min. Makes 4 servings.

Heart

TO BUY AND STORE HEART

Heart is a good buy as it has very little waste. There are 4 kinds of fresh heart. Veal heart is the most delicate in flavor, and the most tender.

Select One of These:

Beef Heart weighs 3 to 3½ lb. and makes 8 to 10 servings.

Veal Heart weighs about ¾ lb. and makes 2 or 3 servings.

Pork Heart weighs about ½ lb. and makes 2 servings.

Lamb Heart weighs about ¼ lb. and makes 1 serving.

Frozen Lamb Hearts packed by well-known meat packers are excellent. Cook as label directs.

To Store: Wrap fresh hearts loosely; refrigerate; use within 24 hr. if possible. Keep frozen hearts frozen until time to use.

SIMMERED HEART

Trim off coarse fibers at top and inside of heart. Wash well; drain. Cover with water; add 1 teasp. salt, pinch dried thyme, 1 sliced onion. Simmer veal or lamb heart, covered, about 1½ hr., beef or pork heart about 2 hr., or until fork-tender.

Nice ground, chopped, or cut up as meat in a hash, meat pie, or casserole. Or you may serve veal or lamb heart sliced, hot or cold.

BRAISED HEARTS

Trim 2 pork, or 4 lamb, hearts as in Simmered Heart above. Quarter pork hearts; or halve lamb hearts. Coat with Seasoned Flour, p. 10. In 3 tablesp. hot fat or salad oil in skillet, brown hearts well with 2 thinly sliced onions. Add 2 teasp. salt, ½ cup water. Simmer, covered, over low heat, 1½ to 2 hr., or until fork-tender. Nice with Spanish or tomato sauce. Makes 4 servings.

BRAISED, STUFFED VEAL OR LAMB HEARTS

3 veal hearts	drippings
Buttery Bread Stuffing, p. 208	1 clove garlic; or ¼ cup sliced onion
Seasoned Flour, p. 10	Salt
¼ cup fat or bacon	⅛ teasp. pepper

Trim off coarse fibers at top and inside of hearts. Wash well; drain. Fill cavities with stuffing; close openings with skewers; tie. (Any leftover stuffing is nice toasted lightly in a little hot butter or margarine in skillet.) Roll in Seasoned Flour; brown well in hot fat in Dutch oven or deep kettle. Add enough boiling water, or part water and part tomato juice, to come halfway up hearts; add garlic, 1 teasp. salt per 1 qt. water, and pepper. Simmer, covered, adding water if necessary, until fork-tender—2 to 2½ hr.

Serve hot, sliced, with gravy made by thickening broth as on p. 7, or with Spanish Sauce, p. 376. Or slice; serve cold. Makes about 6 servings.

Sweetbreads

TO BUY AND STORE SWEETBREADS

This delicate, tender meat is the thymus gland of a calf, young beef, or lamb. Each animal has two kinds of sweetbreads: heart sweetbreads, which are rounded, and throat, or neck, sweetbreads, which are elongated.

Select One of These:

Veal Sweetbreads are the most popular and highest priced. Like lamb sweetbreads, they are white and tender.

Beef Sweetbreads are usually only neck sweetbreads. They are reddish in color, and are inclined to be tough when pressed with fingers.

Frozen Sweetbreads packaged by well-known meat packers are excellent. Cook as label directs.

Amount to Buy: 1 lb. sweetbreads makes about 4 servings.

To Store: Use fresh sweetbreads as soon as they're purchased. Or precook, p. 114, then refrigerate; use within 24 hr. Keep frozen sweet-breads frozen until time to use.

TO PRECOOK SWEETBREADS

Precook sweetbreads this way before using them: Drop sweetbreads into boiling water; add 1 teasp. salt. Simmer veal and lamb sweetbreads, covered, 25 min.; beef sweetbreads 35 min. Drain. Then holding sweetbreads under cold running water, slip off membrane with fingers. With knife, cut out dark veins and thick connective tissue. Split very thick sweetbreads in halves lengthwise. Use at once; or refrigerate.

BROILED SWEETBREADS

Preheat broiler 10 min., or as manufacturer directs. Precook sweetbreads, above; then split. Brush with melted fat or salad oil; sprinkle with salt and pepper; then broil about 3" from heat until golden brown—about 5 to 7 min. on each side. Spread with soft butter or margarine, or Lemon Butter, p. 377. Sprinkle with slivered almonds; or serve with canned pineapple chunks.

PAN-FRIED SWEETBREADS

Precook sweetbreads, above; then split. Dip into packaged dried bread crumbs, then into 1 beaten egg, then again into crumbs. In hot butter or margarine in skillet, pan-fry until delicate brown on all sides.
Serve with tomato sauce, fried ham or bacon, or lemon quarters.

CREAMED SWEETBREADS

Precook 1 lb. sweetbreads as above. Meanwhile, make 2 cups Béchamel Sauce, p. 376, or Medium White Sauce, p. 376, using 3 tablesp. flour instead of ¼ cup. Break precooked sweetbreads into pieces; combine with sauce.
Serve on toast or in Toast Cups, p. 344. Makes 4 servings.

To Vary: To sauce, add 2 teasp. white wine, sherry or cooking sherry; or fresh, frozen, or canned lemon juice, with a little snipped parsley.
Or add 1 cup cooked peas or cut-up asparagus.
Or add ⅓ cup slivered, toasted, blanched almonds.
Or substitute equal amounts of diced, cooked

chicken and sweetbreads, or sautéed sliced mushrooms and sweetbreads, for sweetbreads.

Brains

TO BUY AND STORE BRAINS

Brains are a very delicate, tender meat.

Select One of These:

Veal Brains: These are the most popular, and highest priced. They weigh ½ lb. each.

Beef Brains: These weigh about ¾ lb. each.

Lamb and Pork Brains: These weigh ¼ lb. each.

Frozen Brains packaged by well-known packers are excellent. Cook as label directs.

Amount to Buy: Allow about 1 lb. brains for 4 servings.

To Store: Use brains as soon as they're purchased. Or precook as below; refrigerate; then use within 24 hr. If brains are frozen, keep frozen until ready to use.

TO PRECOOK BRAINS

Precook brains this way before using them: Soak brains in salted water (1 tablesp. salt per 1 qt. water) about 15 min.; drain. Remove membrane with tip of paring knife. Then simmer, covered, 15 min. in boiling water to cover, with 1 teasp. salt and 1 tablesp. lemon juice. Drain; drop into cold water; drain again.
To serve: Reheat in Quick Mushroom Sauce, p. 372; Tomato Sauce, p. 376; Drawn Butter Sauce, p. 376; or Lemon Butter, p. 377. Or cut up and substitute for part of chicken in Susan's Creamed Chicken De Luxe, p. 157.

Broiled Brains: Precook brains as above. Then brush well with melted butter or margarine and broil 10 to 15 min., turning occasionally. Serve with lemon wedges; Quick Tartar Sauce, p. 373; Broiled Bacon, p. 93; Broiled Tomatoes, p. 274; or Beet and Horse-radish Relish, p. 291.

Sautéed Brains: Precook brains as above. Then dip into beaten egg, then into packaged dried bread crumbs or corn meal. Sauté in hot fat in skillet until brown on all sides. Serve as above.

Tongue

Uncooked tongues may be bought fresh, smoked, corned, or pickled. There are also ready-to-eat whole tongues, as well as canned whole or sliced. Thus tongue can provide a variety of tasty main dishes.

TO BUY AND STORE TONGUE

Uncooked Tongues:

Beef Tongue: A beef tongue weighs 2 to 5 lb. and comes fresh, smoked, or cured. Smoked beef tongue often comes in a transparent wrapping and carries a packer's brand name.

Veal Tongue: Veal tongue weighs ½ to 2 lb. and comes fresh.

Lamb Tongue: Lamb tongue weighs 3 to 4 oz. and comes fresh or pickled.

Cooked and Canned Tongues:

Ready-to-Eat Smoked Beef Tongue: This fully cooked whole smoked tongue comes packed in a vacuum package. It has been completely skinned, and boned and is all ready to slice and serve cold, or to heat as label directs. It comes in sizes weighing 1½ to 2½ lb.

You can also buy cooked trimmed beef tongues in cans and jars.

Lamb Tongue: Comes canned in jars.

Pork Tongue: Weighs ½ to 1¼ lb. and usually comes in cans or jars as "lunch tongue."

Amount to Buy: Allow 1 lb. for 4 or 5 servings.

To Store: Refrigerate fresh tongue, loosely wrapped; use within 24 hr. if possible.

Refrigerate smoked tongue, and use within 3 days if possible.

Refrigerate pickled tongue, covered; use within 7 days.

COOKED TONGUE
(fresh, smoked, cured, or pickled)

1. Wash tongue. (If tongue is highly cured, soak 2 hr. in cold water to cover; then drain before cooking.) Place in large deep kettle or Dutch oven; cover with cold water; bring to boil. (To fresh tongue, also add 1½ teasp. salt.)
2. Then add either of these groups of seasonings if desired:
   a. 1 bay leaf, 2 or 3 whole cloves, 1 sliced large onion, and 1 tablesp. grated orange or lemon rind
   b. Or 2 cloves garlic, 2 stalks celery, 1 sliced onion, 1 pared carrot, 1 teasp. whole black peppers
3. Simmer tongue, covered, until fork-tender, allowing about 3 to 3½ hr. for a beef tongue, 1 to 1½ hr. for veal, lamb, or pork tongue. Remove from water; cool slightly.
4. Trim off bone and gristle at thick end. To remove skin, slit skin on underside from thick end to tip; then, with paring knife, loosen skin all around thick end. Turn tongue, top side up, with tip toward you. Grasp skin at thick end; pull off like glove, all in one piece. (With pork tongue, it may be necessary to slice off most of skin.)

Serve tongue, hot or cold, with Horse-radish Sauce I or II, p. 375; barbecue sauce; Tartar Sauce, p. 373; Spanish Sauce, p. 376; Mustard Sauce, p. 375; or California Raisin Sauce, p. 377. Or serve with horse-radish, prepared mustard, chili sauce, pickle relish, pickled beets, or cranberry sauce.

Tongue Dinner: About 45 min. before tongue is done, add 5 pared small white potatoes. Simmer, covered, 10 min. Add 10 small white onions. Simmer, covered, 5 min. Place ½ medium cabbage, quartered, with most of core removed, on top of tongue. Cook, covered, until vegetables are tender. Serve with Horse-radish Sauce I or II, p. 375, or horse-radish or mustard pickle.

With Pickle Sauce: Make 1 cup Drawn Butter Sauce, p. 376, using 1 cup tongue liquid for water and browning butter slightly before adding flour. Add 2 tablesp. minced sweet pickle, ¼ cup pickle juice. Serve over or with sliced, cooked tongue.

Tripe

TO BUY AND STORE TRIPE

Tripe is the inner lining of the stomach of beef. There are 3 kinds of tripe: honeycomb, pocket, and plain (or smooth); honeycomb tripe is considered the greatest delicacy. All 3 come fresh, pickled, or canned.

Fresh Tripe is cooked before you buy it but needs more cooking.

Pickled Tripe is usually thoroughly cooked but should be soaked before using.

Canned Tripe is ready to heat and serve.

Amount to Buy: Allow about 1 lb. for 4 or 5 servings.

To Store: Keep in refrigerator. Use fresh tripe within 24 hr.

COOKED FRESH TRIPE

Cover fresh tripe with water; add 1 tablesp. salt. Simmer, covered, 1 hr., or until fork-tender. Drain; dry between paper towels; then cut into serving pieces. Serve with Tomato Sauce, p. 376, or Spanish Sauce, p. 376.

SAUTEED TRIPE

Cook fresh tripe as above; then cut into serving pieces. Dip pieces into 1 beaten egg mixed with 2 tablesp. water, then into packaged dried bread crumbs. In small amount of hot fat in skillet, sauté tripe until golden brown on both sides.

Serve with lemon wedges, hot canned tomato sauce, or Mustard Sauce, p. 375.

BROILED TRIPE

Preheat broiler 10 min., or as manufacturer directs. Use fresh tripe, cooked as above. Cut into serving pieces. Brush with melted butter or margarine. Broil about 3″ from heat 5 min. Turn; brush with butter; broil 5 min., or until golden brown. Brush with melted butter; sprinkle with salt, pepper, and paprika, or seasoned salt; then serve.

Kidneys

The delicacy and flavor of kidneys are highly prized by epicures; veal, lamb, and beef kidneys are special favorites.

TO BUY AND STORE KIDNEYS

Select One of These:

Veal Kidneys weigh 8 to 12 oz. each and are so tender they need very little cooking. They are usually broiled or sautéed.

Lamb Kidneys weigh 2 oz. each, are very tender, and are delightful broiled or sautéed.

Beef Kidneys weigh about 1¼ lb. each and need thorough braising or simmering.

Amount to Buy: 1 veal or lamb kidney makes 1 serving; 1 beef kidney makes 4 servings.

To Store: Keep, loosely wrapped, in refrigerator. Use within 24 hr.

MAC'S SAUTEED KIDNEYS

Remove any outer membrane from lamb or veal kidneys. Then split kidneys in halves lengthwise; or slice ¼″ to ½″ thick. With scissors, remove fat and white veins; wash; dry between paper towels.

Rub skillet lightly with cut clove garlic; then melt ¼ cup butter or bacon fat in skillet. Sauté kidneys in butter, turning them frequently, 10 to 15 min., or until tender. Season with a little fresh, frozen, or canned lemon juice or sherry. Sprinkle with parsley. Serve as is or on toast.

P.S. Before adding kidneys, you may sauté ¼ cup sliced onion in butter till tender. Omit garlic. A few caraway seeds may be added.

BROILED KIDNEYS ON TOAST

Preheat broiler 10 min., or as manufacturer directs. Remove any outer membrane from lamb or veal kidneys. Split in halves lengthwise; then, with scissors, remove fat and white veins; wash; dry between paper towels.

Brush kidneys with melted butter or margarine, salad oil, or French dressing; sprinkle with salt and pepper. Broil 3″ from heat about 5 to 7 min. on each side, or until well browned.

Serve on buttered toast, with melted butter or margarine to which a little salt, pepper, cayenne, and fresh, frozen, or canned lemon juice have been added.

Kidneys en Brochette: Arrange split kidneys and squares of bacon alternately on skewers; place on greased broiler rack; broil as above. Or wrap kidneys in bacon slices; then broil.

LAMB KIDNEYS PIQUANT

8 lamb kidneys	1 beef-bouillon cube
2 tablesp. fat or salad oil	½ cup boiling water
4 teasp. flour	¼ cup tomato juice
2 tablesp. snipped parsley	⅛ teasp. salt
1 tablesp. minced onion	2 teasp. Worcestershire
	4 slices toast

Remove any outer membrane from lamb kidneys. Split kidneys in halves lengthwise; then, with scissors, remove fat and white veins; wash; dry between paper towels.

In hot fat in skillet, sauté kidneys over medium heat 10 to 15 min., or until tender, turning them often. Reduce heat. Sprinkle kidneys with flour; stir until flour blends with fat. Add parsley and rest of ingredients except toast. Cook over low heat until thickened.

Serve on toast. Makes 4 servings.

BEEF-KIDNEY STEW

1 beef kidney	⅛ teasp. pepper
6 cups boiling water	⅛ teasp. paprika
¼ cup all-purpose flour	3 tablesp. butter or margarine
6 tablesp. cold water	1 chopped, hard-cooked egg
1½ teasp. salt	

Remove any outer membrane from kidney. Split kidney in half lengthwise; with scissors, remove fat and white veins. Cut into ¼″-thick crosswise slices, then into pieces. Cover with cold water; press meat to squeeze out blood; drain; repeat. Now let meat soak 2 hr. in cold water; then drain.

Add boiling water to kidney; simmer, uncovered, 1 hr. Cover; simmer ½ hr., or until kidney is tender and broth is reduced to 3 cups.

Mix flour and cold water to a smooth paste; add to stew gradually, stirring constantly; simmer until thickened. Add salt and rest of ingredients; heat. Makes 4 servings.

Serve as is, on toast, or with mashed or hashed-brown potatoes. A grand dish for Sunday breakfast or supper.

P.S. This dish tastes even better if kidney is simmered and refrigerated day before, then thickened and seasoned just before serving. If desired, add 2 tablesp. minced onion before simmering kidney; or add sherry to taste or a few cooked peas just before serving.

Oxtails

Though oxtails (the tails of cattle) have much bone, they also have a good share of sweet, rich-flavored meat. They need long, slow simmering.

TO BUY AND STORE OXTAILS

Fresh Oxtails come whole or disjointed into 1½″ to 2″ lengths.

Frozen Disjointed Oxtails, packaged by well-known packers, are excellent. Cook as label directs.

Amount to Buy: Allow about 1 lb. oxtails for 2 servings.

To Store: Keep fresh oxtails loosely wrapped in refrigerator; use within 24 hr. Keep frozen oxtails frozen until time to use.

BRAISED OXTAILS

2 lb. oxtails, cut into 2″ lengths	1 tablesp. vinegar
3 tablesp. fat or salad oil	½ teasp. minced garlic
1 cup minced onions	2 teasp. salt
2 cups hot water	⅛ teasp. pepper
	1 tablesp. sugar

Preheat broiler 10 min., or as manufacturer directs. Broil oxtails about 10 min., turning them frequently, until browned on all sides. Meanwhile, in hot fat in Dutch oven, sauté onions until tender. Add meat and rest of ingredients; simmer, covered, 3 to 4 hr., or until meat is tender, adding more boiling water if necessary.

Remove meat to heated platter; keep warm. Thicken gravy as on p. 7. Pour over or serve with meat.

Serve with buttered noodles or mashed potatoes. Makes 4 servings.

OXTAIL RAGOUT

¼ cup all-purpose flour	carrots
2 teasp. salt	1 cup sliced celery
⅛ teasp. pepper	½ lb. small mushrooms
3 oxtails, cut into 2″	2 teasp. salt
lengths	⅛ teasp. pepper
¼ cup fat	¼ teasp. paprika
1 bay leaf	¼ cup flour
4 whole black peppers	4 cups oxtail liquid
3 sliced large onions	¼ lb. medium noodles
6 cups water	(2 cups)
2 cups sliced, pared	

In paper bag or bowl, combine ¼ cup flour, 2 teasp. salt, ⅛ teasp. pepper. Toss oxtails with flour mixture; then sauté in hot fat in Dutch oven or kettle till browned on all sides. Add bay leaf, black peppers, onions, water; simmer slowly, covered, till very tender—3 to 4 hr. Remove meat from bones. (For best flavor, do this day before; refrigerate meat and liquid until used.)

Make sauce: With spoon, skim all fat from oxtail liquid. In 2 tablesp. of this fat in skillet, sauté carrots and celery 5 min. Halve mushrooms; sauté with carrots and celery 1 min. Sprinkle with combined 2 teasp. salt, ⅛ teasp. pepper, paprika, ¼ cup flour; toss well. Slowly stir in oxtail liquid; simmer, covered, ½ hr., or till vegetables are done.

Meanwhile, cook noodles as label directs; drain. Add oxtail meat to sauce; heat. Add salt and pepper to taste.

Serve on noodles. Makes 4 to 6 man-size servings.

P.S. Instead of plain noodles, use fine noodles, tossed with poppy or caraway seeds; mashed potatoes; cubed, boiled potatoes; or fluffy rice.

Curried: Before tossing oxtails with flour, add 1 teasp. curry powder.

Burgundy: Substitute ⅓ cup Burgundy wine or sherry for ⅓ cup water.

Italian Style: Add 1 minced clove garlic with onions.

With Herbs: Add ½ teasp. dried thyme with bay leaf and whole black peppers. Before serving, sprinkle generously with snipped parsley.

To Freeze Meats

See How To Freeze Meats, p. 536, for freezing and cooking directions.

LET'S HAVE READY-COOKED MEATS

TO BUY AND STORE READY-COOKED MEATS

The many delicious ready-cooked meats available today are a boon to menu planners. For short-order occasions, they're a blessing, too!

Select a Meat:

Bologna has a mild, pleasing flavor. There are dozens of varieties, including veal, beef, and ham bologna. Most common kinds are large bologna and ring bologna. Buy by the piece or sliced.

Cervelat (Summer Sausage) is a combination of beef and pork, mildly spiced, then smoked or dried. It has no garlic. Buy by the piece or thinly sliced.

Cooked Hams and Picnics: See p. 86.

Liver Cheese (Liver Loaf) is fine for those who want sandwich-shaped slices of liver sausage. It's generally firm, made in a loaf shape, and covered with fresh white pork fat to keep it moist. Use hot or cold.

Liver Sausage (Liverwurst) varies from soft, light-pink braunschweiger (smoked) to darker, firmer sausage. Delicately spiced and seasoned, the smoked varieties are most popular. Liver sausage is particularly rich in iron and vitamin A and B vitamins, and is best bought by the piece, as all types discolor when sliced.

Luncheon Loaf comes in a square, round, or loaf shape. It has hamlike flavor. Serve cold, sautéed, or baked.

Meat Loaf is a combination of the same meats and seasonings that are used in homemade meat loaf. Buy it sliced for sandwiches and cold plates, as a whole or half loaf to bake as a main dish.

Salami comes in these 2 varieties:

Hard: This is a firm, smoked or unsmoked sausage with a snappy, garlicky flavor. Nice to eat as a nibbler, in sandwiches or salads, or to add, diced and chopped, to scalloped potatoes, spaghetti sauce, etc. Buy by the piece or thinly sliced.

Cooked: This is made and seasoned like hard salami but is softer (semidry). It's preferred for sandwiches because it's less chewy.

Souse (Headcheese) consists of cooked, jellied pork products in a round sausage shape or loaves.

Specialty Loaves include meat, with cubes of cheese throughout; pickle-and-pimento loaves; pepper loaves of many varieties, etc.

Thuringer is another type of cervelat, known as soft cervelat. It contains more beef than pork, is highly seasoned, smoked, and air-dried.

Fully Cooked Tongue: See p. 115.

Jellied Tongue is cured whole beef, pork, or veal tongue, with gelatine added. Or it is chopped or cubed, jellied tongue.

Amount to Buy: For a cold-meat platter, allow about 2 to 3 oz. meat per serving. For salads and sandwiches, allow 1 to 2 oz. per serving.

To Store: Make sure meat slices lie flat; keep prepackaged meats in wrapper. Wrap sliced meat in waxed paper, saran, or aluminum foil. Refrigerate.

To enjoy the fine flavor, use unsliced dry or semidry sausage within 2 or 3 weeks. For others, check storage time guide, p. 48.

TO SERVE READY-COOKED MEATS

Serve Them Cold:

1. Use in cold platter combinations, with or without home-cooked or canned meats and assorted cheese slices or balls.

For platter choose meats that give a variety of flavors, colors, shapes, textures.

Arrange meats in an orderly design. Cut larger slices in two (sometimes from corner to corner). Fold some to make cones; roll others around cooked asparagus stalks, green beans seasoned with French dressing, or pieces of cheese.

Garnish platter in center, at ends, or down sides with pickled fruits, etc. See The Gay Garnish, p. 296.
2. Serve in sandwiches.
3. Add to one of Chef's Salad Bowls, p. 307.
4. Serve as nibbler; see p. 22.

Serve Them Hot:

1. Add meat, cut up, to scalloped potatoes, macaroni with cheese, Spanish rice, etc.
2. Use snipped cervelat or salami as meat in Italian spaghetti. See Salametti, p. 241.
3. Slice, then sauté, liver sausage, bologna, or luncheon loaf until hot; serve with creamed or scalloped vegetables.
4. Use as meat in stuffed peppers, stuffed tomatoes, etc.
5. Slice; quickly broil or sauté and serve with broiled or sautéed tomatoes, sweet potatoes, or peach halves. Or serve with potato salad.
6. Sauté or broil, to fill buttered toasted split buns. Serve with coleslaw.
7. Heat in barbecue sauce; serve on buttered toasted split rolls.
8. Pan-fry with thinly sliced onions.
9. Simmer ½- to 1-lb. piece cervelat in hot water to cover about 8 min.; serve as hot meat at dinner.
10. Sauté bologna slices until they curl up into cup shapes. Fill "cups" with hot baked beans or hot potato salad.
11. Place slices of canned luncheon meat in pie plate; cover with seasoned, mashed sweet potatoes. Sprinkle with brown sugar. Bake at 350°F. about 30 min., or till steaming hot in center.

Franks
(hot dogs)

Today's hot dog is one of America's finest meats. It's a combination of tender, lean, juicy meats and aromatic spices and seasonings, which are encased, then smoked over hickory or other hardwood.

If simply served, franks are as fine for children as for grownups. They supply the same high-quality protein and meat values as roasts, chops, and steaks, and are a very thrifty buy.

TO BUY AND STORE FRANKS

You can't tell a good hot dog just by looking at it! A well-known brand name is your best guide, a packaged hot dog your best buy. Every frank in the cellophane-wrapped packages is full of tender, lean beef and juicy pork—and sometimes tasty veal. Some are all-beef. They have no waste.

Some franks are sold by the link or portion of a pound. If they've been government-inspected, several franks out of each 5-lb. carton carry a little band giving the packer's name and exact ingredients. Ask to see this label.

There are also franks containing some wheat or soy flour; the label usually declares such additions.

Choose a Style (skinless or natural casing): There are all-meat franks, all-beef franks, and kosher franks.

Choose a Pack: Franks come in ½-lb. and 1-lb. cellophane packages, 2- or 3-lb. cartons with cellophane windows, as well as in cans and jars—some with a sack of barbecue or relish sauce inside.

Choose a Size: Regular franks average 9 to 10 per lb.; dinner franks (larger) 5 per lb.; cocktail franks (smaller) 26 to 28 per lb.

Amount to Buy: Allow 1 or 2 regular-sized franks per serving for lunch; 2 or 3 for dinner.

To Store: Keep in original cellophane package in coldest part of refrigerator. Wrap bulk franks loosely in waxed paper. Use within 3 or 4 days.

To Freeze: You may freeze very fresh franks in their original package a week or so in the home freezer. If you plan to freeze them up to a month, wrap in freezer wrapping material.

TO SERVE FRANKS

Serve Them Cold: Franks are cooked, so use them right from the package—whole or cut up, in salads, sandwiches, etc.

Serve Them Hot:

Simmered: Heat franks in water just below boiling point 5 to 8 min. (Do not boil or pierce skins; franks will split.) Remove from water with tongs.

Broiled: Preheat broiler 10 min., or as manufacturer directs. Brush or rub each frank with melted butter or margarine or salad oil. Broil about 2″ to 3″ from heat, allowing about 5 min. on each side.

Or split franks lengthwise, not quite through; arrange, with cut sides up, on broiler rack. Place cheese strip and ½ bacon slice on each frank. Broil.

Pan-broiled: In 1 tablesp. hot fat in skillet, sauté whole franks, turning them occasionally, until just brown. If franks are split, sauté cut side first, then skin side.

Franks for Dinner

FRANKS, COUNTRY STYLE

3 tablesp. bacon fat	½″ thick
8 sliced medium onions	½ teasp. salt
4 sliced green peppers	⅛ teasp. pepper
1 lb. franks, sliced	

In large skillet, heat bacon fat; add onions, green peppers, franks, salt, pepper. Simmer, covered, stirring occasionally, 30 min., or until all are tender. Makes 4 servings.

Succotash Style: Before simmering, add 1 12-oz. can vacuum-packed whole-kernel corn; 2 tomatoes, quartered; ¾ teasp. salt.

FRANKS ITALIAN

1 medium eggplant	2 8-oz. cans tomato
⅓ cup flour	sauce
½ teasp. salt	1 cup grated process
⅛ teasp. pepper	sharp American
⅓ cup salad oil	cheese (¼ lb.)
8 franks	Snipped parsley

Start heating oven to 350°F. Wash eggplant; cut into 8 ½″-thick slices. Coat with mixture of flour, salt, pepper. In hot salad oil in skillet, sauté eggplant slices until golden on both sides. In greased 12″ x 8″ x 2″ baking dish, place 4 eggplant slices side by side. On top of each, place 1 frank, halved lengthwise. Spread with 1 can tomato sauce; then sprinkle with half of cheese. Repeat layers. Bake 30 min., or until cheese is bubbly. Top with parsley. Makes 4 servings.

Hamburger: Substitute 8 sautéed thin hamburger patties for franks. Add ¼ teasp. orégano to cheese.

HARVEST TWOSOME

3 medium zucchini, sliced ½″ thick	⅛ teasp. pepper
4 franks, sliced	1 cup grated process American cheese (¼ lb.)
1 tomato, cut into wedges	2 tablesp. butter or margarine
½ teasp. salt	

Start heating oven to 350°F. Cook zucchini in 1″ boiling salted water, covered, 5 to 7 min., or until tender-crisp. In greased 8″ or 9″ pie plate, arrange zucchini, then franks; tuck in tomato wedges; then sprinkle with salt, pepper, and cheese. Lastly dot with butter. Cover with second pie plate or aluminum foil. Bake 20 min. Makes 2 servings.

FRANK RICE

For an easy dinner dish, top hot fluffy rice with broiled or pan-broiled franks. Pour on Mustard Sauce, p. 375; barbecue sauce; or Zippy Cheese Sauce, p. 374. If desired, garnish with canned peach halves, browned with franks, and parsley.

FRANK SUEY

¼ cup butter, margarine, or salad oil	½ lb. franks, cut into ½″ slices
¾ cup diced onions	1 tablesp. cornstarch
2 cups diced celery	3 tablesp. soy sauce
2 cups boiling water	3 to 4 cups hot fluffy rice
1 cup shredded cabbage	

In hot butter in large skillet, sauté onions and celery until soft; add boiling water, cabbage, franks. Simmer, covered, 10 min. Mix cornstarch with soy sauce; stir into frank mixture. Cook, stirring, until mixture thickens and clears.
Serve on rice. Makes 4 servings.

BARBECUE-BUFFET STEW

⅓ cup salad oil	3 cups drained canned whole-kernel hominy
2 sliced medium onions	1 tablesp. chili powder
1 minced small clove garlic	2 teasp. salt or celery salt
1 doz. franks, sliced ½″ thick	1¾ cups tomato juice
1½ cups pitted ripe olives	1½ cups grated process American cheese
2 cups drained canned or cooked kidney beans	Buttered French-bread slices

Early in day: In hot salad oil in skillet, sauté onions and garlic until golden. Add franks; sauté 5 min. Meanwhile, cut ¾ cup ripe olives into large pieces, leaving remaining olives whole; add to franks, along with beans, hominy, chili, salt, tomato juice; heat till boiling. Blend in cheese. Turn into 12″ x 8″ x 2″ baking dish. Refrigerate.
About 50 min. before dinner: Start heating oven to 400°F. Cover casserole mixture with bread. Bake 40 min. Makes 8 to 10 servings.

P.S. If you make this stew just before dinner, bake 20 min.

BARBECUED FRANKS—3 STYLES

¾ cup catchup	1 teasp. sugar
1 tablesp. Worcestershire	Dash tabasco
1 teasp. chili powder	1 cup water
½ teasp. salt	8 to 12 franks

Start heating oven to 350°F. In saucepan, combine all ingredients except franks; bring to boil; reduce heat and simmer 15 to 20 min. Place franks in casserole; pour on sauce. Bake, uncovered, 30 min., turning occasionally.
Serve in toasted split buns, on hot fluffy rice, buttered noodles, or creamy mashed potatoes; or with baked or boiled potatoes. Makes 4 to 6 servings.

Skillet-Barbecued: Make sauce in skillet; bring to boil; add franks; simmer 15 to 20 min.

Picnic Style: Let sauce simmer 15 to 20 min. Put broiled, pan-broiled, or outdoor-grilled franks in split frank buns; spoon on sauce.

Savory Barbecue Sauce: Before combining sauce ingredients in saucepan, sauté 1 minced medium onion in 2 tablesp. butter or margarine; add rest of sauce ingredients.

TWENTY-MINUTE BOILED DINNER

1 head cabbage, cut into 6 wedges	2 tablesp. flour
1 lb. franks	1½ cups milk or liquefied nonfat dry milk
1 qt. boiling water	1 teasp. salt
1 teasp. salt	2 to 3 tablesp. prepared mustard
2 tablesp. butter or margarine	

In Dutch oven or large kettle, place cabbage wedges; top with franks. Add boiling water, 1 teasp. salt. Boil, covered, 10 min., or until cabbage is tender-crisp.

Meanwhile, make mustard sauce as follows: In saucepan, melt butter. Add flour; stir till smooth. Remove from heat. Add milk, stirring constantly. Then add 1 teasp. salt, mustard. Stir over low heat until thickened.

Remove cabbage wedges and franks to heated platter. Spoon on some of sauce; pass rest. Makes 6 servings.

TOP-HATTER FRANKS

2 tablesp. butter or margarine	mustard
1 minced medium onion	1 can undiluted condensed bean-and-bacon soup
1 sliced green pepper	1 soup can milk or diluted evaporated milk
½ cup minced celery	
1 lb. franks, sliced ½" thick	1 pkg. corn-muffin mix
2 tablesp. prepared	

Start heating oven to 350°F. In hot butter in skillet, sauté onion, green pepper, and celery until tender. Stir in franks, mustard, soup, milk. Turn into 12" x 8" x 2" baking dish. Prepare muffin mix as label directs; pour over frank mixture. Bake 35 min., or until corn bread is done. Makes 8 servings.

Mammy's Way: Substitute the following corn-bread batter for corn-muffin mix: Into mixing bowl, sift 1 cup corn meal, ¼ cup sifted all-purpose flour, 2 tablesp. sugar, ½ teasp. salt, 1½ teasp. baking powder. Add 2 tablesp. salad oil, 1 egg, ½ cup milk. With egg beater, beat until smooth—about 1 min. Pour over frank mixture; then bake as above.

BARBECUED FRANK KABOBS

1 cup chili sauce	½ teasp. salt
1 tablesp. brown sugar	1 tablesp. snipped parsley
3 tablesp. vinegar	
3 drops tabasco	2 tablesp. butter or margarine
1 sliced small onion	
1½ cups boiling water	3 bacon slices
1⅓ cups packaged precooked rice	6 franks, quartered crosswise

Preheat broiler 10 min., or as manufacturer directs. In saucepan, combine chili sauce, sugar, vinegar, tabasco, onion; simmer 5 min. To boiling water in another saucepan, add rice, salt, parsley; cook as rice label directs. Stir in butter.

Cut each bacon slice into 6 pieces. On each of 4 skewers, arrange frank pieces alternately with bacon. Broil till light brown, turning. Spread with half of sauce. Broil 5 min.; turn; spread with remaining sauce. Broil 5 min.

Serve kabobs atop rice. Makes 4 servings.

VIRGINIA FRANKS

Preheat broiler 10 min., or as manufacturer directs. Score top of each frank just as you would score ham, then stud with about 5 whole cloves. Drizzle on dark corn syrup or molasses; then sprinkle lightly with brown sugar. Broil until golden.

Franks for Luncheon

BLANKET FRANKS

12 white-bread slices, with crusts removed	2½ cups milk or liquefied nonfat dry milk
6 franks, split	
6 thick process-sharp-American-cheese slices	1 teasp. salt
	⅛ teasp. pepper
2 eggs, beaten	¼ teasp. dry mustard

About 2¼ hr. before baking: In greased 12" x 8" x 2" baking dish, place 6 bread slices. Cover with split franks, then with cheese. Top with rest of bread. With fork, beat eggs with milk, salt, pepper, mustard; pour over bread. Refrigerate 1 hr.

About 1¼ hr. before serving: Start heating oven to 350°F. Bake franks 1 hr. Makes 6 servings.

FRANK CURRY BAKE

¼ lb. wide noodles	powder
(2 cups)	½ teasp. salt
1 cup commercial sour	⅛ teasp. pepper
cream	5 franks
¾ to 1 teasp. curry	Celery or poppy seeds

Start heating oven to 400°F. Cook noodles as label directs; drain. Add sour cream, curry, salt, pepper; toss lightly. Turn into 10″ x 6″ x 2″ baking dish. Arrange franks on top; sprinkle lightly with celery seeds. Bake 15 min., or until heated through. Makes 2 or 3 servings.

FRANK-STUFFED SQUASH

Start heating oven to 400°F. Scrub 2 medium acorn squash; halve lengthwise; scrape out seeds and stringy portion. Arrange in baking pan, with cut sides down. Bake 30 min.

Turn cut sides up; brush with melted butter or margarine; sprinkle with salt, pepper, brown sugar. Into each squash shell, slice 1 frank, on angle; spread lightly with prepared mustard. Bake 15 min. longer, or until squash is tender. Makes 4 servings.

Sausage-Stuffed: Prepare and bake 2 acorn squash 30 min. as above. Then turn cut sides up; brush generously with mixture of 2 tablesp. melted butter or margarine and ¼ cup honey. Bake 15 min.

Meanwhile, heat 8 fully-cooked brown-and-serve sausages in skillet as label directs. Place 2 sausages in center of each squash half; bake 15 min. longer. Makes 4 servings.

FRANKS AND SAUERKRAUT

Peasant Style: Start heating oven to 350°F. In 2-qt. casserole, mix 1 undrained No. 303 can sauerkraut with 1 undrained No. 2 can peas, ½ teasp. salt, and ⅛ to ¼ teasp. pepper. Arrange 1 lb. franks on top. Bake, covered, 15 min.; uncover; bake 15 min. longer. Makes 4 servings.

Barbecue Fashion: Just make up barbecued franks, p. 121, placing 1 No. 2½ can sauerkraut, drained, in casserole before adding franks and sauce.

Mother's Best: In saucepan, heat 1 undrained No. 2½ can sauerkraut with 1 teasp. caraway seeds. Make Mustard Sauce, p. 375. Top sauerkraut with heated, broiled, or pan-broiled franks; pour sauce over all.

CORN PUPPIES

1 cup sifted all-purpose	evaporated milk
flour	plus ½ cup water
2 tablesp. sugar	⅓ cup salad oil
2 teasp. baking powder	½ cup minced onions
1 teasp. salt	6 franks
¾ cup corn meal	1 tablesp. prepared
1 egg	mustard
1 cup milk; or ½ cup	1 tablesp. salad oil

Start heating oven to 375°F. Into bowl, sift flour, sugar, baking powder, salt. Stir in corn meal. Add egg combined with milk, ⅓ cup salad oil, onions. Stir just enough to dampen flour. Turn into greased 12″ x 8″ x 2″ baking dish. Cut 4 slashes, ¼″ deep, in each frank; place franks, with cut sides up, in row on top of batter. Bake 20 min. Then brush with combined prepared mustard and 1 tablesp. salad oil. Bake 20 min. longer, or till cake tester inserted in corn bread comes out clean. Cut into 6 "puppies," with frank in center of each.

Especially nice served with hot canned tomato sauce; diluted canned condensed tomato soup; Spanish Sauce, p. 376; or barbecue sauce. Makes 6 servings.

LET'S HAVE CANNED MEATS

The timesaving virtues of reliable brands of canned meat make them a staple must in many homes. But other features should place them high on your list of menu aids too.

There's a kind and flavor of canned meat to suit every taste.

Canned meats meet budget needs because they are so reasonably priced. And since they are pre-cooked, their preparation involves no trimming, shrinkage, or kitchen waste.

They team up with other foods and flavors.

Some canned meats, such as luncheon meat, corned beef, chopped ham, tongue, franks, dried beef, Vienna sausage, etc., are ready to open and eat. Or they may be heated or used in combination dishes.

Other canned meats, such as corned-beef hash, beef stew, chili con carne, tamales, etc., need brief heating before serving.

TO BUY CANNED MEATS

Canned Ham: There are 1½-lb. cans containing a solid, boneless piece of ham. There are also canned full-sized boned whole hams of 6¾ to 12 lb., as well as smoked picnics of 4½ to 8 lb.

Canned Meat Loaves: These handy 12-oz. cans contain all chopped ham, cured-pork luncheon meat, or cured-pork-and-beef loaf. There are also smaller cans of beef loaf and veal loaf.

Canned Corned Beef, Tongue, Franks, etc.: You can buy:
1. A solid pack of delicately cured corned beef or corned-beef brisket
2. Small luncheon tongues; larger beef tongues
3. Franks (some with sack of sauce inside); Vienna sausage (little sausages with open ends); pork sausage
4. Beef in natural juices; roasted beef; beef patties; sandwich steaks and gravy; tripe; etc.

Canned Meat Combinations: You have a choice of:
1. Corned-beef hash
2. Beef or lamb stew, with fine flavor
3. Chili con carne (with or without beans) or tamales
4. Spaghetti with meat or meat balls; spaghetti sauce with meat, etc.
5. Chop suey or chow mein, to serve over rice or chow-mein noodles
6. Ham à la king, chicken à la king, etc.

Canned Meat Spreads: These include deviled ham (2¼- and 4½-oz. sizes); liver, chicken, or ham *pâté*, tongue, etc.

Canned Meats for Babies and Juniors: These are nice to add to sandwich fillings, creamed dishes, casseroles, etc.

TO STORE CANNED MEATS

Read can label for storage directions; follow them to the letter.

Full-sized Canned Hams and Smoked Picnics must be refrigerated at all times, as the label very prominently directs.

Small 1½-lb. Canned Ham Pieces may be stored on the pantry shelf.

Other canned meats may be kept in a cool dry place.

Once canned meats are opened, treat them like cooked meat: Cover; refrigerate; use within 1 or 2 days.

Unopened Canned Hams may be frozen for about 3 months.

TO SERVE CANNED MEATS

Serve Them Hot: Open can; turn out contents. Heat slowly just until hot enough to serve; don't overcook or stir; shape and texture of meat may be harmed.

Or serve as below, as in To Serve Ready-Cooked Meats, p. 119, or as in Let's Have the Last of the Meat, p. 127.

Never try to heat any canned food in the unopened can; the can may explode.

Luncheon Meat or Chopped Ham: Broil or sauté slices. Or shred, coarsely grate, or cut up; then use as ham in macaroni, potato, or other casseroles. Or use in creamed eggs, chef's salad, etc.

Corned Beef: Slice; then sauté in butter. Or add to casserole dishes. Or heat with cabbage as in Skillet-Boiled Dinner, p. 126.

Corned-Beef Hash: Bake in casserole at 350°F. Or sauté in butter or margarine till brown. Or slice; then sauté, broil, or bake till brown on both sides. Or heat, and use as sandwich or toast spread. Serve with Tomato Sauce, p. 376; Mustard Sauce, p. 375; Zippy Cheese Sauce, p. 374; chili sauce; chutney; etc.

Chili con Carne: Heat; serve with crackers, or in ring of hot fluffy rice or macaroni.

Pork Sausage: Sauté or broil. Serve with scalloped potatoes, scrambled eggs, etc.

Vienna Sausage: Sauté or broil; then serve as nibblers to dunk into hot chili sauce, etc. Or serve with eggs, cut up in salads, etc.

Spaghetti with Meat, Ravioli with Meat Sauce, etc.: Heat; top with cheese.

Beef Stew: Heat with a little red wine or pinch of dried thyme. Or add sautéed mushrooms or sautéed, sliced onion while heating.

Serve Them Cold: Refrigerate unopened cans of meat or meat loaves 1 to 2 hr. To remove from can, open both ends completely; push meat out; slice.

Use in cold-meat platters, in sandwiches, cut up in tossed salads, or as nibblers—see To Serve Ready-Cooked Meats, p. 119.

CANNED HAMS AND PICNICS

Serve canned ham or smoked picnic sliced as it comes from the can as in To Serve Ready-Cooked Meats, p. 119.

Or heat as label directs. Or remove from can to wire rack in shallow pan. Heat at 325°F. as follows:

Piece of ham: about 10 min. per lb.
6¾-lb. ham: about 20 min. per lb.
10- to 12-lb. ham: about 15 min. per lb.
4½- to 8-lb. picnic: about 10 to 15 min. per lb.

Glaze, p. 87, may be applied ½ hr. before heating time is up. Or heat; then glaze at 450°F. until brown.

CANNED LUNCHEON MEAT

Start heating oven to 350°F. Place 2 cans luncheon meat or 2 cans chopped ham together to form 1 long loaf in baking dish; score as in step 6, p. 87. Bake, uncovered, 30 min.

Serve with barbecue sauce; Savory Jelly Sauce, p. 372; Horse-radish Sauce I or II, p. 375; Mustard Sauce, p. 375; California Raisin Sauce, p. 377. Makes 8 servings.

Spicy Baked: After scoring luncheon meat or chopped ham, spread with mixture of ¼ cup brown sugar, packed; 1 tablesp. vinegar; 1 teasp. prepared mustard; 2 teasp. flour. Bake at 375°F. about 30 min.

Clove Midget: Stud scored luncheon meat or chopped ham with whole cloves. Spread with ½ recipe Marmalade Glaze or other glaze, p. 88. Bake as in Spicy Baked above, basting often.

Stuffed: Split 2 luncheon-meat or chopped-ham loaves lengthwise; place in 8" x 8" x 2" pan. Into 2 cups mashed potatoes, stir ¼ cup minced

onion and 2 tablesp. snipped parsley. Spread over meat; sprinkle with paprika. Bake as above.

Peach Dinner Loaf: Start heating oven to 375°F. Drain 1 No. 2½ can peach slices, reserving syrup. Slice loaf of luncheon meat crosswise into 4 sections, almost, but not quite, through. Arrange peaches between and around meat slices in shallow pan. Blend 2 tablesp. brown sugar with ¼ cup peach syrup; spoon over loaf. Stud with cloves. Bake 35 min. Makes 4 servings.

DUTCH PANTRY PIE

Flaky Pastry IV, p. 409	pimento
4 packaged process-American-cheese slices	¼ to ½ teasp. salt
	¼ teasp. pepper
1 cup undiluted evaporated milk	1 can luncheon meat, cubed
2 cups chopped, cooked potatoes	1 can undiluted condensed cream-of-mushroom, -chicken, or -celery soup, or tomato soup
¼ cup snipped scallions	
2 tablesp. chopped green pepper or	½ cup undiluted evaporated milk

Prepare pastry; then roll half into round as directed. Place pastry, with paper side up, in 9" pie plate. Peel off paper; fit into plate. Roll out top crust same way.

Start heating oven to 425°F. In saucepan, melt cheese in 1 cup evaporated milk, stirring. Add potatoes, scallions, green pepper, salt to taste, pepper; spread in pastry-lined pie plate. Top with luncheon meat. Trim bottom crust. Place top crust over pie; gently peel off paper. Turn edge of top crust under lower crust; seal by pressing edges together; flute edges. Make 3 or 4 slashes in top crust. Bake 35 to 40 min.

Serve hot, with sauce made by heating together soup and ½ cup evaporated milk. Makes 6 to 8 servings.

CELERY-STYLE CORNED BEEF

½ cup undiluted canned condensed cream-of-celery soup	American cheese
	1 1-lb. can corned beef, broken into pieces
1 cup milk	4 slices toast
½ cup grated process	Snipped parsley

In saucepan, combine soup, milk; add cheese; stir over low heat until melted. Add corned beef; heat.

Serve on toast; sprinkle with parsley. Makes 4 servings.

SKILLET-BOILED DINNER

8 scraped small new potatoes	beef, chilled, then quartered
3 pared medium carrots, halved crosswise	¼ cup melted butter or margarine
1 teasp. salt	⅓ cup snipped parsley
1 1½-lb. head cabbage, quartered	⅓ cup mayonnaise
¼ teasp. salt	1 tablesp. prepared mustard
1 12-oz. can corned	1 tablesp. drained horse-radish

In large skillet, chicken fryer, or Dutch oven, place ½″ water; heat. Add potatoes, carrots, 1 teasp. salt; cook, covered, 10 min. Push potatoes and carrots to side of skillet; place cabbage wedges in bottom of skillet; sprinkle with ¼ teasp. salt. Cook, covered, 10 to 15 min., or until almost tender. Top with corned beef. Cook, covered, 5 min.; drain. Pour melted butter or margarine over all. Sprinkle with parsley.

Serve with mustard sauce made by combining mayonnaise, mustard, and horse-radish. Makes 4 servings.

DEVILED HASH

Prepare Deviled Eggs, p. 229 using 4 or 6 eggs. Start heating oven to 400°F. Pour ¼ cup melted butter or margarine into 12″ x 8″ x 2″ baking dish. Spread 3 1-lb. cans corned-beef hash over butter; pour ½ cup light cream over hash. Top with 1 cup chili sauce. Bake 30 min., or until hot and bubbly.

Arrange eggs, with filled sides up, on hash; then serve. (If desired, run hash under broiler to brown eggs.) Makes 8 servings.

HASH CHEESEBURGERS

1 1-lb. can corned-beef hash	8 to 10 packaged process-American-cheese slices
⅓ cup chili sauce	
⅓ cup sliced stuffed olives	8 to 10 stuffed olives
4 or 5 English muffins	Snipped parsley

Preheat broiler 10 min., or as manufacturer directs. Combine hash, chili sauce, olives; mix

well. Split muffins; place under broiler; toast split sides lightly. Spread with hash mixture; place under broiler just long enough to heat hash slightly; then top with cheese slices, quartered if necessary, to fit muffins. Broil just till cheese melts. Press 1 whole olive into cheese on each muffin; sprinkle with parsley. Serve at once. Makes 8 to 10.

CORNED-BEEF-HASH PUFFS

2 eggs, separated	Dash salt and pepper
1 1-lb. can corned-beef hash	4 teasp. pickle relish or sliced stuffed olives
½ teasp. salt	
⅛ teasp. pepper	Snipped parsley
4 tomato slices	

Preheat broiler 10 min., or as manufacturer directs. Beat yolks until lemon-colored. Beat whites till stiff. Mash hash. Add yolks, ½ teasp. salt, ⅛ teasp. pepper. Fold in whites. Drop by spoonfuls onto greased cookie sheet, making 4 patties. Broil until brown—about 7 min.

Meanwhile, sprinkle tomato slices with dash salt and pepper; top with relish. When puffs are brown, top with tomato slices. Broil 5 min., or till hot. Arrange on platter. Sprinkle with parsley. Delicious too with mushroom or mustard sauce instead of tomato slices. Makes 4 patties.

HASH-STUFFED TOMATOES

6 medium tomatoes	½ cup grated process American cheese
1 1-lb. can corned-beef hash	
½ teasp. salt	

Start heating oven to 350°F. Cut ¼″ to ½″ slice from stem end of each tomato. With teaspoon, scoop out pulp, forming cups. Combine tomato pulp, hash, salt; use to stuff tomatoes. Arrange in 10″ x 6″ x 2″ baking dish; top tomatoes with cheese. Bake 35 min. Makes 6 servings.

CHILI CON CORN

Start heating oven to 375°F. Into 4 small casseroles, empty 2 cans chili con carne. Top with rows of packaged corn-muffin-mix batter; place ripe olives between rows. Bake 20 to 25 min. Makes 4 servings.

Dried Beef

TO BUY AND STORE DRIED BEEF

National packers supply dried beef in packages or glass jars. When fresh, the meat is bright red with no brown spots and is moist, not brittle.

To Store: Keep packaged dried beef in refrigerator, tightly wrapped; use within 6 to 7 days. Store unopened jars on a cool shelf; plan to use within 4 to 6 weeks.

To Prepare: Tear dried beef into medium shreds. Pour boiling water over beef; let stand 1 min.; then drain.

Or use beef right from package or jar if you prefer a full flavor.

CREAMED DRIED BEEF

¼ lb. dried beef	milk plus 1 cup
¼ cup butter or mar-	water
garine	1 teasp. bottled thick
3 tablesp. flour	meat sauce, p. 9
2 cups milk; or	(optional)
1 cup evaporated	

Tear dried beef into medium pieces; then prepare as in To Prepare, above.

In double-boiler top over direct heat, melt butter. Add dried beef; cook until edges curl. Stir in flour. Place over boiling water. Add milk slowly, stirring. Cook, stirring, until smooth and thickened. Add meat sauce.

Serve on toast, small baked potatoes, waffles, fluffy white rice, or split hot baking-powder biscuits. Or serve over Baked or Broiled Tomatoes, p. 273, or over hot whole hard-cooked eggs on toast. Makes 4 servings.

To Vary: If desired, simmer ¼ cup minced onion and 2 tablesp. minced green pepper in butter. Or add 1 chopped, hard-cooked egg to sauce.

With Mushrooms: Add ¼ lb. sautéed, sliced fresh mushrooms to sauce.

Curried: Add ¼ to ½ teasp. curry powder to sauce.

FRIZZLED DRIED BEEF

Tear ½ lb. dried beef into medium pieces; then prepare as above. In a little hot butter or margarine, sauté dried beef until edges curl and beef is slightly browned.

Serve as is or as garnish for creamed eggs, scrambled eggs, etc. Makes 4 servings.

DRIED-BEEF SOUFFLE

¼ lb. dried beef	1 pimento, cut into
¼ cup butter or mar-	strips
garine	1 3-oz. can sliced
3 tablesp. flour	mushrooms
Dash pepper	¼ teasp. salt
2 cups milk	3 eggs, separated

Start heating oven to 375°F. Prepare dried beef as in To Prepare, above. Melt butter in large skillet or saucepan. Heat dried beef in butter, stirring, until slightly crisp. Stir in flour, pepper. Add milk; cook, stirring, until smooth and thickened. Add pimento, drained mushrooms. Pour into 1½-qt. casserole. Put casserole in oven. Then make this topping: Add salt to egg whites; beat till stiff. With same beater, beat egg yolks till light-colored; then fold into beaten whites. Pour over hot creamed dried-beef mixture. Bake, uncovered, 20 to 25 min., or until cake tester or toothpick inserted in topping comes out clean.

Serve at once from casserole. Makes 4 or 5 servings.

LET'S HAVE THE LAST OF THE MEAT

Refrigerate Leftover Meat at Once. Leftover cooked roasts, meats, etc. should be loosely covered and refrigerated *at once* (see p. 48). Plan to use them up within a day or two, while they're at their best.

Leftover gravy should also be refrigerated at once, and used within 2 days.

Or Freeze Leftover Meat. You may freezer-wrap and freeze unsliced portions of leftover roast (trimmed of excess fat); sliced leftover roast, meat loaf, etc.; leftover stew; scaloppine, etc. (See p. 542.) Don't keep them in the freezer longer than 1 to 3 months.

If the Meat Can Be Sliced

With roast beef, pork, lamb, or veal—or with pot roast, meat loaf, ham, smoked picnic, corned beef, tongue, etc.—there are likely to be leftovers for 1 or 2 more meals. If the meat is sliceable, serve it in one of these ways:

Serve It Cold:

1. On cold-meat platters. Add garnishes as in The Gay Garnish, p. 296.
2. With hot or cold sauce. Try:

Currant-Mint, p. 372
Savory Jelly, p. 372
Creamy Mustard, p. 375
Horse-radish I or II, p. 375
California Raisin, p. 377
Dilly, p. 373
Jiffy Barbecue, p. 372
Whole-cranberry (your own or canned)

3. Stretched with one of these:

Cheese slices, one or several varieties
Cottage-cheese mounds, in lettuce cups
Deviled Eggs, p. 229
Other home-cooked, canned, or ready-cooked meats
Salad—coleslaw; molded fruit or vegetable salad; marinated tomato slices; a main-dish salad such as egg, potato, chicken
Susan's Raw Relishes, p. 291

4. On hot-and-cold platter. Arrange cold meat slices around one of these:

A casserole—Cheese Soufflé for 4, p. 212; Elena's Macaroni Bake, p. 239; Spanish Rice, p. 235, etc.
Fruit—broiled canned fruit, sautéed bananas, fried apple rings, etc.
Omelet or scrambled eggs
Vegetables—your choice of hot cooked vegetables; cooked broccoli with cheese sauce; cheese-topped, broiled tomatoes, etc.

Serve It Hot:

1. With gravy. Reheat roast lamb, veal, or pork slices in gravy. Serve roast beef cold, with hot gravy.
2. With sauce. Reheat meat in one of these sauces; or pass sauce separately.

Bert's Superb Barbecue, p. 374
Curry, p. 372
Italian Tomato, p. 373

Mustard, p. 375
Onion, p. 372
Quick Mushroom, p. 372
Red Barbecue, p. 375
Spanish, p. 376
Tomato, p. 376
Zippy Cheese Sauce, p. 374

3. In hot sandwiches. See Lunch and Supper Hearties, p. 357. Or try one of these:

a. Add a few sliced mushrooms to gravy or sauce in Hot (or Cold) Meat Sandwiches, p. 360.
b. Reheat meat slices in Bert's Superb Barbecue Sauce, p. 374; serve on toasted buns.
c. Substitute sliced pork, veal, ham, or tongue for chicken in Baked Chicken Sandwiches, p. 358.

If the Meat Is in Small Pieces

When only tag ends remain of a roast, pot roast, steak, ham, etc., cut them up and try them in one of these:

Tongue-Spaghetti: Add slivered tongue or cut-up meat loaf to canned spaghetti in tomato sauce with cheese. Or add to your favorite spaghetti sauce during last 10 min. of heating.

Chef's Salad Bowls: See p. 307.

Salads Plus: Add to salads such as kidney bean, potato, egg, etc.

Fritters: Add to batter for corn fritters.

Savory Omelet: Use as filling for French Omelet, p. 226.

Soups: Top cream soups with slivers of cooked meat.

Stew Encore: Stew usually tastes even better the second day. It can be given a new look with the addition of a different cooked vegetable—corn, peas, tomatoes, mushrooms, okra, etc.

Vegetables: Add strips of meat to hot cooked, buttered or creamed vegetables.

P.S. Cold veal tastes much like chicken in salads and sandwiches.

If the Meat Is in Bits

1. Use ground, chopped, or bits of meat in:

Wonderful Hash, below
Dinner Croquettes, below
Sandwich fillings (See Make It Meat or Poultry, p. 362)
Stuffed peppers
Omelet filling

2. Use bones and bits in:

Soup from Leftover Bones, p. 36
Old-fashioned Split-Pea Soup, p. 40

WONDERFUL HASH

2 cups chopped, cooked roast beef, lamb, veal, ham, or pork *	¼ teasp. pepper
	¼ cup nonfat dry milk (optional)
3 cups chopped, cold cooked potatoes	⅓ cup milk or undiluted evaporated milk
½ cup minced onions	
1 teasp. salt	2 tablesp. salad oil

Coarsely chop meat and potatoes, separately, in chopping bowl; combine. Then stir in onions, salt, pepper, dry milk, milk. Heat salad oil in large skillet; spread hash evenly in bottom of skillet; cook over low heat 30 to 40 min., or until underside is brown and crusty. Do not stir, but occasionally lift edge of hash to check browning. Run spatula around edge of hash to loosen; fold one half onto other half; remove hash to platter. *Serve* with chili sauce, piccalilli, or horse-radish. Or serve with Easy Poached Eggs, p. 225; Broiled Tomatoes, p. 274; canned tomato sauce; or Creamy Mustard Sauce, p. 375. Makes 4 servings.

* Or use cooked or canned corned beef, tongue, or luncheon meat.

To Vary: To hash mixture, add snipped parsley, green pepper, horse-radish, or pickle relish. Or reduce potatoes to 2 cups; then add 1 cup chopped, cooked beets or carrots. Or substitute tomato juice for milk. Or add 1 to 2 tablesp. chutney and a little curry powder.

Corned-Beef Hash and Tomato Bake: Use corned beef as meat. Instead of cooking in skillet, turn into greased 1½-qt. casserole or shallow dish. Press tomato halves into top of mixture;

spread each half with a little prepared mustard; sprinkle with salt, pepper, minced onion, Worcestershire, a few fresh bread crumbs, and bits of butter. Bake at 375°F., uncovered, 30 to 35 min., or until brown.

DINNER CROQUETTES

1 cup Thick White Sauce, p. 376	juice
	Salt
1 teasp. snipped parsley	Speck pepper
1 teasp. minced onion	Pinch dried sage (optional)
2 cups ground, cooked roast lamb, veal, beef, ham, chicken, or turkey *	
	1 egg
	1 tablesp. water
½ teasp. fresh, frozen, or canned lemon	Packaged dried bread crumbs
	Fat or salad oil

1. Combine white sauce, parsley, onion, meat, lemon juice; mix well. Add salt and pepper if needed, plus sage. Refrigerate until well chilled—several hours or overnight.
2. Divide chilled mixture into 8 portions. (Mixture is soft to handle but will make delightfully tender croquettes.) Spoon out each portion; shape into cylinder, cone, or ball.
3. With fork, beat egg and water just till blended. Put bread crumbs on piece of waxed paper.
4. Roll croquettes first in crumbs, then in egg, then again in crumbs, making sure all surfaces are well coated. Refrigerate again.
5. Deep-fry as on p. 7, or shallow-fry as on p. 8, at 390°F. on deep-fat frying thermometer. Fry, turning occasionally, 2 min., or until golden.
6. When croquettes are done, remove with slotted spoon; drain on paper towels. If necessary, keep warm in 300°F. oven.
Serve alone, or with ½ recipe Spanish Sauce, p. 376; canned tomato sauce; Quick Mushroom Sauce, p. 372; or Horse-radish Sauce I or II, p. 375. Makes 8.

* Or use canned ham, chicken, turkey, or luncheon meat.

► **For 2:** Use 1 egg; halve rest of ingredients.

Skillet: If preferred, form croquette mixture into patties; brown on both sides in a little hot salad oil in skillet.

MEAT A LA KING

¼ cup butter or margarine	⅛ teasp. pepper
¼ cup flour	½ teasp. Worcestershire
1½ cups milk	2 teasp. prepared mustard
1 cup diced, cooked roast beef, veal, lamb, or pork or baked ham *	1 cup drained cooked or canned vegetables, or cooked frozen mixed vegetables
2 tablesp. minced celery	
1 teasp. salt	4 slices buttered toast

In saucepan, melt butter; stir in flour. Gradually stir in milk; cook, stirring, until thickened and smooth. Add meat, celery, salt, pepper, Worcestershire, mustard, vegetables; heat thoroughly.

Serve on toast or between buttered, split hot biscuits. Makes 4 servings.

* *Or use canned ham, chopped ham, tongue, or luncheon meat.*

To Vary: Add diced, hard-cooked eggs, or canned or sautéed fresh mushrooms.

Or serve on toasted, split English muffins or corn bread; chow-mein noodles; waffles; or mashed or baked potatoes.

Casserole-Style: Turn meat mixture into casserole; top with crumbled potato chips and a little grated cheese. Bake at 350°F. until bubbly.

SHEPHERD'S PIE

½ recipe hot Mashed Potatoes, p. 268	Leftover gravy
2 cups cut-up, cooked roast beef, lamb, veal, or pork	6 drained cooked small onions
1 tablesp. flour	1 cup drained cooked, quartered carrots
2 tablesp. fat or salad oil	1 cup drained cooked or canned peas
	1 egg, beaten

Grease 1½-qt. casserole. Prepare mashed potatoes. Start heating oven to 425°F.

In bowl, lightly roll meat in flour until coated. In hot fat in skillet, brown meat lightly on all sides. Add 2½ cups leftover gravy (or as much gravy as you have on hand, adding enough hot water to make 2½ cups in all; season to taste; thicken if necessary). Add onions, carrots, peas. Heat; then pour into casserole.

Fold egg into potatoes; arrange in ring on top of meat. Bake until gravy bubbles and potato

ring is light golden brown—about 10 to 15 min. Makes 4 servings.

BEEF-AND-POTATO CAKES

2½ cups ground, cooked roast beef *	1 teasp. bottled thick meat sauce, p. 9
1½ cups cold seasoned, mashed potatoes	2 teasp. minced onion
½ teasp. salt	Flour
Speck pepper	2 tablesp. melted fat or salad oil

Mix all ingredients except flour and fat. Shape into 6 patties. Roll lightly in flour; sauté in hot fat until brown on all sides. Makes 4 to 6 servings.

* *Or use ground cooked roast veal, ham, lamb, or pork.*

SKILLET CORNED BEEF WITH SAUERKRAUT

1 tablesp. bacon fat	4 slices cooked or canned corned beef
1 No. 2 can sauerkraut	
2 tablesp. water	¼ cup light cream

Heat fat in skillet. Spread drained sauerkraut in skillet; add water. Top with corned-beef slices. Simmer, covered, 10 min., or until hot. Uncover; pour cream over sauerkraut. Heat, covered, 2 or 3 min. longer.

Serve meat on top of sauerkraut. Makes 2 servings.

TANGY COLD BEEF-AND-ONION PLATTER

¾ teasp. salt	olive oil
Pinch seasoned salt	8 thin slices cooked or canned corned beef or tongue
1 teasp. dry mustard	
1 teasp. brown sugar	
1 teasp. mixed whole pickling spices	2 thinly sliced onions
3 tablesp. wine vinegar	Shredded lettuce
1 tablesp. salad or	Tomatoes, quartered

At your convenience: Make marinade by mixing well salt, seasoned salt, mustard, sugar, spices, vinegar, oil. Arrange meat slices in shallow open pan; top with onion slices; pour marinade over both. Refrigerate.

At serving time: Arrange meat and onions on bed of shredded lettuce on platter. Garnish with tomato quarters. Makes 4 servings.

SWEET-SOUR ROAST PORK

3 tablesp. butter or margarine	1 cup canned crushed pineapple, undrained
¼ cup green pepper, cut into strips	2 tablesp. vinegar
¼ cup coarsely chopped onion	1 tablesp. soy sauce
1 tablesp. cornstarch	4 ½″-thick slices cooked roast pork

Preheat broiler 10 min., or as manufacturer directs. In hot butter in skillet, sauté green pepper and onion about 5 min.; stir in cornstarch, then pineapple. Heat, stirring, until thickened. Add vinegar, soy sauce. Pour over pork in shallow open pan. Broil about 4½″ below heat about 5 min. Makes 4 servings.

CHEF'S LAMB AND MUSHROOMS

1 tablesp. butter or margarine	1 cup cut-up, cooked roast lamb
1 tablesp. minced onion	1 teasp. grated Parmesan cheese
1 3-oz. can whole mushrooms, undrained	1 teasp. sherry or cooking sherry
½ cup lamb gravy	

In hot butter in saucepan, sauté onion until golden. Add mushrooms, gravy, lamb. Heat, stirring, until piping hot. Just before serving, stir in cheese, sherry.

Serve over mashed potatoes, fluffy rice, noodles, etc. Makes 2 or 3 servings.

LAMB BARBECUE

1 tablesp. butter or margarine	shire
1 sliced small onion	1 cup cut-up, cooked roast lamb
1 to 2 tablesp. vinegar	1½ cups uncooked medium noodles
2 teasp. brown sugar	
½ cup catchup	Melted butter or margarine
¼ cup water	
1 teasp. Worcester-	

In hot butter in small saucepan, sauté onion until lightly browned. Add vinegar, brown sugar, catchup, water, Worcestershire; simmer, covered, 15 min. Add lamb; simmer until heated.

Meanwhile, cook noodles as label directs. When tender, drain and toss with melted butter.

Serve lamb and sauce over noodles. Makes 2 servings.

LAMB CURRY I

4 cups hot cooked rice, p. 233	1 teasp. curry powder
	Salt
2 tablesp. butter or margarine	2 cups lamb gravy, diluted with water; or 2 chicken- or beef-bouillon cubes, dissolved in 2 cups hot water
¾ cup sliced onions	
1 cup diced celery	
1 minced clove garlic	
1½ cups cut-up, cooked roast lamb	
	Snipped parsley

While rice cooks, in hot butter in skillet, sauté onions, celery, and garlic until lightly browned. Add lamb, curry powder, salt to taste, gravy. Simmer, covered, 30 min. If necessary, thicken as on p. 7.

To serve: Arrange hot rice in ring on platter. Sprinkle with parsley. Turn lamb curry into center. Pass choice of Curry Accompaniments, p. 193, if desired. Makes 4 servings.

Veal Curry I: Make as above, substituting cut-up, cooked roast veal for lamb.

MONDAY PIE

Start heating oven to 400°F. In 1½-qt. casserole, mix 2 cups cut-up, cooked roast lamb or beef; 1 cup gravy; 1 pkg. thawed frozen green beans; 1 drained No. 2 can white potatoes; ¼ teasp. monosodium glutamate; ¼ cup red wine; and 1 tomato, sliced, then halved. Crisscross top with ½″ strips of any Flaky Pastry, pp. 407 to 410, pressing ends to edge of casserole. Bake 40 min., or until brown. Makes 4 servings.

DEVILED TONGUE MOLD

2 env. unflavored gelatine	1 tablesp. prepared mustard
1 cup cold water	¼ cup chopped sour pickle
1¼ cups boiling water	
¼ cup mayonnaise	2 cups chopped, cooked or canned tongue
2 tablesp. horse-radish	
1 teasp. salt	2 chopped, hard-cooked eggs
¼ teasp. pepper	

Sprinkle gelatine on cold water to soften; add boiling water; stir until dissolved; cool. Beat in mayonnaise, horse-radish, salt, pepper, mustard. Refrigerate until slightly thickened. Fold in rest of ingredients. Pour into 9″ x 5″ x 3″ loaf pan. Refrigerate until firm. Unmold; slice. Makes 8 servings.

Deviled Ham Mold: Substitute cooked or canned ham or canned luncheon meat for tongue.

STUFFED PEPPERS WITH CABBAGE

3 tablesp. fat or salad oil	⅛ teasp. pepper
½ cup minced onions	8 large cabbage leaves
1 minced green pepper	2 cups ground, cooked
2 6-oz. cans tomato	or canned ham *
paste (1⅓ cups)	½ cup grated raw
2 cans water	potatoes
½ teasp. ground ginger	1 minced medium
2 teasp. brown sugar	onion
⅓ cup fresh, frozen,	½ teasp. dry mustard
or canned lemon	⅛ teasp. ground cloves
juice	1 egg, beaten
2 bay leaves	4 small green peppers
½ teasp. salt	

In hot fat in Dutch oven or kettle, sauté ½ cup onions and green pepper until golden. Add tomato paste and water measured in paste can. Add ginger, sugar, lemon juice, bay leaves, salt, pepper; simmer, covered, 30 min. Cook cabbage leaves in boiling salted water, covered, 2 min.; drain. Combine meat, potatoes, 1 minced onion, mustard, cloves, egg. Place 1 tablesp. meat mixture in cup part of each cabbage leaf; loosely fold sides of leaf over; roll up. Use rest of meat mixture to stuff seeded whole green peppers.

Arrange peppers and cabbage rolls in tomato mixture; simmer, covered, 1¼ hr., or until done. Makes 4 servings.

* Or use ground canned luncheon meat, chopped ham, tongue or corned beef.

▶ **For 2:** Use 1 egg; halve rest of ingredients. Use greased 1-qt. casserole.

SUSAN'S PINEAPPLE HAM LOAF

3½ cups ground cooked	¼ cup catchup
ham *	2 finely snipped celery
½ lb. veal shoulder,	stalks
ground	¾ cup milk
½ lb. round, ground	1 medium onion
2 cups day-old bread	2 tablesp. snipped
crumbs	parsley
¼ teasp. poultry	½ cup brown sugar,
seasoning	packed
½ teasp. salt	4 canned pineapple
¼ teasp. pepper	slices (1 No. 1 flat
1 egg, slightly beaten	can)

1. Start heating oven to 350°F. When grinding cooked ham, use medium blade of food chopper.
2. Put ham, veal, and beef in large mixing bowl. Add crumbs, poultry seasoning, salt, pepper, egg, catchup, celery, milk.
3. Mince onion onto meat (p. 6). Add parsley. With 2-tined fork, lightly mix meat with other ingredients in bowl.
4. Sprinkle bottom of 9″ x 9″ x 2″ baking dish with brown sugar. Arrange pineapple slices on top of sugar. With spoon and spatula, carefully press some of meat mixture around pineapple slices; then pat rest on top. Bake 1 hr.
5. When loaf is done, carefully pour off all drippings. To unmold, place platter or board on top of baking dish; invert so loaf rests, with pineapple side up, on board. Spoon a little of drippings over top. Makes 6 to 8 servings.

* Or use canned ham, chopped ham, or luncheon meat.

ORANGE UPSIDE-DOWN HAM LOAVES

6 tablesp. brown sugar	½ cup fresh bread
½ teasp. dry mustard	crumbs
6 thin unpeeled	1 egg
orange slices	½ cup orange juice
2 cups ground, cooked	½ teasp. paprika
ham or smoked	½ teasp. Worcester-
picnic	shire
1 lb. fresh-pork-sausage	½ teasp. dry mustard
meat	Pinch ground cloves
1 minced small onion	

Start heating oven to 350°F. In each of 6 custard cups or individual casseroles (about 3½″ in diameter), place 1 tablesp. brown sugar; sprinkle with a little mustard; top with 1 orange slice. Combine ham with rest of ingredients; pack lightly into cups. Bake, uncovered, 45 min.; let stand 5 min. Pour off drippings; then invert onto serving platter. Makes 6 servings.

P.S. This dish may also be baked in 9″ x 5″ x 3″ loaf pan 1¼ hr., using 3 or 4 orange slices.

INDIAN HAM BAKE

Start heating oven to 350°F. Place 2½ cups ground, cooked or canned ham, luncheon meat, or corned beef in bottom of greased 12″ x 8″ x 2″ baking dish. Combine 4 cups cooked or canned whole-kernel corn with 1 cup fresh bread crumbs, 2 teasp. prepared mustard, 1¾ cups milk, 2 beaten eggs, 1 teasp. salt, 2 teasp. horse-radish. Pour over ham.

Slice 3 medium tomatoes into ½″-thick slices; arrange on top of corn. Sprinkle tomatoes with salt or seasoned salt; brush with 1 tablesp. melted butter or margarine. Bake 50 min. Makes 6 generous servings.

THIRTY-MINUTE GLAZED HAM PATTIES

4 cups medium-ground, cooked ham *	⅛ teasp. dried thyme
⅓ cup fine cracker crumbs	¼ cup minced onion
1 egg, beaten	⅓ cup brown sugar, packed
⅔ cup undiluted evaporated milk	1 tablesp. vinegar
Dash pepper	½ teasp. dry mustard
	1½ tablesp. flour

Start heating oven to 350°F. Combine ham, crumbs, egg, milk, pepper, thyme, onion; pack into 6 greased 3″ muffin-pan cups. Bake 20 min. Meanwhile, in saucepan, blend brown sugar, vinegar, mustard, flour; boil 1 min., stirring occasionally. Spoon over hot baked patties; broil 2 min. Makes 6 patties.

* Or use canned ham, chopped ham, luncheon meat, or corned beef.

SCALLOPED HAM, POTATOES, AND CHEESE

¾ lb. thinly sliced cooked ham; or 1 can luncheon meat, thinly sliced	¼ teasp. pepper
	1 cup grated process sharp American cheese (¼ lb.)
1 minced small onion	1 cup milk
4 to 6 thinly sliced, pared raw potatoes	2 tablesp. butter or margarine
3 tablesp. flour	¼ cup catchup
½ teasp. salt	

Start heating oven to 350°F. In greased 1½- or 2-qt. casserole, arrange ham. Top with onion. Then top with half of potatoes; sprinkle with half of flour, salt, pepper, cheese; repeat. Meanwhile, heat milk with butter; pour over all. Bake, covered, 40 min. Uncover; dot with catchup. Bake 30 min., or until potatoes are tender. (It curdles a little, but tastes so good!) Makes 4 to 6 servings.

HAM-BANANA ROLLS

½ cup milk	Prepared mustard
½ lb. process-American-cheese slices	4 all-yellow or slightly green-tipped bananas
4 thin slices boiled or baked ham	1½ tablesp. melted butter or margarine

Start heating oven to 350°F. In double boiler, combine milk, cheese; heat, stirring occasionally, until smooth. Meanwhile, lightly spread ham slices with mustard.

Peel bananas; roll up each banana in ham slice. Brush tips of bananas with butter; place in shallow casserole or 12″ x 8″ x 2″ baking dish. Pour cheese sauce over rolls. Bake 30 min. Makes 4 servings.

CRANBERRY-GLAZED HAM ROLLS

1 can whole-cranberry sauce	margarine
	¼ cup minced onion
2 tablesp. fresh, frozen, or canned lemon juice	¼ cup minced celery
	2 cups cooked rice
½ cup brown sugar, packed	¼ teasp. salt
	⅛ teasp. pepper
¼ cup butter or	8 thin slices boiled or baked ham

Start heating oven to 350°F. With fork, break up cranberry sauce; mix with lemon juice, brown sugar. In skillet, melt butter; add onion, celery; sauté until onion is yellow. Add rice, salt, pepper; spread some of this mixture on each ham slice. Roll up; fasten with toothpick; place in greased shallow baking dish. Spoon half of cranberry sauce over rolls. Bake 10 min. Spoon on rest of sauce. Bake 5 to 10 min. Makes 4 servings.

HAM-AND-NOODLE CASSEROLE

1½ cups medium-wide noodles	2 tablesp. catchup
	1 tablesp. horse-radish
2 tablesp. butter or margarine	2 cups cut-up, cooked ham *
2 tablesp. flour	1 cup drained canned or cooked peas
1 cup milk	1 tablesp. melted butter or margarine
1 cup grated process American cheese (¼ lb.)	¼ cup fresh bread crumbs
1 teasp. salt	

Start heating oven to 350°F. Cook noodles as label directs; drain. Meanwhile, in saucepan over low heat, melt 2 tablesp. butter; stir in flour until smooth. Gradually stir in milk; cook, stirring, until smooth and thickened. Remove from heat.

Add cheese, stirring until melted. Add noodles, salt, catchup, horse-radish, ham, peas. Turn into 1½-qt. casserole. Top with combined 1 tablesp. butter and crumbs. Bake, uncovered, 30 min., or until crumbs are browned. Makes 4 servings.

Or use canned ham, chopped ham, tongue, or luncheon meat.

ISLAND-STYLE HAM AND SWEET POTATOES

6 medium sweet potatoes or yams	cooked ham *
1 tablesp. butter or margarine	½ cup green-pepper or pimento strips
½ teasp. salt	1 No. 2 can pineapple chunks, drained
⅛ teasp. pepper	2 tablesp. brown sugar
Pinch nutmeg	1 tablesp. cornstarch
Milk	¾ cup syrup drained from pineapple
2 tablesp. butter or margarine	2 tablesp. vinegar
2 cups coarsely cut-up,	

Cook potatoes as on p. 283; then mash, adding 1 tablesp. butter, salt, pepper, nutmeg, and enough milk to give potatoes a creamy consistency.

Start heating oven to 400°F. In 2 tablesp. hot butter in skillet, sauté ham, stirring, until golden. Add green pepper, pineapple chunks; cook 2 or 3 min. Stir in combined brown sugar and cornstarch, then pineapple syrup and vinegar. Cook, stirring, until clear and thickened. Pour mixture into 9″ pie plate; drop spoonfuls of potato on top. Bake 20 to 25 min., or till bubbling hot. Makes 4 servings.

Or use canned ham, chopped ham, or luncheon meat.

SAVORY HAM AND CAULIFLOWER

1 medium head cauliflower	2 cups cut-up, cooked ham
1 can undiluted condensed cream-of-chicken soup	⅛ teasp. dried savory
	1 cup grated process sharp American cheese (¼ lb.)
¼ cup milk	

Break cauliflower into flowerets; cook till tender-crisp as on p. 280; drain.

Start heating oven to 350°F. Combine soup and milk in 10″ x 6″ x 2″ baking dish. Fold in cauliflowerets, ham, savory, ½ cup cheese. Sprinkle top with ½ cup cheese. Bake 30 min. Makes 4 servings.

HAM-AND-CHICKEN PIE

1 cup sifted all-purpose flour	chicken soup
	¼ cup milk
1 teasp. baking powder	1 cup diced, cooked ham *
½ teasp. salt	
1 cup unseasoned mashed sweet potatoes or yams	1 cup diced, cooked chicken
	⅛ teasp. pepper
⅓ cup melted shortening	⅛ teasp. ground cloves
1 egg, beaten	2 teasp. snipped fresh or dried parsley
1 can undiluted condensed cream-of-	1 cup drained cooked peas

Several hours ahead: For crust, sift flour, baking powder, and salt into bowl; add potatoes, shortening, egg; stir until well blended. Refrigerate several hours.

About 45 min. before serving: Start heating oven to 425°F. Heat soup with milk; remove from heat. Add ham, chicken, pepper, cloves, parsley. Turn half of chicken mixture into 9″ pie plate; scatter peas on top; top with rest of chicken mixture. On very well floured board, gently roll out crust into 10″ circle. Lift onto pie plate; crimp edge; make slits in top. Bake 25 to 30 min. Serve at once. Makes 4 or 5 servings.

Or use canned ham, tongue, corned beef or luncheon meat.

CALIFORNIA HAM SUPREME

2 tablesp. butter or margarine	mustard
	½ teasp. Worcestershire
¼ cup minced green pepper	¼ teasp. salt
2 tablesp. minced onion	⅛ teasp. pepper
3 tablesp. flour	1 tablesp. fresh, frozen, or canned lemon juice
1 cup boiling water	
1⅔ cups undiluted evaporated milk	6 slices white bread, with crusts removed
1½ cups diced, cooked or canned ham or canned luncheon meat	Melted butter or margarine
	1 slivered, peeled avocado
1½ tablesp. prepared	

Start heating oven to 500°F. In saucepan, melt 2 tablesp. butter; add green pepper, onion; cook, stirring occasionally, until tender. Gradually stir in flour and boiling water; cook, stirring, until thickened. Stir in milk; cook until slightly thickened. Add ham, mustard, Worcestershire, salt, pepper, lemon juice; keep warm.

Meanwhile, press each bread slice into muffin-pan cup; brush with melted butter. Toast in 500°F. oven until light brown. Remove from pans.

Fold avocado into ham mixture; use to fill toast cups. Makes 6 servings.

HAM GALA

¼ cup butter or margarine	1½ cups milk
1 diced large green pepper	2 cups slivered, cooked or canned ham
1 tablesp. minced onion	½ cup canned slivered blanched almonds
¼ cup flour	4 egg yolks
½ teasp. salt	½ cup light cream
Dash pepper	Toast

In hot butter in saucepan, cook green pepper and onion 5 min., stirring often. Gradually stir in flour, salt, pepper, milk; cook, stirring, until thickened and smooth. Add ham, almonds. Beat egg yolks; beat in cream; slowly stir into ham mixture. Cook, stirring, until thickened.

Serve on toast. Makes 6 to 8 servings.

USING THE LAST DELICIOUS BITS
(cooked or canned ham, chopped ham, tongue, corned beef, or luncheon meat)

Meat Scramble: In small amount of butter or margarine in skillet, brown bits of meat; pour in scrambled-egg mixture. Scramble as usual.

Pickle Buns: In hot butter in skillet, lightly brown thin pieces of cooked meat; place between buttered, toasted, split hamburger buns. Top with pickle relish or chutney.

Creamed Potatoes Plus: Fold slivered, cooked meat into creamed potatoes (bake extra potatoes night before). Sprinkle with snipped chives.

Savory Beans: In small amount of fat or salad oil, sauté slivers of cooked meat with a little minced onion, green pepper, and celery until golden. Add canned baked beans; heat.

Spaghetti Roll Ups: On each thin slice of cooked (or boiled) ham, arrange some canned spaghetti in tomato sauce with cheese. Sprinkle well with grated Parmesan cheese. Roll up lengthwise; fasten with toothpick. Broil slowly 10 to 15 min., or until golden and hot, brushing occasionally with melted butter or margarine.

Club Special: Top toasted, split corn-bread squares with thin pieces of cooked ham or tongue, then with hot chicken à la king. (You may use frozen chicken à la king, adding sherry to taste.) Sprinkle with sliced ripe olives or slivered, toasted almonds.

Poultry

Time was when turkey appeared on the table only at holidaytime and fried chicken was a summer-only treat. These days, however, production and marketing methods make it possible to serve fine poultry of all kinds at all seasons of the year.

Like meat, poultry is a rich source of important food values. Serve it often, for good health and good eating.

Before using these recipes, refer to Pots and Pans, p. 692, and How to Use Our Recipes, p. 3. Always use standard measuring cups and measuring spoons; measure level.

CHICKEN

TO BUY

How Chicken Is Sold: In most markets, you'll find chicken prepared for you in the following 3 styles:

Ready-to-Cook Chicken: These meaty, tender, top-quality birds come either fresh, ice-chilled, with a tag identifying the brand, or quick-frozen, in a branded package. They have been fully drawn, pinfeathered, cleaned inside and out—are all ready for the oven or pan.

You can buy them whole, with the cleaned giblets and neck, wrapped separately, in the body. Or you can buy them cut up, or as chicken parts such as breasts, drumsticks, wings, thighs, backs.

Ready-to-cook birds have another plus: Their tag, wrapper, or package is your buying guide. It carries the packer's name, the bird's weight, the price, as well as the U.S. inspection mark, or U.S. grade and inspection mark, denoting a high-quality, wholesome bird. The wrapper of quick-frozen chicken also carries cooking directions.

Dressed Chicken: These birds have been plucked but head and feet are still on, viscera still in. Usually the meatman will draw (remove viscera from) a dressed bird for you after purchase, but you will still have considerable cleaning to do at home. If you're planning to roast the bird, be sure to ask the meatman to weigh it after he has drawn it, so you can compute the roasting time.

Cooked Ready-to-Serve Chicken: What a convenience is chicken in handy cans, all ready to heat! You can choose whole chicken, boneless fricassee, fricassee with vegetables, boned chicken, chicken à la king, noodle-chicken dinner, etc. And there's luscious canned cream-of-chicken soup, chicken broth, and chicken-bouillon cubes too.

Cooked ready-to-serve chicken comes frozen too. Don't wait for company to try quick-frozen chicken à la king, individual chicken pies, chicken chow mein, etc.

Kinds of Chicken: Four kinds are available; they differ in size, tenderness, age.

Broiler-Fryers are small tender birds of 1½ to 3 lb. ready-to-cook weight.

Roasters are small tender birds of up to 5 lb. ready-to-cook weight.

Stewing Chickens (formerly called fowl) are mature, less tender 2½- to 5-lb. hens, with more fat than other kinds of chicken.

Capons are young unsexed male birds of 4 to 7 lb. ready-to-cook weight. They have exceptional tenderness and flavor.

Price: When comparing the prices of ready-to-cook and dressed (undrawn) chickens, don't forget that you pay more *per pound* for ready-to-cook chicken because you get the eatable portions *only*. When you buy a dressed bird, you pay for about 25 to 30 per cent waste, which the meatman discards when he draws the bird for you after purchase.

HOW MUCH CHICKEN TO BUY PER SERVING*

	Ready to Cook	Dressed
For Broiling	¼ to ½ bird	¼ to ½ bird
For Sautéing or Frying	⅔ to ¾ lb.	¾ to 1 lb.
For Roasting	⅔ to ¾ lb.	¾ to 1 lb.
For Stewing	¼ to ⅔ lb.†	⅓ to ¾ lb.†

* Per serving, not per person. Some persons take more than 1 serving.

† Buy smaller amount if serving chicken with rice, macaroni, or biscuits.

TO STORE

Quick-frozen, Ready-to-Cook Chicken: Put bird in freezer or refrigerator-freezer combination as quickly as possible. Keep frozen until time to thaw for cooking. Stored at 0°F. or lower, frozen chicken may be held several months.

If you must store bird in freezer compartment of conventional refrigerator, do not hold longer than a month.

To Thaw: Completely thaw bird (except stewing chicken) before cooking, following label directions. (Cook stewing chicken unthawed.) Or leave bird in original wrapper in food compartment of refrigerator 12 to 24 hr. Or to use same day, unwrap bird; then thaw in running cold water until pliable—about 3 hr. As soon as bird is pliable enough, remove bag of giblets and neck inside body. Once bird is thawed, cook at once exactly as if it were fresh.

Fresh, Ice-Chilled, Ready-to-Cook Chicken: Buy only from a meatman who keeps birds refrigerated. Once home, quickly remove wrapper. Remove giblets and neck from body. Then wrap bird loosely, with ends open, in waxed paper, aluminum foil, or saran. Store in coldest part of food compartment of refrigerator. Use whole bird within 1 or 2 days; use cut-up bird within 24 hr. Clean and cook giblets as on p. 138.

Dressed Chicken: Be sure meatman has drawn bird. Remove giblets. Singe hairs by holding bird over flame. Remove oil sac at tail end of bird. Remove pinfeathers with tweezers, or catch between thumb and paring knife. Feel inside bird, along rib section, to be sure all lung has been removed. With cold water, rinse bird well, inside and out; dry well, standing bird upright to drain. Then refrigerate, loosely wrapped as above. Use whole bird within 1 or 2 days; use cut-up bird within 24 hr. Clean and cook giblets as on p. 138.

TO CARE FOR COOKED CHICKEN

Roasted Bird: For safety's sake, always put leftover cooked chicken in the refrigerator *at once.* Remove stuffing from body and neck cavities of roasted bird. If most of bird has been carved, remove rest of meat from bones, so you can make broth from bones to use in leftover-chicken dishes. (Broth will have fuller flavor made now than if you wait until carcass is bare.) Immediately refrigerate meat, stuffing, and gravy in separate containers.

When reheating stuffing or gravy, heat only as much as is needed; keep rest in refrigerator. Both uncooked and cooked stuffings and gravies spoil quickly if kept warm very long.

Plan to use up stuffing within 2 days, gravy within 3 days; heat both thoroughly to serve. Use up cooked chicken within 3 days.

Simmered Bird: If you have simmered a chicken to use later as on pp. 150 to 151, cool it quickly this way: Lift bird from hot broth to wire rack to cool. Cool kettle of broth in cold water in sink, changing water and stirring broth often. At the end of ½ hr. (no longer), put both bird and broth in refrigerator at once. Use within 3 days.

TO COOK GIBLETS

To Clean: Giblets include the heart, gizzard, and liver; with a ready-to-cook, whole bird, the neck is often included too. You can also buy packaged quick-frozen livers, hearts, and gizzards.

Be sure the gizzard has been split open, the inner sac removed, the lining well scraped. Wash all giblets *thoroughly;* refrigerate at once.

Cook giblets within 12 hr. after buying.

To Cook: In saucepan, place heart, gizzard, neck. Add 1 celery stalk, 2 peppercorns, tip of bay leaf, 1 sliced small onion, and water to cover. Simmer giblets, covered, until easily pierced with fork—about ½ hr. if they're from a young chicken; about 1 hr. if they're from an older chicken; about 3 to 4 hr. if they're from a turkey. Add liver with ½ teasp. salt last 15 min. If giblets are not to be used at once, refrigerate promptly. Plan to use within 2 days.

To Use: Use coarsely chopped, cooked giblets in Susan's Chicken Gravy, p. 145, sandwich fillings, stuffings, or as the meat in Italian spaghetti, rice dishes, etc.

Use giblet broth as part of liquid in gravy or to moisten stuffing.

Chicken in About an Hour

SAUTEED CHICKEN

To Buy: Buy cut-up, halved, or quartered small ready-to-cook broiler-fryers. Or buy chicken parts. (See To Buy, p. 136.)

Allow ½ chicken per serving.

Store as in To Store, p. 137.

To Sauté:

1. Dust cut-up chicken lightly with flour if desired. In large skillet or chicken fryer, heat 3 to 4 tablesp. butter, margarine, or bacon fat until bubbling. In it, brown chicken, uncovered, quickly but well on all sides, turning with tongs. (If you're cooking 2 chickens, use 2 skillets.)

2. When chicken is nicely browned, turn heat low. Then add any of these seasonings:

Dried or fresh basil, thyme, or rosemary	glutamate
	Sliced and lightly floured mushrooms
Minced celery	
Curry powder	Minced onion, chives, shallots, or garlic
Garlic, celery, or onion salt	
	Minced pimento
Minced green pepper	Salt and pepper
Monosodium	Seasoned salt

3. Now cover skillet. Let chicken cook slowly, turning it occasionally to brown evenly, 25 to 35 min., or until fork-tender. For crisp-crusted chicken, uncover last 10 min. Just before removing chicken to platter, sprinkle with snipped parsley and paprika.

To Serve: Arrange on heated platter; pour pan juices over all.

Superb Variations: After chicken has cooked, covered, 15 min., as in step 3 above, you may add one of these:

Slivered, blanched almonds
Pinch dried or fresh chervil or dill
Sliced green, ripe, or stuffed olives
Cut-up canned peaches, pears, or pineapple
2 or 3 peeled, chopped tomatoes

Or into pan juices, stir ½ cup heavy or commercial sour cream, ¼ cup white wine, dash lemon juice, or a little grated lemon rind.

Or sprinkle chicken with chopped crisp bacon.

BROILED CHICKEN

To Buy: You may broil any tender, small chicken, but 1½- to 2½-lb. ready-to-cook broiler-fryers are especially nice.

Have meatman halve birds lengthwise and remove backbone, neck, and keel bone (larger birds may be cut crosswise after broiling, to quarter them). Or buy chicken parts. (See To Buy, p. 136.)

Allow ½ broiler-fryer per serving.

Store as in To Store, p. 137.

To Broil:

1. Preheat broiler 10 min., or as manufacturer directs. To make washing easy, line broiler pan with aluminum foil. Arrange chicken, with skin sides down, in bottom of broiler pan, *without rack* (juices in pan keep chicken moist).
2. Sprinkle chicken with salt or seasoned salt and paprika, or monosodium glutamate. Brush with melted butter or margarine, or salad oil.
3. Place pan in broiler so surface of chicken is 7″ to 9″ from heat and chicken can broil slowly. If it is impossible to place broiler pan this low in your range, lower heat (if oven is thermostatically controlled, turn temperature control to about 350°F.).
4. Turn chicken every 15 min., brushing it with melted butter each time. Broil until fork-tender, nicely browned, and crisp—45 to 60 min.

   Test for Doneness: Drumsticks and wing joints should move easily, and thickest part of chicken should yield easily to pressure from fork.
5. If you wish, brush whole mushrooms or un-cooked chicken livers and cooked hearts, giz-zards, and necks with butter. (See To Cook Giblets, p. 138.) Broil with chicken last 15 min.

To Serve: Serve chicken, skin sides up, with pan juices; Bert's Superb Barbecue Sauce, p. 374; or bottled barbecue sauce. Nice with baked white or sweet potatoes or waffles.

Special Touches: Choose any of these:

   Barbecue: Before broiling chicken, brush with one of barbecue sauces, pp. 374 to 375, instead of melted butter.

   Herb: To melted butter for brushing chicken, add one of these: minced garlic or onion, snipped chives or parsley, sliced scallions, white wine, or pinch dried thyme or tarragon.

   Delmarva: Before broiling chicken, rub well with cut lemon. Then, after brushing with melted butter, lightly sprinkle with granu-lated sugar.

   Under Cover: For each chicken, mix ¼ cup snipped parsley, 1 tablesp. snipped chives, bit of fresh or dried tarragon, 3 tablesp. soft butter or margarine, and ¼ teasp. salt. With tip of paring knife, loosen skin on breast of chicken. Then, with small spatula, spread flesh under skin with butter mixture. While broiling chicken, brush skin often with salad oil.

   Anne's Glaze: Sprinkle 2 2½- to 3-lb. broiler-fryers with 2 teasp. salt; then brush with mix-ture of 2 tablesp. crab-apple jelly, mashed; ¼ cup white wine; and ½ cup melted butter or margarine. While broiling chicken, baste with rest of jelly mixture. Serve with pan juices. Makes 6 to 8 servings.

SKILLET-FRIED CHICKEN

To Buy: Buy 2- to 3-lb. ready-to-cook broiler-fryers. Have them halved, quartered, or dis-jointed and cut up. Or buy chicken parts. (See To Buy, p. 136.)

Allow ⅔ to ¾ lb. ready-to-cook chicken per serving.

Store as in To Store, p. 137.

To Coat: Coat chicken in one of these ways:

Seasoned Flour: For every 2 lb. chicken, in paper bag, combine ¼ cup flour, 1 teasp. paprika, ¾ teasp. salt, ⅛ teasp. pepper. Drop in chicken, 2 or 3 pieces at a time; shake until coated. (If there's time, let dry on cake rack ½ hr. before frying.) Save leftover flour for gravy.

Corn Meal and Flour: Substitute 2 tablesp. corn meal and 2 tablesp. flour for each ¼ cup flour in Seasoned Flour, above.

Egg and Seasoned Flour: For every 2 lb. chicken, blend 1 beaten egg, 2 teasp. water, 1½ teasp. salt. Dip chicken into egg mixture; then coat with Seasoned Flour, above. Save leftover flour for gravy.

To Fry:

1. In chicken fryer or large skillet, place ½″ of your favorite shortening or salad oil. Heat until drop of water in shortening sizzles.

2. First brown meaty pieces of chicken, uncovered, turning with tongs or 2 spoons so chicken will brown lightly, evenly. (Don't use a fork; it pierces skin, causes loss of juices.)

3. As first pieces of chicken brown, slip in less meaty pieces; or use second skillet. Browning may take 15 to 20 min.

4. When all chicken has browned, reduce heat and cook, tightly covered, turning chicken to continue even browning, until meatiest pieces are fork-tender—20 to 40 min., depending on size and thickness of pieces. (If cover doesn't fit tightly or chicken pieces are large, add 1 to 2 tablesp. water, uncovering last 10 min. to re-crisp skin.)

   Test for Doneness: Cut into thickest part of drumstick. It should cut easily and should show no pink at bone.

5. Uncooked liver and cooked heart, gizzard, and neck (see To Cook Giblets, p. 138) may be rolled in flour and added last 15 min.

To Serve: Serve chicken hot or cold. Or after removing chicken to heated platter, make Susan's Cream Gravy, below. Pour over chicken, or serve separately. Or serve chicken with your favorite barbecue sauce.

Nice with Corn Fritters, Northern Style, p. 255; Fluffy Hot Rice, p. 234; Libby's Hot Waffles, p. 336; or Candied Sweet Potatoes, p. 266. Pass fresh or canned cranberry sauce of course.

SUSAN'S CREAM GRAVY

1. After chicken is skillet-fried, pour fat from skillet. Return ¼ cup fat to skillet; add 3 to 4 tablesp. flour (left over from coating chicken, plus more flour if needed). Stir over low heat, loosening brown bits from skillet, till smooth.

2. After browning flour slightly, with spoon or pancake turner, stir in 2½ cups milk (or 1 cup milk and 1½ cups light cream; or 1 cup chicken broth and 1½ cups light cream; or 1½ cups chicken broth and 1 cup evaporated milk, undiluted).

3. Cook, stirring, until thickened. Season, adding a little bottled sauce for gravy, p. 9, and 1 tablesp. snipped parsley or sherry to taste. (If gravy gets too thick, stir in a little water.) Serve with chicken.

OVEN-EASY CHICKEN

1 2½- to 3-lb. ready-to-cook broiler-fryer, cut up	Seasoned Flour, p. 139 ¼ cup butter or margarine

Start heating oven to 425°F. Coat chicken with Seasoned Flour. In shallow open pan in oven, melt butter. Remove pan from oven; in it, arrange chicken in single layer, with skin sides down. Bake, uncovered, 30 min.; turn chicken; bake 15 min., or until brown and fork-tender.

Serve with Susan's Cream Gravy, above, if desired. Makes 3 or 4 servings.

With Biscuits: Prepare and bake chicken 30 min. as above; then turn. Meanwhile, make biscuit dough, using 2 cups packaged biscuit mix as label directs. Roll dough ½" thick; cut out biscuits. Place biscuits in single layer, alongside chicken in single layer, in pan. Bake 15 min., or until biscuits are lightly browned and chicken is tender.

Maryland: Coat chicken with Seasoned Flour; dip into 1 egg, beaten with ¼ cup milk, then into 1 cup packaged dried bread crumbs. Bake and serve as above.

FRIED CHICKEN SUPERB

1 2½- to 3-lb. ready-to-cook broiler-fryer, quartered or cut up Seasoned Flour, p. 139 1 egg, beaten 2 tablesp. water	½ cup packaged dried bread crumbs ½ cup grated Parmesan cheese ½ cup butter or margarine

Coat chicken with Seasoned Flour. Dip chicken into combined egg and water; then roll in combined bread crumbs and cheese. In hot butter in large skillet or chicken fryer, sauté chicken, uncovered, until golden on all sides. Then lower heat; cook, uncovered, turning occasionally, 30 to 45 min., or till fork-tender and brown. Makes 4 servings.

Crunchy Style: For bread crumbs and cheese, substitute 1 cup crushed corn flakes combined with ½ cup flour.

Curry Style: Omit cheese. To bread crumbs, add ½ teasp. curry powder and 1 teasp. poultry seasoning.

Deviled Style: To egg, add 1 tablesp. prepared mustard, 1 teasp. vinegar. Omit cheese. To bread crumbs, add ½ teasp. paprika.

SKILLET HERB CHICKEN

1 2½- to 3-lb. ready-to-cook broiler-fryer, cut up	densed cream-of-mushroom soup
Seasoned Flour, p. 139	½ cup milk
¼ cup fat or salad oil	1 sliced medium onion
1 can undiluted con-	½ teasp. dried thyme

Coat chicken with Seasoned Four. In hot fat in skillet, sauté chicken until golden on all sides. Add combined soup and milk; top with onion; sprinkle with thyme. Simmer, covered, basting often, 30 min., or until fork-tender. Makes 4 servings.

CHICKEN PAPRIKA

¼ cup fat or salad oil	2 tablesp. hot water
1 2½- to 3-lb. ready-to-cook broiler-fryer, cut up	1 tablesp. flour
	1½ tablesp. cold water
½ cup minced onions	¼ teasp. lemon juice
1 teasp. paprika	Grated lemon rind
1 teasp. salt	1 cup commercial sour cream

In hot fat in skillet, brown chicken slightly on all sides. Add onions; sauté until onions are tender. Add paprika, salt, hot water. Simmer, covered, 30 min., or until fork-tender. Remove chicken to heated platter; keep hot.

Into liquid remaining in skillet, stir flour blended with cold water. When thickened, stir in lemon juice and a little grated lemon rind. At last minute, add sour cream. Heat, but do not boil; pour over chicken. Makes 4 servings.

► **For 2:** Use 1 1½-lb. ready-to-cook broiler-fryer. Do not thicken gravy with flour and cold water.

FRIED CHICKEN CURRY

1 2½- to 3-lb. ready-to-cook broiler-fryer, quartered or cut up	¾ lb. sliced mushrooms
	⅓ cup minced onion
¼ cup salad oil	1 cup diced, pared, cored cooking apples
1 cup raw regular or processed white rice; or 1⅓ cups packaged precooked rice	3 tablesp. flour
	2 teasp. salt
	1½ teasp. curry powder
	¾ cup light cream
¼ cup butter or margarine	¼ cup snipped parsley

Simmer backbone, neck, wing tips, and giblets of chicken in 2 cups cold water, covered, about ½ hr., or until tender; strain; reserve broth. Meanwhile, in hot oil in skillet, sauté chicken until golden on all sides. Reduce heat; cook slowly, covered, turning occasionally, 30 to 40 min., or until fork-tender.

Meanwhile, cook rice as label directs; drain; keep hot. Melt butter in saucepan; add mushrooms, onion, apples; sauté until mushrooms and onion are tender. Stir in flour, salt, curry, then cream, and ¾ cup reserved broth. Heat, stirring, until thickened.

To serve: Toss parsley with rice; arrange in center of heated platter. Surround with chicken; pour curry sauce over chicken. Pass Curry Accompaniments, p. 193, if desired. Makes 4 servings.

CHICKEN CHASSEURS

1 2- to 2½-lb. ready-to-cook broiler-fryer, cut up	1 teasp. sugar
	1 teasp. salt
Seasoned Flour, p. 139	2 tablesp. fresh, frozen, or canned lemon juice
¼ teasp. dried thyme	
3 tablesp. butter or margarine	⅓ cup apple juice
	2 diced tomatoes
4 chopped scallions or small onions	2 tablesp. snipped parsley
¼ lb. chopped mushrooms	2 tablesp. snipped chives

Coat chicken with Seasoned Flour to which thyme has been added. In hot butter in large skillet, sauté chicken until golden on all sides. Add scallions, mushrooms, sugar, salt, lemon juice, apple juice, tomatoes. Cook slowly, covered, 35 to 45 min., or until chicken is fork-tender. Sprinkle with parsley and chives. Makes 3 or 4 servings.

POULET A LA CREME JOUBINE

¼ cup butter or margarine	cups)
	2 tablesp. white wine
1 2½- to 3-lb. ready-to-cook broiler-fryer, cut up	2 sprigs parsley
	1 stalk celery
	1 tablesp. brandy
1 lb. thinly sliced onions (about 2	½ cup heavy cream

Heat butter in Dutch oven. Generously sprinkle chicken with salt, pepper; sauté in hot butter until golden on all sides, removing pieces when done. Place onions in Dutch oven; add wine, then chicken, parsley, celery, brandy. Cook slowly, covered, 30 to 40 min., or until fork-tender.

Remove chicken to heated serving dish; keep hot. Discard parsley and celery. Bring onion mixture to boil. With back of spoon, break up onions into as little pieces as possible. Slowly add cream, stirring constantly; cook until of desired thickness. Taste; season if necessary; pour over chicken. Garnish with more parsley. Makes 4 servings.

CHICKEN SAUTE BRAZILIAN

1 cup raw regular or processed white rice; or 1⅓ cups pack-aged precooked rice	¼ cup snipped parsley
	½ cup chopped, cooked ham
6 chicken breasts (buy parts)	1 tablesp. flour
	1 cup canned chicken broth
½ teasp. salt	¾ cup white wine
⅛ teasp. pepper	1 tablesp. chili powder
⅔ cup salad oil	½ teasp. salt
3 chopped shallots, scallions, or small onions	¼ teasp. paprika
	⅛ teasp. pepper
	Diced pimento
2 quartered medium tomatoes	Shredded coconut

Cook rice as label directs; keep hot. Meanwhile, season chicken breasts with ½ teasp. salt, ⅛ teasp. pepper. In hot oil in large skillet, sauté chicken, covered, 12 min. Add shallots, tomatoes, parsley, ham. Simmer, covered, 6 min.

Mix flour with ¼ cup broth to form smooth paste; then add to skillet with rest of broth, wine, chili, ½ teasp. salt, paprika, ⅛ teasp. pepper. Simmer, covered, 10 min.

Serve chicken on rice. Garnish with pimento and coconut. Pass sauce. Makes 4 or 5 servings.

CHICKEN LIVER SAUTE

1 lb. fresh or thawed frozen chicken livers	2 cups hot water
	1 teasp. salt
¼ cup butter or margarine	Sherry or cooking sherry to taste; or
1 minced small onion	2 teasp. bottled thick meat sauce, p. 9
¼ cup flour	

Halve livers. In hot butter in skillet over low heat, sauté livers with onion about 5 min., turn-

ing often. Remove livers. Into butter, stir flour; then gradually stir in water; cook, stirring, until thickened. Add salt, sherry, livers.

Serve on toast; toasted, split English muffins; or pancakes. Or serve with omelet. Makes 6 servings.

Mushroom: Sauté a few sliced mushrooms with livers.

Curried: Substitute curry to taste for sherry.

CHICKEN CACCIATORE

6 tablesp. fat or salad oil	1 8-oz. can tomato sauce
2 2½- to 3-lb. ready-to-cook broiler-fryers, cut up	½ cup Chianti wine
	3¾ teasp. salt
1 cup minced onions	½ teasp. pepper
¾ cup minced green peppers	½ teasp. allspice
	2 bay leaves
4 minced cloves garlic	½ teasp. dried leaf thyme
1 No. 2½ can tomatoes (3½ cups)	Dash cayenne pepper

In hot fat in large skillet, sauté chicken until golden on all sides. Add onions, green peppers, garlic; brown lightly. Add rest of ingredients. Simmer, uncovered, 30 to 40 min., or until chicken is fork-tender.

To serve: Pour sauce over chicken. Pass French bread. Makes 8 servings.

▶ **For 2:** Use 1 1½-lb. ready-to-cook broiler-fryer. Halve rest of ingredients.

CHICKEN LIVERS WITH RICE

¼ cup butter or margarine	Seasoned Flour, p. 10
3 tablesp. minced onion	1 can undiluted con-densed cream-of-chicken soup
1⅓ cups packaged pre-cooked rice	½ cup milk
½ lb. fresh or thawed frozen chicken livers, cut into 1" pieces	1 tablesp. snipped parsley
	Pinch dried basil

Start heating oven to 375°F. In 1 tablesp. hot butter in saucepan, sauté onion until tender. Add onion to rice; cook as label directs. Meanwhile, lightly roll chicken livers in Seasoned Flour; sauté in remaining 3 tablesp. butter in skillet until browned on all sides.

In 1½-qt. casserole, combine livers, rice, soup,

milk, parsley, basil. Bake, uncovered, 30 min. Makes 5 or 6 servings.

CHICKEN IN WINE

¼ cup butter or margarine	½ teasp. salt
1 3-lb. ready-to-cook broiler-fryer, cut up	¼ teasp. pepper
	1 chicken-bouillon cube
1 sliced medium onion	1 cup hot water
1 minced clove garlic	10 small new potatoes
2 tablesp. flour	¼ cup red wine
	Snipped parsley

In hot butter in chicken fryer or Dutch oven, sauté chicken until golden on all sides. (As some of chicken browns, add more pieces, a few at a time, heaping those that are done at side of pan.) Then add onion, garlic. Meanwhile, combine flour, salt, pepper; slowly stir in bouillon cube, dissolved in hot water; pour over browned chicken. Add well-scrubbed potatoes. Cook over low heat, covered, 30 min., or until chicken and potatoes are tender. Then stir in red wine.

Serve at once, garnished with snipped parsley. Makes 4 servings.

ARROZ CON POLLO

1 4-lb. ready-to-cook roaster, cut up	olives
½ cup flour	2 cups raw regular or processed white rice
½ cup shortening	1 tablesp. salt
1 minced large onion	¼ teasp. pepper
1 No. 2 can tomatoes (2½ cups)	2 bouillon cubes
2 small cans pimentos, cut up	½ lb. fresh pork sausage links
1 small jar stuffed	1 pkg. frozen peas

In paper bag, shake chicken with flour until coated. In hot shortening in Dutch oven, sauté chicken, a few pieces at a time, until golden on all sides; set chicken aside.

In same fat in Dutch oven, sauté onion until golden. Drain tomatoes, adding enough water to tomato liquid to make 2¼ cups. To onions, add tomato liquid; tomatoes; pimentos and their liquid; olives and their liquid; rice; salt; pepper; bouillon cubes; and sausages, cut into ½" pieces. Place chicken on top. Simmer, covered, 30 min., lifting rice occasionally with fork to avoid sticking. Then uncover and add thawed peas. If there is any liquid left in pan, cook

mixture, uncovered, 10 min. (If mixture seems dry, cook, covered; mixture should be moist, not soggy.) Makes 8 generous servings.

CHICKEN MARENGO

1 2½- to 3-lb. ready-to-cook broiler-fryer, cut up	margarine
	¼ lb. sliced mushrooms
	2 minced cloves garlic
½ teasp. salt	½ cup water
⅛ teasp. pepper	¼ cup sherry
¼ cup flour	4 quartered tomatoes;
¼ cup salad oil	or 1 cup drained
12 small white onions	canned tomatoes
¼ cup butter or	1 teasp. salt

Lightly coat chicken with combined ½ teasp. salt, pepper, flour. In hot oil in skillet, sauté chicken until golden on all sides. Cook slowly, covered, 40 min., or until fork-tender. Meanwhile, cook onions as on p. 283 till nearly tender—about 12 min.; drain.

In hot butter in another skillet, cook onions with mushrooms and garlic, covered, 15 min., stirring often. Stir in 2 tablesp. flour (use up any flour left over from coating chicken), water, sherry, tomatoes, 1 teasp. salt. Heat, stirring, until smooth and thickened. Cook, covered, 10 min.; taste; add more seasonings if needed.

To serve: Remove chicken to heated platter; pour sauce over chicken. Makes 4 servings.

▶ **For 2:** Use 1 1½-lb. broiler-fryer and same amount of other ingredients.

Chicken That Takes Longer

ROAST CHICKEN OR CAPON

To Buy: Buy ready-to-cook roaster, capon, or broiler-fryer. (See To Buy, p. 136.)

Allow ⅔ to ¾ lb. ready-to-cook weight per serving.

Store as in To Store, p. 137.

Preliminaries:
1. Compute roasting time, using ready-to-cook weight of bird. If chicken is of a national brand, follow roasting directions on wrapper or package. Otherwise follow timetable on p. 144. Plan to have bird done 20 to 30 min. before serving. This will give you time to make gravy and remove trussing cords. Bird will be easier to carve too.

2. Choose roasting pan. It should be an open, shallow pan (2″ to 3″ deep) with a wire rack.

3. Check supply of poultry pins (they come in sets in houseware stores). Or you can use thin skewers or new nails. You'll need white twine too.

4. Clean and cook giblets; then refrigerate with broth until needed. (See To Cook Giblets, p. 138.)

5. For safety's sake, never make stuffing or stuff bird the day before. However, you may prepare stuffing ingredients the day before, refrigerating such perishables as chopped giblets, giblet broth, celery, etc.

See Stuffings for Chicken, Duckling, or Pheasant, p. 208, and What You Should Know about Stuffings, p. 206.

To Prepare Chicken for Oven:

1. Just before roasting bird, rub neck and body cavities lightly with salt and monosodium glutamate. Make stuffing.

2. Then stuff bird as follows: Stuff neck cavity lightly (stuffing expands during cooking). Pull neck skin to back, over stuffing; fold ends of skin under neatly; with long skewer or black-headed pin (to make pin easy to find), secure skin to back.

3. Now turn bird, breast side up, on flat table surface. Lift each wing up and out, forcing tip back until it rests flat against neck skin. (This eliminates need for skewers and gives bird a platform on which to rest in roasting pan and on serving platter.)

4. Next stuff body cavity loosely.

5. Now truss bird: With 4 or 5 poultry pins, draw body opening together at regular intervals. Now, with long piece of white twine, lace cavity shut as you would a boot. Tie with knot, leaving long ends of twine. Then cross ends of twine on bird; wind around leg ends; draw close; then tie around tail. Bird should be trussed even if it's roasted unstuffed.

6. If you prefer to bake stuffing separately, pile lightly into greased casserole or loaf pan. Bake, uncovered, with bird during last half hour of roasting.

To Roast:

1. Start heating oven to 325°F. Place bird, with breast side up, on wire rack in *shallow open pan.* If you have a roast-meat thermometer, insert into inside thigh muscle adjoining body of bird. Cover top and sides of bird with piece of cheesecloth dipped into melted butter, margarine, or shortening, or salad oil.

2. Roast bird, as directed on wrapper or package. Or use timetable below as an approximate guide. Remember, chickens vary in type so you may have to increase or decrease indicated time.

If cheesecloth dries, remoisten it with some of drippings in pan.

TIMETABLE FOR ROASTING STUFFED CHICKEN OR CAPON *

Refrigerated till roasted at 325°F. Use shallow open pan. Don't add water; don't baste or turn.

Ready-to-Cook Weight (lb.)	Oven Temperature	Approximate Time (hr.)
1⅓ to 2½	325°F.	1¼ to 2
2½ to 3½	325°F.	2 to 3
3½ to 4¾	325°F.	3 to 3½
4¾ to 6	325°F.	3½ to 4

If chicken or capon is being roasted unstuffed, deduct about 5 min. per lb. from approximate roasting time for stuffed bird.

3. *Test for Doneness:* Start testing about 25 min. before bird is supposed to be done. Grasp end of drumstick. If it moves up and down, if leg joints break or move easily, and if fleshy parts of drumsticks feel very soft when pressed with fingers (protect fingers with paper towel), bird is done. Meat thermometer should read 190°F.

4. When bird is done, remove skewers and string; place bird on heated platter.

To Serve: Garnish chicken with a few sprigs of parsley, mint, or water cress; slices of orange or canned jellied-cranberry-sauce; pickled or canned pear, peach, or apricot halves.

To Make Gravy: See Susan's Chicken Gravy, p. 145.

To Carve: See p. 167.

If There Are Leftovers: See To Care for Cooked Chicken, p. 137; The Last of the Bird, p. 156; and Soup from Leftover Bones, p. 36.

SUSAN'S CHICKEN GRAVY

1. Remove chicken from roasting pan to heated platter; keep warm in oven, with heat off. Pour fat from pan into cup.
2. For 2 cups gravy, return 3 tablesp. fat to pan. Place over low heat. Blend in 3 tablesp. flour, stirring with spoon or pancake turner. Add pinch nutmeg, paprika, or curry.
3. Have ready 2 cups giblet or chicken broth, water, milk, or vegetable liquid (you may use part thin cream or evaporated milk). Pour 1 cup into roasting pan, scraping and stirring until brown bits are loosened. Add rest of liquid; then stir until velvety smooth.
4. If desired, add a little bottled sauce for gravy, p. 9, to add color. Season with salt and pepper.
5. To step up flavor, you may add one of the following; then serve gravy piping hot.

Lemon juice or grated lemon rind
Worcestershire
Prepared mustard
Monosodium glutamate
Seasoned salt
Few whole cloves

Extra Touches: To completed gravy, you may add one of these:

Few bottled capers
Minced chives, onion, or celery
Minced chutney
Canned whole-cranberry sauce
Chopped, cooked giblets
Sautéed fresh or drained canned mushrooms
Sherry to taste
1/3 cup commercial sour cream
1/4 cup canned tomato sauce or catchup
Chopped walnuts

A MAN'S BARBECUED CHICKEN

2 teasp. salt	1 teasp. sugar
1/4 teasp. pepper	3 minced cloves garlic
1 1/2 cups tomato juice	3 tablesp. butter, margarine, or salad oil
1/4 teasp. cayenne pepper	2 2 1/2- to 3-lb. ready-to-cook broiler-fryers, halved or quartered
1/4 teasp. dry mustard	
1 bay leaf	
4 1/2 teasp. Worcestershire	3 thinly sliced medium onions
3/4 cup vinegar	

Early in day or day before: Make barbecue sauce by combining, in saucepan, salt, pepper, tomato juice, cayenne, mustard, bay leaf, Worcestershire, vinegar, sugar, garlic, butter. Simmer, uncovered, 10 min. Refrigerate.

About 2 1/4 hr. before serving: Start heating oven to 350°F. Arrange chicken, with skin sides up, in single layer in shallow open pan. Sprinkle lightly with some salt and pepper; pour in enough hot water to cover bottom of pan, no more. Arrange onions on chicken, tucking a few slices under wings, legs. Bake, uncovered, 1/2 hr.; turn; bake 1/2 hr.

Remove chicken from oven; pour off all but 3/4 cup liquid. Turn chicken, skin sides up; pour on barbecue sauce. Bake, basting often with sauce in pan, 1 hr., or until fork can be inserted easily into legs. Makes 4 to 6 servings.

▶ **For 2:** Use 1 1 1/2-lb. broiler-fryer and same amount of sauce.

NAPA VALLEY BARBECUED CHICKEN

1 3-lb. ready-to-cook broiler-fryer, cut up	or canned lemon juice
Seasoned Flour, p. 139	1 minced medium onion
1/4 cup butter, margarine, or bacon fat	1 tablesp. Worcestershire
1 cup catchup	
1/2 cup sherry	2 tablesp. melted butter or margarine
1/3 cup water	
2 tablesp. fresh, frozen,	1 tablesp. brown sugar

Coat chicken with Seasoned Flour. In hot butter in large skillet, sauté chicken until golden on all sides. Remove to 2-qt. casserole. Start heating oven to 325°F. In same skillet, combine catchup and rest of ingredients; bring to boil; pour over chicken. Bake, covered, 1 1/4 hr., or until fork-tender. Makes 4 servings.

BARBECUED FRIED CHICKEN

1/4 cup salad oil or fat	1 tablesp. vinegar
1 2 1/2- to 3-lb. ready-to-cook broiler-fryer, quartered or cut up	1 tablesp. bottled thick meat sauce, p. 9
	1 tablesp. sugar
2 tablesp. Worcestershire	1/4 cup catchup
	Dash tabasco sauce

Start heating oven to 350°F. In hot oil in skillet, sauté chicken until golden on all sides. Remove to shallow open pan. Pour rest of ingredients, combined, over chicken. Bake, uncovered, 1 hr., or until fork-tender, basting every 10 min. with sauce in pan. (If sauce becomes too thick, stir in a little water.) Remove chicken to heated platter; pour remaining sauce over chicken. Makes 4 servings.

▶ **For 2:** Use 1 1½-lb. broiler-fryer and same amount of other ingredients.

CASSEROLE-BARBECUED CHICKEN

1 3- to 3½-lb. ready-to-cook roaster, cut up	1 cup catchup
	1 cup water
½ cup flour	2 tablesp. Worcestershire
2 teasp. salt	2 tablesp. brown sugar
½ cup fat or salad oil	⅛ teasp. pepper
1 sliced medium onion	1 pkg. frozen whole-kernel corn, thawed just enough to separate (optional)
½ cup chopped celery	
¼ cup minced green pepper	

Early in day: Dip chicken into flour mixed with salt. In hot fat in skillet, sauté chicken until golden on all sides; remove to 3-qt. casserole. Pour off all but 2 tablesp. fat from skillet; in skillet, sauté onion until golden and tender. Add celery, green pepper, catchup, water, Worcestershire, brown sugar, pepper; pour over chicken. Refrigerate.

About 2 hr. before serving: Start heating oven to 350°F. Bake chicken, covered, 1 hr. 20 min. Add corn. Bake, covered, 25 min., or until chicken is fork-tender. Makes 6 servings.

COQ AU VIN

½ cup diced salt pork	½ lb. small mushrooms
2 tablesp. butter or margarine	3 shallots; or ½ cup sliced scallions
1 3½-lb. ready-to-cook broiler-fryer, quartered	1 minced clove garlic
	2 tablesp. flour
1 teasp. salt	1½ to 2 cups red wine
⅛ teasp. pepper	3 sprigs parsley
½ lb. small white onions	½ bay leaf
	⅛ teasp. dried thyme
	Snipped parsley

Early in day: In Dutch oven, cook salt pork in boiling salted water to cover 5 min.; drain. Add butter to pork in Dutch oven; sauté pork until browned; remove; reserve. Sauté chicken in Dutch oven until golden on all sides; sprinkle with salt, pepper. Add onions, mushrooms. Sim-

mer, covered, 15 min., or until onions are partly tender and golden.

Pour off all but 2 tablesp. fat from Dutch oven; add shallots, garlic; simmer 1 min. or so. Stir in flour, then wine; cook, stirring, until thickened. Sprinkle with parsley sprigs, bay leaf, thyme, diced pork. Refrigerate.

About 1 hr. 40 min. before serving: Start heating oven to 400°F. Bake chicken, covered, 1½ hr., or until fork-tender. Sprinkle with snipped parsley. Makes 4 servings.

BAKED BROILERS SAUTERNE

2 2-lb. ready-to-cook broiler-fryers, halved	2 tablesp. snipped scallions
¾ cup sauterne or other white wine	¼ cup melted butter or margarine
2 tablesp. snipped parsley	Salt and pepper
	Paprika

Early in day: Let chickens stand in sauterne in refrigerator 3 to 4 hr.

About 1 hr. before serving: Start heating oven to 450°F. Pour wine from chickens; to wine, add parsley, scallions, butter. Sprinkle chickens with salt, pepper, paprika. Place, with skin sides down, in shallow open pan. Pour wine mixture over chicken. Bake, uncovered, 25 min., basting frequently. Turn skin sides up; bake 20 min., or until fork-tender and brown. Makes 4 to 6 servings.

SALLY'S BATTER CHICKEN

1 4-lb. ready-to-cook stewing chicken, cut up	1 teasp. salt
	¼ cup undiluted evaporated milk
3 cups chicken gravy	1 cup lard or other shortening
3 egg whites	
3 egg yolks	2 tablesp. butter or margarine
3 tablesp. flour	

Day before: Cook chicken as in Simmered Chicken, p. 150. Remove meat from bones in serving-size pieces. Refrigerate meat and broth.

About ½ hr. before serving: (Make 3 cups gravy from chicken broth as in Mom's Chicken Stew, steps 2 and 3, p. 151, keep hot.) Beat egg whites till stiff; with same beater, beat egg yolks with flour, salt, milk; fold in whites. In large skillet, heat lard with butter. Dip chicken meat into fluffy batter. Sauté in hot fat about 5 min., or until brown on both sides.

Serve at once with spoon bread or mashed potatoes and chicken gravy. Makes 6 servings.

CHICKEN TETRAZZINI

1 3- to 4-lb. ready-to-cook stewing chicken, cut up	rooms
	1 egg yolk, slightly beaten
¼ cup chicken fat	3 tablesp. light cream
2 tablesp. flour	1 cup fine noodles
½ teasp. salt	2 tablesp. grated Parmesan cheese
Speck cayenne pepper	
Chicken broth	1 teasp. butter or margarine
½ lb. sliced mush-	

Day before: Cook chicken as in Simmered Chicken, p. 150. Cut meat from bones in strips. Refrigerate meat and broth.

About 30 min. before serving: Skim ¼ cup chicken fat from broth. In double boiler, melt 2 tablesp. chicken fat; stir in flour, salt, cayenne, 1 cup chicken broth; cook, stirring, until thickened. Sauté mushrooms in 2 tablesp. chicken fat 5 min. Into sauce, slowly stir combined egg yolk and cream. Add chicken, mushrooms; heat. Meanwhile, cook noodles in remaining chicken broth (add water if necessary) 10 min., or till tender; drain. Arrange noodles in shallow baking dish; pour on chicken mixture; sprinkle with Parmesan; dot with butter. Brown under broiler. Makes 4 or 5 servings.

SUSAN'S CHICKEN PIE

1 4-lb. ready-to-cook stewing chicken	shire
	Pinch dried tarragon
12 small onions	1 cup light cream
7 tablesp. butter, margarine, or chicken fat	2 cups chicken broth
	2 tablesp. sherry (optional)
7 tablesp. flour	2 cups drained, cooked or canned peas (optional)
Speck pepper	
Dash mace	
½ teasp. Worcester-	

1. *Day before:* Cook chicken as in Simmered Chicken, p. 150. Slice meat from bones in large pieces. Refrigerate meat and broth.
2. *About 1 hr. before serving:* Cook onions as on p. 283 till tender; drain. Meanwhile, start heating oven to 425°F.
3. In saucepan, melt butter; stir in flour, pepper, mace, Worcestershire, tarragon. Then stir in cream and chicken broth; cook over medium heat, stirring, until thickened. Add sherry.

4. Arrange chicken meat and onions in 2-qt. casserole; pour sauce over them. On top, attractively arrange any of Smart Toppings, below. Bake, uncovered, 25 to 30 min., or as directed.

Serve garnished with hot peas if desired. Makes 6 servings.

Smart Toppings:

Biscuit Wheels: Pat biscuit dough (made with 2 cups flour or biscuit mix) ½" thick; cut out 9 2½" rings. Brush with light cream.

Corn Crisp: Split 3 or 4 packaged corn muffins crosswise into thirds. Brush with melted butter or margarine. Bake until golden.

Pie Crusties: Make ½ recipe any Flaky Pastry, pp. 407 to 410. Cut pastry dough into diamonds, squares, or circles; or with cookie cutter, cut into fancy shapes. Brush lightly with cream. Bake until golden.

Toppers: Brush 2" bread rounds with melted butter or margarine. Bake until golden.

Fluffy Potatoes: Heap fluffy mashed white or sweet potatoes (about 4) on top of pie. Brush with melted butter or margarine. Bake at 350°F. about 25 min., or until golden.

Crunchy: Use corn or potato chips, corn flakes, or crisp round scalloped crackers. Use as is, or coarsely crumble and mix with grated cheese. Bake 15 min.

Chicken and Ham: Arrange a few thin cooked ham slices with chicken in casserole.

CHICKEN DINNER DIVAN

1 5-lb. ready-to-cook roaster*	3 tablesp. sherry or cooking sherry
1 tablesp. salt	1 teasp. Worcestershire
2 cups Medium White Sauce, p. 376	2 pkg. frozen broccoli; or 1 large bunch fresh broccoli
¼ teasp. nutmeg	
½ cup mayonnaise	1 cup grated Parmesan cheese
½ cup heavy cream, whipped	

In kettle, cover chicken halfway with water; add salt. Simmer, covered, about 2 hr., or until fork-tender. Cool quickly as in To Care for Cooked Chicken, p. 137; then remove skin; cut breast and leg meat into large slices. Refrigerate rest of bird and use next day (see The Last of the Bird, p. 156).

Meanwhile, make white sauce; stir in nutmeg, mayonnaise, whipped cream, sherry, Worcestershire. Cook broccoli till just tender; drain.

Preheat broiler 10 min., or as manufacturer directs. Arrange broccoli in large casserole or baking dish; sprinkle with half of cheese; arrange chicken slices over broccoli. Pour sauce over all; sprinkle with rest of cheese. Broil till brown and bubbly—about 5 min. Makes 6 to 8 servings.

You may substitute 6 to 8 servings roast- or smoked-turkey slices.

PRESSED CHICKEN

2 4-lb. ready-to-cook roasters	2 bay leaves
4 cups water	¼ teasp. whole cloves
1 cup sherry or cooking sherry*	1 teasp. dried savory
1 sliced, pared carrot	10 sprigs parsley
Green tops of 2 celery stalks	1 halved clove garlic
1 cup sliced celery	¾ cup minced onions
1 leek, halved lengthwise	¼ teasp. whole black peppers
	1 tablesp. salt
	3 tablesp. snipped parsley

Day before: In kettle, place whole chickens with rest of ingredients except snipped parsley. Gently simmer, tightly covered, about 2 hr., or until very tender. Skim off fat. Remove chicken to tray.

Into saucepan, strain broth through fine sieve or piece of cheesecloth. Boil, uncovered, until only 2 cups remain. Meanwhile, remove chicken meat from bones in *good-sized* pieces.

Add chicken to broth; simmer, covered, 10 min. Stir in snipped parsley. Turn chicken and broth into 9″ x 5″ x 3″ loaf pan. Weigh down chicken with refrigerator dish (set 2 tea cups filled with water in dish), or with another 9″ x 5″ x 3″ loaf pan. Refrigerate overnight, or until firm.

To serve: With spatula, loosen pressed chicken from pan; unmold. Cut with *sharp* knife into ¾″ slices. Nice served with tart jelly or mayonnaise. Makes 8 servings.

Or use 1 cup water plus 1 bouillon cube and 1 tablesp. vinegar.

CHICKEN-SPAGHETTI PLATTER

¼ cup fat or salad oil	1 teasp. paprika
1 3-lb. ready-to-cook roaster, cut up	¼ cup chopped pimento
1 veal knuckle	12 oz. thin spaghetti
2 teasp. salt	1 cup slivered ripe olives
¼ teasp. pepper	
¼ cup minced onion	1½ cups grated process American cheese
¼ cup minced green pepper	

In hot fat in skillet, brown chicken well on all sides. Remove to deep kettle. Add knuckle, just enough boiling water to cover chicken, salt, pepper. Simmer, covered, until very tender—about 2 hr. Then remove meat from chicken and veal bones; cut into strips or cubes.

Skim fat from broth; measure broth; add enough water to make 2 qt. In skillet in which chicken was browned, cook onion, green pepper, paprika, until light brown. Add to broth, with pimento and cut-up chicken; heat till boiling. Add spaghetti; cook, uncovered, 15 to 20 min., or until spaghetti is tender; do not drain. Add olives, 1 cup cheese. Heat well.

Serve on large, deep platter or serving dish; top with rest of cheese. Makes 8 to 10 servings.

DIFFERENT CHICKEN CURRY

1 4- to 5-lb. ready-to-cook stewing chicken, cut up*	powder
	½ teasp. salt
	½ teasp. allspice
1½ cups raw regular or processed white rice; or 2⅔ cups packaged precooked rice	½ teasp. mace
	½ teasp. ginger
	Speck cayenne pepper
	¼ cup flour
	1½ cups chicken broth
¼ cup butter or margarine	1 cup heavy cream
2 to 3 teasp. curry	½ cup applesauce

Day before: Cook chicken as in Simmered Chicken, p. 150. Cut meat from bones. Refrigerate meat and broth.

About 30 min. before serving: In double boiler, heat cut-up chicken. Meanwhile, cook rice as label directs; keep hot. In saucepan, melt butter; stir in curry, salt, allspice, mace, ginger, cayenne, flour. Add broth, cream; cook, stirring, until smooth and thickened. Add applesauce; cook about 5 min. Taste; add more seasonings if needed; mix with chicken. Heat 20 to 25 min.

Serve with hot fluffy rice. Pass Curry Accompaniments, p. 193, if desired. Makes 8 servings.

* Or use 4 to 5 cups cooked or canned chicken or turkey and canned chicken broth.

CHICKEN BAKE

1 3½- to 4-lb. ready-to-cook stewing chicken, cut up*	mushrooms, drained
	2 tablesp. flour
	1 cup chicken broth
3 sliced, hard-cooked eggs	1 cup light cream
	1 teasp. salt
1 6-oz. can sliced	⅛ teasp. pepper

Day before: Cook chicken as in Simmered Chicken, p. 150. Cut meat from bones. Refrigerate meat and broth.

About 1 hr. 10 min. before serving: Start heating oven to 350°F. In greased 1½-qt. casserole, arrange one third of chicken meat, then 1 sliced hard-cooked egg, and one third of mushrooms. Repeat until all are used. Mix flour with ¼ cup broth until smooth. Heat remaining broth with cream; stir in flour mixture, salt, pepper; cook until thickened and smooth; pour into casserole. Bake, uncovered, 35 min. Makes 6 to 8 servings.

* Or use 3 cups firmly packed, cut-up or canned chicken or turkey.

CHICKEN CHOP SUEY

1 3½- to 4½-lb. ready-to-cook stewing chicken, cut up*	packaged precooked rice
	6 whole black peppers
6 cups boiling water	1 sliced medium onion
3 chicken-bouillon cubes	1½ cups sliced celery
	¼ cup soy sauce
1½ cups raw regular or processed white rice; or 2⅔ cups	1 1-lb. can bean sprouts, drained
	3 tablesp. cornstarch

Day before: Simmer chicken in water with bouillon cubes, covered, about 3 to 4 hr., or until fork-tender. Cool quickly as in To Care for Cooked Chicken, p. 137. Cut meat from bones. Refrigerate meat and broth.

About ½ hr. before serving: Cook rice as label directs; keep hot. Measure broth (there should be about 6 cups); reserve 1 cup. In rest of broth, cook peppers, onion, and celery, uncovered, 10 min., or until tender but still crunchy. Add soy sauce; chicken; and bean sprouts, rinsed in cold water. Cook 3 to 4 min.

Mix cornstarch with reserved 1 cup broth; add to chicken mixture; cook, stirring, until smooth, slightly thickened.

Serve at once on hot rice. Makes 8 servings.

* Or use 3 cups firmly packed, cut-up canned or cooked chicken or turkey.

▶ **For 2:** Use one third of each ingredient.

To Vary: Substitute 3 to 4 cups cooked veal or pork, in thin strips, for chicken.

Chow-Mein Style: Serve chicken on deep, heated platter, garnished with scallions. Substitute canned chow-mein noodles for rice.

P.S. Excellent Chinese vegetables, cooked rice, chow mein, and chop suey now come canned or frozen.

CHICKEN HICKMANO

½ cup butter or margarine	1 teasp. salt
	1 teasp. pepper
¼ cup olive oil	8 to 10 whole boned chicken breasts
4 minced cloves garlic	
3 minced medium onions	⅓ cup flour
	1 teasp. salt
2 grated, pared carrots	¼ teasp. pepper
¼ cup snipped parsley	¼ cup butter or margarine
1 No. 2½ can Italian tomatoes (3½ cups)	
	¼ cup olive oil
4 6-oz. cans tomato paste (2⅔ cups)	1 lb. Mozzarella cheese
	Grated Parmesan cheese
1 teasp. orégano	

In Dutch oven, heat ½ cup butter and ¼ cup oil. Add garlic, onions, carrots, parsley; sauté until tender. Add tomatoes, tomato paste; simmer, uncovered, ½ hr. Add orégano, 1 teasp. salt, 1 teasp. pepper; simmer ½ hr. longer.

Meanwhile, start heating oven to 350°F. Coat chicken with combined flour, 1 teasp. salt, ¼ teasp. pepper. In skillet, heat ¼ cup butter and ¼ cup olive oil. Add chicken; sauté slowly until golden on all sides and quite tender. Place 1 chicken piece in each individual casserole; or divide pieces between 2 shallow baking dishes. Top each with several slices Mozzarella cheese. Bake, uncovered, 15 min., or until cheese is melted. Spoon generous helpings of hot sauce over chicken. Serve at once. Pass Parmesan cheese. Makes 8 to 10 servings.

GEN'S SCALLOPED CHICKEN

1 4- to 5-lb. ready-to-cook stewing chicken, cut up	crumbs
	2 egg yolks, beaten
	½ cup chicken broth
Salt and pepper	2 egg whites, stiffly beaten
½ cup butter or margarine	
	1 6-oz. can sliced mushrooms, drained
½ cup flour	
2 cups chicken broth	2 tablesp. butter or margarine
1½ cups milk	
½ teasp. salt	½ cup sliced stuffed olives
⅛ teasp. pepper	
2 cups fresh bread	

Day before: Cook chicken as in Simmered Chicken, below. Cut meat from bones. Refrigerate meat and broth.

About 1½ hr. before serving: Arrange chicken meat in greased 13″ x 9″ x 2″ baking dish; sprinkle with salt and pepper. Start heating oven to 325°F. In saucepan, melt ½ cup butter; stir in flour, 2 cups broth, milk; cook until thickened. Remove from heat. Stir in ½ teasp. salt, ⅛ teasp. pepper, crumbs, egg yolks, ½ cup chicken broth. Fold in egg whites. Pour over chicken. Bake 1 hr. Meanwhile, sauté mushrooms in 2 tablesp. butter 3 or 4 min.; add olives; heat.

Serve chicken, topped with mushroom-olive mixture. Makes 8 to 10 servings.

CHICKEN FRICASSEE

1. Buy 4½- to 5-lb. ready-to-cook stewing chicken, cut up. Coat chicken pieces, giblets, and neck with Seasoned Flour, p. 139.
2. In thin layer of hot fat or salad oil in skillet or Dutch oven, brown chicken pieces slowly, turning them with tongs as they brown. Remove chicken; drain off fat.
3. Return chicken to skillet. Add 1 cup water (or a substitute, below) and one or more added extras, below.
   Substitutes for 1 Cup Water: canned tomatoes, tomato juice, wine, or diluted canned condensed cream-of-celery, -mushroom, -chicken, or -tomato soup.
   Added Extras: chopped shallots, onions, or scallions; a few whole cloves or celery tops; a little lemon juice; or dash nutmeg, curry powder, or dried thyme or rosemary.
4. Simmer chicken, covered, over low heat (or in casserole in 325°F. oven) until largest,

meatiest pieces are fork-tender—about 3 to 4 hr. Time will vary with the bird. Peek now and then, adding more water or liquid as needed.
5. When fricassee is done, taste; add more seasonings if necessary; serve.

Or if you prefer a thickened gravy, remove chicken from skillet when done; set aside. Skim fat from surface of broth as on p. 9. Measure broth, adding milk if needed to make desired amount of gravy; return to skillet.

For each cup of broth, blend 1½ tablesp. flour with 3 tablesp. water, milk, or cream until smooth. Gradually stir into broth; then simmer, stirring, until smooth and thickened. Replace chicken in gravy; season well. Makes 6 servings.

Serve chicken fricassee on, with, or in ring of:

Buttered noodles, with poppy seeds and snipped parsley added
Fluffy rice, with toasted, slivered almonds
Canned chow-mein noodles
Baked white or sweet potatoes
Fluffy mashed potatoes
Toast points, hot waffles, or dumplings
Parsley new potatoes or potato pancakes
Toasted, split English or corn muffins
Toasted, split corn-bread squares
Thick slices French bread, sautéed until golden in butter or margarine
Hot buttered split biscuits

White Chicken Fricassee: Omit flouring and browning in steps 1 and 2.

SIMMERED CHICKEN
(nice for cold sliced chicken, salad, etc.)

To Buy: Buy 1 4½-lb. ready-to-cook stewing chicken, cut up. (See To Buy, p. 136.)
Store as in To Store, p. 137.

To Simmer:
1. To chicken, add 3 cups hot water, 1 clove-studded onion, 3 celery tops, 1 tablesp. salt, 1 bay leaf, 1 carrot. Cook as below.
   In Pressure Cooker: Place chicken, water, and seasonings in pressure cooker. Cook at 15 lb. pressure 25 to 35 min., or as manufacturer directs; reduce pressure slowly.
   Or in Deep Kettle or Dutch Oven: Simmer chicken in water with seasonings, covered,

about 3 to 4 hr., or until fork-tender (time will vary with the bird). Peek now and then, adding more water if needed.

2. Cool chicken and broth quickly as in To Care for Cooked Chicken, p. 137. If meat is to be used later in salads, sandwiches, creamed chicken, etc., remove meat from bones in as large pieces as possible; wrap. Refrigerate meat and broth (strained if desired) at once.

Yield: A 4½-lb. ready-to-cook chicken yields about 3 cups firmly packed, coarsely diced, cooked chicken for salads, creamed chicken, etc.

MOM'S CHICKEN STEW

1. Prepare Simmered Chicken, p. 150, browning pieces first if desired. (Substitute canned tomato sauce or tomato juice, or white wine, for 1 cup water if you wish.)
2. Arrange hot cooked chicken in serving dish; keep warm. Skim fat from strained broth. Measure broth, adding milk if needed to make desired amount of gravy; return to cooker or kettle. For each cup broth, blend 1½ tablesp. flour and 3 tablesp. water, milk, or cream to form smooth paste; gradually stir into broth.
3. Simmer, stirring, until smooth and thickened. Season, adding 1 teasp. curry powder, pinch dried tarragon, or some slivered green pepper and tiny whole canned mushrooms if desired.
4. Pour gravy over chicken. Around edges, tuck Susan's Hot Baking-Powder Biscuits, p. 323 (add a little grated carrot to biscuit flour mixture if desired). Makes 4 to 6 servings.

Chicken Stew with Dumplings: When broth for Mom's Chicken Stew is thickened, return chicken to it; bring to boil; turn heat low.

Make Dumplings for Stew, below; drop on top of chicken pieces in boiling stew; cook as recipe directs. When dumplings are done, arrange on rim of platter, with stew in center. Or carry stew to table in Dutch oven.

DUMPLINGS FOR STEW

2 cups sifted all-purpose flour	thyme or savory (optional)
3 teasp. baking powder	¼ cup shortening
1 teasp. salt	1 cup milk; or ½ cup
1 teasp. snipped parsley; or ¼ teasp. dried	evaporated milk plus ½ cup water

Sift flour, baking powder, salt; add parsley. With pastry blender or 2 knives, scissor-fashion, cut in shortening until like very coarse corn meal. With fork, lightly mix in milk to form soft dough (stir as little as possible). Drop dough by tablespoonfuls onto chicken pieces or vegetables in boiling stew. Simmer dumplings 10 min., *uncovered;* then cover and simmer 10 min.

Serve at table, right from Dutch oven if you like. Or with slotted spoon, remove dumplings from stew; arrange around edge of heated platter; place stew in center. Makes about 12.

Note: If stew provides only a little broth, stir in about ½ cup boiling water before adding dumplings.

▶ **For 2:** Halve ingredients.

Speedy: Use packaged biscuit mix to make dumplings, following label directions.

Pan-Ready: Place refrigerated pan-ready biscuits on top of stew; simmer, covered, 15 to 20 min.

TURKEY

TO BUY

How Turkey Is Sold: In most markets, you'll find turkey prepared for you in the following 3 styles:

Ready-to-Cook Turkey: These tender top-quality birds come either fresh, ice-chilled, with a tag identifying the brand, or quick-frozen, in a branded package. They have been fully drawn, pinfeathered, cleaned inside and out—are all ready for the oven or pan.

You can buy them whole, with the cleaned giblets and neck, wrapped separately, in the body. Or you can buy them cut up, or as turkey parts such as breasts, drumsticks, wings, thighs, etc.

So-called "tucked," wrapped quick-frozen turkeys need no trussing or sewing after stuffing. A slit, already made in flesh of bird, holds legs in place.

Ready-to-cook birds have another plus: Their tag, wrapper, or package is your buying guide. It carries the packer's name, the bird's weight, price, as well as the U.S. inspection mark, or U.S. grade and inspection mark, denoting a high-quality, wholesome bird. The wrapper of quick-frozen turkey also carries cooking directions.

Dressed Turkey: These birds have been plucked, but head and feet are still on, viscera still in. So 13 to 16 per cent of the weight you pay for is discarded when the meatman draws the bird (removes viscera) for you.

Be sure to ask meatman to weigh the bird after he has drawn it, so you can use this ready-to-cook weight to compute roasting time.

Cooked Ready-to-Serve Turkey: Boned turkey now comes in cans. There are also quick-frozen turkey pies, turkey dinners, etc.

Sizes: Today's turkeys come in sizes for any family. For roasting, allow about ½ lb. ready-to-cook turkey per serving (not per person).

Small Broiler-Fryer or Roaster Turkeys are of 2 to 8 lb. ready-to-cook weight.

Larger Young Hen or Tom Turkeys are of 8 to 24 lb. ready-to-cook weight.

TO STORE

Quick-frozen, Ready-to-Cook Turkey: Put turkey in freezer or refrigerator-freezer combination as quickly as possible. Keep frozen until time to thaw for cooking. Stored at 0°F. or lower, frozen turkeys may be held several months.

To Thaw: Follow label directions. Or thaw in original wrapper in food compartment of refrigerator, allowing:

Ready-to-Cook Weight	Approximate Thawing Time
4 to 12 lb.	1 to 2 days
12 to 20 lb.	2 to 3 days
20 to 24 lb.	3 to 4 days

Or thaw wrapped bird rapidly in pan set under cold, running water, allowing:

Ready-to-Cook Weight	Approximate Thawing Time
4 to 12 lb.	4 to 6 hr.
12 to 20 lb.	6 to 8 hr.
20 to 24 lb.	8 to 12 hr.

As soon as turkey is pliable enough, to speed up thawing, remove bag of giblets inside body. Once bird is thawed, roast at once exactly as if it were fresh.

Fresh, Ice-Chilled, Ready-to-Cook Turkey: Remove giblets and neck from body. Refrigerate bird, loosely wrapped, in original wrapper, waxed paper, or aluminum foil; plan to roast within 2 days. Clean giblets and cook as on p. 138.

Dressed Turkey: Be sure meatman has drawn bird. Clean as in Dressed Chicken, p. 137, then refrigerate, loosely wrapped as above. Clean and cook giblets promptly as on p. 138. Plan to roast bird within 2 days.

ROAST TURKEY

Preliminaries: See Preliminaries, p. 143, and Stuffings for Turkey or Goose, p. 206.

To Prepare Turkey for Oven: See To Prepare Chicken for Oven, p. 144.

To Roast:
1. Start heating oven to 325°F.
2. Place turkey, with breast side up, on wire rack in *shallow open pan.* If you have a roast-meat thermometer, insert in inside thigh muscle adjoining body of bird.
3. Cover top and sides of bird with piece of cheesecloth dipped into melted butter, margarine, shortening, or salad oil.

    With birds over 12 lb., some cooks like to wrap a strip of clean cloth around the end of each leg bone and tie it with string—to prevent drying.
4. Roast bird as directed on wrapper or package of bird. Or use timetable, p. 153, as an approximate guide. Remember, turkeys vary in type so you may have to increase or decrease indicated time.

    If cheesecloth dries, remoisten it with some of drippings in pan.

When turkey is about two thirds done according to timetable, cut string between drumsticks.

TIMETABLE FOR ROASTING STUFFED TURKEY*

Refrigerated till roasted at 325°F. Use shallow open pan. Don't add water; don't baste or turn.

Ready-to-Cook Weight (lb.)	Oven Temperature	Approximate Time (hr.)
4 to 6	325°F.	3 to 3¾
6 to 8	325°F.	3¾ to 4½
8 to 10	325°F.	4 to 4½
10 to 12	325°F.	4½ to 5
12 to 14	325°F.	5 to 5¼
14 to 16	325°F.	5¼ to 6
16 to 18	325°F.	6 to 6½
18 to 20	325°F.	6½ to 7½
20 to 24	325°F.	7½ to 9

* If turkey is being roasted unstuffed, deduct about 5 min. per lb. from approximate roasting time for stuffed bird.

5. *Test for Doneness:* (Start testing about 25 min. before bird is supposed to be done.) Move drumstick up and down. If it moves easily and fleshy parts of drumstick feel very soft when pressed with fingers (protect fingers with paper towel), bird is done. Meat thermometer should read 190°F.
6. When bird is done, remove skewers and string; place bird on heated platter. To garnish, see To Serve, Roast Chicken or Capon, p. 144.

To Make Gravy: See Susan's Chicken Gravy, p. 145.

To Carve: See p. 167.

Caution: For safety's sake, never partially roast a large turkey one day, leaving it out of refrigerator overnight, and complete the roasting the next day.

If There Are Leftovers: See To Care for Cooked Chicken, p. 137; The Last of the Bird, p. 156; Soup from Leftover Bones, p. 36.

Small meal-size units of leftover roast turkey may be frozen and held up to 1 month before serving. Never try to freeze an uncooked stuffed turkey or a roast stuffed turkey.

P.S. To cook turkey completely wrapped in aluminum foil, refer to Consumer Service Dept. of Reynolds Metal Co., 19 East 47th Street, New York, N.Y.

BROILED TURKEY

1. Buy 2- to 3-lb. ready-to-cook broiler-fryer or roaster turkey, split lengthwise. Have backbone, neck, keel bone, and wing tips removed. Cut into quarters or into 6 to 8 serving-size pieces.
2. Prepare, then broil slowly, as in Broiled Chicken, p. 138. Baste often, and turn at end of 40 to 45 min. Broil 1¼ to 1½ hr. altogether. *Serve* as in Broiled Chicken, p. 138.

FRIED TURKEY

1. Buy cut-up 4- to 6-lb., ready-to-cook broiler-fryer or roaster turkey, or young-turkey parts.
2. Coat, then fry in skillet, as in Skillet-Fried Chicken, p. 139, browning pieces lightly, about 20 min.; then cook slowly, covered, about 50 to 60 min., or until tender.
3. Uncooked liver and cooked gizzard, heart, and neck (see To Cook Giblets, p. 138) may be rolled in flour and fried with turkey last 20 min. Make gravy as in Susan's Cream Gravy, p. 140.

TURKEY FRICASSEE

Buy cut-up 4- to 5-lb. ready-to-cook broiler-fryer or roaster, or young turkey parts. Coat, then cook, as in Chicken Fricassee, p. 150.

SMOKED TURKEY

Smoked turkey is cooked turkey, so treat it like any cooked meat. Have it delivered close to party time; unwrap; refrigerate. Don't plan to keep leftovers more than 10 to 14 days.

For Dinner: Serve cold, thinly sliced. Or reheat in covered roasting pan, with 1 to 2 cups water, at 325°F., allowing about 5 to 10 min. per lb.

Buffets, Suppers, Parties: Serve, sliced and cold, like any roast turkey. Or slice thin; pass in hot buttered biscuits. Or alternate slices of roast chicken and smoked turkey on platter.

Nibblers: Serve slices with punch. Or spread buttered bread fingers with cream cheese; top with smoked-turkey slices; sprinkle with pepper.

Or grind ½ cup each white and dark smoked-turkey meat; add mayonnaise and pepper to taste; use for tiny sandwiches.

Or spread thin slices of smoked turkey with cream cheese; roll up; tuck cress in one end.

Brunch Treat: Thinly slice smoked turkey; sauté slightly in butter; accompany with scrambled or fried eggs, hot biscuits, and coffee.

In Creamed Dishes, etc.: Use in any dish that calls for cooked turkey or chicken—but omit salt and go easy on other seasonings.

DUCKLING

TO BUY

Ready-to-Cook Duckling: Long Island and other specially raised, tender, meaty ducklings come to market ready to cook—that is, plucked, cleaned, and pinfeathered. They may be packaged quick-frozen or fresh, ice-chilled.

Allow at least ¾ to 1 lb. ready-to-cook duckling per serving. A 4-lb. ready-to-cook bird makes about 3 or 4 servings.

Dressed Duckling: These birds, with only their feathers removed, must be drawn (viscera removed) and cleaned by meatman.

TO STORE

Quick-frozen, Ready-to-Cook Duckling: Keep frozen until time to thaw for cooking as in To Store Chicken, p. 137. Then puncture wrapper, and place bird in food compartment of refrigerator. Allow 1 to 1½ days for thawing. Use promptly after thawing.

Fresh, Ice-Chilled, Ready-to-Cook Duckling: Wrap loosely in waxed paper, aluminum foil, or saran; then refrigerate until roasting time. Use within 2 days.

Dressed Duckling: Clean well; then wrap loosely. Refrigerate until roasting time. Use within 2 days.

ROAST DUCKLING

1. Start heating oven to 325°F. Rub body cavity of bird lightly with salt, monosodium glutamate, and any other seasonings (pepper, thyme, etc.) if desired.
2. Stuff bird with one of these: quartered, cored unpared cooking apples; halved onions; celery stalks; Buttery Bread Stuffing, p. 208; ½ recipe Crumbly Celery Stuffing, p. 207, or Orange Stuffing, p. 207.
3. With poultry or black-headed pin, fasten neck skin over back. Close body opening with poultry pins or thin skewers or nails; lace with white twine. If you tie legs, leave 3″ or 4″ between them.
4. Place bird, with breast side up, on rack in shallow open pan. *Do not add water; do not cover; do not baste.*

   Roast at 325°F. until thick portion of legs feels soft when pressed and legs can be easily moved up and down.

   For 3- to 4-lb. ready-to-cook bird, allow about 2½ to 2¾ hr.

   For 4- to 5-lb. ready-to-cook bird, allow 2¾ to 3 hr.
5. About ½ hr. before removing duckling from oven, brush with mixture of 2 tablesp. honey and 1 teasp. bottled sauce for gravy, p. 9. Duckling will have a beautiful glaze.

To Serve: With poultry or kitchen scissors and sharp knife, cut duckling into quarters. Serve with gravy made from drippings as in Susan's Chicken Gravy, p. 145. Or serve with Orange Glaze, p. 155.

If There Are Leftovers: See To Care For Cooked Chicken, p. 137, and The Last of the Bird, p. 156.

ROAST DUCKLING WITH ORANGE GLAZE

1 4- to 5-lb. ready-to-cook duckling	¼ cup minced green pepper
1 teasp. caraway seeds	½ cup minced celery
1 qt. day-old bread crumbs	1 teasp. salt
¼ cup minced onion	⅛ teasp. pepper
	1 tablesp. crushed dried sage

Start heating oven to 325°F. Sprinkle cavity of duckling with caraway seeds. Combine rest of ingredients; use to stuff bird. Fasten neck skin to back; close body opening as on p. 144.

Roast duckling as in Roast Duckling, p. 154, at 325°F. 2¾ to 3 hr.

To serve: With kitchen scissors and sharp knife, halve duckling lengthwise, then crosswise. Arrange with stuffing on large platter. Pour some of Orange Glaze, below, over duckling; pass rest. Makes 4 servings.

Orange Glaze: In saucepan, combine ⅓ cup brown sugar, packed; ⅓ cup granulated sugar; and 1 tablesp. cornstarch. Add 1 tablesp. grated orange rind, 1 cup orange juice, and ¼ teasp. salt; stir over low heat until sugars dissolve. Simmer until transparent and thickened—about 3 min. Makes about 1½ cups.

BROILED DUCKLING

Quarter duckling; remove neck, backbone, and wing tips. Broil as in Broiled Chicken, p. 138, omitting brushing with melted butter. About 3 min. before bird is done, brush with mixture of 2 tablesp. honey, 1 teasp. bottled sauce for gravy, p. 9, and 1 teasp. Worcestershire. Makes 4 servings.

GOOSE

Geese, like chicken, come packaged, quick-frozen, and ready to cook. Or you can buy them dressed. There are smaller birds now.

ROAST GOOSE

Prepare goose for roasting as in Roast Turkey, p. 152, but do not dip cheesecloth into fat.

Roast 5- to 8-lb. ready-to-cook bird at 325°F. 3 to 3¼ hr. (If bird is very fat, prick skin lightly after roasting 1 hr.) If goose is larger, follow time periods for roast turkey of similar weight on p. 153.

SQUAB

Squabs are very young pigeons, averaging about 1 lb. apiece. Allow 1 squab per person.

BROILED SQUAB

Wash, dry, and split cleaned squabs. Season with salt and pepper. Broil as in Broiled Chicken, p. 138, until *well done*—30 to 45 min.

ROAST SQUAB

4 1-lb. cleaned squabs	⅛ teasp. nutmeg
½ cup butter or margarine	½ teasp. celery salt
½ lb. minced mushrooms	Dash cayenne pepper
	4 cups fresh bread crumbs
2 teasp. minced onion	½ cup melted butter or margarine
½ cup melted butter or margarine	½ teasp. salt
2 teasp. snipped chives	1 cup water
2 tablesp. snipped parsley	¼ teasp. dried sage
	¼ teasp. dried savory
2 teasp. salt	¼ teasp. dried thyme
½ teasp. pepper	

Start heating oven to 500°F. Wash and dry squabs. In ½ cup hot butter in skillet, sauté mushrooms and onion until tender; add ½ cup melted butter, chives, parsley, 2 teasp. salt, pepper, nutmeg, celery salt, cayenne, crumbs; mix. Use mixture to stuff squabs; close openings with poultry pins; lace with white twine.

Place, with breast sides up, on rack in shallow open pan; top with ½ cup melted butter, ½ teasp. salt, water, sage, savory, thyme. Bake, uncovered, at 500°F. 15 min., then at 400°F. 30 min., basting every 10 min. with drippings. Makes 4 servings.

SAUTEED SQUAB

Season cleaned, split squabs with salt and pepper. In hot butter or margarine in skillet, sauté squabs until golden brown on both sides and very well done—about 20 to 30 min.

GUINEA HEN

Guinea hens have a gamey flavor and are tenderer, but drier, than chicken. They average about 1½ to 2¼ lb. each after cleaning. The choice meat is on the breast; it is white, thick, tender. One hen makes 2 or 3 servings.

ROAST GUINEA HEN

1 1½- to 2-lb. cleaned guinea hen	1 medium onion
2 tablesp. butter or margarine	1 pared carrot
⅛ teasp. pepper	1 stalk celery, cut up
1 teasp. salt	4 salt-pork or bacon strips

Start heating oven to 350°F. Rub body cavity of guinea hen with butter, pepper, salt. Place onion, carrot, and celery in cavity. Close body opening with poultry pins; lace with white twine; with ends of twine, tie legs to tail.

Place bird, with breast side down, on rack in shallow open pan. Place pork strips across back. Bake, uncovered, 45 min. Turn bird; place pork strips across breast. Bake 45 min. longer, or until tender.

Serve with or without gravy (see Susan's Chicken Gravy, p. 145). Makes 2 or 3 servings.

THE LAST OF THE BIRD

This is what you can do with your leftover or canned chicken or turkey. Or try leftover duckling or goose in these recipes.

In About an Hour

ELLEN'S TURKEY-OLIVE CURRY

2 tablesp. butter or margarine	1½ cups milk
½ cup sliced onions	1 cup pitted whole ripe olives
1 cup diced celery	1 cup diced, cooked or canned turkey or chicken
2½ tablesp. flour	
½ teasp. salt	
¼ teasp. curry powder	
1 chicken-bouillon cube	1 3-oz. can chow-mein noodles

In hot butter in saucepan or skillet, cook onions and celery until tender. Add flour, salt, curry powder, crumbled bouillon cube; cook until bubbling. Slowly add milk, stirring; cook over medium heat until thickened. Add olives, turkey; heat.

Serve over noodles. Makes 4 servings.

TURKEY CASHEW CASSEROLE

1 cup cut-up, cooked or canned turkey or chicken	¼ lb. coarsely chopped cashew nuts, salted or unsalted
1 can undiluted condensed cream-of-mushroom soup	Dash pepper
	Salt
1½ cups coarsely cut celery	30 crisp round scalloped crackers, coarsely crumbled (about 2 cups crumbs)
1 tablesp. minced onion	

Start heating oven to 325°F. Mix turkey, soup, celery, onion, nuts, pepper. Taste; add salt if

unsalted nuts are being used. In 1½-qt. casserole, place layers of turkey mixture and crumbs, ending with crumbs. Bake, uncovered, 40 min. Makes 4 servings.

EASY CHICKEN DIVAN

1 pkg. frozen broccoli spears	or margarine
6 slices cooked or canned chicken or turkey	1 can undiluted condensed cream-of-chicken soup, heated
1 tablesp. melted butter	½ cup grated process American cheese

Cook broccoli as label directs. Arrange chicken in 12" x 8" x 2" baking dish; top with broccoli and butter. Then combine heated soup and cheese; pour over broccoli. Brown lightly under broiler. Makes 4 servings.

Asparagus Divan: Substitute 1 lb. hot cooked fresh asparagus for broccoli.

MINUTE CHICKEN PIE

2 tablesp. fat or salad oil	cream
4 thinly sliced small onions	1 cup cooked or canned chicken or turkey, in large pieces
1 tablesp. minced green pepper	½ cup cooked vegetables
1 can undiluted condensed cream-of-mushroom soup	Baking-powder-biscuit dough (made with 1 cup packaged biscuit mix or flour)
½ cup milk or light	

Start heating oven to 450°F. In hot fat in skillet, sauté onions and green pepper until tender; add soup, milk, chicken, vegetables. Pour into 8" pie plate. Roll dough into 9" circle; arrange on chicken; flute edge; prick. Bake 15 min., or until biscuit dough is done. Makes 4 servings.

BAKED CHICKEN CURRY

2 tablesp. butter or margarine	¼ cup mayonnaise
1 cup minced celery	1 3-oz. can whole mushrooms
1 cup leftover cooked rice	2 teasp. grated onion
2 cups cooked or canned chicken or turkey, in large pieces	1 teasp. curry powder
	¼ teasp. salt
	1 tablesp. fresh, frozen, or canned lemon juice

Start heating oven to 350°F. In hot butter in skillet, sauté celery until tender; add rest of ingredients. Turn into 4 individual casseroles. Bake, uncovered, 20 min., or until bubbling.

Serve with Cran-Apple-Lemon Relish, p. 288. Makes 4 servings.

OVEN-BAKED CHICKEN HASH

2 cups diced, cooked potatoes	or margarine plus 3/4 cup milk
2 cups diced, cooked or canned chicken or turkey	2 1/2 teasp. onion salt; or 2 teasp. salt plus 1 tablesp. grated onion
1 cup heavy cream; or 1/4 cup melted butter	1/4 teasp. pepper

Start heating oven to 375°F. In 10" x 6" x 2" baking dish, combine all ingredients. Bake 20 min., or until bubbling hot.

Serve this moist, creamy hash with corn sticks. Makes 4 servings.

CHICKEN FINALE

4 oz. medium-wide noodles (2 cups)	1 can undiluted condensed cream-of-chicken soup
1 tablesp. butter or margarine	1 cup cooked or canned chicken or turkey, in large pieces
2 tablesp. minced green pepper	

Cook noodles as label directs; drain. In hot butter in skillet, sauté green pepper until tender; then add soup, chicken, noodles. Cook over low heat 10 min. If desired, garnish with green-pepper rings and a few chicken slices. Makes 4 servings.

INDIAN CHICKEN CURRY

Make Indian Shrimp Curry, p. 192, substituting 4 cups cut-up, cooked or canned chicken or turkey for shrimp.

SUSAN'S CREAMED CHICKEN DE LUXE

1/3 cup butter or margarine	Dash pepper
2/3 cup sliced mushrooms	1 1/3 cups chicken broth*
5 tablesp. flour	1/2 cup light cream
1/2 teasp. salt	2 cups cut-up, cooked or canned chicken or turkey

1. In double-boiler top over direct heat, melt butter; add mushrooms; sauté 5 min. Stir in flour, salt, pepper, till smooth.
2. Place over boiling water; slowly stir in broth, cream; cook, stirring, until thickened. Add chicken; heat well. Makes 4 servings.

Serve on or with:

Toast	Baked potatoes
Waffles	Broiled pineapple slices
Baking-powder biscuits	Chow-mein noodles
Split hot corn muffins	Toasted, split English muffins
Mashed potatoes	Pancakes
Buttered noodles, with croutons, almonds, or poppy seeds added	Deviled-ham pin wheels
	Scrambled eggs or omelet
	Cooked broccoli or asparagus
Fluffy rice, tossed with snipped parsley or chutney	

Or serve in Croustades, p. 344, patty shells, or avocado halves.

* *You may use canned broth.*

Creamed Chicken and Ham: Substitute cut-up, cooked ham for part of chicken.

Chicken à la King: Increase mushrooms to 1/4 lb. Add 1 cut-up pimento and sherry to taste.

VERY QUICK CREAMED CHICKEN

1 tablesp. butter or margarine	2 cups cut-up, cooked or canned chicken or turkey
1/4 cup minced green pepper	1/4 cup diced pimento
1 can undiluted condensed cream-of-chicken soup	6 toast slices
	Snipped parsley or paprika
1/4 cup milk	

In hot butter in skillet, sauté green pepper until tender. Stir in soup, milk; heat slowly, stirring constantly. Then add chicken, pimento; cook 10 min. longer. Pour over toast; garnish with parsley. Makes 4 to 6 servings.

P.S. If preferred, serve creamed chicken on buttered, split hot baking-powder biscuits; toasted, split corn-bread squares; fluffy rice; or mashed potatoes.

LUSCIOUS TURKEY HASH

2 cups cut-up, cooked turkey or chicken	¼ cup diced pimento
4 pared medium potatoes	1 teasp. salt
½ seeded green pepper	⅛ teasp. pepper
1 medium onion	3 tablesp. butter or margarine

Put turkey, potatoes, green pepper, and onion through food chopper, using medium blade. Mix in pimento, salt, pepper. In large skillet, melt butter. Pour in hash mixture; cook over low heat, covered, 15 min., or until potatoes are cooked and hash is browned on bottom. Uncover; let stand 1 min. to dry out a bit. Then loosen edge with spatula; turn one half onto other half; turn onto serving platter. Serve with chili sauce. Makes 4 servings.

CREAMED CHICKEN, CHINESE STYLE

3 tablesp. cornstarch	1 8-oz. can water chestnuts, drained, sliced
2 cups milk	
2 cups diced, cooked or canned chicken or turkey	⅛ teasp. each salt, pepper, dried marjoram, and monosodium glutamate
1 can undiluted condensed cream-of-mushroom soup	
	½ teasp. paprika
1 3-oz. can chopped mushrooms, undrained	1 tablesp. sherry or cooking sherry
	2 3-oz., or 1 6-oz., can chow-mein noodles

In saucepan, mix cornstarch with some of milk to form smooth paste; add rest of ingredients except noodles. Cook over low heat till hot.

To serve: Arrange noodles on large platter; spoon on chicken. Makes 6 servings.

CHICKEN A LA QUEEN

2 tablesp. butter or margarine	1 egg yolk, beaten
¼ cup slivered, blanched almonds	2 cups cut-up, cooked or canned chicken or turkey
¼ cup butter or margarine	1 No. 2 can pineapple tidbits, drained
2 tablesp. flour	Toast slices, canned chow-mein noodles, or mashed sweet potatoes
Speck pepper	
1½ teasp. salt	
Dash paprika	
2 cups light cream	

In 2 tablesp. hot butter in skillet, sauté almonds until light golden; set aside. Then, in double boiler, melt ¼ cup butter; add flour, pepper, salt, paprika, stirring, until blended and smooth. Slowly stir in cream. Then pour small amount of sauce over egg yolk; return yolk mixture to remaining sauce, continuing to stir until smooth and thickened. Add chicken, pineapple. Pour over toast; top with sautéed almonds. Makes 6 servings.

Half-and-Half: Substitute cut-up, cooked ham for 1 cup chicken. If desired, substitute chopped walnuts or pecans for slivered almonds.

CHICKEN CASSEROLE SUPREME

1 pkg. frozen chicken à la king	3 tablesp. sherry or cooking sherry
½ cup light cream	¼ lb. packaged process-American-cheese slices
2 tablesp. butter or margarine	
¼ lb. sliced mushrooms	Toast points

In saucepan over low heat, heat frozen chicken à la king with cream 20 min., stirring often. In hot butter in skillet, sauté mushrooms 5 min. Add, with sherry, to chicken à la king. Pour into 10″ x 6″ x 2″ baking dish; top with cheese; put under broiler a few seconds.

Serve on toast points. Makes 4 servings.

CHICKEN CRUNCH

¾ cup raw regular or processed white rice; or 1⅓ cups packaged precooked rice	1 tablesp. soy sauce
	2 cups cut-up, cooked or canned chicken or turkey
2 tablesp. butter or margarine	1 3-oz. can mushrooms, drained
1 sliced medium onion	2 tablesp. cornstarch
1 medium green pepper, cut into strips	3 tablesp. liquid drained from mushrooms
1¼ cups chicken broth*	½ cup coarsely broken walnuts or almonds
3 cups sliced celery	

Cook rice as label directs; keep hot. Meanwhile, in hot butter in skillet, sauté onion until tender. Stir in green pepper, chicken broth, celery, soy sauce. Simmer, covered, 10 min. Add chicken, mushrooms. Mix cornstarch with mushroom liquid; stir into chicken mixture; bring to boil. Add nuts.

Serve on rice. Makes 6 servings.

* You may use canned broth.

TURKEY BUFFET CASSEROLE

4 oz. medium-wide
  noodles (2 cups)
1 pkg. frozen broccoli
  spears
2 tablesp. butter or
  margarine
2 tablesp. flour
1 teasp. salt
¼ teasp. prepared
  mustard

¼ teasp. pepper
2 cups milk
1 cup grated process
  American cheese
  (¼ lb.)
2 cups cut-up, cooked
  or canned turkey
  or chicken
⅓ cup slivered, toasted
  or salted almonds

Start heating oven to 350°F. In separate sauce-pans, cook noodles and broccoli as labels direct until *just* tender. Meanwhile, in saucepan over low heat, melt butter; stir in flour, salt, mustard, pepper, milk. Cook, stirring constantly, until thickened. Remove from heat. Stir in cheese until melted.

Drain noodles and broccoli. Dice broccoli stems; leave flowerets whole. Arrange noodles, broccoli stems, and turkey in shallow casserole or 8″-square baking dish; pour cheese sauce over all. Arrange broccoli flowerets on top, pressing them lightly into sauce; sprinkle with almonds. Bake, uncovered, 15 min., or until bubbling hot. Makes 4 to 6 servings.

Ham Buffet Casserole: For turkey, substitute 2 cups cut-up, cooked or canned ham (or tongue), or 1 cup cooked or canned ham plus 1 cup cooked turkey or chicken.

TURKEY POMPONS

5 cups 2- or 3-day-old
  1″ bread squares
¾ cup diced celery
½ cup chopped walnuts
2 tablesp. minced onion
½ teasp. salt
½ teasp. poultry
  seasoning
⅛ teasp. pepper
1½ cups chopped,
  cooked or canned
  turkey or chicken
½ cup melted butter or
  margarine

About ¼ cup hot
  turkey or chicken
  broth* or water
3 tablesp. coarsely
  chopped walnuts
1 teasp. butter or
  margarine
Hot leftover turkey
  gravy; or 1 can un-
  diluted condensed
  cream-of-chicken
  soup plus ½ cup
  milk

Start heating oven to 375°F. Combine bread squares, celery, walnuts, onion, salt, poultry seasoning, pepper, turkey. Add ½ cup melted butter and enough broth to moisten. Shape into

10 balls. Place in greased shallow pan. Bake about 30 min., or till crisp.

About 10 min. before serving: Put walnuts in small shallow pan; dot with 1 teasp. butter; toast in oven, with turkey balls, stirring once.

Serve turkey balls with hot turkey gravy or cream-of-chicken soup heated with milk; garnish with toasted walnuts. Makes 5 servings.

* You may use canned chicken broth.

TURKEY AND PEAS THERMIDOR

1 pkg. frozen peas
¼ cup butter or
  margarine
3 tablesp. flour
1 teasp. salt
¼ teasp. pepper
½ teasp. dry mustard
2 cups milk

¾ cup grated natural
  American cheese
2 cups slivered, cooked
  or canned turkey or
  chicken
1 tablesp. sherry or
  cooking sherry
  (optional)

Cook peas as label directs. In saucepan or skillet, melt butter. Stir in flour, salt, pepper, mustard. Slowly add milk; cook, stirring constantly, until thickened. Add cheese; stir until melted. Add turkey, peas; heat. Stir in sherry. Makes 4 to 6 servings.

DELMONICO TURKEY SANDWICHES

3 tablesp. butter or
  margarine
3 tablesp. flour
¾ teasp. salt
¼ teasp. prepared
  mustard
Dash cayenne pepper
2 cups milk
2 cups grated process
  sharp American

cheese (½ lb.)
4 toast slices
8 medium slices cooked
  or canned turkey or
  chicken
Dash paprika
4 crisp bacon slices
2 sliced medium
  tomatoes

Start heating oven to 450°F. In saucepan over low heat, melt butter. Gradually add flour, salt, mustard, cayenne, then milk. Cook, stirring, until thickened. Remove from heat. Stir in cheese until melted. Arrange toast in 10″ x 6″ x 2″ baking dish; top with turkey; pour cheese sauce over turkey. Sprinkle with paprika. Bake 10 min. Garnish with bacon and tomato slices. Makes 4 servings.

HOT OR COLD CHICKEN OR TURKEY SANDWICHES, see Lunch and Supper Hearties, p. 357

TURKEY PIE, BROILER STYLE

2 cups Medium White Sauce, p. 376	turkey or chicken slices
2 cups hot mashed sweet or white potatoes	1 cup drained, cooked, sliced carrots
Cooked or canned	1 cup drained, cooked or canned peas

Make white sauce. Spread mashed potatoes in buttered 10" x 6" x 2" baking dish. Cover with turkey slices. To white sauce, add carrots and peas; pour over turkey. Broil until golden—about 5 min. Makes 6 servings.

▶ **For 2:** Halve ingredients; use 8" x 8" x 2" baking pan.

In More Than an Hour

JULIA'S CHICKEN CHOP

2 tablesp. butter or margarine	½ teasp. salt
3 tablesp. flour	Speck pepper
1 cup milk or chicken broth	1 tablesp. snipped parsley
2 cups chopped, cooked or canned chicken or turkey	1 egg, beaten
	2½ cups coarse fresh bread crumbs

In saucepan, melt butter. Stir in flour, then milk; cook, stirring, until thick; cool. Add chicken, salt, pepper, parsley. Refrigerate until cold. Then shape into large balls. Roll balls first in beaten egg, then in bread crumbs. Refrigerate several hours, or until egg-and-bread coating has dried.

Deep-fry balls at 370°F. on deep-fat frying thermometer until golden brown as on p. 7; drain on paper towels.

Serve hot, with Mushroom Sauce, below. Makes 6 servings.

MUSHROOM SAUCE

2 tablesp. butter or margarine	½ teasp. salt
½ lb. chopped mushrooms	Speck pepper
3 tablesp. flour	2 cups milk or chicken broth
	Snipped parsley

In hot butter in saucepan, sauté mushrooms 3 to 4 min. Stir in flour, salt, pepper, then milk; cook, stirring, until thickened. Add parsley.

INDIAN CHICKEN PUDDING

1 can undiluted condensed cream-of-chicken soup	⅛ teasp. pepper
1 cup cut-up, cooked or canned chicken or turkey	2 tablesp. butter or margarine
2 eggs	1 cup undiluted evaporated milk
¼ teasp. salt	1½ cups canned or cooked frozen whole-kernel corn

Start heating oven to 350°F. In 2-qt. casserole, combine soup, chicken. Beat eggs slightly; stir in salt, pepper, butter, milk, then corn. Pour over chicken. Bake, uncovered, 1 hr., or until silver knife inserted in center comes out clean. Makes 4 generous servings.

CHICKEN CORN SQUARES

1 No. 2 can cream-style corn	½ cup minced onions
2 cups tomato juice	½ minced green pepper
1 cup grated process American cheese (¼ lb.)	3 eggs, beaten
	1 cup undiluted evaporated milk
1 cup yellow corn meal	Twice recipe Susan's Creamed Chicken de Luxe, p. 157
1 teasp. salt	
¼ teasp. pepper	

Day before: Mix corn, tomato juice, cheese, corn meal, salt, pepper, onions, green pepper. Refrigerate.

About 1½ hr. before serving: Start heating oven to 300°F. To corn mixture, add eggs, milk. Pour into well-greased 13" x 9" x 2" baking pan; set in pan of hot water. Bake 1¼ hr., or till firm and silver knife inserted in center comes out clean. Loosen edges with pancake turner. Cut into squares. Remove with turner.

To serve: Top with creamed chicken. Makes 12 servings.

BAKED CHICKEN PUFF

1 can undiluted condensed cream-of-mushroom soup	turkey chunks
	2 cups cooked peas, green beans, or chopped broccoli
⅓ cup milk	
½ teasp. salt	4 eggs, separated
1 cup diced, cooked or canned chicken or	⅓ cup grated process American cheese

Start heating oven to 375°F. In 1½-qt. casserole, combine soup, milk, salt. Add chicken, peas. Bake, uncovered, 10 min. Meanwhile, beat egg whites until stiff. Then, with same beater, thoroughly beat egg yolks; add cheese. Lightly fold yolks into whites; pile on top of chicken mixture. Bake, uncovered, 30 min. Makes 4 servings.

Meat Puff: Substitute cut-up, cooked lamb, veal, or ham for chicken. Add ½ teasp. horse-radish.

CROUTON-TOPPED TURKEY BAKE

1½ cups fresh bread crumbs	1 4-oz. can pimentos, drained and diced
½ lb. medium-wide noodles (4 cups)	4 cups cut-up, cooked or canned turkey or chicken
2 tablesp. butter or margarine	½ lb. slivered, cooked or canned tongue
1½ cups grated process sharp American cheese (6 oz.)	2 cups turkey or chicken broth*
1 minced medium onion	3 tablesp. butter or margarine
	1 cut clove garlic

Day before: Start heating oven to 300°F. On cookie sheet in oven, toast crumbs about 15 min., or until golden; set aside. Meanwhile, cook noodles until barely tender as label directs; drain; rinse; toss with 2 tablesp. butter, cheese, onion, pimentos. In 3-qt. casserole, place one third of noodle mixture; top with half of turkey and tongue. Repeat, ending with noodles. Pour chicken broth over all. Melt 3 tablesp. butter with garlic; discard garlic; toss butter with toasted crumbs. Sprinkle over noodles. Refrigerate.

About 1¾ hr. before serving: Start heating oven to 350°F. Bake casserole, uncovered, 1½ hr., or until bubbling hot. Makes 8 servings.

* *You may use canned chicken broth.*

▶ **For 4:** Halve ingredients; bake 1 hr.; let stand a few minutes before serving.

TURKEY PASTIES

Pastry:

1½ cups sifted all-purpose flour	2 tablesp. grated Parmesan cheese
½ teasp. salt	3 tablesp. cold water
½ cup shortening	

Pastry: Sift flour with salt. With pastry blender or 2 knives, scissor-fashion, cut in shortening

until like corn meal. Add cheese. Sprinkle with water, mixing lightly until dough sticks together. Form into ball. Wrap in waxed paper, aluminum foil, or saran. Refrigerate while preparing turkey filling.

Turkey Filling:

2 tablesp. butter or margarine	cooked or canned turkey or chicken
¼ cup chopped onion	½ teasp. caraway seeds
¼ cup chopped celery	¼ teasp. salt
¼ cup chopped nuts	Turkey gravy or cheese sauce
1½ cups chopped,	

Turkey Filling: In hot butter in skillet, lightly brown onion, celery, nuts. Add turkey, caraway seeds, salt. Cool slightly.

To Assemble: Start heating oven to 400°F. Roll out pastry into 16″ square; cut into 4 8″ squares. In center of each square, place one fourth of turkey filling; bring opposite corners of pastry together, sealing edges. Arrange in baking dish. Bake 45 min.

To serve: Serve with turkey gravy or cheese sauce. Makes 4 servings.

SUSAN'S TURKETTI

1¼ cups 2″ spaghetti pieces (not thin)	1 can undiluted condensed cream-of-mushroom soup
1½ to 2 cups cooked or canned turkey or chicken, in 1″ chunks	½ cup turkey or chicken broth*
½ cup diced, cooked ham (optional)	⅛ teasp. celery salt
¼ cup minced pimento	⅛ teasp. pepper
¼ cup minced green pepper	½ grated small onion
	1½ cups grated natural or process sharp American cheese (6 oz.)

1. *Early in day or night before:* Cook spaghetti until barely tender as label directs; drain; rinse with hot water; drain well.
2. Add rest of ingredients except ½ cup grated cheese. Toss lightly; taste; add more seasonings if needed.
3. Pour into 1½-qt. casserole. Sprinkle with ½ cup grated cheese. Refrigerate.
4. *About 1 hr. before dinner:* Start heating oven to 350°F. Bake casserole, covered, 45 min., or until hot. Makes 4 servings.

* *You may use canned chicken broth.*

► **For 8 to 12:** Double ingredients. Use 3-qt. casserole. Bake 1 hr.

HOLIDAY TURKEY CASSEROLE

6 tablesp. butter or margarine	2 cups diced, cooked ham
1½ cups diagonally sliced celery	2 cups sliced or diced, cooked or canned turkey or chicken
1 minced medium onion	2 tablesp. minced pimento
6 tablesp. flour	¼ teasp. dried basil
1 teasp. salt	3 tablesp. sherry or cooking sherry
Speck pepper	½ cup grated natural sharp American cheese
3 cups milk or liquefied nonfat dry milk	
1 can undiluted condensed cream-of-mushroom soup	Parsley sprigs

Day before or early in day: In hot butter in large saucepan, sauté celery and onion until just tender. Stir in flour, salt, pepper, then milk. Cook, stirring constantly, till sauce is thickened. Add soup, ham, turkey, pimento, basil, sherry. Taste; add more seasonings if needed. Turn into 2-qt. casserole; top with cheese. Refrigerate.

About 1 hr. before serving: Bake casserole, uncovered, at 350°F. 1 hr. Garnish with parsley. Especially nice with Baked Consommé Rice, below. Makes 8 servings.

BAKED CONSOMME RICE

Leftover turkey bones	1 sliced medium onion
1 small piece bay leaf	7 cups hot water
½ teasp. celery salt	2 cups raw regular or processed white rice
1½ teasp. salt	2 tablesp. shortening
⅛ teasp. pepper	

Day before: In large kettle, place leftover turkey bones with bay leaf, celery salt, salt, pepper, onion, water. Simmer, covered, 1½ hr. Strain; taste; add more seasonings if needed. There should be 6 cups of broth; if less, add water to make 6 cups. Refrigerate.

On the day: In hot shortening in skillet, brown rice; add to turkey broth in 2-qt. casserole. Refrigerate till 1½ hr. before dinner. Then bake, covered, at 350°F. 1½ hr. Makes 8 servings.

When He Carves

IF IT'S A STANDING RIB ROAST

1. It will be much easier for host to carve a standing rib roast if you have the meatman cut backbone from ribs when you buy the roast. Place roast on platter, with broader cut surface down; set it before host, with rib side to his left and ends of ribs pointing toward him, as shown at right. Be sure knife is razor sharp.

2. To carve the roast, host inserts carving fork securely, with guard up, between two top ribs, as shown. Then, starting at right outside edge, at broadest point, he slices across face of roast toward rib side, as shown above, making slices about ¼" thick.

3. When knife blade meets rib bone, he loosens slice by cutting along full length of rib bone with point of knife, as shown above, left. As each slice is cut, he slides knife blade under it, steadies it with fork, and lifts it to platter, as shown at right.

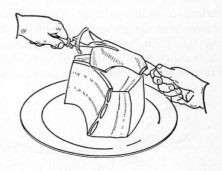

IF IT'S TONGUE

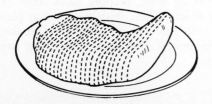

Place trimmed, skinned tongue, p. 115, before host, with tip to his right. With fork inserted at top, at his left, host starts slicing thin part, straight down, at whichever angle produces the largest slices. He keeps slices parallel.

IF IT'S A ROLLED RIB ROAST

1. Place rolled rib roast on platter with broader cut surface down and smaller end up, so roast rests firmly on platter. (Don't remove cords before carving, or roast will fall apart.) Host inserts carving fork securely, with guard up, into left side of roast, about 1″ or 2″ below top.

2. Then he slices across grain, from far side of roast toward fork, making first slice a little thicker than rest, to get a level surface right away. As each slice is cut, he slides knife blade under it, steadies it with fork, and lifts it to platter. He re-inserts fork lower in meat for each slice, severing each cord as it is reached.

IF IT'S A LEG OF LAMB

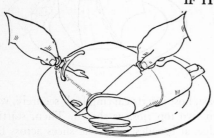

1. On one side of the lamb's leg bone is a thick meaty section; on the other is a thinner, less meaty section. Place leg before host with shank to his right and thinner, less meaty section facing him. He inserts fork securely, with guard up, in large end of leg and cuts 2 or 3 lengthwise slices from thin side near him, as shown at left.

2. Now he turns leg of lamb so it rests firmly on cut surface, as shown at right. This puts the thick meaty section in an upright position, with the shank end pointing up. Then, with fork in large end of roast, host starts slicing from right end of roast, close to shank end. He cuts straight down to leg bone, as shown at right.

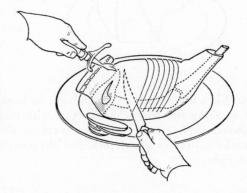

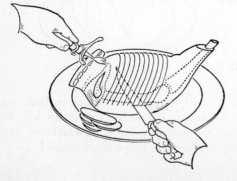

3. He continues to cut parallel slices (as many as are needed), down to leg bone, keeping slices about ¼″ thick, as shown at left. Then, with fork still in place, he runs carving knife under slices, parallel to and along leg bone. This releases all slices at one time. Now lamb is ready to serve.

IF IT'S A PORTERHOUSE STEAK

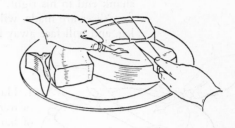

1. Set steak before host, with tapered end at left, as shown above. With point of knife, he cuts around bone closely, freeing it from meat; he lifts bone to side of platter.

2. Then, with knife at right angles to platter, he slices across full width of steak, making slices 1″ wide. He cuts across width of tapered end in same way.

IF IT'S A LOIN OF PORK

To make carving easy, have meatman saw across base of ribs of loin of pork, close and parallel to backbone, to loosen backbone.

1. As soon as loin is roasted, place it, with rib side up, on cutting board. Then remove backbone: With fork astride rib bones, run blade of knife along backbone, close and parallel to it, as shown below. Once this preparation is done, carving the roast will be much easier.

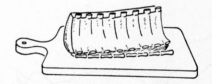

2. Now place roast on platter, with rib ends up and cut surface, from which backbone has just been removed, facing down. Set platter before host, with rib side facing toward him and meaty side facing those at table, as shown below. Now host can use ribs as slicing guide.

3. Host inserts fork securely in top of roast. He starts cutting at right end of loin, carving vertical slices and progressing toward left end as he slices. For first slice, he keeps blade close to left side of first rib. Next slice will probably be thin and boneless. Then he will get either a boneless slice or one with a rib.

IF IT'S A WHOLE HAM

Place whole ham before host, with scored side up and shank end to his right. Thin side of ham, from which first slices are made, will face host if the ham is a left leg, and will face away from him if ham is a right leg.

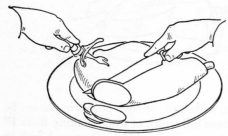

1. Ham shown here is a left leg of ham, with thin side nearer host. Host inserts carving fork securely in heavy part of ham, to the left, and cuts 2 or 3 thin oval slices, parallel to length of ham, from nearer side, as shown at left.

2. Then he turns ham upright so it rests on cut surface. Next, about 6″ in from shank end, he makes a straight cut to leg bone, as for slicing. He makes another cut at an angle to this, close to shank end, and removes this wedge of meat. Now ham is easy to carve into slices.

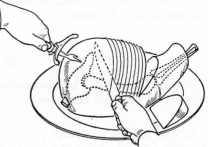

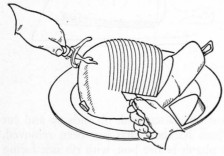

3. With carving fork steadying ham, host cuts thin slices (as many as are needed) down to leg bone. Then he runs carving knife along leg bone, at right angles to slices, releasing all slices at one time, as shown at left.

4. If more servings are required, host turns ham back to its original position on platter, with scored-fat side up. He then carves at right angles to bone, as shown at right. Though these slices are not so large as cushion slices, they make nice servings.

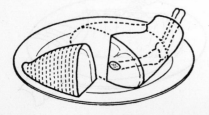

If It's a Shank End of Ham: First, host removes meaty cushion in 1 piece: Starting at meat's face, he cuts close to leg bone, straight along to shank end. Then he lays cushion, flat side down, and slices it thinly. Next he severs joint between shank and leg bones, cuts out leg bone, then slices boned piece like cushion.

IF IT'S A CHICKEN OR TURKEY

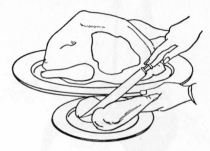

1. Place roast bird before host, with legs to right. Starting at side facing him, host cuts leg from body, bending it back with left hand.

2. Next he lifts leg to side plate nearby. While holding leg with left hand, he severs thighbone from drumstick, just over round bone, as shown above.

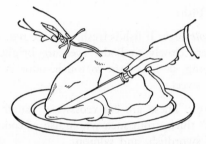

3. He slices all meat from leg. Then, with fork astride breastbone, he cuts down sharply where wing joins body, severing wing completely.

4. Now starting just above joint from which wing was removed, he cuts thin slices of white meat, working upward, always cutting parallel to breastbone.

5. After breast has been sliced, it's easy to reach stuffing. For second servings, host turns platter and carves other side of bird. And he doesn't forget that choice bit of dark meat, the oyster, in a cavity near the tail.

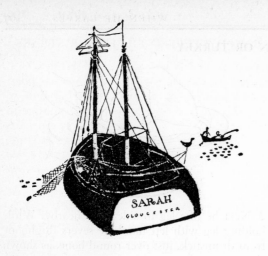

Fish

Don't wait till Friday to serve fish. Packaged quick-frozen, canned, and fresh varieties are so widely distributed today that you can serve a fish dinner any day of the week and be sure the fish is ocean fresh. Furthermore, there's no disagreeable cleaning or washing; all that work has been done for you. Do cook fish properly, though, for it's delicious eating when treated with respect.

Before using these recipes, refer to How to Use Our Recipes, p. 3, and Pots and Pans, p. 692. Always use standard measuring cups and measuring spoons; and measure level.

Off to Market

Packaged Quick-Frozen Fish:

Quick-Frozen Fish Fillets and Steaks, including perch, cod, haddock, flounder, mackerel, sole, etc., of well-known packers, are so quickly frozen that their delicious fresh flavor and fine food value are retained. They need no cleaning or handling, for they are all ready to put into the pan.

Frozen Precooked Fish is also a boon to busy cooks. Fish sticks, for example, are cleaned fish, cut into "sticks," dipped into a special batter, breaded, fried until crisp and brown, then quick-frozen. All you have to do is heat them up in the oven 15 to 20 min. Other frozen precooked fish are also on the market.

Care after Purchase: Be sure fish is frozen when you buy it; keep it frozen; use as soon as thawed.

Fresh Fish:

Whole Fish: If fish is fresh, gills are red, scales adhere closely to body, eyes are bright and bulging, flesh is firm to touch, odor is fresh and sweet.

Steaks: These are cut crosswise, usually ¾" to 1" thick, from such whole fish as cod, halibut, swordfish, and salmon.

Fillets: These are sides or parts of fish cut lengthwise and boned, with all or most of skin removed.

Care after Purchase: Keep fresh fish wrapped in waxed paper, covered, in coldest part of refrigerator. Use same day.

Amount to Buy:

For 2 Servings	Cut of Fish	For 4 Servings
About ¾ lb.	Fillets	About 1½ lb.
About 1 lb.	Steaks	About 2 lb.
About 1½ lb.	Whole	About 3 lb.

BAKED WITH EASE

EASY BAKED FILLETS OR STEAKS

Choose Fish: Buy one of packaged quick-frozen or fresh fish fillets or steaks listed below. For 4 servings, allow about 1½ lb. fillets, or 2 lb.

steaks, 1″ thick. Cut into serving pieces if desired.

If fish is frozen, thaw in food compartment of refrigerator about 1 day before cooking. Or cook, unthawed, as label directs.

Fish Fillets		Fish Steaks	
Cod	Mackerel	Cod	Pollack
Flounder	Ocean perch	Haddock	Salmon
Haddock	Sole	Halibut	Swordfish
Hake	Whitefish		

Prepare It:

1. Season (p. 6) both sides of fish.
2. Dip fish into this **Butter Mixture:** Combine ¼ cup melted butter or margarine; 1 tablesp. fresh, frozen, or canned lemon juice; and 1 teasp. minced onion. To mixture, add a little Worcestershire or chopped sweet pickle or parsley if desired.
3. Arrange fish in baking dish or on broil-and-serve platter. (Placing fish on bed of parsley sprigs, celery leaves, or mixture of chopped celery, parsley, and onion helps prevent sticking and adds flavor.)

Bake It: Start heating oven to 350°F. Pour any leftover Butter Mixture over top of fish. Bake, uncovered, 25 to 30 min., or until easily flaked with fork *but still moist.* Sprinkle with paprika.

Serve It: Serve right from dish, garnished as on p. 296. Pass one of Just for Fish sauces, p. 373, or one of these hot sauces:

Caper Butter, p. 372	Lemon Butter, p. 377
Any barbecue sauce, pp. 374 to 375	Louis, p. 373
Cheese, p. 373	Quick Mushroom, p. 372
Curry, p. 372	Mustard, p. 375
Egg, p. 376	Newburg, p. 376
Easy Hollandaise, p. 374	Parsley Butter, p. 376
Horse-radish I or II, p. 375	Shrimp, p. 376
Italian Tomato, p. 373	Quick Tartar, p. 373
	Canned tomato sauce, p. 373

Pickled Beets, p. 291, Olive Coleslaw, p. 303, Zesty Onion Relish, p. 290, marinated cucumbers, chili sauce, etc., go with fish too.

BAKED, STUFFED FILLETS OR STEAKS

Baked, Stuffed Fillets: Buy thin fish fillets (list, above). Season (p. 6) both sides of each fillet; spread with one of stuffings under For Fish, p. 210; roll up; fasten with toothpicks; arrange in baking dish. (Or spread stuffing between pairs of fish fillets.) Brush with Butter Mixture, above; then bake, uncovered, at 350°F. 25 to 30 min., or until easily flaked with fork *but still moist.*

Baked, Stuffed Steaks: Place ¾″-thick fish steak (list, above) on greased baking dish. Season (p. 6); spread with one of stuffings under For Fish, p. 210, or cover with well-seasoned tomato slices and a little minced onion. Top with another ¾″-thick fish steak. Brush with Butter Mixture, above; then bake, uncovered, at 350°F. 50 to 60 min., or until easily flaked with fork *but still moist.*

Baked Fresh Tuna*: Wipe fresh tuna steaks with cloth moistened in vinegar; arrange on rack in baking pan. Bake, uncovered, at 350°F. 20 min. Remove and discard skin and outer fat (this helps reduce oiliness). Continue baking until tender, allowing 15 min. per lb. Serve with Egg Sauce, p. 376.

* Raw tuna is rather soft, almost mushy. Cooking makes it firm.

Baked Fish Rolls: Season (p. 6) thin fillets; then dip into Butter Mixture, above. Roll up each fillet; secure with toothpick. Bake rolls, standing on end, in pie plate at 400°F. 25 to 30 min. Serve with one of sauces for baked fish, above.

BAKED FILLETS IN SOUR CREAM

Thin lemon or onion slices	⅔ cup commercial sour cream
1 to 1½ lb. fish fillets; or 2 lb. fish steaks, 1″ thick (list, above)	⅛ teasp. salt Paprika

Start heating oven to 400°F. Cover bottom of shallow baking dish with lemon slices; arrange fish on top. Season lightly (p. 6); cover; then bake 30 min., or until easily flaked with fork *but still moist.* Uncover; spread lightly with combined sour cream and salt; sprinkle with paprika. Broil low in broiler until lightly browned. Makes 3 or 4 servings.

Tangy Fish Fillets: To sour cream, add 1 tablesp. minced onion and ½ teasp. prepared mustard.

BAKED FILLETS WITH CHEESE DRESSING

Start heating oven to 350° F. Arrange 2 to 2½ lb. cod or haddock fillets in greased 12″ x 8″ x 2″ baking dish. Heap Cheese Stuffing, p. 210, on top. Pour ¾ cup light cream around fish. Bake, uncovered, 45 min., or until fish is easily flaked with fork *but still moist.* Makes 5 or 6 servings.

SURPRISE TOMATO FILLETS

6 thin fish fillets (list, p. 169)	1 8-oz. can tomato sauce
2 tablesp. bottled tartar sauce	⅔ cup ½″ fresh bread squares
¼ lb. process American cheese	2 tablesp. butter or margarine

Start heating oven to 375° F. Spread fillets with tartar sauce. Cut cheese into 6 pieces; roll each fillet around piece of cheese; fasten with toothpick; place in baking dish. Pour on tomato sauce; top with bread squares; dot with butter. Bake, uncovered, 30 min. Makes 6 servings.

BAKED HADDOCK OR HALIBUT IN CHEESE SAUCE

Start heating oven to 325° F. Season (p. 6) 1½ lb. haddock fillets or 1 halibut steak, 1″ thick. Arrange in greased 10″ x 6″ x 2″ baking dish. Pour on 1 cup Zippy Cheese Sauce, p. 374. Bake, uncovered, 45 min., or till easily flaked with fork *but still moist.* Makes 4 servings.

CURRY-BAKED HADDOCK FILLETS

2 to 2½ lb. haddock fillets	margarine
1 cup sliced celery	1 teasp. salt
1 cup sliced onions	Dash pepper
3 tablesp. butter or	1 teasp. curry powder
	¾ cup light cream

Start heating oven to 350° F. Place fillets in greased 12″ x 8″ x 2″ baking dish. Sauté celery and onions in butter 5 min.; stir in salt, pepper, curry, cream; heat; pour over fish. Bake, uncov-

ered, 30 min., or until easily flaked with fork *but still moist.* Makes 5 or 6 servings.

BAKED FILLETS PARMESAN

1 lb. fish fillets (list, p. 169)	¼ teasp. paprika
2 tablesp. fresh, frozen, or canned lemon juice	¼ teasp. salt
	¼ teasp. pepper
	1 3-oz. can chopped mushrooms
1 tablesp. butter or margarine	Milk
1 tablesp. flour	¼ cup grated Parmesan cheese
¼ teasp. nutmeg	

Start heating oven to 350° F. Place fish in greased baking dish. Sprinkle with lemon juice. In saucepan, melt butter; stir in flour, nutmeg, paprika, salt, pepper. Drain mushrooms; measure juice; add milk to make ½ cup; add to flour mixture, stirring till smooth, thickened; pour over fish. Sprinkle with mushrooms, cheese. Bake, uncovered, 25 to 30 min. Makes 3 servings.

LEON'S BAKED STRIPED-BASS FILLETS

2 lb. striped-bass or other fish fillets (list, p. 169), or 1″ fish slices	margarine
	2 seasoned, sliced, peeled tomatoes; or 1 8-oz. can tomato sauce
1 thinly sliced large onion	½ sliced green pepper
1 cup white wine	2 teasp. Worcestershire
3 tablesp. butter or	

Season (p. 6) fish; place in shallow baking dish; cover with onion slices; pour on wine. Cover; refrigerate overnight or several hours.

About 45 min. before serving: Start heating oven to 375° F. Melt butter in large shallow baking pan; lift fish and onion from wine to pan. Top with tomatoes, green pepper. Bake, uncovered, 35 min., or until easily flaked with fork *but still moist,* basting often with leftover wine mixed with Worcestershire. Makes 5 or 6 servings.

CREAMY BAKED FILLETS OR STEAKS

1 to 1½ lb. fish fillets (list, p. 169); or 2 lb. halibut steak, 1″ thick	½ to 1 cup light cream
	1 cup fresh bread crumbs
½ cup flour	2 tablesp. melted butter or margarine
1 teasp. salt	1 tablesp. snipped parsley
½ teasp. paprika	

Start heating oven to 375°F. Coat fish with combined flour, salt, paprika. Arrange in single layer in greased shallow baking dish. Pour in cream until it almost covers fish. Sprinkle with crumbs tossed with butter and parsley. Bake, uncovered, 30 min., or until golden and easily flaked with fork *but still moist.* Makes 3 or 4 servings.

Halibut, Oregon Style: Bake halibut as above, topping with about 3 halved bacon slices and reserving crumb mixture. When fish is done, remove bacon. Sprinkle fish with 1 cup grated process sharp American cheese (¼ lb.) tossed with crumb mixture; top with bacon. Bake, uncovered, 10 min., or until cheese melts.

SWORDFISH OR TUNA PROVENCAL

1¾- to 2-lb. slice fresh swordfish or tuna, 2" thick	1 stalk celery, 3 sprigs parsley, and 1 bay leaf, tied together
¼ cup salad oil	Pinch dried thyme
2 tablesp. minced onion	1 tablesp. soft butter or margarine
4 chopped, peeled tomatoes (or 1 cup canned)	1½ teasp. flour
2 minced cloves garlic	1 tablesp. bottled capers
½ cup white wine	1 tablesp. snipped parsley
½ teasp. lemon juice	

Start heating oven to 400°F. Season (p. 6) fish; brown on both sides in hot oil in skillet. Remove to 9" x 9" x 2" baking dish; add onion, next 6 ingredients. Bake, uncovered, 25 min., or till easily flaked with fork *but still moist.*

Remove fish to heated platter; discard celery, parsley, bay leaf. Pour sauce into skillet; heat. Add butter blended with flour; heat, stirring; pour over fish. Top with capers, parsley. Makes 4 or 5 servings.

SUSAN'S FILLETS THERMIDOR

FOR 8:	INGREDIENTS:	FOR 4:
3 lb.	Fish fillets (list, p. 169)	1½ lb.
2¼ cups	Milk	1½ cups
1½ teasp.	Salt	1 teasp.
⅛ teasp.	Pepper	Speck
½ lb.	Process sharp cheese	¼ lb.
½ cup	Butter or margarine	3 tablesp.
½ cup	Flour	3 tablesp.
½ cup	Lemon juice or sherry; or cooking sherry to taste	3 tablesp.

1. Start heating oven to 350°F. Roll up each fillet (split lengthwise if 8" or longer); stand on end in shallow 2-qt. casserole (or in 10" x 6" x 2" baking dish if "For 4").
2. Pour milk over fish; sprinkle with salt, pepper. Bake, uncovered, about 30 min., or until easily flaked with fork *but still moist.* (Thick fillets may take 40 min.) Meanwhile, coarsely grate process (or natural) cheese.
3. When fish is done, remove from oven; turn oven up to "broil." Spoon some of milk from fish into large measuring cup, to avoid spilling, then carefully pour in rest of milk. Melt butter in double boiler; stir in flour; then slowly stir in milk.
4. Cook, stirring, until thickened. Add cheese; stir until melted. Add lemon juice. Pour over baked fillets; sprinkle with paprika. Brown quickly under broiler.

With Shrimp or Lobster Sauce: Add 1 lb. cooked, cleaned shrimp, or 2½ cups cooked lobster chunks, to cheese sauce.

To Vary: Sprinkle fillets with dried tarragon before rolling.

BAKED FISH CREOLE

1 4-lb. dressed whole fish (list, p. 169)	⅛ teasp. orégano (optional)
½ cup tomato juice	⅛ teasp. pepper
1 teasp. minced onion	Few grains garlic salt
1 chopped green pepper	1 tablesp. cornstarch
1 sliced small onion	2 tablesp. water
2 tablesp. salad oil	2 cups fresh bread crumbs
1 No. 2½ can tomatoes (3½ cups)	2 tablesp. melted butter or margarine

Start heating oven to 400°F. Rub fish with a little salad oil; season (p. 6). Place in greased baking dish; add tomato juice; sprinkle with minced onion. Bake, uncovered, 30 min., basting occasionally.

Meanwhile, sauté green pepper and sliced onion in 2 tablesp. hot salad oil 2 or 3 min. Add tomatoes, orégano, pepper, garlic salt; simmer about ½ hr. Combine cornstarch, water; stir into tomato sauce. Cook, stirring, until thickened; pour over fish. Sprinkle with crumbs tossed with butter. Bake 10 min., or until golden. Makes 4 or 5 servings.

BAKED SPLIT WHOLE FISH

Order 2- to 4-lb. mackerel, whitefish, bluefish, or similar fish—dressed, split, with backbone removed.

Start heating oven to 450°F. Place fish, with skin sides down, in greased shallow baking dish. Sprinkle with salt, pepper, bit of dried tarragon. Pour ½ to 1 cup hot milk around fish. Bake, uncovered, 20 min., or until easily flaked with fork *but still moist*. Makes 3 to 5 servings.

BAKED, STUFFED WHOLE FISH

Choose Fish: Order dressed 3- to 5-lb. whole fish, with backbone removed if desired. Choose from:

Bluefish	Mackerel
Cod	Shad
Haddock	Whitefish, etc.
Hake	

Bake It: Make one of stuffings under For Fish, p. 210. Season (p. 6) fish; stuff (don't lace); place in baking dish. Bake, uncovered, at 500°F. 10 min.; then at 400°F. 20 to 40 min., allowing about 10 min. per lb. total time, or until easily flaked with fork *but still moist*.

Serve It: Serve right from baking dish or on heated platter, garnished as on p. 296. Or pass one of sauces for baked fish, p. 169. Makes 4 to 6 servings.

MUSHROOM-STUFFED SALMON

Make Mushroom Stuffing, p. 210. Start heating oven to 350°F. Insert skewers; then with string, lace together 2 sides of 4- to 6-lb. salmon shoulder*; stuff. Place on bed of parsley and celery leaves in baking dish; brush with melted butter; season (p. 6). Bake, uncovered, 1¼ to 1¾ hr. (about 18 min. per lb.), or until thick area near backbone is easily flaked with fork *but still moist*. Makes 6 to 8 servings.

* *Small dressed salmon may be used instead.*

HIS LAKE TROUT

2- to 3-lb. dressed trout	margarine
6 bacon slices	2 tablesp. flour
1 thinly sliced onion	½ cup fine cracker
1 crumbled bay leaf	crumbs
3 tablesp. soft butter or	

Start heating oven to 375°F. Season (p. 6) trout. Spread 3 bacon slices along center of shallow pan; cover with onion; sprinkle with bay leaf; place trout on top. Blend butter with flour; spread on fish; sprinkle with crumbs. Place 3 more bacon slices on fish. Bake, uncovered, 35 to 45 min., or until easily flaked with fork *but still moist*. Makes 3 or 4 servings.

BAKED FINNAN HADDIE

Cut tail and fins from finnan haddie; or use fillets. Place, with skin sides down, in large shallow baking pan. Cover with cold water; let soak 2 hr.; drain. Start heating oven to 375°F. Cover fish with equal parts milk and water. Bake, uncovered, 30 min., or until easily flaked with fork *but still moist*. Remove backbone. Drain 2 cups liquid from pan; use as liquid to make 2 cups Medium White Sauce, p. 376. Serve over fish.

BROILED TO A TURN

EASY BROILED FISH

Choose Fish: Buy one of packaged quick-frozen or fresh fish listed below. For 4 servings, allow about 1½ lb. fillets, 2 lb. steaks, or 3-lb. whole or split fish.

If fish is frozen, thaw in food compartment of refrigerator about 1 day before cooking. Or cook, unthawed, as label directs.

Fillets

Sea bass	Haddock	Pollack
Bluefish	Hake	Porgy
Carp	Mackerel	Sole
Cod	Ocean perch	Weakfish
Flounder	Pike	

Steaks

Striped bass	Halibut	Swordfish
Cod	Muskellunge	Fresh tuna
	Salmon	

Dressed Whole

Sea bass	Flounder	Shad
Bluefish	Mackerel	Smelts
Butterfish	Mullet	Weakfish
Carp (up to	Pike	Whitefish
3 lb.)	Porgy	Whiting

Split

Sea bass	Carp	Porgy
Bluefish	Hake	Weakfish
Bonito	Mackerel	Whitefish
mackerel	Mullet	Whiting
	Pike	

Choose Pan: Line bottom of regular broiler pan with aluminum foil before putting fish on rack. (Roll up and discard foil after fish is done.) This makes washing broiler-pan an easy job.

Or use broil-and-serve platter.

Prepare Fish:

1. Preheat broiler 10 min., or as manufacturer directs, with broiler pan in place.
2. Season (p. 6) fish; if desired, lightly dust with flour. Arrange on greased broiler rack or broil-and-serve platter (if fillets or split whole fish, place skin sides down).

Make Basting Sauce: For each 1 lb. fish, combine 2 tablesp. melted butter or margarine, or salad oil; 1 to 2 teasp. fresh, frozen, or canned lemon juice; ¼ teasp. salt; and speck pepper.

If desired, add one or more of seasonings below. Spoon or brush mixture over fish.

1 tablesp. minced onion	¼ teasp. dried savory,
1 teasp. prepared mustard	thyme, or marjoram
	1 tablesp. pickle relish
1 teasp. Worcestershire	1 to 2 tablesp. chopped
1 tablesp. chopped ripe	dill pickle
or green olives	½ teasp. horse-radish
2 tablesp. white wine	1 tablesp. catchup

Broil Fish: Place broiler pan under heat as directed below. Broil fish as below, basting several times, until easily flaked with fork *but moist*.

Fish	Distance From Heat	Approximate Broiling Time
Fillets (¼″ to 1″ thick)	2″	6 to 10 min. (don't turn)
Steaks (½″ to 1½″ thick)	2″	6 to 16 min. (turn once)
Whole (dressed)	3″ if thin, like flounder; 6″ if thick, like mackerel	5 min. on one side; 5 to 8 min. on other side
Split	2″ to 3″	6 to 12 min. (don't turn)

Serve It: Garnish broiled fish as suggested on p. 296. Pass one of savory sauces for baked fish, p. 169.

SAUCE-STYLE BROILED FISH

Barbecue: For 4 or 5 servings, broil 1½ to 2 lb. fish fillets or steaks as in Easy Broiled Fish, p. 172. For basting sauce, substitute this one: Simmer together the following ingredients 5 min.:

3 tablesp. salad oil	or canned lemon
1 teasp. dry mustard	juice
1 teasp. Worcestershire	1 thinly sliced small
½ teasp. salt	onion
⅛ teasp. pepper	1 tablesp. diced celery
¼ cup catchup	¼ cup water
1 teasp. fresh, frozen,	

Golden Puffy: For 3 or 4 servings, broil 1 to 1½ lb. fish fillets or steaks as in Easy Broiled Fish, p. 172, basting several times with melted butter or margarine.

Last 2 min. of broiling time, spread fish with sauce made as follows, and broil until puffy and golden: Into 1 stiffly beaten egg white, fold ¼ cup mayonnaise, dash pepper, 1 tablesp. snipped parsley, 2 tablesp. chopped pickle.

Sour Cream: For 3 or 4 servings, broil 1 to 1½ lb. fish fillets or steaks as in Easy Broiled Fish, p. 172, basting with melted butter or margarine.

Last 2 min. of broiling time, spread with this sauce: Mix ½ cup commercial sour cream with 1 teasp. lemon juice; 1 tablesp. each minced pimento, parsley, and onion; ½ teasp. salt; ⅛ teasp. pepper.

BROILED FILLETS AU GRATIN

2 pkg. frozen, or 3 lb. fresh, broccoli	or canned lemon juice
1½ to 2 lb. cod or haddock fillets	½ cup milk
2 tablesp. butter or margarine	2 cups grated process American cheese (½ lb.)
2 teasp. fresh, frozen,	

Preheat broiler 10 min., or as manufacturer directs. Cook broccoli until just tender. Place fillets, side by side, in greased shallow baking pan (if very thin and small, place 2 together, sandwich style). Dot with butter; sprinkle with lemon juice. Broil 2″ below heat, without turning, 8 to 10 min., or until easily flaked with fork *but still moist.*

Meanwhile, in double boiler, heat milk with cheese until a smooth sauce. Transfer fish to 12″ x 8″ x 2″ baking dish; arrange broccoli over fish; pour sauce over all. Broil low in broiler until golden. Makes 6 servings.

A la Florentine: For broccoli, substitute 2 pkg. frozen chopped spinach; cook; then add ¼ cup minced onion, sautéed till tender in 2 tablesp. butter or margarine.

Summer Style: For broccoli, substitute 2 pkg. frozen, or 2½ lb. fresh, asparagus.

MIXED FISH GRILL

Be smart! Broil the whole main course—fish, vegetable, and garnish—at the same time. Turn to Mixed Grill, p. 55, for suggestions.

BROILED SHAD AND ROE

1 boned shad (3 lb. before boning and cleaning)	margarine
	1 tablesp. fresh, frozen, or canned lemon juice
1 shad roe	
½ lb. sliced small mushrooms; or 1 3-oz. can drained mushrooms	1 to 2 tablesp. white wine (optional)
	1 tablesp. snipped parsley
¼ cup melted butter or	

Preheat broiler 10 min., or as manufacturer directs. Remove head and tail from shad; cut shad into 4 to 6 serving pieces. Arrange, with skin sides down, on lightly greased broiler pan or broil-and-serve platter, with roe and mushrooms around fish. Season (p. 6); brush with some of combined butter and lemon juice. Broil, with top of fish 2″ below heat, 8 to 10 min., basting occasionally with butter mixture; after 4 min., turn roe, mushrooms.

To serve: Brush with rest of butter mixture; then slowly drizzle on wine; sprinkle with parsley. Makes 4 to 6 servings.

POACHED TO PERFECTION

Gourmets extol poached fish fillets for their delicate flavor and texture. And any homemaker can duplicate these results in her own home kitchen. The four recipes that follow give you the know-how.

Two Points to Remember: Soft fish, such as flounder, Boston sole, ocean perch, haddock, and cod, should be poached and served in the same skillet. This does away with the danger of fillets' breaking when moved from pan to platter. However, sea bass, English sole, and pompano are firm enough to be transferred from skillet to platter if you like.

After you've added liquid to fillets, cover with a circle of waxed (or buttered white) paper, with small hole in the center. (The hole allows steam to escape.) By using this paper, you can cook fillets without drowning them in liquid, and you don't have to boil down liquid after fillets are done.

FILLETS OF FISH DUGLERE
(superb poached fish with tomato)

1½ lb. fish fillets*	¾ cup well-drained canned tomatoes
1 teasp. salt	
⅛ teasp. pepper	Snipped parsley
1 clove garlic (optional)	¼ cup white wine; or ¼ cup water plus ½ teasp. lemon juice
1 tablesp. butter or margarine	
1 minced medium onion	¼ cup light cream
2 minced shallots (optional)	1 tablesp. soft butter or margarine
	1 teasp. flour

To Poach:

1. Set out large skillet (about 10″) with cover. Tear or cut circle of waxed paper to fit skillet; tear small hole in center; set aside. Sprinkle fish with salt and pepper. Stick toothpick in garlic.
2. Melt 1 tablesp. butter in skillet; add onion, shallots, garlic; top with fish, then tomatoes, then 1 tablesp. snipped parsley; pour in wine. Place paper circle on fish.
3. Bring to boil; cover; cook over high heat 5 to 10 min., or until easily flaked with fork *but still moist.* Remove cover, paper, garlic.
4. Complete as in Skillet or Platter Style, below. Makes 4 servings.

Skillet Style: Pour cream around fish. Mix 1 tablesp. butter with flour; stir into cream; move skillet in circular motion to combine and thicken sauce. Spoon some sauce onto fish; sprinkle with parsley. Serve from skillet.

Platter Style: Gently remove fish, with tomatoes on top, to broil-and-serve platter or shallow casserole. Then, into skillet, pour cream mixed with 1 egg yolk, then butter-flour mixture. Cook over medium heat, stirring, till thickened; taste; add seasoning if needed. Pour sauce over fish; then, if desired, broil until just golden.

* Use bass, cod, flounder, haddock, pompano, perch, or sole.

FILLETS OF FISH BONNE FEMME
(poached fish with mushrooms)

Poach fish as in Fillets of Fish Duglere, p. 174, but increase wine to ½ cup. Substitute ½ lb. thinly sliced mushrooms for tomatoes, placing half of them in skillet with onion, the rest on top of fish. Complete as in Skillet Style. Or, if Platter Style, fold 2 tablesp. cream, whipped, into sauce just before pouring over fish.

FILLETS OF FISH PAYSANNE
(poached fish with carrots and onions)

Thinly slice 2 pared medium carrots and 2 medium onions; cook with 1 teasp. butter or margarine in small amount of water until tender-crisp; drain. Place on top of fish instead of tomatoes and onion in Fillets of Fish Duglere, p. 174. Complete as in Skillet Style.

FILLETS OF FISH VERONIQUE
(poached fish with grapes)

Poach fish as in Fillets of Fish Duglere, p. 174, omitting tomatoes, parsley; increase wine to ½ cup. Complete as in Skillet Style, adding 2 cups fresh or drained canned seedless grapes after sauce has thickened. Or if Platter Style, place grapes around fish; fold 2 tablesp. cream, whipped, into sauce just before pouring over fish.

POACHED FISH, U.S.A.
(nice for fish fillets or steaks, 1″ thick)

To Buy: Use same varieties of fish fillet and steak as for Easy Broiled Fish, p. 172.

To Poach: Place fillets or steaks in skillet with enough boiling water to just barely cover. Season water with snipped parsley, minced celery or onion, a little garlic, white wine, or a few whole black peppers. Simmer, covered, until fish is easily flaked with fork—10 min. or less.

To Serve: Remove fish to heated platter; sprinkle with salt; serve at once, with one of sauces for baked fish, p. 169.

STEAMED FISH, NEW ENGLAND STYLE
(nice for large chunks of fish like salmon)

Use deep saucepan, Dutch oven, or pressure cooker with greased rack in bottom. Fill with 1½″ to 2″ water, adding snipped parsley, minced celery or onion, a little garlic, white wine, or a few whole black peppers. When water boils, place chunk of fish (you may wrap it in cheese-cloth) on rack; cover tightly. (If using pressure cooker, use cover without pressure gauge.) Steam about 1 min. per ounce, or until easily flaked with fork *but still moist,* turning once if fish is very thick.

To serve: Lift fish to heated platter; sprinkle with salt; serve with one of sauces for baked fish, p. 169. Or chill; serve with Quick Tartar Sauce, p. 373. Or flake for salads, sandwiches, etc.

FRIED TO GOLDEN CRISPNESS
SUSAN'S SAUTEED FISH

Here are 3 easy rules, which insure delicious sautéed fish with a minimum of cooking odor.

1. Cook fish last, when rest of dinner is about done.
2. Don't overcook fish; sautéed fish is done in jig time.
3. Serve it at once, while it's still juicy, crisp, and hot.

Choose Fish: Buy any packaged quick-frozen or small dressed whole fresh fish, fish fillet, or steak listed on p. 176. Cut into serving-size pieces if desired. For 4 servings, allow about 1 to 1½ lb. fish fillets or 2 lb. steaks, ½″ to ¾″ thick.

If fish is frozen, thaw in food compartment of refrigerator about 1 day before cooking. Or cook, unthawed, as label directs.

Dressed Small Whole Fish

Bass	Mackerel	Smelts
Butterfish	Perch	Trout
Flounder	Pike	Whitefish
Lake herring	Pompano	Whiting

Fillets or Steaks

Cod	Ocean perch	Shad (and/or
Flounder	Pickerel	Shad roe)
Haddock	Pollack	Sole
Halibut	Red snapper	Swordfish

Prepare It: Dip small fish, or cut-up fillets or steaks, into one of these:

Milk	Cold water	Egg, beaten with
Evaporated	French	2 tablesp. water
milk	dressing	or white wine

Sprinkle fish well with salt, pepper, paprika, monosodium glutamate, or seasoned salt. Now coat with one of these or blend of two:

Flour	Packaged dried	Crushed corn
Corn meal	bread or cracker	or wheat
Pancake mix	crumbs, or ready	flakes
Biscuit mix	mixed breading	

Sauté It:

1. For large amount of fish, use 2 skillets; or wash single skillet between batches, to avoid brown crumb specks on fish and to keep fish from sticking. Add fresh fat or salad oil for each batch.
2. In skillet, heat enough shortening, salad oil, butter, margarine, or bacon fat to cover bottom well; *never let fat smoke.*
3. Place fish in skillet; quickly fry over moderate heat until underside has crisp golden crust—about 2 or 3 min.
4. Turn carefully with broad spatula; then sauté fish only until golden brown on underside and easily flaked with fork *but still moist*— about 2 or 3 min. *Don't let fish get dry.* Then lift onto heated platter.

Serve It at Once:

1. Sprinkle with snipped parsley, mint, or chives; or bit of fresh or dried basil, rosemary, dill, or tarragon. Garnish with lemon or lime wedges. Nice with Hush Puppies, below.
2. Or serve with one of sauces for baked fish, p. 169.
3. Or pour off fat from skillet in which fish fried; with paper towel, wipe out crumbs. Melt ¼ cup butter or margarine in same skillet; quickly stir in bit of one or more of following; then pour over fish:

Worcestershire	Prepared mustard
or horse-radish	Bottled capers
Anchovy paste	Chopped green, ripe,
Snipped chives	or stuffed olives
	Catchup

4. Or after wiping out fish skillet, in it melt, but do not brown, ¼ cup butter or margarine. Add about ¼ cup sliced, slivered, or chopped almonds; sauté until golden. Add ¼ cup white wine, pinch dried tarragon. Heat; pour over fish.

HUSH PUPPIES

Into bowl, sift 1 cup white corn meal (water ground if possible), 2 teasp. baking powder, 1½ teasp. salt. Stir in ½ cup minced onions, 1 egg, ¼ cup buttermilk (if mixture doesn't hold together, add a little water).

Heat ¼″ fat or salad oil in skillet. Shape mixture into ¼″-thick patties, oyster-size. Fry till golden on both sides. Makes 25 patties. Nice with fried fish.

SAUTEED KIPPERED HERRING

Use 1 smoked kippered herring for each serving. Soak herring in boiling water to cover 10 min.; drain; dry. In a little hot salad oil in skillet, sauté herring about 5 min., turning once.

Serve with Lemon Butter Sauce, p. 377.

KIPPERED HERRING WITH CREAM

2 tablesp. butter or	herring, drained
margarine	½ cup light cream
½ cup onion rings	Paprika
1 14-oz. can kippered	

In butter in skillet, sauté onion till delicate brown; remove. In same skillet, lightly sauté herring on both sides. Add cream; heat.

Serve garnished with onion rings and paprika. Makes 6 servings.

FROGS' LEGS MEUNIERE

2 lb. medium frogs' legs	1/8 teasp. pepper
1/2 cup milk	2 teasp. lemon juice
1/2 cup flour	3 tablesp. butter or
Salad oil or melted but-	margarine
ter or margarine	Snipped parsley
1/2 teasp. salt	Lemon slices

Pull off skin and cut off feet from frogs' hind legs if not already prepared. Soak in cold water 2 hr.; drain. Dip into milk, then flour.

In 1/4" hot salad oil in skillet, sauté frogs' legs 6 to 8 min., or until brown on all sides. Remove to heated platter; sprinkle with salt, pepper, lemon juice. Pour off oil from skillet; then, in same skillet, heat 3 tablesp. butter until hazelnut brown; pour over frogs' legs.

Serve garnished with snipped parsley and lemon slices. Makes 4 servings.

Sautéed Frogs' Legs: In 1/4 cup butter or margarine in skillet over medium heat, sauté drained, prepared frogs' legs with 1/2 minced clove garlic and 1 tablesp. snipped parsley until tender and brown—6 to 8 min. Serve with sauce in skillet, lemon wedges.

SHALLOW-FRIED FISH

Shallow frying produces the same crisp crust as deep frying, but you use a deep skillet or saucepan instead of a kettle. For 4 servings, allow about 1 to 1 1/2 lb. fish fillets or small fish (list, p. 176).

1. Dip cut-up fillets or small fish into 1 egg beaten with 2 tablesp. cold water, then into packaged dried bread crumbs.
2. In deep skillet or saucepan, heat 1 1/2" fat or salad oil (not butter or margarine) to 370°F. on deep-fat thermometer, or till hot enough to brown 1" bread square in 1 min. (See Shallow Frying, p. 8.)
3. Immerse fish in hot fat; fry quickly until nicely browned on all sides and easily flaked with fork *but still moist*—about 3 to 4 min. Drain on paper towels.

Serve at once, piping hot, with one of sauces for baked fish, p. 169.

OVEN-FRIED FISH

It's hard to believe, but true! No pot watching, no turning, no odor—when you oven-fry fish.

1. Choose fish fillets, steaks, or small fish (list, p. 176), allowing about 1 lb. for three persons. In flat dish, mix 1/4 cup milk and 2 teasp. salt with bit of dried thyme, tarragon, dill, or rosemary; or minced onion or garlic; or Worcestershire.
2. In second dish, place 1/2 cup packaged dried bread crumbs, or crushed wheat or corn flakes (flour, corn meal, or cracker crumbs don't brown as evenly). Add 1/2 teasp. paprika and bit of one of these: dry mustard, grated cheese, chili powder, snipped parsley. Start heating oven to 525°F.
3. Now, with one hand, dip 1 piece of fish into milk; with other hand, roll fish in crumbs; place in greased shallow baking dish. Repeat, placing pieces side by side in dish. Drizzle bit of salad oil or melted butter or margarine onto fish.
4. Bake 15 to 20 min., or until golden, easily flaked with fork *but still moist.*

Serve with one of sauces for baked fish, p. 169.

PANTRY-SHELF SPECIALS

OUR BEST CREAMED FISH

Fish:

2 cups flaked canned or cooked tuna, salmon, cod, halibut, etc.	Or 2 cups flaked finnan haddie

Sauce:

1/4 cup butter or margarine	1/2 teasp. salt (omit with finnan haddie)
1/4 cup flour	1/8 teasp. pepper
2 cups milk	2 tablesp. chopped green pepper
2 eggs, beaten	

In saucepan, melt butter; stir in flour. Gradually add milk; cook slowly, stirring, until thickened. Add fish; heat. Add eggs; heat quickly, stirring; then add rest of ingredients.

Serve Over:

1. Hot fluffy rice, plus grated carrot and snipped parsley
2. Buttered noodles, plus a little grated cheese; garlic, celery, or onion salt; dried thyme; or few poppy seeds
3. Hot toast cut into rounds, squares, triangles, or fingers and brushed lightly with melted

butter or margarine. Sprinkle with a little curry powder; garlic, onion, or celery salt; or dried herb. Or spread lightly with prepared mustard, horse-radish, or catchup

4. Heated crackers, sprinkled with grated cheese if desired
5. Mixed frozen or canned vegetables, or left-over cooked vegetables
6. Mashed or baked potatoes

Creamed Shrimp, Crab, Lobster or Scallops: For fish, substitute 2 cups cut-up, cleaned, cooked or canned shrimp; flaked, cooked or canned crab or lobster meat; or cooked scallops; or mixture of these.

SUPERB FISH SCALLOP

¼ cup butter or margarine	1 teasp. bottled thick meat sauce, p. 9
½ teasp. salt	1½ cups flaked canned or cooked fish
2 tablesp. minced green pepper	⅓ cup grated process American cheese
1 tablesp. minced onion	½ cup fresh bread crumbs
2 tablesp. flour	
1 cup milk	

Start heating oven to 400°F. In double-boiler top over direct heat, melt butter. Add salt, pepper, onion; cook till tender. Stir in flour, then milk, meat sauce. Cook over boiling water, stirring, until thickened. Alternate layers of fish and sauce in greased 1-qt. casserole. Top with mixed cheese and crumbs. Bake, uncovered, 20 min., or until brown. Makes 4 servings.

Fish-and-Egg Scallop: Use part fish, part cut-up, hard-cooked eggs.

Shellfish Scallop: For fish, substitute cleaned, cooked or canned shrimp; or flaked, cooked or canned crab or lobster meat.

"OLD SALT" CHEESE CASSEROLE

1½ cups milk	1½ cups grated process American cheese
2 tablesp. butter or margarine	½ teasp. salt
1 cup fresh bread crumbs	⅛ teasp. pepper
1 chopped pimento	Dash paprika
2 tablesp. snipped parsley	3 eggs, well beaten
2 tablesp. minced onion	2 cups flaked canned or cooked fish

Start heating oven to 325°F. Heat milk with butter; pour over bread crumbs. Add pimento, parsley, onion, cheese, salt, pepper, paprika; mix well. Slowly stir in eggs. Arrange fish in greased 1½-qt. casserole; pour cheese mixture over fish. Set casserole in pan filled with warm water to 1″ of top. Bake, uncovered, 1¼ hr., or until silver knife inserted in center comes out clean.

Serve as is or with Quick Mushroom Sauce, p. 372. Makes 6 servings.

TUNA-CASHEW CASSEROLE

1 3-oz. jar chow-mein noodles	(1 cup)
1 can undiluted condensed cream-of-mushroom soup	¼ lb. cashew nuts, salted or unsalted
	1 cup finely diced celery
¼ cup water	¼ cup minced onion
1 can chunk-style tuna	Dash pepper
	Salt

Start heating oven to 325°F. Set aside ½ cup chow-mein noodles. In 1½-qt. casserole, combine rest of noodles with soup, water, tuna, nuts, celery, onion, pepper. Taste; add salt if nuts were unsalted. Sprinkle reserved noodles over top. Bake, uncovered, 40 min. Makes 5 servings.

TUNA SUPPER CASSEROLE

1 pkg. frozen spinach; or 1 lb. washed fresh spinach	1 tablesp. minced onion
	2 tablesp. flour
	½ teasp. salt
1 3-oz. can sliced mushrooms	⅛ teasp. pepper
	1 crushed bay leaf
2 tablesp. fresh, frozen, or canned lemon juice	1 egg, slightly beaten
	1 can solid-pack tuna, drained (1 cup)
2 tablesp. butter or margarine	1 tablesp. butter or margarine

Start heating oven to 350°F. Cook spinach until tender-crisp; drain well; season. Drain mushrooms; to mushroom liquid, add lemon juice with enough water to make 1 cup liquid.

In small saucepan, melt 2 tablesp. butter; stir in onion, flour, salt, pepper, bay leaf, then mushroom liquid; cook, stirring, until thick and smooth. Beat sauce into egg; add mushrooms. Arrange spinach in greased 1½-qt. shallow casserole; top with tuna in big chunks, sauce. Dot with 1 tablesp. butter. Bake, uncovered, 30 min. Makes 4 servings.

SAVORY TUNA ON TOAST

2 tablesp. butter or margarine	1 peeled, firm ripe tomato, cut into wedges
1 tablesp. flour	
1 3-oz. can sliced or chopped mushrooms	4 slices toast, cut into triangles
2 tablesp. minced onion	1 cup light cream
1 can solid-pack tuna, drained (1 cup)	1 teasp. snipped chives
	1 teasp. snipped parsley

Start heating oven to 400°F. In saucepan, melt butter; stir in flour, mushrooms with juice, onion; simmer 5 min., stirring occasionally. Add tuna, in chunks, tomato.

Arrange toast in small baking dish; top with tuna mixture. Then, in saucepan used for tuna, heat cream; pour over all. Sprinkle with chives, parsley. Bake, uncovered, 10 to 15 min. Makes 3 or 4 servings.

ELENA'S TUNA-SALAD BISCUITS

Start heating oven to 450°F. Drain 1 can solid-pack tuna (1 cup). Break into chunks. Toss with 1 tablesp. fresh, frozen, or canned lemon juice; ¼ to ½ cup finely diced celery; and ⅓ to ½ cup mayonnaise (or enough to hold mixture together).

Prepare 2 cups packaged biscuit mix as label directs; roll into ⅓"-thick square. Spread tuna mixture over half of biscuit square; fold over other half, making "sandwich." Cut into 2" or 2½" squares; place on baking sheet. Bake 12 to 15 min., or until done.

Serve with Cheese Sauce, p. 374. Or make smaller biscuit squares and serve hot with vegetable or fruit salad. Makes 6 servings.

TUNA TOMATOES

¾ cup cooked rice	2 teasp. chili powder
6 large tomatoes	½ teasp. salt
2 tablesp. salad oil	⅛ teasp. pepper
¼ cup minced onion	½ cup grated process American cheese
1 can solid-pack tuna, drained (1 cup)	

Start heating oven to 375°F. Keep cooked rice hot. Slice thin slice from stem end of each tomato. Scoop out pulp (reserve). In hot oil in skillet, sauté onion 3 min. Add tomato pulp; rice; tuna, in chunks; chili; salt; pepper. Heat, stirring occasionally, till well blended. Heap in tomatoes; sprinkle with cheese. Bake in 10" x

6" x 2" baking dish, uncovered, 15 min., or till cheese is melted. Makes 6 servings.

▶ **For 2:** Use 4 medium tomatoes (2 each). Halve rest of ingredients. (Save rest of tuna for salad.)

CHIP-TUNA CASSEROLE

2 cans solid-pack tuna (2 cups)	⅓ cup sherry or cooking sherry; or
2 tablesp. flour	2 teasp. Worcestershire
½ teasp. salt	
Speck pepper	1 cup crumbled potato chips
2 cups milk	

Start heating oven to 375°F. Into double boiler, measure 2 tablesp. oil from tuna. Gradually stir in flour, salt, pepper, milk; cook, stirring, until smooth and thickened. Add sherry.

Cover bottom of greased 1½-qt. casserole with ¼ cup potato chips. Top with one third of tuna, in chunks, then one third of sauce. Repeat, making 3 layers; top with rest of potato chips. Bake, covered, 20 min. Uncover; bake 10 min., or until brown. Makes 4 servings.

To Vary: Add ¾ cup sautéed, sliced mushrooms to sauce.

'FRISCO TUNA

¼ lb. medium noodles (about 2 cups)	1 teasp. salt
	¼ teasp. pepper
1 minced medium onion	¼ cup snipped parsley
	1 can chunk-style tuna (1 cup)
2 tablesp. butter or margarine	½ lb. packaged process-American-cheese slices
1 No. 2 can tomatoes (2½ cups)	
¼ teasp. garlic salt	

Start heating oven to 350°F. Cook noodles as label directs, adding minced onion; drain; add butter. Combine tomatoes, salts, pepper, parsley. In 8" x 8" x 2" baking dish, place half of noodles, then half of tuna, then half of cheese slices; pour on half of tomato mixture. Repeat. Bake, uncovered, 40 min. Makes 4 servings.

QUICK-CURRIED TUNA

⅓ cup milk	mushroom soup
1 teasp. curry powder	1 can solid-pack tuna, drained (1 cup)
1 can undiluted condensed cream-of-	

In saucepan, stir milk and curry powder into soup. Add tuna, in chunks; heat.

Serve on buttered toast or hot rice. Makes 4 servings.

TOPSY-TURVY TUNA-LEMON PIE

1 sliced, unpeeled lemon	2 tablesp. fresh, frozen, or canned lemon juice
1 can chunk-style tuna (1 cup)	1/3 cup catchup
2 tablesp. minced onion	1 egg, well beaten
1 tablesp. minced green pepper	About 1/4 lb. sliced process American cheese
1/4 cup fresh bread crumbs	6 tablesp. milk
1/2 teasp. dry mustard	1 cup packaged biscuit mix

Start heating oven to 400°F. Grease 8" round shallow casserole. Arrange lemon slices in bottom of dish. Mix tuna, onion, green pepper, crumbs, mustard, lemon juice, catchup, egg; spread over lemon slices. Top with cheese slices. With fork, stir milk into biscuit mix to make soft dough. Spread dough over cheese layer.

Bake, uncovered, 15 to 20 min., or until light brown. Loosen edges; quickly invert onto serving dish; cut into wedges.

Serve hot, as is or with Thin White Sauce, p. 376. Makes 6 to 8 servings.

CREAMED TUNA SUPREME

2 cans chunk-style tuna (2 cups)	mushroom soup
2 tablesp. cut-up pimento	3/4 cup milk
	6 eggs, separated
2 cans undiluted condensed cream-of-	1/8 teasp. salt
	1 tablesp. heavy cream
	1/8 teasp. pepper

Start heating oven to 400°F. Fold tuna and pimento into combined soup and milk. Pour into greased 12" x 8" x 2" baking dish. Bake until bubbling hot—about 12 min. Meanwhile, beat egg whites with salt until they form peaks when beater is raised. Beat yolks well until light and fluffy; beat in cream, pepper. Fold whites into yolks; then pour this omeletlike mixture over hot tuna. Bake, uncovered, 15 min., or until firm when tested with cake tester.

Serve at once in baking dish. Makes 6 to 8 servings.

▶ **For 2:** Halve ingredients; use 10" x 6" x 2" dish.

SHERRY TUNA

2 cans solid-pack tuna, well drained (2 cups)	1/8 teasp. pepper
	1 tablesp. butter or margarine
1/2 teasp. coarsely grated lemon rind	2 teasp. flour
1 tablesp. lemon juice	1 tablesp. snipped parsley
1/3 cup sherry or dry sauterne	1/2 cup ripe olives, drained

About 30 min. before serving: In saucepan, gently heat together tuna, lemon rind, lemon juice, sherry, pepper.

Meanwhile, in small saucepan, melt butter; stir in flour; cook till bubbling hot and lightly browned. Drain hot liquid from tuna into measuring cup; add more sherry, if necessary, to make 1/2 cup; add to flour mixture; cook, stirring, until smooth and thickened.

Turn hot tuna into serving or chafing dish; pour sauce over tuna. Sprinkle with parsley; garnish with olives. Makes 4 servings.

SARDINE-SANDWICH BAKE

12 bread slices, crusts removed	1 cup water
	6 tablesp. nonfat dry milk*
2 tablesp. melted butter or margarine	1 teasp. salt
2 cups grated process sharp American cheese (1/2 lb.)	1/2 teasp. dry mustard
	1/4 teasp. Worcestershire
1 can small sardines	1/8 teasp. pepper
1 minced small onion	2 eggs

Start heating oven to 350°F. In 12" x 8" x 2" baking dish, arrange 6 bread slices. Brush bread with half of butter; sprinkle with cheese. Arrange drained sardines on cheese; sprinkle with onion, rest of butter. Cover with rest of bread.

To water in bowl, add dry milk, salt, mustard, Worcestershire, pepper. With beater, beat until blended. Add eggs; beat until blended; pour over sandwiches. Bake, uncovered, 40 min., or until brown. Makes 6 servings.

Burger Bake: Substitute 1/2 lb. chuck, ground, browned in skillet, for sardines.

* You may substitute 1 cup milk for water and nonfat dry milk.

TOP-HAT SALMON PIE

Start heating oven to 450°F. Drain 1 1-lb. can salmon (2 cups); break salmon into large pieces;

pile in center of 9″ pie plate. Surround with ring of hot mashed potatoes (6 medium). Pour 2 tablesp. milk over salmon; sprinkle with ½ cup grated process American cheese. Dot with 1 tablesp. butter or margarine. Bake 20 min. Makes 4 servings.

QUICK SALMON PLATTER

1 1-lb. can salmon (2 cups)	⅛ teasp. tabasco
2 tablesp. butter or margarine	1 cup milk
	½ cup grated process American cheese
2 tablesp. flour	Hot cooked, seasoned broccoli, green beans, or asparagus
¼ teasp. dry mustard	
⅛ teasp. salt	

Heat salmon gently in its own liquid. Meanwhile, melt butter; add flour, mustard, salt, tabasco; stir till smooth. Add milk; cook, stirring, until mixture thickens and comes to boil. Remove from heat. Add cheese; stir until melted. Arrange salmon, in large pieces, on hot platter, with broccoli around it.

Serve with sauce. Makes 4 servings.

SALMON LOAF, WEST-COAST STYLE

1 1-lb. can salmon (2 cups)	2 tablesp. melted butter or margarine
¾ cup fresh bread crumbs	3 tablesp. fresh, frozen, or canned lemon juice
1 egg, slightly beaten	
¾ cup milk	¼ cup melted butter or margarine
2 tablesp. minced onion	
½ teasp. salt	¼ cup lemon juice
⅛ teasp. pepper	⅛ teasp. salt

Start heating oven to 350°F. To drained salmon, add bread crumbs, egg, milk, onion, salt, pepper, 2 tablesp. butter, 3 tablesp. lemon juice; toss with fork. Turn into greased 9″ x 5″ x 3″ loaf pan. Bake 40 to 55 min., or until done. Meanwhile for sauce, combine ¼ cup butter, ¼ cup lemon juice, ⅛ teasp. salt.

To serve: Pour sauce over salmon in pan. Or serve loaf and sauce separately. Makes 4 servings.

BUTTER-BROILED SALMON

1 1-lb. can salmon (2 cups)	1 tablesp. minced onion; or ½ teasp. onion salt
2 teasp. fresh, frozen, or canned lemon juice	
	¼ cup commercial sour cream; or 3 tablesp. butter or margarine
Salt and pepper	

Preheat broiler 10 min., or as manufacturer directs. Drain salmon; break into large chunks. Arrange in shallow baking dish or on broil-and-serve platter. Sprinkle with lemon juice, salt, pepper, onion; spread with sour cream. Place low in broiler; broil slowly 7 to 10 min., or until hot and tinged with brown. Makes 4 servings.

Tuna Broil: Substitute 2 cans solid-pack tuna (2 cups) for salmon.

BAKED SALMON LOAF

1 1-lb. can salmon (2 cups)	¼ teasp. monosodium glutamate
2 cups fresh bread crumbs	¼ teasp. poultry seasoning
1 egg, well beaten	
½ cup milk	2 tablesp. melted butter or margarine
2 tablesp. snipped parsley	2 tablesp. fresh, frozen, or canned lemon juice
2 tablesp. minced onion	
½ teasp. salt	A few potato chips
¼ teasp. tabasco	

Start heating oven to 375°F. To salmon, add crumbs and rest of ingredients except potato chips; toss with fork. Lightly turn mixture into greased 9″ x 5″ x 3″ loaf pan; smooth top. Sprinkle with crushed potato chips. Bake 40 min., or until firm in center.

To serve: When loaf is done, loosen edges with spatula; unmold onto heated platter. Serve as is, with lime or lemon wedges, or with Egg Sauce, p. 376. Makes 4 servings.

Fish Loaf: Substitute any flaked, cooked or canned fish for salmon.

Salmon Casserole: Bake in greased 1-qt. casserole as above.

► **For 2:** Halve ingredients, using 1 egg. Use 2 custard cups.

SALMON SCALLOP DIVAN

1 pkg. frozen broccoli, thawed just enough to separate	(2½ cups), drained
	½ cup grated process sharp American cheese
3 tablesp. butter or margarine	
3 tablesp. flour	1½ cups day-old bread crumbs
½ teasp. salt	
⅛ teasp. pepper	1 1-lb. can salmon (2 cups)
2 cups milk	
1 No. 2 can tomatoes	2 hard-cooked eggs, sliced lengthwise

Start heating oven to 375°F. Place broccoli in 2-qt. casserole; cover; bake while preparing rest of dish—about 10 min. In saucepan, melt butter; stir in flour, salt, pepper, then milk. Cook, stirring, until thick and smooth; remove from heat. Fold in tomatoes, cheese, crumbs. Remove casserole from oven; arrange salmon in chunks over broccoli; pour on tomato mixture. Arrange egg slices on top, pressing them down into sauce. Bake, uncovered, 25 min. Makes 4 servings.

TUNA PUFFS

4 eggs, slightly beaten	mustard
1 can chunk-style tuna (1 cup)	1 tablesp. minced onion
2 cups milk	1 can undiluted condensed cream-of-mushroom soup
2 cups fresh bread crumbs	
1 teasp. salt	2 tablesp. butter or margarine
1 tablesp. prepared	

Early in day: Combine eggs, tuna, milk, bread crumbs, salt, prepared mustard, onion. Turn into 6 individual casseroles or 8 custard cups. Refrigerate.

About 50 min. before serving: Start heating oven to 400°F. Set casseroles in pan of warm water. Bake, uncovered, 35 to 40 min. Meanwhile, heat soup; add butter; stir until melted. Use as sauce for puffs. Makes 6 to 8 servings.

SALMON-OLIVE CASSEROLE

1⅓ cups packaged precooked rice	Dash pepper
½ cup milk	1 7¾-oz. can salmon, flaked
½ lb. process American cheese, thinly sliced	¼ cup chopped stuffed olives
¾ teasp. salt	

Start heating oven to 350°F. Cook rice as label directs. Meanwhile, in double boiler, combine milk, cheese, salt, pepper. Heat, stirring occasionally, until well blended and smooth. In 1½-qt. casserole, alternate layers of cooked rice, salmon, olives, and cheese sauce, ending with sauce. Bake, uncovered, 30 min. Makes 6 servings.

Tuna-Olive Casserole: Substitute 1 cup solid-pack tuna, flaked (1 cup), for salmon.

TUNA-EGG SCALLOP

1 can chunk-style tuna (1 cup)	(optional)
1 tablesp. fresh, frozen, or canned lemon juice	Dash tabasco or cayenne pepper
	Dash pepper
2 tablesp. butter or margarine	3 sliced, hard-cooked eggs
¼ cup all-purpose flour	1 tablesp. snipped parsley
¼ teasp. dry mustard	1 cup fresh bread crumbs
¼ teasp. celery salt	2 tablesp. melted butter or margarine
2½ cups milk	
Pinch dried tarragon	

Start heating oven to 375°F. Drain oil from tuna into saucepan. To tuna, add lemon juice. To oil, add 2 tablesp. butter; stir in flour, mustard, celery salt, then milk; cook, stirring, until smooth and thickened. Add tarragon, tabasco, pepper. Lightly fold in eggs, tuna, parsley. Pour into 4 to 6 individual baking dishes or 1½-qt. baking dish; top with crumbs tossed with melted butter. Bake, uncovered, about 25 min., or until browned. Makes 6 servings.

TUNA-BACON BOWL

Toss I can (1 cup) chunk-style tuna or salmon with 4 crisp bacon slices, crumbled; 3 chopped, hard-cooked eggs; ½ cucumber, thinly sliced; ½ teasp. salt; ¼ teasp. pepper; 2 tablesp. mayonnaise. Makes 4 servings.

Shellfish

WHEN IT'S CLAMS

To Buy:

Hard-shell Clams: Large size (quahogs) is used for broth and Manhattan-style clam chowder. Smaller sizes (littlenecks and cherry stones) are served raw on shell, or in clam cocktails.

Soft-shell Clams: Soft-shell clams are usually small and are popular for broth, steaming, New England clam chowders, frying, fritters, etc.

Pacific-Coast Clams: These clams range from little butter clams to 1½-lb. Pismo clams to giant 6-lb. geoducks. Nice for stews, bisques, etc.

Clams in Shell: Sold by peck, dozen, or quart. Shells of live clams are tightly closed, or close quickly when touched. Reject clams with opened or broken shells.

Shucked Clams: Sold by quart, for chowders, frying, etc.

Canned Minced Clams: Fine for quick clam chowders, etc.

Bottled Clam Juice: A delicious first course.

Canned Clam Chowders: For lunch or supper.

STEAMED CLAMS

Use about 1 qt. soft-shell clams in shell per person. Scrub under running cold water until free of sand. Place in large kettle with ½ cup boiling water for every 4 qt. clams. Cover; steam till shells *just* open.

Heap clams in soup dishes. Serve with individual paper cups or custard cups of melted butter or margarine, with a little lemon juice added. Strain hot broth from kettle through fine cheesecloth; serve in cups, with thin lemon slices on top. Guests dip clams into broth, then into butter. Provide paper napkins or bibs.

CLAMS OR OYSTERS ON HALF SHELL*

Serve at table as on p. 689. Or arrange several dozen clams or oysters on half shell (about 6 per person) on large tray, with bowl of cocktail sauce in center; serve as first course in living room. Guests spear clams with picks or oyster forks, then dip them into sauce.

See To Open Oysters in the Shell, p. 189.

FRIED CLAMS

Beat 1 egg with 2 tablesp. water. Drain 1 qt. shucked raw soft-shell clams, removing bits of shell; dip into egg, then into packaged dried bread crumbs, corn meal, or fine cracker crumbs.

Fry as in Shallow Frying, p. 8, at 365°F. on deep-fat frying thermometer, until nicely browned on all sides. Drain on paper towels.

Serve with Quick Tartar Sauce, p. 373, chili sauce, or chutney. Makes 4 servings.

Nice, too, heaped on toast and served with lemon wedges, or with tartar or chili sauce in lettuce cups.

CLAM FRITTERS

1 pt. shucked raw soft-shell clams	⅛ teasp. pepper
1⅓ cups sifted all-purpose flour	½ cup juice drained from clams
2 teasp. baking powder	2 eggs, slightly beaten
¾ teasp. salt	Fat or salad oil

Drain clams through sieve, reserving juice. Coarsely chop clams. Sift flour, baking powder, salt, pepper; stir into chopped clams, with combined clam juice and eggs. Drop by tablespoonfuls into a little hot fat or salad oil in skillet; sauté until golden brown on both sides. Drain on paper towels. Makes about 2 doz.

CLAM BURGERS

2 eggs, beaten	crackers
1 7½-oz. can minced clams	¼ teasp. salt
	Dash pepper
1 cup finely rolled	3 tablesp. bacon fat

Combine eggs, clams with liquid, crackers, salt, pepper. Drop by tablespoonfuls into hot bacon fat in skillet. Brown on both sides.

Serve with Quick Tartar Sauce, p. 373. Garnish with lemon wedges. Makes 6.

CLAM STEW, see Oyster Stew, p. 42

LUNCHEON CLAMBAKE

4 eggs	clams, with liquid
2 cups milk	¼ cup minced onion
2½ cups soda-cracker crumbs (about 20 large or 30 small)	2 tablesp. minced green pepper
	½ teasp. salt
⅓ cup melted butter or margarine	½ teasp. Worcestershire
	Pepper to taste
2 10½-oz. cans minced	

Early in day: In mixing bowl, beat eggs well. Add milk, cracker crumbs; let stand 20 min. Add butter, rest of ingredients. Taste; add more salt if needed (crackers and clams vary somewhat in saltiness). Pour into greased 8″ x 8″ x 2″ or 9″ x 9″ x 2″ pan; refrigerate.

One hour before lunch: Bake mixture at 350°F. about 1 hr. Cut into squares.

Serve as is. Or top with spoonful of Anchovy Sauce, p. 376. Or garnish with crisp bacon. Makes 9 servings.

WHEN IT'S CRAB

To Buy:

Hard-shell Crabs: Available throughout the year, but more plentiful in summer. They should be alive when purchased. Allow 2 per person.

Soft-shell Crabs: When a crab molts (sheds its hard shell), it is called soft-shell. Available from June through September. Allow 2 per person.

Crab Meat: Fresh cooked crab meat comes in pry-open cans; 1 lb. yields about 3 cups. A 6½-oz. can crab meat yields about 1¼ cups. Remove any cartilage before using.

HARD-SHELL CRABS

To Boil: Order live hard-shell crabs; 6 crabs yield about 1 cup meat.

1. Pick up crabs with tongs or by back feelers; place in colander in sink full of cold water. Plunge colander in and out of water until crabs seem clean; drain.
2. Plunge crabs, head first, into enough rapidly boiling water to cover completely. (Let water return to boiling before adding each crab.) Add 1 tablesp. salt per 1 qt. water, 1 sliced onion, 1 bay leaf, 1 tablesp. vinegar. Cover; boil 15 to 20 min., or until red.
3. Drain; plunge into cold water. Drain; allow to cool on tray.

To Remove Meat: When crabs are cool, scrub shells under running water. Twist off claws and legs close to body; with nutcracker or hammer, crack all over. With pointed knife, pick out meat.

Lay each crab on its back shell. Slip knife under point of segment ("apron") that folds under body from rear; lift up, bend backward; break off. Take crab in both hands, with thumbs at tail; pull upper and lower shells apart. (Discard top shell, or scrub well and use in Deviled Crabs, p. 186.)

Hold crab under running water until loose matter is washed away. Break body in half, down center. With scissors, cut off membranous covering along edges. With nutpick, remove meat between sections, keeping meat whole if possible. Remove any cartilage.

SOFT-SHELL CRABS

To Buy: Order cleaned soft-shell crabs, allowing 2 per person. Or if you must clean them:

1. With scissors, remove head of each crab, cutting across crab ½″ behind eyes.
2. Back of soft-shell crab tapers to a point at each side. Lay crab on its back shell; then take one of these points between thumb and forefinger of left hand; pull shell back halfway. Scrape off lungs or spongy substance thus exposed. Do same on other side.
3. Remove segment ("apron") that folds under body from rear and spongy substance under it. Wash crabs under running cold water.

To Boil: Plunge cleaned soft-shell crabs into boiling water to cover, adding 1 teasp. salt per 1 qt. water. Cover; boil 15 min.; drain. Serve, hot or cold, on platter with mayonnaise and lemon wedges, or with Quick Tartar Sauce, p. 373.

To Broil: Combine ¼ cup melted butter or margarine; 1 tablesp. fresh, frozen, or canned lemon juice; pinch salt; speck pepper; dash cayenne pepper. Roll 6 cleaned soft-shell crabs in this mixture, then in flour. Broil under medium heat 8 to 10 min., turning once and basting with rest of butter mixture. Serve on toast with Quick Tartar Sauce, p. 373, and lemon wedges. Makes 3 servings.

SAUTEED SOFT-SHELL CRABS

Sprinkle 8 cleaned soft-shell crabs with salt, pepper. In ½ cup butter or margarine in skillet, sauté crabs, a few at a time, 3 min. on each side, or until just golden brown. Keep warm while sautéing rest of crabs.

Then, to butter left in skillet, add 1 tablesp. snipped parsley; 1 teasp. fresh, frozen, or canned lemon juice; and dash Worcestershire. Pour over crabs. Or serve crabs on or between toast slices, with Quick Tartar Sauce, p. 373. Makes 4 servings.

Almondine: Add ¼ cup slivered, blanched almonds to butter before sautéing crabs.

CRAB-CORN BAKE

1 cup flaked fresh or canned crab meat	3 tablesp. butter
1 12-oz. can vacuum-packed whole-kernel corn	2 tablesp. flour
	1 teasp. dry mustard
	1 cup milk
3 finely chopped, hard-cooked eggs	½ teasp. salt
	½ teasp. Worcestershire
1 tablesp. snipped parsley	1 tablesp. butter
	½ cup fresh bread crumbs
2 teasp. fresh, frozen, or canned lemon juice	¼ cup grated Parmesan cheese
1 tablesp. minced onion	

Start heating oven to 375°F. In 1½-qt. casserole, toss crab meat with corn, eggs, parsley, lemon juice. In saucepan, cook onion in 3 tablesp. butter 3 min.; stir in flour, mustard, milk; cook, stirring, until thickened; add salt, Worcestershire. Turn into casserole; toss with fork. Melt 1 tablesp. butter; stir in crumbs, cheese; sprinkle on top of casserole. Bake, uncovered, 20 to 25 min. Makes 6 servings.

To Do Ahead: Refrigerate unbaked casserole until 40 min. before serving. Then bake at 375°F. 25 to 30 min., or till hot and bubbly.

CRAB MEAT MARYLAND

¼ cup butter or margarine	Dash tabasco
3 tablesp. flour	2 tablesp. sherry or cooking sherry
2 cups milk	1 egg, beaten
2 tablesp. minced onion	1 teasp. salt
½ teasp. celery salt	Speck pepper
⅛ teasp. grated orange rind	3 cups flaked fresh or canned crab meat
1 tablesp. snipped parsley	½ cup fresh bread crumbs
1 tablesp. minced green pepper	1 tablesp. melted butter or margarine
1 minced pimento	

Start heating oven to 350°F. In double boiler, melt ¼ cup butter; stir in flour, milk; cook, stirring, until thickened. Add onion, celery salt, rind, parsley, green pepper, pimento, tabasco. Remove from heat; add sherry. Stir some of sauce slowly into egg; stir egg mixture into rest of sauce. Add salt, pepper, crab meat; turn into greased 1½-qt. casserole. Sprinkle with crumbs mixed with 1 tablesp. butter. Bake, uncovered, 15 to 20 min., or until brown. Makes 6 servings.

▶ **For 2:** Halve ingredients; use 1-qt. casserole.

PIQUANT CRAB CASSEROLE

1 pkg. frozen, or 1 lb. washed fresh, spinach	1 minced small onion
1½ cups grated process sharp American cheese	1 6-oz. can tomato paste (⅔ cup)
1 cup flaked fresh or canned crab meat	1 cup commercial sour cream
1 tablesp. fresh, frozen, or canned lemon juice	½ teasp. salt
	Dash pepper
	Dash nutmeg
	1 tablesp. sherry or cooking sherry

Start heating oven to 350°F. Cook spinach until barely tender; drain; with scissors, snip coarsely. Spread in greased 1- or 1½-qt. casserole, or in 4 individual baking dishes; sprinkle with half of cheese; crab meat, then with lemon juice. Mix onion, tomato paste, sour cream, salt, pepper, nutmeg, sherry; pour over all in casserole. Top with rest of cheese. Bake, uncovered, 30 min. Makes 4 servings.

To Do Ahead: Refrigerate unbaked casserole until 50 min. before serving. Then bake at 350°F. 40 min., or till hot and bubbly.

SOUTHERN CRAB CAKES

3 cups flaked fresh or canned crab meat	2 teasp. snipped parsley
1½ teasp. salt	Flour
1 teasp. dry mustard	1 egg, slightly beaten
½ teasp. pepper	2 tablesp. water
1 egg yolk	Packaged dried bread crumbs
2 teasp. Worcestershire	Butter or margarine
1 tablesp. mayonnaise	

Mix crab meat, salt, mustard, pepper, egg yolk, Worcestershire, mayonnaise, parsley; press mixture firmly into 8 small cakes. Chill well.

To serve: Dip cakes into flour, then into combined egg and water, then into crumbs. Melt bit of butter (or bacon fat) in skillet; quickly sauté cakes over high heat until golden.

Nice served with potato salad, coleslaw, or French fries. Or serve in hot toasted rolls for lunch or supper. Makes 4 servings.

CREAMED CRAB MEAT, see Our Best Creamed Fish, p. 177

DEVILED CRABS

¼ cup butter or margarine	1 cup milk
2 tablesp. flour	2 cups flaked fresh or canned crab meat
1 tablesp. snipped parsley	2 minced, hard-cooked eggs
2 teasp. lemon juice	½ cup fresh bread crumbs
1 teasp. prepared mustard	2 tablesp. melted butter or margarine
½ teasp. horse-radish	
1 teasp. salt	

Start heating oven to 400°F. In double boiler, melt ¼ cup butter; stir in flour, then parsley, lemon juice, mustard, horse-radish, salt. Slowly stir in milk. Cook, stirring, until thickened. Add crab meat, eggs. Use to fill 6 individual casseroles or crab shells; sprinkle with crumbs combined with 2 tablesp. butter. Bake, uncovered, 10 min. Makes 6 servings.

▶ **For 2:** Use 1 egg, one third of rest of ingredients.

QUICK-CURRIED CRAB

1½ cups raw regular or processed white rice; or 2⅔ cups packaged precooked rice	orated milk
	1 teasp. curry powder
2 cans undiluted condensed chicken-gumbo soup	2 cups flaked fresh or canned crab meat
	2 tablesp. minced onion
½ cup undiluted evap-	3 crumbled crisp bacon slices

About 30 min. before supper: Start cooking rice. Meanwhile, in saucepan, combine soup, milk, curry, crab meat; cook over low heat until hot.

Serve on hot fluffy rice; sprinkle with onion and bacon bits. Makes 6 servings.

LIVE LOBSTERS

To Buy: Live lobsters from East-coast waters are available the year round but are most abundant in summer.

The lobster shell is bluish-green with touches of red; after cooking, it turns bright red. The meat is in the 2 large claws and the tail section.

The most desirable lobsters are from 1 to 2 lb. each. The female, preferred by many, is recognized by the softness of its two uppermost finlike appendages.

When buying lobster to cook at home be sure it is alive. When buying a cooked lobster, make sure its tail is curled toward body and that tail springs back into place after being straightened.

Amount to Buy: When serving lobster in shell, allow 1 small, or ½ large, lobster per person.

For recipes calling for lobster meat, remember that 1 lb. lobster in shell yields about ⅔ cup diced, cooked meat. Fresh lobster meat sometimes comes in pry-open cans. One 6-oz. can lobster yields about 1 cup.

BOILED LIVE LOBSTER

To Prepare:

1. Allow 1 small, or ½ large, lobster per person. Grasp each live lobster by body, with claws away from you (so it can't nip you); or use tongs.
2. Plunge lobster, head first, into rapidly boiling salted water—3 tablesp. salt to 3 qt. water. (You may also add a few whole black peppers, onion slice, bay leaf, celery tops, parsley sprig, some lemon juice or slices.)
3. Cover; boil 12 to 15 min.

To Serve Hot in Shell:

1. When lobster is done, remove from water; place on back shell. With sharp knife or kitchen scissors, slit center of thin undershell from head to tail.
2. Spread open; remove dark vein and small sac about 2″ long just below head. Leave in the delicious green liver (tomalley), if any. Or remove it; season well; serve in lettuce cups. Crack large claws.
3. Serve hot, with cut side up, garnished with lemon wedges, parsley. Serve small side dishes of melted butter (if lobster contains any red roe, or "coral," it may be sprinkled on butter). Furnish nutcrackers and finger bowls. Nice with French fries.

To Serve Cold in Shell: When lobsters are done, refrigerate. To serve, split and serve as above, substituting mayonnaise, horse-radish, or tartar sauce for butter.

To Remove Lobster Meat for Salads, etc.:

1. Place boiled lobster on back shell. Twist off claws close to body.
2. With sharp knife or scissors, slit center of thin undershell from head to tail. Spread open with left hand; then insert fingers of right hand under tail meat and force it out in one piece.
3. Place tail meat on table, with striped side down. Run sharp knife down center to expose dark vein; remove and discard.
4. In female lobsters you may find red roe, or "coral." Remove; crumble, as garnish, over mayonnaise, lobster salad, etc.

    Green liver is also a delicacy; see To Serve Hot in Shell, Step 2, above.
5. Cut tail shell from body shell. Hold body shell in left hand; with first two fingers and thumb of right hand, draw out body, leaving in shell the small sac about 2″ long just below head. Discard sac and spongy, grayish lungs covering sides of body.
6. Break body into several pieces and, with nutpick or fork, pick out flesh around cartilage. Tweezers are also good for this job.
7. Crack large claws with hammer or nutcracker; remove meat. Use small claws as garnish.
8. Body and tail shells, if not broken, may be washed, dried, and fitted together. Use to hold lobster salad or Lobster Thermidor, p. 189.

BROILED LIVE LOBSTER

To Prepare: Allow 1 small, or ½ large, lobster per person. Order lobster split lengthwise and cleaned, with large claws cracked. Or do it yourself this way (be sure to cook same day):

1. Lay lobster on back shell on board. Where tail and body come together, insert point of knife through to back shell. (Or place in cold water over low heat until lobster reddens.) With heavy mallet or hammer, crack large part of each large claw.
2. Then cut down through center of thin undershell from head to tail, just to back shell, which should be left intact.
3. Spread lobster open as wide as possible. Discard dark vein down center, also small sac

about 2″ long just below head. Leave in green liver and "coral." Crack large claws.

To Broil:

1. Preheat broiler 10 min., or as manufacturer directs. Place lobster, with meat side up, on broiler rack, 3″ from heat. Brush with melted butter or margarine, or melted butter mixed with green liver.
2. Sprinkle with salt, pepper, snipped parsley, and bit of garlic (optional).
3. Broil 15 to 20 min., depending on size of lobster and desired doneness, brushing with butter now and then. If broiling several lobsters, cut off large claws; arrange around sides of broiler pan, with body sections in center.

To Serve: Serve hot as in Boiled Live Lobster, p. 187.

Broiled Stuffed Lobster: Prepare lobster as on p. 187. Combine 5 tablesp. fresh bread crumbs, 2 tablesp. snipped parsley, ¼ teasp. salt, 2 tablesp. melted butter or margarine, speck pepper, pinch dried herb, and a little grated onion. Broil lobster 10 min. as in step 3 above; then sprinkle with crumbs and broil 5 min., or until golden.

ROCK-LOBSTER TAILS

To Buy: In rock lobsters, the meat lies in the tail section and is delicious. Because these lobsters are usually sold quick-frozen, and are wrapped individually or 2 to a carton, you can always keep a few on hand in your freezer.

They weigh ¼ to 1 lb. apiece; the ½-lb. size makes 1 generous serving.

To thaw lobster tails, unwrap; let stand at room temperature *just* until thawed.

Rock-lobster meat also comes canned.

To Boil: Boil unthawed frozen rock-lobster tails in boiling salted water to cover (1 teasp. salt per 1 qt. water), allowing 3 min. longer than ounce weight of largest tail—for example, 11 min. for 8 oz. tail. If thawed, allow only 1 min. longer than ounce weight of largest tail.

To Serve: Drain; with scissors, cut away thin undershell. Serve as in Boiled Live Lobster, p. 187.

To Remove Meat for Salads, etc.: Boil lobster tails as above; chill. Cut away undershell. Insert fingers between shell and meat; pull out tail meat in one piece. Use as is, or cut up for any of lobster recipes that follow.

BROILED ROCK-LOBSTER TAILS

Thaw frozen rock-lobster tails; cut away undershell. Grasp tail in both hands and bend it backward toward shell side to crack and prevent curling. Preheat broiler 10 min., or as manufacturer directs. Broil tails, with shell side up, 5″ below heat 5 min. Turn; spread with butter or margarine; broil 6 to 9 min. Serve as in Boiled Live Lobster, p. 187.

LOBSTER TAILS A LA BARBER

4 10-oz. frozen rock-lobster tails	¾ cup light cream
	Salt to taste
¼ cup melted butter or margarine	2 cups fresh bread crumbs
¼ cup sherry or cooking sherry	¼ cup melted butter
	¼ cup snipped chives
2 tablesp. flour	¼ teasp. salt
1 teasp. paprika	⅛ teasp. pepper

Boil frozen lobster tails as above; remove meat, keeping shells intact. Cut meat into chunks; refrigerate.

About 15 min. before serving: In saucepan, heat lobster meat with ¼ cup butter and sherry 3 min. Stir in flour, paprika, cream, salt; cook, stirring, until thickened. Use to stuff lobster shells; top with crumbs mixed with rest of ingredients. Broil 2 or 3 min., or until brown. Makes 4 servings.

LOBSTER NEWBURG

6 tablesp. butter or margarine	Dash paprika
	1 teasp. salt
2 tablesp. flour	3 tablesp. sherry or cooking sherry
3 cups cut-up, cooked or canned lobster meat	3 egg yolks
	2 cups light cream
⅛ teasp. nutmeg	Toast points

In double-boiler top, melt butter; stir in flour, lobster, nutmeg, paprika, salt, sherry. Beat yolks slightly; add cream; mix well. Slowly stir yolks into lobster; cook over hot water, stirring, till just thickened.

Serve at once on toast, in patty shells, or in Croustades, p. 344. Or place in individual baking dishes; top with buttered fresh bread crumbs; brown under broiler. Makes 6 servings.

Crab, Shrimp, or Oyster Newburg: For lobster, substitute 2 cups flaked fresh or canned crab meat; cleaned, cooked or canned shrimp; or raw oysters in their liquid, heated until edges *just* curl, then drained.

Lobster Thermidor: Remove meat from 4 boiled 1- or 2-lb. lobsters (about 3 cups). Prepare as above, omitting egg yolks and increasing flour to ¼ cup. Use to fill lobster shells. Sprinkle with ¼ cup grated cheese; brown lightly under broiler. Garnish with lemon wedges.

LOBSTER-TAIL FEAST

With Butter: Boil frozen rock-lobster tails as on p. 188. Remove meat; leave whole, or cut up; reheat in melted butter or margarine, adding lemon juice to taste.

With Hollandaise: Boil frozen rock-lobster tails as on p. 188; remove meat in one piece; plunge into boiling water 1 min.; drain. Serve on platter with bowl of Easy Hollandaise, p. 374, in center.

JANE'S COMPANY LOBSTER

3 cups cut-up, cooked or canned lobster meat	¼ teasp. dry mustard
3 tablesp. fresh, frozen, or canned lemon juice	¾ teasp. salt
	Speck pepper
	2 cups milk
½ teasp. mace	2 cups grated process
¼ lb. elbow macaroni (1 cup)	American cheese (½ lb.)
4 teasp. minced onion	¼ cup sherry or cooking sherry
2 tablesp. butter or margarine	⅓ cup crushed crisp round scalloped crackers
1 tablesp. flour	

Start heating oven to 400°F. Sprinkle lobster with lemon juice, mace. Cook macaroni as label directs; drain. In double boiler, combine onion, butter, flour, mustard, salt, pepper; stir in milk. Cook, stirring, until smooth. Add 1½ cups cheese; stir until melted. Add lobster, sherry. Arrange macaroni in 12″ x 8″ x 2″ baking dish; pour on lobster mixture; sprinkle with rest of cheese, then with crackers. Bake, uncovered, 20 min. Makes 4 to 6 servings.

MUSSELS

Mussels are a neglected, yet delicious, shellfish. They can be had the year round, but are at their best in winter.

MUSSELS MARINIERE

3 to 4 doz. mussels	1 teasp. flour
1 tablesp. minced shallots or onion	Salt and pepper
	1 teasp. snipped parsley
½ cup white wine	½ teasp. snipped chives
3 tablesp. butter or margarine	(optional)

With brush, scrub mussel shells well. Place in saucepan with shallots, wine. Boil, covered, 6 to 8 min., or until mussels open. Take off top shell of each; arrange in serving plates. Strain liquid left in saucepan; cook till reduced to one third original amount. Blend butter with flour; stir into liquid. Bring to boil; add salt and pepper to taste, parsley, chives. Pour over mussels. Makes 5 servings.

WHEN IT'S OYSTERS

To Buy: East-coast and Gulf of Mexico shucked oysters are sold by the dozen, or in ½-pt., 1-pt., and 1-qt. containers.

Pacific-coast oysters are a smaller variety but are tasty.

Oysters in the shell are sold by the dozen. Oysters on the half shell are also sold by many fish dealers.

When using canned or frozen oysters, follow label directions.

To Open Oysters in the Shell: Scrub shells well; rinse in cold water. Insert point of sharp thin knife into hinged end of oyster; push blade between shells until muscle at center is cut and valves begin to separate. Run knife around shell; separate valves; loosen oyster from shell.

To Remove Bits of Shell: Put oysters in sieve to drain; pick over oysters, taking each between finger tips, to remove bits of shell.

BROILER-FRIED OYSTERS

¾ cup packaged dried bread crumbs
½ teasp. dry mustard
Dash cayenne pepper
¼ teasp. paprika
½ teasp. salt

2 doz. shucked raw oysters, drained
¼ cup melted butter or margarine
Lemon wedges

Preheat broiler 10 min., or as manufacturer directs. Combine crumbs, mustard, pepper, paprika, salt. Remove any bits of shell from oysters. Drain oysters; roll in crumb mixture; place, in single layer, in greased baking pan. Sprinkle with half of melted butter. Broil quickly till golden brown. Turn; sprinkle with rest of melted butter. Broil quickly till golden brown. Serve with lemon wedges. Makes 4 servings.

PANNED OYSTERS

3 tablesp. butter or margarine
2 doz. shucked large raw oysters, drained
2 teasp. minced onion
½ teasp. salt

⅛ teasp. pepper
⅛ teasp. paprika
¼ cup light cream
1 teasp. snipped parsley
6 halved slices buttered toast

In skillet, melt butter; add oysters, onion, salt, pepper, paprika. Cook over low heat until oyster edges just begin to curl—3 to 5 min. Add cream, parsley. Heat. Serve on toast. Makes 4 servings.

SKILLET-FRIED OYSTERS

3 tablesp. butter or margarine
3 tablesp. shortening
2 doz. shucked large raw oysters, drained
Finely crushed crisp round scalloped

crackers
¾ to 1 teasp. salt
¼ teasp. pepper
Snipped parsley or paprika
Lemon wedges

Melt butter and shortening in skillet. Roll oysters in cracker crumbs; sauté in butter until golden brown, turning once and sprinkling with salt and pepper.

Serve as is or on buttered toast. Sprinkle with snipped parsley or paprika; garnish with lemon. Makes 4 servings.

FRIED OYSTERS

Prepare and serve as in Fried Clams, p. 183, substituting drained, shucked large raw oysters for clams.

Oyster Club Sandwiches: Use fried oysters, with lettuce, thin tomato slices, and crisp bacon, as filling for hot buttered-toast sandwiches.

OYSTERS IN CREAM

2 doz. shucked raw oysters
2 tablesp. butter or margarine
2 tablesp. flour
¼ cup white wine

½ teasp. salt
⅛ teasp. paprika
Pinch nutmeg
¾ cup light cream
2 egg yolks, beaten

Warm up oysters in their liquor over very low heat. Meanwhile, in double boiler, melt butter; stir in flour, wine, salt, paprika, nutmeg. Stir in cream; cook until thickened. Stir a little cream mixture into yolks; stir into rest of sauce. Add oysters and enough liquid to make sauce consistency; heat.

Serve on toast, or in tart shells, p. 422, Croustades, p. 344, or Toast Cups, p. 344. Sprinkle with snipped parsley. Makes 4 servings.

TARANTINO'S HANGTOWN FRY

8 bacon slices
5 eggs
2 tablesp. water
¼ teasp. salt
Dash pepper

1 doz. shucked small raw oysters, drained
½ cup packaged dried bread crumbs
¼ cup bacon fat

In skillet, fry bacon until crisp; drain on paper towels. Beat eggs with water, salt, pepper. Dip oysters into egg mixture; roll in crumbs. Quickly brown in hot bacon fat, turning once. Top oysters with bacon; pour rest of egg mixture over all. Cook, without stirring, until firm and slightly browned on bottom. Turn out onto hot platter; serve at once. Makes 4 servings.

SUSAN'S SCALLOPED OYSTERS

2 cups coarse toast crumbs
¼ cup melted butter or margarine
2 doz. shucked raw oysters, drained
¼ cup oyster liquid

½ teasp. salt
¼ teasp. pepper
2 tablesp. light cream
1 teasp. Worcestershire
Dash cayenne pepper
2 tablesp. sherry or cooking sherry

1. To make toast crumbs, toast 4 white bread slices. With kitchen scissors, snip into pieces.
2. Start heating oven to 425°F. Combine crumbs and butter; use one third of mixture to cover

bottom of greased 12″ x 8″ x 2″ baking dish.

3. Arrange half of oysters on crumbs. Combine oyster liquid with salt, pepper, cream, Worcestershire, cayenne, sherry; spoon half of this sauce over oysters.

4. Sprinkle with one third of crumbs; top with rest of oysters, then sauce, then crumbs. Bake, uncovered, 20 min. Makes 4 servings.

OYSTER STEW, see p. 42

WHEN IT'S SCALLOPS

To Buy: There are 2 kinds of scallop (the muscle that opens and shuts scallop shells): Allow 1 lb. scallops for 3 or 4 servings.

Bay scallops are tiny, pinkish white cubes, about ¾″ in size; they are especially delicate.

Sea scallops are larger cubes, of 2″ or more. They may be split across the grain.

Some quick-frozen plain and breaded scallops are also available.

GOLDEN SCALLOPS

In large skillet, heat 2 tablesp. butter or margarine, ½ teasp. salt, ⅛ teasp. pepper, and ¼ teasp. paprika till bubbling hot. Add 2 tablesp. minced onion or 1 slivered clove garlic. Using 1 lb. bay scallops (1 pt.) in all, drop in enough scallops to cover bottom of skillet (don't crowd). Sauté over high heat, tossing occasionally, 5 to 7 min., or until golden; remove to heated platter. Repeat. Sprinkle scallops with snipped parsley.

Serve with lemon wedges. Or top with sautéed, sliced mushrooms or crumbled crisp bacon. Makes 3 or 4 servings.

SCALLOP SAUTE

Dip 1 lb. sea scallops first into milk, then into Seasoned Flour, p. 10. In hot melted butter or margarine in skillet over low heat, sauté scallops, a few at a time, until just cooked but juicy—about 8 min.

Serve sprinkled with melted butter or margarine combined with snipped parsley or chives; garnish with lemon wedges. Makes 3 or 4 servings.

SCALLOP BROIL

Preheat broiler 10 min., or as manufacturer directs. Arrange 1 lb. sea scallops in 1 layer in shallow pan; sprinkle with garlic salt, pepper, paprika. Broil about 4 min., turning often and sprinkling with ¼ cup melted butter or margarine mixed with 1 tablesp. lemon juice. Sprinkle *lightly* with packaged dried bread crumbs; broil 1 min. longer. Makes 3 or 4 servings.

SAUTEED SCALLOPS WITH SCALLIONS

1 lb. bay scallops (1 pt.)	margarine
½ cup packaged dried bread crumbs	⅓ cup finely sliced scallions or minced onion
¼ teasp. paprika	½ teasp. salt
6 tablesp. butter or	⅛ teasp. pepper

Roll scallops in combined crumbs and paprika. In skillet, heat butter with scallions, salt, pepper; add scallops and sauté over high heat until scallops are golden on all sides. Makes 3 or 4 servings.

WHEN IT'S SHRIMP

To Buy: Today delicious quick-frozen or fresh raw shrimp (some come deveined) are widely distributed. Sold by size, they vary from 15 to 42 shrimp per pound.

You may also buy frozen cooked, deveined shrimp, as well as frozen ready-to-fry breaded fantail shrimp and canned shrimp. (If canned shrimp is salty, rinse before using.)

One pound frozen or fresh raw shrimp yields 1⅓ to 1⅔ cups (or ½ lb.) after cooking and shelling, and makes 2 or 3 servings. One 5-oz. can yields about 1 cup.

To Shell*: Raw shrimp may be shelled either before or after boiling. We prefer to shell them raw, for, after cooking, they seem plumper. To shell, hold tail end of shrimp in left hand; slip thumb of right hand under shell between feelers, and lift off several segments of shell. Then, holding firmly to tail, pull out shrimp from rest of shell and tail.

To Devein*: The black vein in raw shrimp is harmless, but removing it, before or after cooking, makes the shrimp more attractive. To devein, with sharp knife, cut about ⅛″ deep along outside curve of shrimp; then lift out black vein, washing shrimp under running water.

To Cook: Shell and devein shrimp before cooking. Drop shrimp into boiling salted water to cover, using 1 tablesp. salt per 1 qt. water (if desired, also add 1 sliced small onion, a few parsley sprigs, 4 whole black peppers). Simmer, covered, 2 to 5 min.—never longer—or until pink and tender. Drain. (Now shell and devein if not done before.) Refrigerate.

Special devices for shelling and deveining shrimp are now available.

SHRIMP BROIL

Shell, then devein, 2 lb. raw shrimp; arrange in layer in shallow pan or piepan. Sprinkle well with seasoned salt, monosodium glutamate, then with 3 tablesp. melted butter or margarine mixed with 2 to 3 tablesp. fresh, frozen, or canned lemon juice. Broil until shrimp turn pink—about 5 min. Serve as is or on toast. Makes 4 to 6 servings.

In Bacon Curls: Sprinkle shrimp with seasoned salt, pepper, lemon juice. Wrap each in ½ bacon slice. Secure with wooden toothpick. Broil, turning once, about 6 min., or until bacon is crisp.

SHRIMP SAUTE

Shell, then devein, 2 lb. raw shrimp. In 2 tablesp. butter or margarine in skillet, sauté shrimp with 3 sliced scallions, 1½ teasp. salt, and ⅛ teasp. pepper, tossing to cook all sides, till opaque— 3 to 5 min. Add 2 tablesp. sherry or cooking sherry (or a little lemon juice) and snipped parsley. Makes 4 to 6 servings.

FRIED SHRIMP (JU HAR-KOW)

Batter:

1 egg, beaten	1 lb. deveined, shelled
2 tablesp. flour	large raw shrimp
½ teasp. salt	½ cup salad oil
Dash pepper	

Sauce:

⅔ cup minced onions	1 teasp. soy sauce
1 tablesp. cornstarch	¾ cup chicken bouillon

For Batter: Combine egg, flour, salt, pepper. Add shrimp; stir to coat well. Heat oil in skillet until very hot. Using fork, lift shrimp, one by one, from batter; drop into oil; sauté until golden— 5 to 7 min. Drain on paper towels. Remove to heated platter.

For Sauce: Sauté onions in 2 tablesp. oil left in skillet; add combined cornstarch, soy sauce, bouillon. Cook, stirring, *just* until thickened. Pour over shrimp. Serve with hot fluffy rice. Makes 4 servings as appetizer.

Sweet Pungent: To sauce, add 2 tablesp. each vinegar and sugar, 1 No. 1 can pineapple tidbits, and 1 sliced medium green pepper.

BUTTERFLY SHRIMP

Shell, then devein raw shrimp, leaving tails on. Split along back curve, cutting deep, almost to inner edge; open; then press flat with bottom of measuring cup. Prepare batter for Fried Shrimp, above; add shrimp; stir to coat well. Lift out, one by one, with fork. Fry as in Shallow Frying, p. 8, at 365°F. on deep-fat frying thermometer until golden.

Serve with bowl of soy sauce or chutney for dunking.

INDIAN SHRIMP CURRY

1 to 1½ cups raw regular or processed white rice; or 1½ to 2 cups packaged precooked rice	6 tablesp. flour
	2½ teasp. curry powder
	1¼ teasp. salt
	1½ teasp. sugar
	¼ teasp. ground ginger
1 chicken-bouillon cube	2 cups milk
1 cup boiling water	3 lb. cooked, cleaned shrimp (4 cups)
5 tablesp. butter or margarine	1 teasp. fresh, frozen, or canned lemon juice
½ cup minced onions	

Cook rice as label directs; keep hot. Dissolve bouillon cube in water. In double-boiler top over direct heat, melt butter. Add onions; simmer till tender. Stir in flour, curry, salt, sugar, ginger. Gradually stir in bouillon, milk. Cook over boiling water, stirring, until thickened. Add shrimp, lemon juice; heat.

Serve ring of hot rice on heated platter, with curry in center. Serve with some of Curry Accompaniments, p. 193. Makes 6 to 8 servings.

Curry Accompaniments: A curry dish is at its best served with one or more of these accompaniments, arranged in separate bowls:

Chutney
Tomato wedges
Raisins
Salted almonds
Salted peanuts
Snipped parsley
Sautéed onion rings
Pineapple chunks

Crisp bacon bits
Currant jelly
Chopped, hard-
    cooked eggs
Sweet or sour pickles
Shredded coconut
Sliced avocado
Grated orange rind

Peppers - Mem

Lobster, Crab, or Scallop Curry: For shrimp, substitute 4 cups flaked, cooked or canned lobster or crab meat, or cooked scallops.

SHRIMP FLORADORA

2 tablesp. butter or
    margarine
3 minced shallots or
    ¼ cup minced onion
2 minced cloves garlic
¼ lb. sliced cooked,
    cleaned shrimp
1 tablesp. snipped
    chives
2 tablesp. fresh bread
    crumbs
1 minced large mush-
    room
2 tablesp. tomato purée
Salt

Pepper
3 large fish fillets
    (about 2 lb.)
1 cup hot water
¼ cup white wine
1 tablesp. lemon juice
2 tablesp. butter or
    margarine
1 tablesp. flour
1 cup milk
¼ cup white wine
1 tablesp. soy sauce
3 egg yolks, beaten
Grated Parmesan cheese

Start heating oven to 400°F. In 2 tablesp. hot butter in small skillet, sauté shallots and garlic 2 min. Add shrimp; sauté 1 min. Add next 4 ingredients, ¼ teasp. salt, dash pepper; cook, stirring, 2 min. Sprinkle fillets lightly with salt, pepper; spread with shrimp mixture; roll up. Place in shallow baking dish. Mix water, ¼ cup wine, lemon juice; pour over fish. Bake ½ hr. or until easily flaked with fork.

Meanwhile, in double boiler, melt 2 tablesp. butter; stir in flour then milk; cook, stirring, until smooth and thickened. Add ¼ cup wine, soy sauce, ½ teasp. salt, speck pepper; cook a few minutes; then stir in egg yolks. Cook, stirring, until smooth and thick. Lift fish rolls onto platter. Spoon on sauce. Sprinkle with cheese. Makes 6 servings.

SHRIMP CASSEROLE HARPIN

2 lb. large raw shrimp
1 tablesp. fresh, frozen,
    or canned lemon
    juice
3 tablesp. salad oil
¾ cup raw regular or
    processed rice; or 1⅓
    cups packaged pre-
    cooked rice
2 tablesp. butter or
    margarine
¼ cup minced green
    pepper

¼ cup minced onion
1 teasp. salt
⅛ teasp. pepper
⅛ teasp. mace
Dash cayenne pepper
1 can undiluted con-
    densed tomato soup
1 cup heavy cream
½ cup sherry or cook-
    ing sherry
½ cup slivered almonds
Paprika

Early in day: Shell, devein, then cook shrimp in boiling salted water 5 min.; drain. Place in 2-qt. casserole; sprinkle with lemon juice, oil. Meanwhile, cook rice as label directs; drain. Refrigerate all.

About 1 hr. 10 min. before serving: Start heating oven to 350°F. In butter in skillet, sauté green pepper and onion 5 min. Add to shrimp in casserole, along with rice, salt, and rest of ingredients except ¼ cup almonds and paprika. Top with reserved almonds; sprinkle with paprika. Bake, uncovered, 55 min., or till bubbly. Makes 6 to 8 servings.

SHRIMP CREOLE

¼ cup butter or
    margarine
1 chopped large onion
½ cup minced green
    peppers
1 minced clove garlic
1 teasp. salt
Dash pepper
⅛ teasp. dried rosemary

(optional)
⅛ teasp. paprika
2 cups cooked or
    canned tomatoes
1 lb. cooked, cleaned
    shrimp (1⅓ cups)
2 to 3 cups hot cooked
    rice

Melt butter in saucepan. Add onion, green peppers, garlic; sauté 10 min., or until tender. Add salt, pepper, rosemary, paprika, tomatoes. Bring to boil; reduce heat and simmer 15 min. Add shrimp; heat thoroughly. Serve on hot fluffy rice. Makes 4 servings.

To Vary: If you like a "hot" Shrimp Creole, add 1¼ teasp. chili powder and 2 dashes tabasco with tomatoes.

SHELLFISH SCALLOP, see p. 178

Pressure

Cooking

Have you ever wished you could spend a few more sunshine hours outdoors? Well, if you let your pressure cooker play the starring role in your dinner, you can keep kitchen time to a minimum and so have more time for fun.

Before using these recipes, refer to How to Use Our Recipes, p. 3, and Pots and Pans, p. 692. Always use standard measuring cups and spoons; measure level.

Pressure-Cook Because . . .

1. Cooking time is speeded up. Foods are cooked in steam at temperatures higher than 212°F. boiling temperature.
2. Vegetables taste so good, are so nutritious— the small amount of water used and the short cooking time are responsible.
3. Two or three vegetables can be cooked at the same time, and each will retain its distinctive flavor.
4. Less tender cuts of meat and soups and chowders cook in unbelievably short time.

When You Choose a Pressure Cooker

Look for stainless steel and aluminum pressure cookers. They're made in both metals, in a variety of sizes. There's a skillet-shaped pan available too.

Meet the newest in the field: It's a completely automatic pressure cooker that has its own electric base and controls the time, pressure, and even the venting.

Know that in many cookers you have a choice of several pressures: 15 lb. for general cooking, 10 lb. for canning purposes, etc.

Pay particular attention to the way the cover seals. Some designs may appeal to you more than others.

When You Use a Pressure Cooker

Read the manufacturer's directions carefully. Always follow directions. Pay particular attention to the following:

1. Never use more or less water than the amount called for.
2. Check steam vent before covering. Make sure it is clean and free from food particles.
3. Count cooking time accurately.
4. Regulate heat so cooking pressure won't be exceeded.
5. When cooking vegetables, start with hot water, to save time needed to reach proper pressure.
6. Brown meats *well* in pressure cooker first, to bring out color and flavor.
7. To be sure no steam pressure remains in cooker when you are ready to remove cover, *always follow* manufacturer's directions for reducing pressure. Never force cover off or try to open until you are sure there is no pressure in cooker.

Caution: We do not recommend pressure-cooking applesauce, dried beans or peas, rhubarb, cranberries, or pearl barley. These foods have a tendency to froth or sputter, which may block the vent pipe, with serious consequences. Avoid trouble by using regular cooking utensils for these foods.

Cooking Fresh Vegetables

Pour into pressure cooker amount of water that manufacturer directs, adding ¼ teasp. salt, then vegetables. Cover; over high heat, bring to cooking pressure as manufacturer directs; then reduce heat to maintain same pressure throughout cooking.

Cook for time periods manufacturer directs. Or follow our Vegetable Chart, p. 278; these cooking times start after cooking pressure is reached and are for 15 lb. pressure only. At end of cooking time, reduce pressure immediately as manufacturer directs.

DUTCH POTATO SALAD

4 bacon slices	½ teasp. celery seeds
½ cup minced onions	4 cups sliced, pared
1 teasp. flour	potatoes
1 tablesp. brown sugar	⅓ cup water
2 teasp. salt	¼ cup vinegar
⅛ teasp. pepper	Snipped parsley

Cut bacon into 1″ pieces; sauté in pressure cooker until crisp; add onions and sauté until golden. Stir in flour; add remaining ingredients except parsley; mix well. Cook at 15 lb. pressure 14 min. as manufacturer directs. Reduce pressure immediately. Serve hot, sprinkled with parsley. Makes 4 servings.

PRESSURE-CREAMED POTATOES

4 cups diced, pared	2 tablesp. flour
potatoes (1″ cubes)	1½ teasp. salt
1 small minced onion	¼ teasp. pepper
(optional)	1 cup grated process
1¼ cups milk	American cheese
2 tablesp. soft butter	(¼ lb.)
or margarine	

In pressure cooker, place potatoes, onion, milk. Blend butter with flour, salt, pepper; add, in one lump, to cooker (do not stir). Bring to 15 lb. pressure as manufacturer directs. Remove from heat immediately. Reduce pressure slowly. Then stir until well blended, adding cheese if desired. Makes 6 servings.

QUICK CHEESY MACARONI

1½ lb. cut-up, peeled,	⅛ teasp. pepper
very ripe tomatoes	½ teasp. Worcester-
¼ lb. uncooked elbow	shire
macaroni (1 cup)	¼ cup water
2 tablesp. butter or	1 cup grated process
margarine	American cheese
1 sliced small onion	(¼ lb.)
1 teasp. salt	

Place rack in pressure cooker. Arrange all ingredients except cheese on rack; stir. Cook at 15 lb. pressure 5 min. as manufacturer directs. Reduce pressure immediately. Stir in cheese until melted. Makes 3 or 4 servings.

PRIZE BEEF STEW

2 lb. round steak, cut	1 teasp. dried thyme
into 1½″ pieces	1½ teasp. salt
½ cup red wine	⅛ teasp. pepper
2 tablesp. salad oil	2 or 3 sprigs parsley
¼ lb. lean salt pork,	1 No. 2 can tomatoes
cut into ½″ cubes	(2½ cups)
1 minced large onion	12 halved stuffed olives
1 finely chopped large	1 3-oz. can whole
carrot	mushrooms, drained
1 minced celery stalk	Buttered, cooked
½ minced clove garlic	noodles; or small
1 bay leaf	boiled potatoes

Night before: Cover beef with wine and salad oil; refrigerate until cooking time. Then remove beef from wine mixture. Sauté salt pork in pressure cooker until golden brown; add beef and brown *well*. Mix in onion and rest of ingredients except mushrooms and noodles. Cook at 15 lb. pressure 20 min. as manufacturer directs. Reduce pressure immediately. Add mushrooms; heat. Remove parsley and bay leaf. Thicken, if desired, as on p. 7. Serve over noodles. Makes 5 or 6 servings.

BARBECUED SHORT RIBS

3 lb. beef short ribs,	1 tablesp. brown sugar
cut into 3″ pieces	1 tablesp. Worcester-
1½ to 2 teasp. salt	shire
½ cup minced onions	1 teasp. paprika
½ cup catchup	1 teasp. dry or prepared
½ cup water	mustard
¼ cup wine vinegar	

In pressure cooker, brown ribs on all sides, sprinkling with salt. Drain off most of fat. Combine onions with rest of ingredients; pour over meat. Cook at 15 lb. pressure 25 to 30 min. as manufacturer directs. Reduce pressure immediately. Makes 4 servings.

BEEF BIRDS

1 lb. round steak, cut ½" thick	¼ cup chopped onion
¼ teasp. pepper	¼ cup sliced celery
¼ teasp. salt	1 bouillon cube, dissolved in ¾ cup hot water
¼ teasp. garlic salt	
¼ teasp. celery salt	½ cup flour
1 cup cooked rice; or 2 cups fresh bread crumbs	5 tablesp. fat
	⅓ cup chopped ripe olives

Sprinkle beef with pepper and salts; pound both sides with edge of heavy saucer. Cut into 3" pieces and pound again. Mix rice, onion, celery, and enough bouillon to moisten; place about 2 tablesp. mixture as stuffing on each piece of beef; roll up; tie. Coat beef birds with flour; brown *well* in hot fat in pressure cooker. Add rest of bouillon. Cook at 15 lb. pressure 20 min. as manufacturer directs. Reduce pressure immediately. Remove birds to heated serving dish. Add chopped olives to gravy, plus a little boiling water if too thick. Heat; pour over birds. Nice with noodles. Makes 4 servings.

SWISS STEAK

1½ lb. round steak, cut 1½" thick	¼" thick
¼ cup flour	4 onion slices, ¼" thick
1 teasp. salt	4 tomato slices, ½" thick
⅛ teasp. pepper	
2 tablesp. fat or salad oil	3 tablesp. tomato juice, water, or cooking sherry
4 green pepper rings,	

Trim excess fat from beef; score beef on both sides with sharp knife; cut into 4 equal pieces. Mix flour, salt, pepper; pound into beef, using edge of heavy saucer. In hot fat in pressure cooker, brown beef quickly. On each piece of beef, place 1 pepper ring with onion slice inside it and tomato slice on top. Sprinkle vegetables lightly with more salt and pepper. Add tomato juice. Cook at 15 lb. pressure 25 to 30 min. as manufacturer directs. Reduce pressure immediately. Thicken gravy if desired. Makes 4 servings.

GOULASH, PRESSURE-COOKER STYLE

2 tablesp. salad oil	1 teasp. caraway seeds
2 lb. boned chuck, cut into 1½" cubes	1 teasp. dried marjoram
8 medium white onions	2 bay leaves
4 pared medium carrots	⅓ cup sherry or cooking sherry
2 teasp. salt	⅓ cup water
1 tablesp. paprika	¼ lb. wide noodles (2 cups)
1 tablesp. vinegar	

In hot salad oil in pressure cooker, brown beef. Add rest of ingredients except noodles. Cook at 15 lb. pressure 12 min. as manufacturer directs. Reduce pressure immediately. Push beef to one side of cooker; add noodles, pushing them down well into liquid. Cook at 15 lb. pressure 8 min. Reduce pressure immediately. Makes 4 servings.

MEAT-LOAF DINNER

1½ lb. chuck, ground	3 tablesp. catchup
¼ lb. bulk pork sausage	1 cup finely diced celery
¼ cup minced onion	1 grated, pared medium carrot
1⅓ cups fresh bread crumbs	2 tablesp. water
2 teasp. salt	2 tablesp. fat
1 egg	⅓ cup water
¾ teasp. dry mustard	4 or 5 halved, pared medium potatoes

Lightly mix all ingredients except fat, ⅓ cup water, potatoes. Shape into 6 small oblong loaves, 2" thick. Wrap in waxed paper; refrigerate ½ hr. In hot fat in pressure cooker, brown meat loaves on all sides. Slip rack under meat; add ⅓ cup water, potatoes. Cook at 15 lb. pressure 20 min. as manufacturer directs. Reduce pressure immediately.

Remove potatoes and meat to heated platter. Remove rack. Skim off fat from juice in pan; thicken, if necessary, with 2 tablesp. flour mixed with 3 tablesp. water till smooth. Serve gravy over potatoes; garnish with parsley if desired. Makes 6 servings.

Note: If gravy is too highly flavored, dilute with water.

CHILI CON CARNE

2 tablesp. fat or salad oil	(2½ cups)
1 lb. chuck, ground	2 tablesp. chili powder
1 cup minced onions	2 teasp. salt
1 No. 2 can tomatoes	2 1-lb. cans red kidney beans, drained

In hot fat in pressure cooker, brown beef, onions. Add tomatoes, chili powder, salt, kidney beans; stir. Cook at 15 lb. pressure 20 min. as manufacturer directs. Reduce pressure slowly. Makes 4 or 5 servings.

If desired, serve on crisp crackers, potato chips, or Melba toast.

EASY BEEF-NOODLE CASSEROLE

1 tablesp. fat	½ lb. sliced mushrooms
½ lb. chuck, ground	1 cup uncooked wide
1 teasp. salt	noodles
¼ teasp. pepper	1 8-oz. can tomato sauce
¼ teasp. garlic salt	1 can water (measure
1 teasp. Worcestershire	in sauce can)
¼ cup sliced onion	

In hot fat in pressure cooker, brown beef; add remaining ingredients. Cook at 15 lb. pressure 6 min. as manufacturer directs. Reduce pressure immediately. Makes 4 servings.

SPANISH PORK CHOPS

4 loin or shoulder pork	pepper
chops, ¾″ thick	2 teasp. salt
½ cup raw regular	¼ teasp. pepper
or processed white	½ teasp. paprika
rice	1 teasp. sugar
1 cup sliced onions	1 No. 2 can tomatoes
¼ cup minced green	(2½ cups)

Brown chops *well* in pressure cooker; add rest of ingredients. Cook at 15 lb. pressure 15 to 20 min. as manufacturer directs. Reduce pressure immediately. Makes 4 servings.

CHINESE SWEET-SOUR SPARERIBS

1 tablesp. fat or	1 teasp. salt
salad oil	¼ teasp. pepper
3 lb. spareribs, cut	1½ tablesp. sugar
into serving pieces	¾ cup white vinegar
1 minced clove garlic	2 tablesp. soy sauce
¼ teasp. ginger	

In hot fat in pressure cooker, brown ribs, a few at a time, until golden brown. Return all ribs to cooker; add rest of ingredients. Cook at 15 lb. pressure 15 min. as manufacturer directs. Reduce pressure immediately. Simmer, uncovered, several min., or until all ribs are well coated with sauce. Skim off fat. Remove ribs to heated platter. Thicken gravy slightly as on p. 7; pour over ribs. Makes 4 to 6 servings.

CREAMY LAMB STEW

1½ lb. lamb shoulder or	½ cup water
shank, cut into 2″	2 thickly sliced
cubes	large onions
½ cup flour	4 pared large carrots,
2 teasp. salt	cut into 1″ pieces
¼ teasp. pepper	½ cup frozen peas
3 tablesp. fat or	½ teasp. salt
salad oil	½ cup commercial
4 pared medium	sour cream
potatoes	Snipped parsley

Coat lamb with combined flour, salt, pepper; reserve 1 tablesp. flour mixture. In hot fat in pressure cooker, brown lamb *well* on all sides; add potatoes, water. Cook at 15 lb. pressure 25 min. as manufacturer directs. Reduce pressure immediately. Add onions, carrots. Cook at 15 lb. pressure 3 min. Reduce pressure immediately.

Push lamb and cooked vegetables to one side. Add peas, salt; cook, uncovered, 2 min. Stir reserved 1 tablesp. flour with sour cream until smooth; stir into stew. Cook a few minutes, or until thickened. Garnish with parsley. Nice with biscuits or thin crisp toast. Makes 6 servings.

QUICK SPANISH HAM

1 tablesp. butter or	peppers
margarine	1 cup raw regular or
1 cup diced, cooked	processed white rice
ham	1 No. 2 can tomatoes
1 cup sliced onions	(2½ cups)
½ minced clove	1½ teasp. salt
garlic (optional)	2 teasp. paprika
⅔ cup minced green	

In hot butter in pressure cooker, brown ham slightly. Add onions, garlic, green peppers; sauté 5 min. Add rice; brown lightly. Stir in tomatoes, salt, paprika. Cook at 15 lb. pressure 10 min. as manufacturer directs. Reduce pressure immediately. Makes 4 servings.

PINEAPPLE-HAM ROUNDS

2 to 2½ lb. smoked	orange rind
boneless butt, cut	5 whole cloves
into 1″ slices	1 can vacuum-packed
1 No. 2 can pineapple	sweet potatoes
chunks	3 tablesp. brown sugar
1 tablesp. grated	

Place sliced butt on rack in pressure cooker. Drain ½ cup juice from pineapple chunks. To meat, add this ½ cup juice, plus orange rind, cloves. Cook at 15 lb. pressure 20 min. as manufacturer directs. Reduce pressure immediately. Arrange sweet potatoes on meat; sprinkle with brown sugar. Cook at 15 lb. pressure 3 min. Reduce pressure immediately. Heat pineapple chunks in rest of juice. Lift potatoes to heated platter; surround with meat slices and pineapple chunks. Makes 4 to 6 servings.

VEAL PAPRIKA

1 lb. veal steak, about ½″ thick	3 tablesp. fat or salad oil
¼ cup flour	¼ cup commercial sour cream
1 teasp. salt	
1½ teasp. paprika	1 3-oz. can sliced mushrooms
1 egg, slightly beaten	

Cut veal into 8 to 10 pieces. On waxed paper, mix flour, salt, paprika. Dip veal first into flour mixture, then into beaten egg, then again into flour. In hot fat in pressure cooker, brown veal slowly on both sides. Add sour cream mixed with mushrooms and their liquid. Cook at 15 lb. pressure 10 min. as manufacturer directs. Reduce pressure immediately. Serve with boiled noodles or hot fluffy rice. Makes 4 servings.

SAVORY BURGUNDY CHICKEN

1 2½- to 3-lb. ready-to-cook roasting chicken, cut up	1 teasp. salt
	½ cup sliced mushrooms
¼ cup flour	1 tablesp. snipped parsley
1 teasp. salt	
¼ teasp. pepper	¼ cup Burgundy wine
¼ cup fat or salad oil	2 chicken-bouillon cubes
1 thinly sliced medium onion	1½ cups hot water
¼ cup thinly sliced celery	2 tablesp. sherry or cooking sherry

Coat chicken with combined flour, 1 teasp. salt, pepper. In 2 tablesp. hot fat in pressure cooker, sauté onion and celery until tender; remove. In remaining 2 tablesp. fat in cooker, brown chicken *well*. Combine sautéed vegetables with 1 teasp. salt, mushrooms, parsley, wine, and bouillon cubes dissolved in water; pour over chicken. Cook at 15 lb. pressure 15 min. as manufacturer directs. Reduce pressure slowly. Just before serving, add sherry. Nice with hot fluffy rice. Makes 4 to 6 servings.

COMPANY CHICKEN SUPREME

⅓ cup flour	½ cup sliced onions
1 teasp. salt	½ teasp. salt
¼ teasp. pepper	¼ teasp. pepper
1 teasp. paprika	¼ teasp. paprika
1 2-lb. ready-to-cook broiler-fryer, cut up	¼ cup hot water
	½ cup commercial sour cream
¼ cup shortening	
½ lb. sliced mushrooms	Parsley sprigs

Mix flour with 1 teasp. salt, ¼ teasp. pepper, and 1 teasp. paprika; use to coat chicken pieces well. In hot shortening in pressure cooker, brown chicken well on all sides. Add mushrooms and rest of ingredients except sour cream and parsley. Cook at 15 lb. pressure 10 to 15 min. as manufacturer directs. Reduce pressure immediately. Stir in sour cream. Arrange chicken on heated platter; spoon on sauce; garnish with parsley. Makes 4 servings.

ROAST DUCKLING

1 2½- or 3-lb. ready-to-cook duckling, cut up	¼ cup thin strips lemon rind
	¼ cup thin strips orange rind
1 teasp. salt	
¼ teasp. pepper	1 teasp. meat-extract paste
3 tablesp. butter, margarine, or salad oil	1 tablesp. red jelly
	2 oranges, sectioned
½ cup hot water	
½ teasp. brown sugar	2 tablesp. sherry or cooking sherry
2 tablesp. lemon juice	
2 tablesp. orange juice	Water cress

Sprinkle duckling with salt, pepper. In hot butter in pressure cooker, brown duckling *well* on all sides. Remove duckling; place rack in cooker; then place duckling on rack; add water. Cook at 15 lb. pressure 20 min. as manufacturer directs. Reduce pressure immediately.

Meanwhile, make sauce by cooking together a few min. brown sugar, lemon and orange juices and rinds, meat-extract paste, jelly. When duckling is done, place with skin sides up, on broil-and-serve platter; arrange orange sections on top; keep warm. Carefully skim fat from liquid in cooker; add ½ cup liquid and sherry to sauce; heat; then pour over duckling. Run platter under broiler until piping hot. Garnish with water cress. Makes 4 servings.

Note: For flaming duckling, pour 2 tablesp. cognac over duck after broiling; serve aflame.

PRESSURE-CURRIED SHRIMP

1 tablesp. butter or margarine	1 teasp. Worcestershire
2 sliced large onions	1 bay leaf
2 minced cloves garlic	⅔ cup diced celery
2 tablesp. flour	3 sprigs snipped parsley
2½ teasp. curry powder	1 bouillon cube, dissolved in 1 cup water
1 cup chopped fresh tomatoes	1 teasp. salt
¾ cup chopped green peppers	Pinch brown sugar
	1½ lb. cooked, cleaned shrimp
	Hot fluffy rice

In hot butter in pressure cooker, sauté onions and garlic until golden; mix in combined flour and curry powder. Stir in rest of ingredients except shrimp and rice. Cook at 15 lb. pressure 5 min. as manufacturer directs. Reduce pressure immediately. Remove bay leaf. Add shrimp; heat until shrimp are hot. Serve on heated platter, with border of hot fluffy rice. Pass chutney and grated coconut if desired. Makes 4 to 6 servings.

SHRIMP AND RICE PARMESAN

¼ cup salad oil	1 cup coarsely shredded, pared carrots
⅔ cup raw regular or processed white rice	
1¾ cups water	1 teasp. Worcestershire
2 teasp. salt	1 lb. deveined, shelled raw shrimp
⅛ teasp. pepper	
1 No. 2 can tomatoes (2½ cups)	Grated Parmesan or sharp cheese
1 minced small onion	

In hot oil in pressure cooker, cook rice, stirring constantly, until lightly browned. Add rest of ingredients except shrimp and cheese. Cook at 15 lb. pressure 8 min. as manufacturer directs. Reduce pressure immediately. Add shrimp; place cover on cooker without pressure gauge. After steam appears, cook 3 min. without gauge. Serve topped with Parmesan cheese. Makes 4 servings.

FISH CHOWDER

⅛ lb. salt pork	1 tablesp. salt
2 sliced medium onions	¼ teasp. pepper
1 lb. fresh or thawed frozen haddock or cod fillets, cut into 1″ pieces	4 cups hot milk
	1 12-oz. can vacuum-packed whole-kernel corn
1 lb. diced, pared potatoes	¼ cup butter or margarine
3 cups hot water	

Cut pork into cubes; brown in pressure cooker; set aside bits. Add onions; brown slightly. Add fish, potatoes, hot water, salt, pepper. Cook at 15 lb. pressure 5 min. as manufacturer directs. Reduce pressure immediately. Add milk, corn, butter. Heat until very hot; do not boil. Serve topped with salt-pork bits. Makes 4 servings.

TUNA PEPPERS

1 can undiluted condensed cream-of-chicken soup	¼ cup minced onion
	1 12-oz. can vacuum-packed whole-kernel corn
1 teasp. Worcestershire	
4 medium green peppers	½ teasp. salt
	¼ teasp. pepper
1 can chunk-style tuna (1 cup)	1 egg, beaten

Combine soup and Worcestershire in pressure cooker; place over low heat, so soup heats slowly and thins a bit. Cut tops off peppers; scoop out cores and seeds; rinse under hot water. Toss tuna with onion, corn, salt, pepper, egg; use to stuff peppers. Place tops on peppers, and secure with toothpicks. Put rack in cooker; place peppers on rack. Cook at 15 lb. pressure 4 min. as manufacturer directs. Reduce pressure immediately. Makes 4 servings.

DRIED FRUITS DE LUXE

Night before: Place dried fruit and water in pressure cooker (allow 1 cup water for each 1 cup dried fruit except apples; use 1¾ cup water for apples). Bring to 15 lb. pressure as manufacturer directs; immediately remove from heat. Reduce pressure slowly. Let fruit stand in unopened cooker overnight. Then open and serve. Delicious!

Game and Rabbit

Of course you can cook game! If you can roast a leg of lamb or chicken or make beef stew, you can just as easily roast venison or wild duck or make a *civet,* or game stew.

Don't expect game to taste like other meat. Its unique flavor is one of the reasons so many hunting licenses are issued each year.

Before using these recipes, refer to How to Use Our Recipes, p. 3, and Pots and Pans, p. 692. Always use standard measuring cups and measuring spoons; measure level.

GAME

Prepare Game Birds This Way

Let huntsman or meatman pluck, draw, and clean game birds. Refrigerate 2 or 3 days before cooking. If pheasant, tuck celery stalk inside bird before refrigerating it.

ROAST PHEASANT

Use a young pheasant—one whose spur at back of foot is pliable and has rounded end.

Start heating oven to 450°F. Heat shallow open pan in oven. Finish cleaning bird; with string, tie legs and wings close to body. Sprinkle with salt, pepper. Completely cover breast with slices of fat salt pork or bacon; tie in place with string. Place bird on its side in heated pan; pour ¼ cup salad oil over all.

Roast bird, uncovered, 15 min., basting often. Turn onto other side; roast 15 min. Then turn bird onto its back and roast 10 to 15 min., basting

often. (Bird is done when juice, which runs out when bird is lifted and held tail down is clear and without pink tinge.)

Remove bird from pan; cut away string. Pour off fat from pan. Add about ¾ cup water to pan; simmer, stirring to loosen brown bits that cling to pan, until liquid is reduced to about ½ cup. Season with salt, pepper; quickly stir in 1 tablesp. butter or margarine; remove gravy from heat as soon as butter is melted.

Slice meat from pheasant; serve on toast spread with Rouennaise, p. 204. Top with gravy.

Especially nice with cabbage, braised celery, wild rice, or tart jelly. One pheasant makes 2 to 4 servings.

Note: If you roast several birds in one pan, increase oven heat to 500°F. and increase water for gravy accordingly.

BRAISED PHEASANT WITH CABBAGE

¼-lb. piece fat salt pork	sprig of thyme, tied
1 pheasant (an older	together)
one)	2 cups hot water
2 slices fat salt pork	1 medium head cab-
1 teasp. salt	bage (savoy pre-
⅛ teasp. pepper	ferred)
1 onion, studded with	1 pared carrot
cloves	1 Knockwurst or
1 faggot (2 stalks	frank
celery, 4 sprigs	1 cup hot water
parsley, ½ bay leaf,	

Simmer salt-pork piece in water to cover a few min. Finish cleaning bird; cut into quarters. In Dutch oven, brown salt-pork slices; set aside. In Dutch oven, brown quartered bird. Then add salt, pepper, onion, faggot, simmered salt-pork piece, browned salt-pork slices, 2 cups hot water. Simmer, covered, 40 min.

Meanwhile, separate cabbage leaves; put into kettle with water to cover; simmer 5 min. Drain; dip into cold water; drain. To pheasant, add cabbage, carrot, Knockwurst, 1 cup hot water. Cook, covered, 45 to 60 min., or until meat is tender and leg separates from body.

To serve: Remove cabbage; drain thoroughly; place on heated platter with pheasant quarters. Remove and slice salt-pork piece. Surround pheasant with carrot, onion, Knockwurst, salt pork. Makes 4 servings.

Braised Partridge with Cabbage: Substitute 2 whole partridge for pheasant. To serve: Split each partridge in half, allowing ½ bird per serving.

SALMI OF PHEASANT

1 pheasant (an older one)	1 cup canned tomatoes
2 tablesp. salad oil	½ teasp. salt
1 chopped medium onion	3 whole black peppers
1 chopped shallot (optional)	1 faggot (2 stalks celery, 4 sprigs parsley, ½ bay leaf, sprig thyme, tied together)
1 mashed clove garlic	
4½ teasp. flour	12 mushrooms
⅔ cup red or white wine	3 tablesp. butter or margarine

Day before: Roast cleaned pheasant as on p. 200; refrigerate.

Next day: Cut breasts and legs from roast pheasant; cut up carcass; set aside. For sauce, in saucepan, heat salad oil; add onion; cook until golden. Add shallot, garlic, flour; cook 2 min. Stir in wine; cook, stirring, until thickened. Add tomatoes, salt, peppers, faggot, cut-up carcass, pheasant legs. Simmer, covered, 1 hr.

Remove legs; remove and discard skin; slice meat from bone. Slice breast meat. Place leg and breast meat in skillet; strain sauce over them; heat over low heat until meat is hot. Meanwhile, sauté mushrooms in butter 5 min.

To serve: Top pheasant and sauce with mushrooms. If desired, garnish with toast spread with Rouennaise, p. 204. Makes 2 or 3 servings.

Salmi of Partridge: Substitute 2 cleaned partridge for pheasant. To roast, see Roast Partridge, below.

ROAST PARTRIDGE

Use young partridge—one with breastbone that breaks easily when bent and leg bone that is plump and round near foot.

Finish cleaning bird; with string, tie legs and wings close to body. Roast, uncovered, as in Roast Pheasant, p. 200.

Serve on toast spread with Rouennaise, p. 204. Accompany with sauerkraut or cabbage. One small partridge makes 1 serving; split large bird to make 2 servings.

ROAST GUINEA HEN

Finish cleaning small young guinea hen; with string, tie legs and wings close to body. Roast, uncovered, as in Roast Pheasant, p. 200. One hen makes 2 to 4 servings.

Note: If bird is old, cook as in Chicken Fricassee, p. 150, and serve with sauerkraut.

ROAST WILD DUCK

Start heating oven to 475°F. Heat shallow open pan in oven. Finish cleaning wild duck; with string, tie legs and wings close to body. Place in heated pan. For very rare bird, roast, uncovered, 12 to 15 min.; for medium rare, 20 to 25 min. Remove from oven; let stand at least 5 min.

Make Sauce au Sang, p. 204, up to adding juices from roast duck. Sauté 3 bread slices in butter or margarine till golden on both sides.

Cut breast meat from duck and slice if desired. Also remove legs; if too rare, broil a short time; slice off meat. Now add juices from duck to Sauce au Sang.

Arrange breast and leg meat on 2 sautéed bread slices; pour on sauce; garnish with third bread slice, cut into triangles.

Serve with turnips, peas, or wild rice and cranberry or currant jelly. Makes 2 servings.

WILD DUCK, TEXAS STYLE

1 cup diced celery	2 2- to 2½-lb. wild ducks
1 cup minced onions	6 bacon slices
1 cup seeded raisins	1 cup catchup
1 cup coarsely chopped pecans	½ cup chili sauce
1 qt. fresh bread crumbs (4 cups)	¼ cup Worcestershire
1½ teasp. salt	Water cress or parsley
2 eggs, beaten	Thin orange slices
½ cup scalded milk	Currant jelly

Start heating oven to 500°F. Combine celery, onions, raisins, pecans, crumbs, salt; add eggs; mix well. Stir in milk. Finish cleaning ducks; weigh; compute roasting time, allowing 60 min. per lb. (use weight of heavier bird). Stuff neck and body cavities with bread mixture; close opening as in Roast Chicken, 5, p. 144. Place 3 bacon slices across breast of each duck. Place ducks on wire rack in shallow open pan.

Roast ducks, uncovered, at 500°F. 15 min.; then reduce heat to 350°F. for remaining time. About ½ hr. before removing ducks from oven, mix catchup, chili sauce, Worcestershire; pour over ducks. Complete roasting.

To serve: Arrange ducks on heated platter. Garnish with water cress and orange slices topped with jelly. For spicy sauce, use sauce in pan, skimming off fat; if necessary, thicken as on p. 7; pass. Makes 4 to 6 servings.

ROAST QUAIL

Start heating oven to 450°F. Heat shallow open pan in oven. Finish cleaning quail; wrap in grape leaves if available. Cover with slices of fat salt pork; tie in place with string. Place quail, with breast side up, in heated pan; spread with a little butter or margarine. Roast, uncovered, basting often, 15 to 20 min., depending on degree of rareness desired. When quail is roasted, remove from pan; remove leaves; place under broiler a few min. to brown.

Meanwhile, add about ½ cup water to pan; simmer, stirring to loosen all browned bits that cling to pan. If desired, add 1 tablesp. dry sherry, ¼ cup seedless grapes. Taste; add salt if needed.

Serve bird on toast spread with Rouennaise, p. 204. Top with some of gravy; pass rest. Serve with potato chips, cranberry or currant jelly, or Bread Sauce, p. 203. Allow 1 bird per serving.

BROILED QUAIL

Preheat broiler, with broiler pan in place, 10 min., or as manufacturer directs. Finish cleaning quail; split. Sprinkle with salt; spread with soft butter or margarine. Place, with skin sides up, on heated broiler pan. Broil 5 min. Turn; broil 6 to 7 min. Remove to heated platter. Make Quick Cream Sauce for Game, p. 203.

Serve birds on toast spread with Rouennaise, p. 204; top with sauce. Allow 1 bird per serving.

ROAST WOODCOCK

Start heating oven to 475°F. Heat shallow open pan in oven. Finish cleaning bird; wrap in slices of fat salt pork; tie in place with string. Spread with a little butter or margarine. Place in heated pan. Roast, uncovered, 8 to 15 min., depending on rareness desired. Remove bird; keep warm.

Add about ½ cup water to pan; simmer till liquid is reduced to about half. Add 1 tablesp. butter or margarine; heat until just melted. (For de luxe taste, add a few dry juniper berries—you can buy them at a drugstore.) Taste gravy; add salt if needed.

Serve bird on toast, with gravy. Allow 1 bird per serving.

Roast Grouse: Roast cleaned grouse as above, allowing 10 to 20 min., depending on rareness desired. Make gravy as above. Serve with Bread Sauce, p. 203, dried bread crumbs sautéed in butter or margarine, gravy, and currant jelly. Allow 1 bird per serving.

ROAST VENISON

Cover 5- to 7-lb. leg of venison with Cooked Marinade, p. 203; then refrigerate at least 24 hr., or longer if convenient.

To roast: Start heating oven to 450°F. Heat shallow open pan in oven. Remove venison from marinade; remove skin and tough sinews. Sprinkle venison with salt; cover with slices of fat salt pork. Place in heated pan; add enough salad oil to cover bottom of pan. Roast, uncovered, basting with salad oil, allowing about 15 min. per lb. for medium-rare meat. Or roast 45 to 60 min. for very rare meat.

Serve with Quick Poivrade Sauce, p. 204, or Quick Cream Sauce for Game, p. 203, wild rice, and currant jelly. Makes 6 to 8 servings.

GRENADIN OF VENISON

Cut 1½″-thick slices from loin of venison. (They will look like *filet mignon.*) Cover with Raw Marinade, p. 203; store in refrigerator 2 days or longer.

To cook: Remove venison from marinade; drain well; dry thoroughly with paper towels. Strain marinade; reserve. Cover bottom of skillet with salad oil; heat till very hot. Cook slices of venison 8 to 10 min. on each side. (If you have several slices, use 2 skillets, to insure browned, sautéed surface.)

Serve with Quick Poivrade Sauce, p. 204, or Quick Cream Sauce for Game, below.

CIVET OF VENISON

3 lb. venison shoulder, neck, or other less tender part	(quartered if large)
Raw Marinade, below	2 tablesp. flour
½ cup salad oil	1 mashed clove garlic
1 cup diced fat salt pork	⅔ cup red wine
12 to 15 small onions	1 faggot (2 stalks celery, 4 sprigs parsley, ½ bay leaf, sprig thyme, tied together)
2 sliced, pared carrots	
2 tablesp. brown sugar	
½ lb. mushrooms	Snipped parsley

Remove skin, tough sinews, and bones from meat; cut into pieces as for stew. Cover with Raw Marinade; refrigerate 24 hr. or longer.

To cook: Remove meat from marinade; strain marinade; reserve. Dry meat with paper towels. In hot oil in skillet, brown salt pork; set pork aside. To skillet, add onions; when onions are partially brown, add carrots; sprinkle with brown sugar; cook until vegetables are brown; set aside.

Sauté mushrooms in same skillet until brown all over; set aside. Then brown meat (don't crowd skillet); remove to large saucepan. Sprinkle meat with flour; cook until flour browns. Add garlic, wine, faggot, reserved marinade, and just enough water to cover meat; simmer 1 hr., or until quite tender. Add salt pork, onions, carrots, mushrooms; cook 40 min. Remove faggot; taste stew; season to taste. Serve sprinkled with parsley. Makes 8 servings.

RAW MARINADE

2 thinly sliced medium onions	1 teasp. salt
1 thinly sliced, pared carrot	¼ teasp. dried thyme
2 minced shallots (optional)	2 bay leaves
2 stalks celery	12 whole black peppers
1 clove garlic	2 whole cloves
	2 cups red or white wine
	½ cup salad oil

Mix all ingredients; pour over venison or any furred game as recipe directs. Refrigerate 24 hr. or longer before cooking. Makes enough to cover 2 to 3 lb. meat.

COOKED MARINADE

1 qt. water	1 teasp. dried thyme
1½ cups vinegar	4 sprigs parsley
2 chopped onions	12 whole black peppers
1 diced, pared carrot	1 tablesp. salt
1 clove garlic	

Put all ingredients in saucepan; bring to boil; simmer, covered, 1 hr. Cool. Pour over venison or any furred game as recipe directs. Refrigerate 24 hr. or longer before cooking. Makes enough to cover 5- to 7-lb. venison roast.

GAME SAUCES

QUICK SAUCE FOR FURRED GAME

2 teasp. minced onion or shallots	⅔ cup red wine
2 tablesp. butter or margarine	1⅓ cups strained Raw Marinade, above
2 tablesp. flour	2 teasp. currant jelly
	Salt

After removing cooked venison or other furred game from pan, pour off fat. Stir in onion, butter, flour; cook about 2 min. Add wine; mix well. Slowly stir in marinade; cook, stirring constantly, until thickened. Add jelly. Taste; add salt if needed. Pour over venison—chops, *grenadin,* or sliced roast. Makes 1½ cups.

QUICK CREAM SAUCE FOR GAME

2 teasp. minced onion or shallots	Marinade, above; or 1 teasp. lemon juice
2 tablesp. butter or margarine	1½ cups heavy cream
2 teasp. flour	2 teasp. currant jelly
½ cup strained Raw	Salt

After removing roast venison or other furred game from pan, pour off fat. Stir in onion, butter, flour; cook about 2 min. Add marinade if available. Slowly add cream; cook, stirring, until blended and thickened. (Now add lemon juice if used instead of marinade.) Add jelly. Taste; add salt if needed. Pour over venison. Makes 1¾ cups.

BREAD SAUCE

1 medium onion	1 cup fresh bread crumbs
2 whole cloves	
2 cups milk	1 tablesp. butter or margarine
Dash cayenne pepper	
¼ teasp. salt	

Stud onion with cloves. Place in saucepan with milk, cayenne, salt. Bring to boil; simmer about 5 min.; strain. Add bread crumbs; stir in butter. Use with grouse or other game birds. Makes 2 cups.

SAUCE AU SANG

¼ cup red wine	**1 tablesp. butter or margarine**
5 whole black peppers	**½ teasp. flour**
1 small bay leaf	**Juices collected when roast duck is done**
¼ teasp. dried thyme	**Salt**
1 minced medium onion; or 2 minced shallots	**Pepper**

In saucepan over low heat, cook wine, peppers, bay leaf, thyme, and onion until reduced to 2 tablesp. Blend butter with flour; stir into wine mixture until melted and mixed; strain through fine sieve. Briskly stir all juices from carved duck into sauce. (Do not boil or sauce will curdle.) Taste; add salt and pepper if needed. Pour over duck. Makes enough for 1 duck.

ROUENNAISE

2 tablesp. diced fat salt pork	**1 teasp. salt**
1 cup chicken or duck livers	**⅛ teasp. pepper**
Pinch dried thyme	**1 to 2 tablesp. sherry, cooking sherry, or brandy**
1 bay leaf	

Fry salt pork in skillet until very crisp. Add livers, thyme, bay leaf, salt, pepper. Cook over high heat 3 to 4 min.; stir in sherry. Place in wooden bowl; pound with mallet until soft. Rub through sieve to make paste. To use, spread on toast, served with game. Makes about ½ cup.

QUICK POIVRADE SAUCE FOR VENISON

2 tablesp. fat and pan drippings	**½ cup strained Raw Marinade, p. 203**
1 teasp. minced onion or shallot	**2 cups red wine**
1 tablesp. flour	**Salt**
3 tablesp. vinegar; or	**Pepper**
	2 tablesp. currant jelly

After removing cooked venison from pan, pour off all fat and drippings. Return 2 tablesp. fat and drippings to pan; add onion or shallot. (If onion is used, brown slightly; if shallot, do not brown.) Add flour; blend well. Add vinegar and wine; cook, stirring, until reduced to half. Taste; add salt and pepper if needed. Stir in currant jelly. Pour over venison—chops, *grenadin,* or sliced roast. Makes 1½ cups.

RABBIT

Domestic ready-to-cook rabbit—fresh or packaged quick-frozen—is becoming increasingly available all year round. Its meat, which is practically all-white, is fine-grained and mild-flavored and can be used in many of the ways chicken is used.

BAKED RABBIT

2 2-lb. ready-to-cook rabbits, cut up	**¼ cup sliced onion**
¼ cup flour	**2 bouillon cubes**
2 teasp. salt	**2 cups boiling water**
⅛ teasp. pepper	**2 tablesp. flour**
¼ cup fat or salad oil	**¼ cup water**

Start heating oven to 350°F. Roll rabbit pieces in ¼ cup flour combined with salt, pepper. In fat in Dutch oven, cook onion until tender. Remove onion; brown rabbit in same fat. Arrange onion over rabbit; add bouillon cubes, boiling water; stir till cubes dissolve. Bake, covered, 1½ hr., or till tender. Thicken gravy with 2 tablesp. flour mixed with ¼ cup water. Season to taste. Makes 5 or 6 servings.

BARBECUED RABBIT

Use 1 3-lb. ready-to-cook rabbit, cut up. Substitute for chicken in Napa Valley Barbecued Chicken, p. 145; bake 1 hr., or until fork-tender. Makes 6 servings.

FRIED RABBIT

Use 1 1½- to 2½-lb. ready-to-cook rabbit, cut up. Prepare as in Skillet-Fried Chicken, p. 139. Makes 3 or 4 servings.

FRICASSEED RABBIT

Use 1 3-lb. ready-to-cook rabbit, cut up. Prepare as in Chicken Fricassee, p. 150; simmer 1 hr. 20 min. (or bake about 2 hr.), or until fork-tender. Thicken gravy if desired; serve as in Chicken Fricassee. Makes 4 servings.

RABBIT SUPREME

2 2-lb. ready-to-cook rabbits, cut up	½ cup milk
3 tablesp. flour	1 cup thinly sliced onions
1 teasp. salt	1 minced clove garlic
Speck pepper	1 teasp. salt
¼ cup fat or salad oil	1 tablesp. flour
1 cup commercial sour cream	2 tablesp. cold water

Start heating oven to 350°F. Roll rabbit pieces in 3 tablesp. flour combined with 1 teasp. salt, pepper. Brown in hot fat in Dutch oven; add sour cream, milk, onions, garlic, 1 teasp. salt. Bake, covered, 1½ hr., or until tender. Arrange on heated platter. Blend 1 tablesp. flour with cold water; stir into sauce; cook until thickened. Pour over rabbit. Makes 6 servings.

HASENPFEFFER

1 2½- to 3-lb. rabbit, cut up	1 tablesp. mixed pickling spices
2 qt. cold water	½ cup vinegar
½ cup salt	1 teasp. salt
1½ qt. boiling water	⅛ teasp. pepper
1 cup minced onions	½ cup flour
2 teasp. salt	¾ cup cold water

Wash and dry cleaned rabbit. Cover with 2 qt. cold water and ½ cup salt for 1 hr. Drain; rinse with cold water. Cover with boiling water. Add onions, 2 teasp. salt, and spices tied in cheesecloth. Cover; bring to boil; simmer 2 hr., or until rabbit is almost tender. Add vinegar; simmer, covered, ½ hr. longer, or until rabbit is tender. Remove spice bag. Add 1 teasp. salt, pepper. Place flour in skillet over low heat and stir until golden brown. Stir in ¾ cup cold water; add to rabbit mixture; cook until thickened. Serve with boiled potatoes. Makes 4 servings.

RABBIT STEW

1 2½- to 3-lb. rabbit, cut up	2 cups diced, pared potatoes
6 small white onions	½ lb. sliced fresh mushrooms
1 bay leaf	½ cup flour
1½ cups diced celery	¾ cup cold water
4½ teasp. salt	1 tablesp. snipped parsley
⅛ teasp. pepper	Dash tabasco
2 qt. boiling water	
2 cups diced, pared carrots	

Wash and dry cleaned rabbit. Place in kettle with onions, bay leaf, celery, salt, pepper, water. Simmer, covered, 2 hr., or until rabbit is nearly tender. Add carrots, potatoes, mushrooms. Simmer, covered, 30 min., or until all is tender. Blend flour with water. Stir into stew. Cook until thickened. Add parsley, tabasco. Makes 6 to 8 servings.

Stuffings

A handsome turkey, chicken, fish, or roast, suitably stuffed, makes any meal a feast. Choose the stuffing that will best do three jobs—complement flavor, preserve shape, make the servings bigger and better.

Before using these recipes, refer to How to Use Our Recipes, p. 3, and Pots and Pans, p. 692. Always use standard measuring cups and measuring spoons; measure level.

What You Should Know about Stuffings

For crumbs, use bread, 2 or 3 days old. If you're starting with sliced bread, stack several slices; cut off crusts; cut bread into strips, then into ½″ squares.

If you're starting with an unsliced loaf, cut it in two; fork out inside of loaf, leaving crust. With fork or finger tips, pick bread pieces apart to make fine and even crumbs.

Allow about 1 cup stuffing per 1 lb. ready-to-cook bird. Any extra stuffing can be baked in greased casserole or loaf pan during last half hour of roasting bird.

Are two stuffings popular at your house? Make both if you're roasting a large bird; use one to stuff neck, other to fill body cavity.

Packaged ready-to-use stuffings are a cinch to use and are excellently seasoned. Just follow directions on package.

Wait to stuff bird until just before roasting it. You may prepare stuffing ingredients the day before, refrigerating such perishables as liquid, celery, etc.

Stuffing bird or combining stuffing ingredients a day ahead is not advised because it is almost impossible to chill adequately a stuffed bird or a large amount of stuffing.

Stuff bird loosely to prevent bird's splitting. During roasting, stuffing absorbs juices and expands.

Partially cooking either the turkey and stuffing together, or each separately, is a risk. The cooking process, once started, should be completed.

Never freeze either cooked or uncooked stuffed poultry.

Freezing prepared stuffing is not recommended. Frozen stuffings lose fluffy texture; seasonings change flavor.

FOR TURKEY OR GOOSE

CRUMBLY BREAD STUFFING

1⅛ cups butter, margarine, or salad oil	¼ cup diced celery
¾ cup minced onions	1½ teasp. poultry seasoning
4½ qt. day-old bread crumbs or ½″ squares (18 cups), lightly packed	½ cup snipped parsley (optional)
	¼ teasp. pepper
	2¼ teasp. salt

In hot butter in deep kettle, sauté onions till tender. Combine rest of ingredients; add to onions; heat well without browning, stirring frequently.

Stuffs neck and body cavity of 10-lb. ready-to-cook turkey.

Giblet: Add coarsely chopped, cooked giblets; see To Cook Giblets, p. 138.

Mushroom: Sauté ½ lb. sliced mushrooms and 6 tablesp. minced green pepper (optional) with onions in butter, covered.

For Small Turkey: To stuff turkey of 4 to 5 lb. ready-to-cook weight, use Buttery Bread or Buttery Celery Stuffing, pp. 208 and 209.

MOIST BREAD STUFFING

1½ cups boiling water	2 tablesp. snipped
½ to ¾ cup butter,	parsley
margarine, or salad	2 tablesp. diced celery
oil	3 qt. day-old bread
½ cup minced onions	crumbs or ½″
¼ teasp. pepper	squares (12 cups),
1 teasp. poultry	lightly packed
seasoning	2 tablesp. dry or pre-
1½ teasp. salt	pared mustard

In large kettle, combine water, butter, onions; simmer 5 min. Add rest of ingredients; mix well.

Stuffs body cavity of 8-lb. ready-to-cook turkey.

CRUMBLY CELERY STUFFING

4 cups finely diced	ing
celery	1 tablesp. salt
2 cups boiling water	1 teasp. pepper
½ cup minced onions	4 qt. day-old bread
½ to ¾ cup butter,	crumbs or ½″
margarine, or salad	squares (16 cups),
oil	lightly packed
2 teasp. poultry season-	

Simmer celery in boiling water, covered, 15 to 20 min., or until tender. Drain, reserving 1 cup liquid. Cook onions in butter over low heat until tender but not brown. In large bowl, combine seasonings, crumbs. Add celery, reserved liquid, onions; mix well with fork.

Stuffs neck and body cavity of 10-lb. ready-to-cook turkey.

Orange: Omit 1 cup celery liquid. To crumb mixture, add 2 cups diced oranges with juice and 2 tablesp. grated orange rind.

Oyster: To crumb mixture, add 1⅓ cups chopped, drained, shucked raw oysters. Use oyster liquid as part of celery liquid.

MUSHROOM-RICE STUFFING

½ cup butter or	leaves
margarine	1 tablesp. salt
2⅔ cups packaged	⅛ teasp. pepper
precooked rice	½ teasp. dried mar-
½ cup chopped onions	joram
1 lb. chopped mush-	⅛ teasp. dried sage
rooms	⅛ teasp. dried thyme
2 cups diced celery	2½ cups water
½ cup snipped celery	⅔ cup chopped pecans

In large saucepan, melt butter; add rest of ingredients except water, pecans; sauté, stirring, until onions are golden. Mix in water. Bring to boil over high heat; simmer 2 min., gently fluffing rice once or twice with fork. Remove from heat; add pecans.

Lightly stuffs body cavity of 6- to 7-lb. ready-to-cook turkey.

SAUSAGE STUFFING

1 lb. pork sausage meat	squares (8 cups),
1 cup diced celery	lightly packed
1 cup minced onions	2 tablesp. snipped
2 qt. day-old bread	parsley
crumbs or ½″	

In skillet over medium heat, cook sausage meat, celery, and onions together about 10 min., or until sausage is cooked. Add crumbs, parsley.

Stuffs body cavity of 8-lb. ready-to-cook turkey.

CORN STUFFING

3 cups diced celery	crumbs or ½″
2 cups boiling water	squares (8 cups),
⅔ cup minced onions	lightly packed
½ to 1 cup butter,	2¼ teasp. salt
margarine, or salad	¾ teasp. pepper
oil	3 12-oz. cans vacuum-
1 teasp. dried sage	packed whole-kernel
2 qt. day-old bread	corn

Cook celery in boiling water, covered, 15 to 20 min., or until tender; drain. Sauté onions in butter until transparent; add, with celery, to rest of ingredients in large bowl.

Stuffs neck and body cavity of 7-lb. ready-to-cook turkey.

CHESTNUT STUFFING

½ lb. chestnuts (1 cup boiled)	1 teasp. dried sage
1 tablesp. butter, margarine, or salad oil	1½ teasp. salt
	⅛ teasp. pepper
½ lb. pork sausage meat	2 cups toasted bread crumbs, lightly packed
¼ cup minced onion	2 tablesp. sherry or cooking sherry (optional)
½ cup hot water	

Wash chestnuts; make long slit on both sides of each shell. Bake at 500°F. 15 min. Shell and skin nuts; then boil in salted water to cover, covered, 20 min. Drain; chop medium fine.

In butter in skillet, sauté sausage meat and onion about 10 min., or until sausage is cooked, onion is tender. Combine hot water, sage, salt, pepper, crumbs, sherry. Then add chestnuts, sausage mixture.

Stuffs neck cavity of 8-lb. ready-to-cook turkey. Fill body cavity with any other desired stuffing.

DOWN-SOUTH STUFFING

½ cup butter or margarine	bread (made without sugar)
¾ cup minced onions	½ lb. fresh-pork-sausage links, cut up
½ cup minced green peppers	¼ teasp. salt
½ cup minced celery	⅛ teasp. pepper
1 chicken-bouillon cube	½ teasp. poultry seasoning
5 cups day-old white-bread crumbs	2 eggs, beaten
5 cups crumbled corn	¾ cup chopped pecans

In hot butter in skillet, sauté onions, green peppers, celery until tender. Dissolve bouillon cube in about ⅔ cup hot water; sprinkle over white- and corn-bread crumbs. Add sautéed vegetables. In same skillet, sauté sausages until browned. To crumb mixture, add salt, pepper, poultry seasoning, eggs, pecans, then sausages and drippings; toss.

Divide one third of stuffing between crop and tail end of 10-lb. ready-to-cook turkey (this helps to plump bird). Place rest of stuffing in 8" x 8" x 2" pan. Refrigerate; then bake, uncovered, with turkey at 325°F. last 45 min.

Tasty note: Baste bird with ¼ cup butter or margarine heated with ¾ cup red wine; use liquid left in pan to make gravy; serve over bird and stuffing.

APPLE-RAISIN STUFFING

3 cups diced, pared, cored cooking apples	squares, lightly packed
1 cup light or dark raisins	⅛ teasp. pepper
1 cup minced onions	¼ cup granulated sugar
1½ teasp. salt	¾ cup melted butter, margarine, or salad oil
7 cups day-old bread crumbs or ½"	

Combine all ingredients; mix well.

Stuffs neck and body cavity of 10-lb. ready-to-cook goose.

SAGE-AND-ONION STUFFING

12 medium onions	¼ to ½ teasp. pepper
1 to 2 tablesp. dried sage	2 qt. day-old bread crumbs or ½" squares (8 cups), lightly packed
1 teasp. poultry seasoning	
2 teasp. salt	

Boil onions till tender-crisp; drain; chop fine. Add rest of ingredients; mix well.

Stuffs neck and body cavity of 10-lb. ready-to-cook goose.

FOR CHICKEN, DUCKLING, OR PHEASANT

BUTTERY BREAD STUFFING

1½ qt. day-old bread crumbs or ½" squares (6 cups), lightly packed	⅛ teasp. pepper
	¾ teasp. salt
½ teasp. poultry seasoning; or ½ teasp. dried thyme, marjoram, or sage	½ cup butter, margarine, or salad oil
	¼ cup minced onion
1 teasp. celery seeds	3 tablesp. snipped parsley

Combine bread crumbs, poultry seasoning, celery seeds, pepper, salt. In large skillet, melt butter. Add onion; simmer until tender but not browned. Add crumb mixture, parsley; heat well without browning, stirring often.

Stuffs neck and body cavity of 4-lb. ready-to-cook bird.

Moist Giblet: Add, with crumb mixture, ½ cup giblet water, milk, or cream and coarsely chopped, cooked giblets, p. 138.

Mushroom: Sauté ¼ lb. sliced mushrooms with onion in butter, covered.

Corn: Increase onion to ½ cup, salt to 1 teasp., pepper to ¼ teasp. Add, with crumb mixture, 1 12-oz. can vacuum-packed whole-kernel corn, drained.

Fruit: Reduce bread crumbs to 3 cups. Add, with crumb mixture, 1 cup cut-up, drained, cooked dried apricots or pitted prunes.

Corn Bread: Substitute corn-bread crumbs for bread crumbs. Bacon fat may replace part of butter; or add 4 diced crisp bacon slices.

BUTTERY CELERY STUFFING

1½ cups finely diced celery	seasoning
⅔ cup boiling water	1 teasp. salt
7 cups day-old bread crumbs or ½″ squares, lightly packed	¼ teasp. pepper
	¼ cup minced onion
	⅓ to ½ cup butter, margarine, or salad oil
½ teasp. poultry	

Simmer celery in boiling water, covered, 15 to 20 min., or until tender. Drain, reserving ⅓ cup liquid. In large bowl, combine bread crumbs with poultry seasoning, salt, pepper.

Slowly cook onion in butter till tender but not brown. Add, with celery and celery liquid, to crumbs.

Stuffs neck and body cavity of 5-lb. ready-to-cook bird.

Oyster: Add, to crumbs, ½ cup chopped, drained, shucked raw oysters. Substitute oyster liquid for celery liquid.

SAVORY RICE STUFFING

¼ cup butter or margarine	1 teasp. salt
¾ cup minced onions	¼ teasp. pepper
1½ cups diced celery	¼ teasp. dried sage
1⅓ cups cooked rice	¼ teasp. dried thyme

In skillet, melt butter. Add onions, celery; sauté till tender—about 3 min. Add rice, rest of ingredients; toss.

Stuffs neck and body cavity of 4-lb. ready-to-cook bird.

Apricot: With rice, add 1 cup snipped dried apricots. Omit sage.

Rice and Olive: Use only 1 cup diced celery, ¼ teasp. salt. With rice, add 1 cup chopped stuffed olives. (Double recipe to stuff dressed 6- to 8-lb. fish.)

TINA'S WILD-RICE STUFFING

¼ cup bacon fat, butter, or margarine	1 cup seedless grapes
	¼ cup sherry or cooking sherry
2 minced medium onions	2 cups cooked wild rice
½ cup minced celery	

In hot bacon fat in skillet, sauté onions until tender; add rest of ingredients.

Stuffs body cavity of 4- to 5-lb. ready-to-cook roasting chicken, or 4 1- to 1½-lb. ready-to-cook broiler-fryers.

WILD-RICE STUFFING

½ cup raw wild rice	oil
Giblets from wild pheasant	¼ lb. pork sausage meat
1 small onion	1 teasp. salt
1 tablesp. butter, margarine, or salad	½ teasp. dried sage

Night before: In double-boiler top, soak rice overnight in cold water to cover.

In morning: Drain rice; cook, covered, over boiling water 10 min. Meanwhile, clean and wash giblets; put, with onion, through food chopper, using medium blade.

In butter in skillet, sauté giblets, onion, and sausage 10 min. Add rice, salt, sage; cook 2 min.

Stuffs body cavity of 1½-lb. ready-to-cook wild pheasant.

BAKED STUFFING BALLS

2 qt. day-old ½″ bread squares (8 cups), firmly packed	½ cup snipped parsley (optional)
	1 cup minced celery
1 teasp. poultry seasoning	½ cup butter or margarine
1½ teasp. salt	½ cup water
½ teasp. pepper	2 beef-bouillon cubes
2 tablesp. minced onion	2 egg whites

Early in day: Toss bread squares with poultry seasoning, salt, pepper, onion, parsley, celery. Heat butter with water and bouillon cubes, stirring; toss well with crumbs. Beat egg whites until just foamy; mix with crumbs. Lightly press handful of mixture into ball; if it doesn't hold its shape, add a little more water.

Shape mixture into balls a little larger than golf-ball size—about ½ cup mixture per ball. Place on greased baking sheet; refrigerate till needed.

About 1 hr. before serving: Bake at 325°F. 1 hr., or till crisp and lightly browned. Nice with hot or cold chicken, turkey, ham, or pork. Makes 8.

FOR FISH

CAPTAIN'S STUFFING

1 cup minced celery	lightly packed
½ cup water	3 tablesp. minced onion
6 tablesp. butter or margarine	1 to 1½ teasp. dried sage
1 qt. day-old bread crumbs or ½" squares (4 cups),	¾ teasp. salt
	½ teasp. pepper

Cook celery, water, and butter until butter is melted; pour over rest of ingredients combined.

Stuffs dressed 3-lb. shad, with backbone removed. Or halve recipe to stuff dressed 3-lb. fish or to fill pairs of 1½- to 2-lb. fillets.

Mushroom: Add ½ lb. chopped mushrooms.

Cucumber: Add ½ cup coarsely chopped cucumber.

RICE-AND-OLIVE STUFFING, see p. 209

MUSHROOM-CRACKER STUFFING

¼ cup butter or margarine	1 tablesp. snipped parsley
¼ cup minced celery	2 cups coarsely crushed crackers
¼ cup minced onion	¼ teasp. poultry seasoning
¼ to ½ lb. sliced mushrooms; or 1 3-oz. can mushrooms, drained	½ teasp. salt (unless crackers are salty)

In hot butter in large skillet, cook celery and onion till golden. Add mushrooms; cook 3 min. Add parsley, rest of ingredients.

Stuffs 4- to 6-lb. dressed salmon or salmon shoulder. Or halve recipe to stuff dressed 2- to 3-lb. fish or to fill pairs of 1½- to 2-lb. fillets.

GARDEN STUFFING

1 small clove garlic	½ cup chopped celery
1 teasp. salt	2 coarsely chopped, peeled tomatoes
⅓ cup minced scallions	3 tablesp. snipped parsley
½ cup chopped green peppers	

With 4-tined fork, mash garlic with salt in bottom of bowl; add rest of ingredients.

Stuffs and tops dressed 6- to 7-lb. fish.

CHEESE STUFFING

½ cup sliced onions	1½ cups fresh bread crumbs
¼ cup butter or margarine	½ cup grated process American cheese
¾ teasp. salt	
Dash pepper	

Sauté onions in butter till tender. Toss with salt, pepper, bread crumbs, cheese.

Use to top 2-lb. cod or haddock fillets or to fill pairs of 1- to 1½-lb. fillets.

Cheese

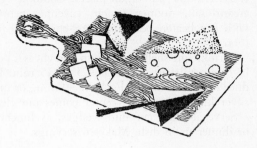

Versatile cheese finds a place in any meal, any course. It's superb for eating as is or for adding flavor to other foods. Because it is so adaptable, and because there's a type for every taste, cheese is the good cook's stand-by for dishes from soup to dessert.

Many of the cheese recipes that follow are especially suitable for luncheon or supper main dishes. Check the index for other appearances of cheese throughout the book.

Before using these recipes, refer to How to Use Our Recipes, p. 3, and Pots and Pans, p. 692. Always use standard measuring cups and measuring spoons; measure level.

Care after Opening Cheeses

If It's Process Cheese or a Cheese Spread: Open packaged kind with care, so that unused cheese can be carefully rewrapped in original wrapping and refrigerated. If wrapper is not usable again, wrap cheese tightly in double thickness of waxed paper, aluminum foil, saran, etc.

If it's a jar spread, refrigerate, with lid tightly in place, after using.

If it's a loaf process cheese, do not remove all of wrapper. Simply cut off what cheese you need; then cover exposed surface with foil.

If It's Natural Cheese: To store small pieces, wrap tightly in double thickness of waxed paper, aluminum foil, saran, etc.; then refrigerate.

To store large pieces, cover cut surfaces with coating of melted paraffin; then wrap tightly in foil; refrigerate.

To store ends of cheese, grate; then refrigerate in covered jar; use in casseroles, etc.

To store cheese with very strong aroma, like Limburger, etc., use covered container; plan to use within reasonable time after refrigerating.

Mold on natural cheeses is not harmful. Cut or scrape off mold; then use cheese beneath.

If It's Cottage or Cream Cheese (soft cheeses): Refrigerate, tightly covered, and plan to use soon after purchase.

To Freeze Cheese: Research indicates that, in general, cheeses do not freeze satisfactorily. The only cheeses that can be frozen without damaging the texture are perfectly ripened Camembert and liederkranz. These can be frozen several months. Serve promptly after thawing.

Grate with Ease

If cheese is soft, like process cheese, use a coarse grater, which insures long flakes of grated cheese. Many times you can merely slice or dice a soft cheese and add it to sauce.

If cheese is very dry, use a fine grater.

CHEESE AS THE MAIN DISH

SUPERB SWISS-CHEESE PIE
(Quiche Lorraine)

1 9″ unbaked pie shell, well chilled	¾ teasp. salt Pinch nutmeg
1 tablesp. soft butter or margarine	Pinch sugar Pinch cayenne pepper
12 bacon slices*	⅛ teasp. pepper
4 eggs	1 cup grated natural
2 cups heavy cream	Swiss cheese (¼ lb.)

Start heating oven to 425°F. Rub butter over surface of unbaked pie shell. Fry bacon until

211

crisp; crumble into small pieces. Combine eggs, cream, salt, nutmeg, sugar, cayenne, pepper; with egg beater, beat just long enough to mix thoroughly.

Sprinkle pie shell with bacon and cheese; pour in cream mixture. Bake at 425°F. 15 min. Reduce oven heat to 300°F.; bake 40 min., or until silver knife inserted in center comes out clean.

Serve at once, cut into wedges, as luncheon or dinner main dish. Makes 6 servings.

* *If you prefer, save 6 bacon slices as garnish. Fry them until done but not too crisp. Immediately roll up each slice; arrange, with seam side down, in bed of parsley around pie plate.*

Nibbler Lorraine: Substitute 11″ unbaked pie shell, well chilled, for 9″ shell. To serve, cut into about 20 wedges.

SUSAN'S SWISS PIE

1 qt. toasted ½″ bread squares	2 eggs
2 sliced tomatoes	¾ teasp. salt
Salt and pepper	½ teasp. paprika
2 cups grated natural Swiss cheese (½ lb.)	½ teasp. dry mustard
	⅛ teasp. pepper
	1½ cups milk

1. Start heating oven to 350°F. Place bread squares in 9″ pie plate; top with tomato slices; sprinkle with salt, pepper, cheese.
2. With fork, mix eggs with rest of ingredients; pour over cheese. Bake 40 min., or until puffy and brown. Makes 4 servings.

CHEESE-ONION PIE

1½ cups coarse cracker crumbs	1 teasp. salt
¼ teasp. curry powder	¼ teasp. paprika
¼ teasp. salt	Speck cayenne pepper
6 tablesp. melted butter or margarine	½ to 1 teasp. curry powder
1½ cups sliced onions	1 tablesp. cold milk
2 tablesp. butter or margarine	1½ cups grated process sharp American cheese
1¼ cups milk	2 eggs, beaten

Start heating oven to 325°F. Combine cracker crumbs, ¼ teasp. curry, ¼ teasp. salt, melted butter; use to line 9″ pie plate, reserving ¼ cup mixture for top. In double-boiler top over direct heat, sauté onions in 2 tablesp. butter until tender but not brown; arrange in bottom of pie plate.

Using same double boiler, heat 1¼ cups milk over boiling water.

Blend 1 teasp. salt, paprika, cayenne, ½ to 1 teasp. curry, 1 tablesp. cold milk; add, with cheese, to hot milk; stir until cheese is melted. Slowly stir in beaten eggs; pour over onions. Sprinkle top with reserved crumb mixture. Bake 35 to 40 min. Makes 4 servings.

SUSAN'S CHEESE SOUFFLE FOR 6

1½ cups milk; or ¾ cup evaporated milk plus ¾ cup water	¼ cup flour
	1 teasp. salt
	Speck cayenne pepper
6 eggs	½ lb. process sharp American cheese
¼ cup butter or margarine	

1. Start heating oven to 300°F. In saucepan, heat, but do not scald, milk. Separate eggs, putting whites in large bowl, yolks in smaller one.
2. In double boiler, melt butter. Stir in flour, then heated milk, salt, cayenne; cook, stirring, until smooth and thickened. Thinly slice cheese right into sauce. Stir until cheese melts completely and sauce is velvety smooth; remove from heat.
3. With fork, beat egg yolks until well blended. Stir in a little of cheese sauce. Slowly stir this mixture back into rest of cheese sauce.
4. With electric mixer or egg beater, beat egg whites until stiff but not dry. Slowly pour in cheese sauce, folding until no large areas of egg white remain.
5. Pour mixture into *ungreased* 2-qt. casserole till ¼″ from top. (Bake any extra mixture in small *ungreased* casserole.)
6. To form crown, with teaspoon, make shallow path in soufflé mixture about 1″ in from edge of casserole all the way around. Bake, uncovered, 1¼ hr.; *don't open oven while soufflé is baking.*

Serve at once, as is or with Quick Mushroom Sauce, p. 372. Sautéed tomato halves and crisp bacon are nice accompaniments. Makes 6 servings.

CHEESE SOUFFLE FOR 4

1 cup milk; or ½ cup evaporated milk plus ½ cup water	¼ cup flour
	½ teasp. salt
	Speck cayenne pepper
4 eggs	¼ lb. process sharp American cheese
3 tablesp. butter or margarine	

Make as in Susan's Cheese Soufflé for 6, p. 212. Bake in *ungreased* 1½-qt. casserole at 300°F., uncovered, 1¼ hr. Makes 4 servings.

CHEESE SOUFFLE FOR 3

3 tablesp. flour	orated milk
2 tablesp. butter or margarine	1 cup grated process sharp American cheese (¼ lb.)
½ teasp. salt	
1 cup undiluted evap-	3 eggs, separated

Start heating oven to 350°F. In saucepan over low heat, blend flour, butter, salt. Add milk; cook, stirring, until thickened. Stir in cheese. Beat egg yolks; stir in a little of cheese sauce. Slowly stir this mixture back into rest of cheese sauce. Cook over low heat, stirring, 1 min.

Beat egg whites until stiff but not dry; fold into cheese mixture. Turn into buttered 1½-qt. casserole; set in pan of water. Bake, uncovered, 1 hr.

Serve at once. Makes 3 servings.

SUSAN'S CHEESE-AND-RICE SOUFFLE

¼ cup raw regular or processed white rice; or ½ cup packaged precooked rice	¾ cup milk
	½ lb. process sharp American cheese
	4 eggs
2 tablesp. butter or margarine	½ teasp. salt
3 tablesp. flour	Dash cayenne pepper

1. Cook rice as label directs. Start heating oven to 325°F. In double boiler, melt butter; stir in flour, then milk. Cook, stirring, until thickened. Slice cheese right into sauce; cook, stirring occasionally, until thickened.
2. Separate eggs, placing whites in large bowl, yolks in small one. To yolks, add salt and cayenne; beat with fork; slowly add to cheese sauce, stirring constantly. Remove sauce from heat; fold in rice.
3. With electric mixer or egg beater, beat whites until stiff but not dry. Gently fold in cheese-rice mixture. Turn into a 1½-qt. greased casserole. To form crown, with spoon, make shallow path about 1″ in from edge all the way around. Bake, uncovered, 40 min.

Serve at once. Or if dinner is delayed, leave in oven with heat turned down to 250°F. Makes 5 servings.

Vegetable Style: Just before folding in egg whites, add 1 cup chopped, cooked broccoli or cooked green beans.

FOUR CHEESE-SOUFFLE VARIATIONS

Bacon: Into Susan's Cheese Soufflé for 6, p. 212, fold ¾ cup crumbled crisp bacon with egg whites. Into Cheese Soufflé for 4, p. 212, or Cheese Soufflé for 3, above, fold ½ cup bacon.

Ham and Cheese: Into Susan's Cheese Soufflé for 6, p. 212, fold ¾ cup ground, cooked ham with egg whites. Into Cheese Soufflé for 4, p. 212, or Cheese Soufflé for 3, above, fold ½ cup ham.

Garden: For Susan's Cheese Soufflé for 6, p. 212, place in bottom of casserole, before pouring in soufflé, 1½ cups cooked frozen mixed vegetables or any favorite vegetable. For Cheese Soufflé for 4, p. 212, or Cheese Soufflé for 3, above, use 1 cup vegetables.

Swiss Cheese: For Susan's Cheese Soufflé for 6, p. 212, substitute 2½ cups grated natural Swiss cheese (10 oz.) for process American cheese. For Cheese Soufflé for 4, p. 212, or Cheese Soufflé for 3, above, substitute 1½ cups (6 oz.) Swiss cheese.

SURPRISE SOUFFLES

3 tablesp. butter or margarine	1 cup grated process sharp American cheese (¼ lb.)
3 tablesp. flour	
1 teasp. salt	4 medium eggs, separated
¼ teasp. cayenne pepper	
½ teasp. dry mustard	4 whole eggs
¾ cup milk	

Start heating oven to 400°F. In saucepan, melt butter; stir in flour, salt, cayenne, mustard, then milk. Cook over medium heat, stirring constantly, until thickened; remove from heat. Stir in cheese, then 4 unbeaten egg yolks. Beat 4 egg whites until stiff but not dry; fold in cheese mixture.

Half fill 4 greased 1-cup ramekins with soufflé mixture. Break 1 egg into center of each ramekin; cover with rest of mixture. Bake, uncovered, 20 min.

Serve at once. Makes 4 servings.

OLD-TIME WELSH RABBIT

3 tablesp. butter or margarine	¾ teasp. Worcestershire
½ cup flour	3 cups milk
½ teasp. salt	2 cups grated sharp natural American cheese (½ lb.)
⅛ teasp. dry mustard	
Dash cayenne pepper	Crisp crackers or toast

In double boiler, melt butter. Stir in flour, salt, mustard, cayenne, Worcestershire, then milk; cook, stirring, until thickened and smooth. Add cheese; cook, stirring occasionally, until melted.
Serve over crisp crackers. Makes 6 servings.

WELSH RABBIT WITH BEER

¼ teasp. paprika	tershire
½ teasp. dry mustard	1 lb. process sharp American cheese
1 or 2 dashes cayenne pepper	Hot crisp crackers; toast; or toasted, split English muffins
⅔ cup beer or ale, or light or heavy cream	
1½ to 2 teasp. Worces-	

In skillet, mix paprika, mustard, cayenne; stir in beer, Worcestershire. Place over *very low* heat. When beer is hot, slice cheese into it; stir until cheese is melted.
Serve at once over crackers. Top with pickles if desired. Makes 6 servings.

Hearty Style: Set sliced tongue, few sardines, spoonful of kidney beans, or poached egg on crackers before pouring on rabbit.

SWISS FONDUE
(a dish that's fun for all)

2 cups grated natural Swiss cheese (½ lb.)	¼ teasp. salt
	Speck pepper
1½ teasp. flour	Nutmeg
1 clove garlic (optional)	2 tablesp. kirsch or cognac (optional)
¾ cup Chablis or sauterne	French bread, cut into bite-size chunks

Toss cheese with flour. Rub skillet or blazer of chafing dish with garlic; pour in wine; heat over low heat till almost boiling. Add cheese; stir until melted. Add salt, pepper, nutmeg, kirsch. When fondue bubbles, lower heat; serve.
To serve: Let each person spear bread with fork or toothpick, then dunk it into fondue, stirring. (If fondue becomes too thick, add a little heated wine.) Makes 3 or 4 servings as

main dish, 6 to 8 as nibbler, served kitchen, living-room, or dining-room style.

CHEESE DITTY

2 cups grated process American cheese (½ lb.)	1 tablesp. catchup
	¼ teasp. dry mustard
	¼ teasp. salt
1 can undiluted condensed tomato soup	⅛ teasp. pepper
	1 egg, beaten
1 tablesp. minced onion	6 slices toast; or 6 rusks

Melt cheese in double boiler. Meanwhile, heat soup with onion, catchup, mustard, salt, pepper; add to cheese, along with beaten egg. Cook 5 min., stirring constantly.
Serve on crisp toast or rusks. Makes 4 servings.

CHEESE FONDUE

2¼ cups milk	Dash cayenne pepper
2 cups coarse day-old bread crumbs	1 tablesp. bottled thick meat sauce, p. 9
2⅔ cups grated process American cheese (⅔ lb.)	2 tablesp. minced onion
	1 teasp. dry mustard
1 teasp. salt	4 eggs

Start heating oven to 325°F. Scald milk in double boiler; then cool. In large bowl combine rest of ingredients except eggs; add milk; stir well. Separate eggs. Beat yolks until thick and lemon-colored; slowly stir into bread mixture. Beat whites till stiff but not dry; fold into bread mixture. Pour into greased 2-qt. casserole; set in pan filled with warm water to 1″ from top of casserole. Bake, uncovered, 1½ hr., or until delicate brown and firm when touched in center.
Serve at once, as is or with Tomato Sauce, p. 376. Makes 6 servings.

► **For 2:** Halve ingredients; use 1-qt. casserole.

POLENTA WITH TOMATO SAUCE

¾ cup corn meal	onions
2 cups milk or water	1 6-oz. can tomato paste (⅔ cup)
1 egg, unbeaten	
½ cup grated Parmesan cheese	1 No. 2 can tomatoes (2½ cups)
1½ teasp. salt	1 teasp. salt
⅛ teasp. pepper	¼ teasp. pepper
½ cup salad oil	½ cup grated Parmesan cheese
2 cloves garlic	
½ cup finely minced	

Place corn meal in saucepan; gradually stir in milk. Cook over *very low heat,* stirring constantly, until mixture thickens and comes to boil. Boil 3 min., stirring often; remove from heat. Stir in egg; beat well. Add ½ cup cheese, 1½ teasp. salt, ⅛ teasp. pepper, ¼ cup salad oil. Turn into 9" x 5" x 3" loaf pan. Refrigerate overnight, or until firm.

Start heating oven to 400°F. Cut corn-meal mixture into 8 squares; arrange in 10" x 6" x 2" baking dish. In ¼ cup hot salad oil in skillet, sauté garlic 3 min.; remove from heat; discard garlic. Stir in rest of ingredients except ½ cup cheese; pour around squares. Sprinkle with ½ cup cheese. Bake, uncovered, ½ hr.; let stand 5 to 10 min. before serving. A nice luncheon dish. Makes 6 servings.

BAKED CHEESE PUDDING

6 bread slices, cut into 1½" squares	¼ teasp. dry or prepared mustard
½ lb. packaged process-American-cheese slices	2½ cups milk; or 1¼ cups evaporated milk plus 1¼ cups water
3 eggs	Few sliced stuffed olives (optional)
½ teasp. salt	
½ teasp. paprika	

Start heating oven to 325°F. In greased 1½-qt. casserole, arrange alternate layers of bread and cheese, ending with cheese. Beat eggs till frothy; stir in rest of ingredients; pour over cheese. Bake, uncovered, 1 hr. Makes 6 servings.

Note: For attractive topping, arrange last layer of bread squares with points sticking upward. Arrange remaining cheese over all.

▶ **For 2:** Use 2 eggs; halve rest of ingredients. Use 1-qt. casserole. Bake, uncovered, 50 to 60 min., or until golden brown.

Baked Cheese Shrimp: Arrange 2 cups cleaned, cooked or canned shrimp in layers with bread and cheese in greased 2-qt. casserole.

CHEESE STRATA

12 day-old bread slices	plus 1¼ cups water
½ lb. thinly sliced process American cheese	½ teasp. dry or prepared mustard
4 eggs	1 tablesp. minced onion
2½ cups milk; or 1¼ cups evaporated milk	1 teasp. salt
	⅛ teasp. pepper

Remove crusts from bread. Arrange 6 bread slices in greased 12" x 8" x 2" baking dish; cover with cheese slices, then with rest of bread. Beat eggs; blend in milk and rest of ingredients; pour over bread. Let stand 1 hr. Bake, uncovered, at 325°F. about 50 min., or until puffy and brown. *Serve at once.* Makes 6 servings.

Note: Use bread crusts to make Dried Bread Crumbs, p. 9.

▶ **For 2:** Halve ingredients; use 10" x 6" x 2" baking dish.

Cheese Pudding: Omit mustard and onion. Serve with jelly.

Corn-Cheese Bake: Spread 1½ cups cooked frozen or canned vacuum-packed whole-kernel corn on top of cheese. Bake 1 hr.

SUSAN'S CHEESE-AND-ONION CASSEROLE

1 cup minced onions	½ teasp. dry mustard
¼ cup fat or salad oil	7 day-old white-bread slices
2 cups grated process sharp American cheese (½ lb.)	2 tablesp. butter or margarine
½ teasp. salt	2 cups milk
⅛ teasp. pepper	

1. Start heating oven to 350°F. Sauté onions in fat till golden. Add cheese, salt, pepper, mustard; cook, stirring, until cheese is melted; remove from heat.
2. Spread bread slices with butter. In 1½-qt. casserole, alternate layers of bread and cheese. Pour on milk. Bake, uncovered, 1 hr. Makes 4 servings.

CHEESE TOAST WITH BACON

4 to 6 bacon slices	½ teasp. dry mustard
4 slices leftover toast or day-old bread	½ teasp. salt
2 eggs	2 cups grated process American cheese (½ lb.)
½ cup milk or light cream	Paprika

Start heating oven to 400°F. Place bacon slices in shallow pan; heat in oven 2 or 3 min., or until bacon softens enough to separate. Then arrange in shallow pan. Halve bread slices diagonally; arrange in another greased shallow pan. With fork, beat eggs well; stir in milk, mustard, salt, cheese. Pour over bread; sprinkle with paprika.

Bake, uncovered, in oven with bacon 10 min., or until bacon is crisp and toast is puffy and brown. Drain bacon.

Serve cheese toast on hot plates, topped with bacon. Makes 4 servings.

TOMATO CHEESIES

6 slices toast	2¼ cups heated tomato
2 cups grated process	or vegetable juice
sharp American	¼ teasp. onion salt
cheese (½ lb.)	⅛ teasp. pepper

Start heating oven to 375°F. Cover bottom of shallow casserole or baking dish with 3 slices toast; sprinkle with half of cheese. Cover with remaining toast and cheese. Pour on tomato juice combined with onion salt and pepper. Bake, uncovered, 30 min. Makes 3 or 4 servings.

TOASTED CHEESE CASSEROLE FOR 1

1 cup grated process	¼ teasp. dry mustard
American cheese	¼ teasp. paprika
(¼ lb.)	1 egg
½ teasp. salt	½ cup milk

Start heating oven to 375°F. Place cheese in individual casserole (about 1½ cups capacity). Sprinkle with combined salt, mustard, paprika. Break egg over cheese; add milk; mix with fork until blended. Set in pan of hot water. Bake, uncovered, 35 min., or until set.

WONDER CHEESE CUSTARD

2 eggs	½" squares
¾ teasp. salt	¾ lb. diced process
⅛ teasp. pepper	sharp American
¼ teasp. dry mustard	cheese
2 cups milk	2 tablesp. butter or
3 bread slices, cut into	margarine

Start heating oven to 350°F. In greased 1½-qt. casserole, beat eggs, salt, pepper, and mustard with fork until blended; then stir in milk. Add bread, cheese; press down into liquid. Dot with butter. Set casserole in pan of hot water. Bake, uncovered, 1 hr., or until silver knife inserted in center comes out clean. Makes 4 servings.

▶ **For 2:** Use 1¼ cups milk; halve rest of ingredients. Use 1-qt. casserole. Bake 50 min., or until done.

CHEESE AS A GARNISH

From the first to the last of the meal, a little cheese can enhance many everyday dishes.

Cheese Croutons: Cut cheese into small cubes; drop into bowls or cups of soup just before serving.

Cheese Popcorn: Mix equal parts grated cheese and melted butter or margarine; pour over freshly popped corn.

Easy Stuffed Tomatoes: Marinate cheese cubes in French dressing; use to stuff hollowed-out tomatoes; serve on lettuce as salad.

Cheese-Salad Curls: Run vegetable parer down side of ½-lb. piece packaged process cheese. Roll up each thin shaving. Use as garnish for fruit or tossed green salad.

Cheese and Chicken: Add grated cheese to frozen chicken à la king. Or frost each serving of creamed chicken with generous mound of grated cheese.

Cheese Scramble: Just before scrambled eggs are done, sprinkle with grated cheese.

Crunchy Cheese Topping: After tossing fresh bread crumbs with melted butter or margarine, toss with some grated cheese (Parmesan or process American). Use to top main-dish casseroles or scalloped vegetables. Or just sprinkle over hot seasoned vegetables before serving.

Cheese Pickups for Vegetables: Stir a little grated cheese into canned- or home-stewed tomatoes.

Top creamed onions with grated cheese tossed with chopped nuts.

Stir a little grated cheese into creamed potatoes—just enough to give a subtle flavor.

Real-Cheese Apple Pie: Before adjusting top crust, place a few slices of process sharp cheese on top of apples.

CHEESE AS DESSERT

One of the easiest desserts or evening refreshments to serve—and such a favorite with every-

one, especially men—is cheese, with or without crackers, with or without fruit.

Just remember, *cheese is at its best at room temperature,* so remove it from the refrigerator at least 1 hr. ahead (cottage cheese is exception).

FIVE WAYS TO SERVE IT

1. *On tray, arrange 1 or 2 choice cheeses, crackers, and bowl of fruit.* Tuck in green leaves here and there. Set dessert plate and fruit knife before each person.
2. *Or arrange fruit on dessert plates,* with fruit knives if needed. Pass tray of assorted cheeses and crackers.
3. *Or make fruit your centerpiece.* At dessert-time, pass tray of assorted cheeses and cheese spreads.
4. *Or group cheese, crackers, and 1 or 2 kinds of jam or jelly on tray.* Pass at table, or serve in living room.
5. *Or serve cheese, crackers, and one of sippers below:*

    Hot coffee

    Well-chilled juice (cranberry, prune, apricot nectar, orange, pineapple, grapefruit, etc.)

    Sweet wine, such as port, muscatel, etc.; or champagne or sauterne

FOURTEEN SURE-TO-PLEASE COMBINATIONS

1. Blue cheese, spread on thin apple slices that have been dipped into lemon juice. Put together sandwich-fashion. Pass salted nuts or hot crackers
2. Blue or Roquefort cheese, with juicy fresh pears (whole or sectioned)
3. Blue, Roquefort, or cream cheese, with preserved or fresh kumquats
4. Camembert, with tart plums and cracked, roasted walnuts
5. Camembert, with apple rings (dipped into citrus-fruit juice) placed around wedges of cored pears (also dipped into juice) that have been arranged petal-fashion
6. Camembert or chantelle, with crisp red and yellow apples and shredded-wheat wafers
7. Cheese spreads in jars (a choice), with unpared crisp apples cut part-way through into quarters, then arranged with peeled whole oranges (sections separated) and small bunches of grapes
8. Cheese—one, two, or more—with crisp crackers and one of fruit salads, p. 311 (omit salad with main course)
9. Chunks of cheese, apples, and pears (dipped into citrus-fruit juice), strung on toothpicks
10. Cottage cheese or cream cheese fluffed with milk, served in bowl; assorted jellies, crackers, and salted nuts around it
11. Edam in center, with wedges of Roquefort, cream cheese, and some American cheese too. Pass fruits and crackers separately
12. Liederkranz or other soft ripened cheese, with Tokay grapes
13. Roquefort-cheese spread, sandwiched between halves of cored ripe juicy pears
14. Swiss-cheese slices and/or cream cheese, with sectioned oranges and tangerines

CHEESE DICTIONARY

*Varieties so marked are made in U.S.A. and are normally available

NATURAL CHEESES

Kind, origin, shape	Description	Uses
*American Cheddar Circular cake or cylindrical	Surface: Waxed yellow brown Interior: Light cream to orange Close texture. Few, if any, irregular small openings Flavor: Mild when fresh; pronounced, pleasing, when cured or aged	Sandwiches — a favorite filling With pies and cobblers Salads — adds heartiness to tossed salads In salad dressings In dishes such as soufflés, casseroles, etc.
*Bel Paese Circular cake	Surface: Slate gray Interior: Light yellow. Soft to solid consistency Flavor: Mild	Dessert — with fruit or crackers
*Blue (blue-vein cheese) Cylindrical	Made from cows' milk by methods similar to those used around Roquefort, France, in making Roquefort from sheep's milk. Blue veins formed by a blue mold Flavor: Piquant	Dessert — with crackers or fruit Salads — popular in tossed ones Salad dressings Appetizers — as a spread
*Brick Rectangular	Surface: Yellowish brown Interior: White to light cream. Pliable body and somewhat open texture Flavor: Mild to pronounced	Sandwiches — especially for lunch or lunch box With cold cuts — use sliced, to round out meat platters
*Caciocavallo (originally from Italy) Made in a number of unusual shapes, often in pairs	Surface: Light brown and paraffined Interior: Rather hard, dry. Very solid body and texture Flavor: Somewhat salty, smoky	As table cheese when fresh For grating and cooking when fully cured
*Camembert (originally from France) Portion servings	Surface: Thin, whitish crust Interior: Soft, creamy, yellowish. Before serving, soften at room temperature until almost fluid. Eat crust Flavor: Luscious flavor all its own	Dessert or salad — the universal favorite with crackers or such fruits as pears, apples, etc.
*Chantelle (Trade-mark name) Wheel shape	Surface: Red-coated Interior: Cream to light orange. Semihard. Rather open texture Flavor: Mild to pronounced, depending on age	With cold meats As dessert or party refreshment — with crackers or fruit, etc.

*Cottage Bulk or packages	Made from skim milk, coagulated by pure lactic-acid bacteria culture. Some has cream added. White *Flavor:* Pleasing, slightly acid	Salads — adds heartiness to fruit and vegetable ones. Season with chives, pickle relish, diced tomatoes, etc.
*Cream Packages or loaf	Made from a mixture of cream and milk with minimum fat content of 33 per cent. Comes with chives, relish, pimento, and pineapple added. White. Smooth *Flavor:* Delicate, slightly acid	Sandwiches Salads — adds heartiness to fruit and vegetable ones Salad dressings Dessert — with crackers and jelly
*Edam (originally from Holland) Round ball	*Surface:* Red-coated *Interior:* Body and texture usually somewhat grainy *Flavor:* Mild. Slightly salty when fresh, pronounced when cured	Dessert — popular in wedges, with fruit or salad Appetizer or nibbler. To serve, cut off top; hollow out center; dice; refill. Or let each person scoop out his own
*Gorgonzola Cylindrical	Blue-mold cheese made from cows' milk *Surface:* Clay color *Interior:* Blue streaks produced by mold spores *Flavor:* Rich, piquant, when fully cured	Salads and salad dressings — add cheese crumbled Dessert — with fruit, salad, or crackers
*Gouda (originally from Holland) Ellipsoid	Made from partly skimmed milk *Surface:* Usually red *Interior:* If imported, solid; often contains small round holes. If domestic (baby Gouda), softer, closer body *Flavor:* Often slightly acid	Same as Edam
*Liederkranz (Trade-mark name) Rectangular packages	*Surface:* Russet *Interior:* Creamy, yellow, soft *Flavor and odor:* Robust	Appetizer — on crackers, toast, etc. With salad, crackers Dessert — with crackers, fruit
*Limburger (originally from Belgium) Cubical; rectangular; in jars	*Surface:* Grayish brown *Interior and flavor:* When fresh, white, odorless, and tasteless. As curing progresses, odor, flavor, and color develop	Sandwiches — especially good with rye, pumpernickel, or other dark breads; or on crackers Nice appetizer
*Mozzarella (originally from Italy) Irregularly spherical in shape	Made from cows' milk. Semisoft. Light cream-colored *Flavor:* Mild	Especially enjoyed in main dishes such as eggplant or veal *parmigiano*, pizza, etc., because of elastic quality of melted cheese *(cont'd.)*

CHEESE DICTIONARY — (continued)

Varieties so marked are made in U.S.A. and are normally available

NATURAL CHEESES

Kind, origin, shape	Description	Uses
*Munster (originally from Germany) Cylindrical	Surface: Yellowish tan Interior: White when fresh. Turns light cream when fully cured Flavor: Mild to pronounced	Sandwiches — good with rye or pumpernickel bread Appetizers or nibblers — nice with scallions, carrot or cucumber sticks, radishes, etc.
*Mysost (Gjetost or primost) Cubical; rectangular	Made from whey. White to brown Flavor and odor: Sweet flavor, distinct odor	Serve thin slices on bread or crackers, at lunch, supper, etc.
*Neufchâtel (originally from France) 2- or 3-lb. loaves	A cream-cheese-type product with lower fat content than cream cheese — 20 per cent minimum. White. Soft Flavor: Mild	Sandwiches Salads Nibblers or light refreshments — good on crackers
Oka (Port du Salut) (made in Canada) Circular cakes, 1 and 5 lb.	Made from cows' milk Surface: Russet Interior: Creamy yellow. Semisoft Flavor: Robust	Dessert — an excellent choice. Especially good with port wine
*Parmesan (Reggiano) Cylindrical	Surface: Black or very dark green Interior: Light yellow, with green tinge. Very hard Flavor: Mild unless cheese is old	Grated — serve with Italian spaghetti; on soups such as onion and minestrone, in all kinds of cookery
*Provolone (originally from Italy) Pear, ball, or sausage shape, tied with rope	Includes such styles as Provolette, Provolone, Provoloni, Salami, etc.	Dessert or nibbler — with crackers
*Ricotta (originally from Italy)	Made from whey, with whole or skim milk added. Soft texture Flavor: Mild	Popularly used in ravioli, lasagna, etc.

Kind	Description	Uses
Roquefort (made in France) Cylinders, 4½ to 6 lb.	Made from sheeps' milk *Surface:* Yellowish-brown rind *Interior:* White, with blue-green mold. Semisoft *Flavor:* Spicy	Dessert — superb with pears or other fruit, crackers, nuts, etc. Salad dressings — crumble into French dressing; or blend with mayonnaise Appetizers, nibblers — blend with cream or cream cheese to make spread, filling for stuffed celery, etc.
*****Swiss — Domestic** (originally from Switzerland) Wheels or blocks	*Surface:* Grayish brown *Interior:* White or slightly glossy cream color. Round, shiny holes throughout *Flavor:* Mild, sweetish to sharp	Sandwiches Sliced — with cold meats Salads — adds heartiness to fruit or vegetable ones In dishes such as Swiss-cheese pies, fondue, etc.

Note: Natural cheeses such as Cheddar, Swiss, Brick — usually pasteurized — may now be purchased in factory-wrapped packages in a variety of sizes.

The flavor of all natural cheeses, except cream and cottage cheeses, is enhanced if the cheese stands at room temperature a while before serving.

PROCESS CHEESES

Kind	Description	Uses
*****Packaged Process Cheese** (¼- to 5-lb. packages)	Made by mixing 2 or more "wheels" of same variety of cheese, or of 2 or more varieties (except cream or Neufchâtel cheese), into a homogeneous mass, with aid of heat and with (or without) water, salt, harmless coloring, and emulsifying agent. Must be heated to pasteurizing temperature during manufacturing, and labeled "process cheese" *Flavors:* American, white American, pimento, Swiss, brick, Limburger, sharp, etc.	Cookery — because it melts easily, it's excellent for all cheese cookery Sandwiches — process cheeses slice well
*****Packaged Process-Cheese Slices** (8-oz. packages)	The same cheese as packaged process cheese, but sold in sliced form. Packaged for easy separation *Flavors:* American (mild and sharp), Swiss, etc.	Sandwiches Any dish calling for process cheese

(cont'd.)

CHEESE DICTIONARY — (continued)

Varieties so marked are made in U.S.A. and are normally available

PROCESS CHEESES

Kind	Description	Uses
*Process-Cheese Spreads Jars and packages	These flavored process-cheese spreads and blends have a soft spreading consistency *Flavors:* pineapple, pimento, blue, relish, olive-pimento, Swiss, American, sharp, Limburger, smoked, cheese and bacon, etc.	Sandwiches Salads Nibblers, etc.
*Process-Cheese Foods (or cheese-food compounds) Packages	*Flavor:* Deliciously mild to sharp process-cheese foods are made of American cheese with milk solids added. Pimento is sometimes added	Sauces Sandwich spreads — they melt smoothly and evenly
*Process Grated Cheese In canisters or glass jars	Two types: American and Italian	American — for au gratin dishes, soups, etc. Italian — for sprinkling on dishes
*Process Smoked Cheese	A process-cheese food that is hickory-smoked or has smoke-flavored solids added	Appetizer or nibbler — delicious served thinly sliced or cubed
*Triple-Use Cheese Spread or Sauce In jars or glasses	A pasteurized process-cheese spread. Can be spread, spooned, or heated	Sauce — delicious on vegetables, meats, etc. Spread — tasty on bread, crackers, etc.

Eggs

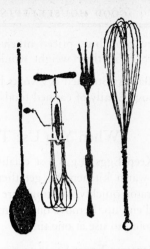

Eggs can be served at any meal (not just breakfast), any day. The wise homemaker knows that smart egg buying and cooking pay off in good eating at comparatively small cost.

Before using these recipes, refer to How to Use Our Recipes, p. 3, and Pots and Pans, p. 692. Always use standard measuring cups and measuring spoons; measure level.

WHAT YOU SHOULD KNOW ABOUT EGGS

When You Buy Them

Be a Choosy Buyer: If possible, buy from a dealer who keeps eggs in refrigerated display cases. Heat lowers egg quality rapidly. For example, eggs left 4 days in a warm store or kitchen (70° to 80°F.) lose as much freshness as those kept several weeks in a refrigerator.

Buy Only Graded, Cartoned, Refrigerated Eggs: The carton should carry a label with a trusted brand name or trade-mark or the letters "U.S." Such eggs have been graded for quality and size. If they have been properly stored, their label is a reliable buying guide.

Check Shell Color: Shell color does not indicate food value or quality of contents, yet it influences egg prices in some localities. There is absolutely no reason for paying a higher price for a particular shell color. Often you can save money by buying brown eggs where white ones are in greater demand, and vice versa.

Consider Egg Quality: Cartoned eggs are graded in 4 ways, according to freshness.

Grade AA or Grade A eggs are top quality, with a large amount of firm white and a well-rounded, high-standing yolk. While good for all uses, their high quality and freshness are most appreciated for poaching, frying, or cooking in the shell.

Grade B and Grade C eggs have thinner whites and somewhat flatter yolks, which may break easily. But many families find it pays to buy these lower-grade, less expensive eggs for making omelets and salad dressings, scrambling, thickening sauces, baking, and combining with such other foods as tomatoes, cheese, onions, etc. They offer the same food value as top-grade eggs.

Check Egg Size: Graded, cartoned eggs are also sorted for size, based on their weight per dozen. These sizes fall into the 6 weight classes below, although Jumbos and Peewees are not too often available.

One Dozen Eggs Must Weigh at Least

Jumbo	30 oz., or 1 lb. 14 oz.
Extra-Large	27 oz., or 1 lb. 11 oz.
Large	24 oz., or 1 lb. 8 oz.
Medium	21 oz., or 1 lb. 5 oz.
Small	18 oz., or 1 lb. 2 oz.
Peewee	15 oz.

In summer and early fall, when medium and small eggs are plentiful, they are likely to be a very good buy, priced much lower than the difference in their weight would imply.

For Babies: Strained egg yolks have now joined the huge family of canned foods for babies.

When You Use Them

To Keep Eggs: Eggs lose quality rapidly if left in a warm kitchen. So get them into your refrigerator quickly, making sure each rests with broad end up. Remove only as many eggs as you are going to use at one time.

To Separate Eggs: Separate eggs as soon as you remove them from refrigerator unless otherwise directed. (Cold yolks are less likely to break.) Break shell with sharp tap at center—with knife blade or on edge of bowl. Press thumb tips into crack; pull shell apart, retaining yolk in one half, letting white pour out of other half. Rock yolk from one half of shell to other, so rest of white pours off.

If Any Yolk Gets into White: Egg whites will not beat up to full volume if there's even a speck of yolk in them. So if a yolk should break when you're separating eggs, you'll find it easy to remove every trace of it with egg shell or paper towel.

When Beating Eggs: Egg whites beat up better if eggs are somewhat warm. So it helps to let whites warm up to room temperature before beating.

When combining beaten eggs with a hot mixture, stir hot mixture very slowly into eggs, otherwise flecks of egg may appear in mixture.

Leftover Yolks or Whites: If yolks are not to be used immediately, refrigerate, covered with cold water. Use within 2 or 3 days, drained. Refrigerate egg whites in covered dish; use within 10 days. See pp. 550 to 551 for Leftover Egg Whites, Leftover Egg Yolks.

For Easier Dishwashing: Before washing egg beater or dish in which eggs or yolks have been beaten or cooked, always rinse with cold water. If you use hot water at the start, egg or yolk will cook on dish and be much more difficult to remove.

TO BRIGHTEN BREAKFAST

FRIED EGGS, SUNNY SIDE UP

1. In skillet over low heat, heat butter or margarine (1 tablesp. per 2 eggs) till hot enough to make drop of water sizzle.
2. Break egg into cup; lower cup close to fat; slide egg into skillet. Repeat, arranging eggs side by side. Lower heat.
3. Gently cook eggs over low heat, spooning hot fat over them, 3 to 4 min., or until of desired firmness. (Instead of basting, you may cover skillet.) Sprinkle with salt (seasoned salt is wonderful!) and pepper.
4 Remove eggs with pancake turner, tilting them against side of skillet to drain well.
   Serve alone or with crisp bacon, sausage, or ham. Season at table if necessary.

Fried Eggs, Over: Fry eggs as in steps 1, 2, and 3 above. Then, with broad spatula, turn carefully so yolks do not break; fry to desired firmness.

Bacon or Ham and Eggs: Pan-fry bacon as on p. 92, or pan-broil ham as on p. 90; keep hot. Drain all but 2 tablesp. fat from skillet; use to fry eggs as above. Serve eggs circled with bacon or ham. Sautéed bananas, canned pineapple slices, or peach or apricot halves go well with them too.

Sauce for Ham and Eggs: Pour off most of ham fat left in skillet. Pour in 2 tablesp. bottled thick meat sauce, p. 9. Add ¼ cup heavy cream, ¼ teasp. paprika. Pour over ham.

SCRAMBLED EGGS

6 eggs	Pinch mixed dried herbs
½ teasp. salt	(optional)
⅛ teasp. pepper	2 tablesp. butter, mar-
6 tablesp. milk or light	garine, or salad oil
cream	

In Skillet:

1. Break eggs, one at a time, into cup; then, before breaking next egg, turn egg into mixing bowl. Add salt, pepper, milk, herbs. With

fork, mix thoroughly if uniform yellow is preferred; mix slightly if streaks of white and yellow are desired.

2. In 9″ skillet, melt butter, tilting skillet so bottom and side are well covered. When hot enough to make drop of water sizzle, pour in egg mixture; reduce heat.
3. Cook slowly, gently lifting from bottom and sides with spoon as mixture sets, so liquid can flow to bottom. *Avoid constant stirring.*
4. Cook until set *but still moist* and slightly underdone. Remember, heat in skillet, after skillet is removed from range, completes cooking. Makes 3 or 4 servings.

In Double Boiler: Melt butter in double boiler; tilt top so butter covers bottom, side; pour in egg mixture. Cook as in steps 3 and 4, above.

To Serve: Serve promptly, as is or:

On toast, spread with deviled ham or anchovy paste
With sausages, ham, or bacon
On toast, topped with chicken à la king or creamed chicken
In Toast Cups, p. 344, or on split, toasted buns or muffins

▶ **For 2:** Make in 8″ skillet, using 4 eggs, ¼ teasp. salt, speck pepper, ⅓ cup milk or light cream, 1½ tablesp. butter or margarine, pinch herbs.

Additions: When eggs are partly cooked, you may add: snipped parsley or chives; minced, cooked ham, liver, or tongue; rinsed, shredded dried beef; sautéed mushrooms; grated cheese; or cream cheese in pieces.

Top Sprinkles: Sprinkle with grated cheese, or snipped chives, parsley, or fresh tarragon.

Chili-Sauce Style: As eggs start to set in step 3 above, quickly stir in 1 tablesp. melted butter or margarine blended with ¼ cup chili sauce and 1 teasp. minced onion.

Spanish: Substitute canned stewed tomatoes for milk.

Quickie Scramble: Stir well 1 can undiluted condensed cream-of-celery soup; add 8 eggs, ¼ teasp. pepper; beat until just blended. Scramble in saucepan as in steps 2, 3, and 4 above.

Susan's Cheesy Scramble: To scrambled-egg mixture, add 1 6-oz. (or 2 3-oz.) pkg. crumbled chive cream cheese; cook as directed.

EASY POACHED EGGS

In Skillet:

1. Butter skillet. Fill with enough water to cover eggs 1″. Bring to boil; then lower heat so water is *just at* simmering point.
2. Break egg into cup; lower cup close to surface of water; quickly slip egg into water. Repeat, placing eggs side by side.
3. Cover skillet; keep water hot, not simmering. Cook eggs until whites are solid, yolks of desired firmness—3 to 5 min.
4. When eggs are done, slip slotted spoon or pancake turner under each; lift out of water; tilt slightly against side of skillet to drain well. Sprinkle with monosodium glutamate.

In Egg Poacher: Today you can buy egg poachers for 1, 2, or more eggs. These do the poaching easily, perfectly; see label's directions.

Serve on:

Hot buttered toast or toasted English muffin	Toasted split corn-bread
Toast, topped with baked-ham slices or deviled ham	Hot asparagus on toast
Hot seasoned spinach	Split hot franks on toast
	Sautéed corned-beef-hash slices

Top with:

Black Butter, p. 377	Cheese Sauce, p. 374
Hot chili sauce	Shrimp Sauce, p. 376
Quick Mushroom Sauce, p. 372	Easy Hollandaise, p. 374

Chili-Poached: For each egg, melt 1 tablesp. butter or margarine in small skillet; add 2 tablesp. chili sauce or catchup. Heat well; then carefully slide in eggs. Cover; cook over low heat until of desired doneness. Serve on toast.

Eggs Benedict: Arrange thin slices of fried ham on buttered, toasted, split English muffins. Top with poached eggs, then with Easy Hollandaise, p. 374.

COUNTRY POACHED EGGS

1 tablesp. butter or margarine	cracker crumbs
¾ to 1 cup light cream	4 slices hot buttered toast
4 eggs	Seasoned salt
2 tablesp. crushed corn or wheat flakes, or	Pepper
	Paprika

In skillet, melt butter; add cream; heat till bubbling. Break eggs, one by one, into cup; slip, side by side, into skillet. Cook over low heat until whites are firm around edges. Sprinkle with corn flakes; cover; cook until eggs are of desired doneness.

Arrange eggs, with cream from skillet, on toast. Sprinkle with seasoned salt, pepper, paprika. Makes 2 to 4 servings.

SOFT-COOKED EGGS

1. Have unshelled eggs at room temperature; place in saucepan; add enough cold water to cover tops by at least 1″. Cover; rapidly bring to boil.
2. Remove from heat, or, if cooking more than 4 eggs, turn heat very low. Let stand, covered, as below:

   Very soft-cooked eggs....2 min.
   Medium soft-cooked eggs....3 to 3½ min.
   Firm soft-cooked eggs....about 4 min.

3. Promptly cool eggs in cold water a few seconds to prevent further cooking and to make them easy to handle.
Serve immediately in shells in egg cups, cracking shells near large end.

Or remove from shells as follows: Hold egg over heated saucer or cup. Hit sharply at center with cutting edge of knife. Insert thumbs in crack. Pull shell apart. With spoon, scoop out egg; sprinkle with salt and pepper; dot with butter or margarine.

HARD-COOKED EGGS

1. Follow directions in steps 1 and 2 of Soft-cooked Eggs, above. Let eggs stand 15 min.
2. Cool promptly and thoroughly in cold water —this makes shells easier to remove and prevents dark surface on yolks.
3. To remove shells, tap entire surface of each egg to crackle it. Roll egg between hands to loosen shell, then peel, starting at large end. Dipping egg into bowl of cold water will help ease off shell.

BAKED (SHIRRED) EGGS

Start heating oven to 325°F. Butter individual shallow baking dishes. Pour 1 tablesp. light cream into each dish if you wish. Carefully break 1 or 2 eggs into each dish. Sprinkle with monosodium glutamate, salt, pepper, paprika; dot with butter or margarine. Bake, uncovered, 12 to 18 min., or until of desired doneness.

Serve from baking dishes, garnished with snipped chives, parsley, or water cress.

To Vary:

1. First circle strip of partially cooked bacon around inside edge of each dish.
2. Or line bottom of each baking dish with buttered crumbs; top with slice of cheese, then with eggs. Top with grated cheese. Proceed as above.
3. Or line each baking dish with ¼ cup minced, cooked ham or corned-beef hash.

FRENCH OMELET

1 to 1½ tablesp. butter or margarine	1 tablesp. cold water
8 eggs	1½ teasp. salt
	Speck pepper

1. In 10″ skillet over low heat, melt butter; tilt skillet back and forth to grease well. With electric mixer or blender, or egg beater, beat eggs with water, salt, and pepper just until blended.
2. Pour eggs into skillet over low heat. As mixture sets at edge, with fork, draw this portion toward center so that uncooked portions flow to bottom. Tilt skillet as necessary to hasten flow of uncooked eggs to bottom. Shake skillet to keep omelet sliding freely. Keep mixture as level as possible. When eggs are set and surface is still moist, increase heat to brown bottom quickly.
3. With spatula, loosen edge of omelet all around. Tilt skillet. With help of spatula, carefully roll up omelet from skillet handle toward opposite side; or fold in half.
4. Hold skillet with one hand, heated platter with other hand, so that bottom edge of skillet

rests on edge of platter. Slowly tip the two together until omelet rolls out onto platter. Makes 4 servings.

▶ **For 2:** Make in 8″ skillet as above, using 1½ tablesp. butter or margarine, 4 eggs, ¼ cup water, ½ teasp. salt, ⅛ teasp. pepper. If using a filling, divide in half.

Individual Omelets: Make each omelet in 8″ skillet, using 1½ tablesp. butter, 2 eggs, 2 tablesp. water, ¼ teasp. salt, pinch pepper.

TEN OMELET FILLINGS

At end of step 2 in French Omelet, p. 226, you may arrange one of fillings below over that half of omelet which is opposite skillet handle. Then proceed with steps 3 and 4.

Or fold one of fillings below into omelet mixture in step 1 before making as directed.

1. 6 crumbled crisp bacon slices
2. ⅓ cup grated sharp cheese
3. ½ cup hot minced, cooked ham or tongue, plus ½ teasp. prepared mustard and 1 teasp. minced onion (omit salt in omelet)
4. 1 cup sautéed mushrooms plus a little sherry
5. ½ recipe Spanish Sauce, p. 376 (use some as filling; place rest on top)
6. Favorite jelly or marmalade (in omelet, omit pepper, reduce salt to 1 teasp., add 1 tablesp. sugar)
7. ¼ teasp. dried thyme, or mixed herbs and 1 teasp. snipped parsley and chives
8. Strawberries or raspberries, sugared and warmed a little
9. Snipped fresh tarragon and parsley or scallions, or sautéed, minced leeks
10. ½ to 1 cup hot chopped, cooked chicken, or lamb, plus pinch curry and onion salt

PUFFY OMELET

6 eggs, separated	⅛ teasp. pepper
6 tablesp. water	2 tablesp. fat or salad
1 teasp. salt	oil

1. Start heating oven to 325°F. In large bowl, with electric mixer or egg beater, beat egg whites with water and salt until whites are stiff and shiny but still moist, and peaks form when beater is raised.

2. With same beater, beat well yolks and pepper until thick and lemon-colored. Lightly but *completely,* fold yolk mixture into whites.
3. Heat fat in 10″ skillet (choose one with handle that will withstand oven heat) until just hot enough to make drop of water sizzle; tip skillet to grease bottom and side. Pour in omelet mixture.
4. Cook over low heat about 5 min., or until omelet is puffy and golden on underside when gently lifted at edge with spatula.
5. Then bake omelet in same skillet about 12 to 15 min., or till surface feels dry and center springs back when pressed lightly with fingertips.
6. Now quickly run spatula around inside of skillet to loosen omelet. With 2 forks, tear gently into pie-shaped wedges. Invert wedges onto serving platter, with brown side up.
7. Or, with spatula, cut down through center of omelet, *only part-way through,* at right angles to handle. Tip handle up and, with aid of spatula, fold upper half over lower half. Hold skillet with left hand so bottom edge rests on heated platter held with right hand. Slowly tip skillet and platter together until omelet rolls out onto platter.

▶ **For 2:** Halve ingredients; use small 8″ skillet.

To Vary: See French Omelet, p. 226.

FOR LUNCH

EGG-SALAD CASSEROLE

6 to 8 coarsely chopped, hard-cooked eggs	½ teasp. salt
	⅔ cup mayonnaise
1½ cups diced celery	1 cup grated process
¼ cup broken pecans	sharp American
1 teasp. minced onion	cheese (¼ lb.)
¼ teasp. pepper	1 cup crushed potato
2 tablesp. snipped parsley	chips

Start heating oven to 375°F. Combine all ingredients except cheese and potato chips, tossing lightly. Turn into 4 individual casseroles; sprinkle with cheese and potato chips. Bake, uncovered, 25 min. Makes 4 servings.

BAKED EGG SANDWICHES DE LUXE

4 hamburger buns	natural American
4 tomato slices,	cheese
¼″ thick	¼ cup light cream
Salt and pepper	3 tablesp. snipped
4 eggs	scallions
⅓ cup grated sharp	

Start heating oven to 375°F. Cut thin slice from top of each bun; with fork, remove most of crumbs, leaving shell about ½″ thick. Arrange shells in shallow baking pan. In bottom of each shell, place tomato slice; sprinkle with salt and pepper; carefully break egg over tomato. Sprinkle with salt and pepper, then with cheese, cream, scallions. Bake, uncovered, 20 to 30 min., or until eggs are of desired doneness. Makes 4 servings.

SWISS EGGS

½ lb. sliced natural	¼ teasp. salt
Swiss cheese	⅛ teasp. pepper
1 cup heavy cream	Dash paprika
4 to 6 eggs	6 slices buttered toast

Start heating oven to 425°F. Line well-buttered, deep, fluted 9″ pie plate with overlapping slices of cheese. Pour in ½ cup heavy cream. Carefully break eggs, one by one, into cup; then slide, side by side, into pie plate. Pour in remaining cream; sprinkle with salt, pepper, and paprika. Bake, uncovered, 10 to 15 min., or until of desired doneness. Serve at once on toast. Wonderful for brunch. Makes 6 servings.

INDIVIDUAL EGG-AND-CHEESE CASSEROLES

3 eggs	1½ cups grated process
½ teasp. salt	American cheese
½ teasp. dry mustard	(6 oz.)
2 tablesp. minced onion	1 cup milk
¼ teasp. paprika	

Start heating oven to 325°F. In bowl, combine eggs, salt, mustard, onion, paprika; with fork, beat well. Add cheese, milk; beat well. Pour into 4 greased custard cups. Set in square cake pan; pour warm water into pan till nearly to top of cups. Bake, uncovered, 30 to 35 min. Makes 4 servings.

MAN-STYLE BAKED EGGS

3 tablesp. butter or	2 tablesp. packaged
margarine	dried bread crumbs
2 thinly sliced medium	4 packaged sharp-
onions	process-American-
Salt and pepper	cheese slices
4 eggs	

Start heating oven to 350°F. In hot butter in skillet, cook onions about 5 min., or until just tender. Arrange in 8″ pie plate; sprinkle lightly with salt, pepper. Carefully break eggs, one by one, into cup; then slide, side by side, on top of onions. Sprinkle with salt and pepper, then with crumbs; top with cheese slices. Bake, uncovered, 10 min., or until eggs are of desired firmness. Makes 4 servings.

THE BEST CREAMED EGGS

6 eggs	1 teasp. Worcestershire
3 tablesp. butter or	(optional)
margarine	2 cups milk
1 tablesp. minced	1 tablesp. snipped
onion (optional)	parsley
3 tablesp. flour	Pinch mixed dried herbs
½ teasp. salt	(optional)
Speck pepper	

1. Hard-cook eggs; then shell.
2. In double-boiler top over direct heat, melt butter. Add onion; simmer till tender; remove from heat. Stir in flour, salt, pepper, Worcestershire.
3. Slowly stir in milk. Cook over boiling water, stirring, until thickened. Add parsley, herbs. Cut eggs into slices, halves, or quarters; fold into sauce; heat.

Serve in one of following ways. Makes 6 breakfast, or 4 luncheon servings.

On toast, topped with crisp bacon
On toast, spread with deviled ham
On hot cooked asparagus or rice
In Toast Cups, p. 344

With Cheese: After adding milk, add ¼ to ½ cup grated process American cheese.

With Ham: On toast or toasted corn bread, arrange thin slices of cooked ham, luncheon meat, crisp bacon, or tongue. Top with creamed eggs.

A la King: Before adding eggs, to sauce, add 1 cup sautéed, sliced fresh mushrooms; ½ cup cooked or canned peas; and 1 pimento, cut into strips.

With Tomatoes: Sauté or broil 1″-thick tomato slices. Arrange 1 or 2 tomato slices on each slice buttered toast; top with creamed eggs.

Creamed Deviled Eggs: Substitute Deviled Eggs, below, for hard-cooked eggs; add ½ cup grated cheese to sauce.

DEVILED EGGS

6 hard-cooked eggs	¼ teasp. prepared mustard
¼ cup melted butter or mayonnaise	1 teasp. minced onion
¼ teasp. salt	¼ teasp. curry powder (optional)
Speck pepper	

1. Cut shelled eggs into lengthwise halves. With teaspoon, carefully remove yolks to small bowl; set whites aside.
2. Mash yolks until very fine and crumbly; blend in butter, rest of ingredients.
3. Generously refill hollows in whites with yolk mixture, slightly rounding each. If desired, garnish with strips of pimento, ripe or green olives, parsley, water cress, or capers. Makes 12 halves.

Serve as hors d'oeuvres; as salad, on salad greens; as garnish for chicken, meat, fish, or vegetable salad; or on cold-meat platter.

Cheese Style: To mashed yolks, add ¼ cup mayonnaise; dash each salt, pepper, and Worcestershire; 1 tablesp. each minced onion and celery; ¼ teasp. prepared mustard; ⅓ cup grated process American cheese. Use to refill whites as above.

Chicken Curry: To mashed yolks, add ¼ cup mayonnaise; ¼ teasp. salt; speck pepper; ½ cup finely chopped, cooked or canned chicken; 1 tablesp. minced celery; and 1 teasp. curry powder. Use to refill whites as above.

Crab or Shrimp: To mashed yolks, add ¼ cup mayonnaise; 1 teasp. fresh, frozen, or canned lemon juice; 1½ teasp. onion salt; 2 crumbled crisp bacon slices; dash tabasco; ½ cup flaked fresh or canned crab meat, or cleaned cooked, or canned shrimp. Use to refill whites as above.

De Luxe: To mashed yolks, add ¼ cup mayonnaise, ¼ teasp. salt, speck pepper, 1 tablesp. grated onion, 1 teasp. minced celery, and 1 tablesp. anchovy paste or 6 small mashed sardines. Use to refill whites as above.

Nordic: To mashed yolks, add ¼ cup melted butter or margarine; ¼ teasp. each salt and prepared mustard; speck pepper; 1 teasp. minced onion; and ⅓ cup flaked tuna, cut-up shrimp, or fresh or canned crab meat. Use to refill whites as above.

Picnic: When stuffing eggs, level off filling. Put eggs together in pairs; wrap in waxed paper; twist ends of paper.

EGG-AND-CHEESE FLAPJACKS

4 eggs	1 teasp. baking powder
1 tablesp. grated onion	1⅓ cups grated process American cheese (⅓ lb.)
⅓ cup all-purpose flour	
½ teasp. salt	
⅛ teasp. pepper	⅓ cup fat or salad oil

Beat eggs; add onion; sift in flour, salt, pepper, baking powder; blend well. Stir in cheese. In skillet, heat some of fat; drop in large spoonfuls of egg mixture and brown on both sides, turning once. Add more fat as needed.

Serve at once, with canned cranberry sauce, marmalade, or sautéed bananas. Makes 8.

PICTURE-FRAME EGGS

With biscuit cutter, remove centers from bread slices. Heat some butter or margarine in skillet; fit in bread slices, one layer deep; cook until brown on underside; turn.

Slip egg into each center. Add more butter if needed to keep bread and eggs from sticking. Cook until eggs are of desired doneness.

Serve topped with pasteurized process cheese spread (cheese sauce).

TO KEYNOTE DINNER

EGGS DIVAN

Deviled Eggs:

6 hard-cooked eggs	½ teasp. salt
1 2¼-oz. can deviled ham	½ teasp. dry mustard
	Dash pepper
¼ teasp. Worcestershire	1 to 2 tablesp. light cream or milk
½ teasp. grated onion	

Broccoli and Sauce:

1 pkg. frozen broccoli	Dash pepper
1½ tablesp. butter or margarine	¾ cup milk
1½ tablesp. flour	½ cup grated process sharp American cheese
⅛ teasp. dry mustard	
½ teasp. salt	

Prepare Deviled Eggs as follows: Cut ¼″ slice from one end of each shelled egg; carefully remove yolk. Mash yolks and end slices; add ham, Worcestershire, onion, salt, mustard, pepper, light cream. Mix well; then use to fill egg whites.

Cook broccoli as label directs. Start heating oven to 400°F. In saucepan, make this sauce: Melt butter; stir in flour, mustard, salt, pepper, then milk; cook until thickened. Add cheese; stir until smooth.

Arrange broccoli in 10″ x 6″ x 2″ baking dish. Stand eggs, with stuffed ends up, between and on broccoli pieces. Pour sauce over all. Bake, uncovered, 40 min., or until bubbly. Makes 4 or 5 servings.

LEE'S SPANISH CHILI WITH EGGS

2 tablesp. fat or salad oil	1¾ teasp. salt
½ cup minced onions	1 teasp. sugar
1 minced clove garlic	1 teasp. chili powder
½ lb. chuck, ground	6 eggs
1 8-oz. can tomato sauce	¼ cup milk

In hot fat in skillet, sauté onions and garlic until tender. Push to one side; then brown beef. Add tomato sauce, ¾ teasp. salt, sugar, chili. Heat, stirring, till boiling.

Make Scrambled Eggs as on p. 224, using eggs, milk, and 1 teasp. salt. Arrange in center of hot platter with hot chili around them. Keep warm. Makes 4 servings.

DINNER CASSEROLE DE LUXE

5 hard-cooked eggs	¼ teasp. salt
1 3-oz. can sliced mushrooms	¼ teasp. onion salt
Milk	½ cup minced celery
3 tablesp. butter or margarine	½ cup packaged poultry stuffing
2 tablesp. flour	½ cup grated process American cheese

Start heating oven to 375°F. Slice shelled eggs into 10″ x 6″ x 2″ baking dish. Drain juice from mushrooms into measuring cup; add milk to make 1 cup.

In 1 tablesp. butter in saucepan, heat mushrooms 2 or 3 min.; scatter over eggs. In saucepan, melt rest of butter; stir in flour, salt, onion salt, then milk mixture. Cook, stirring, until thickened. Add celery; pour over eggs. Scatter stuffing, mixed with cheese, over top. Bake, uncovered, 20 min., or until bubbly. Makes 4 servings.

SPICY HAM AND EGGS

6 eggs	shire
3 tablesp. butter or margarine	1 tablesp. chili sauce
	Dash tabasco
3 tablesp. flour	2 cups diced, cooked ham
1 teasp. dry mustard	½ cup cut-up ripe olives
¾ teasp. salt	
⅛ teasp. pepper	¾ cup diced process sharp American cheese
1½ cups milk	
1 teasp. horse-radish	
1 tablesp. Worcester-	

Hard-cook eggs; shell; slice. Start heating oven to 400°F. In saucepan, melt butter; stir in flour, mustard, salt, pepper, then milk; cook, stirring, until thickened. Stir in horse-radish, Worcestershire, chili sauce, tabasco.

In 1½-qt. casserole, arrange layers of eggs, ham, olives, cheese, and sauce. Bake, uncovered, 25 to 30 min. Makes 4 or 5 servings.

EGGS FOO YOUNG

Sauce:

2 teasp. soy sauce	1 teasp. vinegar
1 teasp. cornstarch	¾ teasp. salt
1 teasp. sugar	½ cup cold water

Eggs:

1 cup drained canned bean sprouts	coarsely cut up (or chopped leftover roast pork)
⅔ cup thinly sliced onions	6 eggs
1 cup cleaned, cooked or canned shrimp,	2 tablesp. bacon fat or salad oil

About 50 min. before supper: Make this sauce: In saucepan, combine soy sauce, cornstarch, sugar, vinegar, salt; stir in water; cook over low heat until thickened.

Combine bean sprouts with onions and shrimp. Then, with fork, beat eggs; add bean-sprout mixture. In hot fat in skillet, fry, as pancake, about ¼ cup mixture at a time, turning once. Fold pancake over; keep hot until all mixture is cooked. Arrange on hot platter; cover with heated sauce.

Nice with canned chow-mein noodles or hot fluffy rice. Makes 3 or 4 servings.

WESTERN CURRIED EGGS

6 eggs	1 teasp. salt
2 tablesp. butter or	¼ teasp. pepper
margarine	2 teasp. grated orange
2 tablesp. minced onion	rind
2 tablesp. flour	¼ cup orange juice
1 teasp. curry powder	3 cups hot fluffy rice
2 cups milk	Parsley

Hard-cook eggs; shell; quarter. In butter in skillet, sauté onion until tender. Stir in flour and curry powder until bubbly. Stir in milk. Cook, stirring, until thickened. Add salt, pepper, orange rind and juice, then eggs. Heat, stirring gently to avoid breaking eggs. Spoon over rice; garnish with parsley.

Serve with choice of Curry Accompaniments, p. 193. Makes 4 to 6 servings.

BENEDICT-STYLE POACHED EGGS

2 tablesp. butter or	-chicken soup
margarine	⅓ cup milk
½ cup minced onions	6 eggs
1 can undiluted con-	3 split English muffins
densed cream-of-	6 thin slices cooked
mushroom or	ham

In butter in skillet, cook onions till tender; blend in soup and milk; heat till boiling; then lower heat. Carefully break eggs, one by one, into saucer; then slide into sauce, side by side. Cook, covered, about 10 min., or until eggs are of desired doneness. Meanwhile, toast and butter muffins.

To serve: Top each muffin half with ham slice, then with egg and some of sauce. Makes 6 servings.

SUSAN'S BAKED EGGS IN CHEESE SAUCE

3 tablesp. butter or	mustard
margarine	1½ cups milk
3 tablesp. flour	1 cup grated process
Speck pepper	American cheese
¾ teasp. salt	(¼ lb.)
1 teasp. prepared	6 eggs

1. Melt butter in double boiler; stir in flour, pepper, salt, mustard, then milk. Cook stirring, until smooth and thickened.
2. Add cheese; stir until melted. Start heating oven to 325°F.
3. Cover bottom of greased 10″ x 6″ x 2″ baking dish with half of sauce. Carefully break eggs, one by one, into cup; then slide into sauce, side by side; cover with rest of sauce.
4. Bake, uncovered, until eggs are set—about 20 to 25 min.

Serve from dish or on toast. Makes 6 servings.

NEW ZEALAND-STYLE EGGS

3 tablesp. butter or	Dash pepper
margarine	2 tablesp. snipped
¼ cup minced onion	parsley
1 cup diced, cold	4 quartered tomatoes
cooked potatoes	Salt
5 eggs	Pepper
½ cup light cream or	Granulated sugar
milk	1 tablesp. butter or
¾ teasp. salt	margarine

In 3 tablesp. butter in skillet, sauté onion and potatoes until golden. With fork, beat eggs with cream, ¾ teasp. salt, dash pepper, parsley, just until blended; pour over potatoes. Cook over medium heat, gently scraping mixture from bottom as it cooks, until set but still moist. Meanwhile, sprinkle tomatoes with salt, pepper, sugar; sauté till tender in 1 tablesp. butter in another skillet.

To serve: Attractively arrange tomatoes around eggs. Makes 4 servings.

DEVILED-EGG CASSEROLE

12 deviled-egg halves	1 No. 2½ can tomatoes
¾ cup raw regular or	(3½ cups)
processed white rice	1 teasp. sugar
⅓ cup butter or	1 teasp. salt
margarine	¼ teasp. garlic salt
½ cup minced onions	¼ teasp. pepper
⅓ cup minced celery	½ cup buttered fresh
3 tablesp. flour	bread crumbs

Prepare Deviled Eggs as in Eggs Divan, p. 229, halving eggs lengthwise, mashing yolks only, and omitting deviled ham. Cook rice as label directs. Start heating oven to 425°F. In butter in saucepan, sauté onions and celery until tender; blend in flour, then tomatoes; cook, stirring, until thickened. Add sugar, salts, pepper. Arrange rice in 12" x 8" x 2" baking dish; pour on sauce; arrange eggs on top. Sprinkle with crumbs. Bake 10 to 15 min., or until bubbly. Makes 4 to 6 servings.

SHORTCAKE OMELET

6 egg whites	2 tablesp. snipped
¾ teasp. salt	parsley
6 egg yolks	2 cups cheese sauce or
¼ teasp. pepper	creamed chicken,
1 tablesp. grated onion	shrimp, or dried beef
3 tablesp. flour	

Start heating oven to 350°F. Grease 2 8" layer pans; set in oven. Beat egg whites with salt until stiff but still glossy. With same beater, beat egg yolks; add pepper, onion, flour, parsley; beat until thick and thoroughly blended; fold into egg whites. Spread mixture in hot pans. Bake 15 min., or until knife inserted in center comes out clean.

To serve: Invert 1 layer onto serving dish; spread with some cheese sauce; invert second layer on top. Serve in wedges with rest of sauce. Makes 6 servings.

RABBIT SCRAMBLE

1 tablesp. butter or	¼ cup undiluted evap-
margarine	orated milk
1 cup grated sharp	½ teasp. salt
natural American	Dash pepper
cheese (¼ lb.)	3 tablesp. catchup
4 eggs	2 teasp. Worcestershire

In double boiler, melt butter; add cheese, stirring occasionally, until melted. With fork, beat eggs, milk, salt, and pepper just until blended; stir into cheese. Cook, lifting mixture from bottom and sides with spoon, until partially scrambled. Add catchup, Worcestershire. Cook until set *but still moist.*

Serve on toast. Makes 3 or 4 servings.

VEGETABLE-CHEESE BAKE

4 eggs, separated	2 cups finely chopped,
1 cup milk	cooked vegetables
3 slices white bread,	1 minced small onion
crusts removed	2 tablesp. minced green
¾ teasp. salt	pepper or snipped
½ teasp. dry mustard	parsley
¼ teasp. monosodium	1 can undiluted con-
glutamate	densed tomato soup
⅛ teasp. pepper	2 tablesp. butter or
1 cup cottage cheese	margarine

Day before: In mixing bowl, beat egg yolks with fork. Add milk and next 5 ingredients. Let bread soften; break up with fork; add cottage cheese, cooked vegetables, onion, green pepper. Refrigerate.

About 1 hr. before serving: Start heating oven to 350°F. Beat egg whites till stiff; fold into cheese mixture. Pour into greased 10" x 6" x 2" or 8" x 8" x 2" baking dish. Bake 45 min., or till firm. Cut into squares. For sauce, heat soup with butter.

Serve with hot sauce. Makes 4 servings.

Rice and Macaroni

Rice and macaroni make important contributions to menu planning. They are delicious, inexpensive, and versatile. They make pleasant substitutes for potatoes or combine with meat, cheese, fish, etc., in hearty main dishes. Since they have a long life on the pantry shelf, they can always be kept available. Besides the dishes in this chapter, there are many other recipes, in other parts of this book, that use rice and macaroni. For these, see Index.

Before using these recipes, refer to How to Use Our Recipes, p. 3, and Pots and Pans, p. 692. Always use standard measuring cups and measuring spoons; measure level.

RICE FAMILY

Here are the varieties of packaged rice you are likely to see on your grocer's shelf:

Regular White Rice, packaged in both long-grain and regular-grain styles, has entire outer coating of bran removed. It may be polished or unpolished. To some white rice, vitamin B and iron have been added.

Long-grain rice is especially nice to serve instead of potatoes or in a main dish—because it is plump and flaky when cooked.

Regular grain is popular for rice pudding and other dishes in which creaminess is desired.

Processed White Rice is a long-grain, packaged rice that's been processed to retain a large percentage of the natural vitamins and minerals present in the bran of the whole grain.

Packaged Precooked Rice is made of long-grain rice. It's completely cooked, then dehydrated and dried. You get fluffy white rice in a jiffy—without washing, rinsing, draining, or steaming.

Canned Cooked Rice is all cooked, ready to heat and serve.

Regular Brown Rice is natural rice with just the hull removed. It is richer in vitamins and minerals than white rice.

How Much Rice to Cook

Regular or processed rice swells to about 4 times its original measure; i.e., 1 cup raw rice makes about 4 cups cooked. So if you allow a scant ¼ cup raw rice per person you should have enough.

Packaged precooked rice will slightly more than double its volume in preparation; i.e., 1⅓ cups precooked rice makes about 3 cups after preparation. So allow about ⅓ cup rice, before preparation, per person.

Rice As a Vegetable

FLUFFY HOT RICE

If Raw Regular White Rice:

1 cup rice	water
1¾ cups boiling	1 teasp. salt

If Raw Processed White Rice:

1 cup rice	water
2¼ cups boiling	1 teasp. salt

In saucepan with tight cover, combine rice, water, salt. Cook, covered, over low heat 20 to 25 min., or until rice feels tender between fingers and all water is absorbed.

To serve: With 2-tined fork (*never* stir rice with spoon), fluff up rice. Season with butter or margarine and one of these. Makes 4 servings.

> Bit of snipped parsley
> Bit of minced pimento or grated cheese
> Few sliced ripe or stuffed olives
> Sautéed canned or fresh mushrooms
> Slivered, toasted almonds

Green: When rice is done, stir in ¼ cup sliced scallions sautéed in ¼ cup butter or margarine till tender-crisp.

Rosy: Substitute chicken broth for water. Sprinkle with paprika before serving.

Oriental: When rice is done, toss in about ¼ cup dark or light raisins and, if desired, a generous sprinkling of curry. Especially nice with lamb, veal, or chicken dishes.

Green-Gold: When rice is done, stir in 1 grated, pared medium carrot and ½ cup snipped parsley.

To Reheat Leftover Rice: Place cooked rice in strainer over boiling water; cover; steam 10 min.

FLUFFY HOT RICE
(packaged precooked kind)

For 4 servings, prepare 1⅓ cups packaged precooked rice as label directs. Before serving, with fork, lightly mix in any of these:

Chive: 2 tablesp. snipped chives or minced onion and 2 tablesp. butter or margarine

Olive: ¼ cup sliced or chopped stuffed olives and 2 tablesp. butter or margarine

Parsley: 2 tablesp. snipped parsley and 2 tablesp. butter or margarine (if desired, sauté ¼ cup minced onion in butter; then add parsley)

Cheese: ¾ cup grated natural American cheese or 1 cup grated process American cheese

Mint: 3 tablesp. mint jelly and 1½ tablesp. butter or margarine

RAISIN RICE

For 4 servings, prepare 1⅓ cups packaged precooked rice as label directs, adding ¼ cup raisins or currants with water.

Before serving: With fork, lightly mix in 2 tablesp. butter or margarine. Perfect accompaniment for chicken, lamb, or shrimp curry.

HERB RICE

For 4 servings, prepare 1⅓ cups packaged precooked rice as label directs, adding to water one of these:

> ⅛ teasp. dried thyme, orégano, sage, rosemary, basil, or savory
> About ½ teasp. celery seeds or dried dill
> About ¾ teasp. dried marjoram
> About 2 teasp. poppy seeds
> 1 small bay leaf

Before serving: With fork, lightly mix in 1½ tablesp. butter or margarine. Especially nice with creamed tuna, beef stew, or on a vegetable plate.

TOMATO-RICE QUICKIE

2 cups tomato juice	½ teasp. sugar
1⅓ cups packaged precooked rice	Dash onion salt (optional)
½ teasp. salt	

In saucepan, bring tomato juice to boil. Add rice, salt; mix just till all rice is moistened. Cover and remove from heat; let stand 13 min. With fork, lightly mix in sugar and onion salt. Makes 4 servings.

RICE RING

Cook 1¼ cups raw regular or processed white rice as in Fluffy Hot Rice, p. 233. Or prepare 2⅓ cups packaged precooked rice as label directs.

When rice is done, stir in 2 tablesp. butter or margarine; with spoon, gently pack into buttered 1-qt. ring mold.* Let stand about 1 min. or so; invert onto heated platter.

To serve: Sprinkle ring with snipped parsley; fill with any creamed mixture. Makes 4 generous, or 6 small, servings.

Note: To keep rice ring hot a few minutes before unmolding, set mold in pan containing a little water; simmer on top of range.

* If no ring mold is available, spoon rice onto heated platter in a ring.

OVEN DINNER RICE
(regular or processed kind)

1 cup raw regular or processed white rice	margarine
2 tablesp. butter or	2 cups boiling water*
	1 teasp. salt

Start heating oven to 350°F. In greased 1½-qt. casserole, combine all ingredients. Bake, covered, 30 min., or until rice feels tender between fingers and all water is absorbed. Uncover at once.

To serve: Fluff up rice with 2-tined fork. Makes 4 servings.

* For processed rice, use 1¾ cups water.

Pilaff: Before combining butter with rice, sauté 1 minced medium onion in butter until golden. Dilute 1 can condensed consommé with ⅔ cup water; bring to boil; substitute for boiling water. Omit salt. Bake as above or at 400°F. 25 min. For special touch, sprinkle with pine nuts or slivered almonds.

Risotto Style: Sprinkle Pilaff with grated Parmesan cheese.

Curried: First brown rice lightly in 2 tablesp. salad oil. Omit butter. Add 1½ teasp. curry powder and 1 minced medium onion. Bake as above or at 400°F. 30 min.

OVEN DINNER RICE
(packaged precooked kind)

1⅓ cups packaged precooked rice	1½ tablesp. butter or margarine (optional)
1 teasp. salt	
1½ cups cold water	

Start heating oven to 325°F. In 1-qt. casserole, combine rice, salt, water. Bake, covered, 30 min. If desired, add butter before serving, mixing lightly with fork. Makes 4 servings.

SUSAN'S FEATHERED RICE

1½ cups raw regular white rice	3½ cups boiling water
1½ teasp. salt	

1. Start heating oven to 400°F. Spread rice in shallow baking pan.
2. Bake rice 30 min., or until golden brown, stirring occasionally with long-handled spoon. (Rice may smoke a bit.)
3. Turn browned rice into fine-mesh strainer; rinse under running cold water.
4. Place in 1½-qt. casserole. Add salt, boiling water. Bake, covered, 25 min. Uncover at once. With 2-tined fork, fluff up feathery rice.

Serve right from casserole; or arrange around chicken fricassee, shrimp creole, etc. Makes 4 to 6 servings.

SPANISH RICE
(regular or processed kind)

½ cup raw regular or processed white rice	1 No. 2 can tomatoes (2½ cups)
2 tablesp. butter or margarine	3 tablesp. minced green pepper
1 cup sliced onions	2 whole cloves
1⅛ teasp. salt	1 small bay leaf
	2 teasp. sugar

Cook rice as label directs; drain. In hot butter in skillet, cook onions until golden and tender. Add salt and rest of ingredients except rice. Simmer, uncovered, 15 min.; remove bay leaf, cloves. Add rice; mix well; turn into greased 1-qt. casserole. Bake, uncovered, at 375°F. 30 min. Makes 4 servings.

P.S. If desired, top with packaged cheese slices before baking.

▶ **For 2:** Halve ingredients; use 3 custard cups.

SPEEDY SPANISH RICE
(packaged precooked kind)

¼ cup salad oil or fat	2 8-oz. cans tomato sauce
1⅓ cups packaged precooked rice	1 teasp. salt
½ cup thinly sliced onions	¼ teasp. monosodium glutamate
⅓ cup diced green pepper	Dash pepper
1¾ cups hot water	1 teasp. prepared mustard (optional)

In hot salad oil in skillet, quickly brown rice with onions and green pepper; add water and rest of ingredients. Bring to boil; simmer, covered, 10 min. Makes 4 servings.

Pantry-Shelf Kind: Canned Spanish rice just needs to be heated in skillet or double boiler. Nice topped with grated sharp cheese or crumbled crisp bacon.

ORANGE RICE
(regular or processed kind)

¼ cup butter or margarine	orange rind
	1 cup orange juice
⅔ cup diced celery with leaves	1 teasp. salt
	⅛ teasp. dried thyme (optional)
2 tablesp. minced onion	
1½ cups water	1 cup raw regular or
2 tablesp. grated	processed white rice

In hot butter in saucepan, cook celery and onion until tender but not brown. Add water, orange rind, juice, salt, thyme. Bring to boil; slowly add rice. Cook, covered, over low heat 25 min., or until tender.

Delicious served with ham, duckling, chicken, etc. Makes 6 servings.

TANGY ORANGE RICE
(packaged precooked kind)

¼ cup butter or margarine	1 cup water
	¾ cup orange juice
1 cup diced celery	1½ teasp. salt
3 tablesp. minced onion	½ teasp. sugar
1⅓ cups packaged precooked rice	1 to 2 teasp. grated orange rind

In hot butter in saucepan, cook celery and onion until tender but not brown. Add rice, water, orange juice, salt, sugar; mix just till all rice is moistened. Bring quickly to boil over high heat; cover and remove from heat; let stand 13 min. Add orange rind; then fluff gently with fork before serving.

Serve with ham, duckling, or chicken. Makes 4 servings.

Main Dishes with Rice
SPANISH BEEF-RICE

2 tablesp. fat or salad oil	1 tablesp. salt
	2 8-oz. cans tomato sauce
1⅓ cups packaged precooked rice	1 bouillon cube
2 tablesp. minced onion	1 cup hot water
½ cup minced green peppers	1 teasp. soy sauce
	1 teasp. sugar
3 tablesp. diced celery	Snipped parsley
1 lb. chuck, ground	

In hot fat in skillet, cook rice with onion, peppers, celery, and beef until golden brown. Add salt and rest of ingredients except parsley; simmer, covered, 10 min., or until rice is tender. Sprinkle with parsley. Makes 4 servings.

RICE WITH SHRIMP

Rinse, then devein, 2 5-oz. cans shrimp (or use 1 lb. deveined, shelled raw shrimp).

In large saucepan, brown 1 clove garlic in ⅓ cup hot salad oil; discard garlic. Add ⅔ cup raw regular or processed white rice; heat, stirring often, till golden brown. Add 2 tablesp. minced onion, 2 tablesp. canned tomato sauce, shrimp, 1½ cups boiling water, ½ teasp. salt. Cover tightly; reduce heat, and cook slowly 30 min. without lifting lid. Makes 4 servings.

SAVORY RICE AND CHEESE

¾ cup raw regular or processed white rice	2 tablesp. minced onion
	1¼ teasp. salt
2 tablesp. fat or salad oil	¼ teasp. pepper
	2 cups grated process sharp American cheese (½ lb.)
½ cup diced celery	
¼ cup minced green pepper	⅔ cup milk

Cook rice as label directs; drain. Start heating oven to 425°F. In hot fat in skillet, sauté celery, pepper, and onion until tender-crisp; stir in salt, pepper.

In greased 1½-qt. casserole, arrange layers of rice, sautéed vegetables, and cheese, ending with cheese. Pour on milk. Bake, uncovered, 35 min., or until golden brown. Makes 4 servings.

▶ **For 2:** Halve ingredients; use 1-qt. casserole.

FRIDAY RICE SPECIAL

1⅓ cups packaged precooked rice	Dash pepper
	1 7¾-oz. can salmon (1 cup); or 1 can solid-pack tuna
½ cup milk	
½ lb. thinly sliced process American cheese	
	¼ cup chopped stuffed olives
¾ teasp. salt	

Start heating oven to 350°F. Cook rice as label directs. Meanwhile, in double boiler, combine milk, cheese, salt, pepper; heat, stirring occasionally, until well blended and smooth. In 1½-qt. casserole, arrange layers of cooked rice, flaked fish, olives, and cheese sauce, ending with sauce. Bake, uncovered, 30 min. Makes 6 servings.

WILD RICE

Wild rice is the seed of a shallow water grass. The grains are long, spindly, and grayish, and they require a special method of cooking. Wild rice is more expensive than white rice. Especially nice with game.

BOILED WILD RICE

¾ cup raw wild rice   2 teasp. butter or
1 teasp. salt   margarine
3 cups boiling water   Dash pepper

Wash rice well in 3 or 4 changes of cold water, removing foreign particles. Add salt to boiling water; add rice very slowly so that water keeps boiling. Boil, covered, stirring occasionally with fork, 30 to 45 min., or until rice is tender and all water is absorbed. Add butter, pepper. Nice with game or poultry. Makes 2¼ cups, or 3 servings.

WILD RICE BAKED IN CONSOMME

1 cup raw wild rice   rooms
1 can undiluted con-   1 tablesp. butter or
   densed consommé   margarine
½ lb. sliced mush-

Wash rice well in 3 or 4 changes of cold water, removing foreign particles. Place in greased 1½-qt. casserole; add consommé. Let stand 3 hr. Bake, covered, at 350°F. 45 min., adding a little water if rice becomes too dry. Meanwhile, sauté mushrooms in butter about 5 min., or until tender; stir into rice. Leave rice uncovered and allow to dry out a little (but not to crust) in 300°F. oven. Should be moist, with all liquid absorbed. Especially nice with poultry or game. Makes 4 servings.

MACARONI FAMILY

The macaroni family includes macaroni, spaghetti, and egg noodles in an astonishing number of shapes and sizes. The most frequently used shapes are:

Macaroni—the tubular shape, in short elbows and long lengths

Spaghetti—the solid-rod form, available in varying degrees of thickness

Egg Noodles—the ribbonlike pieces, in varying widths

Other Shapes—corrugated elbows, coiled or bunched rods, alphabets, shells, bows, stars, seeds, etc.

Ingredients: Best-quality macaroni and spaghetti are made from a mixture of semolina (from durum wheat) and water.

Egg noodles may be made from the same mixture of semolina and water, but they also contain at least 5.5 per cent egg solids, as required by law. Only egg yolks are used; whites tend to make noodles tough.

Some manufacturers are enriching macaroni products with vitamins B_1, B_2, niacin, and iron. The label indicates this enrichment.

Macaroni as a Vegetable

BUTTERED MACARONI, SPAGHETTI, OR NOODLES

Cook 6 to 8 oz. macaroni, spaghetti, or noodles (break up if necessary) as label directs; drain quickly. If to be used for salad, rinse in cold water.

To serve: Season with salt and pepper, or as on p. 6. Add 3 to 4 tablesp. butter or margarine.

If preferred, simmer a little minced onion and green pepper in butter till tender. Then add to macaroni.

Yield: Makes about 4 to 5 cups cooked macaroni, 3 to 4 cups cooked spaghetti or noodles—enough for 4 to 6 servings.

Crunchy: Sprinkle hot seasoned macaroni, spaghetti, or noodles with a few fresh bread crumbs browned in butter or margarine.

Cheesy Macaroni: After draining macaroni, stir in ⅔ cup milk, ½ teasp. prepared mustard, and 1½ cups grated process American cheese. Heat slightly; season if needed.

Or stir in 2 to 4 tablesp. butter or margarine and 1 6-oz. pkg. crumbled pimento-cheese spread. Heat till cheese melts.

Golden Noodles: After draining noodles, heat 2 tablesp. butter or margarine in skillet. Add noodles, ½ teasp. salt, ⅛ teasp. paprika, ⅛ teasp. pepper, ⅓ cup grated Parmesan cheese. Sauté over medium heat, stirring occasionally, till slightly browned.

Poppy or Caraway Noodles: After draining noodles, stir in 3 to 4 tablesp. butter or margarine, 2 to 2½ teasp. poppy or caraway seeds, salt and pepper to taste. (For crunchy effect, first sauté ⅓ cup chopped, blanched almonds in butter until light brown.)

White Spaghetti: After draining spaghetti, blend in ⅔ cup hot canned chicken broth and 5 tablesp. melted butter or margarine. Arrange in serving dish and sprinkle generously with grated Parmesan cheese.

Spaghetti Parmesan: After draining spaghetti, stir in ¼ cup minced onion, ¾ teasp. dried savory (optional), 2 tablesp. butter or margarine, and ½ cup grated Parmesan cheese.

MACARONI SAUTE

⅓ cup fat or salad oil	1 minced clove garlic (optional)
½ lb. elbow macaroni (2 cups)	3 cups tomato juice
½ cup minced onions	1 teasp. salt
½ cup minced green peppers	¼ teasp. pepper
	2 tablesp. Worcestershire

In hot fat in skillet, sauté uncooked macaroni, onions, peppers, garlic about 10 min., or until macaroni turns yellow. Stir in tomato juice, salt, pepper, Worcestershire. Bring to boil over high heat; turn heat low and cook, covered, without stirring, 20 min. Makes 6 servings.

NANCY'S CURRIED SPAGHETTI

½ lb. spaghetti	1 3-oz. can whole mushrooms, undrained
1½ cans undiluted condensed cream-of-chicken soup	1½ teasp. grated onion
1 can undiluted condensed cream-of-mushroom soup	¼ teasp. dried thyme
½ cup milk	⅛ teasp. dried basil
¼ cup water	⅛ teasp. dried orégano
2 teasp. curry powder	¼ cup grated Parmesan cheese
2 tablesp. warm water	

Cook spaghetti as label directs but only until barely tender; drain. Meanwhile, in saucepan, stir together soups, milk, ¼ cup water; simmer, stirring, 10 min. Combine curry, 2 tablesp. water; add to soup mixture, along with rest of ingredients except cheese. Simmer, stirring, 10 min. longer. Arrange spaghetti in 2-qt. casserole; pour on soup mixture; toss lightly with fork; then sprinkle with cheese.

Serve at once. Or keep warm in 300°F. oven, covered, as long as 1 hr. Makes 9 or 10 servings.

Dinner-in-a-Dish Spaghetti: When adding curry, add 2 cups cooked or canned turkey, chicken, or other meat except ham. Or use tuna.

Buffet Style: Double recipe. Use 3-qt. casserole. Makes 18 to 20 servings.

Main Dishes with Macaroni

SUSAN'S BAKED MACARONI AND CHEESE

1 tablesp. salt	¾ teasp. salt
½ lb. macaroni, in 2½" pieces, or elbow macaroni (about 2 cups)	Speck pepper
	2 cups milk
	½ lb. process American cheese
1 small onion	¾ cup fresh bread crumbs
2 tablesp. butter or margarine	4 teasp. butter or margarine
1 tablesp. flour	
¼ teasp. dry mustard	

1. In large kettle, bring to boil 3 qt. water with 1 tablesp. salt. Start heating oven to 400°F. Grease 1½-qt. casserole.
2. Drop macaroni into boiling water; boil, uncovered, stirring often with fork, about 9 min., or until piece rubbed between fingers parts fairly easily.
3. Meanwhile, mince onion (about 4 teasp.); put in double boiler with 2 tablesp. butter. When butter is melted, stir in flour, mustard, salt, pepper. Slowly stir in milk; cook until smooth and hot, stirring often.
4. Slice about three fourths of cheese right into sauce; stir until cheese is melted. (If preferred, grate cheese ahead, using medium grater, or slice it.)
5. When macaroni is tender, drain into colander; turn into casserole. Pour cheese sauce over macaroni, tossing lightly with fork so

that all macaroni gets nicely coated. Top with rest of cheese.

6. Toss bread crumbs with 4 teasp. melted butter. Sprinkle over cheese.

7. Bake, uncovered, 20 min. Makes 4 servings as main dish, or 6 when served instead of potatoes. Nice with crisp bacon.

▶ **For 2:** Use following ingredients: ⅓ lb. cheese, 1⅓ cups raw macaroni in 2½" pieces, 1 tablesp. minced onion, 4 teasp. butter or margarine, 2 teasp. flour, ¼ teasp. dry mustard, ½ teasp. salt, speck pepper, 1⅓ cups milk, ½ cup fresh bread crumbs, and 1 tablesp. butter or margarine. Bake in 1-qt. casserole at 400°F. 20 min.

Baked Tomato Macaroni: Arrange 2 or 3 sliced, peeled tomatoes in layers with macaroni and sauce.

Baked Macaroni with Green Beans: With cheese in step 4, add 2 cups cooked green beans.

Baked Macaroni with Ham: With cheese in step 4, add ½ to 1½ cups slivered, cooked ham, tongue, chicken, or corned beef, or luncheon meat. (If tongue or ham, reduce salt to ½ teasp.)

ELENA'S MACARONI BAKE

½ lb. macaroni, in 1½" pieces, or elbow macaroni (about 2 cups)	¼ cup butter or margarine
½ lb. diced process American cheese	¾ teasp. salt
	¼ teasp. pepper
	1 cup commercial sour cream

Start heating oven to 350°F. Cook macaroni as label directs; drain. In 1½-qt. casserole, place one third of macaroni and one third of cheese; dot with some butter; sprinkle with some of salt and pepper; add one third of sour cream. Repeat till all ingredients are used, ending with sour cream. Bake, covered, 30 min. Makes 5 servings.

▶ **For 2:** Halve ingredients; use 1-qt. casserole.

MARDI GRAS MACARONI AND CHEESE

6 oz. elbow macaroni (about 1½ cups)	½ teasp. dry mustard
1⅔ cups undiluted evaporated milk	1½ teasp. Worcestershire
½ teasp. salt	¼ cup chopped pimento
½ lb. cubed process sharp American cheese	¼ cup chopped green pepper

Start heating oven to 350°F. Cook macaroni as label directs; drain. Meanwhile, in saucepan over low heat, heat milk with salt to just below boiling point. Add cheese; stir until thickened and smooth. Stir in mustard, Worcestershire. In greased 2-qt. casserole, combine macaroni, pimento, green pepper; pour on cheese sauce. Bake, uncovered, 25 to 30 min. Makes 4 servings.

▶ **For 2:** Halve ingredients; use 1-qt. casserole.

MARTHA'S COMPANY CASSEROLE

½ lb. noodles (4 cups)	cheese
1 tablesp. butter or margarine	¼ cup commercial sour cream
1 lb. chuck, ground	⅓ cup snipped scallions
2 8-oz. cans tomato sauce	1 tablesp. minced green pepper
½ lb. cottage cheese (1 cup)	2 tablesp. melted butter or margarine
1 8-oz. pkg. soft cream	

Start heating oven to 375°F. Cook noodles as label directs; drain. Meanwhile, in 1 tablesp. hot butter in skillet, sauté beef until browned. Stir in tomato sauce. Remove from heat.

Combine cottage cheese, cream cheese, sour cream, scallions, green pepper. In 2-qt. casserole, spread half of noodles; cover with cheese mixture; then cover with rest of noodles. Pour on melted butter, then meat mixture. Bake, uncovered, 30 min. Makes 6 servings.

To Do Ahead: Make casserole early in day; refrigerate. To serve, bake at 375°F. 45 min., or until hot.

▶ **For 2:** Halve ingredients; use 1-qt. casserole.

MINA'S ITALIAN SPAGHETTI

1 No. 2½ can tomato purée (3½ cups)	1 teasp. salt
1 lb. Italian sausage	¼ teasp. pepper
Meat Balls, p. 240	1 minced small onion
1 6-oz. can tomato paste (⅔ cup)	1 tablesp. sugar
	1½ lb. thin spaghetti
	Grated Parmesan cheese

In large kettle, combine tomato purée and 1 can water (measured in purée can); start simmering, uncovered, over low heat. Cut sausages into serving-size pieces; prick. Cook in large skillet over low heat until brown on all sides; remove sausages. Add Meat Balls to fat in skillet; cook until golden brown and crusty. Add sausages. Cool; refrigerate.

While meat cooks, to simmering purée, add tomato paste, 4 cans water (measured in paste can), salt, pepper, onion. Continue simmering, uncovered, 1½ hr. Add Meat Balls and sausages; simmer, uncovered, 2 to 3 hr., or until sauce is of consistency of heavy cream. Add sugar about 15 min. before sauce is done.

Meanwhile, cook spaghetti as label directs; drain. Pour sauce over spaghetti on platter or on individual plates; sprinkle generously with cheese. Makes 9 generous servings.

To Do Ahead: Make sauce day before; refrigerate. Reheat while cooking spaghetti.

Meat Balls:

1 lb. chuck, ground	¼ cup grated Parmesan
½ cup packaged dried	cheese
bread crumbs	1 egg
1 minced clove garlic	½ teasp. salt
2 tablesp. snipped	⅛ teasp. pepper
parsley	

Combine all ingredients; mix well. Shape into golf-ball-size balls. Use as directed in Mina's Italian Spaghetti, p. 239, or Italian Spaghetti, California Style, below.

ITALIAN SPAGHETTI, CALIFORNIA STYLE

2 tablesp. bacon fat	drained
½ cup sliced onions	1½ teasp. salt
1 lb. chuck, ground	⅛ teasp. pepper
1 minced clove garlic	1 teasp. dried sage
1 minced green pepper	¼ teasp. dried thyme
1 No. 2½ can tomatoes	1 teasp. dried rosemary
(3½ cups)	1 bay leaf
2 8-oz. cans tomato	1 cup water
sauce	2 tablesp. salad oil
1 6-oz. can whole	Meat Balls, above
mushrooms, un-	1 lb. spaghetti

In bacon fat in large kettle, sauté onions until tender. Add beef; cook, stirring often, until meat loses red color. Add garlic and rest of ingredients except oil, Meat Balls, spaghetti. Simmer, uncovered, stirring occasionally, 1½ hr., or until as thick as you like.

Meanwhile, in hot oil in skillet, brown Meat Balls quickly on all sides. About 20 min. before sauce is done, add Meat Balls. Also cook spa-

ghetti as label directs; drain. Pour sauce over spaghetti on platter or individual plates. Makes 6 generous servings.

SPAGHETTI WITH ITALIAN MEAT SAUCE

¼ cup salad or olive oil	½ teasp. pepper
½ cup minced onions	¼ teasp. sugar
1 lb. chuck, ground	Tiny bit fresh or dried
2 minced cloves garlic	basil or thyme
2 3-oz. cans chopped	1 cup Burgundy,
mushrooms, un-	claret, or other red
drained	wine
¼ cup snipped parsley	1 lb. spaghetti, or shell
1 8-oz. can tomato	or elbow macaroni
sauce	¼ lb. diced sharp
1 No. 2 can tomatoes	American cheese
(2½ cups)	½ to 1 cup grated
2½ teasp. salt	Parmesan cheese

In hot oil in skillet or kettle, simmer onions 5 min. Add beef, garlic; cook, stirring, until meat loses red color. Add mushrooms, parsley, tomato sauce. Force tomatoes through sieve; add to sauce, with salt, pepper, sugar, basil. Simmer, covered, 1 hr. Add wine; simmer, covered, 1 hr.

About 20 min. before serving: Cook spaghetti as label directs; drain. Add hot sauce and diced cheese; toss. Turn onto large platter; sprinkle generously with Parmesan cheese. Makes 6 to 8 generous servings.

To Do Ahead: Make sauce day before; refrigerate. Reheat while cooking spaghetti.

SPAGHETTI WITH CLAM SAUCE

2 tablesp. olive oil	½ chopped green
1 split clove garlic	pepper
2 doz. shucked cherry-	2 cups canned Italian
stone clams	tomatoes
¼ cup butter or marga-	1½ teasp. salt
rine	⅛ teasp. pepper
Snipped parsley sprig	¼ cup snipped parsley
½ teasp. dried orégano	1 lb. thin spaghetti

In hot oil in skillet, cook garlic until brown; discard garlic. Drain clams, saving 1 cup liquid. Add liquid to skillet, along with butter, parsley sprig, orégano, green pepper, tomatoes, salt, pepper. Cook, uncovered, 30 min. Add clams, finely cut up, and ¼ cup snipped parsley; cook 3 min.

Meanwhile, cook spaghetti as label directs; drain. Pour sauce over spaghetti on platter or individual plates; toss. Makes 6 to 8 servings.

FORTY-FIVE-MINUTE SPAGHETTI

¼ lb. bacon slices, cut into 1″ pieces	1 teasp. Worcestershire
¾ cup sliced onions	2 teasp. sugar
½ lb. chuck, ground	3 8-oz. cans tomato sauce
1 teasp. salt	¼ cup sliced stuffed or ripe olives
⅛ teasp. pepper	½ lb. thin spaghetti
1 minced clove garlic (optional)	Grated Parmesan cheese

In large skillet, cook bacon until light brown, pouring off excess fat. Add onions, beef; cook, stirring with fork, until brown. Add salt, pepper, garlic, Worcestershire, sugar, tomato sauce. Simmer, covered, 20 min. Add olives; simmer, covered, 15 min.

Meanwhile, cook spaghetti as label directs; drain. Pour sauce over spaghetti on platter or on individual plates; sprinkle lightly with cheese. Makes 4 servings.

TUNA SPAGHETTI

3 tablesp. salad oil	sauce
1 minced medium onion	1 bay leaf
1 minced clove garlic	1 can chunk-style tuna (1 cup)
1 3-oz. can mushrooms, undrained	6 sliced or chopped green olives
1 No. 2 can tomatoes (2½ cups)	1 lb. spaghetti
1 8-oz. can tomato	½ cup grated Parmesan cheese

In hot oil in skillet, sauté onion and garlic until golden. Add mushrooms, tomatoes, tomato sauce, bay leaf. Simmer, covered, about 1½ hr., or until thickened. Add tuna, olives; simmer 10 min.

Meanwhile, cook spaghetti as label directs; drain. Pour sauce over spaghetti on platter; sprinkle with cheese. Makes about 6 servings.

SALAMETTI

3 tablesp. salad oil	2 tablesp. snipped parsley
1 cup chopped onions	1 6-oz. can sliced mushrooms, drained
1 tablesp. flour	
½ lb. slivered salami	¼ cup chopped green pepper
2 cups tomato juice	
2 tablesp. Worcestershire	1 lb. spaghetti
¼ teasp. pepper	Grated Parmesan cheese

In hot oil in large skillet, sauté onions until golden. Stir in flour, salami, tomato juice, Worcestershire, pepper. Simmer, uncovered, 25 min.

Add parsley, mushrooms, green pepper; simmer 5 min. Meanwhile, cook spaghetti as label directs; drain.

Serve sauce over spaghetti on platter or on individual plates; sprinkle with Parmesan cheese. Makes 4 servings.

SAVORY BAKED SPAGHETTI

3 tablesp. bacon fat or salad oil	1 No. 2½ can tomatoes (3½ cups)
2 coarsely chopped medium onions	1 teasp. chili powder
	1 cup water
1 clove garlic (optional)	½ lb. spaghetti
½ lb. chuck, ground	1 cup grated process American cheese (¼ lb.)
1½ teasp. salt	
⅛ teasp. pepper	

In fat in large skillet, slowly cook onions and garlic 5 min. Add beef; cook, stirring occasionally, until meat loses red color. Stir in salt, pepper, tomatoes. Simmer, covered, 30 min.; discard garlic. Add chili, water.

Start heating oven to 325°F. Break half of uncooked spaghetti into greased 2-qt. casserole; pour on half of sauce; sprinkle with half of cheese. Break in rest of spaghetti; add rest of sauce and cheese. Bake, covered, 35 min. Uncover; bake 15 min. longer, or until brown. Makes 6 servings.

► For 2: Halve ingredients; use 1-qt. casserole.

ITALIAN HAM AND SPAGHETTI

¼ cup salad or olive oil	¼ teasp. pepper
2 tablesp. minced onion	1 No. 2 can tomatoes (2½ cups)
1 tablesp. minced green pepper	
1 minced clove garlic	1 3-oz. can sliced mushrooms, drained
¼ cup snipped parsley	
2 teasp. mixed dried herbs (rosemary, marjoram, thyme)	1 cup liquid (mushroom liquid plus water to fill cup)
2 cups diced, cooked or canned ham or luncheon meat	½ lb. spaghetti, broken into 2″ lengths
	½ cup grated Parmesan or process American cheese
2 teasp. salt	

In hot oil in skillet, cook onion, green pepper, garlic, parsley, and herbs until brown. Add ham; brown. Add salt, pepper, tomatoes, mushrooms and liquid. Simmer, covered, 20 min.

Start heating oven to 350°F. Cook spaghetti as label directs; drain. Add to meat mixture.

Pour into 2-qt. casserole; sprinkle with cheese. Bake, covered, 40 min., or until bubbly. Makes 8 servings.

▶ **For 4, or 2 with leftovers:** Halve all ingredients except mushrooms; use 1-qt. casserole.

JANE'S BUFFET LASAGNA

2 No. 2½ cans Italian-style peeled tomatoes	2 lb. chuck, ground
4 8-oz. cans tomato sauce	2 teasp. monosodium glutamate
2 teasp. salt	2 teasp. salt
2 teasp. onion salt	1 lb. lasagna (very broad noodles)
1 tablesp. dried orégano	1½ lb. ricotta cheese
¼ teasp. pepper	1 lb. Mozzarella cheese, thinly sliced
⅓ cup salad oil	1 cup grated Parmesan cheese
2 cups minced onions	
2 minced cloves garlic	

In large saucepan or kettle, combine tomatoes, tomato sauce, 2 teasp. salt, onion salt, orégano, pepper; start simmering, uncovered. In hot oil in skillet, sauté onions and garlic until lightly browned; add beef, monosodium glutamate, 2 teasp. salt; cook until meat loses red color. Add to tomato sauce; simmer, uncovered, 2½ hr., or until thickened. Meanwhile, cook lasagna as label directs, stirring occasionally; drain, separating pieces.

Start heating oven to 350°F. In bottoms of 2 12" x 8" x 2" baking dishes, place several spoonfuls of sauce; top with crisscross layer of lasagna, then with half of ricotta (divide between two dishes). Top with one third of Mozzarella and half of Parmesan (divide between two dishes). Repeat, ending with sauce. Top with remaining Mozzarella. Bake, uncovered, 50 min., or until bubbly. Remove from oven; let stand 15 min. Makes 16 servings.

THOR'S COMPANY CASSEROLE

2 tablesp. salad oil	½ cup commercial sour cream
1 clove garlic	¼ lb. Swiss cheese, sliced
1 lb. veal round (thin slice cut into 6 pieces)	2 sliced tomatoes
Salt and pepper	½ cup dry white wine
2 3-oz. cans sliced mushrooms	½ cup grated Parmesan cheese
¼ lb. noodles	

Start heating oven to 400°F. In hot oil in skillet, brown garlic with veal, sprinkling veal with ½

teasp. salt, ⅛ teasp. pepper. Remove garlic. Add undrained mushrooms. Simmer, covered, 15 to 20 min. Meanwhile, cook noodles as label directs; drain; toss with sour cream.

In 1½-qt. casserole, place half of noodle mixture, half of veal and mushrooms, then half of Swiss cheese and tomato slices. Sprinkle with ½ teasp. salt, ⅛ teasp. pepper. Repeat. Into gravy in skillet, stir wine, Parmesan. Pour into casserole. Bake, uncovered, about 25 min. Makes 6 servings.

GOLDEN GATE LASAGNA

2 tablesp. salad oil	1 8-oz. can tomato sauce
½ cup minced onions	½ cup grated Parmesan cheese
1 lb. chuck, ground	
2 cloves garlic	½ lb. lasagna (1½"-wide noodles)
1½ teasp. salt	
¼ teasp. black pepper	¾ lb. thinly sliced Mozzarella or natural Swiss cheese
¼ teasp. orégano	
3 tablesp. snipped parsley	1 lb. ricotta or cottage cheese
1 No. 2 can tomatoes (2½ cups)	

Day before or early in day: In hot oil in skillet, sauté onions. Add beef; cook until red color disappears. Slice garlic; mash with salt; add to meat, with pepper, orégano, parsley, tomatoes, tomato sauce, 2 tablesp. Parmesan. Simmer, covered, 30 min. Refrigerate until ready to use.

About 45 min. before serving: Start heating oven to 350°F. Cook lasagna as label directs. Drain; cover with cold water. Now, in 12" x 8" x 2" baking dish, arrange one third of meat sauce; then single layer of drained lasagna, placed lengthwise (leave rest in water); layer of Mozzarella; layer of ricotta; 2 tablesp. Parmesan. Repeat, ending with remaining sauce and Parmesan. Bake 30 min. Makes 8 servings.

Especially Easy Macaroni Dishes

The list of macaroni-family favorites that come in cans or packages to keep on your pantry shelf grows all the time. Here are examples of what you'll find on the grocer's shelves—they need only heating or short cooking. Or they can be combined quickly with meat or fish, as in Top-Stove or Oven Macaroni Specials, p. 243.

In Cans or Jars:

Spaghetti in tomato sauce with cheese
Spaghetti and meat balls in tomato sauce
Macaroni in cheese sauce
Macaroni creole
Spaghetti sauce—with or without meat, or
    with mushrooms
Marinara sauce
Ravioli in meat sauce
Cheese ravioli in mushroom sauce
Noodle-chicken or -giblet dinner
Tuna-noodle dinner

Packaged:

Macaroni and cheese, in one handy package
Spaghetti, grated cheese, and spaghetti sauce
    with meat or mushrooms, in one package
Spaghetti sauce mix

TOP-STOVE MACARONI SPECIALS

Savory Spaghetti: In skillet, sauté ½ to 1 lb. bulk
pork sausage until nicely browned; pour off all
but 1 tablesp. fat. Add 1 3-oz. can sliced mushrooms, drained; 1 sliced medium onion; 1
minced clove garlic; ½ teasp. salt; ⅛ teasp.
pepper. Sauté until onion is tender. Add 2 cans
spaghetti in tomato sauce with cheese; heat over
low heat, covered, stirring occasionally. Makes 4
servings.

Beef and Spaghetti: In 1 tablesp. hot fat in skillet, sauté 1 minced small onion until tender; add
½ lb. chuck, ground. Cook, stirring occasionally,
until meat loses red color. Add ½ teasp. salt or
1 teasp. garlic salt and 1 can spaghetti in tomato
sauce with cheese. Heat, uncovered, stirring often, till bubbling. Makes 4 servings.

Chicken-Noodle Bake: Cook ¼ lb. (2 cups)
medium noodles as label directs; drain. In 1
tablesp. hot butter or margarine in skillet, sauté
2 tablesp. minced green pepper until tender. Stir
in 1 can undiluted condensed cream-of-chicken
soup and 1 cup cooked or canned chicken, in
large pieces. Add noodles. Cook over low heat,
uncovered, 10 min. If desired, garnish with
green-pepper rings and few chicken slices. Makes
4 servings.

OVEN MACARONI SPECIALS

Beef-and-Chili Bake: Start heating oven to
350°F. In 2 tablesp. hot fat or salad oil in skillet,
sauté 1 lb. chuck, ground, till red color disappears; stir in 1 teasp. chili powder. Grate ½ lb.
process sharp American cheese. Open 3 cans
spaghetti in tomato sauce with cheese. Place 1
can spaghetti in 2-qt. casserole; top with one
third of meat and one third of cheese. Repeat
twice. Bake 45 min. Pass grated Parmesan cheese
if desired. Makes 4 or 5 generous servings.

Cheesy Spaghetti Omelet: Mix 3 egg yolks, ¼
teasp. salt, and ⅛ teasp. pepper with 1 can spaghetti in tomato sauce with cheese. Beat 3 egg
whites till stiff; fold into spaghetti mixture.

Start heating oven to 375°F. Heat 2 tablesp.
butter or margarine in medium iron skillet;
pour in spaghetti mixture. Cook over medium
heat about 10 min., or until brown around edge
when lifted with fork or spatula.

Sprinkle top with ¾ cup grated process sharp
American cheese. Bake 10 to 12 min., or until
cheese is melted and top is brown. To serve, cut
into wedges. Makes 4 servings.

Macaroni-Tuna Bake: Start heating oven to
375°F. In small saucepan, melt 2 tablesp. butter
or margarine; toss with ½ cup fresh bread
crumbs. In 1½-qt. casserole, combine 2 cans
macaroni in cheese sauce with 1 can chunk-
style tuna (1 cup); top with crumbs. Bake 20
min. Makes 6 servings.

Vegetables

Want to hear requests for "More, please!" when you serve vegetables? Then do as master chefs do:

1. Cook them gently, to retain vitamins and flavor and to produce delectable tender crispness.
2. Season them subtly; bring out, don't conceal, the wonderful vegetable flavor.
3. Add sauce or garnish carefully, choosing the finishing touch that provides the best possible combination of flavors in the most eye-catching way.

Before using these recipes, refer to How to Use Our Recipes, p. 3, and Pots and Pans, p. 692. Always use standard measuring cups and measuring spoons; measure level.

Shop Wisely

Market Fresh Vegetables: These are available all year long but are the best buy when in their growing season in your locality. Keep these points in mind when buying:

1. Check on vegetable supplies in local markets through newspaper and radio reports.
2. Buy from a dealer who has a quick turnover and who keeps vegetables under refrigeration or on crushed ice. Market fresh vegetables begin to lose flavor, tenderness, and vitamins as soon as they're picked.
3. Buy only enough for 1 or 2 days' supply whenever possible; use promptly.

4. Go to market yourself whenever you can. In today's markets vegetables are so attractively displayed you can quickly see daily specials and be reminded of vegetables that seldom appear on your menus.

Frozen Vegetables: These are available all year long. They are always in season, so you always have a wide variety to choose from. The best of the crop is harvested at the peak of quality and rapidly frozen within a few hours; thus nutritional losses are negligible. Keep these points in mind when buying:

1. Buy frozen vegetables from a grocer who keeps them in a freezer cabinet that maintains near 0°F. temperature. They should be frozen solid, not beginning to soften.
2. Watch for specials of the week—they'll be especially advantageous if you have freezer space available.

Canned Vegetables: These offer a wonderful variety to choose from too. To buy, see p. 515.

Store with Care

Market Fresh Vegetables:

Potatoes, Onions, Yellow Turnips: Store where cool air can circulate around them. Do not clean until ready to use.

All Other Vegetables: To reduce vitamin losses, store *at once* in food bags, waxed paper, or vegetable crisper in refrigerator. Before storing, clean with dry cloth. Or if washing seems necessary, *dry well.*

Garden Vegetables: Pick home-grown vegetables just before cooking so they will be at their peak of freshness and food value. Or refrigerate them at once; then cook as soon as possible.

Frozen Vegetables: Don't waste time—once you select them, get them home and store at once; keep frozen solid until ready to use.

Canned Vegetables: Store in a cool dry place until used. If for salads, chill before using.

Leftover Cooked Vegetables: Store, covered, in refrigerator; plan to use next day if possible. See Leftovers, p. 552.

Cook with Care

For specific instructions on buying, preparing, and cooking vegetables, see charts, pp. 278 to 285.

Check these nine tips for further help in serving attractive, wholesome vegetables.

1. *Cook only enough for one meal*—unless you have plans for using leftovers next day.
2. *When paring vegetables,* use a vegetable parer that makes thin parings.
3. *Avoid presoaking;* it dissolves out vitamins and minerals.
4. *Keep cooking utensil tightly covered.* This shortens cooking time.
5. *Stir as little as possible.* Stirring adds air to vegetables, increases loss of vitamin C.
6. *Do not overcook.* Cook only until vegetable is just tender-crisp, no more. The longer the cooking, the greater the vitamin loss.
7. *Serve vegetables as soon as they're cooked.* Keeping vegetables hot for a long period reduces vitamins.
8. *Don't throw away cooking liquid.* Refrigerate it; use as part of liquid in sauces, soups, gravies, or stews. Or combine with tomato- or vegetable-juice cocktails.
9. *Avoid using more than a pinch of baking soda* in cooking vegetables. Although soda helps bring out green color, it usually makes texture

and flavor less desirable, may destroy vitamins.

MARKET FRESH OR GARDEN VEGETABLES

There are several excellent ways to cook market fresh or garden vegetables. Take your pick, depending on the vegetable, the amount of time you have, the type of meal you're serving.

In Covered Saucepan: Cook vegetable quickly in small amount of water—not more than 1″. Start with boiling water; after adding vegetables, cover; quickly bring water back to boil over high heat; then reduce heat just enough to keep water boiling. With this method, you'll save food value, for when a lot of water is used, valuable minerals cook out into the water, which, all too often, is then poured down the sink.

In Pressure Cooker: See p. 195.

In Skillet: This method is especially nice for asparagus, shredded cabbage, kale, spinach, sliced young summer squash or zucchini, etc. Put prepared vegetable in large covered skillet, with a few tablespoonfuls of water, salt, and a little butter; cook, stirring once in a while, until tender but not mushy.

In Oven: Many vegetables can bake along with the main dish, at the same temperature. If baking times vary, plan to put each dish into oven so that all come out together. Here are some to choose from:

Baked Beets with Onions, p. 251
Carrots:
    Baked, p. 253
    Buffet Cheese-Scalloped, p. 253
Corn:
    Custard Corn Pudding, p. 255
    Southern Corn Pudding, p. 256
Eggplant:
    Eggplant-and-Tomato Bake, p. 258
    Scalloped, p. 258
Karen's Green Limas, p. 260
Baked Onions de Luxe, p. 263
Sweet Potatoes:
    Orange Candied, p. 266
    Puffy Mallow, p. 265
    Special Candied, p. 266
    Sweet-Potato Surprises, p. 265

CANNED VEGETABLES

To preserve the delicious flavor and food value in canned vegetables, treat as follows:

Peas, Green Limas, Green Beans, Carrots, etc.: Drain liquid from can or jar into saucepan. Boil it down till half or one third in volume; add vegetables; heat. Season with salt and pepper (or as on p. 6), then with butter or margarine.

Tomatoes, Cream-Style Corn, and Squash: Heat contents of can; season; serve.

Vegetables to Be Used Cold in Salads: Drain. Toss with, or arrange on, greens. (Use liquids in stews, soups, gravies, sauces, etc.)

FROZEN VEGETABLES

Saucepan-Cooked: Packaged frozen vegetables can be cooked quickly and easily. Just follow label directions. Be careful not to overcook; time carefully once water boils.

Oven-Cooked: Another easy way to cook frozen vegetables is to bake them. When baking a casserole, meat loaf, etc., just bake frozen vegetable right along with it, placing it in oven so it will be done same time as main dish. Follow chart below.

TO OVEN-COOK FROZEN VEGETABLES

Place 1 box frozen vegetables, 1 to 2 tablesp. butter or margarine, and ¼ teasp. salt in casserole. (Cut block of spinach or chopped broccoli into 6 or 8 pieces.) Bake, covered, as below.

Vegetable	Oven-Cooking Time at 350°F.*	Number Of Servings
Asparagus cuts	55 to 60 min.	3
Asparagus spears	55 to 60 min.	3
Broccoli, chopped	45 to 50 min.	3
Broccoli, spears	40 to 45 min.	3
Brussels sprouts	40 to 45 min.	3
Cauliflower	50 to 55 min.	3
Corn, whole kernel	45 to 50 min.	3 or 4
Green beans, cut	55 to 60 min.	3 or 4
Green beans, French style	55 to 60 min.	3 or 4
Green limas, small†	55 to 60 min.	3
Green limas, Fordhook ‡	45 to 50 min.	3
Mixed vegetables	60 min.	3
Peas	45 to 50 min.	3
Peas and carrots	55 to 60 min.	3
Spinach	45 to 50 min.	3
Spinach, chopped	45 to 50 min.	2 or 3
Squash	45 min.	3
Succotash	55 to 60 min.	3
Wax beans, cut	60 min.	3 or 4

* *If baking at 325°F., increase time about 10 min.*
* *If baking at 375°F., decrease time about 10 min.*
† *Add ¼ cup water with butter and salt.*
‡ *Add 2 tablesp. water with butter and salt.*

SERVE WITH A FLAIR

SEASON TO TASTE

Use imagination when adding that lump of butter or margarine, that extra salt and pepper, to cooked vegetables. Try adding seasoned, garlic, or onion salt, (omit regular salt), or monosodium glutamate, etc. (See Shaker Seasonings, p. 521.)

BUTTERY BUT DIFFERENT

To melted butter or margarine, heated till golden brown if desired, add any of the following. Pour over any hot cooked vegetable. Or pass in small pitcher.

Celery seeds
Chili sauce
Snipped chives
Curry powder
Generous pinch
   dried or fresh
   herbs
Horse-radish

Lemon juice and
   grated lemon rind
Prepared mustard
Grated Parmesan or
   other cheese
Snipped scallions
   (sauté in butter
   until tender)

CRUMB STYLE

Sauté ½ cup to 1 cup fresh bread crumbs in 2 to 4 tablesp. butter or margarine until light brown. Add pinch salt; speck each pepper and paprika; 1 tablesp. fresh, frozen, or canned lemon juice. If desired, add ½ cup grated cheese instead of lemon juice.

Especially nice sprinkled over cauliflower, asparagus, broccoli, or Brussels sprouts.

CRUNCHY OR COLORFUL

Just before serving vegetables, season with salt, pepper, and butter or margarine; sprinkle with any of these:

Slivered, toasted almonds. Especially nice on peas, green beans, green limas, asparagus, cauliflower, broccoli, Brussels sprouts

Crumbled crisp bacon bits. Especially nice on cabbage, spinach, carrots, broccoli

Sliced ripe or stuffed olives. Especially nice on carrots, peas, green beans, green limas, cauliflower

Chopped, hard-cooked egg. Especially nice on spinach, asparagus, broccoli

Snipped parsley. Nice on any vegetable

Diced pimento. Especially nice on peas, asparagus, cauliflower, green beans, green limas

QUICK CREAM STYLE

Heat light cream. Season with salt, pepper, butter or margarine, and, if desired, some grated cheese. Pour over any of these hot cooked vegetables:

Asparagus
Brussels sprouts
Cabbage
Carrots
Cauliflower

Celery
Whole-kernel corn
Green beans
Green limas
Peas

OLD-FASHIONED CREAMED

Use one, or a combination of two or more, cooked vegetables. Make Vegetable or Cheese Sauce, p. 376. (Allow about ½ cup sauce per 1 cup vegetables.)

If creaming canned vegetables, boil down can liquid till one third in volume; use as part of milk.

Add hot sauce directly to vegetables; reheat. Or pour sauce over vegetable in serving dish and sprinkle with paprika. Three cups vegetables with 1½ cups sauce makes 4 servings.

SCALLOPED

For 4 servings, arrange 3 cups cooked vegetables and 1½ cups hot Vegetable or Cheese Sauce, p. 376, in alternate layers in greased 1½-qt. casserole. Top with ⅓ cup buttered fresh bread crumbs (if desired, mix ¼ to ⅓ cup grated cheese with crumbs); sprinkle with paprika. Bake at 450°F. 5 to 10 min., or until vegetables are hot and crumbs are brown.

DIFFERENT COMBINATIONS

Combine two or more vegetables after cooking. (Or combine before cooking if they cook in about the same time.) Then season; toss lightly. Try:

Asparagus, cut up, with peas, green limas, or whole-kernel corn

Green Limas, with cauliflowerets, peas, slivered carrots, or sliced celery (cut on angle)

Brussels Sprouts, with peas, small onions, cauliflowerets, green beans, or sliced celery

Carrots, with diced celery, sliced onions, green limas, peas, green beans, or cauliflower

Cauliflower, with peas, green limas, or slivered carrots

Whole-Kernel Corn, with peas, slivered carrots, green beans, or sliced zucchini

Green Beans, with small whole onions, green limas, peas, whole-kernel corn, or sliced celery or carrots (cut on angle)

Small Whole Onions, with green limas, peas, slivered carrots, summer squash, green beans, or mushrooms

Parsnips, with peas or slivered carrots

Peas, with diced white or yellow turnips, summer squash, whole-kernel corn, sliced celery, green beans, or mushrooms

Summer Squash, with peas, green limas, whole-kernel corn, green beans, or sliced zucchini

GLAMOROUS SERVING

Arrange 2 or 3 vegetables on one heated large chop plate or platter or in attractive 3-qt. casserole or oversized vegetable dish—they'll stay hot longer and look handsome. And you'll have one dish to wash instead of several.

Broccoli bunchlets down one side of platter; whole carrots down other

Cauliflower head in center of platter; slivered carrots and green beans in groups, radiating from it

Cauliflower head in center of platter; green beans and onions around it

Cauliflower head, studded with almonds or topped with cheese sauce, in center of platter; green beans around it

Corn (Mexican-style), in center of heated casserole; green beans and small whole onions around it

Mashed potatoes or yellow turnips in mound in center of chop plate; peas and onions around it

Rice in center of platter (place hot cooked rice in buttered 2-qt. casserole; unmold); peas and mushrooms around it

Acorn squash, filled with peas and onions, down one side of platter; braised celery down other

Mashed turnips or squash in ring (form with spoon); peas, with slivered almonds added, in center

ARTICHOKES—ITALIAN OR FRENCH

To Buy, to Prepare: See chart, p. 278.

To Cook: Stand artichokes upright (do not tip) in deep saucepan that's just big enough to hold them snugly. For each artichoke, add 1 tablesp. salad oil, small clove garlic, 1 thick lemon slice. Pour in 1″ boiling salted water.

Boil artichokes gently, covered, 20 to 45 min., or until leaf can be easily pulled from stalk, or stem can be easily pierced with fork. (Add a little more boiling water if needed.) With 2 spoons, lift out artichokes; let drain upside down; cut off stubs of stems.

To Serve: Arrange artichokes on salad plates, so waste leaves won't clutter dinner plates.

Serve with one of sauces below. If sauce is thick, serve in small lettuce cup on each salad plate; if thin, put in tiny bowl or paper cup. If serving ½ artichoke per person, place on dinner plate, with sauce poured over it.

Caper Butter, p. 372	374 (use ½ recipe)
Drawn Butter, p. 376	
Easy Hollandaise, p. 374	Lemon Cocktail, p. 21
Spur-of-the-Moment Hollandaise, p.	Louis, p. 373 (use ½ recipe)

Or for sauce, melt ½ cup butter or margarine. Add 2 tablesp. each snipped parsley and fresh, frozen, or canned lemon juice. Makes 4 servings.

Or for sauce, sauté ¼ cup minced onion or 1 minced clove garlic in ½ cup butter or margarine. Makes 4 servings.

To Eat: Pluck off leaves, one by one; dip base (light-colored end) of each leaf into sauce; scrape off pulp at base with teeth; discard rest. When all outer leaves have been eaten, cut away fuzzy center, or "choke," with fork and knife; discard, exposing heart. Cut heart, or bottom, into chunks; dip into sauce; eat.

JERUSALEM ARTICHOKES

To Buy, to Prepare, to Cook: See chart, p. 278.

To Serve: Drain artichokes. Season with salt, pepper. Add Lemon Butter, p. 377, or butter or margarine and snipped parsley. Serve instead of potatoes.

ASPARAGUS

To Buy, to Prepare: See chart, p. 278.

To Cook: Spread stalks in 2 layers in 9″ or 10″ skillet. Sprinkle with 1½ teasp. salt. Pour on 1″ boiling water. Boil, covered, 12 to 15 min., or until lower part of stalks tested with fork is just tender-crisp. With 2 forks or perforated pancake turner, lift out asparagus. Or drain; turn onto platter.

To Serve: Sprinkle with salt, pepper. Melt ¼ cup butter or margarine, browning it slightly if desired. Pour over asparagus, as is or with one of following added:

Toasted, blanched almonds	rooms
Crisp bacon bits	Prepared mustard or horse-radish
Bottled capers or celery seeds	Sprinkling of nutmeg
Grated cheese	Minced onion or garlic
Fresh or dried herbs	
2 or 3 tablesp. lemon juice	Snipped parsley or chives
Sautéed, sliced mush-	

Or spoon on one of these sauces:

Béarnaise, p. 374	Hollandaise, p. 374
Drawn Butter, p. 376	
Chive Cheese, p. 372	Louis, p. 373
Saucepan Cheese, p. 373	Quick Mushroom, p. 372
Dilly, p. 373	Sour Cream, p. 373
Easiest of All, p. 374	Thousand Island, p. 374
Easy Hollandaise, p. 374	Vinaigrette, p. 373
Spur-of-the-Moment	

Asparagus on Toast: Arrange hot cooked asparagus on buttered toast; toasted, split buns; or Holland rusks. Pour on melted butter or margarine, a little asparagus liquid, or one of sauces,

p. 249. Or place fried ham slice under asparagus. Or top asparagus with poached or creamed eggs.

Marinated Asparagus: Chill cooked asparagus. Top with French dressing and snipped parsley.

BEST-EVER QUICK-COOKED ASPARAGUS

Wash 1½ lb. asparagus, removing, with knife, scales that hold sand and grit. Lay 1 or 2 asparagus stalks together on cutting board; with sharp knife, cut on very long, slanting diagonal to end of green length of stalk, making bias slices not more than ¼″ thick and 1½″ long.

Put 3 tablesp. butter or margarine and ¼ cup water in large skillet with tight cover; heat. Then add asparagus, about ½ teasp. salt, dash pepper. Cook, covered, over high heat 5 min., shaking skillet occasionally and checking once to see whether a bit more water is needed. Test asparagus with fork; if not tender-crisp, cook 1 min. more. Uncover at once; serve quickly. Makes 4 servings.

OLD-FASHIONED CREAMED ASPARAGUS

2 lb. fresh asparagus; or 2 pkg. frozen asparagus cuts	4½ teasp. flour ¾ cup undiluted evaporated milk
3 tablesp. butter or margarine	½ teasp. salt ⅛ teasp. pepper

Prepare and cook fresh asparagus, cut up, as on p. 278; or cook frozen asparagus as label directs.

Meanwhile, in saucepan, melt butter; blend in flour. When asparagus is done, drain liquid into measuring cup (there should be ¾ cup; if less, add water; if more, discard excess). Stir asparagus liquid and evaporated milk into flour mixture; cook, stirring, until thickened. Add salt, pepper, asparagus. Heat just till boiling (stir as little as possible, to avoid mashing asparagus). Makes 4 servings.

BEETS

To Buy, to Prepare, to Cook: See chart, p. 278.

To Serve: Drain beets. If cooked whole, hold under running cold water; slip off skins, stems, and root end. (Leave beets whole; or slice or dice them.) Season with salt, pepper, and butter

or margarine. Add a little lemon juice, sautéed onion, pinch of cloves or allspice, or a little sour cream. Or add a little horse-radish and a little cream.

Or mix one of these sauces with sliced beets. Or serve beets whole; pass sauce in small bowl.

Avery Butter, p. 372	374
Black Butter, p. 377	Sour Cream, p. 373
Easy Hollandaise, p.	Vinaigrette, p. 373

BEET-AND-CABBAGE SCRAMBLE

3 or 4 pared medium beets	or margarine ¼ teasp. salt
½ small head cabbage, finely shredded	⅛ teasp. pepper 2 teasp. sugar
1 minced small onion	2 tablesp. vinegar
¼ cup bacon fat, butter,	2 tablesp. water

On medium-coarse grater, shred beets; toss with cabbage and onion (they should make 4 or 5 cups). In large skillet, melt bacon fat; add vegetables, then salt, pepper, sugar, vinegar, water. Cook slowly, covered, 10 min., tossing occasionally. Makes 4 servings.

BUTTERY SHREDDED BEETS

6 pared medium beets	⅛ teasp. pepper
½ teasp. salt	2 tablesp. butter or
⅛ teasp. garlic salt	margarine

On medium grater, grate beets; arrange in skillet. Sprinkle with salt, garlic salt, pepper; dot with butter. Simmer, covered, 20 to 30 min., or until tender. Pass vinegar or lemon wedges at table. Makes 4 to 6 servings.

SWEET-SOUR BEETS

2 tablesp. butter or margarine	radish 2½ cups diced or sliced,
1 tablesp. minced onion	cooked or canned
2 tablesp. brown sugar	beets (No. 2 can)
2 teasp. cornstarch	½ teasp. salt
¼ cup vinegar	⅛ teasp. pepper
1 to 2 tablesp. horse-	

In hot butter in saucepan, cook onion 2 or 3 min. Stir in sugar mixed with cornstarch, then vinegar, horse-radish; cook, stirring, until smooth and clear. (If too thick or vinegary, thin with little beet liquid.) Add beets, salt, pepper; heat. Makes 4 servings.

BAKED BEETS WITH ONIONS

4 cups diced, pared beets	1½ teasp. salt
1 cup coarsely chopped onions	¼ cup boiling water
	¼ cup butter or margarine

Start heating oven to 375°F. Arrange beets and onions in greased 1½-qt. casserole. Add salt, boiling water, butter. Bake, covered, 1 hr. 10 min. Makes 6 servings.

BEETS IN ORANGE SAUCE

8 small beets	¼ cup milk
1 tablesp. butter or margarine	¼ cup beet liquid
2 tablesp. flour	1 teasp. grated orange rind
1¼ teasp. salt	½ cup orange juice
Speck pepper	

Prepare, then cook beets whole as on p. 278. Drain, reserving liquid; peel. In double boiler, melt butter; stir in flour, salt, pepper. Slowly stir in milk, beet liquid, orange rind and juice. Cook, stirring, until thickened. Add beets; heat. Makes 4 servings.

HARVARD BEETS

⅓ cup granulated sugar	margarine
½ teasp. salt	1 teasp. minced onion
1 tablesp. cornstarch	3 cups hot diced or sliced, cooked or canned beets
½ cup vinegar	
2 tablesp. butter or	

In double boiler, blend sugar, salt, cornstarch; stir in vinegar; cook, stirring constantly, until smooth and thickened. Add butter, onion, beets; heat 20 min. Makes 5 servings.

YOUNG BEETS WITH BEET GREENS

Use beet greens with tiny beets attached. Clean; wash in several changes of cold water. To ½″ boiling salted water in saucepan (½ teasp. salt per cup water), add greens. Boil, covered, 20 to 25 min., or until tender. Drain *well*. Cut off beets; slip off skins. Cut up greens (scissors make this easy). Add beets; season. Add butter or margarine and a little lemon juice, vinegar, or French dressing. Heat.

BROCCOLI

To Buy, to Prepare, to Cook: See chart, p. 278.

To Serve: With 2 forks or perforated pancake turner, lift out broccoli; drain; arrange on heated platter. Spoon on melted butter or margarine seasoned with salt, pepper, lemon juice.

Or spoon one of these sauces over upper part of hot cooked broccoli; pass rest of sauce.

Chive, p. 372	Louis, p. 373
Egg, p. 376	Creamy Mustard, p. 375
Easy Hollandaise, p. 374	Sour Cream, p. 373
Spur-of-the-Moment Hollandaise, p. 374	Thousand Island, p. 374
Horse-radish I, p. 375	Vinaigrette, p. 373

Also see Serve with a Flair, p. 247.

BRUSSELS SPROUTS

To Buy, to Prepare, to Cook: See chart, p. 279.

To Serve: Drain sprouts. Season with salt, pepper, butter or margarine, and lemon juice.

Or sauté sliced mushrooms in butter; then add to sprouts.

Or spoon one of these sauces over sprouts:

Drawn Butter, p. 376	Thousand Island, p. 374
Easy Hollandaise, p. 374	Vinaigrette, p. 373

Also see Serve with a Flair, p. 247.

BRUSSELS-SPROUT MEDLEY

Prepare 1 cup diced celery (or ½ lb. green beans, crosscut) and 1 lb. Brussels sprouts. Cook together as for Brussels Sprouts, p. 279. Drain. Season with salt, pepper, and butter or margarine. If desired, add a little cream or some grated process American cheese.

CABBAGE
(green, savoy, Chinese, or red)

To Buy, to Prepare, to Cook: See chart, p. 279.

To Serve Shredded Green, Savoy, or Chinese

Cabbage: Drain cooked cabbage. Season with salt, pepper, and butter or margarine.

Or melt butter; then add to cabbage, along with one of these:

Diced crisp bacon	Prepared mustard
Dried basil	and a little lemon
Celery seeds	juice
Grated cheese	Minced onion
Chili sauce	Snipped parsley or
Hot cream	chives
Lemon juice	

Also see Serve with a Flair, p. 247.

To Serve Wedges of Green or Savoy Cabbage: Drain cooked wedges. Season with salt, pepper; then drizzle on melted butter or margarine.

Or spoon one of these sauces over wedges:

Mustard, p. 375	374
Thousand Island, p.	Vinaigrette, p. 373

To Serve Shredded Red Cabbage: Drain cooked cabbage. Add salt, pepper, butter or margarine.

DOUBLE-BOILER-SCALLOPED CABBAGE

4 cups shredded cabbage	crumbs
¾ cup canned or diced fresh tomatoes	1 cup grated process sharp American cheese (¼ lb.)
Salt and pepper	2 tablesp. melted butter or margarine
1 cup fresh bread	

Cook cabbage in small amount of boiling water until tender-crisp—about 5 min. In buttered double boiler, place half of cabbage, then half of tomatoes; sprinkle very lightly with salt and pepper; add half of crumbs and half of cheese. Repeat. Drizzle butter over all. Cook over hot water, covered, about 30 min., or until cheese is melted. Makes 4 servings.

If you prefer, you may cook this in covered saucepan over low heat about 30 min., or bake in covered casserole at 350°F. 30 min.

QUICK-COOKED CABBAGE

Prepare 5 cups finely shredded cabbage as on p. 279. In 10″ skillet, heat 2 tablesp. bacon fat; add shredded cabbage, ¾ to 1 teasp. salt, dash pepper. Toss several times—until cabbage is coated with bacon fat. Cook, covered, about 3 min. Makes 4 servings.

CABBAGE SCRAMBLE

1 tablesp. butter or margarine	onion
3 cups shredded green or Chinese cabbage	½ green pepper, cut into strips
1 cup thinly sliced celery	2 cups diced, peeled tomatoes
1 thinly sliced medium	1 teasp. salt
	⅛ teasp. pepper

In large skillet, heat butter. Add rest of ingredients. Cook, covered, 5 to 8 min., or until tender, stirring twice. Makes 4 servings.

DUTCH HOT SLAW

6 cups shredded cabbage	½ teasp. salt
1 tablesp. butter or margarine	1½ tablesp. sugar
	½ teasp. dry mustard
2 eggs	⅛ teasp. paprika
¼ cup vinegar	¼ cup water
	¼ cup light cream

Cook cabbage as on p. 279. Drain; keep hot. Meanwhile, melt butter in double boiler; add eggs beaten with vinegar, salt, sugar, mustard, paprika, water. Cook, stirring, until thickened. Remove from heat. Add cream; beat till smooth. Pour over cabbage. Makes 4 or 5 servings.

PANNED CURRIED CABBAGE

2 tablesp. butter, margarine, or salad oil	1 teasp. curry powder
1 minced small clove garlic	6 cups finely shredded cabbage
	1 teasp. salt

In butter in large skillet, sauté garlic 2 min. Stir in curry, cabbage, salt. Cook, covered, stirring occasionally, until tender—about 10 min. Makes 4 or 5 servings.

To Vary: Add 1 cup canned tomatoes just before cabbage is done. Season to taste.

RED CABBAGE WITH APPLES

1 2½-lb. head red cabbage, shredded	¼ cup vinegar
¾ cup boiling water	1½ teasp. flour
3 sliced, pared, cored large cooking apples	¼ cup brown sugar, packed
3 tablesp. melted butter or margarine	2 teasp. salt
	Speck pepper

Put shredded cabbage in kettle. Add water; cook, covered, 10 min. Add apples; cook 10 min., or until tender. Add rest of ingredients combined. Heat. Makes 6 servings.

▶ **For 2:** Use 1-lb. head cabbage, 3 small apples; halve rest of ingredients.

SKILLET CHINESE CABBAGE

7 tablesp. butter, margarine, or salad oil	(1 medium head)
	6 tablesp. light cream
7 cups finely shredded Chinese cabbage	½ teasp. salt
	Speck pepper

In skillet, melt butter. Add cabbage. Cook over medium heat, covered, 5 min. Stir in rest of ingredients. Cook, covered, 5 min., or until tender. Makes 4 servings.

SOUR-CREAM CABBAGE

3 tablesp. butter, margarine, or salad oil	⅓ cup commercial sour cream
½ minced clove garlic	1 tablesp. lemon juice
8 cups finely shredded cabbage, firmly packed	1 tablesp. sugar
	1 tablesp. salt
	½ teasp. celery seeds
¼ cup boiling water	1 egg, beaten

In hot butter in large skillet, sauté garlic over low heat 5 min. Add cabbage, water. Simmer, covered, 8 to 15 min., or until tender. Add rest of ingredients combined; toss. Makes 4 or 5 servings.

▶ **For 2:** Use 1 egg; halve rest of ingredients.

CARROTS

To Buy, to Prepare, to Cook: See chart, p. 279. For a savory touch, along with each 1 lb. carrots, cook 1 cup thinly sliced onions, ½ cup snipped scallions, or 1 cup diced celery.

To Serve: Drain carrots. Season with salt (or seasoned salt), pepper, butter or margarine, and snipped parsley.

Or add ¼ teasp. dried tarragon or savory to each 1 lb. carrots.

Or mash or whip carrots with electric mixer; then season, adding pinch nutmeg.

Also see Serve with a Flair, p. 247.

BAKED CARROTS

Start heating oven to 375°F. In 1½-qt. casserole, arrange 1 lb. pared medium carrots, halved lengthwise or shredded medium coarse. Add 1 minced small onion, ¼ cup hot water, 2 tablesp. butter or margarine, 1½ teasp. salt, and ½ teasp. celery seeds or dried basil. Bake, covered, 45 min., or until tender. Makes 4 servings.

GLAZED CARROTS

Cook pared small whole carrots till almost tender as on p. 279. Drain well; then dry. Roll in granulated sugar. In same saucepan, simmer carrots in melted butter or margarine, turning often, until glazed.

BUFFET CHEESE-SCALLOPED CARROTS

12 sliced, pared medium carrots	2 cups milk
	⅛ teasp. pepper
¼ cup butter or margarine	¼ teasp. celery salt
1 minced small onion	½ lb. packaged process-sharp-American-cheese slices
¼ cup flour	
1 teasp. salt	3 cups buttered fresh bread crumbs
¼ teasp. dry mustard	

Start heating oven to 350°F. Cook carrots as on p. 279. Drain. Meanwhile, in butter in saucepan, gently cook onion 2 to 3 min. Stir in flour, salt, mustard, then milk; cook stirring, until smooth. Add pepper, celery salt.

In 2-qt. casserole, arrange layer of carrots, then layer of cheese. Repeat until both are used, ending with carrots. Pour on sauce; top with crumbs. Bake, uncovered, about 25 min., or until crumbs are golden. Makes 8 servings.

To Do Ahead: Make early in day; refrigerate. To serve, bake, uncovered, at 350°F. 35 to 45 min., or until hot.

CREAMY CARROTS AND CORN

6 sliced, pared medium carrots	corn
	2 tablesp. butter or margarine
1 sliced medium onion	
½ cup milk	1 tablesp. flour
1 12-oz. can vacuum-packed whole-kernel	About ¼ teasp. salt
	About ⅛ teasp. pepper

Cook carrots with onion as on p. 279. Drain. Add milk, corn; heat till boiling. Meanwhile, mix butter with flour until smooth; drop into vegetables; cook, stirring gently, until smooth and thickened. Add salt, pepper, and any other desired seasonings. Makes 4 servings.

BACON-FRIED CARROTS

In skillet, cook 3 bacon slices until crisp; remove; set aside. To bacon fat, add 1 lb. sliced, pared carrots and 1 sliced medium onion. Sprinkle with ½ teasp. salt, ⅛ teasp. pepper. Cook over low heat, covered, about 10 min., or until barely tender. Uncover; cook, turning occasionally, until carrots are slightly brown. Add crumbled bacon. Makes 4 servings.

CARROTS IN CREAM

8 pared small carrots	2 tablesp. snipped
¼ cup butter or	parsley
margarine	1 teasp. salt
2 teasp. sugar	⅓ cup light cream

Cut carrots into matchsticklike slivers. In saucepan with tight cover, melt butter. Add carrots, sugar, parsley, salt. Simmer, covered, till tender —about 10 min. Add cream. Heat. Makes 4 servings.

▶ For 2: Use 3 tablesp. cream; halve rest of ingredients.

PARSLEY CARROTS AND POTATOES

2 cups slivered, pared	¾ cup boiling water
carrots	6 tablesp. melted butter
2 cups slivered, pared	or margarine
potatoes	⅛ teasp. pepper
1¼ teasp. salt	½ cup snipped parsley

Cook carrots and potatoes with salt in boiling water, covered, 10 min., or until tender. Drain; add rest of ingredients; toss. Or drain; mash; then add butter, pepper, parsley. Makes 4 servings.

CAULIFLOWER

To Buy, to Prepare, to Cook: See chart, p. 280.

To Serve: Drain cauliflower; season with salt, pepper, and butter or margarine.

Or pour one of these sauces over cauliflower in serving dish.

Saucepan Cheese, p. 373	Quick Mushroom, p. 372
Tomato Cheese, p. 373	Creamy Mustard, p. 375
Easy Hollandaise, p. 374	Thousand Island, p. 374
Spur-of-the-Moment Hollandaise, p.	Vinaigrette, p. 373

Also see Serve with a Flair, p. 247.

CAULIFLOWER SUPREME

2 pkg. frozen	2 tablesp. flour
cauliflower	1 teasp. salt
2 tablesp. butter or	⅛ teasp. pepper
margarine	1 teasp. bottled thick
½ lb. thickly sliced	meat sauce, p. 9
mushrooms	1 cup light cream

Cook cauliflower as label directs until just tender-crisp. Meanwhile, in hot butter in skillet, sauté mushrooms 10 min. Sprinkle with flour; add salt, pepper, meat sauce, cream. Cook, stirring occasionally, until smooth and thickened. When cauliflower is done, drain well. Serve topped with mushroom sauce. Makes 4 or 5 servings.

CHINESE CAULIFLOWER

Wash and remove lower stalks from small or medium *firm, crisp* head of cauliflower. With coarse shredder, shred entire head. Place in skillet; sprinkle lightly with salt; add ⅓ cup hot water. Cook, covered, 5 to 7 min., or until tender but still slightly crisp. Do not drain.

To cauliflower, add 2 tablesp. each butter or margarine and heavy cream; heat, tossing with fork, 1 to 2 min. Serve at once, sprinkled with paprika or snipped chives or parsley. Makes 3 or 4 servings.

CELERIAC
(knob celery)

To Buy, to Prepare, to Cook: See chart, p. 280.

To Serve: Season with salt, pepper, and butter or margarine.

Or reheat in thin cream.

Or mash, season, and add enough hot milk to beat until fluffy.

Or serve as salad: Pour a little French dressing over hot cooked celeriac at once so it won't discolor; refrigerate. Serve on salad greens.

CELERY

To Buy, to Prepare: See chart, p. 280. Use hearts and center stalks as relish or in salads. Use fresh leaves in soups, stews, salads, stuffings, sauces, etc.

To Cook: Cook outer stalks, slivered or diced, as on p. 280. Or use in soups.

To Serve Cooked Celery: Drain celery. Season with salt, pepper, butter or margarine, and snipped parsley or paprika.
Or reheat in light cream.
Also see Serve with a Flair, p. 247.

BRAISED CELERY AND TOMATOES

2 tablesp. butter or margarine	¼ teasp. onion salt
2 cups cleaned celery, cut into 1″ pieces	2 cups quartered, peeled tomatoes; or 1 No. 2 can tomatoes, drained*
¾ teasp. salt	
⅛ teasp. pepper	

In saucepan or small skillet with tight cover, melt butter. Add celery, salt, pepper, onion salt. Simmer, covered, 10 min., or till tender-crisp. Add tomatoes; cook, covered, 5 min., or till celery is tender, tomatoes are hot. Makes 4 servings.

Save tomato juice to use later in soup.

CORN

To Buy, to Prepare: See chart, p. 280.

To Cook: Cook only enough ears of corn to serve everyone once. Drop into plenty of boiling salted water (1 teasp. salt per 1 qt. water). Boil, covered, until milk in corn is just set—about 5 to 6 min.

To Serve: With fork or tongs, remove corn from water to heated platter; cover with napkin (now start to cook second servings). Serve at once with butter or margarine, or butter in which cut clove of garlic, snipped chives, or celery seeds have been standing.

▶ **For 2:** If desired, use large covered skillet for boiling a few ears of corn.

CORN IN CREAM

Boil corn on the cob as above. Slice off kernels, being careful not to cut too close to cob. Add light cream, salt, pepper, butter or margarine, and paprika. Heat.

CORN FRITTERS, NORTHERN STYLE

3 egg yolks	¼ cup sifted all-purpose flour
1⅔ cups cooked or canned whole-kernel corn	3 egg whites, stiffly beaten
½ teasp. salt	6 tablesp. fat or salad oil
⅛ teasp. pepper	

Beat egg yolks until light; mix in corn, salt, pepper, flour. Fold in egg whites. Drop by tablespoonfuls into hot fat in skillet. Cook on both sides until brown and done.
Serve as vegetable, with chicken, meat, or fish. Or serve as main dish, with butter and syrup or crisp bacon. Makes 6 servings.

▶ **For 2:** Use 1 egg; halve rest of ingredients.

Hickory Corn Fritters: Add 1 cup grated franks (about 3) with corn. Substitute seasoned salt for salt.

CORN FRITTERS, SOUTHERN STYLE

1 cup sifted all-purpose flour	¼ cup milk
1 teasp. baking powder	2 teasp. salad oil
1 teasp. salt	2½ cups cooked or canned whole-kernel corn
2 eggs	

Sift flour with baking powder, salt. Beat eggs; add milk, 2 teasp. salad oil. Stir in flour mixture, then corn. Drop by tablespoonfuls into fat heated to 365°F. on deep-fat frying thermometer as in Shallow Frying, p. 8. Fry 3 to 5 min., turning once. Makes 5 or 6 servings.

CUSTARD CORN PUDDING

2 cups chopped, cooked or canned whole-kernel corn	1½ tablesp. melted butter or margarine
2 eggs, slightly beaten	2 cups scalded milk
1 teasp. sugar	1¾ teasp. salt
	¼ teasp. pepper

Start heating oven to 325°F. Combine all ingredients; pour into greased 1½-qt. casserole. Set in pan of warm water. Bake, uncovered, 1 hr. 15 min. Makes 5 or 6 servings.

To Vary: Before baking pudding mixture, add ½ cup minced, cooked ham or grated cheese, or 2 tablesp. minced onion.

▶ **For 2:** Halve ingredients; use 3 individual casseroles.

SOUTHERN CORN PUDDING

8 to 12 ears corn	1¼ cups light cream
1½ teasp. salt	

Start heating oven to 350°F. Husk corn. With sharp knife, split corn kernels, cutting lengthwise of ears. Then, with back of knife, scrape out kernels until you have 2 cups corn pulp. Combine with salt, cream; pour into greased 1½-qt. casserole. Bake, uncovered, 1 hr.

Serve hot, with butter. Makes 4 servings.

▶ **For 2:** Halve ingredients; use 1-qt. casserole. Bake at 350°F. 40 min.

SUCCOTASH

1½ cups hot cooked or canned whole-kernel corn	canned green beans, green limas, or shell beans
2 tablesp. butter or margarine	½ cup light cream
1½ cups hot cooked or	Salt
	Pepper

Combine all ingredients, adding salt and pepper to taste. Heat. Makes 6 servings.

CUCUMBERS

To Buy, to Prepare, to Cook: See chart, p. 280.

To Serve: Drain cucumbers. Season with salt, pepper, and butter or margarine.

Or reheat in Vegetable Sauce, p. 376.

DRIED BEANS

To use dried beans, peas, and lentils in well-balanced main dishes, see p. 563.

Note: If beans are quick-cooking, follow label directions.

OLD-FASHIONED BOSTON BAKED BEANS

1 lb. pea or navy beans	¼ cup molasses
5 cups water	2 tablesp. sweet-pickle juice; or 2 tablesp.
2 teasp. dry mustard	
¼ teasp. pepper	vinegar, with speck
1 tablesp. salt	ground cinnamon
3 quartered medium onions	and cloves
	¼ lb. piece salt pork
¼ cup brown sugar	Pepper

Pick over beans; wash. Cover with 3 cups water; soak 8 hr. or overnight; then add 2 cups water, mustard, and rest of ingredients except salt pork and pepper. Boil, covered, about 1 hr., or until skins of beans begin to wrinkle.

Start heating oven to 250°F. Cut salt pork at ½″ intervals almost all the way through; place in 2-qt. bean pot; cover with hot beans and their liquid. Generously sprinkle with pepper. Bake 6 to 8 hr., covered, or until tender. When beans are two thirds baked, add about ¾ cup water, or enough to just cover. Uncover last ½ hr. of baking. Makes 4 to 6 servings.

Serve instead of potatoes, or with a baked ham, franks, crisp bacon, etc. Or serve as breakfast, luncheon, or supper main dish, with brown bread, corn bread, etc.

As accompaniment, serve pickle relish, tomato catchup, chili sauce, or mustard pickle, etc.

SAVORY LIMA-BEAN POT

4 cups large California dry limas, rinsed	½ cup molasses
	2 tablesp. vinegar
4 teasp. salt	½ teasp. tabasco
2 tablesp. butter or margarine	2 teasp. dry mustard
	1 to 3 cups diced,
2 sliced medium onions	cooked ham
1 diced green pepper	3 tablesp. butter or
½ cup catchup	margarine

Place rinsed limas and salt in 2-qt. boiling water; simmer, covered, 2 hr., or until tender (add more boiling water if needed). Start heating oven to 325°F. In 2 tablesp. butter, sauté onions and green pepper until tender. Mix catchup with molasses, vinegar, tabasco, mustard. When limas are tender, drain, reserving 1 cup liquid. Add this reserved liquid to catchup mixture.

In 3-qt. casserole or large bean pot, arrange, in layers, limas, onion-and-pepper mixture, ham; pour on catchup mixture. Dot with 3 tablesp.

butter. Bake, uncovered, 1½ hr. Wonderful for a buffet. Makes 10 to 12 servings.

Boston Style: Substitute 4 cups dried pea beans, soaked overnight, for dry limas; simmer only 1 hr. Use 2¾ cups liquid drained from cooked beans instead of 1 cup. (When arranging layers, place beans on top.) Bake 2½ hr., or until beans are tender.

BLACK-EYED PEAS

1 cup dried black-eyed peas	2 tablesp. minced onion
6 cups hot water, left-over meat broth, or vegetable water	1 minced small clove garlic
	1 tablesp. snipped parsley
½ lb. salt pork, in ½" cubes or in one piece	1 tablesp. minced celery
	1 teasp. salt

Pick over peas; wash. Place in kettle with hot water and rest of ingredients. Cover; bring to boil slowly; simmer over low heat 2½ hr., or until tender. Drain. Makes 4 servings.

P.S. Have you tried frozen fresh black-eyed peas? Look for them in your local market—they're delicious. Cooking directions are on the label.

BAKED-BEAN CASSEROLE

2 tablesp. fat or salad oil	1 tablesp. prepared mustard
1 cup sliced onions	2 sliced, peeled tomatoes
2 1-lb. cans Boston-style baked beans	1 teasp. salt
1 2¼-oz. can deviled ham	2 teasp. brown sugar

Start heating oven to 400°F. In hot fat in skillet, sauté onions until tender. Combine beans, ham, mustard; arrange half in 2-qt. casserole. Place half of onions and tomatoes over beans; sprinkle with half of salt and sugar. Repeat. Bake, covered, 30 min. Uncover; bake 5 min. Makes 4 servings.

SAVORY BAKED BEANS AND HAMBURGER

2 tablesp. fat or salad oil	kidney beans, un-drained
⅓ cup sliced onion	2 teasp. Worcestershire
⅔ cup diced celery	¾ teasp. salt
½ lb. chuck, ground	¾ teasp. dried sage
2⅔ cups canned baked beans or cooked	⅓ cup water or tomato juice

Heat fat in skillet. Add onion, celery, beef; cook, uncovered, about 10 min. Add rest of ingredients; heat. Makes 4 servings.

QUICK HOME-STYLE BAKED BEANS

Start heating oven to 375°F. In 1-qt. casserole, combine 1 1-lb. can baked beans (Boston style or in tomato sauce), 2 tablesp. molasses or dark-brown sugar, 1 tablesp. dry or prepared mustard, ½ cup water. Top with 3 or 4 bacon slices or 4 or 5 fresh pork sausage links, cut into 2 or 3 pieces each. Bake, uncovered, 30 to 40 min. Makes 3 servings.

MOTHER'S EASY CHILI BEANS

¼ lb. suet, cut into small pieces	1 red pepper (from pickling spice)
1 chopped onion	1 8-oz. can tomato sauce
1 lb. chuck, ground	2 No. 2 cans kidney beans
2½ teasp. chili powder	
1½ teasp. salt	Grated process Amer-ican cheese
⅛ teasp. pepper	

In large skillet, sauté suet until golden. Add onion and sauté until golden. Add beef; cook, stirring, until brown. Sprinkle with chili powder, salt, pepper; add red pepper; stir in tomato sauce. Cook, covered, 20 min. Add undrained beans; cook, covered, 1 to 3 hr., depending on how you like your beans (stir every ½ hr. and add a little water if mixture seems dry). Top with cheese. Makes 4 to 6 servings.

KIDNEY-BEAN SOPHISTICATE

2 tablesp. butter or margarine	beans
½ cup minced onions	¼ teasp. dried rosemary
1 No. 2 can kidney	1 teasp. salt
	¼ cup red wine

In butter in skillet, sauté onions until tender. Add undrained beans, rest of ingredients; simmer, uncovered, stirring occasionally, until enough liquid has evaporated to make mixture of desired consistency. Makes 4 servings.

KIDNEY-LIMA CASSEROLE

Start heating oven to 350°F. Drain 1 No. 2 can green limas and 1 No. 2 can kidney beans, reserving liquid from kidney beans. In 2-qt. casserole, mix limas and beans with 1 cup diced, cooked ham or canned luncheon meat. Blend 1 can undiluted condensed cream-of-mushroom soup with 1 teasp. Worcestershire and ¼ cup reserved kidney-bean liquid; pour over beans. Slice 1 medium green pepper and 1 small onion into very thin rings. Arrange on beans. Bake, uncovered, 35 min., or until hot. Makes 8 servings.

EGGPLANT

To Buy, to Prepare: See chart, p. 281.

SAUTEED EGGPLANT

Pare large eggplant; cut into ¼″ crosswise slices. Sprinkle with salt, pepper, and a little flour. Or dip into beaten egg, then into cracker crumbs. In hot bacon fat or salad oil in skillet, sauté eggplant till golden brown on both sides—about 6 to 8 min.

Serve alone or with Spanish Sauce, p. 376. Makes 6 servings.

EGGPLANT PARMESAN

1 large eggplant	cheese
3 eggs, beaten	2 teasp. dried orégano
1 cup packaged dried	½ lb. sliced Mozzarella
bread crumbs	cheese
¾ cup olive or salad oil	3 8-oz. cans tomato
½ cup grated Parmesan	sauce

Start heating oven to 350°F. Pare eggplant if desired; cut into ¼″-thick slices. Dip each slice first into eggs, then into crumbs. Sauté in hot olive oil until golden brown on both sides. Place layer of eggplant in 2-qt. casserole; sprinkle with some of Parmesan, orégano, and Mozzarella; then cover well with some of tomato sauce. Repeat until all eggplant is used, topping last layer of sauce with several slices of Mozzarella. Bake, uncovered, ½ hr., or until sauce is bubbly and cheese is melted. Makes 4 to 6 servings.

SCALLOPED EGGPLANT

1 medium eggplant	1 teasp. salt
½ cup minced onions	Dash pepper
2 teasp. salt	1¼ cups milk
1½ cups crumbled soda	6 tablesp. melted butter
crackers	or margarine

Start heating oven to 375°F. Pare eggplant; cut into 1″ cubes. Boil with onions and 2 teasp. salt

in 1″ boiling water, covered, until tender but not mushy—about 5 min. Drain.

Spread half of crumbs in greased 10″ x 6″ x 2″ baking dish; arrange eggplant and onions on top; sprinkle with 1 teasp. salt, pepper. Top with rest of crumbs. Pour milk into corners of baking dish, to cover bottom. Pour butter over top. Bake, uncovered, 45 min. Makes 4 servings.

► **For 2:** Use ¾ lb. eggplant; halve rest of ingredients. Use 1-qt. casserole.

EGGPLANT-AND-TOMATO BAKE

1 medium eggplant	2 tablesp. snipped
¼ cup salad oil	parsley
3 peeled large tomatoes	1 minced clove garlic
Salt and pepper	1 tablesp. salad oil
2 cups ½″ fresh bread	¼ cup grated Parmesan
squares	cheese

Start heating oven to 400°F. Cut eggplant into ½″-thick slices; pare. Sauté in ¼ cup salad oil until golden on both sides (add more oil as needed). Cut tomatoes into ½″-thick slices; sauté in same skillet. In 10″ x 6″ x 2″ baking dish, alternate layers of eggplant and tomato slices (4 layers in all), sprinkling each layer with ¼ teasp. salt, ⅛ teasp. pepper.

Combine bread squares with parsley, garlic, 1 tablesp. salad oil, cheese; sprinkle over eggplant. Bake, uncovered, 20 min., or until bread squares are golden, eggplant is tender. Makes 4 or 5 servings.

GREEN, WAX, OR SNAP BEANS

To Buy, to Prepare, to Cook: See chart, p. 281.

To Serve: Drain beans, reserving liquid. Boil liquid down to a few tablespoonfuls; add to beans, with salt, pepper, butter or margarine.

Or spoon on, or toss drained beans with, one of these sauces:

Tomato-Cheese, p. 373	Mustard, p. 375
Quick Cream, p. 374	Thousand Island, p. 374
Quick Mushroom, p. 372	Vinaigrette, p. 373

Also see Serve with a Flair, p. 247.

GREEN BEANS LYONNAISE

1¼ lb. green beans   1 teasp. tarragon
4 diced bacon slices   vinegar
¼ cup minced onion   Speck pepper
½ teasp. salt

Prepare beans, French cut, then cook as on p. 281. Meanwhile, fry bacon in skillet until crisp. Remove bacon bits; reserve. To bacon fat, add onion; sauté until tender. Add salt, vinegar, pepper, bacon bits; pour over drained beans. Toss with fork. Makes 4 servings.

GREEN BEANS WITH HERB SAUCE

1 lb. green beans   ¼ cup minced celery
¼ cup butter or   ¼ cup snipped parsley
   margarine   ¼ teasp. dried rosemary
¾ cup minced onions   ¼ teasp. dried basil
1 minced clove garlic   ¾ teasp. salt

Prepare beans, crosscut, then cook as on p. 281. Meanwhile, melt butter in saucepan. Add onions, garlic, celery; sauté 5 min. Add rest of ingredients. Simmer, covered, 10 min. Toss well with drained beans. Makes 4 servings.

GREEN BEANS DE LUXE

1 lb. green beans   sliced mushrooms*
2 tablesp. bacon fat,   ½ teasp. salt
   butter, or margarine   Pepper to taste
1 coarsely chopped   ¼ cup light cream or
   small onion   undiluted evaporated
1 3-oz. can chopped or   milk

Prepare, then crosscut beans into 1″ lengths as on p. 281. Heat bacon fat in skillet. Add beans, onion, mushrooms with their liquid, salt, pepper. Turn heat very low; cook, covered, 20 to 25 min. (If liquid cooks away so you can hear beans sizzle, add 1 or 2 tablesp. water.) When beans are barely tender, add cream; heat. Makes 4 servings.

If desired, substitute ¼ lb. sliced mushrooms and ¼ cup water.

SWEET-SOUR GREEN BEANS

1 lb. green beans   3 tablesp. vinegar
2 tablesp. bacon fat   1 tablesp. soy sauce
1 cup boiling water   ¼ cup cold water
½ teasp. salt   ¼ cup sweet pickle
1 teasp. cornstarch   relish
3 tablesp. sugar

Prepare, then crosscut beans into 1″ lengths as on p. 281. Place beans in large skillet or saucepan with tight cover; add bacon fat, boiling water, salt. Heat quickly, covered, until beans steam; then turn down heat and cook 15 to 20 min., or till tender-crisp. Do not drain. Mix cornstarch with rest of ingredients; pour over beans; cook, stirring, until slightly thickened and smooth. Makes 4 servings.

GREEN LIMAS

To Buy, to Prepare, to Cook: See chart, p. 281.

To Serve: Drain limas. Season to taste with salt (try monosodium glutamate too, or celery, garlic, onion, or seasoned salt), pepper, and butter or margarine.

Or sauté sliced mushrooms or minced onion in butter until tender; then add to limas.

Or toss limas with one of these sauces:

Saucepan Cheese, p. 373   Quick Mushroom, p. 372
Tomato-Cheese, p. 373   Italian Tomato, p. 373
Curry, p. 372

Also see Serve with a Flair, p. 247.

GREEN LIMAS A LA CREME

2 lb. green limas (about   margarine
   2 cups shelled)   ¼ cup light cream
½ teasp. minced onion   ¼ cup milk
¼ cup grated process   Salt
   American cheese   Pepper
1 tablesp. butter or

Prepare, then cook, limas as on p. 281. Drain. Add onion, cheese, butter, cream, milk. With fork, toss lightly over low heat until cheese is melted. Season to taste. Makes 4 servings.

GREEN LIMAS AND SCALLIONS

2 lb. green limas (about   1 tablesp. flour
   2 cups shelled)   ¼ teasp. paprika
2 tablesp. butter or   ½ teasp. salt
   margarine   Speck pepper
6 snipped scallions

Prepare, then cook, limas as on p. 281. Drain, reserving ½ cup liquid. In butter in saucepan, simmer scallions 2 min. Stir in flour, then lima liquid; cook, stirring, until thickened. Add limas, paprika, salt, pepper; heat. Makes 4 to 6 servings.

DOUBLE-BOILER GREEN LIMAS AND CORN

Put 1½ cups water in double-boiler bottom, ½ cup light cream in top; heat. When water boils, drop 1 pkg. frozen limas and ½ teasp. salt into bottom. Replace double-boiler top; drop 1 pkg. frozen whole-kernel corn and ½ teasp. salt into cream; cover. Bring limas to boil; cook till tender—about 12 to 15 min. (Corn cooks in same time.) Drain limas; season. Serve corn and limas separately or combined. Makes 4 to 6 servings.

KAREN'S GREEN LIMAS

Start heating oven to 350°F. Place 1 pkg. frozen Fordhook limas in 1-qt. casserole. Sprinkle with ½ teasp. salt, speck pepper. Pour on ¾ cup light cream. Bake, covered, 45 min., or until tender. Makes 4 servings.

GREEN PEPPERS

To Buy, to Prepare: See chart, p. 281.

STUFFED-PEPPER TWINS

4 large green peppers, halved lengthwise	margarine
1½ cups cooked rice	2 eggs
¼ cup undiluted evaporated milk or light cream	¼ cup light cream or milk
1 cup grated sharp American cheese (¼ lb.)	2 tablesp. melted butter or margarine
½ teasp. monosodium glutamate	1½ cups cooked or canned corn (cream style or whole kernel)
Salt and pepper	1 cup coarsely crumbled crackers
2 peeled medium tomatoes	½ teasp. salt
4 teasp. butter or	Speck pepper

Start heating oven to 375°F. Boil green peppers in boiling salted water 5 min.; drain.

For rice stuffing, mix rice, evaporated milk, cheese, monosodium glutamate, salt and pepper to taste. Cut tomatoes into thick slices; sprinkle with more salt and pepper; stand slice at one end, or at each end, of 4 pepper halves; then fill halves with rice stuffing; top each with 1 teasp. butter.

For corn stuffing, beat eggs with fork. Add light cream, melted butter, corn, crackers, ½ teasp. salt, speck pepper. Heap in remaining 4 pepper halves.

Arrange all stuffed-pepper halves in greased shallow baking dish. Bake, uncovered, about 30 min., or until corn stuffing is firm when tested with tip of knife. Add dash of paprika to corn stuffing. Serve 1 pepper half of each kind on each plate. Makes 4 servings.

CHILI PEPPERS

¼ lb. diced bacon	peppers
1 minced medium onion	4 diced, peeled large tomatoes
1 minced clove garlic	½ teasp. salt
2 quartered large green	

In skillet, fry bacon until crisp. Add onion and garlic; sauté 3 to 4 min. Add peppers and heaping spoonful of diced tomatoes. Sauté, covered, 5 min. Add rest of tomatoes, salt. Cook, covered, 10 min. Makes 4 servings.

ITALIAN GREEN PEPPERS

4 large green peppers	1 sliced medium onion
3 tablesp. olive or salad oil	2 minced cloves garlic
¼ cup boiling water	2 cups canned tomatoes
1 teasp. salt	2 teasp. sugar
1 tablesp. olive or salad oil	1 teasp. salt
	⅛ teasp. pepper
	½ teasp. dried basil

Cut green peppers into 1½" strips; then halve each strip crosswise. Heat 3 tablesp. olive oil in large skillet; add peppers; sauté 10 min., or until slightly browned. Add boiling water, 1 teasp. salt; simmer, covered, 20 min., or until tender.

Meanwhile, in 1 tablesp. olive oil in saucepan, sauté onion and garlic until golden. Add tomatoes, and the next 4 ingredients. Simmer, uncovered, 30 min., or until thickened. Put drained peppers in serving dish; pour on sauce. Makes 4 servings.

GREENS

Beet tops	Mustard greens
Collards	Spinach
Dandelion greens	Swiss chard (young)
Kale	Turnip greens, etc.

To Buy, to Prepare, to Cook: See chart, p. 281.

To Serve: Drain greens well several times. If desired, with scissors or 2 knives, slash through greens. Add salt, pepper, and butter or margarine. If desired, sauté a little minced onion in butter or margarine before adding to greens.

Or after seasoning, toss one of following with, or sprinkle over, greens.

Crumbled crisp bacon	French dressing
	Horse-radish
Chopped, cooked beets	Lemon juice
	Nutmeg
Chili sauce	Fresh or dried rosemary
Chopped, hard-cooked egg	Flavored vinegar

Also see Serve with a Flair, p. 247.

PANNED SPINACH

2 lb. spinach	⅛ teasp. pepper
1 tablesp. bacon fat, butter, or margarine	½ cup milk
1 minced clove garlic	1 teasp. fresh, frozen, or canned lemon juice
1 teasp. salt	1 tablesp. flour

Prepare spinach as on p. 281. Meanwhile, heat bacon fat in kettle. Add garlic; sauté till tender. Add spinach, salt, pepper. Cook, covered, over medium heat, stirring occasionally, until tender —about 5 min. Slowly add milk and lemon juice to flour, stirring till smooth; pour over spinach. Cook, tossing with fork, until sauce is smooth and thickened. Makes 4 servings.

VINAIGRETTE SPINACH

2½ lb. spinach	or canned lemon juice; or 2 tablesp. vinegar
6 tablesp. butter or margarine	
1 teasp. minced onion	¾ teasp. salt
½ teasp. prepared mustard	⅛ teasp. pepper
2 tablesp. fresh, frozen,	2 chopped, hard-cooked eggs

Prepare and cook spinach as on p. 281. Drain well; chop. In 1 tablesp. butter, sauté onion till tender. Add rest of ingredients except spinach; heat. Pour over spinach; toss. Makes 4 servings.

MATURED SWISS CHARD

To Buy: Matured Swiss chard usually comes tied in bunches and has large, ribbed leaves and broad, cream-colored stalks.

To Cook Stalks: Cut stalks from 2 lb. large Swiss chard leaves; wash both well. Cut stalks into 2″ pieces; cook in 1″ boiling water with 1 teasp. salt, covered, 15 min., or until tender. Drain; add 2 tablesp. butter or margarine, speck pepper, and salt if necessary. Or cream as in Old-fashioned Creamed Vegetables, p. 247.

To Cook Leaves: While stalks cook, cook washed leaves in ½″ boiling water with ¾ teasp. salt, covered, 10 min., or until tender. Drain; add 2 tablesp. butter or margarine, speck pepper, and salt if necessary.

To Serve: Place cooked leaves in center of serving dish, with stalks around them. Or toss together. Pass lemon wedges. Makes 4 servings.

CHEESY SWISS CHARD

2 lb. matured Swiss chard	2 tablesp. flour
2 teasp. salt	½ cup milk
2 tablesp. butter or margarine	¼ lb. diced process American cheese

Start heating oven to 325°F. Cut stalks from washed chard into 1″ pieces; cook in ½″ boiling water with salt, covered, 5 min. Then add torn leaves; cover; cook 5 min. Drain well, using saucer to press out excess liquid.

Meanwhile, melt butter in saucepan; stir in flour; slowly add milk; cook, stirring, over medium heat until thickened. Add cheese; toss with chard. Turn into 1½-qt. casserole. Bake, uncovered, 45 min. Makes 4 servings.

▶ **For 2:** Halve ingredients; use 2-cup casserole.

KOHLRABI

To Buy, to Prepare, to Cook: See chart, p. 282.

To Serve: Drain kohlrabi. Season with salt, pepper, butter or margarine, and few drops lemon juice or a little snipped parsley or chives.

Also see Serve with a Flair, p. 247.

MUSHROOMS

To Buy, to Prepare: See chart, p. 282.

Remember too the wonderful canned mushrooms; they come broiled—whole, sliced, or chopped; or plain—as slices, buttons, or stems and pieces.

BROILED MUSHROOMS

Allow 3 or 4 mushrooms per person. Wash mushrooms well; remove stems and reserve for Cream-of-Mushroom Soup, p. 38. In shallow baking pan, place mushroom caps, with rounded sides down; in each upturned cavity, place ½ teasp. butter or margarine. Sprinkle lightly with salt, pepper, dash of nutmeg, a little lemon juice; brush with melted butter. Broil 5 to 8 min. Also see Mixed Grill, p. 55.

Serve with steaks, chicken, etc., or on vegetable plate. Or serve on toast with bacon.

CREAMED MUSHROOMS

1 lb. mushrooms	1 teasp. lemon juice
2 tablesp. butter or margarine	¾ teasp. celery salt
2 tablesp. minced onion	1½ cups milk
2 tablesp. flour	3 tablesp. sherry or cooking sherry
1 teasp. salt	(optional)
⅛ teasp. pepper	

Slice or halve washed mushrooms (caps and stems) lengthwise. In butter in large skillet over low heat, sauté onion until tender; add mushrooms. Sauté over medium heat, covered, stirring occasionally, 8 to 10 min. Stir in flour, salt, pepper, lemon juice, celery salt, then milk. Cook over low heat, stirring, until thickened. Add sherry.

Serve as is or on toast. Or serve as main dish, on toast, topped with Baked Tomatoes, p. 273, or with bacon. Makes 4 servings.

SAUTEED MUSHROOMS

1 lb. mushrooms	1 teasp. fresh, frozen, or canned lemon juice
¼ cup butter or margarine	½ teasp. salt
2 tablesp. minced onion	⅛ teasp. pepper

Cut washed whole mushrooms into thick slices. Meanwhile, in butter in large skillet over low heat, sauté onion until tender. Add mushrooms. Sauté over medium heat, covered, stirring occasionally, 10 min. Turn off heat; let stand, covered, 4 to 5 min., to absorb juice in pan. Sprinkle with lemon juice, salt, pepper; toss.

Serve as is, or on toast, with steaks, chops, chicken, vegetable dinner, etc. Makes 4 servings.

P.S. If you prefer to leave mushrooms whole, sauté as above 12 min.

Mushrooms in Cream: Omit lemon juice. Stir in 2 tablesp. sherry or cooking sherry, then ⅓ cup light cream.

STUFFED MUSHROOMS

1 lb. medium mushrooms	¼ cup finely minced celery
Butter or margarine	1 teasp. Worcestershire
¼ cup finely minced onion	½ teasp. salt
	Speck pepper

Wash mushrooms; drain. Remove stems; chop fine. In large skillet, heat ¼ cup butter; add onion, celery, mushroom stems. Simmer until celery is tender. Stir in Worcestershire, salt, pepper. Brush mushroom caps with melted butter; then fill with onion mixture. Arrange caps, with stuffed sides up, in same skillet. Simmer 5 min., or until lightly browned (cover first 2 or 3 min.).

Serve with steak, chops, chicken, etc. Makes 4 servings.

OKRA

To Buy, to Prepare, to Cook: See chart, p. 283.

To Serve: Drain okra. Add salt, pepper, and butter or margarine. Also add a little lemon juice, herb vinegar, French dressing, chili sauce, or commercial sour cream.

Or first sauté snipped scallions or finely minced onion in butter; then add to okra.

Or serve one of these sauces in small dishes. Dip okra into sauce.

Drawn Butter, p. 376
Easy Hollandaise, p. 374

Thousand Island, p. 374
Vinaigrette, p. 373

OKRA MEDLEY

1½ cups sliced summer squash
1½ cups okra, cut into ½" slices
1 cup thinly slivered, pared carrots

1¼ teasp. salt
1 cup scallions (1 bunch)
Speck pepper
3 tablesp. butter or margarine

If squash is large, cut in half lengthwise; then slice. Cook squash, okra, and carrots with salt in 1" boiling water, covered, about 7 min. Meanwhile, cut scallions (green tops and all) into 1" pieces. Add to okra; cook 3 to 5 min., or until all vegetables are just tender-crisp. Season with pepper, butter, and more salt if needed. Makes 4 servings.

ONIONS

To Buy, to Prepare, to Cook: See chart, p. 283.

To Serve: Drain onions. Season with salt, pepper, and butter or margarine.

Or cream onions as in Old-fashioned Creamed Vegetables, p. 247, adding sherry or cooking sherry, nutmeg, or curry powder to taste.

Or toss onions with one of these sauces:

Saucepan Cheese, p. 373
Quick Cream, p. 374
Curry, p. 376
Quick Mushroom, p.

372

Thousand Island, p. 374

Tomato-Cheese, p. 373

Also see Serve with a Flair, p. 247.

BAKED ONIONS DE LUXE

8 medium onions (1½ lb.)
1 tablesp. melted butter or margarine
¼ cup tomato juice

2 tablesp. honey
1 teasp. salt
½ teasp. paprika
Parsley sprigs

Start heating oven to 350°F. Prepare onions as on p. 283; cut in halves crosswise; place in greased 1-qt. casserole. Combine butter, tomato juice, honey, salt, paprika; pour over onions. Bake, covered, 1 hr., or until onions are tender.

Serve garnished with parsley. Makes 4 servings.

▶ **For 2:** Halve ingredients; use 2-cup casserole.

GLAZED ONIONS

Prepare and cook 1½ lb. onions till almost tender as on p. 283. Drain. In large skillet over low heat, blend 2 tablesp. butter or margarine, 6 tablesp. granulated sugar, 2 teasp. water. Add onions; cook until golden and glazed, turning often. Makes 4 servings.

BERMUDA ONIONS PIQUANT

4 Bermuda onions
½ cup onion liquid
2 cups grated process American cheese (½ lb.)

3 tablesp. butter or margarine
1 teasp. Worcestershire
Speck pepper

Prepare onions, slice ¼" thick, and cook as on p. 283. Drain. To ½ cup onion liquid, add cheese, rest of ingredients. Stir gently over low heat till cheese is melted. Pour over onions.

Serve as is or on toast. Makes 6 servings.

To Vary: Use 18 small onions.

SAUTEED ONIONS

12 medium onions
¼ cup butter or

margarine
Salt

Slice onions ¼" thick. In hot butter in large skillet, sauté slowly, turning often, 25 to 30 min., or until tender and golden. Sprinkle with salt. Or add bottled thick meat sauce, p. 9, or soy sauce to taste. Or add curry powder and lemon juice to taste.

Serve with chops, steak, hamburgers, liver, etc. Makes 6 servings.

FRENCH-FRIED ONIONS

3 large onions
⅓ cup milk

⅓ cup flour
¼ teasp. salt

Slice onions ¼" thick; separate into rings. Dip into milk, then into combined flour and salt. Fry until light brown, a few rings at a time, as in Shallow Frying, p. 8, at 380°F. on deep-fat frying thermometer. Drain on paper towels; sprinkle with salt.

Serve hot, with steak, liver and bacon, etc. Makes 4 servings.

PARSNIPS

To Buy, to Prepare, to Cook: See chart, p. 283.

To Serve: Drain parsnips. Season with salt, pepper, butter or margarine, and snipped parsley or paprika.

Or mash well; then season, adding a little hot milk or cream; beat until fluffy.

Or sauté parsnips in a little hot fat in skillet until golden brown on all sides, sprinkling with salt and pepper.

Or spoon one of these sauces over parsnips:

Béchamel, p. 376   Easy Hollandaise, p.
Drawn Butter, p. 376   374

PARSNIP PATTIES

4 cups thinly sliced,   ½ cup coarse fresh
 pared, cored parsnips   bread crumbs
⅓ cup sliced onions   Speck pepper
1¾ teasp. salt   Packaged dried bread
1¼ cups boiling water   crumbs
¼ cup snipped parsley   2 tablesp. fat
1 egg, beaten

Cook parsnips with onions and salt in boiling water, covered, 15 min., or until tender. Drain; mash. Add parsley, egg, fresh bread crumbs, pepper. Chill well. Form into 8 patties. Roll in packaged crumbs. In hot fat in skillet, sauté patties on both sides until brown. Makes 8 servings.

PEAS

To Buy, to Prepare, to Cook: See chart, p. 283. For variety, add one of the following before cooking peas:

2 or 3 lettuce leaves
Pinch dried marjoram or savory
Fresh mint sprigs
Sliced or minced onions
Snipped scallions

To Serve: Drain peas, reserving liquid. Boil liquid down to a few tablespoonfuls; add to peas, with salt, pepper, butter or margarine. If desired, add a little cream and snipped fresh mint.

Or sauté sliced mushrooms in butter or margarine before adding to peas.

Or spoon one of these sauces over peas:

Saucepan Cheese, p.   372
 373   Creamy Mustard, p.
Quick Cream, p. 374   375
Quick Mushroom, p.   Sour Cream, p. 373

Also see Serve with a Flair, p. 247.

PEAS AND SCALLIONS

2 tablesp. butter or   1 teasp. sugar
 margarine   ⅛ teasp. pepper
12 to 14 scallions   ¼ teasp. nutmeg
 snipped into 1"   ¾ cup liquid drained
 pieces   from peas
2 teasp. flour   2 cups drained hot peas
½ teasp. salt

In hot butter over medium heat, sauté scallions 3 min. Stir in flour, salt, sugar, pepper, nutmeg; then add pea liquid. Cook, stirring, until thickened. Add peas. Makes 4 servings.

PEAS CONTINENTAL

2 tablesp. butter or   ⅛ teasp. dried
 margarine   marjoram
1 cup sliced fresh or   2 tablesp. sherry or
 canned mushrooms   cooking sherry
¼ cup minced onion   (optional)
¼ teasp. salt   2 cups drained hot
Speck pepper   cooked or canned
¼ teasp. nutmeg   peas

In hot butter in skillet, sauté mushrooms and onion about 5 min., or until tender. Add salt, pepper, nutmeg, marjoram, sherry, then peas. Makes 4 servings.

BETTER-THAN-EVER PEAS

In saucepan over medium heat, cook ¾ cup minced onions in 1 cup boiling water with ½ teasp. salt, covered, 20 min. Add 3 tablesp. butter or margarine and 1 pkg. frozen peas. Cover; bring to boil; cook peas 8 to 12 min., or until tender, stirring once or twice and adding more boiling water if needed. Season to taste. Serve liquid with peas. Or drain peas; boil liquid down to ¼ cup; pour over peas in serving dish. Makes 4 servings.

SWEET POTATOES AND YAMS

Sweet potatoes and yams may be used interchangeably in recipes.

To Buy, to Prepare: See chart, p. 283.

BAKED SWEET POTATOES

Start heating oven to 350°F. Scrub and dry 4 unpared medium or large sweet potatoes as nearly the same size as possible, so they will bake in same time. Rub each with a little salad oil. Arrange on small baking sheet or oven rack. Bake 45 to 50 min., or till tender when tested with fork.

To serve: Remove potatoes from oven at once; with fork, prick to let out steam. Immediately cut 1½″ cross in top of each. Then, holding potato with clean towel, press from bottom until tender interior partially bursts through cross. Break up lightly with fork. Top with butter or margarine, salt, and paprika. Serve at once, to avoid sogginess. Makes 4 servings.

For Oven Meals: If oven is set for another dish at a temperature other than 350°F., bake sweet potatoes along with it until tender.

Stuffed, Baked Sweet Potatoes: Bake sweet potatoes. Immediately cut slice from top of each. With spoon, scoop out potatoes (do not break skins); mash well. Beat in enough hot milk to make potatoes creamy. Add butter or margarine; season to taste (p. 6). Pile back into shells.

BOILED SWEET POTATOES

Prepare and cook unpared sweet potatoes as on p. 283. Drain. Hold each potato on fork; peel off skin. Serve whole, with butter or margarine; sprinkle with paprika or snipped parsley.

Mashed Sweet Potatoes: Peel cooked sweet potatoes; mash well. Add hot milk or cream; beat with masher until creamy. Add salt, pepper, and butter or margarine to taste. If desired, also add a few tablespoonfuls of drained canned crushed pineapple or chopped pecans, or dash of nutmeg or cinnamon.

Broiled Sweet Potatoes: Peel cooked sweet potatoes; halve lengthwise. Brush with melted butter or margarine; sprinkle with salt, pepper, and a little sugar if desired. Broil without turning 8 min., or till golden brown.

Or slice peeled, cooked sweet potatoes lengthwise in halves or thirds; arrange in baking pan. Pour on combined melted butter or margarine and brown sugar, allowing ¼ cup butter and ½ cup brown sugar for every 4 medium potatoes. Broil as above.

PUFFY MALLOW SWEET POTATOES

4 or 5 medium sweet potatoes	margarine
1 cup pineapple or orange juice	1 egg, slightly beaten
¼ cup butter or	1 teasp. salt
	¼ teasp. cinnamon
	8 marshmallows

Pare sweet potatoes; cut into large chunks. Cook, covered, in pineapple juice about 20 min., or until tender. Drain, reserving juice.

Start heating oven to 350°F. Mash potatoes well; add butter, egg, salt, cinnamon, and about ⅓ cup reserved juice. With spoon or electric mixer, beat until creamy; spoon into 8″ round baking dish. Lightly press marshmallows into top. Bake, uncovered, 30 min., or until marshmallows are golden brown. Makes 6 servings.

SWEET-POTATO SURPRISES

1 1-lb. 2-oz. can vacuum-packed sweet potatoes	⅛ teasp. pepper
1 teasp. grated orange rind	
⅓ cup milk	4 marshmallows
1 tablesp. butter or margarine	1 egg, beaten
1 cup crushed cereal flakes	
½ teasp. salt	

Start heating oven to 425°F. In saucepan, place sweet potatoes, milk, butter. Heat till butter is melted and milk is hot. Then mash potatoes, adding salt, pepper, orange rind. Form into 4 balls, with marshmallow in center of each. (Be sure marshmallows are completely covered.) Roll balls in egg, then in cereal. Bake in pie plate 20 to 25 min., or until crusty. Makes 4 servings.

▶ **For 2:** Halve ingredients.

QUICK-CANDIED SWEET POTATOES

In large skillet, simmer together 5 min. ¾ cup brown sugar, packed; ½ cup water; ½ teasp.

salt; 2 tablesp. butter or margarine; dash cinnamon. Add 1 1-lb. 2-oz. can vacuum-packed sweet potatoes. Turn heat low; cook, uncovered, turning occasionally, 15 to 20 min., or until potatoes are well glazed. Or place potatoes in greased shallow baking pan; add syrup. Bake, uncovered, turning now and then, at 400°F. 20 to 25 min. Makes 5 or 6 servings.

CANDIED SWEET POTATOES

6 medium sweet potatoes	½ cup dark corn syrup
¼ cup butter or margarine	2 tablesp. water
	¼ cup brown sugar, packed

Cook unpared scrubbed sweet potatoes in boiling water 15 min. Cool; peel; halve lengthwise.

In skillet,* place butter, corn syrup, water, brown sugar. Arrange potatoes on top, with cut sides down. Cook over very low heat, uncovered, basting occasionally, about 1 hr., or until potatoes are tender and well glazed. Makes 6 servings.

If preferred, use shallow baking dish instead of skillet. Then bake, uncovered, basting occasionally, at 375°F. 1 hr., or until well glazed.

SPECIAL CANDIED SWEET POTATOES

2 lb. peeled, cooked sweet potatoes	margarine
1 cup drained, cooked dried apricots	¼ cup liquid drained from cooked apricots
1 cup brown sugar, packed	1 teasp. grated orange rind
¼ cup melted butter or	¼ cup chopped walnuts

Start heating oven to 375°F. Cut sweet potatoes into thick slices; arrange layer of some of potatoes in greased 10″ x 6″ x 2″ baking dish. Cover with layer of some of apricots; sprinkle with some of brown sugar. Repeat layers. Combine butter, apricot liquid, orange rind. Pour over layers. Bake, uncovered, 45 min., basting once or twice with liquid in bottom of dish. Top with nuts last 5 min. Makes 8 servings.

Baked Sweet Potatoes and Apples: Substitute 2 cups thinly sliced, pared cooking apples for apricots and their liquid.

Quickie Sweets: Substitute 1 No. 2 can vacuum-packed sweet potatoes for fresh potatoes, 1 No. 2 can applesauce for apricots and their liquid.

ORANGE CANDIED SWEET POTATOES

8 pared medium sweet potatoes	packed
¼ cup butter or margarine	2 tablesp. honey
1 cup brown sugar,	1 teasp. grated orange rind
	½ cup orange juice

Start heating oven to 450°F. Halve sweet potatoes lengthwise; brown in butter in skillet. Place in 2-qt. casserole, along with any butter left in skillet. Add sugar, rest of ingredients. Bake, covered, 30 min. Uncover; bake, basting often, 20 min., or until potatoes are tender and golden brown. Makes 8 servings.

To Do Ahead: Assemble casserole early in day; refrigerate. To serve, bake at 450°F. 45 min.; then uncover and bake 20 min.

Pineapple Sweets: Substitute 1 buffet-size can crushed pineapple, undrained, for honey, orange rind, and juice.

PAN-ROASTED SWEET POTATOES

Substitute sweet potatoes for white potatoes in Franconia, or Pan-Roasted, Potatoes, p. 267.

FRIED SWEET POTATOES

Make Susan's Hashed Brown Potatoes, p. 268, using cold cooked sweet potatoes cut into ¼″ cubes and stirring cubes often so they will brown on all sides.

WHITE POTATOES

To Buy, to Prepare: See chart, p. 284.

BAKED POTATOES

Start heating oven to 450°F. Wash, then dry, medium or large unpared potatoes as nearly the same size as possible, so they will bake in same time. Rub each with salad oil. Arrange on small baking sheet or oven rack. Bake 45 to 60 min., or till tender when tested with fork.

To serve: Remove potatoes from oven at once; with fork, prick to let out steam. Immediately cut 1½″ cross in top of each. Then, holding potato with clean towel, press from bottom until snowy white interior partially bursts through cross. Break up lightly with fork. Top with salt, butter or margarine, and paprika. Serve at once, to avoid sogginess.

For Oven Meals: If oven is set for another dish at temperature lower than 450°F., bake potatoes along with it until tender.

Stuffed, Baked Potatoes: Bake 7 unpared medium or large potatoes. Immediately cut slice from top of each. Scoop out potatoes (do not break skins); mash well. Beat in enough light cream to make potatoes fluffy. Add butter or margarine; season to taste. Pile into 6 shells; round slightly. Brush with melted butter or margarine; dust with paprika. Serve at once. Or lightly brown at 450°F. Makes 6 servings.

To vary: Before piling mashed potatoes in shells, add 1 tablesp. grated cheese, or snipped chives or parsley, or minced onion.

Cheese-Stuffed Baked Potatoes: Prepare Stuffed Baked Potatoes, above, adding to mashed potatoes 2 to 4 tablesp. crumbled blue cheese.

REBAKED POTATOES

Start heating oven to 350°F. With fork, mash 1 minced clove garlic to pulp with ½ teasp. salt (or use garlic press); blend with 3 tablesp. soft butter or margarine, 2 tablesp. grated Parmesan cheese, ½ teasp. paprika, dash pepper. (Or substitute ½ cup cheese spread—sharp, blue, or pimento—for this mixture.)

Slash 4 unpeeled, cold baked medium potatoes into ½" slices almost all the way through. Spread garlic mixture between slices. Bake 20 min. Makes 4 servings.

CASSEROLE-ROASTED POTATOES

Start heating oven to 350°F. Wash, and pare 4 medium potatoes; roll in 2 tablesp. melted butter or margarine, then in combined ¼ teasp. salt and ¼ cup packaged dried bread crumbs. Place in 2-qt. casserole. Bake, covered, 45 to 60 min., or until tender. Makes 4 servings.

▶ **For 2:** Halve ingredients; use 1-qt. casserole.

FRANCONIA, OR PAN-ROASTED, POTATOES

About 1¼ hr. before roast meat is done, boil 8 pared medium potatoes 10 min. Drain; arrange around roast in roasting pan. Bake 40 to 60 min., or until tender, turning occasionally and basting with fat in pan. Plan so roast and potatoes are done at same time.

When roast is done, remove to heated platter. If potatoes are not brown enough, place in pan under broiler; turn as they brown.

To serve: Sprinkle potatoes with paprika, snipped parsley, or dried thyme. Arrange around roast. Makes 5 or 6 servings.

To Vary: If no roast is available, after draining boiled potatoes, arrange in shallow pan, in 1 tablesp. butter, margarine, or salad oil for each potato. Bake at 400°F., turning often, 40 min., or until tender and brown.

BOILED MATURE POTATOES

Prepare, then cook potatoes, unpared or pared very thinly as on p. 284. Drain; then hold each potato on fork and peel if necessary. Return to saucepan; heat, uncovered, over very low heat, shaking pan gently, 2 min., or until potatoes become mealy. Sprinkle with salt, pepper; pour on melted butter or margarine. If desired, to butter, add snipped parsley and a little lemon juice.

Creamed Potatoes: After potatoes are drained and peeled, dice. Pour on Vegetable Sauce, p. 376 or Quick Cream Sauce, p. 374. (Allow 1½ cups sauce per 3 to 3½ cups diced potatoes.) Sprinkle with snipped parsley or chives.

BOILED NEW POTATOES

Prepare, then cook, new potatoes as on p. 284 (leave skins on and scrape lightly; or pare off narrow strip from center of each). Drain. Peel off skins if desired. Season with salt, pepper; pour melted butter or margarine over all. Sprinkle with snipped parsley or paprika. Or add sautéed minced onion, basil, or snipped chives or mint.

Creamed New Potatoes: After draining cooked potatoes, heat in thin cream; season to taste. Or pour on one of these sauces; then sprinkle with paprika or snipped parsley. Allow 1 cup sauce for every 8 hot small new potatoes.

Quick Cream, p. 374   Sour Cream, p. 373
Quick Mushroom, p. 372   Vegetable, p. 376

Creamed New Potatoes and Peas: Toss hot peas with potatoes before adding sauce.

Delmonico Potatoes: Turn Creamed New Potatoes made with Vegetable Sauce into greased casserole. Sprinkle with grated cheese, then with a few buttered fresh bread crumbs. Bake at 400°F. until brown.

MASHED POTATOES

9 medium potatoes   diluted evaporated
  (3¼ lb.)   milk
6 tablesp. butter or   Speck pepper
  margarine   Salt
¾ cup hot milk or

Prepare, then cook, unpared potatoes as on p. 284. Drain; peel. Place over low heat 1 or 2 min. to dry out, shaking pan gently. With potato masher or electric mixer, mash potatoes thoroughly until no lumps remain. With masher, mixer, or spoon, beat, gradually adding enough combined butter and milk to make potatoes fluffy, creamy. Season to taste.

To serve: Heap potatoes at once in heated serving dish; top with lump of butter or margarine; sprinkle with paprika or snipped parsley, mint, water cress, or chives. Makes 6 servings.

To keep warm: If mashed potatoes cannot be served at once, cover them and set in pan of hot water over low heat.

Duchess or Plank-Border Potatoes: Mash potatoes, adding 2 beaten eggs and enough milk to make mixture smooth. Arrange with spoon, in mounds, on greased cookie sheet. Brush with melted butter or margarine; brown under broiler, or in 450°F. oven.

Mashed Potatoes à la Phyfe: To Mashed Potatoes, add ½ minced clove garlic sautéed 5 min. in 1 teasp. olive or salad oil, paprika, and ⅛ teasp. celery seeds. Serve with Veal Paprika, p. 105, Danish Goulash, p. 62, etc.

Mashed Potato Cakes: Shape cold leftover mashed potatoes into flat cakes. With flour dust on both sides; then sauté in butter, margarine, bacon fat, or salad oil till delicate brown on both sides.

Savory Mashed Potatoes: To Mashed Potatoes, add a few snipped mint leaves or some snipped water cress just before serving.

NOISETTE POTATOES

In 10″ skillet, melt 6 tablesp. butter or margarine; add 2 teasp. salt and 1½ lb. washed, dried unpared tiny new potatoes. Sauté very slowly, covered, 30 min., or until tender, turning often. Serve as is. Or remove to hot dish; to butter left in skillet, add 2 tablesp. each grated Parmesan cheese and snipped parsley; pour over potatoes. Makes 4 servings.

COUNTRY (OR COTTAGE FRIED) POTATOES

6 peeled, cold cooked   garine, or bacon fat
  potatoes (boiled or ¾ teasp. salt
  baked)   ⅛ teasp. pepper
3 tablesp. butter, mar-

Slice or dice potatoes. Heat butter in skillet; add potatoes; sauté, without stirring, until golden on underside; turn; brown other side. Sprinkle with salt and pepper. Makes 4 to 6 servings.

Lyonnaise: Sauté a little minced or thinly sliced onion with potatoes.

SUSAN'S HASHED BROWN POTATOES

4 peeled, chilled,   Dash pepper
  cooked medium   3 tablesp. butter or
  potatoes   margarine
1 tablesp. grated onion 3 tablesp. bacon fat
1 teasp. salt

1. Using medium grater, grate potatoes onto waxed paper till you have 4 cups. On paper, toss with onion, salt, pepper.
2. In 10″ skillet over medium high heat, heat butter and bacon fat. Add potatoes, pressing down well with turner. Shape potatoes into circle, leaving ½″ trough of fat around edge.
3. Cook about 20 min., or until crisp and brown on underside. (After 12 to 15 min., lift edge to test brownness.)
4. When potatoes are brown on bottom, hold skillet with left hand; with turner, cut through them from far edge to center. Fold 2 cut quarters onto uncut half.
5. Carefully run turner under potatoes, so they'll slide out of skillet easily. Then, holding skillet firmly in left hand, turn potatoes onto platter, with uncut side on top. Makes 4 servings.

FRIED RAW POTATOES

¼ cup bacon fat or salad oil
1 cup sliced onions (optional)
4 cups sliced, pared potatoes, ¼" thick
1¼ teasp. salt
⅛ teasp. pepper
Snipped parsley

Heat bacon fat in skillet. Arrange onions and potatoes in layers in fat. Sprinkle with salt, pepper. Sauté, covered, over low heat 15 min. Then uncover; turn heat up slightly and sauté 10 min., or until brown and crispy on underside (do not stir). Sprinkle with parsley; then fold in half like omelet. Makes 3 or 4 servings.

To Vary: Use coarsely grated potatoes.

CRISPY NEW POTATOES

Fry 4 bacon slices till crisp but not dry; remove slices. To hot bacon fat, add sliced, washed unpared new potatoes. Cook, covered, a few minutes, to steam. Uncover; season with salt and pepper; cook very slowly, stirring and turning frequently, until tender and flecked with crusty golden-brown bits—about 20 min. Crumble crisp bacon over top.

CRUMBED POTATOES

12 medium potatoes
¼ cup melted butter or margarine
½ cup fine cornflake crumbs
1 tablesp. salt
2 tablesp. butter or margarine

Prepare and cook unpared potatoes, as on p. 284. Drain; cool; peel. Roll potatoes in melted butter, then in crumbs mixed with salt. In butter in skillet, sauté potatoes over medium heat until golden on all sides. Makes 6 servings.

QUICK GOLDEN POTATO BALLS

In skillet, melt 2 tablesp. butter, margarine, bacon fat, or salad oil; add ½ teasp. paprika and 1 drained can small whole white potatoes. Sauté till golden, tossing occasionally. Season to taste. Makes 3 or 4 servings.

FRENCH-FRIED POTATOES
(two-step method)

Precooking: Several hours before serving, wash and pare 2 lb. potatoes. Cut into ⅜" slices, then into ⅜"-wide lengthwise strips. Wash in cold water; dry well between towels. Fry as in Shallow Frying, p. 8, or Deep Fat Frying, p. 7, at 370°F. on deep-fat frying thermometer, 5 to 7 min., or until potatoes are tender but not brown. Drain on paper towels in baking pan. Cover with waxed paper; set aside until just before mealtime.

Browning: Just before serving, fry potatoes at 390°F. until crisp and brown. Drain on paper towels; sprinkle with salt. Keep warm at 300°F. until all are browned.

To Serve: Serve at once. Makes 4 servings.

P. S. If you have an automatic electric deep fryer, p. 7, closely follow manufacturer's directions for French-Fried Potatoes—they are excellent.

Shoestring or Julienne Potatoes: Cut potatoes into ¼" strips. Fry until tender.

Quick Oven French Fries: You can buy excellent packaged frozen French fries, which need only heating in oven or broiler. Follow label directions.

CHEESE-POTATO MOUND

3 tablesp. butter or margarine
¼ cup flour
1½ teasp. salt
⅛ teasp. pepper
1 cup milk
2 cups sliced, cooked potatoes (about 4 medium)
1 tablesp. snipped parsley
1 tablesp. minced onion
¾ cup grated process sharp American cheese

Early in day: Grease 1-qt. casserole; line bottom with waxed paper. In saucepan, melt butter; stir in flour, salt, pepper, then milk; cook, stirring, until smooth and very thick. Stir in potatoes, parsley, onion; pack firmly into casserole. Refrigerate several hr. or overnight.

About 45 min. before serving: Start heating oven to 400°F. Loosen sides of casserole with spatula; turn onto cookie sheet; peel off paper. Sprinkle with cheese. Bake, uncovered, 25 min., or until lightly browned and thoroughly heated. Loosen bottom. Then slide mound onto serving platter. Garnish with parsley and radish roses if desired. Makes 2 or 3 generous servings.

▶ **For 4:** Multiply each ingredient 1½ times; use 1½-qt. casserole.

OLIVE POTATOES

3 tablesp. butter or margarine	American cheese (¼ lb.)
3 tablesp. flour	4 cups diced, cooked potatoes
½ teasp. salt	
Dash pepper	½ cup sliced ripe olives
¾ cup undiluted evaporated milk	½ cup fresh bread crumbs
¾ cup water	2 tablesp. melted butter or margarine
1 cup grated process	

Start heating oven to 350°F. Melt butter in saucepan. Remove from heat. Blend in flour, salt, pepper. Gradually stir in milk and water; cook over medium heat, stirring constantly, till thickened. Add cheese; continue cooking and stirring until cheese is melted.

Combine potatoes and olives in 1½-qt. casserole; pour cheese sauce over them. Toss crumbs with butter; sprinkle on top. Bake, uncovered, 30 min., or until golden. Makes 8 servings.

POTATOES IN CREAM

4 cups diced, cooked potatoes	margarine
½ teasp. salt	⅛ teasp. pepper
¼ cup butter or	2 cups light cream
	Snipped parsley

In large skillet, combine all ingredients except parsley; cook slowly until cream is slightly thickened and potatoes are hot. Sprinkle with parsley and a little grated cheese if desired. Makes 6 servings.

SUSAN'S SCALLOPED POTATOES

2 tablesp. snipped parsley	3 tablesp. butter or margarine
1½ cups thinly sliced onions	7 teasp. flour
	1 teasp. salt
4½ cups thinly sliced, pared white potatoes	⅛ teasp. pepper
	⅛ teasp. paprika
2 teasp. salt	1¾ cups milk

1. Start heating oven to 400°F. Bring 1″ water to boil in covered saucepan. Grease 1½-qt. casserole. (Prepare parsley, onions, potatoes.)
2. To boiling water, add onions, potatoes, 2 teasp. salt; boil, covered, 5 min. Drain.
3. Meanwhile, melt butter in double boiler or

skillet over very low heat. Stir in flour, salt, pepper, paprika, then milk. Cook, stirring constantly, until smooth and thickened.

4. In casserole, arrange one third of potatoes and onions; sprinkle with half of parsley; pour on one third of sauce. Repeat with another third of potatoes and onions, rest of parsley, and half of remaining sauce. Now add rest of potatoes and sauce. Bake, uncovered, 35 min., or until tender and brown. Makes 4 or 5 servings.

▶ **For 2:** Use 4 teasp. flour, 1 cup milk. Halve rest of ingredients; use 1-qt. casserole. Bake 25 min.

OLD-TIME SCALLOPED POTATOES

4 cups thinly sliced, pared potatoes	⅛ teasp. pepper
	2 tablesp. butter or margarine
⅔ cup minced onions	
2 tablesp. flour	1½ cups scalded milk
1 teasp. salt	Paprika

Start heating oven to 375°F. Arrange layer of potatoes in greased 2-qt. casserole. Cover with some of onions. Sprinkle with some of combined flour, salt, and pepper. Dot with some of butter. Repeat layers until all are used, ending with butter. Pour milk over all; sprinkle with paprika. Bake, covered, 45 min. Uncover; bake 15 min. longer, or until tender. Makes 4 servings.

▶ **For 2:** Halve ingredients; use 1-qt. casserole.

Curried: Add ½ teasp. curry powder to flour.

With Ham: Arrange 2 cups cooked ham strips in layers between potatoes and onions.

QUICK SCALLOPED POTATOES

In ½ cup boiling water in saucepan, cook 4 cups diced, pared potatoes, 1 cup minced onions, 2 teasp. salt, covered, 10 min. Uncover; simmer, stirring occasionally, until water is almost evaporated. Add ½ cup each light cream and grated cheese, plus speck pepper. Heat; add 2 tablesp. snipped parsley. Makes 5 or 6 servings.

POTATO PANCAKES

5 tablesp. flour	1 egg, unbeaten
1½ lb. pared potatoes	1 teasp. salt
1 grated small onion	⅛ teasp. pepper

Plan to fry pancakes *as soon as mixture is made* to prevent darkening. Measure flour into bowl. Over flour, grate potatoes on very fine grater; stir in rest of ingredients.

Lightly grease medium skillet; place over medium heat. Drop potato mixture, by heaping tablespoonfuls, into hot skillet. Fry until crisp and golden brown on underside. Turn; brown other side. Drain on paper towels.

Serve as vegetable, or with applesauce as luncheon or supper main dish. Nice with pot roast or short ribs. Makes about 16.

▶ **For 2:** Omit egg; add 3 tablesp. milk. Divide each remaining ingredient by 3.

Quick Potato Pancakes: Packaged potato pancake mix is so good, so easy to use.

PUMPKIN

To Buy, to Prepare, to Cook: See chart, p. 284.

To Use: Drain pumpkin well; mash; drain again. Use in Pilgrim Pumpkin Pie, p. 415.

SALSIFY
(oyster plant)

To Buy, to Prepare, to Cook: See chart, p. 284.

To Serve: Drain salsify. Season with salt and pepper; then add butter or margarine. Or reheat in a little cream.

SAUERKRAUT

To Buy: Sauerkraut comes canned in 3 sizes; choose whichever you prefer.

To Cook: Turn can of sauerkraut, with all of its liquid, into a saucepan. Then heat it, covered, 30 min. or longer if desired. Drain. (Serve drained liquid as juice cocktail.)

To hot sauerkraut, add butter or margarine, salt, and pepper to taste. Also add caraway or celery seeds. Or add a little minced onion sautéed in butter till tender.

Nice with roast pork, pork chops, spareribs, pigs' knuckles, franks, goose or duckling.

TOMATO SAUERKRAUT

½ cup sliced onions	sauerkraut
2 tablesp. butter or margarine	1½ cups tomato juice
	1 bay leaf
1 tablesp. flour	½ teasp. salt
4 cups drained canned	1 tablesp. honey

Cook onions in butter until tender. Add flour; cook until lightly browned. Add rest of ingredients except honey. Simmer, covered, 30 min. Remove bay leaf; stir in honey. Makes 3 or 4 servings.

KRAUT-NOODLE CASSEROLE

4-oz. medium-wide noodles (2 cups)	drained (2½ cups)
	Pepper
2 tablesp. butter or margarine	¼ lb. packaged process-American-cheese
1 No. 2 can sauerkraut,	slices

Start heating oven to 300°F. Cook noodles as label directs until barely tender; drain. Add butter; toss until well mixed. Spread three fourths of sauerkraut in 1½-qt. casserole or 10″ x 6″ x 2″ baking dish. Sprinkle with pepper. Top with noodles, cheese, rest of sauerkraut. Bake, covered, 1 hr. Makes 4 or 5 servings.

▶ **For 2:** Halve ingredients, using 1 1-lb. can sauerkraut. Leftovers may be reheated.

ACORN SQUASH

To Buy, to Prepare, to Cook: See chart, p. 284.

To Serve: Drain squash halves well. With fork, mash squash in shells a little; season to taste with salt, pepper, and butter or margarine. Serve in shells.

STUFFED ACORN SQUASH

Prepare and cook 3 halved acorn squash as on p. 284. Sauté 6 tablesp. minced onion in ¼ cup butter or margarine until tender but not brown. When squash are done, remove from kettle; do not break shells.

With spoon, carefully scoop squash from shells. Reserve 4 shells. To squash, add sautéed onion, 1½ teasp. salt, ¼ teasp. pepper, 2 tablesp. light cream; beat well with fork. Lightly pile mixture into shells; sprinkle with paprika. Broil

10 min., or until delicate brown. Makes 4 servings.

BAKED ACORN SQUASH

Start heating oven to 400°F. Prepare 2 medium acorn squash as on p. 284. Brush cut surface of each half with melted butter or margarine; then sprinkle each with ¼ teasp. salt. Arrange, with cut sides down, in baking pan. Bake 30 min.

Turn squash, with cut sides up; brush with combined ¼ cup melted butter or margarine and ¼ cup corn syrup. Bake until tender, brushing often with syrup—about 30 min. Makes 4 servings.

To Vary: Omit corn syrup. About 10 min. before squash are done, sprinkle centers with thin, small pieces of sharp cheese.

With Vegetables: As soon as squash are baked, fill each half with ½ cup hot seasoned peas, onions, or Brussels sprouts.

HUBBARD SQUASH

To Buy, to Prepare, to Cook: See chart, p. 284.

To Serve: Drain squash well; with spoon, scoop squash from shell. Mash well with potato masher; add salt, pepper, butter or margarine, and a little cream; beat well. Sprinkle with paprika, snipped parsley, grated cheese, ginger, or a little minced onion sautéed in butter.

WINTER SQUASH WITH CRANBERRIES

4 cups mashed, cooked Hubbard squash; or 2 pkg. thawed frozen squash	¼ cup granulated sugar 1½ cups halved raw cranberries ½ teasp. salt
2 eggs, beaten	⅛ teasp. pepper
⅓ cup melted butter or margarine	Dash nutmeg

Start heating oven to 400°F. With egg beater, beat squash with eggs and 3 tablesp. melted butter. Stir in sugar, cranberries, salt, pepper (taste and season more if needed). Spoon into 2-qt. casserole. Drizzle on rest of melted butter; sprinkle with nutmeg. Bake, uncovered, 30 min. Makes 8 servings.

To Do Ahead: Make early in day; refrigerate. Bake at 400°F. 45 min.

SAVORY SQUASH

2- to 2½-lb. piece Hubbard squash	⅛ teasp. pepper ¼ cup butter or
1 sliced medium onion	margarine
2 teasp. salt	1 8-oz. can tomato sauce

Start heating oven to 375°F. Remove seeds and stringy portion from squash; cut squash into 8 pieces; pare. Place in 2-qt. casserole; cover with onion slices. Sprinkle with salt, pepper; dot with butter; pour on tomato sauce. Bake, covered, 1 hr., or until tender. Makes 4 servings.

SQUASH SAUTE

Remove seeds and stringy portion from 2- to 2½-lb. piece unpared Hubbard squash. Cut into 2″ cubes. Cook, covered, in ½″ boiling salted water until just tender—about 15 min. Drain well. In skillet, melt 3 tablesp. butter or margarine; add 1 tablesp. minced onion, 2 teasp. salt, and squash (with skin sides up). Cook over medium heat until squash is golden brown. Serve with skin sides down. Makes 4 servings.

BAKED HUBBARD-SQUASH SQUARES

2½-lb. piece Hubbard squash	or margarine 1½ teasp. salt
3 tablesp. melted butter	¼ teasp. pepper

Start heating oven to 400°F. Scrub squash. With long sharp knife, cut squash into serving-size pieces about 4″ x 2″. With spoon, scrape out seeds and stringy portion. Brush with some of melted butter; sprinkle with some of salt and pepper.

Arrange squash pieces, side by side, with cut sides down, in greased baking pan. Bake, uncovered, 30 min. Turn cut sides up; brush with melted butter; sprinkle with rest of salt, pepper. Bake 30 min., or until tender, brushing often with melted butter. When squash is done, mash in shell with fork. Makes 4 servings.

SUMMER SQUASH

To Buy, to Prepare, to Cook: See chart, p. 285.

To Serve: Drain squash thoroughly. Season with salt, pepper, butter or margarine, and a little cream. Heat; sprinkle with snipped parsley. Or add sautéed, minced onion and grated cheese. Or before seasoning, mash thoroughly.

Also see Serve with a Flair, p. 247.

SKILLET SQUASH AU GRATIN

¼ cup butter or margarine	Dash pepper
4 cups thinly sliced summer squash or zucchini	¼ cup water; or 2 sliced, peeled tomatoes
1 sliced onion	½ cup grated process American cheese
1 teasp. salt	Soy sauce (optional)

Melt butter in skillet. Add summer squash, onion, salt, pepper, water. Cook, covered 10 to 15 min., or till squash is tender. Sprinkle with cheese and soy sauce if desired. Makes 4 generous servings.

CHICKEN-BAKED SQUASH

3 cups cubed summer squash	½ cup chopped nuts
2 tablesp. butter or margarine	2 tablesp. chopped pimento
1 can undiluted condensed cream-of-chicken soup	¼ cup ¼"-squares fresh bread
	2 tablesp. melted butter or margarine

Start heating oven to 375°F. In 1½-qt. casserole, arrange layers of squash, bits of butter, soup, nuts, and pimento. Top with bread squares and melted butter tossed together. Bake, uncovered, 50 min. Makes 8 servings.

SUMMER SQUASH EN CASSEROLE

2 lb. summer squash	2 tablesp. butter or margarine
1 teasp. salt	
⅛ teasp. pepper	

Start heating oven to 400°F. Wash squash; cut into ½" slices. Place in layers in greased 2-qt. casserole, sprinkling each layer with some of salt and pepper and dotting with some of butter, until all is used. Bake, covered, 1 hr., or until tender. Makes 4 servings.

SUMMER-SQUASH MEDLEY

Buy 1 lb. small squash of mixed varieties: summer squash, white pattypan, and dark-green zucchini.

Wash squash; cut into ¾" cubes. Cook in 1" boiling salted water, covered, until just tender—about 10 to 15 min. Meanwhile, cut 2 bread slices into small squares. Heat 2 tablesp. butter or margarine in skillet; add bread squares; heat, stirring, until crisp and brown.

When squash are done, drain; shake over heat to dry off. Add salt and pepper to taste, plus 2 tablesp. butter or margarine. With fork, toss gently. Then add bread squares; toss. Serve promptly. Makes 4 servings.

TOMATOES

To Buy: See chart, p. 285.

To Peel: Dip each tomato into boiling water for 1 min.; remove. Cut out stem end; with knife, pull off skin; refrigerate. Or hold tomato on fork over heat until skin wrinkles and splits; then pull off skin; refrigerate.

SCALLOPED TOMATOES

3 tablesp. butter or margarine	Dash cayenne pepper
¼ cup minced onion	1 No. 2½ can tomatoes (3½ cups)
2 cups fresh bread crumbs	¼ cup fresh bread crumbs
½ teasp. sugar	1 tablesp. melted butter or margarine
1 teasp. salt	
¼ teasp. pepper	

Start heating oven to 375°F. In 3 tablesp. butter in small saucepan, sauté onion until tender. Add 2 cups bread crumbs, sugar, salt, pepper, cayenne. Arrange layer of tomatoes in greased 1½-qt. casserole. Top with layer of onion-bread mixture. Continue until all is used, ending with tomatoes on top. Combine ¼ cup bread crumbs with 1 tablesp. butter; sprinkle over tomatoes. Bake, uncovered, 45 min. Makes 5 or 6 servings.

▶ **For 2:** Halve ingredients; use 1-qt. casserole.

BAKED TOMATOES

3 medium tomatoes	shire
¾ teasp. prepared mustard	Salt
1 tablesp. minced onion	3 tablesp. buttered fresh bread crumbs
1½ teasp. Worcester-	

Start heating oven to 375°F. Wash tomatoes; cut out stem ends; then halve crosswise. Arrange, with cut sides up, in baking pan. Spread with prepared mustard; top with minced onion, Worcestershire; sprinkle well with salt, then with crumbs. Bake, uncovered, 30 min.

Serve with meat, fish, or poultry, on vegetable plate, with omelets, etc. Makes 6 tomato halves.

Broiled Tomatoes: Prepare Baked Tomatoes; sprinkle with a little curry powder if desired. Broil, without turning, 15 min., or until nicely browned. Serve with meat, fish, on vegetable plate, with omelets, etc.

Cheese Tomatoes with Bacon: Arrange Baked or Broiled Tomatoes on toast; top with Cheese Sauce, p. 374, and crisp bacon. Nice luncheon dish.

STEWED TOMATOES

2¼ teasp. sugar	1 teasp. minced onion
4 teasp. flour	1 teasp. salt
1 No. 2 can, or 2½ cups, quartered, peeled fresh, tomatoes	4 teasp. butter or margarine
	Pepper to taste

Mix sugar with flour; add rest of ingredients. Simmer 10 min. Makes 4 servings.

To Vary: Add 1 minced small white onion, 1 teasp. Worcestershire, or 1 tablesp. chili sauce, or all three. Or add a little grated cheese. Or sprinkle tomatoes with ⅓ cup crisp croutons just before serving.

With Mushrooms: Add ¼ lb. sautéed, sliced, or quartered mushrooms.

Quick: Stewed tomatoes now come canned— onions, green peppers, and celery have been added. Just heat and serve.

TOMATOES STUFFED WITH MACARONI AND CHEESE

4 large firm tomatoes	4 teasp. melted butter or margarine
¾ cup elbow macaroni	
1 cup Thin White Sauce, p. 376	¼ cup buttered day-old bread crumbs
2 tablesp. grated process American cheese	1 tablesp. grated process American cheese

Start heating oven to 375°F. Scoop out pulp and juice from tomatoes (use pulp and juice for stewed tomatoes, tomato sauce, etc.). Sprinkle insides of tomatoes *well* with salt. Cook macaroni as label directs; drain. Mix well with white sauce and 2 tablesp. cheese. Put 1 teasp. melted butter in each tomato; fill with macaroni mixture. Sprinkle with bread crumbs mixed with 1 tablesp. grated cheese. Bake 20 min. Makes 4 servings.

Tomatoes Stuffed with Succotash: Combine 1 cup cooked green limas, 1 cup cooked or canned whole-kernel corn, 2 tablesp. butter or margarine, ⅛ teasp. pepper, ½ teasp. salt, ¼ cup light cream. Use to fill 6 tomatoes, scooped out as above. Top each with small square of bacon. Bake as directed.

CREAMY FRIED TOMATOES

6 large tomatoes	1½ cups milk
1 tablesp. flour	¾ teasp. salt
¾ teasp. salt	1½ teasp. sugar
⅛ teasp. pepper	¾ teasp. bottled thick meat sauce, p. 9
¼ cup butter or margarine	
2 tablesp. flour	1½ teasp. prepared mustard

Cut out stem end of each tomato; then halve crosswise. Combine 1 tablesp. flour, ¾ teasp. salt, pepper; sprinkle over tomato halves. In butter in skillet, sauté tomatoes until golden on both sides and just tender. Arrange 10 halves on heated platter. To 2 tomato halves left in skillet, add 2 tablesp. flour, milk, ¾ teasp. salt, sugar, meat sauce, mustard. Cook until creamy. Pour over tomatoes.

Serve for breakfast or lunch, as is, or on toast. Makes 5 servings.

TOMATO-CHEESE CASSEROLE

4 medium tomatoes, cut into ½″ slices	onion
	½ teasp. salt
1 cup grated process American cheese (¼ lb.)	⅛ teasp. pepper
	1 cup crushed potato chips
⅓ cup thinly sliced	

Start heating oven to 350°F. Arrange half of tomato slices in 1½-qt. casserole. Arrange half of cheese and onion slices in layers over tomatoes; sprinkle with half of salt and pepper. Repeat. Top with potato chips. Bake, uncovered, 30 min., or until cheese is melted and bubbly. Makes 4 servings.

SPEEDY CREAM-FRIED TOMATOES

Wash and cut out stem ends of 2 or 3 large firm tomatoes. Halve crosswise. Sprinkle cut surfaces with salt, pepper; dip into flour. Place, with floured sides down, in small amount of hot bacon fat; brown over medium heat; then turn.

Pour ⅓ to ½ cup undiluted evaporated milk or light cream over tomatoes. Cook, covered, 5 min., or until tomatoes are just heated through. Serve on toast rounds if desired, spooning rich cream gravy over tomatoes. Makes 4 servings.

VEGETABLE MEDLEY

1 large (or 2 small) coarsely diced, peeled tomatoes	1 pkg. frozen mixed vegetables
1 tablesp. minced onion	½ teasp. salt
2 tablesp. melted butter or margarine	⅛ teasp. pepper
	1 tablesp. snipped parsley

Simmer tomatoes and onion in butter 3 to 4 min. Add mixed vegetables, salt, pepper. Simmer, covered, stirring occasionally, about 12 min., or until barely tender. Just before serving, add parsley; toss. Makes 4 servings.

TOMATO-CORN CASSEROLE

1 No. 2 can tomatoes (2½ cups)	½ teasp. cornstarch
2 bacon slices, cut into squares	½ teasp. salt
¼ cup coarsely chopped onion	Dash pepper
½ coarsely chopped small green pepper	1 12-oz. can vacuum-packed whole-kernel corn
½ teasp. sugar	1 toast slice
	1 small clove garlic (optional)

Start heating oven to 350°F. Drain tomatoes; set aside. Fry bacon until lightly browned; add to drained tomatoes. To fat in skillet, add onion and green pepper; cook over medium heat about 5 min. Stir in sugar, cornstarch, salt, and pepper, then tomatoes and bacon; cook, stirring, 3 to 4 min. Add corn.

Rub toast with garlic. Cut toast into cubes. Add to tomato mixture. Pour into 1-qt. casserole. Bake, covered, about 30 min., or till bubbling hot. Makes 4 servings.

SCOOPED TOMATOES

4 whole medium tomatoes	1 teasp. fresh, frozen, or canned lemon juice
¼ cup sharp-cheese spread	1 tablesp. butter or margarine
1 teasp. minced onion	1 tablesp. snipped chives or parsley
Dash tabasco	
½ teasp. salt	
Dash pepper	

Start heating oven to 375°F. Cut thin slice from top and bottom of each tomato; cut each tomato in half horizontally. From center of each half, scoop out about 1 teasp. seeds and pulp. Combine cheese, onion, tabasco. Sprinkle centers of tomatoes with some of salt and pepper; fill centers of 4 halves with spoonful of cheese mixture; top with unfilled halves; press firmly together. Score top of each tomato about ¼″ deep; sprinkle with remaining salt, pepper, lemon juice; dot with butter. Bake in shallow pan 15 to 20 min. Garnish with chives. Makes 4 servings.

WHITE TURNIPS

To Buy, to Prepare, to Cook: See chart, p. 285.

To Serve: Drain turnips. Season with salt, pepper, and butter or margarine. Add a little lemon juice or light cream if desired. Garnish with snipped parsley or paprika.

Or before seasoning, toss with hot peas. Or before seasoning, mash well.

TOP-STOVE SCALLOPED TURNIPS

1 cup water	¼ cup diced green pepper
1 cup milk	1 tablesp. butter or margarine
1 teasp. salt	1 cup grated process American cheese (¼ lb.)
3 cups thinly sliced, pared white turnips	
2 cups sliced, pared carrots	5 tablesp. finely crumbled saltines
½ cup sliced onions	
¼ cup diced celery	

Bring water and milk to boil; add salt, turnips, carrots, onions, celery, green pepper. Simmer, covered, about 20 min., or until tender. *Do not drain.* Add butter, cheese, saltines. Heat, covered, until cheese is melted. Makes 5 servings.

TURNIP BUTTER BALLS

4 large white turnips	½ teasp. salt
3 tablesp. butter or margarine	Dash pepper

Pare turnips. Using melon-ball scoop, cut turnips into balls. Or quarter turnips. (Save bits of raw turnip left over from making balls to chop and sprinkle over green salad or to add to soup.) In 1″ salted water in covered skillet, boil turnips about 3 min., or until almost tender; drain well in strainer. In same skillet, melt butter; add turnip balls; sauté until golden on all sides. Sprinkle with salt and pepper. Makes 4 servings.

TURNIP FLUFF

6 to 8 medium white turnips	Dash pepper
2 tablesp. shortening or meat drippings	2 teasp. sugar
	½ teasp. flour
1 teasp. salt	2 eggs, separated

Prepare, cube, then cook turnips as on p. 285. Start heating oven to 350°F. Drain turnips; mash well over low heat. Add shortening, salt, pepper, sugar, flour. Beat egg whites until stiff; set aside. With same beater, beat egg yolks until light; stir gradually into hot turnips. Fold in beaten whites. Pour into greased 1½-qt. casserole. Bake, uncovered, 30 to 35 min., or until puffy and lightly browned. Makes 6 servings.

TURNIPS DE LUXE

4 cups hot cooked, diced white turnips	1 tablesp. minced pimento
1 cup Vegetable Sauce, p. 376	1 tablesp. minced onion
2 tablesp. minced green pepper	½ teasp. Worcestershire
	½ cup grated process American cheese

Combine hot turnips with rest of ingredients; heat. Makes 4 servings.

YELLOW TURNIPS
(rutabaga)

To Buy, to Prepare, to Cook: See chart, p. 285.

To Serve: Drain turnips. Season with salt, pepper, butter or margarine, then snipped parsley. Or before seasoning, mash well.

Savory Mashed Turnips: To 3 cups hot unseasoned mashed yellow or white turnips, add 1 teasp. salt, ⅛ teasp. pepper, 2 tablesp. butter or margarine, ⅔ cup grated process American cheese, 1 tablesp. minced onion, and ½ teasp. bottled thick meat sauce, p. 9. Mix well. Makes 4 servings.

Mashed Turnips with Potatoes: Combine 1½ cups hot unseasoned mashed yellow turnips with 3 cups hot mashed potatoes. Season with salt, pepper, and 6 tablesp. melted butter or margarine. Makes 4 to 6 servings.

BAKED TURNIP PUFF

1½ cups hot mashed potatoes	⅛ teasp. pepper
1½ cups hot mashed yellow turnips	2 tablesp. butter or margarine
1½ teasp. salt	2 tablesp. minced onion
	1 egg, well beaten

Start heating oven to 400°F. Combine all ingredients; heap in greased 1-qt. casserole. Bake, uncovered, 30 min. Makes 4 servings.

ZUCCHINI

To Buy, to Prepare, to Cook: See chart, p. 285.

To Serve: Drain zucchini well. Season with salt, pepper, butter or margarine, and a few chopped, sautéed almonds if desired.

Or before seasoning, mash well. Drain again. Then season, adding a little soy sauce if desired.

STUFFED ZUCCHINI

1½ lb. small zucchini	1¼ teasp. salt
1½ cups fresh bread crumbs	⅛ teasp. pepper
½ cup grated process American cheese	2 eggs, beaten
	2 tablesp. butter or margarine
¼ cup minced onion	¼ cup grated process American cheese
2 tablesp. snipped parsley	

Scrub zucchini well. Cut off ends; do not pare. Cook whole with 1 teasp. salt in 1″ boiling water, covered, about 5 to 7 min. Start heating oven to 350°F.

Cut squash in halves lengthwise. With tip of spoon, carefully remove squash from shells. Chop into small pieces; then combine with bread crumbs and rest of ingredients except butter and ¼ cup cheese. Pile mixture lightly into zucchini shells; dot with butter. Sprinkle with ¼ cup grated cheese. Arrange filled shells in large baking pan. Bake, uncovered, 30 min., or until brown on top. Makes 4 servings.

TOMATO ZUCCHINI

3 tablesp. fat or salad oil	1 teasp. salt
⅓ cup minced onion	⅛ teasp. pepper
1 minced clove garlic	1½ lb. unpared zucchini, cut into ¼" slices
2 8-oz. cans tomato sauce	
¼ cup water	¼ teasp. dried marjoram

In hot fat in saucepan, sauté onion and garlic till tender. Add tomato sauce, water. Heat until sauce begins to boil. Add salt, pepper, zucchini, marjoram. Simmer over low heat, uncovered, until zucchini are tender—about 20 min. Makes 4 to 6 servings.

Note: Summer squash (crookneck squash) are delicious cooked this way.

ZUCCHINI, ITALIAN STYLE

Scrub 2 lb. zucchini. Cut off ends; do not pare. Cut in halves lengthwise; cut crosswise into 3"-long pieces. In skillet, heat ¼ cup olive or salad oil. Add zucchini, with green sides up; sprinkle with 1½ cups sliced onions; lightly brown cut sides over low heat. Turn cut sides up; add 1½ teasp. salt, ¼ teasp. pepper, and 3 cups tomato juice. Cook, covered, over low heat 40 min., or until zucchini are tender and tomato juice forms thick sauce. Makes 4 servings.

ZUCCHINI, CHINESE STYLE

In skillet, heat ¼ cup bacon fat or salad oil. Add 1 lb. thinly sliced, washed unpared zucchini or summer squash; 1 thinly sliced small onion; 1 clove garlic; and ¼ cup water (do not add salt); stir. Cook, covered, until zucchini is almost tender—10 min. Discard garlic. Sprinkle 2 tablesp. soy sauce over zucchini. Cook, turning occasionally, 5 min., or till zucchini are tender. Makes 4 servings.

ZUCCHINI CASSEROLE AU GRATIN

1½ lb. zucchini, cut into ½" slices	evaporated milk
1 thickly sliced medium onion	¼ cup liquid drained from cooked vegetables
1 cup boiling water	¼ teasp. salt
½ teasp. salt	¼ teasp. pepper
2 cups grated process American cheese (½ lb.)	¾ cup tiny fresh bread squares
½ cup undiluted	2 tablesp. melted butter or margarine

Start heating oven to 350°F. Cook zucchini with onion in boiling water with ½ teasp. salt, covered, 5 min., or until tender. Drain. Alternate layers of vegetables and cheese in 1½-qt. casserole. Pour on milk combined with vegetable liquid, ¼ teasp. salt, pepper. Sprinkle with bread squares combined with butter. Bake, uncovered, 30 min., or until lightly browned. Makes 6 servings.

CHEESY-VEGETABLE GOULASH

¼ cup butter or margarine	ends trimmed
2 medium green peppers, cut into strips	½ teasp. salt
	Dash pepper
2 sliced medium onions	1 12-oz. can vacuum-packed whole-kernel corn
3 coarsely cut-up, peeled large tomatoes; or 3 drained canned tomatoes	½ cup grated process sharp American cheese
6 small zucchini, with	

In melted butter in skillet or saucepan, sauté green peppers and onions about 10 min., or until tender. Add tomatoes, whole zucchini (if desired, gash each zucchini in 3 or 4 places), salt, pepper. Simmer, covered, about 15 min., or until zucchini are tender. Add corn; heat over low heat just till boiling. Stir in grated cheese. Serve at once. Makes 6 servings.

VEGETABLE CHART — BUYING, PREPARING, AND COOKING

Note: The following time periods are only approximate; exact cooking time varies with age of vegetables.

VEGETABLE	AMOUNTS TO BUY		TO BUY, TO PREPARE (Wash all vegetables thoroughly before cooking or as directed)	APPROXIMATE COOKING TIME Use 1″ boiling water with ½ teasp. salt per cup water. Add vegetable; cover; boil as below.	In a pressure cooker (see p. 195)
	For 2	For 4			
Artichokes, French or Italian	Allow 1 per person — unless artichokes are large; then split lengthwise to serve 2.		Buy compact, tightly closed heads. Cut 1″ off top, cutting straight across with sharp knife. Cut off stem about 1″ from base, leaving stub. Pull off outside bottom leaves. With scissors, clip of any thorny tips on leaves.	20–45 min. (see p. 249)	6–10 min.
Artichokes, Jerusalem	¾ lb.	1½ lb.	Buy artichokes free from blemishes. Scrub well. Pare thinly. Leave whole, dice, or slice.	15–35 min.	Sliced: 8 min. Whole: 14 min.
Asparagus	1 lb.	2 lb.	Buy straight, green brittle stalks with close compact tips. Break off each stalk as far down as it snaps easily. Remove scales with knife. Scrub with soft brush to remove sand. (Or scrub; then thinly pare length of stalk with vegetable parer.) Leave stalks whole; or break into 1″ lengths.	Cut up: 10–15 min. Whole: see p. 249	Cut up: 1–2 min. Whole: 2 min. (lay stalks crosswise)
Beets	1 lb., topped	2 lb., topped	Buy smooth small or medium beets. Leave whole; cut off tops, leaving 1″ of stem and root end. Or for quick cooking, pare; then slice, dice, or sliver.	Use boiling salted water to cover. Whole, young: ½ — 1 hr. Old: 1–2 hr. Quick: 20–30 min.	10–12 min. 12–18 min. 5 min.
Broccoli	1 lb.	2 lb.	Buy broccoli with tender firm stalks and tightly closed green flowerets, with no yellow color evident.	Lay in 9″ or 10″ skillet. Cook in 1″ boiling salted	1½–2 min.

				water, covered, 10–15 min.	2 min.
BROCCOLI— *cont'd*	½ lb.		Cut off large leaves and bit of lower stalk. Wash well. If stalks are more than ½″ in diameter, make lengthwise slits (about 4 or 6) almost to flowerets.		
Brussels Sprouts	½ lb.	1 lb.	Buy green fresh-looking sprouts. Avoid yellow spots or worm holes. Remove imperfect leaves; cut off bit of stem end.	10–25 min.	2 min.
Cabbage:					
Green and Savoy, shredded	½ lb.	1 lb.	Buy heads with fresh crisp-looking leaves. Remove any wilted leaves; wash. *To shred:* Cut into quarters. Remove most of core. With sharp knife, thinly slice cut surface of each quarter into medium shreds. Or use shredder.	5–8 min.	2 min.
Green and Savoy, in wedges	1 lb.	2 lb.	*To quarter:* Cut into wedges; then core each wedge, leaving just enough core to retain shape.	8–12 min.	4–6 min.
Chinese, shredded	1 small head	1 medium head	*To shred:* Remove root end. With sharp knife, slice thinly into shreds.	4–5 min.	1–1½ min.
Red, shredded	½ lb.	1 lb.	*To shred:* See Green and Savoy.	15–25 min. (add 1–2 tablesp. lemon juice to water, to preserve color).	2 min.
Carrots	½ lb.	1 lb.	Buy bright crisp carrots. Remove tops at once. Scrub. Scrape or pare thinly. Then leave whole. Or cut into halves or quarters. Or sliver, slice, or dice. Whole carrots · Halved carrots · Quartered carrots · Thin slivers or strips of carrot · Sliced large carrots · Sliced small carrots (Use shorter time for tender-crisp carrots, longer time for well-done carrots.)	20–40 min. · 15–25 min. · 12–20 min. · 10–14 min. · 15–20 min. · 6–10 min.	Whole: 5–6 min. Sliced or slivered: 2–3 min.

(cont'd.)

VEGETABLE CHART — BUYING, PREPARING, AND COOKING — (continued)

VEGETABLE	AMOUNTS TO BUY		TO BUY, TO PREPARE	APPROXIMATE COOKING TIME	
	For 2	For 4	(Wash all vegetables thoroughly before cooking or as directed)	Use 1″ boiling water with ½ teasp. salt per cup water. Add vegetable; cover; boil as below.	In a pressure cooker (see p. 195)
Cauliflower	1 small head	1 large head	Buy compact, crisp white head, as free from blemishes as possible, with fresh green outer stalks.		
			Remove outer leaves and stalks; cut off any blemishes on flowerets. Wash well. Leave whole, removing as much of core as possible without altering shape.	20–30 min.	
			Or break into flowerets.	8–15 min.	2 min.
Celeriac (variety of celery with root like turnip)	¾ lb.	1½ lb.	Buy firm crisp roots. Cut away leaves and root fibers. Scrub well. Pare; then slice or dice.	25–27 min.	5 min.
Celery	Allow ½ to ¾ cup diced celery per serving		Buy crisp stalks with fresh green leaves. Pascal celery with its green stalks is especially tasty. Remove leaves; trim roots. Using soft brush, wash well. With knife, scrape off any discoloration. Dice or sliver outer stalks.	15–20 min.	3 min.
Corn on the cob	Allow 1 or 2 ears per person		Buy young corn that spurts milk when kernels are pressed. Refrigerate until ready to cook. Just before cooking, remove husks, all silk, and any blemishes or discoloration.	Boil in boiling water to cover 5–6 min. (see p. 255)	4–5 min.
Cucumber	1 medium cucumber yields about 1½ cups, diced		Buy firm cucumbers — not too plump or seedy. Cut off and discard ends down to where seeds begin. Pare. Then cut into thick slices; or dice.	15 min., or until tender	

	Amount	Preparation	Cooking	Time
Eggplant	1 medium (about 1½ lb.) makes 4 servings	Buy well-shaped, purple, firm, shiny eggplant with no rust spots. Use soon after buying. Wash. Pare if necessary when ready to use. Eggplant discolors upon standing. Do not soak in salted water.	Cook as in recipes, p. 258	
Green Beans (Snap or Wax)	½ to ¾ lb.	Buy crisp slender green or yellow pods that snap. Wash. Remove ends and string if any. Then fix in one of these ways:		
	1 to 1½ lb.	*Snapped:* Snap or cut into 1″ or 2″ pieces.	15–30 min.	
		Crosscut: Cut crosswise into thin slanted slices.	10–20 min.	2–3 min.
		French Cut: Cut lengthwise into thin strips.	10–20 min.	1–2 min.
		One lb. fresh green beans yields 3 cups cooked.		
Green Limas	2 to 3 lb.	Buy crisp green full pods. Snap open pods; remove beans. If necessary, with knife, cut off thin strip from inner edge of pod; push out beans. One lb. green limas makes about 1¼ cups shelled.	20–30 min.	Small: 2 min. Large: 3–5 min.
Green Peppers	4	Buy peppers that are thick-fleshed, crisp, and bright green. Buy wide, chunky ones for stuffing. Use hot and green peppers in relishes.	Cook as in recipes, p. 260	
	2	Cut thin slice from stem end. Remove seeds and fibrous portion. Wash inside; then cut as recipe directs.		
Greens	1 to 1¼ lb.	Buy greens that have crisp, clean, leaves with good color. Avoid seedy or woody stems. Discard ends, tough stems, and yellowed leaves. Wash 3 times in warm water, lifting greens out of water each time and shaking well so sand sinks to bottom.	Cook in ½″ boiling water, covered. (If very young and tender, use no water; greens will cook in water clinging to leaves after washing.) Add ½ teasp. salt per 1 lb. greens. 5–15 min.	
	2 to 2½ lb.			
Beet Tops			3 min.	

(cont'd.)

VEGETABLE CHART — BUYING, PREPARING, AND COOKING — (continued)

VEGETABLE	AMOUNTS TO BUY — For 2	AMOUNTS TO BUY — For 4	TO BUY, TO PREPARE (Wash all vegetables thoroughly before cooking or as directed)	APPROXIMATE COOKING TIME — Use 1″ boiling water with ½ teasp. salt per cup water. Add vegetable; cover; boil as below.	APPROXIMATE COOKING TIME — In a pressure cooker (see p. 195)
GREENS— cont'd					
Dandelion Greens				10–20 min.	4 min.
Mustard Greens					
Spinach				7–10 min.	1 min.
Swiss Chard, Young				6–10 min. 3–10 min.	3–5 min.
Turnip Greens				8–15 min.	
Kale or Collards	1 to 1¼ lb.	2 to 2½ lb.	Buy fresh, crisp leaves. Strip veins from leaves; discard. Wash rest of leaves in several changes of water, lifting leaves out of water each time.	Cook in ½″ boiling salted water, covered, 10–15 min.	3½–5 min.
Kohlrabi	4 medium	8 medium	Buy small or medium kohlrabi with fresh tops and rind that can be easily pierced with fingernail. Discard stems and leaves; wash. Pare thinly; then cut into slices, slivers, or quarters.	25–40 min.	5 min.
Mushrooms	½ lb.	1 lb.	Buy firm, plump, cream-colored mushrooms with short stems. For safety's sake, buy only cultivated ones. Wash well, scrubbing if necessary with soft brush. Do not peel if fresh and tender. Cut thin slice off stem end; use rest. To slice whole, slice parallel to stem.	Cook as in recipes, p. 262	Small: 3–4 min. Large: 7 min.

Okra	½ lb.	1 lb.	Buy young tender, crisp pods. Wash. Leave whole (do not cut off stems or tips). Or cut into ½" pieces.	Lay in 9" or 10" skillet. Use 1 teasp. salt and 1" boiling water. Cook, covered, 7–12 min., or until tender.	Whole: 3 min. Cut up: 2 min.
Onions Yellow or Red Globe Small White Spanish Bermuda	¾ lb.	1½ lb.	Buy clean, hard, well-shaped onions with brittle skins. Avoid any with developed stems. Cut slice from stem and root ends. Peel thinly, slipping off only first and second layers (do this under cold running water to prevent tears). Or slice onion; then pull off skin. Especially nice for seasonings. Excellent as whole cooked vegetable. Delicious French fried or raw. Good raw or cooked.	Small white: 23–25 min. Yellow or white (2"): 28–30 min. Sliced, ¼" thick: 10 min.	5–6 min. 6–7 min. 3–4 min.
Parsnips	¾ lb.	1½ lb.	Buy smooth, firm, well-shaped small to medium parsnips. Soft or shriveled ones are apt to be pithy. Wash. Cut thin slice off top and bottom. Pare; halve; cut out center core. Cut into quarters or slices.	7–15 min.	Diced: 2 min. Small whole: 8 min.
Peas	1½ lb.	3 lb.	Buy well-filled fresh, green pods. Just before cooking, shell by pressing pods between thumbs to open; then remove peas. Discard any with shoots.	Add 1 teasp. sugar to water. 8–25 min.	Add a few pods for flavor. 1 min.
Sweet Potatoes or Yams	¾ to 1 lb.	1½ to 2 lb.	Sweet potatoes have yellowish, fawn-colored skins and are mealy when cooked. Yams have white to reddish skins, are moist when cooked. Buy smooth-skinned potatoes with bright appearance. Buy in small quantities as they're perishable. Scrub well.	Cook in jackets or skins. 30–35 min.	8–10 min.

(cont'd)

VEGETABLE CHART — BUYING, PREPARING, AND COOKING — (continued)

VEGETABLE	AMOUNTS TO BUY		TO BUY, TO PREPARE	APPROXIMATE COOKING TIME	
	For 2	For 4	(Wash all vegetables thoroughly before cooking or as directed)	Use 1" boiling water with ½ teasp. salt per cup water. Add vegetable; cover; boil as below.	In a pressure cooker (see p. 195)
White Potatoes (mature or new)	¾ to 1 lb.	1½ to 2 lb.	Buy uniform, well-shaped potatoes. Scrub with brush; remove blemishes and eyes. To save food value, cook in jackets or skins. Scrape or pare thinly if necessary.	Whole: 35–40 min. Cut up: 20–25 min.	Whole: 10–20 min. Slices: 1½ min.
Pumpkin	3 lb. raw yields 3 cups cooked and mashed.		Buy bright-colored, unblemished, firm pumpkins. Halve; remove seeds and stringy portion. Cut into small pieces; then pare.	25–30 min.	To pressure cook, leave on rind; cut into desired lengths. Cook 15 min.
Salsify	¾ lb.	1½ lb.	Buy firm, well-shaped medium roots. Scrub; then scrape or pare. Slice or sliver. Plunge into cold water containing a little vinegar to prevent discoloration.	15–20 min.	4–9 min.
Spinach			See Greens		
Squash, Acorn	1 large	2 large	Buy ridged, acorn-shaped squash that are green, firm, and oval or round. Scrub well. Cut in half lengthwise; remove seeds and stringy portion.	25 min.	10 min.
Butternut	1½ lb.	3 lb.	Scrub well. Cut into serving pieces; remove seeds and stringy portion.	12–15 min.	12–13 min.
Hubbard	1 to 1½ lb.	2 to 3 lb.	Buy with hard, warted rind. Scrub well. Cut into serving pieces; remove seeds and stringy portion.	25–30 min.	

SQUASH — cont'd Summer Crookneck or Yellow	1 lb.	2 lb.	Buy squash with curved neck, deep-yellow color, and tender warted rind. Rind becomes rough and less tender as it matures. Scrub well. Cut slice from stem and blossom ends. (Do not pare or remove seeds if squash is young and tender.) Cut into pieces or thin slices.	15–20 min.	2–3 min.
Cymling or Pattypan Zucchini	1 lb.	2 lb.	This type is flat, scalloped, and disk-shaped. Prepare as in crookneck or yellow squash. See Zucchini.	15–20 min.	2–3 min.
Tomatoes	1 lb.	2 lb.	Buy large or small oval red and yellow tomatoes. Sometimes they are purchased green. Regardless of type, look for firm, plump, smooth tomatoes with good color and no blemishes.	Cook as in recipes, pp. 273 to 275	
Turnips, White	1 lb.	2 lb.	Buy white turnips with fresh green tops. Turnips should be firm and heavy. Avoid those that are lightweight for their size; they may be woody, pithy, or strong in flavor. Scrub; pare thinly; then: Cut into ¼″ slices Cut into strips or ½″ cubes	9–12 min. 15–20 min.	5–6 min. 3–5 min.
Yellow, or Rutabaga	1 lb.	2 lb.	Buy heavy, firm yellow turnips. Avoid light-weight ones; they may be woody, pithy, strong in flavor. Scrub well; pare thinly; then: Cut into 2″ pieces Cut into strips or ½″ cubes	35–40 min. 20–25 min.	15 min. 8–12 min.
Zucchini, or Italian, Squash	1 lb.	2 lb.	Buy small or medium-sized squash. Zucchini looks like a cucumber but is striped and may be longer, more irregular. Scrub well. Cut off dark spots and stem end, but do not pare. Cut into ¼″ or ½″ slices.	5–10 min.	

Relishes and Garnishes

As the name implies, relishes add savor to eating, making many good things taste even better. They sometimes take the place of salad (remember this on busy days).

Most of the following relishes you'll make to serve right away or within a few days. But when the supply of fresh vegetables and fruits is too plentiful to resist, put up some of the fine old favorites in Relishes to Keep for Later Use, p. 292. Then you can have summer's goodness on your table all year long.

Before using these recipes, refer to How to Use Our Recipes, p. 3, and Pots and Pans, p. 692. Always use standard measuring cups and measuring spoons; measure level.

RELISHES TO MAKE AND SERVE

SPEEDY PICKLED PEACHES

1 No. 2½ can peach halves, drained	peaches
Whole cloves	½ cup vinegar
1 cup peach syrup, drained from	1 3″ stick cinnamon
	½ cup granulated sugar

Day or more ahead: Stud each peach half with 3 or 4 cloves. Simmer with rest of ingredients 3 or 4 min. Cool; refrigerate.

Serve with poultry, meat, or fish. Nice, too, as dessert, with vanilla ice cream. Makes 8 servings.

Speedy Pickled Pears: Substitute canned pears and pear syrup for peach halves and syrup.

Quick Spiced Pears: Turn can of pears, syrup and all, into saucepan; stud pears with a few cloves. To syrup, add 3″ cinnamon stick, strip of lemon peel. Simmer 5 min.; remove pears from syrup. (Use syrup over cut-up fresh fruit.) Serve hot, with poultry, lamb, etc.

SAUTEED PEACHES

Peel, pit, and quarter peaches. Sprinkle lightly with salt and flour; sauté in butter until tender. Serve with meat or fish.

SAUTEED PINEAPPLE

Dry canned pineapple slices on paper towels. Sauté in butter in skillet until golden brown, turning once. Serve with ham, sautéed or baked fish, or poultry.

QUICK PICKLED PINEAPPLE

1 No. 2½ can pineapple chunks or slices	sugar
	Pinch salt
¾ cup vinegar	6 to 8 whole cloves
1¼ cups granulated	1 4″ stick cinnamon

Week or so ahead: Into saucepan, drain syrup from pineapple. Add vinegar, sugar, salt, cloves, cinnamon; simmer, uncovered, 10 min. Add pineapple. Bring to boil. Cool; refrigerate. Nice with poultry, meat, or fish, or as hors d'oeuvres. Makes about 8 servings.

RHUBARB-PINEAPPLE RELISH

1⅓ cups minced unpeeled pink rhubarb	⅔ cup minced fresh pineapple
⅓ cup minced celery	⅔ cup granulated sugar

Combine rhubarb with rest of ingredients. Refrigerate ½ to 1 hr. Serve as accompaniment for lamb or chicken. Makes 4 servings.

GLAZED PINEAPP[LE]

In skillet, melt bit of butte[r]
drained canned pineapple c[hunks]
dash of catchup; sprinkle [with]
sugar. Heat 5 min., or unti[l]
casionally. Serve with meats[.]

PICKLED PINEAP[PLE]

In pie plate, toss 1 No. 2 can[,]
drained; 3 tablesp. brown sug[ar; vine]gar. Dot with 1 tablesp. bu[tter.]
Bake at 350°F. 30 min. Serve[as a side]
course. Makes 6 servings.

CURRIED FOUR-FRU[IT]

1/3 cup butter or
margarine

3/4 cup brown sugar,
packed

4 teasp. curry powder

1 No. 303 can pear
halves

5 ma[raschino cherries]
(o[ptional])

1 No. [303 can]
pe[ach halves]

hal[ves]

1 No. [303 can peach]
slic[es]

Start heating oven to 325°F. M[ix brown]
sugar and curry. Drain and dry [fruits; in]
1½-qt. casserole; add butter mixture. Bake 1 hr.,
uncovered. Serve warm, from casserole, with
ham, lamb, poultry, etc. Makes 12 servings.

To Do Ahead: Flavor will be even better if dish
stands, covered, in refrigerator and is then reheated. It may be reheated several times. Any
leftover juice may be used as baster when baking
ham slice or served, thickened, as sauce over
ham.

To Vary: For 4 fruits, substitute 1 1-lb. 13-oz.
jar fruits for salad. Use ¼ cup butter and 1
tablesp. curry powder. Bake in 1-qt. casserole.

Curried Apricots: In pie plate, arrange 1 No. 303
can apricot halves, drained. Combine 2 tablesp.
melted butter or margarine; ¼ cup brown
sugar, packed; and 1½ teasp. curry powder.
Spoon mixture over fruit. Bake at 350°F. 30
min. Serve warm. Makes 6 servings.

SPICED JELLIED APRICOTS

1 No. 2½ can
apricot halves

¼ cup vinegar

½ cup granulated
sugar

12 cloves

1 stick cinnamon

1 pkg. orange-flavored
gelatin

[before:] Into saucepan, drain syrup from
[aprico]ts; add vinegar, sugar, cloves, cinnamon.
[Bring] to boil. Add apricots; simmer 10 min. Re-
[move] apricots to 6 custard cups or individual
[molds.] Strain syrup; add hot water to make 2
[cups. P]our over gelatin; stir until dissolved; pour
[over ap]ricots. Refrigerate until set.

[To se]rve: Unmold apricots onto relish tray.
[Serve w]ith meat, poultry. Makes 6 servings.

[Spiced] Apricot Salad: Unmold apricots onto
[waterc]ress or curly chicory. Place spoonful of
[cream c]heese beside each mold.

[J]ELLIED CRANBERRY SAUCE

[4 cups fres]h cranberries
[(1 lb.)

[2 cups wa]ter

2 cups granulated
sugar

[Cook cr]anberries in water 5 to 10 min., or until
[skins] pop open. Strain through fine sieve to
[remove sk]ins and seeds, pressing pulp through
[sieve.] Stir sugar into pulp; boil about 3
[min. Pour] into mold; refrigerate until set; un-
[mold, or] pour into bowl; refrigerate until set,
then spoon into serving dish. Makes 1 qt.

SPEEDY WHOLE-CRANBERRY SAUCE

2 cups granulated
sugar

2 cups water

1 lb. fresh cranberries
(4 cups)

In saucepan, combine sugar, water. Boil 3 to 5
min. Add cranberries. Bring to boil, uncovered.
Cook, without stirring, until skins of berries pop
open—about 5 min. Cool; refrigerate until
served. Makes 1 qt.

Quick: In saucepan, combine all ingredients.
Boil rapidly until skins of berries pop open—
about 5 min. Cool; refrigerate until served.
Makes 1¼ qt.

Quickest of All: You'll find it at your grocer's—
delicious jellied or whole-cranberry sauce, in
large and small cans. Especially wonderful with
chicken, turkey, and ham.

FRESH CRANBERRY RELISHES

These delightfully crisp, crunchy cranberry relishes give a nice lift to breakfast, luncheon, or
dinner. Start making them in October, when the

Overlaid recipe card:

If convenient, prepare the fruits
a couple of days ahead of time
and put in the refrigerator to
chill.

Spiced Brandied Fruits.

1 No. 2 can (1 pound) apricots

1 No. 2 can (1 pound) peach
halves

1 No. 2½ can (20 ounces)
sliced pineapple

1½ cup each, red and green
maraschino cherries

½ cup brown sugar

¾ cup cider vinegar

¼ teaspoon salt

3 sticks (2 inches long) whole
cinnamon

1½ teaspoons each, whole cloves,
whole allspice

½ cup brandy

Drain fruit syrups into a saucepan. Add sugar, vinegar, salt, and
cinnamon. Tie cloves and allspice
in a bag and add. Heat to rolling
boil. Boil 5 minutes. Add fruit.
Simmer 15 minutes. Do not boil.
Cool, remove spices. Add brandy.
Cover and chill at least 24 hours.
Makes 10 to 12 servings.

Bake cup cakes made from your
favorite recipe or a mix in fluted
paper cups. Frost with white
frosting and decorate with colored sugar, chocolate shot and
silver dragees.

new crop is so good. These relishes keep well in refrigerator.

Cran-Orange: *Same day or several days before:* Put 1 lb. fresh cranberries (4 cups) and 2 seeded, quartered unpeeled oranges through food chopper, using medium blade. Stir in 2 cups granulated sugar. Refrigerate several hours or longer. Makes 2 pt.

Good news: 1-lb. cans of frozen cranberry-orange relish, similar to that above, are now available.

Cran-Tangerine: *Same day or several days before:* Put 1 lb. fresh cranberries, plus pulp (seeds removed) and rind (membrane removed) of 3 tangerines, through food chopper, using medium blade. Add 2 cups granulated sugar. Refrigerate several hours. Makes 2 pt.

Cran-Pineapple: *Same day or several days before:* Put 1 lb. fresh cranberries and 1 seeded, quartered unpeeled lemon through food chopper, using medium blade. Stir in 1 8-oz. can (1 cup) crushed pineapple and 2 cups granulated sugar. Refrigerate several hours. Makes 2 pt.

Cran-Apple: *Same day or several days before:* Put 1 lb. fresh cranberries (4 cups) and 2 cored, unpared cooking apples through food chopper, using medium blade. Quarter and remove seeds from 2 unpeeled oranges and 1 lemon; put through food chopper. Add to cranberries with 2½ cups granulated sugar; blend. Refrigerate several hours. Makes 3 pt.

SHIRL'S JELLIED CRANBERRY RELISH

½ lb. fresh cranberries (2 cups)	1¾ to 2 cups granulated sugar
1 seeded, quartered unpeeled orange	3 cups hot water
½ cup chopped celery	2 pkg. lemon-flavored gelatin

On the day: Put cranberries and orange through food chopper, using coarse blade; add celery, sugar. Add hot water to gelatin; stir until dissolved; refrigerate until as thick and syrupy as unbeaten egg white. Add cranberry mixture. Refrigerate until served. Let guests help themselves to partially set relish. Makes about 10 servings.

Molded Raw-Cranberry Relish: Make day before. Refrigerate in 1¼-qt. mold. Unmold and serve as relish or salad.

NO-COOK CRANBERRY RELISHES

Day before: Into 1 1-lb. can whole-cranberry sauce, stir any of the following. Refrigerate until served. Wonderful with chicken, ham, pork, fish, turkey, etc. Makes about 2 cups.

Cranberry-Grape: 2 teasp. grated orange rind, ½ cup seedless grapes

Cranberry-Chutney: ½ cup light or dark raisins; ½ cup chopped, cored unpared cooking apple; ½ cup chopped celery; 1 teasp. ground ginger

Crisp Cranberry: 2 grated, pared carrots; ½ cup diced celery; ½ teasp. mace or nutmeg; 1 teasp. fresh, frozen, or canned lemon juice

Cranberry-Pear: 1 or 2 diced, cored pears; ½ seeded unpeeled lemon, put through food chopper; 1 teasp. ground ginger

Tangy Orange-Cranberry: 2 tablesp. each grated orange rind, coarsely chopped walnuts, and pickle relish

Cran-Apple-Lemon: 1 cored unpared large cooking apple and ¼ seeded unpeeled lemon, put through food chopper

Cranberry Butter: ½ cup applesauce, ½ teasp. cinnamon. Extra nice if jellied cranberry sauce is used

SPICED FRUIT COCKTAIL

1 No. 2½ can fruit cocktail, drained	sugar
1 cup syrup drained from fruit cocktail	⅔ cup cider vinegar
	¼″ stick cinnamon
1⅓ cups granulated	1 teasp. whole cloves

Spread fruit cocktail in flat pan. In saucepan, combine syrup, sugar, and vinegar with cinnamon and cloves tied together in small piece of cheesecloth. Boil 5 min.; remove spice bag. Pour sauce over fruit cocktail (sauce will not be thick). Let stand in refrigerator at least 1 hr. or overnight. Drain syrup from fruit; spoon fruit around meat loaf. Makes 8 servings.

For Special Occasions: Halve 4 small or medium oranges; scoop out orange pulp (save fruit for breakfast). Fill shells with Spiced Fruit Cocktail; arrange around meat loaf, roast, poultry, etc., with parsley sprigs between shells.

SPICED PRUNES

1 lb. large prunes	1 cup water
1 cup vinegar	1 teasp. ground cloves
1 cup granulated sugar	1 teasp. cinnamon

Week or so ahead: Rinse prunes; cover with cold water; boil 10 to 12 min.; drain. Combine vinegar, sugar, water, spices; boil 1 min. Add prunes; bring to boil. Cool; refrigerate. Nice with poultry or roasts, or as garnish for fruit salads. Makes about 10 servings.

BARBECUED BAKED APPLES

Start heating oven to 350°F. Wash 4 cooking apples; cut in halves crosswise; remove cores. Place halves, with cut sides up, in shallow baking pan. On each half, put 1 tablesp. brown sugar and 1 tablesp. catchup; dot with butter or margarine. Pour ¼" hot water around apples in pan; bake about 30 min. Serve hot, spooning liquid from pan over apples. Serve as meat accompaniment. Makes 8 servings.

ROSY CINNAMON APPLES

1 cup red cinnamon candies	pared, cored cooking apples
2⅔ cups boiling water	½ cup granulated sugar
8 small or medium	

In saucepan, dissolve candies in boiling water. Add apples. Simmer until tender, turning often. Remove to shallow dish. Add sugar to syrup; boil 3 min. Pour over apples, turning each apple to glaze it. Cool. Serve with meat. Makes 6 to 8 servings.

BROILED APPLE RINGS

Wash and core large cooking apples; cut into ¼" slices. Place on broiler rack; brush with melted butter or margarine mixed with fresh, frozen, or canned lemon juice (1 teasp. lemon juice to each 1 tablesp. melted butter). Broil 4 to 5 min., or until slices begin to soften. Turn with broad spatula. Brush second side with butter and lemon juice; sprinkle with cinnamon and sugar. Broil 3 to 5 min., or until golden brown. Serve as garnish for meat or vegetable plate.

FRIED APPLE RINGS

Select 3 large cooking apples. Wash; core; cut into ½" to ¾" slices. Sprinkle lightly with granulated or brown sugar. In a little hot butter or margarine in skillet, sauté apple slices until tender on both sides. Serve with pork, sausages, etc. Makes 18.

GLAZED APPLE QUARTERS

In saucepan or skillet, combine 2 teasp. grated orange rind, ½ cup orange juice, ½ cup granulated sugar. Arrange 4 quartered, cored unpared red cooking apples, with skin sides up, in mixture. Simmer, covered, over low heat 10 to 15 min., or until apples are tender but still hold their shape. Use as garnish for Braised Pork Chops, p. 79, or other pork dish. Cook orange sauce until thickened; spoon over apples. Makes 4 servings.

BROILED FRUIT

Canned Peaches, Pears, Pineapple, or Apricots: Preheat broiler 10 min., or as manufacturer directs. Place well-drained fruit on broiler rack. Sprinkle with a little lemon juice. Brush with melted butter or margarine or salad oil. Sprinkle with a little granulated or brown sugar, then with more lemon juice and pinch of ground cloves, cinnamon, or nutmeg. Broil 3" to 4" from heat 8 min., or until golden. Serve as garnish for meat, fish, or poultry. Or top with vanilla ice cream for dessert.

Fresh Peaches or Pears: Pare, halve, and pit or core fruits. Proceed as above. If you like, put ½ teasp. chili sauce in center of each peach or pear half; then broil.

Bananas: Peel firm, all-yellow or slightly green-tipped bananas. Proceed as above, broiling bananas about 5 min. on each side, or until brown and fork-tender.

SAUTEED BANANAS

¼ cup butter or margarine	4 firm bananas*
	Salt

In large skillet, melt butter. Peel bananas; leave whole, or cut crosswise into halves. Sauté slowly until easily pierced with fork, turning to brown bananas evenly. Sprinkle lightly with salt. Serve as vegetable, with meat, fish, poultry, etc. Makes 4 servings.

Use all-yellow or slightly green-tipped bananas.

BANANA SCALLOPS

1½ teasp. salt	½ cup fine corn
1 egg, slightly beaten;	flakes, packaged
or ¼ cup undiluted	dried bread or
evaporated milk	cracker crumbs, or
4 firm bananas*	corn meal

Add salt to egg. Peel bananas; slice crosswise into chunks ¾" to 1" thick. Dip into egg; drain. Roll in crumbs. Deep-fry as on p. 7, or Shallow-fry as on p. 8, at 375°F. on deep-fat frying thermometer, until brown and tender. Drain well. Serve hot, as vegetable, with meat, fish, etc. Makes 4 servings.

Use slightly green-tipped or all-yellow bananas.

BAKED BANANAS

4 firm bananas*	butter or margarine
2 tablesp. melted	Salt

Start heating oven to 450°F. Peel bananas; place in well-greased baking dish. Brush well with butter; sprinkle lightly with salt. Bake 10 to 12 min., or till bananas are tender and easily pierced with fork. Serve hot, as vegetable, with ham, hamburgers, poultry, etc. Makes 4 servings.

Use slightly green-tipped or all-yellow bananas.

P.S. For a golden-brown tint, broil baked bananas about 1 min.

Cranberry: Pour ¾ cup canned whole-cranberry sauce over bananas before baking. Serve hot, with beef, ham, chicken, duckling, or turkey.

FROSTED GRAPES OR CURRANTS

Beat 1 egg white till frothy; dip small bunches of grapes or large currants into white. Let grapes or currants stand until nearly dry; then sprinkle with granulated sugar. Refrigerate until dry. Nice as garnish for baked ham, pie wedges, fruit salads, steamed puddings, etc.

MARINATED TOMATOES

Slice peeled ripe tomatoes into shallow dish. Cover lightly with thinly sliced scallions and green tops. Sprinkle with salt and, if desired, with bit of dried basil. Pour French dressing over all (about ½ cup dressing per 1½ lb. tomatoes). Refrigerate. Drain. Serve instead of salad.

With Olives: Substitute whole ripe olives for scallions.

With Avocado: Substitute sliced avocado or cucumber for scallions.

TWO-IN-ONE RELISH

1 cup grated, pared	sour cream
raw white turnips	Dash pepper
¼ cup sliced radishes	1 tablesp. French
¼ teasp. salt	dressing
2 tablesp. commercial	

Combine all ingredients. Refrigerate. Serve with fish. Makes 1¼ cups.

ZESTY ONION

½ cup vinegar	or 1 tablesp. celery
1 tablesp. confectioners'	seeds
sugar	1 cup thinly sliced
¾ cup chopped	small onions
fresh mint leaves;	

Combine vinegar, sugar, mint; heat gently, or let stand 30 min. Add onions. Refrigerate until crisp. Serve with fish. Makes 6 servings.

FRESH TOMATO RELISH

Several hours before serving: Chop 2 lb. tomatoes, 2 medium green peppers, 2 medium onions; drain slightly. Add 2 teasp. salt, 1 teasp. dry mustard, 1 teasp. celery seeds, ¼ cup vinegar, ¼ cup salad oil. Mix. Refrigerate. Makes 1 qt.

APPLE DILL

½ cup finely minced	pickle
unpared apple	1 tablesp. French
⅓ cup minced dill	dressing

Toss together all ingredients. Refrigerate 30 min. Serve with fish. Makes 4 to 6 servings.

Garlic Dills: Drop 2 or 3 garlic cloves into liquid in jar or can of dill pickles or ripe olives. Refrigerate several days before serving.

PICKLED BEETS

½ teasp. dry mustard	½ clove garlic
1 tablesp. sugar	6 tablesp. vinegar
½ teasp. salt	¼ cup water
½ teasp. ground cloves	2 cups sliced drained cooked or canned beets

Combine mustard, sugar, salt, cloves, garlic. Slowly stir in vinegar, water. When mixture is smooth, pour over beets. Refrigerate until well chilled. Remove garlic. Serve with meat or fish. Makes 6 servings.

P.S. Add pinch of fennel if desired.

BEET AND HORSE-RADISH RELISH

1 No. 2 can beets	2 teasp. salt
1 tablesp. sugar	⅛ teasp. pepper
1 tablesp. minced onion	½ cup vinegar
	½ cup horse-radish

Drain beets; reserve liquid. Cut beets into small cubes; add sugar, onion, salt, pepper, vinegar, horse-radish. Add enough beet liquid to cover. Refrigerate overnight. Serve with meat or fish. Makes 6 servings.

SUSAN'S RAW RELISHES

Susan serves her relishes on a tray, right along with the meat course, so no separate salad is necessary. For those who crave it, there's a tiny pitcher of French dressing in the center of the tray.

Radishes: Wash crisp radishes; then remove all but tuft of leaves. With sharp knife, cut off roots.

Roses: Cut thin slice from each side of each radish, making slices equally distant; next cut thin slices, not quite through to stem, behind each white spot. Refrigerate on ice until red-rimmed petals open. Pat dry on towel.

Fans: Cut each radish crosswise into thin slices, not quite through to stem end. Refrigerate on ice. Pat dry on towel.

Carrots:

Curls: With vegetable parer, shave lengthwise strips from pared long straight carrot. Curl each strip around forefinger; then place on ice, tucking it in tightly. Let stand 1 hr. Pat dry on towel.

Fans: With very sharp thin knife, cut pared, chilled young carrots into ¼"-thick lengthwise slices. Cut each slice in half crosswise. Then make lengthwise cuts ¼" apart, almost to end of each slice.

Celery:

Hearts: Break off heavy outer stalks, then cut tops from bunch of celery (Pascal, the all-green kind, is nice). Wash; pare root; halve bunch lengthwise through root. Cut each half lengthwise into 2 or 3 strips; then make 3 or 4 gashes along outside stalk of each. Refrigerate on ice. Pat dry on towel.

Curls: Cut each large tender stalk of celery into 3" lengths; slit each, almost to end, into narrow, parallel strips. Or slit both ends almost to center. Refrigerate on ice until ends curl. Pat dry on towel.

Cauliflowerets: Remove outside stalks from well-chilled cauliflower. Wash and break head into small flowerets. Serve raw.

Cucumber Slices: Pare cucumber; then score by running sharp-tined fork down length of cucumber from end to end. Cut crosswise into very thin slices; refrigerate on ice; pat dry on towel. Sprinkle with snipped parsley.

Or pat finely snipped parsley or chives into grooves of scored, pared cucumber. Refrigerate. Then slice. Or slice unpared cucumbers.

Beet, Cucumber, Carrot, Turnip Sticks: Cut each washed, pared, chilled raw vegetable lengthwise into ⅛" slices; cut each slice into thin sticks. (If carrot or cucumber is very long, first cut it in half.) If desired, string ripe pitted olives on sticks.

Scallions (spring or green onions): Wash; cut off all but 2" of green tops. Cut off roots; remove loose skin. Wrap in damp cloth; refrigerate. Use green tops in soup.

Stuffed Raw Mushrooms: Wash 1 doz. medium mushrooms (about ¼ lb.); dry; remove stems. Mix ½ 3-oz. pkg. soft cream cheese, 1 teasp. Worcestershire, 2 tablesp. minced onion or chives. Use to fill mushroom caps.

Susan's Relish Nibblers: Arrange assortment of raw relishes on tray, with one of dunks, p. 28, in bowl in center of tray. Serve as first course in living room; let guests dip relishes into dunk.

RELISHES, PRETTY AS A PICTURE

It's so easy to add a bit of drama to your relish tray or dish. Let these suggestions start you off.

Green and White: Make two rows, side by side —one of watermelon pickle, other of celery hearts.

Nibbler: Set bowl of mixed olives on small tray, carrot and dill-pickle sticks near bowl.

Lazy Susan: Set 4 or 5 small bowls of assorted relishes on tray, with flower in low bowl in center of tray.

Parsley Bed: Top bed of parsley with carrot curls and green, ripe, and stuffed olives.

Help Yourself: Place basket of salted nuts on one side of tray; radiate raw turnip chips, carrot sticks, green-pepper rings, and radish roses from basket on tray.

Black-and-White: Serve bowl of plump ripe olives, with fringed celery tucked here and there.

Homemade: Roll pickled peaches in snipped celery leaves.

Take Your Choice: Place coleslaw in hollowed-out cabbage head on one end of tray, canned jellied-cranberry-sauce slices at other end.

In Pewter Bowl: Serve Quick Pickled Pineapple, p. 286, and ripe and green olives.

Ring-around-a-rosy Bowl: Pile olives or pickle slices in center of bowl; circle with carrot curls, then with cauliflowerets.

Tray Style: In center of tray, set sherbet glass of homemade jelly; on one side, place celery curls; on other side, ripe olives.

Yellow and White: In shallow glass bowl, place bed of carrot curls; top with celery fans.

Two Rows: Down one side of oblong dish, place overlapping slices of canned jellied cranberry sauce; down other side, pickles studded with almonds.

Grapefruit "Bowl": Use grapefruit shell as "bowl" for cranberry-orange relish (it comes frozen).

Black and Yellow: Serve bowl of ripe olives, with lemon slices tucked in here and there.

Relish Twosome: Serve canned jellied-cranberry-sauce slices, with pickled apricots in center of tray.

MORE GO-ALONGS FOR MEAT, FISH, POULTRY

See Coleslaw Quartet, p. 303; Rhubarb Sauce, p. 402; Buttery Baked Peaches, p. 401; Buttery Baked Pears, p. 401; Baked Applesauce, p. 389.

QUICKEST-OF-ALL RELISHES

The cans and jars of relishes on your grocer's shelves are chock-full of old-time goodness. Here are a few:

Applesauce	Horse-radish
Barbecue sauce	Bottled meat sauce
Brandied fruits	Prepared mincemeat
Catchup	Prepared mustard
Chili sauce	Pickle relish
Chowchow	Pickled beets
Chutney	Pickled onions
Cocktail sauce	Pickles of all kinds
Corn relish	Spiced fruits
Cranberry sauce	Tomato sauce
Hamburger relish	Watermelon pickle
Hot-dog relish	Worcestershire

RELISHES TO KEEP FOR LATER USE

Good Things to Know

Equipment: Use a *big* kettle so mixture won't bubble over. A long-handled wooden spoon is a must. Keep mixtures that must stand overnight in a large mixing bowl or enamel kettle. Use a wide-mouthed funnel to keep mixture from spilling as you pour it into jars.

The Jar: Preserve jars for storing relish mixtures must be sterilized just before filling—*unless* mixture is to be processed. In that case, they need only be clean and hot.

To Sterilize Jars: Wash jars in soapy water; rinse. Place on wire rack in kettle; add warm water to cover. Cover. Boil 20 min. Remove jars from boiling water, one by one, just before filling.

Glass covers should be sterilized with jars. Covers with sealing composition should be handled as manufacturer directs.

Rubbers for jars should be dipped into boiling water just before being adjusted on jars. Never re-use jar rubbers; buy new ones for each use.

To Fill and Seal Jars: Follow manufacturer's directions, setting jars on towel to fill.

CHILI SAUCE

4 teasp. whole cloves	2½ cups chopped, seeded green or sweet red peppers (6)
3 tablesp. whole allspice	
4 qt. chopped, peeled ripe tomatoes (8 lb.)	1½ cups granulated sugar
2½ cups chopped medium onions (6)	2 tablesp. salt
	1 qt. cider vinegar

Tie spices in cheesecloth; add to rest of ingredients combined in kettle. Cook, uncovered, stirring often, 2½ to 3 hr., or until quite thick. Remove spice bag. Pour sauce at once into clean hot preserve jars; adjust covers as manufacturer directs.

To process: Set jars on wire rack in covered deep kettle, with boiling water to cover tops of jars 1″. Boil 30 min., counting time from moment active boiling resumes. Remove; then seal jars at once as manufacturer directs. Makes 4 to 5 pt.

SUSAN'S PICCALILLI

8 qt. green tomatoes	½ cup salt
12 sweet red peppers	1 cup mustard seeds
12 green peppers	3 tablesp. celery seeds
1 qt. small onions	1 tablesp. cinnamon
3 qt. cider vinegar	1 tablesp. ground allspice
7 cups granulated sugar	

1. Sterilize 12 pint preserve jars as above. Keep in boiling water until ready to be filled.

2. Wash tomatoes; cut out stem ends; quarter lengthwise. Wash and seed peppers; quarter lengthwise. Peel and quarter onions.

3. Put all vegetables through food chopper, using medium-fine blade; then pour vegetables into colander; drain off liquid and discard it.

4. Turn drained vegetables into large kettle; add 2 qt. vinegar; boil, uncovered, 30 min., stirring often. Again drain vegetables, discarding liquid.

5. Into vegetables, stir 1 qt. vinegar, sugar, and rest of ingredients. Simmer, uncovered, 3 min.

6. Pour at once into sterilized jars to within 1″ of top. Pour ½″ layer of hot new paraffin into each. Then seal jars at once as manufacturer directs; cool. Makes about 12 pt.

GREEN-AND-RED-PEPPER RELISH

7½ cups chopped, seeded sweet red peppers (18)	5 cups chopped onions (12)
	3 tablesp. salt
2½ cups chopped, seeded green peppers (6)	2 cups granulated sugar
	2 cups cider vinegar

To chop peppers and onions, put through food chopper, using medium blade; or chop in chopping bowl.

Combine all ingredients in kettle; bring to boil; cook, uncovered, 2 min. Pour at once into clean hot preserve jars; adjust covers as manufacturer directs. Process as in Chili Sauce, above. Makes 5 to 6 pt.

MIXED MUSTARD PICKLES

1 large cauliflower	1 qt. cold water
3 green peppers	1½ qt. vinegar
1 sweet red pepper	2 cups granulated sugar
3 cups small white onions	
2 lb. green tomatoes	2 teasp. celery seeds
3 cups tiny whole cucumbers	¾ cup sifted all-purpose flour
1 qt. unpared cucumber slices, ⅛″ thick	¼ lb. dry mustard (1¼ cups)
1 cup salt	1½ teasp. turmeric
	2 cups cold water

Wash cauliflower; break into small flowerets. Wash, seed, and halve peppers; cut in ¼″ crosswise slices. Pour boiling water over onions; let stand 5 min.; skin. Wash and cut tomatoes into eighths. In large bowl, mix cauliflower, peppers, onions, tomatoes, whole and sliced cucumbers. Cover with salt and 1 qt. cold water combined. Let stand 16 hr.; bring just to boil in same water; drain.

Meanwhile, heat vinegar, sugar, and celery seeds till boiling. Mix flour, mustard, turmeric, water, to form paste; stir into vinegar mixture. Add to drained vegetables; cook, uncovered, 20 min., stirring. Turn at once into hot sterilized preserve jars; seal at once as manufacturer directs. Makes about 9 pt.

CORN RELISH

8 cups raw corn, cut from cob	¾ cup brown sugar, packed
3 cups chopped onions	½ cup white or dark corn syrup
½ cup chopped green peppers	7 teasp. salt
½ cup chopped red peppers	1 tablesp. dry mustard
2 tablesp. celery seeds	3 cups cider vinegar

Combine all ingredients; mix thoroughly. Cover; bring to boil; simmer 15 min., stirring occasionally. Pour at once into clean hot preserve jars; adjust covers as manufacturer directs. Process as in Chili Sauce, p. 293. Especially nice served with ham. Makes 4 to 5 pt.

WATERMELON PICKLE

3 qt. trimmed watermelon rind	½ teasp. oil of cloves
Boiling water	½ teasp. oil of cinnamon
7 cups granulated sugar	1 small unpeeled orange
2 cups vinegar	1 unpeeled lemon

First day: Use rind from firm but not overripe watermelon. Trim off green skin and any pink flesh; cut rind into 1″ cubes. (There should be 2½ qt.) Place rind in large saucepan; cover with boiling water; boil till tender but *not* soft—about 10 min. Drain well. In saucepan, combine sugar, vinegar, oil of cloves, cinnamon; bring to boil. Pour over rind. Let stand overnight at room temperature.

Next day: In morning, drain syrup from watermelon rind; heat to boiling point and pour over rind. Let stand overnight.

Third day: In morning, slice unpeeled orange and lemon crosswise; quarter each slice. Add orange and lemon to watermelon rind in syrup; heat to boiling point. Turn at once into 4 to 6 hot sterilized pt. preserve jars; seal as manufacturer directs. Store in cool dry place. Makes 4 to 6 pt.

PRESERVED KUMQUATS

1½ cups granulated sugar	1½ cups water
	1 qt. kumquats

At your convenience: Boil sugar and water 5 min.; cool. Meanwhile, wash kumquats; cut small cross in blossom end of each. Place in cooled syrup. Cover; bring to boil; simmer 1 hr., or until clear. *Do not remove cover at end of cooking time or fruit will shrink.* Remove covered saucepan from heat; cool, with cover on, to room temperature. Pack in hot sterilized jars; cover with syrup; seal as manufacturer directs. Or refrigerate. Serve as relish with poultry or meat. Or serve as dessert, with cheese and crackers or cookies. Or serve on vanilla ice cream. Makes about 2 pt.

SPICED SECKEL PEARS

8 lb. Seckel pears	7 3″ sticks cinnamon
8½ cups granulated sugar	2 tablesp. whole cloves
1 qt. cider vinegar	2 tablesp. whole allspice
2 cups water	

Wash pears; leave stems on, but scrape out blossom ends. Boil pears in water to cover 10 min.; then drain; prick skins.

For syrup: Combine sugar, vinegar, water, and spices tied in cheesecloth. Cook, covered, 5 min. Add pears; boil, covered, 10 min., or until tender. Let pears stand in syrup overnight. Drain, reserving syrup; remove spice bag. Pack pears at once in clean hot jars. Bring syrup to boil. Pour at once over pears; adjust covers as manufacturer directs. Process as in Chili Sauce, p. 293. Makes 4 to 5 qt.

Spiced Citron Melon: Remove seeds, pare, then dice 2 5½-lb. citron melons (there should be 4 qt. prepared fruit). Add 2 qt. cold water; simmer ½ hr. Drain. Make syrup as above; add melon; proceed as directed. Makes about 2 qt.

Spiced Crab Apples: Wash 8 lb. crab apples; leave stems on; scrape out blossom ends. Make syrup as above; add crab apples; proceed as directed. Makes about 4 to 5 qt.

Spiced Kieffer or Bartlett Pears: Wash 8 lb. pears; pare; cut into halves or quarters; core. Boil pears 10 min. in water to cover; then drain. Make syrup as above; add pears and proceed as directed. Makes about 3 qt.

Spiced Peaches: Pour boiling water over 8 lb. cling peaches; let stand until skins can be removed easily. Dip into cold water; peel. Stick 3 whole cloves in each peach. Make syrup as above; add peaches; proceed as directed. Makes about 3 qt.

Note: Store any leftover syrup in refrigerator; use next day to make second lot of same spiced fruit, adding vinegar and spices to taste if necessary.

PEAR CHUTNEY

4½ lb. firm ripe pears	½ teasp. salt
½ cup minced green peppers	1 cup water
½ lb. seeded raisins (1½ cups)	¼ teasp. ground cloves
4 cups granulated sugar	½ teasp. cinnamon
1 cup crystallized ginger, cut small	¼ teasp. nutmeg
3 cups vinegar	¼ teasp. allspice
	6 bay leaves
	½ cup bottled liquid fruit pectin

Pare, core, and slice pears. Mix pears with green peppers, raisins, sugar, ginger, vinegar, salt, water. Tie cloves, cinnamon, nutmeg, allspice, and bay leaves in cheesecloth bag; add to pears. Simmer until pears are tender and mixture is thick—about 2 hr. Remove bag. Add liquid pectin; boil 1 min. Pour at once into hot sterilized

preserve jars; seal at once as manufacturer directs. Makes 3 pt.

APPLE CHUTNEY

4 lb. chopped onions (2 qt.)	1 lb. light or dark raisins
3 lb. chopped, pared green cooking apples	2 teasp. ginger
	2 teasp. ground cloves
4½ cups brown sugar, packed	1 tablesp. cinnamon
	1 tablesp. salt
3 tablesp. molasses	Dash cayenne pepper

Combine all ingredients in large kettle; simmer, uncovered, stirring occasionally, about 2 hr., or until mixture becomes thick and dark. Pour at once into hot sterilized preserve jars; seal at once as manufacturer directs. Makes about 6 pt.

PEACH CHUTNEY

4 cups granulated sugar	citron
	2 cups seedless raisins
1½ pt. cider vinegar	
5 lb. peaches	2 minced cloves garlic
2 medium seedless oranges	2 cups chopped onions
	3 chopped, green peppers
4 lemons	
½ lb. preserved	

In large kettle, bring sugar and vinegar to boil. Add peeled, quartered peaches; oranges and lemons, sliced paper-thin; citron, cut fine; rest of ingredients. Simmer, uncovered, 30 min. Pour into clean hot preserve jars; adjust covers as manufacturer directs. Process as in Chili Sauce, p. 293. Makes about 7 to 8 pt.

DILL, MIXED, SOUR, OR SWEET PICKLES

Additional pickle and relish recipes may be found in first 6 booklets listed on p. 544.

THE GAY GARNISH

Let your garnish provide color contrast. Make it pretty but not gaudy.

Choose the plate carefully. The dish, as well as the food, can be effective.

Always leave some plate showing. It provides a frame for the food.

Arrange food with imagination. Often the way you place the food on the plate or platter is all the garnish that's needed.

Don't overgarnish, especially if you're serving buffet style or if someone is carving or dishing out the food.

Last but *not* least, use your imagination. Don't stick just to conventional garnishes.

IF IT'S MEAT, POULTRY, OR FISH

Roasts, Chops, Steaks
Roast Chicken or Duckling
Roast Turkey
Baked, Broiled, or Poached Fish
Pan-Fried Fish
Broiled or Fried Shellfish

Apricots* (studded with almonds)
Beet cups (with horse-radish)
Carrots (sticks or curls)
Celery (cheese-stuffed)
Celery (fans or sticks)
Chutney (in lettuce cups)
Currant jelly (spoonfuls)
Cucumber slices (fluted)
Dill sprigs or celery leaves
Green grapes (tiny bunches)
Green peppers (in rings)
Jellied cranberry sauce*
Kumquats (fresh or preserved: nest in cress)
Lemons, limes (halved lengthwise, then crosswise; dipped into snipped parsley or chives, or paprika)
Mushrooms (sautéed or broiled)
Ripe olives
Stuffed olives (in rows)
Onions (overlapping rings)
Orange or lemon shells (filled with crushed pineapple)
Peaches* (pickled)
Pear halves* (filled with chili sauce or pickle relish)
Pickles* (dill, sour, sweet)
Pineapple chunks* (rolled in

snipped mint)
Pineapple slices* (topped with coleslaw or whole or halved apricots*)
Mashed potatoes (nests, with peas)
Spinach (tender leaves)
Tomato slices (with pickle relish)
Tomatoes (tiny ones, filled with horse-radish)
Tomato wedges (dipped into snipped chives)
Turnips (thin slices, chilled on ice)
Water cress (perky sprigs)
Zucchini (cooked slices)

Baked Ham
Broiled or Fried Chicken

Baked small apples (filled with brown-and-serve sausages)
Apricots, peaches, pears, or pineapple* (sautéed or broiled)
Banana halves (sautéed or broiled)
Bing cherries*
Corn fritters
Crab apples*
Jellied cranberry sauce*
Orange slices
Peaches* (pickled)
Pineapple chunks* (rolled in snipped mint)
Sweet-potato halves
Prunes (plain or stuffed)

Chops, Steaks
Hamburgers

Blue cheese (crumbled)
Capers, bottled (just a few)
Chives (snipped)
Pickle relish
Banana halves (sautéed or broiled)
French fries
Onions (overlapping rings)
Peaches, pears, or apricots* (heated in syrup)
Peach halves* (topped with chili sauce)

Meat or Chicken Pie
Chicken Fricassee
Savory Stew

Blue cheese (crumbled)
Carrots (grated raw)
Capers, bottled (just a few)
Cheese (grated or shredded)
Chives (snipped)
Parsley (snipped)
Pimento* (diced or in strips)

Fried Oysters, Shrimp, Fish
Broiled Scallops, etc.

Avocado balls
French fries
Pineapple slices* (sautéed)
Potato chips or sticks
Tomato slices (with tartar sauce)

* Canned

IF IT'S SALAD

Tossed Green: See Salad Extras, p. 299.

Tossed Vegetable: See Extras, p. 302.

Potato, Macaroni, Rice: See Extras, p. 302.

Dill (sprigs)
Celery leaves

Onions (rings)
Pickles (fans, chunks, slices)
Tomato aspic (cubes)
Tomato wedges (dipped into snipped chives)

Meat, Fish, or Fruit

Apricots* (studded with almonds)
Crab apples*

Jellied cranberry sauce*
Grapes (small bunches)
Peaches* (pickled)
Pineapple cubes* (rolled in snipped mint)
Spinach (tender leaves)
Water cress (perky sprigs)

Poultry: See Our Best Chicken Salad, p. 305.

IF IT'S SOUP: See A Bit of Garnish, p. 33.
IF IT'S A DRINK: See The Ice, p. 498, and Glamour Touches, p. 497.
IF IT'S A VEGETABLE: See Serve With a Flair, p. 247.
IF IT'S ICE CREAM: See Sundae Toppings, p. 436.

HOLIDAY PRETTIES

New Year's

Shredded coconut
Confectioners' sugar
Whipped cream (in drifts)
Silver *dragées*

St. Valentine's Day
Lincoln's Birthday
Washington's Birthday

Bing cherries*
Cinnamon candies (heart-shaped)
Jellied cranberry sauce* (cut into shapes)
Maraschino cherries (with stems)
Radishes (sliced, grated, or halved)

St. Patrick's Day

Coconut* (tinted green)
Crushed pineapple* (tinted green)
Melted mint jelly
Pickle relish*

* *Canned*

Shamrocks (instead of cress or mint)

Easter

Coconut* (tinted pink, green, or yellow)
Eggs (hard-cooked, chopped or quartered)
Strawberry, vanilla, pistachio ice cream (scoopfuls)
Jelly beans
Fresh posies

Fourth of July

Celery fans (ends dipped into paprika)
Jellied cranberry sauce* (cut into stars)
Pimento* (strips)
Radishes (chopped or grated)
Strawberries and blueberries
Peppermint candies (striped)
Sugar (tinted red)
Watermelon (balls)

Halloween

Dried apricots and prunes
Cheese (pumpkin cutouts)
Chocolate (grated)
Blue grapes
Ripe olives
Oranges (slices)

Thanksgiving

Cheese pumpkins
Chrysanthemums (button)
Jellied cranberry sauce*
Salted nuts* and raisins
Peaches* (halves and slices)
Walnuts (in shell, cracked)

Christmas

Cinnamon drops
Currant and mint jelly
Red and green grapes (small bunches)
Holly sprigs
Preserved fruits
Snipped parsley and paprika

Salads

What is more deliciously attractive than a salad of crisp greens, piquant dressing, and perhaps an added attraction of meat, fish, vegetable, or fruit? Remember that salad is one of the most appealing ways of fitting necessary leafy, green, and yellow vegetables into the day's plan for good healthful eating.

Before using these recipes, refer to How to Use Our Recipes, p. 3, and Pots and Pans, p. 692. Always use standard measuring cups and measuring spoons; measure level.

Salad Suggestions

Salad Greens: Iceberg and Boston lettuce are the salad greens used most often. Serve the following, too, when they are plentiful:

Beet greens, young	Belgian
Cabbage, green or red	Escarole
	Field salad
Celery, green tops	Kale
Chicory or American endive	Lettuce, bibb or leaf
	Mustard greens
Chinese cabbage	Romaine
Dandelion greens, young	Spinach, young raw
	Turnip greens
Endive, French or	Water cress (cress)

Vitamin Roundup: Don't discard the outer green leaves of lettuce, romaine, etc. Though they're not as tender as the inner leaves, they're especially rich in vitamins and minerals. So if leaves aren't bruised, wash them *very thoroughly;* dry; shred with scissors; use in salads, sandwiches, etc.

Lettuce-Cup Lore: The family will be less likely to leave greens on the plate if you sprinkle greens with dressing, or toss in French dressing before arranging salad on top. Keep bed of greens small.

Tomato Touch: Tomatoes are wonderful in tossed salad, but they tend to thin the dressing. So add at last minute. Also, cut them the French way—in vertical slices; they'll lose less juice.

Salad-Bowl Treatment: Never soak a wooden salad bowl in water. After use, rinse it quickly in clear lukewarm water, then in cold water. Wipe dry with clean paper towel; store in dry place. In time, garlic and other flavorings from salads will season bowl.

Care of Salad Greens

To Store: Buy crisp, young salad greens. Remove bruised leaves, but keep heads whole. Rinse under running water; shake off excess water; then refrigerate in crisper.

Just before using: Take out greens needed; prepare as below; dry; then refrigerate if preparing ahead.

To Prepare:

Iceberg Lettuce:

For Cups: Cut out core. To loosen leaves, hold lettuce head, with cored side up, under running water. Slip leaves off. Shake off excess water. Then gently pat dry between paper towels; or shake dry in tea towel; or whirl dry in lettuce basket. Water left clinging to leaves makes dressing watery, weakens its flavor.

For Wedges: Just before serving, cut chilled, washed heads of lettuce into quarters or sixths.

To Tear: Tear or break chilled, washed lettuce into bite-size pieces. (Or for quick job, use scissors.) Use in tossed salads.

To Shred: Cut head of lettuce in half; then, with sharp knife, shred very fine. Good as base for "patterned" salads.

Boston Lettuce: Prepare as for iceberg lettuce.

Romaine, Endive, Escarole, Leaf Lettuce, etc.: Separate, leaf by leaf; wash; dry *well* as for iceberg lettuce.

Chicory, Young Spinach, etc.: Wash in several changes of water and dry well as in Greens, p. 281.

Water Cress, Parsley, Mint: Open up bunch; pick over; wash under running cold water. Drain well; store loosely—separate from other salad greens—with stem ends down, in covered jar in refrigerator.

THE GREAT GREEN SALAD

The most popular salad of all is the tossed green salad. It can be economical of time and dishes and couldn't be easier to make or more wonderful to eat—as an accompaniment or as a course by itself. Here's our favorite:

HELEN'S TOSSED GREEN SALAD

Greens: one, two, or more, p. 298	Tarragon-wine, wine, malt, or other vinegar; or lemon juice
1 clove garlic	Salad oil
Salt	
Whole black peppers	

Early in day: Wash and drain greens. (A nice combination is iceberg or Boston lettuce, esca-role, endive, and water cress.) Tear leaves (no tough centers, please!) into bite-size pieces—about 2 qt. Dry well; wrap in towel; refrigerate in vegetable crisper.

When starting dinner: Get out roomy salad bowl. Cut tiny checkerboard pattern across top of garlic clove; then, right into bowl, cut off 2 or 3 thin slivers (this makes lots of tiny garlic bits). Add about ½ teasp. salt and generous grinding (¼ teasp.) of whole black peppers from pepper mill. Add bit of dry mustard too if you like.

With back of spoon, mash seasonings together (all that remains of garlic is delicate flavor). Into seasonings, with fork, stir 1 tablesp. vinegar, then ¼ cup salad oil. Place greens on top of dressing, *but don't toss.* Set salad bowl on top of pile of salad plates; refrigerate.

At salad-serving time, not before: Remove salad bowl and plates from refrigerator. Whisk them to table, and toss greens lightly. (Or toss salad in kitchen.) Every leaf should be coated, but not dripping, with dressing. Serve at once. Makes 4 to 6 servings.

SALAD EXTRAS

Just before tossing Helen's Tossed Green Salad, add one or more of these for color:

Apples (sticks or wedges)
Artichoke bottoms (canned)
Avocado (slivers)
Bacon (crispy bits)
Cauliflowerets (raw)
Celery (sliced diagonally)
Cheese, any kind (crumbled, grated, or slivered)
Chicken, ham, luncheon meat, salami, turkey, tongue, or franks (in thin strips)
Chives or scallions (snipped)
Cucumber (chunks or slices)
Eggs (chopped, hard-cooked)
Grapefruit, orange, or tangerine sections
Grapes
Mushrooms (raw caps or slices)
Olives (green or ripe)
Pineapple (fresh, canned, or frozen: in tidbits or chunks)
Potato chips or corn chips (coarsely broken)
Radishes (sliced or grated)
Sweet onions (sliced paper-thin)

Tomatoes (tiny wedges)
Tuna, sardines, shrimp, salmon, crab meat, lobster
Vegetables (cold cooked)
Walnuts, pecans, or almonds

DRESSING EXTRAS

When mixing dressing for Helen's Tossed Green Salad, add one or more of these:

Anchovy (cut-up fillets or paste)
Bottled thick meat sauce, p. 9 (a few dashes)
Cheese (crumbled blue, or grated sharp or Parmesan)
Chili sauce (a little)
Curry powder (a pinch)
Horse-radish (a little)
Monosodium glutamate (a pinch)
Onion, celery, seasoned, or garlic salt (a sprinkling)
Onions (minced)
Paprika (a pinch)
Parsley, chervil, or tarragon (fresh or dried)
Pickles (chopped)
Seeds—poppy, dill, celery, caraway, sesame, or fennel (a sprinkling)
Tabasco or Worcestershire (a few dashes)

Two Other Ways to Toss Green Salad

1. To table, take cruet of favorite ready-to-use salad dressing, p. 317, and bowl of greens. Shake dressing; drizzle over greens (about 1 tablesp. per serving); toss. Or do all this in kitchen.
2. To table, take bowl of greens and tray of favorite salad-dressing ingredients, p. 319. Over greens, drizzle about 1 tablesp. salad oil per person; add seasonings; toss gently. Then sprinkle lightly with vinegar or lemon juice (about one fourth to one third as much as oil used); toss again. Or do all this in kitchen.

HEARTS OF LETTUCE

Cut chilled head of iceberg lettuce into wedges. Arrange on cold salad plates; top with Roquefort French Dressing, p. 320; Russian Dressing, p. 318; or Puff Sour-Cream Dressing, p. 318.

ROMAINE OR ENDIVE SALAD

Arrange chilled romaine or endive on salad plates. Top with radish, cucumber or celery slices; snipped chives; or grated cheese. Drizzle on dressing (see French Dressing Plus, p. 317).

SLICED GREEN SALAD

Cut chilled, cored iceberg lettuce or Chinese cabbage into 1"-thick rounds. Top with onion rings and Tarragon Sour-Cream Dressing, p. 318.

HI'S CAESAR SALAD

1 clove garlic	cheese
1/4 cup salad oil	1/2 cup salad oil
2 cups 1/4" bread squares	1 tablesp. Worcestershire
1 large head each romaine and iceberg lettuce (3 qt. bite-size pieces)	3/4 teasp. salt
	1/4 teasp. freshly ground black pepper
	1 egg
1/4 cup grated Parmesan cheese	1/4 cup fresh, frozen, or canned lemon juice
1/4 cup crumbled blue	

Early in day: Quarter garlic; drop into 1/4 cup oil; set aside. Toast bread squares in shallow pan at 300°F. 20 min., or until golden, tossing often with fork. Tear lettuce into bite-size pieces into salad bowl. Refrigerate all.

Just before serving: Sprinkle greens with cheeses; drizzle on 1/2 cup salad oil mixed with Worcestershire, salt, pepper. Toss gently until every leaf glistens. Break whole raw egg onto greens; pour lemon juice over all; toss until egg specks disappear.

Now pour the 1/4 cup oil you set aside (remove garlic) over bread squares; toss; sprinkle over greens. If desired, add 8 cut-up anchovies. Toss salad; serve at once. Makes 4 or 5 servings.

GREEN GODDESS SALAD

1 minced clove garlic	1/2 cup commercial sour cream
1/2 teasp. salt	
1/2 teasp. dry mustard	1/8 teasp. pepper
1 teasp. Worcestershire	1 qt. mixed greens, in bite-size pieces
2 tablesp. anchovy paste	
3 tablesp. tarragon-wine vinegar	1 cup cooked, cleaned shrimp or flaked fresh or canned crab meat (optional)
3 tablesp. snipped chives or scallions	
1/3 cup snipped parsley	2 quartered tomatoes
1 cup mayonnaise	

Combine all ingredients except greens, shrimp, tomatoes. Add about ⅓ cup of this dressing to greens and shrimp; toss. Garnish with tomatoes. (Refrigerate rest of dressing; nice as dunk for potato chips.) Makes 4 servings.

V.I.P.'S TOSSED SALAD

1 sliced clove garlic	1 medium head lettuce
1 teasp. salt	½ small bunch ro-
2 tablesp. fresh, frozen,	maine; or 1 bunch
or canned lemon	water cress
juice	½ cup sliced, toasted,
¼ teasp. sugar	blanched almonds
¼ teasp. pepper	1 cup tiny raw cauli-
⅛ teasp. celery seeds	flowerets
½ teasp. paprika	½ diced, peeled avo-
¾ teasp. dry mustard	cado
5 tablesp. salad oil	1 sliced tomato
1 clove garlic	

With 4-tined fork, mash sliced garlic with salt; blend in lemon juice, sugar, pepper, celery seeds, paprika, mustard. Add oil; beat well. Refrigerate.

Rub salad bowl with clove garlic; tear lettuce and romaine into bowl; add almonds, cauliflowerets, avocado, tomato, then salad dressing; toss. Makes 4 servings.

To Vary: Add bits of blue cheese or chopped, hard-cooked egg.

OLD-FASHIONED LETTUCE

½ cup light cream	1 medium head iceberg
1 teasp. sugar	or Boston lettuce
¼ cup vinegar	½ cup snipped scal-
¼ teasp. salt	lions

Combine cream, sugar, vinegar, salt. Into bowl, tear lettuce into bite-size pieces; add scallions, cream mixture. Toss; serve at once. Makes 4 servings.

MAC'S SPINACH-BACON SALAD BOWL

6 quartered cloves gar-	1 lb. young spinach
lic	(2 qt.)
¾ cup French dress-	3 chopped, hard-
ing	cooked eggs
8 bacon slices	

Add garlic to French dressing; refrigerate 2 hr. Meanwhile, in skillet over low heat, fry bacon until crisp, pouring off fat as it cooks. Drain

bacon; crumble. Into salad bowl, tear spinach into pieces; sprinkle with eggs, bacon. Remove garlic from French dressing; pour over salad. Toss; serve at once. Makes 6 servings.

WILTED LETTUCE

1 head Boston lettuce,	¼ cup bacon fat
in bite-size pieces	¼ cup vinegar
¼ cup thinly sliced	1 teasp. dry mustard
scallions; or 2	⅛ teasp. garlic salt
tablesp. minced	1½ teasp. sugar
onion	¼ teasp. salt
1 tablesp. snipped	¼ teasp. pepper
fresh herbs	2 chopped, hard-
5 diced bacon slices	cooked eggs

In salad bowl, combine lettuce, scallions, herbs. Fry bacon over low heat until crisp, pouring off fat as it cooks. Drain bacon; add to salad bowl. Return ¼ cup bacon fat to skillet; add vinegar and rest of ingredients except eggs. Bring to boil, stirring; pour over salad; toss. Sprinkle with eggs. Serve at once. Makes 4 servings.

Wilted Chinese Cabbage: For lettuce, substitute 1 thinly sliced medium head Chinese cabbage.

Hot Winter Salad: For lettuce, substitute 2 cups young spinach, in bits; 1 grated, pared raw white turnip; and 2 grated, pared carrots.

TANGY WILTED SPINACH

Tear ½ lb. young spinach into bowl. Fry 3 bacon slices until crisp; drain, reserving fat. In double boiler, combine 1 beaten egg, 1 teasp. dry mustard, 2 tablesp. cornstarch, 2 tablesp. sugar, ⅓ cup vinegar, ¼ cup water, 1 teasp. salt, ⅛ teasp. pepper. Cook until thick enough to mound. Add 1 tablesp. bacon fat, ¼ cup light cream. Pour over spinach; toss. Top with crumbled bacon. Makes 4 servings.

HEARTS-OF-PALM BUFFET SALAD

3 large heads iceberg	palm, drained and
lettuce, in bite-size	cut into ¼″ slices
pieces	¼ cup vinegar
2 diced, peeled avo-	¾ cup salad oil
cados	1 teasp. salt
3 14-oz. cans hearts of	¼ teasp. pepper

In salad bowl, toss lettuce, avocados, hearts of palm. In another bowl, mix vinegar, salad oil, salt, pepper; pour over greens; toss well. Makes 15 servings.

SUPERB VEGETABLE SALADS

These vegetable salads go well with the main course. Or they may be served as a separate course, alone or with oven-toasted, buttered crackers; Cheese Straws, p. 327; pretzels; assorted crisp crackers; or thin wheat, rye, or shredded-wheat crackers.

THE TOSSED VEGETABLE SALAD

For 4 hungry people, toss about 1-qt. torn, chilled salad greens with 3 cupfuls of two or more vegetables listed below. Add enough French dressing or Half-and-Half Mayonnaise, p. 318, to coat greens but not leave pool in bowl—about ¼ to ⅓ cup.

Add one or more extras, below, if you wish.

Raw Vegetables:

Beets (coarsely grated)
Broccoli or cauliflower (tiny buds)
Carrots (thinly slivered or coarsely grated)
Cucumbers (slices or cubes)
Green pepper (rings or cubes)
Leeks or scallions (slices)
Mushrooms (slices or cubes)
Onions (thinly sliced)
Parsnips (coarsely grated)
Radishes (sliced or grated)
Tomatoes (small wedges or cubes)
Turnips (slivers)
Zucchini (thinly sliced or grated)

Cooked Vegetables (fresh, frozen, or canned):

Artichoke hearts	Lentils
Asparagus (cut up)	Limas
Beans, green	Mixed vegetables
Carrots	Peas
Corn	Sweet or white
Hearts of palm	potatoes, etc.

Or use leftover cooked vegetables. (It's better to serve them cold than to reheat them—reheating robs them of more vitamins.)

Extras:

Anchovies (3 or 4 cut-up fillets)
Bacon bits (crumbled crisp slices)
Blue cheese (to taste)
Capers (1 or 2 tablesp.)
Cheese (grated or slivered)
Dill pickle (small one, diced)
Eggs (chopped, hard-cooked)
Lemon rind (grated)
Nuts (broken up)
Olives (ripe, green, or stuffed)
Pickle relish (1 or 2 tablesp.)
Sardines (cut up)

CUCUMBERS IN SOUR CREAM

Pare, then thinly slice, 3 cucumbers. Add 1½ teasp. salt; ⅛ teasp. pepper; 3 tablesp. minced chives or onion; 1 cup commercial sour cream; and 2 tablesp. fresh, frozen, or canned lemon juice. Refrigerate until served. Makes 4 to 6 servings.

FLOATING ISLAND

In bowl, arrange layers of thinly sliced onions, green-pepper rings, thick tomato slices, and, if desired, thinly sliced cucumber. Sprinkle layers lightly with salt and freshly ground black pepper.

Cover with flavored vinegar (wine, herb, garlic, etc.) diluted with equal quantity of cold water; refrigerate. Serve floating in vinegar.

GREEN BEANS PARMESAN

2 lb. green beans	¼ teasp. pepper
1 minced small onion	½ cup grated Parmesan cheese
½ cup salad oil	mesan cheese
¼ cup wine vinegar	2 tablesp. chopped
1 teasp. salt	anchovies (optional)

Cut beans on angle into 2″ pieces; cook until tender as on p. 281. Drain; cool; toss with rest of ingredients. Refrigerate. Makes 6 to 8 servings.

Frosted Green-Bean Salad: Omit Parmesan. Serve bean mixture topped with spoonfuls of Chunky Egg Salad, p. 307.

Lima Supper Salad: Substitute 2 pkg. cooled, cooked frozen Fordhook limas for green beans. Omit Parmesan and anchovies. Just before serving, toss in 5 crumbled crisp bacon slices. Serve on greens.

DUNK-IT SALADS

On each salad plate, place mound of one of dressings below. Surround with one or more crisp raw relishes. Let each person dunk his own. Nice with main course or as salad course.

Dressings:

Cream cheese, mixed with blue or Roquefort cheese, then thinned with mayonnaise

Mayonnaise, mixed with a little curry powder, dried dill, catchup, or horse-radish

Cottage cheese, mixed with commercial sour cream, then seasoned

One of Salad Dressings, p. 317

Crisp Raw Relishes:

Chunks of lettuce or avocado, Chinese cabbage or romaine leaves

Carrot or celery sticks

Cucumber or green-pepper strips

Scallions or radishes

Tomato wedges or cauliflower buds

P.S. The raw relishes above, without dressing, can double as salad too.

COLESLAW QUARTET

Susan's Coleslaw: Gently toss 4 cups finely shredded green or Chinese cabbage with 1 tablesp. minced onion, ⅓ cup diced celery, ⅓ cup slivered green peppers or raw green beans, ⅓ cup grated carrot, and ¼ cup sliced radishes. Toss with Susan's Coleslaw Dressing, p. 321; hot Cooked Salad Dressing, p. 320; or Tarragon Sour-Cream Dressing, p. 318. Makes 4 servings.

To Vary: Substitute ½ cup diced tomatoes for carrot and radishes.

Olive Coleslaw: Toss 4 cups finely shredded green or Chinese cabbage with ¾ teasp. celery seeds, ½ cup sliced stuffed olives, 1 tablesp. minced onion. Toss with Susan's Coleslaw Dressing, p. 321; ½ cup hot Cooked Salad Dressing, p. 320; or Mustard Coleslaw Dressing, p. 320. You may add 5 coarsely grated franks.

Chopped Coleslaw: Toss 3 cups chopped green cabbage and ¼ cup chopped green pepper with 1 teasp. salt, ¼ teasp. pepper, ½ teasp. dry mustard, 1 teasp. celery salt, 2 tablesp. sugar, 1 tablesp. chopped pimento, 1 teasp. grated onion,

3 tablesp. salad oil, and ⅓ cup vinegar. Garnish with sliced olives or tomatoes. Makes 4 servings.

Waldorf Coleslaw: Toss 4 cups shredded green or Chinese cabbage with ½ cup diced unpared red apple; ¼ cup broken nut meats; and ½ cup light or dark raisins, or diced oranges, pineapple, or peaches, or grapes. Toss with Susan's Coleslaw Dressing, p. 321.

Bowl Style: Slice off top half or third of green cabbage head; with knife, carefully scoop out center of core end, leaving "bowl" intact. Use cutout cabbage and top to make any coleslaw above; heap in "bowl."

GUACAMOLE

In chopping bowl, place 1 small onion, 1 small dried red pepper (optional), 1 tomato; chop fine. Add 6 peeled avocados; 2½ teasp. salt; 2 teasp. fresh, frozen, or canned lemon juice; 2 tablesp. mayonnaise; 1 teasp. salad oil; 4 drops tabasco. Chop fine (don't mash). Serve in bowl or on greens. Makes 8 servings.

STUFFED TOMATOES—3 STYLES

Cut ¼″ slice from stem end of each chilled, peeled tomato. With teaspoon, scoop out pulp from tomato, leaving cup (save pulp for sauce, stewed tomatoes, etc.). Or cut each tomato into 5 or 6 sections almost to stem end; spread apart slightly.

Sprinkle inside of each tomato cup well with salt; then fill with one of fillings below. Serve on salad greens.

Our Best Chicken Salad, p. 305   mesan, p. 302

Shrimp Salad, p. 308

Chunky Egg Salad, p. 307   Crunchy Tuna Salad, p. 309

Green Beans Par-

Easy Stuffed Tomatoes: Cut ¼″ slice from stem end of each chilled, peeled tomato. Halve crosswise; season. Firmly pack one of salads below into custard cups; unmold onto each tomato half. Or place green-pepper ring on each tomato half; fill with salad.

Best-Ever Macaroni Salad, p. 304   Chunky Egg Salad, p. 307

Fan-tans: Allow 1 chilled, peeled tomato per serving. Slice tomatoes vertically (French way) not quite through. Fill space between slices with Best-Ever Macaroni Salad, below; drained Cucumbers in Sour Cream, p. 302, or roll of chilled process-cheese food, sliced ⅛″ thick. Top with favorite dressing.

CURRIED VEGETABLE SALAD

1⅓ cups packaged precooked rice	¾ teasp. curry powder
1½ cups water	½ teasp. salt
½ teasp. salt	⅛ teasp. pepper
¼ cup French dressing	½ teasp. dry mustard
¾ cup mayonnaise	1 cup diced celery
1 tablesp. minced onion	1⅓ cups chilled, cooked frozen green peas

In saucepan, combine rice, water, ½ teasp. salt; cook as label directs. Lightly toss in French dressing; let cool to room temperature.

About 1 hr. before serving: In large bowl, mix mayonnaise, onion, curry, ½ teasp. salt, pepper, mustard. Add celery, peas, and rice; lightly toss. Refrigerate. Serve on lettuce. Nice with sliced ham. Makes 6 servings.

GUESS-WHAT SALAD

1½ cups coarsely shredded, pared raw parsnips	½ teasp. salt
	Dash pepper
¾ cup diced celery	¼ cup French dressing
3 tablesp. minced onion	Mayonnaise
8 to 10 sliced small stuffed olives	1 small head lettuce

Combine parsnips, celery, onion, olives, salt, pepper; toss with French dressing, then with mayonnaise to moisten. Arrange in bowl lined with lettuce. Makes 4 servings.

To Vary: Omit olives; add cubes of oranges and unpared red apples.

SUSAN'S SKILLET POTATO SALAD

2 lb. potatoes (6)	mustard
6 bacon slices	2 sliced celery stalks
¼ cup bacon fat	1 small head romaine
1½ tablesp. flour	1 thinly sliced cucumber; or 2 cups cooked green beans or peas
1 cup water	
⅓ cup vinegar	
1¾ teasp. salt	
⅛ teasp. pepper	2 sliced small onions
1 tablesp. sugar	6 sliced red radishes
1 teasp. prepared	

1. Cook unpared potatoes *just* until tender as on p. 284. Meanwhile, in cold 10″ skillet over low heat, fry bacon until crisp, pouring fat into measuring cup. Remove skillet from heat; drain bacon on paper towels; crumble.
2. Return ¼ cup bacon fat to skillet; stir in flour, then water, until smooth; add vinegar, salt, pepper, sugar, mustard. Cook over low heat, stirring, until thickened; remove from heat.
3. When potatoes are just tender, drain; peel; slice. Put skillet back over low heat; add layer of potatoes, then layer each of celery, romaine in bite-size pieces, cucumber, and onions, repeating till all are used. Toss gently. Top with radishes, bacon bits.

Nice with cold sliced meats and rye bread. Makes 6 servings.

Skillet Luncheon Salad: Brown 6 franks, sliced on angle, in bacon fat before stirring in flour, water, etc.

OLD-FASHIONED POTATO SALAD

4 cups diced, cooked potatoes	1 cup mayonnaise
	1 tablesp. vinegar
1½ cups sliced celery	2 teasp. prepared mustard
½ cup cut-up scallions	
¼ cup sliced radishes	½ teasp. celery seeds
2 tablesp. snipped parsley	1½ to 2 teasp. salt
	⅛ teasp. pepper

Several hours ahead: Combine all ingredients; refrigerate. Serve on lettuce; garnish with tomato or hard-cooked-egg wedges, sliced olives, grated carrots, or pickles. Makes 6 servings.

Individual Style: Press potato salad into custard cups; refrigerate. Then turn each cupful onto thick, peeled tomato slice.

Best-Ever Macaroni: Substitute 4 cups cooked elbow macaroni (½ lb. uncooked) for potatoes; increase vinegar to 2 tablesp. You may substitute 1 cup slivered process American cheese for ½ cup celery.

Best-Ever Rice: Substitute 4 cups cold cooked rice for potatoes.

De Luxe Potato or Macaroni: For ½ cup celery, substitute ½ cup sliced green olives, diced pared cucumber, or diced green pepper; or 4 chopped, hard-cooked eggs. Add 1 lb. franks, in chunks, if desired.

HOT BAKED-POTATO SALAD

8 baking potatoes	6 tablesp. vinegar
8 bacon slices	4 teasp. sugar
½ cup minced onions	½ cup minced green
2 teasp. salt	peppers
¼ teasp. pepper	

About 1¼ hr. ahead: Start heating oven to 400°F. Rub potatoes with salad oil; bake 1 hr., or till done. Meanwhile, fry bacon till crisp; drain; crumble. Measure bacon fat (add salad oil to make ⅔ cup); return to skillet; add onions, salt, pepper, vinegar, sugar; heat.

Cut thin slice from top of each baked potato; scoop out; blend with vinegar mixture, green peppers, bacon. Stuff back into potato shells. Makes 8 servings.

SOME SPECIAL VEGETABLE SALADS

Serve these on salad greens, with your favorite or suggested dressing.

Tomato Deckers: Between 2 tomato slices, place one of these, sandwich-fashion:

Susan's Coleslaw, p. 303, or Cottage-Cheese Salad, p. 307

Soft cream cheese, mixed with mashed avocado, then seasoned

Blue cheese or chive-cheese spread

Tomato Cart Wheels: Cut thin slice from stem end of each peeled tomato. With small spoon, hollow out tomato, leaving ribs of tomato intact. Fill with smoky-, bacon-, or pimento-cheese spread. Refrigerate overnight. Slice thick; place 2 slices on each bed of greens.

Broccoli: Top hot broccoli with Tarragon Sour-Cream Dressing, p. 318.

Dandelion Green: Heap chopped, cooked dandelion greens and scallions on tomato slices; pass Blue-Cheese French Dressing, p. 320.

Green Bean with Radish: Toss chilled, cooked or canned green beans or limas with minced onion and sliced radishes.

Zucchini: Sprinkle chilled, cooked zucchini halves or slices with minced, hard-cooked eggs, then with favorite French dressing.

Okra: Chill cooked okra pods; top with French dressing with a little horse-radish added.

Super-Stuffed Celery: Prepare as on p. 24. Serve cut into ½″ slices.

Mushroom: Cut raw mushrooms into thin vertical slices; let stand in French dressing about 1 hr. Drain before serving. (Save dressing to use again.)

Asparagus: Top hot asparagus with Puff Sour-Cream Dressing, p. 318.

Scallion-Tomatoes: Cover sliced, peeled tomatoes with thin scallions and stuffed- or green-olive or avocado slices. Sprinkle with salt, bit of dried basil; pour French dressing over all. Refrigerate. Drain before serving. (Save dressing to use again.) Nice with meat or fish.

Green Lima and Apple: Toss chilled, cooked green limas with coarsely chopped, unpared red apples and French dressing.

Manero's Roquefort: To mixed greens, add diced tomatoes and minced green pepper. Toss with French dressing. Grate ¼ lb. Roquefort cheese over all.

SALADS THAT MAKE A MEAL

Hearty salads such as the ones that follow can be the main dish of a luncheon, supper, or hot-weather dinner. Make servings generous. With them, you may serve such hot breads as:

Hot Cheese Biscuits, p. 324	Toasted English muffins or crumpets
Hot Corn Sticks, p. 329	Savory Garlicky
Hot Popovers, p. 328	Bread, p. 341
Hot Brown-and-Serves, p. 343	Grilled Cheese Sandwiches, p. 361
Susan's Blueberry Muffins, p. 327	Chicken or ham sandwiches

OUR BEST CHICKEN SALAD
(or turkey)

4 to 5 cups cooked chicken or turkey, in large chunks	¼ cup light cream
	⅔ cup mayonnaise or cooked salad dressing
2 teasp. grated onion	
1 cup celery, cut on angle	1 teasp. salt
	⅛ teasp. pepper
1 cup minced green peppers	2 tablesp. vinegar

Combine chicken, onion, celery, peppers. Mix cream with mayonnaise, salt, pepper, vinegar; toss with chicken. Refrigerate till served.

To serve: Arrange salad on greens on chop plate. Makes 6 to 8 servings.

Circle with your choice of these if desired:

Asparagus tips	Seeded or seedless
Avocado slices	grapes
Cheese-stuffed celery	Ripe and stuffed
Spoonfuls of cran-	olives
berry jelly	Pickled peaches
Sliced hard-cooked	Pineapple chunks
eggs	Spiced prunes

Or sprinkle with one of these:

Slivered almonds	Snipped parsley
Water cress or dill	Walnuts
Snipped mint	

Exotic Chicken: Add ⅔ cup slivered, toasted almonds or chopped pecans. Also add 2 cups halved, seeded green grapes or orange sections.

New Chicken: Omit celery, green peppers. Add 2 cups diced cucumbers, 1 cup drained canned pineapple tidbits. Top with ripe olives.

Ham and Chicken: Substitute 2 cups cut-up cooked ham for 2 cups chicken. Add 1 to 2 cups fresh or drained canned pineapple chunks.

Top Hat: Arrange chicken salad on canned pineapple slices.

Waldorf: Add 2 cups diced unpared red apples and ⅔ cup chopped walnuts or peanuts.

Gladys': In 2 teasp. butter, sauté ½ cup broken walnuts with pinch salt 3 or 4 min., or until crisp. Cool. Add to chicken.

Ham, Veal, or Lamb: Halve ingredients, substituting 2 cups cut-up cooked ham, veal, or lamb for chicken. Makes 3 or 4 servings.

GOURMET CHICKEN SALAD

Mix ½ cup mayonnaise; 1 tablesp. fresh, frozen, or canned lemon juice; ¼ teasp. salt; ⅛ teasp. pepper; 2 tablesp. cream; ⅛ teasp. dried marjoram. Use to coat 4 large thick pieces cold chicken or turkey.

Serve on greens, garnished with tomato, cucumber, and snipped parsley. Makes 2 to 4 servings, depending on size of chicken pieces.

CHICKEN FRUIT BUFFET

Add 1 cup slivered, toasted almonds to Our Best Chicken Salad, p. 305. Arrange on half of large serving dish. On other half, arrange chilled honeydew-melon strips, grapefruit and orange sections, and balls made from chilled canned jellied cranberry sauce.

Or serve chicken salad in avocado or canned peach halves. Makes 8 servings.

HOT BAKED CHICKEN SALAD

Start heating oven to 450°F. Toss 1½ cups cut-up, cooked (or 2 5-oz. cans) chicken or turkey with 1½ cups sliced celery, ½ cup chopped walnuts, ½ teasp. salt, dash pepper, 2 teasp. minced onion, 2 tablesp. lemon juice, ¾ cup mayonnaise. Heap in 4 individual baking dishes or 1 deep 9″ pie plate. Sprinkle with 1 cup crushed potato chips. Bake 15 min., or until light brown. Makes 4 servings.

CHICKEN-CURRY SALAD

3 cups cooked or canned chicken or turkey, in large pieces	1½ teasp. salt
	2 cups drained, cooked or canned peas
	¾ cup French dressing
3 cups cold cooked rice	½ to 1 teasp. curry
2 cups slivered celery	powder
½ cup chutney	

Combine ingredients; toss; refrigerate. Serve on greens. Makes 6 servings.

Shrimp, Lobster, or Tuna: Substitute cooked, cleaned shrimp, flaked cooked or canned lobster, or canned tuna for all or half of chicken.

CHICKEN SHORTCAKE SALAD

Susan's Hot Baking-Powder Biscuit dough, p. 323	⅛ teasp. celery salt
	1 tablesp. fresh, frozen, or canned lemon
1 cup coarsely cut-up, cooked or canned chicken, turkey, or tuna	juice
	⅓ to ½ cup cooked salad dressing
1 tablesp. butter or margarine	2 chopped, hard-cooked eggs
1 tablesp. water	½ cup diced celery
¼ teasp. salt	and/or ¼ cup
⅛ teasp. pepper	toasted almonds

From biscuit dough, cut 4 biscuits extra large, the rest regular-sized. Bake at 450°F. 12 to 15 min. Meanwhile, heat chicken with butter and water over low heat. Just before serving, add rest of ingredients. Split large biscuits; fill with hot chicken mixture.

Serve at once. Pass rest of biscuits. Makes 4 servings.

CHUNKY EGG SALAD

6 hard-cooked eggs	½ teasp. Worcestershire
1 cup sliced celery	Dash tabasco
2 tablesp. minced green pepper	1 tablesp. vinegar
	1 teasp. salt
1 teasp. minced onion	⅛ teasp. pepper
¼ cup mayonnaise	

Cut eggs into big pieces; add rest of ingredients; refrigerate. Serve on greens. Makes 6 servings.

Bacon and Egg: Add 3 crumbled crisp bacon slices or coarsely grated franks and 2 chopped stuffed olives. Serve on thick tomato slices.

Kelly's Baked Bean and Egg: Add 1 No. 2 can Boston-style baked beans, drained. Reduce mayonnaise to 1 tablesp. Add 1 tablesp. chili sauce. Garnish with 4 sliced franks, sautéed in 1 tablesp. salad oil.

Coast Style: For 3 hard-cooked eggs, substitute 1 can chunk-style tuna (1 cup) and 4 crumbled crisp bacon slices or 1 cup diced, cooked ham.

ZIPPY HOT EGG SALAD

6 hot hard-cooked eggs	parsley
¼ teasp. salt	¼ cup mayonnaise
⅛ teasp. pepper	2 tablesp. chili sauce
3 tablesp. snipped scallions	1 teasp. prepared mustard
3 tablesp. snipped	

Into warm bowl, slice eggs. Toss with salt, pepper, scallions, parsley. Then toss with combined mayonnaise, chili sauce, mustard.

Serve on lettuce on hot buttered, toasted, split rolls or toast. Makes 3 or 4 servings.

CHEF-SALAD BOWLS

Make Helen's Tossed Green Salad, p. 299. After placing greens in salad bowl, top with one of the following chef combinations. Toss well just before serving. Makes 4 to 6 servings.

Tongue and Cheese: Use 6 slivered slices canned tongue, corned beef, or luncheon meat; ¼ lb. slivered Swiss cheese; 2 sliced, hard-cooked eggs; ½ cup sliced cucumbers; 2 coarsely grated carrots or ½ cup radish slices; and 1 thinly sliced medium onion. Makes 4 servings. Sharp-Cream Mayonnaise, p. 318, may replace dressing.

Salami and Bologna: Use ¼ lb. each slivered salami and bologna; ¼ lb. coarsely grated process American cheese; and ½ cup tiny raw cauliflowerets or 2 chilled, peeled tomatoes, cut into strips.

Chicken and Ham: Use ½ cup slivered, cooked or canned chicken or turkey; ½ cup cooked-ham strips; ⅔ cup slivered Swiss cheese; and 1 sliced, hard-cooked egg or 1 cup cooked green limas.

Ham Club: Use 1 cup diced, peeled avocado; 1 cup diced tomatoes; 1 cup thinly sliced cucumbers; and 1½ cups diced, cooked ham.

HOT FRANK-AND-POTATO-SALAD CASSEROLE

4 cups thinly sliced, cooked potatoes	1½ cups canned or cooked green beans
1½ teasp. salt	¼ cup thinly sliced onion
Speck pepper	4 sliced franks
⅓ cup salad oil	
3 tablesp. vinegar	

Start heating oven to 400°F. Combine potatoes, salt, pepper, oil, vinegar. In greased 1½-qt. casserole, arrange beans, then, in layers, potato mixture, onion, franks. Bake, covered, 30 min. Makes 4 servings.

TOP-HAT TOMATO SALAD

1 cup cottage cheese	¼ teasp. dried basil (optional)
6 chopped, hard-cooked eggs	⅛ teasp. Worcestershire
¾ teasp. salt	1 tablesp. minced onion
½ teasp. prepared mustard	4 chilled, peeled large tomatoes

Combine all ingredients except tomatoes. Slice tomatoes; arrange on individual beds of crisp greens; top with mounds of cheese-egg mixture. Pass French dressing. Makes 4 servings.

COTTAGE-CHEESE SALAD

To ⅔ cup chilled cottage cheese, add one or more of these:

Celery or caraway seeds
Pickle relish or chili sauce
Minced dill pickle or horse-radish
Minced chives, scallions, or onion
Chopped celery, olives, or nuts
Cut-up radishes or tomatoes
Grated raw carrots
Mayonnaise or French dressing
Commercial sour cream or cream

Heap mixture in lettuce cup. Or heap in hollowed-out tomato (you may first spread inside of tomato with deviled ham). Or press into wet custard cup; invert onto greens. Top with French dressing. Makes 1 serving.

"CHILLY" CON CARNE

1 1-lb. can kidney beans	Dash pepper
¾ cup coarsely diced celery	½ teasp. chili powder
	2 tablesp. vinegar
¾ cup coarsely diced, cooked or canned luncheon meat or ham	¼ cup mayonnaise
	1 clove garlic
	¼ teasp. salt
	1 grated small onion

Early in day: Drain beans. Add celery, meat. In small bowl, mix pepper, chili powder, vinegar; stir in mayonnaise, garlic crushed with salt, onion. Add to bean mixture; mix lightly. Refrigerate until serving time. Serve on lettuce. Makes 4 or 5 servings.

BAKED SEA-FOOD SALAD

¾ lb. cooked, cleaned shrimp (1 cup)	1 cup mayonnaise
1 cup flaked fresh or canned crab meat	1 teasp. Worcestershire
	½ teasp. salt
½ to ¾ cup chopped green peppers	¼ teasp. pepper
	½ cup fresh bread crumbs
¼ cup minced onion	1 tablesp. melted butter or margarine
1 cup sliced celery	

Start heating oven to 350°F. Split shrimp lengthwise. Add crab meat, green peppers, onion, celery, mayonnaise, Worcestershire, salt, pepper. Spread in 10″ x 6″ x 2″ baking dish. Toss crumbs with butter; sprinkle over salad. Bake, uncovered, 30 min., or until brown. Nice with parsley and lemon quarters. Makes 4 servings.

To Do Ahead: Make salad early in day; refrigerate. Before serving, bake 30 to 40 min.

SHRIMP SALAD NEW ORLEANS

1 cup cold cooked rice	scallions or onion
¾ lb. cut-up, cooked, cleaned shrimp (1 cup)	2 tablesp. French dressing
¾ teasp. salt	1 tablesp. chopped stuffed olives
1 tablesp. fresh, frozen, or canned lemon juice	¾ cup diced raw cauliflower
¼ cup slivered green pepper	Speck pepper
	⅓ cup mayonnaise or cooked salad dressing
1 tablesp. minced	

Toss together all ingredients. Serve on lettuce. Makes 4 servings.

SHRIMP SALAD

1⅛ lb. cooked, cleaned shrimp (1½ cups)	olives
	½ teasp. minced onion
1 cup sliced celery	½ cup mayonnaise
½ cup chopped walnuts (optional)	¼ cup French dressing
	Salt and lemon juice
¼ cup sliced stuffed	to taste

Combine all ingredients; refrigerate a short time. Serve on greens. Makes 4 servings.

Or serve with:
  Tomato Aspic, p. 314, in 1¼-qt. ring mold (heap salad in center)
  Pineapple slices (arrange salad between split slices)
  Peach halves (fill fresh or canned halves with salad)
  Jellied cranberry sauce (slice or spoon out as salad garnish)
  Avocado halves (sprinkle with lemon juice, salt; fill with salad)
  Tomato slices (arrange salad between slices)
  Asparagus (heap salad on 3 or 4 cold cooked asparagus tips)

Pineapple-Shrimp: Use cooked, cleaned shrimp, split lengthwise. Substitute 1 cup fresh, frozen, or canned pineapple chunks for celery. Omit nuts.

Lobster or Crab Meat: Substitute 1½ cups cooked or canned lobster or crab-meat chunks for shrimp.

Tuna: Substitute 2 cans drained solid-pack tuna (2 cups) for shrimp.

Salmon: Substitute 1 1-lb. can salmon (2 cups), in chunks, for shrimp; substitute 2 hard-cooked eggs, in large pieces, for nuts.

First-Course Sea Food: Make salad servings small. Pass crisp crackers if you wish.

CRUNCHY TUNA SALAD

¼ cup mayonnaise	chicken or turkey
2 tablesp. diced sweet pickle	½ cup sliced celery
1 tablesp. pickle juice	½ cup chilled, cooked or canned peas
1 cup canned tuna or salmon, or cut-up, cooked or canned	1 cup coarsely crushed corn or potato chips

Toss mayonnaise with pickle, pickle juice, tuna, celery, peas. Add chips.

Serve at once on greens. Makes 4 servings.

CURRIED SEA-FOOD SALAD

1 can drained solid-pack, or chunk-style tuna (1 cup)	½ cup mayonnaise
¾ lb. cooked, cleaned shrimp (1 cup)	2 tablesp. lemon juice
½ cup chopped celery	1 teasp. curry powder
¼ cup cut-up ripe or stuffed olives	3 cups cold cooked rice
	2 or 3 tablesp. French dressing
	½ cup snipped parsley

Refrigerate tuna and shrimp (or use all tuna or all shrimp).

Just before serving: To sea food, add celery, olives, then mayonnaise mixed with lemon juice and curry powder. Toss rice with French dressing and parsley; spoon onto serving platter; top with salad. Makes 4 to 6 servings.

FRUIT-SALAD PLATES
(for lunch or supper)

Medley: For each salad plate, select 3 or 4 fruits below. Arrange on crisp greens, with lettuce cup of Golden Cream-Cheese Topping, p. 319, in center. At side, place dainty tongue sandwiches.

Peach or pear halves	Melon strips
Bing cherries	Banana chunks or
Small bunches red or green grapes	frozen or canned pineapple chunks
Grapefruit sections	Orange slices
Strawberries	

Melon Ring: For each serving, place 2″-thick pared crosswise slice of seeded cantaloupe on crisp lettuce. Fill with raspberries or strawberries and seedless grapes. Top with favorite sherbet. At side, place buttered hot biscuits filled with thin ham slices.

West-Coast Special: For each serving, slice avocado onto nest of water cress; flank with finger sandwiches filled with chicken salad. Around these, arrange horseshoe of overlapping orange slices. Place cheese- and nut-stuffed celery in center. Pass Pineapple French Dressing, p. 318.

Big Fruit: For each serving, prepare 2 or 3 pared slender strips of cantaloupe or honey dew melon or both. On top and beside melon, arrange pitted Bing cherries, canned or frozen pineapple chunks, banana cubes, walnuts, water cress. At side, place dainty egg-salad sandwiches. Pass Lemon-Cream Mayonnaise, p. 318.

Golden: For each serving, fill ½ seeded cantaloupe with canned or frozen pineapple chunks; top with chive cream cheese and water cress. Beside melon, place hot toasted corn muffins. Pass French dressing.

Fruit Chef Salad: Tear 1 medium head iceberg lettuce or romaine into bite-size pieces. Toss with 1 cup cottage cheese; 1 cup fresh, canned, or frozen pineapple chunks; ¼ cup chopped walnuts; ¼ cup light or dark raisins; 3 sectioned oranges; 2 tablesp. French dressing. At side, place deviled-ham-and-egg sandwiches. Makes 4 servings.

Fruit-Cheese: Many other all-fruit salads can serve as a luncheon main dish if you couple them with such protein-rich cheeses as these:

Cottage Cheese Salad mixture, p. 307 (on peach or pear halves, or orange or pineapple slices)

Camembert or blue-cheese wedges

Sticks of natural or process American or Swiss cheese (about 4 or 5)

Slices of favorite cheese or spoonfuls of cheese spread

Or serve fruit salad with cheese and crackers, grilled cheese sandwiches; or hot Filled Butterflake Rolls, p. 342.

FRUIT-DESSERT SALADS

After a hearty main course, a fruit salad makes a welcome top-off. It's equally welcome at a dessert bridge, as an evening snack, with a hot bread or sandwich and a hot drink, or as a main-dish accompaniment.

Whatever the occasion, try some of these.

TWENTY-FOUR-HOUR DESSERT SALAD

1 egg	quartered
2 tablesp. fresh, frozen, or canned lemon juice	1 cup drained canned pineapple tidbits
	1 cup diced oranges
2 tablesp. sugar	1 cup seedless grapes
Pinch salt	1 cup sliced bananas
½ cup heavy cream, whipped	8 maraschino cherries
	½ cup toasted, slivered almonds
12 marshmallows,	

In double boiler, beat egg with fork; stir in lemon juice, sugar, salt. Cook over hot water, stirring, 5 min., or until mixture thickens. Remove from heat; cool. Fold in cream, marshmallows, fruits. Refrigerate overnight.

To serve: Fold in almonds; arrange on greens. Makes 6 servings.

FREEZER STRAWBERRY-DESSERT SALAD

1 pt. strawberries	pkg. soft cream cheese
2 teasp. lemon juice	
6 tablesp. granulated sugar	½ cup heavy cream, whipped
1½ 8-oz. (or 4 3-oz.)	Lettuce

Day or so ahead: With fork, crush hulled strawberries with lemon juice and sugar. Stir into cream cheese. Fold in whipped cream. Pour into ice-cube tray; freeze until firm. Remove from tray; freezer-wrap and freeze.

To serve: Cut into slices; arrange on lettuce; let stand in food compartment of refrigerator until eatable—about 1 hr. Makes 6 servings.

WINTER-PEAR WALDORF

2 cups diced, pared pears; or 1 cup each diced pears and unpared red apples	1 teasp. sugar
	½ cup mayonnaise
	1 cup thinly sliced celery
2 tablesp. fresh, frozen, or canned lemon juice	½ cup broken walnuts or shredded coconut

Toss fruits with lemon juice, sugar, 1 tablesp. mayonnaise. Just before serving, add celery, walnuts, rest of mayonnaise; toss.

Serve on lettuce. Top with **French** dressing. Makes 4 servings.

To Vary: For pears, substitute fresh, frozen, or canned pineapple; banana cubes; or 1 cup orange sections and 1 cup grapes.

Waldorf Salad: For pears, substitute 2 cups diced unpared red apples and ½ cup light or dark raisins.

H.R.M.'S DESSERT SALAD

1 honeydew, casaba, or Persian melon	cheese
	Chopped nuts
2 tablesp. milk	6 cups fruit *
2 3-oz. pkg. soft cream	Water cress or mint

Pare whole melon; cut slice from top and reserve; scoop out seeds; shave bottom slightly so melon stands up well. Blend milk with cheese; use to frost melon and reserved top; sprinkle with nuts. Set melon in center of deep serving platter. Fill with some of fruit; surround with rest. Set top in place. With thread, tie water cress to toothpick; insert in top. Garnish with water cress. Refrigerate.

To serve: Remove top; cut melon into wedges, from top to bottom, like layer cake; spoon fruit onto each wedge. Pass French dressing if desired. Makes 6 to 8 servings.

* Use berries, pineapple chunks, pear slices, melon balls, seedless grapes, tangerine sections, pitted cherries, and/or apple cubes.

FROSTY HALF-AND-HALF SALAD

2 3-oz. pkg. soft cream cheese	½ cup chopped pecans
	1 drained No. 2½ can peach halves
2 tablesp. cream	
¼ teasp. paprika	1 drained No. 2½ can pear halves
Dash salt	

Combine cheese, cream, paprika, salt, pecans; use to fill centers of peach halves. Top each peach half with pear half; press together. Wrap separately in waxed paper; place in ice-cube trays. Freeze just until firm.

To serve: Unwrap; arrange on greens. Pass Fluffy Mayonnaise, p. 318. Makes 8 servings.

MORE FRUIT SALADS

Serve any of these on greens, with suggested or your favorite dressing. Use as first course, with main course, or as dessert.

Autumn Salad: Toss slivered unpared apples and pineapple with halved seeded grapes, cut-up celery and walnuts. Arrange on canned jellied-cranberry-sauce slices if desired.

Banana Roll-Ins: Roll banana chunks in minced salted peanuts.

Filled Avocado: Halve, peel, and pit each avocado. Brush with lemon juice; sprinkle with salt. Set each avocado half on crisp greens; fill with one of combinations listed below; top with French dressing, to which curry powder, chutney, horse-radish, or blue cheese has been added if desired.

   Pineapple chunks and unpared apple cubes
   Cut-up oranges
   Cut-up grapefruit and cooked cleaned shrimp
   Canned fruit cocktail with diced orange
   Cottage cheese with bits of Roquefort cheese
   Seedless or seeded grapes

Melon Bowl: Halve watermelon lengthwise, making one half larger than other. Cut red meat from both halves into chunks. Heap, with choice of added fruits, in larger half. Serve on large tray; pass French dressing.

Orange Kabobs: On skewers, string, alternately, orange and banana chunks, or orange slices and dates, or pear or apple slices. End each with grape or cherry. Dip into Lemon French Dressing, p. 319.

Pear-Orange: Fill fresh or canned pear halves with cut-up oranges.

Frosted Honeydew: Quarter honeydew melon; hollow out each quarter. Fill with berries, melon meat, and grapefruit or orange sections. Top with spoonfuls of favorite sherbet; tuck water cress or chicory along inside edge.

Susies: Arrange grapefruit or orange sections around cut-up nuts and dates.

Strawberry: Toss strawberries with grapefruit or orange sections, grated orange rind, Manhattan French Dressing, p. 318.

Grape: Toss red, white, and blue grapes with Lorenzo French Dressing, p. 318.

FRUIT-AND-CHEESE DESSERT SALADS

These are nice served on crisp greens with suggested or your favorite dressing. Also serve as first course, or with main course.

Cantaloupe Circles: Fill each 1"-thick pared ring of seeded cantaloupe with cut-up water cress, tossed with Lemon French Dressing, p. 319. Serve with Camembert cheese at room temperature.

   Or place each cantaloupe slice on lettuce; pass Roquefort French Dressing, p. 320.

Orange-Nut: Put 2 orange slices together with cream cheese; sprinkle with peanuts.

June Ring: Frost each pineapple slice with cottage cheese, cream cheese, or sour cream. Heap strawberries on top. Garnish with water cress. Pass Lorenzo French Dressing, p. 318.

Pineapple Cheese: Mix cottage cheese with pineapple chunks; heap on lettuce; top with pineapple chunks and Honolulu French Dressing, p. 318.

Banana Split: Toss cottage cheese with pineapple chunks; set big spoonful on each peeled banana, halved lengthwise. Top with currant jelly.

Stuffed Peaches: Fill canned peach halves with cream cheese or cottage cheese mixed with chopped celery and nuts.

Pineapple-Cheese Ring: Top pineapple slices with chunks of Roquefort cheese. Pass Cranberry French Dressing, p. 318.

Prune and Grapefruit: Stuff pitted, cooked prunes with cream cheese and sliced stuffed olives. Set on grapefruit sections.

Pineapple: Top pineapple slices with grated cheese, then with bit of tart jelly. Or top slices with shredded coconut or raspberries.

Grapefruit Half Shells: Prepare grapefruit halves as on p. 389; tuck chicory around edges. Sprinkle with grated cheese, then with French dressing.

Frosted Fruit Bowls: Fill soup bowls or individual casseroles with mixture of chilled cut-up oranges, 1 can fruit cocktail (juice and all), strawberries, and seedless grapes. Top each with mound of cottage cheese.

Melon Rings: Place each 2″-thick pared ring of seeded cantaloupe on bed of lettuce. Fill with berries and seedless grapes. Top with sherbet. Garnish with sharp-cheese-and-nut balls.

Citrus: To several orange or grapefruit sections, with or without bit of avocado, add French dressing or Roquefort French Dressing, p. 320.

MOLDED SALADS

CHEESE-SALAD RING

2 teasp. unflavored gelatine	½ cup mayonnaise
¼ cup cold water	1½ teasp. Worcestershire
2 cups cottage cheese	¼ teasp. salt
¼ lb. crumbled blue cheese	2 tablesp. minced onion
2 tablesp. snipped parsley	½ cup heavy cream, whipped

Sprinkle gelatine over cold water in glass measuring cup to soften; stir over hot water until dissolved. Blend into cheeses, then add parsley, mayonnaise, Worcestershire, salt, and onion. Fold in whipped cream. Turn into 1¼-qt. ring mold. Refrigerate until set.

To serve: Unmold onto greens. Fill with The Tossed Vegetable Salad, p. 302. On one side, place marinated asparagus; on the other, sliced tongue. Or fill with favorite fruit salad. Makes 8 servings.

CHICKEN-TONGUE SUPPER LOAF

1 3½- to 4-lb. ready-to-cook stewing chicken, cut up	relish
Chicken broth	2 cups slivered, cooked or canned tongue
1 cup ripe olives	¼ cup diced green pepper
4 teasp. unflavored gelatine	¼ cup diced pimento
¼ cup cold water	⅛ teasp. pepper
1 teasp. grated onion	1 teasp. salt
¼ cup sweet pickle	Pickled peaches

Early day before: Simmer chicken till tender as on p. 150; quickly refrigerate meat and broth as on p. 138.

Later day before: Chop chicken meat. Boil broth down to 2 cups. Cut olives from pits into large pieces. Sprinkle gelatine over cold water to soften; then dissolve in hot broth. Add chicken, olives, onion, and rest of ingredients except peaches. Taste; season if necessary. Turn into 10″ x 5″ x 3″ loaf pan; refrigerate till next day.

To serve: Unmold; slice with sharp knife; garnish with pickled peaches. Makes 8 servings.

CHICKEN-ALMOND SUPPER MOLD

½ teasp. butter or margarine	½ teasp. salt
½ cup slivered almonds	¼ teasp. paprika
1 env. unflavored gelatine	Dash cayenne pepper
1½ cups chicken broth	1 cup diced, cooked or canned chicken or turkey
2 egg yolks, slightly beaten	½ cup heavy cream, whipped

In advance: Start heating oven to 300°F.; in butter in shallow pan, toast almonds 15 to 20 min., stirring often. Sprinkle gelatine over ½ cup cold chicken broth to soften. Heat rest of broth; stir a little into yolks; then stir yolks into rest of broth, along with salt, paprika, cayenne. Cook over low heat, stirring, until slightly thickened. Remove from heat; stir in gelatine until dissolved; then stir in chicken. Cool until partially thickened; fold in almonds, cream. Pour into greased 9″ x 5″ x 3″ loaf pan or 6 small molds. Refrigerate till set.

To serve: Unmold; garnish with greens. Makes 6 servings.

PRESSED CHICKEN SPECIAL

1½ cups cold chicken broth	2 cups cooked or canned peas
2 env. unflavored gelatine	½ cup chopped, blanched almonds
2 cups diced, cooked or canned chicken or turkey	2 tablesp. pickle relish
	1 cup mayonnaise

In advance: Skim fat from cold chicken broth. Sprinkle gelatine over broth in glass measuring cup to soften; then stir over hot water until dissolved. Cool slightly; stir into chicken, rest of ingredients. Pour into 2-qt. mold or 10″ x 5″ x 3″ loaf pan. Refrigerate till set.

To serve: Unmold; slice with sharp knife; serve on greens. Makes 10 servings.

MOLDED CHICKEN SALAD

1 env. unflavored gelatine	1/3 cup mayonnaise
1/2 cup cold water	Pinch grated lemon rind
2 chicken-bouillon cubes	1 diced, peeled avocado
1/2 teasp. salt	1 cup diced, cooked or canned chicken or turkey
1 1/4 cups boiling water	
2 tablesp. lemon juice	3/4 cup diced apples

Sprinkle gelatine over cold water to soften. Dissolve bouillon cubes and salt in boiling water; stir in gelatine until dissolved; then stir in lemon juice. Cool till consistency of unbeaten egg white. Fold in mayonnaise, lemon rind, avocado, chicken, apples. Pour into 6 individual molds. Refrigerate till firm.

To serve: Unmold onto greens. Makes 6 servings.

TURKEY-AND-RICE SALAD

1 env. plus 1 1/2 teasp. unflavored gelatine	2 tablesp. chopped green pepper
2 cups cold water	1 tablesp. pickle relish
1/2 teasp. salt	1/4 cup chopped pecans
Dash pepper	2 tablesp. chopped stuffed olives
Dash paprika	
1 1/2 cups cooked or canned turkey or chicken chunks	1 tablesp. snipped parsley
	2/3 cup mayonnaise
1 cup cold cooked rice	2/3 cup heavy cream, whipped
3/4 cup minced celery	

Sprinkle gelatine over cold water in glass measuring cup to soften. Add salt, pepper, paprika. Stir over hot water until dissolved. Add to turkey; then fold in rest of ingredients. Pour into 8" x 8" x 2" pan. Refrigerate till firm.

To serve: Cut into squares; serve on greens. Sprinkle with snipped parsley, paprika. Makes 6 servings.

To Vary: For turkey, substitute cooked, cleaned shrimp; flaked fresh or canned crab meat, tuna, or lobster; or cooked ham.

JELLIED TUNA SALAD

Combine 2 cans chunk-style tuna (2 cups); 2 chopped, hard-cooked eggs; 1/2 cup chopped stuffed olives; 2 tablesp. bottled capers; 1 tablesp. minced onion. Sprinkle 1 env. unflavored gelatine over 1/4 cup cold water in glass measuring cup to soften. Stir over hot water until dissolved.

Stir into 2 cups mayonnaise. Add tuna mixture.

Pour mixture into 1 1/4-qt. ring mold. Refrigerate until firm. Unmold; garnish with greens. Fill center with tomato quarters and avocado slices (or cold cooked vegetables) seasoned with French dressing. Makes 6 to 8 servings.

Jellied Salmon: Substitute 1 1-lb. can (2 cups) flaked salmon for tuna.

TUNA-CUCUMBER MOLD

1 env. plus 1/2 teasp. unflavored gelatine	2 to 4 tablesp. granulated sugar
1/2 cup cold water	1/2 teasp. salt
3/4 cup boiling water	2 or 3 drops green food color
1/4 cup vinegar	
2 tablesp. fresh, frozen, or canned lemon juice	1 large cucumber
	Shrimp Salad, p. 308

Sprinkle gelatine over cold water to soften; add boiling water; stir until dissolved. Add vinegar, lemon juice, sugar, salt, and food color to tint mixture delicate green. Refrigerate till consistency of unbeaten egg white.

Lightly oil 1-qt. bowl or casserole. Wash and pare cucumber; flute surface by drawing tines of sharp fork down length of cucumber. Cut off 12 to 16 thin even slices; then dice rest fairly fine (about 1 cup). Arrange slices around sides and outer edge of bottom of bowl. Fold diced cucumber into thickened gelatine; pour into bowl; refrigerate till firm.

To serve: Unmold onto cold plate. Arrange Shrimp Salad around mold. Garnish with tomato wedges if desired. Makes 4 servings.

MOLDED SEA-FOOD SALAD

1 env. unflavored gelatine	commercial sour cream
1/4 cup cold water	1/4 cup vinegar
1 1/2 teasp. salt	1 1/2 cups flaked fresh or canned crab meat (or lobster, salmon, halibut, or white fish)
1 1/2 teasp. dry mustard	
2 tablesp. sugar	
2 eggs or 3 yolks, unbeaten	
1 cup sweet cream or	Marinated Tomatoes, p. 290

Sprinkle gelatine over cold water to soften. In double boiler, mix salt, mustard, sugar, eggs, cream, vinegar. Cook, stirring, until thickened. Remove from heat; stir in gelatine until dissolved. Pour over crab meat; toss; then turn into 1-qt. mold. Refrigerate till set.

To serve: Unmold; garnish with Marinated Tomatoes. Makes 8 servings.

OLIVE RELISH MOLD
(perfection salad)

2 env. unflavored gelatine	¾ cup diced celery
1 cup cold water	1½ cups shredded green or Chinese cabbage
1½ cups boiling water	
⅓ cup granulated sugar	
1¼ teasp. salt	¾ cup shredded, pared carrot
¼ cup vinegar	
¼ cup fresh, frozen, or canned lemon juice	¼ cup chopped green pepper
⅔ cup cut-up ripe olives	2 tablesp. diced pimento

Sprinkle gelatine over cold water to soften; add boiling water; stir until dissolved. Stir in sugar, salt, vinegar, lemon juice; cool. Add olives and rest of ingredients; mix well. Pour into 1¼-qt. mold or 8" x 8" x 2" pan. Refrigerate until firm.

To serve: Unmold, or cut into squares; garnish with greens. Pass Half-and-Half Mayonnaise, p. 318. Makes 10 to 12 servings.

Olive-Relish Ring: Make in 1¼-qt. ring mold. Refrigerate until firm. Unmold. Fill with Tuna Salad, p. 308, or Shrimp Salad, p. 308.

▶ **For 5 or 6:** Halve ingredients; use 8" x 8" x 2" pan.

COLESLAW SOUFFLE SALAD

1 cup hot water	Dash pepper
1 pkg. lemon-flavored gelatin	2 cups finely chopped cabbage
½ cup cold water	2 tablesp. minced green pepper
2 tablesp. vinegar	
½ cup mayonnaise	1 tablesp. minced onion
¼ teasp. salt	¼ teasp. celery seeds

Pour hot water over gelatin; stir until dissolved. Add water, vinegar, mayonnaise, salt, pepper. With egg beater, beat until well blended. Pour into ice-cube tray; quick-chill in freezing unit (without changing control) 15 to 20 min., or until firm about 1" in from edges but soft in center. Turn into bowl; with egg beater, beat until fluffy. Fold in cabbage, pepper, onion, celery

seeds. Pour into 1-qt. mold or 7 or 8 individual molds. Refrigerate until firm.

To serve: Unmold onto greens. Makes 7 or 8 servings.

TOMATO ASPIC
(jellied tomato salad)

3 cups tomato juice	⅔ cup cold tomato juice
1 stalk celery	
1 sliced small onion	¼ cup vinegar
2 lemon slices	About 1½ cups chopped mixed raw vegetables or mixed cooked or canned vegetables (optional)
1 small bay leaf	
1 teasp. salt	
⅛ teasp. pepper	
2 env. unflavored gelatine	

Combine 3 cups tomato juice, celery, onion, lemon, bay leaf, salt, pepper. Simmer, uncovered, 10 min.; strain. Meanwhile, sprinkle gelatine over cold tomato juice and vinegar to soften; stir in hot mixture until dissolved. (If adding vegetables, chill tomato mixture, stirring occasionally, till consistency of unbeaten egg white; fold in vegetables.) Pour into 7 individual molds. Refrigerate till firm.

To serve: Unmold onto greens; serve with Half-and-Half Mayonnaise, p. 318, or Creamy Blue-Cheese Dressing, p. 321. Makes 7 servings.

Tomato-Cheese: When tomato mixture in each mold is partially set, drop in spoonful of cottage cheese.

Tomato Ring: Pour tomato mixture into 1¼-qt. ring mold. When set, unmold; fill with tuna, shrimp, or chicken salad. Serve with Cucumber Mayonnaise, p. 318.

Two-Tone: Pour half of tomato mixture into 7 individual molds; refrigerate till almost set. Refrigerate rest until consistency of unbeaten egg white; fold in 1 cup cottage cheese, 1 tablesp. snipped chives, 1 tablesp. diced celery; pour into same molds. Refrigerate till set.

Ham or Sea-Food Tomato Aspic: Refrigerate tomato mixture till consistency of unbeaten egg white. Fold in ¼ cup pickle relish and 1 cup slivered, cooked ham; 1 cup cooked, cleaned shrimp; or 1 cup canned tuna. Refrigerate in molds till firm.

Tomato-Olive Aspic: Place stuffed-olive slice (or hard-cooked-egg slice) in bottom of each individual mold; cover with small amount of Tomato Aspic mixture. Refrigerate till firm; fill with rest of aspic mixture. Refrigerate till firm.

Canned Tomato Aspic: A delicious canned tomato aspic on the market requires no refrigeration. Use as is; or melt over low heat; add flaked tuna, cut-up chicken, etc., and rejell in just a few minutes.

SPEEDY BARBECUE SALAD MOLDS

Dissolve 1 pkg. lemon-flavored gelatin in 1¼ cups hot water. Add 1 8-oz. can tomato sauce, 1½ tablesp. vinegar, ½ teasp. salt, speck pepper, and a little horse-radish or minced onion. Pour into 4 to 6 individual molds. Refrigerate until firm.

FROSTED LIME-CHEESE SALAD

1 cup hot water	½ cup chopped walnuts
1 pkg. lime-flavored gelatin	1 3-oz. pkg. cream cheese
1 No. 2 can crushed pineapple, undrained	1 tablesp. mayonnaise
1 cup cottage cheese	1 teasp. fresh, frozen, or canned lemon juice
½ cup minced celery	A little grated lemon rind
1 tablesp. chopped pimento	

Pour hot water over gelatin; stir until dissolved. Refrigerate, stirring occasionally, till consistency of unbeaten egg white. Add pineapple, cottage cheese, celery, pimento, walnuts. Pour into 8″ x 8″ x 2″ pan. Refrigerate till firm.

To serve: Frost with combined cream cheese, mayonnaise, lemon juice and rind. Serve cut into squares on greens; top with walnut halves. Makes 6 servings.

SPICY PEACH-CRANBERRY RING

1 No. 2½ can peach halves	1 cup fresh cranberries
1 teasp. whole cloves	½ unpeeled orange
3″ stick cinnamon	⅓ cup granulated sugar
¼ cup vinegar	1¾ cups hot water
1 pkg. lemon-flavored gelatin	1 pkg. cherry-flavored gelatin

Drain peaches; to syrup, add water to make 1¾ cups. Add cloves, cinnamon, vinegar; simmer, uncovered, 10 min. Add peaches; heat slowly 5 min. Remove peaches; place, with cut sides up,

in 3-qt. ring mold. Strain peach syrup; measure; add hot water to make 1⅔ cups. Add to lemon gelatin, stirring until dissolved; pour over peaches. Refrigerate till almost firm.

Put cranberries and orange through food chopper, using medium blade. Stir in sugar. Add hot water to cherry gelatin; stir until dissolved; cool. Stir in cranberry-orange mixture. Pour over almost firm peach layer. Refrigerate till firm. Unmold; fill center with greens.

Serve with Lemon-Cream Mayonnaise, p. 318. Makes 10 to 12 servings.

P.S. One cup of packaged frozen cranberry-orange relish may replace cranberries, orange, and sugar.

ORANGE-GINGER-ALE RING

2 env. unflavored gelatine	2 cups ginger ale
½ cup fresh, frozen, or canned lemon juice	2 cups orange sections
	⅔ cup chopped walnuts or pecans
½ cup granulated sugar	Cottage cheese
½ teasp. salt	Orange slices
1¼ cups orange juice	

Sprinkle gelatine over lemon juice in glass measuring cup to soften; stir over hot water until dissolved. Stir into sugar, salt, orange juice, ginger ale. Refrigerate, stirring often, till consistency of unbeaten egg white. Fold in orange sections, nuts. Pour into 1¼-qt. ring mold. Refrigerate till firm.

To serve: Unmold. Fill with cottage cheese; garnish with orange slices, greens. Makes 6 to 8 servings.

Cherry-Peach: For orange sections, substitute 1 cup pitted, drained canned Bing cherries and 1 cup sliced fresh or drained, thawed frozen or canned sliced peaches.

HEAVENLY FROZEN FRUIT SALAD

1 teasp. unflavored gelatin	whipped
2 tablesp. fresh, frozen, or canned lemon juice	¼ cup chopped nuts
	¼ cup quartered maraschino cherries
1 3-oz. pkg. soft cream cheese	1 drained No. 2 can crushed pineapple; or
¼ cup mayonnaise	1 drained No. 303 can fruit cocktail; or
¼ teasp. salt	1¾ cups mixed, sliced fresh fruit
2 tablesp. sugar	
½ cup heavy cream,	

Turn temperature control of refrigerator to coldest setting. Sprinkle gelatine over lemon juice in glass measuring cup to soften. Stir over hot water until dissolved. Add to combined cheese, mayonnaise, salt, and sugar. Fold in rest of ingredients. Pour into ice-cube tray; freeze just till firm. Then reset temperature control.

To serve: Slice; serve on greens. Makes 8 servings.

SHERRY-STRAWBERRY MOLD

1 cup hot water	drained, thawed
1 pkg. strawberry-	frozen strawberries
flavored gelatin	or raspberries
½ cup cold water	¼ cup snipped
½ cup sherry	shredded coconut
1 diced small banana	(optional)
1 cup sliced fresh or	

Pour hot water over gelatin; stir until dissolved. Add water, sherry. Refrigerate, stirring occasionally, till consistency of unbeaten egg white. Fold in fruits, coconut. Pour into 4 to 6 individual molds. Refrigerate till firm.

To serve: Unmold. Serve on greens with Fruity Cream-Cheese Topping, p. 319. Makes 4 to 6 servings.

Sherry Peach or Orange: For berries, substitute 1 cup sliced fresh or drained canned or thawed frozen sliced peaches; or 1 cup orange sections.

Cranberry-Nut: Omit sherry, strawberries, coconut. Fold in 1 1-lb. can jellied cranberry sauce, broken up with fork, and ¼ cup chopped walnuts. Pour into 1-qt. mold. Serve with Coconut Cream-Cheese Topping, p. 319.

PEACH-JELLY LAYER MOLD

2 pkg. lemon-flavored	cheese
gelatin	1 tablesp. fresh, frozen,
3 cups hot water	or canned lemon
1 pkg. frozen sliced	juice
peaches	1 tablesp. sugar
1 or 2 plums	Chicory
1 to 2 cups cottage	French dressing

Early in day: Dissolve gelatin in hot water. Add frozen fruit; with fork, break fruit apart. Turn into 2 8″ layer-cake pans. Cut plums into 6 to 8 thin slices; arrange, spoke-fashion, on center top of each jelly layer; refrigerate until firm.

To serve: Unmold 1 layer onto large plate. Stir cheese with lemon juice and sugar until smooth; spread over gelatin layer. Unmold second layer on top of cheese. Cut into 8 wedges and serve on beds of chicory as dessert salad. Pass French dressing. Makes 8 servings.

MOLDED GRAPE SUPREME

1 env. unflavored	3 tablesp. fresh, frozen,
gelatine	or canned lemon
¼ cup cold water	juice
1 cup boiling water	¾ cup halved seedless
⅓ cup granulated	grapes
sugar	2 diced medium-sized
Dash salt	bananas
1 6-oz. can frozen	¼ cup chopped wal-
grape-juice concen-	nuts
trate	Salad greens

Day before: Sprinkle gelatin over cold water to soften. Add boiling water, sugar, salt; stir until dissolved. Stir in grape juice, lemon juice. Refrigerate until partially thickened. Fold in fruits, nuts. Pour into 6 individual molds. Refrigerate until firm enough to unmold. Serve as dessert salad on greens, plain or with Half-and-Half Sour-Cream Dressing, p. 319. Makes 6 servings.

Salad Dressings

Salad can be a grand-slam success when it's teamed with the right dressing. From the many salad dressings that follow—French, mayonnaise, cooked, sour cream, and the like—choose the type and variation that best complement the taste and texture of your salad.

Before using these recipes, refer to How to Use Our Recipes, p. 3, and Pots and Pans, p. 692. Always use standard measuring cups and measuring spoons; measure level.

QUICK-AND-EASY DRESSINGS

Popular Ready-to-Use Salad Dressings

Just take your pick! Today wise homemakers keep these and other salad dressings—of national brands—on hand. They're delicious right from the jar or bottle, so easy to season to special tastes.

French: This comes creamy thick or clear and thin, mild or flavored with onion, garlic, wine, Caesar style, etc.

Mayonnaise: This is usually more bland than cooked salad dressing.

Cooked: This is a cross between old-fashioned boiled dressing and mayonnaise. One kind is Thousand Island dressing.

Meat: This is the zesty dressing that's so good on cold sliced meats, etc.

Low Calorie: This comes in several varieties.

FRENCH DRESSINGS PLUS

Into ½ cup ready-to-use or homemade French dressing, stir one of the following. You'll have 24 exciting variations.

For Green or Vegetable Salads:

Anchovy: 2 teasp. finely cut anchovies

Bombay: ¼ teasp. curry powder; 1 chopped, hard-cooked egg; ½ teasp. minced onion

Cheese and Pickle: 1 tablesp. each cottage cheese, pickle relish, and snipped parsley

Chiffonade: 2 teasp. each minced pimento and parsley; ½ chopped, hard-cooked egg

Curry: ¼ teasp. curry powder

Florentine: 1 tablesp. minced raw spinach

Herb: 2 teasp. snipped parsley, ½ teasp. minced fresh or dried tarragon or basil

Mustard: 1 tablesp. prepared mustard

Parmesan: * 2 tablesp. grated Parmesan cheese

Roquefort or Blue: * 1 to 2 tablesp. crumbled Roquefort or blue cheese

Vinaigrette: 1 teasp. snipped chives; 1 chopped, hard-cooked egg

Zesty: 1 tablesp. Worcestershire or bottled thick meat sauce, p. 9.

* Use on fruit too.

For Fruit Salads:

Chutney: * 2 tablesp. cut-up chutney

317

Cranberry: * 2 tablesp. canned whole-cranberry sauce

Creamy: 2 or 3 tablesp. heavy cream

Currant-Nut: * 1 tablesp. lemon or lime juice, ¼ cup currant jelly, ¼ cup chopped walnuts

Honey: 1 tablesp. honey, 2 teasp. lemon juice, 1 teasp. grated lemon rind

Honolulu: 3 whole cloves, 1 clove garlic, 2 tablesp. brown sugar, 1 teasp. Worcestershire. Let stand 1 hr.; remove cloves, garlic

Lorenzo: * 2 teasp. chili sauce, 2 tablesp. snipped water cress, 2 tablesp. currant jelly

Manhattan: 1 teasp. angostura bitters

Mint: * 2 tablesp. snipped mint, 2 teasp. sugar

Pineapple: * 3 tablesp. canned crushed pineapple

Superb: ¼ cup honey, ½ teasp. celery seeds

Two Fruit: 1 tablesp. lemon juice, ¼ teasp. grated orange rind, 2 tablesp. orange juice, 1 teasp. sugar, ¼ teasp. dry mustard

* *Use on greens too.*

MAYONNAISE PLUS

Into ½ cup ready-to-use or homemade mayonnaise or cooked salad dressing, stir one of the following. Keep a choice on hand.

For Green or Vegetable Salads:

Celery: ¼ cup minced celery, 1 tablesp. snipped chives

Cheese: 1 cup grated process American cheese (¼ lb.), 1 tablesp. vinegar, ½ minced clove garlic, ¼ teasp. salt, ½ teasp. Worcestershire

Cucumber: ½ cup minced cucumber, ¼ teasp. salt

Half-and-Half: ½ cup French dressing

Herb: Few drops lemon juice, 1 teasp. each snipped parsley and chives (or minced onion)

Horse-radish: 3 tablesp. horse-radish

Mustard: 1 tablesp. prepared mustard

Roquefort or Blue: ½ cup French dressing, ¼ cup crumbled Roquefort or blue cheese

Russian: ½ cup French dressing, 1 minced green pepper, 2 tablesp. chili sauce, 1 tablesp. minced onion

Sharp Cream: 1 teasp. minced onion, 1 teasp. vinegar, ½ teasp. sugar, ½ cup light cream

Thousand Island: 1 tablesp. chopped stuffed olives; 1 teasp. minced onion; 1 chopped, hard-cooked egg; 1 tablesp. minced green pepper; a little snipped parsley

Tomato: 1 diced tomato, 2 chopped scallions, ¼ teasp. salt, 2 tablesp. vinegar or lemon juice

For Fruit Salads:

Chutney: * 2 tablesp. cut-up chutney

Curry: * ½ teasp. curry powder, ¼ teasp. minced garlic

Fluffy: 1 egg yolk, lightly beaten; 1 tablesp. confectioners' sugar. Then fold in 1 egg white, beaten stiff

Lemon-Cream: 3 tablesp. lemon juice (or pineapple or orange juice), 3 tablesp. confectioners' sugar, 3 tablesp. heavy cream, dash salt. Or omit cream; fold in ½ cup heavy cream, whipped

Party Cream: 2 tablesp. currant jelly, beaten with fork; ¼ cup heavy cream, whipped

Raisin-Nut: 1 tablesp. snipped raisins, 2 tablesp. chopped nuts, ¼ cup orange juice

* *Use on greens too.*

SOUR-CREAM DRESSINGS

Into ½ cup commercial sour cream, stir one of the following:

For Green or Vegetable Salads:

Celery: ¼ cup minced onion, 1 tablesp. vinegar, ½ to 1 teasp. celery seeds, ¾ teasp. salt

Piquant: 2 teasp. horse-radish, ¼ teasp. salt, ½ teasp. sugar, ½ teasp. curry powder

Puff: 1 tablesp. minced onion, 1 teasp. sugar, 1 tablesp. vinegar, ½ teasp. bottled capers, ¼ teasp. paprika, ½ teasp. salt. Just before serving, fold in ½ cup croutons

Tarragon: 1 tablesp. tarragon vinegar, 1 teasp. minced onion, ¼ teasp. sugar, ¼ teasp. salt

Half-and-Half: ½ cup mayonnaise and seasonings to taste

Casa Grande: 1 minced scallion, 1 tablesp. mayonnaise, 1 tablesp. lemon juice, ¼ cup blue cheese, salt and pepper to taste

For Fruit Salads:

Festive: ¼ cup beaten currant jelly; ⅛ teasp. salt

Mint: 1 tablesp. snipped mint, ½ teasp. sugar, ½ teasp. lemon juice, ¼ teasp. salt

COTTAGE-CHEESE TOPPINGS

To ½ cup cottage cheese, add one of the following:

For Fruit, Green, or Vegetable Salads:

Chive: 1 tablesp. lemon juice, 1 tablesp. salad oil, ½ teasp. salt, 2 teasp. snipped chives or minced onion

Savory Thin: 3 tablesp. lemon juice, ⅓ cup undiluted evaporated milk, ½ teasp. salt, 2 teasp. sugar, 1 tablesp. snipped chives or minced onion

CREAM-CHEESE TOPPINGS

To 1 3-oz. pkg. soft cream cheese, add one of the following combinations; then whip smooth with fork.

For Fruit Salads Especially:

French: Thin with French dressing to sauce consistency

Fruity: ¼ cup orange juice, 4 teasp. lemon juice, ¼ teasp. salt, 1 teasp. sugar, dash paprika

Golden: ⅓ cup chopped walnuts, ¼ cup mayonnaise, ⅓ cup orange juice, 2 tablesp. lemon juice, 1 tablesp. sugar, ¼ teasp. salt

Coconut: ¼ cup milk or cream, dash salt. Add ¾ cup shredded coconut just before serving

FOR THE HOMEMADE-DRESSING FAN
Important Ingredients

Fine Salad Oil Is a Must. Choose one of the national brands of corn, cottonseed, olive, peanut, or soy oil; or use a blend of these. Do not use mineral oil; it may rob the body of important vitamins.

Lemon Juice Gives a Nice Accent. Fresh, canned, or frozen, it not only adds the tartness you crave but vitamin C as well. Use interchangeably with vinegar.

Vinegar comes in a dozen or more exciting flavors, as described on p. 525.

Packaged Salad-Dressing Bases—these contain a just-right amount of seasonings, spices, etc. You add salad oil, vinegar, and water.

FRENCH DRESSINGS

Choose one of dressings below, doubling or tripling recipe if you use it often.

Combine all ingredients in jar, bowl, or bottle. Shake or beat till blended; or mix in electric blender. Refrigerate, covered. Shake well before using. (For variations, see French Dressings Plus, p. 317.)

Simple (makes 1 cup):

¾ teasp. salt	vinegar
Speck pepper	¾ cup salad oil
Dash paprika	1 clove garlic; or 1
¼ teasp. sugar	tablesp. minced
¼ cup lemon juice,	onion
lime juice, or	

Lemon (makes 1⅔ cups):

1 cup salad oil	1½ teasp. salt
¼ to ⅓ cup granu-	2 teasp. paprika
lated sugar	1 teasp. minced onion
⅔ cup lemon juice	

Creamy (makes 1¼ cups):

½ cup undiluted	½ teasp. salt
evaporated milk	⅛ teasp. pepper
½ cup salad oil	⅛ teasp. Worcestershire
¼ cup vinegar	⅛ teasp. tabasco
½ teasp. sugar	(optional)
½ teasp. dry mustard	1 egg white, unbeaten

Fruit (makes ½ cup):

½ teasp. salt	2 tablesp. vinegar
1 teasp. sugar	2 teasp. honey
Speck pepper	2 teasp. lemon juice
Dash paprika	¼ teasp. grated lemon
⅓ cup salad oil	rind

Roquefort or Blue Cheese (makes 1⅔ cups):

1 cup salad oil
1 teasp. sugar
1 teasp. salt
2 teasp. paprika
3 tablesp. lemon juice or vinegar
3 oz. Roquefort or blue cheese
½ minced small onion

Wine (makes about 1½ cups):

1 tablesp. sugar
1 teasp. salt
½ teasp. dry mustard
1 teasp. Worcestershire
¼ cup catchup
¼ cup claret wine
¼ cup vinegar
¾ cup salad oil
1 gashed clove garlic

De Luxe (makes about 1½ cups):

1¼ cups salad oil
7 tablesp. vinegar or lemon juice
2¼ teasp. salt
¼ teasp. pepper
½ teasp. paprika
1 teasp. sugar
3 tablesp. chili sauce
1 teasp. horse-radish
1 teasp. prepared mustard
2 gashed cloves garlic

RASPBERRY FRENCH DRESSING

½ cup thawed frozen raspberries
¼ cup granulated sugar
1½ tablesp. vinegar
½ teasp. dry mustard
¼ teasp. salt
2 tablesp. vinegar
¾ cup salad oil

Press raspberries through sieve. Add sugar, 1½ tablesp. vinegar. Let stand 1 hr. Mix mustard, salt, 2 tablesp. vinegar. Gradually add oil, beating with egg beater till slightly thickened. Add raspberry mixture in thirds, beating constantly. A treat on fruit salads. Makes 1½ cups.

MAYONNAISE

2 teasp. dry mustard
1 tablesp. lemon juice
1 teasp. salt
1 teasp. sugar
Dash cayenne pepper
2 egg yolks
1¾ cups salad oil
2 tablesp. vinegar
1 tablesp. lemon juice

1. In cold bowl, with egg beater or electric mixer at medium speed, beat mustard, 1 tablesp. lemon juice, salt, sugar, cayenne.
2. Beat in egg yolks; then beat in oil, drop by drop, until ¼ cup has been added.
3. Continue beating in oil slowly; when mixture is thick, beat in vinegar and 1 tablesp. lemon juice alternately with oil until all are used.
4. Store, *covered, in least cold part of refrigerator.* (If too cold, mayonnaise may separate.) Makes 2 cups.

To Vary: See Mayonnaise Plus, p. 318.

BIG THOUSAND ISLAND DRESSING

1 halved clove garlic
½ cup mayonnaise
2 tablesp. light cream
2 tablesp. chili sauce
2 tablesp. chopped green pepper
½ cup coarsely cut-up stuffed olives
1 coarsely cut-up, hard-cooked egg
½ teasp. salt
½ teasp. paprika

Rub garlic well on inside of small bowl; discard. In bowl, blend mayonnaise with cream and chili sauce; add rest of ingredients; stir lightly. Refrigerate. Makes 1¼ cups.

COOKED SALAD DRESSING

2 tablesp. flour
2 tablesp. sugar
3 tablesp. salad oil
1¼ teasp. salt
Speck cayenne pepper
1 teasp. prepared mustard
1 cup water
2 eggs
6 tablesp. lemon juice or vinegar

1. In double boiler, thoroughly combine flour, sugar, oil, salt, cayenne, mustard, water. Cook, stirring, until consistency of medium white sauce.
2. Beat eggs slightly; gradually stir in lemon juice, then half of hot sauce; now stir this mixture *very slowly* into rest of sauce in double boiler. (If added too quickly, it may curdle.)
3. Cook mixture over *hot, not boiling,* water, stirring constantly, until thick enough to mound. Remove from heat *at once.*
4. Pour into bowl or jar; cover; cool. Refrigerate. Makes about 1½ cups.

Fluffy: Use 2 egg yolks instead of 2 eggs. After cooling mixture, fold in 2 stiffly beaten egg whites.

Horse-radish: After removing dressing from heat, add 1 to 2 tablesp. horse-radish.

Mustard Coleslaw: Increase mustard to 2 tablesp.

COOKED SALAD DRESSING PLUS

To ½ cup Cooked Salad Dressing, above, add one of these:

Cottage Cheese: 2 tablesp. cottage cheese, ½ teasp. snipped parsley, ¼ teasp. minced onion

Cucumber: ¼ cup minced, seeded cucumber and 2 teasp. snipped chives

Egg: 1 chopped, hard-cooked egg; ½ teasp. snipped parsley; 1 teasp. snipped chives

Sour Cream: 2 tablesp. commercial sour cream, ½ teasp. snipped parsley, ¼ teasp. minced onion

CREAMY BLUE-CHEESE DRESSING

¼ lb. soft blue or Roquefort cheese	⅛ teasp. salt
3 tablesp. light cream	⅛ teasp. pepper
½ cup mayonnaise or cooked salad dressing	1 teasp. prepared mustard
	¼ cup wine vinegar
	6 tablesp. salad oil

With fork, mash cheese with cream till creamy. Add rest of ingredients. Beat until very creamy. Refrigerate. Wonderful on tossed green salad. Makes about 1 cup.

SEA-FOOD DRESSING

¼ cup mayonnaise or cooked salad dressing	3 minced small sweet pickles
½ cup chili sauce	2 tablesp. snipped parsley
2 tablesp. snipped scallions	1 teasp. Worcestershire
2 tablesp. minced celery	1 teasp. horse-radish

Combine mayonnaise and chili sauce; then add rest of ingredients. Refrigerate. Nice on shrimp, tuna, or other fish salads. Makes ¾ cup.

SUSAN'S COLESLAW DRESSING

½ cup mayonnaise or cooked salad dressing	Dash paprika
	½ teasp. sugar
¾ teasp. salt	1 tablesp. vinegar
Speck pepper	1 tablesp. milk

Blend all ingredients. Refrigerate. Especially nice on cabbage salad. Makes ½ cup.

TART AND TASTY FRUIT DRESSING

2 eggs	⅛ teasp. salt
¼ cup granulated sugar	½ cup heavy cream, whipped
¼ cup lemon juice	
¼ cup pineapple or orange juice	½ teasp. grated lemon rind

In double boiler, beat eggs. Stir in sugar, juices, salt; cook over *hot, not boiling,* water till thickened. Cool; fold in cream, rind. Makes 2 cups.

LEMON-WALNUT SALAD DRESSING

Put 6 tablesp. chopped walnuts and ¼ cup granulated sugar on waxed paper; cover with more waxed paper; crush nuts well with rolling pin. Just before serving, mix with ¼ cup lemon juice and ¼ cup mayonnaise. Wonderful on fruit salad. Makes ⅔ cup.

COFFEE-FRUIT DRESSING

1½ teasp. instant-coffee	condensed milk
½ teasp. dry mustard	¼ cup fresh, frozen, or canned lemon juice
½ teasp. salt	
¼ cup melted butter or margarine	⅓ cup pineapple juice
⅔ cup sweetened	1 egg yolk

Blend together coffee, mustard, salt; stir into butter. Combine milk, juices, egg yolk; stir in butter mixture. Beat until thickened. For a thicker consistency, chill before serving. Makes 1½ cups.

TOMATO SALAD DRESSING

3 tablesp. corn syrup	(½ cup plus 2 tablesp.)
2 teasp. dry mustard	
1 teasp. salt	½ soup can salad oil (½ cup plus 2 tablesp.)
1 teasp. paprika	
½ teasp. pepper	
1 can undiluted condensed tomato soup	2 tablesp. minced onion
½ soup can vinegar	

In jar or bowl, combine corn syrup, mustard, salt, paprika, and pepper, in order listed. Add rest of ingredients. Shake. Refrigerate. Shake before using. Makes about 2⅔ cups.

LOW-CALORIE DRESSINGS

LOW-CALORIE FRENCH DRESSING

¾ cup water	1¼ teasp. prepared mustard
2 teasp. cornstarch	
¼ cup lemon juice	½ teasp. paprika
¾ teasp. salt	1 clove garlic
1½ teasp. sugar	½ teasp. Worcestershire
2 tablesp. salad oil	¼ cup catchup
1 teasp. horse-radish	

Simmer water with cornstarch over low heat, stirring, until clear and thickened—about 5 min. Cool. Add lemon juice and rest of ingredients; with egg beater or electric mixer, beat until smooth and blended. Refrigerate. Shake before using. Makes about 1¼ cups (20 calories per tablespoon).

Egg: Add 1 finely chopped, hard-cooked egg (25 calories per tablespoon).

Fruit: Substitute ¼ cup pineapple juice for ¼ cup water; omit sugar. Or add ¼ cup diced orange, peach, pear, apricot, grapefruit, etc. (25 calories per tablespoon).

Garden: Add 2 tablesp. minced onion, 3 tablesp. minced cucumber, 2 tablesp. minced green pepper (20 calories per tablespoon).

YOGHURT DRESSING

1 cup yoghurt	¼ teasp. salt
2 tablesp. vinegar	¼ teasp. sugar
1 tablesp. minced onion	Speck pepper

Combine all ingredients. Refrigerate. Makes 1¼ cups (about 10 calories per tablespoon).

LOW-CALORIE TOMATO-JUICE DRESSING

½ cup tomato juice	1 teasp. salt
2 to 4 tablesp. salad oil	1 teasp. minced onion
2 tablesp. lemon juice	1½ teasp. bottled thick
½ teasp. dry mustard	meat sauce, p. 9

Combine all ingredients. With egg beater or electric mixer, beat until well blended. Refrigerate. Makes about 1 cup (25 calories per tablespoon).

LOW-CALORIE BUTTERMILK DRESSING

1½ teasp. sugar	pepper
1½ teasp. dry mustard	1 egg, slightly beaten
½ teasp. salt	½ cup buttermilk
⅛ teasp. paprika	1 tablesp. melted butter
1½ teasp. cornstarch	or margarine
⅛ teasp. onion salt	½ cup vinegar
Few grains cayenne	

In double boiler, mix sugar, mustard, salt, paprika, cornstarch, onion salt, cayenne. Add egg, buttermilk; stir till smooth. Cook over *hot, not boiling,* water until mixture begins to thicken. Add butter and vinegar, a little at a time; beat well. Refrigerate. Makes 1 cup (15 calories per tablespoon).

LOW-CALORIE FRUIT-SALAD DRESSING

1 minced clove garlic	1 teasp. sugar
¼ cup vinegar	½ teasp. salt
½ cup orange juice	⅛ teasp. pepper
¼ teasp. paprika	

Let garlic stand in vinegar 1 hr. Strain. Add rest of ingredients; shake or beat well. Refrigerate. Shake before using. Makes about 1 cup (10 calories per tablespoon).

Quick Breads

Homemade quick breads give a wonderful lift to even the simplest meal. And they're easy to make, whether you work from scratch or use one of today's mixes. They have another plus too: The enriched flour you use contains more dietary essentials than ever before. So serve quick breads often, at or between meals.

Before using these recipes, refer to How to Use Our Recipes, p. 3, and Pots and Pans, p. 692. Always use standard measuring cups and measuring spoons; measure level.

Unless a specific kind of baking powder is specified, any kind, in the amount called for in these recipes, will give satisfactory results. For milk called for, you may use regular, evaporated (diluted with an equal amount of water), or liquefied instant nonfat dry milk.

Serve with Style

Line a basket or plate with a pretty napkin or bun cozy. When hot bread is done, remove at once from pans and arrange on napkin. Bring corners of napkin up and over bread, to keep it warm. Serve at once.

Some hot breads are pretty served right in the dish in which they were baked—they stay hot longer that way too.

HOT BISCUITS AND MUFFINS

SUSAN'S HOT BAKING-POWDER BISCUITS

2 cups sifted all-purpose flour	6 to 7 tablesp. shortening
3 teasp. baking powder	About ⅔ to ¾ cup milk
1 teasp. salt	

1. Start heating oven to 450°F. Into bowl, sift flour, baking powder, salt. With pastry blender or 2 knives, used scissor-fashion, cut in shortening until mixture is like coarse corn meal.
2. Make well in center; pour in ½ cup milk. With fork, mix lightly and quickly. Add enough more milk to form dough that's just moist enough to leave sides of bowl and cling to fork as ball. Turn onto lightly floured surface.
3. Knead this way: Pick up side of dough farthest from you; fold over toward you; with palms, press down, pushing dough away *lightly.* Turn dough around part way; repeat process 6 or 7 times, working *gently.*
4. Lightly roll dough out from center, lifting rolling pin as you near edges. Roll dough ½" to ¾" thick for high, fluffy biscuits, ¼" for thin crusty ones.
5. With floured 2" biscuit cutter, cut out biscuits, using straight, *not twisting,* motion and cutting biscuits as close together as possible. Between cuttings, dip cutter into flour.
6. With spatula, lift biscuits to ungreased baking sheet. Place about 1" apart for crusty biscuits, or nearly touching for soft-sided ones.
7. Lightly press dough trimmings together; roll and cut as before. With pastry brush, brush biscuit tops with milk, melted butter or margarine, or light cream. Bake 12 to 15 min., or until delicate brown. Serve *hot.* Makes about 19 2" biscuits.

Piping Hot: Bake biscuits in oven-glass pie plate or baking dish; rush them to table in same plate.

Extra Rich: Increase shortening to ½ cup.

Speedy: Roll biscuit dough into oblong; cut into squares, triangles, or diamonds; then bake.

Drop: Increase milk to 1 cup. Drop biscuits 1″ apart onto greased cookie sheet; or fill greased muffin-pan cups two thirds full. Bake at 450°F. 12 to 15 min. Makes about 12.

HOT BAKING-POWDER BISCUITS
(with salad oil)

2 cups sifted all-purpose flour	1 teasp. salt
3 teasp. baking powder	⅓ cup salad oil
	⅔ cup milk

Start heating oven to 450°F. or 475°F. Sift flour, baking powder, salt. Measure oil, then milk, into 1 measuring cup (don't stir together). Pour, all at once, over flour mixture. With fork, mix to make soft dough that cleans side of bowl. With hands, shape lightly into ball.

Dampen table surface; cover with waxed paper. Place dough on paper; knead lightly, without additional flour, 10 times, or until smooth. Pat dough ¼″ to ½″ thick (or roll between 2 sheets of waxed paper; then remove top sheet).

Cut with unfloured biscuit cutter. Bake on ungreased cookie sheet 10 to 15 min., or until golden brown. Makes 12 large biscuits, or 18 small ones.

Shortcakes: Sift 2 tablesp. granulated sugar with dry ingredients. If desired, add 1 egg to oil in measuring cup; then pour in enough milk to make 1 cup liquid. Proceed as directed, cutting with 2½″ cutter. Bake as above. Serve as in Susan's Strawberry Shortcake, p. 383. Makes 8.

HOT BISCUITS PLUS

Before adding liquid to Susan's Hot Baking-Powder Biscuits, p. 323, Hot Baking-Powder Biscuits, above, or 2 cups packaged biscuit mix, add one of these:

Cheese: ¼ to ½ cup grated sharp American cheese; or ⅓ cup crumbled blue cheese

Chive: ¼ cup snipped chives

Piquant: ¼ teasp. dry mustard, ½ teasp. sage, 1¼ teasp. caraway seeds

Curry: ¼ teasp. curry powder

Orange: Grated rind of 1 orange

Ham: ⅔ cup chopped, cooked ham

CUT BISCUITS PLUS

Make Susan's Hot Baking-Powder Biscuit dough, p. 323, Hot Baking-Powder Biscuit dough, above, or packaged biscuit-mix dough (2-cup recipe). Then choose:

Orange: Roll or pat dough ½″ thick; cut out biscuits. Place close together, or 1″ apart, on baking sheet. Rub halved sugar lumps on rind of 1 orange; dip quickly into orange juice; press ½ lump into top of each biscuit. Bake at 450°F. 12 to 15 min. Or instead of orange treatment, dip halved sugar lumps into strong cold coffee.

Cheese Triangles: Roll or pat dough into 8″ circle. Cut into 8 wedge-shaped pieces. Reassemble in circle on cookie sheet, leaving space between wedges. Mix 1 3-oz. pkg. soft pimento cream cheese with 1 tablesp. mayonnaise, 2 teasp. minced onion, and 1 tablesp. snipped parsley; spread on top of wedges. Bake at 450°F. 12 to 15 min.

Date or Cheese: Roll or pat dough ¼″ thick. Cut out 2″ biscuits. Set pitted date or piece of cheese on each. Fold over; press edges together. Bake at 450°F. 12 to 15 min.

BISCUIT PIN WHEELS

Make Susan's Hot Baking-Powder Biscuit dough, p. 323, Hot Baking-Powder Biscuit dough, above, or packaged biscuit-mix dough (2-cup recipe). Roll into rectangle ¼″ thick; then complete as below:

Party: Spread dough with soft cheese spread, deviled ham or tongue, or thick marmalade. Roll up from long side, jelly-roll-fashion; cut into ½″- to 1″-thick slices. Place, with flat sides down, in greased muffin-pan cups. Bake at 450°F. about 12 min., or until nicely browned and done.

Butterscotch: Spread dough with 2 tablesp. soft butter or margarine. Sprinkle with mixture of ¼ cup granulated sugar and 1 teasp. cinnamon, then with raisins if desired. Roll up from long side, jelly-roll-fashion. Cut into ½″ to 1″ slices;

place, with flat sides down, in greased muffin-pan cups. Bake at 425°F. about 15 min.

Pecan: Make Butterscotch Pin Wheels, p. 324. In bottom of each greased muffin-pan cup, put 1 teasp. melted butter or margarine, 1 teasp. brown sugar, 2 or 3 pecan halves. Top with pin wheels. Bake at 425°F. about 15 min.

DROP BISCUITS PLUS

Make Susan's Hot Drop Baking-Powder Biscuit dough, p. 324, or drop-biscuit dough from packaged biscuit mix (2-cup recipe). Complete in one of the following ways; then bake at 450°F. 12 to 15 min.

Blueberry: To dough, add 1 cup drained, washed fresh blueberries. Sprinkle biscuit tops with sugar. Bake.

Nut-Butter: Mix ½ cup brown sugar, packed, with ¼ cup honey, 2 tablesp. butter or margarine, few chopped nuts. Place 1 tablesp. of this mixture in each greased muffin-pan cup. Drop biscuit dough, by spoonfuls, on top. Bake.

Hot Pimento: Over hot water, melt 1 3-oz. pkg. pimento cream cheese with 2 tablesp. butter or margarine. Place spoonful on each drop biscuit on cookie sheet. Bake.

Top Up: Drop biscuit dough, by spoonfuls, into greased muffin-pan cups. Make slight impression in top of each biscuit. Top with one of the following combinations. Bake.

About 1 teasp. raspberry jam
Pitted, cooked prune; then a little brown sugar, honey, and butter or margarine
Pickle relish and dab of chili sauce
Grated orange or lemon rind with sugar
Melted butter or margarine, plus a little garlic salt or mixed herbs
Honey, brushed on; sprinkling of nutmeg
Drained canned crushed pineapple and sprinkling of brown sugar
Brown sugar mixed with butter or margarine, then with shredded coconut or chopped nuts

PAN-READY BISCUITS

These light, fluffy biscuits (some are the buttermilk type) come all rolled and cut, in tubelike packages. They must be kept refrigerated in the store and at home. *Never* store on pantry shelf or in freezer.

They're good baked just as is. Or you may vary them as below. (Or if you prefer, use Susan's Hot Baking-Powder Biscuit dough, p. 323, Hot Baking-Powder Biscuit dough, p. 324, or packaged biscuit-mix dough; roll ¼" thick; cut into rounds.)

Puffs (soufflé-topped): In 8" pie plate, arrange about 10 biscuits (1 pkg.), overlapping them slightly. With fork, beat 1 egg with 2 tablesp. light cream, ⅛ teasp. dry mustard, ¼ teasp. salt, ½ cup grated process sharp American or pimento cheese. Pour over biscuits. Bake at 450°F. 15 min.

Quick Coffeecakes: Dip biscuits into melted butter or margarine; sprinkle with cinnamon and sugar. Bake at 425°F. 10 min., or until done.

Frosties: Combine 1 3-oz. pkg. pimento cream cheese with ½ teasp. cream and 1 tablesp. chopped pimento. Spread on top of about 10 biscuits (1 pkg.). Bake at 425°F. 10 min., or until done.

Upside-down: In bottom of each of 10 muffin-pan cups, place some of one of mixtures below. Top with biscuit in each cup. Bake at 425°F. 15 to 18 min.; let stand in cups ½ min.; then invert pan onto waxed paper. Cool 5 min.; then lift off pan.

Honey-Pecan: In each muffin cup, put 3 canned pecan halves, then some of ¼ cup honey mixed with ½ teasp. cinnamon.

Butterscotch-Nut: In each of 10 muffin cups, place ½ teasp. melted butter or margarine and 1 teasp. corn syrup; stir; top with 3 pecans, with flat sides up.

Pineapple: In each of 10 muffin cups, place ½ teasp. melted butter or margarine or salad oil and 1 teasp. brown sugar; stir; top with 2 teasp. drained canned crushed pineapple.

Orange: Cook ½ cup granulated sugar with ¼ cup orange juice, ¼ cup butter or margarine, and 2 teasp. grated orange rind 5 min. Pour into 10 muffin cups.

Coffee-ettes: Use about 20 biscuits (2 pkg.). Dip first into ¼ cup melted butter or margarine, then into combined ¾ cup granulated sugar, ¾ teasp. cinnamon, ⅓ cup chopped nuts. Arrange biscuits, overlapping them, in greased 9″ layer-cake pan or on greased cookie sheet. Bake at 425°F. 20 to 25 min.

Cheese Top Up: Place about 10 biscuits (1 pkg.) close together in 9″ pie plate. Stir ¼ lb. grated process sharp American cheese with ¼ cup melted butter or margarine until smooth. Spread over biscuits. Bake at 450°F. 15 min.

Cheese Upside-down: Place 2 tablesp. butter or margarine and ¼ cup pimento- or blue-cheese spread in 8″ pie plate. Place in oven till partly melted; stir. Arrange about 10 biscuits close together in mixture. Bake at 450°F. 15 min. Turn out of pan.

Leftover Biscuits

Reheat baking-powder biscuits in one of these ways:

In Aluminum Foil: Snugly wrap biscuits in aluminum foil. Bake at 375°F. about 20 min., or till heated. If served in foil wrappings (turn foil edges down to form basket), they'll keep hot to the last delicious crumb.

In Covered Skillet: Put 2 tablesp. water in large skillet. Place round trivet in bottom, with biscuits on it. Cover; leave over low heat 10 min., or until biscuits are hot.

In Paper Bag: Moisten biscuits by passing them quickly through running water from faucet. Bake in tightly closed paper bag at 350°F. about 15 to 18 min., or till heated.

In Broiler: Split biscuits. Butter. Then sprinkle with a little grated cheese; celery, poppy, or caraway seeds; or cinnamon and sugar. Or spread with cheese spread. Then toast under broiler.

AFTERNOON TEA SCONES

2⅓ cups sifted cake flour	6 tablesp. shortening
2½ teasp. baking powder	5 tablesp. milk or light cream
½ teasp. salt	2 eggs
2 teasp. sugar	2 tablesp. sugar

Start heating oven to 450°F. Into bowl, sift together the first 4 ingredients. With pastry blender or 2 knives, scissor-fashion, cut in shortening until like corn meal. Add milk. Separate 1 egg; reserve 1 tablesp. white; beat rest of egg with second egg; add to flour.

On lightly floured surface, roll dough ½″ thick. Cut into 3″ squares; cut each square into 2 triangles. Arrange on greased cookie sheet; brush with 1 tablesp. egg white, slightly beaten; sprinkle with 2 tablesp. sugar. Bake 10 to 15 min., or until done.

Serve hot, for luncheon, supper, or tea. Makes about 10.

Blueberry: With eggs, add 1 cup well-drained, washed fresh blueberries. Makes about 18.

Jam: Increase flour to 2½ cups. Roll dough ¼″ thick; cut into 2½″ squares. Place 1 teasp. plum or other jam in center of each square; fold opposite corners toward center; with moistened finger tips, pinch together firmly. Makes about 12.

Dainty Tea: Cut dough into 1½″ to 2″ rounds.

Toasted: Make scones day before. On the day, split; brush with melted butter or margarine; toast under broiler until golden brown.

HONEY BUNS

⅓ cup brown sugar, packed	cuit mix
¼ cup honey	2 tablesp. soft butter or margarine
2 tablesp. butter or margarine	⅓ cup brown sugar, packed
1 egg	⅓ cup chopped nuts
About ⅓ cup milk	⅓ cup light or dark raisins
2 cups packaged bis-	

Start heating oven to 400°F. Grease 8 3″ muffin-pan cups. For honey mixture, in pan, slowly heat ⅓ cup brown sugar, honey, 2 tablesp. butter. Put egg in measuring cup; add milk to make ⅔ cup liquid; add to biscuit mix; mix as label directs.

Roll dough into rectangle about 14″ x 10″. Spread with 2 tablesp. butter; sprinkle with ⅓ cup brown sugar, nuts, raisins. Roll up from long side, jelly-roll-fashion. Cut into 8 slices.

In each muffin-pan cup, place 1 tablesp. honey mixture; top with biscuit, with flat side down.

Date Muffins -

1 c. flour sifted
1/4 c. sugar
3 tsps. B.P.
1/2 tsp. salt
1 c. Quaker Oats, uncooked

1/2 c. dates chopped
3 Tbsps. liquid shortening -
1 egg, unbeaten
3/4 c. milk
6 pitted dates, sliced long
Orange powd. sugar icing

Sift flour, sugar, B.P., and salt. Stir in Oats + dates. Add shortening, egg + milk. Stir only until moistened. Fill greased muffin cups (12) 2/3 full. Place half date on batter in each muffin cup. Bake in hot oven 425° about 15 min. Drizzle with orange frosting.

Lazy daisy Oatmeal Cake

1¼ cups boiling water
1 cup Quaker Oats, uncooked
½ cup butter or margarine, softened
1 cup granulated sugar
1 cup firmly-packed brown sugar
1 teaspoon vanilla
2 eggs
1½ cups sifted all-purpose flour
1 teaspoon soda
½ teaspoon salt
3/4 teaspoon cinnamon
¼ teaspoon nutmeg

Frosting:

¼ cup butter or margarine, melted
½ cup firmly-packed brown sugar
3 tablespoons half and half
1/3 cup chopped nutmeats
3/4 cup shredded or flaked coconut

For cake, pour boiling water over oats;
cover and let stand 20 minutes. Beat butter
until fluffy; gradually add sugars and beat
until creamy. Blend in vanilla and eggs.
Add oats mixture: mix well. Sift together
flour, soda, salt, cinnamon and nutmeg. Add
to creamed mixture. Mix well. Pour batter
into well-greased and floured 9-inch square
pan. Bake in preheated moderate oven 350
degrees for 50 to 55 minutes. Do not
remove cake from pan. For frosting, combine
all ingredients. Spread evenly over cake.

Broil until frosting becomes bubbly. Cake
may be served warm or cold.

Brush tops with any remaining honey mixture. Bake 15 to 20 min., or until golden brown. Immediately place buns on cake rack; dribble syrup remaining in muffin cups over sides of buns. Makes 8.

CHEESE STRAWS

1 cup sifted all-purpose flour	2 tablesp. shortening
1½ teasp. baking powder	½ cup finely grated American cheese
½ teasp. salt	⅓ cup milk or water
	Paprika

Start heating oven to 425°F. Into mixing bowl, sift flour, baking powder, salt. With pastry blender or 2 knives, scissor-fashion, cut in shortening and cheese until like coarse corn meal. Add milk; mix well.

Roll dough ⅛″ thick; sprinkle with paprika; cut into 3″ x ¼″ strips. Bake 8 to 10 min. Nice with soup or salad. Makes about 90.

HOT MUFFINS

2 cups sifted all-purpose flour	1 egg
3 teasp. baking powder	1 cup milk
½ teasp. salt	¼ cup salad oil or melted shortening
2 tablesp. sugar	

1. Start heating oven to 425°F. Grease 14 2½″ muffin-pan cups well. Into mixing bowl, sift flour, baking powder, salt, sugar.
2. Beat egg till frothy; add milk and salad oil; mix well. Make small well in flour mixture; pour in milk mixture all at once. Stir quickly and lightly—*don't beat*—until just mixed but still lumpy.
3. Quickly fill muffin cups two thirds full; wipe off any spilled drops of batter. (If batter does not fill all cups, fill empty ones with water to keep grease from burning.) Bake about 25 min., or until wire cake tester inserted in center of muffin comes out clean.

To serve: Run spatula around each muffin to loosen it; lift out onto heated dish. Makes about 14.

Note: If muffins are done before rest of meal, loosen; then tip slightly in pans; keep warm. Then they won't steam and soften.

► **For 2:** Use 1 egg; halve rest of ingredients.

Susan's Blueberry:

1. Wash and drain 1 cup fresh blueberries; pat dry on paper towels; sweeten to taste with 2 to 3 tablesp. sugar. (Or use 1 cup frozen blueberries; don't sweeten.)
2. Make muffin batter, increasing salt to 1 teasp. and using 6 tablesp. salad oil.
3. Just before filling muffin-pan cups, quickly stir berries into batter. Before baking muffins, sprinkle with 4 teasp. granulated sugar.

Orange: Increase sugar to ¼ cup. Reduce milk to ¾ cup. With milk, add ¼ cup orange juice, ¼ cup grated orange rind.

Whole-wheat: Decrease flour to ¾ cup. Add 1 cup unsifted whole-wheat flour. Increase sugar to ¼ cup, baking powder to 4 teasp. Bake at 375°F. 35 min. Makes about 16.

Muffins Plus: You may like to bake half of muffins plain. To rest of batter, add one of following, then bake; serve toasted next day.

Caraway: 1 tablesp. caraway seeds

Fruit: ½ cup light or dark raisins; or 1 cup cut-up, pitted dates

Nut: 1 cup finely chopped nuts

Leftover Muffins: Split, butter, and toast leftover muffins under broiler.

HOT MUFFINS—QUICK

Make muffin batter, using packaged muffin or biscuit mix. Now complete as below. Makes luscious muffins.

Filled: Fill greased muffin-pan cups half full with muffin batter. Top with one of fillings below; then add more batter to fill each cup two thirds full. Bake as label directs.

Jam-Dandy: ½″ cube of cream cheese and 1 teasp. raspberry, strawberry, or peach jam (extra nice for small muffins)

Candied: Several bits of preserved orange or lemon rind or citron

Fruitful: 1 drained, cooked dried apricot or pitted prune. Or 1 teasp. applesauce and sprinkling of cinnamon. Or 1 teasp. canned whole-cranberry sauce or drained crushed pineapple mixed with a little grated orange rind. Or 1 banana slice. Or a few blueberries, blackberries, or drained canned Bing cherries. Or a few cut-up pitted dates or raisins

Tip-Topped: Turn all of batter into about 14 2½″ muffin-pan cups; top with one of the following; then bake as label directs.

Sugar mixed with a little grated orange or lemon rind, or cinnamon
Honey, brushed on batter, and sprinkling of nutmeg or poppy seeds
Shredded coconut or chopped nuts, plain or mixed with brown sugar and butter or margarine
Grated process American cheese; or caraway or poppy seeds (for corn or plain muffins)
Small dot jelly
Cube of cream cheese
Dab of canned cranberry sauce

P.S. You can also buy packaged blueberry or date-muffin mix.

HOT PINEAPPLE MUFFINS

¼ cup brown sugar, packed	Muffin batter
¼ teasp. cinnamon	About ½ cup drained canned crushed
2 tablesp. melted butter or margarine	pineapple

Start heating oven to 400°F. Grease 12 2½″ muffin-pan cups. Mix brown sugar, cinnamon, butter. Prepare muffin batter, using packaged muffin mix, 2 cups biscuit mix, or Hot Muffin batter, p. 327. Fill muffin cups two thirds full. Make depression in each muffin; in it, place 1 teasp. brown-sugar mixture. Top each muffin with 1 teasp. drained pineapple. Bake 20 to 25 min., or until browned and done. Makes 12.

HOT BRAN MUFFINS

1 cup sifted all-purpose flour	1 cup milk
½ teasp. salt	2 tablesp. soft shortening
3 teasp. baking powder	¼ cup granulated sugar
1 cup ready-to-eat bran	1 egg, beaten

Start heating oven to 400°F. Grease well about 12 2½″ muffin-pan cups. Sift flour, salt, baking powder. In medium bowl, soak bran in milk 5 min. Meanwhile, in small bowl, with spoon,

beat shortening with sugar until light; add beaten egg; stir till smooth. Stir into bran. Add flour mixture, *stirring only until just mixed, no longer*. Fill muffin cups two thirds full. Bake 25 min., or until done. Makes about 12.

▶ **For 2:** Use 1 egg; halve rest of ingredients.

Orange Glaze: Just before baking, sprinkle muffins with combined 2½ teasp. grated orange rind and ¼ cup granulated sugar.

Raisin-Nut: To flour mixture, add ½ cup chopped walnuts and ½ cup raisins.

HOT 40-MINUTE ORANGE ROLLS

1 tablesp. orange juice	flour
2 teasp. grated orange rind	4 teasp. baking powder
½ cup strained honey	½ teasp. salt
¼ cup margarine	¼ cup margarine
2 cups sifted all-purpose	About ¾ cup milk

In small saucepan over low heat, cook orange juice, rind, honey, and ¼ cup margarine until margarine is melted; simmer 2 to 3 min.; remove from heat. Meanwhile, start heating oven to 450°F. Grease 8 custard cups; divide orange mixture between custard cups.

Into mixing bowl, sift flour, baking powder, salt. With pastry blender or 2 knives, scissor-fashion, cut in ¼ cup margarine until like corn meal. Stir in enough milk to form soft dough; blend.

Divide dough between custard cups. Bake 15 min., or until done. Remove from cups; invert. Serve hot. Makes 8.

POPOVERS AND CORN BREAD

POPOVERS

1 cup sifted all-purpose flour	2 or 3 eggs
¾ teasp. salt	1 cup milk
1 tablesp. shortening (optional)	

1. Grease 8 large, or 12 medium, custard cups; place on baking sheet. Start heating oven to 375°F.
2. Into mixing bowl, sift flour, salt. With pastry blender or 2 knives, scissor-fashion, cut in shortening until like corn meal.

3. In small bowl, beat eggs slightly with egg beater; beat in milk. Add to flour mixture; with egg beater, beat until smooth. Fill cups one third full.
4. Bake 50 min. Then remove from oven; quickly cut slit in side of each popover to let out steam; return to oven for 10 min.
5. Promptly remove popovers from cups so bottoms do not steam and soften. Serve promptly. Makes 12 medium, or 8 large, popovers.

Giant Popovers: With egg beater beat 3 eggs well, then beat in 1 cup milk and 3 tablesp. melted butter or margarine. Now with egg beater slowly beat in 1 cup sifted all-purpose flour which has been sifted with ½ teasp. salt. Turn into 6 custard cups which have been greased with 1 tablesp. butter or margarine. Bake at 400°F. 50 min. Makes 6.

YORKSHIRE PUDDING

When roast beef is done (p. 50), remove from oven and keep warm. Increase oven heat to 450°F. Pour ¼ cup hot drippings from roasting pan into 11″ x 7″ x 1½″ pan. Make popover batter, p. 328; pour into pan. Bake 25 to 30 min.

Cut into squares; serve *at once* with roast beef. Makes 6 servings.

QUICK POPOVERS

Delightfully light popovers can be made quickly from packaged popover mix. Just follow label directions.

SKILLET CUSTARD CORN BREAD

2 tablesp. butter or margarine	lated sugar
1⅓ cups yellow corn meal	1¼ teasp. salt
⅓ cup sifted all-purpose flour	1 cup milk
1 teasp. baking soda	2 eggs, unbeaten
3 to 4 tablesp. granu-	1 cup buttermilk or sour milk
	1 cup milk

Start heating oven to 400°F. Place butter in 9″ iron skillet or 9″ x 9″ x 2″ pan. Heat in oven.

Meanwhile, into bowl, sift corn meal, flour, soda, sugar, salt. Stir in 1 cup milk and eggs, then buttermilk. Pour into skillet; then pour 1 cup milk *over top* of corn mixture; do not stir. Bake 35 min.

Serve hot from skillet, cut into wedges, with lump of butter on each wedge. Corn bread will have layer of custard. Or serve with tart jelly or table syrup. Eat with fork. Makes 6 servings.

YANKEE-STYLE GOLDEN CORN BREAD

1¼ cups sifted all-purpose flour	powder
	1 teasp. salt
¾ cup yellow corn meal	1 egg
	⅔ cup milk
2 to 4 tablesp. granulated sugar	⅓ cup melted butter, margarine, or fat, or salad oil
4½ teasp. baking	

1. Start heating oven to 425°F. Grease 8″ x 8″ x 2″ pan. Into medium mixing bowl, sift flour, corn meal, sugar, baking powder, salt.
2. In small bowl, beat egg well with fork; stir in milk, butter; pour, all at once, into flour mixture, stirring with fork until flour is *just moistened*. (Even if mixture is lumpy, do not stir any longer or holes or tunnels in corn bread will result.)
3. Quickly turn batter into greased pan; spread evenly with spatula.
4. Bake 25 to 30 min., or until done. Serve hot, cut into squares. Makes 9 servings.

▶ **For 2:** Use 1 egg; halve rest of ingredients; bake in 6″ pie plate or in muffin-pan cups.

To Do Ahead: Bake corn bread day before. Before mealtime, cut into squares. Split; butter; then quickly toast under broiler.

Leftover Corn Bread or Muffins: Split; butter; toast as in Toasted Corn-Bread Cuts, p. 330.

Blueberry Corn Muffins: To flour mixture, add 1 cup sugared fresh berries. Fill 16 greased muffin-pan cups two thirds full. Bake at 425°F. 25 to 30 min., or until done. Serve hot. Makes 16 2½″ muffins.

Corn-Bread Ring: Bake as directed in greased 8½″ (3-pt.) ring mold. Serve as hot bread, cut into wedges. Or fill center of ring with creamed ham, chicken, dried beef, oysters, etc.

Corn Sticks: Melt ¼ cup shortening; use to grease corn-stick pans *very well*. Fill three fourths full with corn-bread batter. Bake as directed. Makes about 14.

Corn Muffins: Fill about 12 well-greased 2½″ muffin-pan cups two thirds full. Bake as directed.

QUICK CORN BREAD

You can buy excellent corn-muffin and corn-bread mixes, which are as good as they are quick. Just make as label directs.

Cheese-Corn Strips: Pour corn-muffin- or corn-bread-mix batter into greased 12″ x 8″ x 2″ pan. Sprinkle with 1 cup grated process American cheese. Bake at 375°F. 25 min.

When corn bread is cool, cut in half, lengthwise; then cut into ¾″ crosswise strips.

Toasted Corn-Bread Cuts: Bake corn-muffin- or corn-bread-mix batter in greased 8″ x 8″ x 2″ pan at 375°F. 25 min.

When corn bread is cold, cut into squares; split squares. Spread with soft butter or margarine; sprinkle with poppy seeds, grated cheese, or dried thyme; or spread lightly with molasses or jelly. Broil till golden.

MARJIE'S FLUFFY SPOON BREAD

1 qt. milk	2 tablesp. butter or
1 cup corn meal	margarine
(yellow or white)	4 eggs
1½ teasp. salt	

In double boiler, heat milk; gradually stir in corn meal mixed with salt; cook, stirring, until smooth and thick. Cover; cook till mushy. Meanwhile, start heating oven to 425°F. Remove the mush from heat; add butter. In bowl, beat eggs till well blended; slowly stir into mush. Pour into well-greased 1½-qt. casserole. Bake, uncovered, 50 to 55 min.

Serve from casserole, spooning some onto each plate. Eat instead of bread, with lots of butter or margarine. Makes 4 or 5 servings.

CORN-MEAL CRISPS

1 cup yellow corn meal	¼ teasp. baking soda
½ cup sifted all-	2 tablesp. melted
purpose flour	shortening
½ teasp. salt	⅓ cup milk

Early in day: Start heating oven to 350°F. Sift corn meal, flour, salt, soda; stir in shortening, milk. On lightly floured surface, knead dough 6 to 8 times, or until it just holds together. Break off nickel-size pieces; roll each into very thin 4″ round (leave edges ragged). Bake on ungreased cookie sheet 15 min., or until golden.

Just before serving: Brush with melted butter or margarine; sprinkle with salt. Makes 24.

To Vary: Sprinkle a little grated cheese, celery seeds, or chili powder on top of salted, buttered, baked crisps.

COFFEECAKES AND TEA BREADS

RAISIN-SPICE COFFEECAKE

2 tablesp. melted butter or margarine	1 teasp. salt
	½ cup granulated sugar
2 tablesp. sugar	1 teasp. cinnamon
½ teasp. cinnamon	¼ teasp. mace
½ cup crushed cereal flakes or packaged dried bread crumbs	⅓ cup shortening
	½ cup snipped light or dark raisins
2 tablesp. chopped nuts	1 egg, well beaten
2 cups sifted all-purpose flour	½ cup milk
	1 tablesp. melted butter or margarine
3 teasp. baking powder	

1. Combine 2 tablesp. melted butter, 2 tablesp. sugar, ½ teasp. cinnamon, cereal flakes, nuts; set aside.
2. Start heating oven to 400°F. Grease 8″ x 8″ x 2″ pan or 9″ pie plate. Into large bowl, sift flour, baking powder, salt, ½ cup sugar, 1 teasp. cinnamon, mace. With pastry blender or 2 knives, scissor-fashion, cut in shortening until like coarse corn meal; add raisins.
3. Combine egg, milk; stir into flour mixture until just mixed, *no longer*. Turn into pan.
4. With pastry brush or crumbled waxed paper, brush batter with 1 tablesp. melted butter; then spread nut mixture on top. Bake 25 to 30 min., or until cake tester inserted in center comes out clean.

Serve hot or warm, cut into squares or wedges, as breakfast or dessert bread, or as snack with coffee. Makes 8 to 10 servings.

▶ **For 2:** Use 1 egg yolk; halve rest of ingredients. Bake in 6″ pie plate.

Crumbcake: Omit the 1 teasp. cinnamon, mace, and raisins.

Leftover Coffeecake: Split, butter, and toast leftover coffeecake under broiler.

BEST-EVER COFFEECAKE

3 cups sifted all- purpose flour	sugar, packed
3 teasp. double-acting baking powder	3 tablesp. flour 2½ to 3 tablesp. cinna- mon
1 teasp. salt	¾ cup melted butter or margarine
1 cup soft shortening	
1 cup granulated sugar	1½ cups light or dark raisins, rinsed in hot water
2 eggs, unbeaten	
1 cup milk	
1 teasp. vanilla extract	1½ cups coarsely chopped walnuts
1½ cups light-brown	

Start heating oven to 350°F. Grease bottoms of 2 8" x 8" x 2" pans. Sift the first 3 ingredients. With electric mixer at medium speed, or "cream" (or with spoon), thoroughly mix shortening with granulated sugar, then with eggs, until *very light and fluffy*—about 4 min. altogether. Then, at low speed, or "blend," beat in alternately, just until smooth, flour mixture in fourths and combined milk and vanilla in thirds. Spread one fourth of batter in each pan; top with one fourth of combined brown sugar, 3 tablesp. flour, and cinnamon; pour on one fourth of melted butter; then sprinkle with one fourth of raisins and nuts. Repeat. Bake 50 min., or until done. Makes 16 to 20 servings.

Note: Cake may also be baked in 1 13" x 10" x 2" pan 50 min., or until done.

BROWN FRUIT BREAD

2 cups sifted all- purpose flour	1 tablesp. grated orange or lemon rind
1 teasp. salt	1 cup milk
1 teasp. baking soda	¼ cup vinegar
1 tablesp. soft butter or margarine	1 tablesp. orange juice
½ cup brown sugar, packed	½ cup finely chopped nuts
1 egg	⅔ cup light or dark raisins

Start heating oven to 350°F. Wash and dry 2 empty No. 2 food cans; grease well. Sift flour, salt, soda; reserve about ¼ cup. In large bowl, with spoon, cream butter and sugar until fluffy; add egg and orange rind; beat till smooth. Combine milk, vinegar, orange juice; add alternately with flour mixture to sugar mixture. Combine nuts and raisins with reserved flour mixture; carefully fold into batter. Turn batter into cans; now tie on greased waxed or brown paper. Bake

1¼ hr. Run spatula around inside of can to loosen bread. Invert onto cake rack.

CHRISTMAS-TREE FRUIT BREAD

Filling:

½ cup chopped light or dark raisins	¼ cup chopped citron
¼ cup chopped candied cherries	⅓ cup granulated sugar ⅓ cup boiling water 1 tablesp. lemon juice

Tree:

2 cups sifted cake flour	shortening
2½ teasp. double-acting baking powder	1 teasp. grated lemon rind
¾ teasp. salt	1 egg, slightly beaten
3 tablesp. sugar	About ⅓ cup light cream
5 tablesp. soft	

Filling: Combine filling ingredients in order listed. Cook, stirring, over low heat until sugar melts and mixture is thick—about 10 min. Cool. *Tree:* Into mixing bowl, sift flour, baking powder, salt, sugar. With pastry blender or 2 knives, scissor-fashion, cut in shortening until like coarse corn meal; add lemon rind. Combine egg and cream; add to flour mixture, stirring only till soft dough is formed (about 20 strokes). Turn onto lightly floured surface; knead 20 times.

Start heating oven to 400°F. Divide dough in half; with hands, shape each half into triangle; roll each into ⅛"-thick fir-tree shape. Cut narrow strip off base of each triangle; cut strips in half crosswise. Lightly fold 1 triangle in half; lift to greased baking sheet; unfold. Fasten 2 strips at bottom to resemble trunk. Spread entire tree with filling almost to edges; moisten edges. Place remaining triangle, with remaining 2 strips, on top of filling. Press edges together.

On each side of tree, cut 4 slanting slits almost to center, to resemble branches; twist "branches" so filling shows. Bake 20 min. Let stand about 5 min.; then loosen with broad spatula. Mix confectioners' sugar with enough water to make thin frosting; drizzle over warm tree. Makes 8 to 10 servings.

P.S. This makes a pretty buffet bread when served on a piece of cardboard covered with aluminum foil.

EASY CHERRY-NUT BREAD

½ cup granulated sugar	¾ cup cut-up candied
1 egg	cherries
1¼ cups milk	3 cups packaged bis-
1 cup chopped nuts	cuit mix

Start heating oven to 350°F. Grease 10" x 5" x 3" loaf pan. In large mixing bowl, stir together sugar, egg, milk, nuts, cherries. Add biscuit mix; beat briskly 30 sec. (just count to 30); turn into pan.

Bake 45 to 50 min., or until done. (There will be a slight crack in top.) Cool slightly before slicing.

Nut Bread: Increase nuts to 1½ cups; omit cherries.

Orange-Nut Bread: Use ¾ cup sugar, 1 egg, 1¼ cups orange juice, ¾ cup chopped nuts, 1 tablesp. grated orange rind, 3 cups packaged biscuit mix.

Date-Nut: Substitute cut-up, pitted dates for cherries.

DATE-AND-NUT BREAD

¾ cup chopped walnuts	¾ cup boiling water
1 cup cut-up, pitted	2 eggs
dates	1 teasp. vanilla extract
1½ teasp. baking soda	1 cup granulated sugar
½ teasp. salt	1½ cups sifted all-
3 tablesp. shortening	purpose flour

With fork, mix walnuts, dates, soda, salt. Add shortening, water; let stand 20 min. Start heating oven to 350°F. Grease 9" x 5" x 3" loaf pan. With fork, beat eggs; beat in vanilla, sugar, flour. Mix in date mixture until just blended; turn into pan. Bake 1 hr. 5 min., or until done. Cool in pan 10 min.; remove. Cool overnight before slicing.

BANANA TEA BREAD

1¾ cups sifted all-	⅓ cup soft shortening
purpose flour	⅔ cup granulated sugar
2 teasp. baking powder	2 eggs, unbeaten
¼ teasp. baking soda	1 cup mashed ripe
½ teasp. salt	bananas (2 or 3)

Start heating oven to 350°F. Grease 9" x 5" x 3" loaf pan. Sift flour, baking powder, soda, salt. With electric mixer at medium speed, or "cream"

(or with spoon), thoroughly mix shortening with sugar, then with eggs, until *very light and fluffy*—about 4 min. altogether. Then, at low speed, or "blend," beat in flour mixture alternately with bananas just until smooth; turn into pan. Bake 1 hr., or until done. Cool in pan 10 min.; remove. Cool overnight before slicing.

Banana-Apricot: To flour mixture, add 1 cup finely cut-up dried apricots. (If apricots are very dry, first soak in warm water until soft; drain; dry well.)

Banana-Date: To flour mixture, add ½ cup chopped, pitted dates.

Banana-Nut: To flour mixture, add ½ cup coarsely chopped Brazil nuts.

Banana-Prune: To flour mixture, add 1 cup finely cut dried prunes. (If prunes are very dry, first soak in warm water until soft; drain; dry well.)

Banana-Raisin: To flour mixture, add 1 cup light or dark raisins.

APPLESAUCE NUT BREAD

2 cups sifted all-	1 cup coarsely chopped
purpose flour	walnuts
¾ cup granulated sugar	1 egg
3 teasp. baking powder	1 cup canned apple-
½ teasp. cinnamon	sauce
1 teasp. salt	2 tablesp. melted
½ teasp. baking soda	shortening

Start heating oven to 350°F. Grease 9" x 5" x 3" loaf pan. Onto waxed paper, sift flour, sugar, baking powder, cinnamon, salt, soda; add walnuts. In mixing bowl, beat egg; add applesauce, shortening. Add flour mixture; stir just until blended; turn into pan. Bake 1 hr. Cool in pan 10 min.; remove. Cool overnight before slicing.

BRAN-DATE BREAD

⅔ cup hot water	1 teasp. salt
1 cup pitted dates,	1 teasp. cinnamon
finely cut up	½ cup chopped nuts
1 cup ready-to-eat bran	2 tablesp. shortening
1½ cups sifted all-	⅔ cup granulated sugar
purpose flour	2 eggs, beaten
3 teasp. baking soda	

Start heating oven to 350°F. Grease 9″ x 5″ x 3″ loaf pan. Pour hot water over dates and bran; let stand. Sift flour, soda, salt, cinnamon; add chopped nuts. With spoon, cream shortening with sugar until fluffy; add eggs. Add flour mixture alternately with date mixture until just combined; turn into pan. Bake about 1 hr., or until done. Cool in pan 10 min.; remove. Cool overnight before slicing.

Gift Size: Halve each ingredient; bake in greased 5″ x 3″ x 2″ pan 40 min., or until done. *Or* grease 3 empty frozen-orange-juice-concentrate cans; fill with ½ recipe; bake 15 to 20 min., or until done.

CRANBERRY-RELISH BREAD

2 cups sifted all-purpose flour	3 tablesp. white vinegar plus enough water to make ⅔ cup
1 teasp. baking soda	
1 teasp. salt	¼ cup melted shortening
¾ cup granulated sugar	
1 egg	1 cup halved or coarsely chopped raw cranberries
⅓ cup orange juice	
1 teasp. grated orange rind	1 cup chopped nuts

Start heating oven to 350°F. Grease 9″ x 5″ x 3″ loaf pan. Into mixing bowl, sift flour, soda, salt, sugar. With fork, beat egg; stir in orange juice and rind, vinegar, water, shortening. Add, all at once, to flour mixture; stir just until all flour is moistened. Add cranberries and nuts; turn into pan. Bake 60 to 70 min., or until done. Cool in pan 10 min.; remove. Cool overnight before slicing.

FIG-NUT BREAD

1 cup hot water	3 teasp. double-acting baking powder
1 teasp. grated lemon rind	
	¾ cup granulated sugar
1 cup finely snipped dried figs	½ cup chopped walnuts
	1 egg, well beaten
3 cups sifted all-purpose flour	¼ cup melted shortening
1½ teasp. salt	

Start heating oven to 350°F. Grease bottom of 9″ x 5″ x 3″ loaf pan. Add water and lemon rind to figs; set aside for 10 min. Into mixing bowl, sift flour, salt, baking powder, sugar. To fig mixture, add walnuts, then egg and shortening; thoroughly blend with flour; turn into loaf

pan. Bake 1 hr. 10 min., or until done. Cool in pan 10 min.; remove. Cool overnight before slicing.

PRUNE BREAD

1 cup uncooked dried prunes	2 tablesp. sugar
	¼ cup shortening
3 cups sifted all-purpose flour	2 tablesp. grated orange rind
4 teasp. baking powder	2 eggs, beaten
½ teasp. baking soda	1 cup milk
1½ teasp. salt	

Start heating oven to 350°F. Grease 10″ x 5″ x 3″ loaf pan. If prunes are very dry, boil in water to cover, 5 min.; drain. Pit prunes; put prunes through food chopper, using medium blade. Sift flour, baking powder, soda, salt, sugar. Cut in shortening with pastry blender or 2 knives, scissor-fashion, until like coarse corn meal. Stir in prunes, rind. Combine eggs, milk; add to flour mixture; mix well; turn into pan. Bake 1 hr., or until done. Cool in pan 10 min.; remove. Cool overnight before slicing.

WALNUT BREAD

3 cups sifted all-purpose flour	powder
	1 egg, beaten
½ cup granulated sugar	1½ cups milk
1 teasp. salt	1 cup chopped walnuts
3¾ teasp. baking	3 tablesp. salad oil

Start heating oven to 375°F. Grease 9″ x 5″ x 3″ loaf pan. Sift flour, sugar, salt, baking powder. Combine egg with milk, then with walnuts, salad oil. Add to flour mixture; blend thoroughly; turn into pan. Bake 1 hr., or until done. Cool in pan 10 min.; remove. Cool overnight before slicing.

APRICOT-WALNUT BREAD

2 cups packaged biscuit mix	baking powder
	½ cup snipped dried apricots
1 cup uncooked rolled oats	1 cup broken walnuts
¾ cup granulated sugar	1 egg, well beaten
¼ teasp. salt	1¼ cups milk
1 teasp. double-acting	

Start heating oven to 350°F. Grease 9″ x 5″ x 3″ loaf pan. Stir biscuit mix with oats, sugar, salt, baking powder; add apricots, nuts. Combine egg, milk; add to dry ingredients. With spoon, beat hard 30 sec.; turn into pan. Bake 1 hr., or till done. Cool in pan 10 min.; remove. Cool overnight before slicing.

OATMEAL-RAISIN BREAD

2 cups sifted all-purpose flour	1 cup light or dark raisins
2 teasp. baking powder	1/3 cup shortening
3/4 teasp. baking soda	1/3 cup brown sugar, packed
1 1/2 teasp. salt	
1 cup uncooked rolled oats	1 egg
	1 1/4 cups buttermilk

Start heating oven to 350°F. Grease 9" x 5" x 3" loaf pan. Sift flour, baking powder, soda, salt; add oats, raisins. With electric mixer at medium speed, or "cream" (or with spoon), thoroughly mix shortening with sugar, then with egg, until *very light and fluffy*—about 4 min. altogether. Add buttermilk; then add this mixture in thirds to flour mixture, stirring after each addition until blended; turn into pan. Bake 1 hr., or until done. Cool in pan 10 min.; remove. Cool overnight before slicing.

STEAMED BOSTON BROWN BREAD

1 cup unsifted whole-wheat flour	1 1/2 teasp. salt
	3/4 cup molasses
1 cup unsifted rye flour	2 cups buttermilk or sour milk
1 cup yellow corn meal	
1 1/2 teasp. baking soda	

Grease and flour 2-qt. mold. Combine flours, corn meal, soda, salt. Stir in molasses, buttermilk. Turn into mold; cover tightly. Place on trivet in deep kettle. Add enough boiling water to kettle to come halfway up sides of mold; cover. Steam 3 1/2 hr., or until done. Remove from mold to cake rack.

Serve hot, with baked beans, boiled tongue, franks, etc. Makes 1 loaf.

Raisin: To flour mixture, add 1 cup seeded raisins.

Toasted: Butter slices of leftover brown bread; toast under broiler.

So Quick: Canned brown bread is delectable. To heat it for serving, *remove bread from can;* heat, covered, in colander set over boiling water.

IRISH SODA BREAD

4 cups sifted all-purpose flour	2 cups light or dark raisins
1/4 cup granulated sugar	1 1/3 cups buttermilk
1 teasp. salt	1 egg, unbeaten
1 teasp. baking powder	1 teasp. baking soda
2 tablesp. caraway seeds	1 egg yolk, or a little cream
1/4 cup butter or margarine	

Start heating oven to 375°F. Grease 2-qt. casserole. Into mixing bowl, sift flour, sugar, salt, baking powder; stir in caraway seeds. With pastry blender or 2 knives, scissor-fashion, cut in butter till like coarse corn meal; stir in raisins. Combine buttermilk, egg, soda; stir into flour mixture till just moistened.

Turn dough onto lightly floured surface; knead lightly till smooth; shape into ball. Place in casserole. With sharp knife, make 4" cross, 1/4" deep, in center. Brush with yolk, beaten with fork. Bake 1 hr. 10 min., or until done. Cool in pan 10 min.; remove. Cool before slicing.

PANCAKES, WAFFLES, DOUGHNUTS

Your Pancake Griddle

Greaseless griddles have a smooth, polished surface that helps keep batter from sticking. Greasing is not necessary if medium or low heat is used and fat is added to batter.

We recommend low heat for all griddles. Heat griddle until drops of cold water dance in small beads on surface. Then pour on batter.

Electric skillets are ideal for griddlecakes, because the heat is controlled. They can be used for cooking at table too.

HOMEMADE PANCAKES

1 1/4 cups sifted all-purpose flour	1 egg
	1 1/4 cups milk *
2 1/2 teasp. baking powder	3 tablesp. melted butter, margarine, or fat, or salad oil
2 tablesp. sugar	
3/4 teasp. salt	

1. Set griddle over low heat to warm up. Into medium bowl or wide-mouthed pitcher, sift flour, baking powder, sugar, salt.

Boston Brown Bread

1 c. enriched corn meal	1 c. rye flour
1 tsp. soda	¾ c. molasses
1 tsp. baking powder	2 c. buttermilk
1 tsp. salt	1 c. raisins, plumped and
1 c. whole wheat flour	drained

Sift together corn meal, soda, baking powder and salt. Stir in whole wheat and rye flours. Add molasses, butter-milk and raisins, stirring until blended. Pour batter into three well-greased cans (approximately 1 lb. 4-oz. cans or 2½-cup capacity). Cover with aluminum foil and tie with string. Place cans on trivet or rack in large kettle which has tight-fitting cover. Pour enough boiling water into kettle to cover bottom half of cans. Cover; bring water to boil. Reduce heat; gently boil three hours. (If necessary, add more water during steaming.) Remove foil. Place cans in preheated very hot oven (450 degrees) five minutes; cool five minutes. Loosen edges and remove from cans. Wrap cooled loaves in plastic wrap or aluminum foil and store in cool place. Makes 3 small loaves.

NOTE: Breads can be baked instead of steamed. To bake, place covered pans in preheated oven (400 degrees) about one hour. Cool five minutes; loosen edges and remove from cans.

step 1. To batter, add 1 cup finely chopped, pared, cored cooking apples.

Blueberry: To batter, add ½ cup sweetened blueberries. Or before turning each pancake, sprinkle with 1 teasp. fresh or unthawed frozen blueberries.

Corn: Substitute ½ cup yellow or white corn meal for ½ cup flour.

QUICK PANCAKES

Packaged mixes for pancakes, muffins, biscuits, corn muffins, and buckwheat cakes all make wonderful pancakes in jig time. Make as label directs, and vary pancakes or pancake batter in any of these delightful ways:

Vary the Batter:

Nutty: To batter, add ¾ to 1 cup finely chopped nuts. Or sprinkle nuts on top of stack of pancakes. Serve with syrup or ice cream.

Apfel Pfannkuchen: To batter, add about 1 cup grated, pared, cored tart cooking apples;

1 tablesp. lemon juice; and 2 tablesp. sugar. Serve with sugar and cinnamon or syrup.

Pineapple: To batter, add ½ cup well-drained canned crushed pineapple and dash of ground cloves. Serve with fried ham, sausages, etc.

Cheese: To batter, add ½ cup grated sharp process cheese. Serve with creamed meats or vegetables, or with syrup.

Corn: To batter, add 1 cup canned vacuum-packed whole-kernel corn and ½ teasp. paprika. Serve with creamed dried beef or ham, or with syrup.

Frank: Before turning pancakes, dot with thin frank slices. Serve with honey, stirred into soft butter or margarine, or with creamed vegetables.

Blueberry: Before turning pancakes, sprinkle with unthawed frozen or fresh blueberries. Serve with honey stirred into soft butter or margarine.

Vary the Cakes:

Peach: Top pancakes with sliced or halved canned peaches in their syrup, to which bit of nutmeg has been added.

Mexicana: Spoon heated canned chile con carne over each pancake; sprinkle with 1 tablesp. each minced onion and grated process American cheese. Roll up each pancake; sprinkle with 1 tablesp. more cheese. Serve 2 cakes per person.

Tropical: Top each stack of pancakes with heated canned pineapple slice. Nice with sausages, etc.

A la Washington: Make 8″ or 9″ pancakes; spread with butter or margarine, then with tart jelly or jam or canned jellied cranberry sauce. Stack cakes. Top stack with sifted confectioners' sugar; then cut stack into wedge-shaped pieces. Serve as dessert.

Curried Tuna: Stir ⅓ cup milk and 1 teasp. curry powder into 1 can undiluted condensed cream-of-mushroom soup. Add 1 can chunk-style tuna; heat. Spoon over pancakes.

Strawberry: Put pancakes together in stacks of 3, with lumps of butter or margarine and thawed frozen sliced strawberries as filling; top with butter and berries. (One 12-oz. pkg. frozen strawberries provides 4 servings.)

Ham-Filled: Put spoonful of deviled ham between and on top of each stack of hot cakes. Serve with maple or maple-blended syrup, or with brown sugar.

CORN-MEAL PANCAKES

½ cup sifted all-purpose flour	1 tablesp. sugar
3 teasp. baking powder	½ cup boiling water
½ cup sifted water-ground corn meal	¼ cup milk
	¼ cup melted shortening
½ teasp. salt	1 egg, well beaten

Sift flour with baking powder. Into bowl, sift corn meal, salt, sugar. Slowly stir in boiling water; beat well. Stir in flour. Slowly stir in milk, shortening; fold in egg.

Drop batter by tablespoonfuls onto hot griddle, spreading each cake with back of spoon into round. Cook until cakes are puffy, full of bubbles, and edges are cooked. Turn; cook other side.

Serve as in Homemade Pancakes, p. 334. Makes about 20 small thin cakes.

To Vary: Reduce flour to ¼ cup; with flour and baking powder, sift ¼ cup additional water-ground corn meal.

BUTTERMILK GRIDDLECAKES

1 cup sifted all-purpose flour	1 cup buttermilk or sour milk
½ teasp. baking soda	1 tablesp. melted butter or margarine
¼ teasp. salt	
1 egg, separated	

Sift flour, soda, salt. In small bowl, with egg beater, beat egg white until it forms moist peaks; set aside. In medium bowl, using same beater (do not wash), beat egg yolk and buttermilk just till blended. Stir in flour mixture, then melted butter; stir till smooth. Fold in egg white. Drop by tablespoonfuls onto hot griddle. Cook until cakes are puffy, full of bubbles, and edges are cooked. Turn; cook other side.

Serve as in Homemade Pancakes, p. 334. Makes about 10.

Your Waffle Iron

1. *Carefully read and follow directions* that come with the waffle iron.
2. *Season grids of waffle iron* before using them, to prevent waffles from sticking, unless manufacturer advises to the contrary. To season, brush *cold* grids well with vegetable shortening or salad oil. Heat to baking temperature; let cool again.
3. *When making waffles for the first time* in waffle iron, discard first waffle; it will be very greasy. After that, waffles made according to our recipes should not stick.

If Waffles Stick

Once waffle grids have been seasoned, *never wash them.* If waffle particles stick to grids, before baking any more waffles, brush off particles with a wire brush.

LIBBY'S HOT WAFFLES

1½ cups sifted all-purpose flour	2 cups milk
3 teasp. double-acting baking powder	2 eggs, separated
	¼ cup melted butter or margarine, or salad oil
½ teasp. salt	
2 teasp. sugar	

1. Start heating waffle iron as manufacturer directs.
2. Into large bowl or wide-mouthed pitcher, sift flour, baking powder, salt, sugar.
3. Slowly stir in milk, beaten egg yolks, then melted butter.
4. Fold in egg whites, beaten stiff.
5. When waffle iron is ready to use, pour batter into center of lower half until it spreads about 1″ from edges. Bring cover down gently. Cook as manufacturer directs. *Do not raise cover during baking.*
6. When waffle is done, lift cover; loosen waffle with fork; serve at once. Reheat iron before pouring in next waffle. Makes about 6.

Serve as:
Breakfast main dish, with butter and favorite syrup, honey, apple butter, or molasses
Accompaniment for sausages, bacon, creamed

dried beef, creamed chicken, creamed mushrooms, creamed fish, chicken curry, etc.
Dessert, topped with fruit or ice cream

Berry: Just before folding in beaten egg whites, fold in 1 cup fresh blueberries, sweetened to taste.

Cheese: Just before adding butter, add 1 cup grated process American cheese (¼ lb.). Serve topped with any creamed vegetable or with creamed ham, etc.

Corn: After adding butter, add 1 cup canned vacuum-packed whole-kernel corn. Nice with fried chicken, chicken fricassee, creamed chicken or ham, etc.

Curry: To batter, add ½ teasp. curry powder. Serve with creamed chicken or turkey.

Ham: Spread hot baked waffles with deviled ham. Serve with favorite syrup.

Pecan: To dry ingredients, add ½ to ¾ cup finely chopped pecans.

Coconut: To batter, add 1 cup snipped shredded coconut. Serve with butterscotch sauce.

DE LUXE WAFFLES

2 cups sifted all-purpose flour	sour milk
3 teasp. baking powder	4 eggs, well beaten
1 teasp. baking soda	1 cup melted butter, margarine, or fat, or salad oil
1 teasp. salt	
2 cups buttermilk or	

Sift flour, baking powder, soda, salt. Combine buttermilk, eggs; add to flour mixture. With egg beater or electric mixer at high speed, beat until smooth; stir in butter. Bake in waffle iron as manufacturer directs.
Serve as in Libby's Hot Waffles, p. 336.

SPEEDY WAFFLES

Packaged frozen waffles are delicious. To heat, let stand at room temperature 15 min. Then toast in electric toaster or in broiler, until hot.

You can make luscious waffles from packaged waffle, pancake, biscuit, muffin, or corn-muffin mix too. Just follow label directions.

FRENCH DOUGHNUTS

¼ cup granulated sugar	1 cup hot water
1 teasp. salt	1 cup sifted all-purpose flour
1 tablesp. grated orange rind	
¼ cup shortening	3 eggs

In medium saucepan, place sugar, salt, orange rind, shortening. Add hot water; bring to boil. Add flour, all at once; stir until smooth. Cook, stirring, until mixture leaves sides of pan in ball and spoon pressed into mixture leaves clear impression. Remove from heat; add eggs, one at a time, beating after each addition till smooth.

Cut 10 3″ squares of aluminum foil or waxed paper; grease each. Using cookie press and rosette tube, or teaspoon, form dough into 2½″ rings, placing 1 ring on each square of foil. Let stand 15 min.

Heat fat to 370°F. as in To Fry, Old-fashioned Doughnuts, below. Then hold 1 ring of dough close to surface of fat; slip off foil into fat. Repeat. Fry as directed; drain on paper towels. When doughnuts are cool, spread tops with Sugar Glaze, p. 465. Makes 10.

OLD-FASHIONED DOUGHNUTS

3½ cups sifted all-purpose flour	2 eggs
2 teasp. baking powder	3 tablesp. soft shortening
1 teasp. baking soda	1 cup granulated sugar
½ teasp. cinnamon	¾ cup buttermilk or sour milk
½ teasp. nutmeg	
½ teasp. mace	½ cup minced nuts (optional)
1 teasp. salt	

Sift flour, baking powder, soda, cinnamon, nutmeg, mace, salt. In large electric-mixer bowl, with mixer at medium speed, or "cream" (or with spoon), beat eggs well; beat in shortening, sugar, then buttermilk. Add flour mixture, all at once; beat just until smooth. Quickly mix in nuts. Refrigerate 1 hr. or longer. On floured surface, roll dough ½″ thick. With floured doughnut cutter, cut out doughnuts. Form dough trimmings into ball; roll; then cut.

To Fry: Fry doughnuts in 1½″ fat or salad oil, heated to 370°F. on deep-fat frying thermometer, or until square of day-old bread browns in 60 sec. (See Shallow Frying, p. 8.) Fry only as many doughnuts at one time as will float easily on fat. As soon as doughnuts rise to surface, turn with long-handled fork (don't pierce). Turn often thereafter until golden and done. Remove with fork; hold over fat 1 sec.; drain on paper towels. Or deep-fry as on p. 7.

Serve as is. Or dust with sugar, or sugar and cinnamon. Or shake, a few at a time, in paper bag containing sugar. Makes about 2½ doz.

"Holes": Use centers cut out from doughnuts; or using small biscuit cutter, cut all dough into "holes." Fry and sugar. Nice with tea or fruit compote.

Chocolate: Omit spices; increase sugar to 1¼ cups. After adding sugar, add 1½ sq. melted unsweetened chocolate and 1 teasp. vanilla extract.

Drops: With rubber scraper, push heaping teaspoonfuls of dough into hot fat; then fry and sugar.

SO-EASY GOLDEN PUFFS

2 cups sifted all-purpose flour	1 teasp. salt
¼ cup granulated sugar	1 teasp. nutmeg or mace
3 teasp. double-acting baking powder	¼ cup salad oil
	¾ cup milk
	1 egg

Combine all ingredients. With fork, stir until well mixed. Fry teaspoonfuls of mixture at 375°F. until golden brown—about 3 min.—as in To Fry, Old-fashioned Doughnuts, p. 337. Drain; then roll in cinnamon-sugar mixture; or spread top with Sugar Glaze, p. 465. Makes about 2½ doz.

QUICK DOUGHNUT PUFFS

1 can refrigerated pan-ready biscuits	Cinnamon sugar
	Confectioners' sugar

Fry pan-ready biscuits at 370°F. as in To Fry, Old-fashioned Doughnuts, p. 337.

Serve warm, letting guests dip doughnut puffs into cinnamon or confectioners' sugar. Makes 10. If preferred, halve biscuits; fry.

RAISED DOUGHNUTS

1 cup milk	3 tablesp. butter or margarine
1 pkg. active dry, or 1 cake compressed, yeast	¾ cup granulated sugar
¼ cup warm (not hot) or lukewarm water	1 egg
1 tablesp. sugar	1½ teasp. nutmeg
1½ cups sifted all-purpose flour	1 teasp. salt
	3 cups sifted all-purpose flour

Scald milk; cool in large electric-mixer bowl till lukewarm. Sprinkle or crumble yeast onto warm water (for compressed yeast, use lukewarm water); stir until dissolved. Stir into milk, with 1 tablesp. sugar. Add 1½ cups flour; with mixer (or egg beater), beat well. Cover with clean towel; let rise in warm place (about 85°F.) about 1 hr.

In small mixer bowl, with mixer at medium speed, or "cream" (or with spoon), beat butter with ¾ cup sugar, then with egg, nutmeg, and salt, until light and fluffy. Beat into yeast mixture. Beat in 3 cups flour; place in well-greased bowl.

Brush dough with salad oil. Cover with clean towel; let rise in warm place (about 85°F.) until doubled in bulk. Turn onto lightly floured surface; roll ½" thick. Cut with floured doughnut cutter. Place on floured board. Cover with towel; let rise in warm place until doubled in bulk.

Fry and serve as in To Fry, Old-fashioned Doughnuts, p. 337. Makes about 2½ doz.

Jelly: On floured surface, roll dough ¼" thick. With floured cookie cutter, cut into 2½" rounds. Place ½ teasp. jelly or jam in center of half of rounds. Moisten edges with cold water; top with remaining rounds, pinching edges together firmly. Cover with towel; let rise; fry.

Raised Crullers: Roll dough ½" thick. Cut into strips, about 8" x 1". Fold each strip in half lengthwise; twist several times; pinch ends together. Cover; let rise; fry.

Yeast Breads

Even though today's busy life leaves little time for breadmaking, you can serve superb breads and rolls on short notice. There's a delectable assortment to choose from—ready-to-eat or brown-and-serve—at your baker's or grocer's. And you can make them distinctively yours by glamorizing them as suggested in Bread and Rolls You Buy, p. 340.

When you do have time, try The Rolls You Make, p. 346, Coffeecakes You Make, p. 349, and The Breads You Make, p. 345. Every recipe is guaranteed to bring back fond memories of Grandmother's kitchen on baking day!

Before using these recipes, refer to How to Use Our Recipes, p. 3, and Pots and Pans, p. 692. Always use standard measuring cups and measuring spoons; measure level.

When You Store Bread

First Choice: In Home Freezer or Freezer of Refrigerator-Freezer Combination. The best place to store bread is in the home freezer or freezer of your refrigerator-freezer combination, at 10°F. or lower. Properly cooled bread, wrapped airtight in moistureproof material and stored in the freezer, will retain its moisture, remain free of mold, and keep its freshness for several weeks.

Second Choice: In Ventilated Breadbox. The next best place to store bread is in a ventilated breadbox at room temperature. Wrapped in waxed paper, bread will stay acceptably fresh several days, but is more subject to mold than when stored in refrigerator or home freezer.

Third Choice: In Refrigerator. The least desirable place to store bread is in the food compartment of the refrigerator. Here wrapped bread retains its moisture and is less subject to mold but stales more rapidly than in the breadbox.

Reheating Bread

In Aluminum Foil: Snugly wrap bread slices or rolls in aluminum foil. Bake at 375°F. about 20 min., or till heated. If they're served in foil wrappings (turn foil edges down to form basket), they'll keep hot to the last delicious crumb.

In Covered Skillet: Put 2 tablesp. water in large skillet. Place round trivet in bottom, with rolls on it. Cover; leave over low heat 10 min., or until rolls are hot.

In Paper Bag: Moisten rolls by passing them quickly through running water from faucet. Bake in tightly closed paper bag at 350°F. about 15 to 18 min., or till heated.

In Original Package: Heat bakers' rolls in 350°F. oven about 15 min.

Toasted: Split rolls or muffins; spread with butter or margarine; sprinkle with grated cheese, seasoned salt, poppy seeds, etc. if desired; broil until golden.

To reheat frozen bread, toast slices, unthawed, right in electric toaster. Or if you're reheating a quantity of slices, broil until golden, turning.

Coffeecake: Reheat in aluminum foil, covered skillet, or paper bag as on p. 339; serve cut into strips. Or split, brush with butter or margarine; then broil till golden.

BREAD AND ROLLS YOU BUY

FAN-TAN LOAF

In 10″ x 5″ x 3″ loaf pan, place day-old loaf of bakers' sliced bread, with top side up. Fill, then top, as below. Bake at 425°F. 15 min., or until hot and toasty. If baking only part of a loaf, use inverted custard cup to prop it up in pan.

Serve in loaf form; or cut apart with scissors.

Cheesy: Between slices, spread soft butter or margarine mixed with a little prepared mustard; then spread with some grated cheese or cheese spread (or insert halved cheese slices). Spread top of loaf with a little mayonnaise or soft butter. Sprinkle with grated cheese, then with a little grated onion, snipped chives, or a few sliced scallions, tossed with melted butter.

Relish: Between slices and over top of loaf, spread soft butter or margarine mixed with a little garlic salt and one of these: prepared mustard, horse-radish, snipped parsley, or blue cheese.

Savory: Between slices and over top of loaf, spread soft butter or margarine mixed with one of these: celery, garlic, seasoned, or onion salt; dried thyme; curry or chili powder plus garlic salt. Sprinkle with celery or poppy seeds or paprika.

TOASTED ROLLS IN LOAF

1. Buy loaf of unsliced bread (it's wise to place order a day ahead). Trim crusts from top and sides of loaf. (For rounded top, peel off top crust.)
2. Cut *almost* through to bottom crust of loaf in any of 5 ways below.

Squares: Cut crosswise into 1½″ slices, then lengthwise through middle.
Jumbo Slices: Cut crosswise into 1″ slices.
Thinsies: Cut crosswise into as thin slices as possible.
Tipsy Slices: Cut crosswise into ¾″ slices,

drawing knife on extreme slant down through bread.
Diamonds: Cut diagonally into 2″ crosswise slices. Then cut diagonally in opposite direction, to form diamonds.

3. Spread cut surfaces, top, and sides of loaf with one of mixtures below. Bake in shallow pan at 400°F. 18 min., or until golden.
To serve: Snip apart.

Savory Cheese: Mix ½ cup soft butter or margarine, ¼ cup minced onion, 1 tablesp. each prepared mustard and poppy seeds. Arrange halved or quartered Swiss-cheese slices between cuts; top loaf with 2 halved bacon slices.

Butter Crust: Cream ½ cup soft butter or margarine with one of these:

Blue cheese and a little minced onion
Grated process sharp American cheese (2 to 3 cups)
Snipped parsley or chives, or grated onion (¼ cup)
Dried savory and thyme (½ teasp. each), plus some snipped parsley and garlic salt
Light-brown sugar and cinnamon

Fluffy Cheese: Cream ¼ cup soft butter or margarine with 1 cup grated process sharp American cheese. Beat in 2 egg yolks. Fold in 2 egg whites, beaten stiff.

Ham and Cheese: Mix 1 4½-oz. can deviled ham with 2 3-oz. pkg. soft cream cheese and 1 teasp. each lemon juice and horse-radish.

Cream Cheese: Mix 1 3-oz. pkg. soft cream cheese; 2 tablesp. milk; 1 cup grated process sharp American cheese; 1 tablesp. each snipped parsley, horse-radish, and pimento; 1 teasp. each grated onion and lemon juice; and ¼ teasp. salt. After spreading mixture on loaf, wrap loaf in aluminum foil, leaving top open.

Celery: Mix ½ cup soft butter or margarine, ¼ teasp. salt, dash cayenne pepper, ¼ teasp. paprika, ½ teasp. celery seeds. Salad oil or vegetable shortening may replace butter; if so, double salt and paprika.

SUPPER CUTS

Cut loaf of day-old unsliced bread as in Quick Coffeecake, p. 341. Then spread cut surfaces, top, and sides with one of mixtures suggested in Toasted Rolls in Loaf, p. 340.

SAVORY FRENCH BREAD

Use yard-long or junior-size loaf of French bread. Slash into thin, thick, or diagonal slices, *almost* through to bottom crust. If desired, rub garlic very lightly over crust.

Spread cut surfaces with one or more of the spreads below. (If desired, wrap in aluminum foil, leaving foil partially open at top.) Bake at 375°F. 15 to 20 min.

Buttery Spreads: Cream ½ cup soft butter or margarine with one of these:

¼ teasp. each paprika and salt
2 tablesp. each snipped chives or minced onion, plus snipped parsley
2 tablesp. anchovy paste or prepared mustard
½ cup crumbled blue cheese, plus 2 tablesp. snipped chives
Generous pinch dried herbs

Creamy Spreads: To ½ cup commercial sour cream, add ¼ teasp. each salt and horse-radish, plus dash pepper. Then add one of these:

½ 6-oz. pkg. flavored cream cheese
½ teasp. celery or poppy seeds
½ teasp. garlic, celery, or onion salt
1 teasp. paprika or curry powder
Pinch herbs and a little prepared mustard

Cheese Spreads: Use one of these:

Soft chive cream cheese, with salt and milk to moisten
Smoky-, sharp-, or pimento-cheese spread
Soft cream cheese, seasoned with horse-radish and garlic salt, with milk to moisten
Any flavored process-cheese-food roll, cut into thin rings (tuck into slashes)
Grated cheese, mixed with snipped parsley, garlic salt, and a little lemon juice
Grated cheese, mixed with caraway seeds, onion salt, and mayonnaise to moisten

Garlicky Spread: To ½ cup salad oil or soft butter or margarine, add bit of minced or mashed garlic, or garlic salt, plus snipped parsley or fresh or dried herbs if desired. Before baking loaf, sprinkle with grated Parmesan cheese.

Note: Now you can buy a delicious, ready-to-use garlic spread in jars.

French Onion-Cheese Loaf: Use one of Buttery Spreads above. Before baking loaf, into each gash, insert 1 thin cheese slice and 1 thin onion slice.

FRENCH HALF-AND-HALF

Split long loaf of French bread lengthwise in half. Slash each half into 1¼″ diagonal slices, *almost* through to bottom crust. Top each half with one of spreads for Savory French Bread, above. Bake at 375°F. 10 to 15 min., until golden.

JUNIOR LOAVES
(from hard or soft rolls)

Use hard or soft white, wheat, French, or frankfurter rolls. Slash each, almost through to bottom crust, into 2 or 3 thick chunks. Spread with one of spreads in Savory French Bread, above. Bake at 425°F. 10 min.

TOASTY SWEET BREADS
(nice with tea, coffee, or cocoa)

Raisin Rolls in Loaf: Cut loaf of unsliced raisin bread crosswise into 1½″ slices, *almost* through to bottom crust; then cut lengthwise through center *almost* to bottom. Brush cut surfaces and top with melted butter or margarine. Sprinkle with mixture of sugar and cinnamon. Bake at 375°F. 15 min., or until golden.

Quick Coffeecake: From loaf of day-old unsliced white bread, trim crusts. Cut loaf lengthwise in half. Cut each half into 1½″ slices, *almost* through to bottom crust; then cut each half lengthwise, *almost* through to bottom, to form squares.

Spread cut surfaces, top, and sides with soft butter or margarine, or salad oil. Then cover each half with one of mixtures below. Bake at 375°F. 15 to 20 min. To serve, break "rolls" apart.

Nutted: Mix brown sugar, chopped nuts.
Coconut: Mix sweetened condensed milk, shredded coconut, chopped nuts.
Honey: Mix honey with brown sugar; top with chopped nuts.

Rum-Raisin: Mix ¼ cup white corn syrup with 1 tablesp. rum; top with 2 tablesp. each raisins and chopped nuts, 1 tablesp. sugar, ¼ teasp. cinnamon.

Sugar and Spice: Mix sugar, cinnamon.

SLICETTES

To Bake: Use all white-, or half white- and half wheat-bread slices. Cut slices in half. Stand, with cut edges up, in loaf pan or shallow "box" made of folded aluminum foil.

Between slices and over top of "loaf", spread one of mixtures below. Bake at 450°F. 15 min., or until toasted.

Cheesy (with soup or salad): Mix grated cheese with mayonnaise. Or thin chive cream cheese with milk.

Savory (for dinner): Substitute mayonnaise for butter in Savory Fan-tan Loaf, p. 340.

Crispy (for lunch): Use soft butter or margarine, alone or mixed with one of these:

Celery, garlic, or onion salt	Dried thyme or rosemary
Prepared mustard	Curry powder
Horse-radish	Snipped parsley

Tealets (with hot drinks): Spread bread first with butter or margarine; then top with one of these:

Cinnamon-sugar	cranberry sauce
Brown sugar and coconut	Marmalade
Cream cheese and marmalade or canned jellied	Honey and grated orange rind or cinnamon

To Broil:

Pizza Style: Toast bread slices on one side in broiler. Turn; spread with butter or margarine; top with cheese spread, a little anchovy paste, then with chili sauce and pinch orégano. Broil till bubbly.

Imitation Onion Focaccia: Slice scallions medium fine. Add equal parts of soft pimento cream cheese and butter or margarine. Season (p. 6). Spread on ½" slices French bread. Broil until bubbly. Cut into strips.

EASY BREAD STICKS

From Frankfurter or Hard Rolls: Quarter rolls lengthwise. Spread cut sides, or all sides, with soft butter or margarine or salad oil. Roll in one of these: snipped parsley or chives; minced nuts; poppy, caraway, or celery seeds; grated Parmesan cheese; bit of dried rosemary or thyme. Bake at 425°F. 5 to 10 min. Or broil till golden brown.

From Unsliced Bread: From loaf of day-old unsliced bread, trim crusts. Cut lengthwise into ¾" slices; then cut each slice into 4" x ¾" strips. Brush strips on all sides except bottom with melted butter or margarine, or salad oil. Then roll in, spread, or sprinkle with one of mixtures below. Bake at 350°F. 20 min., or until golden. Or broil till golden brown.

Poppy, celery, or caraway seeds
Finely chopped nuts
Grated process pimento or sharp American cheese, mixed with celery seeds, snipped parsley, or minced garlic
Finely chopped stuffed olives and nuts

PULLED BREAD

From loaf of day-old unsliced bread, peel crusts. Then, with 2 forks, pull off 1½" slices. With fork, tear each slice into thirds. Bake on rack in shallow pan, turning often, at 350°F. 20 to 25 min., or until golden.

MELBA TOAST

Melba: Cut day-old unsliced bread into ⅛" slices. If you like, remove crusts; then cut bread slices diagonally into triangles. Bake at 325°F. 15 min., or until golden crisp and curled, turning once. Serve hot or cold, with soup, salad, or main course.

Easy Melba: Your grocer carries delicious packaged Melba toast.

FILLED BUTTER-FLAKE ROLLS

Partly separate leaves of packaged butter-flake rolls. Spread *all* leaves with soft butter or margarine; then spread *a few* leaves with one of fillings below.

For toasted rolls, set rolls in muffin-pan cups;

for soft rolls, wrap in aluminum foil. Bake at 425°F. 5 to 10 min.

Fillings:

Marmalade or preserves, mixed with chopped nuts

Blue cheese or grated Parmesan, mixed with butter

Mayonnaise, mixed with garlic salt (omit butter)

Brown sugar and cinnamon or nuts, mixed with butter

Curry powder and snipped parsley, added to butter

Peanut butter, mixed with honey and bit of grated orange rind

Cottage cheese, in half of each roll; strawberry or other jam in other half. Bake in foil

Deviled ham, alternated with grated cheese

Cheese spread, mixed with bit of prepared mustard or chili sauce

Chive cream cheese, or smoky- or pimento-cheese spread, thinned with milk

Grated tuna or mashed sardines, mixed with mayonnaise, chili sauce, and snipped parsley. Bake in foil

BROWN-AND-SERVE STICKIES

Packaged bakers' brown-and-serve rolls come completely "raised" and almost completely baked. The golden crust appears with the last-minute baking you give them.

In bottom of 9″ x 5″ x 3″ loaf pan, spread one of mixtures below. Place 8 brown-and-serve soft rolls (such as clover leafs or fan-tans) upside down, on mixture. Bake at 400°F. 25 min. Let stand 1 min.; invert pan; remove rolls.

Nut: Mix 3 tablesp. melted butter or margarine; ⅓ cup brown sugar, packed, and 3 tablesp. chopped nuts.

Caramel-Orange: Mix ¼ cup granulated sugar, 1 teasp. grated orange rind, 1½ tablesp. orange juice, ¼ teasp. mace, and 1 tablesp. melted butter or margarine.

GLAZE-TOPPED BROWN-AND-SERVES

In each greased muffin-pan cup, place one of mixtures below. Arrange brown-and-serve soft rolls, upside down, on mixture in cups. Bake at 400°F. 15 min. Let stand 1 min.; invert pan; remove. Serve at once.

Coconut: Mix 2 teasp. brown sugar, 1 teasp. shredded coconut, 1 teasp. melted butter or margarine, ½ teasp. water.

Butterscotch: Boil, 8 to 10 min., ¼ cup butter or margarine; ½ cup brown sugar, packed; and 1 tablesp. water. Place tablespoonful of this syrup in each greased muffin cup. Sprinkle with chopped nuts.

Orange: Mix ¼ teasp. orange juice and pinch grated orange rind. (When rolls are baked, drizzle on icing made by mixing ½ cup confectioners' sugar with about 1 tablesp. orange juice.)

TOASTED ENGLISH MUFFINS
(plus variations)

Buy packaged English muffins. For toasting, they're best broken apart, *not cut;* the uneven inner surfaces and porous texture hold the butter well. To split, make small cut with knife near edge of muffin; then insert fingers into cut, and gently pull muffin apart.

Spread torn surfaces with butter or margarine. Toast under broiler.

To Vary: After spreading muffins with butter, top with one of these; then toast under broiler.

Soft cream cheese, then bit of jelly
Caraway, celery, or poppy seeds
Grated cheese or crumbled blue cheese
Cinnamon and sugar, then chopped nuts
Grated Parmesan cheese, then garlic salt
Soft sharp-cheese spread, then a little catchup, grated Parmesan cheese, snipped anchovies, garlic salt, and dried thyme

CINNAMON TOAST

Mix 1 teasp. cinnamon with 3 tablesp. sugar. Or use packaged cinnamon-sugar mixture. Sprinkle generously over hot buttered toast. Serve hot, as is, or cut into strips or triangles.

Or toast bread on one side in broiler. Then turn; butter untoasted side; sprinkle with cinnamon-sugar mixture; broil until bubbly. Serve hot.

To Vary: For cinnamon mixture, substitute brown or maple sugar; honey; grated cheese; or blend of 1 tablesp. orange juice, 1 tablesp. grated orange rind, and ½ cup granulated sugar.

CINNAMON-PUFF TOAST

From loaf of unsliced bread, cut 3 1″-thick slices. Remove crusts; cut each slice into 3 strips.

Quickly dip strips into ⅓ cup heavy cream. Brush with 2 tablesp. melted butter or margarine; then coat thickly on all sides with 1 tablesp. cinnamon mixed with 3 tablesp. sugar. Arrange on rack set in shallow baking pan. Bake at 400°F. 20 min. Makes 9 toast fingers.

MILK TOAST

Toast, then butter, white-, whole-wheat-, or rye-bread slices. Arrange 2 slices in each heated soup plate or bowl. Pour on about 1 cup hot milk seasoned with a little salt and pepper.

FRENCH TOAST

2 eggs	Butter, margarine, or
½ teasp. salt	bacon fat
1 tablesp. sugar	6 white- or whole-
¼ cup milk	wheat-bread slices

Break eggs into shallow dish; with fork, beat lightly; stir in salt, sugar, milk. Heat a little butter in skillet. *Quickly* dip bread slices, one at a time, into egg mixture; turn until just well coated. In hot butter, brown at once on both sides. Makes 6 servings.

Serve immediately with one of these:

Crisp bacon or fried ham
Butter and syrup, molasses, jelly, jam, marmalade, honey, or applesauce
Confectioners' sugar; sprinkling lemon juice

Fluffy: Separate eggs. Beat whites with salt and sugar until stiff. Beat yolks until thick and lemon-colored; add milk. Fold whites into yolks. Dip bread into mixture; brown as above.

De Luxe: Substitute light or heavy cream for milk; add 2 teasp. sherry.

Petite: Slice hard rolls or French bread ½″ or ¾″ thick. Dip and sauté as above. Or dip slices into maple or maple-blended syrup; then sauté in butter or margarine till golden on both sides.

Sandwich Style: Butter 1 slice hot French toast; cover with one of fillings below; place second slice of toast on filling; add topping.

Cranberry: Fill with canned jellied cranberry slices. Sprinkle with confectioners' sugar.
Banana: Fill with sliced bananas. Top with maple-blended syrup.
Marmalade: Fill with orange marmalade. Top with orange slices or sections.

Oven-Style: Arrange dipped bread slices on well-greased cookie sheet. Bake at 500°F. 5 min. on each side.

TOAST

In Oven: Butter thinly sliced bread. Top with one of the following. Bake at 425°F. as directed.

Cream cheese, topped with marmalade, canned jellied cranberry sauce, or bits of blue cheese. Bake 8 min.
Snipped parsley or chives. Bake 5 min.

Broiler: Toast bread on one side in broiler. Then turn; butter; top with one of the following; finish toasting in broiler.

Prepared mustard and thin onion rings
Cheese spread, dots of anchovy paste, chili sauce, then orégano
Honey, then sprinkling of cinnamon
Honey, mixed with grated orange rind
Brown sugar, then chopped nuts or coconut

In Skillet: Melt butter or margarine in skillet. Sprinkle with paprika or celery, garlic, or onion salt. Sauté bread slices in this mixture till golden on both sides.

In Waffle Iron: Bake unbuttered bread slices in waffle iron till golden.

In Electric Toaster: Just pop bread into toaster. Today's toasters are better than ever.

MOCK PATTY SHELLS

Toast Cups: Brush thinly sliced bread (crusts removed) with melted butter or margarine. Press each slice into 3″ muffin-pan cup. Bake at 375°F. about 12 min., or until golden.

Use as patty shells to hold creamed mixture.

Croustades or Toast Cases: Cut unsliced bread 2″ thick; remove crusts. Cut into squares or

oblongs; or with cutter, cut into rounds or hearts. Hollow out, leaving ⅜"-thick wall. Brush with melted butter or margarine. Bake at 375°F. about 12 to 15 min., or until golden. Use as patty shells to hold creamed mixture. Use leftover crumbs as on p. 554.

Cheese Croustades: When Croustades, p. 344, are partially toasted, brush with melted butter or margarine; then sprinkle with grated cheese.

Cracker Toast: Mix 2 cups fine saltine crumbs (about 30) with 6 tablesp. butter or margarine and 2 teasp. grated onion until crumbly. Press into 11" x 7" x 1½" baking pan; cut into 8 squares. Bake at 400°F. 15 min. Serve hot, topped with any creamed mixture. Makes 8 servings.

THE BREADS YOU MAKE

Bread—from Dough to Loaf

Before you begin, be sure that utensils, work surface, and your hands are clean. This is a must for good bread.

INGREDIENTS

Flour: Read about All-Purpose Flour, p. 517.

Liquid: Milk and water are the liquids ordinarily used in yeast breads. The milk may be whole, diluted evaporated, or nonfat dry.

Temperature Is Important: Because yeast is a living plant, too much heat can kill the yeast's action, while not enough heat can slow it down.

For best results, soften active dry yeast in *warm* (not hot) water (105°F.) and compressed yeast in *lukewarm* water (95°F.). To test temperature of liquid, drop a little on inside of wrist. Warm, not hot, water feels comfortably warm. Lukewarm water feels neither warm nor cool.

Active Dry Yeast: This new, modern dry yeast stays fresh for several months if kept on cool shelf and gives uniformly fine results until expiration date on package. If it's refrigerated, it performs efficiently well beyond expiration date stated on label.

When dissolved, 1 pkg. dry yeast equals 1 cake compressed yeast. Use dissolved active dry yeast as you would dissolved compressed yeast in any favorite recipe.

Compressed Yeast: Compressed yeast must be kept in refrigerator—not longer than a week or two. It can be frozen but must be thawed at room temperature, then used immediately. To determine whether it's usable, crumble it between fingers; if it crumbles easily, even though edges are slightly brown from drying, it is still good.

KNEADING

After mixing dough as recipe directs, turn it onto lightly floured surface. Measure about ½ cup flour; use to sprinkle, little by little, on surface as you knead—the exact amount depends on the dough.

With floured hands, flatten dough very slightly by pressing it firmly; shape into round, flat ball. Now you are ready to knead as follows:

1. Pick up edge of dough at point farthest from you; fold over toward you, with rolling motion, using fingers of both hands.
2. With heels of hands, press down, pushing ball of dough away from you.
3. Turn dough one quarter way around on board.
4. Repeat first 3 steps until dough is full and rounded, smooth, satiny, and tightly stretched —about 8 to 10 min.

RISING

Temperature Needed: When dough has been kneaded, place it in lightly greased bowl (twice size of dough). Grease top of dough with thin film of salad oil; cover with clean towel. Let rise, away from drafts in warm place at about 85°F., until doubled in bulk.

In hot weather, keep dough out of direct sunlight and away from extra heat of kitchen. *In cold weather,* warm bowl before putting in dough. Place bowl of dough in warm place— near range or radiator, but never on top of either. If the room is cold, you can place dough in an unheated oven, with a large pan of hot water on the shelf beneath it, or on the broiler rack, with hot water in broiler pan. Or set bowl of dough in deep pan of water that's comfortably warm to hand.

Approximate Rising Time: Dough should double its original size, becoming "doubled in bulk." The time varies with the temperature, kind and amounts of ingredients, etc.

To test, press 2 fingers deep into dough. If holes remain when fingers are withdrawn, dough is probably doubled in bulk.

Punching Down: When dough is doubled in bulk, punch it down by first pressing gently into middle of dough. Then pull edges of dough into center and turn dough over, with rounded side up. If directed to do so, let dough rise again; otherwise turn out onto lightly floured surface.

SHAPING LOAVES

1. Form dough into smooth, round ball. With sharp knife, cut into portions—one for each loaf desired. Cover with towel and let rest on board 10 to 15 min.—so they will be easier to handle. Lightly grease desired number of 9″ x 5″ x 3″ loaf pans.
2. With fingers, flatten each piece of dough; then press flattened dough into oblong about 9″ x 7″ x 1″. Width will be almost length of bread pan.
3. Fold each end of oblong to center, overlapping ends slightly. Press each fold down firmly. (Working with both hands helps to shape loaf evenly.) Pinch center overlap, then narrow sides, to seal dough into shape. Place loaf, with sealed edge down, in greased loaf pan; brush with melted fat or salad oil. Repeat with other pieces of dough.
4. Cover loaves with clean towel. Set in warm place (about 85°F.); let rise until sides of dough have reached top of pan and center is well rounded above pan. At this stage dough will be puffy and light, and if pressed very gently with finger tip, slight indentation will remain.

SHAPING ROLLS

See Shaped Rolls, p. 348.

BAKING

To bake 2 loaves or 2 pans of rolls, place on center shelf in oven with 2″ between pans to allow heat to circulate. For 4 loaves, use 2 shelves;

place at right front, left back, left front, and right back.

CRUST TREATMENT

1. Remove bread or rolls from pans as soon as they're baked.
2. Then grease or not as follows, depending on crust desired:

   Crisp crust: Do not grease loaves again.

   Soft tender crust: Brush loaves with soft shortening just after removing them from oven.

   Glazed crust: Before baking loaves, brush with milk; or for every 4 loaves, mix 1 tablesp. egg yolk with ¼ cup water; brush on loaves.
3. To cool bread, place, uncovered, on cake racks or across tops of pans; keep away from drafts, to prevent cracking.

The Rolls You Make

LAST-MINUTE ROLLS

1¼ cups scalded milk	cakes compressed,
2½ tablesp. gran-	yeast
ulated sugar	¼ cup warm (not hot)
1½ teasp. salt	or lukewarm water
¼ cup soft shortening	3¼ cups sifted all-
2 pkg. active dry, or 2	purpose flour

About 1½ hr. before dinner: Into scalded milk in large bowl, stir sugar, salt, shortening; cool till lukewarm. In small bowl, sprinkle or crumble yeast onto warm water (for compressed yeast, use lukewarm water); stir until dissolved. Stir into lukewarm milk mixture. Add flour; stir until well blended—about 1 min.

Cover with clean towel; let rise in warm place (about 85°F.) until doubled in bulk. Stir batter well; then beat vigorously about ½ min. Fill greased 3″ muffin-pan cups about two thirds full. Bake at 400°F. about 25 min. Remove rolls from pans while hot. Makes 1 doz.

TWINKLING ROLLS

¾ cup scalded milk	1 cake compressed,
1 teasp. salt	yeast
¼ cup soft shortening	¼ cup warm (not hot)
3 to 4 tablesp. gran-	or lukewarm water
ulated sugar	3½ to 4 cups sifted all-
1 egg, slightly beaten	purpose flour
1 pkg. active dry, or	

In large bowl, cool scalded milk till lukewarm; stir in salt, shortening, sugar, egg. In small bowl, sprinkle or crumble yeast onto warm water (for compressed yeast, use lukewarm water); stir until dissolved. Stir into lukewarm milk mixture. Add half of flour; beat till smooth. Stir in rest of flour to form stiff dough; beat well.

Place dough in large greased clean bowl. Brush top with salad oil. Cover with clean towel; let rise in warm place (about 85°F.) until doubled in bulk. Turn out onto lightly floured surface; knead until smooth and elastic, adding flour if needed. Cut into 18 equal pieces; form each into ball. Place 1 ball in each greased 2½″ muffin-pan cup. Cover with towel; let rise in warm place until doubled in bulk. Bake at 425°F. 15 min., or until done. Makes 1½ doz.

Butterscotch Pecan: Make and raise dough as above. Meanwhile, boil ¾ cup water with 1 cup plus 2 tablesp. brown sugar, packed, 5 min. Place 1 tablesp. of this syrup in each greased 2½″ muffin-pan cup. Put 4 pecan halves, with rounded sides down, on top of syrup in each cup.

Turn dough out onto lightly floured surface; cut into 18 equal pieces. Form each into ball; place 1 ball in each muffin-pan cup. Cover with towel; let rise in warm place until doubled in bulk. Bake at 425°F. 12 to 15 min. Invert pan at once. Remove rolls, turning pecan sides up. Makes 1½ doz.

Cheese: Add 1 cup grated process American cheese (¼ lb.) with first 2 cups flour.

Williamsburg Buns: Decrease milk to ½ cup. Reduce flour to 2¼ cups, sifting it with ½ teasp. each nutmeg and mace. After first rising, beat well. Fill 12 greased 3″ muffin-pan cups two thirds full. Cover with towel; let dough rise in warm place until it rounds slightly above tops of cups. Bake at 400°F. 15 min., or until done. (You may replace 2 tablesp. milk with 2 tablesp. sherry.) Makes 1 doz.

Sugar-and-Spice Buns: Bake Williamsburg Buns, above; dip tops and sides *at once* into 6 tablesp. melted butter or margarine; then roll in combined ½ cup granulated sugar and 1 teasp. cinnamon.

Whole-wheat Rolls: Substitute 1½ cups unsifted whole-wheat flour for 1½ cups all-purpose flour.

SOUR-CREAM BATTER ROLLS

1 cup commercial sour cream	4 cups sifted all-purpose flour
½ cup granulated sugar	½ cup chopped, toasted almonds
1½ teasp. salt	½ cup cut-up candied cherries, lemon peel, or pineapple
6 tablesp. shortening	2½ teasp. rum extract
2 pkg. active dry, or 2 cakes compressed, yeast	½ cup chopped, toasted almonds
¼ cup warm (not hot) or lukewarm water	½ cup granulated sugar
3 eggs, beaten	

Bring sour cream to boil; stir in ½ cup sugar, salt, shortening; cool till lukewarm. In large bowl, sprinkle or crumble yeast onto warm water (for compressed yeast, use lukewarm water); stir until dissolved. Stir in lukewarm sour-cream mixture. Add eggs, flour, ½ cup almonds, cherries, extract; stir until well blended.

Fill greased 3″ muffin-pan cups about half full. Cover with clean towel; let rise in warm place (about 85°F.) until doubled in bulk. Mix ½ cup almonds with ½ cup sugar; sprinkle on top of muffins. Bake at 400°F. about 25 min. Remove from pans while warm. Makes 20.

BRAN REFRIGERATOR ROLLS

½ cup shortening	yeast
6 tablesp. granulated sugar	½ cup warm (not hot) or lukewarm water
1½ teasp. salt	1 egg, beaten
½ cup boiling water	About 3 to 3¼ cups sifted all-purpose flour
½ cup ready-to-eat bran	
1 pkg. active dry, or 1 cake compressed,	

In large bowl, combine shortening, sugar, salt, boiling water. Stir in bran; cool till lukewarm. In small bowl, sprinkle or crumble yeast onto warm water (for compressed yeast, use lukewarm water); stir until dissolved; add with egg to bran mixture. Stir in enough flour to make soft dough; beat well. Brush dough with soft shortening; cover tightly with aluminum foil or waxed paper, then with towel; refrigerate overnight.

Turn dough out onto floured surface; form into 2″ balls. Place 1 ball in each greased 2½″ muffin-pan cup. Brush lightly with melted butter or margarine. Cover with towel; let rise in warm place (about 85°F.) until doubled in bulk. Bake at 425°F. 15 to 20 min., or until done. Makes about 2 doz.

Oatmeal Refrigerator Rolls: Reduce sugar to 3 tablesp.; substitute 1 cup uncooked rolled oats for bran; reduce flour to about 2½ cups. Bake at 450°F. 15 to 20 min.

REFRIGERATOR ROLLS DE LUXE

1 pkg. active dry, or 1 cake compressed, yeast	¾ cup granulated sugar
	1 cup unseasoned hot mashed potatoes
½ cup warm (not hot) or lukewarm water	1 cup cold water
	1½ teasp. salt
½ cup soft butter or margarine	About 6 to 6½ cups sifted all-purpose flour
½ cup soft shortening	

In large bowl, sprinkle or crumble yeast onto warm water (for compressed yeast, use lukewarm water); stir until dissolved. Stir in butter, shortening, sugar, potatoes, then cold water, salt, and enough flour to make stiff dough. Place dough in large greased clean bowl. Brush top with salad oil; cover tightly with waxed paper or aluminum foil, then with clean towel; refrigerate.

To use dough, cut off only as much as you need, returning rest to refrigerator, covered (dough keeps 2 or 3 days in refrigerator). Shape dough as in Shaped Rolls, below. Brush lightly with melted butter or margarine. Cover with towel; let rise in warm place (about 85°F.) until doubled in bulk. Bake at 425°F. 20 to 25 min., or until done. Makes 3 doz.

SUSAN'S REFRIGERATOR ROLLS

½ cup granulated sugar	2 cakes compressed, yeast
1½ teasp. salt	
2 cups hot water drained from cooked potatoes	1 egg, beaten
	7 cups sifted all-purpose flour
2 pkg. active dry, or	½ cup melted fat

1. In large mixing bowl, combine sugar, salt, potato water; stir until sugar dissolves.
2. Cool mixture till just warm (for compressed yeast, cool till lukewarm); sprinkle or crumble yeast onto it; stir until dissolved. Stir in egg.
3. With spoon, beat in 3½ cups flour until batter is very elastic and almost smooth. Then beat in fat until well blended.

4. Gradually add 3½ cups more flour, working it in with hands if necessary until dough is no longer sticky. Turn dough out onto lightly floured surface; let rest, covered, 10 min.
5. With floured hands, knead dough 8 to 10 min., or until smooth and elastic. Then put dough into greased clean bowl. Cover with clean towel; let rise in warm place (about 85°F.) until doubled in bulk and very light to touch—2 to 4 hr.
6. Punch down dough; turn dough over, with rounded side up; brush with melted butter or margarine. Cover bowl tightly with waxed paper and damp towel; store in refrigerator. (You may keep dough 2 to 3 days in refrigerator. Occasionally redampen towel and punch down dough.)
7. To use, remove dough from refrigerator; cut off amount needed. Form into long rolls, about 1″ thick, then cut into 1″ pieces. Shape each piece into ball; then place 3 balls in each greased muffin-pan cup. Brush rolls with melted butter or margarine. Cover with clean towel; let rise in warm place until doubled in bulk.
8. Bake at 425°F. 15 to 18 min., or until golden brown. Brush with melted butter or margarine. Makes about 4 doz.

SHAPED ROLLS

Make dough for Refrigerator Rolls De Luxe, above; Twinkling Rolls, p. 346; or Whole-wheat Rolls, p. 347. Or use packaged hot-roll mix.

Turn dough onto lightly floured surface. Shape as below; brush with melted butter or margarine; let rise; then bake as recipe directs.

Clover-leaf Rolls (Fig. 1): Form dough into long rolls, 1″ in diameter. Cut off 1″ pieces. Form each piece into smooth ball; dip into melted butter or margarine. Place 3 balls in each greased muffin-pan cup, with balls touching bottom of pan.

Bread Sticks (Fig. 2): Roll dough ½″ thick. Cut into 6″ x ½″ strips. Pinch each strip into pencillike shape. Then place fingers on ends of each strip; gently roll strip back and forth, moving fingers to center, then out to ends again, to form evenly shaped 10″ x ⅜″ stick. Place sticks 1″ apart on greased cookie sheet.

Crescents (Fig. 3): Roll dough ¼″ thick. Cut into 9″ circles, using 9″ pie plate as guide. Cut circle into 12 wedges. Brush with melted butter or margarine. Starting at wider edge, roll up each wedge. Place with center point down, 2″ apart on greased cookie sheet. Curve ends to form crescents.

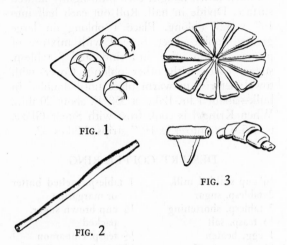

FIG. 1

FIG. 3

FIG. 2

Dinner Rolls (Fig. 4): Shape pieces of dough into 2″ balls. With floured hands, roll each ball 4″ long, making ends taper. Place 1″ apart on greased cookie sheet. (Make finger or salad rolls smaller.)

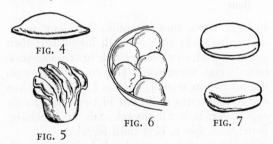

FIG. 4

FIG. 6   FIG. 7

FIG. 5

Vienna Rolls: Make Dinner Rolls, above; brush with slightly beaten egg white mixed with 1 tablesp. water. Sprinkle with caraway seeds.

Fan-Tans (Fig. 5): Roll dough into rectangle ⅛″ thick. Brush with melted butter or margarine. Cut into 1½″-wide strips. Stack 6 or 7 strips together. Cut into 1½″-wide pieces; place, with cut sides up, in greased muffin-pan cups.

Old-fashioned Pan Rolls (Fig. 6): Cut off pieces of dough; shape into 2″ balls. Dip into melted butter or margarine. Place in greased 8″ layer pan, letting balls just touch each other.

Parkerhouse Rolls (Fig. 7): Roll dough ¼″ thick. Cut with 2¾″ floured biscuit cutter. Flour handle of wooden spoon; in each round, make crease to one side of center; roll handle of spoon toward edge, flattening half of round slightly. Brush lightly with melted butter or margarine. Fold thicker half of round over thinner half, pressing edges together. Place rounds 1″ apart on greased cookie sheet.

Coffeecakes You Make

CRUNCHY-TOP COFFEECAKE

2 pkg. active dry yeast	1 large egg, beaten
¼ cup warm (not hot) water	2¾ to 3 cups sifted all-purpose flour
¾ cup buttermilk	½ cup granulated sugar
3 tablesp. granulated sugar	2 tablesp. brown sugar
1 teasp. salt	½ teasp. cinnamon
3 tablesp. soft shortening	2 tablesp. melted butter or margarine
	¼ cup chopped nuts

Sprinkle yeast onto water; stir until dissolved. Heat buttermilk just till warm; pour into large mixing bowl, with 3 tablesp. sugar, salt; blend; cool till lukewarm. Stir in yeast, then shortening, egg, half of flour; with spoon, beat until smooth. Add more flour until dough begins to clean sides of bowl.

Turn dough onto lightly floured surface. Knead lightly until smooth—about 30 sec. Cover with damp cloth; let rest 5 min. Place in lightly greased 9″ x 9″ x 2″ layer pan, or in 2 8″ layer pans; pat evenly into pans. Let rise in warm place (about 85° F.) until doubled in bulk—30 to 40 min.

For topping: Mix ½ cup sugar, brown sugar, cinnamon, melted butter, nuts. With fingers, make several dents in coffeecake; cover top with sugar mixture. Bake at 375°F. 35 to 45 min. Cool on rack.

Early-Breakfast: Day before, make dough; place in pans; sprinkle with topping; cover with waxed paper or aluminum foil; refrigerate. Next morning, remove from refrigerator; bake.

SUPERB DANISH COFFEE TWIST

¾ cup scalded milk	1 cup melted shortening
2 pkg. active dry, or 2 cakes compressed, yeast	1 teasp. ground cardamom seeds
¼ cup warm (not hot) or lukewarm water	1 cup seedless raisins
	1 cup cut-up citron
	1 egg
About 5 cups sifted all-purpose flour	½ cup confectioners' sugar
½ cup granulated sugar	½ cup chopped, blanched almonds
1½ teasp. salt	
3 eggs	

In medium bowl, cool milk till lukewarm. Sprinkle or crumble yeast onto warm water (for compressed yeast, use lukewarm water); stir until dissolved. Stir into milk. Sift flour with sugar, salt. Stir about 1 cup flour mixture into milk mixture. Beat in 1 egg. Stir in 1 cup flour; add 2 eggs, beating well after each addition. Add shortening and remaining 3 cups flour; stir till smooth. Mix in cardamon, raisins, citron.

Turn dough into large greased bowl; knead several minutes, turning dough over and over in bowl. Cover with clean towel; let rise in warm place (about 85°F.) until doubled in bulk. Punch down; turn out onto lightly floured surface; knead about 8 min.; divide in half. Roll each half into long sausagelike roll; twist each into pretzel shape. Place on greased cookie sheets. Flatten top of each twist slightly. Brush with beaten egg; sprinkle thickly with confectioners' sugar and chopped almonds. Let rise in warm place until doubled in bulk. Bake at 375°F. 25 to 30 min. Makes 2.

COFFEE KRINGEL

¼ cup scalded milk	or lukewarm water
¼ cup granulated sugar	1 egg, beaten
½ teasp. salt	1½ cups chopped, drained, pitted, cooked prunes
2¼ cups sifted all-purpose flour	
¼ cup soft shortening	3 tablesp. lemon juice
1 pkg. active dry, or 1 cake compressed, yeast	½ teasp. grated lemon rind
	3 tablesp. granulated sugar
¼ cup warm (not hot)	

Cool milk till lukewarm. Mix ¼ cup sugar, salt, flour. With pastry blender or 2 knives, scissor-fashion, cut in shortening. In large bowl, sprinkle or crumble yeast onto warm water (for com-

pressed yeast, use lukewarm water); stir until dissolved. Stir in milk. Add egg, flour mixture; stir until well blended—about 2 min. Place in greased bowl. Brush top with soft shortening. Cover with clean towel; let rise in warm place (about 85°F.) until doubled in bulk—about 1½ hr.

Punch down dough; turn onto lightly floured surface. Divide in half. Roll out each half into 16″ x 12″ oblong. Place 1 oblong on large greased cookie sheet. Spread with mixture of prunes, lemon juice and rind, and 3 tablesp. sugar; cover with other oblong. Cover with towel; let rise in warm place until doubled in bulk—about 1 hr. Bake at 350°F. about 20 min. When Kringel is cool, frost with Sugar Glaze, p. 465. Cut into 4″ x 1½″ strips. Makes 32.

DESSERT COFFEE RING

¼ cup scalded milk	1 tablesp. melted butter or margarine
2 tablesp. sugar	¼ cup brown sugar, packed
2 tablesp. shortening	
½ teasp. salt	½ teasp. cinnamon
1 egg, beaten	¼ cup light or dark raisins
½ pkg. active dry, or ½ cake compressed, yeast	3 tablesp. confectioners' sugar
¼ cup warm (not hot) or lukewarm water	1 teasp. warm water
2 cups sifted all-purpose flour	¼ cup pecan halves

In large bowl, combine milk, 2 tablesp. sugar, shortening, salt; stir; cool till lukewarm; then stir in egg. Meanwhile, sprinkle or crumble yeast onto ¼ cup warm water (for compressed yeast, use lukewarm water); stir until dissolved; then add to lukewarm milk. Stir in 1 cup flour; with egg beater, beat till smooth. Stir in remaining flour; with spoon, beat until blended.

Brush top of dough with salad oil. Cover with clean towel; let rise in warm place (about 85°F.) until doubled in bulk. Punch down dough; turn out onto lightly floured surface; roll into rectangle about 13″ x 7″.

Brush dough with melted butter; then sprinkle with brown sugar, cinnamon, raisins. Roll up from long side, jelly-roll-fashion, pulling edges to keep them even. Pinch seam to roll; then place, with seam side down, in semicircle on greased cookie sheet. With scissors, cut through ring, almost to center, making 1″-thick slices.

Turn each slice slightly so cut side lies almost flat on sheet. Brush lightly with melted butter or margarine. Cover with towel; let rise in warm place until doubled in bulk.

If glaze is desired, brush top and sides of ring with slightly beaten egg white mixed with 1 tablesp. water. Bake at 400°F. 15 min., or until done. Cool slightly; frost with confectioners' sugar and 1 teasp. warm water, mixed till smooth. Top with pecans.

Serve at brunch or as dessert. Or slice and toast for breakfast. Makes 1 ring.

QUICK COFFEE RING

1 cup scalded milk	or lukewarm water
½ cup granulated sugar	1 egg, well beaten
1 teasp. salt	3¾ cups sifted all-
¼ cup shortening	purpose flour
2 pkg. active dry, or	¼ cup granulated sugar
2 cakes compressed,	¼ teasp. cinnamon
yeast	¼ cup chopped nuts
¼ cup warm (not hot)	

In large bowl, combine milk, ½ cup sugar, salt, shortening; cool till lukewarm. Sprinkle or crumble yeast onto warm water (for compressed yeast, use lukewarm water); stir until dissolved. Stir into milk mixture, with egg and 1 cup flour. With spoon, beat till smooth. Add rest of flour; beat 3 min.

Line bottom of greased 9″ tube pan with waxed paper. Spoon in batter.

For topping: Combine ¼ cup sugar, cinnamon, nuts. Sprinkle over batter. Cover with clean towel; let rise in warm place (about 85°F.) until doubled in bulk. Bake at 375°F. 40 min., or until done. Makes 1 cake.

BERT'S BRIOCHE

¼ cup scalded milk	2 cups plus 6 tablesp.
1 pkg. active dry, or	sifted all-purpose
1 cake compressed,	flour
yeast	⅓ cup soft butter or
¼ cup warm (not hot)	margarine
or lukewarm water	1 egg
¼ cup granulated sugar	2 egg yolks*
¼ teasp. salt	½ teasp. lemon extract

Cool milk till lukewarm. Sprinkle or crumble yeast onto warm water (for compressed yeast, use lukewarm water); stir until dissolved. Add to milk, with sugar, salt, 1 cup flour; with spoon,

beat till smooth. Beat in butter, then egg and yolks, one at a time. Add 1 cup plus 6 tablesp. flour and extract; beat 5 min. Brush with salad oil. Cover with clean towel; let rise in warm place (about 85°F.) until doubled in bulk. Cover with waxed paper and damp towel; refrigerate 12 hr.

Turn onto lightly floured surface; form into 2″ balls. Place 1 ball in each 3″ muffin-pan cup. Brush tops with salad oil. Cover with towel; let rise in warm place until doubled in bulk. Bake at 375°F. 15 min., or until done. Makes 18 to 20.

* *For ways to use egg whites, see p. 551.*

Brunch Brioche: In morning, after dough has been refrigerated 12 hr., turn onto lightly floured surface. Roll into rectangle 14″ x 6″ x ½″. Cut off lengthwise strips, ½″ wide. Braid 3 strips together; cut into thirds; then pinch ends to prevent separating. Set on greased cookie sheet. Cover with towel; let rise in warm place until doubled in bulk. Bake at 375°F. 12 min., or until done. Remove; while brioche are warm, frost with Sugar Glaze, p. 465. Makes about 12.

CHRISTMAS STOLLEN

1 cup milk	1 cup slivered, blanched
½ cup granulated sugar	almonds
½ teasp. salt	Grated rind of 1 lemon
1 pkg. active dry yeast	1 cup seedless raisins
¼ cup warm (not hot)	2 eggs, well beaten
water	¾ cup soft butter or
5 cups sifted all-purpose	margarine
flour	¼ teasp. nutmeg
½ cup finely cut-up	¼ cup melted butter or
citron	margarine
½ cup finely cut-up	½ teasp. cinnamon
candied cherries	2 tablesp. sugar

In large saucepan, scald milk; add ½ cup sugar, salt; cool till lukewarm. Meanwhile, sprinkle yeast onto water; stir until dissolved. Add to lukewarm milk, with 1 cup flour; with egg beater, beat to remove lumps. Cover with clean towel; let rise in warm place (about 85°F.) until doubled in bulk—about 2 hr.

Now stir in citron, cherries, almonds, lemon rind, raisins, eggs, soft butter, nutmeg, then 3 cups flour. On lightly floured surface, knead 1 cup flour into dough until dough is smooth and elastic. Roll into large 18″ x 12″ oval, about ½″

thick. Brush with some of melted butter; sprinkle with combined cinnamon and 2 tablesp. sugar.

Make lengthwise crease down center of dough; fold over. Remove to large greased cookie sheet. Push into crescent shape; then, with palm of hand, press down along crease to shape. Brush with rest of melted butter. Cover with waxed paper, then with towel; let rise in warm place until nearly doubled in bulk. Bake at 350°F. 45 to 50 min., or until golden. Cool; sift confectioners' sugar over top. Keeps well. Makes 1 large stollen.

P.S. If desired, shape dough into 2 stollens.

DANISH PASTRY

1 pkg. active dry, or 1 cake compressed, yeast	½ teasp. lemon extract
	¼ teasp. mace
	3½ to 4 cups sifted all-
¼ cup warm (not hot) or lukewarm water	purpose flour
	1 cup shortening
⅓ cup granulated sugar	1 egg
1 teasp. salt	2 tablesp. sugar
¼ cup shortening	⅓ cup chopped un-
1 cup scalded milk	blanched almonds, or
2 eggs	pecans or walnuts
¼ teasp. vanilla extract	

Sprinkle or crumble yeast onto warm water (for compressed yeast, use lukewarm water); stir until dissolved. In large bowl, place ⅓ cup sugar, salt, ¼ cup shortening, milk; stir until blended. Cool till lukewarm; then beat in 2 eggs. Add yeast, extracts, mace, 3 cups flour; stir till smooth. Stir in enough more flour to make soft, easy-to-handle dough. Cover with clean towel; let rise in warm place (about 85°F.) until doubled in bulk.

Meanwhile, let 1 cup shortening soften at room temperature. On lightly floured surface, roll dough into ¼″-thick square. Dot with half of shortening, leaving 2″ border. Fold dough in half; press edges together. Dot with rest of shortening, leaving 2″ border. Fold in half; seal edges. Roll dough into ⅓″-thick square; fold in half, then crosswise in half. Repeat rolling and folding 3 times. Place dough in greased bowl; cover with towel; let stand 20 min.

Now, on lightly floured surface, roll dough ⅓″ thick. Cut into 3″ squares; place spoonful of jam, or Cheese, Almond, or Prune Filling, below, in center of each square. Fold 2 opposite

corners to center; press to seal. Place on cookie sheet. Cover with towel; let rise in warm place until half double in size; brush with egg combined with 2 tablesp. sugar. Sprinkle with nuts. Bake at 475°F. 8 to 10 min., or until done. Makes 24. If desired, drizzle on Sugar Glaze, p. 465.

Cheese Filling: Combine 1 egg yolk, slightly beaten; 1 cup cottage cheese; ⅓ cup granulated sugar; ½ teasp. vanilla extract; 1 teasp. grated lemon rind.

Almond Filling: Cream together ¼ cup butter or margarine, ¼ cup granulated sugar. Blend in 1 egg, ½ cup (¼ lb.) almond paste, ¾ teasp. almond extract.

Prune Filling: Combine 1 jar or can (½ cup) baby-pack strained prunes, 2 tablesp. granulated sugar, 1 teasp. lemon juice, ¼ teasp. cinnamon. Simmer, stirring, until thick enough to mound when dropped from spoon.

QUICK COFFEE ROLLS

Make batter for Quick Coffee Ring, p. 351. Spoon into greased 2½″ muffin-pan cups. Sprinkle with topping. Cover with towel; let rise in warm place (about 85°F.) until doubled in bulk. Bake at 375°F. 20 to 25 min., or until done. Makes 2 doz.

ORANGE PIN WHEELS

1 pkg. hot-roll mix	or margarine
½ cup granulated sugar	2 tablesp. orange juice
1 tablesp. grated orange rind	¼ cup granulated sugar
	1 tablesp. grated orange rind
2 tablesp. melted butter	

Prepare roll mix as label directs. Cover with clean towel; let rise in warm place (about 85°F.) until doubled in bulk—30 to 60 min. Combine ½ cup sugar, 1 tablesp. orange rind, butter, orange juice. Spread evenly in bottoms of about 18 greased 2½″ muffin-pan cups.

On lightly floured surface, roll dough into 20″ x 12″ rectangle. Combine ¼ cup sugar, 1 tablesp. orange rind. Sprinkle over dough. Roll up from long side, jelly-roll-fashion. Cut into 1″ slices. Place 1 slice, with cut side down, in each muffin-pan cup. Let rise in warm place until light—30 to 60 min. Bake at 375°F. 20 to 25 min. Makes 1½ doz.

NUT TWISTS

1 pkg. hot-roll mix	¾ cup chopped walnuts
2 tablesp. melted short- ening or salad oil	½ cup granulated sugar 1 teasp. cinnamon

Prepare roll mix as label directs, adding shortening to yeast-water liquid. Cover with clean towel; let rise in warm place (about 85°F.) about 30 min.

Combine nuts, sugar, cinnamon. Divide dough into small pieces. Stretch each piece about 8" long; roll in nut mixture; twist into **S** or other shape. Place on greased cookie sheet. Sprinkle with nut mixture. Let rise in warm place until light—30 to 60 min. Bake at 400°F. 12 to 15 min. Makes 1½ doz. rolls.

SUSAN'S HOT CROSS BUNS

¾ cup scalded milk	½ teasp. mace
½ cup shortening	About 3½ to 4 cups
⅓ cup granulated sugar	sifted all-purpose
1 teasp. salt	flour
1 pkg. active dry, or	1 egg white, slightly
1 cake compressed,	beaten
yeast	1 cup confectioners'
¼ cup warm (not hot)	sugar
or lukewarm water	2 tablesp. hot water
1 egg, beaten	½ teasp. vanilla extract
¾ cup currants	

1. In large bowl, combine milk, shortening, granulated sugar, salt; cool till lukewarm.
2. In small bowl, sprinkle or crumble yeast onto warm water (for compressed yeast, use lukewarm water); stir until dissolved. Add to milk mixture, with egg, currants, mace, and as much flour as can be stirred into dough—about 3½ cups.
3. Place in greased clean bowl. Brush top with salad oil. Cover with clean towel; let rise in warm place (about 85°F.) until doubled in bulk.
4. Turn onto lightly floured surface; knead 1 min.; shape into 18 2" balls. Arrange, side by side, in 2 greased 8" x 8" x 2" pans.
5. With greased scissors, snip deep cross in each bun. Brush with egg white. Cover with towel; let rise in warm place until doubled in bulk.
6. Bake at 425°F. 25 min., or until done. Cool on wire rack; frost with combined confectioners' sugar, hot water, and vanilla extract. Makes 1½ doz.

To Vary: With egg and milk, add 3 tablesp. finely chopped preserved orange or lemon peel and 3 tablesp. finely chopped citron.

Homemade Loaf Breads

LEMON DROP LOAF

⅓ cup granulated sugar	1 egg
Grated rind of 2 lemons	2 tablesp. soft
1 pkg. active dry yeast	shortening
¼ cup warm (not hot)	2½ to 2¾ cups sifted
water	all-purpose flour
½ cup scalded milk	2 tablesp. butter or
¼ cup granulated sugar	margarine
½ teasp. salt	

Mix ⅓ cup sugar with half of lemon rind; let stand while dough is being made.

Sprinkle yeast onto water; stir until dissolved. Into large bowl, pour scalded milk; add ¼ cup sugar, salt, rest of lemon rind; stir until sugar dissolves. Cool till lukewarm; stir in yeast. Stir in egg, shortening, half of flour; beat until smooth. Add rest of flour, a little at a time, until dough just begins to clean sides of bowl.

Turn dough onto lightly floured surface; knead a few minutes until smooth and elastic. Place in greased bowl; brush top with salad oil. Cover with damp cloth; let rise in warm place (about 85°F.) until doubled in bulk—50 to 60 min.

Punch down dough; turn onto lightly floured surface; cover with towel; let rest 5 to 10 min. Melt butter. Shape dough into 20 1" balls. Place 10 balls in greased 10" x 5" x 3" loaf pan (make 2 rows, with 5 balls in a row). Brush with half of melted butter; sprinkle with half of lemon-sugar mixture. Repeat. Let rise in warm place until doubled in bulk—45 min. Bake at 350°F. 25 to 30 min. Remove from pan. Cool on rack.

To serve: Slice or pull apart. Makes 1 loaf.

CHEESE BREAD

1 pkg. active dry, or	sugar
1 cake compressed,	2 teasp. salt
yeast	About 6 cups sifted
¼ cup warm (not hot)	all-purpose flour
or lukewarm water	½ lb. wedge natural
1 cup milk	sharp American
1 tablesp. shortening	cheese
2 tablesp. granulated	1 cup lukewarm water

Sprinkle or crumble yeast onto ¼ cup warm water (for compressed yeast, use lukewarm water); stir until dissolved. In saucepan, scald milk with shortening; pour into large bowl. Add sugar, salt; cool till lukewarm. Add 2 cups flour; beat till smooth. Grate cheese over dough. Add yeast and 1 cup lukewarm water; mix well. Add about 4 cups flour all at once; with spoon, beat till smooth. Add a bit more flour to make medium-stiff dough.

Turn dough onto lightly floured surface. Knead until smooth and elastic. Shape into ball. Place in greased bowl; brush top with salad oil. Cover with clean towel; let rise in warm place (about 85°F.) until doubled in bulk. Punch down; fold edges in; turn dough over.

Place dough on lightly floured surface; cut in half. Turn under all edges till top of each half is rounded; let rest 10 min. Mold each ball into loaf as in Shaping Loaves, p. 346. Place in 2 greased 9″ x 5″ x 3″ loaf pans. Cover with clean towel; let rise in warm place until center is slightly higher than pan edge. Bake at 400°F. about 40 min. Makes 2 loaves.

WHITE BREAD

1 cup scalded milk	1 cake compressed,
3 tablesp. granulated	yeast
sugar	1 cup warm (not hot)
2½ teasp. salt	or lukewarm water
6 tablesp. shortening	About 6 cups sifted all-
1 pkg. active dry, or	purpose flour

Into scalded milk, stir sugar, salt, shortening. Cool till lukewarm. Sprinkle or crumble yeast onto warm water in large bowl (for compressed yeast, use lukewarm water); stir until dissolved. Stir in lukewarm milk mixture. Add 3 cups flour; with spoon, beat until smooth. Stir in remaining 3 cups flour.

Turn onto lightly floured surface. Knead until smooth and elastic. Place in greased bowl; brush top with salad oil. Cover with clean towel; let rise in warm place (about 85°F.) until doubled in bulk. Punch down; then turn onto lightly floured surface.

Divide dough in half; let rest 15 to 20 min. Then shape into 2 loaves, as in Shaping Loaves, p. 346. Place in 2 greased 9″ x 5″ x 3″ loaf pans. Cover with clean towel; let rise in warm place until center is slightly higher than edges of

pan. Bake at 400°F. about 50 min., or until done. Makes 2 loaves.

For 1 loaf: Use 1 pkg. or cake yeast; halve rest of ingredients.

For 4 loaves: Double each ingredient.

WHOLE-WHEAT BREAD

¾ cup scalded milk	water
3 tablesp. granulated	2 pkg. active dry, or
sugar	2 cakes compressed,
4 teasp. salt	yeast
⅓ cup shortening	4½ cups whole-wheat
⅓ cup molasses	flour
1½ cups warm (not	2 cups sifted all-purpose
hot) or lukewarm	flour

Into scalded milk, stir sugar, salt, shortening, molasses; cool till lukewarm. Sprinkle or crumble yeast onto warm water in large bowl (for compressed yeast, use lukewarm water); stir until dissolved. Stir in lukewarm milk mixture. Add half of combined whole-wheat and all-purpose flours. Beat until smooth. Stir in rest of flour mixture.

Turn dough onto lightly floured surface. Knead until smooth and elastic. Place in greased bowl; brush top with salad oil. Cover with clean towel; let rise in warm place (about 85°F.) until doubled in bulk.

Punch down; turn onto lightly floured surface. Divide in half; shape into loaves, as in Shaping Loaves, p. 346. Place in 2 greased 9″ x 5″ x 3″ loaf pans. Cover with towel; let rise in warm place until center is slightly higher than edges of pan. Bake at 400°F. about 50 min. Makes 2 loaves.

OLD-TIME SALLY LUNN

¼ cup scalded milk	or lukewarm water
6 tablesp. shortening	2 cups sifted all-purpose
1 pkg. active dry, or	flour
1 cake compressed,	2 tablesp. sugar
yeast	½ teasp. salt
¼ cup warm (not hot)	2 eggs

Combine milk, shortening; cool till lukewarm. Meanwhile, sprinkle or crumble yeast onto warm water (for compressed yeast, use lukewarm water); stir until dissolved. In large bowl, combine flour, sugar, salt; make well in center; stir in yeast, then milk mixture. Let rise in warm place (about 85°F.) about 20 min.; stir in 1 egg, beaten; mix well. Cover with clean towel; let rise until doubled in bulk.

Turn dough onto lightly floured surface; knead lightly. Cut in half; mold each piece into round, flat loaf. Place loaves in 2 greased 8″ layer pans, pressing with knuckles to fit dough into pans. Cover with clean towel; let rise in warm place until doubled in bulk. Brush tops with beaten egg. Bake at 425°F. 15 to 20 min., or until done.

Serve hot, cut into wedges. Or next day, split; then toast wedges. Makes 2 loaves.

ITALIAN-STYLE PIZZA

1 pkg. hot-roll mix	¼ teasp. orégano
½ lb. sliced mushrooms	⅛ teasp. garlic salt
2 tablesp. butter	½ lb. Mozzarella or
1 to 2 lb. fresh pork	natural sharp Amer-
sausage meat or links	ican cheese, grated
½ cup minced onions	Grated Parmesan or
1 8-oz. can tomato sauce	sharp American
1 6-oz. can tomato paste	cheese
(⅔ cup)	Snipped parsley

Prepare roll mix as label directs; let rise in warm place (about 85°F.) until light—30 to 60 min.

Meanwhile, sauté mushrooms in butter until tender; remove. In same skillet, pan-fry sausage meat until pink color disappears (if using links, pan-fry until lightly browned; slice). Remove sausage; pour off drippings; return 1 tablesp. drippings to skillet; use to sauté onions until tender. Add tomato sauce and paste, orégano, garlic salt.

When dough is light, divide into 4 parts. Flatten each piece; pat into bottom of 4 9″ or 10″ pie plates. (Or divide dough in half; roll out 2 12″ x 8″ rectangles; place on cookie sheets.) Brush with olive oil or sausage drippings.

Arrange half of Mozzarella cheese on dough; cover with tomato mixture. Top with rest of cheese and sausage. Sprinkle with grated Parmesan cheese, parsley, and mushrooms. Bake at 450°F. 15 to 20 min. Serve hot, cut into wedges. Makes 8 servings.

Speedy: Packaged pizza mix is easy to use and delicious!

Sandwiches

What wonderful variety there is in sandwiches! There are hearty sandwiches you can plan a meal around—knife-and-fork or finger style, hot or cold. There are good-traveler sandwiches, just right for the lunch box or picnic chest. And there are eye-catching partytime sandwiches that are as much fun to make as they are good to eat.

Here are recipes for our favorite sandwiches. When you make them, be sure to make enough. Remember, an invitation to "have another sandwich" is not often turned down.

Before using these recipes, refer to Pots and Pans, p. 3, and How to Use Our Recipes, p. 692. Always use standard measuring cups and measuring spoons; measure level.

Sandwich Breads and Crackers

Kind to Use:

For everyday sandwiches, fresh or day-old bread slices

For sandwich loaves, day-old unsliced bread

For roll-up, envelope, or pin-wheel sandwiches, very fresh unsliced or sliced bread (so bread won't break in rolling)

For cracker sandwiches, packaged crackers. Today they're crisper than ever. Some packages contain crackers wrapped in several packets, so you can open and use one packet at a time

Choose From:

Breads:

Canned brown, date-nut, etc.
Cheese
Cinnamon
Cracked wheat
French or Italian
Nut
Pumpernickel
Raisin
Caraway rye
Party rye
Swedish or plain rye
Square sandwich
Enriched white
Whole-wheat

Rolls, etc.:

Biscuit or roll mix

Brown-and-serve rolls
Corn muffins
Crumpets
English muffins
Frankfurter rolls
Hamburger buns
Hard rolls
Refrigerated pan-ready biscuits

Crackers:

Cheese crackers
Crisp round scalloped crackers
Rye wafers
Shredded-wheat wafers
Soda crackers, etc.

Production-Line Techniques

Soften butter or margarine. For easy spreading, let butter or margarine soften at room temperature; or work it with spoon or electric mixer until spreadable.

If you must "stretch" butter or margarine:

1. Be sure it's soft, so you can spread it thin.
2. Or mix it with salad dressing, peanut butter, or jelly, etc.

3. Or spread half of bread slices with salad dressing.

4. Or to 1 lb. soft butter or margarine, slowly add ½ cup evaporated milk, beating with wooden spoon or egg beater. Makes 1½ lb.

Make fillings next. If you're making pack-and-carry sandwiches, choose fillings that will not soak into bread. Wrap separately items that wilt easily—lettuce, tomatoes.

For safety's sake, refrigerate all fillings until used—especially meat, fish, poultry, or eggs.

Line up bread slices. Use a good sharp knife for slicing and trimming bread. Place bread slices two by two, in vertical rows, on work surface. Pair slices that lie next to each other in loaf, so edges will match.

Butter all slices to very edges, using flexible spatula. This keeps bread moist, prevents filling from soaking through.

Place filling on slices in every other row; spread from edge to edge. (Be generous, but not so lavish that filling oozes out.) Then close sandwiches.

Leave crusts on all but daintiest sandwiches; crusts help sandwiches stay moist.

When wrapping sandwiches, set each, cut into halves or thirds, in center of square of waxed paper, saran, or aluminum foil. Bring opposite sides of paper together, directly over center. Fold edges over and over until fold rests against sandwich. Dog-ear ends; tuck under. Or use sandwich bags.

A word of warning: Completed sandwiches are as perishable as the fillings alone. So, to avoid any possibility of food poisoning, refrigerate sandwiches right up to time of eating. Never cover them with a damp towel; use waxed paper, saran, foil, or dry towel.

If sandwiches are for picnic or lunch boxes, refrigerate them until just before packing. Plan to eat within 4 hr. Or freeze sandwiches; let them thaw en route.

To freeze sandwiches ahead for parties, lunch boxes, picnics, etc., see p. 541.

LUNCH AND SUPPER HEARTIES

Here's a choice selection of those wonderful broiled, baked, toasted, and untoasted sandwich hearties that make lunch or supper a feast.

BROILED OPEN-FACE SANDWICHES

Use buttered or toasted bread; or use buttered, toasted, split rolls, English muffins, or crumpets; or use buttered, split hot baking-powder biscuits. On top, arrange makings of any combination below, in order given. Then broil until bubbly and toasted.

1. Cheese and tomato slices (or chili sauce), semibroiled bacon slices
2. Chicken, Crab, Tuna, or Egg Salad, p. 364; cheese slices
3. Cheese slices, prepared mustard or barbecue sauce
4. Creamed chicken or turkey, cheese slices. Serve with tomato slices and broiled bacon or beef bacon
5. Franks, split lengthwise; sharp-cheese slices; tomato slices
6. Deviled-ham spread, scrambled eggs (unsalted), grated cheese
7. Chicken or turkey slices, cheese sauce (bought in jar or homemade)
8. Turkey and tomato slices, semibroiled bacon slices, cheese slices
9. Chicken slices, cooked asparagus spears, cheese sauce

OTHER BROILED SANDWICHES

Onion-Cheese: In 2 tablesp. butter or margarine, sauté 2 or 3 thinly sliced medium onions until tender and light brown. Add ½ teasp. salt, ⅛ teasp. pepper. Spread on 4 slices of hot toast; top with 4 packaged process-American-cheese slices. Broil till cheese is melted. Makes 4.

Salad Burgers: Split hamburger buns. Spread half with cheese spread, rest with any of salad fillings, p. 364, doubling recipe if necessary. Then broil all till bubbly. Serve halves open style; or top salad buns with cheese buns.

Salad Rolls: Hollow out frankfurter rolls. Fill with any of salad fillings, p. 364, doubling recipe if necessary. Top with grated cheese. Toast in broiler. Or split, toast, then butter rolls; top with salad, cheese; then broil.

Frank Burgers: Place heated franks in split frankfurter rolls. Spread with prepared mustard; top with cheese slices. Broil 3 min., or until cheese is melted. Spread pickle relish on cut edges of rolls.

Au Gratin Corned-Beef Hash: In 1 tablesp. butter or margarine, sauté 2 teasp. minced onion till tender. Add 1½ cups canned corned-beef hash, 2 tablesp. catchup; heat well. Spread on 8 slices hot buttered toast. Sprinkle each with ¼ cup grated process American cheese. Broil till cheese is melted. Makes 8.

DEVILED HAMBURGER TOAST

1 lb. chuck, ground	1 teasp. salt
⅓ cup chili sauce	1½ teasp. Worcester-
1½ teasp. prepared	shire
mustard	Speck pepper
1½ teasp. horse-radish	8 bread slices
1 teasp. minced onion	

Combine all ingredients except bread. Toast bread on one side in broiler. Spread untoasted side with beef mixture. Broil 6 min., or until nicely browned. Makes 8.

Finger Style: Cut each sandwich into 3 strips.

MARIETTA'S CHICKEN-CHEESE SANDWICHES

2 tablesp. butter or	(¼ lb.)
margarine	6 slices hot toast
2 tablesp. flour	1 sliced, peeled large
½ teasp. salt	avocado or tomato
¼ teasp. dry mustard	12 slices cooked chicken
1 cup milk	or turkey
1 cup grated process	Paprika
American cheese	

Melt butter. Stir in flour, salt, mustard, then milk; cook, stirring, until thickened. Add cheese; stir over very low heat until melted. Arrange toast in shallow pan; top with avocado,

then chicken. Pour on sauce. Sprinkle with paprika. Broil until golden. Makes 6.

BAKED CHICKEN SANDWICHES

4 bread slices	chicken, -mushroom,
Cheese spread	or -celery soup
Cold sliced, cooked	½ cup milk
chicken or turkey	½ cup crushed potato
1 can undiluted con-	chips
densed cream-of-	

Start heating oven to 425°F. Spread bread slices with cheese spread; arrange, close together, in baking pan; top with chicken. Pour on soup mixed with milk; top with potato chips. Bake 15 min., or until light brown. Makes 4.

Stuffing Sandwiches: Omit cheese. Spread bread with very thin layer of leftover stuffing; top with chicken. Complete as above.

CHILI-EGG BUNWICHES

3 chopped, hard-cooked	2 tablesp. butter, mar-
eggs	garine, or salad oil
3 tablesp. chopped	2 tablesp. chili sauce
green pepper	⅛ teasp. salt
1 tablesp. minced onion	Dash pepper
Bit of minced garlic	2 tablesp. grated process
1 tablesp. chopped	American cheese
pimento	6 frankfurter rolls

Day ahead: Mix all ingredients except rolls. With fork, scoop out center of each roll; fill with egg mixture. Wrap in aluminum foil or waxed paper. Refrigerate.

To serve: Bake wrapped rolls at 400°F. 8 min. Makes 6.

BAKED HAM-AND-EGG SANDWICHES

2 thin slices fully	2 tablesp. soft butter or
cooked or ready-to-	margarine
eat ham (1 lb.)	4 eggs, slightly
12 slices white, French,	beaten
or Vienna bread	½ teasp. salt
1 cup grated process	1 teasp. dry mustard
sharp American	1 qt. milk
cheese (¼ lb.)	Dash paprika

Early in day: In hot skillet, fry ham slices till golden. Remove ham and cool slightly; reserve drippings. Then cut ham into small cubes or strips. Use drippings to grease 12″ x 8″ x 2″ baking dish or shallow 2-qt. casserole.

Arrange 6 bread slices in bottom of baking dish. Scatter ham and cheese over bread; top with matching slices of bread; lightly spread with butter. Mix eggs with salt, mustard, milk, paprika; pour over sandwiches. Refrigerate.

About 1 hr. 15 min. before serving: Start heating oven to 325°F. Bake sandwiches, uncovered, 60 to 70 min., or until egg mixture is firm in center and sandwiches are puffy and lightly browned.

To serve: Cut around each sandwich and lift onto heated plates. Nice with tomato slices. Makes 6.

STUFFED ROLLS

6 chopped, hard-cooked eggs	2 teasp. prepared mustard
1 12-oz. can corned beef, chopped	Salt and pepper to taste
¼ cup sweet pickle relish	12 frankfurter rolls; or 1½ doz. finger rolls
½ cup mayonnaise	Soft butter or margarine

Early in day: Combine eggs, corned beef, pickle relish, mayonnaise, mustard, salt, pepper. Cut off tops of rolls; hollow out slightly. Lightly brush inside of each roll with soft butter. Fill with egg filling; replace top. Wrap in aluminum foil or waxed paper. Refrigerate.

Serve cold. Or bake wrapped rolls at 350°F. 10 to 15 min. Makes 12.

Frank Style: Mix 3 minced franks; ¼ cup grated cheese; 1 coarsely grated, hard-cooked egg. Use as filling for 4 hamburger rolls; wrap; then bake as above. Makes 4.

BAKED TUNA-CHEESE BUNS

¼ lb. cubed process American cheese	pepper
3 chopped, hard-cooked eggs	2 tablesp. minced onion
2 tablesp. pickle relish	½ cup mayonnaise
1 can chunk-style tuna (1 cup)	3 tablesp. chopped stuffed olives
1 tablesp. minced green	6 buttered, split hamburger buns

Early in day: Combine all ingredients except buns. Spoon mixture between bun halves; wrap in aluminum foil or waxed paper. Refrigerate.

To serve: Bake wrapped buns at 400°F. 15 min. Makes 6.

To Vary: For tuna, substitute 1 cup cut-up, cooked or canned chicken or turkey, sardines, ham, tongue, or flaked canned salmon.

FRANK ROLLS

Start heating oven to 325°F. Place each frank diagonally across fresh bread slice, with crusts removed. Spread with prepared mustard or cheese spread. Roll up; insert toothpick. Brush with melted butter or margarine. Bake 10 min., or until toasted.

FRENCH FRANKWICHES

Start heating oven to 400°F. Make 4 sandwiches, using as filling 4 franks (split lengthwise, then halved crosswise) with prepared mustard.

In pie plate, beat 2 eggs with ¼ cup milk, ¼ teasp. sugar, ½ teasp. salt; dip sandwiches into mixture. Set on greased cookie sheet; sprinkle with ½ cup grated cheese, dash paprika. Bake 10 to 12 min.

CLUBS OR DOUBLE DECKERS

1. For each sandwich, in electric toaster, lightly toast 3 bread slices. (If making several sandwiches, toast in broiler, turning once.)
2. Spread each toast slice lightly with butter, margarine, mayonnaise, cooked salad dressing, or Russian dressing.
3. Choose one of sandwich combinations below. Place lower-layer ingredients (L.L.) on first toast slice. Cover with second toast slice, with buttered side up. Place upper-layer ingredients (U.L.) on second slice. Top with third toast slice, with buttered side down.
4. With toothpicks, fasten layers together at corners. Cut into 2, 3, or 4 triangles. Garnish with potato chips, celery, olives, pickles, etc.

Ham or Luncheon Meat, Cheese, Tomato, Lettuce

    L.L.: Ham slices, process American cheese

    U.L.: Thin tomato slices, lettuce

Cheese, Bacon, Tomato, Lettuce

    L.L.: Swiss-cheese slices, crisp bacon

    U.L.: Thin tomato slices, lettuce

Canadian Bacon, Tomato, Lettuce

    L.L.: Sautéed Canadian-style-bacon slices

    U.L.: Thin tomato slices, lettuce, process-American-cheese slices

Chicken, Egg Salad
L.L.: Sliced chicken
U.L.: Egg Salad, p. 364

Sardine, Tomato, Bacon, Dill Pickle
L.L.: Sardines sprinkled with lemon juice
U.L.: Tomato slices, crisp bacon, dill pickle

Chicken, Tomato, Tongue, Coleslaw (Try on rye toast; spread top slice with chili sauce)
L.L.: Chicken, thin tomato slices
U.L.: Tongue slices, spread with mustard; coleslaw

Frank, Tomato, Pickle
L.L.: Tomato slices
U.L.: Split hot franks, sliced pickles

Crab Salad, Tomato, Egg Salad, Lettuce
L.L.: Crab Salad, p. 364; thin tomato slices
U.L.: Egg Salad, p. 364; lettuce

Tuna Salad, Egg and Tomato Slices, Bacon, Lettuce
L.L.: Tuna Salad, p. 364; hard-cooked-egg slices
U.L.: Thin tomato slices, crisp bacon, lettuce

Turkey, Bacon or Ham, Tomato, Lettuce
L.L.: Turkey and crisp bacon or ham slices
U.L.: Thin tomato slices, lettuce

JUNIOR CLUBS

Make up any of Clubs or Double Deckers, p. 359, omitting center toast slice. Or use one of these fillings:

Chicken: Combine 1 cup minced, cooked or canned chicken; ½ cup minced celery; ¼ cup cooked salad dressing; ½ teasp. salt; ⅛ teasp. pepper; pinch monosodium glutamate; ¼ teasp. prepared mustard. Fills 4 sandwiches.

Tuna-Cranberry: In Chicken Junior Club, above, substitute flaked canned tuna for chicken. Top filling with thin canned jellied-cranberry slices.

Curried: In Chicken Junior Club, above, substitute flaked canned tuna, salmon, or crab meat for chicken. Or use chopped, cooked, cleaned shrimp; cooked ham or tongue; or hard-cooked eggs. Add curry to taste. Or add chopped, buttered, toasted walnuts.

Salami-Bean: Snip ¼ lb. salami into bits. Add 1 1-lb. can baked beans with tomato sauce, 2 tablesp. chili sauce, 2 teasp. prepared mustard, a little minced onion. Mash with fork. Fills 6 sandwiches.

HOT OR COLD MEAT SANDWICHES

Use hearty fillings of thinly sliced meat or poultry on, or between, hot buttered toast slices; buttered, toasted split buns; or buttered bread slices. Serve this way:

Roast Chicken, Turkey, or Duckling:
1. *Hot,* with hot giblet gravy, barbecue sauce, or diluted canned cream-of-mushroom or -chicken soup
2. *Cold,* with slices of Swiss cheese, salami, ham, tongue, or crisp bacon. Also canned cranberry sauce, dill pickles, or coleslaw

Roast Beef:
1. *Hot,* with bottled thick meat sauce, p. 9; Worcestershire; hot gravy; or Quick Mushroom Sauce, p. 372
2. *Cold,* with pickle relish, chili sauce, barbecue sauce, or horse-radish

Roast Pork:
1. *Hot,* with hot applesauce, gravy or barbecue sauce
2. *Cold,* with applesauce, dill pickle, horse-radish, or barbecue sauce

Roast Lamb:
1. *Hot,* with hot gravy (add sautéed, sliced mushrooms or cooked vegetables) or barbecue sauce
2. *Cold,* with mint jelly, curry mayonnaise, or barbecue sauce

Corned Beef:
1. *Hot,* with Mustard Sauce, p. 375, or dill pickle
2. *Cold,* with coleslaw, pickles, olives, or sauerkraut

Tongue:
1. *Hot,* with horse-radish sauce, or canned tomato sauce or soup, as gravy
2. *Cold,* with chili sauce or barbecue sauce

Baked or Canned Ham:

1. *Hot,* with horse-radish, mushroom gravy, or barbecue sauce
2. *Cold,* with prepared mustard, catchup, chili sauce or canned cranberry sauce

Steak (or cube steaks):

1. *Hot,* alone or with thin sweet onion slices or Steak Sauce, p. 373
2. *Cold,* with Quick Mushroom Sauce, p. 372

Bacon:

1. *Hot,* alone
2. *Cold,* with sliced, hard-cooked egg; sliced scallions; chopped stuffed olives; or chili sauce

OTHER SANDWICH HEARTIES

Western: For each sandwich, to 1 beaten egg, add 1 tablesp. each minced onion and green pepper; 2 tablesp. each minced, cooked ham and milk; speck salt and pepper. Pour into greased 8″ skillet. Cook till set on both sides, shaping mixture into round with spatula as it cooks.

Bacon-Chicken Liver: Fry 3 bacon slices till crisp; remove from skillet. In bacon fat, sauté ½ lb. chicken livers and ¼ lb. chopped mushrooms till tender; chop fine, along with bacon. Add 1 tablesp. minced onion, ¾ teasp. salt, dash pepper. Fills 4 sandwiches.

Grilled Cheese Sandwiches: Cover half of bread slices with cheese slices or cheese spread. Spread with prepared mustard, deviled ham, or barbecue sauce. Top with bread slices. Toast in broiler, skillet, or sandwich toaster.

Crab Rolls: Use Southern Crab Cakes, p. 186, or Sautéed Soft-shell Crabs, p. 185, to fill bread-and-butter sandwiches (plain or toasted).

Hamburgers: Use sautéed or broiled hamburgers with thin onion or tomato slices, or hot baked or chili beans, to fill bread-and-butter sandwiches. Nice, too, in toasted buns that have been spread with blue cheese, cheese spread, barbecue sauce, chutney, pickle relish, catchup, or mustard.

SUSAN'S STROGANOFF BUNS

Prepare Hamburger Stroganoff, p. 70. Cut thin slice from top of each of 6 hard rectangular bakers' or baked brown-and-serve club rolls. Hollow out rolls; fill with meat mixture. Garnish with snipped parsley, chives, or dill. Nice with spiced peaches. Makes 6.

SUSAN'S BEANIES

2 tablesp. butter or margarine	½ teasp. Worcestershire
1 chopped green pepper	¼ teasp. salt
2 tablesp. minced onion	Dash pepper
1 drained No. 2 can kidney beans	2 cups grated process sharp American cheese (½ lb.)
2 tablesp. catchup	6 split frankfurter rolls

In hot butter in skillet, sauté green pepper and onion until tender. Stir in beans, catchup, Worcestershire, salt, pepper, cheese; cook till bubbly. Serve in split rolls. Makes 6.

HI-YI SPECIALS

1½ cups chopped, cooked ham or coarsely grated canned luncheon meat	2 tablesp. mayonnaise
	1 teasp. chili powder
	⅔ cup chopped ripe olives
	12 bread slices
1 cup grated process American cheese (¼ lb.)	2 eggs, beaten
	¼ cup milk

Combine ham, cheese, mayonnaise, chili powder, olives. Spread on half of bread slices. Cover with remaining bread slices. Cut from corner to corner into triangles.

In pie plate, combine eggs, milk. Dip sandwiches into egg mixture; place on cookie sheet. Broil till brown on both sides. Makes 6 servings.

WAFFLE-TOASTED SANDWICHES

1 cup grated process American cheese (¼ lb.)	mustard
	½ teasp. salt
	½ teasp. grated onion
⅓ cup chopped stuffed olives	12 white-bread slices
	⅓ cup melted butter or margarine
2 teasp. prepared	

About 20 min. before supper: Preheat waffle iron as manufacturer directs. Combine cheese, olives, mustard, salt, onion; spread on 6 bread slices; top with rest of bread.

Brush outside surfaces of sandwiches with butter. Toast in waffle iron until golden brown. Serve immediately. Makes 6.

Susan's Waffle Devils: Spread half of bread slices with deviled ham, the rest with cream cheese. Put together, sandwich-fashion; then brush with butter; toast as above.

Other Fillings: Use cream cheese; peanut butter; sliced or chopped, cooked ham or chicken; flaked canned salmon or tuna; or one of salad fillings, p. 364.

If You Have a Freezer: After toasting sandwiches in waffle iron, cool; then wrap for freezing. Freeze 2 weeks or less. To serve, toast twice in electric toaster. Or heat at 400°F.

FRENCH-TOASTED SANDWICHES

Make up sandwiches, using one of fillings below:

> Thin ham and cheese slices
> Chicken, Tuna, Ham, Egg, or Crab Salad, p. 364 (double recipe if necessary)
> Turkey or chicken slices
> Sharp cheese or cheese spread
> Corned-beef and Swiss-cheese slices
> Cream cheese or deviled ham
> Franks, split lengthwise and crosswise

About 15 min. before supper: For every 6 sandwiches, combine 3 beaten eggs, ½ cup milk, 1 teasp. sugar, ¼ teasp. salt. Dip each sandwich into egg mixture. Then, in ¼ cup hot butter, margarine, or salad oil in skillet, brown each sandwich on both sides. Cut each sandwich in half.

Serve on heated platter, with bowl of canned cranberry sauce, pickle relish, or pickled watermelon, pineapple, or peaches in center.

PACK-AND-CARRY SANDWICHES

Nine times out of ten the mainstay of a box lunch or picnic is sandwiches. So don't let yours be humdrum. Vary them from day to day with new fillings and breads. (Be sure to read Production-Line Techniques, p. 356.) Or pack fillings and crisp crackers separately; each person spreads his own.

MAKE IT MEAT OR POULTRY

Add salad dressing, if desired, and seasonings to one of these meat combinations:

1. Sliced bologna, coleslaw
2. Chopped chicken or turkey, apple, and celery
3. Chopped chicken, walnuts, and olives
4. Sliced corned beef, chopped green pepper, horse-radish
5. Chopped franks, baked beans, catchup, minced onion
6. Ground ham or canned luncheon meat, American cheese, and dill pickle
7. Ground ham, drained canned crushed pineapple, a little brown sugar, and ground cloves
8. Chopped ham and pickle, cottage cheese
9. Chopped corned beef, minced onion and pickle
10. Chopped liver and crisp bacon, pickle relish
11. Sliced meat loaf, chopped green olives
12. Chopped roast pork, green pepper, and celery
13. Sliced roast pork, apple butter
14. Sliced turkey or ham, canned cranberry jelly

MAKE IT EGG

Mix chopped, hard-cooked eggs with mayonnaise, desired seasonings, and one of these:

1. Chopped crisp bacon, snipped chives
2. Grated carrots, sliced ripe olives
3. Chopped celery, onion, and chicken
4. Chopped, cooked chicken giblets; catchup
5. Chopped corned beef or salami, mustard pickle
6. Sliced franks, chili sauce
7. Deviled ham, chopped pickle, mustard
8. Chopped tongue, grated cheese, mustard
9. Tuna or salmon, chopped celery, pickle relish

MAKE IT CHEESE

Add mayonnaise, if desired, to one of these:

1. Grated cheese, shredded dried beef, chili sauce
2. Blue-cheese spread, chopped crisp bacon, chili sauce
3. Cheese and egg slices, chili sauce

4. Swiss-cheese slices, deviled ham, sweet pickle
5. Chopped dates or figs, chopped peanuts, cream cheese
6. Cream cheese, sliced radishes
7. Any package or jar of cheese spread
8. Cottage cheese, chopped peanuts, peach jam
9. Sharp-cheese spread, sliced salami, prepared mustard
10. Swiss-cheese and tongue slices, pickle relish
11. Cream cheese; chopped, cooked dried apricots and prunes
12. Cream cheese; chopped green pepper, olives, and celery
13. Cream cheese, peanut butter, orange juice, grated orange rind

MAKE IT PEANUT BUTTER

Mix peanut butter with one of these:

1. Chopped crisp bacon and apple, a little cream
2. Chopped crisp bacon, catchup
3. Grated carrot, chopped raisins or celery
4. Minced ham, pickle relish
5. Chopped dates and figs, lemon juice
6. Deviled ham, chopped dill pickle, mayonnaise
7. Chopped nuts, honey
8. Applesauce, sliced dates
9. Cream cheese and apple butter or chopped, cooked dried prunes
10. Marshmallow cream

MAKE IT FISH

Add mayonnaise and seasonings to one of these:

1. Salmon, minced cucumber and onion
2. Cut-up shrimp, chopped green pepper and celery
3. Sardines, chopped celery, lemon juice
4. Tuna, chopped apple, lemon juice
5. Tuna, chopped celery and walnuts
6. Tuna, cottage cheese, pickle relish
7. Tuna, drained canned crushed pineapple, chopped celery

MAKE IT RAW VEGETABLES

Add salad dressing, seasonings, to one of these:

1. Chopped cabbage and walnuts, snipped dried apricots
2. Chopped cabbage and nuts, grated carrot
3. Grated carrot, minced celery and green pepper, chili sauce
4. Grated carrot, chopped peanuts, raisins
5. Chopped radishes, cucumbers, and green pepper

FOR PARTYTIME

At a tea, bridge, shower, garden party, wedding, birthday—at any party, in fact—these pretty sandwiches star.

SUSAN'S PARTY SANDWICH LOAF

Fillings: Ham Salad,	cheese
Chicken Salad, Egg	¼ lb. blue cheese
Salad, p. 364	⅓ to ½ cup light cream
½ 5-oz. jar sharp-cheese	Day-old loaf unsliced
spread	bread
2 tablesp. hot water	6 thin tomato slices
3 3-oz. pkg. soft cream	

1. Night before, if convenient, prepare all 3 fillings; *refrigerate at once.*
2. In morning, blend sharp-cheese spread with hot water. For **Cream-Cheese Frosting:** Blend cream cheese and blue cheese with enough cream to spread easily (omit blue cheese if sandwich fillings are fruity).
3. Then, with sharp knife, trim all crusts from bread. Lay loaf on side and slice lengthwise into 5 even slices, about ½" thick. (You may use ruler as guide to keep slicing straight.)
4. Spread bottom bread slice with sharp-cheese spread. Spread second bread slice with half of Chicken Salad. Top with tomato slices, trimming them so they cover salad evenly. Top with rest of Chicken Salad. Place on cheese-spread slice.
5. Spread third bread slice with Egg Salad; place on Chicken Salad layer. Avoid pressing layers together too firmly lest fillings ooze.
6. Spread fourth slice with Ham Salad; place on Egg Salad layer. Top loaf with last bread slice, with rounded side up; gently shape loaf with hands so all sides are even. Remove any oozing bits.
7. With spatula, "frost" top, sides, with Cream-Cheese Frosting, above.
8. Refrigerate loaf several hours, or till easy to cut.

To serve: Top loaf with sliced radishes; sprinkle with snipped parsley. With sharp knife, cut into 10 1″ slices. Cake server makes serving easy. Makes 10 servings.

Fillings (choose any three of these):

Ham Salad: Mix ½ cup ground, cooked or canned ham or canned luncheon meat with 2 tablesp. minced green pepper, 1 teasp. prepared mustard, 2 tablesp. mayonnaise, 1 tablesp. minced onion. Refrigerate.

Chicken Salad: Mix ½ cup ground or finely chopped, cooked or canned chicken or turkey; ¼ cup minced celery; 2 tablesp. pickle relish; ½ teasp. salt; dash pepper; 2 tablesp. mayonnaise. Add pinch of curry if desired. Refrigerate.

Tuna, Salmon, Shrimp, or Crab Salad: Use flaked fresh or canned tuna, salmon, shrimp, or crab meat for chicken in Chicken Salad above. Refrigerate.

Egg Salad: Mix 2 finely chopped, hard-cooked eggs; 2 tablesp. minced ripe olives; ½ teasp. salt; dash pepper; ½ to ¾ teasp. prepared mustard; 2 tablesp. mayonnaise. Refrigerate.

Canned Deviled Ham or Thin Tomato Slices

Blue- or Pimento-Cheese Spread

DESSERT SANDWICH LOAF

Make Susan's Party Sandwich Loaf, p. 363, spreading alternate slices with fillings below. Frost with Cream-Cheese Frosting, p. 363, adding ½ cup grated orange rind.

Date-Nut Filling: Mix 1 7¼-oz. pkg. pitted dates, snipped fine with scissors; ½ cup chopped walnuts or pecans; 2 3-oz. pkg. cream cheese; ⅓ cup light cream. Refrigerate.

Peanut-Butter-Marmalade Filling: Mix ½ cup peanut butter with ¼ cup orange marmalade. Refrigerate.

MINIATURE SANDWICH LOAVES

Use 12 thin white-bread slices, with crusts removed. Make 3 stacks of 4 slices each, filling with Ham, Chicken Salad, and Egg Salad, above. Cut stacks in halves; frost with Cream-

Cheese Frosting, p. 363. Makes 6. (Or cut bread slices into circles; fill; stack; frost as above.)

SWEET AND SAVORY SANDWICHES

Blend soft butter or margarine with one of the following. Use to fill dainty-shaped sandwiches.

1. Anchovy paste, plus lemon juice, snipped chives
2. Catchup or chili sauce, plus minced onion or seasoned salt
3. Pimento, sharp, smoky, American, blue, or other snappy cheese spread, plus minced onion or chopped nuts
4. Snipped chives, parsley, or mint, plus lemon juice
5. Deviled ham, plus snipped chives, minced onion, or chili sauce
6. Honey, plus a little lemon juice
7. Horse-radish or prepared mustard, plus grated cheese
8. Grated lemon or orange rind and juice, plus nutmeg
9. Mashed pimento, plus a few drops tabasco
10. Sardines or cleaned canned shrimp mashed with lemon juice, plus a little minced onion

DAINTY TEA SANDWICHES

Fill dainty-shaped buttered sandwiches with any of these:

1. Cheese spread, plus very thin tomato slices
2. Applesauce, plus nutmeg or peanut butter
3. Chicken salad, plus orange marmalade
4. Cream cheese, a bit of salad dressing, plus one of these:

Bacon bits, chutney	cherries
Honey, raisins, nuts	Chopped salted
Snipped chives,	peanuts
canned crushed	Chopped, pitted
pineapple	dates; lemon
Sardines, lemon juice	juice
Snipped water cress,	Chopped almonds,
grated onion	lemon juice
Chopped watermelon	Ground salami
pickle	Minced nuts and
Minced maraschino	stuffed olives

5. Chopped, hard-cooked egg, plus minced anchovy fillets; mayonnaise
6. Minced turkey or chicken, plus cream

cheese, olive spread, peanut butter, or marmalade
7. Flaked canned tuna or salmon, plus mayonnaise, lemon juice, and minced onion or
chives
8. Grated Parmesan cheese, plus mayonnaise
9. Liverwurst or canned liver *pâté,* plus dried
thyme, snipped chives, mayonnaise
10. Banana mashed with lemon juice, mayonnaise, speck nutmeg
11. Avocado mashed with a little lemon juice
or tarragon vinegar, salt, pepper, and a little
chili powder or chili sauce
12. Peanut butter, plus deviled ham or ground
corned beef, a little prepared mustard, horse-
radish, and mayonnaise
13. Your favorite bottled sandwich spread

OPEN-FACE PRETTIES

Use single slice of bread; cut into fancy shape.
Or use crisp round scalloped crackers. Spread
with butter or margarine, then with any filling
below; decorate gaily.

Red and White: Spread bread with jelly; sprinkle with coconut.

Paper Stencil: Cut out paper stencil; lay on
open sandwich; sprinkle with snipped parsley;
lift off stencil.

Cheese Strips: With cookie press, decorate bread
strips with sharp- or blue-cheese spread. Top
with poppy seeds or nuts.

Olive Scallops: Halve stuffed olives lengthwise;
slice crosswise. Place, with rounded sides down,
along edge of bread round.

Borders: Spread bread with peanut butter or
jelly; dip edges into chopped peanuts. Or spread
with cheese spread; dip edges into snipped parsley or chives.

Half-and-Half: Spread half of each bread round
with jelly, rest of each round with deviled-ham
or pineapple-cream-cheese spread.

One-Two-Three: Spread bread with favorite filling. Place 3 pecan or walnut halves, or stuffed-
olive or radish slices, along center.

Berry Bright: Spread bread with seasoned cottage cheese. Set halved strawberries or blueberries on top.

Parsley Crusts: Trim crusts from French-bread
slices in oval pieces. Butter crusts; sprinkle with
seasoned or onion salt and snipped parsley.

Cottage Cheese-Peach: Top bread slice with
cottage cheese, then with drained canned peach
slices and nutmeg.

Cucumber-Radish Flowers: Border edges of
bread rounds with sliced radishes. Top each
round with cucumber slice. Dot center with
mayonnaise and snipped parsley.

NOVELTY NUMBERS

Show-offs: With cutter, cut bread slices into
rounds; with smaller cutter, cut hole in center
of half of rounds. Spread whole rounds with
chicken salad; top with remaining rounds; place
dab of cranberry jelly in each center. Or use
cream cheese (flavored with almond extract)
and dab of currant jelly. Or use tomato slice
and dab of chive cream cheese.

Sandwich Sticks: Cut 3″ x ½″ bread fingers.
Spread all sides with butter or margarine; roll
in chopped pecans, grated Parmesan cheese,
snipped chives, or cinnamon and sugar.

Frosted Biscuits: Bake tiny baking-powder biscuits; immediately frost tops with cheese spread;
serve piping hot. Or before baking, roll tiny
biscuits in melted butter and grated cheese.

Teatime Bites: Split tiny hot baking-powder biscuits. Spread with cheese spread or deviled ham
or tongue.

Devonshire Muffins: Split English muffins;
toast. Butter well. Spread with orange marmalade; top with thin cheese slices. Broil.

Peanut Creams: On graham crackers or white
bread, spread peanut butter, then marshmallow
cream, then shaved chocolate.

Cookie Sandwiches: Fill chocolate, ginger, or
molasses cookies; macaroons; or thin gingerbread slices with soft cream cheese.

Choco-Nut Fingers: Melt semisweet-chocolate
pieces; spread on sugar wafers, graham crackers,
bread, or ladyfingers; top with chopped nuts.

Chocolate-Almond Bars: Place bars on white
bread; broil until melted.

Cake Slices: Fill cake slices with frosting or crushed chocolate-mint patties.

Jam Fingers: Spread jam between split ladyfingers or sugar wafers.

Angel-Cake Slices: Fill cake slices with marmalade; sprinkle with coconut.

RIBBON SANDWICHES

1. Use fresh or day-old bread. For each stack, alternate 3 slices whole-wheat and 2 slices white bread, filling with any extra-smooth and creamy filling for Dainty Tea Sandwiches, p. 364.
2. Firmly press together each stack of slices. Then, using sharp knife in sawing motion, slice off crusts from all sides of each stack.
3. Arrange stacks in shallow pan; cover with waxed paper, saran, or aluminum foil. Refrigerate *at least* several hours. Then cut into ½" slices.
4. Cut each ½" slice into thirds, halves, or 2 or 3 triangles.

CHECKERBOARDS

1. Use fresh or day-old bread. For each stack, alternate 2 slices whole-wheat and 2 slices white bread, filling with one or more extra-smooth and creamy fillings for Dainty Tea Sandwiches, p. 364.
2. Firmly press each stack of slices together. Then, using sharp knife in sawing motion, slice off crusts from all sides of each stack. Wrap tightly in waxed paper, saran, or foil; refrigerate several hours.
3. Now cut each stack into 6 ½" slices. Spread cut sides of slices with one of fillings for Dainty Tea Sandwiches, p. 364, or Sweet and Savory Sandwiches, p. 364. Rebuild slices into stacks of 3 layers each, with outside white strips alternating with whole-wheat strips.
4. Wrap tightly in waxed paper, saran, or foil. Refrigerate *at least* several hours. Then, with sharp knife, *immediately* slice into slices, ¼" to ½" thick.

MOSAICS

1. Cut 2 white and 2 whole-wheat-bread rounds. With small, round (or fancy-shaped) cutter, remove center of 1 white and 1 dark round.

Insert small round of dark bread into hole in white ring and small round of white bread into hole in dark ring. This makes 2 "mosaics."
2. Spread 2 plain rounds with one of fillings for Dainty Tea Sandwiches, p. 364, or Sweet and Savory Sandwiches, p. 364. Cover white round with dark mosaic, dark round with white mosaic.

PIN WHEELS

1. Buy unsliced loaf of very fresh white bread. With long sharp knife, cut off all crusts except bottom one.
2. With crust side of loaf to left, cut into lengthwise slices, ⅛" to ¼" thick. Run rolling pin over each slice, starting at narrow end (bread is less likely to crack).
3. Spread each slice with soft butter or margarine to edges, then with any extra-smooth and creamy filling for Dainty Tea Sandwiches, p. 364. Then, if desired, place 3 stuffed olives or gherkins, 1 frank, or 2 Vienna sausages across short end.
4. Starting at end with stuffed olives, *tightly* roll up bread, being careful to keep sides in line.
5. Wrap rolls individually in waxed paper, saran, or foil, twisting ends securely. Refrigerate several hours or overnight. (Or make ahead; wrap; freeze as on p. 541; thaw about 45 min.; slice.)

To serve: Cut chilled rolls into ¼" to ½" slices. With broad spatula, lift onto serving plate. Or fix on trays; cover with waxed paper, foil, saran, or dry towel; refrigerate until served.

P.S. Pin wheels are nice toasted.

ROLL-UPS

Trim crusts from thin fresh bread slices. Roll lightly with rolling pin. Spread each to edge with any of tea-sandwich fillings, p. 364, that is extra smooth and creamy. Lay asparagus tip or stuffed celery stalk across one end; roll up.

Serve whole or cut into halves or thirds, with sprig of water cress, mint, or parsley tucked in one or both ends if desired.

To Toast: Place Roll-ups on cookie sheet; brush with melted butter or margarine or salad oil; broil till golden. Serve hot.

Sauces

A saucy touch does for a good dish what the right accessories do for a pretty dress—makes a wonderful thing even better. But it must be the right sauce, and it must be well made. Choose your sauce with flavor and eye appeal in mind. Then follow recipe directions to the letter, to avoid that culinary tragedy—a sauce that's too thick or too thin.

Before using these recipes, refer to How to Use Our Recipes, p. 3, and Pots and Pans, p. 692. Always use standard measuring cups and measuring spoons; measure level.

EXTRA-EASY DESSERT SAUCES

EIGHT LITTLE SAUCE RECIPES

Simplicity Orange: Stir ½ cup orange juice and ¼ cup granulated sugar till sugar dissolves. Nice on rice, tapioca, or bread pudding, etc. Makes about 4 servings.

Spiced Cream: To heavy cream, add pinch nutmeg, cinnamon, or allspice. Serve in pitcher, to pour over fruit shortcakes or cobblers.

Red and White: Sprinkle canned whole-cranberry sauce with brown sugar mixed with cinnamon. Nice on vanilla pudding, baked custards, etc.

Nectar: Use canned whole-fruit apricot, peach, or pear nectar; sprinkle with shredded coconut. Wonderful on cake squares, ice cream, etc.

Jelly: Add ½ cup orange or pineapple juice to ½ cup heated jelly. Serve on cake squares, baked custard, etc. Makes about 6 servings.

Maple: Slowly stir ¼ cup hot maple-blended syrup into ½ cup heavy cream, whipped. Use on bread pudding, chocolate cake, etc. Makes 6 to 8 servings.

Sundae: Thaw frozen fruit juices, such as grape, pineapple, orange, etc., just enough to pour. Luscious on ice cream, sherbet, Bavarian cream, custards, bread pudding, etc.

Coffee Sundae: Mix 1 to 2 tablesp. instant coffee with 1 cup canned sweetened condensed milk. Nice on ice cream. Makes about 6 servings.

CHOCOLATE SAUCE

In double boiler, heat 1 pkg. semisweet-chocolate pieces (1 cup) with ½ to ¾ cup white corn syrup, stirring, until blended. Stir in ¼ cup light cream, 1 tablesp. butter or margarine, ¼ teasp. vanilla extract.

Serve warm, on chocolate or coffee ice cream. Makes 4 servings.

EGGNOG SAUCE

2 egg yolks	3 tablesp. brandy
¾ cup confectioners' sugar	½ cup heavy cream, whipped

Beat yolks well; stir in sugar, then brandy; fold in whipped cream.

Serve on gingerbread, coffee jelly, canned pears, etc. Makes 6 servings.

EASY CARAMEL SAUCE

In double boiler, place ½ lb. packaged vanilla caramels and ½ cup milk. Cook, stirring, until sauce is smooth.

Serve hot, on vanilla or chocolate ice cream, cream puffs, etc. Makes 4 servings.

CHOCOLATE-PEPPERMINT SAUCE

In double boiler over *hot, not boiling,* water, melt 20 chocolate-covered peppermints with 2 tablesp. butter or margarine. Thin with light cream.

Serve warm, on chocolate, coffee, or vanilla ice cream; white-cake squares, etc. Makes 4 to 6 servings.

FROSTY SAUCE

With fork, stir 1 pt. vanilla ice cream until soft *but not runny.* Add sherry, almond or brandy extract, or bit of spice. Serve at once on warm fruit cobblers, brownies, angel cake, fruit gelatin, etc. Makes 6 to 8 servings.

Coffee-Rum: Use coffee ice cream and 2 teasp. rum extract. Nice on warm fruitcake, bread pudding, baked apples, etc.

Brandy-Pecan: Use butter-pecan ice cream, 1 tablesp. brandy extract. Luscious on warm baked apples or pears, broiled peaches, etc.

Choco-Almond: Use chocolate ice cream and ½ teasp. almond extract. So good on bread pudding.

Fruit: Use vanilla ice cream and 2 tablesp. slightly thawed frozen orange, tangerine, or pineapple juice.

Berry: Use vanilla ice cream and 2 tablesp. strawberry jam.

"Fresh" Strawberry: Use 1 pt. vanilla ice cream; add 1 pkg. slightly thawed frozen strawberries. Stir just enough to blend. Nice on sponge or angel cake, Spanish cream, etc. Makes 8 to 10 servings.

BUTTER-CREAM SAUCE

In saucepan, combine 1 cup granulated sugar, ½ cup butter or margarine, ½ cup light cream, and 1 teasp. vanilla extract. Heat till boiling.

Serve hot, on puddings, gingerbread squares, etc. Makes 6 to 8 servings.

Quick Rum: Just before serving, stir in 2 to 3 tablesp. rum and dash nutmeg.

BUTTERSCOTCH SAUCE

Combine 1 cup brown sugar, packed; ¼ cup light cream; 2 tablesp. white corn syrup; 2 tablesp. butter or margarine. Bring to boil; cook, stirring, 3 to 4 min., or until thickened.

Serve on butter-pecan or other ice cream, warm cake squares, etc. Makes 4 servings.

CHOCOLATE-MARSHMALLOW SAUCE

In saucepan, combine ¼ lb. (16) marshmallows, ⅓ cup honey, ⅓ cup heavy cream, pinch salt, 1½ sq. unsweetened chocolate. Cook, stirring occasionally, till marshmallows are almost melted. Remove from heat; stir till entirely melted.

Delicious on ice cream, cake squares, etc. Makes 10 servings.

Snowy Marshmallow: Omit chocolate.

THREE SPEEDY CUSTARD SAUCES

1. Prepare 1 pkg. custard-dessert mix as label directs. Refrigerate; then beat well. Makes 12 servings (3 tablesp. each).
2. Or into 1 can strained custard pudding (baby pack), fold ⅓ cup heavy cream, whipped, and favorite extract to taste. Refrigerate. Nice on jellied desserts, cut-up fruit, coffee ice cream, etc. Makes 5 or 6 servings (3 tablesp. each).
3. Or into ½ pkg. vanilla pudding (measure package contents; use half) in double boiler, gradually stir 1½ cups milk, or ¾ cup milk and ¾ cup cream. Cook, stirring, until smooth and thick enough to coat spoon. Refrigerate; add 1 teasp. almond, vanilla, or sherry extract. Makes 9 or 10 servings (3 tablesp. each).

BING-CHERRY SAUCE

In skillet, melt ¾ cup currant jelly; add 1 drained No. 2½ can Bing cherries. Heat slowly till boiling, stirring.

Serve warm, on strawberry or vanilla ice cream, baked custards, etc. Makes 6 servings.

DATE-NUT SAUCE

Combine 1 7¼-oz. pkg. pitted dates, snipped; pinch salt; ½ cup water. Heat just till boiling. Remove from heat; stir in ½ cup each white corn syrup and chopped walnuts. Cool.

Serve on coffee or vanilla ice cream. Makes 8 servings.

WHIPPED CREAM

Unsweetened: With egg beater or electric mixer, beat chilled heavy cream until it *just* mounds. (Overbeating causes curdling. In hot weather, chill bowl and beater.)

Sweetened: Allow 2 to 4 tablesp. granulated sugar to ½ pt. (1 cup) heavy cream. Beat cream until it begins to thicken. Gradually add sugar, then ¼ teasp. vanilla or almond extract, or sherry to taste, beating until cream *just* holds shape.

Berry: Fold drained, crushed slightly sweetened berries into whipped cream.

Chocolate: Place 2 tablesp. instant-cocoa mix, or 2 teasp. sugar and 2 tablesp. cocoa, in bowl; add 1 cup heavy cream. Beat until cream *just* mounds. Wonderful on angel-food cake.

Coffee: Place 2 teasp. instant coffee in bowl; add 1 cup heavy cream. Beat until cream *just* mounds. Nice on any chocolate dessert.

Mint: Fold 2 tablesp. beaten mint jelly into ¼ cup heavy cream, whipped. Luscious on chocolate ice cream.

Note: In this book, when recipe calls for "1 cup heavy cream, whipped," first measure 1 cup cream, then whip. One cup heavy cream yields about 2 cups, whipped, or 16 servings of 2 tablesp. each.

WHIPPED MILK TOPPING

½ cup undiluted evap-orated milk
1 tablesp. lemon juice
½ cup confectioners' or granulated sugar
½ teasp. vanilla ex-tract; or ¼ teasp. almond extract; or a little cinnamon or nutmeg

Chill milk in ice-cube tray until soft crystals form throughout milk—about 15 to 20 min. Turn into bowl; whip until stiff enough to form peaks. Add lemon juice; whip just to blend well. Fold in sugar, vanilla. If topping is not to be used at once, refrigerate; it will hold up well 45 min. to 1 hr. Makes 1½ cups, whipped, or 6 servings (4 tablesp. each).

LOW-CAL TOPPING
(use instead of whipped cream)

½ cup ice water
1 tablesp. fresh, frozen, or canned lemon juice
1 teasp. vanilla extract
½ cup nonfat dry milk
3 tablesp. granulated sugar

In bowl, place water, lemon juice, vanilla. Sprinkle dry milk on top. With electric mixer or egg beater, beat until stiff—about 10 min. Beat in sugar; continue beating until stiff enough to hold soft peaks—about 5 min. more.

Use instead of whipped cream to top desserts. Makes about 2½ cups, or 20 servings (2 tablesp. each).

Maple: Substitute ½ teasp. maple flavoring for vanilla.

Coffee: With vanilla, add 1 teasp. instant coffee.

OTHER DESSERT SAUCES

ICE-CREAM SAUCE

1 egg
¼ cup granulated sugar
Pinch salt
⅓ cup melted butter or margarine
1 teasp. vanilla or brandy extract
1 cup heavy cream, whipped

Beat egg until thick and light; beat in sugar and salt. Gradually beat in butter, extract. Fold in cream.

Serve on warm chocolate- or white-cake squares. Makes about 12 servings.

BUTTER-CARAMEL SAUCE

¾ cup granulated sugar
⅛ teasp. salt
½ cup white corn syrup
¼ cup butter or margarine
1 cup light cream
½ teasp. vanilla extract

In saucepan, combine sugar, salt, syrup, butter, ½ cup cream. Cook slowly, stirring frequently, to 250°F. on candy thermometer, or until a little mixture in cold water forms hard ball. Add ½ cup cream; cook to 216°F., or until a little mixture forms thread when dropped from spoon. Remove from heat; add vanilla.

Serve warm, on chocolate ice cream, cream

puffs, baked custard, warm cake squares, etc. Makes 4 servings.

Rum Butter: Add rum to taste.

HOT FUDGE SAUCE

2 sq. unsweetened chocolate	1½ cups corn syrup
½ cup water	⅛ teasp. salt
	1 teasp. vanilla extract

In saucepan over low heat, cook chocolate with water, stirring, 2 min., or until thick. Remove from heat; gradually add syrup, salt. Simmer 10 min., stirring often. Add vanilla.

Serve hot or cold, on favorite ice cream. Or pour over warm cake squares, cream puffs, etc. Makes 10 servings.

CUSTARD SAUCE I
(3 eggs or 6 egg yolks)

2 cups milk; or 1 cup evaporated milk plus 1 cup water	lated sugar
3 eggs; or 6 egg yolks	¼ teasp. salt
3 to 4 tablesp. granu-	1 teasp. vanilla extract; or ½ teasp. almond extract

1. In double boiler, heat milk until tiny bubbles appear around edge.
2. In medium bowl, beat eggs or yolks slightly with fork; stir in sugar (amount depends on taste), salt. Add hot milk *slowly*, stirring constantly to avoid cooked-egg specks.
3. Return mixture to double boiler; cook over *hot, not boiling,* water, stirring constantly, until thick enough to coat spoon with thin film of custard.
4. Pour *at once* into cool bowl; cool; add vanilla. Cover; refrigerate until chilled.

Serve on Susan's Snow Pudding, p. 405, cut-up fruit, cake, coffee ice cream, fruit gelatin, etc. Makes 16 servings (2 tablesp. each).

Important: If custard is not smooth when done, strain. If it curdles, set pan of custard in cold water and beat vigorously with egg beater. This restores smoothness, but custard may be a little thinner.

To Vary: To sauce, add ¼ cup shredded coconut.

Custard Sauce II (2 egg yolks): Make ½ recipe, using 2 egg yolks. If desired, add 2 teasp. grated orange rind. Makes 8 servings (2 tablesp. each).

Custard Sauce de Luxe: Substitute 1 cup heavy cream for 1 cup milk. Use 3 or 4 egg yolks. Add 1 tablesp. flour to sugar. Cook in double boiler until consistency of heavy cream.

Holiday Custard Sauce: Omit vanilla. Add sherry, rum, or brandy to taste. Nice on coffee ice cream, topped with grated chocolate.

VANILLA SAUCE

½ cup granulated sugar	¼ cup butter or margarine
2 tablesp. cornstarch	2 teasp. vanilla extract
¼ teasp. salt	Dash nutmeg or mace
2 cups boiling water	

In saucepan, combine sugar, cornstarch, salt; gradually stir in water. Boil, stirring constantly, 5 min., or until sauce is thickened. Add rest of ingredients.

Serve hot, on warm cake squares, Dutch Apple Cake, p. 387, etc. Makes 10 servings.

Holiday: Omit vanilla, spices. Add brandy, rum, or sherry to taste.

Lemon: Use ½ cup granulated sugar, 1 tablesp. cornstarch, pinch salt, 1 cup boiling water, 2 tablesp. butter or margarine, 1 teasp. grated lemon rind, 3 tablesp. lemon juice. Make as above. Makes 5 servings.

Orange: Use ½ cup granulated sugar, 1 tablesp. cornstarch, dash each salt and cinnamon, ¾ cup boiling water, 2 tablesp. butter or margarine, 1 teasp. grated orange rind, ¼ cup orange juice, 1 tablesp. lemon juice. Combine sugar, cornstarch, salt, cinnamon; gradually stir in water; proceed as above. Makes 5 servings.

SUNSHINE FOAMY SAUCE

Beat 1 egg white with pinch salt until foamy; slowly add 2 tablesp. brown sugar, beating until stiff. To 1 egg yolk, add 2 tablesp. brown sugar; beat until light-colored; fold into egg-white mixture. Fold in ¼ cup heavy cream, whipped, and ½ teasp. vanilla extract.

Serve on warm gingerbread, chocolate- or white-cake squares. Makes 6 servings.

HARD SAUCE

⅓ to ½ cup butter or margarine	sugar
1 cup confectioners'	½ teasp. vanilla or lemon extract

With spoon or electric mixer, beat butter with sugar till fluffy and creamy; beat in extract. Pile in pretty dish. Or make into balls and roll in grated orange rind. Refrigerate until firm.

Serve on fruit cobblers, steamed puddings, bread pudding, etc. Makes 8 servings (2 tablesp. each).

Fluffy: Fold in ¼ cup heavy cream, whipped; refrigerate.

Or use ⅓ cup butter; blend with ⅔ cup confectioners' sugar; substitute 1 teasp. sherry for vanilla. Then beat 1 egg white until it forms peaks when beater is raised; gradually add ⅓ cup confectioners' sugar, beating; fold into sauce. Refrigerate.

Orange: Use ⅓ cup butter. For vanilla, substitute 2 teasp. orange juice, ½ teasp. orange extract, and 1 tablesp. grated orange rind.

Sterling Sauce: Use ½ cup butter. Substitute brown sugar, packed, for confectioners' sugar. After blending butter with sugar, slowly add ¼ cup light cream. Use 1 teasp. vanilla. Add rum to taste if desired.

MELBA SAUCE

1 pkg. thawed frozen raspberries*	1½ teasp. cornstarch
½ cup currant jelly	1 tablesp. cold water

In saucepan, mash raspberries. Add jelly; bring to boil. Add cornstarch mixed with water; cook, stirring, until clear. Strain if desired; cool.

Serve on lemon sherbet or Peach Melba, p. 427. Makes 6 servings.

* Two cups fresh raspberries and ½ cup granulated sugar may replace frozen berries.

MINTED CANTALOUPE SAUCE

⅓ cup granulated sugar	2 teasp. fresh, frozen, or canned lemon juice
¼ cup water	
1 cup diced cantaloupe	
2 sprigs mint	

Cook sugar with water over low heat, stirring constantly, until sugar dissolves; boil 1 min. Add cantaloupe, mint; bring to boil. Remove from heat; add lemon juice. Refrigerate. Remove mint.

Serve on vanilla ice cream, garnished with mint. Makes 4 servings.

FLAMING FRUIT-COCKTAIL SAUCE

1 No. 2½ can fruit cocktail, drained	1 tablesp. cornstarch
½ cup granulated sugar	½ teasp. grated lemon rind
2 tablesp. butter or margarine	¼ cup brandy or light rum

In double boiler or chafing dish, heat fruit, sugar, butter, cornstarch, and lemon rind, stirring, until thickened. Add brandy; don't stir. Light brandy; spoon sauce, over and over, into flame.

When flame expires (alcohol has burned off), spoon over vanilla or coffee ice cream. Makes 8 servings.

ORANGE FLUFF SAUCE

½ cup granulated sugar	concentrate
Dash salt	2 egg yolks
½ cup thawed frozen orange-juice	1 cup heavy cream, whipped

In saucepan, combine sugar, salt, orange juice. Cook over low heat, stirring, until sugar dissolves. Beat egg yolks slightly; gradually pour in some of orange mixture, beating constantly. Return to rest of mixture in saucepan and cook, stirring, until slightly thickened. Cool to room temperature; fold in whipped cream. Refrigerate until well chilled.

Serve on warm waffles (frozen ones heated in toaster are easy to use). Nice too on devil's-food or spicecake squares. Makes 8 to 10 servings.

BLUEBERRY SAUCE

1 tablesp. butter or margarine	1 tablesp. grated lemon rind
1½ teasp. flour	1 tablesp. lemon juice
1 pkg. thawed frozen blueberries	Pinch salt
2 tablesp. sugar	2 tablesp. water

In saucepan, melt butter; blend in flour, then rest of ingredients. Cook, stirring, till thickened.

Serve warm, on vanilla ice cream. Makes 4 servings.

EXTRA-EASY MAIN-COURSE SAUCES

Notes on Sauce Making

If your sauce is:

Too thin: Mix flour and cold water to form smooth paste, using 1 tablesp. flour to 1½ tablesp. water. Add gradually to sauce, stirring, until thickened.

Too thick: Stir or beat in more of liquid used in sauce (or water). Taste; add seasonings if necessary.

Lumpy: Beat with egg beater; or strain.

If sauce must stand before serving, cover to prevent crust forming. If crust has formed, remove with spoon, or beat sauce with egg beater. Sauce may thicken on standing; dilute with more liquid if needed.

For Meat, Poultry, Vegetables, Fish

Jiffy Barbecue: Combine ½ cup catchup, 1 teasp. dry mustard, 3 dashes tabasco, 1 tablesp. Worcestershire. Serve on franks, hamburgers, cube steaks, etc. Makes about ½ cup.

Onion Barbecue: Sauté ½ cup minced onions in ¼ cup butter, margarine, or salad oil until tender. Add 1⅓ cups chili sauce, ⅓ cup bottled thick meat sauce, p. 9. Serve on hamburgers, franks, cube steaks, chicken, etc. Makes about 2¼ cups.

Avery Butter: Melt ¼ cup butter or margarine. Stir in 1 teasp. salt; 1 teasp. dry mustard; 1 teasp. paprika or snipped parsley; 2 teasp. water; 2 tablesp. fresh, frozen, or canned lemon juice or orange juice; ¼ teasp. tabasco. Especially nice on hamburgers or steak. Makes about ⅓ cup.

Caper Butter: Melt ½ cup butter or margarine. Add 4 teasp. vinegar, 2 tablesp. bottled capers, 2 tablesp. snipped parsley. Nice with roast lamb or broiled steak or on asparagus, cauliflower, fish, etc. Makes about ½ cup.

Chive Cheese: Melt ½ pkg. chive cheese with 2 to 4 tablesp. milk. Nice on broccoli. Makes about ½ cup.

Currant-Mint: With fork, break up 1 cup currant jelly; mix in 2 tablesp. each grated orange rind and snipped mint leaves. Nice with roast lamb, ham, or chicken. Try also on broiled fish. Makes about 1 cup.

Curry: In 2 tablesp. butter or margarine, sauté ¼ cup sliced mushrooms 5 min. Stir in 2 tablesp. flour, then 1 cup water, 1 beef-bouillon cube, ½ teasp. curry powder. Cook, stirring, till thickened. Nice on hamburgers or franks. Try also on broiled, baked, or fried fish. Makes about 1⅛ cups.

Savory Jelly: Combine ½ cup currant jelly or sieved canned whole-cranberry sauce; 1 tablesp. vinegar or sherry; ½ teasp. dry mustard; ⅛ teasp. each ground cloves and cinnamon. Cook over low heat, stirring, until jelly melts. Nice over baked, sautéed, or broiled ham. Makes about ½ cup.

Quick Mushroom: Heat 1 can undiluted condensed cream-of-mushroom soup with 2 tablesp. butter or margarine and ⅓ cup milk or sherry or cooking sherry. Add ½ cup drained canned mushrooms, ¼ cup grated cheese or pinch curry. Nice on hamburgers or lamb chops. Try also on chicken, fish, green beans, cauliflower, etc. Makes 1½ cups.

Quick Mustard: Combine ½ cup vinegar; 1 tablesp. butter or margarine; 1 egg, slightly beaten; 1 tablesp. sugar; 2 tablesp. prepared mustard; 1 tablesp. paprika. Cook over low heat, stirring, until just thickened. Serve hot, with baked ham, tongue, etc. Makes about ½ cup.

Onion: Stir ½ cup water into 1 tablesp. cornstarch; add 2 tablesp. butter or margarine and 1 can undiluted condensed onion soup. Heat until thickened.

Or increase water to 1½ cups and substitute ½ pkg. onion-soup mix for canned soup. Nice on hamburgers or cubed steaks. Makes about 1½ cups.

Curried Pineapple Sauce: Simmer 1 9-oz. can crushed pineapple with 2 tablesp. butter or margarine and 1 teasp. curry powder, covered, 5 min. Serve with ham, chicken, or pork. Makes 1 cup.

Sour Cream: Stir 2 tablesp. flour into 2 tablesp. melted butter or margarine. Add ½ cup water, ½ cup commercial sour cream, 1 teasp. horse-radish, ¼ teasp. dried thyme, ¼ teasp. salt, ⅛ teasp. pepper. Heat. Good on hamburgers, broiled steak, or fried chicken. Try also on broccoli, asparagus. Makes about 1 cup.

Steak Sauce: Combine ½ cup melted butter or margarine, 1½ tablesp. catchup, 1½ teasp. Worcestershire, 1 teasp. dry mustard, and 2¼ teasp. fresh, frozen, or canned lemon juice. Serve on broiled steak or chops. Makes about ⅔ cup.

Tomato–Horse-radish: Heat 1 can undiluted condensed tomato soup with 2 tablesp. butter or margarine, 2 tablesp. horse-radish, 2 teasp. prepared mustard, pinch ground cloves, dash pepper. Use on hamburgers or pork or lamb chops. Try too on fried fish. Makes about 1¼ cups.

Just As Is: Canned tomato sauce; chili sauce; bottled thick meat sauce, p. 9; or Worcestershire.

Just for Fish

Saucepan Cheese: In ¼ cup butter or margarine in saucepan, sauté ½ cup minced onions till tender-crisp—about 3 min. Add ½ cup undiluted evaporated milk; 2 dashes tabasco; ½ lb. process sharp cheese, sliced. Heat, stirring occasionally, till blended. Nice with baked or oven- or pan-fried fish. Makes 2 cups.

Cucumber: Mix ¼ cup mayonnaise or commercial sour cream, ½ cup finely diced cucumbers, ¼ teasp. salt, ¼ teasp. celery seeds. Use for dunking cold cooked, cleaned shrimp or lobster chunks. Or serve on sautéed scallops, etc. Makes ⅔ cup.

Dilly: Combine ½ cup mayonnaise, 1 tablesp. dried dill. Nice for dunking cold cooked, cleaned shrimp or lobster chunks, etc. Makes ½ cup.

Louis: Mix 1 cup mayonnaise, ¼ cup French dressing, ¼ cup catchup or chili sauce, 1 teasp. each horse-radish and Worcestershire, and salt and pepper to taste. Serve on sea-food cocktails, broiled or fried fish, or in fish salads. Makes 1½ cups.

Red: Mix ¼ cup catchup, 2 tablesp. cooking sherry. Nice with broiled or fried fish, or on shellfish cocktails. Makes ⅓ cup.

Sherry: Combine 1 cup mayonnaise, ¼ cup cooking sherry, 2 tablesp. snipped chives or scallions. Nice on broiled or fried fish, or as dunk for shrimp or lobster. Makes 1¼ cups.

Quick Tartar: Combine 1 cup mayonnaise and 1 tablesp. each minced pickle, parsley, bottled capers, onion, green olives. Nice with hot or cold fish or shellfish. Makes 1¼ cups.

P.S. Don't forget you can buy fine bottled tartar sauce too.

Tomato-Cheese: Heat 1 can undiluted condensed tomato soup with 1 cup grated process American cheese (¼ lb.) and ¼ teasp. prepared mustard till cheese melts. Nice on baked or oven-fried fish. Makes about 1½ cups.

Italian Tomato: Sauté 2 tablesp. minced onion in 1 tablesp. butter or margarine until tender. Add 1 8-oz. can tomato sauce, 2 tablesp. grated Parmesan cheese; heat. Delicious on broiled or fried fish. Makes 1 cup.

Just for Vegetables
VINAIGRETTE SAUCE

3 tablesp. sweet pickle relish	¾ teasp. sugar
	1 teasp. salt
2 tablesp. snipped parsley	6 tablesp. vinegar
	¾ cup salad oil

Combine all ingredients. Blend with egg beater or electric mixer.

Serve on hot or chilled, cooked asparagus or broccoli, on hot cooked greens or Brussels sprouts, etc. Makes about 1 cup.

SPUR-OF-THE-MOMENT HOLLANDAISE

Carefully heat 1 cup mayonnaise, stirring constantly. Then fold in ¼ cup heavy cream, whipped.

Serve on hot asparagus, broccoli, etc. Makes about 1½ cups.

ZIPPY CHEESE SAUCE

In double boiler, place ⅓ cup milk, ½ lb. sliced process cheese. Add dash cayenne or tabasco, or a little minced onion sautéed till tender in bit of butter. Heat, stirring, until blended and smooth.

Serve on broccoli, cauliflower, asparagus, etc. Nice too on poached or baked fish. Makes 1⅓ cups.

Easiest of All: A wonderful cheese sauce (pasteurized process-cheese spread) comes in jars, all ready to heat and spoon over hot vegetables, spread on sandwiches, etc.

QUICK CREAM SAUCE

Blend 1 can undiluted condensed cream-of-mushroom or cream-of-chicken soup with ⅓ cup milk. Heat. Or blend 1 can undiluted condensed cream-of-celery soup with ½ cup milk; heat.

Serve with or on hot vegetables. Nice too on croquettes, fish, in casseroles, etc. Makes about 1½ cups.

Celery-Mustard: Prepare canned cream-of-celery soup as above; add 2 tablesp. prepared mustard.

OTHER MAIN-COURSE SAUCES

EASY HOLLANDAISE

2 egg yolks	or margarine
¼ teasp. salt	1 tablesp. fresh, frozen,
Dash cayenne pepper	or canned lemon
½ cup melted butter	juice

1. With egg beater or electric mixer, beat egg yolks until thick and lemon-colored; add salt, cayenne.
2. Add ¼ cup melted butter, about 1 teasp. at a time, beating constantly.
3. Combine remaining ¼ cup melted butter with lemon juice. Slowly add, about 2 teasp. at a time, to yolk mixture, beating constantly.
Serve soon after making. Nice with broccoli,

hot asparagus, broiled fish, poached or steamed salmon, etc. Makes ½ cup.

Curry: With salt, add ¾ teasp. curry powder.

Lemon: To sauce, add 1 teasp. grated lemon rind.

Mustard: To sauce, add 1 teasp. prepared mustard.

Béarnaise: To sauce, add 1 teasp. each minced onion and parsley and 1 teasp. minced fresh, or ½ teasp. dried, tarragon, or 1½ teasp. tarragon vinegar.

THOUSAND ISLAND SAUCE

1½ tablesp. butter or	cooked vegetables
margarine	¾ cup undiluted
3 tablesp. flour	evaporated milk
¾ teasp. salt	¼ cup mayonnaise
⅛ teasp. pepper	¼ cup chili sauce
¾ cup liquid from	

In saucepan, melt butter; blend in flour, salt, pepper. Slowly stir in vegetable liquid. Boil 2 min., stirring constantly. Add milk; heat thoroughly. Mix mayonnaise and chili sauce; stir into hot mixture. Thin with a little hot milk if desired.

Superb on hot green beans, onions, cabbage, broccoli, fried fish, etc. Makes 2 cups.

BERT'S SUPERB BARBECUE SAUCE

¼ cup vinegar	1 sliced onion
½ cup water	¼ cup butter or
2 tablesp. sugar	margarine
1 tablesp. prepared	½ cup catchup
mustard	2 tablesp. Worcester-
½ teasp. pepper	shire
1½ teasp. salt	1½ teasp. liquid or
¼ teasp. cayenne	powdered smoke
pepper	(optional)
1 thick lemon slice	

In saucepan, mix vinegar, water, sugar, mustard, pepper, salt, cayenne, lemon, onion, butter. Simmer, uncovered, 20 min. Add catchup, Worcestershire, smoke; bring to boil.

Serve hot, on spareribs, broiled chicken, short ribs, lamb chops, etc. Or use as baster when broiling chicken, roasting lamb or spareribs, braising short ribs, etc. Makes about 1¾ cups.

LEMON BARBECUE SAUCE

1 cup butter or margarine	¼ teasp. pepper
1 minced clove garlic	6 tablesp. fresh, frozen, or canned lemon juice
4 teasp. flour	
⅔ cup water	¼ teasp. tabasco
1 tablesp. sugar	½ teasp. dried thyme
4 teasp. salt	

In hot butter in saucepan, sauté garlic a few min.; stir in flour, then rest of ingredients. Cook, stirring, until slightly thickened. Cool.

Use as baster when broiling or grilling chicken, shrimp, scallops, etc. Makes about 2 cups.

RED BARBECUE SAUCE

3 tablesp. butter, margarine, or salad oil	2 tablesp. brown sugar
	½ cup water
⅓ cup minced onion	2 teasp. prepared mustard
1 cup catchup	
⅓ cup vinegar or fresh, frozen, or canned lemon juice	2 tablesp. Worcestershire
	⅛ teasp. salt

In hot butter in saucepan, sauté onion until tender but not brown. Add rest of ingredients. Simmer, covered, about 10 min.

Serve hot, on hot franks, hamburgers, broiled chicken, pork or lamb chops, broiled or fried fish, etc. Makes 2 cups.

INVERNESS WINE BARBECUE SAUCE

¼ cup salad oil	½ teasp. celery salt
½ cup white wine or lemon juice	½ teasp. pepper
	1 teasp. each chopped fresh, or ¼ teasp. each dried, thyme, marjoram, rosemary
1 grated clove garlic	
1 grated onion	
½ teasp. salt	

Mix all ingredients; refrigerate several hours.

Use as baster when broiling or grilling chicken or veal chops. (Even more delicious when poured over chicken or veal, then refrigerated 3 hr. before cooking.) Makes ¾ cup.

P.S. There are excellent bottled barbecue sauces on the market too.

MUSTARD SAUCE

2 tablesp. butter, margarine, or salad oil	1 tablesp. flour
	1 egg yolk, beaten
Dash pepper	¾ cup milk
1 teasp. salt	1½ to 3 teasp. fresh, frozen, or canned lemon juice
1 tablesp. prepared mustard	

In double boiler, melt butter; stir in pepper, salt, mustard, flour, then combined yolk and milk. Cook, stirring, until smooth and thickened—about 5 min. Remove from heat at once. Add lemon juice just before serving.

Serve on green beans, cauliflower, cabbage, etc. Try too on broiled, fried, or baked fish, hot baked ham, etc. Makes about ¾ cup.

To Vary: Make in saucepan. Omit egg yolk; increase milk to 1 cup. Add onion slice to milk if desired; remove onion before serving.

Onion Mustard: Simmer ¼ cup minced onion in butter in double-boiler top over direct heat. Then complete over boiling water as above.

CREAMY MUSTARD SAUCE

1 cup commercial sour cream	¼ teasp. salt
	⅛ teasp. pepper
1 tablesp. prepared mustard	1 tablesp. chopped scallions (optional)
1 tablesp. minced onion	

Combine cream, mustard, onion, salt, pepper. Heat over low heat. Sprinkle with scallions.

Serve on grilled franks, hamburgers, luncheon meat, fish, etc. Makes about 1 cup.

HORSE-RADISH SAUCE I

½ cup day-old bread crumbs	¼ teasp. salt
	Dash cayenne pepper or tabasco
½ cup light cream	
½ cup horse-radish	½ cup heavy cream

Combine crumbs, light cream, horse-radish, salt, cayenne; let stand until crumbs are soft. Shortly before serving, whip heavy cream till fairly stiff; fold in horse-radish mixture. Refrigerate.

Serve with broiled steak; tongue; roast beef; ham; corned beef; poached, baked, or fried fish. Makes 2 cups.

Horse-radish Sauce II: Mix ½ cup day-old bread crumbs with 3 tablesp. undiluted evaporated milk and ½ cup horse-radish; let stand. Meanwhile, chill ½ cup undiluted evaporated milk in ice-cube tray until ice crystals form around edges. Then whip until stiff, adding 1 tablesp. fresh, frozen, or canned lemon juice or vinegar. Fold in horse-radish mixture, dash cayenne, ¼ teasp. salt. Serve as above. Makes 2 cups.

SPANISH SAUCE

¼ cup butter, margarine, or salad oil	1 No. 2 can tomatoes (2½ cups); or 2½ cups canned tomato juice
1 cup sliced onions	
1 diced green pepper	
2 teasp. salt	1 teasp. sugar
Dash pepper	3 tablesp. flour
1 bay leaf	6 tablesp. water
2 whole cloves	

In hot butter in saucepan, sauté onions till tender. Add rest of ingredients except flour, water. Simmer, covered, 30 min. Stir in flour mixed with water till smooth; cook, stirring, until thickened. Remove bay leaf, cloves; strain if desired.

Serve with meat loaf, hamburgers, omelets, fried fish, etc. Makes about 2 cups.

Creole: Add ½ cup thinly sliced mushrooms during last 15 min. of simmering.

Tomato: Reduce onions to ½ cup, salt to 1 teasp. Omit green pepper. Simmer, uncovered, 20 min.; remove bay leaf, cloves; press through sieve; then thicken as above.

MEDIUM WHITE SAUCE
(cream sauce)

2 tablesp. butter or margarine	Dash paprika
2 tablesp. flour *	1 cup milk, or part milk and part light cream
Speck pepper	
½ teasp. salt	

1. In double boiler (or in saucepan over *low* heat), melt butter; add flour, pepper, salt, paprika; stir until blended, smooth.
2. Slowly add milk, stirring constantly to avoid lumps.
3. Cook, stirring, until smooth and thickened. Makes 1 cup.

* *Some people prefer to reduce flour to 1½ tablesp.*

Thin: Reduce butter and flour to 1 tablesp. each.

Thick: Increase butter and flour to ¼ cup each.

Anchovy: Omit pepper, salt, paprika. To sauce, add ¾ to 1 teasp. anchovy paste, 2 tablesp. minced celery. Good on poached or steamed fish, etc.

Béchamel: Substitute ½ cup chicken broth for ½ cup milk. Serve over croquettes, fried chicken, etc.

Cheese: To sauce, add ½ to 1 cup grated process or natural American cheese and ⅛ teasp. dry mustard. Heat, stirring, until melted.

Curry: To butter, add 2 teasp. curry powder, ¾ teasp. sugar, ⅛ teasp. ginger, ¼ cup minced onion. Just before serving, add 1 teasp. fresh, frozen, or canned lemon juice. Delicious on croquettes, fish, etc.

Egg: Increase butter to ¼ cup; decrease flour to 2 teasp. To sauce, add 2 teasp. prepared mustard and 2 sliced, hard-cooked eggs. Nice on poached fish, croquettes, etc.

Newburg: Just before serving sauce, add 1 cup cooked or canned lobster and 2 tablesp. cream, mixed with 1 beaten egg yolk.

Shrimp or Crab Meat: To sauce, add 1 teasp. Worcestershire and ½ cup diced, cleaned, cooked or canned shrimp or flaked fresh or canned crab meat. Serve with poached, broiled, or baked fish.

Vegetable: For part of milk, substitute leftover liquid from cooked vegetables.

DRAWN BUTTER SAUCE

¼ cup butter or margarine	½ teasp. salt
	Dash paprika
2 tablesp. flour	1 cup water
Speck pepper	1 teasp. lemon juice

In double boiler, melt butter. Stir in flour, pepper, salt, paprika, till smooth. Slowly stir in water. Cook until thickened. Just before serving, stir in lemon juice.

Nice on broiled or fried fish. Makes 1 cup.

Parsley: Add 2 tablesp. snipped parsley.

LEMON BUTTER
(maître d'hôtel butter)

¼ cup soft butter or margarine
½ teasp. salt
Dash cayenne pepper
1 tablesp. fresh, frozen, or canned lemon juice
1 tablesp. snipped parsley

Hot: Melt butter; add rest of ingredients.

Cold: Work soft butter till creamy. Gradually stir in lemon juice, then rest of ingredients.

Serve with broiled or fried fish or hot shellfish. Try too on hot broccoli, spinach, cauliflower, etc. Makes about ½ cup.

Mustard: Stir in 2 tablesp. prepared mustard.

Fine Herb: Substitute 3 tablesp. white wine for lemon juice; stir in 2 tablesp. snipped chives, 1 teasp. snipped fresh dill.

Caper: Add 2 tablesp. bottled capers.

Black: Heat butter till frothy and brown; add rest of ingredients.

Supreme: Make hot Lemon Butter; cool; stir in ¼ cup heavy cream, whipped.

Soy: Add 1 tablesp. soy sauce.

Chili: Add 1 tablesp. chili sauce plus a little prepared mustard and garlic salt.

CALIFORNIA RAISIN SAUCE

½ cup light or dark raisins
⅓ cup orange juice
¼ cup brown sugar, packed
½ cup water
⅓ cup port wine or currant jelly
1 tablesp. cornstarch
Dash salt
½ teasp. grated orange rind
Dash allspice

Rinse raisins. Add water, wine, orange rind and juice; bring to boil. Blend sugar with cornstarch, salt, allspice; stir into orange mixture. Cook, stirring, until clear.

Serve hot, on broiled or baked ham, or on sliced tongue. Makes 1⅓ cups.

SPICY DUNK SAUCE

½ cup chili sauce
1 tablesp. vinegar
¼ cup well-drained horse-radish
2 dashes tabasco
¼ teasp. bottled thick meat sauce, p. 9
1 teasp. Worcestershire
1 teasp. minced onion
1 teasp. celery seeds
¼ teasp. garlic salt
2 tablesp. sugar
½ teasp. salt
1 teasp. celery salt
⅛ teasp. pepper

Two or three days before using: Combine all ingredients. Refrigerate to blend flavors.

Nice for dunking cold cooked, cleaned shrimp or lobster chunks. Or use to top crab, lobster, or shrimp cocktail. Makes about ¾ cup.

SHARP SAUCE

2 egg yolks
¼ teasp. pepper
2½ teasp. prepared mustard
1½ teasp. sugar
½ cup chilled salad oil
½ teasp. salt
1 tablesp. vinegar
1 tablesp. dried dill

Place egg yolks in small bowl. With egg beater or electric mixer, beat in mustard, salt, dill, pepper, and sugar until well blended. Add oil, 1 teasp. at a time, beating continuously. Then beat in vinegar.

Nice for dunking cold cooked, cleaned shrimp or lobster chunks. Makes about ¾ cup.

CHILI–HORSE-RADISH SAUCE

Combine ⅓ cup mayonnaise; ¼ cup chili sauce; 1 tablesp. catchup; 2 teasp. Worcestershire; 1 teasp. bottled thick meat sauce, p. 9; and 2½ tablesp. horse-radish.

Nice for dunking cold cooked, cleaned shrimp. Makes about ¾ cup.

Desserts

Dessert gives you one more chance to fill the day's quota of milk, eggs, fruit, etc. How to choose it? The rule is simple: Keep the rest of the meal in mind when you plan its finale.

If the meal is light, a hearty dessert such as pie or bread pudding will round it out nicely. Fruit gelatin, sherbet, prune whip, or other light fare can end the very satisfying meal. Does dinner feature a vegetable main dish? Then include an egg dessert, such as custard or tapioca cream. Is luncheon short of potatoes, macaroni, or other starchy foods? Top it off with rice or bread pudding, or a cake dessert.

Before using these recipes, refer to How to Use Our Recipes, p. 3, and Pots and Pans, p. 692. Always use standard measuring cups and measuring spoons; measure level.

DESSERTS IN NO TIME

QUICK FRUIT TOP-OFFS

Splits: Split each peeled banana lengthwise. Top with canned or frozen pineapple chunks, canned crushed pineapple, or whole or sliced strawberries. Pass whipped cream with a little spice added.

Or put split bananas together with cream cheese thinned with milk; top with strawberries.

Bananas on the Half Shell: Use unpeeled whole bananas or bananas halved crosswise. Remove top half of peel lengthwise, without removing fruit. Then cut fruit (not through peel) into ½″ slices. Top with whipped cream; sprinkle with nutmeg.

Fruit Cream: Top sliced bananas or peaches, strawberries, or thawed frozen or canned pineapple chunks with spoonful of commercial sour cream. Sprinkle with brown sugar and cinnamon or nutmeg.

Gourmet Grapes: Combine ½ cup commercial sour cream with 2 tablesp. brown sugar; refrigerate at least 1 hr., or until well blended. Just before serving, combine with 1½ to 2 lb. seedless grapes. Stir to coat grapes lightly. Makes 4 or 5 servings.

Melon Array: Serve honeydew, cantaloupe, and watermelon wedges on tray. Tuck in sprigs of mint and lime wedges.

Fruited Melon: Top melon quarters with canned fruit cocktail. Sprinkle with bit of grated orange rind; or pass pitcher of lime, lemon, or orange juice.

Melon Cream: Fill melon halves or quarters with sherbet.

Sugary Oranges: Top cut-up oranges with brown sugar and shredded coconut.

Dessert Oranges: Cut unpeeled oranges into ¼″ slices; halve slices. Eat with fingers.

Or heap soft cream cheese in center of plate; pile quartered orange slices around cheese. Let guests dip orange slices into cheese.

Peaches de Luxe: In each chilled, peeled peach half, place spoonful of brandy; drizzle on honey; top with whipped cream.

Hot Peach Marlow: Fill peach halves with canned crushed pineapple; top with marshmallows; broil until golden.

Glazed Peaches: Top peach or pear halves, rounded sides up, with melted currant jelly.

Pineapple or Melon Sophisticate: Quarter fresh pineapple lengthwise through green top. Or quarter honeydew melon; remove seeds. Run knife between shell and meat, loosening but not removing meat; cut meat into ¼" to ½" slices. If desired, top with a few raspberries or shredded or toasted coconut. Or serve with lime wedges.

Strawberry Dip: Whip cream cheese with a little milk; place mound on plate; circle with unhulled strawberries. To eat, dunk berries.

Florida Ambrosia: Alternate layers of shredded coconut with mixed grapefruit, orange, and tangerine sections; sprinkle each layer with sugar; let stand 1 hr. before serving.

OTHER QUICK FRUIT TOP-OFFS

Cheese Bowl: Top bowlful of cottage cheese with applesauce or fresh, canned, or thawed frozen cherries, peach slices, or berries.

Applesauce Cream: Heat homemade or canned applesauce. Stir in snipped marshmallows; or top with whipped cream, marshmallow cream, or ice cream. Sprinkle with a little nutmeg or cinnamon.

Minted Apricots: Top canned apricot, pear, or peach halves or pineapple slices with whipped cream into which a little mint jelly has been folded.

Hot Apricots: Heat canned apricots—juice and all—with piece of lemon peel. Serve as is; or top with whipped cream or vanilla ice cream.

Cherry-Orange Medley: Serve hot canned Bing cherries over sliced oranges.

Frozen Fruit Sauté: Sauté canned peach halves or pineapple slices in butter or margarine till golden. Top with ice cream, then with some syrup from fruit, with a little sherry added.

Marmalade Peaches: To drained syrup from canned peaches, pears, or pineapple chunks, add spoonful of orange marmalade; heat. Pour over fruit. Serve warm, topped with whipped cream if desired.

Peach Cream: Top canned peach or pear halves or pineapple slices with cream cheese, whipped with a few fresh or thawed frozen raspberries.

Peach-Sherbet Cup: Fill fresh or canned peach halves with seedless grapes; top with raspberry sherbet.

Frosty Peaches: Top fresh, thawed frozen, or canned peach slices with Frosty Sauce, p. 368.

Red Peaches: Boil down syrup from canned peaches with 1 teasp. vanilla extract until quite thick; add 1 pkg. just thawed frozen raspberries. Pour over peaches.

Quick Crème Brûlée: In shallow baking dish, place peach halves, pineapple chunks, or whole berries (chilled fresh, or drained canned or thawed frozen). Spread with chilled commercial sour cream. Sift ½ cup brown sugar, packed, over cream. Broil 3" from heat till sugar caramelizes—about 1 min. Serve at once.

Polka Dots: In sherbet glasses, arrange, in layers, canned-jellied-cranberry-sauce cubes, canned or frozen pineapple chunks, and chopped walnuts.

Broiled Fruit Medley: Sprinkle canned pineapple slices and peach halves with brown sugar; dot with butter or margarine. Broil. Serve hot, topped with whipped cream.

Frosted Pineapple: Toss canned or thawed frozen pineapple chunks with slightly thawed frozen orange-juice concentrate and snipped mint.

Coconut Pineapple: Sprinkle thin slices of fresh pineapple, or split canned pineapple slices, with coconut.

Two-Tone Plum Bowl: Pour drained No. 2½ can purple plums and ½ cup sherry over chilled No. 2½ can greengage plums with syrup.

Fruit Frost: Slice block of frozen raspberries, peaches, or strawberries into ½" slices. Top each with whipped or commercial sour cream, or nuts.

Or about 1 hr. before serving, cut 2 or 3 kinds of frozen fruit into squares. Arrange in sherbet glasses. Top with almond-flavored whipped cream, macaroon or other cookie crumbs, toasted coconut, or chopped nuts.

Berry Rice: Into cold cooked rice, fold whipped cream, thawed frozen raspberries, and a little sugar.

Strawberries with Mock Devonshire Cream: Mash 1 3-oz. pkg. cream cheese; blend in ½ cup chilled heavy cream. Place mound on each dessert dish; spoon on sweetened fresh or thawed frozen strawberries.

Compote de Luxe: Heat 2 or 3 8-oz. cans of different fruits. Flavor with lemon juice, vanilla extract, or nutmeg. Top with commercial sour cream and grated chocolate or slivered nuts.

Two-Tone Fruits: Serve fruit in a tasty juice. Try one of these:

Fresh strawberries in orange juice
Sliced bananas in cranberry-juice cocktail
Canned peach halves or seedless grapes in grape juice
Canned or thawed frozen pineapple chunks in apricot nectar or orange juice

Canned Fruit Plus: To drained canned fruit syrup, add a little almond, vanilla, or lemon extract; sherry; brandy; or lemon, lime, or orange juice. Pour over fruit. Top with whipped or frozen whipped cream.

TEN FRUIT-CUP DESSERTS

Two or more fruits can taste newer than one. Top any of these fruit-cup combinations with sherbet and you'll have a de luxe dessert.
1. Banana chunks and thawed frozen strawberries, sprinkled with nuts
2. Grapefruit sections and pineapple chunks in grape juice
3. Diced oranges, snipped pitted dates, and sliced bananas
4. Sliced bananas in pink rhubarb sauce
5. Fresh or thawed frozen peach slices, raspberries, and slivered almonds
6. Fresh, canned, or thawed frozen pineapple chunks and seedless grapes in apricot nectar
7. Fresh, canned, or thawed frozen pineapple chunks mixed with strawberries
8. Canned peach halves, filled with chopped

nuts; peach syrup, flavored with almond extract, spooned over all
9. Canned fruit cocktail, sliced bananas, and unpared apple cubes
10. Melon cubes and seedless grapes, topped with slightly thawed orange-juice concentrate and fresh mint sprigs

JUST FRUIT DESSERTS

Cherries on Stems: Arrange on green leaves on dessert plates. (Provide spoons for removing pits from mouth.)

Currants: Wash; remove stems. Sprinkle currants with sugar; chill; then serve. Currants and raspberries are a wonderful team too.

Fresh Figs: Wash; pare off outer skins. Serve whole, cut into halves, or sliced. Serve with cream.

Grapes: Place small bunch of each of 2 or 3 kinds of grape on each plate. (Provide spoons for removing pits from mouth.)

Kumquats: Cut into halves; spread with cream cheese. Or serve whole, with cream cheese for dunking. (Eat rind and pulp.) Nice hors d'oeuvre too.

Melons: Cut into wedges; remove seeds; serve in one of these ways:
1. Serve with salt and lemon or lime wedges; or sprinkle with sherry. Nice too as breakfast fruit or first course.
2. Garnish with berries, cherries, mint sprigs, or grapes.
3. Sprinkle with a little ground ginger or nutmeg.
4. Top with lemon or raspberry sherbet.

Peaches: Wash; dry. Serve, unpeeled, in fruit bowl. Or serve, peeled and sliced, with pour cream or ice-cold custard sauce.

Pears: Cut into halves; then cut out cores. Serve with blue-cheese wedges. Provide spoons.

Persimmons: Wash; dry. Cut off stem ends; cut into halves crosswise. Provide spoon or fork.

Pomegranates: Cut into halves; serve with spoon.

Strawberries: Wash berries; do not hull. Place mound of confectioners' sugar, whipped cream, or cream cheese on each plate. Circle with berries. To eat, dunk berries. Nice as breakfast fruit too.

Tangerines: Cut tangerine peel into 6 sections; peel part way down. Spread sections apart, sunburst-fashion. Fill center with salted nuts or raisins.

Watermelon: Cut into crosswise slices or wedge-shaped pieces.

Or with tablespoon, scoop out medium-sized pieces; arrange 3 or 4 pieces, with rounded sides up, on each dessert plate; sprinkle with lime or lemon juice.

CAKE DESSERT QUICKIES

Charlotte Russe: Line sherbet glasses with ladyfingers. In each, place mound of sweetened whipped cream; top with maraschino cherry. Serve at once. Or refrigerate; then serve.

Coconut Fingers: Butter bakers' poundcake slices; cut into fingers; sprinkle with shredded coconut. Broil till toasted.

Toasted Jam Cake: Broil or sauté sponge- or angel-food-cake slices until golden. Spread with jam; top with chopped nuts or shredded coconut.

French-Toasted Slices: Dip bakers' poundcake slices into French Toast mixture, p. 344. Sauté in butter or margarine till golden. Serve with jelly or maple-blended syrup.

Spur-of-the-Moment Shortcakes: Fill, then top bakers' dessert shells, or sponge- or angel-food-cake slices, with:

Berries and/or sliced peaches; commercial sour cream
Whipped cream or marshmallow cream; chocolate sauce; salted nuts
Orange cubes and banana slices; sprinkling of sherry; shredded coconut
Orange sherbet; whipped cream
Sprinkling of rum; ice cream; sliced strawberries or butterscotch sauce
Spiced applesauce or canned crushed pineapple
Sweetened, sliced strawberries with pineapple chunks or sliced bananas

Thawed frozen peach slices; almond-flavored whipped cream
Choco-whipped cream (add a little chocolate sauce and instant coffee to cream before whipping it)

Make-Your-Own Shortcakes: Provide bakers' dessert shells and poundcake slices; plain or whipped cream; and sliced peaches or bananas, blueberries, or strawberries. Guests make their own shortcakes.

Orange Fluff: Whip 1 cup heavy cream; add 1 cup shredded coconut, 2 tablesp. orange juice, 1 teasp. grated orange rind. Heap on warm cake squares, made from packaged mix.

Apricot Cream Torte: Crush 1½ cups drained canned apricots with 2 tablesp. sugar. Spoon onto sponge- or white-cake layer. Circle top of layer with whipped cream.

Doughnut Deckers: Split doughnuts; top each half with cream cheese and canned whole-cranberry sauce.

Or put split doughnut halves together with melted semisweet chocolate as filling.

PEACH CRUMB DESSERT

Drain 1 No. 2½ can peach halves; spoon peaches into dessert dishes. In saucepan, melt 1 tablesp. butter or margarine; stir in ½ teasp. cinnamon, 1 cup day-old bread crumbs; toss until golden. Add 2 teasp. brown sugar; toss well. Spoon hot crumbs into peach halves. Serve at once, with whipped cream.

TWO-BERRY AMBROSIA

Into bowl, turn 1 pkg. each just thawed frozen raspberries and strawberries. Add 1 lb. seedless grapes (or ½ lb. halved, pitted Malaga grapes), 2 cups shredded coconut, 1 to 2 cups commercial sour cream, and confectioners' sugar to taste; toss together lightly.

Serve buffet style, in pretty bowl; top with small blobs of sour cream; sprinkle with coconut. Or spoon into sherbet glasses. Makes 10 servings.

APPLE SNOW

To 1⅔ cups chilled, unsweetened applesauce, add dash nutmeg, pinch salt, 1 teasp. vanilla extract. Fold in 2 egg whites, beaten with ¼ cup granulated sugar till stiff.

Serve with cream, whipped cream, or custard sauce. Makes 5 or 6 servings.

Prune Snow: Substitute 1¾ cups sieved, cooked prunes for applesauce; 2 tablesp. lemon juice, bit of grated lemon rind, and ⅛ teasp. cinnamon for vanilla. Reduce sugar to 3 tablesp.

INSTANT CREAM PUDDINGS

Packaged instant puddings give you luscious vanilla, chocolate, butterscotch, and coconut cream puddings in a matter of minutes—without any cooking. Just add cold milk; mix; let set; then serve.

NO-BAKE CUSTARDS

Packaged custard-dessert mix, which cooks in about 7 min., unmolds and tastes remarkably like old-fashioned baked custard.

Coffee: To mix, add 2 teasp. instant coffee.

QUICK COOKIE DESSERTS

Peanut Marlows: Top graham crackers with peanut butter, then with marshmallows. Broil till bubbly.

Ginger-Cheese Snaps: Fill gingersnaps or chocolate cookies with cream cheese, sandwich style.

Waffles and Fruit: Heat frozen waffles in electric toaster; top with berries or cut-up fruit, plus ice cream or whipped cream. Or top with thawed frozen fruit and squares of cream cheese.

MORE DESSERTS IN NO TIME

See Cheese as Dessert, p. 216; Ice Creams and Sherbets, p. 424; Fruit-Dessert Salads, p. 310; and Drinks—Hot and Cold, p. 494.

DESSERTS TO DO ALONG WITH DINNER

KITCHENETTE CARAMEL PUDDING

1 cup dark-brown sugar, packed	3 eggs
	1 cup milk
3 slices buttered fresh white or raisin bread, cut into ½" squares	Dash salt
	½ teasp. vanilla extract
	Ice cream or whipped cream

Generously butter inside of double-boiler top; pour in brown sugar; then add bread squares. Beat eggs with milk, salt, vanilla; pour over bread; don't stir. Cook over boiling water, covered, 1 hr.

Serve warm, with ice cream. Makes 4 servings.

Kitchenette Chocolate: Melt 1 sq. unsweetened chocolate in buttered double-boiler top. Stir in brown sugar, ¼ cup milk. Stir over boiling water until sugar dissolves. Add bread, then eggs beaten with remaining ¾ cup milk, salt, vanilla; *don't stir.* Cook as above.

MARY'S FUDGE PUDDING

1 cup sifted all-purpose flour	olate, melted
	1 teasp. vanilla extract
1½ teasp. baking powder	¾ cup coarsely chopped nuts
½ teasp. salt	½ cup brown sugar, packed
¼ cup soft butter or margarine	½ cup granulated sugar
⅔ cup granulated sugar	3 tablesp. cocoa
½ cup milk	¼ teasp. salt
1 sq. unsweetened choc-	1½ cups boiling water

Start heating oven to 350°F. Sift flour, baking powder, ½ teasp. salt. With spoon, cream butter with ⅔ cup granulated sugar until light and fluffy. Add flour mixture with milk, stirring just enough to blend. Add chocolate, vanilla, nuts; turn into 8" x 8" x 2" pan.

Combine brown sugar, ½ cup granulated sugar, cocoa, ¼ teasp. salt; sprinkle over batter. Pour boiling water over batter; don't stir. Bake 1 hr. (pudding will separate into cake and sauce layers). Cool slightly in pan.

Serve warm, cut into squares, with sauce over it. Pass cream if desired. Makes 9 servings.

GALA DESSERT FRUIT PLATE

Peaches, peeled and quartered	into chunks
	Thawed frozen raspberries, sieved or mashed if desired
Pears, pared, cored, and quartered	
1 cantaloupe, pared and cut into strips	Soft cream cheese, whipped with a little milk
Bananas, peeled and cut	

Buffet Style: On platter or tray, arrange peaches, pears, melon, bananas, pitcher or bowl of raspberries, and bowl of cream cheese. Let guests help themselves to fruit, top it with raspberries, then take some cream cheese in which to dunk fruit before eating.

Sit-Down Style: On each dessert plate, arrange serving of fruit, topped with raspberries, and mound of cheese. Garnish with mint sprig if desired.

AMBROSIA

Slice 6 to 8 peeled oranges. Arrange in layers with confectioners' sugar and grated fresh or shredded coconut in serving dish or sherbet glasses. Refrigerate until well chilled. Makes 6 to 8 servings.

To Vary: Arrange sliced bananas in layers with oranges. Or add some coarsely snipped dried figs and bit of lime juice.

De Luxe Style: Add 2 tablesp. grated orange rind to ½ cup heavy cream; chill. Whip cream until it forms soft mounds; stir in 3 tablesp. granulated sugar. Pass with Ambrosia.

CRANBERRY-CRUNCH ALAMODE

1 cup uncooked rolled oats	½ cup butter or margarine
½ cup sifted all-purpose flour	1 1-lb. can cranberry sauce (jellied or whole)
1 cup brown sugar, packed	Vanilla ice cream

Start heating oven to 350°F. Grease 8″ x 8″ x 2″ pan. Mix oats, flour, sugar; with 2 knives, scissor-fashion, cut in butter until crumbly. Place half of mixture in pan. Cover with cranberry sauce; top with rest of oat mixture. Bake 45 min.

Serve hot, cut into squares; top with ice cream. Makes 6 to 8 servings.

Rhubarb Crunch: For cranberry sauce, substitute 3 cups diced unpeeled young rhubarb mixed with 1 tablesp. flour, ½ cup granulated sugar, 1 teasp. cinnamon, ⅛ teasp. salt, and 1 tablesp. water.

RICE PEACH MELBA

⅔ cup packaged pre-cooked rice	⅛ teasp. cinnamon
2 cups milk	½ cup heavy cream, whipped
⅓ cup granulated sugar	1 No. 2½ can peach halves, drained
½ teasp. salt	⅓ cup currant jelly, melted
⅛ teasp. nutmeg	

In saucepan, combine rice, milk; bring to boil; boil gently, loosely covered, 15 min., fluffing rice occasionally with fork. Remove from heat; add sugar, salt, nutmeg, cinnamon. Cool 5 min.; chill in ice-cube tray about 20 min., watching mixture to be sure it doesn't freeze. Fold mixture into whipped cream. Pile into 6 sherbet glasses; top with peaches, with cut sides down; pour on jelly. Makes 6 servings.

SUSAN'S STRAWBERRY SHORTCAKE

2 cups sifted all-purpose flour	½ cup shortening
3 teasp. baking powder	1 egg, beaten
¾ teasp. salt	About ⅓ cup milk
3 to 5 tablesp. granulated sugar	Butter or margarine
1 teasp. grated lemon or orange rind (optional)	4 cups sweetened, sliced or crushed strawberries
	1 cup heavy cream

1. Start heating oven to 450°F. Into mixing bowl, sift flour, baking powder, salt, sugar; add rind.
2. With pastry blender or 2 knives, scissor-fashion, cut shortening into flour mixture until like corn meal. Add egg, then enough milk to make easily handled dough.
3. *For Large Shortcake:* Roll or pat dough into ½″-thick round, to fit greased 9″ layer pan. Bake 15 to 20 min., or until done.
   For Individual Shortcakes: Roll or pat dough ½″-thick; cut into 3″ rounds. Place 1″ apart on cookie sheet. Bake 12 to 15 min., or until done.
   To serve: Split hot shortcake; butter well; fill with some of strawberries. Top with rest of berries, then with whipped cream. Or omit whipped cream; make Whipped-Milk Topping, p. 369. Or pass pour cream or commercial sour cream. Makes 6 to 8 servings.

▶ **For 2:** Mix 1 cup packaged biscuit mix, 6 tablesp. cream, and 1 tablesp. sugar to make easily handled dough. Roll and bake as in For Individual Shortcakes, above.

To Do Ahead: Any time before meal, make dough up to point of adding egg and milk; refrigerate. Just before serving, complete and bake.

To Vary Fruit: Substitute one of these fruits for strawberries:

Half-and-half sweetened raspberries and strawberries or sliced bananas

Sweetened crushed raspberries or blackberries

Warm applesauce, topped with cinnamon-flavored whipped cream

Sweetened, sliced fresh or thawed frozen peaches

Sliced bananas and drained canned fruit cocktail

Drop-Biscuit Shortcakes: Increase milk to about ½ cup. Drop dough in 6 to 8 3″ mounds on greased cookie sheet. Bake 12 to 15 min., or until done.

Pin Wheels: Knead dough a little until easy to handle; then roll into 8″ x 6″ rectangle. Spread with 2 tablesp. soft butter or margarine; sprinkle with 1½ tablesp. sugar mixed with ¼ teasp. nutmeg. Roll up from long side, jelly-roll-fashion. Cut into 6 to 8 slices. Bake on greased cookie sheet 12 to 15 min., or until done. Spoon strawberries, whipped cream, over each slice. Makes 6 to 8 servings.

BRIDE'S CHOCOLATE-SOUFFLE CUPS

Start heating oven to 350°F. In saucepan, combine 1 pkg. chocolate-pudding, pinch salt, 1¼ cups milk. Cook over medium heat, stirring, until mixture comes to *full* boil. Cool 5 min., stirring once or twice; add 1 teasp. vanilla extract. Stir into 3 beaten egg yolks.

Beat 3 egg whites until they stand in soft peaks; gently fold in pudding. Pour into 8 greased custard cups; place in pan of hot water. Bake 25 min.

Serve at once with pour or whipped cream. Leftovers are good served cold. Makes 8 servings.

EASY BAKED COFFEE SOUFFLE

2 tablesp. butter or margarine	¾ cup water
2 tablesp. flour	3 eggs, separated
¼ teasp. salt	½ cup granulated sugar
2 tablesp. instant coffee	½ teasp. vanilla extract
	Light cream

Start heating oven to 350°F. Melt butter in saucepan. Stir in flour, salt, coffee, and water

till smooth. Cook, stirring, till thickened; remove from heat. Beat egg yolks till thick and lemon-colored; gradually add sugar, beating. Stir in coffee mixture, vanilla. Beat whites till they form moist peaks; fold in coffee mixture. Turn into greased 1-qt. casserole; place in pan of hot water. Bake, uncovered, 45 to 50 min.

Serve at once with cream. Makes 6 servings.

CHOCOLATE SOUFFLE

1 cup milk	4 eggs, separated
2 sq. unsweetened chocolate	⅓ cup granulated sugar
⅓ cup flour	1 teasp. vanilla extract
¼ teasp. salt	¼ teasp. almond extract

1. Start heating oven to 425°F. With butter, liberally grease 1½-qt. casserole; sprinkle bottom and sides with a little granulated sugar until coated.
2. In double boiler, heat ½ cup milk with chocolate until chocolate is melted; with egg beater, beat till smooth.
3. Stir rest of milk into flour and salt; stir into chocolate. Cook, stirring, until very thick. Remove from heat; beat till smooth.
4. To chocolate mixture, add egg yolks, one by one, beating after each addition until smooth. Cover; let stand.
5. With electric mixer or egg beater, beat egg whites until they form peaks when beater is raised; slowly add sugar, continuing to beat until stiff. Fold in yolk mixture and extracts. Pour into casserole.
6. Bake, uncovered, 22 to 27 min. When 22 min. are up, insert silver knife part way into center of soufflé; if it comes out clean, soufflé is done. If any soufflé adheres to knife, bake 5 min. more.

Serve at once with Frosty Sauce, p. 368; Holiday Vanilla Sauce, p. 370; pour cream; or whipped cream. Makes 6 servings.

GINGERBREAD TOP-OFFS

During dinner, bake your favorite packaged gingerbread mix in square pan or muffin-pan cups as label directs.

Serve hot or warm, topped with one of these:

Canned crushed pineapple, then whipped cream

Applesauce

Lemon sherbet

Ice cream, then Hot Fudge Sauce, p. 370.

Cream cheese, whipped with a little milk, then sprinkling of nutmeg

Speedy Custard Sauce, p. 368; add a little grated orange rind if you wish

Prepared mincemeat, folded into whipped cream

Lemon sauce, with snipped dried figs added

Nut-Topped: Combine ⅓ cup brown sugar, packed; 2 teasp. cinnamon; 3 tablesp. flour; 3 tablesp. butter or margarine; ⅓ cup chopped walnuts. As soon as gingerbread is done, sprinkle top with nut mixture. Return to oven for 5 min.

Broiler-Frosted: Top gingerbread slices with applesauce; sprinkle with sugar and cinnamon. Broil till bubbly.

BANANA-COCONUT ROLLS

Start heating oven to 375°F. Halve 4 peeled firm bananas crosswise; place in greased 10" x 6" x 2" baking dish. Brush with 2 tablesp. melted butter or margarine and 2 tablesp. fresh, frozen, or canned lemon juice, or lime juice; sprinkle with ½ cup shredded coconut. Bake 15 to 20 min., or until easily pierced with fork.

Serve warm, with cream. Makes 4 servings.

▶ **For 2:** Halve each ingredient; use 8" pie plate.

APPLE-ANNAS

Start heating oven to 350°F. Into 1-qt. casserole, slice 1 pared, cored cooking apple; sprinkle with 1½ tablesp. sugar. Slice 1 peeled banana over apple; then slice 2 more apples. Sprinkle with 2 to 3 tablesp. sugar. Dot with 1 tablesp. butter or margarine. Bake, covered, 20 min. Uncover; bake 15 min. longer, or till tender.

Serve warm, with cream. Makes 4 servings.

CHERRY BUBBLES

1 No. 2 can pitted red sour cherries, packed in water	2 tablesp. butter or margarine
½ cup granulated sugar	⅛ teasp. almond extract
⅛ teasp. salt	1 pkg. refrigerated pan-ready biscuits
4 teasp. cornstarch	Light cream

Start heating oven to 400°F. Drain cherries, reserving juice. Combine sugar, salt, cornstarch; stir in cherry juice; cook, stirring, until clear and thickened. Remove from heat; add butter, extract.

Place cherries in 8" x 8" x 2" pan; arrange biscuits on top (quarter the tenth biscuit; place around center biscuit). Pour on sauce. Bake 25 min.

Serve warm, with cream. Makes 5 servings.

HURRY-UP APPLE "PIE"

½ cup brown sugar, packed	sauce (2 cups)
1 cup packaged pie-crust mix	1 tablesp. fresh, frozen, or canned lemon juice
½ teasp. cinnamon	Light cream or ice cream
½ teasp. nutmeg	
1 No. 303 can apple-	

Start heating oven to 375°F. Grease 8" pie plate. Combine sugar, piecrust mix, cinnamon, and nutmeg until crumbly. In pie plate, place applesauce; sprinkle with lemon juice; spread with crumbly mixture. Bake 25 to 30 min., or until tender.

Serve warm, with cream. Makes 4 servings.

CAROLYN'S APPLE PANDOWDY

1 cup brown sugar, packed	3 tablesp. shortening
¼ cup flour	¾ cup milk
¼ teasp. salt	5 cups sliced, pared, cored cooking apples
1 teasp. vinegar	¼ teasp. cinnamon
1 cup water	Dash nutmeg
1 cup sifted all-purpose flour	1 teasp. lemon juice
	1 teasp. vanilla extract
2 teasp. baking powder	2 tablesp. butter or margarine
¾ teasp. salt	

In saucepan, mix sugar, ¼ cup flour, ¼ teasp. salt; stir in vinegar, water; cook over low heat, stirring, until thick. Set aside.

Start heating oven to 375°F. Sift 1 cup flour, baking powder, ¾ teasp. salt. With 2 knives, scissor-fashion, cut in shortening until size of peas; add milk; stir until moistened but still lumpy.

Arrange apples in well-greased 12" x 8" x 2" baking dish. To sauce, add cinnamon, nutmeg, lemon juice, vanilla, butter; pour over apples.

Drop dough on top of apples. Bake 40 min., or until topping is brown.

Serve warm, with pour cream, commercial sour cream, ice cream, or cream cheese thinned with milk. Makes 6 servings.

BUTTER-NUT PANDOWDY

1 cup packaged biscuit mix	fruit
½ cup coarsely chopped walnuts	¾ cup brown sugar, packed
½ cup milk	2 tablesp. butter or margarine
1 cup water or syrup drained from canned	Heavy cream

Start heating oven to 375°F. Grease 10″ x 6″ x 2″ pan. Combine biscuit mix, nuts, milk; spread in pan. Bring water, brown sugar, butter, to boil; pour over dough. Bake 30 min.

Serve warm, with pour or whipped cream. Makes 6 servings.

Rum-Butterscotch: Omit biscuit mix, walnuts, milk. Arrange 1 pkg. refrigerated pan-ready biscuits in 10″ x 6″ x 2″ pan. Bake at 375°F. 6 min. Pour on hot mixture of water, brown sugar, butter, 1 teasp. rum extract. Bake 30 min.

OLD-FASHIONED PEACH DUMPLINGS

Dumplings:

Any Flaky Pastry for Two-Crust Pie, pp. 407 to 410	6 peeled ripe peaches
	2 tablesp. currant jelly
	¾ cup granulated sugar

Syrup:

1 cup hot water	1 tablesp. grated lemon rind
¼ cup granulated sugar	
2 tablesp. butter or margarine	3 tablesp. lemon juice
	1 egg white

For Dumplings: Roll pastry ⅛″ thick; cut into 6 7″ squares. Halve and pit peaches. Place peach half in center of each pastry square; fill each hollow with 1 teasp. currant jelly; top with second peach half; sprinkle each with 2 tablesp. sugar. Moisten edges of squares with cold water; bring points up over peaches; press edges together. Place in greased 12″ x 8″ x 2″ baking dish. Start heating oven to 375°F.

For Syrup: Combine hot water with rest of ingredients except egg white; heat until sugar

dissolves; pour into dumpling dish. Brush dumplings with slightly beaten egg white; sprinkle with sugar. Bake 40 min., or until tender.

Serve warm, with pour cream; Hard Sauce, p. 370; whipped cream; Lemon Sauce, p. 370; or Frosty Sauce, p. 368. Makes 6 servings.

Apple Dumplings:

For Dumplings: Use 6 pared, cored, medium cooking apples (save peel) instead of peaches. Instead of jelly, mix ½ cup granulated sugar with 1 teasp. cinnamon; use to fill apples; then dot each with bit of butter or margarine (1 tablesp. in all). Wrap in pastry, and place in baking dish as above; then refrigerate.

For Syrup: Pour 1½ cups boiling water over apple peel; simmer, covered, 20 min. Drain peel; stir liquid with 2 tablesp. sugar, ¼ cup butter or margarine, ¼ teasp. cinnamon, 1 tablesp. grated lemon rind, and 3 tablesp. lemon juice until sugar dissolves. Pour into dumpling dish. Bake at 375°F. 40 min., or until tender.

Quick Apple Dumplings: Make Apple Dumplings, using ¼ cup butter or margarine to dot apples. Omit syrup.

Biscuit Apple Dumplings: Make Apple Dumplings, substituting Susan's Hot Baking-Powder Biscuit dough, p. 323, or dough made from 2 cups packaged biscuit mix for pastry. Roll into rectangle 21″ x 14″; cut into 6 7″ squares. Omit syrup.

EASY APPLE OR PEACH DUMPLINGS

¾ cup granulated sugar	ready biscuits
1 teasp. cornstarch	2 diced, pared, cored cooking apples; or
½ teasp. cinnamon	
1 cup water	2 diced, peeled ripe peaches
1 tablesp. fresh, frozen, or canned lemon juice	2 tablesp. butter or margarine
1 pkg. refrigerated pan-	Light cream

Start heating oven to 400°F. Combine sugar, cornstarch, cinnamon, water; cook 5 min., or until clear. Remove from heat; add lemon juice.

Stretch each biscuit into 4″ circle; place a little diced apple in center of each; dot with butter; gather up dough over apple and seal at center. Place in 10″ x 6″ x 2″ baking dish; pour syrup over dumplings. Bake 25 min.

Serve warm, with cream. Makes 5 servings.

Mincemeat: Reduce sugar to ½ cup. Substitute 1 cup prepared mincemeat for apples and butter.

DUTCH PLUM CAKE

1 cup sifted all-purpose flour	halved, prune plums
1½ teasp. baking powder	1 teasp. cinnamon
½ teasp. salt	¼ teasp. nutmeg
3 tablesp. sugar	3 tablesp. sugar
¼ cup shortening	3 tablesp. melted butter or margarine
1 egg	⅓ cup currant jelly or apricot jam
¼ cup milk	About 1 tablesp. hot water
5 pitted plums, cut into eighths; or 16 pitted,	

Start heating oven to 400°F. Sift flour, baking powder, salt, 3 tablesp. sugar. With 2 knives, scissor-fashion, or pastry blender, cut in shortening until like coarse corn meal. With fork, stir in combined egg and milk.

Spread dough in greased 12″ x 8″ x 2″ baking dish. On top, arrange plums, slightly overlapping, in parallel rows, with pointed edges down. Sprinkle with combined cinnamon, nutmeg, 3 tablesp. sugar, butter. Bake 35 min., or until plums are tender.

Beat jelly with enough hot water to make syrup; brush over fruit when it's done.

Serve warm, cut into squares, as is or with Sunshine Foamy Sauce, p. 370; Vanilla Sauce, p. 370; or Frosty Sauce, p. 368. Makes 6 servings.

▶ **For 2:** Use 1 egg; halve rest of ingredients. Use greased 8″ pie plate. Bake 20 min.

Dutch Medley: For plums, substitute 2 sliced, peeled, ripe peaches; 3 sliced, pitted plums, and a few seedless grapes. Cover one third of dough with each fruit. Or use all grapes.

Dutch Peach: For plums, substitute 5 thinly sliced, peeled ripe peaches.

Dutch Apple: For plums, substitute 3½ to 4 cups sliced, pared, cored cooking apples.

Quick Dutch Plum: For dough, add 3 tablesp. sugar to 1 cup packaged biscuit mix; stir in 1 egg, beaten slightly with ¼ cup heavy cream.

PEACH DESSERT CAKE

1 cup sifted cake flour	rind
1 teasp. baking powder	2 eggs, unbeaten
¼ teasp. salt	4 peeled ripe peaches*
½ cup granulated sugar	⅓ cup granulated sugar
½ cup soft shortening	½ teasp. cinnamon
1 teasp. grated lemon	¼ cup chopped walnuts

Start heating oven to 350°F. Sift flour, baking powder, salt. Beat ½ cup sugar with shortening until light and creamy. Add lemon rind, then eggs, one at a time, beating well. Add flour in fourths, beating after each addition.

Spread half of batter in greased 8″ x 8″ x 2″ pan; top with peaches. Spread rest of batter on top. Mix ⅓ cup sugar, cinnamon, walnuts; sprinkle over all. Bake 50 min.

Serve warm, cut into squares, as is or topped with pour cream, whipped cream, or ice cream. Makes 9 servings.

* *Or use 2 cups canned or thawed frozen peach slices.*

CREPES SUZETTE

Crepes, below	sugar
6 sugar lumps	¼ cup Cointreau or curaçao
1 orange	
1 lemon	2 tablesp. rum or Benedictine
⅓ cup orange juice	
½ cup butter	⅓ cup brandy or Grand Marnier
2 tablesp. granulated	

Make crepes; fold each in half, then in quarters; keep warm. Rub lump sugar on rinds of orange and lemon. Add lump sugar to orange juice; crush until dissolved.

In chafing dish, melt butter; add orange-juice mixture and granulated sugar; heat. Lift crepes into this sauce; ladle sauce over crepes until saturated. Mix Cointreau and rum; pour over crepes; then pour on brandy but do not stir. When mixture is heated, tilt pan to flame, so sauce catches fire. Spoon flaming sauce over crepes.

Serve crepes and sauce on heated plates. Makes 6 servings.

CREPES

2 eggs	½ cup sifted all-purpose flour
⅔ cup milk	
1 tablesp. melted shortening	¼ teasp. salt
	1 teasp. sugar

Beat eggs thoroughly; add milk, shortening. Sift flour with salt, sugar; add to egg mixture; with egg beater, beat until smooth. On griddle or in chafing dish, heat a little salad oil or shortening. Drop crepe batter, in 5″ rounds, on griddle; cook, turning once, until a light brown on both sides.

For dessert: Spread with jelly or jam; roll up; sprinkle with sugar.

Or omit jelly; roll up; sprinkle with sugar; serve with lemon wedge.

Or serve, unrolled, in piles of 3, with sweetened strawberries between; cut into wedges.

For main dish: Omit sugar.

ZABAGLIONE

3 egg yolks	rind
¾ cup granulated	5 teasp. lemon juice
sugar	½ cup sherry or
2 teasp. grated lemon	Marsala wine

In double-boiler top, beat egg yolks slightly. Add rest of ingredients. Cook over boiling water, beating constantly with egg beater, until as thick and fluffy as whipped cream. Remove from water at once.

Serve hot or chilled, in parfait, sherbet, or champagne glasses. Or use to top spongecake or fruit. Makes 4 servings.

CAMILLE'S PEACH COCONUT

1 No. 2½ can peach	packed
slices	½ cup shredded
2 tablesp. butter or	coconut
margarine	¼ cup brown sugar,
1 cup fresh bread	packed
crumbs, lightly	¼ teasp. cinnamon

Start heating oven to 450°F. Drain peaches, reserving syrup. Spread peaches in buttered 9″ pie plate. In hot butter in skillet, heat crumbs, stirring, till tinged with brown. Add coconut, sugar, cinnamon; heat, stirring, till sugar begins to melt. Spread over peaches. Bake 9 min., or until crisply toasted and bubbling.

Serve warm, with hot Peach Sauce, below. Makes 4 servings.

Peach Sauce: In saucepan, combine 1 cup peach syrup with ½ cup brown sugar, packed; dash salt; 1 tablesp. fresh, frozen, or canned lemon juice; 2 tablesp. butter or margarine; ¼ teasp. nutmeg. Boil, stirring, 4 min.

▶ **For 2:** Halve ingredients; use 6″ pie plate.

QUICK APPLE CRISP

1 No. 2 can apples; or	cracker crumbs (8
2½ cups thinly	crackers) or all-
sliced, pared, cored	purpose flour
cooking apples	½ teasp. cinnamon
1 tablesp. fresh, frozen,	½ teasp. nutmeg
or canned lemon	¼ cup soft butter or
juice	margarine
½ cup brown sugar,	Light cream or ice
packed	cream
½ cup fine graham-	

Start heating oven to 375°F. Grease 10″ x 6″ x 2″ baking dish. Arrange apples in dish; sprinkle with lemon juice. Mix sugar with next 4 ingredients until crumbly; spread over apples. Bake 25 to 30 min., or until tender.

Serve warm, with cream. Makes 4 servings.

Quick Peach: Substitute 1 drained No. 2½ can peach slices for apples.

Pear-Butter: Substitute 1 drained No. 2½ can pear halves for apples. Bake at 425°F. 20 min.

APPLE BROWN BETTY

⅓ cup melted butter	brown sugar
or margarine	½ teasp. nutmeg
2 cups fresh bread	¼ teasp. cinnamon
crumbs	1 tablesp. grated
6 cups sliced, pared,	lemon rind
cored cooking	2 tablesp. lemon juice
apples	¼ cup water
½ cup granulated or	

Start heating oven to 375°F. Toss butter with crumbs; arrange one third of this mixture in greased 1½-qt. casserole. Cover with half of apples and half of combined sugar, nutmeg, cinnamon, and lemon rind. Cover with one third of crumbs, rest of apples, and rest of sugar mixture. Spoon on combined lemon juice and water. Top with rest of crumbs. Bake, covered, ½ hr. Uncover; bake ½ hr. longer, or until apples are done.

Serve warm, with pour cream; whipped cream, sprinkled with cinnamon or grated cheese; Hard Sauce, p. 370; Sterling Sauce, p.

371; cream cheese softened with a little milk; or ice cream. Makes 6 servings.

▶ **For 2 or 3:** Halve each ingredient; use 1-qt. casserole. Bake, covered, at 350°F. ½ hr.; uncover; bake ½ hr.

Peach: Substitute peaches for apples.

FRUITFUL COBBLER

1 qt. sliced, peeled peaches; sliced, pared, cored cooking apples; or sliced, pitted plums	½ cup corn syrup or honey
½ teasp. salt	1 cup packaged biscuit mix
1 tablesp. flour	2 tablesp. sugar
	½ cup milk or water
	1½ teasp. sugar

Start heating oven to 425°F. In 1½-qt. casserole, toss peaches with salt, flour, corn syrup. Mix biscuit mix with 2 tablesp. sugar, milk. Pour over peaches; top with 1½ teasp. sugar. Bake, uncovered, 40 min., or until golden and tender. Makes 8 servings.

Cherry: Substitute 1 qt. drained canned pitted red sour cherries for peaches. Use honey instead of syrup.

BAKED APPLESAUCE

Start heating oven to 350°F. Pare, core, and thickly slice 4 cooking apples. Mix ½ cup granulated sugar with ¼ teasp. cinnamon. Spread layer of apple slices in 1½-qt. casserole; sprinkle with part of cinnamon-sugar; repeat until both are used. Dot top with 1 tablesp. butter or margarine. Bake, covered, 1 to 1½ hr., or until apples are completely soft.

Serve hot, topped with ice cream. Nice too with pork, ham, or other meat. Makes 4 servings, with a little left over to serve cold for breakfast, with ready-to-eat cereal.

LUSCIOUS LEMON-BAKED APPLES

1 or 2 seeded, quartered, unpeeled oranges	garine
¾ cup prepared mincemeat	½ cup granulated sugar
6 cored cooking apples	1 egg, well beaten
½ cup butter or mar-	1 tablesp. grated lemon rind
	3 tablesp. lemon juice
	3 tablesp. water

Start heating oven to 350°F. Put enough oranges through food chopper, using coarse blade, to make ¾ cup. Combine with mincemeat; use to pack into cored apples. Arrange apples in baking dish. Mix butter with sugar until light and fluffy; add egg, then lemon rind and juice, water. Pour over apples. Bake, uncovered, about 40 min., or until done.

Serve warm, with sauce spooned over apples. Makes 6.

CHILLED GRAPEFRUIT

1. Wash and dry chilled grapefruit. Halve crosswise. Remove seeds with tip of sharp knife.* If desired, cut out core.
2. Then, with sharp knife, cut around each section to loosen flesh from membrane and skin (do not cut around entire outer edge of fruit). Remove remaining seeds.
3. If desired, sprinkle with a little sugar; then serve. Or refrigerate until served.

Serve as dessert or first course, topped with one of these:

Grape juice	Crushed after-dinner mints
Bottled grenadine	
Dash of bitters	Melon balls
A red or green cherry	Jelly cubes
Diced oranges	Sherbet
Seeded grapes	Madeira wine
Canned crushed pineapple	Sherry or *crème de menthe*

* *If grapefruit contains many seeds, before freeing fruit from membrane, with scissors, cut around seeds, removing core and seeds all at once.*

BROILED GRAPEFRUIT

Prepare grapefruit as in Chilled Grapefruit, above. Sprinkle each half with 1 teasp. granulated sugar and 2 teasp. brown sugar. Brush with 1½ teasp. melted butter. Broil 10 min., or until golden. If desired, just before serving, pour on a little sherry or rum. Serve at once. Nice too as first course.

P.S. All-brown sugar, honey, or maple-blended syrup may replace sugars. Sprinkle with ground cloves or nutmeg if desired.

Baked: Instead of broiling grapefruit, bake at 450°F. 20 min.

Skillet Style for 2: Melt 1 tablesp. butter or margarine in skillet; sprinkle lightly with brown sugar; then, in this mixture, lightly brown 2 prepared grapefruit halves, with cut sides down. Serve syrup in skillet over fruit.

MINTED GRAPEFRUIT

Drain well fresh, canned, or thawed frozen grapefruit sections. Roll each section in sugar, then in snipped mint. Arrange, spoke-fashion, on chilled glass plates, with a few cherries or strawberries in center. Nice, too, as appetizer.

PEAR-BUTTERSCOTCH CRISP

1 No. 2½ can pear halves, drained	¼ teasp. salt
	¼ teasp. cinnamon
½ cup brown sugar, packed	¼ cup butter or margarine
½ cup flour	

Start heating oven to 425°F. Arrange pear halves, with cut sides down, in greased pie plate. Mix sugar, flour, salt, cinnamon; with fork or pastry blender, work in butter until crumbly. Sprinkle thickly over and around pears. Bake 15 to 20 min., or until crumbs are golden brown.

Serve warm, with cream, ice cream, or chilled custard sauce. Makes 4 servings.

BAKED LEMON CAKE PUDDING

2 eggs, separated	2 tablesp. melted butter or margarine
¼ teasp. salt	
½ cup granulated sugar	¼ cup granulated sugar
1 tablesp. grated lemon rind	3 tablesp. flour
	1 cup milk
5 tablesp. lemon juice	

Start heating oven to 350°F. Grease 1-qt. casserole. Beat egg whites with salt until moist peaks form when beater is raised. Gradually add ½ cup sugar, beating until stiff. With same beater, beat yolks with lemon rind and juice, melted butter. Stir in ¼ cup sugar mixed with flour; add milk. Fold into beaten egg whites.

Pour batter into casserole. Set in pan containing ½″ hot water. Bake, uncovered, 55 to 65 min., or until top is firm and browned. (Pudding will separate into cake layer and sauce layer.)

Serve slightly warm or chilled, as is or topped with whipped cream, berries, or other fruit if desired. Makes 4 to 6 servings.

Individual Baked Lemon Puddings: Pour into 6 greased custard cups; bake at 350°F. 50 to 60 min.

FEATHERWEIGHT DESSERT PANCAKES

Beat 3 egg whites until stiff but not dry. With same beater, beat 3 yolks until thick and lemon-colored; stir in ¼ teasp. salt, ¼ cup all-purpose flour, ¾ cup cottage cheese. Fold in whites. Drop by small spoonfuls onto hot, lightly greased griddle. Cook until golden on both sides.

Serve at once with butter, brown sugar, and maple-blended syrup. Or serve with canned whole-cranberry sauce and brown sugar. Makes 16 small pancakes, which are creamy and cheesy inside.

DESSERTS TO DO AHEAD

MOUSSE AU CHOCOLAT

½ pkg. semisweet-chocolate pieces (½ cup)	3 eggs, separated
	1 teasp. vanilla extract

Melt chocolate over *hot, not boiling,* water. Remove from heat. With spoon, beat in egg yolks, then vanilla. Beat egg whites until stiff but not dry; fold into chocolate mixture. Spoon into sherbet glasses; refrigerate.

Serve with pour cream or whipped cream, flavored with rum or almond extract, or cinnamon. Makes 4 servings.

P.S. Nice with a few chopped nuts added.

MALLOW-CREAM WHIP

¼ lb. marshmallows (16)	¾ cup orange juice
	½ cup heavy cream

In saucepan over low heat, melt marshmallows in orange juice, stirring; refrigerate till consistency of unbeaten egg white. Whip cream. Beat orange mixture until foamy; fold in whipped cream; pour into sherbet glasses. Refrigerate several hours.

Serve garnished with orange sections if desired. Makes 6 servings.

Coffee: For orange juice, substitute ¾ cup cold coffee. If desired, with cream, fold in ¾ cup drained canned fruit cocktail.

Pineapple: For orange juice, substitute 1 cup canned crushed pineapple and 1½ teasp. lemon juice.

HEAVENLY PRUNE WHIP

1¼ cups well-cooked dried prunes	½ teasp. grated orange rind
2 tablesp. confectioners' sugar	1 cup heavy cream, whipped

Cut prunes from pits; press prunes through coarse sieve; add sugar, orange rind. With spoon, gradually fold mixture into whipped cream. Spoon into sherbet glasses. Refrigerate several hours. Garnish with more grated orange rind. Makes 4 servings.

PEACH FLUFF

½ cup heavy cream	lows
1 tablesp. sugar	2 tablesp. chopped, toasted almonds or snipped coconut
4 or 5 diced canned peach halves (No. 303 can)	
6 snipped marshmal-	1 cup cubed 2-day-old cake

Whip cream with sugar till stiff. Fold in rest of ingredients. Spoon into sherbet glasses. Refrigerate several hours. Makes 4 or 5 servings.

SUSAN'S CUSTARD BREAD PUDDING

1 qt. milk	¼ teasp. nutmeg
2 cups 2-day-old bread crumbs or ½" squares	1 tablesp. vanilla extract; or 1 teasp. almond extract
2 eggs	2 to 4 tablesp. melted butter or margarine
¼ cup granulated sugar	
½ teasp. salt	

1. Start heating oven to 350°F. Grease 1½-qt. casserole. In double boiler, heat milk until tiny bubbles appear around edges. Remove from heat; stir in bread crumbs; set aside.
2. Break eggs into casserole; beat slightly with fork. Stir in sugar, salt, then milk mixture, nutmeg, vanilla, butter.
3. Set casserole in baking pan; fill baking pan

with warm water to 1" from top of casserole.
4. Bake, uncovered, 1 hr. 15 min., or until silver knife inserted in center of pudding comes out clean.

Serve warm or cold, with pour cream; whipped cream; Lemon Sauce, p. 370; Hard Sauce, p. 370; or sweetened crushed strawberries, flavored with almond extract. Or top with bits of jelly. Makes 6 to 8 servings.

► **For 2 or 3:** Halve each ingredient; use 1-qt. casserole or 4 custard cups. Bake as directed 45 to 50 min., or until done.

Cake Crumb: Substitute stale cake crumbs for bread crumbs.

Chocolate Nut: In heated milk, melt 2 sq. unsweetened chocolate; with egg beater, beat until blended; add ½ cup chopped walnuts.

Coconut: Before baking pudding, sprinkle top with ½ cup shredded coconut.

Fruit: With milk mixture, add ½ cup light or dark raisins, or snipped, pitted dates.

Individual: Use 8 greased custard cups; bake as directed 45 to 50 min.

Queen of Puddings: Use 2 eggs and 2 egg yolks. Use 6 to 8 greased custard cups; bake as directed 45 to 50 min. Remove from oven.

Beat 2 leftover egg whites until they form peaks when beater is raised; slowly add ¼ cup granulated sugar, beating till stiff. Heap on top of puddings, leaving depression in center of each. Bake in pan of warm water 12 to 15 min., or until golden. Serve warm or cold, with dab of currant jelly in center of each. Or spread jelly on puddings before topping with meringue. Makes 6 to 8 servings.

SUSAN'S RICE CUSTARD

½ cup raw regular or processed white rice	½ cup light or dark raisins
2½ cups boiling water	1½ teasp. grated lemon rind
¾ teasp. salt	3½ cups milk
3 eggs	1 teasp. nutmeg
⅓ cup granulated sugar	2 tablesp. butter or margarine
2 teasp. vanilla extract	

1. Start heating oven to 300°F. Add rice to boiling water and salt. Cook, uncovered, stirring

occasionally with fork, 15 to 20 min., or until a grain, pressed between finger tips, feels tender. Drain.

2. Into 2-qt. casserole, break eggs; beat slightly with fork. Stir in sugar, vanilla, raisins, rind.
3. Add milk to rice; stir into egg mixture. Sprinkle with nutmeg; then dot with butter. Set casserole in baking pan; fill pan with hot water to 1″ from top of casserole.
4. Bake, uncovered, 1 hr. 25 min., stirring once after ½ hr. (To avoid breaking top, insert spoon at edge of pudding; draw gently back and forth along bottom of casserole.) Near end of baking time, insert silver knife in center of custard. When knife comes out clean, custard is done. Remove casserole from baking pan; cool.

Serve slightly warm or cold, with pour cream; whipped cream; maple or maple-blended syrup; Hot Fudge Sauce, p. 370; or Butterscotch Sauce, p. 368. Makes 6 to 8 servings.

▶ **For 2 or 3:** Use 3 tablesp. rice, 2 small eggs, 3 tablesp. sugar; halve rest of ingredients. Use 1-qt. casserole. Bake 55 min.

CREAMY BAKED RICE PUDDING

1 qt. milk	¼ teasp. salt
¼ cup granulated sugar	¼ teasp. nutmeg
¼ cup raw regular white rice*	1 teasp. vanilla extract
1 tablesp. butter or margarine	½ cup light or dark raisins (optional)

Start heating oven to 325°F. In greased 1½-qt. casserole, combine milk, sugar, rice, butter, salt, nutmeg, vanilla. Bake, uncovered, stirring often, 2½ hr., or until rice is done. Add raisins after first hour.

Serve warm or cold, with pour cream; whipped cream; Custard Sauce II, p. 370, flavored with rum; Hot Fudge Sauce, p. 370; Butter Caramel Sauce, p. 369; berries; fruit; or maple sugar. Makes 4 to 6 servings.

* For thicker pudding, increase the rice to 5 tablesp.

FRUIT FLOAT

In sherbet glasses, arrange one or more of the following. Top with chilled Custard Sauce de Luxe, p. 370, or Speedy Custard Sauce, p. 368. Then, if desired, top with sprinkling of mace or nutmeg, grated chocolate, whipped cream, or macaroon crumbs.

Sliced bananas	Baked apple
Pineapple chunks	Orange slices and
Peach slices	shredded coconut
Pitted, cooked dried prunes	Fruit-flavored gelatin
Any berries	Canned or frozen fruit

Fruit Custard Trifle: Line sherbet glasses with thin pieces of spongecake, ladyfingers, or crumbled macaroons; top with Fruit Float.

FRESH STRAWBERRY TAPIOCA

1 pt. sliced strawberries	2 tablesp. fresh, frozen, or canned lemon juice
¾ cup granulated sugar	⅓ cup heavy cream, whipped
¼ cup quick-cooking tapioca	
¼ teasp. salt	

Sprinkle berries with ¼ cup sugar; let stand 30 min. Drain; add enough water to juice to make 2 cups. In saucepan, combine juice with ½ cup sugar, tapioca, salt; cook over medium heat, stirring, until mixture comes to boil. Cool, stirring occasionally. Add berries, lemon juice; refrigerate.

Just before serving: Fold in cream. Makes 6 to 8 servings.

TAPIOCA CREAM

For dreamy tapioca cream, just follow directions on package of quick-cooking tapioca. (The jiffy double recipe gives you 2 desserts with just one fixing.) Then dress it up in one of the ways below. Try these suggestions too with the easy-to-make packaged prepared tapioca pudding.

Ripple Style: Fold in any of these:

Whipped cream, alone or with cut-up maraschino cherries and snipped marshmallows
Salted nuts and a little chocolate or butterscotch sauce
Drained canned Bing cherries
Drained fresh, frozen, or canned peach slices or pineapple tidbits
Raspberry, strawberry, or peach preserves
Chopped unpared red apple or banana chunks

Parfait Fashion: In sherbet, parfait, or tall glasses, alternate layers of tapioca cream with one of these:

> Canned crushed pineapple, flavored with mint extract, then tinted green
>
> Whipped cream, beaten with some bright jelly until fluffy and thick
>
> Canned whole-cranberry sauce, as is or mixed with slivered almonds
>
> Melted currant jelly, tossed with shredded coconut
>
> Melted semisweet-chocolate pieces and chopped nuts
>
> Brown sugar and butter or margarine, melted together until syrupy
>
> Cut-up oranges and snipped fresh mint

Sundae Best: Spoon tapioca cream into sherbet glasses; top with one of these:

> Just thawed frozen raspberries, strawberries, or pineapple chunks
>
> Bright jelly, sprig of mint
>
> Shredded coconut tossed with grated orange rind
>
> Crushed peanut brittle or peppermint candy
>
> Chocolate Sauce, p. 367, or Butterscotch Sauce, p. 368; then whipped cream
>
> Just thawed frozen orange- or grape-juice concentrate
>
> Vanilla, chocolate, or strawberry ice cream
>
> Pink rhubarb sauce
>
> Snipped, pitted dates or dried figs and chopped nuts, moistened with thawed frozen orange-juice concentrate

DE LUXE RENNET CUSTARD

Choose your favorite flavor of packaged rennet-custard dessert. Make as label directs, substituting light cream for milk. Serve topped with one of these:

Toasted, shredded coconut	Partially thawed frozen or fresh raspberries or strawberries
Orange sections	
Canned apricot nectar	
Chopped walnuts	Canned pineapple tidbits

Chocolate-Almond: To chocolate rennet, add ¼ teasp. almond extract.

Rum-Mocha: To chocolate rennet, add 1 teasp. instant coffee and rum to taste.

Trifle: Sprinkle bakers' poundcake slices with rum, sherry, or brandy. Pour vanilla or lemon rennet over slices. Refrigerate till set.

DANISH CREAM

Prepare 1 pkg. vanilla rennet-custard dessert as label directs, substituting light cream for milk; pour into 8 sherbet glasses. Prepare 1 pkg. Danish dessert as label directs; when rennet is set, spoon Danish dessert over it. Refrigerate.

Serve topped with toasted shredded coconut. Makes 8 servings.

Note: Danish dessert is delicious served with light cream or custard sauce. See label for more dessert suggestions.

CHOCOLATE-ALMOND CREAM
(old-fashioned blancmange)

1¾ cups milk	2 tablesp. sugar
2 tablesp. cocoa	⅛ teasp. almond extract
¼ teasp. salt	
2 tablesp. sugar	½ teasp. vanilla extract
1½ tablesp. cornstarch	½ cup heavy cream, whipped
¼ cup milk	
1 egg, well beaten	

In double boiler, scald 1¾ cups milk. Combine cocoa, salt, 2 tablesp. sugar, cornstarch. Mix with ¼ cup milk till smooth; stir into scalded milk. Cook, stirring, until smooth and thickened.

Combine egg with 2 tablesp. sugar; slowly add chocolate mixture. Return to double boiler; cook, stirring, until smooth and thickened—about 2 min. Cool. Fold in extracts, then half of whipped cream. Turn into serving dish or sherbet glasses. Top with remaining whipped cream. Refrigerate until served. Makes 4 servings.

TODAY'S BLANCMANGE

Delectable butterscotch, chocolate, vanilla, coconut cream, lemon, peppermint chocolate, and other flavored puddings (or blancmanges) can be made in a jiffy with today's packaged pudding mixes. Serve hot or cold. Vary thus:

Any Flavor:

1. For delicate pudding, increase milk to 2¼ to 2½ cups; before serving, beat with egg beater.
2. Or fold in diced bananas; shredded coconut; cut-up, pitted dates or marshmallows; chopped nuts; or a little cooked rice.
3. Or swirl spoonful of melted semisweet-chocolate through each serving.
4. Or serve warm, topped with vanilla ice cream.
5. Or chill; then fold in ½ cup heavy cream, whipped.
6. Or fold in cookie crumbs or toasted nuts.

Vanilla:

1. Alternate layers of pudding with sweetened fresh or thawed frozen berries or pineapple chunks, diced bananas, or canned Bing cherries.
2. Or flavor with almond extract, sherry, or brandy to taste. Fold in ¼ cup heavy cream, whipped.
3. Or top with whipped cream, to which cocoa or instant coffee has been added.
4. Or top with chocolate or butterscotch sauce.
5. Or flavor with almond extract; fold in 1 drained No. 2 can crushed pineapple.

Chocolate:

1. Before cooking, add 1 sq. unsweetened chocolate or ⅓ cup semisweet-chocolate pieces. Gives fuller flavor.
2. Or substitute 1¼ cups coffee for 1 cup milk.
3. Or flavor with sherry, rum, or brandy to taste.
4. Or serve in layers with peppermint-flavored whipped cream, tinted delicate green.

SNOW CUSTARD

2 cups milk	4 egg yolks
4 egg whites	3 tablesp. granulated
⅛ teasp. salt	sugar
6 tablesp. granulated	½ teasp. vanilla extract
sugar	

In double boiler, scald milk (use shallow saucepan type, not deep kind; or make double boiler of 2 saucepans). Beat egg whites till foamy; gradually add salt and 6 tablesp. sugar, beating

until stiff but not dry. Drop by heaping tablespoons (5 or 6) onto milk; cook, covered, 5 min., or until meringues have set and lost their stickiness. With slotted spoon, lift them out of milk into bowl.

Lightly beat egg yolks with 3 tablesp. sugar; stir in a little hot milk; stir into rest of milk in double boiler. Cook, stirring, until custard thickens and coats spoon; add vanilla; cool. Pour over meringues; then refrigerate.

Serve sprinkled with toasted almonds, shredded coconut, or grated chocolate. Makes 5 or 6 servings.

Fruited: Refrigerate custard and meringues separately. To serve, arrange one of the following fruits in bottom of serving dish or sherbet glasses. Top with meringues; pour custard on top; then sprinkle with chopped nuts, shredded coconut, or shaved chocolate:

Sliced peaches, pineapple, oranges, or bananas
Strawberries or raspberries
Pitted, cooked prunes

SUSAN'S BAKED CUSTARD

4 eggs	2 to 2½ cups milk*
¼ cup granulated	1 teasp. vanilla extract
sugar	Nutmeg or shredded
¼ teasp. salt	coconut

Individuals:

1. Start heating oven to 300°F. Butter 5 or 6 custard cups. Into large bowl, break eggs; with electric mixer or egg beater, beat until fluffy.
2. Add sugar, salt; beat until *thick and lemon-colored.* Add milk, vanilla; beat again until thoroughly combined.
3. Pour mixture through fine strainer into custard cups, filling each to about ½" from top; top with nutmeg or coconut. Set custard cups in shallow baking pan; place on oven rack. Fill pan with hot water to ¾" from top of cups.
4. Bake about 1 hr. Near end of baking time, insert silver knife in center of custard. When knife comes out clean, custards are done. Remove at once from oven; then cool on wire rack. Refrigerate.

To serve: Serve right in custard cups. Or run

spatula all around inside of each cup; place dessert plate, upside down, on top of each cup; then invert. Remove cup.

Serve custards with whipped cream; maple-blended syrup; Chocolate Sauce, p. 367; or Butter Caramel Sauce, p. 369. Or surround with fresh, canned, thawed frozen, or stewed dried fruits, or applesauce flavored with bit of lemon rind. Or garnish with jam. Makes 5 or 6 servings.

For a richer custard, use part cream.

Large: Turn custard mixture into buttered 1-qt. casserole. Place in baking pan; fill with hot water to ¾″ from top of casserole. Bake at 300°F. 1¼ hr., or until knife inserted in center comes out clean. Remove from water. Cool on wire rack. Refrigerate until cold.

To serve: Unmold. Or spoon into sherbet glasses. Makes 5 or 6 servings.

Baked Caramel: In skillet over medium heat, melt ¼ cup granulated sugar, stirring constantly, until it forms caramellike syrup. Immediately pour into 6 buttered custard cups. Slowly pour custard mixture into cups; if desired, sprinkle with shredded coconut or chopped pecans; bake as directed. Refrigerate until cold; unmold. Caramel becomes sauce over custard.

Baked Custard Surprises: When serving individual custards, lift spoonful of custard from center of each; drop in bit of jelly; replace custard. Top with whipped cream if desired.

Baked Maple: Before pouring in custard mixture, place 1 tablesp. maple or maple-blended syrup in each cup.

Baked Marshmallow: Before pouring in custard mixture, place marshmallow in bottom of each custard cup. Or cover bottom of large casserole with marshmallows.

SUSAN'S CREAM PUFFS

½ cup boiling water	½ cup sifted all-
¼ cup butter, mar-	purpose flour
garine, or salad oil*	2 eggs, unbeaten
⅛ teasp. salt	

1. Start heating oven to 375°F. Bring water, butter, salt to boil. Add flour, *all at once;* then beat over low heat until mixture leaves sides of pan and forms compact ball.

2. Remove from heat; continue beating to cool mixture slightly—about 2 min.
3. Add eggs, one at a time, beating well after each addition. After last egg has been added, beat until mixture has satinlike sheen.
4. Onto greased baking sheet, drop 5 or 6 mounds of batter, 2″ apart, swirling top of each mound.
5. Bake until well browned and puffy—about 50 min. Remove from oven; immediately cut 1 or 2 slits in side of each puff; return to oven for 10 min.
6. Cool on cake rack.

To serve: Split cream puffs almost all the way around. Or slice off top of each.

Fill with Cream Puff Filling, p. 461; Chocolate Cream Filling, p. 461; sugared strawberries; ice cream; or sweetened whipped cream, flavored with almond, vanilla, or rum extract. Set tops back on.

Top with confectioners' sugar, Bittersweet Frosting, p. 464, and nuts; hot Butterscotch Sauce, p. 368; Hot Fudge Sauce, p. 370; crushed, sweetened berries; or sliced peaches. Makes 5 or 6 puffs.

If using salad oil, increase salt to ¼ teasp.

To Do Ahead: Make Cream Puffs one day. Next day, reheat in 325°F. oven 5 min.; cool; split; fill.

Petite: Drop cream-puff mixture by rounded ½ teaspoonfuls, about the size of a quarter, onto ungreased baking sheet. Bake at 375°F. until well browned and puffy—about 30 min. Remove from oven; cut slit in side of each; bake 5 min. more. Cool. Fill and top as you wish. Serve 2 per person. Makes 30 to 35.

ECLAIRS

Start heating oven to 375°F. Make Susan's Cream Puff mixture, above. Drop by rounded tablespoonfuls, about 2″ apart, in rows 6″ apart onto ungreased baking sheet. Now, working carefully with small spatula, spread each ball of dough into 4″ x 1″ rectangle, rounding sides and piling dough on top.

Bake about 50 min., or until well browned and puffy. Remove from oven; immediately cut 1 or 2 slits in side of each éclair; return to oven for 10 min. Cool on cake rack. Make lengthwise slit in side of each. Fill and top as in Susan's Cream Puffs, p. 395. Makes 8.

Chocolate Eclairs: Fill éclairs with Cream-Puff Filling, p. 461; top with Bittersweet Frosting, p. 464.

GRANNY'S INDIAN PUDDING

1 qt. milk	margarine
¾ cup corn meal	1 teasp. cinnamon
¾ cup finely chopped, not ground, suet	½ teasp. ground cloves
	¼ teasp. nutmeg
¾ cup light molasses	½ teasp. ginger
1 egg, beaten	1½ cups light or dark raisins
1 teasp. salt	
½ cup butter or	2 cups milk

Start heating oven to 300°F. Bring 1 qt. milk just to boiling point over low heat. Gradually stir in corn meal; boil over low heat, stirring, till thickened. Add suet, rest of ingredients except milk. Turn into greased 3-qt. casserole. Bake, uncovered, in pan of hot water 30 min. Pour on 2 cups milk; *don't stir.* Bake 3 hr.

Serve warm or cold, topped with vanilla ice cream. Makes 12 servings.

To Do Ahead: Bake pudding day before; then refrigerate. To serve, reheat in pan of hot water at 300°F. about 45 min.

NO-BAKE CHEESECAKE

2 env. unflavored gelatine	1 teasp. vanilla extract
1 cup granulated sugar	2 tablesp. melted butter or margarine
¼ teasp. salt	1 tablesp. sugar
2 eggs, separated	½ cup graham-cracker crumbs
1 cup milk	
1 teasp. grated lemon rind	¼ teasp. cinnamon
	¼ teasp. nutmeg
3 cups creamed cottage cheese, sieved	1 cup heavy cream, whipped
1 tablesp. lemon juice	

In double-boiler top, mix gelatine, 1 cup sugar, salt. In bowl, beat egg yolks with milk; add to gelatine mixture. Cook over boiling water, stirring constantly, about 10 min., or until gelatine dissolves and mixture thickens. Remove from heat; add lemon rind; cool.

Stir in cottage cheese, lemon juice, vanilla. Refrigerate, stirring occasionally, about 1 hr., or

until mixture mounds slightly when dropped from spoon.

Meanwhile, mix butter, 1 tablesp. sugar, crumbs, cinnamon, nutmeg.

Beat egg whites until stiff; fold into gelatine mixture with cream. Turn into 9" clampless spring-form pan with flat bottom insert in place.* Sprinkle with crumb mixture. Refrigerate until firm.

Nice topped with strawberries, blueberries, peaches, chopped nuts, canned crushed pineapple, or cherry preserves. Makes 10 to 12 servings.

Note: For family-size cheesecake, halve each filling ingredient, but use full amount of crumb mixture. Use 8" or 9" layer pan or pie plate. Makes 5 or 6 servings.

* Or if desired, with waxed paper, line bottom of 8" x 8" x 2" or 9" x 9" x 2" pan or 9" x 5" x 3" loaf pan; then press crumb mixture to bottom of pan. Turn in gelatine mixture. Refrigerate until firm. Unmold. Serve cut into squares. Garnish as above.

DE LUXE CHEESECAKE

1 cup sifted all-purpose flour	1¾ cups granulated sugar
¼ cup granulated sugar	¼ teasp. vanilla extract
1 teasp. grated lemon rind	½ teasp. grated orange rind
¼ teasp. vanilla extract	3 tablesp. flour
½ cup soft butter or margarine	¼ teasp. salt
	½ teasp. grated lemon rind
3 egg yolks	
5 8-oz. pkg. soft cream cheese	5 medium eggs
	¼ cup heavy cream

Cookie Mixture: Mix 1 cup flour, ¼ cup sugar, 1 teasp. lemon rind, vanilla. With pastry blender or 2 knives, scissor-fashion, cut in butter and 1 egg yolk. Shape into ball; wrap in waxed paper; refrigerate 1 hr. Start heating oven to 400°F. Roll about one third of dough between floured pieces of waxed paper into 9½" circle. Place on bottom of 9" spring-form pan; trim to fit. Bake at 400°F. about 10 min., or till golden; cool.

Grease side of spring-form pan; fit over filled base. Roll rest of dough into 15" x 4" rectangle; cut in half lengthwise; use to line side of pan, patching if necessary.

Cheese Filling: Increase oven temperature to 500°F. With electric mixer or spoon, beat cheese until fluffy. Combine 1¾ cups sugar with vanilla, orange rind, 3 tablesp. flour, salt, ½ teasp. lemon rind; slowly add to cheese, beating till smooth. Add eggs and 2 yolks, one at a time, beating after each addition. Stir in cream. Turn into lined pan. Bake at 500°F. 12 min., or till dough is golden. Reduce oven temperature to 200°F.; bake 1 hr. Cool on rack away from drafts. Remove side of pan; refrigerate until cold.*

To serve: Sprinkle cake with chopped, toasted nuts. Or cover with ¼" layer of commercial sour cream; refrigerate.

Or spread strawberry, peach, apricot, or cherry jam or preserves on top.

Or top wedges with canned crushed pineapple, sliced peaches, or fresh or thawed frozen strawberries. Makes 12 servings.

* *Even better if refrigerated 24 hr.*

DATE-NUT ROLLS

½ lb. pitted dates, snipped into pieces	1⅓ cups graham-cracker crumbs
½ lb. marshmallows, snipped into pieces	1 cup heavy cream, whipped
½ cup chopped walnuts	1 teasp. grated orange rind
½ cup light cream	

Combine dates, marshmallows, nuts, cream; mix well. Add 1 cup crumbs; mix well; then work in rest of crumbs. Form into rolls, 2" or 3" in diameter; wrap in waxed paper or saran. Refrigerate 24 hr.

Serve sliced, with whipped cream to which rind has been added. Makes 6 servings.

MERINGUE GLACEE

⅛ teasp. salt	1 teasp. vinegar
6 egg whites	1 teasp. vanilla extract
2 cups granulated sugar	

Day or so before: Add salt to egg whites. With electric mixer at high speed, beat until stiff enough to hold shape. At low speed, add sugar, about 2 tablesp. at a time, beating about 2 min. after each addition. (This takes about 30 min.)

Start heating oven to 275°F. Add vinegar and vanilla to meringue; beat at high speed about 10 min. longer. Drop by heaping spoonfuls onto buttered baking sheet. Bake at 275°F. 45 min. Reduce heat to 250°F.; bake 15 min., or until creamy white and delicately firm. Remove to rack; cool.

Cover meringues lightly with waxed paper, saran, or aluminum foil; store in covered container until needed—they keep well.

To serve: Break each meringue apart like a biscuit. Fill lower part with ice cream or whipped cream; add spoonful of fruit or chocolate, butterscotch, or caramel sauce; replace top. Makes 18 to 24.

BRAZIL-NUT TORTE

½ cup sifted all-purpose flour	¾ cup chopped Brazil nuts
2 teasp. double-acting baking powder	1 teasp. vanilla extract Milk*
2 cups fine graham-cracker crumbs	3 egg whites
½ cup soft shortening	1 pkg. vanilla pudding
1 cup granulated sugar	1½ cups milk
3 egg yolks	½ cup heavy cream, whipped

Day before: Start heating oven to 375°F. With waxed paper, line bottoms of 2 1¼"-deep 8" layer pans. Sift flour, baking powder; add cracker crumbs.

With electric mixer at medium speed, or "cream" (or with spoon), thoroughly mix shortening with sugar, then with egg yolks, until very light and fluffy—about 4 min. altogether. Add nuts, vanilla.

At low speed, or "blend," beat in flour mixture alternately with milk, beating just until smooth. Beat egg whites until stiff but not dry; quickly fold into nut mixture. Turn into pans. Bake 30 min., or till cake tester inserted in center comes out clean. Cool in pans on wire rack. Meanwhile, combine vanilla pudding with 1½ cups milk. Cook over medium heat, stirring, until mixture comes to boil. Remove from heat; pour into bowl; place waxed paper directly on surface of pudding. Refrigerate.

The day: Beat pudding until smooth; fold in whipped cream. Split each cake layer; spread filling between layers and on top. Refrigerate at least 1 hr.

* *With butter, margarine, or lard, use 1 cup milk. With vegetable or any other shortening, use 1 cup plus 2 tablesp. milk.*

STRAWBERRY DELIGHT

1 lb. packaged filled sugar wafers	2 large, or 3 small, eggs, separated
¾ cup soft butter or margarine	2 12-oz. pkg. thawed frozen strawberries
1 cup sifted confectioners' sugar	½ cup coarsely chopped walnuts
½ teasp. vanilla extract	1½ cups heavy cream, whipped
¼ teasp. almond extract	

Two days before: Crush wafers medium fine; spread half in 12″ x 8″ x 2″ baking dish. With electric mixer at medium speed, or "cream" (or with spoon), thoroughly mix butter, sugar, extracts. Add yolks, one at a time, beating well after each addition. Beat egg whites until stiff but not dry; fold into butter mixture; drop, making thin layer over crumbs. Spoon on drained berries; sprinkle with nuts. Spread with whipped cream; sprinkle with rest of crumbs. Refrigerate 36 to 48 hr.

To serve: Cut into squares; top with any crumbs left in dish. Makes 12 to 16 servings.

▶ **For 6:** Halve each ingredient; place in 8″ x 8″ x 2″ pan.

CHOCO-MOUSSE CAKE

1½ teasp. unflavored gelatine	1 teasp. vanilla extract
½ cup granulated sugar	4 egg whites
Pinch salt	½ cup heavy cream, whipped
⅓ cup water	½ cup finely chopped walnuts
3 sq. unsweetened chocolate	2 doz. ladyfingers, split
4 egg yolks, unbeaten	

Day before: In double-boiler top, combine gelatine, sugar, salt, water, chocolate. Cook over *hot, not boiling,* water, stirring, until chocolate is melted and gelatine dissolves. Remove from heat; add egg yolks, one at a time, beating well after each addition. Cook over boiling water, stirring, 2 min. Add vanilla; cool.

Beat egg whites until stiff but not dry; fold into chocolate mixture; refrigerate 15 min. Fold in whipped cream, nuts.

With waxed paper, line bottom, sides, of 2-qt. casserole or mold; arrange split ladyfingers on bottom and sides; add thin layer of chocolate mixture, then more ladyfingers. Repeat until all are used, ending with chocolate. Refrigerate 12 to 24 hr.

To serve: Unmold; decorate with whipped cream; cut into wedges. Makes 8 to 10 servings.

LEMON-COCONUT CAKE

About 24 hr. ahead: Mix 1 pkg. lemon pie filling as label directs; cool. Fold in 2 teasp. grated lemon rind; 1 cup heavy cream, whipped; 1 cup shredded coconut.

Split 2 bakers' or homemade sponge-, white-, or yellow-cake layers, making 4 layers in all. (Or use 1 12″ loaf of bakers' angel-food cake; split into 3 layers.) Fill and frost with lemon filling. Refrigerate 24 hr. Makes 8 to 10 servings.

CHOCOLATE WHIPPED-CREAM CAKE

Split 2 8″ or 9″ cake layers, making 4 layers in all. Whip 1 cup heavy cream till it thickens; add ½ cup canned chocolate sauce, all at once; beat until mixture mounds. Use to fill and frost cake layers. Top with toasted, slivered almonds. Refrigerate 24 hr. Makes 8 to 10 servings.

▶ **For 2:** Use 1 8″ cake layer; halve rest of ingredients. Cut layer in half; then split each half, making 4 layers in all.

Mocha: In double boiler over *hot, not boiling,* water, melt ½ pkg. semisweet-chocolate pieces (½ cup). Remove from heat; stir in ¼ cup water; cool. Add 1 cup heavy cream and 1 to 2 tablesp. instant coffee. Beat until stiff enough to mound. Use to fill and frost layers.

EDNA'S PICCADILLY TRIFLE

1 pkg. vanilla pudding	½ cup syrup drained from pears
3 cups milk	
1 teasp. sherry extract; or sherry to taste	1 No. 2½ can pear halves, drained
2 6″ bakers' sponge-cake layers	⅔ cup heavy cream, whipped (optional)
⅔ cup seedless black-raspberry jam	Candied cherries (optional)

Early in day: To make custard sauce, prepare pudding as label directs, using 3 cups milk; cool; add sherry. In attractive 2-qt. bowl, set 1 cake layer. Spread with half of jam. Sprinkle with ¼ cup pear syrup. Arrange half of pears on top of jam. Gently crush pears with 2-tined fork. Pour on half of custard sauce. Repeat. Refrigerate.

To serve: Spread whipped cream on top of cake; garnish with cut-up cherries. Cut into wedges; spoon on sauce from bowl. Makes 9 servings.

CRANBERRY ANGEL

Open 1 can jellied cranberry sauce. Remove sauce in one piece; press into hole in center of 9" or 10" angel-food or chiffon cake (enlarge hole with knife if necessary). Cut off any jelly that protrudes above top. Whip ½ cup heavy cream with ½ teasp. almond extract; spread over top of cake. Makes 10 to 12 servings.

GALA RAINBOW DESSERT

1 10" chiffon or angel-food cake	pineapple, well drained
2 cups heavy cream	Green food color
¼ cup sifted confectioners' sugar	¼ cup thick raspberry jam
1 No. 303 can apricot halves, drained and mashed	Chopped pistachio nuts; or slivered, toasted almonds
2 9-oz. cans crushed	

Make or buy cake. Whip cream until stiff; stir in sugar. Fold ½ cup whipped cream into apricots; ½ cup whipped cream into pineapple, tinted delicate green; and ½ cup whipped cream into jam. Cut cake into 4 even layers. On bottom layer, spread apricot filling. Top with second layer; spread with pineapple filling. Top with third layer; spread with raspberry filling.

Place fourth layer on top of all. Spread top and side of cake with rest of whipped cream; sprinkle outer top edge with pistachio nuts. Refrigerate several hours before serving. Makes 12 servings.

MOCHA ANGEL FOOD

Make or buy 10" angel-food cake.

Two hours or so before serving: Whip 1½ cups heavy cream with 1 tablesp. instant coffee. Cut cake into 2 even layers. Place bottom layer on cake plate; spread with small amount of coffee whipped cream; firmly replace top layer. With very sharp, thin-bladed knife, cut cake into 12 or more servings, using sawing motion to prevent crushing and leaving wedges in place.

Frost entire cake with rest of whipped cream; sprinkle with shaved unsweetened chocolate. Refrigerate till served. Makes 12 servings.

TWIN ANGEL-FOOD PIES

1 10" angel-food cake	2 egg whites
1 env. unflavored gelatine	⅛ teasp. salt
½ cup cold water	1 cup heavy cream, whipped
2 10-to-12-oz. pkg. thawed frozen sliced strawberries or raspberries	½ cup heavy cream, whipped
4 teasp. lemon juice	2 cups shredded coconut

Make or buy angel-food cake; cut into 2 even layers. Hollow out both layers, leaving shell not quite 1" thick. Place each cake shell on serving plate. Fill in tube hole in each with bits of cake.

Sprinkle gelatine over cold water in glass measuring cup to soften; stir over hot water until dissolved; stir into berries with lemon juice. Refrigerate until partially thickened. Beat egg whites with salt until stiff. Fold into fruit mixture with 1 cup cream, whipped. Refrigerate a few minutes; then heap in cake shells. Refrigerate several hours.

To serve: Decorate tops with ½ cup cream, whipped, and coconut. Makes 16 to 18 servings.

COFFEE-MARSHMALLOW REFRIGERATOR CAKE

Day before: In saucepan, dissolve 2 tablesp. instant coffee in 1 cup hot water. With scissors, snip ½ lb. marshmallows into coffee. Cook over low heat, stirring, until marshmallows are melted. Refrigerate until slightly thickened; then fold in 1 cup heavy cream, whipped. Split 18 ladyfingers; use to line bottom of 10" x 8" x 2" baking dish or 9" clampless spring-form pan with flat bottom insert in place; cover with half of coffee mixture. Repeat. Refrigerate.

At serving time: Spread top with ½ cup heavy cream, whipped. Cut into squares or wedges. Makes 8 servings.

BUTTERSCOTCH ICEBOX COOKIE CAKE

1 pkg. butterscotch pudding	gelatine
1¾ cups cold water	1 pt. vanilla ice cream
1 env. unflavored	36 to 40 packaged coconut-bar cookies

In saucepan, combine pudding, water, gelatine; cook over medium heat, stirring, until mixture comes to full boil. Cool 5 min., stirring once or twice. Add ice cream by spoonfuls, stirring until melted. Refrigerate 10 to 15 min., or until slightly thickened.

Arrange about 12 cookies in bottom of greased 9″ x 5″ x 3″ loaf pan; spoon on one third of pudding. Repeat, making 3 layers of each. Refrigerate until firm—about 2 hr.

To serve: Loosen all around with knife; then unmold; slice. Makes 8 servings.

Chocolate: Substitute chocolate pudding for butterscotch, chocolate ice cream for vanilla.

COTTAGE PUDDING

Make Miracle Cake, p. 440; or use your favorite cake mix to make layer or square cake.

Serve warm, cut into wedges or squares, with Lemon Sauce, p. 370; Vanilla Sauce, p. 370; Hot Fudge Sauce, p. 370; Butterscotch Sauce, p. 368; or crushed sweetened berries or fruit on top.

Jiffy: Keep squares of unfrosted cake in freezer. Warm in double boiler. Serve as above.

Favorite Fruit Desserts

SAUCEPAN APPLESAUCE

8 cored, quartered, unpared cooking apples (2 lb.)	About ½ cup granulated sugar or brown sugar, packed
½ cup water	

In saucepan, simmer apples with water, covered, 15 to 20 min., or until fork-tender. (Stir occasionally, adding water if necessary, to keep apples from scorching.) Put through food mill or coarse sieve. Stir in sugar (amount depends on desired sweetness) until dissolved. Adding a few drops of lemon juice or bit of butter will perk up the flavor.

Serve warm or cold, with cream, whipped cream, custard sauce, ice cream, etc.

Or use as breakfast fruit or meat accompaniment. Makes 6 servings.

To Vary: Pare and core apples before cooking. When cooked, beat smooth with spoon. Or add vanilla or almond extract or brandy to taste.

Fruity: Before cooking, add 2 teasp. grated orange, lemon, or lime rind; or ½ cup canned crushed pineapple; or bit of canned whole-cranberry sauce.

Spiced: Before cooking, add lemon juice to taste, plus ⅛ teasp. cinnamon or mace, or 8 whole cloves. To serve, remove cloves.

Cinnamon: Chill applesauce well. Just before serving, add a few tiny red cinnamon candies. Nice for breakfast.

BAKED APPLES

6 medium red cooking apples	1 cup water
	2 tablesp. sugar
¾ cup granulated sugar	

1. Start heating oven to 350°F. Wash and core apples.
2. Starting at stem end, pare apples one third of way down. (This helps keep skins from bursting.) Arrange in shallow baking pan, with pared sides up.
3. Boil ¾ cup sugar with 1 cup water 10 min. Pour over apples. (For color, cook a few parings with syrup; remove before using.)
4. Bake apples, spooning syrup from pan over them frequently, ½ to 1 hr., or until easily pierced with fork. (Time varies with apples.)
5. When apples are tender, remove from oven; sprinkle each with 1 teasp. sugar. Broil under low heat, basting often, till brown.

Serve cold or warm, as is or with pour cream, whipped cream, or ice cream. Or sprinkle with port or sherry. Also nice as breakfast fruit with cream. Makes 6.

To Vary: Before sprinkling sugar in step 5, place one of these in each baked apple:

Pitted, cooked prune	Currant jelly
Marshmallow	Orange marmalade
Cut-up pitted dates	A few raisins with
1 teasp. grated orange or lemon rind	chopped nuts
	Coconut mixed with
1 tablesp. prepared mincemeat	butter and brown sugar

Cranberry: Substitute 1 can whole-cranberry sauce for ¾ cup sugar. Combine sauce with water; pour over apples; bake as above. Omit sprinkling with sugar and broiling. Nice as dessert.

TOP-OF-RANGE "BAKED" APPLES

Cut 3 small cooking apples into halves, cross-wise; remove cores. Dissolve ⅓ cup granulated sugar in 1 cup water; add 1 teasp. butter or margarine, 1 teasp. lemon juice. Pour into heavy skillet; add apple halves. Turn heat very low; simmer, covered, about 15 min., or till tender, turning apples once or twice and basting occasionally with syrup.

Serve as in Baked Apples, p. 400. Makes 6 servings.

BAKED BANANA DESSERT

Prepare Baked Bananas, p. 290. Serve with cream; Lemon or Orange Sauce, p. 370, or Frosty Sauce, p. 368.

STEWED PEACHES

6 ripe peaches	1 cup water
¾ cup granulated sugar	4 whole cloves (optional)

Peel fruit; halve and pit if desired. Simmer sugar, water, and cloves 5 min. Add peaches; simmer, covered, 10 min., or until just tender. Refrigerate.

Serve topped with Frosty Sauce, p. 368; whipped cream cheese; cottage cheese; or commercial sour cream. Nice at breakfast too. Makes 6 servings.

To Vary: Substitute ¼ cup white wine for ¼ cup water, or small piece of stick cinnamon for cloves.

BUTTERY BAKED PEACHES OR PEARS

½ cup granulated sugar	margarine
2 tablesp. fresh, frozen, or canned lemon juice	1 cup boiling water
	3 peeled, halved ripe peaches or pears
2 tablesp. butter or	Currant or mint jelly

Start heating oven to 350°F. Simmer sugar, lemon juice, butter, and boiling water 5 min. Arrange peaches in 1½-qt. casserole; add sauce. Bake, covered, 45 min., or until tender. Refrigerate. Place a little jelly on each.

Serve with whipped cream. Or drain and use as meat garnish. Makes 6 servings.

Spiced: Omit lemon juice, jelly; sprinkle with nutmeg or sherry.

CINNAMON PEACHES OR APRICOTS

1 lb. peeled ripe peaches or halved, pitted, unpeeled apricots	⅓ cup granulated sugar
	1 teasp. cinnamon
	⅓ cup water
	¼ cup light cream

Night before: Start heating oven to 375°F. Place fruit in 1-qt. casserole. Combine sugar, cinnamon, water; pour over peaches. Bake, uncovered, basting occasionally, 30 to 40 min. Then pour on cream. Bake 5 min. Refrigerate till needed.

Serve, with juice poured over fruit. Nice too at breakfast. Makes 4 servings.

TANGERINE DELIGHT

8 medium tangerines	6 whole cloves
1½ cups water	2 tablesp. fresh, frozen, or canned lemon juice
½ cup granulated sugar	
5 2″ cinnamon sticks	

Day before: Wash, peel, and section tangerines; place peel from 3 tangerines in saucepan. Remove all white fiber from fruit; add fiber to peel, along with water, sugar, spices, lemon juice. Bring to full, rolling boil; boil, uncovered, 10 min. Remove peel; add tangerine sections; bring to boil again; boil 1 min.; cool. Refrigerate.

Serve with cream cheese and crackers. Makes 4 servings.

STEWED PLUMS OR FRESH PRUNES

Select firm plums or fresh prunes. Wash; prick skins; place in saucepan; half cover with water. Simmer, covered, 20 to 25 min., or until soft. Add sugar to taste; cook, uncovered, 5 min. Refrigerate.

To serve: Top with lemon sherbet; sprinkle with nutmeg, shredded coconut, or slivered almonds.

ROSY PEAR SAUCE

Cut 4 large pears in halves; remove cores. In saucepan, combine ¾ cup granulated sugar, 1½ cups water, ½ teasp. cinnamon. Bring to boil, stirring. Gently cook 2 or 3 pear halves in syrup at a time until tender; remove; cook rest of pears.

About 10 min. before all pears are cooked, add 1 cup fresh cranberries; cook till tender. Pour syrup and cranberries over pears; cool; then refrigerate. Makes 4 servings.

RHUBARB SAUCE

1½ lb. rhubarb	½ to ⅔ cup granu-
½ cup water	lated sugar
⅛ teasp. salt	

Saucepan Method: Wash rhubarb; cut off root and leaf ends; cut into 1″ or 2″ pieces, without peeling. In saucepan, combine all ingredients; simmer, covered, 10 min., or until tender, stirring gently once or twice. Refrigerate.

Double-Boiler Method: Prepare rhubarb as above. Omit water. Place rhubarb in double boiler with salt and sugar. Cook, covered, 25 min., or until tender, occasionally stirring with 2-tined fork.

Oven Method: Start heating oven to 375°F. Reduce water to 1½ tablesp.; increase sugar to 1 cup. Place all ingredients in 1½-qt. casserole. Bake, covered, 30 to 40 min., or until tender, stirring once.

Serve with or without whipped cream. Also nice as breakfast fruit. Makes 4 or 5 servings.

Rhubarb-Strawberry Delight: Use ¾ cup sugar. Just before removing from heat, add 1 pt. halved, hulled strawberries. Makes 6 to 8 servings.

With Pineapple: Just before serving, add ¾ cup drained canned or fresh pineapple wedges.

Gelatin Desserts

Unflavored Gelatine: Unflavored gelatine is sold 4 envelopes to the package. Follow recipes on label or those that follow here. Generally, 1 env. (about 1 tablesp.) gelatine is used for every 2 cups liquid.

Gelatine desserts made with fresh pineapple will not set unless the pineapple is first brought to a boil, to destroy enzymes present in the fresh fruit. Canned pineapple may be used without boiling.

Fruit-Flavored Gelatin: Fruit-flavored gelatin is sweetened and comes in many delectable flavors. Follow recipes on label or those that follow here.

To Chill Quickly: Half fill large bowl with ice cubes; add some water and 2 tablesp. salt. In ice, set bowl containing gelatin mixture. Stir gelatin often until of proper consistency.

To Unmold Gelatin Desserts: Lower mold, almost to rim, in bowl of warm water for 10 sec. (if mold is glass, use hot water); remove. Gently loosen gelatin with paring knife. (If it's not easy to loosen after one dipping, repeat dipping.) Then place chilled serving dish, upside down, on top of mold; invert. Carefully lift off mold, leaving jelly on dish.

P.S. If you rinse the serving dish in cold water before unmolding the gelatin, you can move gelatin to center of dish more easily if it is askew.

JIFFY JELLIED FRUIT

1 pkg. fruit-flavored	juice
gelatin	1 unthawed 12-oz. pkg.
1 cup hot water	frozen raspberries,
½ cup cold water or	or sliced strawber-
fruit juice	ries or peaches
1 tablesp. fresh, frozen,	1 cup seedless grapes
or canned lemon	

Dissolve gelatin in hot water; add rest of ingredients. Refrigerate, stirring occasionally, until fruit thaws and gelatin sets—about 30 min. for soft jelly, 1 hr. for firm jelly. Spoon into sherbet glasses.

To serve: Top with Speedy Custard Sauce, p. 368, or Low-Cal Topping, p. 369. Makes 6 servings.

Date-Nut: Substitute ½ cup chopped walnuts and ½ cup snipped, pitted dates for grapes.

Pine-Mallow: Substitute drained canned pineapple chunks for grapes. When gelatin is slightly thickened, fold in 4 snipped marshmallows.

FRUITED JELLY

Using unflavored gelatine, make orange or lemon jelly as label directs.

Or prepare your favorite fruit-flavored gelatin as label directs (substitute fruit syrup drained from canned or frozen fruit for part of liquid if desired).

Refrigerate gelatin mixture until consistency of unbeaten egg white. Beat until fluffy; or leave as is. Fold in one, or a combination of two or three, of these:

Fresh or thawed frozen strawberries	Fresh or canned grapefruit sections
Sliced fresh or canned peaches	Canned apricot halves
Sliced or diced bananas	Diced fresh or canned pears
Fresh or thawed frozen raspberries	Diced raw apples
Seeded or seedless grapes	Cream-cheese balls
	Chopped nuts
Canned pineapple chunks or tidbits	Snipped marshmallows
Shredded coconut	Snipped, pitted dates or dried figs
Diced oranges	Pitted, cooked dried prunes or apricots

Leave in bowl; or turn into 1-qt. mold or individual molds. Refrigerate until set; spoon into sherbet glasses or unmold.

Serve as is or with pour cream; whipped cream; custard sauce; Low-Cal Topping, p. 369; or cream cheese whipped with a little milk until creamy.

Fruit Cream: Just before folding in fruit, beat in 1 pt. vanilla ice cream until well blended. Refrigerate until set.

Red-and-White Sundaes: When Fruited Jelly is set, break up with fork; spoon into sherbet glasses; top with vanilla ice cream; sprinkle with cinnamon.

GRAPE COOLER

1 pkg. lemon-flavored gelatin	or honeydew-melon balls
1 cup hot water	1 3-oz. pkg. soft cream cheese
1 cup cold grape juice	2 to 3 tablesp. milk
1½ cups seedless grapes	

Dissolve gelatin in hot water. Add grape juice. Refrigerate until consistency of unbeaten egg white. Fold in grapes. Pour into 6 to 8 dessert dishes. Refrigerate until set.

To serve: Unmold; top with mounds of cream cheese thinned with milk. Garnish with whole or sliced grapes. Makes 6 to 8 servings.

CHERRY-SHERRY JUBILEE

1 No. 2½ can Bing cherries	½ cup sherry
1 pkg. cherry-flavored gelatin	⅓ cup slivered toasted almonds

Drain cherries. Add enough water to cherry syrup to make 1¾ cups. Heat syrup; pour over gelatin; stir until dissolved. Add cherries, sherry, almonds. Refrigerate till set. Break up gently with fork; spoon into sherbet glasses.

Serve with custard sauce, whipped cream, or ice cream. Makes 6 servings.

CHERRY COLA

½ cup water	½ cup chopped walnuts
1½ cups cola beverage	
1 pkg. cherry-flavored gelatin	½ cup snipped, pitted dates

Heat water with ¾ cup cola; pour over gelatin; stir until dissolved. Add rest of cola. Refrigerate until consistency of unbeaten egg white. Fold in nuts, dates. Turn into sherbet glasses. Refrigerate until firm.

Serve garnished with whipped cream or Low-Cal Topping, p. 369. Makes 6 servings.

FRUIT-WINE JELLY

1 cup Chianti wine	1 pkg. raspberry-flavored gelatin
1 cup orange segments, sweetened	1 cup hot water

Pour wine over oranges; let stand a few min. Dissolve gelatin in hot water; cool. Stir in oranges and wine. Leave in bowl; or turn into individual molds or custard cups. Refrigerate until firm.

To serve: Spoon into sherbet glasses or unmold. Top with whipped cream, if desired. Makes 5 servings.

BAVARIAN CREAM

1 env. unflavored gelatine	¼ cup granulated sugar
Pinch salt	1 cup heavy cream
2 tablesp. sugar	1 teasp. vanilla extract;
2 eggs, separated	½ teasp. almond extract; or rum to taste
1¼ cups milk	

In double-boiler top, combine gelatine, salt, 2 tablesp. sugar. Stir in egg yolks; then slowly stir in milk. Cook over boiling water, stirring, until mixture coats spoon. Remove at once. Refrigerate until slightly thicker than unbeaten egg whites.

Beat egg whites until they form moist peaks when beater is raised; gradually add ¼ cup sugar, beating until stiff. Fold into yolk mixture, along with whipped cream, vanilla. Leave in bowl; or turn into 1½-qt. mold, or 6 to 8 custard cups or molds. Refrigerate till set.

To serve: Spoon into sherbet glasses or unmold. Nice as is or topped with shredded coconut and green *crème de menthe;* crushed strawberries or raspberries; sliced peaches; canned Bing cherries, flavored with brandy; Hot Fudge Sauce, p. 370; Rum Butter Sauce, p. 370; or Bing-Cherry Sauce, p. 368. Makes 6 to 8 servings.

Bavarian Charlotte: Line bowl, mold, or custard cups with spongecake strips or ladyfingers; spoon in Bavarian Cream mixture.

Coffee Bavarian: To milk, add 1 to 2 tablesp. instant coffee.

Grenadine Bavarian: Refrigerate Bavarian Cream mixture in bowl. To serve, heap in sherbet glasses; spoon on bottled grenadine syrup.

HEAVENLY PINEAPPLE DESSERT

1 No. 2 can crushed pineapple	or other flavored gelatin
1½ cups pineapple syrup plus water	2 tablesp. sugar
1 pkg. lemon, orange,	1 cup heavy cream, whipped

Drain crushed pineapple; add enough water to syrup to make 1½ cups. Bring syrup to boil; pour over gelatin mixed with sugar; stir until dissolved. Refrigerate until slightly thickened. Fold in pineapple, whipped cream. Pour into sherbet glasses. Refrigerate until set. Makes 6 servings.

For Calorie Counters: Omit sugar. Substitute Low-Cal Topping, p. 369, for whipped cream.

Jellied Rice Supreme: Reduce pineapple syrup to 1 cup. Omit sugar. When gelatin is slightly thickened, beat till light and fluffy. Fold in 16 snipped marshmallows, 1 cup cooked rice, then pineapple, whipped cream. Pour into 9″ x 5″ x 3″ loaf pan. Refrigerate till firm. Unmold; slice. Makes 6 to 8 servings.

DELMONICO PUDDING

1 pkg. raspberry-flavored gelatin	1 qt. fresh raspberries or hulled strawberries
¾ cup hot water	
½ cup cold water	3 to 4 sliced bananas
1 cup heavy cream, whipped	About 3 cups cake cubes

Dissolve gelatin in hot water; add cold water. Refrigerate till consistency of unbeaten egg white. Beat till fluffy. Fold in whipped cream, fruits. Pour one third of mixture into 10″ x 5″ x 3″ loaf pan; top with half of cake cubes; repeat. Pour on rest of gelatin mixture. Refrigerate till firm.

To serve: Unmold; slice. Makes 10 generous servings.

SUSAN'S SNOW-PUDDING BALLS

2½ teasp. unflavored gelatine	¾ cup boiling water
½ cup cold water	1 teasp. grated lemon or lime rind
¾ cup granulated sugar	¼ cup lemon or lime juice
Pinch salt	2 or 3 egg whites

1. In large bowl, sprinkle gelatine over cold water to soften; add sugar, salt, boiling water; stir until gelatine dissolves. Add lemon rind and juice; stir until blended. Refrigerate, stirring often, until consistency of unbeaten egg white.

2. Add egg whites; with electric mixer or egg beater, beat until mixture begins to hold its shape.

3. Turn mixture into 5 or 6 custard cups. Refrigerate until set. Unmold onto dessert dishes, or pile in serving dish.

Serve with Custard Sauce II, p. 370, or ½ recipe Custard Sauce I, p. 370, made with yolks. Top with sliced berries, peaches, bananas, etc., if desired. Or sprinkle with mace. Or drizzle on maple-blended or maple syrup. Makes 4 or 5 servings.

▶ **For 2 or 3:** Use 2 egg whites; halve rest of ingredients.

Susan's Snow Pudding: Pour Snow-Pudding-Ball mixture into bowl or 1-qt. mold. Refrigerate until set. Spoon into sherbet glasses or unmold. Serve as on p. 404.

SPANISH CREAM

1 env. unflavored gelatine	3 eggs, separated
¼ cup granulated sugar	3 cups milk
	1 teasp. vanilla extract
¼ teasp. salt	¼ cup granulated sugar

1. In double-boiler top, mix gelatine, ¼ cup sugar, salt. Stir in egg yolks; then slowly stir in milk. Cook over boiling water, stirring, until mixture coats spoon.
2. Refrigerate mixture until slightly thicker than unbeaten egg white. Stir in vanilla. Beat egg whites until they form moist peaks when beater is raised; gradually add ¼ cup sugar, beating until stiff. Fold in gelatine mixture.
3. Leave in bowl; or turn into 12 individual molds or custard cups. Refrigerate until set.

To serve: Spoon into sherbet glasses or unmold. Serve plain or top with Chocolate Sauce, p. 367; Butter-Caramel Sauce, p. 369; Butterscotch Sauce, p. 368; crushed strawberries or raspberries; or whipped cream. Makes 12 small molds, or 6 generous servings.

▶ **For 2 or 3:** Use 2 eggs; halve rest of ingredients.

Two-Layer: If you prefer Spanish Cream that separates into 2 layers (custard on top, jelly below), do not chill gelatine mixture. Add vanilla and fold in beaten egg whites while gelatine is still hot.

COFFEE JELLY

1 env. unflavored gelatine	⅛ teasp. salt
½ cup cold water	1 cup hot coffee
⅓ cup granulated sugar	1 teasp. fresh, frozen, or canned lemon juice

In medium bowl, sprinkle gelatine over cold water to soften. Add sugar, salt, hot coffee; stir until gelatine dissolves. Stir in lemon juice. Leave in bowl; or pour into 3 or 4 individual molds or custard cups. Refrigerate until set.

To serve: Spoon into sherbet glasses, or unmold. Top with cream; whipped cream; Custard Sauce I, p. 370; Eggnog Sauce, p. 367; Frosty Sauce, p. 368; or sliced bananas or peaches. Makes 3 or 4 servings.

Coffee Cream: Refrigerate coffee jelly until consistency of unbeaten egg white. Fold in ½ cup heavy cream, whipped, and ¼ teasp. almond extract. Pour into sherbet glasses. Refrigerate until set.

Steamed Puddings

To save work on busy days, make these puddings ahead; then reheat them at serving time as directed. Of course, they can be made and steamed just before serving too.

For a Flaming Pudding: For large pudding, heat ½ cup brandy till lukewarm; for individual puddings, heat 2 teasp. brandy per pudding. Immediately pour brandy over and around hot pudding. Touch lighted match to brandy; carry to table ablaze.

Or soak cubes of sugar in lemon extract; place around pudding; light with match.

CRANBERRY HOLIDAY PUDDING

3 cups raw cranberries	purpose flour
¾ cup light or dark raisins	3 teasp. baking soda
	¾ cup light molasses
2¼ cups sifted all-	½ cup hot water

Rinse cranberries and raisins; drain; place in mixing bowl. Sift flour, soda, over fruit. Add molasses, water; stir until batter is smooth. Turn into 2 1-lb. greased, lightly sugared coffee cans; replace covers. Place on trivet in deep kettle. Add enough boiling water to come halfway up sides of cans. Steam, covered, 1¼ hr., or until done.

Serve with Butter Cream Sauce, p. 368. Makes about 12 servings.

To Do Ahead: Make pudding several days ahead. After steaming it, remove from cans; cool; wrap; refrigerate. To serve, wrap pudding in aluminum foil; bake at 325°F. about 45 min., or until hot. Or steam in same coffee cans about 1 hr.

COCONUT STEAMED PUDDING

½ cup sifted all-purpose flour	1 cup grated, pared carrots
1 teasp. double-acting baking powder	1 cup grated raw potatoes
¾ teasp. salt	1 cup finely diced, pared, cored cooking apples
1 teasp. baking soda	
½ teasp. nutmeg	
1 teasp. cinnamon	½ cup light or dark raisins
⅛ teasp. ground cloves	
¾ cup shredded coconut, snipped fine	¼ cup currants
	¼ cup diced preserved orange peel
1 cup brown sugar, packed	
	½ cup salad oil or melted shortening
1 cup packaged dried bread crumbs	
	1 egg, slightly beaten

Into large bowl, sift flour, baking powder, salt, soda, nutmeg, cinnamon, cloves. Add rest of ingredients; mix well. Turn into well-greased 2-qt. mold; cover tightly. Place on trivet in deep kettle. Add enough boiling water to come halfway up sides of mold. Steam, covered, 2 hr., or until done.

Serve with Sunshine Foamy Sauce, p. 370, or any favorite sauce. Makes about 10 servings.

To Do Ahead: Make pudding several days ahead. After steaming it, remove from mold; cool; wrap; refrigerate. To serve, wrap pudding in aluminum foil; bake at 325°F. about 1 hr., or until hot.

FLUFFY STEAMED FIG PUDDING

1 lb. dried figs	1 teasp. nutmeg
1¾ cups milk or liquefied nonfat dry milk	1 teasp. cinnamon
	¾ teasp. salt
	3 eggs
1½ cups sifted all-purpose flour	1½ cups ground suet
	1½ cups fresh bread crumbs
2½ teasp. baking powder	
	3 tablesp. grated orange rind
1 cup granulated sugar	

With scissors, snip stems from figs. Into double boiler, snip figs into small pieces; add milk; cook, covered, 20 min. Sift flour, baking powder, sugar, nutmeg, cinnamon, salt. In bowl, beat eggs; add suet, bread crumbs, rind, fig mixture, then flour mixture; mix well.

Turn into well-greased 2-qt. mold; cover tightly. Place on trivet in deep kettle. Add enough boiling water to come halfway up sides of mold. Steam, covered, 2 hr., or until done. Let stand 2 min. before removing from mold.

Serve with Hard Sauce, p. 370, or other sauce. Makes about 10 servings.

To Do Ahead: Make pudding several days ahead. After removing it from mold, cool; then refrigerate. To serve, wrap pudding in aluminum foil; bake at 325°F. about 1 hr., or until hot. Or steam in same mold about 1 hr.

GRANDMOTHER'S PLUM PUDDING
(double-boiler style)

2 cups packaged dried bread crumbs	1½ cups milk or liquefied nonfat dry milk
1 teasp. cinnamon	
1 teasp. allspice	½ cup diced candied citron or mixed preserved fruit
¼ teasp. ground cloves	
1 cup finely ground suet	
	1 15-oz. pkg. seeded raisins
¾ cup molasses	
2 eggs, unbeaten	1 tablesp. flour

In large bowl, combine crumbs, cinnamon, allspice, cloves, suet, molasses, eggs, milk, blending well after each addition. Then toss together citron, raisins, flour; stir into batter.

Turn batter into well-greased 2-qt. double boiler. Cook, covered, over boiling water (adding more water as needed) 5 hr. Run spatula around pan and unmold pudding.

Serve hot, with Hard Sauce, p. 370. Makes 8 servings.

To Do Ahead: Make and steam pudding day before; then refrigerate. To serve, reheat in double boiler about 1 hr.

PANTRY-SHELF STEAMED PUDDINGS

Delicious plum, date, and fig puddings come canned, in small and large sizes. Just open them; place in colander; steam over hot water until piping hot.

Pies

Easy as pie! That very expression describes today's pastry making. Top-notch ingredients and streamlined techniques make it possible to turn out masterpieces with little effort and no guesswork at all. You can start from scratch or use one of the excellent packaged mixes—either way you're certain of a mouth-watering dessert.

Before using these recipes, refer to How to Use Our Recipes, p. 3, and Pots and Pans, p. 692. Always use standard measuring cups and measuring spoons; measure level. Also see Shortenings, p. 524.

Remember, an 8″ pie serves 4 or more people; a 9″ pie serves 6 or more.

THE ALL-IMPORTANT CRUST

FLAKY PASTRY I

2¼ cups sifted all-purpose flour	shortening (except butter, margarine, or salad oil)
1 teasp. salt	
¾ cup plus 2 tablesp.	⅓ cup cold water

Two-Crust Pie:

To Make Pastry:

1. In bowl, mix flour and salt. With pastry blender or 2 knives, scissor-fashion, cut two thirds of shortening into flour until like corn meal—for tenderness. Cut in rest of shortening until like large peas—for flakiness. (Or cut in all *at once* until like coarse meal.)
2. Sprinkle water, 1 tablesp. at a time, over different parts of mixture, tossing quickly with fork until particles stick together when pressed gently and form dough that clings to fork. (Use only enough water to make flour particles cling together—dough should not be wet or slippery.)
3. With cupped hands, lightly form dough into smooth ball. (If very warm day, wrap in waxed paper, saran, or aluminum foil and refrigerate up to ½ hr.) Then divide in half; form into 2 balls. Makes enough for 8″ or 9″ pie.

Bottom Crust:

1. On lightly floured surface, place ball of pastry. With stockinet-covered rolling pin, flatten gently. Then roll lightly from center out to edge, in all directions, forming circle about 1½″ wider all around than inverted 8″ or 9″ pie plate (11″ to 12″ in diameter).
2. Be sure to lift rolling pin near edge of circle, to keep edge from splitting or getting thin. If edge splits, pinch cracks together. If pastry sticks, loosen gently with spatula; then lift and lightly flour surface.
3. Fold pastry circle in half; lift onto ungreased pie plate, with fold at center; unfold. Use bent right index finger to fit pastry gently into plate. (Be sure there are no cracks or holes for juices to seep through.)

Top Crust:

1. Roll top crust as in Bottom Crust, 1 and 2, above. Arrange filling in lined pie plate. Trim bottom crust even with edge of plate. Now fold top crust in half; with knife, make several slits of your own design near center fold, so steam can escape.
2. Moisten edge of lower crust with water (use

fingers). Lay top crust over filling, with fold at center; unfold. (Or roll pastry circle over rolling pin; then unroll onto filled pie.)

3. With scissors, trim upper crust ½″ beyond edge of plate; fold edge of upper crust under edge of lower crust; press together. Finish pastry edge as in Handsome Edgings, p. 411.
4. To insure nicely browned crust, glaze top of pie as in Glazed, p. 411. Then bake as specific recipe directs.

Baked Pie Shell:

1. Use 1 cup plus 2 tablesp. sifted all-purpose flour, ½ teasp. salt, 7 tablesp. shortening, and 2 tablesp. plus 1 teasp. water. Make pastry as for Two-Crust Pie, p. 407, forming it into 1 ball.
2. On lightly floured surface, place ball of pastry. With stockinet-covered rolling pin, flatten gently. Then roll lightly from center out to edge, in all directions, forming circle about 1½″ wider all around than inverted 8″ or 9″ pie plate (11″ to 12″ in diameter).
3. Be sure to lift rolling pin near edge of circle, to keep edge from splitting or getting thin. If edge splits, pinch cracks together. If pastry sticks, loosen gently with spatula; then lift and lightly flour surface.
4. Fold pastry circle in half; lift onto ungreased pie plate, with fold at center; unfold. Use bent right index finger to fit pastry gently into plate. (Be sure there are no cracks or holes for juices to seep through.)
5. Trim pastry about 1″ beyond edge of plate. Flute or finish pastry edge as in Handsome Edgings, p. 411. With 4-tined fork, prick close and deep on bottom, side. Refrigerate ½ hr.
6. Bake at 450°F. 12 to 15 min., or till golden. Peek after 5 min.; if bubbles appear, prick at once. Cool before filling.

Unbaked Pie Shell: For pie in which filling is baked in shell, omit pricking and baking in Baked Pie Shell, above. Fill and bake as specific recipe directs.

Cheese Pastry: After cutting shortening into flour in Flaky Pastry I, p. 407, add ½ to 1 cup grated process American cheese.

FLAKY PASTRY II

2¼ cups sifted all-purpose flour	cept butter, margarine, or salad oil)
1 teasp. salt	5 tablesp. cold water
¾ cup shortening (ex-	

Two-Crust Pie:

To Make Pastry:

1. In bowl, mix flour and salt. With pastry blender or 2 knives, scissor-fashion, cut in shortening until size of peas.
2. Blend ⅓ cup flour-shortening mixture with water. Add to rest of flour mixture; with fork or fingers, mix until dough holds together.
3. Shape into flat round. (If very warm day, wrap in waxed paper, saran, or aluminum foil and refrigerate up to ½ hr.) Then divide in half; form into 2 balls. Makes enough for 8″ or 9″ pie.

Bottom and Top Crusts: Make as Bottom and Top Crusts in Flaky Pastry I, p. 407.

Baked Pie Shell:

1. Use 1½ cups sifted all-purpose flour, ½ teasp. salt, ½ cup shortening, and 3 tablesp. water. Make pastry as for Two-Crust Pie, above, forming it into 1 ball.
2. Make pie shell as in Baked Pie Shell, Flaky Pastry I, above.
3. Bake at 450°F. 12 to 15 min., or till golden. Peek after 5 min.; if bubbles appear, prick at once. Cool before filling.

Unbaked Pie Shell: For pie in which filling is baked in shell, omit pricking and baking in Baked Pie Shell, above. Fill and bake as specific recipe directs.

FLAKY PASTRY III

¾ cup shortening (except butter, margarine, or salad oil)	1 tablesp. milk
	2 cups sifted all-purpose flour
¼ cup boiling water	1 teasp. salt

Two-Crust Pie:

To Make Pastry:

1. Put shortening in medium bowl. Add boiling water, milk; with 4-tined fork, break up

shortening. Tilt bowl; then, with fork, beat in rapid cross-the-bowl strokes until mixture is smooth and thick like whipped cream and holds soft peaks when fork is lifted.

2. Sift flour and salt onto shortening. With vigorous, round-the-bowl strokes, stir quickly, forming dough that clings together and cleans bowl. Pick up dough and work into smooth flat round. Then divide in half; form into 2 balls. Makes enough for 8" or 9" pie.

Bottom and Top Crusts: Make as in Bottom and Top Crusts, Flaky Pastry IV, below. (If you prefer, pastry may be rolled out on lightly floured surface rather than between sheets of waxed paper.)

Baked Pie Shell:

1. Use ½ cup minus 1 tablesp. shortening, 3 tablesp. boiling water, 1 teasp. milk, 1¼ cups sifted all-purpose flour, and ½ teasp. salt. Make pastry as in Two-Crust Pie, above, forming it into 1 ball.
2. Make pie shell as in Baked Pie Shell, Flaky Pastry IV, below.
3. Bake at 450°F. 14 to 19 min., or till golden. Peek after 5 min.; if bubbles appear, prick at once. Cool before filling.

Unbaked Pie Shell: For pie in which filling is baked in shell, omit pricking and baking in Baked Pie Shell, above. Fill and bake as specific recipe directs.

FLAKY PASTRY IV

2¼ cups sifted all-purpose flour	⅓ cup cold milk
1½ teasp. salt	½ cup plus 1 tablesp. salad oil

Two-Crust Pie:

To Make Pastry:

1. In bowl, mix flour, and salt. Pour milk and salad oil into same measuring cup (don't stir); add, *all at once,* to flour. With fork, stir lightly until well mixed.
2. With hands, press dough into smooth ball. Then divide in half; form into 2 balls. Makes enough for 8" or 9" pie.

Note: You may substitute ice water for milk. With fork, beat water with salad oil until thick and creamy. Immediately pour, *all at once,* over flour; proceed as directed.

Bottom Crust:

1. Wipe table with damp cloth (so paper won't slip). Place half of pastry, flattened slightly, between 2 12"-square sheets of waxed paper. With rolling pin, roll out gently until pastry circle reaches edges of paper. Then peel off top sheet of paper. If pastry tears, mend by pressing edges together; or press piece of pastry lightly over tear.
2. Lift bottom sheet of paper and pastry by far corners (they will cling together). Place, with paper side up, in ungreased 8" or 9" pie plate. Carefully peel off paper. Gently ease and fit pastry into plate.

Top Crust:

1. Roll top crust as in Bottom Crust, 1 and 2, above. Arrange filling in pastry-lined pie plate. Trim bottom crust even with edge of plate. Lay top crust, with paper side up, over filling. Gently peel off paper.
2. Trim upper crust to about ½" beyond edge of plate; fold edge of upper crust under edge of lower crust; press together. Finish pastry edge as in Handsome Edgings, p. 411. Cut 3 or 4 small slits near center. Bake as specific recipe directs.

Baked Pie Shell:

1. Use 1⅓ cups sifted all-purpose flour, 1 teasp. salt, ⅓ cup salad oil, and 3 tablesp. milk or ice water. Make pastry as in Two-Crust Pie, above, forming it into 1 ball.
2. Wipe table with damp cloth (so paper will not slip). Place ball of pastry, flattened slightly, between 2 12"-square sheets of waxed paper. With rolling pin, roll out gently until pastry circle reaches edges of paper. Then peel off top sheet of paper. If dough tears, mend by pressing edges together; or press piece of pastry lightly over tear.
3. Lift bottom sheet of paper and pastry by far corners (they will cling together). Place, with paper side up, in ungreased 8" or 9" pie plate. Carefully peel off paper. With bent right index finger, gently ease and fit pastry into plate.
4. Trim pastry about 1" beyond edge of plate.

Flute or finish pastry edge as in Handsome Edgings, p. 411. With 4-tined fork, prick close and deep on bottom, side.

5. Bake at 475°F. 8 to 12 min., or till golden. Peek after 5 min.; if bubbles appear, prick at once. Cool before filling.

Unbaked Pie Shell: For pie in which filling is baked in shell, omit pricking and baking in Baked Pie Shell, p. 409. Fill and bake as specific recipe directs.

PACKAGED PIECRUST MIX

You can make delicious, uniformly excellent pastry quickly and easily with nationally known brands of packaged piecrust mix. Just add water or milk as label directs; mix quickly; roll out as in Two-Crust Pie or Baked or Unbaked Pie Shell, Flaky Pastry I, p. 407.

One package makes pastry for 1 8" or 9" two-crust pie, or 2 8" or 9" pie shells. You can use half of package and store the rest for later use—see directions on label.

BAKED CRUMB CRUST

Kind	Crumbs	Granulated Sugar	Butter or Margarine
Graham crackers (about 16)	1⅓ cups	¼ cup	¼ cup
Vanilla wafers (about 24 2")	1⅓ cups	none	¼ cup
Chocolate wafers (about 18 2¾")	1⅓ cups	none	3 tablesp.
Gingersnaps (about 20 2")	1⅓ cups	none	6 tablesp.
Corn or wheat flakes (about 3 cups)	1⅓ cups	2 tablesp.	¼ cup

Let butter soften. Place long piece of waxed paper on pastry board; stack crackers, or pour cereal, along center. Wrap, making double fold in paper; tuck ends under. Roll fine with rolling pin. Or roll out in plastic bag.

In 2-cup measuring cup, with fork, mix 1⅓ cups crumbs, sugar, and soft butter until crumbly. Set aside 3 tablesp. mixture. With back of spoon, press rest to bottom and side of 9" pie plate, forming small rim. Bake at 375°F. 8 min. Cool; fill as specific recipe directs; top with reserved crumbs.

Nut-Crumb Crust: Reduce crumbs to 1 cup; add ½ cup finely chopped walnuts, pecans, almonds, or Brazil nuts.

Marble-Crumb Crust: Reduce crumbs to 1 cup. Add 2 sq. grated unsweetened chocolate.

UNBAKED CRUMB CRUST

Graham Cracker: Mix till crumbly 1⅓ cups graham-cracker crumbs, ⅓ cup brown sugar, ½ teasp. cinnamon, ⅓ cup melted butter or margarine. Set aside 3 tablesp. mixture. With back of spoon, press rest to bottom and side of well-greased 9" pie plate; do not spread on rim. Chill well. Fill as recipe directs; top with reserved crumbs. Refrigerate.

Pretzel: With rolling pin, crush enough pretzel sticks to make ¾ cup *coarse* crumbs. In 9" pie plate, blend crumbs with ¼ cup soft butter or margarine and 3 tablesp. sugar. Press to bottom and side of plate; chill; then fill as above.

NUT CRUST

Mix 1 cup finely ground Brazil nuts, pecans, walnuts, blanched almonds, or peanuts with 2 tablesp. granulated sugar. With back of spoon, press to bottom, side, of 9" pie plate; *do not spread on rim*. Bake at 400°F. about 8 min. Cool. Fill as recipe directs.

MERINGUE CRUST

1 cup granulated sugar	tartar
¼ teasp. cream of	4 egg whites

Start heating oven to 275°F. Sift sugar, cream of tartar. With electric mixer or egg beater, beat egg whites until stiff but not dry. Slowly add sugar mixture, beating until meringue makes stiff, glossy peaks. Spread over bottom and up side just to rim of *well-greased* 9" pie plate, making bottom ¼" thick, side 1" thick. Bake about 1 hr., or until light brown and crisp to touch. Cool away from drafts (don't worry if meringue cracks and falls in center—it's supposed to behave that way).

Budget Version: Halve ingredients; bake in 9″ pie plate.

TOASTED COCONUT CRUST

See Toasted Coconut Pie, p. 421.

CHOCOLATE-COCONUT CRUST

See Chocolate-Coconut Bavarian Pie, p. 421.

HANDSOME EDGINGS

Coin (for one-crust pie): Trim overhang even with edge of plate. From trimmings, cut penny-size pastry rounds (about 45 for 9″ pie). Moisten pastry rim. Place rounds on rim, overlapping them slightly; press lightly with finger tips.

Fluted (for one- or two-crust pie): Fold overhang under; turn pastry up to make stand-up rim. Firmly place right index finger on inside of pastry rim; with left thumb and index finger, pinch pastry at that point. Repeat every ¼″. Leave flutings rounded; or pinch into points.

Scalloped (for one- or two-crust pie): Make Fluted edging above, leaving ½″ between flutes; don't pinch into points. Flatten each flute with floured 4-tined fork, forming scallop.

Fork (for one- or two-crust pie): Fold overhang under; turn pastry up to make stand-up rim. With floured 4-tined fork, press pastry to plate rim at ½″ intervals.

Rope (for one- or two-crust pie): Fold overhang under; turn pastry up to make stand-up rim. Press right thumb into pastry rim *at angle*. Then pinch pastry between this thumb and knuckle of index finger. Repeat around edge.

PRETTY PIETOPS

Double Trellis, or Twisted Lattice (for two-crust pie): Line pie plate with pastry as in Bottom Crust, Flaky Pastry I, p. 407, fill. Trim overhang to 1″. Roll rest of pastry into 12″ circle; cut into ½″ strips.

Moisten rim of bottom crust with water. Attach 1 pastry strip to this rim; press; twist strip across filling; attach to pastry rim on opposite side; press firmly. Repeat with 4 strips about 1¼″ apart. Repeat with 5 more strips placed across first ones to make trellis design. Turn

bottom-crust overhang up over rim and ends of pastry strips; with fingers, press firmly all around to seal strips tightly to rim. Make Fluted edge, above; or press with floured fork. Brush pastry rim and strips with melted butter or cream. Bake as specific recipe directs.

Single Trellis (for two-crust pie): Make as for Double Trellis, above, using 7 twisted ½″ pastry strips, placing all in same direction.

Lattice: Make as for Double Trellis, above, leaving pastry strips untwisted.

Wedge (for one-crust pie): With knife or pastry wheel, cut 8″ pastry circle into 6 wedges. Prick. Bake wedges while shell bakes. Place wedges on top of such fillings as fresh strawberry, peach, or cream.

Glazed: Before baking two-crust pie, brush top with one of these: slightly beaten egg white; undiluted evaporated milk; cream; ice water; salad oil; or melted butter, margarine, or shortening. For sparkling effect, sprinkle with granulated sugar.

FRUIT TWO-CRUST PIES

To Assemble and Bake: Start heating oven to 425°F. Make any Flaky Pastry for Two-Crust Pie, pp. 407 to 410. Line 9″ pie plate with pastry. Roll out top crust. Arrange filling in lined pie plate. Adjust top crust. Glaze, if desired, as above.

Bake at 425°F. 40 to 50 min., or until filling is tender, crust nicely browned. Especially nice served warm.

SUSAN'S FRESH APPLE PIE

⅔ to ¾ cup granulated sugar (or half granulated and half brown sugar)
1 to 2 tablesp. flour (if fruit is very juicy)
⅛ teasp. salt
½ teasp. grated lemon rind

1 to 2 teasp. lemon juice
¼ teasp. nutmeg
½ teasp. cinnamon
6 to 7 cups thinly sliced, pared, cored cooking apples (2 lb.)*
1 tablesp. butter or margarine

1. See To Assemble and Bake, above.
2. Combine all ingredients except apples and

butter (amount of sugar depends on tartness of apples).

3. Place half of apples in lined pie plate, with sharp edges facing inward; sprinkle with half of sugar mixture.

4. Top with rest of apples, heaping them in center, then with rest of sugar mixture. Dot with butter.

Use firm, tart, juicy cooking apples—see list on p. 525.

To Vary: To sugar mixture, add ½ cup chopped nuts or raisins. Or before adjusting top crust, pour ⅔ cup heavy cream, slightly whipped, over apples. Or when pie is done, pour 3 tablesp. brandy through slits in crust.

BETTER-THAN-EVER APPLE PIE

4 or 5 diced, pared, cored cooking apples	4 crushed drained canned pear halves
¾ to 1 cup granulated sugar	2 tablesp. white rum
2 tablesp. flour	2 tablesp. butter or margarine
½ teasp. cinnamon	

See To Assemble and Bake, p. 411. Combine apples, sugar, flour, cinnamon. Spread pears in lined pie plate; sprinkle with rum; top with apple mixture. Dot with butter.

SPEEDY APPLE PIE

⅓ to ½ cup granulated sugar	¼ teasp. cinnamon
½ to 1 tablesp. flour (optional)	¼ teasp. nutmeg
	Pinch salt
½ teasp. grated lemon rind	1 No. 2 can apples*
	1½ teasp. butter or margarine
1 teasp. lemon juice	

See To Assemble and Bake, p. 411. Combine all ingredients except apples, butter. Place half of apples in lined pie plate; sprinkle with half of sugar mixture. Repeat. Dot with butter.

Canned apple slices are already pared and cored. One No. 2 can apples makes a fine 8″ pie.

SUPERB CHEESE-APPLE PIE

¾ cup granulated sugar	5 cups sliced, pared, cored cooking apples
2 tablesp. flour	2 teasp. fresh, frozen, or canned lemon juice
⅛ teasp. salt	
1 cup grated process sharp American cheese (¼ lb.)	3 tablesp. heavy cream

See To Assemble and Bake, p. 411. Combine sugar, flour, salt, ⅔ cup cheese; sprinkle lined pie plate with half of mixture. Heap apples on top; sprinkle with lemon juice, rest of sugar mixture, then remaining ⅓ cup cheese and cream.

CRAN-APPLE PIE

¾ cup granulated sugar	1½ teasp. grated orange rind
3 tablesp. cornstarch	2 tablesp. butter or margarine
¼ teasp. salt	
¾ cup corn syrup	1½ cups chopped, pared, cored cooking apples
¼ cup water	
1½ cups washed cranberries	

See To Assemble and Bake, p. 411. In saucepan, mix sugar, cornstarch, salt; gradually add corn syrup, water. Cook, stirring, until mixture thickens slightly and boils. Add cranberries; cook till skins break. Add orange rind, butter; cool. Add apples; pour into lined pie plate.

RHUBARB PIE

1½ cups granulated sugar	or 2 to 4 tablesp. quick-cooking tapioca
2 tablesp. grated orange rind (optional)	4 cups rhubarb, in 1″ pieces
¼ teasp. salt	2 tablesp. butter or margarine
4 to 6 tablesp. flour	

See To Assemble and Bake, p. 411. Combine all ingredients except rhubarb, butter. Place half of rhubarb in lined pie plate; sprinkle with half of sugar mixture. Repeat. Dot with butter.

AUNT JANE'S GRAPE PIE

4 cups Concord grapes	lemon juice
¾ cup granulated sugar	1 tablesp. grated orange rind
1½ tablesp. fresh, frozen, or canned	1 tablesp. quick-cooking tapioca

See To Assemble and Bake, p. 411. Slip grapes from skins; save skins. Cook pulp until seeds loosen; press through coarse sieve. Mix sieved pulp, skins, and rest of ingredients; let stand 5 min. Place in lined pie plate. Nice too with Double-Trellis Pietop, p. 411.

MINCE PIE

See To Assemble and Bake, p. 411. Place 3 cups prepared mincemeat in lined pie plate.

Mince-Apple: Use 2 cups thinly sliced, pared, cored cooking apples and 2 cups mincemeat.

Pineapple-Mince: Spread 1 drained No. 2 can crushed pineapple over 2 cups mincemeat in lined pie plate.

FRESH BERRY PIE

⅔ to ¾ cup granu- lated sugar	juice ¼ teasp. nutmeg
2 tablesp. flour; or 1½ tablesp. quick- cooking tapioca	½ teasp. cinnamon ⅛ teasp. salt 4 cups berries*
½ teasp. grated lemon rind	1 tablesp. butter or margarine
1 to 2 teasp. lemon	

See To Assemble and Bake, p. 411. Combine all ingredients except berries, butter. Place half of berries in lined pie plate; sprinkle with half of sugar mixture. Repeat. Dot with butter.

Use fresh blueberries, blackberries, raspberries, loganberries, or boysenberries.

Peach or Plum: Substitute sliced, peeled peaches or plums for berries.

PRUNE-AND-APRICOT PIE

2½ cups cooked dried prunes and apricots, pitted (1¼ cups each)	Dash salt ¼ teasp. cinnamon ¼ teasp. nutmeg 2 tablesp. fresh,
½ cup prune and apricot liquid	frozen, or canned lemon juice
1 tablesp. cornstarch ½ cup granulated sugar	1 tablesp. butter or margarine

See To Assemble and Bake, p. 411. Arrange fruit in lined pie plate. Heat fruit liquid; add cornstarch combined with sugar, salt, cinnamon, nutmeg; boil, stirring, until clear and thickened. Add lemon juice, butter; pour over fruit.

FRENCH APPLE PIE

Make any Unbaked 9″ Pie Shell, pp. 408 to 410, with Fluted edge, p. 411. Start heating oven to 425°F. Fill pie shell with Susan's Fresh Apple Pie, p. 411, or Mince-Apple Pie, above. Sprinkle with Crumbly Crust or Coconut Streusel, below. Cover with aluminum foil or 9″ pie plate. Bake 20 min.; uncover; bake 20 min. longer, or until fruit is tender.

Crumbly Crust:

½ cup brown sugar, packed	⅓ cup sifted all- purpose flour
¼ cup butter or margarine	¼ teasp. cinnamon

With fork, blend together all ingredients.

Coconut Streusel: Make Crumbly Crust, adding ½ cup each chopped nuts and shredded coconut.

DE LUXE RED-CHERRY PIE

2 tablesp. quick- cooking tapioca	packed in water (2 No. 2 cans)
1 cup granulated sugar	¼ teasp. almond extract
⅛ teasp. salt	1 tablesp. butter or margarine, in bits
3½ cups drained canned pitted red sour cherries,	Red food color (to make cherry red)

See To Assemble and Bake, p. 411. Combine all ingredients; let stand about 15 min. Turn into lined pie plate. Also very attractive made with Double-Trellis Pietop, p. 411.

For 8″ Pie: Halve ingredients.

TOPPINGS FOR FRUIT PIES

If the occasion calls for a special topping, we suggest:

Vanilla ice cream, sprinkled with cinnamon or nutmeg	Hard sauce Shaved maple sugar Commercial sour cream
Cheese food (rolls, individual wedges, etc.)	Whipped cream cheese
Whipped cream	Sharp or mild Amer- ican cheese

PRIZE PRUNE PIE

Unbaked 9″ Pie Shell, pp. 408 to 410	⅛ teasp. salt 1 tablesp. fresh,
2¾ cups cooked dried prunes, pitted	frozen, or canned lemon juice
1 egg	½ cup prune juice
⅓ cup granulated sugar	Crumbly Crust, above

Start heating oven to 425°F. Arrange prunes in pie shell. Beat egg with sugar, salt, lemon juice, prune juice; pour over prunes. Sprinkle with Crumbly Crust. Bake 40 min.

Storing Leftover Fruit Pies

Fruit pies are best when fresh. So, assuming that what's left won't last longer than a day or two, cover pie well and store on pantry shelf. Freshen by warming pie a few minutes at 325°F. If you want to store pie in refrigerator, crust will taste better if pie is removed 20 min. before serving, then warmed at 325°F.

DEEP-DISH PIES

Big Deep Dish: Make any Flaky Pastry or Cheese Pastry for Baked Pie Shell, pp. 407 to 410. Roll ⅛″ thick, to fit top of baking dish with ½″ overhang; fold in half; cut several slits at center fold. Fill dish as below; then unfold pastry over filling; turn overhang under; press firmly to side of dish; flute or mark with floured tines of fork. Glaze, if desired, as on p. 411. Bake as directed.

SPICY APPLE

6 to 8 pared, cored medium cooking apples, cut into eighths	¼ cup granulated sugar
1 tablesp. cornstarch	1 teasp. grated lemon rind
1 teasp. cinnamon	1 teasp. lemon juice
¼ teasp. nutmeg	¼ cup melted butter or margarine
¼ teasp. salt	½ cup corn syrup

Start heating oven to 450°F. Arrange apples in 2-qt. casserole. Mix rest of ingredients; pour evenly over apples. Adjust crust as in Big Deep Dish, above. Bake 45 min., or until apples are tender. Makes 6 servings.

PLUM

4 cups halved, pitted plums (about 2½ lb.)	⅛ teasp. salt
	¼ teasp. almond extract
1¼ cups granulated sugar	2 tablesp. butter or margarine
3 tablesp. flour	

Start heating oven to 425°F. Arrange plums in 10″ x 6″ x 2″ (1½-qt.) baking dish. Mix rest of ingredients; sprinkle over plums. Adjust crust as in Big Deep Dish, above. Bake 45 to 50 min. Makes 6 servings.

Berry or Fresh Peach: Make Plum Deep-Dish Pie, using as filling 4 cups berries or sliced peaches; ⅔ to ¾ cup granulated sugar; 3 tablesp. flour; ⅛ teasp. salt; ¼ teasp. nutmeg; ¼ teasp. cinnamon; 1 teasp. fresh, frozen, or canned lemon juice; 2 teasp. butter or margarine.

YEAR-ROUND PEACH

2 No. 2½ cans sliced peaches	½ teasp. mace
½ cup granulated sugar	2 tablesp. fresh, frozen, or canned lemon juice
2½ tablesp. cornstarch	2 tablesp. butter or margarine
½ teasp. salt	
½ teasp. nutmeg	

Start heating oven to 425°F. Drain peaches, reserving 1⅓ cups syrup. Combine reserved peach syrup, sugar, cornstarch, salt, spices; cook until thickened, stirring. Stir in lemon juice, butter, peaches; turn into 10″ x 6″ x 2″ (1½-qt.) baking dish. Adjust crust as in Big Deep Dish, above. Bake 45 to 50 min. Makes 6 servings.

INDIVIDUAL DEEP-DISH PIES

Among 5 individual round baking dishes (1¼ cups each), divide filling for Spicy Apple, Berry, Year-Round Peach, or Plum Deep-Dish Pie, above, or for De Luxe Red-Cherry Pie, p. 413. Top with circles of pastry (cut pastry to allow ½″ overhang); fold overhang under; press firmly to edge of dish; flute or mark pastry edge with floured tines of fork. Bake at 425°F. 40 min.

TOPPINGS FOR DEEP-DISH PIES

Any of these are delicious on a warm deep-dish pie.

Pour cream or ice cream, with dash of nutmeg or mace

Whipped cream, topped with brown sugar and nutmeg, cinnamon and sugar, chopped nuts, or grated orange rind

Hard sauce, with rum extract, chopped nuts, or raisins folded in

Cream or cottage cheese, with bit of grated orange rind folded in

LUSCIOUS ONE-CRUST PIES

PILGRIM PUMPKIN OR SQUASH PIE

Unbaked 9″ Pie Shell, pp. 408 to 409	½ teasp. allspice
1 cup granulated sugar	½ teasp. ground cloves
½ teasp. salt	1½ cups canned pumpkin or thawed frozen squash
1½ teasp. cinnamon	
½ teasp. ground ginger	1⅔ cups undiluted evaporated milk
½ teasp. nutmeg	2 eggs, well beaten

Refrigerate pie shell several hours. Start heating oven to 425°F. Combine sugar, salt, spices; add pumpkin, milk, eggs; beat till smooth. Pour into shell. Bake at 425°F. 15 min.; reduce heat to 350°F. and bake 35 min., or until custard is set. Cool.

To serve: Top each wedge with whipped cream, with honey, chocolate curls, or drained canned crushed pineapple in center. Or top with spoonfuls of ice cream. Or top with whipped cream cheese and chopped nuts.

Nut-Pumpkin Pie: About 10 min. before pie is done, sprinkle with ½ cup sliced Brazil nuts, almonds, filberts, peanuts, pecans, or walnuts.

DE LUXE PECAN PIE

Unbaked 9″ Pie Shell, pp. 408 to 410	1 cup granulated sugar
2 eggs, beaten	2 tablesp. melted butter or margarine
1 cup dark corn syrup	1 cup coarsely broken pecans*
⅛ teasp. salt	
1 teasp. vanilla extract	

Start heating oven to 400°F. Mix eggs with syrup, salt, vanilla, sugar, butter; add pecans; pour into shell. Bake at 400°F. 15 min.; reduce heat to 350°F. and bake 30 to 35 min. Cool.

Serve cut into small wedges, with whipped cream or small bunches of grapes.

* *If salted nuts are used, omit salt.*

RICH WALNUT PIE

Unbaked 9″ Pie Shell, pp. 408 to 410	¼ cup corn or maple-blended syrup
½ cup light-brown sugar, packed	½ cup milk or light cream
½ cup soft butter or margarine	1 cup coarsely chopped walnuts
¾ cup granulated sugar	½ teasp. vanilla extract
3 eggs	¼ cup broken walnuts
¼ teasp. salt	

1. Start heating oven to 350°F.
2. In double-boiler top, with electric mixer at medium speed, or "cream" (or with spoon), mix brown sugar and butter until well blended.
3. Add granulated sugar; mix well. Add eggs, one at a time, beating after each addition to blend. Add salt, corn syrup, milk; mix well.
4. Cook over boiling water, stirring, 5 min. Remove from water; stir in 1 cup walnuts and vanilla. Pour into lined pie plate.
5. Bake 1 hr.; scatter broken walnuts on top; bake 5 min. Cool.

Note: Pie puffs during baking and shrinks slightly during cooling.

Susan's Fudge-Nut Pie: Start heating oven to 350°F. In double boiler, melt 2 sq. unsweetened chocolate; remove from water; add ½ cup brown sugar, packed, and ¼ cup soft butter or margarine. Then beat until well blended.

Proceed as in steps 3 and 4, above. Bake 55 min.; scatter broken walnuts on top; then bake 5 min. longer. Serve warm. Or make day before; refrigerate; then, to serve, warm at 350°F. about 15 min. (This pie has a moist filling similar to that of pecan pie.)

MAX'S SUPER CHEESE PIE

Unbaked Graham-Cracker Crumb Crust, p. 410	2 eggs
	½ cup granulated sugar
1½ 8-oz. pkg. soft cream cheese	½ teasp. vanilla extract
	1 cup commercial sour cream

Start heating oven to 350°F. With electric mixer or egg beater, beat cheese, eggs, sugar, and vanilla until smooth and creamy. Turn into shell. Bake 35 min. Spread sour cream on top. Cool. Serve as is or topped with sliced strawberries or peaches.

Cherry- or Pineapple-Cheese Pie: Omit sour cream. Top cooled cheese pie with Cherry or Pineapple Glaze, below.

Cherry Glaze: Mix 2½ teasp. cornstarch with 2 tablesp. sugar; slowly stir in ½ cup liquid drained from canned pitted red sour cherries, packed in water. Simmer until clear and thickened. Add 1 cup drained, pitted cherries; 1 teasp. fresh, frozen, or canned lemon juice; ¼ teasp. almond extract; few drops red food color. Cool.

Pineapple Glaze: Combine 1 cup canned crushed pineapple and 1 teasp. cornstarch. Simmer until clear and thickened; add 1 tablesp. fresh, frozen, or canned lemon juice. Cool.

Mince-Cheese Pie: Substitute Unbaked 9″ Pie Shell, pp. 408 to 410, for graham-cracker crust. Spread 1⅓ cups prepared mincemeat in bottom of shell. Bake at 450°F. 10 to 12 min. to brown crust lightly. Remove from oven. Top with cheese mixture and bake as above. Omit sour-cream topping.

WALNUT-RAISIN PIE

Start heating oven to 400°F. Cream ½ cup butter or margarine with ¾ cup granulated sugar. Add 3 eggs, one at a time, beating well. Add 1 cup light or dark raisins, 1 cup broken walnuts, 1 teasp. vanilla extract. Turn into Unbaked 9″ Pie Shell, pp. 408 to 410. Bake at 400°F. 10 min.; reduce heat to 375°F. and bake 30 min.

FLUFFY APRICOT PIE

Baked 8″ Pie Shell, pp. 408 to 410
½ lb. dried apricots
1½ cups water
2 teasp. unflavored gelatine
¼ cup granulated sugar
3 egg yolks
2 tablesp. fresh, frozen, or canned lemon juice
3 egg whites
⅛ teasp. salt
½ cup granulated sugar
4 drops almond extract
¼ cup heavy cream, whipped
½ cup heavy cream, whipped (optional)

Soak apricots in water 1 hr.; then cook in same water, covered, 10 min., or until tender. Press apricots and juice through food mill or sieve; then measure 1 cup purée. Combine gelatine, ¼ cup sugar.

In double-boiler top, beat egg yolks; stir in lemon juice, purée, then gelatine mixture. Cook over boiling water, stirring, 5 min., or till thickened. Refrigerate until as thick and syrupy as unbeaten egg white. Beat egg whites with salt till fairly stiff; gradually add ½ cup sugar and extract, beating until stiff; fold in apricot mixture and ¼ cup cream, whipped. Turn into shell. Refrigerate until set.

To serve: Top with ½ cup cream, whipped, and, if desired, with grated chocolate.

PUMPKIN CHIFFON PIE

Baked 9″ Pie Shell, pp. 408 to 410
1 env. unflavored gelatine
½ cup dark-brown sugar, packed
½ teasp. salt
½ teasp. nutmeg
½ teasp. cinnamon
¼ teasp. ginger
2 egg yolks
1 cup undiluted evaporated milk
½ cup cold water
1¼ cups canned pumpkin
2 egg whites
¼ cup dark-brown sugar, packed
½ cup heavy cream, whipped (optional)

Combine gelatine, ½ cup brown sugar, salt, spices. In double-boiler top, beat egg yolks; stir in milk, water, pumpkin, then gelatine mixture. Cook over boiling water, stirring, 10 min. Refrigerate, stirring occasionally, until as thick and syrupy as unbeaten egg white. Beat egg whites until fairly stiff; gradually add ¼ cup brown sugar, beating until very stiff; fold in pumpkin mixture. Turn into shell. Refrigerate until set.

To serve: Spread whipped cream on pie.

LEMON CHIFFON PIE

Baked 9″ Pie Shell, pp. 408 to 410; Baked Crumb Crust, p. 410, or Unbaked Crumb Crust, p. 410
1½ teasp. unflavored gelatine
⅓ cup granulated sugar
4 egg yolks
1 tablesp. grated lemon rind
¼ cup lemon juice
⅓ cup cold water
4 egg whites
¼ teasp. salt
½ cup granulated sugar
½ cup heavy cream, whipped

Combine gelatine, ⅓ cup sugar. In double-boiler top, beat egg yolks; stir in lemon rind and juice, water, then gelatine mixture. Cook over boiling water, stirring, 5 min., or till thickened. *Remove from heat.* Beat egg whites with salt till fairly stiff; gradually add ½ cup sugar, beating until stiff; fold in lemon mixture. Turn into shell. Refrigerate until set.

To serve: Spread whipped cream on pie. Garnish with blueberries or sliced strawberries or bananas.

Lime-Swirl: Omit the ⅓ cup sugar. Substitute 1 teasp. grated lime rind for lemon rind, lime juice for lemon juice. Swirl whipped cream through filling in shell. Top with ½ teasp. grated lime rind.

Orange: Reduce lemon juice to 1 tablesp.; to juice, add ¼ cup thawed frozen orange-juice concentrate. Reduce the ½ cup sugar, beaten with whites, to ⅓ cup.

CHOCOLATE-FLAKE BAVARIAN PIE

Baked Crumb Crust, p. 410; Nut Crust, p. 410; or Baked 9″ Pie Shell, pp. 408 to 410
1 env. unflavored gelatine
¼ cup granulated sugar
⅛ teasp. salt
3 egg yolks

1¼ cups milk
1 teasp. vanilla extract
3 egg whites
¼ cup granulated sugar
½ to 1 cup heavy cream, whipped
¼ teasp. nutmeg
½ sq. unsweetened chocolate

Combine gelatine, ¼ cup sugar, salt. In double-boiler top, beat egg yolks; stir in milk, gelatine mixture. Cook over *hot, not boiling,* water, stirring, until custard coats spoon. Stir in vanilla. Refrigerate, stirring occasionally, until mixture mounds when dropped from spoon. Beat until *just* smooth.

Beat egg whites till fairly stiff; gradually add ¼ cup sugar, beating until stiff; fold in custard, whipped cream. Turn into shell; sprinkle with nutmeg. Refrigerate until set.

To serve: Shave on chocolate.

Note: If preferred, use whipped cream as topping rather than to fold into filling.

Frosted Coffee: Add 2 tablesp. instant coffee to egg whites before beating. Omit whipped cream and shaved chocolate. Melt ¾ pkg. semisweet-chocolate pieces (¾ cup) over *hot, not boiling,* water; stir in ¼ cup water; drizzle on top of pie.

To vary: With egg whites, fold in ½ cup sliced, pitted dates and ¼ cup chopped pecans. Omit semisweet-chocolate topping; sprinkle with cocoa.

Strawberry: Fold 1 cup sliced strawberries into filling. Garnish with berries instead of shaved chocolate.

Nesselrode: Substitute 2 tablesp. rum (or rum extract to taste) for vanilla. With whipped cream, fold in ¼ cup diced, mixed preserved fruits.

Susan's Christmas: Subsitute 2 tablesp. rum for vanilla. With whipped cream, fold in ½ cup thinly sliced candied cherries. Turn into Nut Crust made with Brazil nuts, p. 410.

Eggnog: Omit chocolate. For vanilla, substitute brandy or rum to taste. Increase nutmeg to 1 teasp. Especially nice in Unbaked Pretzel Crumb Crust, p. 410.

Coconut: Omit nutmeg. With whipped cream, fold in ½ cup shredded coconut. Try, too, with grated fresh coconut, adding ¼ teasp. almond extract with vanilla.

Cranberry: Substitute almond extract for vanilla. Use ½ cup heavy cream. Omit nutmeg and chocolate. Heat 1 can whole-cranberry sauce with 1 tablesp. cornstarch till clear and thickened; cool; spread on pie when filling is set. Refrigerate pie till served.

ROYAL CHOCOLATE CHIFFON PIE

Baked Crumb Crust, p. 410; or Baked 9″ Pie Shell, pp. 408 to 410
1 env. unflavored gelatine
¾ cup granulated sugar
⅛ teasp. salt
1 egg yolk
¾ cup milk

3 sq. unsweetened chocolate
1 cup undiluted evaporated milk
1 teasp. vanilla extract
1 cup heavy cream, whipped
½ sq. unsweetened chocolate

Combine gelatine, sugar, salt. In double-boiler top, beat egg yolk; stir in milk, then gelatine mixture. Add 3 sq. chocolate. Cook over boiling water, stirring, until chocolate is melted. Remove from heat. With egg beater, beat until smooth. Refrigerate, stirring occasionally, until mixture mounds when dropped from spoon.

Store evaporated milk in ice-cube tray of refrigerator until soft ice crystals form around edges—15 to 20 min.; then beat until stiff. Fold in chocolate mixture and vanilla. Turn into shell. Refrigerate until set.

To serve: Spread whipped cream on pie. Shave on ½ sq. chocolate, making attractive curls.

REFRIGERATOR PINEAPPLE-CHEESE PIE

Baked Crumb Crust made with corn flakes, p. 410	crushed pineapple
1 tablesp. unflavored gelatine	1 teasp. grated lemon rind
¼ cup granulated sugar	2 tablesp. lemon juice
3 egg yolks	1 cup cottage cheese
¼ cup cold water	3 egg whites
1 cup undrained canned	¼ teasp. salt
	½ cup granulated sugar

Combine gelatine, ¼ cup sugar. In double-boiler top beat egg yolks; stir in gelatine mixture, water, pineapple, lemon rind and juice. Cook over boiling water, stirring, until thick. Remove from heat.

Press cheese through fine sieve; stir into hot mixture. Cool mixture until it begins to thicken. Beat egg whites with salt till fairly stiff; gradually add ½ cup sugar, beating until stiff; fold in cheese mixture. Turn into shell. Refrigerate till set.

PEACH GLACE PIE

Baked 9″ Pie Shell, pp. 408 to 410	¼ cup sherry
1½ teasp. unflavored gelatine	Pinch salt
	1 No. 2½ can peach halves, well drained
2 tablesp. cold water	½ cup heavy cream, whipped
1 cup apricot preserves	

Sprinkle gelatine over cold water to soften. Bring preserves to boil; stir in gelatine until dissolved; then add sherry, salt. Cool mixture until it begins to thicken. Place peach halves in pie shell, with cut sides down; pour on cooled mixture. Refrigerate till set.

To serve: Garnish with whipped cream.

PINEAPPLE FROST PIE

Baked 9″ Pie Shell, pp. 408 to 410	½ cup granulated sugar
1¼ cups *undrained* canned crushed pineapple	1 cup undiluted evaporated milk
1 pkg. lemon-flavored gelatin	1 tablesp. fresh, frozen, or canned lemon juice

Bring crushed pineapple to boil; stir in gelatin until dissolved; then stir in sugar. Cool until

almost stiff. Chill evaporated milk in ice-cube tray until soft ice crystals form around edges—15 to 20 min.; add lemon juice; beat until stiff. Pour on top of gelatin mixture; with egg beater or electric mixer at low speed, beat in slowly until well blended. Pour into shell. Refrigerate at least 1 hr.

To serve: Garnish with *drained* crushed pineapple if desired.

Note: For a high, fluffy pie, be sure gelatin mixture is almost stiff and evaporated milk is whipped until it stands in stiff peaks.

SUSAN'S LEMON PARFAIT PIE

Baked 8″ Pie Shell, pp. 408 to 410	1 teasp. grated lemon rind
1 pkg. lemon-flavored gelatin	3 tablesp. lemon juice
1¼ cups hot water	1 pt. vanilla ice cream

1. In 2-qt. saucepan, dissolve gelatin in hot water; add lemon rind and juice.
2. Add ice cream by spoonfuls, stirring until melted. Refrigerate until thickened but not set—25 to 30 min.
3. Turn into shell. Refrigerate until firm—25 to 35 min.

LEMON MERINGUE PIE

Baked 8″ or 9″ Pie Shell, pp. 408 to 410	¼ cup lemon juice
1 cup granulated sugar	3 egg yolks, slightly beaten
¼ cup cornstarch	1 tablesp. butter or margarine
⅛ teasp. salt	Pie Meringue (3 eggs), p. 419
1¼ cups warm water	
Grated rind of 1 lemon	

In double boiler, combine sugar, cornstarch, salt. Slowly stir in water, then lemon rind and juice, egg yolks, butter. Cook, stirring, until smooth and thick enough to mound when dropped from spoon. Remove from heat. Cool thoroughly. Start heating oven to 350°F. Spoon filling into cooled pie shell. Top with meringue. Bake 12 to 15 min.

Lemon Snow Pie: Use Baked 9″ Pie Shell, pp. 408 to 410. Fold meringue into hot filling. Turn into shell. Refrigerate until set.

Orange Meringue: Reduce sugar to ¾ cup, water to ½ cup, lemon juice to 1 tablesp. Substitute grated rind of 1 orange for lemon. Add 1 cup orange juice with water.

Pineapple Meringue: Reduce sugar to ¾ cup, lemon juice to 1 tablesp. Add ⅔ cup well-drained canned crushed pineapple to hot filling.

Quick Lemon: For pie filling, use packaged lemon-pudding pie-filling mix, following label directions. To hot filling, add 1 tablesp. each butter or margarine and grated lemon rind. Complete as on p. 418.

HURRY-UP LEMON MERINGUE PIE

Baked 8″ Pie Shell, pp. 408 to 410; or Baked Crumb Crust, p. 410	rind
	½ cup lemon juice
	2 egg yolks
1⅓ cups sweetened condensed milk	Pie Meringue (2 eggs), below
1 teasp. grated lemon	

Start heating oven to 350°F. Blend milk with lemon rind, juice, and egg yolks until thickened. Pour into shell. Top with meringue. Bake 12 to 15 min.

Hurry-Up Lime: Substitute lime rind and juice for lemon.

PIE MERINGUE

	3 eggs (9″ pie)	2 eggs (8″ pie)
Egg whites	3	2
Salt	¼ teasp.	¼ teasp. (scant)
Extract	¼ to ½ teasp.	¼ teasp.
Granulated sugar	6 tablesp.	4 tablesp.

1. Have eggs at room temperature. (Whites beat to greater volume when not too cold.) Start heating oven to 350°F.
2. Place whites in medium bowl; add salt and extract; with electric mixer at high speed, or with egg beater, beat until frothy throughout (don't wait until whites begin to stiffen).
3. Add sugar, a little at a time, beating well after each addition. (Since sugar dissolves better, this method helps prevent beading.)
4. Continue beating until stiff peaks are formed. To test, slowly withdraw beater and hold up; meringue should form pointed peaks that are so stiff they stand upright and don't curl over.
5. With spoon, place mounds of meringue around edge of filling; spread meringue so it touches inner edge of crust *all around,* to prevent shrinking. Heap rest of meringue in center; push out to meet meringue border.
6. With back of spoon, pull up points on meringue, to make attractive top. Bake 12 to 15 min.*
7. Cool on rack *away from drafts.* To cut meringue neatly when serving, first dip sharp knife into water; then shake off excess drops.

* Bake meringue at 425°F. about 4 min. if preferred.

SUSAN'S SLIPPED CUSTARD PIE

Baked 9″ Pie Shell, pp. 408 to 410	½ teasp. salt
	1 teasp. vanilla extract
4 eggs, slightly beaten	2 cups milk
½ cup granulated sugar	½ teasp. nutmeg

1. Start heating oven to 350°F. Combine eggs, sugar, salt, vanilla, milk; beat well.
2. Butter 9″ pie plate; set in shallow baking pan. Pour in egg mixture; sprinkle with nutmeg.
3. Set in oven; pour enough hot water into baking pan to come three quarters up side of pie plate. Bake 35 min., or till silver knife inserted in center comes out clean.
4. *Cool well on rack at room temperature.*
5. When shell and custard are cool, tilt custard a bit. With small spatula, gently pull custard away from side of pie plate; then holding plate level with both hands, shake gently. Now holding plate, tilted, over pie shell with far edge of custard just above and close to far edge of shell, shake gently; as custard slips out, pull plate back toward you till custard is in shell.
6. Let settle a few minutes; serve at once.
   Serve pie as is. Or top with fruit or berries and whipped cream; toasted coconut; or drizzling of maple-blended syrup and nuts.

Chocolate-Crested Custard Pie: Melt 1 sq. unsweetened chocolate over very low heat. Stir in 2 tablesp. granulated sugar and 2 tablesp. hot water, a little at a time. Spread over custard in pie shell.

Coconut Custard Pie: Sprinkle custard with ½ cup shredded coconut just before or after baking.

BUTTERSCOTCH CREAM PIE

Baked 9″ Pie Shell,
  pp. 408 to 410
½ cup light-brown
  sugar, packed
⅓ cup all-purpose flour
¼ teasp. salt
2 cups milk
3 egg yolks

¼ cup light-brown
  sugar, packed
3 tablesp. butter or
  margarine
1 teasp. vanilla extract
Pie Meringue (3 eggs),*
  p. 419

In double boiler, combine ½ cup brown sugar, flour, salt. Gradually stir in milk. Cook, stirring, until thick. Cook, covered, stirring occasionally, 10 min. longer. Beat egg yolks with ¼ cup brown sugar; stir in a little sauce; add to rest of sauce in double boiler. Cook, stirring, 2 min., or until mixture mounds when dropped from spoon. Add butter, vanilla; cool. Start heating oven to 350°F. Turn filling into shell. Cover with meringue. Bake 12 to 15 min.

Or omit meringue. Top with ½ cup heavy cream, whipped; sprinkle with shaved chocolate.

Butterscotch-Date: With vanilla, add ½ cup sliced, pitted dates. Omit meringue. Just before serving, top with whipped cream.

SATIN-SMOOTH CREAM PIE

Baked 9″ Pie Shell, pp.
  408 to 410; or Baked
  Crumb Crust, p. 410
1 pkg. vanilla-pudding
  pie-filling mix
2 cups milk
2 tablesp. butter or

margarine
¼ teasp. vanilla, lemon,
  rum, or almond
  extract
½ cup heavy cream,
  whipped

Prepare pudding as label directs, using 2 cups milk; add butter, extract. Cover surface of pudding with waxed paper. Refrigerate till cold.* Then, with spoon, beat till smooth; turn into shell. Refrigerate.

To serve: Top with whipped cream. Garnish with grated chocolate or orange rind, chopped nuts, banana slices dipped into citrus-fruit juice, toasted coconut, crushed peanut brittle, or chopped chocolate mints.

Note: You may reduce milk to 1½ cups; fold whipped cream into beaten cold filling.

If time is short, omit waxed paper and chilling. Cool filling 5 min.; then pour into shell.

De Luxe Topped: Add 1½ teasp. instant coffee or cocoa to cream while it's being whipped.

Meringue-Topped: Omit whipped cream. Add 2 egg yolks to milk. Top with Pie Meringue (2 eggs), p. 419, sprinkling meringue with shredded coconut or nuts before baking it. Or spread filling with 1 cup sieved, stewed apricots before topping with meringue.

Banana: Arrange ½″ layer of banana slices in shell just before filling. Circle whipped cream with banana slices dipped into citrus-fruit juice and, if desired, with toasted coconut.

Coconut: Fold ½ cup shredded or grated fresh coconut into hot filling. Sprinkle whipped cream or Pie Meringue, p. 419 (before baking meringue), with ¼ cup coconut. Or garnish with any canned, fresh, or frozen fruit. Packaged coconut-cream-pudding pie-filling mix makes delicious pie too.

P.S. Packaged instant pudding makes a delicious cream pie filling too. Use as label directs.

CHOCOLATE CREAM PIE

Baked 9″ Pie Shell,
  pp. 408 to 410
¼ cup granulated sugar
2 to 2½ sq. unsweet-
  ened chocolate, cut
  up
⅓ cup all-purpose flour
¼ teasp. salt

2 cups milk
3 egg yolks
¼ cup granulated sugar
2 tablesp. butter or
  margarine
1 teasp. vanilla extract
Pie Meringue (3 eggs),
  p. 419

Make as in Butterscotch Cream Pie, above, combining ¼ cup sugar and chocolate with flour and salt. When chocolate is melted, beat with egg beater until smooth.

Warning

It is most important that cream, custard, and whipped-cream pies be stored in refrigerator before and after serving to avoid any possibility of food poisoning.

SUSAN'S HEAVENLY PIE

Meringue Crust, p. 410
4 egg yolks
½ cup granulated sugar
1 tablesp. grated lemon

rind
3 tablesp. lemon juice
⅛ teasp. salt
2 cups heavy cream

1. Make Meringue Crust.
2. In double-boiler top, beat egg yolks slightly;

stir in sugar, lemon rind and juice, salt. Cook over boiling water, stirring, 8 to 10 min., or till very thick. Cool.

3. Whip 1 cup cream; fold into lemon mixture. Fill crust. Refrigerate 12 to 24 hr.

To serve: Top with 1 cup cream, whipped. If desired, garnish with strawberries and chocolate curls.

STRAWBERRY TRIUMPH PIE

Baked 9″ Pie Shell or Baked Crumb Crust, pp. 408 to 410	2 tablesp. fresh, frozen, or canned lemon juice
1 qt. hulled strawberries	½ cup heavy cream, whipped
3 tablesp. cornstarch	
1 cup granulated sugar	

With fork or pastry blender, crush half of strawberries; stir in cornstarch, sugar, lemon juice. Cook over moderate heat, stirring, until clear and thickened; cool. Cut rest of berries in halves; fold into cooled mixture. Turn into crust. Refrigerate until well chilled.

To serve: Garnish with whipped cream.

CHOCOLATE MOUSSE PIE

Baked 9″ Pie Shell, pp. 408 to 410; or Baked Crumb Crust made with chocolate wafers, p. 410	1 teasp. rum; or rum extract to taste
1 pkg. semisweet-chocolate pieces (1 cup)	2 egg whites
1 egg	1 cup heavy cream, whipped
2 egg yolks	¼ cup heavy cream, whipped
	½ sq. unsweetened chocolate

Melt chocolate pieces over *hot, not boiling,* water. Remove from water. Beat in whole egg and yolks, one at a time; add rum. Beat whites till they form peaks when beater is raised; fold in 1 cup cream, whipped, and chocolate mixture. Spoon into shell. Refrigerate until well chilled.

To serve: Top with ¼ cup cream, whipped; shave on chocolate.

Marvel: Substitute Meringue Crust, p. 410, for piecrust. Halve all filling ingredients except the 1 egg. Refrigerate 12 to 24 hr.

STRAWBERRY-MARSHMALLOW PIE

In saucepan, melt 24 marshmallows in ¼ cup warm water; refrigerate till *completely cool* but *not* set. Butter 9″ pie plate; sprinkle with ⅔ cup graham-cracker crumbs. Stir marshmallows; fold in 1 cup heavy cream, whipped; then fold in 3 cups halved, hulled strawberries. Pile into shell. Arrange 1 cup whole hulled strawberries on top; sprinkle 2 tablesp. crumbs around edge. Refrigerate until thoroughly chilled.

TOASTED COCONUT PIE

Toasted Coconut Crust: Spread 2 tablesp. soft butter or margarine evenly in 8″ or 9″ pie plate. Pat 1½ cups shredded coconut evenly into butter. Bake at 300°F. 15 to 20 min., or until golden. Cool.

Filling: Fill crust with ice cream or fruit; add topping as in Sundae Pies, p. 428. Serve at once.

Or fill with filling for any of the following pies and refrigerate until set.

1. *Chiffon Pies:* Fluffy Apricot, Lemon, or Royal Chocolate, pp. 416 to 417
2. *Bavarian Pies:* Chocolate Flake, Frosted Coffee, Strawberry, or Coconut, p. 417
3. *Cream Pies:* Satin Smooth, Banana, Chocolate, or Butterscotch, p. 420.

CHOCOLATE-COCONUT BAVARIAN PIE

Chocolate-Coconut Crust:

2 sq. unsweetened chocolate	or water
2 tablesp. butter or margarine	⅔ cup sifted confectioners' sugar
2 tablesp. hot milk	1½ cups snipped shredded coconut

Filling:

Coconut Bavarian Pie filling, p. 417	nut
½ cup shredded coco-	½ sq. unsweetened chocolate, grated

Grease 8″ or 9″ pie plate. For crust, in double boiler, melt chocolate with butter; stir till blended. Combine milk, sugar; stir into chocolate mixture. Add snipped coconut; mix well. Press to bottom and side of plate. Refrigerate 1 hr.

Fill with Coconut Bavarian Filling; refrigerate until serving time. (For 8″ pie, reserve one third of filling; refrigerate pie until almost set; then heap reserved filling on center top of pie.)

To serve: Remove pie from refrigerator about

15 min. before serving. Garnish top with combined ½ cup coconut and grated chocolate.

To Vary: Substitute any chiffon or cream filling listed in Toasted Coconut Pie, p. 421, for Coconut Bavarian Pie filling. Omit coconut topping.

Chocolate-Coconut Ice-Cream Pie: Refrigerate crust until firm; remove 15 min. before serving. Just before serving, heap with ice cream.

TARTS AND TURNOVERS

PRETTY TART SHELLS

Make Flaky Pastry I or II for Two-Crust Pie, pp. 407 to 408, or use packaged piecrust mix, p. 410. Roll out; then shape as below. Prick well. Refrigerate ½ hr. Bake (set on cookie sheet if desired) at 450°F. 10 to 15 min., or until golden brown. Cool; carefully lift from pan.

Petal: For each tart shell, cut 6 2¼" pastry rounds. Place 1 round in bottom of each custard cup or 2¾" muffin cup. Wet edge of round; press 5 rounds to side and bottom of cup, overlapping rounds slightly.

Big Floweret: Cut 5" pastry squares. Snugly fit 1 square inside each muffin cup (about 3"), letting corners stand upright.

Little Floweret: Make Big Floweret, using 4" pastry squares in muffin cups (about 3").

Pleated: Invert muffin pan. With piece of cord, measure one of cups—up one side, across bottom, down other side; cut cord to this length. Cut desired number of pastry rounds, using as guide saucer or small pie plate with diameter equal to length of string. Fit pastry round over outside of 1 inverted muffin cup, pinching it into pleats to fit snugly. Repeat on alternate cups.

QUICK FRUIT TARTS

Just before serving, fill baked Pretty Tart Shells, above, with:

Sliced berries or peaches—fresh, frozen, or canned.
Sliced or cut-up oranges, or sliced bananas, dipped into citrus-fruit juice
Pineapple chunks—canned or frozen

Applesauce or apple butter
Fruit cocktail—canned, as is, or tossed with fresh fruit
Grapes, or grapes and cut-up oranges
Apricots or prunes—canned or stewed dried

Top with:

Sweetened whipped cream (flavored, if desired, with orange rind, vanilla or almond extract, sherry, brandy, or rum)
Vanilla ice cream, with chopped nuts, cinnamon, flaked chocolate, or shredded coconut
Commercial sour cream, whipped cream cheese, or cottage cheese, sprinkled, if desired, with cinnamon sugar

Or about 1 hr. before serving, glaze with one of these; then refrigerate:

1. Heat ¼ to ½ cup currant or apple jelly with 1 tablesp. water till melted. Spoon over fruit. Glazes 8 to 10 tarts.
2. Blend 1 tablesp. cornstarch with 1 tablesp. water. Stir into ⅔ cup juice from canned or cooked fruit. Boil till clear; add 1 teasp. fresh, frozen, or canned lemon juice. Glazes 8 to 10 tarts.

SCRUMPTIOUS FILLED TARTS

Several hours ahead: Fill baked Pretty Tart Shells, above, with filling for any of the following pies:

Fluffy Apricot Pie, p. 416
Pumpkin Chiffon Pie p. 416
Lemon or Orange Chiffon Pie, pp. 416 to 417
Royal Chocolate Chiffon Pie, p. 417
Chocolate-Flake, Strawberry, Frosted Coffee, or Coconut Bavarian Pie, p. 417
Lemon, Orange, or Pineapple Meringue Pie, pp. 418 to 419

SUSAN'S STRAWBERRY TARTS

Make filling for Strawberry Triumph Pie, p. 421, folding whole rather than halved berries into cooled mixture. Whip soft cream cheese with a little milk and grated lemon or orange rind; spoon into baked Pleated Tart Shells, above; top with berry mixture. Refrigerate 1 to 2 hr. before serving. Makes 6.

SHERRY-PRUNE TARTS

6 to 8 baked Big Floweret Tart Shells, p. 422	3 lemon slices
	¾ cup sherry
2 cups large dried prunes	1 tablesp. cornstarch
	1 tablesp. water
	½ cup heavy cream

Cook prunes with lemon as label directs; drain. Boil down prune liquid to ¾ cup; add sherry; pour over prunes; refrigerate 4 hr. Drain liquid into saucepan; stir in cornstarch mixed with water. Cook, stirring, until thick and clear. Add pitted prunes. Refrigerate till well chilled. Spoon into tart shells; top with whipped cream. Serve at once. Makes 6 to 8.

PARTY TARTS

3 cups crisp rice cereal	Vanilla ice cream
2 tablesp. butter or margarine	Berries or chocolate sauce
¼ lb. marshmallows	

Place cereal in greased large bowl. In double boiler, heat butter with marshmallows until syrupy; pour over cereal, stirring briskly. With buttered hands, quickly press enough of mixture into each 3¾" fluted tart pan to line bottom and sides. Let set at least 1 hr.; lift out. Fill with ice cream. Top with berries. Makes 6 to 8.

SHORTCAKE TARTS

Make any Flaky Pastry, pp. 407 to 409; or use packaged piecrust mix. Cut into 3½" pastry rounds; with 1½" biscuit cutter, remove center from half of rounds. Arrange on ungreased cookie sheet. Bake at 450°F. 10 to 15 min. Cool. For each tart, put 2 rounds (1 solid and 1 cutout) together with filling of apple butter, sliced peaches, or berries. Or use filling for Lemon Meringue Pie, p. 418, Satin-Smooth Cream Pie, p. 420, or Strawberry Triumph Pie, p. 421. Top with whipped cream or whipped cream cheese.

LUNCH-BOX TURNOVERS

Make Flaky Pastry I or II for Two-Crust Pie, pp. 407 to 408; or use packaged piecrust mix. Roll pastry ⅛" thick. Cut into 4" squares or 4½" rounds.

Place 1 tablesp. of any filling below in corner of each square or on half of each round. Moisten pastry edges with water; fold from corner to opposite corner so edges come together. Firmly seal edges with floured fork. Slit top; or prick with skewer. Glaze as on p. 411. Bake at 450°F. 15 min., or until golden. Serve with cheese cubes. Makes about 12.

Fillings:

1. Mix 1 cup finely chopped, pitted dates or cooked dried prunes, with ¼ cup chopped walnuts and ¼ cup orange juice.
2. Use orange marmalade mixed with chopped nuts.
3. Mix apple butter or applesauce with chopped nuts or raisins.
4. Use strawberry, raspberry, peach, cherry or apricot jam.
5. Mix ½ cup each cooked, dried, pitted prunes and apricots with ¼ cup granulated sugar; 1 tablesp. cornstarch; ¼ teasp. salt; and 1 tablesp. fresh, frozen, or canned lemon juice.
6. Use prepared mincemeat, plain or mixed with chopped apple.

CREAM-CHEESE TURNOVERS

Make and bake Lunch-Box Turnovers, above, using this pastry: With spoon, blend 3 3-oz. pkg. cream cheese with ½ cup butter or margarine. Blend in 1½ cups sifted all-purpose flour. Refrigerate overnight.

FREEZING PIES

Pies—chiffon, double crust, and deep-dish fruit—freeze beautifully. See p. 539.

Ice Creams and Sherbets

Ice cream is universally popular however you serve it. You can buy it and eat it just as it comes from the carton or dress it up in many ways. Or you can make your own in delicious variety.

Before using these recipes, refer to How to Use Our Recipes, p. 3; and Pots and Pans, p. 692. Always use standard measuring cups and measuring spoons; measure level.

WHEN YOU BUY ICE CREAM

These days your grocer, supermarket, and drugstore are all making it easy for you to buy delicious ice creams, sherbets, and frosty novelties in quality brands. You can buy whatever amount you like, prepackaged—half pints, pints, thrifty handy half gallons, or gallons—all ready to use or store.

Serve them straight from the carton. Or, even better, convert them into the production numbers beginning on this page.

To Store Ice Cream at Home

In a refrigerator-freezer combination, the freezer temperature will be close to 0°F. when the temperature control is at the normal setting. Pints, quarts, or even half gallons of ice cream may be stored up to a month if necessary. Keep partly used cartons tightly covered.

In conventional refrigerators, you may be able to store ice cream in its original carton for short periods of time.

Ice cream stays firmer when it is removed from the carton and turned into an ice-cube tray. Cover tray with waxed paper or foil; place on freezing surface. Turn control to a colder setting if necessary, but return it to normal as soon as possible or fresh food may freeze. Use ice cream within 2 days.

The home freezer is the place to keep ice cream in quantity—a month's supply if you wish. You will save money if you buy half-gallon or gallon containers. Store unopened containers in coldest part of freezer. Reseal opened containers tightly to prevent loss of flavor and formation of ice crystals. Store away from freezing surface to keep nearer serving consistency.

P.S. See your refrigerator or freezer instruction booklet for more detailed information on storing ice cream.

Ways to Serve Ice Cream You Buy

ICE-CREAM SNOWBALLS

With big spoon or ice-cream scoop, spoon or scoop out balls of ice cream. Roll each in coating; top with sauce, fruit, or jelly, as below.*

1. Roll in fine cake crumbs; top with Hot Fudge Sauce, p. 370.
2. Roll in grated fresh or shredded coconut; top with Chocolate Sauce, p. 367.
3. Roll in chopped walnuts, pecans, or almonds; top with Rum-Butter Sauce, p. 370.
4. Roll in crumbled sugar-coated cereal flakes

424

or shredded coconut; top with Hot Fudge Sauce, p. 370.

5. Roll in grated chocolate; top with thawed frozen, canned, or fresh peaches.
6. Roll in tinted or toasted shredded coconut; top with favorite sauce.
7. Roll in shredded coconut; top with canned whole-cranberry sauce.
8. Roll in salted peanuts; top with Butterscotch Sauce, p. 368.
9. Roll in sugar-coated cereal; top with crushed berries.
10. Roll in semisweet chocolate; top with custard sauce.
11. Roll in crushed peppermint candy; top with Chocolate Sauce, p. 367.
12. Roll in shredded coconut; top with grape juice.
13. Roll in crushed peanut brittle or chopped nuts; top with favorite sauce.

If you have a home freezer or combination refrigerator-freezer, you can make ice-cream balls (without topping) ahead; then freezer-wrap and freeze them. Or make them several hours ahead; arrange on tray; store in freezer.

EASY PARFAITS

You don't have to own parfait glasses to serve this impressive dessert! Just use your sherbet, pilsner, or small iced-tea glasses, instead. Or make half-size parfaits, using fruit-juice glasses.

To start you off, here are a few parfait combinations you can put together just before dessert time. Then make up some combinations of your own, alternating layers of your favorite sauces (pp. 367 to 371), with layers of ice cream, or ice cream and sherbet. Top with whipped cream and a few nuts or bit of fruit if you like.

Pineapple-Orange: For sauce, to 1 6-oz. can thawed frozen orange-juice concentrate, add No. 1 flat can crushed pineapple. In glasses, alternate layers of vanilla ice cream and some of sauce.

Fruit: Alternate layers of vanilla ice cream with crushed sweetened berries or fruit. Garnish with whipped cream, shaved chocolate.

Sundae: Alternate layers of 2 ice creams such as vanilla and coffee, or coffee and orange sherbet, with fudge, marshmallow, or other sauce.

Cocktail: Alternate layers of vanilla ice cream with chilled canned fruit cocktail mixed with seedless grapes and grated orange rind.

Pineapple-Mint: For sauce, drain 1 No. 2 can crushed pineapple. Measure syrup; add water to make 1 cup; simmer with ½ cup granulated sugar 5 min.; cool. Add pineapple, a few drops peppermint extract; tint delicate green. In glasses, alternate layers of vanilla ice cream with some of sauce.

Red and White: Alternate layers of raspberry-flavored gelatin with vanilla ice cream; sprinkle with cinnamon.

Chocolate: Make layers of chocolate ice cream, whipped cream, and canned crushed pineapple.

Orange: Alternate vanilla ice cream with orange sections, strawberry jam, or berries.

RIPPLED ICE CREAM

Turn temperature control of refrigerator to coldest setting. Turn 1 pt. ice cream, slightly softened, into ice-cube tray. Fold in, or swirl through ice cream, one of flavors below. Freeze until firm; then reset temperature control. Makes 4 servings.

Coffee-Rum: Melt ½ cup chocolate-rum wafers over hot water; add 2 tablesp. hot water, 1½ teasp. rum. Swirl through coffee ice cream.

Fudge: Melt ½ pkg. semisweet-chocolate pieces (½ cup) over *hot, not boiling,* water; add 4 teasp. boiling water, 2 tablesp. milk; stir till smooth. Cool, but don't refrigerate. Swirl through vanilla ice cream.

Berry: With fork, swirl 1 cup slightly crushed fresh or just thawed frozen strawberries or raspberries through vanilla ice cream.

Quick Biscuit Tortoni: Combine ⅓ cup fine macaroon crumbs, 2 tablesp. diced candied cherries, and ¼ cup chopped salted almonds. Fold into vanilla ice cream. (May also be frozen in small paper cups.)

Snap: Fold 1 cup coarsely broken gingersnaps or chocolate wafers into vanilla ice cream.

Apple Surprise: Mix ½ cup applesauce; 1 tablesp. fresh, frozen, or canned lemon juice; and ¼ teasp. cinnamon. Swirl through vanilla ice cream.

Fig Delicious: Cook 8 crumbled fig cookies with ½ cup light cream over low heat until blended. Add ½ cup chopped salted peanuts and ¼ cup peanut butter; cool. Fold into vanilla ice cream.

TRAY ICE-CREAM CAKES

Frozen Ladyfingers: Pack ice-cube tray two thirds full with vanilla ice cream. Split ladyfingers; sprinkle generously with rum; arrange crosswise on ice cream, with flat sides down. Freeze until firm. To serve, spread whipped cream over ladyfingers; then slice.

Butter-Almond Slices: Line bottom of ice-cube tray with strips of bakers' poundcake or cake from cake mix. Spread with 1 pt. vanilla, coffee, or chocolate ice cream. Freeze until firm. Serve sliced, with butterscotch sauce and toasted almonds.

Susan's Ripple Pie: Mix 1⅓ cups graham-cracker crumbs with ¼ cup granulated sugar and ¼ cup soft butter or margarine. Press mixture to bottom, sides, of ice-cube tray; fill with 1½ pt. slightly soft pistachio ice cream; swirl thawed frozen grape-juice concentrate through ice cream. Freeze until firm. To serve, cut into wedges.

Chocolate Charlotte: Line bottom and sides of ice-cube tray with ¼″-thick spongecake slices. Sprinkle with 2 tablesp. sherry; then spread with ½ pt. chocolate ice cream. Top with layer of spongecake slices, 1½ tablesp. sherry, and another ½ pt. chocolate ice cream. Freeze until firm. Serve sliced, with whipped cream.

Tray Trifle: In ice-cube tray, alternate layers of spongecake strips with vanilla, coffee, chocolate, butter-pecan, or strawberry ice cream, ending with cake. Sprinkle with ¼ cup rum. Freeze until firm. Serve sliced, with crushed berries and custard sauce flavored with rum.

Sundae Roll: See p. 430.

ONE-APIECE SPECIALTIES

Serve any of these ice-cream treats at once to eat out of hand. Or freezer-wrap; then freeze for later use. Nice served from basket or large plate.

Cookie Sandwiches: For each serving, spread 2 graham crackers or large chocolate, sugar, or ginger cookies with jelly or with chocolate or butterscotch sauce. Put together, sandwich-fashion, with slice of firm ice cream.

Ice-Cream Bars: Place 1 slice ice cream between 2 slices cake, sandwich-fashion; cut in half crosswise.

Sundae Cones: Fill ice-cream cones with ice cream; dip tops into chocolate or butterscotch sauce; then dip into nuts, shredded coconut, or chocolate sprinkles. Try:

> Peach ice cream, chocolate sauce, slivered almonds
> Coffee ice cream, butterscotch sauce, chocolate sprinkles
> Chocolate ice cream, fudge sauce, shredded coconut
> Vanilla ice cream, butterscotch sauce, chopped nuts

ICE-CREAM-CAKE SUNDAES

Melba: Spoon 1 pt. ice cream onto spongecake layer or square; top with 6 canned pear or peach halves; then spoon on Melba Sauce, p. 371.

Chocolate Ripple: Spoon 1 pt. pistachio ice cream onto devil's-food-cake layer made from cake mix; drizzle chocolate sauce over ice cream. Serve, cut into wedges.

Speedy: Top squares of warm yellow, white, or devil's-food cake, made from packaged mix, with ice cream and your favorite sauce.

ICE-CREAM SHORTCAKES

Individual: For each serving, put 2 thin slices toasted or plain angel, sponge, or white cake together with ice cream. Top with Hot Fudge Sauce, p. 370, or fresh, frozen, or canned fruit.

Berry Layer: Place 1 8″ white- or yellow-cake layer on serving plate. Spoon on about 1 pt. lemon or other ice cream and several spoonfuls of strawberries or raspberries. Top with second cake layer, another 1 pt. ice cream, then more berries. Garnish with whipped cream. Serve, cut into wedges.

Luxuro: Split 1 spongecake layer into 2 layers. Fill with favorite ice cream. Sprinkle top with chopped salted pecans or almonds. Serve, cut into wedges; pass Hot Fudge Sauce, p. 370.

Sponge Berry: Split 2 spongecake layers to form 4 layers. Fill with sweetened berries. Serve, cut into wedges and topped with ice cream, whipped cream, or custard sauce.

ICE-CREAM CUPCAKES

Top Hat: From center of cupcake, cut out cone-shaped piece; fill cupcake with ice cream. Top with "cone" and chocolate sauce.

Black and White: Split chocolate cupcake into 3 layers. Spread vanilla ice cream between layers; top with fudge sauce.

PRALINE ICE-CREAM RING

½ cup butter or margarine	2½ cups corn, bran, or wheat flakes
1 cup brown sugar, packed	Ice cream
½ cup broken pecans or walnuts	

Chill 1¼ qt. ring mold. In saucepan, boil butter, sugar *just 2 min.* Add pecans, cereal flakes; with fork, toss to coat. Press lightly into mold. Refrigerate 10 min.; unmold onto serving dish. Place spoonfuls of your favorite ice cream, with rounded sides up, in center. Makes 6 servings.

Praline Crunch: Make Praline Ice-Cream Ring mixture; cool; then crumble. Serve over vanilla or coffee ice cream.

PEACH MELBA

Top each serving of vanilla ice cream with canned or ripe fresh peach half; pour on Melba Sauce, p. 371.

Quick: Fill canned or fresh peach halves with vanilla ice cream. Top with thawed frozen raspberries.

MINCEMEAT AFLAME

Spoon heated prepared mincemeat around vanilla or coffee ice cream. Top ice cream with sugar lump dipped into lemon extract; light; rush to table.

CHERRIES FLAMBE

In skillet or chafing dish over direct heat, melt ¾ cup currant jelly, stirring gently. Quickly drain 1 No. 2½ can pitted Bing cherries; add cherries to jelly; heat slowly till simmering, stirring occasionally. Pour ½ cup brandy into center of cherries; heat undisturbed; then light with match. Spoon flaming cherries over 8 servings (1½ qt.) vanilla ice cream.

Peach: Substitute 1 No. 2½ can peach halves for cherries. When peaches are heated, turn cut sides up; pour brandy in center; don't stir. Light. Spoon over 6 servings ice cream.

FRUIT AND ICE CREAM

Susan's Banana Split: For each serving, split 1 peeled banana lengthwise; place halves, with cut sides up, on plate. Top with 3 scoops of vanilla ice cream. Top 1 scoop with drained canned crushed pineapple, 1 with chocolate sauce, 1 with crushed strawberries. Sprinkle with nuts.

Streamlined Banana Split: For each serving, slice part of banana into sherbet glass. Top with favorite ice cream or sherbet and spoonful of thawed frozen strawberries or raspberries.

Frosted Pineapple: For each serving, top 1 drained canned pineapple slice with raspberry sherbet and spoonful of thawed frozen strawberries or raspberries.

Chocolate Pears: For each serving, top 1 drained canned pear half with vanilla ice cream and spoonful of chocolate sauce; sprinkle with chopped walnuts.

Pineapple Split: For 6 to 8 servings, halve fresh pineapple lengthwise, right through green top; hollow out. Fill with ice cream; sprinkle with coconut and pineapple bits.

BAKED ALASKAS

1. Start heating oven to 450°F. For cake base, choose one of Alaskas, p. 428; set cake base on brown paper (½" larger than cake) on cookie sheet.

2. Make meringue: With electric mixer or egg beater, beat 3 egg whites until they stand in peaks when beater is raised. Slowly add 6 tablesp. granulated sugar, beating until stiff and glossy.

3. Quickly fill or top cake base with about 1 qt. very firm ice cream, as directed below. Quickly cover ice cream and base completely with meringue. If desired, sprinkle with slivered almonds, shaved chocolate, or shredded coconut. Bake 4 to 5 min., or until delicate brown.

4. Remove from oven at once; slip 2 spatulas between Alaska and paper; transfer Alaska to chilled serving dish. Garnish with berries or fresh, frozen, or canned peach slices, etc. Serve at once.

5. To serve ablaze, pour a little lemon extract over 3 sugar cubes; set on top of meringue; light; carry to table.

Alaskas:

Igloo: Use bakers' spongecake layer as base. Pile ice cream on top, leaving ½″ free around edge.

Brownie: Use panful of uncut brownies as base. Top with brick ice cream.

Little Baked: Use 6 bakers' dessert shells as base. Top each with well-drained canned pineapple slices. Place scoop of ice cream on each.

Traditional: Use 1 piece thin spongecake, 8″ x 6″ x 1″. Top with brick ice cream.

Surprise: Use 9″ tube spongecake as base. Hollow out as in Frozen Ice-Cream Angel, p. 429. Fill trough with 2 to 3 pt. ice cream. (Use leftover cake crumbs in Susan's Cake Crumb Pudding, p. 391.)

P.S. You can have baked Alaska on short notice if you keep cake and ice cream on hand in your freezer.

SUNDAE PIES

1. *Make a baked pie shell*—any on pp. 408 to 410.
2. *At serving time,* fill with 1, 2, or 3 flavors of ice cream—1 to 2 pt. for 8″ shell, 2 to 3 pt. for 9″ shell.
3. *Top with* shaved unsweetened chocolate, plain or toasted shredded coconut, chopped nuts, or one of toppings in Sundae Toppings, p. 436.

We Suggest:

Baked Crumb Crust, p. 410; vanilla ice cream; chocolate sauce; whipped cream

Baked Crumb Crust made with gingersnaps, p. 410; vanilla ice cream; canned crushed pineapple

Chocolate-Coconut Crust, p. 421; coffee ice cream

Baked Pie Shell, pp. 408 to 410; peach ice cream; Melba Sauce, p. 371

Meringue Crust, p. 410; vanilla ice cream; sliced peaches, strawberries, or raspberries, or canned whole-cranberry sauce

Toasted Coconut Crust, p. 421; vanilla ice cream; crushed pineapple

Unbaked Pretzel-Crumb Crust, p. 410; vanilla ice cream; favorite topping

Frozen Sundae Pies: Make and fill as above. Freezer-wrap; freeze. To serve, unwrap; let set in refrigerator until easy to cut.

SUNDAE TARTS

Fill Pretty Tart Shells, p. 422, with your favorite ice cream; top as in Sundae Pies, above. Serve at once.

Or fill tart shells with ice cream; top, then cover completely, with Pie Meringue (2 egg), p. 419. Bake at 500°F. about 2 min.

BAKED-ALASKA PIE

Choose any Baked Crumb Crust, p. 410. Refrigerate until well chilled. Start heating oven to 500°F. Make Pie Meringue (3 egg), p. 419.

Working quickly, fill shell with 1 qt. firm ice cream. Cover entire surface of ice cream with meringue. Bake about 2 min., or until delicate brown. Serve at once.

STRAWBERRY ICE-CREAM PIE

1 Baked 9″ Pie Shell, pp. 408 to 410	¼ cup granulated sugar
16 marshmallows	¼ teasp. salt
2 tablesp. strawberry juice	1 qt. firm vanilla ice cream
Few drops red food color	1 cup drained, thawed frozen sliced strawberries
2 egg whites	

Refrigerate pie shell until well chilled. Preheat broiler 10 min., or as manufacturer directs. Over low heat, heat marshmallows with strawberry juice, folding constantly, until melted. Fold in food color. Beat egg whites until fairly stiff; gradually add sugar and salt, beating until very stiff; fold in marshmallow mixture. Fill chilled shell with ice cream; cover with strawberries; completely top with meringue. Broil several inches below heat until lightly browned. Serve at once. Makes 6 servings.

If You Have a Freezer or Refrigerator-Freezer Combination

ICE-CREAM ANGELS

Frozen: Hollow out 9″ or 10″ angel cake this way: Cut down into cake along top, all the way around, about ½″ to 1″ in from outer edge (don't cut through to bottom). Then repeat all the way around, cutting same distance in from center edge of cake. Gently pull out cake between cuts, leaving deep trough all around.

Fill cake with 2 or 3 pt. pistachio ice cream; frost entire cake with Orange Butter Cream, p. 462. Freeze till frosting is set; freezer-wrap; freeze. To serve, thaw in refrigerator about 1 hr. Cut into wedges.

Black and White: Make Frozen Angel above, filling with chocolate ice cream. Just before serving, frost with whipped cream.

Frozen Layer: Split angel cake into 3 layers. Fill with ice cream. Freezer-wrap; freeze to use later. Or serve at once, cut into wedges, with chocolate sauce.

Double Chocolate: Make or buy 9″ or 10″ angel cake. With fork, tear off large, irregular pieces. Alternate cake pieces and spoonfuls of chocolate ice cream in 9″ x 5″ x 3″ loaf pan, pressing them into pan to form loaf shape. Freezer-wrap; freeze. To serve, thaw in refrigerator about 1 hr. before unmolding. Slice. Pass chocolate sauce.

Frosty Angel: Enlarge hole in center of angel or chiffon cake to 4″ in diameter. Use some of cake to fill bottom of hole. Spoon vanilla ice cream into hole; drizzle chocolate sauce over cake. Freezer-wrap; freeze until firm. To serve, unwrap; let stand a few minutes; slice.

ICE-CREAM CAKES

Berry: Split 6″ or 8″ square spongecake into 3 layers. Fill with 1 pt. or 1 qt. strawberry ice cream. Freezer-wrap; freeze. To serve, thaw in refrigerator 1 hr. Cut into squares; spoon thawed frozen berries over each square.

Sweetheart: In 2 waxed-paper-lined heart-shaped layer pans, make and bake white cake from packaged mix; cool; remove from pans. Press 1 qt. raspberry sherbet into same 2 waxed-paper-lined heart-shaped layer pans; freeze until firm. Unmold each sherbet layer onto cake layer; then set one on top of other. Freezer-wrap; freeze. To serve, thaw in refrigerator about 1 hr.; frost sides with 1 pt. heavy cream, whipped. Serve, cut into wedges.

Partytime: *Two days ahead:* Press 1 qt. vanilla ice cream into waxed-paper-lined 9″ layer pan; freezer-wrap; freeze.

Day ahead: Whip 1 cup heavy cream. Split 1 9″ yellow- or white-cake layer into 2 layers; place 1 cake layer on waxed paper; unmold ice-cream layer onto cake; spread with ¼ cup jelly, jam, or drained canned crushed pineapple; top with second cake layer.

Now, working quickly, spread sides of cake with whipped cream. On top, spread thin layer of jelly; then decorate cake with whipped cream in cake decorator. Freeze till cream is set; freezer-wrap; freeze. To serve, thaw in refrigerator about 1 hr. Cut into wedges.

Susan's Seven Layer: Bake 9″ x 9″ x 2″ cake from packaged devil's-food or white-cake mix. Cool cake; cut in half, making 2 rectangles; split each rectangle into 2 layers.

If it's devil's-food cake, spread one layer with coffee ice cream, one with pistachio, one with cherry-vanilla. If it's white cake, use raspberry sherbet, butter-pecan, then chocolate ice cream.

Set layers, one on top of the other, pressing them into shape and ending with plain cake layer. Freezer-wrap; freeze. To serve, unwrap, let stand a few minutes; slice.

Strawberry: Into 9″ clampless spring-form pan, with round insert in place, spoon 2 qt. vanilla ice cream. While placing split ladyfingers around inside of pan, spread ice cream over bottom and up sides, to hold ladyfingers upright. Freezer-wrap; freeze.

Before serving, unmold cake onto cake plate and set in freezer to firm up. To serve, fill center with sliced berries. Cut cake into wedges at table.

ICE-CREAM ROLLS

Jelly-Roll Torte: Cut 5″ bakers' jelly roll into ½″-thick slices; use to line bottom and side of ungreased 9″ tube pan. Fill with 3 pt. ice cream. Freezer-wrap; freeze until firm. To serve, un-mold; cut into wedges.

Ice-Cream Jelly Roll: Gently unroll 1 6″ bakers' jelly roll; spread with more red jelly, then with 1 pt. slightly soft ice cream. Roll up. Freezer-wrap; freeze until firm. To serve, let set in refrigerator about 1 hr.; slice. Pass crushed berries or chocolate sauce.

Cookie Roll: *Day before serving,* slice 1-pt. round carton vanilla ice cream into ½″ slices. Alternate about 8 2¾″ packaged chocolate wafers with ice-cream slices (standing them on edge), to form long roll. Wrap in waxed paper; shape and press into even roll. Remove waxed paper; roll in crumbs made from 6 chocolate wafers. Freezer-wrap; freeze overnight. To serve, slice diagonally. Makes 4 servings.

Sundae Roll: Leave Jelly Roll, p. 454, or Susan's Chocolate Roll, p. 454, rolled up until cooled. Then unroll; spread with 1-qt. slightly soft ice cream; drizzle on ¼ cup butterscotch or chocolate sauce; sprinkle with ¼ cup chopped nuts. Roll up; freezer-wrap. Store, with roll resting on seam side, in freezer, or ice-cube tray until firm. To serve, cut into slices.

ICE-CREAM BOMBE

Fill 1-qt. mold with 1 qt. ice cream. With back of spoon, smooth ice cream so it is equally distributed over bottom and side of mold, leaving center hollow. Spoon 1 pt. sherbet into hollowed center, packing it down. Freezer-wrap; freeze. Try any of these combinations:

Chocolate or coffee ice cream; orange sherbet or green-tinted, mint-flavored whipped cream in center

Vanilla ice cream; orange sherbet in center

Pistachio ice cream; lemon sherbet in center

Strawberry ice cream; raspberry sherbet in center

To serve: Dip mold into cool water 5 to 10 sec.; unmold.

ICE-CREAM PUFFS

Twin Frozen: Make Petite Cream Puffs, p. 395. When puffs are cool, split from top almost to bottom; fill half of puffs with one flavor of ice cream, rest with another. Carefully pack puffs in containers; freeze.

Just before dinner: Place 2 puffs on each dessert plate; let stand in food compartment of refrigerator 20 to 30 min. To serve, top with Hot Fudge Sauce, p. 370. Makes 12 to 15 servings.

Ice-Cream Puffs or Eclairs: Fill Susan's Cream Puffs, p. 395, or Eclairs, p. 395, with favorite ice cream. Freeze as above; then serve with favorite sauce.

P.S. Cream puffs or éclairs may be filled with ice cream, topped with sauce, and served at once if preferred.

WHEN YOU MAKE ICE CREAM

There are still a lot of people (and you may be one) who like to make their own ice creams and sherbets. And there are several nice ways of doing it. On these pages are some of our favorite recipes.

In Ice-Cube Tray of Refrigerator

VANILLA ICE CREAM
(uncooked base)

⅔ cup canned sweet-
　ened condensed milk
½ cup cold water
⅛ teasp. salt

1½ teasp. vanilla
　extract
1 cup heavy cream

Turn temperature control of refrigerator to coldest setting. Combine milk, water, salt, vanilla; refrigerate until well chilled. Whip cream to custard-like consistency. Fold into chilled mixture. Turn into ice-cube tray; freeze until frozen

1″ in from edges of tray. Turn into chilled bowl; with electric mixer or egg beater, beat until smooth but not melted. Quickly return mixture to ice-cube tray; freeze until just firm enough to spoon out. Then reset temperature control. Makes 3 or 4 servings.

Butter Pecan: In 2 tablesp. butter or margarine in skillet, sauté ½ cup broken pecan meats until golden brown. Add, with ¼ teasp. salt, to milk mixture.

Chocolate: In double boiler, melt 1 sq. (1 oz.) unsweetened chocolate. Add condensed milk; stir over boiling water 5 min., or until thick. Add water; mix well. Refrigerate until well chilled. Add salt, vanilla, then whipped cream.

Peach: To milk mixture, add 2 cups sieved fresh or thawed frozen peaches; 1 or 2 drops almond extract; 1 tablesp. fresh, frozen, or canned lemon juice.

Strawberry: Combine 1½ cups crushed strawberries; 2 tablesp. fresh, frozen, or canned lemon juice; and ¼ cup granulated sugar. Add to milk mixture. Makes 4 or 5 servings.

Toasted Coffee-Nut: Increase sweetened condensed milk to 1 can, water to ¾ cup. Add 3 tablesp. instant coffee to cream before whipping. In 2 teasp. butter or margarine, sauté ⅓ cup coarsely chopped walnuts until toasted. After last beating, fold in 1 tablesp. brandy (optional) and nuts.

FROZEN PUDDING

⅔ cup granulated sugar	canned pineapple
¾ cup water	tidbits
3 egg whites *	¼ cup candied cherries,
1 pt. heavy cream	coarsely cut
1 teasp. vanilla extract	¼ cup light raisins,
¼ cup coarsely chopped	snipped fine

Turn temperature control of refrigerator to coldest setting. Boil sugar and water to 230°F. on candy thermometer, or until a little of mixture forms thread when dropped from spoon. Beat egg whites and cream in separate bowls until stiff.

Slowly pour sugar syrup over beaten egg whites, beating until cool. Fold in whipped cream, vanilla, fruits. Turn into ice-cube tray; freeze, without stirring, until just firm enough

to spoon out. Then reset temperature control. Makes 8 to 10 servings.

* *For ways to use egg yolks, see p. 550.*

PINEAPPLE ICE CREAM

2 eggs	1 cup syrup drained
½ cup granulated sugar	from pineapple
1 tablesp. cornstarch	1 cup heavy cream
1 cup milk	2 drops lemon extract
1½ cups drained	2 teasp. grated lemon
canned crushed	rind
pineapple	

In double-boiler top, mix eggs, sugar, cornstarch, milk, pineapple, syrup; cook, stirring, until smooth and thickened. Refrigerate until well chilled.

Turn temperature control of refrigerator to coldest setting. Whip cream; fold, with extract and rind, into chilled pineapple mixture. Turn into ice-cube tray; freeze until very firm. Turn into chilled bowl; with electric mixer or egg beater, beat until smooth but not melted. Quickly return mixture to ice-cube tray; freeze, stirring once, until just firm enough to spoon out. Then reset temperature control. Makes 6 servings.

PISTACHIO MOUSSE

2 cups milk	2 teasp. vanilla extract
3 egg yolks	½ teasp. almond extract
1 cup granulated sugar	½ cup chopped pista-
¼ teasp. salt	chio nuts
1⅓ cups heavy cream	Green food color

Turn temperature control of refrigerator to coldest setting. Scald milk. Beat egg yolks; add sugar, salt; slowly stir in milk. Cook over low heat until mixture thickens—about 3 min. Cool; then add cream, extracts, nuts. Tint delicate green with food color. Turn into ice-cube tray; freeze, stirring once, until just firm enough to spoon out. Then reset temperature control. Makes 8 to 10 servings.

STRAWBERRY MOUSSE

1 12-oz. pkg. thawed	juice
frozen sliced straw-	¼ teasp. salt
berries	2 egg whites
1 teasp. fresh, frozen,	1½ cups heavy cream
or canned lemon	

Turn temperature control of refrigerator to coldest setting. Press strawberries through sieve. Add lemon juice, salt. Beat egg whites till they form soft peaks; fold into berries. Whip cream; fold into berry mixture. Turn into ice-cube tray. Freeze, stirring once, until just firm enough to spoon out. Then reset temperature control. Makes 8 to 10 servings.

CHOCO-NUT TORTONI

1 egg white	**½ pkg. semisweet-chocolate pieces (½ cup)**
2 tablesp. granulated sugar	**1 teasp. shortening**
1 cup heavy cream, whipped	**¼ cup canned finely chopped, toasted almonds**
2 tablesp. granulated sugar	
1 teasp. vanilla extract	

Turn temperature control of refrigerator to coldest setting. Beat egg white until fairly stiff; gradually add 2 tablesp. sugar, beating until stiff. Combine whipped cream, 2 tablesp. sugar, vanilla; fold into beaten egg white. Turn into ice-cube tray; freeze until frozen ½" in from edges of tray. Melt chocolate with shortening over *hot, not boiling,* water. Turn frozen mixture into chilled bowl; stir until smooth but not melted; quickly fold in melted chocolate, then almonds. Turn into 8 2-oz. paper cups; freeze until just firm. Then reset temperature control. Makes 8 servings.

WILLIE MAE'S FRESH CRANBERRY SHERBET*

1 env. unflavored gelatine	**2 cups granulated sugar**
½ cup cold water	**⅓ cup fresh, frozen, or canned lemon juice**
4 cups fresh cranberries	
2½ cups water	

Turn temperature control of refrigerator to coldest setting. Sprinkle gelatine over cold water to soften. Cook cranberries in 2½ cups water, covered, until skins pop open; force through sieve; then add sugar, gelatine. Heat until gelatine dissolves; cool. Add lemon juice.

Turn into ice-cube tray; freeze until firm. Turn into chilled bowl; with electric mixer or egg beater, beat until thick and mushy. Quickly return mixture to ice-cube tray; freeze until just firm enough to spoon out. Then reset temperature control. Makes 4 servings.

* *This is a tart sherbet, and is especially nice with meats or poultry.*

LIME MILK SHERBET

1 env. unflavored gelatine	**2 cups light cream**
½ cup milk	**¼ cup fresh, frozen, or canned lemon juice**
½ teasp. salt	**½ cup lime juice**
1½ cups milk	**2 tablesp. grated lime rind**
1⅓ cups granulated sugar	

Turn temperature control of refrigerator to coldest setting. Sprinkle gelatine over ½ cup milk in glass measuring cup to soften; stir over hot water until gelatine dissolves. Combine rest of ingredients; stir in gelatine. Turn into ice-cube tray; freeze until frozen 1" in from edges of tray. Turn into chilled bowl; with electric mixer or egg beater, beat until smooth but not melted. Quickly return mixture to ice-cube tray; freeze until just firm enough to spoon out. Then reset temperature control. Makes 5 or 6 servings.

Note: Mixture may curdle, but sherbet will be creamy when frozen.

Libby's Lemon Sherbet: Substitute ¾ cup fresh, frozen, or canned lemon juice for lime juice, 1 teasp. grated lemon rind for lime rind.

PANTRY-SHELF ORANGE SHERBET

1 14½-oz. can undiluted evaporated milk (1⅔ cups)	**½ cup orange juice**
1 cup granulated sugar	**2 tablesp. lemon juice**
⅛ teasp. salt	**1 tablesp. grated lemon rind**

Turn temperature control of refrigerator to coldest setting. Combine evaporated milk, sugar, salt. Gradually stir in orange juice, lemon juice, rind. Pour into ice-cube tray; freeze until firm. Turn into chilled bowl; with electric mixer or egg beater, beat until smooth and fluffy. Quickly return mixture to ice-cube tray; freeze, stirring once, until just firm enough to spoon out. Then reset temperature control. Makes 3 or 4 servings.

Pineapple: Substitute ⅓ cup canned pineapple juice for orange juice.

Lemon: Omit orange juice; increase lemon juice to ⅓ cup.

DIFFERENT PINEAPPLE SHERBET

1 env. unflavored gelatine	rind
	2 tablesp. lemon juice
1 cup syrup drained from 1 No. 2 can crushed pineapple	Dash salt
	2 cups cold milk
½ cup granulated sugar	¾ cup drained canned crushed pineapple
1 teasp. grated lemon	

Turn temperature control of refrigerator to coldest setting. Sprinkle gelatine over pineapple syrup to soften; stir over hot water until gelatine dissolves. Stir in sugar, lemon rind, lemon juice, salt; remove from heat. Gradually stir into cold milk. Pour into ice-cube tray; freeze till partially firm. Turn into chilled bowl; with electric mixer or egg beater, beat until smooth but not melted. Fold in pineapple. Quickly return mixture to ice-cube tray; freeze until just firm enough to spoon out. Then reset temperature control. Makes 6 servings.

LEMONADE CREAM SHERBET

1 env. unflavored gelatine	¼ cup granulated sugar
⅓ cup cold water	1 cup heavy cream, whipped
1 can frozen lemonade concentrate *	Few drops yellow food color
2 cups milk	

Turn temperature control of refrigerator to coldest setting. Sprinkle gelatine over cold water in glass measuring cup to soften. Stir over hot water until gelatine dissolves. Combine lemonade concentrate, milk, sugar, gelatine; beat well. Turn into ice-cube tray; freeze until partially firm. Turn into chilled bowl; with electric mixer or egg beater, beat well. Add whipped cream and food color; beat well. Quickly return mixture to ice-cube tray; freeze until just firm enough to spoon out, stirring occasionally. Then reset temperature control. Makes 4 servings.

* For other flavors, use frozen limeade, orange, or pineapple-juice concentrate.

APRICOT SHERBET

2 cans apricot nectar (1½ cups)	2 teasp. almond extract

Turn temperature control of refrigerator to coldest setting. Mix together nectar and almond. Turn into freezing tray; freeze, stirring occasionally, until just mushy. Serve at once. Makes 6 servings.

THREE-FRUIT SHERBET

1 cup granulated sugar	frozen raspberries
	¼ cup orange juice
2 cups water	¼ cup fresh, frozen, or canned lemon juice
1 pkg. raspberry-flavored gelatin	
2 12-oz. pkg. thawed	

Turn temperature control of refrigerator to coldest setting. Combine sugar, water; boil 5 min. Add gelatin dessert; stir until dissolved. Chill until slightly thickened. Meanwhile, sieve berries; add, with orange and lemon juices, to gelatin. Pour into freezing tray; freeze until firm. Turn into chilled bowl; with electric mixer or egg beater, beat until smooth. Quickly return mixture to tray; freeze until just firm, stirring once. Then reset temperature control. Makes 8 servings.

WONDERFUL PINEAPPLE SHERBET

1 No. 2 can crushed pineapple	lemon rind
	2 tablesp. lemon juice
½ cup granulated sugar	Dash salt
	2 cups milk
1 teasp. grated	

Turn temperature control of refrigerator to coldest setting. Drain pineapple; combine syrup with sugar, lemon rind, juice, salt. Slowly stir in milk. Pour into freezing tray; freeze until firm. Turn into chilled bowl; with electric mixer or egg beater, beat until fluffy. Fold in drained pineapple. Quickly return mixture to tray; freeze until just firm. Then reset temperature control. Makes 6 servings.

CRANBERRY MOUSSE

1 1-lb. can jellied cranberry sauce	1 cup heavy cream, whipped
2 tablesp. granulated sugar	½ teasp. almond extract

Turn temperature control of refrigerator to coldest setting. With fork, beat together cranberry sauce and sugar until well blended. Fold in cream and extract. Turn into freezing tray; freeze until just firm, stirring once. Then reset temperature control. Makes 6 servings.

Ice-Cream-Mix Tricks

Don't fail to scan your grocer's shelves for those packaged mixes and concentrates you can so easily whip up into frozen desserts, ice creams, and sherbets. The vanilla flavor can be used as a basic mix and varied in a number of interesting ways as suggested on the label. Also try chocolate, strawberry, black raspberry.

Lemon, raspberry, lime, and orange sherbet mixes speak for themselves. For tastiest results, always follow package directions to the letter.

In Crank Freezer
(hand-turned or electric)

GRANDMA'S VANILLA ICE CREAM

1½ cups milk	2 eggs; or 3 egg yolks
¾ cup granulated sugar	1½ teasp. vanilla
2 tablesp. flour	extract
Few grains salt	1½ cups heavy cream

In double boiler, scald milk. Mix sugar, flour, salt; stir in enough milk to make smooth paste. Stir into rest of milk in double boiler. Stir until thickened; cook, covered, 10 min. Beat eggs slightly; stir in milk mixture; return to double boiler; cook 1 min. Cool; add vanilla, cream. Freeze in 2-qt. or larger crank freezer until difficult to turn, using 8 parts crushed ice to 1 part ice-cream salt.

To ripen: When ice cream is firm, draw off water from freezer; wipe off and remove lid. Take out dasher; plug opening in lid. Pack ice-cream mixture down; re-cover. Repack freezer as follows: If serving within 2 hr., use 1 qt. crushed ice to each 1 cup ice-cream salt; if holding ice cream longer, use 2 qt. ice to each 1 cup salt; cover with heavy cloth. Makes 1¼ qt.

Bisque: Substitute 3 tablesp. sherry for vanilla. When ready to freeze mixture, add 1 cup fine macaroon crumbs.

Burnt Almond: Caramelize half of sugar as on p. 5. Stir into scalded milk until caramel dissolves. Just before freezing mixture, add ¼ lb. finely chopped, toasted, blanched almonds.

Butter Pecan: In ¼ cup hot butter, margarine, or salad oil in skillet, sauté 1 cup broken pecan meats until golden. Add, with ¼ teasp. salt, just before freezing.

Chocolate: Add 2 sq. unsweetened chocolate to milk before scalding. When chocolate is melted, with egg beater, beat till smooth.

Coffee: Substitute ¾ cup cold **strong** coffee beverage for ¾ cup milk.

French Vanilla: Substitute 6 egg yolks for eggs.

Peach: Just before freezing mixture, add 1½ cups sieved fresh peaches combined with ¼ cup additional sugar (or enough to sweeten) and few drops almond extract.

Peppermint: Omit vanilla; add 1 drop oil of peppermint. Or add 1½ cups very finely crushed peppermint-stick candy to milk before scalding; omit sugar. Tint delicate pink or green with food color.

Pineapple: Substitute 1 tablesp. fresh, frozen, or canned lemon juice for vanilla. Just before freezing mixture, add 2 cups well-drained canned crushed pineapple.

Pistachio: With vanilla, add ¾ teasp. almond extract and ½ cup chopped, blanched pistachio nuts. Tint delicate green with food color.

Raspberry: Just before freezing mixture, add 1½ cups crushed raspberries mixed with about ¼ cup additional sugar, and a few drops almond extract.

Strawberry: Reduce milk to 1 cup. When milk-and-egg mixture has cooled, add 1 qt. washed, hulled strawberries, mashed and sweetened with ¼ cup additional sugar; blend well. Then add cream.

LEMON MILK SHERBET

¾ cup lemon juice	rind
1½ cups granulated sugar	4 cups milk
1 tablesp. grated lemon	¼ teasp. salt

Combine lemon juice, sugar, rind; add very slowly to milk, stirring constantly till sugar dissolves. Add salt and more sugar if desired. Freeze in 2-qt. or larger crank freezer until difficult to turn, using 8 parts crushed ice to 1 part ice-cream salt. Ripen as on p. 434. Makes 1½ qt.

Note: Mixture may curdle, but sherbet will be creamy when frozen.

BANANA ICE CREAM

2 cups mashed ripe bananas (5 or 6 bananas)	2 eggs, beaten
1½ tablesp. fresh, frozen, or canned lemon juice	1 cup milk; or ½ cup evaporated milk plus ½ cup water
½ cup granulated sugar	1½ teasp. vanilla extract
½ teasp. salt	2 cups heavy cream

Mix together bananas, lemon juice, sugar. Add salt, eggs, milk, vanilla. Stir in cream. Freeze in 2-qt. or larger crank freezer until difficult to turn, using 8 parts crushed ice to 1 part ice-cream salt. Ripen as on p. 434. Makes about 2 qt.

ORANGE MILK SHERBET

2 cups orange juice	1 tablesp. grated orange rind
¼ cup fresh, frozen, or canned lemon juice	1¾ cups milk
½ cup granulated sugar	⅛ teasp. salt

Combine orange juice, lemon juice, sugar, orange rind. Add very slowly to milk, stirring till sugar dissolves. Add salt. Freeze in 2-qt. or larger crank freezer until difficult to turn, using 8 parts crushed ice to 1 part ice-cream salt. Ripen as on p. 434. Makes 1½ qt.

Note: Mixture may curdle, but sherbet will be creamy when frozen.

PHILADELPHIA ICE CREAM

1 qt. light cream	5 teasp. vanilla extract
¾ cup granulated sugar	Few grains salt

Mix all ingredients; stir till sugar dissolves. Freeze in 2-qt. or larger crank freezer until difficult to turn, using 8 parts crushed ice to 1 part ice-cream salt. Ripen as on p. 434. Makes about 1 qt.

CIDER ICE

4 cups cider	½ cup fresh, frozen, or canned lemon juice
1 cup granulated sugar	
1 cup orange juice	

Simmer cider with sugar 5 min. Add orange and lemon juices. Freeze in 2-qt. or larger crank freezer until difficult to turn, using 8 parts crushed ice to 1 part ice-cream salt. Ripen as on p. 434. Makes about 1½ qt.

Lemon: Simmer 4 cups water with 1½ cups granulated sugar 5 min. Add ¾ cup lemon juice, 1 tablesp. grated lemon rind, ¼ teasp. salt, and a few chopped mint leaves (optional). Cool. Freeze. Makes about 1½ qt.

Orange: Simmer 2 cups water with 1 cup granulated sugar 5 min. Add 2 cups orange juice; ¼ cup fresh, frozen, or canned lemon juice; ⅛ teasp. salt; 1 tablesp. grated orange rind. Freeze. Makes 1½ qt.

Pineapple: Simmer 2 cups water with ½ cup granulated sugar 5 min. Add 1 No. 2 can pineapple juice; ⅓ cup fresh, frozen, or canned lemon juice; and ⅛ teasp. salt. Freeze. Makes about 2 qt.

Raspberry, Strawberry, or Loganberry: Simmer 1 cup granulated sugar with 2 cups water 5 min. Pour over 2 cups crushed berries; cool. Rub through sieve. Then add 1 tablesp. lemon juice (or lemon juice to taste). Freeze. Makes about 1 qt.

SUNDAE TOPPINGS

TOP VANILLA ICE CREAM WITH:

Applesauce, warmed, and sprinkling of nutmeg or cinnamon

Canned whole-fruit apricot nectar and sprinkling of plain or toasted coconut

Banana slices and sprinkling of nutmeg

Bing-Cherry Sauce, p. 368

Heated canned Bing cherries

Blueberry Sauce, p. 371, or Date-Nut Sauce, p. 368

Minted Cantaloupe Sauce, p. 371

Easy Caramel Sauce, p. 367

Chocolate-Peppermint Sauce, p. 368

Cocoa or *crème de menthe*

Coconut, tinted green, and lemon wedges

Coconut, tinted pink, and lime wedges

Cranberry-juice cocktail and melon balls

Canned whole-cranberry sauce, mixed with drained canned crushed pineapple and bit of peppermint extract

Dates, dried figs, or raisins, snipped, then soaked in brandy

Flaming Fruit Cocktail Sauce, p. 371

Hot fudge sauce with crumbled pretzels

Frozen grape-juice concentrate, slightly thawed; seedless grapes; and sprinkling of cinnamon

Crumbled macaroons or chocolate wafers

Maple or maple-blended syrup, warmed, and sprinkling of salted almonds, peanuts, etc.

Prepared mincemeat, heated

Molasses, honey, or Chocolate Sauce, p. 367, mixed with crunchy peanut butter or salted nuts

Frozen orange- or tangerine-juice concentrate, slightly thawed, and sprinkling of grated chocolate

Orange marmalade, or berry or apricot jam, heated

Peanut brittle, crushed

Canned peach half and Melba Sauce, p. 371

Fresh, frozen, or canned peach slices and sprinkling of cinnamon

Chocolate-covered peppermint patties, crumbled

Frozen pineapple-juice or lemonade concentrate, slightly thawed, and sprinkling cinnamon or nutmeg

Praline Crunch, p. 427

Pitted stewed prunes and sprinkling of ground cloves

Rum-Butter Sauce, p. 370

Frozen strawberries or raspberries, slightly thawed

TOP CHOCOLATE ICE CREAM WITH:

Canned crushed pineapple

Chocolate sauce and crumbled pretzels

Honey, mixed with crunchy peanut butter

Grated orange rind, mixed with sugar

Hard peppermint candy, crushed

Peanut brittle, crushed

Butterscotch Sauce, p. 368

Chocolate Sauce, p. 367, mixed with crunchy peanut butter and a little corn syrup

Marshmallow cream, thinned to sauce consistency, and grated chocolate

Chocolate-Peppermint Sauce, p. 368

Butter-Caramel Sauce, p. 369

Toasted shredded coconut

TOP COFFEE ICE CREAM WITH:

Date-Nut Sauce, p. 368

Peanut brittle, crushed

Prepared mincemeat, warmed

Custard sauce and shaved chocolate

Sliced peaches and custard sauce

Chocolate Sauce, p. 367, mixed with crunchy peanut butter and a little corn syrup

Maple or maple-blended syrup; few salted nuts

Marshmallow cream, thinned to sauce consistency, and sprinkling of grated chocolate

Praline Crunch, p. 427

Fudge Sauce, p. 370, hot or cold

Chocolate-Peppermint Sauce, p. 368

Rum-Butter Sauce, p. 370

TOP ORANGE OR LEMON SHERBET WITH:

Grated orange rind, mixed with sugar

Whipped cream, plus drained crushed berries

Slightly thawed frozen raspberries or orange-juice concentrate

Canned crushed pineapple and mint sprigs

Seedless grapes and cut-up oranges or pineapple

Crème de menthe or triple sec

Cakes and Cupcakes

Cakes can be the proudest product of your oven. No matter what kind—creamed, quick-method, chiffon, angel, sponge—they should be tender, high, rich in flavor—and should invite immediate sampling. Our carefully checked recipes will give you such cakes if you follow directions to the letter.

To Make a Good Cake

1. First read carefully How to Use Our Recipes, p. 3, and Pots and Pans, p. 692.
2. Next read cake recipe all the way through. Then assemble the necessary utensils and ingredients. Always use standard measuring cups and measuring spoons; measure level.
3. Follow directions; otherwise even the best recipes can go wrong.
   a. *Use pans that are the exact size and depth indicated.* (Read Measuring Pan Sizes, p. 13.) Bigger, smaller, or shallower pans than those called for can cause a cake to fail. If pans aren't the right size, fill only half full with batter, so cake will rise to, but not over, top of pan; use rest of batter for cupcakes.
   b. *Be sure metal cake pans are bright and shiny* inside and out, so cakes will brown evenly, delicately. Dull, dark pans cause cakes to brown too fast, too unevenly. To keep cake pans shiny, clean with steel-wool soap pads.

   If **you're** using oven-glass cake dishes and cakes are overbrowning, try reducing oven temperature 25°F.
   c. *Follow recipe exactly.* No substitutions of ingredients, *no* changes in amounts, *no* changes in directions are allowed.
   d. *Use exact ingredients called for*—double-acting baking powder, cake flour, etc. This can mean the difference between a masterpiece and a mediocrity.
   e. *Bake at temperature and for time period specified.*
4. Do these little jobs before you mix a cake:
   a. *If cake pans are to be lined with paper,* set pan on large piece of waxed paper. Trace around bottom of pan with point of scissors or sharp knife. Cut out; place in bottom of cake pan. Paper should fit snugly. Making several liners at once saves time. You can also buy cake liners, already cut.
   b. *If cake pans are to be greased,* apply thin film of salad oil or soft shortening with paper or pastry brush.
   c. *If cake pans are to be floured,* sprinkle each greased pan with a little flour; then shake pan to coat it evenly. Remove excess flour by gently knocking inverted pan on work surface.
   d. *Start heating oven in time* to have it heated to specified temperature when cake batter is ready.
   e. *Chop nuts, prepare fruit, etc. ahead.*
   f. *Sift flour just before you measure it.*
5. Most cakemaking troubles can be traced to:

a. *Not using ingredients called for.* Substitutes are not the same, even though they may look so.

b. *Not using accurate, level measurements.* Small variations in amounts of ingredients may affect volume, texture, or crust.

c. *Not baking in right pan, at right temperature for right time.*

If You Live at a High Altitude

The cake recipes in this chapter have been perfected for use at sea level. They probably need no modification up to an altitude of 2,500 or 3,000 feet. Above that, it is often necessary to adjust slightly the proportions of flour, eggs, leavening, sugar, etc. These adjustments, however, vary from recipe to recipe, and only repeated experiments can give the most successful proportions for each.

If high altitude seems to be causing trouble with your baking and cooking, write to the following sources for recipes developed especially for, and perfected at, high altitudes.

General Foods, Consumer Service Dept., 250 North Street, White Plains, New York

General Mills, Home Service Dept., 400 Second Avenue S., Minneapolis, Minnesota

Colorado Agricultural Experiment Station, Colorado A. & M. College, Fort Collins, Colorado

University of Wyoming, Agricultural Experiment Station, Laramie, Wyoming

Your local utility company

Your state extension service

When using cake mixes at a high altitude, *be sure* to check label for specific baking directions. Some mixes are manufactured especially for use at high altitudes.

To Cut a Cake

Angel, Chiffon, or Spongecake: For fluffy, high wedges, with cake breaker or 2 forks, gently pull pieces apart. Or "saw" cake lightly with very sharp knife.

Layer Cake: Use long, thin, sharp knife. Cut with gentle sawing motion; don't press down. If cutting cake in kitchen, after each cut, wipe off crumbs clinging to knife; rinse knife in hot water.

Cutting Ways: To cut your cake to best advantage, try one of ways diagrammed below. Dotted lines show first cuts to be made.

To Store Cakes

Any cake is at its best served the day it's made. However, if it's stored well, it will still be delicious the second and often the third day. Keep these pointers in mind:

1. *If cake has a cream or whipped-cream filling,* or is frosted with whipped cream, serve at once. Or store in the refrigerator until served, and after serving—it's the safest place.

2. *Wrap fruitcake tightly* in waxed paper, saran, or aluminum foil; then refrigerate. If desired, brush occasionally with fruit juice, cider, port, sherry, or brandy. Or you may saturate a cloth

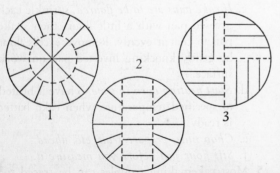
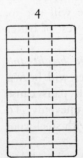
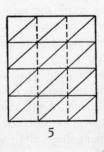

with brandy, etc., and wrap cake in it first.

A home freezer or refrigerator-freezer combination is ideal for storing fruitcake, just be sure cake is freezer-wrapped.

3. *Store all other plain or frosted cakes* in clean covered box, or in a "cake keeper" that has a roomy cover, which fits over plate or tray. Or invert large deep bowl over cake so that bowl rests on cake-plate edge.

4. *After serving cake, keep unserved portion* fresher by covering cut surface with strip of waxed paper held in place with a few toothpicks. As a rule frosted cakes keep more moist than unfrosted layers or squares.

5. *To freeze cakes,* see p. 539.

CAKES YOU CREAM

Here are cake favorites—all made with shortening, all made by the old familiar creaming method, all the kind of cake you make when you have time to enjoy every minute.

Important How-Tos

1. *Where shortening is called for,* you may use any shortening you like except salad oil.

2. *Have shortening at room temperature,* soft enough to mix in easily.

3. *Use any baking powder,* unless recipe indicates a specific kind.

4. *Measure sifted flour, baking powder, and/or soda, salt, and spices into sifter;* sift onto large piece of waxed paper or into bowl.

5. *When cake recipe calls for milk,* use milk, diluted evaporated, or liquefied nonfat dry milk.

6. *If you have an electric mixer—regular or portable—*cakemaking is a special joy. Set dial on mixer at speed recipe suggests. Beat for time indicated, using a timer so you won't underbeat or overbeat. With rubber spatula, scrape bowl and beaters as needed.

7. *If you prefer to mix cake with a spoon,* here's an easy way:
   a. To soft shortening, add sugar in thirds, beating with spoon after each addition until *very light and fluffy.*
   b. Then, if whole eggs or egg yolks are to be added, drop them in, *unbeaten,* one at a time, beating thoroughly after each addition. Batter should be *very creamy.*
   c. Now, unless otherwise directed, add, alternately, flour mixture in fourths and combined milk and extract in thirds, stirring only until batter is smooth. *Do not overmix* at this point; overmixing reduces volume, causes poor texture. Scrape down batter in bowl with rubber spatula as needed; scrape spoon.
   d. When recipes call for beaten egg whites, nuts, or raisins, they are usually folded in last. See Fold In, p. 6.

8. *Pour batter into prepared pan or pans,* dividing it equally if you're using more than one pan. Spread evenly with rubber spatula.

9. *Place cake in oven in this position:*
   a. *Single cake:* Bake on rack in center of oven.
   b. *Two layers:* Bake on rack in center of oven. Don't let pans touch sides of oven or each other.
   c. *Three layers:* Bake on 2 racks, placed so they divide oven in thirds; don't place one pan directly over another.

10. *To test doneness of cake:* When baking time is up (not before), open oven door just enough to test cake quickly. Insert cake tester or toothpick in center of cake; if it comes out clean and dry, cake is done. Or lightly touch center of cake with finger; if cake springs back and leaves no imprint, it's done. If cake is not quite done, bake it a little longer; test again.

11. *To cool cake:* Set it, in pan, on cake rack for 10 to 15 min., depending on size and tenderness of cake. With spatula, loosen cake around edges. Place rack over top of cake; invert pan and rack together; then place rack on table. Lift off pan; peel off paper, if any. Place second rack lightly on bottom of cake; invert both racks with cake to turn cake right side up. Finish cooling.

MIRACLE CAKE

2 cups sifted cake flour	beaten
2½ teasp. baking powder	1 cup minus 2 tablesp. milk
¾ teasp. salt	1 teasp. vanilla extract;
⅓ cup soft shortening	or 1 tablesp. grated
1 cup granulated sugar	orange or lemon
1 medium egg, un-	rind

Start heating oven to 350°F. Grease, then line with waxed paper, bottom of 8″ x 8″ x 2″ pan. Sift flour, baking powder, and salt 3 times.

* In large electric-mixer bowl, with mixer at medium speed, or "cream," mix shortening with sugar, then with egg, until *very light and fluffy* —about 4 min. altogether. At low speed, or "blend," beat in alternately, *just until smooth,* flour mixture in fourths and combined milk and vanilla in thirds. Turn into pan. Bake 45 to 50 min., or until cake tester inserted in center comes out clean. Cool cake as in step 11, p. 439.

This cake may be baked in:

2 1¼″-deep 8″ layer pans at 375°F. 25 min., or until done.
1 9″ x 9″ x 2″ pan at 375°F. 25 to 30 min., or until done.

* *To mix with spoon, see step 7, p. 439.*

Frostings: Choose Sugar-Top, p. 467; Harvest Moon, p. 467; Jiffy Chocolate, p. 463; Dreamy Coffee, p. 462; or Orange Butter Cream, p. 462.
Or fill with Clear Orange or Lemon Filling, p. 461; frost with Snow Peak, p. 462.

Nut: Substitute ¼ teasp. almond extract for vanilla. Quickly fold into batter 1 cup *very finely chopped* walnuts, pecans, Brazil nuts, almonds, or black walnuts. Bake in 8″ x 8″ x 2″ pan. Frost with Quick Fudge Frosting, p. 464, or Harlequin Frosting, p. 462.

Chocolate Layer: Split 2 layers to make 4 layers. Fill and frost with Bittersweet Frosting, p. 464. Or fill and frost 2 layers with Easy Fudge Frosting, p. 462.

Mocha Spice: With flour, sift 2 teasp. cinnamon, ½ teasp. allspice, 1 teasp. nutmeg, and ¼ teasp. ground cloves. Frost with Mocha Butter Cream, p. 462.

Praline: Bake in 9″ x 9″ x 2″ pan. While cake is still warm, frost with Broiled Praline Topping, p. 465.

Caramel Fudge: To egg mixture, add 2 sq. melted unsweetened chocolate. Bake in 2 1¼″-deep 8″ layer pans. Fill and frost with Quick Caramel Frosting, p. 465.

Choco-Nut: Combine ⅓ cup semisweet-chocolate pieces, melted; 1⅓ cups snipped shredded coconut; and ¼ cup water. Turn half of cake batter into prepared 9″ x 9″ x 2″ pan. Sprinkle with half of chocolate mixture; top with rest of batter, then with rest of chocolate mixture. Bake at 375°F. 35 min., or until done.

SILVER WHITE CAKE

2½ cups sifted cake flour	½ cup soft shortening
3 teasp. double-acting baking powder	1 cup granulated sugar
1 teasp. salt	1 cup plus 2 tablesp. milk
4 medium egg whites	1 teasp. vanilla extract
½ cup granulated sugar	¼ teasp. almond extract (optional)

Start heating oven to 375°F. Grease, then line with waxed paper, bottoms of 2 1¼″-deep 8″ or 2 1½″-deep 9″ layer pans. Sift flour, baking powder, and salt 3 times.

* In small electric-mixer bowl, with mixer at high speed, beat egg whites until foamy. Gradually add ½ cup sugar, beating only until mixture holds soft peaks. Set aside. In large bowl, with mixer at medium speed, or "cream," mix shortening with 1 cup sugar until *very light and fluffy*—about 2 min. altogether. Next, at low speed, or "blend," beat in alternately, *just until smooth,* flour mixture in fourths and combined milk and extracts in thirds; then thoroughly beat egg-white mixture into batter. Turn into pans. Bake 25 min., or until cake tester inserted in center comes out clean. Cool as in step 11, p. 439.

* *To mix with spoon, see step 7, p. 439; beat and fold egg-white mixture into batter last.*

Frostings: Fill and frost with Hungarian, p. 464, or Mocha Butter Cream, p. 462. Or fill with Almond-Creamy Custard Filling, Quick Chocolate-Cream Filling, or Clear Lemon Filling, p. 461; frost with Snow Peak, p. 462.

Three-Layer Coconut: Double recipe. Bake in 3 1½″-deep 9″ layer pans at 375°F. 30 to 35 min., or until done. Fill and frost with Princess Frosting, p. 467.

Lady Baltimore: Fill and frost 2 1¼"-deep 8" layers with Lady Baltimore Frosting, p. 466.

Chocolate Marble: Blend 1 sq. melted unsweetened chocolate with 1 tablesp. sugar, 2 tablesp. water, and ¼ teasp. baking soda; cool. Add to one third of Silver White Cake batter, mixing only enough to blend. Alternate plain and chocolate mixtures, by tablespoonfuls, in layer pans. With knife, cut carefully through batter in wide zigzag, to give marbleized effect. Bake at 375°F. 30 to 35 min., or until done. Serve as is; or frost with Jiffy Chocolate Frosting, p. 463.

DEVIL'S-FOOD CAKE

2 cups sifted cake flour	beaten
1 teasp. baking soda	3 sq. unsweetened
¾ teasp. salt	chocolate, melted
½ cup soft shortening*	1¼ cups minus 2
1⅓ cups granulated	tablesp. milk
sugar; or 1½ cups	1 teasp. vanilla extract;
brown sugar, packed	or ¼ teasp. pepper-
2 medium eggs, un-	mint extract

Start heating oven to 350°F. Grease, then line with waxed paper, bottoms of 2 1½"-deep 9" layer pans. Sift flour, soda, and salt 3 times.

† In large electric-mixer bowl, with mixer at medium speed, or "cream," mix shortening with sugar, then with eggs, until *very light and fluffy* —about 4 min. altogether; mix in chocolate. At low speed, or "blend," beat in alternately, *just until smooth,* flour mixture in fourths and combined milk and vanilla in thirds. Turn into pans. Bake 25 to 30 min., or until cake tester inserted in center comes out clean. Cool as in step 11, p. 439.

* With butter, margarine, or lard, decrease milk to 1 cup.

† To mix with spoon, see step 7, p. 439.

Frostings: Fill and frost with Snow Peak, p. 462; Quick Fudge, p. 464; Mocha Butter Cream, p. 462; Dreamy Orange, p. 462; or Penuche, p. 467.

Chocolate-Nut: Quickly fold into batter ¾ cup *very finely chopped* walnuts, pecans, or other nuts. Bake as above.

Or bake in 13" x 9" x 2" pan at 350°F. 45 min., or until done. Frost with Quick Caramel Frosting, p. 465.

Chocolate-Almond: Split each layer into 2 layers; fill with Whipped-Cream Frosting, p. 463; frost with Velvety Frosting, p. 464; top with chopped, toasted almonds.

PECAN CAKE

2 cups pecans	¼ teasp. salt
1 cup seeded raisins	3 egg whites
½ cup sifted all-	⅓ cup granulated
purpose flour	sugar
2 teasp. nutmeg	½ cup soft shortening
½ cup bourbon	¾ cup granulated
1 cup sifted all-	sugar
purpose flour	3 egg yolks, unbeaten
1 teasp. double-acting	20 pecan halves
baking powder	

Day before: Start heating oven to 325°F. Grease, then line with waxed paper, 3½"-deep 9" tube pan. Finely chop pecans; snip raisins in half; mix both with ½ cup flour. Add nutmeg to bourbon. Sift 1 cup flour, baking powder, salt.

* In small electric-mixer bowl, with mixer at high speed, beat egg whites until quite stiff; gradually add ⅓ cup sugar, beating until stiff. Set aside.

In large bowl, with mixer at medium speed, or "cream," mix shortening with ¾ cup sugar and egg yolks until *very light and fluffy* —about 4 min. altogether. At low speed, or "blend," beat in alternately, in 2 parts, *just until smooth,* bourbon and flour mixture. Fold in nut mixture, then beaten whites. Turn into pan; decorate with pecan halves. Bake 1¼ hr., or until cake tester inserted in center comes out clean. Cool in pan on wire rack 30 min.; remove from pan; peel off paper. Keeps well. Needs no frosting. Nice served with grape clusters.

* To mix with spoon, see step 7, p. 439.

PENNY-WISE GOLD CAKE

2 cups sifted cake flour	3 medium egg yolks,
2 teasp. double-acting	beaten very thick
baking powder	1 cup minus 2 tablesp.
½ teasp. salt	milk
½ cup soft shortening*	1 teasp. vanilla extract;
1 cup plus 2 tablesp.	or ½ teasp. orange
granulated sugar	extract; or ¼ teasp.
	nutmeg

Start heating oven to 375°F. Grease, then line with waxed paper, bottom of 9" x 9" x 2" pan. Sift flour, baking powder, and salt 3 times.

† In large electric-mixer bowl, with mixer at medium speed, or "cream," mix shortening with sugar, then with beaten egg yolks, until *very light and fluffy*—about 4 min. altogether. At low speed, or "blend," beat in alternately, *just until smooth,* flour mixture in fourths and combined milk and extract in thirds. Turn into pan. Bake 35 to 40 min., or until cake tester inserted in center comes out clean. Cool as in step 11, p. 439. Nice unfrosted.

This cake may be baked in:

8" x 8" x 2" pan at 350°F. 55 to 60 min., or until done.

2 1¼"-deep 8" layer pans at 375°F. 25 to 30 min., or until done.

* *With butter or margarine decrease milk to ¾ cup.*

† *To mix with spoon, see step 7, p. 439.*

Frostings: Choose Chocolate "Seven Minute," p. 466, or Jiffy Chocolate, p. 463. Or serve slices topped with berries or ice cream and fudge sauce.

WALNUT-CHIP POUNDCAKE

2 cups sifted cake flour	1 cup soft shortening
¼ teasp. salt	1 cup granulated sugar
1 teasp. baking powder	5 eggs, unbeaten
¼ teasp. mace (optional)	1 teasp. vanilla extract
1 pkg. well-chilled semisweet-chocolate pieces	½ cup chopped walnuts

Start heating oven to 300°F. Grease, then line with waxed paper, 10" x 5" x 3" loaf pan. Sift flour, salt, baking powder, mace. Finely grind chocolate, 3 or 4 pieces at a time, in food chopper.

* In large electric-mixer bowl, with mixer at medium speed, or "cream," mix shortening with sugar until *very light and fluffy,* then with eggs, one at a time, until very creamy—about 8 min. altogether. At low speed, or "blend," beat in flour mixture, vanilla, walnuts, and chocolate just until smooth. Turn into pan. Bake 1½ hr., or until cake tester inserted in center comes out

clean. Cool as in step 11, p. 439. Needs no frosting.

* *To mix with spoon, see step 7, p. 439.*

Luxury Loaf: Use ungreased waxed-paper-lined 10" x 5" x 3" loaf pan. Substitute sifted all-purpose flour for cake flour; increase salt to ½ teasp. Add grated rind of 1 orange and ¼ cup orange juice alternately with flour mixture; reduce nuts to ¼ cup. Bake at 300°F. 1 hr. 40 min., or until done.

ELSA'S POUNDCAKE

3 cups sifted cake flour	1 cup soft butter
1½ teasp. double-acting baking powder	1½ cups granulated sugar
⅛ teasp. salt	1 teasp. vanilla extract
¼ to ½ teasp. mace	3 eggs, unbeaten
	½ cup milk

Day before: Start heating oven to 350°F. Grease 3 qt. ring mold on bottom and sides. Sift flour, baking powder, salt, and mace 3 times.

In large electric-mixer bowl, with mixer at medium speed, or "cream," mix butter with sugar and vanilla, then with eggs, until *very light and fluffy*—about 4 min. altogether. Then, at low speed, or "blend," beat in flour mixture alternately with milk in small amounts, beating well after each addition. Turn into ring mold. Bake 50 to 60 min., or until cake tester inserted in center comes out clean. Cool as in step 11, p. 439. Delicious as is or dusted with confectioners' sugar.

Old-fashioned Loaf: Bake in greased 10" x 5" x 3" loaf pan at 350°F. 1 hr. and 10 min., or until done.

HARVEST PRUNE CAKE

2¼ cups sifted all-purpose flour	sugar
	3 medium eggs, unbeaten
2¼ teasp. baking powder	¾ cup buttermilk or sour milk
¾ teasp. baking soda	
1 teasp. salt	1¼ teasp. vanilla extract
½ cup soft shortening	
½ cup soft butter or margarine	1¼ cups finely cut, drained, cooked prunes
1½ cups granulated	

Start heating oven to 375°F. Grease, then line with waxed paper, bottoms of 2 1½"-deep 9" layer pans. Sift flour, baking powder, soda, salt.

* In large electric-mixer bowl, with mixer at medium speed, or "cream," mix shortening and butter with sugar, then with eggs, until *very light and fluffy*—about 4 min. altogether. At low speed, or "blend," beat in alternately, *just until smooth,* flour mixture in fourths and combined buttermilk and vanilla in thirds. With spoon, quickly stir in prunes. Turn into pans. Bake 35 to 40 min., or until cake tester inserted in center comes out clean. Cool as in step 11, p. 439.

* *To mix with spoon, see step 7, p. 439.*

Frostings: Fill and frost with Harvest Moon, p. 466, or Whipped-Cream Frosting, p. 463. Or top wedges with whipped cream to which shredded packaged or fresh grated coconut has been added.

JIM'S APPLESAUCE CAKE

2 cups sifted all-purpose flour	½ teasp. cinnamon
1½ teasp. baking soda	½ teasp. ground cloves
¾ teasp. salt	½ teasp. nutmeg
¾ cup snipped, pitted dates	½ teasp. allspice
¾ cup light or dark raisins	2 tablesp. cocoa
¾ cup chopped walnuts or pecans	1½ cups granulated sugar
½ cup soft shortening	2 eggs, unbeaten
	1½ cups canned applesauce

Day or so before: Start heating oven to 350°F. Grease 3 qt. ring mold on bottom and sides. Sift flour, soda, salt. Toss 2 tablesp. flour mixture with dates, raisins, nuts.

* In large electric-mixer bowl, with mixer at medium speed, or "cream," mix shortening, cinnamon, cloves, nutmeg, allspice, cocoa. Gradually add sugar, beating until fluffy. Add eggs, one at a time, beating well after each addition. At low speed, or "blend," beat in alternately, *just until smooth,* flour mixture and applesauce. Stir in date mixture. Turn into ring mold. Bake 55 to 60 min., or until cake tester inserted in center comes out clean. Cool as in step 11, p. 439. Nice as is or frosted with Orange Butter Cream, p. 462.

* *To mix with spoon, see step 7, p. 439.*

SUSAN'S PINEAPPLE UPSIDE-DOWN CAKE

1¼ cups sifted all-purpose flour	1 No. 2 can pineapple chunks
2 teasp. baking powder	5 maraschino cherries
¼ teasp. salt	⅓ cup soft shortening
3 tablesp. butter or margarine	½ cup granulated sugar
½ cup brown sugar, packed	1 egg, unbeaten
	1 teasp. vanilla extract
	½ cup syrup drained from pineapple

1. Start heating oven to 350°F. Sift flour, baking powder, salt. Melt butter in 8″ x 8″ x 2″ aluminum cake pan over low heat on top burner; remove from heat; sprinkle with brown sugar.

2. Meanwhile, drain pineapple chunks, reserving syrup. On brown-sugar mixture, arrange 6 pineapple chunks to form small daisy. Repeat, making 5 daisies in all. (Extra chunks may be placed between daisies and at edges of pan.) Place drained maraschino cherry in center of each daisy.

3. * In large electric-mixer bowl, with mixer at medium speed, or "cream," mix shortening with sugar, then with egg and vanilla, until *very light and fluffy*—about 4 min. altogether. At low speed, or "blend," beat in alternately, *just until smooth,* flour mixture in thirds and pineapple syrup in halves. Spread batter carefully over pineapple daisies, keeping design intact.

4. Bake cake 1 hr., or until cake tester inserted in center comes out clean. Remove from oven; cool on cake rack 10 min. Then, with spatula, loosen cake from sides of pan. Invert serving plate onto pan; then, with one hand under pan, other on top of plate, turn both until cake rests, with fruit side up, on serving plate. Remove pan. If fruit sticks to pan, lift off with spatula and return to its place on cake.

Serve cake warm; top with cream, whipped cream, or vanilla ice cream. Makes 6 to 8 servings.

* *To mix with spoon, see step 7, p. 439.*

Pineapple Spice: With flour, sift 1 teasp. cinnamon, ½ teasp. nutmeg, ⅛ teasp. ground cloves.

More Upside-down Cakes: In place of pineapple chunks and pineapple syrup, use:

Peach: 1 No. 2½ can peach slices or halves, or apricots, and ½ cup of their syrup

Cocktail: 1 No. 303 can fruit cocktail and ½ cup of its syrup

Cherry: 1 drained No. 2 can pitted sour cherries, packed in water. Substitute milk for ½ cup pineapple syrup

Two Fruit: 1 No. 2 can crushed pineapple, or 1 No. 2 or 2½ can sliced pineapple (4 to 6 slices), and ½ cup pineapple syrup. Decorate with well-drained maraschino cherries, pitted dates, or cooked prunes

P.S. On the label of a nationally known packaged biscuit mix is an excellent recipe for a speedy upside-down cake.

SPICY GINGERBREAD

2½ cups sifted all-purpose flour	½ cup soft shortening
1½ teasp. baking soda	½ cup granulated sugar
½ teasp. ground cloves	1 medium egg, unbeaten
1 teasp. cinnamon	
1 teasp. ginger	1 cup molasses
¾ teasp. salt	1 cup hot water

Start heating oven to 350°F. Grease, then line with waxed paper, bottom of 9″ x 9″ x 2″ pan. Sift flour, soda, cloves, cinnamon, ginger, salt.

*In large electric-mixer bowl, with mixer at medium speed, or "cream," mix shortening with sugar, then with egg, until *very light and fluffy* —about 4 min. altogether; beat in molasses. At low speed, or "blend," beat in alternately, *just until smooth,* flour mixture in fourths and hot water in thirds. Turn into pan. Bake 50 to 55 min., or until cake tester inserted in center comes out clean. Cool as in step 11, p. 439.

* *To mix with spoon, see step 7, p. 439.*

Frostings: Choose Dreamy Chocolate, p. 462; Orange Glaze, p. 465; "Four Minute," p. 466; Sugar Top, p. 467; or Broiled Praline Topping, p. 465. Or split cake to make 2 layers; fill with spicy applesauce; top with whipped cream. Or serve with Gingerbread Top-Offs, p. 384.

Quick Gingerbread: There are excellent packaged gingerbread mixes on the market. Simply add liquid; then bake as directed.

HOLIDAY WHITE FRUITCAKE

2 cups sifted all-purpose flour	1 cup diced preserved citron
1 teasp. baking powder	½ cup diced preserved orange peel
¼ teasp. salt	1½ cups halved candied cherries
1 cup soft shortening	
1 cup granulated sugar	1½ teasp. grated lemon rind
5 medium eggs, unbeaten	
1 tablesp. lemon juice	½ cup sifted all-purpose flour
1 cup slivered, blanched almonds	

Start heating oven to 300°F. Grease, then line with waxed paper, bottom of 10″ x 5″ x 3″ loaf pan. Sift flour, baking powder, salt.

*In large electric-mixer bowl, with mixer at medium speed, or "cream," thoroughly mix shortening with sugar, then with eggs, until *very light and fluffy*—about 4 min. altogether. At low speed, or "blend," beat in flour mixture and lemon juice; then add almonds combined with rest of ingredients, beating just until mixed. Turn into pan. Bake 1¾ hr., or until cake tester inserted in center comes out clean. Cool as in step 11, p. 439. Store as on p. 438.

* *To mix with spoon, see step 7, p. 439.*

DARK CHRISTMAS FRUITCAKE

1 cup currants	purpose flour
3 cups light or dark raisins	1 teasp. nutmeg
	1½ teasp. cinnamon
½ cup diced preserved orange peel	1½ teasp. ground cloves
½ cup diced preserved lemon peel	½ teasp. baking soda
1½ cups diced preserved citron	1 cup soft shortening
	1 cup brown sugar, packed
1 cup halved candied cherries	6 eggs, separated
1 cup diced preserved pineapple	½ sq. unsweetened chocolate, melted
1 cup pecan halves	¼ cup fresh, frozen, or canned lemon juice
1 cup blanched almonds, cut lengthwise	
2 cups sifted all-	¼ cup orange juice

Thoroughly grease 3½″-deep 9″ or 4″-deep 10″ tube pan. Cut heavy waxed paper to fit bottom and sides of pan. Line pan with waxed paper (be sure paper fits snugly), and lightly grease paper. Or use aluminum foil without greasing. In large bowl, thoroughly mix currants, raisins, peels, citron, cherries, pineapple, and nuts with 1 cup flour until all are coated with flour. Start heating oven to 300°F. Sift remaining 1 cup flour with spices and soda.

In large electric-mixer bowl, with mixer at medium speed, or "cream," blend shortening with sugar *until light and fluffy.* Add egg yolks, one at a time, beating thoroughly after each addition. Then add melted chocolate. At low speed, or "blend," beat in alternately, *just until smooth,* flour mixture and fruit juices. When mixture is thoroughly blended, stir by hand into fruit mixture. Beat egg whites until stiff; fold into cake mixture. Turn into tube pan. Bake 2 hr. 20 min., or until cake tester inserted in center comes out clean. Cool completely in pan; remove paper; then store as on p. 430.

FRUITCAKE CONFECTION

½ cup sifted all-purpose flour	3½ cups pecan halves
½ teasp. salt	1 cup diced preserved pineapple
½ teasp. baking powder	½ cup diced preserved orange peel
⅛ teasp. allspice	
⅛ teasp. nutmeg	½ cup diced preserved lemon peel
⅓ cup soft shortening	
3 tablesp. brown sugar	¼ cup diced preserved citron
3 tablesp. honey	
2 eggs, unbeaten	1 cup candied cherries
2 tablesp. orange juice	

Start heating oven to 300°F. With 2 thicknesses waxed paper, line 1¼″-deep 8″ layer pan; then grease. Sift flour, salt, baking powder, allspice, nutmeg.

In large electric-mixer bowl, with mixer at medium speed, or "cream" (or with spoon), mix shortening with sugar, then with honey and eggs, until *very light and fluffy*—about 4 min. altogether. Then, at low speed, or "blend," beat in alternately, *just until smooth,* flour mixture and orange juice.

Spread one third of batter in cake pan. To remaining batter, add pecans and rest of ingredients, reserving a few pecans and cherries; spoon onto batter in pan, packing down batter and leveling top. Decorate with reserved nuts and cherries. Cover with brown paper; tie

securely. Set in shallow pan of hot water (water should be only one fourth depth of layer pan). Bake 1 hr.; remove from water; bake 1 hr. longer, or until cake tester inserted in center comes out clean. When cake is done, brush top with hot corn syrup. Cool completely in pan on wire rack; remove from pan; peel off paper. Keeps up to 2 months wrapped in foil and refrigerated.

BRAZIL-NUT SENSATION

¾ cup sifted all-purpose flour	shelled)
	2 pkg. pitted dates (about 1 lb.)
¾ cup granulated sugar	
½ teasp. baking powder	1 cup well-drained maraschino cherries
½ teasp. salt	
3 cups shelled Brazil nuts (2 lb. un-	3 eggs
	1 teasp. vanilla extract

Start heating oven to 300°F. Grease, then line with waxed paper, 9″ x 5″ x 3″ loaf pan. In sifter, place flour, sugar, baking powder, salt.

In large bowl, place nuts, dates, cherries; sift flour mixture over these; with hands, mix until nuts and fruits are well coated. Beat eggs until foamy; add vanilla; stir well into nut mixture; spread evenly in pan. Bake 1 hr. 45 min., or until cake tester inserted in center comes out clean. Cool as in step 11, p. 439. Wrap in aluminum foil. Refrigerate. Keeps 5 or 6 weeks.

EASY-TO-BAKE FRUITCAKE

Packaged fruitcake mix—complete except for egg and liquid—can be baked in the pan it comes in. It makes a delicious fruitcake. Just follow manufacturer's directions.

QUICK-METHOD CAKES

These cakes are made with shortening too. But they're made by a quick-and-easy, one-bowl method that produces especially fine-grained, rich, and tasty cakes.

Important How-Tos

1. *Have all ingredients at room temperature.* Take eggs, milk, etc., out of refrigerator an hour or so ahead of time. (In hot weather, use eggs and milk right from refrigerator.)

2. *For soft emulsifier-type shortening,* use one of shortenings that come in 3-lb. or 1-lb. cans and whose labels recommend use in quick-method, one-bowl, or quick-mix cakes. Store such shortenings on pantry shelf.

3. *Use exact kind and amount of baking powder called for.* To identify kind, check can label.

4. *Use pans that are of exact size and depth indicated.* See 3a and b, p. 437.

5. *If you're using an electric mixer—regular or portable—*set dial at speed recipe suggests. Beat for time indicated, using a timer so you won't underbeat or overbeat. With rubber spatula, scrape bowl and beaters as needed.

6. *If you prefer to mix cake with a spoon,* while turning bowl, beat briskly with sweeping, round-the-bowl strokes for same time periods as for making cake with an electric mixer. End each stroke with a strong upward movement; take time out to scrape down batter as needed, but count only actual beating time and strokes.

7. *Fill pans; bake cake; then cool as in steps 8 through 11, p. 439.*

Caution: Never try to make cakes that call for creaming by the quick method.

SIMPLICITY 1-EGG CAKE

1¼ cups sifted cake flour	type shortening (see step 2, above)
¾ cup granulated sugar	½ cup milk
2 teasp. double-acting (or 2½ teasp. tartrate or phosphate) baking powder	1 teasp. vanilla extract; or 1 tablesp. grated orange or lemon rind
½ teasp. salt	1 medium egg, unbeaten
⅓ cup soft emulsifier-	

Start heating oven to 375°F. Grease, then line with waxed paper, bottom of 8" x 8" x 2" pan.

Into large electric-mixer bowl, sift flour, sugar, baking powder, salt. Drop in shortening; pour in milk, vanilla. *With mixer at low to medium speed, beat 1½ min., scraping bowl and beaters as needed. Add egg; beat 1½ min. Turn into pan. Bake 25 min., or until cake tester inserted in center comes out clean. Cool as in step 11, p. 439.

* *To mix with spoon, beat briskly for same time periods as above, allowing 100 full, round-the-bowl strokes per minute.*

Frostings: Choose Broiled Honey-Coconut, p. 465; Dreamy Orange, p. 462; Sugar-Top, p. 467; or Penuche, p. 467.

Chocolate-Walnut: Substitute ¼ teasp. almond extract for vanilla. Into batter, fold ½ cup *very finely chopped* walnuts. Frost with Dreamy Chocolate Frosting, p. 462.

LUSCIOUS COCONUT-LAYER CAKE

2¼ cups sifted cake flour	½ cup soft emulsifier-type shortening (see step 2, above)
1½ cups granulated sugar	¾ cup milk
4 teasp. double-acting (or 5½ teasp. tartrate or phosphate) baking powder	1 teasp. vanilla extract
	¾ teasp. orange extract
	4 medium egg whites, unbeaten
1 teasp. salt	¼ cup milk

Start heating oven to 350°F. Grease, then line with waxed paper, bottoms of 2 1½"-deep 9" layer pans.

Into large electric-mixer bowl, sift flour, sugar, baking powder, salt. Drop in shortening; pour in ¾ cup milk and extracts. *With mixer at low to medium speed, beat 2 min., scraping bowl and beaters as needed. Add egg whites and ¼ cup milk; beat 2 min. Turn into pans. Bake 20 min., or until cake tester inserted in center comes out clean. Cool as in step 11, p. 439.

* *To mix with spoon, beat briskly for same time periods as above, allowing 100 full, round-the-bowl strokes per minute.*

Frostings: Fill and frost with Princess, p. 467. Or fill with Clear Lemon Filling, p. 461, or Quick Pineapple-Cream Filling, p. 461; frost with Snow Peak, p. 462.

CARNIVAL CAKE

2¼ cups sifted cake flour	type shortening (see step 2, above)
1½ cups granulated sugar	½ cup milk
2½ teasp. double-acting baking powder	1 teasp. orange extract
	½ teasp. almond extract
1 teasp. salt	3 medium eggs, unbeaten
¾ cup soft emulsifier-	¼ cup milk

Start heating oven to 375°F. Grease, then line with waxed paper, bottoms of 2 1½″-deep 9″ layer pans.

Into large electric-mixer bowl, sift flour, sugar, baking powder, salt. Drop in shortening; pour in ½ cup milk, extracts; add 1 egg. * With mixer at low to medium speed, beat 2 min., scraping bowl and beaters as needed. Add ¼ cup milk, 2 eggs; beat 2 min. Turn into pans. Bake 25 min., or until cake tester inserted in center comes out clean. Cool as in step 11, p. 439.

To mix with spoon, beat briskly for same time periods as above, allowing 100 full, round-the-bowl strokes per minute.

Frostings: Fill and frost with Penuche, p. 467, or Quick Caramel, p. 465.

LIGHT-GOLDEN CAKE

2¼ cups sifted cake flour	type shortening (see step 2, p. 446)
1½ cups granulated sugar	¾ cup milk
1 teasp. salt	1½ teasp. vanilla extract
3 teasp. double-acting baking powder	¼ cup milk
½ cup soft emulsifier-	2 medium eggs, unbeaten

Start heating oven to 350°F. Grease, then line with waxed paper, bottoms of 2 1½″-deep 9″ layer pans.

Into large electric-mixer bowl, sift flour, sugar, salt, baking powder. Drop in shortening; pour in ¾ cup milk, vanilla. *With mixer at medium speed, beat 2 min., scraping bowl and beaters as needed. Add ¼ cup milk, eggs; beat 2 min. Turn into pans. Bake 25 to 30 min., or until cake tester inserted in center comes out clean. Cool as in step 11, p. 439.

This cake may be baked in:

13″ x 9″ x 2″ pan at 350°F. 35 to 40 min., or until done.

To mix with spoon, beat briskly for same time periods as above, allowing 150 full, round-the-bowl strokes per minute.

Frostings: Fill and frost with Marshmallow "Seven Minute," p. 466, or Easy Fudge, p. 463.

Spicecake: With flour, sift 1 teasp. cinnamon, ½ teasp. ground cloves, ¼ teasp. allspice. When you drop in shortening, pour in 1 tablesp. molasses. Bake in 2 1½″-deep 9″ layer pans at 375°F. 25 min., or until done. Or bake in 13″ x 9″ x 2″ pan at 375°F. 35 min., or until done.

Fill and frost with Lemon Butter Cream, p. 462, or Quick Caramel Frosting, p. 465.

Fresh Orange: With flour, sift ¼ teasp. baking soda. Substitute 1 teasp. grated orange rind for vanilla, ¼ cup unstrained orange juice for ¼ cup milk. Bake in 2 1½″-deep 9″ layer pans at 350°F. 25 to 30 min.

Fill with Quick Orange-Cream Filling, p. 461; frost with Snow-Peak Frosting, p. 462. Or fill and frost with Tropical Whip Frosting, p. 463.

APRICOT FUNNY CAKE

1 unbaked 9″ or 10″ pie shell, pp. 408 to 410	baking powder
	½ teasp. salt
1 cup dried apricots	¾ cup granulated sugar
½ cup granulated sugar	¼ cup soft emulsifier-type shortening (see step 2, p. 446)
2 tablesp. butter or margarine	
1¼ cups sifted cake flour	½ cup milk
	1 teasp. vanilla extract
1 teasp. double-acting	1 egg, unbeaten

Day before if desired: Make unbaked 9″ or 10″ pie shell with high fluted edge. Refrigerate.

On the day: Cover apricots with water; cook until very tender; drain well, reserving liquid. Press apricots through food mill or sieve; measure ½ cup purée; combine with ½ cup apricot liquid, ½ cup sugar; boil 1 min. Stir in butter; set aside to cool to lukewarm.

Start heating oven to 350°F. Into large electric-mixer bowl, sift flour, baking powder, salt, ¾ cup sugar. Drop in shortening; pour in milk, vanilla. * With mixer at low to medium speed, beat 2 min., scraping bowl and beaters as needed. Add egg; beat 1 min.

Turn batter into unbaked pie shell; gently pour lukewarm apricot sauce over top of batter. Bake 50 to 55 min. (Sauce will form layer between cake and pie shell.)

Serve warm, as is or topped with ice cream or whipped cream.

To mix cake with spoon, beat briskly for same time periods as above, allowing 150 full, round-the-bowl strokes per minute.

Chocolate: Replace apricot sauce with this sauce: Cook 1 sq. unsweetened chocolate with ½ cup water over low heat, stirring, until melted. Stir in ⅔ cup granulated sugar. Bring to boil. Remove at once from heat; stir in ¼ cup butter or margarine and 1 teasp. vanilla extract until blended.

Butterscotch: Replace apricot sauce with this sauce: Combine ¼ cup butter or margarine; ½ cup brown sugar, packed; 2 tablesp. white corn syrup. Bring to boil over low heat, stirring. Add 3 tablesp. water; then boil 1 to 2 min. Remove from heat; stir in ½ teasp. vanilla extract.

SUSAN'S WALNUT CAKE

3 cups sifted cake flour	(see step 2, p. 446)
2 teasp. double-acting baking powder	4 medium eggs, unbeaten
1¾ cups granulated sugar	¾ cup milk
1½ teasp. salt	2 teasp. vanilla extract
1 cup soft emulsifier-type shortening	1 cup very finely chopped walnuts

1. Start heating oven to 375°F. Grease, then line with waxed paper, bottom of 3½"-deep 9" tube pan.
2. Into large electric-mixer bowl, sift flour, baking powder, sugar, salt. Drop in shortening, 2 eggs; pour in milk, vanilla.
3. *With electric mixer at medium speed, beat 2 min., scraping bowl and beaters as needed. Add 2 eggs; beat 2 min. Fold in chopped nuts.
4. Turn into pan. Bake 1 hr., or until cake tester inserted in center comes out clean. Cool as in step 11, p. 439.
5. Brush with Fruit Glaze, p. 465. Or serve unfrosted.

To mix cake with spoon, beat briskly for same time periods as above, allowing 150 full, round-the-bowl strokes per minute.

WONDER GOLD CAKE

2¼ cups sifted cake flour	type shortening (see step 2, p. 446)
2 teasp. double-acting baking powder	5 medium egg yolks, unbeaten
¾ teasp. salt	1 teasp. vanilla extract; or 2 teasp. grated orange rind
1 cup granulated sugar	
½ teasp. mace	
½ cup soft emulsifier-	¾ cup milk

Start heating oven to 350°F. Grease, then line with waxed paper, bottom of 10" x 5" x 3" loaf pan.

Into large electric-mixer bowl, sift flour, baking powder, salt, sugar, mace. Drop in shortening, egg yolks; pour in vanilla, half of milk. *With mixer at low to medium speed, beat until all flour is dampened; then beat 2 min., scraping bowl and beaters as needed. Add rest of milk; beat 1 min. Turn into pan. Bake 1 hr. to 1 hr. 10 min., or until cake tester inserted in center comes out clean. (Top of cake will crack.) Cool as in step 11, p. 439.

Serve unfrosted, sprinkled with confectioners' sugar; or frost top with ½ recipe Orange or Chocolate Butter Cream, p. 462.

To mix with spoon, beat briskly for same time periods as above, allowing 150 full, round-the-bowl strokes per minute.

SUSAN'S 3-LAYER FUDGE CAKE

2 cups sifted cake flour	chocolate, melted
2 cups granulated sugar	¾ cup milk
1 teasp. salt	1 teasp. vanilla extract
1½ teasp. baking soda	½ teasp. double-acting baking powder
½ cup soft emulsifier-type shortening (see step 2, p. 446)	½ cup milk
3 sq. unsweetened	3 medium eggs, unbeaten

1. Start heating oven to 350°F. Grease, then line with waxed paper, bottoms of 3 1¼"-deep 8" layer pans.
2. Into large electric-mixer bowl, sift flour, sugar, salt, soda. Drop in shortening; pour in chocolate, ¾ cup milk, vanilla.
3. *With electric mixer at medium speed, beat 2 min., scraping bowl and beaters as needed. Stir in baking powder. Add ½ cup milk, eggs; beat 2 min.
4. Turn into pans. Bake 35 to 40 min., or until cake tester inserted in center comes out clean. Cool as in step 11, p. 439.

To mix with spoon, beat briskly for same time periods as above, allowing 150 full, round-the-bowl strokes per minute.

Frostings: Fill and frost with "Seven-Minute," p. 466, or double recipe of Mocha Butter Cream, p. 462.

Two-Layer Fudge Cake: Bake in 2 1½"-deep 9" layer pans at 350°F. 35 to 40 min., or until done. Fill and frost with Chocolate Fluff, p. 464.

CHOCOLATE POUNDCAKE

2¾ cups sifted cake flour	Milk*
¾ teasp. cream of tartar	1 teasp. vanilla extract
½ teasp. baking soda	3 medium eggs, unbeaten
1½ teasp. salt	1 egg yolk, unbeaten
1¾ cups granulated sugar	3 sq. unsweetened chocolate, melted
1 cup soft shortening	Confectioners' sugar

Start heating oven to 350°F. Line with waxed paper bottom of 3½"-deep 9" tube pan.

Into large electric-mixer bowl, sift flour, cream of tartar, soda, salt, sugar. Drop in shortening; pour in milk, vanilla. †With mixer at low to medium speed, beat 2 min., scraping bowl and beaters as needed. Add eggs, egg yolk, chocolate; beat 1 min. Turn into pan. Bake 1 hr. 10 min., or until cake tester inserted in center comes out clean. Cool as in step 11, p. 439.

Just before cutting: Spoon confectioners' sugar into ridges on top of cake.

* *With butter, margarine, or lard, use ⅔ cup milk; with other shortenings, use 1 cup minus 2 tablesp. milk.*

† *To mix with spoon, beat briskly for same time periods as above, allowing 150 full, round-the-bowl strokes per minute.*

Chocolate-Nut: Into batter, fold ¾ cup *finely chopped* walnuts, pecans, or other nuts.

BANANA CREAM CAKE

2¼ cups sifted cake flour	½ cup soft emulsifier-type shortening (see step 2, p. 446)
1¼ cups granulated sugar	2 medium eggs, unbeaten
2½ teasp. double-acting baking powder	1½ cups well-mashed ripe bananas (4 or 5)
½ teasp. baking soda	1 teasp. vanilla extract
½ teasp. salt	

Start heating oven to 375°F. Grease, then line with waxed paper, bottoms of 2 1¼"-deep 8" layer pans.

Into large electric-mixer bowl, sift flour, sugar, baking powder, soda, salt. Drop in shortening, eggs; add ½ cup mashed bananas. *With mixer at low to medium speed, beat 2 min., scraping bowl and beaters as needed. Add 1 cup mashed bananas, vanilla; beat 1 min. Turn into pans. Bake 25 min., or until cake tester inserted in center comes out clean. Cool as in step 11, p. 439.

* *To mix with spoon, beat briskly for same time periods as above, allowing 150 full, round-the-bowl strokes per minute.*

Frosting: Fill and frost with Whipped-Cream Frosting, p. 463; garnish with thin slices of fully ripe bananas dipped into fruit juice.

Banana-Spice Layer: With flour, sift ⅛ teasp. ground cloves, 1¼ teasp. cinnamon, ½ teasp. nutmeg.

Note: To mash bananas, slice them; then beat with fork, egg beater, or electric mixer till smooth and creamy.

HARVEST RIBBON CAKE

2½ cups sifted cake flour	½ cup milk
1 teasp. salt	5 egg whites, unbeaten
1⅔ cups granulated sugar	Yellow food color
⅔ cup soft emulsifier-type shortening (see step 2, p. 446)	1 tablesp. grated orange rind
¾ cup milk	½ teasp. cinnamon
4½ teasp. double-acting baking powder	⅛ teasp. ground cloves
1 teasp. vanilla extract	⅛ teasp. baking soda
	2 tablesp. cocoa
	2 tablesp. water

Start heating oven to 360°F. Grease, then line with waxed paper, bottoms of 3 1¼"-deep 8" layer pans.

Into large electric-mixer bowl, sift flour, salt, sugar. Drop in shortening; pour in ¾ cup milk. *With mixer at low to medium speed, beat 2 min., scraping bowl and beaters as needed. Stir in baking powder. Add vanilla, ½ cup milk, egg whites; beat 2 min.

Divide batter into three parts. For *yellow layer,* add a few drops yellow food color and grated orange rind. For *chocolate layer,* add cinnamon; cloves; soda; and cocoa, blended with water. Turn the 3 batters into the 3 layer pans. Bake 20 to 25 min., or until cake tester inserted in center comes out clean. Cool as in step 11, p. 439.

* To mix with spoon, beat briskly for same time periods as above, allowing 150 full, round-the-bowl strokes per minute.

Frosting: Fill and frost with Harvest Moon, p. 466.

Christmas Ribbon: Substitute pink food color for yellow, ½ teasp. almond extract for orange rind. Fill and frost with "Seven-Minute" Frosting, p. 466, tinted green.

ELEGANT DEVIL'S-FOOD CAKE

2 cups sifted cake flour	1 teasp. salt
1¾ cups granulated sugar	¾ cup soft emulsifier-type shortening
¾ cup cocoa	(see step 2, p. 446)
1¼ teasp. baking soda	¾ cup milk
½ teasp. double-acting (or ¾ teasp. tartrate or phosphate) baking powder	1 teasp. vanilla extract
	½ cup milk
	3 medium eggs, unbeaten

Start heating oven to 350°F. Grease, then line with waxed paper, bottoms of 2 1½"-deep 9" layer pans.

Into large electric-mixer bowl, sift flour, sugar, cocoa, soda, baking powder, salt. Drop in shortening; pour in ¾ cup milk, vanilla. *With mixer at low to medium speed, beat 2½ min., scraping bowl and beaters as needed. Add ½ cup milk, eggs; beat 2½ min. Turn into pans. Bake 35 min., or till cake tester inserted in center comes out clean. Cool as in step 11, p. 439.

* To mix cake with spoon, beat briskly for same time periods as above, allowing 100 full, round-the-bowl strokes per minute.

Frostings: Fill and frost with Princess, p. 467, or Dreamy Coffee, p. 462.

CHIFFON, SPONGE, AND ANGEL-FOOD CAKES

These cakes are all favorites in the spongecake family—chiffon being the newest member. All are wonderfully light and lovely.

Important How-Tos

1. *Be sure to use ungreased cake pan* if recipe so directs. Then batter can cling to sides of pan, rise to full, glorious height. Keep pans well scrubbed and free from grease.

2. *About an hour before using, remove eggs from refrigerator* and separate. (If you're not using egg yolks, cover with water; refrigerate. If you're not using egg whites, just refrigerate.) Whites beat up more easily and produce a finer-textured, lighter cake when at the temperature of a cool room.

3. *Use any type of baking powder* unless recipe indicates a specific kind.

4. *For correct way to fold one ingredient into another,* see Fold In, p. 6.

5. *To test chiffon, sponge, or angel cake for doneness* at end of baking time, see step 10, p. 439. When cake is done, remove from oven immediately.

6. *To cool cake,* invert it and let hang in tube pan for 1 hr., or until cold, resting pan on center tube, which protrudes above top edge of pan, or on side "ears." If pan has neither "ears" nor extended center tube, place tube over funnel or neck of bottle. Or rest edges of inverted pan on other pans to allow air to circulate. Cake will shrink if removed from pan while warm.

7. *To remove cooled cake,* turn pan right side up. Insert spatula between cake and side of pan until tip touches bottom. Then press gently against side of pan, cutting away clinging cake. Pull spatula out; repeat all around edge and tube. (Use slender knife to loosen cake from center tube.) Then invert cake on cake rack and lift off pan.

Serving Chiffon, Sponge, and Angel-Food Cakes

1. Tube cake:
   a. Frost with Strawberry, Pineapple, or Orange Glaze, p. 465.
   b. Frost with Snow-Peak Frosting, p. 462.
   c. Sprinkle with confectioners' sugar mixed with a little mace or nutmeg.
   d. Serve cake wedges topped with Frosty Sauce, p. 368; custard sauce; crushed berries; sliced fruit; or fudge or butterscotch sauce.

2. Cake layers or tube cake, split into 2 or 3 layers:

   a. Fill and frost with Whipped-Cream Frosting or a variation, p. 463. Sprinkle with grated chocolate, chopped nuts, drained canned crushed pineapple, or shredded coconut.

   b. Fill with jam or jelly; frost with whipped cream or Snow-Peak Frosting, p. 462.

   c. Fill with crushed berries; Clear-Lemon Filling or a variation, p. 461; or Dark-Chocolate Filling, p. 461. Frost with whipped cream.

BIG ORANGE CHIFFON

5 medium egg yolks, unbeaten	3 teasp. baking powder
1 cup egg whites (7 or 8 medium eggs)	1 teasp. salt
2¼ cups sifted cake flour*	½ cup salad oil
1½ cups granulated sugar	3 tablesp. grated orange rind
	¾ cup orange juice
	½ teasp. cream of tartar

1. About 1 hr. ahead, set out yolks, whites.
2. When ready to make cake, start heating oven to 325°F. Into large electric-mixer bowl, sift flour, sugar, baking powder, salt. Make well in flour mixture; pour salad oil in well. Add egg yolks, orange rind, orange juice. With mixer at medium speed (or with spoon), beat until smooth.
3. Measure egg whites into another large bowl; add cream of tartar. With mixer at high speed (or with egg beater), beat whites until they hold *very stiff peaks. Do not underbeat.* (They should be stiffer than for angel-food cake or meringue.)
4. Slowly pour egg-yolk mixture over whites, folding in mixture gently with rubber spatula or spoon. *Do not stir.* Continue folding until yolk mixture is just blended.
5. Turn batter into *ungreased* 4″-deep 10″ tube pan. Bake at 325°F. 55 min., then at 350°F. 10 to 15 min., or until cake tester inserted in center comes out clean. Cool and remove as in steps 6 and 7, p. 450.

You may substitute 2 cups sifted all-purpose flour for cake flour; if so, use 7 egg yolks instead of 5.

Frostings: Serve unfrosted; or frost with Orange Butter Cream, p. 462. Or serve as on p. 450.

Almond Chiffon: Substitute 1 teasp. each vanilla and almond extracts for orange rind, water for orange juice.

Lemon Gold: Use 6 egg yolks and 6 egg whites. Substitute 1 teasp. grated lemon rind and 2 teasp. lemon juice for orange rind, water for orange juice. Bake at 325°F. 1 hr. 10 min. Frost with Lemon Butter Cream, p. 462.

Banana Chiffon: Substitute 1 cup mashed ripe bananas (2 or 3 bananas) for ¾ cup orange juice. Substitute 1 tablesp. lemon juice for grated orange rind.

Pineapple Chiffon: Substitute 2 teasp. grated lemon rind for orange rind, ¾ cup pineapple juice for orange juice. Just before pouring batter into pan, fold in 1 cup shredded coconut. Frost top with Pineapple Glaze, p. 465, letting it run down sides.

LITTLE ORANGE CHIFFON

2 egg yolks	½ teasp. salt
½ cup egg whites (4 eggs)	¼ cup salad oil
1 cup plus 2 tablesp. sifted cake flour	1½ tablesp. grated orange rind
¾ cup granulated sugar	¼ cup plus 2 tablesp. orange juice
1½ teasp. baking powder	¼ teasp. cream of tartar

Make and cool as in Big Orange Chiffon, above. This cake may be baked in:

   1 8″ x 8″ x 2″ pan at 350°F. 30 to 35 min., or until done.

   1 9″ x 9″ x 2″ pan at 350°F. 30 to 35 min., or until done.

   1 3½″-deep 9″ tube pan at 325°F. 50 to 55 min., or until done.

LOVELIGHT CHIFFON LAYER CAKE

2 eggs, separated	baking powder
1½ cups granulated sugar	1 teasp. salt
2¼ cups sifted cake flour	⅓ cup salad oil
3 teasp. double-acting	1 cup milk
	1½ teasp. vanilla extract

1. About 1 hr. ahead, set out separated eggs.
2. When ready to make cake, start heating oven to 350°F. Grease generously, then dust with flour, 2 1½"-deep 8" or 9" layer pans.
3. Beat egg whites until frothy. Gradually beat in ½ cup sugar; continue beating until stiff and glossy enough to stand in peaks.
4. Into large electric-mixer bowl, sift remaining 1 cup sugar, flour, baking powder, salt. Pour in oil, half of milk. *With mixer at medium speed, beat 1 min., scraping sides and bottom of bowl as needed. Add remaining milk, egg yolks, extract; beat 1 min.
5. Fold beaten egg whites into batter. Turn into pans. Bake 30 to 35 min. Cool in pans on wire racks about 10 min. Remove from pans; cool on racks.

This cake may be baked in:

13" x 9" x 2" pan at 350°F. 35 to 40 min., or until done.

To mix cake with spoon, beat briskly for same time periods as above, allowing 150 full, round-the-bowl strokes per minute.

Frostings: Fill with Clear Orange Filling, p. 461; frost with Snow Peak, p. 462; sprinkle generously with shredded coconut. Or split each layer into 2 layers; fill with Luscious Cream Filling, p. 461; frost with Yummy Chocolate, p. 464.

Chocolate 2-Egg Chiffon Layer: Decrease flour to 1¾ cups. Substitute ¾ teasp. baking soda for baking powder. Decrease salt to ¾ teasp. Substitute buttermilk for milk. Omit extract. With egg yolks, add 2 sq. melted unsweetened chocolate. Bake in 2 1½"-deep 8" or 9" layer pans as above. Or bake in 13" x 9" x 2" pan at 350°F. 40 to 45 min. Split each layer into 2 layers; fill and frost with Chocolate Fluff, p. 464.

LUSCIOUS SPONGECAKE

¾ cup egg whites (6 eggs)	½ teasp. salt
½ cup egg yolks (6 eggs)	1½ cups sifted granulated sugar
1⅓ cups sifted cake flour	1 teasp. cream of tartar
½ teasp. double-acting baking powder	¼ cup water
	1 teasp. vanilla extract
	1 teasp. lemon extract

1. About 1 hr. ahead, set out whites, yolks.
2. When ready to make cake, start heating oven

to 375°F. Into small bowl, sift flour, baking powder, salt, 1 cup sugar.
3. In large electric-mixer bowl, combine egg whites and cream of tartar. With mixer at high speed (or with egg beater or flat wire whip), beat whites until soft mounds begin to form. Then beat in remaining ½ cup sugar, 2 tablesp. at a time; beat until very stiff peaks are formed. Do not underbeat.
4. Combine yolks, water, extracts. With spoon, stir into sifted flour mixture; beat ½ min., just to blend (about 75 beating strokes).
5. Then, with spoon, fold yolk mixture into beaten whites until blended (about 40 folding strokes). Turn batter into ungreased 4"-deep 10" tube pan; cut gently through batter to remove large air bubbles.
6. Bake about 35 min. Cool and remove as in steps 6 and 7, p. 450. Serve as on p. 450.

HOT-MILK SPONGECAKE

3 eggs	1 cup granulated sugar
1 cup sifted cake flour	¼ teasp. grated lemon rind
1 teasp. double-acting baking powder	2 teasp. lemon juice
¼ teasp. salt	6 tablesp. hot milk

1. About 1 hr. ahead, set out eggs.
2. When ready to make cake, start heating oven to 350°F. Sift flour, baking powder, and salt 3 times.
3. In large electric-mixer bowl, with mixer at high speed (or with egg beater), beat eggs until *very thick and light*—about 5 min. Gradually add sugar, beating constantly. Beat in lemon rind and juice.
4. With rubber spatula or spoon, fold in flour mixture, a small amount at a time. Quickly stir in hot (not boiling) milk.
5. *Immediately* turn batter into *ungreased* 3½"-deep 9" tube pan or 10" x 5" x 3" loaf pan. Bake 35 min., or until cake tester inserted in center comes out clean. Cool and remove as in steps 6 and 7, p. 450.

This cake may also be baked in the following pans, lined on bottom with waxed paper:

2 1¼"-deep 8" layer pans at 375°F. 20 min., or until done.
1 9" x 9" x 2" pan at 375°F. 20 min., or until done.

Frostings: Serve unfrosted; or frost with one of glazes, p. 465. Or fill and top with sweetened sliced peaches or strawberries and whipped cream.

Spice Spongecake: With flour, sift 1 teasp. cinnamon, ½ teasp. nutmeg, and ¼ teasp. ground cloves.

Boston Cream Pie: Bake in 2 1¼″-deep 8″ layer pans as above. Fill with Luscious Cream Filling, p. 461; frost top with Thin Chocolate Coating, p. 465.

Washington Pie: Bake in 2 1¼″-deep 8″ layer pans as above. When cake is cool, fill with jelly. Sprinkle top with confectioners' sugar.

DAFFODIL CAKE

1¼ cups egg whites (about 10 medium eggs)	tartar
	½ teasp. vanilla extract
4 medium egg yolks	1 cup sifted granulated sugar
1¼ cups sifted cake flour	1 teasp. grated orange rind
½ cup sifted granulated sugar	2 tablesp. orange juice
¼ teasp. salt	2 tablesp. granulated sugar
1½ teasp. cream of	

1. About 1 hr. ahead, set out whites, yolks.
2. When ready to make cake, start heating oven to 375°F. Sift flour with ½ cup sugar 4 times.
3. In large electric-mixer bowl, with mixer at high speed (or with egg beater or flat wire whip), beat egg whites with salt, cream of tartar, and vanilla until stiff enough to hold soft, moist peaks. With mixer at same speed, beat in 1 cup sugar, sprinkling ¼ cup at a time over egg whites. Beat until sugar is just blended. (To beat by hand, beat 25 strokes, or turns, after each addition.)
4. Next sift in flour mixture by fourths, folding in each addition with 15 complete fold-over strokes of spoon or rubber spatula and turning bowl often. After all flour has been folded in, give batter 10 to 20 extra strokes.
5. In another bowl, beat egg yolks with orange rind and juice and 2 tablesp. sugar until *very thick and light*. With 15 fold-over strokes of rubber spatula or spoon, fold in one third of white batter.
6. In *ungreased* 4″-deep 10″ tube pan, alternate

yellow and white batters to give marbleized effect, with white batter on top. Bake 35 to 40 min., or until cake tester inserted in center comes out clean. Cool and remove as in steps 6 and 7, p. 450.

Frostings: Sprinkle top with confectioners' sugar. Or thinly frost with Orange Butter Cream, p. 462; or frost with Snow Peak, p. 462, tinted pale yellow.

SUSAN'S ANGEL-FOOD CAKE

1¼ cups egg whites (10 to 12 eggs)	1¼ teasp. cream of tartar
1 cup plus 2 tablesp. sifted cake flour	1 teasp. vanilla extract
½ cup sifted granulated sugar	¼ teasp. almond extract
¼ teasp. salt	1 cup sifted granulated sugar

1. About 1 hr. ahead, set out egg whites.
2. When ready to make cake, start heating oven to 375°F. Sift flour with ½ cup sugar 4 times.
3. In large electric-mixer bowl, combine egg whites, salt, cream of tartar, extracts. With electric mixer at high speed (or with egg beater or flat wire whip), beat whites until stiff enough to hold soft, moist peaks.
4. With mixer at same speed, beat in 1 cup sugar, sprinkling ¼ cup at a time over egg whites. Beat until sugar is just blended. (To beat by hand, beat 25 strokes, or turns, after each addition.)
5. Stop mixer. Sift in flour mixture by fourths, folding in each addition with 15 complete fold-over strokes of spoon, rubber spatula, or wire whip and turning bowl often. After all flour has been folded in, give batter 10 to 20 extra strokes.
6. Gently push batter into *ungreased* 4″-deep 10″ tube pan. With spatula, cut through batter once without lifting spatula out of batter.
7. Bake 30 to 35 min., or until cake tester inserted in center comes out clean. Cool and remove as in steps 6 and 7, p. 450. Serve as on p. 450.

Macaroon: After sifting flour with sugar, add ⅓ cup finely snipped coconut; toss with fork. Omit vanilla; increase almond extract to 1¼ teasp.

Orange: After sifting flour with sugar, add 3 tablesp. grated orange rind; toss with fork. Substitute 1 teasp. orange extract for vanilla and almond.

JELLY ROLL

4 eggs	¼ teasp. salt
¾ cup sifted cake flour	¾ cup granulated sugar
¾ teasp. double-acting baking powder	1 teasp. vanilla extract
	1 cup tart jelly or jam

1. About 1 hr. ahead, set out eggs.
2. When ready to make cake, start heating oven to 400°F. With waxed paper, line bottom of 15″ x 10″ x 1″ jelly-roll pan. Sift flour, baking powder, salt.
3. In small electric-mixer bowl, with mixer at high speed (or with egg beater), beat eggs until foamy. Beat rapidly, adding sugar slowly; continue beating until *very thick and light-colored.* With rubber spatula or spoon, fold in flour, vanilla. Turn into pan, spreading batter evenly. Bake 13 min., or until light brown.
4. Lightly dust clean dish towel with confectioners' sugar. When cake is done, with spatula, loosen it from sides of pan; invert onto towel. Lift off pan; carefully peel off paper; with very sharp knife cut crisp edges from cake. Roll up cake very gently, from narrow end, rolling towel up in it (this prevents cake's sticking). Cool about 10 min.
5. Unroll so cake will be on towel. Spread cake with jelly to within ½″ of edges. Start rolling up cake from narrow end by folding edge of cake over, then tucking it under; continue rolling cake, lifting towel higher and higher with one hand as you guide roll with other hand. Finish with open end of cake on underside. Wrap towel tightly around roll to shape it. Finish cooling jelly roll on wire rack. Sprinkle with more confectioners' sugar.

Serve cut into 1″ crosswise slices, just as is or topped with vanilla ice cream. Makes 6 to 8 servings.

Cranberry Cake Roll: Leave jelly roll rolled up until cold. Meanwhile, make cranberry filling: Combine 1 cup canned whole-cranberry sauce with ½ unpeeled orange, ground fine, and ¼ cup granulated sugar. Sprinkle 2 teasp. un-flavored gelatine over 2 tablesp. cold water in glass measuring cup to soften; place over hot water until gelatine dissolves; then stir into cranberry mixture. Refrigerate until firm. Unroll jelly roll; spread with cranberry mixture; roll up. Refrigerate, with open end on underside, until served (no longer than 1 hr.).

At serving time, frost top with whipped cream or 1 8-oz. pkg. cream cheese, softened.

Susan's Strawberry-Cream Roll: Leave jelly roll rolled up until cold; unroll. Whip 1 cup heavy cream; fold in ¼ cup granulated sugar and ½ teasp. vanilla extract. Spread on cake; sprinkle with 2 cups sliced strawberries (about 1 pt.). Roll up. Refrigerate, with open end on underside, until served (not longer than 1 hr.).

At serving time, sprinkle with confectioners' sugar.

SUSAN'S CHOCOLATE ROLL

4 eggs	1 teasp. vanilla extract
½ cup sifted cake flour	2 tablesp. granulated sugar
½ teasp. baking powder	¼ teasp. baking soda
¼ teasp. salt	3 tablesp. cold water
2 sq. unsweetened chocolate	Confectioners' sugar
¾ cup sifted granulated sugar	1 cup heavy cream
	¼ teasp. almond extract

1. About 1 hr. ahead, set out eggs.
2. When ready to make cake, start heating oven to 375°F. Grease, then line with waxed paper, bottom of 15″ x 10″ x 1″ jelly-roll pan (or large open roasting pan, 17½″ x 11½″ x 2¼″). Sift flour, baking powder, and salt onto piece of waxed paper. Melt chocolate (see p. 6).
3. Break eggs into large electric-mixer bowl; sift ¾ cup sugar over them; with electric mixer at high speed (or with egg beater), beat until *very thick and light.*
4. With rubber spatula or spoon, fold flour mixture and vanilla, all at once, into egg mixture. To melted chocolate, add 2 tablesp. sugar, soda, cold water; stir until thick and light; quickly fold into batter.
5. Turn into pan. Bake 15 to 20 min., or just until cake springs back when gently touched with finger. (If cake is baked in roasting pan, it may take a little longer.)
6. While cake bakes, place clean dish towel on

flat surface; over it, sift thick layer of confectioners' sugar. When cake is done, with spatula, loosen it from sides of pan, invert onto towel. Lift off pan; carefully peel off paper; with very sharp knife, cut crisp edges from cake, to make rolling easier. Cool exactly 5 min.

7. Roll up cake very gently from narrow end, rolling towel up in it (this prevents cake's sticking). Gently lift rolled cake onto wire rack to finish cooling—about 1 hr. (If cake is warm, whipped cream filling will melt.)

8. Just before serving, carefully unroll so cake will be on towel. Quickly spread cake with almond-flavored whipped cream to within 1" of edges. Start rolling up cake from narrow end by folding edge of cake over, then tucking it under; continue rolling cake, lifting towel higher and higher with one hand as you guide roll with other hand. Finish with open end of cake on underside. Cut into crosswise slices.

Serve slices plain; or top with vanilla or coffee ice cream. Makes 8 servings.

CHOCOLATE TORTE

10 medium egg whites	1 teasp. vanilla extract
10 medium egg yolks	1 cup sifted cake flour
¼ teasp. salt	½-lb. cake sweet
2 teasp. cream of tartar	chocolate, grated
1 cup granulated sugar	Unsweetened chocolate

About 1 hr. ahead, set out whites and yolks. When ready to make cake, start heating oven to 325°F.

In large electric-mixer bowl, with mixer at high speed (or with egg beater), beat egg whites with salt and cream of tartar until stiff but still moist.

Slowly add granulated sugar, beating until stiff peaks are formed. With rubber spatula or spoon, fold in vanilla, flour, then grated chocolate. Beat yolks until thick, lemon-colored; fold into chocolate mixture.

Turn batter into *ungreased* 9" clampless spring-form pan, with tube insert in place. Bake 1 hr., or until cake tester inserted in center comes out clean. Cool in pan, upside down, 1 hr.; then remove as in step 7, p. 450.

About 2 hr. before serving: Frost with Choco-

late Fluff, p. 464. Grate unsweetened chocolate on top. Refrigerate 2 hr. Makes 12 servings.

To Do Ahead: Make cake day before. Frost 2 hr. before serving.

CUPCAKES UNLIMITED

The fun of cupcakes is the fascinating variety you can get from just one baking. Whether you start from scratch or use your favorite cake mix, you can individualize each cupcake.

Important How-Tos

1. *Grease and flour just the bottoms of cupcake-pan cups.* This helps keep cupcakes from running over pans.

2. *Or buy packaged paper liners* for cupcake cups. They do away with greasing, scouring, and sticking. Peel them off when cupcakes are cool.

3. *Never fill cupcake cups more than half full* unless directed otherwise. Don't guess. Fill 1 cupcake cup with water; measure water; use half this amount of batter for each cupcake. To pour batter, use cup from graduated measuring-cup set.

MIRACLE CUPCAKES

Make Miracle Cake, p. 440, reducing milk to ¾ cup. Pour batter into cupcake cups, prepared as above. Bake at 375°F. 20 min., or until cake tester inserted in center comes out clean. Makes 24 2½" cupcakes.

Spice: With flour, sift 1 teasp. allspice, 2 teasp. cinnamon, and 1 teasp. nutmeg. Reduce vanilla to ½ teasp.

DEVIL'S-FOOD CUPCAKES

1 cup sifted cake flour	type shortening (see
½ teasp. double-acting	step 2, p. 446)
baking powder	¼ cup water
½ teasp. salt	½ teasp. vanilla extract
½ teasp. baking soda	½ cup minus 2 tablesp.
¼ cup cocoa	buttermilk or sour
¾ cup granulated	milk
sugar	1 egg, unbeaten
¼ cup soft emulsifier-	1 egg yolk, unbeaten

Start heating oven to 350°F. Prepare 12 2½" cupcake cups as on p. 455.

Into large electric-mixer bowl, sift flour, baking powder, salt, soda, cocoa, sugar. Drop in shortening; pour in water, vanilla, 2 tablesp. buttermilk. *With mixer at low to medium speed, beat 2 min., scraping bowl and beaters as needed. Add remaining ¼ cup buttermilk, egg, egg yolk; beat 1 min. Fill cups half full. Bake 25 min., or until cake tester inserted in center comes out clean. Makes 12 cupcakes.

To mix with spoon, beat briskly for same time periods as above, allowing 150 full, round-the-bowl strokes per minute.

OLD-FASHIONED WHITE CUPCAKES

2½ cups sifted cake flour	acting (or 5½ teasp. tartrate or phosphate) baking powder
1⅔ cups granulated sugar	
1 teasp. salt	5 egg whites, unbeaten
¾ cup soft shortening	½ cup minus 2 tablesp. milk
¾ cup milk	
4½ teasp. double-	1 teasp. vanilla extract

Start heating oven to 375°F. Prepare 24 3" cupcake cups as on p. 455.

Into large electric-mixer bowl, sift flour, sugar, salt. Drop in shortening; pour in ¾ cup milk. *With mixer at low to medium speed, mix until all flour is dampened; then beat 2 min., scraping bowl and beaters as needed. Stir in baking powder. Then add egg whites, remaining milk, vanilla; beat 2 min. Fill cups half full. Bake 20 min., or until cake tester inserted in center comes out clean. Makes 24 cupcakes.

To mix with spoon, beat briskly for same time periods as above, allowing 150 full, round-the-bowl strokes per minute.

SHERRY CHRISTMAS CUPCAKES

3 cups sifted all-purpose flour	1 cup diced, mixed preserved fruits
1¼ teasp. baking soda	1 cup chopped nuts
½ teasp. salt	1 cup soft shortening
½ teasp. cinnamon	1½ cups granulated sugar
½ teasp. nutmeg	
¼ teasp. ground cloves	2 eggs, unbeaten
1 cup light or dark raisins	1 cup sherry
	½ cup honey

Start heating oven to 325°F. Grease bottoms of 25 to 30 3" cupcake cups. Sift flour, soda, salt, cinnamon, nutmeg, cloves; stir in raisins, preserved fruits, walnuts.

*In large electric-mixer bowl, with mixer at medium speed, or "cream," mix shortening with sugar, then with eggs, until *very light and fluffy*—about 4 min. altogether. At low speed, or "blend," beat in alternately, *just until smooth,* fruit mixture, sherry, honey. Fill cupcake cups two thirds full. Bake 50 to 60 min., or until cake tester inserted in center comes out clean. Dip into sugar; top with pieces of preserved fruit. Makes 25 to 30 cupcakes.

To mix with spoon, see step 7, p. 439.

SPONGE CUPCAKES

Make Hot-Milk Spongecake batter, p. 452. *Immediately* fill ungreased or paper-lined 2½" cupcake cups half full. Bake 15 min., or until cake tester inserted in center comes out clean. Makes 24 2½" cupcakes.

Also see Tricky Cupcakes, p. 469.

CAKES IN LESS TIME
From a Cake Mix

Today's packaged cake mixes produce superb cakes—high, light, tender, and delicious—all with a great saving of time and work.

When you go to market to pick up a mix, you'll find favorites like these:

Snowy angel food	Fragrant spicecake
Rich devil's food	Fluffy white cake
Spicy gingerbread	Golden yellow cake
Marvel marble cake	

Once you've made your choice, just read, then follow to the letter, those one-two-three label directions. See how quickly you can whip up your cake by hand or with an electric mixer, pour the batter into the pan or pans, and bake it. (Remember, it really is your cake, for you've baked it!)

Tube cake, layers, square, sheet or cup cakes, can all be made with mix. With cake mix and the fillings and frostings on p. 461, you can even reproduce some of the luscious cakes and cupcakes for which we give "from scratch" recipes on previous pages. Or maybe the family will vote for one of the cakes, below.

P.S. If family is small, bake half of batter as a layer, the rest as cupcakes. Then refrigerate or freeze what you don't need that night for serving in a different way a day or so later.

ANGEL-FOOD MIX PLUS

Ripple: Grate 2 sq. unsweetened chocolate. In tube pan, alternate layers of grated chocolate and cake batter, beginning and ending with batter. Or substitute 6 tablesp. instant cocoa mix for chocolate.

Pineapple-Almond: Into cake batter, fold ⅓ cup *minced,* blanched almonds and ⅓ cup finely diced preserved pineapple.

Pistachio-Almond: Into cake batter, fold a few drops green food color, ¼ teasp. almond extract, ¾ cup *minced,* blanched almonds.

Toasted Almond: Pour cake batter into pan; sprinkle top with ⅓ cup *finely* sliced, blanched almonds.

Cherry Angel: Use 2 tablesp. maraschino-cherry juice as part of liquid called for on label. Into cake batter, fold ⅓ cup chopped, *well-drained* maraschino cherries.

Coconut: Into cake batter, fold ½ to 1 cup finely snipped shredded coconut.

Coffee: Stir 1 tablesp. instant coffee into liquid called for on label.

Chocolate Fleck: See Devil's-Food-Cake Mix Plus, below.

DEVIL'S-FOOD-CAKE MIX PLUS

Chocolate Fleck: Into cake batter, fold 1 or 2 sq. unsweetened chocolate, grated.

Coconut: To cake batter, add ½ to ¾ cup finely snipped shredded coconut.

Orange Coconut: To cake batter, add 1 tablesp. grated orange rind and ½ to ¾ cup finely snipped shredded coconut.

Coffee Spice: To dry mix, add 4 teasp. instant coffee, ½ teasp. cinnamon, ¼ teasp. allspice, and ¼ teasp. nutmeg.

Maple-Nut: See Fluffy White-Cake Mix Plus, below.

Nut: To cake batter, add ½ cup *minced* nuts.

Orange: To cake batter, add 1 teasp. grated orange rind. Frost cake with Orange Butter Cream, p. 462.

Peanut: To cake batter, add ¾ cup *minced* salted peanuts.

Peppermint: To cake batter, add a few drops peppermint extract.

FLUFFY WHITE-CAKE MIX PLUS

Maple Nut: To cake batter, add a few drops maple flavoring. After pouring batter into pan, sprinkle with ½ cup *minced* nuts.

Lemon or Orange Coconut: To cake batter, add ¼ teasp. lemon extract, or 1 tablesp. grated orange rind, and ½ cup finely snipped shredded coconut.

Spice: To dry mix, add about 1 teasp. cinnamon, ½ teasp. nutmeg, ¼ teasp. ground cloves. If desired, to cake batter, add ¼ cup *minced* nuts.

Cherry-Nut: To cake batter, add ½ cup *minced* nuts and 8 minced, *well-drained* maraschino cherries.

Chocolate Fleck: See Devil's-Food-Cake Mix Plus, above.

Cinnamon: To dry mix, add ¾ teasp. cinnamon.

Date: To cake batter, add ½ cup finely chopped, pitted dates and 1 teasp. grated lemon rind.

Peanut: To cake batter, add ¾ cup *minced* salted peanuts.

Orange: See Devil's-Food-Cake Mix Plus, above.

Nut: To cake batter, add ½ cup *minced* nuts.

Coffee: To dry mix, add 4 teasp. instant coffee.

Coconut: See Devil's-Food-Cake Mix Plus, above.

GOLDEN YELLOW-CAKE MIX PLUS

Lemon: To cake batter, add 2 teasp. grated lemon rind.

Chocolate Fleck: Into cake batter, fold 1 or 2 sq. unsweetened chocolate, grated.

Spice: To dry mix, add about 1 teasp. cinnamon, ½ teasp. nutmeg, ¼ teasp. ground cloves.

Orange Coconut: To cake batter, add 1 tablesp. grated orange rind and ½ cup finely snipped shredded coconut.

Coffee: To dry mix, add 4 teasp. instant coffee.

Nut: To cake batter, add ½ cup *minced* nuts.

Coconut: To cake batter, add ½ to ¾ cup finely snipped shredded coconut.

SPICY GINGERBREAD MIX PLUS

1. As soon as gingerbread is baked, top, then return to oven, as in Nut-Topped Gingerbread, p. 385.
2. Or as soon as it is baked, top, then broil, as in Broiled Praline Topping, p. 465.
3. Or slice and top gingerbread as in Broiler-Frosted Gingerbread, p. 385.
4. Or serve gingerbread hot or warm, with one of Gingerbread Top-Offs, p. 384.

OTHER CAKE-MIX CAKES

Don't miss any of those cakes, cupcakes, and petit fours in Easy Decorating, pp. 467 to 470. Also see Tray Ice Cream Cakes, p. 426; Ice Cream-Cake Sundaes, p. 426; Ice Cream Angels, p. 429; and Ice Cream Cakes, p. 429.

QUICK UPSIDE-DOWN CAKE

Choose a packaged cake mix—white, yellow, or devil's food. Start heating oven to 375°F.

In 9″ x 9″ x 2″ cake pan, prepare one of toppings below. Then make up cake mix as label directs. Carefully turn batter over topping, to come halfway up sides of pan. (Pour any leftover batter into cupcake cups.)

Bake cake at 375°F. 40 to 50 min., or until cake tester inserted in center of cake comes out clean. Cool in pan on wire rack 10 min.; then invert, with fruit side up, on serving plate. Let stand 1 min.; lift off pan. Serve slightly warm, with or without cream, ice cream, or whipped cream cheese.

Toppings:

Nutted Apricot: In cake pan, melt 3 tablesp. butter or margarine. Sprinkle butter with ¼ cup granulated or brown sugar. On top, arrange, with cut sides down, 1 No. 2 can apricot halves, drained. Sprinkle with ½ cup coarsely chopped nuts.

Caramel Coconut: In cake pan over low heat on top burner, toast 1 cup snipped shredded coconut, tossing coconut with fork. Add ½ cup butter or margarine; melt. Add ⅔ cup brown sugar, packed, and 2 tablesp. water; toss. Especially nice with white- or yellow-cake mix.

Pineapple Chunk: In cake pan, melt ¼ cup butter or margarine. Sprinkle butter with ½ cup brown sugar, packed. On top, arrange 1 No. 2 can pineapple chunks, drained. Also nice with gingerbread mix.

EASY BRIDE'S CAKE
(3 tiers)

Day before: Make up 1 pkg. favorite white- or yellow-cake mix; use batter to fill 1 12″ x 8″ x 2″ cake pan a little less than half full. (Bake rest of batter in cupcake cups.) Bake as label directs, or until cake tester inserted in center comes out clean. Make 3 more 12″ x 8″ x 2″ cakes.

To assemble: For bottom tier, put 2 cakes, side by side (12″ sides together), on wooden board. Thinly frost with Ornamental Frosting, p. 465, or Butter Cream,* p. 462. Center third cake on top of bottom tier, with its 12″ side at right angles to 12″ side of bottom tier. Frost. Use one third of last cake for top tier; center, with 8″ side of this cake parallel to 12″ side of second tier. Frost. Let cake stand until next day.

On the big day: Make another batch of frosting. Refrost cake, frosting board too. At the last minute, with bit of frosting, "glue" fresh yellow or white daisies to corners of each tier, and "glue" small bunch to top of cake; then place smilax around base. Or decorate cake with Susan's Rosebud, Full-blown Roses, or Chrysanthemums, p. 472.

* *If cake is frosted with Butter Cream, it may be made ahead, then frozen.*

CHOCOLATE ANGEL DESSERT

1 pkg. angel-food- cake mix	⅔ cup fudge or chocolate sauce
⅛ teasp. nutmeg	About ½ lb. crushed
2 cups heavy cream	English toffee

Day before: Make 10″ angel-food cake as label directs, adding nutmeg to batter; cool. Then cut cake crosswise into 2 even layers. Whip cream till almost stiff; fold in fudge sauce. Frost lower layer of cake with some of cream mixture; sprinkle with some of toffee. Set top layer in place. Frost top and sides with cream mixture; sprinkle with rest of toffee. Refrigerate at least 8 hr.

To serve: Cut into wedges. Makes 16 servings.

BERRY BASKET CAKE

1 pkg. angel-food- cake mix	or raspberries
¼ teasp. grated lemon rind	¼ teasp. lemon extract ½ cup sifted confec- tioners' sugar
1 qt. fresh strawberries	2 cups heavy cream

Early in day or day before: Make angel-food cake as label directs, adding lemon rind to batter; cool.

About 1 or 2 hr. before serving: Hollow out cake, leaving shell about ¾″ thick. Place on large serving plate. Fill bottom of center tube hole with piece of cut cake. Tear or break rest of cut cake into bite-size pieces. Wash and hull berries, saving some of the prettiest ones as garnish (about 2 cups); slice rest. Add extract and sugar to cream; whip till stiff. Fold in cut-up berries and broken pieces of cake. Heap high in cake shell (fill center hole too). Circle cake with ivy or other pretty greens. Tumble berries over and around cake. Makes 8 servings.

Freezer Note: Cut leftover cake into serving-size pieces. Freezer-wrap each piece; freeze quickly. To serve, let thaw on shelf of refrigerator until just soft.

Cakes You Buy

Don't forget your baker (or grocer) when you want a delicious cake or cake dessert. His unfrosted layers, loaf cakes, angel and chiffon cakes, poundcakes, jelly rolls, cupcakes, dessert shells, etc. make a fine foundation for an easy cake or cake dessert.

For wonderful ways of using these cakes, just turn to Ice Creams and Sherbets, p. 424; Cake-Dessert Quickies, p. 381; Desserts to Do Ahead, p. 390; Tricky Cupcakes, p. 469; Little Cakes and Petit Fours, p. 470; Boston Cream Pie, p. 453; and Washington Pie, p. 453.

Cake Frosting and Decorating

Even the simplest cake becomes a wonderful treat when it's attractively frosted. Choose any of the following frosting recipes (they're all easy, all delicious, all appetizing-looking), read the detailed how-to section; your frosted cake is sure to be a great success.

Two reminders: Frosting is always at its best the day it goes on the cake. For hints on using leftover egg yolks or egg whites, see Leftovers, p. 550.

Before using these recipes, refer to How to Use Our Recipes, p. 3. Always use standard measuring cups and measuring spoons; measure level.

How to Fill and Frost the Cake

Square, Loaf, Sheet, or Tube Cake:

1. Cool cake well if you plan to use a butter frosting (frosting may melt). If an egg-white frosting is your favorite, cake may be slightly warm.
2. Brush or rub off loose crumbs; trim ragged edges with scissors.
3. Place cake, with top side up (if tube cake, place bottom side up), on flat cake plate or tray that extends about 2″ all around cake.
4. To keep cake plate clean while frosting cake, cover outer area of plate with strips of waxed paper, extending them beyond edge of plate.
5. So cake can be turned as you frost, set cake plate on rim of mixing bowl, with plate ex-tending at least 1″ beyond rim of bowl; or place plate on platform of electric mixer (if it's a big cake, detach mixer head).
6. Use a spatula to spread frosting.
7. Working quickly, frost sides of cake first, using upward strokes.
8. Pile rest of frosting on top; spread out in attractive swirls to meet sides. Spread naturally and irregularly, not painfully smooth.
9. Let frosting set slightly; then carefully pull out waxed-paper strips.

Layer Cakes:

1. If there is any difference between layers, make thicker layer the bottom layer; use smooth, crusted layer on top. Place 1 layer, upside down, on cake plate. Adjust strips of paper on plate, as above.
2. Spread filling on bottom layer, almost to edge (if filling is soft, spread only to 1″ from edge). Adjust second layer, with top side up, so edges are even and cake is of uniform height. If top layer slides, insert wire cake tester or slender knitting needle through both layers to anchor them. Remove cake tester before frosting top.
3. Frost as in steps 5 through 9 above.

For Very Special Cakes: It pays to frost cake first with thin, smooth layer of frosting, to hold down crumbs. Let this layer set; then final frosting will spread more easily.

FILLINGS

CREAMY CUSTARD FILLING

⅓ cup granulated sugar
2 tablesp. flour
⅛ teasp. salt
1 egg, slightly beaten
¾ cup scalded milk
1 teasp. vanilla extract
½ cup heavy cream, whipped

In double-boiler top, mix sugar, flour, salt. Stir in egg, then milk; blend thoroughly. Cook over boiling water, stirring constantly, 5 min. Cook, stirring occasionally, 5 min. longer. Refrigerate until cold. Add vanilla; then fold in whipped cream.

Fills 2 8″ or 9″ layers.

Almond: Use ½ teasp. vanilla extract and ½ teasp. almond extract. To cold filling, add ½ cup chopped, toasted almonds.

Cream-Puff: Double ingredients. Fills 6 cream puffs.

CLEAR LEMON FILLING

1 cup granulated sugar
3 tablesp. cornstarch
½ teasp. salt
1 cup boiling water
2 tablesp. grated lemon
rind
½ cup lemon juice
2 tablesp. butter or margarine

Combine ingredients. Bring to full, rolling boil, stirring occasionally. Turn down heat; boil 1 min., stirring. Let cool at room temperature. Before using, beat with egg beater.

Fills 2 8″ or 9″ layers.

Lime: Increase boiling water to 1¼ cups. Substitute grated lime rind for lemon rind, ¼ cup lime juice for lemon juice.

Orange: Reduce boiling water to ¾ cup. Substitute grated orange rind for lemon rind, ¾ cup orange juice for lemon juice. Add 1 tablesp. lemon juice.

RICH PINEAPPLE FILLING

¾ cup granulated sugar
2½ tablesp. cornstarch
⅛ teasp. salt
1 teasp. grated lemon rind
1 tablesp. lemon juice
3 egg yolks, slightly beaten
¾ cup canned pineapple juice
2 tablesp. butter or margarine

In double-boiler top, thoroughly mix sugar, cornstarch, salt. Stir in lemon rind and juice, then rest of ingredients. Cook over boiling water, stirring constantly, until smooth and thick— about 15 min. Refrigerate till cold.

Fills 2 8″ or 9″ layers.

DARK-CHOCOLATE FILLING

1 egg yolk
½ cup granulated sugar
3 tablesp. light cream
1 sq. unsweetened chocolate
1 tablesp. butter or margarine

Combine all ingredients. Cook over medium heat, stirring, until mixture bubbles around edges. Remove from heat. Beat till thick.

Fills 2 8″ or 9″ layers.

WALNUT FILLING

Combine 1 cup ground walnuts, ½ cup light cream, ⅔ cup granulated sugar, ¼ teasp. salt, 2 egg yolks. Cook over low heat, stirring, till mixture thickens and turns brown. Add 2 teasp. butter or margarine. Cool at room temperature.

Fills 2 8″ or 9″ yellow- or white-cake layers. (Frost cake with Snow-Peak Frosting, p. 462; decorate with walnut halves.)

LUSCIOUS CREAM FILLING

Prepare packaged vanilla pudding as label directs, reducing milk to 1½ cups. When pudding is chilled, fold in ½ cup heavy cream, whipped. Flavor with a little vanilla or almond extract.

Fills 2 8″ or 9″ layers.

Quick Orange: Substitute 1½ cups orange juice for milk. With cream, add 1 tablesp. grated orange rind.

Quick Pineapple: Instead of cream, fold in ½ cup drained canned crushed pineapple.

Quick Chocolate: Substitute packaged chocolate pudding for vanilla pudding. Make as label directs, reducing milk to 1½ cups. Into hot filling, stir 2 tablesp. brown sugar. Omit cream, if desired.

Quick Butterscotch: Substitute packaged butterscotch pudding for vanilla pudding. Make as label directs, reducing milk to 1½ cups. Into hot filling, stir 2 tablesp. brown sugar and 3 tablesp. melted butter or margarine. Omit cream, if desired.

Quick Lemon: Substitute packaged lemon pudding for vanilla pudding. Make as label directs. Omit cream.

QUICK-AND-EASY FROSTINGS

WHITE FUDGE FROSTING

½ cup butter or margarine	1¾ to 2 cups sifted confectioners' sugar
1 cup granulated sugar	1 teasp. vanilla extract
¼ cup milk	

In saucepan, melt butter. Add granulated sugar, milk; stir until blended. Then bring to boil, stirring occasionally; cool. Gradually add confectioners' sugar until thick enough to spread, beating well after each addition. Add vanilla; blend.

Fills and frosts 2 8″ or 9″ layers; or frosts 13″ x 9″ x 2″ cake.

DREAMY FROSTING

2 3-oz. pkg. soft cream cheese	4½ cups sifted confectioners' sugar
2 tablesp. milk or light cream	Dash salt
	1 teasp. vanilla extract

Blend cheese with milk. Slowly stir in sugar, then salt, vanilla. Blend well.

Fills and frosts 2 8″ or 9″ layers. Halve recipe to frost 8″ x 8″ x 2″ or 9″ x 9″ x 2″ cake.

Chocolate: To cheese, add 2 sq. slightly cooled, melted unsweetened chocolate; increase milk to 3 tablesp.

Orange: Substitute orange juice for milk, 1 teasp. grated orange rind for vanilla.

Coffee: With sugar, add 4 teasp. instant coffee.

BUTTER CREAM

⅓ cup soft butter, margarine, or shortening	tioners' sugar
	About ¼ cup milk or light cream
⅛ teasp. salt	1½ teasp. vanilla extract
3 cups sifted confec-	

With electric mixer at medium speed, or "cream" (or with spoon), thoroughly mix butter with salt and 1 cup confectioners' sugar until light

and fluffy. Add rest of sugar and milk alternately, beating till very smooth and of spreading consistency; add vanilla.

Fills and frosts 2 8″ or 9″ layers; or frosts 9″ x 9″ x 2″ cake.

Lemon: Substitute lemon juice for milk. Omit vanilla.

Mocha: Increase sugar to a 1 lb. pkg.; sift with ½ cup cocoa. Substitute ⅓ cup hot coffee for milk. Decrease vanilla to ½ teasp.

Orange: Use ½ cup soft butter, ⅛ teasp. salt, 3½ cups sifted confectioners' sugar, 2 unbeaten egg yolks, 1 teasp. grated orange rind, about 2 tablesp. milk. Make as above, adding egg yolks and rind before adding rest of sugar and milk.

Browned: Lightly brown butter in heavy skillet before blending it with salt and sugar.

Chocolate: Increase butter to ½ cup, sugar to 3½ cups. Before adding rest of sugar and milk, add 2 unbeaten egg yolks and 3 sq. melted unsweetened chocolate.

Peppermint: Substitute few drops peppermint extract for vanilla.

Harlequin: Make Butter Cream. To half of frosting, add 2 sq. melted unsweetened chocolate. Cut 8″ x 8″ x 2″ cake into quarters. Frost top and crust sides of 2 quarters with chocolate frosting, 2 with plain frosting. Assemble in checkerboard pattern. Decorate top of cake with walnut halves, sides with chopped walnuts.

Susan's Posy Cream: This is a wonderfully creamy, buttery frosting—especially nice to use in a cake decorator to bedeck birthday, wedding, and other cakes. Keeps soft several days.

To make: Substitute 1 cup vegetable shortening for butter. For milk, *be sure* to substitute ¼ cup soft butter (butter makes frosting flow smoothly from decorating tube).

SNOW-PEAK FROSTING

1¼ cups white corn syrup	Pinch salt
	1 teasp. vanilla extract
2 egg whites	

In small saucepan, heat corn syrup till boiling. With electric mixer at high speed, or with egg beater, beat egg whites until they form soft peaks when beater is raised. Add salt. Slowly pour in syrup, continuing to beat until frosting is fluffy and forms peaks when beater is raised. Fold in vanilla.

Fills and frosts 2 8" or 9" layers.

NO-COOK MARSHMALLOW FROSTING

In small electric-mixer bowl, place ¼ teasp. salt, 2 egg whites. With mixer at high speed, beat until soft peaks form when beater is raised. Add ¼ cup granulated sugar, a tablespoonful at a time, beating until smooth and glossy. Slowly add ¾ cup white corn syrup, beating thoroughly after each addition. Then beat until frosting forms firm peaks when beater is raised. Fold in 1¼ teasp. vanilla extract. Tint if desired.

Fills and frosts 2 8" or 9" layers.

P.S. After frosting cake, store *uncovered*.

MAGIC FROSTING

2 egg whites	⅛ teasp. cream of
⅔ cup granulated	tartar
sugar	½ teasp. vanilla extract;
3 tablesp. white corn	or ¼ teasp. almond
syrup	extract

In double-boiler top, stir together well egg whites, sugar, corn syrup, cream of tartar. Cook over *rapidly boiling* water 5 min., stirring often. Turn into bowl. With electric mixer at high speed, or with egg beater, beat until frosting stands in peaks. Stir in vanilla.

Fills and frosts 2 8" layers.

WHIPPED-CREAM FROSTING

½ teasp. unflavored	Speck salt
gelatine	2 tablesp. confec-
2 tablesp. cold water	tioners' sugar
1 cup heavy cream	½ teasp. lemon juice

Sprinkle gelatine over cold water in small bowl to soften. Scald 2 tablesp. cream; pour over gelatine, stirring till dissolved. Refrigerate until consistency of unbeaten egg white. Then, with egg beater, beat until smooth. Whip remaining cream; add salt, sugar, lemon juice; fold in gelatine mixture.

Fills and frosts tops of 2 8" or 9" layers; or frosts 10" angel cake or spongecake. Stands up well even in warm weather.

Chocolate: Omit lemon juice. After folding in gelatine mixture, fold in 1 pkg. cooled, melted semisweet-chocolate pieces (1 cup).

Coffee: To remaining cream, add 1 teasp. instant coffee.

Orange: Substitute 1 teasp. grated orange rind for lemon juice.

TROPICAL WHIP FROSTING

1 cup shredded coco-	2 tablesp. orange or
nut	pineapple juice
1 tablesp. grated	1 tablesp. lemon juice
orange rind	1 cup heavy cream,
¼ cup granulated	whipped
sugar	

Mix coconut, orange rind, sugar, fruit juices. Let stand 15 min. Whip cream; fold in coconut mixture.

Fills and frosts 2 8" layers.

EASY FUDGE FROSTING

3 sq. unsweetened	6 tablesp. light cream
chocolate	or undiluted evap-
2 tablesp. butter or	orated milk
margarine	Dash salt
2¾ cups sifted con-	1 teasp. vanilla extract
fectioners' sugar	

Melt chocolate with butter over boiling water; blend. Add 1½ cups confectioners' sugar, cream, and salt, all at once; with spoon, beat until smooth. Cook over low heat, stirring, until mixture bubbles well around edges. Remove from heat. Add vanilla and remaining sugar in thirds, beating until smooth after each addition. Set in bowl of ice water until thick enough to spread, stirring occasionally.

Fills and frosts 2 8" layers or frosts 2 8" square cakes.

JIFFY CHOCOLATE FROSTING

2 sq. unsweetened	1 tablesp. water
chocolate	¼ teasp. almond ex-
1 can sweetened con-	tract; or ½ teasp.
densed milk	vanilla extract
Dash salt	

In double boiler, combine chocolate, milk, salt, water. Cook over *rapidly boiling* water, stirring often, till thick—about 10 min. Remove from heat. Cool. Add extract.

Fills and frosts 2 8″ layers; or frosts 9″ x 9″ x 2″ cake.

QUICK FUDGE FROSTING

2 pkg. semisweet-
  chocolate pieces
  (2 cups)
3 cups sifted confec-

tioners' sugar
¼ cup soft shortening
½ cup hot milk

Melt chocolate over *hot, not boiling,* water. Add rest of ingredients. Remove from heat. With spoon, beat till smooth.

Fills and frosts 2 8″ or 9″ layers; or frosts 9″ x 9″ x 2″ cake.

QUICK-AS-A-WINK FROSTING

1 pkg. semisweet-
  chocolate pieces
  (1 cup)
1 cup sifted confec-

tioners' sugar
⅓ cup undiluted evap-
  porated milk

Melt chocolate over *hot, not boiling,* water. Add sugar, evaporated milk. Beat until smooth.

Frosts tops of 2 8″ layers. Nice on Susan's Frosted Brownies, p. 474.

BITTERSWEET FROSTING

2¼ cups sifted con-
  fectioners' sugar
¼ cup hot water
9 sq. unsweetened
  chocolate, melted
3 eggs

½ cup plus 2 tablesp.
  butter or margarine
Dash salt
1½ teasp. vanilla ex-
  tract

Combine sugar, water, melted chocolate; stir only enough to dampen sugar. Add eggs, one at a time, beating vigorously with spoon until smooth. Add butter; beat till melted and smooth. Add salt, vanilla.

Fills and frosts 2 8″ layers, split to make 4 layers.

HUNGARIAN FROSTING

3 sq. unsweetened
  chocolate, melted
1½ cups sifted con-
  fectioners' sugar

2½ tablesp. hot water
3 egg yolks, unbeaten
¼ cup soft butter or
  margarine

Combine melted chocolate, sugar, water. Add egg yolks, one at a time, beating with electric mixer or spoon after each addition. Add butter, 1 tablesp. at a time, beating until thick enough to spread.

Fills and frosts 2 8″ or 9″ layers; or frosts 8″ x 8″ x 2″ or 10″ x 5″ x 3″ cake.

Note: You may substitute 1 whole egg for 3 egg yolks; reduce water to 2 tablesp.

YUMMY CHOCOLATE FROSTING

1 cup sifted con-
  fectioners' sugar
1 egg; or 2 egg yolks*
¼ cup milk
½ teasp. vanilla

extract
4 sq. unsweetened
  chocolate, melted
1 tablesp. soft butter
  or margarine

Combine sugar with rest of ingredients. With electric mixer or egg beater, beat until stiff enough to spread—about 5 min. (If weather is warm, set bowl of frosting in bowl of ice, and beat. Or refrigerate frosting a short while before beating.)

Fills and frosts 2 9″ layers; or frosts 8″ x 8″ x 2″ cake. So nice on Devil's-Food Cake, p. 441, with chopped walnuts on side.

* Yolks make deeper-colored frosting.

To Vary: Substitute almond extract for vanilla.

VELVETY FROSTING

1 pkg. semisweet-
  chocolate pieces
  (1 cup)

½ cup soft butter or
  margarine
2 eggs, unbeaten

Melt chocolate over *hot, not boiling,* water; cool slightly. Mix butter with eggs. Add chocolate, beating with spoon until smooth and creamy.

Fills and frosts 2 8″ layers or tops of 2 9″ layers.

CHOCOLATE EGGNOG FROSTING

3 sq. unsweetened
  chocolate
1½ cups sifted confec-
  tioners' sugar
2 tablesp. hot water

1 egg, unbeaten
¼ cup soft butter or
  margarine
Rum extract to taste

In double boiler, melt chocolate. Remove from heat. Blend in sugar, water (mixture will thicken). Add egg, butter; with spoon, beat well. Add extract. Let stand until thick enough to spread.

Fills and frosts 2 8″ layers.

CHOCOLATE FLUFF

In chilled bowl, with electric mixer or egg beater, beat 2 cups heavy cream with 1 cup sifted confectioners' sugar, ½ cup cocoa, and dash salt until thick enough to spread.

Fills and frosts 2 8″ or 9″ layers, split to make 4 layers.

QUICK CARAMEL FROSTING

½ cup butter or margarine	¼ cup milk
1 cup brown sugar, packed	1¾ to 2 cups sifted confectioners' sugar

In saucepan, melt butter. Add brown sugar; boil over low heat, stirring constantly, 2 min. Add milk; stir until mixture comes to boil. Remove from heat; cool. Slowly add confectioners' sugar, beating well with spoon after each addition, until thick enough to spread.

Fills and frosts 2 8″ or 9″ layers; or generously frosts 8″ x 8″ x 2″ or 9″ x 9″ x 2″ cake.

COOK-ON TOPPINGS

Broiled Praline: Blend ⅓ cup melted butter, margarine, or shortening with ½ cup brown sugar, packed; ¼ cup milk; pinch salt; ½ teasp. vanilla extract; 1 cup snipped shredded coconut; ½ cup chopped nuts.

Spread mixture over top of hot 9″ x 9″ x 2″ Miracle Cake, p. 440. Broil *slowly* until golden —about 5 min.; don't burn.

Broiled Honey Coconut: Combine ⅓ cup honey, ¼ cup melted butter or margarine, 1 cup shredded coconut. Spread and broil as in Broiled Praline, above.

Mint Patty: Place 12 large chocolate-covered peppermint patties on top of hot 8″ x 8″ x 2″ Miracle Cake, p. 440. Return cake to oven for 2 min.; then spread softened patties over cake, or leave as is.

STRAWBERRY GLAZE

2 egg yolks, beaten	tioners' sugar
2 tablesp. soft butter or margarine	About ⅓ cup crushed, thawed frozen strawberries
3 cups sifted confec-	

Stir yolks into butter. Alternately add sugar and berries (there should be enough berries to make thin glaze that will run down sides of cake).

Makes nice thin frosting for 10″ angel cake or spongecake.

Pineapple: Substitute ½ cup drained canned crushed pineapple for strawberries.

Orange: Substitute ¼ cup orange juice and 3 tablesp. grated orange rind for strawberries.

FRUIT GLAZE

In small saucepan, boil 2 tablesp. white corn syrup with 2 tablesp. butter or margarine 3 min.; brush onto Susan's Walnut Cake, p. 448. Decorate with slivered citron and candied cherries, pressing them gently into place. Gives cake a nice gloss.

SUGAR GLAZE

Mix ¾ cup sifted confectioners' sugar, ½ teasp. vanilla extract, and 3 to 4 teasp. water until smooth and of frosting consistency, adding a few more drops of water if needed. Tint with food color if desired. Makes nice thin frosting for cookies; French Doughnuts, p. 337; Danish Pastry, p. 352; etc.

CHOCOLATE GLAZE

Melt ½ pkg. semisweet-chocolate pieces (½ cup) over *hot, not boiling,* water; stir in 1 tablesp. white corn syrup; cool slightly. Use to decorate Melting Moments, p. 479.

THIN CHOCOLATE COATING

2 tablesp. butter or margarine	1 cup sifted confectioners' sugar
2 sq. unsweetened chocolate	2 tablesp. boiling water

Melt butter with chocolate over boiling water. Remove from heat. Blend in sugar and water. With spoon, beat till smooth but not stiff.

Frosts top of 8″ or 9″ layer cake. Nice on Boston Cream Pie, p. 453; French Doughnuts, p. 337; etc.

ORNAMENTAL FROSTING

2 1 lb. pkg. confectioners' sugar	6 egg whites
1 teasp. cream of tartar	1 teasp. vanilla or almond extract

Sift sugar and cream of tartar through very fine sieve. Add egg whites; mix, using electric mixer, slotted spoon, or wire whip. Add vanilla. Beat until so stiff that knife drawn through mixture leaves clean-cut path. (On damp days, you may need to beat in more sugar to stiffen frosting.) Use this frosting to cement together tiers of large cake such as Easy Bride's Cake, p. 458; then spread thinly over entire cake to set crumbs.

Make second batch of frosting; refrost cake. Use rest of frosting to decorate cake (see Decorating with Tubes, p. 471, or your cake-decorator booklet). Or use to make any of Susan's Posies, p. 472; let dry at room temperature until firm; then "glue" to cake with bit of frosting.

P.S. Unlike Susan's Posy Cream, Ornamental Frosting becomes very hard. It's popular for decorating tiered wedding cakes.

SUPERSPEEDY FROSTINGS

You'll find them all on your grocer's shelf. Some are a combination fudge-and-frosting mix—chocolate, penuche, coconut, etc. They make a fine fudgelike frosting in no time.

You can also buy an excellent frosting mix that makes a fluffy, light, white frosting with no cooking. New ones will be coming along, too.

COOKED FROSTINGS

SUSAN'S FLUFFY FROSTING

1¼ cups granulated sugar	6 tablesp. water
⅛ teasp. cream of tartar	Pinch salt
	3 egg whites
	1 teasp. vanilla extract

1. In small saucepan, combine sugar, cream of tartar, water, salt; stir over low heat until sugar dissolves. Cook, *without stirring,* to 260°F. on candy thermometer, or until a little mixture dropped in cold water forms hard ball.
2. Set syrup aside. Using electric mixer at high speed (if you must use egg beater, ask friend to help), beat whites until they form peaks when beater is raised.
3. Now add syrup gradually, beating. When all syrup has been added, add vanilla; continue beating until mixture forms peaks when beater is raised and is thick enough to spread. Fills and frosts 2 8" or 9" layers.

"SEVEN-MINUTE" FROSTING

2 egg whites	1 tablesp. white corn syrup
1½ cups granulated sugar	½ teasp. salt
½ cup water*	1 teasp. vanilla extract

In double-boiler top, combine all ingredients except vanilla. With electric mixer at high speed, beat about 1 min. to blend; then place over *rapidly boiling* water, and beat till mixture forms peaks when beater is raised (don't be surprised if this takes more than 7 min.). Remove from boiling water (for smoothest frosting, empty into large bowl). Add vanilla; continue beating until thick enough to spread.

Generously fills and frosts 2 8" or 9" layers; or frosts 10" sponge, angel, or chiffon cake, or 13" x 9" x 2" cake, or 2 doz. cupcakes.

* For crusty surface, reduce water to ⅓ cup.

"Four Minute": Halve each ingredient, using 1½ teasp. white corn syrup. Make as directed, cooking mixture about 4 min., or until it forms peaks when beater is raised; then complete.

Fills and frosts 2 8" layers; or frosts 8" x 8" x 2" or 9" x 9" x 2" cake.

If making variations below, halve ingredients.

Chocolate: When frosting is done, gently fold in (don't beat) 2 or 3 sq. cooled, melted unsweetened chocolate.

Harvest Moon: Substitute 1½ cups brown sugar, packed, for granulated sugar. While frosting is still soft on cake, you may sprinkle it with chocolate curls or chopped nuts to form 1" border around top.

Lady Baltimore: To one third of completed frosting, add ⅓ cup snipped light or dark raisins, ⅓ cup snipped dried figs, 6 tablesp. chopped walnuts; use to fill 2 8" or 9" white-cake layers.

Frost cake with remaining plain frosting. Sprinkle with snipped candied cherries if desired.

Marshmallow: With vanilla, add 1 cup snipped marshmallows.

Peppermint: Substitute ¼ teasp. peppermint extract for vanilla. Tint frosting pink with red food color.

Princess: Substitute 1½ teasp. vanilla, ½ teasp. orange, and 1 teasp. almond extracts for vanilla. Sprinkle filled and frosted cake with packaged shredded or grated fresh coconut.

PENUCHE FROSTING

1½ cups light-brown sugar, packed	¼ cup shortening
1½ cups granulated sugar	¼ cup butter or margarine
2 tablesp. white corn syrup	¼ teasp. salt
¾ cup milk	1 teasp. orange extract
	1 cup chopped nuts

In large saucepan, combine sugars, syrup, milk, shortening, butter, salt. Bring slowly to rolling boil, stirring constantly. *Boil briskly* 2 min. Cool till *lukewarm*. Add extract; beat* until thick enough to spread. Add nuts.

Fills and frosts 2 8″ or 9″ layers; or frosts 8″ x 8″ x 2″ or 9″ x 9″ x 2″ cake.

* This frosting takes a while to beat. Let your electric mixer do it. The result is worth the effort.

EASY DECORATING

Make cake "from scratch" or from your favorite cake mix; or buy unfrosted layers, or a tube or sheet cake, from your baker. Then, with your choice of the decorating ideas that follow, turn the cake into something special.

GAILY FROSTED CAKES

White Mountain: Generously frost cake with "Seven-Minute" Frosting, p. 466. Lightly press tip of flat side of spatula on frosting; lift off. Frosting follows spatula to form peak. Repeat several times. Sprinkle peaks with shredded coconut, grated chocolate, or chopped nuts.

Shadow: Frost cake with white or light frosting. Melt 2 sq. unsweetened chocolate with 1 teasp. shortening. With spoon, drizzle chocolate mixture along top edge of cake, so that it runs down sides at 1″ intervals.

Sugar Top: On unfrosted cake, lay strips of paper; paper cutout of heart, Easter egg, tulip, etc.; or lace paper doily. Sift confectioners' sugar over all. Now gently lift off paper.

Border: Sprinkle chopped nuts, shredded coconut, grated chocolate, sugar-coated cereal, or crushed peppermint sticks in 2″ border around top of frosted cake.

Shaggy: Toss shredded coconut with grated unsweetened chocolate or chopped, drained maraschino cherries. Press to sides of frosted cake and up over top to make 1″ border.

Polka Dot: Dot frosted cake here and there with walnut halves, small or large round gumdrop slices, semisweet-chocolate pieces, nonpareils, varicolored candy wafers, or thin mints.

Hobnail: Turn tip of spoon in frosting to make indentation; repeat all over top and sides of cake.

Happy New Year: Make white or yellow cake or sponge sheet cake. Cut into 2″ squares. Frost 12 squares with "Seven-Minute" Frosting, p. 466, or Snow-Peak Frosting, p. 462. With red-tinted granulated sugar or silver *dragées* (edible, candy balls), form one of letters of "Happy New Year" on each square. Then group on tray to spell out greeting.

"Hearty" Valentine: Chill well 1 can jellied cranberry sauce. Cut into ½″ slices; then, with small heart-shaped cookie cutter, cut out hearts. Just before serving, place hearts in border around top of white-frosted cake, 1″ in from edge, pointing tip of hearts toward center. Sprinkle sides of cake, up to hearts, with shredded coconut.

Washington's or Lincoln's Birthday: Make Susan's Chocolate Roll, p. 454, or Jelly Roll, p. 454, with plain or flavored whipped cream as filling. Frost with chocolate frosting. Run flat side of spatula along frosted roll in parallel lines to simulate log. Arrange on oblong plate; garnish with huckleberry leaves and maraschino cherries with stems.

St. Patrick's Day: Frost filled layer cake with Snow-Peak Frosting, p. 462. Slice small green gumdrops; arrange here and there on cake in groups of 3 like shamrocks. Dip toothpick in green food color; use to draw stem for each shamrock. Circle cake with green leaves.

Mother's or Father's Day: Frost filled layer cake with Snow-Peak Frosting, p. 462, or Butter Cream, p. 462. Using pink or green frosting and plain tube for writing in cake decorator, make stick figures of Mother (or Dad), children, and pets on top of cake. Write "With Love to Mom" (or "Dad"). Circle cake with carnations; or let each figure hold a taper candle (cut candles so they make steplike row).

Thanksgiving Buffet: Frost filled layer cake with pale-yellow Butter Cream, p. 462, or Snow-Peak Frosting, p. 462. On top, with toothpick, draw outline of large cornucopia. Heap teaspoonfuls of pale-orange frosting within cornucopia; then, with small spatula, smooth frosting out to fill in cornucopia.

Build up mouth of cornucopia with more frosting; smooth. Arrange small uncooked dried apricots and pitted prunes so they seem to tumble out of cornucopia. Insert unblanched almonds here and there, tucking a few in mouth of cornucopia.

Christmas Tree: Frost filled layer cake with Snow-Peak Frosting, p. 462. On top, with toothpick, draw outline of Christmas tree; lay bits of candied cherries or cinnamon drops on outline; then scatter silver *dragées* or mixed candied fruit within tree outline. Sprinkle rest of cake with shredded coconut, tossed with cut-up maraschino cherries.

Baby Shower: Use 2 10" x 5" x 3" loaf cakes. Cut each in half crosswise; cut off crust ends, leaving 4 blocks. (Or use 3 6" x 2½" poundcakes; trim each into block shape.)

Use 3 blocks. Frost sides with Butter Cream, p. 462 (if desired, alternate colors on sides of blocks—white, pink, white, pink). Frost tops of all blocks with a pretty shade of blue. With cake decorator, on sides of blocks, write letters of alphabet in blue, white, and pink, contrasting color of letter with that of block. Arrange 2 blocks on oblong plate; top with third block.

BIRTHDAY AND ANNIVERSARY CAKES

Roly-Poly Birthday Cake (teen-agers' pet): Frost Jelly Roll, p. 454, or 2 bakers' jelly rolls set end to end, with pale-green Snow-Peak Frosting, p. 462, reserving ⅓ cup frosting. Add bit of melted unsweetened chocolate or cocoa to reserved frosting. Use with plain tube for writing in cake decorator to write guests' names on roll; slice roll between names.

Minted Birthday Cake: Fill and frost 2 chocolate-cake layers with pale-green Snow-Peak Frosting, p. 462. Coat all but center top with shredded coconut. Brush mint sprigs with water; dust with granulated sugar; set around top edge. Place candles in center.

Five O'Clock Cake: Fill and frost 2 cake layers with No-Cook Marshmallow Frosting, p. 463. Into side, press chopped walnuts or pecans. Place 1 black gumdrop on center of cake. Then, with point of sharp knife, cut crisscross gash in top of 12 gumdrops; press candle into opening in each gumdrop; arrange around top edge of cake to represent numbers on clock. Place 2 long gumdrops in position to form hour and minute hands, making them point to age of birthday child.

Birthday Year: Draw large paper or cardboard pattern for each numeral of birthday year, making numerals as large as 2 sheet cakes or 2 9" x 9" x 2" cakes will permit.

Place pattern of first number on top of one of cakes. With sharp knife, carefully trace around it, cutting through to bottom of cake; remove excess cake. Then repeat with pattern of second number, using other sheet or 9" x 9" x 2" cake.

Place cake numerals side by side on mirror or rectangular cake plate. Completely frost cakes with Snow-Peak Frosting, p. 462; then, on each numeral, spoon on mound of frosting where you plan to place fresh or frosting roses (see Susan's posies, p. 472). Arrange roses on each cake. Then, using green Susan's Posy Cream, p. 462, and leaf tube in paper cone, tuck green leaves here and there (or use fresh leaves). If desired, save your best posies to place on front of cake plate, between cake numbers. Add leaves of frosting.

Rainbow Cake: Frost tube angel, sponge, or chiffon cake with Snow-Peak Frosting, p. 462. Prepare 1½ cups green-tinted coconut, 1 cup pink-tinted coconut, and 1 cup yellow-tinted coconut as on p. 10.

On cake, alternate panels of tinted coconut. Group candles on cake to match tint of coconut

—pink on pink, green on green, yellow on yellow. Let a guest help light candles.

Corsage Cake: Frost entire 9″ or 10″ angel, sponge, or chiffon cake with pale-pink or green Snow-Peak Frosting, p. 462; sprinkle with silver *dragées*. Around outer top edge, set ring of candles. Set old-fashioned nosegay, which birthday child will wear, in center of cake.

Lollipop Cake: Frost 9″ or 10″ angel, sponge, or chiffon cake with Snow-Peak Frosting, p. 462. Make gumdrop corsage as follows: Insert wooden skewer into each of 8 or 9 large gumdrops. Remove center from paper doily; insert gumdrop lollipops; tie with ribbon. Set in hole in cake. Ring top edge of cake with candles.

Suzy's Christmas Angel: Frost 9″ or 10″ angel, sponge, or chiffon cake with green Snow-Peak Frosting, p. 462. Sprinkle with silver *dragées*. Set Christmas corsage in center of cake. Ring top edge of cake with red candles.

Toothsome Telegram: Frost top and sides of 13″ x 9″ x 2″ cake with some of Dreamy Frosting, p. 462. To remaining frosting, add a little instant coffee; use with plain tube for writing in cake decorator or paper cone.

Print "Western Union" across center top of cake. Draw line underneath this, clear across cake (it should be about one fourth of way down cake). Then print birthday message on rest of cake top. Set candles at top corners.

Calico Cake: Leave top of frosted cake free of decoration. Arrange pink, blue, yellow, green, and white birthday candles in casual disorder on top of cake.

Candle Year Cake: On center top of frosted cake, with candles, write age of birthday child.

One-Candle Cake: Use big red candle for granddad's birthday cake. Use big pink one for baby sister's.

High-Low Cake: Arrange 4 or 5 regular table candles of different colors and heights in hole of frosted angel, sponge, or chiffon cake set on cake plate. (Melt bottom of each candle before setting in place on plate.) Tie candles with big bow.

Candle Wreath Cake: With modeling clay, glue candles to cake plate, around birthday cake.

Golden-Anniversary Ring: Make or buy 3 9″ or 10″ angel cakes. Cut each cake in half vertically. Arrange halves to form scalloped ring on large piece of cardboard, covered with gold paper, or on tray. Frost with twice recipe for "Seven-Minute" Frosting, p. 466, tinted yellow. Scatter silver *dragées* of assorted sizes on frosting. Surround with wreath of smilax.

Silver-Bell Anniversary Cake: Place 2 filled 9″ layer cakes, side by side, on tray. Frost with twice recipe for Snow-Peak Frosting, p. 462, reserving 1 cup frosting. With toothpick, draw outline of bell on top of each cake, letting tops of bells meet where cakes join. Fill in outlines with silver *dragées*. Tint reserved frosting pale green; with cake decorator and ribbon tube, make bow on top of each bell. Retrace bows to get depth.

TRICKY CUPCAKES

From your favorite cake mix, make cupcakes. (The label tells you how.) Then top as below:

Chocolate Butterflies: With paring knife, remove cone-shaped piece from top center of each chocolate cupcake. Fill hollow with whipped cream, ice cream, or Snow-Peak Frosting, p. 462. Cut cake cone in half; press into filling to look like butterfly wings.

Honeycomb: Dip top of cupcake into honey; sprinkle with finely chopped nuts or grated orange rind, or nuts and rind combined.

Lacy Cocoa: Cut out small cardboard pattern of star, tree, etc. Place on top of each cupcake; sift cocoa over top; gently lift off pattern.

Nugget: Just before cupcakes are done, gently press nut-meat half into top of each; or sprinkle with chopped nuts. Finish baking.

Shadow: Drizzle melted unsweetened chocolate over frosted or unfrosted cupcakes. Sprinkle with finely chopped nuts if desired.

Snowball: Frost cupcakes with whipped cream or Snow-Peak Frosting, p. 462. Sprinkle sides generously with shredded coconut, alone or with snipped candied cherries added.

Half-and-Half: Cut white and chocolate or gingerbread cupcakes vertically in halves. Spread cut surfaces with Butter Cream or Mocha Butter Cream, p. 462. Before frosting sets, press 2 contrasting halves together. Or frost top and cut side of chocolate half with Butter Cream; frost top of white half with green-tinted Butter Cream; press together.

Pineapple-Cream: Split each cupcake into 3 layers. Fill with Quick Pineapple Filling, p. 461. Sift confectioners' sugar on top. Or top with whipped cream and bit of drained canned crushed pineapple.

Broiled Praline: Top each cupcake with Broiled Praline, p. 465, omitting nuts. Broil as directed.

CANDLE CUPCAKES

Rainbow: Dip tip end of each almond into melted semisweet chocolate; let dry. Or use Jordan almonds. Tuck tiny candle into top center of each pastel-frosted cupcake; group 3 or 4 almonds around it.

In the Pink: Top each white-frosted cupcake with red maraschino or candied cherry; then insert white candle in cherry.

Sunburst: Into center of unfrosted cupcake, insert yellow carnation with short stem. Insert candle in carnation.

Ringling: Top each pastel-frosted cupcake with 2 hard round candies with holes in center, placing one on top of other. Insert yellow candle in center of candies.

Floweret: Split 2 or 3 small red gumdrops. With fingers, shape into petals. Insert candle into center of each white-frosted cupcake. Surround with gumdrop petals.

LITTLE CAKES AND PETIT FOURS

Fiesta Balls: Cut white or yellow sheet cake made from cake mix into 1¼" squares. Frost all sides with "Seven-Minute" Frosting, p. 466. Roll in coconut, tinted pink or green as on p. 10 or mixed with grated chocolate. Or roll in split pistachio nuts, shaved chocolate, or slivered almonds. For birthday, top with candles.

Checkerboards: Split chocolate and white sheet cake made from cake mix to make 2 layers each. Make Orange Butter Cream, p. 462. Put 1 chocolate layer and 1 white layer together, with half of frosting as filling. Halve lengthwise; then slice each half crosswise into 1" slices. Put these slices together in pairs (black against white) with rest of Orange Butter Cream. Frost sides of each pair with Bittersweet Frosting, p. 464. To serve, slice. Repeat with other chocolate and white sheet-cake layers.

Ribbonets: Cut bakers' poundcake or Wonder Gold Cake, p. 448, into ¼" slices. Spread 5 slices with melted semisweet-chocolate pieces. Stack 6 slices (top slice should be unfrosted) to make tiny 6-layer cake. Cut this into 1"-thick slices; then cut each slice into 1" cubes. Top each cube with blob of "Seven-Minute" Frosting, p. 466, then with chopped nuts, candied cherries, tinted shredded coconut, or bright-colored jelly.

Confettis: Cut white, yellow, or chocolate sheet cake made from cake mix into fingers. Frost with "Seven-Minute" Frosting, p. 466. Pat shredded coconut, tossed with snipped candied cherries, onto sides.

Four-in-Ones: Grease jelly-roll pan or 17½" x 11½" x 2¼" roasting pan. Prepare 1 pkg. white- or yellow-cake mix and 1 pkg. devil's food mix as labels direct. Pour batters into opposite ends of pan, filling pan only half full. (Use any leftover batter for cupcakes.) Bake as label directs, allowing about 10 min. longer, or until cake tester inserted in cake at several points comes out clean. Cool in pan, then frost with "Seven-Minute" Frosting, p. 466.

Now drizzle melted unsweetened chocolate over one fourth of cake; sprinkle one fourth with chopped nuts, one fourth with snipped candied cherries, one fourth with cocoa. Cut white end of cake into tiny squares, chocolate end into small diamond shapes.

Miniature Jelly Rolls: Cut bakers' or homemade spongecake layer into ⅛" slices. Spread each slice with raspberry jam, canned jellied cranberry sauce, or melted semisweet-chocolate pieces. Then roll each up into tiny jelly roll; dust with confectioners' sugar or cocoa, sifted through small strainer.

DECORATING WITH TUBES

Make your own paper-cone decorator as below; check our directions to see which tubes you'll need. Use only Susan's Posy Cream, p. 462, or Ornamental Frosting, p. 465.

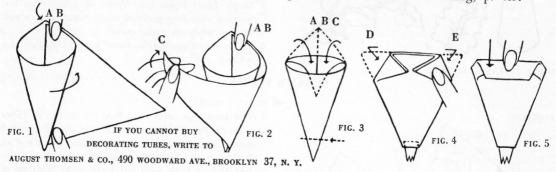

FIG. 1 FIG. 2 FIG. 3 FIG. 4 FIG. 5

IF YOU CANNOT BUY DECORATING TUBES, WRITE TO
AUGUST THOMSEN & CO., 490 WOODWARD AVE., BROOKLYN 37, N. Y.

TO MAKE PAPER-CONE DECORATOR

From bond or parchment paper, cut 11" x 8" x 8" triangle (or fold square of waxed paper into triangle). Hold in right hand with long side at bottom, thumb at center of long side.

With left hand, bring lower left-hand corner A up to corner B to shape cone. Hold points A and B together with left hand. Bring corner C around cone so that points A, B, and C meet; fold points down into cone. Cut off about ¾" of bottom tip. Drop indicated tube into cone.

Half fill decorator with frosting. Fold corners D and E to middle as shown; then fold top down.

HOW TO USE TUBES

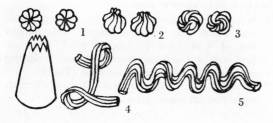

WAYS TO USE STAR TUBE

1. *Rosette:* Hold tube perpendicular to cake; press out a little frosting; lift away.
2. *Bud:* Hold tube at slight angle; press out a little frosting; lift away.
3. *Circlet:* Hold tube perpendicular to cake; press out closed circle.
4. *Writing:* See Fine Writing, below.
5. *Zigzag:* Move tube up and down.

1. *Fine Writing:* With toothpick, lightly mark letters on frosting. Follow these outlines.
2. *Forget-me-nots:* Hold tube perpendicular to cake; press out center dot, then 5 dots around it. For stem and leaves, hold tube at angle; then press.
3. *Lily of the Valley:* Hold tube at angle; make curved stem, then dots, as shown.

WAYS TO USE PLAIN TUBE FOR WRITING

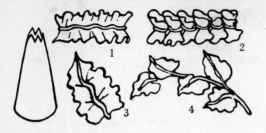

WAYS TO USE LEAF TUBE

◀ 1. *Border:* Hold tube, flat side down, at sharp angle; press out frosting in steady line.
2. *Overlapping Border:* Make Border, above, using overlapping motion.
3. *Single Leaf:* Point tube down at cake; press out frosting, changing pressure to vary width; then pull up and away to make point.
4. *Leaves on Stem:* Make stem with plain tube for writing. Add leaves.

SUSAN'S POSIES

◀ SUSAN'S ROSEBUD

1. Buy large rose-petal tube No. 127 to use in paper cone. Or buy smaller rose-petal tube to use in either paper cone or cake decorator. Make Susan's Posy Cream, p. 462. Reserve some for outer petals; tint rest delicate pink with red food color. With bit of frosting, "glue" 2″ square of waxed paper to 2″ cover of small jar. With wide part of tube opening resting on center of jar cover, hold cone so tube opening is straight up and down (Fig. 1). Press out frosting with one hand, slowly turning jar counter-clockwise with other hand, until tight, bud-like center is formed (Fig. 1).
2. Holding cone in same position, with tube against bud-like center, press out small petal about ½″ long, slowly turning jar as you press. Continue, making 3 or 4 more overlapping petals (Fig. 2).

◀ SUSAN'S FULL-BLOWN ROSE

1. Make rosebud, above. With pink frosting, mixed with a little reserved white frosting, make another row of 4 or more overlapping petals. Press out final row of 4 or more overlapping petals, slanting upper part of tube slightly outward (Fig. 3).
2. Firm up rose in ice-cube tray. Make, chill, more roses. Peel off paper; place on cake.

ROSEBUD

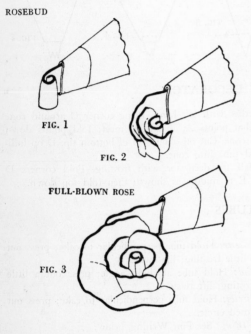

FIG. 1

FIG. 2

FULL-BLOWN ROSE

FIG. 3

SUSAN'S CHRYSANTHEMUM

1. With red and blue food colors, tint Susan's Posy Cream, p. 462, light purple. Use in paper cone with tube No. 80.
2. With bit of frosting, "glue" 3″ piece of waxed paper to 3″ jar cover. Starting at center of jar cover each time, press out 4 petals (Fig. 1). For each stand-up petal end, lift tube as you press out frosting. Now, starting from center each time, press out 12 more radiating petals, or enough to cover entire jar top (Fig. 2). Don't worry if some stand-up petal ends break off; they give flower lifelike look.
3. Make another layer of petals, between petals of first layer. Now, with cone of dark-purple frosting, pile layers of petals until center is filled (Fig. 3).
4. Firm up chrysanthemum in ice-cube tray. Make, chill, more posies. Gently peel off paper. With spatula, group posies on cake.

▶ FIG. 1

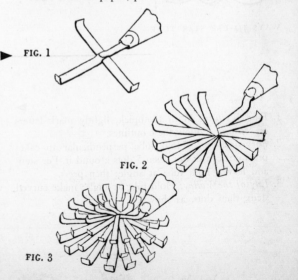

FIG. 2

FIG. 3

CHOCOLATE
POUNDCAKE

BRAZIL-NUT SENSATION

Cookies

Perhaps the only real problem about cookies is keeping the cookie jar filled! They're easy (and fun) to mix, shape, and bake. Modern recipes cut time and effort to a minimum, produce the maximum in goodness. Cookies you make from packaged mixes—cookie or gingerbread—have a homemade flavor. And packaged, ready-to-eat cookies hold their delicious own—just as they come or dressed up. Serve cookies often, serve them in quantity, but do keep that cookie jar filled.

Before you make any of our cookies, refer to How to Use Our Recipes, p. 3, and Pots and Pans, p. 692. Be sure to use standard measuring cups and measuring spoons; measure level.

Helps for the Cookie Maker

1. *For the soft shortening* called for in our cookie recipes, use any shortening that is in condition to be creamed easily. If necessary, let it stand at room temperature until soft enough.
2. *With an electric mixer,* you can whisk a batch of cookies together in no time. Just follow our recipes, using medium speed, or "cream," for mixing shortening, sugar, etc., and using low speed, or "blend," for dry ingredients. Or use a portable electric mixer.
3. *If you're mixing with a spoon,* use a wooden one with a comfortable long handle so you can mix, stir, and beat effectively.
4. *For evenly baked cookies, use cookie sheets about 2" narrower and shorter than oven,* to

allow space around edges for heat circulation. If you bake one sheet at a time, place oven rack in center of oven; if two, place racks so they divide oven into thirds.
5. *If cookie sheet is to be greased,* do it lightly. Inverted baking pans may replace cookie sheet.
6. *Use a broad spatula* to lift cookies onto cookie sheet.
7. *To cool baked cookies,* slide them, with a broad spatula, onto wire cake rack. Never overlap or heap cookies until cold.

Storing Cookies

Soft Cookies: Keep in container with tight-fitting cover. Bar-type cookies may be stored right in baking pan, tightly covered. If cookies tend to dry out, add piece of apple, orange, or bread, replacing it often.

Crisp Cookies: Keep in container with loose-fitting cover. If they soften, heat in 300°F. oven about 5 min. before serving.

Crisper Canisters: Thanks to the container of moisture-absorbing crystals on top, these canisters keep cookies soft or crisp—if each type is stored separately.

How to Freeze Cookies, see p. 540

How to Pack Cookies for Mailing

1. Bake travel-wise cookies that can stand a few knocks. See list on p. 474.

2. Use sturdy cardboard packing box. Line it with waxed paper. Place cushion of crumpled waxed paper or cellophane straw on bottom.

3. In moisture-vaporproof material, wrap flat cookies in pairs, back to back, with waxed paper between. Wrap others snugly; tape well.

4. Snugly arrange layers of cookies in rows in box, with heavy cookies at bottom; tuck enough sugar-coated cereal or popcorn into each crevice to keep cookies from jiggling. Top with crushed waxed paper or folded paper towels. Repeat to within ¼" of top.

5. Add final generous cushioning layer of waxed paper. Tape box shut (use broad brown-paper tape if available). Print address on box. Wrap in heavy brown paper; tie securely.

6. Label front and back with printed address and return address; cover with clear tape. Add "Fragile, Handle with Care" stickers.

7. For overseas mailing, use air express or parcel post if possible. Metal or wooden containers are best.

Some Cookie Travelers*

All Brownies (for short distances)	Peanut-Butter Fingers
	Crinkles-molded kind
Coconut-Butterscotch Squares	No-Bake Cookie Balls
	Walnut Bourbon Balls
Rocky-Road Fudge Squares	Orange Spritz Cookies
	Cinnamon Crisps
Luscious Apricot Bars	Peanut-Butter Bites
Chocolate Date Fingers	Neapolitans
	Susan's Refrigerator
Fruit-Betty Bars	Cookies (¼"
Fresh-Orange Cookies	thick)
Applesauce Cookies	Lemon-Nut
Coconut Macaroons	Refrigerator
Brazil Mincemeat Cookies	Cookies (¼" thick)
Chocolate-Honey Cookies	Sugar Cookies (¼" thick)
Soft Molasses Cookies	Pecan Wafers
Walnut Clusters	Rich Filled Cookies

See Index for page references.

BARS AND SQUARES
SUSAN'S BROWNIES

¾ cup sifted cake flour	2 to 2½ sq. unsweetened chocolate, melted
½ teasp. baking powder	
¾ teasp. salt	
1 cup granulated sugar	1 cup chopped walnuts, almonds, pecans, Brazil nuts, pistachio nuts, or peanuts
½ cup soft shortening	
2 eggs, unbeaten	
1 teasp. vanilla extract	

1. Start heating oven to 350°F. Grease 8" x 8" x 2" pan. Sift flour, baking powder, salt.
2. Gradually add sugar to shortening, mixing until *very light and fluffy*. Add eggs, vanilla; mix till smooth. Mix in chocolate, then flour mixture and nuts. (If desired, save half of nuts to sprinkle on top of batter before baking.)
3. Turn into pan. Bake 30 to 35 min., or until done. Cool slightly; cut into 16 squares or bars; sprinkle with confectioners' sugar if desired. Store right in pan.

Fudgies: Change flour to ½ cup sifted all-purpose; baking powder and salt to ⅛ teasp. Use butter. Bake at 325°F. 30 to 35 min.

Fruit: For part or all of nuts, substitute snipped raisins, pitted dates, or dates and nuts.

Frosted: Frost with Peppermint Butter Cream, p. 462. When frosting is firm, drizzle on 1 sq. unsweetened chocolate melted with 1 tablesp. margarine. Or frost with Quick-As-A-Wink Frosting, p. 464.

Coconut: Substitute shredded coconut for all or half of nuts. Some may be sprinkled on top of batter.

Peanut: Substitute ¼ cup peanut butter for ¼ cup shortening.

Double-decker: Omit chocolate, nuts. Remove one fourth of batter to small bowl; add ⅓ cup shredded coconut and ½ teasp. almond extract. To rest of batter, add 1½ sq. melted unsweetened chocolate; pour into pan. Spread with coconut batter. Bake.

Mocha: Add 1 tablesp. instant coffee to chocolate.

Chocolate-Orange: Add 1 tablesp. grated orange rind to batter. Frost with Orange Butter Cream, p. 462; top with more nuts.

COCONUT-BUTTERSCOTCH SQUARES

¾ cup sifted all-purpose flour
½ teasp. baking powder
½ teasp. salt
¼ cup soft shortening
1 cup brown sugar, packed
1 egg, unbeaten
1 teasp. vanilla extract
1 cup snipped shredded coconut
½ cup shredded coconut
1 tablesp. melted butter or margarine
1 tablesp. granulated sugar

Start heating oven to 350°F. Grease paperlined 8" x 8" x 2" pan. Sift flour, baking powder, salt. Mix shortening, brown sugar, egg, and vanilla until *very light and fluffy;* mix in flour mixture, 1 cup coconut; turn into pan. Mix ½ cup coconut, butter, granulated sugar; sprinkle over batter. Bake 35 min., or until done. Cut into 16 squares while warm. Cool in pan.

CHOCOLATE HALFWAY BARS

1 cup sifted all-purpose flour
⅛ teasp. salt
⅛ teasp. baking soda
½ teasp. baking powder
½ cup soft shortening
¼ cup granulated sugar
¼ cup brown sugar, packed
1 egg, separated
1½ teasp. water
½ teasp. vanilla extract
½ pkg. semisweet-chocolate pieces (½ cup)
½ cup brown sugar, packed

Start heating oven to 375°F. Grease 12" x 8" x 2" baking dish. Sift flour, salt, soda, baking powder. Mix shortening with sugars until *very light and fluffy.* Add egg yolk, water, vanilla; mix well. Thoroughly mix in flour mixture. Pat into baking dish; top with chocolate. Beat egg white until stiff; gradually beat in ½ cup brown sugar. Spread over chocolate. Bake 25 min., or until done. Cut into 32 bars while warm. Cool in dish.

ROCKY-ROAD FUDGE SQUARES

1 cup sifted all-purpose flour
1 cup granulated sugar
½ teasp. salt
⅔ cup soft shortening
2 eggs, unbeaten
1 teasp. vanilla extract
2 sq. unsweetened chocolate, melted
½ cup chopped walnuts or other nuts
24 marshmallows, snipped into quarters
1 pkg. semisweet-chocolate pieces (1 cup)

Start heating oven to 350°F. Grease 11" x 7" x 1½" pan. Sift flour, sugar, salt. Add shortening and eggs; beat until *light and fluffy.* Blend in vanilla and chocolate. Stir in walnuts. Turn into pan. Bake 20 to 25 min., or until done.

Immediately cover with marshmallows; cool in pan. Melt chocolate pieces over *hot, not boiling* water; pour over marshmallows (spread if necessary). Cool. Cut into 24 squares.

LUSCIOUS APRICOT BARS

⅔ cup dried apricots
½ cup soft butter or margarine
¼ cup granulated sugar
1⅓ cups sifted all-purpose flour
½ teasp. baking powder
¼ teasp. salt
1 cup brown sugar, packed
2 eggs, well beaten
½ teasp. vanilla extract
½ cup chopped nuts
Confectioners' sugar

Rinse apricots; cover with water; boil 10 min. Drain; cool; chop. Start heating oven to 350°F. Grease 8" x 8" x 2" pan. Mix butter, granulated sugar, and 1 cup flour until crumbly. Pack into pan. Bake 25 min.

Sift ⅓ cup flour, baking powder, salt. Gradually beat brown sugar into eggs; mix in flour mixture, then vanilla, nuts, apricots. Spread over baked layer. Bake 30 min., or until done. Cool in pan. Cut into 32 bars; roll in confectioners' sugar.

SUSAN'S TOFFEE BARS

½ cup soft butter or margarine
¼ cup granulated sugar
¼ cup brown sugar, packed
¼ teasp. salt
1 teasp. vanilla extract
1 egg, unbeaten
½ cup sifted all-purpose flour
½ cup uncooked rolled oats
1 pkg. semisweet-chocolate pieces (1 cup)
½ cup chopped walnuts

1. Start heating oven to 350°F. Grease 11" x 7" x 1½" pan.
2. Mix butter, sugars, salt, vanilla, and egg until *very light and fluffy.*
3. Mix in flour and rolled oats; then blend well. Spread in pan.
4. Bake 30 min., or until done. Cool 10 min.
5. Meanwhile, melt chocolate over *hot, not boiling,* water; stir until smooth; spread over baked layer; sprinkle with nuts. Cool in pan. Cut into 24 bars.

CHOCOLATE-DATE FINGERS

½ cup sifted all-purpose flour	or margarine
½ teasp. baking powder	2 teasp. hot water
¼ teasp. salt	½ cup snipped, pitted dates
½ cup granulated sugar	1 pkg. semisweet-chocolate pieces (1 cup)
1 egg, unbeaten	
1 teasp. melted butter	⅔ cup chopped walnuts

Start heating oven to 325°F. Grease 8″ x 8″ x 2″ pan. Sift flour, baking powder, salt. Mix sugar with egg till *very light and fluffy*. Mix in butter, water, dates, chocolate, flour mixture. Pour into pan; top with nuts. Bake 30 to 35 min., or until done. Cool in pan. Cut into 24 "fingers."

FRUIT-BETTY BARS

1½ cups sifted all-purpose flour	packed
	½ cup chopped nuts
1 teasp. baking soda	1 cup melted shortening
1 teasp. salt	
2½ cups uncooked rolled oats	Date, Fig, Prune, Raisin, or Mincemeat Filling, p. 484
1½ cups brown sugar,	

Start heating oven to 350°F. Grease 12″ x 8″ x 2″ baking dish. Combine flour, soda, salt, oats, sugar, nuts. Add melted shortening; mix well. Press half of dough firmly into dish. Spread with one of fillings; cover with rest of dough; pat down well. Bake 25 to 35 min., or until done. Cool in dish. Cut into 36 bars.

CHEWY PECAN STICKS

½ cup soft shortening	1 cup brown sugar, packed
1½ cups sifted all-purpose flour	2 tablesp. flour
1 tablesp. granulated sugar	½ teasp. baking powder
¼ teasp. salt	½ teasp. salt
1 egg, unbeaten	½ teasp. vanilla extract
2 tablesp. water	1 cup chopped pecans
2 eggs	

Start heating oven to 350°F. With fork, mix shortening, 1½ cups flour, granulated sugar, ¼ teasp. salt, until consistency of fine corn meal. Mix in 1 egg and water. Press into 12″ x 8″ x 2″ baking dish. Bake 15 min. Beat 2 eggs; add rest of ingredients; mix well. Spread over baked layer. Bake 40 min. Cool in dish. Cut into 32 sticks.

FUDGE CUTS

2 sq. unsweetened chocolate	purpose flour
	¼ teasp. salt
½ cup shortening	1 teasp. vanilla extract
1 cup granulated sugar	½ cup finely chopped walnuts
2 eggs, well beaten	
½ cup sifted all-	

Start heating oven to 400°F. Grease 2 8″ x 8″ x 2″ pans. In double boiler, melt chocolate and shortening; remove from water. Add sugar, eggs, then flour, salt, vanilla; stir well. Pour into pans; sprinkle with nuts. Bake 12 min., or until done. Cool in pan. Cut into 32 2″ squares.

Tea Brownies: Cut Fudge Cuts with small fancy cutter. Or put 2 layers together, with Orange Butter Cream, p. 462, as filling; cut.

DROP-AND-BAKE COOKIES

FROSTED CHOCOLATE JUMBOS

1¾ cups sifted all-purpose flour	2 eggs, unbeaten
	⅓ cup milk
2 teasp. baking powder	½ teasp. vanilla extract
½ teasp. salt	3 sq. unsweetened chocolate, melted
1 cup granulated sugar	
½ cup salad oil	½ cup chopped walnuts

Start heating oven to 350°F. Into large bowl, sift flour, baking powder, salt, sugar. Make well in flour mixture; add salad oil, eggs, milk, vanilla; beat until smooth. Stir in chocolate, nuts. Drop by tablespoonfuls, 2″ apart, onto greased cookie sheet. Bake 20 min., or until done. Frost with ½ recipe Mocha Butter Cream, p. 462. Makes about 2 doz.

FRESH-ORANGE COOKIES

2½ cups sifted cake flour	1 tablesp. grated orange rind
½ teasp. salt	½ cup orange juice
½ teasp. baking soda	½ cup chopped walnuts or shredded coconut
½ cup soft shortening	
1 cup granulated sugar	
2 eggs, unbeaten	

Start heating oven to 400°F. Sift flour, salt, soda. Mix shortening, sugar, eggs, and orange rind until *very light and fluffy*. Mix in flour mixture alternately with orange juice; then mix in nuts. Drop by teaspoonfuls, 2″ apart, onto greased cookie sheet. Bake 10 to 12 min., or until golden.

Frost with Orange or Chocolate Butter Cream, p. 462. Makes 4 doz.

MERINGUE DIPS

3 egg whites	extract
1 tablesp. vinegar	1 cup chopped,
¼ teasp. salt	blanched almonds
1 cup sifted granulated	4 sq. unsweetened
sugar	chocolate, coarsely
1 teasp. vanilla extract	grated
½ teasp. almond	

About 1 hr. ahead, set out egg whites. To make dips, start heating oven to 250°F. With electric mixer or egg beater, beat egg whites with vinegar and salt until they stand in moist peaks; slowly beat in sugar. Then, with spoon, fold in extracts, nuts, chocolate. Drop by teaspoonfuls, 2″ apart, onto greased cookie sheet. Bake 30 min., or until firm to touch. Cool. Dip half of each cookie into Chocolate Dip, below. Let harden on wire rack. Makes about 3 doz.

Chocolate Dip: Melt 1 pkg. semisweet-chocolate pieces (1 cup) with 1 tablesp. shortening (not butter or margarine) over *hot, not boiling,* water; stir till smooth.

APPLESAUCE COOKIES

1¾ cups sifted cake flour	1 teasp. baking soda
½ teasp. salt	½ cup soft shortening
1 teasp. cinnamon	1 cup granulated sugar
½ teasp. nutmeg	1 egg, unbeaten
½ teasp. ground cloves	1 cup light or dark raisins
1 cup canned apple-sauce	1 cup ready-to-eat bran

Start heating oven to 375°F. Sift flour, salt, cinnamon, nutmeg, cloves. Combine applesauce, soda. Mix shortening with sugar and egg until *very light and fluffy.* Mix in flour mixture alternately with applesauce. Fold in raisins, bran. Drop by teaspoonfuls, about 2″ apart, onto greased cookie sheet. Bake 20 min., or until golden brown. If desired, frost with Butter Cream, p. 462. Makes 3 doz.

CHOCOLATE NO-BAKES

In double boiler, melt ½ lb. milk chocolate, 1 pkg. semisweet-chocolate pieces (1 cup), 2 sq. unsweetened chocolate, and 1 tablesp. butter

or margarine; cool. Mix in 1½ cups snipped shredded coconut, then 4 cups corn flakes. Drop in mounds onto cookie sheet. Refrigerate till set. Makes about 4 doz.

LACY RAISIN WAFERS

¾ cup sifted all-purpose flour	½ cup salad oil
½ teasp. baking soda	¼ cup water
½ teasp. salt	1 cup brown sugar, packed
¼ teasp. cinnamon	1 teasp. vanilla extract
¼ teasp. nutmeg	1½ cups uncooked rolled oats
¾ cup light or dark raisins	½ cup chopped nuts

Sift flour, soda, salt, cinnamon, nutmeg. Rinse and drain raisins; mix with salad oil, water; mix in sugar, vanilla, oats, nuts, then flour mixture. Refrigerate 1 hr. Start heating oven to 350°F. Drop dough by teaspoonfuls, about 2″ apart, onto greased cookie sheet. Bake 10 to 12 min., or till crisp around edges. Makes 3½ doz.

Lacy Coconut: Omit raisins, nuts. Fold in 1 cup shredded coconut after adding flour.

Lacy Chocolate: Omit raisins, nuts. Fold in 1 pkg. semisweet-chocolate pieces (1 cup) after adding flour.

Lacy Date-Nut: Omit raisins. Fold in 1 cup chopped, pitted dates after adding flour.

COCONUT MACAROONS

With electric mixer or egg beater, beat 3 egg whites till stiff but not dry. Slowly beat in 1 cup granulated sugar. With spoon, fold in 3 cups shredded coconut mixed with 2 tablesp. cornstarch. Cook, stirring often, in double boiler over hot water 15 min. Add 1 teasp. vanilla extract. Meanwhile, start heating oven to 300°F. Drop mixture by teaspoonfuls, 1″ apart, onto greased cookie sheet. Bake 20 to 25 min., or till golden. Makes 2½ doz.

OLD-FASHIONED SOFT SUGAR COOKIES

2 cups sifted all-purpose flour	1 egg yolk
½ teasp. baking soda	½ cup buttermilk or sour milk
½ teasp. salt	½ teasp. vanilla extract
½ cup soft shortening	1 egg white
1 cup granulated sugar	

Start heating oven to 375°F. Sift flour, soda, salt. Mix shortening, sugar, and egg yolk till *very light and fluffy*. Mix in flour mixture alternately with buttermilk; then mix in vanilla. Fold in egg white, beaten stiff. Drop by rounded tablespoonfuls, 3" apart, onto greased cookie sheet. With spatula, flatten till ½" thick. If desired, sprinkle with sugar mixed with chopped nuts, raisins, or grated lemon rind. Bake 20 min., or until golden brown. Makes 1½ doz.

BRAZIL MINCEMEAT COOKIES

1 cup sifted all- purpose flour	1 egg, unbeaten ½ cup prepared
¼ teasp. baking soda	mincemeat
1 teasp. baking powder	1 teasp. vanilla extract
1 teasp. salt	1 cup uncooked
1 teasp. cinnamon	rolled oats
½ cup soft shortening	1 cup chopped Brazil
1 cup granulated sugar	nuts
1 tablesp. light molasses	

Start heating oven to 350°F. Sift flour, soda, baking powder, salt, cinnamon. Mix shortening, sugar, molasses, and egg until *very light and fluffy*. Mix in mincemeat, then flour mixture, vanilla, oats, nuts. Drop by level tablespoonfuls onto greased cookie sheet. Bake 10 to 12 min. Makes 6 doz.

CHOCOLATE MERINGUES

3 egg whites	saltines
1 cup sifted confec- tioners' sugar	1 pkg. semisweet- chocolate pieces
⅓ cup crumbled	(1 cup), melted

Start heating oven to 350°F. With electric mixer or egg beater, beat egg whites till stiff but not dry. Add sugar slowly, beating constantly. With spoon, fold in saltines, chocolate. Drop by teaspoonfuls, 2" apart, onto greased cookie sheet. Bake 13 min., or until firm to touch. Makes 4 doz.

DATE-AND-NUT MACAROONS

Start heating oven to 350°F. Mix together ⅔ cup canned sweetened condensed milk; 1 cup each shredded coconut, chopped nuts, and chopped, pitted dates; and 1 teasp. vanilla extract. Drop by teaspoonfuls, 1" apart, onto greased cookie sheet. Bake 10 to 12 min., or until golden. Makes about 2 doz.

CHOCOLATE-HONEY COOKIES

1 cup sifted all- purpose flour	½ cup uncooked rolled oats
1 teasp. baking powder	½ cup chopped walnuts
¼ teasp. salt	½ cup light or dark
½ cup soft shortening	raisins
1 egg, unbeaten	1 pkg. semisweet- chocolate pieces
1 teasp. vanilla extract	(1 cup), chopped
½ cup honey	

Start heating oven to 375°F. Sift flour, baking powder, salt. Mix shortening, egg, vanilla, and honey until *very light and fluffy*. Mix in flour mixture, oats, nuts, raisins, chocolate. Drop by teaspoonfuls onto greased cookie sheet; flatten with tines of fork. Bake 10 min. Makes 5 doz.

SOFT MOLASSES COOKIES

2¼ cups sifted all- purpose flour	½ cup soft shortening ½ cup granulated sugar
1 teasp. ginger	½ cup molasses
1 teasp. cinnamon	1 egg, unbeaten
¼ teasp. salt	6 tablesp. cold water
2 teasp. baking soda	½ cup light or dark
2 tablesp. hot water	raisins, or chopped nuts

Start heating oven to 400°F. Sift flour, ginger, cinnamon, salt. Dissolve soda in hot water. Mix shortening, sugar, molasses, and egg until *very light and fluffy*. Mix in flour mixture alternately with cold water; then mix in soda and all but a few raisins. Drop by rounded tablespoonfuls, 2" apart, onto greased cookie sheet. Top with rest of raisins. Bake 12 min., or until done. Makes about 2 doz.

WALNUT CLUSTERS

½ cup sifted all- purpose flour	½ cup granulated sugar 1 egg, unbeaten
¼ teasp. baking powder	1½ teasp. vanilla extract
½ teasp. salt	1½ sq. unsweetened
¼ cup soft butter or margarine	chocolate, melted 2 cups broken walnuts

Start heating oven to 350°F. Sift flour, baking powder, salt. Mix butter, sugar, egg, and vanilla until *very light and fluffy*. Mix in chocolate, then flour mixture. Fold in walnuts. Drop by teaspoonfuls, 1" apart, onto greased cookie sheet. Bake just 10 min.—no longer. Makes 2½ doz.

MOLDED COOKIES

PEANUT-BUTTER FINGERS

1 cup sifted all-purpose flour	2 teasp. grated orange rind
¼ teasp. baking soda	½ cup brown sugar, packed
1½ teasp. baking powder	½ cup granulated sugar
½ teasp. salt	1 egg, unbeaten
½ cup soft shortening	½ cup finely ground or chopped raisins
½ cup peanut butter	

Start heating oven to 350°F. Sift flour, soda, baking powder, salt. Mix shortening, peanut butter, orange rind; beat in sugars, egg, and raisins until *very light and fluffy.* Mix in flour mixture. Pinch off small pieces of dough, rolling each with palms of hands into roll 2″ long; place on ungreased cookie sheet; with tines of fork, press lengthwise. Bake 12 to 15 min., or until golden. Makes 4 doz.

NUT BUTTER BALLS

1 cup soft butter or margarine*	2 cups sifted all-purpose flour
¼ to ½ cup granulated or confectioners' sugar	1 to 2 cups finely chopped or ground walnuts, pecans, almonds, black walnuts, Brazil nuts, or filberts
½ teasp. salt	
1 teasp. almond extract; or 2 teasp. vanilla extract	

Mix butter with sugar until *very light and fluffy.* Add salt, extract, flour, nuts; mix *well.* Refrigerate until easy to handle. Start heating oven to 350°F. Shape dough into 1″ balls or 1″ to 2″ x ½″ rolls, triangles, or crescents. Place on ungreased cookie sheet. (Or drop by level tablespoonfuls onto cookie sheet.) Bake 12 to 15 min., or until light brown. While cookies are warm, roll in granulated or confectioners' sugar, fine cookie crumbs, or cinnamon and sugar. Makes 4 to 5 doz.

* *Or use soft shortening, or half soft butter and half soft shortening.*

Honey-Pecan: Substitute ¼ cup honey for sugar.

Prickly Butter: Omit nuts from dough. Before baking balls, dip into beaten egg white, then into chopped n... or crushed corn or wheat flakes.

Cherryettes: Before baking balls, press candied-cherry half into each.

Coconut Pompons: Omit nuts. Shape each ball of dough around ½ pecan, date, candied cherry, or almond; roll in shredded coconut.

Choco-Butter Crescents: When adding nuts, also add 1 pkg. semisweet-chocolate pieces (1 cup), coarsely chopped.

Melting Moments: Omit nuts. Add 2 teasp. baking powder to flour. With fork dipped into flour, press balls flat on cookie sheet.

If desired, when cookies are cool, turn bottom sides up. Spread with Sugar Glaze, p. 465; then drizzle on Chocolate Glaze, p. 465, in parallel lines; immediately draw toothpick across lines.

Almond Cookies: Increase granulated sugar to 1 cup, flour to 2⅔ cups. With extract, add 2 egg yolks. Use almonds. After shaping dough into 2″ balls, dip into 2 unbeaten egg whites. Place almond in center of each. Bake.

Mexican Wedding Cakes: With bottom of tumbler dipped into flour, flatten each 1″ ball. Bake at 325°F. 12 min. While cookies are warm, sprinkle with confectioners' sugar.

French Dips: Use ½ cup confectioners' sugar. Omit nuts. Add 1 cup uncooked rolled oats to dough (don't refrigerate). Shape into logs or balls; place nut half in center of some cookies. Bake at 325°F. 25 to 30 min.; cool.

Melt 2 pkg. semisweet-chocolate pieces (2 cups) with ¼ cup milk over *hot, not boiling,* water. Using tongs or 2 forks, dip top or ends of each cookie into chocolate, then into chopped nuts, snipped shredded coconut, chocolate sprinkles, or silver *dragées.*

Or make Nut Butter Balls, above; dip as above.

Finnish Butter Strips: Reduce butter to ¾ cup. Omit nuts. Roll chilled dough ⅛″ thick; cut into 2″ x 1″ strips. Brush with beaten egg white; sprinkle with granulated sugar, chopped almonds. Bake.

Chocolate Halfways: Omit nuts. Use ¾ cup confectioners' sugar, 1 teasp. vanilla. Roll chilled dough ⅓″ to ½″ thick; cut into desired shapes. Bake at 300°F. 20 to 25 min. Cool; dip end or side of each cookie into Chocolate Dip, p. 477. Let harden on wire cake rack.

PRALINE COOKIES

½ cup soft butter or margarine	1½ cups sifted all-purpose flour
1½ cups dark-brown sugar, packed	1 teasp. vanilla extract
1 egg, unbeaten	1 cup coarsely chopped pecans

Mix together butter, sugar, and egg until creamy. Mix in rest of ingredients. Refrigerate till easy to handle. Start heating oven to 375°F. Shape dough into 1" balls; place, 3" apart, on greased cookie sheet. Using bottom of tumbler covered with damp cheesecloth, flatten balls till ⅛" thick. Bake 12 min., or until done. Makes 3 doz.

CHRISTMAS WREATHS

1 cup soft shortening	¼ teasp. salt
½ cup brown sugar, packed	2 cups chopped nuts or shredded coconut
2 eggs, separated	½ cup raspberry or strawberry jam
2 cups sifted all-purpose flour	

Start heating oven to 375°F. Mix shortening with sugar until *very light and fluffy*. Mix in egg yolks, flour, salt. Form into 1" balls. Dip into unbeaten egg whites; then remove with fork and drop into nuts. Place, 1" apart, on greased cookie sheet. Make slight depression in center of each cookie. Bake 5 min.; then press center again; bake 10 min. longer. Cool slightly. Remove from cookie sheet. Fill centers with jam. Makes 3 doz.

CRINKLES

2¼ cups sifted all-purpose flour	¾ cup soft shortening
1 teasp. salt	1 cup brown sugar, packed
2 teasp. baking soda	1 egg, unbeaten
1 teasp. cinnamon	¼ cup molasses
½ teasp. ground cloves	Granulated sugar
1 teasp. ginger	

Sift flour, salt, soda, cinnamon, cloves, ginger. Mix shortening with brown sugar and egg until *very light and fluffy*. Mix in molasses, then flour mixture. Refrigerate 1 hr. or longer. Start heating oven to 375°F. Shape dough into walnut-size balls; dip one side of each into granulated sugar. Place, with sugar sides up, 3" apart, on greased cookie sheet. Sprinkle each cookie with 2 or 3 drops water. Bake 12 to 15 min., or until done. Makes 4 to 5 doz.

Pumpkins: Before sprinkling cookies with water, flatten each ball with fork; press bit of citron into top, for stem.

NO-BAKE COOKIE BALLS

1 pkg. semisweet-chocolate pieces (1 cup)	2 teasp. instant coffee
	⅓ cup hot water
3 tablesp. white corn syrup	1¾ cups finely crushed packaged vanilla wafers (about 3 doz.)
3 cups sifted confectioners' sugar	
1 cup chopped walnuts	½ cup sifted confectioners' sugar

In double boiler over *hot, not boiling,* water, melt chocolate; remove from heat. Mix in syrup, 3 cups sugar, nuts, coffee dissolved in hot water, wafer crumbs. Form into 1" balls. Roll in ½ cup sugar. Store in covered container a day or so to ripen. Makes about 5 doz.

Choco-Orange: Substitute ⅓ cup orange juice for instant coffee and hot water.

WALNUT BOURBON BALLS

2½ cups finely crushed packaged vanilla wafers (about 5 doz.)	1 cup finely chopped walnuts, or walnuts and shredded coconut
2 tablesp. cocoa	3 tablesp. corn syrup
1 cup confectioners' sugar	¼ cup bourbon
	Confectioners' sugar

Mix well wafer crumbs, cocoa, 1 cup sugar, nuts. Add corn syrup, bourbon; mix well. Form into 1" balls; then roll in sugar. Store in covered container a day or so to ripen. Makes 3½ doz.

ORANGE SPRITZ COOKIES

2½ cups sifted all-purpose flour	packed
¼ teasp. salt	1 teasp. grated orange rind
¼ teasp. baking soda	2 tablesp. orange juice
1 cup soft shortening	1 medium egg, unbeaten
½ cup granulated sugar	
½ cup brown sugar,	

Start heating oven to 400°F. Sift flour, salt, soda. Mix shortening with sugars, rind, orange juice, and egg until *very light and fluffy*. Gradually add flour mixture, mixing well after each addition. Fill cookie press*; press cookies onto *un-*

greased cold cookie sheet. Bake 10 to 12 min., or until golden. Makes about 7 doz.

A cookie-press set, with several recipes for making fascinating cookies, can be purchased in a housewares' department.

Cinnamon Crisps: Omit orange rind and juice. Add 2 teasp. cinnamon to flour, 1 tablesp. cream to egg.

Peanut-Butter Bites: Omit orange rind. Reduce flour to 2 cups. Substitute ½ cup peanut butter for ½ cup shortening.

CREAM-CHEESE SMOOTHIES

2½ cups sifted all-purpose flour	1 teasp. grated lemon rind
1 teasp. baking powder	1 tablesp. lemon juice
1 cup soft margarine	1 cup confectioners' sugar
1 3-oz. pkg. soft cream cheese	2 tablesp. lemon juice
1 cup granulated sugar	½ cup chopped pecans
1 egg, unbeaten	

Sift flour, baking powder. Mix margarine with cheese; add granulated sugar; mix thoroughly. Add egg, lemon rind, 1 tablesp. lemon juice; mix well. Mix in flour mixture. Refrigerate about ½ hr. Start heating oven to 375°F. Force dough through ribbon disk of cookie press onto *ungreased cold* cookie sheet. Bake 8 to 10 min., or until golden.

Mix confectioners' sugar with 2 tablesp. lemon juice. When cookies are cool, dip one end of each into this frosting, then into pecans. Let set. Makes about 6 doz.

JAM RIBBONS

2½ cups sifted all-purpose flour	1 cup soft margarine
½ teasp. baking powder	⅔ cup granulated sugar
	1 egg, unbeaten
Pinch salt	1 teasp. almond extract
	Jam

Start heating oven to 400°F. Sift flour, baking powder, salt. Mix margarine, sugar, egg, and extract until *very light and fluffy.* Mix in flour mixture. Force dough through ribbon disk of cookie press onto *ungreased cold* cookie sheet. Place jam along center of each strip. Bake 7 to 10 min., or until golden. While cookies are hot, cut into 2½" lengths. Cool on wire rack.

REFRIGERATOR COOKIES
NEAPOLITANS

Dark Dough:

3 cups sifted all-purpose flour	packed
¼ teasp. salt	2 eggs, unbeaten
1 teasp. baking soda	1 cup coarsely ground nuts
½ teasp. cinnamon	1 pkg. well-chilled semisweet-chocolate pieces (1 cup), finely ground
½ teasp. ground cloves	
1 cup soft shortening	
1½ cups brown sugar,	

Sift flour, salt, soda, cinnamon, cloves. Mix shortening with sugar, then with eggs, until *very light and fluffy.* Mix in flour mixture, nuts, chocolate.

Light Dough:

2 cups sifted all-purpose flour	½ teasp. almond extract
½ teasp. salt	2 tablesp. water
¼ teasp. baking soda	¾ cup finely chopped dark raisins
½ cup soft shortening	12 chopped candied cherries
¾ cup granulated sugar	
1 egg, unbeaten	
1 teasp. vanilla extract	

Sift flour, salt, soda. Mix shortening with sugar, then with egg, extracts, and water, until *very light and fluffy.* Mix in flour mixture, then raisins, cherries.

To Assemble: Pack half of dark dough into waxed-paper-lined 10" x 5" x 3" loaf pan. Pack in all of light dough, then remaining dark dough. Refrigerate at least 24 hr.

To Bake: Start heating oven to 400°F. Cut dough lengthwise into thirds; slice crosswise into ¼" slices. Place, 1" apart, on *ungreased cold* cookie sheet. Bake 8 to 10 min., or until done. Makes 8 to 9 doz.

SUSAN'S VANILLA REFRIGERATOR COOKIES

1½ cups sifted all-purpose flour	brown sugar, packed
½ teasp. baking soda	1 egg, unbeaten
¾ teasp. salt	2 to 3 teasp. vanilla extract; or ½ teasp. almond extract
½ cup soft shortening	
1 cup granulated sugar; or ½ cup each granulated sugar and	½ cup chopped nuts (optional)

1. Sift flour, soda, salt. Mix shortening with sugar, egg, and vanilla until *very light and fluffy*. Gradually mix in flour mixture and nuts.
2. Turn dough onto large piece of waxed paper. Shape into roll 1½″ in diameter; then wrap. Refrigerate several hours, overnight, or several weeks if desired.
3. Start heating oven to 375°F. With sharp thin knife dipped into hot water, then wiped dry, slice roll ⅛″ to ¼″ thick. (Slice off only what you need; return rest of roll to refrigerator to bake later.)
4. Place on ungreased cookie sheet. Bake 10 min., or until done. Cool; store in tightly covered container. Makes 5 doz.

Chocolate: Add 3 sq. melted unsweetened chocolate to egg mixture before adding flour. Decrease vanilla to 1 teasp.

Orange: Add 1 tablesp. grated orange rind to egg mixture; substitute orange juice for vanilla.

Date: Add ½ cup chopped, pitted dates to flour mixture.

Spice-Nut: Sift ½ teasp. cinnamon and ¼ teasp. nutmeg with flour mixture.

Coconut: Increase shortening to ¾ cup. Use granulated-brown sugar combination. Add 2 cups shredded coconut.

CHOCOLATE SPECKLE COOKIES

1½ cups sifted all-purpose flour	½ cup peanut butter
1 cup granulated sugar	½ cup water
½ teasp. baking soda	½ cup uncooked rolled oats
1 teasp. salt	½ cup finely chopped walnuts
¼ teasp. nutmeg	
¾ teasp. cinnamon	
½ cup soft shortening	1 pkg. semisweet-chocolate pieces (1 cup), finely chopped
1 egg, unbeaten	

Sift flour, sugar, soda, salt, nutmeg, cinnamon. Mix shortening, egg, peanut butter, and water until *very light and fluffy*. Mix in flour mixture, oats, nuts, chocolate. Shape into roll 2″ in diameter; wrap in waxed paper. Refrigerate till firm.

At baking time: Start heating oven to 375°F. Cut roll into ⅛″ slices; place on ungreased cookie sheet. Bake 12 min., or till done. Makes 8 doz.

LEMON-NUT REFRIGERATOR COOKIES

2 cups sifted all-purpose flour	½ cup granulated sugar
¼ teasp. baking soda	1 egg, well beaten
¼ teasp. salt	1 tablesp. grated lemon rind
1 cup soft shortening	2 tablesp. lemon juice
½ cup brown sugar, packed	½ cup chopped walnuts

Sift flour, soda, salt. Mix shortening with sugars, then with egg, lemon rind and juice, until *very light and fluffy*. Mix in flour mixture, nuts. Shape into roll 2″ in diameter; wrap in waxed paper. Refrigerate several hours, overnight, or several weeks.

At baking time: Start heating oven to 400°F. Cut roll into ⅛″ to ¼″ slices. Place on ungreased cookie sheet. Bake 10 to 12 min., or until done. Makes about 4½ doz.

ROLL-AND-CUT COOKIES

SUGAR COOKIES

4 cups sifted cake flour	1½ cups granulated sugar
2½ teasp. baking powder	2 eggs, unbeaten
½ teasp. salt	1 teasp. vanilla extract
⅔ cup soft shortening	4 teasp. milk

1. Sift flour, baking powder, salt. Mix shortening with sugar, eggs, and vanilla until *very light and fluffy*. Mix in flour mixture alternately with milk.
2. Refrigerate dough until easy to handle (you can hasten this chilling by placing dough in freezing compartment).
3. Start heating oven to 400°F. On lightly floured surface, roll half or third of dough at a time, keeping rest in refrigerator. For *crisp* cookies, roll dough paper-thin. For *softer* cookies, roll ⅛″ to ¼″ thick.
4. With floured cutter or cardboard pattern, cut into desired shapes, keeping cuttings close together.
5. With broad spatula, arrange cookies, ½″ apart, on lightly greased cookie sheet. If desired, brush with cream, or with egg white diluted with a little water. Then, if desired, sprinkle with white or colored sugar, chopped nuts, shredded coconut, cut-up gumdrops, silver *dragées,* cinnamon and sugar, bits of candied fruit, etc.

6. Bake 9 min., or until delicate brown. Then cool. Makes about 6 doz.

Butterscotch-Pecan: Substitute 2 cups brown sugar, packed, for granulated sugar. Add 1 cup finely chopped pecans with flour mixture.

Caraway: Substitute 3 tablesp. brandy for vanilla and milk. Add 1½ teasp. caraway seeds to sugar. Dust cookies with confectioners' sugar.

Chocolate: Add 4 sq. melted unsweetened chocolate to shortening mixture. Add 1 cup chopped walnuts (optional) to flour mixture.

Coconut: Add 1 cup snipped shredded coconut with flour.

Lemon: Substitute 4 teasp. lemon juice and 2 tablesp. grated lemon rind for vanilla.

Two Short Cuts: To save time needed to roll out Sugar Cookie dough, you may do this:

1. Drop level or rounded spoonfuls of well-chilled dough, 2″ apart, onto greased cookie sheet. Flatten by pressing with fork or bottom of tumbler dipped into sugar.
2. Or cut rolled-out dough to fit greased shallow baking pan. Bake as directed. While cookies are still hot and in pan, cut into squares or "fingers."

JELLY TARTS

2½ cups sifted all-purpose flour	½ cup sifted confectioners' sugar
¼ teasp. baking powder	2 tablesp. milk
½ teasp. salt	Top milk
1 cup soft shortening	Blanched almonds
2 teasp. vanilla extract	Currant jelly

Sift flour, baking powder, salt. Mix shortening, vanilla, and sugar until *very light and fluffy*. Mix in flour mixture, 2 tablesp. milk. Refrigerate till easy to handle. Start heating oven to 350°F. On lightly floured surface, roll dough ¼″ thick. Cut into 2½″ rounds. Cut ¾″ circle from center of each of half of rounds; brush with top milk; shave on a few almonds. Place, 1″ apart, on ungreased cookie sheet. Bake 15 min., or till done; cool. Place 1 teasp. jelly in centers of flat sides of whole rounds; top with rings, with right sides up. Makes 1 doz.

SCOTCH SHORTBREAD

2 cups sifted all-purpose flour	1 cup soft butter or margarine
¼ teasp. baking powder	½ cup confectioners' sugar
¼ teasp. salt	

Sift flour, baking powder, salt. Mix butter with sugar until *very light and fluffy*. Mix in flour mixture. Refrigerate until easy to handle. Start heating oven to 350°F. On lightly floured surface, roll dough ¼″ thick. Cut into squares, triangles, etc. Place, 1″ apart, on ungreased cookie sheet. Bake 20 to 25 min., or until done.

If preferred, pat unchilled dough into 9″ x 9″ x 2″ pan; bake; cut into desired shapes while warm. If desired, before baking, sprinkle with cinnamon-and-sugar mixture. Makes about 2½ doz.

Walnut: Substitute ⅔ cup brown sugar, packed, for confectioners' sugar. Add ¾ cup finely chopped walnuts. Decorate cookies with walnut halves or candied cherries. Bake at 300°F. 20 to 25 min.

PECAN WAFERS

1½ cups soft shortening	3 egg whites
1 cup granulated sugar	¼ cup granulated sugar
3 egg yolks	1 teasp. cinnamon
4 cups sifted all-purpose flour	¾ cup chopped pecans

Start heating oven to 375°F. Mix shortening, 1 cup sugar, and egg yolks until *very light and fluffy*. Mix in flour. On lightly floured surface, roll half of dough thin. Beat egg whites till stiff; spread half on rolled dough. Combine ¼ cup sugar, cinnamon, nuts; sprinkle half over whites. Cut into 2″ squares; place, 1″ apart, on ungreased cookie sheet. Repeat with rest of dough. Bake 10 min., or till done. Makes 3 doz.

PEANUT WHIRLIGIGS

2 cups sifted all-purpose flour	1 teasp. vanilla extract
½ teasp. salt	¾ cup ground salted peanuts
½ cup soft butter or margarine	½ pkg. semisweet-chocolate pieces (½ cup), melted
½ cup soft shortening	2 tablesp. melted butter or margarine
1 3-oz. pkg. soft cream cheese	
1 cup granulated sugar	

Sift flour, salt. Mix soft butter with shortening, cheese, sugar, and vanilla until *very light and fluffy*. Mix in flour mixture and peanuts. Refrigerate until easy to handle.

Start heating oven to 400°F. On lightly floured surface, roll half of dough into ⅛″-thick rectangle. Mix chocolate, melted butter; spread half over rolled dough. Roll up like jelly roll. Repeat with rest of dough. With sharp knife or heavy string, slice ⅛″ thick. Place, 1″ apart, on greased cookie sheet. Bake 8 to 10 min. Makes about 8 doz.

RICH FILLED COOKIES

5 cups sifted all-	2 cups granulated sugar
purpose flour	2 eggs, unbeaten
2 teasp. baking powder	1 teasp. vanilla extract
1 teasp. baking soda	1 cup commercial
½ teasp. salt	sour cream
1 cup soft shortening	

Sift flour, baking powder, soda, salt. Mix shortening with sugar, eggs, and vanilla until *very light and fluffy*. Mix in sour cream, then flour mixture, a little at a time. Refrigerate until easy to handle.

Start heating oven to 425°F. On lightly floured surface, roll dough ⅛″ thick; cut with 3″ round, scalloped, or star cutter. Place half of rounds on ungreased cookie sheet; place rounded teaspoonful of one of fillings, below, on center of each. Top with remaining rounds, with centers cut out if desired; press edges together with fingers or floured fork. Brush with cream if desired. Bake 8 to 10 min., or until golden. Makes 4 to 5 doz.

LUSCIOUS COOKIE FILLINGS

Date: Simmer, stirring, until thick, 2 7¼-oz. pkg. pitted dates, ½ cup granulated sugar, ¾ cup white corn syrup, ¼ cup orange juice, 1 tablesp. grated orange rind, ¼ teasp. salt. Cool.

Fig: Simmer, stirring, about 20 min., 1 lb. dried figs, cut or ground; ¾ cup granulated sugar; ¾ cup water; 2 tablesp. lemon juice; ½ teasp. salt. Cool.

Prune: Cook over low heat, stirring, until thick, 3 cups cut, pitted, cooked prunes and ¾ cup

granulated sugar. Add 1 teasp. vanilla extract. Cool.

Raisin: Simmer, stirring, until thick, 1½ cups light or dark raisins, ⅓ cup water, ½ cup granulated sugar, 1 tablesp. cornstarch, pinch salt, 1 tablesp. lemon juice. Cool.

Honey-Coconut: Combine ½ cup granulated sugar, ⅓ cup honey, ½ cup water, ¼ teasp. salt, 3 cups shredded coconut. Cook about 10 min., or until coconut absorbs most of syrup. Stir in ½ teasp. vanilla extract and 1 tablesp. butter or margarine. Cool.

Mincemeat: Simmer, stirring, until thick, ¼ cup granulated sugar, 1 tablesp. cornstarch, ½ teasp. fresh, frozen, or canned lemon juice, 1½ cups prepared mincemeat. Cool.

Quick: Use preserves or jelly, apple butter, a few semisweet-chocolate pieces, raisins and chopped nuts, or mincemeat.

HOLIDAY MOLASSES CRISPS

1¼ cups sifted	½ cup molasses
all-purpose flour	¼ cup soft shortening
¾ teasp. baking soda	1 teasp. grated
½ teasp. ginger	orange rind

Sift flour, soda, ginger. In saucepan, bring molasses and shortening to boil. Cool slightly; mix in flour mixture, orange rind. Chill well.

Start heating oven to 375°F. On lightly floured surface, roll dough ⅛″ thick. With holiday cutters, cut out Santa Clauses, Christmas trees, angels, etc. Arrange, ½″ apart, on greased cookie sheet. Bake 8 to 10 min., or until done.

If desired, when cookies are cool, frost with Sugar Glaze, p. 465; then decorate with silver *dragées,* red or green sugar, or tiny varicolored candies. Makes about 3 doz.

PACKAGED COOKIE MIXES

Indeed they are good, and for a good reason— the finest ingredients go into them! What's more, these mixes couldn't be easier to adapt for a variety of delicious cookies. Just check the label of plain, chocolate chip, peanut, etc.

Packaged gingerbread mixes also carry label directions for making luscious ginger cookies.

Holiday Specials

LEBKUCHEN

2¼ cups sifted all-purpose flour	mixed preserved fruits
½ teasp. salt	3 eggs
1 teasp. baking powder	1 egg yolk
½ teasp. ground cloves	1½ cups dark-brown sugar, packed
1 teasp. cinnamon	
1 cup coarsely broken walnuts	½ cup strong coffee or sherry
½ lb. canned diced	Sugar Glaze, p. 465

Start heating oven to 375°F. Sift flour, salt, baking powder, cloves, cinnamon. Mix with nuts, fruits. With electric mixer at high speed, or with egg beater, beat eggs and egg yolk until thick and lemon-colored. Add sugar gradually, beating well after each addition. With spoon, thoroughly blend in coffee and flour mixture. Turn into greased 15½" x 10½" x 1" jelly-roll pan, spreading batter ½" thick. Bake 25 min., or until cake tester inserted at several points comes out clean. Cool. Frost with Sugar Glaze. Before frosting dries, with wet knife, mark into 2" x 2½" bars; when it's dry, cut. Good with plain or holiday eggnog, coffee, or wine. Makes about 30.

NO-BAKES

1 pkg. semisweet-chocolate pieces (1 cup)	1¾ cups bite-size shredded- rice or -wheat biscuits
¼ cup corn syrup	Shredded coconut

In 2-qt. double boiler, melt chocolate with syrup; blend well. Remove from heat, keeping chocolate mixture over hot water. Gently mix in shredded rice until well coated. Drop by heaping teaspoonfuls onto waxed paper. Sprinkle with shredded coconut. Cool. Makes about 2 doz.

SUPERB BRAZIL-NUT STRIPS

2 cups sifted all-purpose flour	margarine
	½ cup soft shortening
1 teasp. baking powder	1 egg
1⅓ cups granulated sugar	1 egg, separated
	1 cup chopped Brazil nuts
4 teasp. cinnamon	
½ cup soft butter or	

Start heating oven to 350°F. Into bowl, sift flour, baking powder, 1 cup sugar, 3 teasp. cinnamon. Add butter, shortening, egg, egg yolk. With electric mixer at low speed, or "blend" (or with spoon), mix well. Turn into 15½" x 10½" x 1" jelly-roll pan; spread evenly with spatula. With fork, beat egg white slightly; brush over dough. Combine remaining ⅓ cup sugar, 1 teasp. cinnamon, nuts; sprinkle over top of dough. Bake 25 min., or until nuts are golden. Cool in pan; then cut into 2" x 1" bars. Makes 75.

TREATS FROM READY-TO-EATS

Packaged cookies are delightful snacks or desserts, served as they come from the box or dressed up a bit, for novelty. Or try these:

Bittersweets: Sprinkle shredded coconut, then semisweet-chocolate pieces, on saltines. Bake at 425°F. 8 min., or until chocolate melts.

Peanut Puffs: Top graham crackers or saltines with peanut butter, then with marshmallows. Broil till bubbly.

Butterscotch Squares: Blend together 3 tablesp. butter or margarine; ½ cup light-brown sugar, packed; and ¼ cup shredded coconut or chopped nuts. Spread on about 12 graham crackers. Broil slowly until golden.

Homemade Candies

Whether you choose a traditional recipe or one that takes advantage of today's easy-on-the-cook ingredients, you can turn out wonderful candy merely by obeying the rules. In this chapter we've omitted elaborate candies that call for special equipment and skill.

Before using these recipes, refer to How to Use Our Recipes, p. 3, and Pots and Pans, p. 692. Always use standard measuring cups and measuring spoons; measure level.

EASY TO MAKE

FRENCH FUDGE

2 pkg. semisweet-
   chocolate pieces
   (2 cups)
¾ cup sweetened con-
   densed milk
Few grains salt

1 cup chopped walnuts
   (optional)
1 teasp. vanilla extract
   (or rum or rum ex-
   tract to taste)

Line 9" x 5" x 3" loaf pan with waxed paper. Melt chocolate over *hot, not boiling,* water. Stir in milk, salt, nuts, vanilla. Pour into pan. Cool a few hr.; when firm, cut into squares. Makes 1¼ lb.

Truffle Balls: Cool mixture until easy to shape into ¾" balls. Dip each ball into snipped shredded coconut, chopped nuts, instant-cocoa mix, instant coffee, or chocolate shot. Or make fudge without nuts; mold around filberts, or press pecan or walnut half into each ball.

COCONUT PATTIES

Start heating oven to 350°F. Over *hot, not boil-ing,* water, melt 1 pkg. semisweet-chocolate pieces (1 cup). Remove from heat. Slowly stir in ½ cup sweetened condensed milk, ½ teasp. vanilla extract, and 2 cups snipped shredded coconut. With lightly greased hands, form into 1" balls; place on ungreased cookie sheet. Bake 5 min.; at once flatten with fork. Cool on wire rack. Makes 2½ doz.

TING-A-LINGS

1 pkg. semisweet-
   chocolate pieces
   (1 cup)
1 cup corn flakes
½ cup snipped

shredded coconut
1 teasp. vanilla extract
½ cup salted peanuts;
   cut-up, pitted dates;
   or seedless raisins

Melt chocolate over *hot, not boiling,* water; stir until smooth. Remove from heat. Stir in corn flakes, coconut, vanilla, peanuts. Drop by tea-spoonfuls onto waxed paper. Refrigerate until firm. Makes 2 doz.

DELIGHT SQUARES

Dissolve 1 pkg. fruit-flavored gelatin in 1 cup hot applesauce. Add 1 cup granulated sugar; stir over low heat until dissolved. Add ⅔ cup chopped nuts; pour into greased 9" x 5" x 3" loaf pan. Refrigerate until firm; cut into squares; roll in sugar. After 24 hr., sugar again. Makes about 3 doz.

PEANUT-BUTTER BALLS

Combine 2 cups snipped shredded coconut with ½ cup creamy or chunk-style peanut butter and 4 teasp. vanilla extract; mix well. Shape between palms of hands into small balls; arrange on waxed paper in pan. Refrigerate until firm. Makes 2 doz.

MARSHMALLOW DIPS

Mallow Pops: For each candy, stick marshmallow on long kitchen fork. Hold in steam of boiling water until sticky; then roll in finely chopped walnuts until well coated. Let stand on waxed paper until firm. Insert 1 short colored straw in each.

Butterscotch Mallows: In 2-qt. saucepan, combine 1 cup light-brown sugar, packed, with ½ cup light cream, ½ teasp. vanilla extract, ¼ teasp. salt. Cook slowly, stirring often, to 236°F. on candy thermometer, or until a little mixture in cold water forms soft ball. Remove from heat; place over hot water to keep warm. Drop in ½ lb. marshmallows, one by one, turning until well coated. Lift out; roll in finely chopped walnuts (¾ cup in all). Cool on greased cookie sheet. Makes 2½ doz.

Coconut Mallows: Over *hot, not boiling,* water, melt 1 pkg. semisweet-chocolate pieces (1 cup) with 1 tablesp. shortening (not butter or margarine); stir until smooth. Drop in marshmallows, one at a time, turning until well coated. Lift out; roll in chopped nuts or toasted, white or tinted, snipped shredded coconut. Refrigerate on waxed paper till well chilled. Makes about 2½ doz.

SEMISWEET FUDGE BALLS

1 pkg. semisweet-
   chocolate pieces
   (1 cup)
¾ cup undiluted
   evaporated milk
¼ teasp. cinnamon
   (optional)
½ cup finely chopped
   walnuts
½ cup chocolate shot

Melt chocolate over *hot, not boiling,* water; stir in milk, cinnamon. Cook, stirring often, 20 min. (mixture should be very thick). Refrigerate 1 hr., or until easy to handle. Shape into ¾" balls; roll some in walnuts, some in chocolate shot (or in snipped shredded coconut, instant-cocoa mix, or instant coffee). Makes 3 doz.

PEANUT-BUTTER PIN WHEELS

Combine ½ cup cold mashed potatoes (with no milk or seasoning added), ⅛ teasp. salt, and enough sifted confectioners' sugar (about 4 cups) to make easily handled fondant; beat well. Add ½ teasp. vanilla extract. Turn half of mixture onto board that's been lightly dusted with confectioners' sugar; roll into rectangle ¼" thick. Spread with ½ cup peanut butter; roll up from short side, jelly-roll-fashion. Repeat with rest of fondant. Refrigerate until firm; slice ¼" thick. Makes about 4 doz.

LUSCIOUS TEN-MINUTE NUT FUDGE

1⅔ cups granulated
   sugar
2 tablesp. butter or mar-
   garine
½ teasp. salt
⅔ cup undiluted evap-
   orated milk
1½ pkg. semisweet-
   chocolate pieces
   (1½ cups)
¼ lb. snipped marsh-
   mallows
½ cup chopped walnuts
1 teasp. vanilla extract

In 2-qt. saucepan, combine sugar, butter, salt, milk; bring to boil over medium heat; boil 5 min., stirring constantly. Remove from heat. Add chocolate and rest of ingredients. Beat vigorously until marshmallows melt. Pour into greased 8" x 8" x 2" pan; sprinkle with more nuts if desired. Cool; cut into small squares. Makes about 5 doz. squares.

BLACK-AND-WHITE SQUARES

3 cups sifted confec-
   tioners' sugar
2½ cups snipped
   shredded coconut
2 egg whites, slightly
   beaten
1 teasp. vanilla extract
½ cup melted butter or
   margarine
2 sq. unsweetened
   chocolate, melted
1 cup ready-to-eat bran

Line 9" x 5" x 3" loaf pan with waxed paper. Combine sugar, coconut, egg whites, vanilla, butter; press half of mixture into pan. To rest, add chocolate, bran; pack onto first layer. Refrigerate until firm; cut into squares. Makes about 2½ doz. squares.

COCONUT PEAKS

¼ cup butter or
   margarine
2 cups sifted confec-
   tioners' sugar
3 cups snipped
   shredded coconut
¼ cup light cream
1 pkg. semisweet-
   chocolate pieces
   (1 cup)
2 teasp. shortening (not
   butter or margarine)

In saucepan, slowly heat butter until golden; gradually stir in sugar, coconut, cream. Drop by teaspoonfuls onto waxed paper. Refrigerate till easy to handle; then shape into peaks. Over *hot, not boiling,* water, melt chocolate with shortening; stir until smooth. Dip bottoms of peaks into chocolate; harden on rack covered with waxed paper. Makes 3 doz.

PEANUT CHIPPEROOS

1½ cups peanut butter	rind
1 7¼-oz. pkg. snipped pitted dates	1 teasp. lemon juice
	¾ cup confectioners'
½ cup snipped shredded coconut	sugar
	¾ cup finely crushed
½ teasp. grated lemon	potato chips

Night before if desired: Combine peanut butter, dates, coconut, lemon rind and juice. Sift sugar over mixture; blend well. Shape between palms of hands into large marble-size balls.

Just before serving: With rolling pin, crush potato chips between 2 sheets of waxed paper. Roll balls in crushed chips. Makes 3 doz.

DREAM NUT FUDGE

1 3-oz. pkg. cream cheese	½ cup chopped almonds or Brazil
2½ cups sifted confectioners' sugar	nuts, or shredded coconut
½ teasp. almond extract	Pinch salt

With electric mixer at medium speed, or "cream" (or with spoon), beat cream cheese until soft and smooth. Slowly blend in sugar, extract, nuts, salt. Press into greased 9" x 5" x 3" loaf pan. Refrigerate until firm; cut into squares. Makes about 2½ doz. squares.

Chocolate-Nut: Reduce sugar to 2 cups. Add 2 sq. unsweetened chocolate, melted. Substitute vanilla extract for almond, walnuts for almonds.

Peanut Butter: Substitute 2 tablesp. peanut butter for almond extract, ¼ cup chopped salted peanuts for almonds.

NOUGAT BARS

3 tablesp. butter or margarine	¼ cup coarsely chopped walnuts
½ lb. marshmallows	½ teasp. salt
4 cups puffed corn cereal	¾ pkg. semisweet-chocolate pieces
½ cup shredded coconut	(¾ cup)

In double boiler, melt butter with marshmallows; stir until smooth. Remove from heat. Add

cereal, coconut, nuts, salt; press smooth into greased 9" x 9" x 2" pan. Melt chocolate over *hot, not boiling,* water; spread over candy. Cool till firm; then cut. Makes 2½ to 3 doz.

To Vary: Omit chocolate topping.

CARAMEL CRISPIES

In double boiler, place ½ lb. vanilla caramels and 2 tablesp. water; heat, stirring often, until melted and smooth. Add 1 cup broken pecans. In large bowl, place 4 cups bite-size shredded rice or wheat cereal; pour on nut mixture; toss until well coated. Spread on lightly greased cookie sheet. Let stand until surface is dry; then pull apart.

SPUR-OF-THE-MOMENT FUDGE

Smooth, creamy fudge can be made in a jiffy with packaged chocolate-, penuche-, or coconut-fudge-and-frosting mix. Just follow simple label directions.

Fudge Balls or Fingers: When fudge mixture is cool enough to handle, shape, then coat, as in Truffle Balls, p. 486.

EVER-EASY CANDY

You can buy wonderful candy by the bar, package, or pound. The bar kind becomes company candy too when cut into bite-size pieces. And don't overlook creamy caramels, buttery mints, and paper-thin peanut brittle.

CANDIES THAT TAKE MORE TIME

When making the candies in this group, it is important, for best results, that you use a candy thermometer. Be sure to stand thermometer in mixture before you start to cook and leave it in during cooking. The bulb must be completely covered with boiling syrup yet must not rest on bottom of pan.

When reading thermometer, your eyes should be on a level with the mercury. When mixture is ready to be removed from heat, take out thermometer and lay it where it can cool before being washed; otherwise it may break.

COFFEE-CHIP FUDGE

2 tablesp. instant coffee
3 cups granulated sugar
1/8 teasp. salt
1/2 cup light cream
2 tablesp. white corn syrup
1 cup milk
3 tablesp. butter or margarine
1 teasp. vanilla extract
1/2 cup chopped walnuts, pecans, or almonds
1 pkg. semisweet-chocolate pieces (1 cup)

In 3-qt. saucepan, combine coffee, sugar, salt, cream, corn syrup, milk; stir over low heat until boiling. Then cook gently, without stirring, to 236°F. on candy thermometer, or until a little mixture in cold water forms soft ball. Remove from heat; add butter, vanilla; *do not stir.*

Cool, without stirring, to 110°F., or until outside of saucepan feels lukewarm to hand. With electric mixer at medium speed (or with spoon), beat until candy loses gloss and small amount dropped from spoon holds its shape. Add nuts, chocolate. Turn into greased 8″ x 8″ x 2″ pan (don't scrape saucepan; leavings may be sugary). Cool; cut. Makes about 3 doz. squares.

OLD-FASHIONED FUDGE

2 cups granulated sugar
1 cup milk; or 1/2 cup evaporated milk and 1/2 cup water
1/2 teasp. salt
2 sq. unsweetened chocolate
2 tablesp. white corn syrup
2 tablesp. butter or margarine
1/2 teasp. vanilla extract
1/2 cup chopped nuts

In saucepan, combine sugar, milk, salt, chocolate, corn syrup; stir over low heat until sugar dissolves. Cook gently, stirring occasionally, to 238°F. on candy thermometer, or until a little mixture in cold water forms soft ball. Remove from heat; drop in butter; *do not stir.*

Cool, without stirring, to 110°F., or until outside of saucepan feels lukewarm to hand. Add vanilla. With electric mixer at medium speed (or with spoon), beat until candy loses gloss and small amount dropped from spoon holds its shape. Add nuts. Turn into greased 9″ x 5″ x 3″ loaf pan (don't scrape saucepan; leavings may be sugary). Cool; cut. Makes 1 1/4 lb.

Chocolate Marshmallow: Pour half of fudge into pan. Cover quickly with 1 cup halved marshmallows; top with rest of fudge. Or add 1 cup snipped marshmallows to fudge just before turning it into pan.

Peanut Butter: Substitute 1/4 cup peanut butter for butter, adding it after candy cools to 110°F.

NUT PENUCHE

2 tablesp. butter or margarine
3/4 cup liquid, half milk and half heavy cream
1 cup light-brown sugar, packed
1 1/2 cups granulated sugar
1 teasp. vanilla extract
3/4 to 1 cup chopped walnuts or pecans

In 2-qt. saucepan, melt butter; grease side of pan well. Pour in liquid; bring to boil; stir in sugars until dissolved. Cover; boil 1 min., or until all sugar crystals on side of pan have melted. Uncover; cook gently, stirring, to 238°F. on candy thermometer, or until a little mixture in cold water forms soft ball.

Cool, without stirring, to 110°F., or until outside of saucepan feels lukewarm to hand. Add vanilla, nuts. With spoon, beat until mixture loses gloss and small amount dropped from spoon holds its shape. Pour into greased 8″ x 8″ x 2″ pan or 9″ x 5″ x 3″ loaf pan (don't scrape saucepan; leavings may be sugary). Cut while warm. Makes about 2 1/2 doz. squares.

DIVINITY DROPS

2 2/3 cups granulated sugar
2/3 cup white corn syrup
1/2 cup water
1/4 teasp. salt
2 egg whites
1/2 cup chopped Brazil nuts or walnuts (or shredded coconut)
1/2 teasp. vanilla or almond extract

In 2-qt. saucepan, combine sugar, corn syrup, water, salt; stir over low heat until sugar dissolves. Cover; boil 1 min., or until all sugar crystals on side of pan have melted. Uncover; cook gently, without stirring, to 265°F. on candy thermometer, or until a little mixture in cold water forms almost-brittle ball.

Meanwhile, in large electric-mixer bowl, with mixer at high speed (or with egg beater), beat egg whites until stiff. Slowly pour on syrup, beating, until mixture loses gloss and small amount dropped from spoon holds its shape. Add nuts, vanilla. Drop by teaspoonfuls into greased shallow pan (don't scrape saucepan;

leavings may be sugary). If desired, sprinkle with chopped nuts, chocolate shot, or tinted coconut. Makes about 1½ lb.

Divinity Fudge: Pour mixture into greased 9″ x 9″ x 2″ pan. Cool; cut into squares.

CHOCO-NUT CRUNCH

1¼ cups granulated sugar	½ cup Blanched Almonds, p. 521
¾ cup butter or margarine	½ cup chopped walnuts or other nuts
1½ teasp. salt	⅓ cup semisweet-chocolate pieces, melted
¼ cup water	
½ cup unblanched almonds	½ cup finely chopped nuts
½ teasp. baking soda	

In saucepan, mix sugar, butter, salt, water, unblanched almonds. Boil, stirring often, to 290°F. on candy thermometer, or until a little mixture in cold water becomes brittle. Stir in soda, blanched almonds, walnuts; pour into greased 15½″ x 10½″ x 1″ pan. Spread with chocolate; sprinkle with chopped nuts. Cool; break up. Makes 1½ lb.

NUT BRITTLE

2 cups granulated sugar	¼ cup butter or margarine
1 cup brown sugar, packed	1¼ cups walnuts, peanuts, Brazil nuts, pecans, or blanched almonds, in small pieces
½ cup white corn syrup	
½ cup water	
⅛ teasp. baking soda	
Pinch salt	

In saucepan, combine sugars, corn syrup, water. Cook, stirring, until sugar dissolves. Continue cooking, without stirring, to 300°F. on candy thermometer, or until a little mixture in cold water becomes very brittle.

Remove mixture from heat; add soda, salt, butter; stir *only enough* to mix. Add nuts; turn at once into greased 12″ x 8″ x 1″ pan (don't scrape saucepan; leavings may be sugary). After 1 min. or so, take hold of candy at edges; lift from pan onto greased surface; pull quite thin. When cold, break up. Makes about 1½ lb.

BRAZIL-NUT CRUNCH

In heavy skillet, cook 2 cups granulated sugar over low heat, *stirring constantly,* until melted. Add ¼ teasp. baking soda, 1 cup ground Brazil nuts. Immediately turn onto greased cookie sheet; with rolling pin, roll mixture until about ¼″ thick. Before it is cool, mark into squares with knife. When it is cold, spread with ⅔ pkg. semisweet-chocolate pieces (⅔ cup), melted; sprinkle with ½ cup ground Brazil nuts. When chocolate is firm, break crunch into pieces. Makes 1¾ lb.

PLANTATION PRALINES

2 cups granulated sugar	margarine
1 teasp. baking soda	2⅓ cups pecan halves
1 cup buttermilk	⅔ cup perfect pecan halves
Pinch salt	
2 tablesp. butter or	

In large kettle (about 8 qt.), combine sugar, soda, buttermilk, salt. Cook over high heat 5 min., or to 210°F. on candy thermometer, *being sure* to stir mixture often and to scrape bottom and crevices of kettle. Add butter and 2⅓ cups pecans. Cook, stirring constantly, scraping bottom and side of kettle, to 230°F., or until a little mixture in cold water forms very soft ball—about 5 min. Remove from heat.

Cool mixture slightly—just 1 or 2 min. Then, with spoon, beat until thickened and creamy; immediately drop by tablespoonfuls onto waxed paper, aluminum foil, or greased cookie sheet. Dot with ⅔ cup pecans. Makes 7.

PULLED MOLASSES-MINT TAFFY

2 cups light molasses	⅛ teasp. salt
2 teasp. vinegar	½ teasp. baking soda
1½ tablesp. butter or margarine	7 drops oil of peppermint

In 3-qt. saucepan, mix molasses, vinegar. Cook gently, stirring, to 260°F. on candy thermometer, or until a little mixture in cold water becomes brittle. Remove from heat. Add butter, salt, soda. Stir until foaming stops; pour into greased 12″ x 8″ x 1″ pan.

When candy is cool enough to pull, drop peppermint into center. Lift corners; draw to center; press together. Pull, using thumbs and fingers; fold. Repeat until light in color and slightly firm. Pull into 2 long ropes, ¾″ thick; twist. With scissors (dip often into hot water), cut into 1″ pieces; wrap in waxed paper, saran, or foil. Makes about 6½ doz. pieces.

Molasses Taffy: Omit oil of peppermint.

POPCORN CAPERS

Caramel Popcorn: Into very large bowl, put 3 qt. popcorn or puffed cereal (if desired, add 2 cups salted peanuts); sprinkle lightly with salt. In 2-qt. saucepan, heat 1 cup granulated sugar, stirring, until melted and golden. Very carefully, to avoid spattering, stir in ¾ cup hot water until sugar dissolves. Add ½ cup light-brown sugar, packed. Cook to 238°F. on candy thermometer, or until a little mixture in cold water forms soft ball. Pour over popcorn; toss until well coated. (If desired, form into balls at once.) Serve hot or cold. Makes 3 qt.

Christmas Popcorn Balls: In very large bowl, mix 3 qt. popcorn, ½ lb. cut-up candied cherries. In 2-qt. saucepan, combine 2 cups white corn syrup, 1 tablesp. vinegar, 1 teasp. salt; cook, stirring occasionally, to 250°F. on candy thermometer, or until a little mixture in cold water forms hard ball. Add 2 teasp. vanilla extract. Slowly pour over popcorn, tossing until coated. Quickly and gently shape into 3″ balls. Makes about 15.

Molasses Popcorn Balls: In very large bowl, mix 1½ qt. popcorn or puffed cereal with ¼ teasp. salt. In 2-qt. saucepan, combine ½ cup light molasses, ½ cup corn syrup, 1½ teasp. vinegar; cook, stirring occasionally, to 240°F. on candy thermometer, or until a little mixture in cold water forms soft ball. Continue cooking, stirring constantly, to 270°F., or until a little mixture in cold water is slightly brittle. Remove from heat. Add 1½ tablesp. butter or margarine, stirring only enough to mix. Pour over popcorn, tossing until coated. Quickly and gently shape into 2½″ balls. Makes about 10.

CRISP COCONUT BALLS

4 cups sugar-coated wheat cereal	⅛ teasp. salt
½ cup granulated sugar	1 tablesp. butter or margarine
½ cup light molasses	1 cup snipped shredded coconut
¼ cup light cream	
¼ cup white corn syrup	

In shallow pan in 350°F. oven, lightly toast cereal 10 min. In 3-qt. saucepan, combine rest of ingredients except coconut; stir over low heat until sugar dissolves. Boil, stirring occasionally, to 248°F. on candy thermometer, or until a little

mixture in cold water forms firm ball. Remove from heat. Quickly mix in cereal, coconut. Quickly and gently shape into 2″ balls. Makes 2½ doz.

Coconut Squares: Pack into greased 8″ x 8″ x 2″ pan; when mixture is firm, cut into squares.

CARAMEL-TAFFY APPLES

6 washed medium apples	1 can sweetened condensed milk
1 cup granulated sugar	1 teasp. vanilla extract
½ cup white corn syrup	

Insert wooden skewer or clean twig into stem end of each apple. In medium *heavy* saucepan, combine rest of ingredients. Cook slowly, stirring constantly, to 230°F. on candy thermometer, or until a little mixture in cold water forms very stiff ball. Working quickly, away from drafts, dip each apple into caramel, twirling it until well coated. Place, with skewer ends up, on buttered plate; let stand till firm. Serve same day. Makes 6.

Quick Caramel: Use 4 or 5 apples. For caramel, in double boiler, heat 1 lb. packaged vanilla caramels with 2 tablesp. hot water, stirring frequently, until smooth. Dip as above. Refrigerate to firm up.

FRUIT AND NUT SWEETS

SPANISH SWEETS

2 cups walnuts	¾ cup candied cherries
¾ cup almonds	¾ cup dark or light raisins
1 7¼-oz. pkg. pitted dates	Confectioners' sugar
2 cups pecans	

Put all ingredients except sugar through food chopper, using medium blade. On board covered with confectioners' sugar, knead until thick and smooth. Shape into 1″ balls. Refrigerate. Makes about 5 doz.

COCONUT-APRICOT BALLS

1 cup dried apricots	rind
1 cup shredded coconut	1 teasp. grated lemon rind
¼ cup confectioners' sugar	1 tablesp. lemon juice
1 teasp. grated orange	Granulated sugar

Put apricots and coconut through food chopper, using fine blade. Mix in confectioners' sugar, rinds, lemon juice. Form into small balls. Roll in granulated sugar. Let ripen in refrigerator at least a week before serving. Makes 2 doz.

FRUITED DISKS

1 8-oz. pkg. dried figs, ground	2 tablesp. lemon juice
½ cup light or dark raisins	⅓ cup confectioners' sugar
1 teasp. grated lemon rind	1 cup peanut butter
	Chopped nuts

Combine all ingredients except nuts; knead well. Shape into roll about 1½" in diameter. Refrigerate overnight. Cut into ¼" disks; place a few chopped nuts on each. Makes about 1½ doz.

FRUIT PORCUPINES

1 7¼-oz. pkg. pitted dates, ground	coconut
½ lb. dried figs, ground	1 teasp. lemon juice
1 cup snipped shredded	¼ cup finely chopped walnuts

Combine all ingredients except nuts; knead well. Roll into ¾" balls; roll in nuts till well coated. Store, wrapped in waxed paper, in refrigerator. Makes about 3 doz.

STUFFED FRUITS

In colander over boiling water, steam dried prunes, figs, or apricots, covered, 5 min., or until plump but not softened. Pit prunes. Stuff fruits (also stuff pitted dates) with Easy Fondant, below; peanut butter; or coarsely ground candied orange peel and chopped walnuts, moistened with brandy or rum. Decorate with, or roll in, cut-up preserved orange rind, finely chopped nuts, almond halves, snipped shredded coconut, granulated sugar, or chopped candied cherries.

Easy Fondant: Slowly blend ½ cup sweetened condensed milk with 2½ cups sifted confectioners' sugar. Mix in 1 teasp. vanilla extract until smooth. If hard to handle, add more sugar. To tint, drop a few drops food color onto part of fondant, and knead in well.

Apricot Chubbies: Put 2 steamed dried-apricot halves together with Easy Fondant or marshmallow; roll in sugar.

GLAZED APRICOTS

2 cups dried apricots	About 4 doz. walnut quarters
2 cups granulated sugar	
1 cup water	Granulated sugar
⅛ teasp. cream of tartar	

Simmer apricots in water to cover 5 to 10 min., or till tender; drain. In saucepan, stir 2 cups sugar with water and cream of tartar. Cook to 236°F. on candy thermometer, or until a little mixture in cold water forms soft ball. Add apricots. Boil gently 10 min. With slotted spoon, remove fruit from syrup; drain well on paper towel. Roll each apricot around 1 walnut quarter; then roll in granulated sugar. Store in covered container.

To serve: Sugar again if needed. Makes about 4 doz.

CANDIED GRAPEFRUIT PEEL

Cut peel from 2 grapefruit into 4 lengthwise sections. (If white membrane is very thick, remove some of it; otherwise leave intact.) Cover peel with cold water; bring to boil. Boil 10 min.; drain. Repeat 3 times. Cut peel into thin strips.

In 3-qt. saucepan, combine 1 cup granulated sugar, ½ cup white corn syrup, 1 cup water; stir over low heat until sugar dissolves. Add peel; boil gently, uncovered, about 40 min., or until most of syrup is absorbed. Drain in coarse strainer or colander. Roll peel, a few pieces at a time, in granulated sugar. Arrange in single layer on waxed paper or pan; let dry about 2 days. Store in covered container. Makes about ½ lb.

Candied Orange Peel: Substitute 6 thick-skinned oranges for grapefruit; boil peel 5 min. each time instead of 10 min. Increase sugar to 2 cups. Decrease corn syrup to 2 teasp. Makes about 1½ lb.

SPICED BRAZIL-NUT CHIPS

Start heating oven to 350°F. Stir 1½ teasp. water into 1 slightly beaten egg white. Halve lengthwise 2 cups blanched, shelled Brazil nuts, p. 521; roll in egg white, a few at a time, coating well. Then roll in 1 cup granulated sugar mixed with ½ teasp. cinnamon. Arrange on well-greased brown paper on baking sheet. Bake until golden. Makes about 2 cups.

CINNAMON NUTS

Boil 1 cup sugar with ½ teasp. cinnamon, ⅛ teasp. cream of tartar, ¼ cup boiling water, to 240°F. on candy thermometer, or until a little syrup in cold water forms soft ball. Add 1½ cups walnut halves or mixed nuts; cool. Add ½ teasp. vanilla extract; stir until nuts are coated. Turn onto flat surface; separate; cool. Makes ¾ lb.

GOLDEN WALNUTS

Stir 1½ cups granulated sugar with ¼ cup warm water, 3 tablesp. orange juice. Cover; boil 1 min., or until sugar crystals on side of pan have melted. Uncover; cook to 240°F. on candy thermometer, or until a little syrup in cold water forms soft ball. Add ¼ teasp. cinnamon, ½ cup grated orange rind, 2½ cups walnuts. With fork, stir till creamy; turn onto waxed paper; separate; cool. Makes 2½ cups.

SHERRY WALNUTS

1½ cups granulated sugar	½ teasp. cinnamon
½ cup sherry	2 to 3 cups walnut halves

Boil sugar and sherry to 240°F. on candy thermometer, or until a little mixture in cold water forms soft ball. Remove from heat. Add cinnamon and walnuts; stir until cloudy. Turn out onto well-buttered cookie sheet; separate nuts.

PENUCHE NUTS

Over low heat, stir 1 cup light-brown sugar, packed, with ½ cup granulated sugar and ½ cup commercial sour cream until sugars dissolve.

Cover; boil 1 min., or until sugar crystals on side of pan have melted. Uncover; cook over low heat to 246°F. on candy thermometer, or until a little syrup in cold water forms ball that's a little firmer than soft. Add 1 teasp. vanilla extract and 2½ cups walnuts, pecans, or other nuts. Stir until mixture begins to coat nuts; turn onto waxed paper; separate; cool. Makes about 1¼ lb.

NUT DRESS-UPS

Choco-Nut Dips: Over *hot, not boiling,* water, melt 1 pkg. semisweet-chocolate pieces (1 cup) with 1 tablesp. shortening (not butter or margarine); stir until smooth. Dip sides of walnut halves, or ends of almonds or Brazil nuts, into chocolate, then into chopped nuts or chocolate shot. Cool.

Marshmallow Nuts: Melt marshmallows in double boiler. Dip one end of each pecan into marshmallows, then into green- or pink-tinted shredded coconut.

Christmas Cherries: Cut a cross part-way through tops of red candied cherries. Fill centers with tiny balls of Easy Fondant, p. 492, pressing "petals" back to open flower. Into fondant, press pieces of filbert or other nut if desired.

Almond Cherryettes: Cut slice from stem end of each candied cherry. Into cherry, insert rounded end of blanched almond.

Nut Creams: Make Easy Fondant, p. 492; tint part green, part yellow. Put 2 or 3 nut halves together, with fondant ball between. Or press whole nut or nut half into fondant ball.

Drinks—
Hot and Cold

A CUP OF GOOD COFFEE

There's no trick at all to making good coffee. Just follow our rules every time you put the pot on. And make enough to fill those requests for seconds.

Start with a Clean Pot: A stale pot makes poor coffee. So:

1. Wash coffeepot in hot sudsy water, occasionally using a special brush for valves, spouts, tubes, etc.
2. If water is hard, add a water-softener compound or use a dishwashing detergent.
3. Remove stains on aluminum coffeepots and parts with soap-filled steel-wool pads.
4. Do not scour plated interiors; instead, clean them with products made especially for that purpose, such as Maid-Easy Coffee Stain Remover and Dip-It.
5. After washing pot, rinse it thoroughly with very hot water; dry well.

Use Only Fresh Coffee: Oxygen in the air destroys coffee flavor, produces staleness. To be sure your coffee is fresh:

1. Buy it in a vacuum-sealed can.
2. Or, if it's not vacuum-packed, be sure it was roasted and ground within the last few days.
3. Don't stock coffee unless it's in a vacuum-sealed can.
4. After opening can or bag of coffee, *use it up within a week* if possible.
5. If a little coffee is left over at end of week, don't mix it with a fresh supply.

What Grind to Use: We have found that a drip grind makes good coffee in all types of coffee maker. However, if the manufacturer specifies a different grind for his coffee maker, try it and compare.

Measure Coffee Level: Regardless of the coffee maker—drip, vacuum type, percolator, etc.—from 2 to 3 level measuring tablesp. coffee to each 1 measuring cup (8 oz.) water is a popular proportion. The exact amount of coffee will vary with family taste.

Whatever strength you prefer, use a ½-pt. or 1-pt. measuring cup to measure water, a set of measuring spoons to measure coffee. *Be sure to keep measurements accurate, leveling off each spoonful of coffee with spatula.* (The Coffee Brewing Institute, Inc., 120 Wall Street, New York City, distributes a standard coffee-measuring device for 2 level tablespoonfuls.)

Use Right Size of Coffee Maker: Modern coffee makers give best results when filled to capacity. They make from 1 to 10 servings (5 to 6 oz. each). So if your family drinks 4 cups of coffee at a meal, buy a coffee maker for 4 servings. For entertaining, choose at least an 8-serving size. Or buy both a small and large size.

Types of Coffee Maker

There are 4 types of coffee-making device—the old-time coffeepot, drip coffeepot, percolator, and vacuum-type coffee maker. A popular trend is the automatic coffee maker, in either the percolator or vacuum type. It brews for the proper length of time, then automatically switches to a lower "keep warm" heat.

IN AN OLD-TIME COFFEEPOT

1. Measure drip-grind coffee into coffeepot, allowing 2 to 3 level tablesp. coffee to each 1 cup (8 oz.) water.
2. Add water—cold, hot, or boiling.
3. Place over heat; stir well. Just bring to boil; stir again; remove. Add dash of cold water to settle grounds. (Don't let coffee boil—aroma and flavor will escape.)
4. Let coffee stand over *very low heat* about 5 min.; then strain through fine cheesecloth into another utensil. Serve hot.

IN A VACUUM-TYPE COFFEE MAKER

1. Measure drip-grind coffee, allowing 2 to 3 level tablesp. coffee for each 1 cup (8 oz.) water—unless manufacturer directs otherwise.
2. Measure water into lower bowl; start heating.
3. Adjust filter (it may be a cloth, stainless-steel, or glass-rod type). Measure coffee into upper bowl; place snugly on lower bowl.
4. When water in lower bowl is heated, most of it rises to upper bowl. When all but a small amount of water has risen, or when water in upper bowl starts to bubble vigorously, turn off heat. Stir once to mix coffee and water.

5. Let coffee maker stand with heat turned off until brew returns to lower bowl—5 to 7 min.
6. To keep filter cloth clean, rinse it out well after each use. Keep in cold water until used again, or as manufacturer directs.

IN A DRIP COFFEEPOT

1. Measure drip-grind coffee into coffee section of drip pot, allowing 2 to 3 level tablesp. coffee for each 1 cup (8 oz.) water. (If filter paper is used, adjust before putting in coffee.)
2. Pour rapidly boiling water into water section.
3. Immediately put pot over low heat and let water drip through. *Do not let it boil.*
4. Remove coffee and water sections from pot; stir coffee well; serve at once.
5. If coffee cannot be served at once, place pot over *low heat. Do not let it boil.*

IN A PERCOLATOR

1. Measure drip- or percolator-grind coffee, allowing 2 to 3 level tablesp. coffee for each 1 cup (8 oz.) water.
2. Pour cold water into bottom of percolator; place coffee in basket.
3. If you're making 6 or more servings, percolate coffee 10 min. (Start timing when liquid coming through tube shows color.) If you're making less than 6 servings, reduce time to 7 min., so coffee will not get bitter.
4. Remove coffee basket as soon as percolating is completed; grounds absorb flavor, aroma.

INSTANT COFFEE

Instant coffee is a dry soluble extract, obtained by removing the water from a strong coffee brew. Practically all widely distributed brands on the market today consist of just the dehydrated coffee brew, with no added ingredients. Whatever type or brand you use, *make as label directs.*

When only a few cups of coffee are needed, it is convenient to make coffee right in the cup. However, when several cups are to be served, make it, all at once, in a pot. Then you can serve it either in the kitchen or at table.

DECAFFEINATED COFFEE

Decaffeinated coffee is coffee from which practically all the caffein has been removed. It comes in two forms: One you prepare as you would regular coffee, the other as you would an instant type. Follow label directions.

CEREAL BEVERAGES

For those who do not drink coffee or who prefer other types of hot drink, there are cereal beverages. They come in two forms: one you prepare as you would regular coffee, the other as you would an instant type.

DEMITASSE, OR AFTER-DINNER, COFFEE

Make hot coffee, allowing 3 level tablesp. coffee to each 1 cup (8 oz.) water. Serve hot in demitasse cups, with sugar and cream if you wish.

DELICIOUS ICED COFFEE

Do-Ahead Kind: Make hot coffee as on pp. 494 to 496, allowing 2 to 3 level tablesp. coffee for each 1 cup (8 oz.) water. Pour into pitcher or other warm container. Cool not more than 3 hr. Serve with ice cubes in tall glasses. Or to avoid dilution of coffee flavor, use coffee ice cubes made by freezing extra coffee in ice-cube tray.

Hot from the Pot: Make hot coffee as on pp. 494 to 496, using half as much water to your usual quantity of coffee (that is, 4 to 6 level tablesp. coffee to each 1 cup (8 oz.) water). Pour, hot, into ice-filled tall glasses.

Quick Style: For pitcher or glassful of truly delicious iced coffee, use instant coffee or instant decaffeinated coffee as label directs.

SERVING ICED COFFEE

With iced coffee, pass cream and sugar or small pitcher of white corn syrup. Or serve in one of these ways:

Snow-Capped: In each glass, blend 1 cup cool regular-strength coffee with 2 tablesp. chocolate syrup. Add ice and cream. Top with whipped cream.

Topknot: To ½ cup heavy cream, add 1 teasp. sugar and ½ teasp. cinnamon or a few drops mint extract. Beat till stiff. Use to top iced coffee.

Floats: Into each tall glass, put 1 or 2 scoops of coffee or chocolate ice cream. Fill with cool regular-strength coffee. Stir; sweeten.

A CUP OF GOOD TEA

You can count on tea to your taste—fragrantly full-bodied every time you make it—when you follow these directions *to the letter*.

Pick Your Tea: Black, green, and oolong teas are sold loose, in packages, or in tea bags. Always keep tightly covered.

> **Black Tea,** grown in India, Ceylon, and Indonesia, owes its full flavor to the fermenting process the leaves go through before they are heated and dried. It is popular in this country.
> *Flavored and Spiced Teas* are often made from black teas; they are delightfully refreshing too.

> **Green Tea** comes from China and Japan. Leaves are not fermented.

> **Oolong Tea,** from Formosa, is fermented only a short time.

> **Orange Pekoe** indicates a particular size and type of leaf, not a kind or quality of tea.

> **Instant Tea.** Some instant teas are just the dried extract of freshly brewed tea; some are composed of equal parts of the dried extract and carbohydrates added to protect the flavor. Use as label directs.

Use a Clean Teapot: Wash it in heavy suds, but *be sure* to rinse it out thoroughly. Next, heat teapot by filling it with hot water. The hotter the pot, the better it keeps the brew warm. The brew should never come in contact with copper, brass, or iron.

Have Water Boiling Hard: For water, use freshly drawn cold water from the tap, to avoid a metallic taste. Bring to full, rolling boil. The high temperature of boiling water extracts the flavor from the tea leaves. Just very hot water will not do; reheated water will also make tea taste flat.

Measure Carefully: Whether you use tea leaves or tea bags, the rules are the same: Allow 1 teasp. tea, or 1 tea bag, per 1 measuring cup (8 oz.) water. One teaspoonful of tea is equivalent to 1 tea bag.

Time the Brewing: Pour boiling water directly over tea leaves or bags. Then let tea brew (stand) no less than 3 min. and no more than 5 min. *by the clock.* Remember, overbrewing causes bitterness. *Never boil tea.*

Do not judge strength of tea by its color. Some strong teas brew light; some weak teas brew dark. After brewing, stir and serve.

If you like weak tea, you should still follow the rules above for making a cup of good hearty tea; then, after the tea flavor has been extracted from the leaves, weaken it with hot water.

The Serving: Tea experts prefer milk in tea to cream; with milk, you get the full, rich flavor of the tea. But your family may prefer one of our Glamour Touches, below.

SPARKLING ICED TEA

To Please Everyone: For delicious iced tea, follow our basic rules for making tea, p. 496, adding 50 per cent more tea to allow for ice dilution. In other words, use 6 teasp. loose tea, or 6 tea bags, for 4 measuring cups boiling water. To serve, pour hot tea into ice-filled iced-tea glasses; add lemon or sugar to taste. Fills 4 glasses.

When There's Company: To make iced tea in quantity for home use, put 2-qt. cold water in saucepan and bring to full, rolling boil. Remove from heat; immediately add 15 tea bags, or 5 tablesp. loose tea. Brew 4 min. Stir; strain into pitcher. To serve, pour into ice-filled iced-tea glasses. Serve with lemon and sugar to taste. Fills 8 glasses.

P.S. Don't refrigerate hot brewed tea; refrigeration may cause it to cloud, though its flavor will not be impaired. Cloudy tea can be cleared by adding a little boiling water; it brings back the tea's clear amber color.

The Cloudless Way: In covered pitcher or china or glass container, add 3 level teasp. loose tea, or 3 tea bags, to each ¾ measuring cup (1 glass) cold water. Refrigerate 12 to 24 hr.; strain; add ice; serve as usual. Long brewing in cold water does not injure flavor.

Instant Kind: Use instant tea as label directs. Pour into ice-filled glasses.

GLAMOUR TOUCHES
(for hot or iced tea)

To Add When Brewing:

Bit of grated orange rind
Rose-geranium leaf or few whole cloves
Few crushed mint sprigs
Cinnamon stick

To Add When Serving:

Lemon, lime, or orange slices, with cloves if desired
Lemon, lime, or orange wedge
Lemon, lime, pineapple, or orange juice, passed in small pitcher
Strawberry or red-cherry garnish
Lemon rind, cut into corkscrew shape
Pineapple spears or chunks
Mint sprigs, dusted with sugar
Pineapple chunks and strawberries, strung on sippers
Cinnamon stick, as stirrer
Garnished Ice Cubes, p. 498
Flavored Ice Cubes, p. 498
Tiny scoops of lemon sherbet

COCOA AND CHOCOLATE

HOT COCOA

6 tablesp. cocoa	2¼ cups evaporated
6 tablesp. granulated	milk plus
sugar	2¼ cups water
Few grains salt	Few drops vanilla
1½ cups water	extract (optional)
4½ cups milk; or	

In saucepan, mix cocoa, sugar, salt, water. Bring to boil over low heat; boil gently 2 min., stirring.

Add milk; heat thoroughly, but do *not* boil. Just before serving, beat with egg beater until smooth and foamy; add vanilla. Makes 9 servings.

Speedy Hot Cocoa: Use instant-cocoa mix.

Iced Cocoa: Cool cocoa; pour over ice in 5 or 6 glasses. Stir well. Top with whipped cream; dust with nutmeg or cinnamon if desired.

HOT FRENCH CHOCOLATE

2½ sq. unsweetened chocolate	Dash salt
½ cup water	½ cup heavy cream, whipped
½ cup granulated sugar	1½ qt. hot milk

In saucepan, combine chocolate, water. Cook over low heat, stirring, until chocolate is melted and blended. Add sugar, salt; boil, stirring, 4 min. Remove from heat; cool.

Fold cooled chocolate mixture into whipped cream. Place 1 well-rounded tablesp. chocolate mixture in each serving cup; add hot milk to fill cup. Stir to blend. Makes 8 coffee-cup servings, or 18 chocolate-cup servings.

FRUIT COOLERS

Tall cool drinks are the very symbol of summer refreshment. Here are fruit drinks, for any hour of a summer's day or evening, for any occasion from a morning pickup for the youngsters to a full-scale party.

The Ice

Just Ice: Ice cubes are a must for fruit drinks. So store extra cubes in the tray under the refrigerator's freezing compartment. Or keep an extra supply in a plastic bag, heavy treated paper bag, or cardboard tub in home freezer.

Garnished Ice Cubes: If you're having a party, fill ice-cube tray about two thirds full with water (boiled water may aid clarity); then let cubes freeze. Now place one, or combination of several, of the following on top of cubes; then pour on just enough water to cover. Complete freezing.

> Orange, lemon, or lime slices, in small wedges
> Red or green maraschino cherries, halved or sliced
> Canned pineapple tidbits, drained
> Fresh mint sprigs
> Purple grapes, halved, or whole green grapes
> Fresh raspberries, blueberries, or halved unhulled strawberries
> Dried apricot halves
> Fresh sweet cherries
> Fresh cranberries

Flavored Ice Cubes: Into small ice-cube tray, empty thawed contents of 1 can frozen lemonade or limeade, or orange- tangerine- or grape-juice concentrate; set ice-cube section in place; slowly fill tray with water. Freeze.

Tinted Ice Cubes: For concentrate and water, substitute water, delicately tinted with green or red maraschino-cherry juice, grenadine, or food color.

Pineapple Juice: Freeze canned or reconstituted frozen pineapple juice. Add no water.

Golden: Combine 1 cup orange juice; 1 cup fresh, frozen, or canned lemon juice; 1 cup corn syrup; and 2 cups cold water. Pour into ice-cube tray, with ice-cube section in place. Freeze as above.

Frosty Rims: To "frost" rims of your tall glasses, lightly dip edge of each glass into lemon or orange juice, to depth of ½"; then dip into plain or tinted granulated sugar. Refrigerate until sugar looks dry and frosty. Fill glasses carefully.

Off-the-Shelf Coolers

The variety you can serve is endless if you keep on hand some of today's fine branded canned and frozen fruit juices and ades. Just look over the partial list that follows, and read our hints for keeping them at their best.

Canned Juices:

Concentrated:
Grape
Lemonade
Apple
Baby-pack strained
fruits
Cranberry cocktail
Grapeade
Grapefruit
Bottled lemon

Lemon
Whole-fruit nectars
Orange
Orangeade
Orange and grape-
fruit
Pineapple
Prune
Tangerine

There are also liquid and powdered bases in a variety of fruit flavors.

Frozen Juices:

Concentrated:
Grape
Grapefruit
Orange
Orange and
grapefruit
Pineapple

Tangerine
Lemonade
Limeade
Orangeade
Natural Strength:
Lemon

Handle Unopened Canned Juices with Care: The best storage place for canned juices is the coolest, driest spot you have. This way, canned juices will keep their fresh flavor and vitamin content for months. Never store them near a range, pipes, or radiator.

Keep Unopened Frozen Juices in Freezer: Get frozen fruit juices home and into home freezer or freezer of combination refrigerator-freezer as quickly as possible; they'll keep many months at 0°F.

If frozen juices are stored in freezing compartment of conventional refrigerator, they'll keep several weeks. Never let unopened cans of frozen juice stand at room temperature—they may burst.

When You Open Canned Juices: Shake can well to mix juice. Puncture top with regular 3-cor-

nered puncture-type opener. Make second opening on other side; then juice will pour easily. If it's a concentrate, reconstitute as label directs.

To Reconstitute Frozen Juices: Follow label directions. To bring out juice's full fresh bouquet, be sure to shake or stir briskly and thoroughly. For best flavor, use within 24 hr. If using unreconstituted juice as an ingredient in recipes, let thaw until just soft enough to be stirred well; then measure.

Leftovers: Of course you can keep opened cans of juice on hand in your refrigerator. For best results, see p. 516.

MADE WITH FROZEN JUICE

Lemonade Plus: To lemonade, add cranberry juice, grape juice, bottled grenadine, or maraschino-cherry juice to taste. Or add bit of mint extract.

Ade Duet: Mix limeade with orangeade or lemonade. Float a few raspberries, plump red cherries, or strawberries in glasses.

Limeade-Grape: To limeade, add grape or pineapple juice to taste.

Orange-Mint: To orangeade, add a little canned crushed pineapple, a few snipped mint leaves.

Orange Scoop: Float small scoop of vanilla ice cream in orangeade.

Grapefruit Sip: Reconstitute frozen grapefruit juice with ginger ale; top with twist of lemon peel.

Tangerine Sparkle: Mix tangerine juice with some sparkling water or pineapple juice.

Grape Sparkle: Reconstitute frozen grape juice with grapefruit juice, ginger ale, sparkling water, or lemonade. Add lime or lemon juice and sugar to taste.

Grape Ice: Add scoop of lemon or lime sherbet to grape juice. Or use half-and-half grape juice and ginger ale.

Orange-Milk: Reconstitute frozen orange juice with milk instead of water; beat well.

Susan's Orange-Juice Highball: Add 2 cups ginger ale and 1 cup water to 1 can frozen orange-juice concentrate.

MADE WITH CANNED OR FROZEN JUICE

Pineapple Nectar: Mix equal parts pineapple juice and canned apricot nectar.

Pineapple Ale: Mix 2 parts pineapple juice with 1 part ginger ale. Tint delicate pink with maraschino-cherry juice. Or float raspberry sherbet on top.

Pineapple Cream: To pineapple juice, add few drops peppermint extract, bit of green food color, then small scoop of vanilla ice cream.

Orange Duet: Mix equal parts of orange juice and one of these: grapefruit juice, pineapple juice, lemonade, ginger ale. Top with mint sprigs.

Orange Float: Into each glass, pour equal parts of orange juice and ginger ale. Float vanilla ice cream or orange sherbet on top.

Pineapple Dash: Add refreshing tartness to pineapple juice by adding grapefruit juice.

Cranberry Cocktail: Combine cranberry-juice cocktail with twice as much or equal amount of pineapple juice. Float vanilla ice cream on top if you wish.

Apple Spice: Sprinkle apple juice with nutmeg or cinnamon.

Apple Tang: To apple juice, add lemon or lime juice.

Apple-Mint: Top apple juice with snipped mint leaves.

Prune Flip: Pep up prune juice with lemonade or orange, lemon, or lime juice to taste; top with twist of peel.

Prune Cream: To prune juice, add small spoonful of vanilla ice cream.

TAMPA TEA

1 cup boiling water	4 cups ice water
2 teasp. tea; or 2 tea bags	½ cup lime juice 2½ cups orange juice
½ cup granulated sugar	

Pour boiling water over tea; let brew (stand) 3 min.; strain. Stir in sugar until dissolved. Add ice water and fruit juices. Pour into 8 tall ice-filled glasses. If desired, garnish with lime slices and fresh cherries. Makes 8 servings.

PINEAPPLE-LIME NECTAR

½ cup fresh, frozen, or canned lemon juice	¾ cup lime juice ½ cup confectioners' sugar
2½ cups pineapple juice	Ginger ale

Combine fruit juices and sugar. Divide among 6 tall ice-filled glasses. Fill with ginger ale. If desired, garnish with fresh cherries. Makes 6 servings.

SUSAN'S APPLE-LIMEADE

½ cup granulated sugar	½ cup lime juice 2 cups apple juice
½ cup water	¼ teasp. salt
12 snipped mint leaves	Sparkling water

1. Boil sugar and water together 8 min.; pour over mint; cool.
2. Add fruit juices, salt. Divide among 6 tall ice-filled glasses. Fill with sparkling water. Makes 6 servings.

MINT SPARKLE

1 cup warm water	½ teasp. mint extract
1 cup white corn syrup	
½ cup fresh, frozen, or canned lemon juice	Green food color 1 large bottle ginger ale

Combine water, corn syrup; refrigerate. Add lemon juice, mint extract, and enough food color to tint delicate green. Just before serving, add ginger ale. Pour into 6 tall ice-filled glasses. Makes 6 servings.

CRANBERRY PITCHER PUNCH

1 chilled can jellied cranberry sauce	¾ cup chilled orange juice
2¼ cups cold water	1 teasp. almond extract
½ cup fresh, frozen, or canned lemon juice	1 cup chilled ginger ale

With fork, crush cranberry sauce in can; turn into large bowl. Add water; beat until smooth. Stir in juices, extract, ginger ale, and a few ice cubes. Pour into 6 tall glasses. If desired, garnish with mint and clove-studded lemon circles. Makes 6 servings.

LEMONADE

Homemade: Combine 2 cups lemon juice, 4 teasp. grated lemon rind, 1½ cups granulated sugar. Pour into glass jar; cover. Keep on hand in refrigerator.

To serve: Allow ¼ cup syrup for each glass. Fill with ice cubes and water. (Nice tinted pink with bottled grenadine.) Makes 2⅔ cups syrup.

Jiffy: Just open can of frozen or canned lemonade concentrate; add water and ice as label directs; enjoy a pitcherful of luscious lemonade in no time at all.

Limeade: Substitute fresh lime juice for lemon juice in Homemade Lemonade, above. Or make limeade according to directions on can of frozen limeade concentrate.

MINT-ORANGEADE COOLER

1 cup orange juice	1 cup orange juice
½ cup granulated sugar	¼ cup lime juice
12 snipped mint sprigs	1½ cups sparkling water

Bring 1 cup orange juice to boil. Add to sugar and mint; cool; strain. Add 1 cup orange juice, lime juice. Just before serving, add sparkling water. Pour into 4 tall ice-filled glasses. Makes 4 servings.

OLD ENGLISH SPICED CIDER

1 teasp. whole allspice	⅔ cup brown sugar, packed
2 2″ sticks cinnamon	
12 whole cloves	Ground nutmeg
2 qt. cider	

Tie allspice, cinnamon, and cloves together in cheesecloth. In large saucepan, combine cider, brown sugar; heat. Add spice bag; simmer 10 min., or until cider is spicy enough to suit taste. Remove bag.

Serve piping hot in mugs, with dash of nutmeg in each. Makes 7 to 8 servings.

Iced Spiced Cider: Make hot spiced cider; chill before serving.

ICE-CREAM COOLERS

HOME SODA FOUNTAIN

A smart mother keeps the makings of ice-cream drinks on hand and lets the youngsters mix their own. Grownups love them too.

Place your favorite ice cream or sherbet in tall glass; add one of flavors below, then one of coolers. Stir well; insert straws; sip away.

Flavors:
   Chocolate or maple-blended syrup
   Fresh or frozen berries, peach slices, etc.
   Canned whole-cranberry sauce
   Molasses or prepared mincemeat
   Chopped nuts

Ginger ale
Coolers:
   Root beer or cola
   Milk or cream
   Coffee (made from instant coffee)
   Canned or frozen fruit juice or lemonade

CARIBE COOLER

Among 4 tall glasses, divide 2 cups slightly sweetened, cut-up, mixed fresh fruit (berries, peaches, oranges, bananas, etc.). To each portion, add ¼ cup each pineapple and orange juice and 1 big scoop of vanilla ice cream. Fill glasses with chilled sparkling water. Makes 4 servings.

COLA QUICKIES

In tall glass, place 2 tablesp. light cream; add several scoops of chocolate ice cream. Fill glass with chilled cola.

Or try coffee ice cream and root beer; black-raspberry ice cream and ginger ale; or vanilla ice cream and raspberry soda. Makes 1 serving.

NECTAR FREEZE

With temperature control of refrigerator at coldest setting, in ice-cube tray, freeze 2 cups canned whole-fruit apricot nectar until half frozen. Turn into bowl; add ½ pt. vanilla ice cream; beat until light and fluffy. Pour into 3 tall glasses; sprinkle with nutmeg. Makes 3 servings.

ROOT-BEER SPARKLE

In tall glass, mix ½ cup chilled root beer and 1 tablesp. milk. Add 1 big scoop of vanilla or chocolate ice cream; fill glass with root beer. Makes 1 serving.

FLIP-FLOP

In tall glass, place 1 scoop of orange sherbet, 1 teasp. jam, then 1 scoop of vanilla ice cream. Repeat till glass is three fourths full. Fill glass with chilled ginger ale. Eat with spoon. Makes 1 serving.

SUSAN'S PINEAPPLE CREAM

3½ cups chilled pineapple juice	cream
½ pt. orange sherbet	1½ cups chilled ginger ale
1 pt. vanilla ice	

Mix pineapple juice, sherbet, ice cream; with egg beater or electric mixer, beat until well mixed. Pour into punch bowl; gently stir in ginger ale. Makes 12 punch-cup servings.

MOCHA FLOAT

6 tablesp. canned chocolate syrup	4½ cups cold milk
3 cups hot or cold strong coffee	⅛ teasp. salt
	1 pt. vanilla ice cream

Blend chocolate syrup with coffee; add sugar to taste if desired; chill. Blend thoroughly with milk and salt. Pour into 6 tall glasses; top with ice cream. Makes 6 servings.

BANANA SMOOTHIE

Beat 4 ripe bananas until smooth. Add 3 cups cold milk, ½ cup heavy cream, 2 teasp. vanilla

extract; beat until well mixed. Pour into 4 glasses. Float 1 scoop of vanilla ice cream on each. Place banana slice on edge of each glass. Makes 4 servings.

FOUR-FRUIT FROST

1 cup chilled orange juice	lemon juice
½ cup chilled lime juice	1 cup chilled pineapple juice
¼ cup chilled fresh, frozen, or canned	⅔ cup granulated sugar
	1 pt. vanilla ice cream

Mix juices with sugar; add ice cream; beat just until blended. Garnish each glass with thin slice orange, lemon, and lime, with slices touching. Makes 4 servings.

PRUNE VELVET

1 chilled can strained prunes (baby pack)	1 teasp. fresh, frozen, or canned lemon juice
⅓ cup chilled orange juice	1 tablesp. sugar
1 cup cold milk	1 big scoop of vanilla ice cream
Pinch salt	

Mix prunes, orange juice, milk. Add salt, lemon juice, sugar, ice cream. With egg beater, blend thoroughly. Top with twist of orange peel. Makes 2 large, or 4 small, servings.

MILK COOLERS

Remember, everyone in the family, from the youngest to the oldest, needs plenty of milk every day. Here's one way to get each one to drink it: Serve these milk tempters. Use regular, diluted evaporated, or liquefied nonfat dry milk. An electric blender or mixer makes quick work of whipping up the drinks.

BANANA MILK SHAKE

For each tall serving, slice 1 fully ripe banana into bowl; beat until smooth and creamy. Add 1 cup cold milk; beat well. Pour into glass.

If desired, top with whipped cream (or spoonful of ice cream) and grated unsweetened chocolate; or top with sprinkling of cinnamon or nutmeg. Garnish edge of glass with banana slice. Serve at once.

Brown Cow: With milk, add 1½ to 2 tablesp. chocolate malted-milk powder (or homemade or canned chocolate syrup) and ¼ teasp. vanilla extract. Top with ice cream.

Pineana: Substitute pineapple juice for ¼ cup milk.

LEMON SHAKE

2 eggs	juice
½ cup ice water	½ cup granulated
6 tablesp. fresh, frozen,	sugar
or canned lemon	3 cups cold milk

Beat eggs; add water, lemon juice, and sugar, mixing thoroughly. Add slowly to milk, beating constantly. Makes 4 or 5 servings.

CHOCOLATE MILK

Today there's more than one way to make quick work of mixing chocolate milk. In fact, here are five start-offs to which you need only add milk.

Instant-cocoa mix	Melted semisweet-
Chocolate-malted-	chocolate pieces
milk powder	Homemade Choco-
Canned chocolate	late Syrup, below
syrup	

Or use chilled Hot Cocoa, p. 497, or Hot French Chocolate, p. 498, or bottled chocolate-milk drinks.

HOMEMADE CHOCOLATE SYRUP
(to use in chocolate-milk drinks)

4 sq. unsweetened	¼ teasp. salt
chocolate	½ teasp. vanilla
1¼ cups hot water	extract
1 cup granulated sugar	

In saucepan over low heat, cook chocolate with water, stirring, until thick and well blended. Add sugar, salt; boil 2 min., stirring constantly. Remove from heat; add vanilla. Cool; then refrigerate. Makes 2 cups.

To use: Allow 2 to 3 tablesp. chocolate syrup to each cup of milk.

Double-Quick Chocolate Syrup: Stir 1 cup instant-cocoa mix with 6 tablesp. hot water until cocoa dissolves. Makes ⅔ cup.

FOUR CHOCOLATE MILK DRINKS

Mocha: For each serving, beat 1 cup milk with 2 tablesp. homemade or canned chocolate syrup and 2 teasp. instant coffee.

Choco-Nog Special: For each serving, slowly stir 1 cup chilled milk into 3 tablesp. chocolate syrup; add 1 well-beaten egg. Beat or shake well.

Frosted Chocolate: For each serving, beat 1 cup milk with 2 tablesp. chocolate syrup and small spoonful of ice cream.

Chocolate Float: Make Frosted Chocolate, above, floating spoonfuls of ice cream on top.

SUSAN'S HONEY ICED CHOCOLATE

In saucepan, bring 2 cups milk to boil. Remove from heat. Combine ⅓ cup honey, 4 teasp. cocoa, pinch salt. Stir into milk. Pour mixture into 4 small glasses, filled with crushed ice; top with blobs of whipped cream. Makes 4 servings.

MILK TINGLERS

For each serving, into 1 cup cold milk, slowly stir any of the following. If desired, top with dab of whipped cream, marshmallow cream, or spoonful of ice cream.

- ¼ cup canned crushed pineapple
- ¼ cup sweetened, crushed raspberries or strawberries
- 2 to 3 tablesp. maple-blended syrup
- 1 to 2 tablesp. molasses
- 2 to 3 tablesp. strawberry, raspberry, or apricot jam
- 2 to 3 tablesp. thawed frozen grape-, orange-, or pineapple-juice concentrate
- 1 heaping tablesp. raspberry-flavored rennet-dessert powder
- 1 to 2 tablesp. prepared mincemeat
- Vanilla or almond extract
- Cinnamon, nutmeg, or mace

TWO BUTTERMILK COOLERS

1. Sprinkle cold buttermilk with paprika and salt.

2. Fill each glass halfway with thawed frozen sliced strawberries; fill to top with buttermilk; stir.

PEACHY MILK SHAKE

2 cups milk	¼ cup granulated
1 No. 303 can peach	sugar
halves, well chilled	Few grains salt
½ cup light cream	

Pour milk into ice-cube tray; freeze until about half frozen. Meanwhile, drain peaches; with fork, mash to make 1 cup purée. Turn frozen milk into chilled bowl; add peach purée, cream, sugar, salt. Beat until well blended. Sprinkle with nutmeg. Makes 4 servings.

AMBROSIA SHAKE

4 sliced fully ripe	Pinch salt
bananas	¼ teasp. almond
⅓ cup orange juice	extract
6 tablesp. honey	1 qt. cold milk

Beat bananas until smooth and creamy. Beat in orange juice, honey, salt, extract. Add milk; beat well. Garnish with whipped cream and shredded coconut. Makes 6 servings.

CRANBERRY NOG

3 eggs, separated	cocktail
½ cup cold milk	½ teasp. vanilla extract
2 cups chilled	3 tablesp. granulated
cranberry-juice	sugar

Beat egg yolks until light and fluffy. Add milk and cranberry juice; beat until well blended. Add vanilla. Just before serving, beat egg whites until stiff but not dry. Gradually beat in sugar. Fold into cranberry mixture. Sprinkle with nutmeg. Makes 5 servings.

CHOCO-MINT FLUFF

1 qt. cold milk	extract
⅓ cup chocolate	2 tablesp. crushed
syrup	peppermint candy
¼ cup heavy cream	⅓ cup heavy cream,
¼ teasp. peppermint	whipped

Combine milk, syrup, ¼ cup cream, extract; beat well until blended. Pour into 5 glasses. Fold crushed peppermint candy into whipped cream; use to top each drink. Makes 5 servings.

COFFEENOG

1 egg, beaten	Dash salt
4 teasp. instant coffee	2 cups cold milk
2 tablesp. granulated	⅛ teasp. vanilla
sugar	extract

Combine beaten egg, coffee, sugar, salt; beat until coffee and sugar dissolve. Add milk, vanilla; beat well. Refrigerate. Makes 2 servings.

Eggnog: Omit coffee; increase vanilla to ½ teasp.

COOL, COOL, PUNCHES

Turn to pp. 647 to 649 for punches for small or large groups.

ENGAGEMENT-PARTY HEART

PLACE-CARD HEART

SHOWER-PARTY BASKI

HAT FOR ST. PADDY'S DAY

TOY SOLDIER'S DRUM

SWEET FIRECRACKER

EASTER BUNNY

LIBERTY BELL

Wines

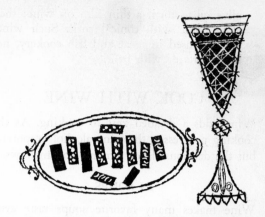

The superb wines produced abroad and in this country can brighten your meals, bring new zest to your cooking, add new smartness to your entertaining.

What Is Wine?

Wine is the fermented juice of freshly gathered, ripe grapes.

The many different species of grapevine grown in different parts of the world, the great variations in soil, aspect, and climate of the various vineyards, and the varying methods of vine growing and wine making result in many different kinds of wine. Even the quality of the grape juice from the same vine differs from year to year according to the weather that prevails during the growth and ripening of the grapes.

In the United States wine is made in 27 states; California produces 90 per cent of the commercial grape crop. California's 8 viticultural sections are planted almost exclusively in European wine grapes. The other states that also produce wines (chiefly New York and Ohio) do so from native American grape varieties.

When You Buy Wines

If you are not too well acquainted with different wines or what you should pay for them, talk to a reliable wine dealer. Let him suggest good wines, notable vintage years for imported wines, etc., in keeping with your tastes and budget.

Also study the Brief U.S.A. Wine Dictionary, pp. 510 to 513.

Store and Keep It Properly

Storing Wine: Ideally wine should be stored in a wine cellar at an even temperature of 50° to 60°F. If this is impossible (as it often is today), the wine bottle can be laid on its side on a pantry shelf. It is especially important that bottles of table and sparkling wines, which are corked, be kept on their sides, so that the corks are kept moist and, therefore, airtight. If the bottle has a screw cap, it may remain upright.

WHEN WINE IS LEFT OVER

Appetizer and Dessert Wines: Once opened, these wines keep well for weeks unless they are exposed to air for very long periods.

Table Wines: Because of their lower alcoholic content, table wines are perishable after opening. Contact with air and heat makes them "go off" (spoil). Care for them as follows:

1. If it's a fifth bottle of wine, cork it tightly; refrigerate; use the next day. If it must be held longer than a day, pour into clean smaller bottles; close with conical cork from drugstore; refrigerate. Plan to use within a week.
2. If it's a gallon jug of wine, pour what is left into clean smaller bottles; cork tightly; refrigerate. Plan to use within a week.
3. If you intend to use leftover wine for cooking, it need not be refrigerated. Just add enough

olive oil to form a thin film on wine; then close bottle with conical cork. Such wines are best used in meat and fish cookery, not in desserts or with fruit.

COOK WITH WINE

Wine adds a decided zest to cooking. As the cooking progresses, the wine alcohol evaporates but the delicious flavor remains and mellows.

IN SOUPS

Wine makes many favorite soups taste even better.

Canned Consommé: Add ½ wineglass white table wine per 4 or 5 servings.

Brown Soups: Soups such as oxtail, lentil, black bean, etc. taste all the better if about 2 teasp. dry or medium sherry is added.

IN MEAT AND FISH DISHES

Beef Roasts, Pot Roasts, etc.: A few tablespoonfuls of any red table wine added to beef as it cooks improves both meat and gravy.

Lamb and Mutton: Pouring ½ cup any white table wine over a shoulder or stuffed breast of lamb or mutton before starting to cook it, and spooning wine over meat during cooking, makes it a delicacy.

Veal and Chicken Dishes: You can perk up sauces for these dishes with a spoonful or more of any white table wine, as in Sautéed Chicken, p. 138.

Stews: A small amount of any red or white table wine gives an added lift to dishes such as lamb stew, beef stew, etc.

Fish: White table wine provides a pleasing foil for the flavor of fish. See Swordfish or Tuna Provençal, p. 171, Fillets of Fish Duglere, p. 174, etc.

Game: Marinating gamey meat, such as venison, in any red table wine 24 hr. or longer removes most of the gaminess, objectionable to some people.

IN SALAD DRESSINGS

For Tossed Green Salads: Use red table wine for part of vinegar in French dressing.

Cold Asparagus and Chicory: Dress with a light French dressing in which white wine replaces vinegar. This is a French classic when served with broiled chicken.

IN SAUCES

One of the best-known cooking uses of wine is in the preparation of sauces. Some sauces using wine include:

Sherry Sauce, p. 373
Inverness Wine Barbecue Sauce, p. 375
Fine Herb Sauce, p. 377
Game Sauces, p. 203
Holiday Sauce, p. 370
Fluffy Hard Sauce, p. 371
Zabaglione, p. 388

IN DESSERTS

Wine adds the master touch, the "French atmosphere," to many desserts, especially to cut-up fruit. Dry-tasting (not sweet) and sweet-tasting table wines (which often eliminate the need for sugar), as well as dessert wines and liqueurs, may be used.

Strawberries, Peaches, and Pears: These fruits—fresh, canned, or frozen—are often served in port.

Bananas: Sliced bananas are good in red wine.

Cooked Unsweetened Raspberries with Cooked Dried Prunes: Add a little port and brown sugar to make a compote men like. Serve it with Mock Devonshire Cream, p. 380.

Fruit combinations: Combine pitted cherries, sliced peaches, mangoes, blackberries. Add sweet sauterne. Chill.

Or try sliced or diced melon, seedless grapes, and sliced or diced pears tossed with the thinnest julienne strips of orange peel. Add sweet sauterne or inexpensive sparkling wine plus, if desired, 1 liqueur glassful of triple sec. Chill.

Sherbet: Heap firmly frozen lemon sherbet, stuck with sprigs of mint, in bowl packed in ice. Pour over it any cold, cut-up fruits—melon, cut into balls; grapes, pears and unpeeled plums, quartered. Just before serving, pour 1 or 2 wineglasses of light wine, or your favorite liqueur, over all.

SERVE WINE AS A BEVERAGE

Wine is as easy to serve correctly as tea or coffee. For greatest enjoyment, there are certain amenities to be observed, but there is no mysterious ritual. These few points should tell you all you need to know.

The Glasses

Unless you go in for elaborate entertaining, 3 standard glass sizes are all you need.

For appetizer and dessert wines: Use 2- to 3-oz. cocktail glass.

For red and white table wines: Use 4- to 6-oz. wineglass.

For sparkling wines: If available, flute glasses are often preferred. Or use saucer or hollow-stemmed champagne, water goblet, or high sherbet glass.

Wine will taste best if you fill glasses only one half to two thirds full. Space left in glass permits you to enjoy wine's aroma.

What Wine To Serve When

It's perfectly correct to serve any wine any time you wish. However, if you want the wine-and-food combinations that many people prefer, here they are:

Alone, as Appetizer: Before the meal, serve either of these appetizer wines:

Sherry	Vermouth

Serve it slightly chilled, living-room style.

With Hors d'Oeuvres or Soup: Serve dry sherry, slightly chilled.

With Sea Food, Chicken, Omelet, or Other Light Dishes: Serve one of these delicate white table wines; their characteristic acidity enhances such foods.

Sauterne	Rhine wine
Sauvignon blanc	Riesling
Semillon	Traminer
Chablis	Sylvaner
Pinot chardonnay	White Chianti
Pinot blanc	Rosé

Refrigerate 2 hr. or more; or chill by standing wine in water containing ice. Never put ice in any wine (except in mixed wine drinks, such as spritzes and claret lemonade).

With Steak; Roast; Chops; Game; Cheese, Spaghetti, or Macaroni Dishes; etc.: Serve one of these red table wines. Their slight tartness goes especially well with red meats.

Burgundy	Zinfandel
Pinot noir	Cabernet
Red pinot	Grignolino
Gamay	Red Chianti
Barbera	Rosé
Claret	

Serve all except rosé at room temperature. Let wine stand in dining room until it takes on temperature of room (unless your room is overheated). *Do not* warm it up quickly. Chill rosé several hours before serving.

P.S. Although some people prefer rosé with red meats, this pink wine's preferred usage is with chicken and other light dishes.

With Fruit, Nuts, Cookies, Cheeses: Serve one of these dessert wines:

Port	Tokay
White port	Angelica
Tawny port	Sweet sherry
Muscatel	Madeira

Serve chilled or at cool room temperature.

P.S. Table wines have dessert uses too. Sweet-tasting white table wines, such as sweet sauterne or sweet Semillon, go best with fruit or a sweet dessert.

Sweet-tasting white table wines also make delicious punches, wine cups, or iced drinks.

With cheeses, the red table wines, as well as port, are favored choices.

With Appetizer, Main Course, or Dessert: Depending on the degree of sweetness, these festive, effervescent wines are served before, during, and after meals:

Champagne Sparkling Burgundy
Pink champagne Sparkling muscat

The dry sparkling wines are appreciated best before and during the meal. Sweet champagnes and sparkling muscats are reserved for dessert-time or between meals.
Serve very well chilled.

The Order of Serving Wine

The order in which wines should be served varies with individual taste and the food.

For informal meals, when one wine is served throughout, it should be chosen to harmonize with the main course as suggested on p. 507.

For more formal meals, the classic order is:

1. *With oysters:* Chablis or champagne (dry)
2. *With soup:* pale sherry or dry Madeira
3. *With fish:* champagne (dry) or dry white table wines
4. *With entrées:* claret
5. *With roast or game:* Burgundy
6. *With sweets:* champagne (sweet) or sweet sauterne
7. *With cheese:* port, sweet sherry, or Madeira

Serve Wine with Style

At the simple one-wine dinner, bring on the wine with the main course. Pour it just before, or at the same time as, the main dish is served. Then everyone can enjoy a sip after his first taste of the food.

Here's How: Before meal begins, have wine bottle on small tray on table. (It's good practice for host to sample the wine beforehand, to be sure of its quality.) Host pours a bit of wine into his glass, to make certain no pieces of cork remain in bottle. Then he goes from person to person, filling glasses. Or let bottle pass from hand to hand, in the age-old European manner.

Here's Why: Guests enjoy knowing the wine they are drinking. So they can examine the label, pass the bottle as is or, if it's chilled, with a cloth wrapped around the lower part only. Wrapping the bottle completely makes guests feel they are expected to guess what the wine is or to believe the wine is better than it is.

Some Notes on Imported Wines

Alsatian: These are white wines from the vineyards on the left bank of the Rhine, from Mulhouse to Strasbourg. Serve as Rhine Wine, p. 510.

White Bordeaux (graves and sauternes): Graves and sauternes are white wines from Bordeaux. Some are fairly dry, others rather sweet. Serve as Sauterne, p. 511.

Burgundy: There are many wines—red and white, still and sparkling—known as Burgundy. They are made in *départements* of France that were formerly part of the old province of Burgundy. The Côte d'Or produces the choicest red Burgundies, particularly in northern part. To the south, the Saône-et-Loire district produces lighter though pleasing, less expensive wines.

The best known white Burgundy is Chablis. The white wines of the Côte d'Or are finer but also more expensive.

Champagne: Champagne is a sparkling wine made from grapes grown within the former boundaries of the ancient province of Champagne. It is always blended, each producer having his own particular blend of old and new wines. A vintage champagne is one bearing the date of the particular year when the grapes from which it was mainly, if not entirely, made, were gathered.

Chianti: Chianti is the best-known Italian red wine. It's light and fairly dry. There are also a few white Chiantis of good quality.

Claret: Claret is the red wine of Bordeaux. In color it should be a brilliant ruby red, never black or pink. It differs very much in bouquet and flavor according to the species of grape, the soil, and aspect of the vineyard, the method of pressing the juice, and length of time it has been kept.

Hock: Hock is Rhenish white wine, deriving its name from Hochheim on the river Main.

Madeira: Madeira is a fortified wine made and matured on the island of Madeira. It is fortified and matured in a different way from port and sherry. The fermented grape juice, or new wine, is subjected to heat and is then racked and rested, after which it is fortified by the addition of cane spirit. At this stage the wines are blended together and left for some years to mature.

Malaga: This is one of the best sweet wines of Spain.

Marsala: This is the best, and best-known, dessert wine of Italy.

Moselle: Moselle comes from vineyards on the river Moselle. Serve as Rhine Wine, p. 510.

Muscatel: This is a white wine made in Spain and Italy from muscat grapes.

Port: Port is a fortified wine made from grapes grown in the Upper Valley of the Douro River in Portugal and shipped from Oporto. It is fortified by brandy, added at time of pressing grapes. There are a number of different types: red, white, or tawny in color, and different in style, age, strength, and sweetness.

A vintage port is the best; that is to say, red port, made from the grapes of a vintage (good and sunny) year. The grapes must also be perfectly sound and ripe when picked. The wine is shipped from Oporto eighteen months to two years afterward, and bottled in England soon after landing. Then it must be given time, twelve to fifteen years or longer, to mature.

Sherry: Sherry is a wine made from white grapes grown in the south of Spain, in the Jerez district. It is allowed to ferment in its own way and may be fortified by the addition of brandy at a much later stage of its existence.

The vintage of sherry does not count for much, nor does any individual vineyard; what matters is the shipper. Sherry is a blend of wines, similar in style but made from grapes of different vineyards and wines of different years. They are blended together to maintain the standards set by the different sherry shippers.

Tokay: This is the best, and best-known, wine of Hungary.

BRIEF U. S. A. WINE DICTIONARY

WINE	CHARACTERISTICS	WHEN TO SERVE (See also pp. 507-508)	TEMPERATURE
Appetizer Wines:			
Sherry	Appetizer or dessert wine, with nutty, or *rancio*, flavor. Color ranges from pale to dark amber. Made dry, medium dry, and sweet. Dry sherry is the most popular appetizer wine	*Dry sherries:* Before meal as appetizer. *Sweet sherries:* Usually served with dessert, with between-meal refreshments, or with biscuits, crackers, etc.	Chilled or at room temperature
Vermouth	Appetizer wine flavored with aromatic herbs. There are two kinds: *Sweet* (Italian type) is dark amber. *Dry* (French type) is pale amber	Before meal as appetizer	Well chilled
White Table Wines:			
Catawba	Made in Eastern and Midwestern states from native hybrid grapes that give it characteristic flavor and aroma. Both dry and semisweet	Same as sauterne	Well chilled
Chablis	Straw-colored wine, similar to Rhine wine but less tart than most wines in that group, and with fruit flavor and body	With main course. Especially good with fish, shellfish, poultry, veal, lamb, etc.	Well chilled
Delaware	Made from Delaware grapes grown in Eastern states	Same as Rhine wine	Well chilled
Folle Blanche	Chablis type. Made from folle blanche grapes	Same as Chablis	Well chilled
Light Muscat	Dry or semisweet. Also called dry muscat. Light wine of muscat grapes with characteristic muscat flavor and aroma	*Dry types:* With white meat or sea food. *Semisweet types:* With or after dessert; or with between-meal refreshments	Well chilled
Pinot Blanc	Chablis type. Made from pinot blanc grapes	Same as Chablis	Well chilled
Rhine Wine (hock or Moselle)	Thoroughly dry. Sometimes on acid side, with delicate pale-gold, slightly greenish color. Eastern Rhine wines are flowery, fruity	With main course, especially white meats or sea foods	Well chilled

Riesling	Rhine-wine type made from Riesling grapes	Same as Rhine wine	Well chilled
Sauterne	*Golden-hued wines*, sometimes dry but often semisweet. *Very sweet sauternes*, also labeled haut sauterne or frequently chateau sauterne. *Eastern sauternes*, often less sweet, with characteristic aroma and grape taste	*Dry:* With white meats and sea food. *Sweet:* With dessert, between meals, or with white meats and sea food. *Very Sweet:* After dessert, often with meals	Well chilled
Semillon	Sauterne-type wine made from semillon grapes. Either dry or semisweet	Same as sauterne	Well chilled
Sylvaner	Made from sylvaner (also called Franken Riesling) grapes. Rhine-wine type, but fruitier and more fragrant. Resembles Alsatian wine	Same as Rhine wine	Well chilled
Red Table Wines: Barbera	Heavy-bodied—typical Italian type. Made from, and with distinct flavor and aroma of, barbera grape. Strong in flavor. Burgundy type	With main course. Delicious with highly seasoned food, rice and spaghetti dishes, etc.	Room temperature or slightly chilled
Burgundy	Dark ruby in color, stronger in flavor, body, and bouquet than claret. (Made from a number of grape varieties.) Eastern Burgundy has characteristic "grapy" perfume and flavor of Eastern native grapes	With main course, especially red meats, turkey, or dark-meated birds	Room temperature or slightly chilled
Cabernet	Made from cabernet sauvignon grapes, famous Bordeaux grape of France and one of the best red wine grapes of California. Has distinctive flavor. Stronger flavor and body than most clarets, sometimes heavier than California Burgundy. Harsh when young, very fine cabernet becomes really great with age	Same as claret	Room temperature or slightly chilled
Chianti	Medium-bodied, ruby-red wine, strongly flavored, dry, fruity, slightly tart	Same as claret	Room temperature or slightly chilled
Claret	Medium-bodied, with tasty dryness. Often less expensive than other red wines	With steaks, roasts, chops, spaghetti, game	Room temperature or slightly chilled *(cont'd)*

BRIEF U. S. A. WINE DICTIONARY—Continued

WINE	CHARACTERISTICS	WHEN TO SERVE (See also pp. 507-508)	TEMPERATURE
Gamay	Made from gamay grapes. Light in body. Often made into rosé wine	Same as Burgundy	*Red:* room temperature *Rosé:* chilled
Pinot Noir	Made from famous pinot noir grapes (Burgundy type). Varies greatly with amount of this grape present (by law, at least 51 per cent). Finest are velvety to taste, beautiful red in color. Can be aged into wonderful wine in bottle	Same as Burgundy	Room temperature or slightly chilled
Rosé	Lightest of red table wines, being light in color, body, and alcoholic content. Dry, fruity wine	Ideal for luncheon or picnic	Chilled
Zinfandel	Claret type. Made from, and has distinct taste and aroma of, zinfandel grape. Somewhat coarse, fruity, medium-bodied	Same as claret	Room temperature or slightly chilled
Dessert Wines: Angelica	Sweet; straw- or amber-colored; mild and fruity in flavor; originated in California	With or after dessert, or with between-meal refreshments	Room temperature or chilled
Madeira	Deep amber. Semisweet. Resembles sherry, but is sweeter and darker. Drier than Tokay	With or after dessert, or with little cakes as refreshments	Room temperature or chilled
Marsala	Deep amber. Resembles sherry but is sweeter and darker. Usually sweeter than Madeira but drier than Tokay. Medium-bodied	With or after dessert, or with cheese and nuts	Room temperature or chilled
Muscatel	Has distinctive flavor, aroma, and sweetness of muscat grapes from which it is made. Ranges in color from golden to amber. Medium-bodied	With or after dessert, or with between-meal refreshments, biscuits, crackers, or cheese and nuts	Room temperature or chilled

Port	Rich, heavy-bodied, sweet wine, ranging from deep-red to tawny color	With or after dessert. Especially good with cheese and nuts	Room temperature or chilled
Tokay	Amber-colored, sweet dessert wine. In no way resembles Hungarian Tokay in flavor. Usually made by blending angelica, port, and sherry	With or after dessert; or with fruitcake, nuts, raisins; or as between-meal refreshments	Room temperature or chilled
White Port	White dessert wine. Usually straw-colored. Sweet, heavy-bodied	With or after dessert, or with between-meal refreshments	Room temperature or chilled
Sparkling Wines: Champagne	Made sparkling by secondary fermentation of finished wine, creating natural effervescence. Comes dry, usually labeled brut; or semidry, labeled dry, extra-dry, or sec. There are pink champagnes	*Dry type:* As appetizer. Or with main course—especially poultry, game, sweetbreads, fish *Sweet type:* With dessert	Very well chilled
Sparkling Burgundy	Red wine made naturally sparkling by same process as champagne. Smooth, slightly sweet, light-bodied	With main course—especially poultry, game, sweetbreads	Very well chilled

Marketing

If you would be a thrifty shopper and know your way around today's serve-yourself food stores, don't wait until you get to market to decide what you're going to buy.

Develop some marketing know-how. Read the pages that follow here for marketing tips. Then take time out to leaf through the To Market and To Buy sections of Meats, Poultry, Fish, Shellfish, Vegetables, etc.

And brush up, too, on the wonderful best buys suggested in Thrifty Meals, p. 560; Cooking for One, p. 625; Quick-and-Easy Meals, p. 569; Cooking for Two, p. 631; etc.

FOODS FOR YOUR PANTRY SHELVES

Perhaps you're a bride planning your first trip to market after moving into a new home. Or maybe you forgot to jot down all those items used up during the past week. In any case, here's a partial list of the fine foods that make meal getting easier. It may serve to jog your memory as to what you need to buy.

Where page references are given, additional information on the product will be found.

Remember that you can often save by purchasing a large, rather than a small, package of a food that you use frequently, providing it keeps well.

If the package label calls for storing the food in the refrigerator, *be sure to do so.*

Baking powder, p. 519
Baking soda, p. 519
Bouillon cubes, meat-extract paste
Bread crumbs, dried
Canned foods:
  Baby pack: fruits, meats, vegetables, etc.
  Baked beans, chili beans, etc.
  Breads: brown, chocolate nut, date and nut, fruit and nut, etc.
  Chicken, p. 136: boned, fricasseed, whole, etc.
  Chinese foods: bean sprouts, chop suey, chow mein, chow-mein noodles, etc.
  Cranberry sauce: jellied or whole
  Cream for coffee: powdered
  Fish: anchovies, crab meat, salmon, sardines, shrimp, tuna, etc.
  Fruit juices: apple, cranberry, grape, grapefruit, lemon, orange, pineapple, prune, tangerine, whole-fruit nectar, etc.
  Fruits: applesauce, cherries, fruit cocktail, grapefruit, peaches, pears, pineapple, purple plums, etc. Also dietetic packs
Gravy, beef
Meats: chopped ham, corned beef, corned-beef hash, deviled ham, ham, luncheon meat, meat *pâtés,* stews, tongue, etc.
Milk, p. 519: evaporated, sweetened condensed
Nuts, p. 521
Pimentos
Popcorn
Preserved fruits and peels
Puddings: date, fig, plum, etc.
Rice: cooked or Spanish
Soups, chowders, etc.
Spaghetti and macaroni dishes
Tomato juice or vegetable-juice cocktail
Tomato aspic, paste, purée, or sauce
Turkey, boned
Vegetables: asparagus, beets, green beans (Blue Lake,

WHEN YOU BUY CANNED FOODS

You Get Fine Cooked Food. Canned foods are delicious just as they come from the can or jar; they are all cooked too, saving you many hours of preparation and assuring no waste.

The fruits and vegetables used are specially grown, picked at just the right point of maturity, sealed in cans, and cooked in the briefest time after harvesting. So, like other quality canned foods, they retain a high degree of the food value of the fresh food.

The Label Is Your Buying Guide. In this age of self-service food stores, we have all become increasingly dependent on labels to guide our buying.

For this reason, well-known canners are wording labels to give you a clear picture of what's inside the can. The can size; variety, style, and amount of food in the can; number of servings; kind of syrup; uses, etc., are noted right on the label. This helps you buy what you want, and the amount you need. Of course, you must judge flavor for yourself. If certain brands satisfy you, remember their names.

Canned Fruits Are of the Best. Your grocer has a wonderful assortment of canned fruits that come not only in larger sizes but also in 8-oz. cans, which are made to order for the family of one or two (see p. 516). Look for pineapple, peaches, purple plums, fruit cocktail, pears, grapefruit, cherries, etc. Then refer to Desserts, p. 378, Relishes and Garnishes, p. 286, Salads, p. 298, etc., for ways to serve them.

Canned Vegetables Are Tasty Timesavers. Today's canned vegetables, such as green peas, green limas, green beans (Blue Lake, etc.), whole-kernel corn, asparagus, etc., are unusually fine in flavor. So it is more important than ever to preserve their flavor and food value when you heat them for the table. For the best heating methods, see Cook With Care, p. 245.

Never rinse canned vegetables under cold water; you'll lose food value and flavor. Don't turn them out of the can to be aerated before using; that simply adds work, does not improve flavor.

There Are Dietetic Packs Too. For those who must count calories, watch their sodium intake, or are diabetic, there are an increasing number of fine dietetic-pack canned foods, including fruits, vegetables, tuna, soups, juices, chicken, meats, prepared dishes, salad dressings, etc.

CAN SIZES

Size	Approximate Weight	Approximate Contents	Chief Uses
6 oz.	6 oz.	¾ cup	Frozen concentrates, natural-strength juice
8 oz.	8 oz.	1 cup	Fruits, vegetables, ripe olives
No. 1 (picnic)	10½ oz.	1¼ cups	Fruits, condensed soups, vegetables, etc.
12 oz.	12 oz.	1½ cups	Vacuum-packed whole-kernel corn
No. 300	1 lb.	1¾ cups	Pork and beans, baked beans, cranberry sauce, etc.
No. 303	1 lb.	2 cups	Vegetables, fruits, etc.
No. 2	1 lb. 4 oz.	2½ cups	Vegetables, fruits, juices, etc.
No. 2½	1 lb. 13 oz.	3½ cups	Fruits, vegetables, etc.
46 oz. (No. 3 cylinder)	1 qt. 14 fl. oz.	5¾ cups	Juices, whole chicken

Know How to Open a Can or Jar Easily. Of course, a good can opener is indispensable, and many fine ones are available today.

For glass jars and tumblers that have pry-off caps, there is now an inexpensive, efficient opener that easily lifts caps without bending or bursting them. The caps may be resealed by pressing with the heels of both hands.

Don't Hesitate to Store Leftovers in Opened Cans. Canned foods may be safely left in the opened can if they're covered and kept in the refrigerator. Of course any leftover cooked food, stored in any type of container, should be refrigerated.

CEREALS

Keep a Variety on Hand. And what a variety there is! Whole-grain or enriched, in ready-to-eat and hot styles, they're all ready to serve or cook in no time. Latest comer to the ready-to-eat field is the presweetened kind—wonderful as both cereal and snack.

Some cereal manufacturers are now marketing an assortment of their ready-to-eat cereals in serving-size packages, allowing you to keep and serve an even greater variety. And don't forget the special ready-to-use cereals for babies.

To Store: Store all cereals in a cool, dry, convenient spot. Packages and inner wrappings should be carefully opened so that they may be resealed after each use. This is particularly important with ready-to-eat cereals, which are only at their best when crisp.

Keep cereals that require cooking in original packages, so label directions may be followed.

CHOCOLATE AND COCOA

Unsweetened Chocolate is made from highly selected beans, with no cocoa butter removed.

Semisweet Chocolate has just enough sweetening added to give a pleasing, half-sweet flavor. Some cocoa butter is removed.

Cocoa is prepared from cocoa beans by removing varying amounts of cocoa butter.

Breakfast Cocoa contains at least 22 per cent cocoa butter.

Dutch Process Cocoa is made from cocoa beans that have been alkalized to give the cocoa more color and flavor.

Instant Cocoa Mix and Ready-to-Serve Cocoas require only the addition of hot or cold water or milk to be served as a beverage. See label directions for making frosting, sauce, etc.

COCONUT

Packaged Shredded: Sweetened coconut in mixed shred lengths comes packed in moisture-retaining cartons.

Canned Shredded: Coconut shreds that are more moist come in vacuum-packed cans. One style has short shreds, another mixed shred lengths.

Fresh: It's easy to open a fresh coconut this way: With a long nail, puncture the 3 indentations at the end of the coconut. Drain milk out of these holes. Then, in shallow pan, bake whole coconut at 350°F. 15 min.; this will crack shell. Complete cracking with hammer; then pry out white meat in as large pieces as possible. With knife or vegetable parer, cut brown skin from white meat; then grate meat, rubbing each piece the full length of the grater.

CREAM, see p. 10

EXTRACTS

Since we use extracts to lend a pleasing flavor to our food, buy well-known, quality brands to insure full, uniform flavor. You may save by buying a large, rather than a small, bottle. Keep bottle tightly closed.

Don't stick to just one or two flavors. Try new ones. Or plan to combine flavors, such as vanilla and almond, lemon and orange.

FLOURS

In cake, cookie, bread, and similar recipes in this book, we indicate the kind of flour to be used. *Never substitute another kind.* The following descriptions will guide you in buying the right flour. Don't buy more than you can use in a reasonable length of time.

All-Purpose: All-purpose flour is sometimes referred to as general-purpose, or family, flour. It comes in bags, and gives good results in all types of home baking.

It may be a blend of hard wheats, soft wheats, or of both. It is generally enriched, and this is indicated on the label of the bag. Enriched flour contains thiamine, niacin, riboflavin, and iron, in addition to excellent, energy-yielding carbohydrates and supplementary protein.

Always sift all-purpose flour just before measuring.

Bread: Bread flour, which also comes in bags, is excellent for yeast breads but is not as satisfactory for general use. It is made from hard wheats and has a higher, stronger gluten than all-purpose flour.

Cake: Cake flour comes in packages and makes especially delicate cakes. It is made from selected soft wheats and is specially milled to give a very fine flour.

Always sift cake flour just before measuring.

Self-rising: Self-rising flour is all-purpose flour to which leavening and salt have been added in proper amounts for most home baking except yeast breads. To use, follow recipes on package.

Self-rising Cake: This flour comes in packages and is cake flour to which salt and leavening have been added in proper amounts for home baking. For best results, follow manufacturer's directions on package.

Whole-wheat, Entire-wheat, and Graham are synonymous terms. Such flour contains, in natural proportions, all the constituents of the entire cleaned wheat grain.

Do not sift before measuring.

FROZEN FISH, MEATS, POULTRY, VEGETABLES, ETC.,
see Index

HERBS

DRIED HERBS

Today you can buy many dried herbs in cans, jars, etc., that add new interest and delightful flavor to your everyday cooking. They should be added to enhance, not overpower, food flavors.

To use dried herbs on your own, start by adding ¼ teasp. to a dish that makes 4 servings. Add as follows:

1. Soups and stews: Add during last hour.
2. Hamburgers, meat loaf, or stuffing: Add when mixing.
3. Roasts: Sprinkle on toward end of roasting time.
4. Steaks or chops: Sprinkle on while meat cooks. Or 1 hr. before cooking, brush meat with salad oil; then sprinkle with herbs.
5. Vegetables, sauces, gravies: Add while cooking.
6. Vegetable juices, salad dressings, cream cheese, etc.: Add dried herb; then refrigerate mixture a few hours.

Of the herbs below, basil, marjoram, savory, tarragon, thyme, and rosemary are especially versatile.

Basil: An herb of west Europe. Cook with or sprinkle on:

Egg dishes	Poultry dishes
Green beans	Salad dressings
Lamb chops	Sauces
Meats	Soups
Peas	Squash
Potatoes	Tomato dishes

Bay Leaves: From a laurel tree grown in eastern Mediterranean countries. Use in:

Fish dishes	Sauces and gravies
Pickling	Stews and soups

Chervil: Resembles parsley. Is slightly peppery. Delicious in:

Egg dishes	Salad dressings
Fish dishes	Salads
Peas or carrots	Summer squash
Poultry dishes	Tomato dishes

Dill: Imported from India. Add to:

Cream- or cottage-cheese mixtures	Sauces
	Spaghetti dishes
Fish dishes	Tomato dishes
Potato dishes	Vegetable salads

Marjoram: Herb of the mint family from France and Chile. Use sparingly in or on:

Cheese and egg dishes	Meat pies, hash, stews
Chicken dishes	Stuffings
Fish or vegetable sauces	Vegetables such as: asparagus, carrots,
Roast lamb	greens, limas, squash

Orégano: Imported from Italy and Mexico. Good in or on:

Cheese dishes	Pork or hamburgers
Chili con carne	Spaghetti sauce
Omelets	Stews
Pizza	Vegetables

Poultry Seasoning: Fragrant herbs combined with sage. Delicious in:

Biscuit dough	Stuffings

Rosemary: Delectable in, with, or on:

Biscuit dough	Sauces for meat or fish
Lamb dishes	
Boiled potatoes	Stews
Poultry dishes	Vegetables
Roasts	

Sage: A favorite used lightly in or on:

Cheese dishes	Poultry dishes
Fish dishes	Sausage dishes
Pork, veal, or ham dishes	Tomato dishes
	Tossed salads

Savory: Herb of the mint family from France and Spain. Try in or on:

Egg dishes

Baked beans

Green limas

Meat loaf, hamburgers, roasts

Potato or squash dishes

Rice dishes

Vegetable soup

Tarragon: Leaf with anise flavor. Good in:

Egg dishes

Poultry dishes

Salads

Sauces

Sea food

Tomato dishes

Vegetables such as beets, greens, mushrooms, peas

Thyme: Many varieties. Use sparingly in or with:

Breads

Cheese dishes

Fish dishes

Stews, chowders

Stuffings

Veal or pork

Vegetables such as carrots, eggplant, peas, tomatoes

FRESH HERBS

Picked Fresh: Use as garnish. Or snip fine with scissors and use as on p. 518, allowing 3 to 4 times as much fresh as dried herbs.

To Dry: When fresh herbs begin to flower, pick off tops and perfect leaves. Wash; spread on cheesecloth on tray. Dry in warm, sunshiny spot, turning occasionally, 2 or 3 days. Then crush leaves (no stems); store in jars.

Bouquet Garni: Tie sprig of thyme, parsley, and celery with piece of carrot and sprig of basil, rosemary, or savory. Add to stew or soup at start of cooking; remove to serve.

Chives: This plant's slender green tops have a delicate onion flavor. Snip fine; add to:

Cheese dishes

Meat or egg dishes

Poultry dishes

Salads

Soups and sauces

Vegetables, etc.

Fines Herbes: Combine equal amounts of minced chives, parsley, and fresh tarragon or thyme. Sprinkle on steak, or egg or chicken dishes.

LEAVENING AGENTS

Baking Powder: Baking powders are classified according to the acid ingredients they contain. There are 3 types. Nationally known brands clearly indicate the type on the label; look for it.

Double-Acting Baking Powder: Reacts very slowly, releasing about one fifth to one third of its leavening in the cold mixture; the rest in the heat of baking.

Phosphate Baking Powder: Reacts slowly and requires heat to liberate about one third of its leavening.

Tartrate Baking Powder: Reacts rapidly and begins its action at room temperature as soon as liquid is added.

If our recipes do not indicate a type of baking powder, you may safely use any of those above. If the recipe calls for a specific type, *be sure to use it.*

Baking Soda: Baking soda is used alone or with baking powder to leaven cakes made with buttermilk, sour milk, chocolate, molasses, fruit juices, etc. Acid from these ingredients reacts with soda to release leavening. When using soda, don't delay mixing or baking.

MILK

Everyone needs milk every day, so *never* skimp on that daily quota!

WHEN IT'S MILK

Check Milk Source. Be sure that the milk you buy comes from a reputable dealer, and be certain it is pasteurized.

In some communities, several grades of milk are sold. Ask your local health department to explain the differences; then buy the best grade you can afford.

Insist That Milk Be Pasteurized. The health of your family is being endangered constantly if you are using raw milk and unpasteurized dairy products. Undulant fever and many streptococcal infections are traceable to raw milk. Pasteurization is a sure way to make milk safe.

Homogenized Milk. This is pasteurized fluid whole milk, now available in nearly all areas of the U.S., in which the fat globules have been reduced in size so they remain evenly distributed throughout the milk. All portions of the milk have the same butter-fat content.

To Care for Milk:

1. *Take delivered milk in promptly* and store at once in coldest part of refrigerator. Refrigerate continuously until used.
2. *Wash top of container and cap* before opening or putting milk away.
3. *Always keep milk covered*.
4. *Never mix new and old milk or cream* except for immediate use. Adding yesterday's milk or cream to today's hastens the souring process.

WHEN IT'S EVAPORATED MILK

Canned unsweetened evaporated milk is pure, fresh, whole cow's milk of excellent uniform quality, with nothing removed except about half the natural water content. And nothing but vitamin D (the sunshine vitamin) is added. It is homogenized to distribute the cream evenly throughout the milk. It is pasteurized before it is put into the can, then sterilized after the can is sealed.

To Use: Evaporated milk offers one of the best ways to cut down your food bills. Just as it comes from the can (undiluted) or with an equal amount of water added (diluted), it may be used in cooking many dishes, such as sauces, casseroles, desserts, etc. It's economical too used as table or whipping cream.

To Store After Opening: Keep evaporated milk in the can after opening it; cover top with food cover or piece of foil pressed close against top edge. Refrigerate when not in use.

WHEN IT'S INSTANT NONFAT DRY MILK

Instant nonfat dry milk is now being marketed for home use. This dairy product is top-quality pasteurized milk with only the fat and water removed. In reliquefied form, it provides the valuable whole milk amounts of calcium, protein, B-vitamins and other protective milk minerals. It's a wonderfully thrifty type of milk. Be sure to keep it in its protective package on a cool, dry pantry shelf; close the package carefully after each use.

To Liquefy It: It's a very good idea to liquefy enough nonfat dry milk to take care of the next day's cooking and drinking needs. To liquefy it, carefully follow the simple label directions. One pound of nonfat dry milk makes 5 qt. fluid nonfat milk. Once it's liquefied, refrigerate it as you would milk. Or if more convenient, liquefy as label directs and use immediately.

To Use It in Dry Form: When making muffins, biscuits, etc., you may sift the nonfat-dry-milk powder with the dry ingredients and then substitute water for milk, if label so directs.

For Extra Nourishment: Oftentimes you can step up the food value of a dish by adding some nonfat-dry-milk powder before the dish is baked. See Two-Day Caramel Ham Loaf, p. 92.

WHEN IT'S CONDENSED MILK

Canned sweetened condensed milk is a mixture of pure, whole cow's milk and sugar, from which about 60 per cent of the water is removed before the mixture is put into cans and sealed. It is used to sweeten coffee, make ice cream, lemon pie filling, etc.

MOLASSES

Molasses is an important source of iron, so use it often.

Dark Molasses has a full, tangy flavor and deep color, and is excellent for all cooking in which many spices are present—gingerbread, Indian pudding, etc.

Light Molasses has a more delicate flavor than dark, a lower iron content, and a golden color, and is excellent for general cooking purposes.

NUTS

KINDS YOU CAN BUY

In the Shell* (in bags or bulk):

Almonds	Walnuts (top-qual-
Black walnuts	ity, large ones are
Brazil nuts	likely to carry
Filberts	a red stamp on
Peanuts	the shell; me-
Pecans	dium ones, a blue
	stamp)

Shelled* (in vacuum-sealed cans):

Almonds	Black walnuts
Blanched	Pecans
Buttered, diced	Salted peanuts
Slivered	Salted nuts
Unblanched	Walnuts

* For number of cupfuls per lb., see p. 15.

WHEN YOU STORE NUTS

Don't store nuts on the pantry shelf unless they're vacuum-packed; otherwise they may get stale. Shelled or in the shell, nuts keep fresh in the refrigerator for weeks on end. Or, even better, store them in a home freezer or refrigerator-freezer combination.

It's a good idea to shell walnuts, Brazil nuts, pecans, almonds, etc. as soon as you buy them. Then, if you're not going to use them at once, pack nut meats in tightly covered containers; store in refrigerator or freezer.

WHEN YOU USE NUTS

To Shell Brazil Nuts Easily: Cover unshelled Brazil nuts with salted water (1 tablesp. salt per 1 qt. water). Boil 3 min.; drain. Let stand in cold water to cover 1 min.; drain. Now they'll crack easily.

To Slice Brazil Nuts Easily: Cover shelled Brazil nuts with cold water. Bring slowly to boil; simmer 2 to 3 min.; drain. Now they'll slice easily.

To Blanch Almonds: Cover shelled almonds with cold water. Bring to boil; then remove from heat at once and drain. Slip off skins by pressing each almond between thumb and forefinger. Then dry almonds on paper towels.

To Toast Nuts: Spread shelled nuts in shallow pan. Bake at 350°F. 10 to 20 min., or until lightly toasted.

To Chop Nuts: Spread nuts on wooden board. With left hand, hold tip of long, sharp knife close to surface of board, moving handle up and down and around in semicircle with right hand so blade contacts uncut nuts.

Today's trick nut choppers do a good job too. So does the electric blender, especially when you have a large quantity of nuts to chop.

SALAD AND OLIVE OILS

Salad Oils: When buying salad oil, choose one of the many brands of corn, cottonseed, or peanut oils, or a blend of two or more oils. They're excellent for sautéing, deep or shallow frying, making salad dressings, preparing dishes that call for melted fat, etc.

Olive Oil: Olive oil, with its unique flavor, is popular for salad dressings, Italian-style dishes, etc.

To Store: After pouring what you need from a bottle of salad or olive oil, before screwing cap back on again, be sure to wipe off neck of bottle and inside of cap with paper towel or tissue. Keep salad and olive oils refrigerated at all times.

SHAKER SEASONINGS

Today several fine seasonings come in shaker-top containers—so handy for adding that just-right bit of seasoning at the range. And some of them spare you the job of mincing onion, garlic, celery, etc., too.

Monosodium Glutamate: A white crystalline seasoning that enhances the natural flavors of many foods. Especially nice in or on meat, fish, poultry, and shellfish dishes, vegetables, salads, etc.

Seasoned or Seasoning Salt: A flavorful blend of many spices with salt—just right for many everyday foods.

Celery Salt: Mixture of ground celery seeds with salt. Gives zest to such dishes as:

Fish	Salad dressings
Oyster stew	Soups
Potato salads	Tomato juice, etc.

Garlic Salt: Mixture of garlic powder with salt. Use with, or instead of salt, in or on:

Ground meats	spaghetti sauce
Salad dressings	Soups
Salads	Steaks or chops
Sauces such as	Tomato juice

Onion Salt: A blend of dehydrated onion and salt. Adds a delicate onion flavor to:

Meats	Spaghetti sauce
Salad dressings	Vegetables (add to
Salads	cooking water)

SPICES

It pays to buy quality brands of spices for full natural flavor. Buy them in small quantities and store them, tightly covered, in a cool place. Give them the nose test occasionally (in other words, smell them). If they lose their delicate aroma, replace them with fresh ones.

Here are some of the fascinating spices that can make triumphs out of everyday cooking.

Allspice (resembles blend of cinnamon, nutmeg, and cloves)	*Use whole in:*	Pickling, gravies, meats, fish dishes, etc.
	Use ground in or on:	Cakes, cookies, puddings, relishes, preserves, tomato sauce, steak, etc.
Aniseed (licoricelike flavor)	*Sprinkle on:*	Coffeecakes, sweet rolls, fruit, etc.
	Use ground in:	Cookies, sweet pickles, candies
Caraway Seeds (from Holland)	*Sprinkle over or use in:*	Sauerkraut, cabbage, asparagus, noodles, French fries, soups, cookies, breads and rolls, cheese spreads, pork, liver, kidneys, loaf cake, etc.
Cardamom Seeds (small pod of brown seeds)	*Use whole in:*	Demitasse, pickling, etc.
	Use ground in or on:	Cookies, coffeecakes, grape jelly, melon, etc.
Cayenne Pepper (most pungent chili pepper)	*Use in:*	Sauces, meat and egg dishes, sea food, etc.
Celery Seeds (tiny seedlike fruit)	*Use in:*	Cheese dishes; fish dishes; salad dressings; sauces; soups; stews; tomato, egg, or potato dishes; vegetables; etc.
Chili Powder (blend of chilies and spices)	*Use in:*	Chili con carne, cocktail sauces, egg dishes, gravies, sea food, stews
Cinnamon (spicy bark of Oriental tree)	*Use whole in:*	Pickling, preserving, canned or stewed fruits, etc.

	Use ground in or on:	Mashed sweet potatoes, toast, blueberries, apple or pineapple dishes, broiled grapefruit, bananas, cakes, ice cream, cookies, puddings, hot biscuits
Cloves (nail-shaped flower, bud of clove tree)	*Use whole in or on:*	Pork and ham roasts; pickling peaches, pineapple, etc.
	Use ground in:	Baked dishes, stews, chocolate puddings, vegetables, beets, broiled grapefruit, potato soup, etc.
Curry Powder (blend of spices)	*Use in:*	Sauce for eggs, fish, meats, poultry, vegetables; in tomato juice, etc.
Dill Seeds (small seeds of dill plant)	*Use in:*	Pickling, gravies, apple pie, soups, potato salad, salads, sauerkraut, cabbage, turnips, cauliflower, etc.
Ginger (root of Oriental plant)	*Use cracked in:*	Chutneys, conserves, pickling, stewed dried fruits, applesauce, etc.
	Use ground in:	Gingerbread, pumpkin pie, Indian pudding, summer squash, melon, canned fruit, chicken dishes, etc.
Mace (dried pulp around nutmeg kernel; has flavor similar to nutmeg)	*Use ground in or on:*	Cherries, chocolate dishes, whipped cream, jellies, canned fruit, gingerbread, poundcake, broiled grapefruit, fish sauces, etc.
Nutmeg (kernel of nutmeg fruit)	*Use ground in:*	Cakes, breads, cabbage, cauliflower, broiled fruit, green beans, greens, puddings, sauces
	Use as topping for:	Eggnog, custards, whipped cream, sauces, etc.
Paprika (mild member of pepper family; adds color, flavor)	*Sprinkle on or use in:*	Canapés, fish, gravies, meats, salad dressings, shellfish, vegetables, etc.
Pepper (world's most popular spice, from East Indies)	*Use whole peppers in:*	Pickling, soups, pepper grinders, etc.
	Use ground (black or white) in:	Eggs, gravies, meats, salads, sauces, soups, many vegetables—in fact, most foods
Poppy Seeds (fragrant seeds from Holland)	*Sprinkle on:*	Breads, rolls, cookies, etc.
	Use in:	Salads, noodles, etc.
Saffron (world's most expensive spice. A little goes a long way)	*Use in:*	Baked goods, rice, etc.

SHORTENINGS

Butter: Butter has always been a favorite because of its popular flavor and its ability to enhance the texture and flavor of so many of our everyday dishes.

It gives us important amounts of vitamin A, as well as a high energy value of 100 calories per tablespoon. Refrigerate, covered, or in butter conditioner.

Margarine: Most of today's fine margarine is made entirely from vegetable oils processed to give them desirable spreading and cooking properties. A culture of skim milk used in the manufacturing process is largely responsible for its appetizing flavor.

Margarine has the same energy value as butter, and since it is fortified with a minimum of 15,000 units of vitamin A per lb., it is nutritionally comparable to butter and is uniform in food value throughout the year. Nationally known, quality brands are excellent and economical for table and cooking use. Buy margarine only from a store that keeps it refrigerated. Store, covered, in refrigerator.

Emulsifier-Type Shortenings: Whether these shortenings are all-vegetable (as many of them are) or a combination of meat fat and vegetable oils, they are specially adapted for the richer, quick-method cakes, as most labels indicate. They're wonderful too for pastry and other forms of baking, sautéing, frying, etc. Creamy white in color, bland in odor and flavor, they are light, workable, easy to blend with other ingredients. They require no refrigeration and come in 1-lb. and 3-lb. cans. Also see 2, p. 446.

New-Type Lard: This type of lard is processed to make it creamy and smooth, slightly hardened to produce a higher melting point. A little antioxidant is added so it may be kept without refrigeration. It is fine for all kinds of cooking.

Regular Lard: Its quick-blending properties make this type of lard excellent for pastry. It is also used for sautéing, shallow and deep frying, baking breads, etc. Keep, covered, in refrigerator.

SUGARS

Brown Sugar: Brown sugar gets its color from its molasses content. There are 2 kinds:

Light-Brown Sugar has a delicate cane flavor, desirable for general cookery.

Old-fashioned Brown Sugar contains more molasses and is, therefore, darker, with more flavor. It is excellent for baked beans, baked hams, and other cookery.

Today's brown-sugar packages are designed to retain the sugar's moisture longer and thus keep it soft and fresh. So after each use, fold down the inner paper liner carefully, and tuck in the flap.

If brown sugar should lump, place it in a jar with a damp piece of cheesecloth over the top of the jar; replace cover. Sugar should be soft again within a few hours.

Granulated Sugar: Granulated sugar is made from sugar cane or from sugar beets. Use either kind, interchangeably, in all cookery.

Confectioners' Sugar: This is a very finely pulverized sugar with a soft, perfectly smooth, fluffy texture. A little cornstarch is added to prevent caking. It is often known as 4XXXX sugar.

Fine Sugar for Fruits, Cereals, Drinks, etc.: This packaged sugar is finer than granulated sugar and dissolves quickly. It is excellent on fruits, cereals, in cold drinks, etc.

Cube and Tablet Sugar: This is a convenient sweetening for hot drinks. Use cubes for demitasse, tea, etc.; tablets for any hot drink.

SYRUPS

Corn Syrup: Corn syrup, used widely in cooking and as a table syrup, comes in 3 styles:

Dark: Deep-amber in color

White or Light: Colorless

Maple-Flavored: Golden

Maple-Blended Syrup: This is a blend of maple and cane syrups. Delightful on pancakes, ice-cream sundaes, etc.

Maple Syrup: This is the pure boiled-down sap from the maple tree. A favorite on pancakes, in candies, on ice cream, etc.

VINEGARS

Today you can buy any number of delightfully flavored vinegars to use in cooking. Here are some of them:

Cider: This fine, all-purpose vinegar is a standby for salads and salad dressings.

Distilled White: This clear-colored vinegar is ideal for pickling, preserving.

Malt: Its rich flavor gives zest to salad dressings, meat and fish sauces, sea foods.

Tarragon: Its herb fragrance is wonderful in salad dressings, salads, sauces, pot roasts.

Wine: Made from select table wines, it adds zest to sauces, salad dressings, etc.

Basil, Herb and Spice, or Mixed Herb: Use lightly in or on cooked greens, slaw, sauces, salad dressings, etc.

Garlic Wine: Use instead of garlic in hamburgers, stews, salads, sauces, etc.

FRESH FRUITS

APPLES

To Buy: Apples are on the market the year round, and are at their peak from October to March. Listed below are some of the commercial leaders. About 3 or 4 apples equal 1 lb.

Variety	Color	Season
For Cooking		
Rhode Island Greening	Green	Oct. to Mar.
Rome Beauty	Red	Nov. to May
For Eating		
Delicious	Striped	Oct. to May
For Cooking and Eating		
Baldwin	Red	Nov. to Apr.
Gravenstein	Striped	July to Sept.
Grimes Golden	Yellow	Sept. to Jan.
Jonathan	Red	Sept. to Feb.
McIntosh	Red	Sept. to Mar.
Northern Spy	Striped	Oct. to Mar.
Winesap	Red	Jan. to Aug.
Yellow Newtown	Greenish-yellow or yellow	Jan. to June

To Store: Keep apples in a cold, dry place.

APRICOTS

To Buy: Fresh apricots, in season from May through August, are at their peak in June and July. Look for orange-yellow, plump, juicy apricots. About 8 to 16, depending on their size, equal 1 lb.

To Store: Keep in refrigerator.

To Prepare: Peel like peaches, p. 530.

AVOCADOS

To Buy, to Store: Avocados, a pear-shaped, dark-green fruit, are available all year long. The peak season for California avocados is February through April; for Florida avocados, September through November.

The avocado flesh when ripe is mellow and soft, yields readily to gentle pressure from palms of hands. If it's firm, you can hasten the softening by keeping the avocado in a warm room;

then refrigerate it until used. Always be sure to soften a firm avocado before refrigerating it.

To Prepare: Just before using avocado, cut in half lengthwise. To open, hold between palms of hands and turn halves in opposite directions. Insert sharp paring knife into pit; lift out and discard it.

Serve avocado halves unpeeled. Or tear glove-like skin from halves; then slice crosswise or lengthwise. Or halve avocado crosswise, turn halves, and pit as above; peel; then slice into rings.

To prevent darkening, dip avocado slices into lemon juice. Wrap any leftover avocado in waxed paper or foil; store in refrigerator.

BANANAS

To Buy: Bananas are available the year round. Buy them by the hand or cluster, at whatever stage of ripeness you find them in the store; they'll finish ripening at home. About 3 bananas equal 1 lb.

For Baking, Broiling, or Frying: Use firm bananas that are all-yellow or slightly green-tipped.

For Eating Out of Hand; Serving in Salads, Desserts, Milk Shakes; or Using as an Ingredient in Baking: Use fully ripe bananas, flecked with brown, or all-yellow bananas.

To Store: Keep bananas in fruit bowl at comfortable room temperature, not in refrigerator. (Low temperatures prevent proper ripening, impair the delicate flavor.) They'll ripen as they stand.

To Prepare: When slicing bananas, you may first run tines of fork down peeled surface, to get fluted effect. Then slice crosswise or diagonally. To prevent darkening, dip banana slices into an acid fruit juice such as lemon or pineapple juice.

BERRIES

To Buy: Fresh-berry time begins in April. The order of appearance is:

Strawberries: April through August; most plentiful in April, May, and June

Gooseberries: April through August; most plentiful in June and July

Raspberries: mid-April through July; at their peak in July

Blackberries: May through August; best in June, July, and August

Blueberries: May to September; most plentiful in July

Loganberries: June and July

Choose berries that are ripe, well-colored, and free from off-color spots.

To Store: Pick over berries, removing spoiled ones; spread out on tray; refrigerate, uncovered.

To Prepare: Just before using, wash as follows: Place berries in colander or sieve; gently run water over them. Drain well; hull. One quart yields about 3½ cups.

CHERRIES

To Buy: Red, white, and black sweet cherries are available from May through August. They're delicious fresh or cooked.

Red sour cherries, in season from late June to mid-August, make fine cherry pies and preserves.

Cherries should be firm, shiny, plump, of fully ripe color, and free of spots.

To Store: Wash, examining any that float for worms. Drain; dry; refrigerate.

To Prepare: To pit, use a new wire paper clip, wire hairpin, metal end of pencil (eraser removed), or tip of vegetable parer.

CRANBERRIES

To Buy: Fresh cranberries, available from September through March, are most plentiful from October through December. Choose berries that are firm, plump, fresh-appearing, and with high luster.

To Store: Refrigerate cranberries. Or freeze as on p. 535; they keep well.

To Prepare: Pick over; wash; drain; use.

CURRANTS

To Buy, to Store: July is the month for currants. Look for bright, plump currants; make sure they are not so ripe they fall off stems. Refrigerate on shallow tray.

Use white or red currants for eating, or in salads, fruit cups, or desserts. Use black currants for jelly or jam.

To Prepare: Wash; serve in clusters, or with stems removed. Or prepare Frosted Currants, p. 290.

FRESH FIGS

To Buy, to Store: Fresh figs, in season from June through November, are most plentiful in September and October. They should be soft. Kadota figs should be greenish yellow; Black Mission, purplish. Buy them slightly underripe; refrigerate until fully ripe, when they're ready to eat.

To Prepare: Wash; pare off outer skin.

GRAPEFRUIT

To Buy, to Store: Grapefruit are especially delicious January through May. They should be firm, well-shaped, heavy with juice, and thin-skinned. The color varies from pale yellow to reddish brown. Rust spots and green tinges do not affect the inner quality.

Very often small grapefruit are sweeter and juicier than the large sizes. Small grapefruit can be easily reamed for fresh juice too. Store grapefruit in a cool place, preferably in refrigerator.

Grapefruit meat is white or pink, with or without seeds. Under U. S. Department of Agriculture rulings, any grapefruit containing fewer than 17 seeds is considered seedless.

Grapefruit Sections: From chilled fresh grapefruit, cut off peel in strips, from top to bottom; or pare like an apple, cutting deep enough to remove white membrane. Now cut slice from top and bottom of grapefruit. Go over fruit again, removing any remaining white membrane. Cut along side of each dividing membrane, from outside down to core. Remove, section by section, over bowl to catch juice from fruit.

P.S. Canned grapefruit sections are excellent. Chill well before serving. Sprinkle, if desired, with ground cinnamon or cloves.

GRAPES

To Buy, to Store: June to April is the grape season. Choose firm, fresh-looking bunches, in which plump grapes cling to stems when gently shaken. Refrigerate.

To Prepare: Wash grapes; drain.

KUMQUATS

To Buy, to Store: Kumquats are in season November through February. They are a small, orangelike fruit, resembling pecans in shape. Choose firm fruit, heavy for its size; refrigerate.

To Prepare: Wash; cut up or slice for salads and fruit cups. Or use whole for Preserved Kumquats, p. 294.

LEMONS

To Buy, to Store: Big juicy fresh lemons are in season the year round. You can keep some on hand in the refrigerator at all times.

To Prepare: A few drops of juice squeezed from a plump lemon wedge brings out the flavor of almost any meat, fish, poultry, vegetable, or salad. And since lemon contains virtually no sodium, it's a fine seasoning for low sodium diets. Fine too as seasoning in low calorie diets. For many other uses, see Index. For lemon juice, see p. 529.

LIMES

To Buy, to Store: Florida limes are most available between June and September; California limes, between October and December.

Look for limes that are green, not yellowish, and heavy for their size. Most of these will be Persians, which are the size and shape of lemons. The small round variety are Key limes. Refrigerate.

To Prepare: Cut limes into wedges to serve in iced tea or to squeeze over melon, ice cream, etc. For lime juice, see p. 529.

MANGOES

To Buy, to Store: Mangoes, in season from May to September, vary in size from a few ounces to 3 or 4 lb. Yellow or red in color, they have a soft, juicy, aromatic flesh. Wrap in waxed paper; refrigerate.

To Prepare: With sharp knife, mark wide band in skin, down one side. Peel skin back slightly; eat flesh with spoon, as dessert, putting skin back in place between bites. Or peel; slice; use in salads or fruit cups.

MELONS

To Buy: Melons must be fully ripe if you are to enjoy their wonderful flavor at its peak. Most ripe melons yield to pressure at the blossom end, and have a typical melon fragrance and yellowish tinge.

Cantaloupes are in season from May to November; imported ones may come in earlier. They may be round, oval, or oblong, usually with over-all netted skins, and are light gray in color.

When ripe, they have a yellow ground color, distinct aroma, and smooth scar on the stem end. Blossom end yields to pressure.

Casabas are in season from July to December. They are large, rough-skinned, roundish, sometimes considerably pointed and deeply ridged.

When fully ripe, their rind is golden yellow; the white flesh is very juicy and sweet. Melon weighs 4 to 10 lb.

Cranshaws are in season from July to November. They have a fairly smooth rind, mottled with gold and green. Flesh is bright-salmon color, thick, juicy. Melon weighs 4 to 8 lb.

Honeyballs are in season from May to October. They are like honeydews but are rounder and smaller, with a slightly netted skin.

Honeydews are in season from January to November. They are large, round or oval, averaging about 6 lb.; their smooth hard skin is without netting.

When vine-ripened, they are creamy or yellowish in color, show softening at the blossom end, have smooth, well-rounded ridges next to stem, and are definitely fragrant. Their green flesh is exceptionally sweet.

Papayas, in season from December through February, are melonlike in their superficial characteristics—thin, smooth skin; spherical to oblong shape; center cavity packed with seeds.

Papayas are ready to eat when the rind is yellow and the fruit feels soft. They taste and look (on the inside) like cantaloupe.

Persians are in season from July to November. They look like large cantaloupes; are round, but have flat ends. They have a green rind with heavy netting.

When ripe, rind has yellowish cast; flesh is pink, not as sweet as honeydew or honeyball but resembling cantaloupe in flavor. Melon may weigh as much as 10 lb.

Santa Claus, or Christmas, melons are winter melons; they look like small, oblong watermelons. They have a hard, thick, slightly netted green rind. Their light-yellow-to-green flesh is sweet.

Signs of ripeness are light yellowing of rind, softness at blossom end.

To Store, to Prepare: Wash melon; dry; place in paper bag or waxed paper; refrigerate. Just before serving, cut into halves, quarters, or wedges; scrape out seeds.

To Make Melon Balls: With fruit-ball cutter or the ½ teasp. in your measuring-spoon set, scoop out balls from edible portion of halved, seeded melon or watermelon wedge.

NECTARINES

To Buy: Nectarines, available in June, July, and August, are a kind of peach with a smooth skin like a plum; skin is greenish white with a faint blush. Choose firm fruit, free from cuts and decayed spots. Refrigerate.

ORANGES

To Buy: Oranges are available all year round. The two important varieties from California are Valencias, available May to November, and navel oranges (seedless), available November to May.

Florida ships Hamlins and Parson Browns (pale, thin-skinned, juice fruit) from October to February. Then comes the Valencia season, which extends from February through May. Florida is growing increasing quantities of Temples, first cousins to tangerines; these peel easily and are available from Christmas through February.

Toward the end of the orange season, the skin near the stem takes on a greenish tinge. This is not a sign of underripeness but is a peculiarity of citrus fruits.

All oranges must pass state maturity requirements before they can be shipped. To enhance the eye appeal of certain varieties, Florida oranges are sometimes colored with harmless color; such fruit is stamped, "Color Added."

Look for oranges that are firm and heavy for their size.

To Store: Keep oranges in a cool place, refrigerating those that will be used for juice or salad the next day. If space is available, and there are several persons in the family, it is economical to buy oranges by the box or bag.

Orange Sections:
1. Peel or pare chilled fruit with knife, leaving some white membrane clinging to fruit if you wish. (This white membrane contains protopectin, minerals, and vitamins valuable to health.)
2. Hold orange over bowl. With sawing motion, cut along side of each dividing membrane from outside down to core.

   Or cut halfway between each membrane instead of just alongside it. This way that white wall with its food value is a part of each orange wedge.
3. Loosen each section with knife; lift out. Remove seeds if any; drop section into bowl. Repeat. Squeeze juice from membranes over sections.

Orange Cart Wheels: For each serving, cut unpeeled or peeled orange into 3 or 4 crosswise slices. Arrange on dessert plates to eat out of hand for breakfast or dessert.

Orange Tidbits: Stack cart wheels; then cut each slice into 4 bite-size wedges.

Hurry-ups: Cut orange in half, starting at top and going almost to bottom peel. Cut each half into quarters; then cut through each quarter to make eighths. Pull each piece apart slightly until orange resembles open flower petals. Then eat "petals," watermelon style!

ORANGE, GRAPEFRUIT, LEMON, OR LIME JUICE

Fresh Juices: For best flavor, squeeze fruit juice just before serving, as loss of flavor is rapid. The vitamin C content is not lost so readily; in fact, if the juice is refrigerated, the vitamin C loss is extremely slow in 24 hr. Covering juice helps retain flavor.

Don't strain out pulp from juice—it contains valuable minerals and vitamins.

If a recipe calls for both juice and grated rind, it's easier to grate rind first, then squeeze juice.

Frozen Juices: See p. 499.

Canned Juices: See p. 499.

PEACHES

To Buy, to Store: Peaches, in season from late May to mid-October, are at their best in July and August. They are white- or yellow-fleshed, either clingstone or freestone. Cling peaches are used for canning; freestones are fine for all uses.

Ripe peaches should be firm but yield to gentle pressure, and should be free from brown spots or other signs of decay. Flesh should be yellow or white, not green. About 4 peaches equal 1 lb. Refrigerate.

To Prepare: If the freestone variety does not peel easily, let stand in boiling water to cover 1 to 2 min.; then plunge into cold water; peel; remove pits. Pare cling peaches.

PEARS

To Buy, to Store: For cooking, slightly under-ripe pears are best. Varieties of pears include:

Bartlett: In season from July through October. Bell-shaped; soft yellow; sweet; juicy

Bosc: In season September through February. Russet variety, with long tapering neck

Comice: In season October through February. Green skin. Famous for size, superb quality, beauty

Anjou: October through May. Green skin, fine grain, spicy

Nelis: February through June. Russet variety. Very sweet, luscious

When buying pears, check ripeness by pressing slightly near stem end. If pears are not quite ripe, let ripen at room temperature in paper bag or fruit bowl. When ripe, store in refrigerator.

To Prepare: Pears need no peeling. Just wash. To eat whole, start at stem end, after removing stem. Or halve, core, and slice. (To slice and hold before serving, coat with fruit juice or French dressing, to prevent darkening.)

PERSIMMONS

To Buy, to Store: Persimmons are in season October, November, and December. Orange-red in color, their pulpy fruit is soft, rich, and very sweet when ripe. Refrigerate.

To Prepare: Wash. Use whole or in halves.

FRESH PINEAPPLE

To Buy, to Store: In season all year long, pineapple is at its peak from March through June. Quality fruit is heavy for its size and has no signs of decay or mold at bottom or around eyes.

When ripe, fruit has sweet fragrance, golden-yellow flesh; center leaves loosen easily when pulled. Keep, wrapped, in refrigerator.

To Prepare: Cut off crown and stem ends. (If using only part of pineapple, cut off as much as is needed.) Stand fruit on one end on board. If using only top end, grasp by crown; if lower end, insert fork into core; hold firmly.

Cut off rind all around, from top down, following curve of fruit. Remove eyes with pointed knife. Then complete as below:

Slices: Cut into ¼″ to ½″ crosswise slices. Remove cores with small biscuit cutter.

Cubes: Cut cored slices into small or large cubes.

Sticks: Stand pared, eyed, whole pineapple upright on board. Cut lengthwise into eighths. Cut out core from each wedge; cut each wedge into ¾″ lengthwise strips, then in half crosswise. Refrigerate. Serve as first course or dessert.

PLUMS AND FRESH PRUNES

To Buy, to Store: Plums are in season May through September; fresh prunes are available July to November. Choose those that are plump and yield slightly to pressure. Refrigerate. About 12 to 15 equal 1 lb.

To Prepare: Wash; eat raw, as is.

POMEGRANATES

To Buy, to Store: Pomegranates are in season September through December. About the size of an orange; they have a red-brown, leathery rind. The seeds, crimson juice, and pulp are all eaten. Refrigerate.

To Prepare: Halve. Eat with spoon; or use as garnish.

RHUBARB

To Buy, to Store: Rhubarb is in largest supply from March through July, and is at its peak May and June.

Early rhubarb has light-pink stalks; late-rhubarb stalks are dark reddish green. Buy fresh crisp stalks; store in cool, dry place.

To Prepare: Before cooking, trim ends; discard leaves (they are not edible); wash well. Don't peel unless rhubarb is tough, stringy.

TANGERINES

To Buy, to Store: Tangerines are in season from November until late February. December and January are their best months. Their deep-orange skin is loose and puffy, peels easily. Refrigerate.

To Prepare: Select firm, heavy fruit for fruit bowls. Use sections in salads, fruit cocktails, etc. Juice and grated rind may be substituted for orange juice and rind.

WATERMELONS

To Buy, to Store: Watermelon is available the year round except for a short period, usually in December. Large melons, weighing 20 to 40 lb., vary from round to long cylindrical types, are green to light green, with stripes.

When ripe, underside is turning yellow, not light green; flesh is crisp, juicy, red. Your best bet in judging ripeness is to have watermelon "plugged," i.e., have a piece cut out so you can examine the flesh.

The small icebox watermelon, sometimes called New Hampshire midget, is available April to September. It may weigh 3 to 5 lb., resembles a cantaloupe in size and shape. Color may vary from light to very dark green, usually with stripes. It ripens close to rind, has texture like that of larger watermelon. Refrigerate until served.

To Serve: Cut into crosswise slices or wedge-shaped pieces. Or with tablespoon, scoop out large spoonfuls; arrange 2 or 3, with rounded sides up, on each plate. Sprinkle with lemon or lime juice.

DRIED FRUITS

Packaged Dried Prunes, Apricots, Peaches, Pears, Apples, etc.: These fruits are so deliciously tender they need no overnight soaking. Their cooking time is cut down too; see label directions. Keep in refrigerator.

Pressure-cooked Dried Fruits de Luxe, p. 199, are wonderfully delicious too. Try them.

You may also eat dried fruits out of hand.

Bulk Dried Prunes, Apricots, etc.: Cover with water; boil 30 to 45 min., or until tender, adding sugar to taste last 5 min. (If sugar is added earlier, fruit may toughen.)

To Vary: Before cooking dried fruit, add a little grated orange or lemon rind, clove, cinnamon stick, a few raisins, or lemon or orange slice.

Canned Cooked Prunes: Several packers market canned cooked prunes, as well as precooked, pasteurized prunes, which need only 10 to 20 min. boiling.

Dried Figs: All American dried figs are grown and packed in California. They are available in the several varieties below. Try them all; then pick your favorite.

Black Mission (black): Equally delicious as confection, for stewing, and other dishes

Calimyrna (large, light brown): Delicious as a confection, for stewing, and for a wide variety of other dishes. Especially favored for eating out of hand

Kadota (light brown): Usually sold canned or fresh

FROZEN FRUITS

Frozen fruits such as peaches, raspberries, strawberries, blueberries, etc. provide summer-fresh flavor all year long. Most of them come sweetened and ready to eat or cook, as is or thawed. Check label for sweetening and thawing directions. Usually it's best to thaw fruit almost, but not quite, completely; a few ice crystals should remain for fruits to be at their best.

Wonderful Ways with Fruit

See Desserts, pp. 378 to 406; Salads, pp. 298 to 316; Wine in Desserts, p. 506; Cheese as Dessert, p. 216; Fruit Beginnings, p. 17; Jellies and Jams, pp. 545 to 549; Relishes and Garnishes, pp. 286 to 297; Pies, pp. 407 to 423; Drinks—Hot and Cold, pp. 494 to 504. Also refer to Index.

Home Freezing
and Canning

HOME FREEZING

Here are the essentials you need to know about freezing food in a home freezer. You will also find helpful the instruction booklet that comes with your freezer and also bulletins from the U.S. Department of Agriculture and your state college of agriculture. Write too to the state extension service in your state for the names of the best varieties of fruits and vegetables for freezing.

Selecting the Right Home Freezer

You'll have to choose from dozens of makes and sizes. If you have no previous experience to draw on, you may find it helpful to talk to friends and neighbors who own freezers.

What Type? Most freezer manufacturers are reputable, so there's little risk if you choose a well-known make. However, you'll have to choose among three types of freezer:

1. *Upright type,* with shelves like a refrigerator
2. *Chest type,* with baskets or dividers
3. *Combination refrigerator-freezer,* with freezer space varying from 2 to 10 or more cubic feet.

The type you should choose depends on the amount of floor or wall space you have available and on which type seems to offer you the most convenience.

If you are about to replace your refrigerator, if you need only limited freezer space, or if you don't have room for separate appliances, the combination may be your choice. In a true combination refrigerator-freezer (see p. 694), where the freezer temperature averages around 0°F., you can keep foods fresh and flavorful for months just as in a true home freezer.

What Size? The answer to this question depends entirely on what use you hope to make of your freezer. Do you grow your own fruits and vegetables? Do you plan to market infrequently and to buy in large quantities? Do you intend to cook and freeze whole meals? All these projects take space, so choose a size large enough to handle all your freezing requirements.

Cutting Food Costs with a Freezer

Here are the ways a freezer can help you cut food costs:

1. You need never waste a scrap of food.
2. You can cook at your leisure and so spend time concocting less expensive, but time-consuming, dishes.
3. You'll have fewer leftovers, because you can package food in amounts to suit your family.
4. When you shop, you can take advantage of every special buy that comes along, whether it's a basket of peaches or a leg of lamb.
5. You can contact the grocer, butcher, locker plant, and nearby farmers about buying in quantity. For example, some stores give quantity discounts on commercially frozen foods.

However, when buying large amounts, you should be even more careful about a food's quality, because the supply will last so long.

6. You can freeze your own garden produce.

Using Your Freezer

Freeze Only Food of Good Quality. While freezing does retain the flavor, texture, and color of food to a remarkable degree, it does not improve quality.

Freeze Foods Promptly. If this cannot be done, refrigerate them a short time. Don't let food stand at room temperature.

Freeze Foods in Small Amounts. Don't buy or prepare more food than can be frozen at one time. Consult your freezer instruction booklet on this point, for overloading results in slow freezing.

Use Only Special Freezer Wrapping Materials. The low temperatures of a freezer tend to draw moisture from foods, causing them to lose flavor, volume, and texture. So home-frozen foods need the special types of moisture-vapor-proof packaging material described below. Commercially packed frozen foods need no additional wrapping.

Sheet Wrappings: There is a wide variety to choose from—aluminum foil, Pliofilm, cellophane, polyethylene, and heavy paper (impregnated with wax or lined with film). When you use these sheet wrappings, remember that edges must be folded over several times and sealed with freezer tape or heat-sealed.

Bags: Polyethylene or paper freezer bags are quick and easy to use. Often they can be re-used.

Glass Jars: These jars are handy for storing soups, fruit juices, other liquid foods. They are made in pint and quart sizes, have wide mouths, straight sides, screw caps.

Containers: Many types of container are available for packing fruits, vegetables, cooked foods, shellfish, etc.

Containers made of aluminum or aluminum foil can be used for both freezing and reheating foods. Others are clear plastic, with plastic lids that seal tight (these can be used for refrigerator storage too); heavily waxed paper cartons, which come in many sizes and shapes; paper cartons lined with moisture-vapor-proof material.

Label and Date All Packages: Labeling is important because it's very hard to identify food once it's frozen. The date will prompt you to use food before it loses quality.

Freeze Packages Quickly: Do not let packaged food stand; place in freezer promptly. Check your instruction booklet to see where you should place packages in freezer.

Storage Time for Frozen Foods: No one can tell you exactly how long you can keep foods in a freezer. Time limits depend on the temperature, kind of food, care taken in packaging, and the original quality of the food. These are general time limits:

Beef, lamb, veal	up to 1 year
Chopped beef	up to 2 or 3 months
Fruits and vegetables	up to 1 year
Pork (fresh), poultry, fish	4 to 6 months
Ham	up to 1 month
Cooked and baked foods	1 to 3 months
Franks	up to 1 month
Sandwiches	2 weeks
Ice cream	up to 1 month

Long storage causes loss of flavor. Use your freezer every day, so that when you serve a food it's still as fresh as the day it was frozen.

Don't Refreeze Thawed Foods: As a general rule, avoid refreezing foods. If food is left standing after it thaws, it may begin to spoil and you might refreeze it without realizing this. Also, refreezing almost always results in loss of texture and flavor. So whenever food is thawed, refrigerate it and use it promptly.

Partially thawed food (except sea food) can be refrozen as long as it still contains ice crystals. Remember this if your freezer is accidentally disconnected or the power fails.

Exception to This Important Rule: You can thaw uncooked food, cook it completely, then refreeze it. For example, if you roast a frozen turkey, you can freeze the leftovers—if you package and freeze them quickly.

Fruits

TO FREEZE FRUITS

General Pointers: Freeze only sound, fully ripe fruits. You can pack them in dry sugar, sugar syrup, or a combination of sugar syrup and corn syrup. (For the last, follow directions given by manufacturer of corn syrup.) Some fruits can be packed unsweetened.

Fruits can be packaged in any liquid-tight container. Leave 1″ at top for expansion.

To Pack Fruit in Dry Sugar: Mix sugar and fruit gently.

To Pack Fruit in Sugar Syrup: Add enough sugar syrup to cover fruit in container.

To Make Sugar Syrup: Heat water with sugar in proportions below until dissolved. Chill well before using.

Light syrup .... 2 cups sugar per 1 qt. water
Medium syrup ...... 3 cups sugar per 1 qt. water
Heavy syrup ..... 4¾ cups sugar per 1 qt. water
Extra-heavy syrup .... 7 cups sugar per 1 qt. water

To Keep Fruit from Darkening: To each 1 qt. sugar syrup (or 1 cup dry sugar), add ½ teasp. ascorbic acid; or add a commercial preparation made just for this purpose. Either will also help protect flavor.

Apples: Peel; core; slice. If apples are to be served as is, add medium syrup. If they're to be used in cooking, add ½ cup sugar per 1 qt. apples. Add ascorbic acid.

Apricots: Wash; peel; pit; halve or slice. Add syrup or sugar as for apples. Or to freeze unpeeled whole apricots, drop fruit into boiling water ½ min., then into ice water until chilled. Add medium syrup. Add ascorbic acid.

Blueberries: Sort; wash. For fruit cup, etc., add medium syrup. For pies, pack unsweetened.

Cherries: Wash; pit if desired. If sweet, add medium syrup. If sour (for pies), add ¾ cup sugar per 1 qt. fruit. Add ascorbic acid.

Cranberries: Sort; wash. Pack unsweetened; or cover with heavy syrup. Or make cranberry sauce or cranberry-orange relish, adding sugar to taste.

Grapefruit and Oranges: Peel; seed; section. Drain off juice; pack, covering with juice mixed with heavy syrup—about 1 part juice to 3 parts heavy syrup. Add ascorbic acid.

Grapes: Wash; remove stems. If they're to be used in making jam or jelly, pack unsweetened. For fruit cups, etc., remove seeds; add medium syrup.

Melons: Remove seeds; pare; slice or cube. Or make balls. Add light syrup. Several kinds of melon can be packed together, for fruit cups.

Peaches: Peel; slice. Add medium syrup. Or add ⅔ cup sugar per 1 qt. peaches. Add ascorbic acid. To keep fruit submerged, place crumpled waxed paper on top of it.

Pineapple: Pare; remove core and eyes; slice or cube. Pack unsweetened. Or add light syrup.

Rhubarb: Wash; trim; cut. Pack unsweetened for pies. Or make rhubarb sauce as usual; then freeze.

Strawberries: Sort; wash; hull. Slice if large. Add ¾ cup sugar per 1 qt. berries (increase or decrease sugar depending on tartness of berries). Or cover with medium or heavy syrup.

TO THAW FROZEN FRUITS

Thaw fruit in container—in refrigerator, at room temperature, or under running cold water—until fruit separates but is still ice-cold. Serve promptly.

Vegetables

TO FREEZE VEGETABLES

General Pointers: Freeze garden-fresh, tender vegetables. Avoid damaged or bruised vegetables.

Before freezing, vegetables must be heated in boiling water, to reduce the action of enzymes and to preserve flavor and appearance. Then they must be quickly chilled. (Heating in steam is recommended by some authorities. For directions and time periods, see U.S. Department of Agriculture bulletins.)

To Heat: Boil 1 gal. or more of water in large kettle; keep heat high at all times. Add vegetables (1 lb. prepared vegetable per 1 gal. water); cover; start timing as indicated under each vegetable. Heat thick pieces or stalks longest time indicated.

To Chill: Plunge heated vegetables into ice water; let stand until cold—about the same number of minutes as directed for heating. Drain well; then pack in any convenient container.

Asparagus: Break off tough ends; wash; sort into narrow, medium, and thick stalks. Cut into pieces; or leave as spears. Heat 2 to 4 min. Chill.

Broccoli: Use compact, dark-green heads. Wash; trim. Cut lengthwise, making heads 1½″ wide. Heat 3 min. Chill.

Brussels Sprouts: Trim, removing coarse outer leaves. Wash thoroughly; sort for size. Heat 3 to 5 min. Chill.

Corn on the Cob: Use young, tender ears of corn. Husk; wash; sort for size. Heat small ears 7 min., medium ears 9 min., large ears 11 min. Chill. Pack in cartons; or wrap individually.

Corn, Whole Kernel: Use young, tender ears of corn. Husk; wash. Heat 4 min. After chilling, drain; cut off kernels (avoid cutting into cob).

Green Beans: Wash; remove ends. Cut into lengthwise strips or 1″ or 2″ pieces. Heat 3 min. Chill.

Green Limas: Shell; sort for size; discard any over-mature, white beans. Heat 2 to 4 min. Chill.

Green Peppers: Wash; remove stems and seeds; cut into halves or slices if desired. Heat halves 3 min., slices 2 min. Chill. If peppers are to be stuffed, freeze whole, without heating.

Mushrooms: Sort for size; wash; trim stem ends. Slice mushrooms if they're larger than 1″. Let stand in 1 pt. water with 1 teasp. lemon juice 5 min.; then heat whole mushrooms 5 min., slices 3 min. Chill.

Peas: Shell; discard immature or tough peas. Heat 1½ min. Chill.

Spinach: Wash; remove tough stems and older leaves. Heat 1½ to 2 min. Chill. Then chop if desired.

Squash: If you're freezing summer squash, wash; cut into ½″ slices; heat 3 min.; chill. If it's Hubbard squash, wash; cut up; remove seeds. Cook till soft as on p. 284; then remove pulp and mash it. Chill by setting pan in cold water.

TO COOK FROZEN VEGETABLES

Do not thaw any vegetable except corn on the cob. Drop frozen vegetable into small amount of salted water; cook, covered, until just tender. Remember that frozen vegetables take about half as long to cook as fresh ones.

Meat

TO FREEZE, THAW, AND COOK MEAT

General Pointers: Because meat is usually the most precious food in a freezer, it requires special, careful attention. Follow these important rules:

1. *Package* in amounts convenient for your family.
2. *Wrap tightly* in freezer wrapping materials or containers; seal securely with freezer tape. See p. 534.

3. *Label clearly,* noting date, kind of meat, cut, and weight or number of servings.

4. *Thaw meat completely* before cooking in most cases. For 1 lb. meat, allow 5 to 6 hr. in food compartment of refrigerator, 2 to 3 hr. at room temperature, or 1 to 1½ hr. in front of electric fan. If meat is thawed at room temperature, cook it as soon as it's thawed but while it's still icy cold; or refrigerate and cook as soon as possible.

Roasts:

To Freeze: Trim off excess fat. Pad sharp bone edges with fat, to avoid puncturing wrapping. Pack in bag or sheet wrapping; seal.

To Cook: Thaw, wrapped; roast as usual.

To cook meat unthawed, roast at usual oven temperature until meat thaws sufficiently to let you insert roast-meat thermometer; then roast to same internal temperature as you would for a regular roast. (See Meats, p. 46.) A roast-meat thermometer is the only reliable guide to the doneness of any roast, and especially an unthawed one.

Steaks and Chops:

To Freeze: Trim as desired. Package together, in bag or sheet wrapping, as many steaks or chops as you'll need for one meal. If there's more than one layer of meat, separate layers with film or foil so they'll come apart more quickly when thawing. Press wrapping flat against meat; seal edges securely with freezer tape.

To Cook: Thaw, wrapped (unwrap if packed in layers); cook as usual. To cook unthawed, allow about twice the usual cooking time; be sure to check for doneness by making small cut close to bone.

Chopped Meat or Cut-Up Meat for Stews:

To Freeze: Use only freshly cut or ground meat. Package chopped meat in bulk or in patties in any convenient freezer wrapping material or container, separating layers of meat with film or foil. Pack meat for stews in recipe amounts in any freezer material.

To Cook: Thaw, wrapped (unwrap if packed in layers); cook as usual. To cook unthawed patties, broil or pan-broil them, sprinkling them with seasonings as they cook.

Poultry

TO FREEZE POULTRY

Broiler-Fryers: Clean thoroughly. Halve, quarter, or cut up for broiling or frying. Package compactly in bag or sheet wrapping, separating halves, quarters, or pieces with foil or film to speed thawing. Wrap giblets separately.

Stewing Chickens: Clean, cut up, and package as for broiler-fryers. (You may wish to package pieces with special uses in mind, putting together pieces for fricassee, necks and gizzards for stock, breasts for a party dish, etc.). Or leave cleaned bird whole; then package as for roasting chicken.

Roasting Chickens or Turkeys: Clean birds as for roasting. Wrap giblets separately; place in body cavity or under wing. Tie wings and legs close to body of bird to make it compact. Package in bag or sheet wrapping.

TO COOK FROZEN POULTRY

Thaw poultry, wrapped. Cook as usual. (See pp. 136 to 162.) Or if they're stewing chickens, unwrap; then cook unthawed.

Sea Food

TO FREEZE SEA FOOD

Fish: Wrap cleaned whole or halved fish, fillets, or steaks individually in sheet wrapping; then place in freezer bag or carton.

Scallops, Oysters, and Clams: Pack washed scallops or shucked oysters or clams in freezer containers. Cover with salt solution, using 1 tablesp. salt per 1 cup water; or substitute their own liquor for part of salt solution. Leave 1″ head space for expansion.

Shrimp: Pack cooked or uncooked, shelled or unshelled, in freezer containers.

Crabs and Lobsters: Cook as usual; then cool. Remove meat from shells; pack tightly in freezer containers.

TO USE FROZEN SEA FOOD

Thaw sea food in wrapping or container. Use promptly. Serve or cook as usual.

Eggs

TO FREEZE EGGS

Place convenient recipe amounts of whole eggs, yolks, or whites in any freezer container (see p. 534) as follows. Store up to 6 months.

Whole Eggs: Break into measuring cup. If eggs are to be used for sweet dishes such as desserts, cakes, etc., add 1 tablesp. sugar or corn syrup per 1 cup eggs. For other kinds of cooking, add 1 teasp. salt per 1 cup eggs. Stir to mix, but do not beat.

Yolks: Freeze as for whole eggs, adding 2 tablesp. sugar or corn syrup, or 1 teasp. salt, per 1 cup yolks.

Whites: Freeze without adding salt or sugar.

TO USE FROZEN EGGS

Thaw in container in refrigerator; use promptly. Substitute for fresh eggs in recipes as follows:
  2½ tablesp. whole eggs for 1 egg
  1 tablesp. yolks for 1 egg yolk
  1½ tablesp. whites for 1 egg white

Other Dairy Products

Butter: Butter may be frozen in original waxed carton. To store longer than 1 month, overwrap with sheet wrapping.

Cheese: See To Freeze Cheese, p. 211.

Heavy Cream: This is the best type of cream to freeze. Freeze in original carton. Or whip; pack in container. Or drop spoonfuls of whipped cream onto foil; freeze; then wrap. Store up to 1 month.

To serve, thaw cream in container until it can be spooned out. Unwrap spoonfuls of whipped cream; place on dessert; let thaw 15 to 20 min. before serving.

Ice Cream: It's an economical buy in 1-gal. or ½-gal. packages. Freeze in original carton. After opening, keep surface of ice cream covered with waxed paper. Store up to 1 month.

Breads

TO FREEZE BREADS

Kinds to Freeze: Biscuits, muffins, fruit-and-nut bread, brown bread, plain and sweet rolls, tea rings, English muffins, popovers, waffles, yeast bread (white, rye, and whole-wheat, etc.)

Bakers' Breads: If they come wrapped, freeze in original wrapper; limit storage to 2 weeks. If unwrapped, place in bag; or wrap in sheet wrapping. Store up to 3 months.

Homemade Breads: Make and bake as usual; cool.

Place loaf breads in bag; or wrap in sheet wrapping.

Place rolls, biscuits, muffins, or popovers in bag or container.

Place coffeecake or pan rolls on foil-covered cardboard or in paper pie plate; then wrap in sheet wrapping.

TO USE FROZEN BREADS

Loaf Breads: Thaw, wrapped, at room temperature 1 to 3 hr.

Sliced Bread: Toast, unthawed (simply drop into toaster, frozen). Or thaw a little if slices cannot be separated easily.

Rolls, Biscuits, Coffeecake, etc.: Place, unthawed, on baking sheet; heat at 400°F. 10 to 15 min. Or thaw, wrapped, at room temperature 30 to 35 min.; then serve.

Frozen Waffles: See Speedy Waffles, p. 337.

Pies

TO FREEZE AND SERVE PIES

Use any regular pie plate, including glass. Or use special paper pie plate.

Chiffon Pies:

To Freeze: Make as usual; let set. Omit whipped-cream topping. Freeze. Then place in freezer bag; or wrap in sheet wrapping.

To Serve: Unwrap frozen pie; let stand in food compartment of refrigerator 1 to 1½ hr. Top with whipped cream.

Cream or Custard Pies: These pies do not freeze well.

Fruit or Mince Pies:

To Freeze: Make as usual. Some juicy fruit pies may require more thickening than usual —¼ cup flour per pie is about enough to thicken the juiciest fruit. Then bake, cool, and freeze; or freeze unbaked. If pie is unbaked, do not slit top crust.

Place baked or unbaked pie in freezer bag; or wrap in sheet wrapping.

Note: If pie seems too tender to handle, freeze before wrapping. For extra protection, cover pie with paper pie plate before wrapping.

To Serve: If pie is unbaked, unwrap, frozen; slit top crust; bake at 425°F. 40 to 60 min.

If it's baked, unwrap, frozen; heat at 375°F. 30 to 50 min., or until center is bubbling hot.

Lemon Meringue Pie:

To Freeze: Make Lemon Meringue Pie, p. 418 (we have found this recipe best for freezing), omitting meringue topping. Then wrap as in Chiffon Pies, above.

To Serve: Spread meringue on unwrapped frozen pie. Bake at 350°F. 20 to 25 min.; let stand 1 hr. before serving.

Pumpkin Pie:

To Freeze: Make and bake pie as usual; cool. Then wrap as in Chiffon Pies, above. Or pour unbaked filling into liquid-tight freezer container.

To Serve: Thaw baked pie, unwrapped, at room temperature 1 to 2 hr. To use unbaked filling, thaw and pour into unbaked pie shell; bake as usual.

Pie Shells:

To Freeze: Freeze pie shells, baked or unbaked, before wrapping. Then place in freezer bag; or wrap in sheet wrapping. (Frozen unbaked shells can be stacked before wrapping if you place crumpled waxed paper between them.)

To Use: If pie shell is unbaked, unwrap; bake at 450°F. 5 min. Prick; bake about 15 min. longer. If pie shell is baked, unwrap. Heat at 375°F. 10 min.; or thaw at room temperature.

Pastry:

To Freeze: Make as usual; roll into circles if desired. Stack unbaked pastry circles, placing 2 sheets of waxed paper between them. Then place in freezer bag; or wrap in sheet wrapping.

If dough is unrolled, wrap in sheet wrapping.

To Use: Thaw at room temperature; then use as usual.

Cakes

TO FREEZE CAKES

Kinds to Freeze: Angel-food and chiffon or lovelight cakes, spongecakes, butter cakes, poundcakes, fruitcakes (any flavor freezes well). Bake as loaf, layers, or cupcakes. Or bake 2 layers; use one layer, freeze other.

Unfrosted Cakes: Make and bake as usual; then cool. Wrap in sheet wrapping. For extra protection, place in cardboard box.

Frosted Cakes: Make and bake as usual. Set cake on cardboard covered with film or foil. Freeze until frosting is set; then wrap. (Butter Cream, p. 462, and Penuche Frosting p. 467, freeze well.)

TO USE FROZEN CAKES

Unwrap frosted cakes. Leave unfrosted cakes wrapped. Thaw on cake rack at room temperature. Cupcakes thaw in about 30 min.; cake layers in 1 hr.; other cakes in 2 or 3 hr.

Cookies

TO FREEZE COOKIES

Kinds to Freeze: Molded or cookie-press, drop, refrigerator, bar, and roll-and-cut cookies

Cookie Dough: Form refrigerator-cookie dough into roll or bar; wrap in sheet wrapping.

Pack other cookie doughs in freezer containers.

Baked Cookies: Make and bake as usual; then cut if necessary; cool thoroughly. Arrange on cardboard covered with waxed paper or foil; then place in plastic bag. Or pack gently in any freezing bag, box, or container of convenient size. Use a sturdy container for fragile cookies— metal or plastic box, or coffee can if you wish. Cushion cookies with crumpled foil or waxed paper.

TO USE FROZEN COOKIES

Thaw refrigerator-cookie dough in refrigerator about 1 hr., or until it slices easily. Then bake as usual.

Thaw any other kind of cookie dough till it can be handled easily; prepare and bake as usual.

Thaw baked cookies, unwrapped, about 15 min. at room temperature.

Cooked Foods

TO FREEZE COOKED FOODS

See chart, page 541, for directions on freezing and serving specific cooked foods. Here are some general pointers to guide you.

To Cook before Freezing:

1. Undercook rather than overcook dishes that will be reheated before serving.
2. When making gravies and sauces for freezing, be sure to beat them until smooth. This helps prevent separation during freezing.
3. Chill hot mixtures quickly before packaging and freezing them. Do this by setting pan, dish, or casserole in cold water or in refrigerator.

To Wrap:

1. If cooked foods are to be baked or reheated in oven before serving, pack in pie plates, baking dishes or pans, or aluminum or aluminum-foil freezer boxes. Then food can go directly from freezer to oven. (If a container does not have its own cover, use aluminum foil.)
2. If cooked foods are to be reheated on top of the range, pack them in straight-sided containers. Then frozen food can be removed from container easily, by dipping container into warm water until contents slip out. (Some paper containers can be peeled off and contents removed.)

TO USE FROZEN COOKED FOODS

1. Don't forget that most cooked foods are perishable; therefore, the way you thaw frozen cooked foods is most important.

    If a food is to be reheated or baked before serving, place it in the oven or on top of the range without thawing whenever possible. (Exceptions to this rule are large pieces of meat and deep casseroles in which the outside layer of food would become dry before the center was heated through; thaw these.)

    If a food is to be thawed and served without heating, thaw in refrigerator or at room temperature; then refrigerate immediately to keep cold until served.
2. Unless otherwise directed, thaw frozen cooked foods wrapped, whether thawed in refrigerator or at room temperature.

TO FREEZE AND SERVE COOKED FOODS

BREADS, SANDWICHES, SOUPS, AND SPREADS

IF YOU WANT	FREEZE THEM THIS WAY	SERVE THEM
Breads	See p. 538.	
Lunch-Box or Picnic Sandwiches	Spread bread with butter or margarine (don't use salad dressing or jelly). Fill with sliced meat or a spread. (Omit lettuce, celery, tomatoes, hard-cooked egg white.) Wrap individually.	Pack frozen—they'll be thawed in time for lunch. Or thaw, wrapped, 2 to 3 hr. at room temperature, 5 to 6 hr. in refrigerator.
Party Sandwiches	Cut day-old bread into shapes as desired; stack and wrap in sheet wrapping. Or make as lunch-box sandwiches, above; stack in layers, with sheet wrapping between layers; wrap.	Thaw bread or sandwiches, wrapped, 1 to 2 hr. in refrigerator. To use bread, make into sandwiches as desired. To use sandwiches, unwrap and serve while still cold.
Soups, Chowders	When making, cut down on water if possible. Omit milk, potatoes. Cool. Freeze in straight-sided freezer jar (or container).	Run warm water over jar. Slip out frozen block. Heat slowly. Add omitted liquid. If potatoes are to be added, cook them first in this liquid.
Spreads (for sandwiches or Nibblers)	Make favorite mixture of meat, fish, etc. as usual, but omit raw vegetables (celery, carrots, lettuce, etc.). Pack in freezer container.	Thaw several hours in refrigerator.

MAIN DISHES

Chicken, Fried	Brown pieces as usual; omit final cooking; cool. Wrap in sheet wrapping or freezer bag.	Unwrap frozen chicken; place in shallow baking dish; bake, uncovered, at 350°F. 30 to 40 min.
Chili con Carne	Make; then cool. Freeze in straight-sided freezer jar or container.	Heat as for soups.
Creamed Dishes	Make as usual, but omit any hard-cooked egg white. Cool. Pack in freezer container.	Thaw enough to remove from container; heat in double boiler.
Croquettes	Make as usual up to the point of frying. For easier handling, freeze first on pan or tray; then place in freezer bag or box, or in any box over-wrapped with freezer material.	Fry, unthawed, in deep fat or salad oil heated to 390°F. until golden brown on all sides.
Franks	Franks are cooked when you buy them. To store them 2 weeks or less, leave in original package. Otherwise wrap in sheet wrapping.	Use frozen if they can be separated. Or thaw and heat as desired.

(cont'd.)

TO FREEZE AND SERVE COOKED FOODS — (continued)

IF YOU WANT	FREEZE THEM THIS WAY	SERVE THEM
Gravy, Meat Stock	Make; then cool. Skim off fat. Pack in straight-sided freezer container or jar.	Heat as for soups.
Ham, Baked	Leave in large pieces if possible. Wrap in sheet wrapping, using foil if ham is to be heated in oven.	Thaw about 5 hr. per lb. in refrigerator; then use as desired. Or heat small packages, unthawed, wrapped in foil, at 350°F. 30 min. to 1 hr.
Macaroni and Cheese, Baked	Make as usual. Place in casserole, but do not bake. Cool; cover.	Thaw about 8 hr. in refrigerator; then bake as usual. Add a little milk toward end of baking period if mixture seems dry.
Meat Balls, Swedish	Make as usual; then cool. Arrange meat balls and gravy in pie or cake pan close to size of your skillet; cover with freezer material.	Set pan in hot water long enough to loosen contents; slip mixture into skillet. Cover and heat slowly—about 25 min.
Meat Loaf	Package, baked or unbaked, in aluminum foil or covered loaf pan or baking dish. Or place layer of baked slices on foil; cover with gravy or canned tomato sauce; fold foil over tightly.	Thaw about 8 hr. in refrigerator. Then serve cold; or heat or bake as usual. Or, if they're slices, reheat, unthawed, in foil package at 400°F. 40 min.
Peppers, Stuffed	Fill uncooked pepper shells with desired mixture; cool. Wrap or place in freezer container.	Bake, unthawed, in covered baking dish at 350°F. until tender.
Pies—Chicken, Beef, etc.	Pour hot filling into large or individual baking dishes; cool. Add top crust; cover.	Thaw large pies about 8 hr. in refrigerator; then bake as usual. Bake individual pies, unthawed, at 425°F. about 30 min.
Potatoes, Baked, Stuffed	Make as on p. 267, but do not brown; cool; place in shallow baking dish; cover.	Bake, unthawed and uncovered, at 350°F. 25 to 35 min., or until hot and slightly brown.
Potatoes, Candied Sweet	Make candied sweets as usual; cool in baking dish. Cover; or pack in freezer container.	Heat, thawed or unthawed, in double boiler or in covered baking dish at 350°F.
Rice, Cooked	Pack tightly in freezer container or greased baking dish; cover.	Thaw several hours at room temperature; then heat in double boiler. Or heat, unthawed, in covered baking dish at 350°F.
Roast Meat—Beef, Lamb, Veal, Pork	Sort into large pieces, slices, and bits. Pack tightly in freezer container; pour on gravy or broth to protect flavor. Large pieces may be wrapped in sheet wrapping.	Thaw 4 to 8 hr. in refrigerator. Heat; or serve cold. Small containers of meat in gravy may be heated without thawing at 350°F.

IF YOU WANT	FREEZE THEM THIS WAY	SERVE THEM
Sauces—Spaghetti, Creole, or Barbecue	Make 2 or 3 batches at a time; pack as for soups.	Heat as for soups.
Stews—Beef, Veal, Lamb	Brown and cook meat in usual amount of liquid until tender-firm. Omit all vegetables; or just omit potatoes. Cool. Pack in freezer container.	Thaw about 8 hr. in refrigerator. Add vegetables in time to simmer till tender (add water if needed).
Swiss Steak Braised Veal Chops Pork Chops Veal Scaloppine Spareribs	Make as usual, but cook only until tender-firm. Cool. Pack in shallow baking dish; cover.	Thaw about 8 hr. in refrigerator; then heat. Or heat, unthawed, in covered baking dish at 350°F. about 1 hr., or until tender and hot. (Time depends on quantity.)
Turnovers—Ham, Chicken	Make as usual, but do not bake. Freeze; then wrap.	Bake, unthawed, unwrapped, on baking sheet at 400°F. 15 min. if bite-size, 25 to 30 min. if dinner-size.

DESSERTS

IF YOU WANT	FREEZE THEM THIS WAY	SERVE THEM
Applesauce	Make as usual without adding spices; cool. Pour into freezer container.	Thaw several hours at room temperature; add desired spices.
Baked Alaska	(See recipe p. 427.) Make on same day you plan to serve Alaska, but do not brown or wrap. Just set cookie sheet level in freezer.	Bake, unthawed, as recipe directs; serve immediately.
Brown Betty Fruit Cobbler	Make as usual; cool. Leave in baking dish; cover.	Heat, unthawed, covered, at 350°F.
Cakes, Cookies	See directions on pp. 539 to 540.	
Eclairs, Cream Puffs	Make cream puffs or éclairs (see p. 395); cool. Slit; fill with ice cream; wrap.	Unwrap; serve at once with sauce.
Ice-Cream Sundaes (in quantity)	For a party, early in day, set paper dishes on tray and fill with scoops of ice cream. Set level in freezer.	Remove tray from freezer and spoon sauce or fruit over ice cream; serve at once.
Other Ice-Cream Desserts	See Ice Creams and Sherbets, pp. 424 to 436.	
Pies—Chiffon, Fruit, Mince, Pumpkin, Lemon	See p. 539.	

HOME CANNING

Without doubt, the U. S. Department of Agriculture is the leading authority on the subject of home canning, and for this reason we feel that this government body is the best source of information on canning procedures and solutions to canning problems. Complete and detailed canning instructions can be obtained as follows:

Canning Fruits and Vegetables

Detailed instructions for canning fruits and vegetables in glass jars or tin cans are included in the U.S. Department of Agriculture's Home and Garden Bulletin No. 8, "Home Canning of Fruits and Vegetables." Individual copies can be obtained (without charge) by writing to the Division of Publications, Office of Information, U. S. Department of Agriculture, Washington 25, D.C.

Canning Meats and Poultry

Detailed instructions for canning pork, beef, and other lean meats (lamb and veal), as well as poultry, rabbit, and small game, are included in the U. S. Department of Agriculture's Home and Garden Bulletin No. 6, "Home Canning of Meat." Individual copies can be obtained in the same manner described in Canning Fruits and Vegetables, above.

Additional Sources

Manufacturers of home-canning equipment offer the following booklets, which also give detailed canning procedures:

"Atlas Book of Recipes" (single copies available without charge)
Hazel-Atlas Glass Co., Wheeling, West Virginia

"Ball Blue Book" (25¢ per copy)
Ball Brothers Co., Inc., Muncie, Indiana

"Bernardin Home Canning Guide" (25¢ per copy)
Bernardin Bottle Cap Co., Inc.
2201 W. Maryland St., Evansville, Indiana

"Burpee Way of Home Canning" (25¢ per copy)
Burpee Can Sealer Co.,
128 W. Liberty St., Barrington, Illinois

"Crown Ideas for Home Canning" (25¢ per copy)
Crown Cork Specialty Corp.,
Div. of Crown Cork and Seal Co., Inc.,
Decatur, Illinois

"Kerr Home Canning Book" (25¢ per copy)
Kerr Glass Manufacturing Corp.,
54 Main St., Sands Springs, Oklahoma

"The Modern Guide to Pressure Cooking and Canning" (50¢ per copy)
National Presto Industries, Inc.,
10 W. Madison St., Eau Claire, Wisconsin

Jellies and Jams

When jelly was made by the old-fashioned, long-boil method, the success of the results depended on the exact proportions of pectin and acid contained in the fruit itself. Since these vary considerably in different fruits in different seasons, the success of the jelly was by no means assured.

Today natural fruit pectin in either liquid or powdered form is added to the juice of ripe fruit according to carefully balanced recipes, and the short-boil method is used with assured success. *Before using these recipes,* refer to How to Use Our Recipes, p. 3, and Pots and Pans, p. 692. Always use standard measuring cups and measuring spoons; measure level.

The Do's and Don't's of Perfect Jelly

Scald Jelly Glasses. Just before starting to make jelly, wash, rinse, and drain jelly glasses and covers. Pour on boiling water to cover; let stand until ready to fill. Then drain well; fill.

Squeeze Juice This Way: Use a 1-yd. square of cheesecloth, several layers thick. Wet cloth; spread over colander in bowl. Place prepared fruit in cloth; bring corners of cheesecloth together and twist while pressing down on bag.

If you prefer a very clear jelly, knot corners of cheesecloth together to make bag. Then suspend bag over bowl, so juice can drip through, *without pressing,* several hours. You'll need 1½ times as much fruit as is called for in our recipes.

Melt Paraffin. Use new paraffin; old paraffin often causes spoilage. Melt paraffin in small pot over hot water over low heat. (Over direct heat, paraffin may smoke or spatter and if it gets too hot, it may flavor jelly objectionably.)

Measure Carefully.

For Jelly: If there's not enough juice, prepare more. Or mix water with pulp left in jelly bag; then squeeze again.

For Jam: Pack fruit and juice solidly into cup to exact measurement; if there's not quite enough, add water to fill.

Add Liquid Pectin Right from Bottle. Remove bottle cap; turn bottle, holding it straight, upside down. For ½ bottle, let pectin drain down to ½ bottle mark; then turn bottle upright.

Fill Glasses Only to Within ½″ of Top. This allows space for paraffin.

Paraffin at Once: Cover hot jam or jelly with ⅛″ layer of hot paraffin. (Jellies contract and expand; a thin layer of paraffin "adjusts" better than a thick layer, and so gives best protection.)

Cover Glasses: When glasses are cool, cover with scalded tin covers. Or if covers are not available, cut out circles of paper large enough to fold over tops of glasses. Label; then store in cool dry place.

JELLIES TO MAKE IN SEASON

Recipes for popular jellies, jams, and marmalades are in the booklet or leaflet that comes with your pectin. If the booklet isn't handy, here are some of our favorite jellies made the same way.

CONCORD-GRAPE JELLY

About 5½ lb. fully ripe Concord grapes (4 cups grape juice)	7 cups (3 lb.) granulated sugar
½ cup water	½ 8-oz. bottle liquid fruit pectin

Scald about 10 jelly glasses as on p. 545. Prepare juice as follows: Remove stems from washed grapes; crush grapes well. Add water; simmer, covered, 10 min. Squeeze out 4 cups juice as on p. 545. (Use fruit pulp for Concord-Grape Butter, below.)

Into large saucepan, measure sugar and juice; mix. Bring to boil over high heat. Stir in pectin at once. Bring to *full, rolling boil; boil hard 1 min.*, stirring constantly. Remove from heat. With metal spoon, skim off foam.

Fill glasses at once; paraffin, cool, and cover as on p. 545. Makes about 10 medium glassfuls.

CONCORD-GRAPE BUTTER

5 cups prepared grape pulp	granulated sugar
7½ cups (3¼ lb.)	½ 8-oz. bottle liquid fruit pectin

Scald 12 jelly glasses as on p. 545. Prepare pulp as follows: Rub grapes left from Concord-Grape Jelly, above, through sieve.

Into large saucepan, measure sugar and prepared pulp; if necessary, fill last cup with excess juice or water; mix. Bring to *full, rolling boil* over high heat; *boil hard 1 min.*, stirring constantly. Remove from heat. Stir in pectin at once. With metal spoon, skim off foam; stir and skim by turns 5 min.

Fill glasses at once; paraffin, cool, and cover as on p. 545. Makes 12 medium glassfuls.

QUINCE JELLY

About 3 lb. fully ripe quince (4 cups quince juice)	¼ cup strained fresh, frozen, or canned lemon juice
4½ cups water	½ 8-oz. bottle liquid fruit pectin
7½ cups (3¼ lb.) granulated sugar	

Scald 13 jelly glasses as on p. 545. Prepare juice as follows: Wash quince; remove blossom and stem ends; core but do not peel. Put through food chopper, using medium blade. Add water; simmer, covered, 15 min. Squeeze out juice as on p. 545.

Into large saucepan, measure sugar and juice. Add lemon juice; mix. Bring to boil over high heat; add pectin at once, stirring constantly. Bring to *full, rolling boil; boil hard 1 min.*, stirring constantly. Remove from heat. With metal spoon, skim off foam.

Fill glasses at once; paraffin, cool, and cover as on p. 545. Makes 13 medium glassfuls.

SUSAN'S STRAWBERRY JAM

About 2 qt. fully ripe strawberries (4 cups crushed)	lated sugar
7 cups (3 lb.) granu-	½ 8-oz. bottle liquid fruit pectin

1. Wash and hull strawberries. Scald 10 medium jelly glasses as on p. 545. Start melting new paraffin in small pot over hot water.
2. With masher, crush berries *well*, a layer at a time.
3. Into large saucepan, measure 4 cups crushed berries. Stir in sugar. Bring to *full, rolling boil* over high heat; *boil hard 1 min.*, stirring constantly.
4. Remove from heat. Stir in pectin at once. With metal spoon, skim off foam. Then stir and skim by turns 5 min., to cool slightly and help prevent fruit's floating.
5. Fill glasses at once; paraffin, cool, and cover as on p. 545. Makes 10 medium glassfuls.

Blackberry: Substitute blackberries for strawberries. Put half of crushed berries through sieve, to remove some of seeds.

APRICOT-AND-PINEAPPLE JAM

¼ lb. dried apricots and 1 ripe medium pineapple (4 cups prepared fruit)	2 cups water
	1 box powdered fruit pectin
	4⅔ cups (2 lb.) granulated sugar

Scald about 8 jelly glasses as on p. 545. Prepare fruit as follows: To dried apricots, add water; cover; let stand 4 hr. or overnight. Drain, reserving liquid. Grind or chop apricots fine; combine with liquid. Pare pineapple; grind or chop very fine. Combine fruits.

Into large saucepan, measure 4 cups fruit. Stir in pectin; mix well. Stir over high heat until mixture comes to hard boil. Stir in sugar at once. Bring to *full, rolling boil; boil hard 1 min.*, stirring constantly. Remove from heat. With metal spoon, skim off foam; stir and skim by turns 5 min.

Fill glasses at once; paraffin, cool, and cover as on p. 545. Makes about 8 medium glassfuls.

BLACK-CHERRY JAM

About 3 lb. fully ripe Bing or other sweet cherries (3¾ cups prepared fruit)	juice
	7 cups (3 lb.) granulated sugar
¼ cup fresh, frozen, or canned lemon	1 8-oz. bottle liquid fruit pectin

Scald about 11 jelly glasses as on p. 545. Prepare fruit as follows: Remove stems and pit cherries; chop cherries fine.

Into large saucepan, measure 3¾ cups fruit. Add lemon juice, sugar; mix well. Bring to *full, rolling boil* over high heat; *boil hard 1 min.*, stirring constantly. Remove from heat. Stir in pectin at once. With metal spoon, skim off foam; stir and skim by turns 5 min.

Fill glasses at once; paraffin, cool, and cover as on p. 545. Makes about 11 medium glassfuls.

Sour-Cherry Jam: Use 4 cups prepared sour cherries; omit lemon juice.

RED-RASPBERRY JAM

About 2 qt. ripe raspberries (4 cups prepared berries)	granulated sugar
	½ 8-oz. bottle liquid fruit pectin
6½ cups (2¾ lb.)	

Scald about 10 jelly glasses as on p. 545. Prepare fruit as follows: Crush washed raspberries. If desired, sieve half of pulp, to remove some of seeds.

Into large saucepan, measure sugar and 4 cups prepared fruit; mix well. Bring to *full, rolling boil* over high heat; *boil hard 1 min.*, stirring constantly. Remove from heat. Stir in pectin. With metal spoon, skim off foam; stir and skim by turns 5 min.

Fill glasses; paraffin, cool, and cover as on p. 545. Makes about 10 medium glassfuls.

ORANGE MARMALADE

3 medium oranges and 2 lemons (3 cups prepared fruit)	6 cups (2 lb. 10 oz.) granulated sugar
1½ cups water	½ 8-oz. bottle liquid fruit pectin
⅛ teasp. baking soda	

Scald about 8 jelly glasses as on p. 545. Prepare fruit as follows: From oranges and lemons, remove peel in quarters. Lay peel flat; shave off and discard about half of white part. With sharp knife, slice remaining peel very fine. Add water, soda; bring to boil; simmer, covered, 20 min., stirring often. Chop peeled fruit, removing any seeds; add pulp and juice to undrained peel. Simmer, covered, 10 min.

Into large saucepan, measure 3 cups prepared fruit. Add sugar; mix well. Bring to *full, rolling boil* over high heat; *boil hard 1 min.*, stirring constantly. Remove from heat. Stir in pectin at once. With metal spoon, skim off foam; stir and skim by turns 7 min.

Fill glasses; paraffin, cool, and cover as on p. 545. Makes about 8 medium glassfuls.

Christmas Conserve: To prepared fruit, add ½ cup minced nut meats; ¼ cup chopped light or dark raisins, packed; and ¼ cup cut-up maraschino cherries. Proceed as directed.

Grapefruit: Use 2 small grapefruit.

Orange and Grapefruit: Use 2 medium oranges and 1 small grapefruit.

Orange, Grapefruit, and Lemon: Use 1 medium orange, 1 small grapefruit, and 1 medium lemon.

CRANBERRY MARMALADE

2 medium oranges, 1 medium lemon, and 1 lb. fully ripe cranberries (5 cups prepared fruit)	⅛ teasp. baking soda
	6½ cups (2¾ lb.) granulated sugar
	½ 8-oz. bottle liquid fruit pectin
1½ cups water	

Scald about 11 jelly glasses as on p. 545. Prepare fruit as follows: Cut unpeeled oranges and lemon into quarters; remove any seeds. Grind (or chop fine; or slice crosswise, wafer-thin) oranges, lemon, and cranberries. Add water, soda. Bring to boil; simmer, covered, 20 min., stirring occasionally.

Into very large saucepan, measure 5 cups prepared fruit. Add sugar; mix well. Bring to *full, rolling boil* over high heat; *boil hard 1 min.,* stirring constantly. Remove from heat. Stir in pectin at once. With metal spoon, skim off foam; stir and skim by turns 5 min.

Fill glasses; paraffin, cool, and cover as on p. 545. Makes about 11 medium glassfuls.

DAMSON-PLUM-AND-ORANGE CONSERVE

About 2 lb. ripe damson plums and 1 orange (4½ cups prepared fruit)	1 box powdered fruit pectin
2 cups water	7 cups (3 lb.) granulated sugar
½ cup light or dark raisins	½ cup coarsely chopped walnuts

Scald about 11 jelly glasses as on p. 545. Prepare fruit as follows: Cut unpeeled plums in halves; pit; chop fine. Chop unpeeled orange very fine; add water; simmer, covered, 20 min. Combine with plums.

Into very large saucepan, measure 4½ cups prepared fruit. Add raisins, then pectin; mix well. Stir over high heat until mixture comes to hard boil. Stir in sugar at once. Bring to *full, rolling boil; boil hard 1 min.,* stirring constantly. Remove from heat. Add nuts. With metal spoon, skim off foam; stir and skim by turns 5 min.

Fill glasses; paraffin, cool, and cover as on p. 545. Makes about 11 medium glassfuls.

SPICED CURRANT RELISH

About 3 lb., or 2 qt., ripe red currants (6 cups prepared fruit)	1 teasp. cinnamon
	¼ cup vinegar
¼ cup water	1 box powdered fruit pectin
1 teasp. ground cloves	7 cups (3 lb.) granulated sugar

Scald about 13 jelly glasses as on p. 545. Prepare fruit as follows: Remove stems and crush currants well. Place in saucepan. Add water, cloves, cinnamon, vinegar. Bring to boil; simmer, covered, 10 min.

Into very large saucepan, measure 6 cups prepared fruit. Add pectin; mix well. Stir over high

heat until mixture comes to hard boil. Stir in sugar at once. Bring to *full, rolling boil; boil hard 1 min.,* stirring constantly. Remove from heat. With metal spoon, skim off foam; stir and skim by turns 5 min.

Fill glasses; paraffin, cool, and cover as on p. 545. Makes about 13 medium glassfuls.

TO MAKE THE YEAR ROUND

Frozen, canned, and dried fruits, and frozen and bottled juices, make excellent jellies and jams—and they're available winter, spring, summer, and fall. Keep glasses and pectin on hand; make a batch whenever you have a few spare minutes, following recipes in pectin booklet. For short storage of 2 months or so, omit paraffin; cover glasses and refrigerate.

ORANGE RHINE JELLY

4 cups (1¾ lb.) granulated sugar	juice
½ cup strained fresh orange juice	¼ teasp. finely grated orange rind
2 tablesp. fresh, frozen, or canned lemon	1½ cups Rhine wine
	½ 8-oz. bottle liquid fruit pectin

Scald about 7 jelly glasses as on p. 545. Into double-boiler top, measure sugar. Add fruit juices, orange rind, wine; mix well. Place over rapidly boiling water; stir until sugar dissolves —about 2 min. Remove from heat. Stir in pectin. With metal spoon, skim off foam.

Fill glasses; paraffin, cool, and cover as on p. 545. Makes about 7 medium glassfuls.

PEACH-RASPBERRY JAM

½ lb. dried peaches (about 1¾ cups)	canned lemon juice
3½ cups water	6 cups (2 lb. 10 oz.) granulated sugar
1 10-oz. box thawed frozen raspberries	½ 8-oz. bottle liquid fruit pectin
¼ cup fresh, frozen, or	

Scald about 10 jelly glasses as on p. 545. In medium saucepan, simmer peaches with water, covered, 10 min. Drain, reserving liquid. Chop peaches fine; mix with reserved liquid.

In large saucepan, combine raspberries and enough peach mixture to make 4 cups prepared fruit. Add lemon juice, sugar; mix well. Bring to *full, rolling boil* over high heat; *boil hard 1 min.*, stirring constantly. Remove from heat. Stir in pectin. With metal spoon, skim off foam; stir and skim by turns 5 min.

Fill glasses; paraffin, cool, and cover as on p. 545. Makes about 10 medium glassfuls.

PEACH-MARASCHINO-ORANGE JAM

2 10-oz. boxes thawed frozen sliced peaches (2¼ cups)	or canned lemon juice
⅓ cup chopped maraschino cherries	½ box (about 3½ tablesp.) powdered fruit pectin*
1 medium orange	3½ cups (1½ lb.) granulated sugar
1 tablesp. fresh, frozen,	

Scald about 6 jelly glasses as on p. 545. Chop peaches into large pieces; add cherries. Peel orange; discard white part and seeds. Put orange peel and pulp through food chopper, using medium blade. Combine all fruits; measure 3 cups into large saucepan. Add lemon juice, then pectin; mix well. Stir over high heat until mixture comes to hard boil. Stir in sugar at once. Bring to *full, rolling boil; boil hard 1 min.*, stirring constantly. Remove from heat. With metal spoon, skim off foam; stir and skim by turns 5 min.

Fill glasses; paraffin, cool, and cover as on p. 545. Makes about 6 medium glassfuls.

Stir contents of box thoroughly before measuring.

RASPBERRY-PINEAPPLE JAM

2 10-oz. boxes thawed frozen red raspberries (2½ cups)	¼ cup water
	5½ cups (2 lb. 6 oz.) granulated sugar
1 No. 2 can crushed pineapple (2⅓ cups)	½ bottle liquid fruit pectin

Scald about 10 jelly glasses as on p. 545. In very large saucepan, combine fruits. Add water, sugar; mix well. Bring to *full, rolling boil* over high heat; *boil hard 1 min.*, stirring constantly. Remove from heat. Stir in pectin at once. With metal spoon, skim off foam; stir and skim by turns 5 min.

Fill glasses; paraffin, cool, and cover as on p. 545. Makes about 10 medium glassfuls.

Leftovers

Leftovers needn't mean waste or a dreary repetition of exactly the same meal. They can easily be worked into dishes that are deliciously different from the food's first appearance. In the lists that follow, you'll find some of the many recipes in this book that put leftovers to good use.

Don't forget you can freeze that leftover bird, roast, etc. Give the family a rest by wrapping and freezing the bird; then bring it out a week or two later, when the family's all enthused again. See p. 542.

LEFTOVER EGG YOLKS

To Store Leftover Egg Yolks: Put them in small bowl; cover with cold water; then refrigerate. Use, drained, within a day or two in any of the recipes below. The figures in parentheses beside each recipe indicate the number of egg yolks called for.

Use in Desserts

Butterscotch-Date Cream Pie (3), p. 420
Chocolate Butter Cream (2), p. 462
Chocolate Poundcake (1), p. 449
Custard Sauce I (6), p. 370
Custard Sauce de Luxe (3 or 4), p. 370
Dark-Chocolate Filling (1), p. 461
De Luxe Cheesecake (3), p. 396
Devil's-Food Cupcakes (1), p. 455

Eggnog Sauce (2), p. 367
Grandma's Vanilla Ice Cream (3), p. 433
Hungarian Frosting (3), p. 464
Orange Fluff Sauce (2), p. 371
Penny-Wise Gold Cake (3), p. 441
Pistachio Mousse (3), p. 431
Queen of Puddings (2), p. 391
Rich Pineapple Filling (3), p. 461
Royal Chocolate Chiffon Pie (1), p. 417
Strawberry Glaze (2), p. 465
Walnut Filling (2), p. 461
Wonder Gold Cake (5), p. 448
Yummy Chocolate Frosting (2), p. 464
Zabaglione (3), p. 388

Use Elsewhere

Bert's Brioche (2), p. 351
Blanquette de Veau (2), p. 104
Chicken à la Queen (1), p. 158
Chicken-Almond Supper Mold (2), p. 312
Easy Hollandaise (2), p. 374
Fillets of Fish Duglere, Platter Style (1), p. 174
Lobster Newburg (3), p. 188
Mayonnaise (2), p. 320
Molded Sea-Food Salad (3), p. 313
Mustard Sauce (1), p. 375
Sharp Sauce (2), p. 377
Southern Crab Cakes (1), p. 186
Superb Biff à la Lundstrom (2), p. 66

Leftover Egg Yolks May Be Hard-Cooked as Follows: Put yolks in strainer; lower into simmering water to cover; simmer until hard-cooked. Remove; mince with fork; then use where hard-cooked eggs are called for, as in:

Sandwich fillings; see Sandwiches, p. 356
Tossed Salads; see

Salad Extras, p. 299
Salad dressings; see

French Dressing Plus, p. 317 and

Mayonnaise Plus, p. 318

LEFTOVER EGG WHITES

To Store Leftover Egg Whites: Turn them into covered jar and refrigerate. Use the whites within 10 days in any of the ways below. The figures in parentheses beside each recipe indicate the number of egg whites called for.

Use in Cakes

Big Orange Chiffon (2 or 3), p. 451
Daffodil Cake (6), p. 453
Little Orange Chiffon (2), p. 451
Luscious Coconut-Layer Cake (4), p. 446
Old-fashioned White Cupcakes (5), p. 456
Silver White Cake (4), p. 440
Susan's Angel-Food Cake (10 to 12), p. 453

Use in Frostings

Magic Frosting (2), p. 463
No-Cook Marshmallow Frosting (2), p. 463
Ornamental Frosting (6), p. 465
"Seven-Minute" Frosting (2), p. 466
Snow-Peak Frosting (2), p. 462
Susan's Fluffy Frosting (3), p. 466

Use Elsewhere

Apple Snow (2), p. 381
Baked-Alaska Pie (3), p. 428
Baked Alaskas (3), p. 427
Black-and-White Squares (2), p. 487
Chocolate Meringues (3), p. 478
Choco-Nut Tortoni (1), p. 432
Coconut Macaroons (3), p. 477
Creamy French Dressing (1), p. 319
Divinity Drops (2), p. 489
Frozen Pudding (3), p. 431
Meringue Crust (4), p. 410
Meringue Dips (3), p. 477
Meringue Glacée (6), p. 397
Pie Meringue (2 or 3), p. 419
Pineapple-Lemon Foam Cocktail (2), p. 19
Strawberry Mousse (2), p. 431
Susan's Hot Cross Buns (1), p. 353
Twin Angel-Food Pies (2), p. 399

LEFTOVER MEATS

Most Meats

The Last of the Meat (36 fine recipes for leftover beef, pork, lamb, veal, ham), pp. 127 to 135
Leftover Bacon, p. 93
Leftover Bacon Fat (or ham or pork-sausage fat), p. 93
Nibblers (check through chapter), p. 22
Scrambled Eggs (see Additions), p. 224

Ten Omelet Fillings, p. 227

Ham

Baked (Shirred) Eggs, p. 226
Baked Macaroni with Ham, p. 239
Benedict-Style Poached Eggs, p. 231
Chicken Sauté Brazilian, p. 142
"Chilly" con Carne Salad, p. 308
Custard Corn Pudding (see To Vary), p. 255
Eggs Benedict, p. 225
Eggs Foo Young (pork), p. 230
Four Cheese-Soufflé Variations: Ham and Cheese, p. 213
Ham-and-Chicken Salad, p. 306
Ham or Sea-Food Tomato Aspic, p. 314
Ham, Veal, or Lamb Salad, p. 306
Holiday Turkey Casserole, p. 162
Hot Biscuits Plus, p. 324
Italian Ham and Spaghetti, p. 241
Kidney-Lima Casserole, p. 257
Quick Spanish Ham, p. 197
Sandwiches (check through chapter), p. 356
Savory Lima-Bean Pot, p. 256
Susan's Turketti, p. 161
The Best Creamed Eggs with Ham, p. 228

LEFTOVER CAKE OR PIE

Baked Alaskas, p. 427
Cake Dessert Quickies, p. 381
How to Freeze Pies, p. 539

Ice-Cream-Cake Sundaes, p. 426
Ice-Cream Cupcakes, p. 427
Ice-Cream Shortcakes, p. 426
Ice-Cream Snowballs, p. 424
Storing Leftover Fruit Pies, p. 414

Tray Ice-Cream Cakes, p. 426

LEFTOVER FISH

Piece out leftover cooked fish with another fresh or canned fish or shellfish. Or mix leftover fish with chopped raw or cooked vegetables, salad dressing, and seasonings to use as a sandwich filling. Or use as below.

Crab-Corn Bake, p. 185
Deviled Eggs: Nordic, p. 229
Make It Fish (sandwiches), p. 363
"Old Salt" Cheese Casserole, p. 178
Our Best Creamed Fish, p. 177
Piquant Crab Casserole, p. 186
Quick-Curried Crab, p. 186
Salad Extras, p. 299
Sea-Food Cocktails, p. 20
Shrimp Creole, p. 193
Superb Fish Scallop, p. 178

LEFTOVER VEGETABLES

In Salads: Add leftover vegetables to green, fish, egg, or meat salads.

In Soups: Add leftover vegetables, cut up if necessary, to soup in time to heat.

With Tomorrow's Vegetable: Add leftovers to next day's hot green beans, limas, carrots, onions, peas, etc.

In Combination: Combine 2 kinds; heat in double boiler.

Leftover Boiled Potatoes: Serve them cut up, then creamed with peas, tuna, salmon, etc. Or toss with greens, vegetables, meat, fish, or poultry for salad. Or fry in skillet.

Leftover Mashed Potatoes: Add them to mashed turnips or squash. Or form into cakes; then sauté.

Vegetable Liquid: Save it. It contains valuable soluble minerals and vitamins. Use it:
  1. Combined with tomato juice
  2. As liquid with which to dilute any canned condensed soup
  3. As part of liquid in sauces, soups, gravies, or stews

Most Any Vegetable

Make It Fish (sandwiches), p. 363
Make It Raw Vegetables (sandwiches), p. 363
Meat à la King, p. 130
Minute Chicken Pie, p. 156
Old-fashioned Creamed, p. 247
Salad Extras, p. 299
Scalloped, p. 248
The Tossed Vegetable Salad, p. 302
Tomato Aspic, p. 314
Vegetable-Cheese Bake, p. 232

Corn

Columbus Casserole, p. 112
Libby's Hot Corn Waffles, p. 336
Pacific-Coast Clam Chowder, p. 44
Quick Corn Pancakes, p. 335

Celery

Orange Rice, p. 236
Tangy Orange Rice, p. 236

Peas

Blender Vichyssoise, p. 37

Ham-and-Chicken Pie, p. 134
Ham-and-Noodle Casserole, p. 133

Potatoes

Cheese-Potato Mound, p. 269
Ham-and-Chicken Pie, p. 134
New Zealand-Style Eggs, p. 231
Potatoes in Cream, p. 270
Refrigerator Rolls de Luxe, p. 348
Susan's Hashed Brown Potatoes, p. 268

Susan's Refrigerator Rolls (water drained from cooked potatoes), p. 348

Tomatoes

Consommé Madrilene, p. 37
Fillets of Fish Duglere, p. 174
Spanish Scrambled Eggs, p. 225

Squash and Pumpkin

Pilgrim Pumpkin or Squash Pie, p. 415
Pumpkin Chiffon Pie, p. 416

LEFTOVER TURKEY OR CHICKEN

LEFTOVER FRUITS AND FRUIT SYRUPS

Fruit: Use in or on fruit gelatin desserts, fruit cups, fruit cocktails, ice cream, sherbets, cake slices etc. Use in *salads*—fruit, meat, or fish salads. Use as a garnish; see The Gay Garnish, p. 296.

Fruit Syrups: Use in cold drinks.

LEFTOVER "EXTRAS"

Olives

Baked Cheese Pudding, p. 215
Barbara's Tamale Pie, p. 73
Big Thousand-Island Dressing, p. 320
Crunchy or Colorful Vegetables, p. 247
Fluffy Hot Rice, p. 234
Gen's Scalloped Chicken, p. 150
Hamburger Spread-Ons, p. 65
Spicy Ham and Eggs, p. 230
Susan's Sautéed Fish, p. 175
Tomato-Olive Aspic, p. 314

Pickles

Apple Dill, p. 290
Chicken-Tongue Supper Loaf, p. 312
Cooked Tongue: with Pickle Sauce, p. 115
Deviled Tongue Mold, p. 131
Hamburger Spread-Ons, p. 65
Pressed Chicken Special, p. 312
Sweet-Sour Green Beans, p. 259

Pimento

Creamed Tuna Supreme, p. 180
Crunchy or Colorful Vegetables, p. 247

"Old Salt" Cheese Casserole, p. 178
Olive Relish Mold (perfection salad), p. 314
Sautéed Chicken, p. 138
Very Quick Creamed Chicken, p. 157

Anchovies

French Dressings Plus, p. 317
Green Beans Parmesan, p. 302
The Tossed Vegetable Salad, p. 302

Cranberry Sauce

Egg-and-Cheese Flapjacks, p. 229

Eight Little Recipes: Red and White Sauce, p. 367
French Dressings Plus: Cranberry, p. 318
Ice-Cream Snowballs (No. 7), p. 424
Other Quick Fruit Top-Offs: Polka Dots, p. 379

Potato Chips

Baked Salmon Loaf, p. 181
Chip Burgers, p. 65
Chip-Tuna Casserole, p. 179
Crunchy Tuna Salad, p. 309
Egg-Salad Casserole, p. 227

LEFTOVER BREAD OR CRUSTS

Use in Main Dishes, etc.

Baked Cheese Pudding, p. 215
Baked Fillets with Cheese Dressing, p. 170
Baked Fish Creole, p. 171
Baked Salmon Loaf, p. 181
Baked Stuffed Pork Chops, p. 80
Cheese Fondue, p. 214
Cheese Strata, p. 215

Cheese Toast with Bacon, p. 215
Chicken à la Queen, p. 158
Chicken Casserole Supreme, p. 158
Creamy Baked Fillets or Steaks, p. 170
Crouton-Topped Turkey Bake, p. 161
Crumb Style Vegetables, p. 247
Salmon Loaf, West-Coast Style, p. 181
Surprise Tomato Fillets, p. 170

Susan's Cheese-and-Onion Casserole, p. 215
Susan's Pineapple-Ham Loaf, p. 132
Susan's Swiss Pie, p. 212
Tomato Cheesies, p. 216
Very Quick Creamed Chicken, p. 157
Wonder Cheese Custard, p. 216

Use in Desserts

Apple Brown Betty,

p. 388
Camille's Peach Coconut, p. 388
Kitchenette Caramel Pudding, p. 382
Peach Crumb Dessert, p. 381
Susan's Custard Bread Pudding, p. 391

Use as

Dried Bread Crumbs, p. 9

EXTRA CHEESE

Almost Any Cheese

Cheese (entire chapter), pp. 211 to 222
Cheese Croustades,

p. 345
Dressing Extras, p. 300
Filled Butter-Flake Rolls, p. 342
Fruit-and-Cheese

Dessert Salads, p. 311
Hot Biscuits Plus: Cheese, p. 324
Nibblers (lots to

choose from), pp. 22 to 32
Make It Cheese (sandwiches), p. 362
Pan-Ready Biscuits:

Cheese Upside-down (cheese spread), p. 326
Rice and Macaroni (lots to choose from), p. 233
Salad Extras, p. 299
Scrambled Eggs: Additions, p. 224
Slicettes, p. 342
Toasted English Muffins, p. 343

American Cheese

Corn-Meal Crisps, p. 330
Cream-of-Onion-and-Cheese Soup, p. 39
Deviled Eggs, Cheese Style, p. 229
Green Limas à la Crème, p. 259
Hamburger Spread-Ons, p. 65
Hot Muffins—Quick:

Tip-Topped, p. 327
Quick Pancakes: Cheese, p. 335
Skillet Squash au Gratin, p. 273
Superb Skillet Burger Loaf, p. 69

Cottage Cheese

Other Quick Fruit Top-Offs: Cheese Bowl, p. 379
Dunk-It Salads, p. 303

Cream Cheese

Ginger-Cheese Snaps, p. 382
Kumquats, p. 380
Peach Cream, p. 379

Blue Cheese

Hot Biscuits Plus, p. 324
Hamburger Go-Betweens: Blue Cheese, p. 65

IF YOU HAVE LOTS OF MILK

Use in Soups

Soups and Chowders (lots to choose from), pp. 33 to 45

Use in Main Dishes

Baked Cheese Pudding, p. 215
Cheese-Onion Pie, p. 212
Cheese Soufflé for 4, p. 212
Cheese Strata, p. 215
Indian Ham Bake, p. 132
"Old Salt" Cheese Casserole, p. 178
Old-time Welsh Rabbit, p. 214
Our Best Creamed Fish, p. 177
Salmon Scallop Divan, p. 181
Scalloped Ham, Potatoes, and Cheese, p. 133
Superb Fish Scallop, p. 178
Susan's Cheese-and-Onion Casserole, p. 215
Susan's Cheese Soufflé for 6, p. 212
Susan's Fillets Thermidor, p. 171
Susan's Swiss Pie,

p. 212
Wonder Cheese Custard, p. 216

Use in Desserts, Dessert Sauces

Bavarian Cream, p. 403
Creamy Baked Rice Pudding, p. 392
Custard Sauce I, p. 370
Edna's Piccadilly Trifle, p. 398
Granny's Indian Pudding, p. 396
Rice Peach Melba, p. 383
Snow Custard, p. 394
Spanish Cream, p. 405
Susan's Baked Custard, p. 394
Susan's Rice Custard, p. 391
Three Speedy Custard Sauces, p. 368
Today's Blancmange, p. 393

Use in Drinks

Hot Cocoa or Iced Cocoa, p. 497
Milk Coolers, p. 502
Prune Velvet, p. 502

Evaporated Milk

Custard Sauce I, p. 370
Dutch Pantry Pie,

p. 125
Extra-Juicy Hamburgers, p. 65
Luscious Ten-Minute Nut Fudge, p. 487
Pineapple Frost Pie, p. 418
Pumpkin Chiffon Pie, p. 416
Quick-as-a-Wink Frosting, p. 464
Royal Chocolate Chiffon Pie, p. 417
Saucepan Cheese Sauce, p. 373
Semisweet Fudge Balls, p. 487
Thirty-Minute Glazed Ham Patties, p. 133
Thousand Island Sauce, p. 374
Whipped Milk Topping, p. 369
Zucchini Casserole au Gratin, p. 276

Buttermilk

Crunchy-Top Coffee-cake, p. 349
Hush Puppies, p. 176
Old-fashioned Soft Sugar Cookies, p. 477
Plantation Pralines, p. 490
Two Buttermilk Coolers, p. 503

Condensed Milk

Coconut Patties, p. 486
Coffee Sundae Sauce, p. 367
Date-and-Nut Macaroons, p. 478
French Fudge, p. 486

Sour Cream, Commercial

Baked Fillets in Sour Cream, p. 169
Butter-Broiled Salmon, p. 181
Compote de Luxe, p. 380
Cottage-Cheese Salad, p. 307
Cucumber Sauce, p. 373
Fruit Cream, p. 378
Fruit Frost, p. 379
Gourmet Grapes, p. 378
Green Goddess Salad, p. 300
Penuche Nuts, p. 493
Quick Crème Brûlée, p. 379
Sour Cream Sauce, p. 373

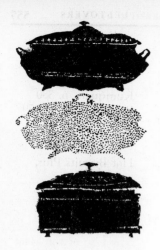

Casserole Dinners

When you're planning a casserole as the main dish, why not have an oven meal? Choose a vegetable, bread, and/or dessert that bakes at the same temperature as the casserole. Then, with the aid of a minute timer, slide each dish into the oven at its correct time.

Here is a list of casserole dishes for which recipes are found in this book (beside each is its baking temperature). Following that list is another list suggesting dishes that may be baked at the same time.

Many of the main dishes listed here are hearty enough to be a meal-in-a-dish for luncheon or supper (serve with a salad or vegetable). Some of these are starred for easy reference.

FISH AND SHELLFISH CASSEROLE DISHES

Fish

Chip-Tuna Casserole (375°F.), p. 179
Creamed Tuna Supreme (400°F.), p. 180
Friday Rice Special (350°F.), p. 236
'Frisco Tuna (350°F.), p. 179
"Old Salt" Cheese Casserole (325°F.), p. 178
Salmon Loaf, West-

Coast Style (350°F.), p. 181
*Salmon Scallop Divan (375°F.), p. 181
*Sardine-Sandwich Bake (350°F.), p. 180
Superb Fish Scallop (400°F.), p. 178
Susan's Fillets Thermidor (350°F.), p. 171
Top-Hat Salmon Pie (450°F.), p. 180
Topsy-Turvy Tuna-

Lemon Pie (400°F.), p. 180
Tuna-Cashew Casserole (325°F.), p. 178
*Tuna Supper Casserole (350°F.), p. 178
Tuna Tomatoes (375° F.), p. 179

Shellfish

*Baked Sea-Food Salad (350°F.), p. 308
Crab-Corn Bake (375°

F.), p. 185
Crab Meat Maryland (350°F.), p. 185
*Jane's Company Lobster (400°F.), p. 189
Luncheon Clambake (350°F.), p. 184
*Piquant Crab Casserole (350°F.), p. 186
Shrimp Casserole Harpin (350°F.), p. 193
Susan's Scalloped Oysters (425°F.), p. 190

EGG CASSEROLE DISHES

*Baked Egg Sandwiches de Luxe (375°F.), p. 228
Deviled-Egg Casserole (425°F.), p. 231
Dinner Casserole de Luxe (375°F.), p.

230
*Egg-Salad Casserole (375°F.), p. 227
*Eggs Divan (400°F.), p. 229
Individual Egg-and-Cheese Casseroles

(325°F.), p. 228
Man-Style Baked Eggs (350°F.), p. 228
Spicy Ham and Eggs (400°F.), p. 230
Susan's Baked Eggs

in Cheese Sauce (325°F.), p. 231
*Swiss Eggs (425°F.), p. 228
Vegetable-Cheese Bake (350°F.), p. 232

MEAT CASSEROLE DISHES

CHEESE CASSEROLE DISHES

POULTRY CASSEROLE DISHES

Baked Chicken Curry (350°F.), p. 156
Baked Chicken Puff (375°F.), p. 160
Baked Chicken Sandwiches (425°F.), p. 358
Casserole-Barbecued Chicken (350°F.), p. 146
Chicken Bake (350°F.), p. 149
Chicken Livers with

Rice (375°F.), p. 142
Coq au Vin (400°F.), p. 146
Crouton-Topped Turkey Bake (350°F.), p. 161
Delmonico Turkey Sandwiches (450°F.), p. 159
Gen's Scalloped Chicken (325°F.), p. 150

Holiday Turkey Casserole (350°F.), p. 162
*Hot Baked Chicken Salad (450°F.), p. 306
Indian Chicken Pudding (350°F.), p. 160
*Minute Chicken Pie (450°F.), p. 156
Napa Valley Barbecued Chicken (325°F.), p. 145

Oven-Baked Chicken Hash (375°F.), p. 157
*Susan's Chicken Pie (425°F.), p. 147
*Susan's Turketti (350°F.), p. 161
*Turkey Buffet Casserole (350°F.), p. 159
Turkey-Cashew Casserole (325°F.), p. 156

RICE, MACARONI, AND DRIED-BEAN CASSEROLE DISHES

Rice, Macaroni, etc.

*Cheesy Spaghetti Omelet (375°F.), p. 243
Elena's Macaroni Bake 350°F.), p. 239
*Italian Ham and Spaghetti (350°F.), p. 241
Jane's Buffet Lasagna (350°F.), p. 242

Macaroni-Tuna Bake (375°F.), p. 243
Mardi Gras Macaroni and Cheese (350°F.), p. 239
Martha's Company Casserole (375°F.), p. 239
Savory Baked Spaghetti (325°F.), p. 241
Savory Rice and

Cheese (425°F.), p. 236
Susan's Baked Macaroni and Cheese (400°F.), p. 238

Dried Beans

Baked-Bean Casserole (400°F.), p. 257
Kidney-Lima Casserole (350°F.), p. 257

Kraut-Noodle Casserole (300°F.), p. 271
Old-fashioned Boston Baked Beans (250°F.), p. 256
Quick Home-Style Baked Beans (375°F.), p. 257
*Savory Lima-Bean Pot (325°F.), p. 256

GO-ALONGS

After you've chosen a casserole main dish, round out your oven meal with dishes that bake at the same temperature.

VEGETABLES TO BAKE

Market Fresh or Garden Vegetables, in Oven, p. 245
Frozen Vegetables, Oven-Cooked, p. 246
Baked Potatoes, for Oven Meals, p. 267
Baked Sweet Potatoes, for Oven Meals, p. 265

325°F.

Franconia, or Pan-Roasted, Potatoes,

p. 267
Oven Dinner Rice (packaged pre-cooked kind), p. 235

350°F.

Oven Dinner Rice (regular or processed kind), p. 235
Rebaked Potatoes, p. 267
Stuffed Zucchini, p. 275
Tomato-Cheese Casse-

role, p. 274
Wild Rice Baked in Consommé, p. 237

375°F.

Candied Sweet Potatoes, p. 266
Old-time Scalloped Potatoes, p. 270
Spanish Rice, p. 235
Stuffed-Pepper Twins, p. 260
Tomatoes Stuffed with Macaroni and

Cheese, p. 274

400°F.

Baked Turnip Puff, p. 275
Curried Rice, p. 235
Quick-Candied Sweet Potatoes, p. 265
Rice Pilaff, p. 235
Rice, Risotto Style, p. 235
Susan's Feathered Rice, p. 235

RELISHES TO BAKE

325°F.

Curried Four-Fruit
Bake, p. 287

350°F.

Barbecued Baked
Apples, p. 289

Pickled Pineapple
Bake, p. 287

450°F.

Baked Bananas, p. 290

BREADS TO BAKE

375°F.

French Half-and-Half,
p. 341
Savory French Bread,
p. 341

Toasty Sweet Breads,
p. 341

400°F.

Brown-and-Serve

Stickies, p. 343
Glaze-Topped Brown-
and-Serves, p. 343
Toasted Rolls in Loaf,

p. 340

450°F.

Slicettes, p. 342

DESSERTS TO BAKE

300°F.

Susan's Baked Cus-
tard, p. 394
Susan's Rice Custard,
p. 391

350°F.

Apple-Annas, p. 385
Baked Applesauce, p.
389
Baked Lemon Cake
Pudding, p. 390
Bride's Chocolate
Soufflé Cups, p. 384
Cranberry Crunch

Alamode, p. 383
Easy Baked Coffee
Soufflé, p. 384
Luscious Lemon
Baked Apples, p.
389
Mary's Fudge Pud-
ding, p. 382
Susan's Custard Bread
Pudding, p. 391

375°F.

Apple Brown Betty, p.
388
Banana-Coconut Rolls,

p. 385
Butter-Nut Pandowdy,
p. 386
Carolyn's Apple Pan-
dowdy, p. 385
Hurry-up Apple
"Pie," p. 385
Old-fashioned Peach
Dumplings, p. 386
Quick Apple Crisp,
p. 388

400°F.

Cherry Bubbles, p. 385

Dutch Plum Cake, p.
387
Easy Apple Dumpl-
ings, p. 386

425°F.

Fruitful Cobbler, p.
389
Pear-Butterscotch
Crisp, p. 390

450°F.

Camille's Peach Coco-
nut, p. 388

PIES TO BAKE

300°F.

Toasted Coconut Pie,
p. 421

350°F.

Rich Walnut Pie, p.

415
Susan's Fudge-Nut
Pie, p. 415

425°F.

Deep-Dish Pies (ex-

cept Spicy Apple),
p. 414
French Apple Pie, p.
413
Fruit Two-Crust Pies,
p. 411

Individual Deep-Dish
Pies, p. 414
Prize Prune Pie, p. 413

Thrifty Meals

Thrifty homemaking doesn't just happen. It takes time and effort, planning and thinking ahead.

SAVE BY PLANNING

The less money you have, the more planning you'll have to do.

How much should you spend? There's no perfect pattern for everyone. This is just a guide: Spend one fourth of your food budget on milk and milk products (cheese, ice cream, etc.); one fourth on meat, fish, poultry, eggs; one fourth on fruits and vegetables; one eighth on breads and cereals; one eighth on sugar and fats, including butter and margarine.

Be forehanded. Plan ahead. Menus planned after you get to the grocer's are likely to cost more.

Buy family favorites. Plan meals your family will enjoy so they will eat every last bite.

And splurge on a steak or turkey occasionally. The family will co-operate better in economizing if they know it means more money for special treats.

Do a balancing act. If a treat makes costs mount one day, plan on thriftier foods the next.

Classify costs. Jot down food expenses under such headings as meat, poultry, fish, dairy products, staple groceries, fruits, and vegetables.

Don't account for every penny, but do keep track of what you spend.

Discover what causes high-expense months. Compare total monthly food expenditures.

Keep a menu book. It helps in planning future menus and food budgets.

Pep up your meals with new recipes. Check the list of recipes at the end of this chapter for delicious, thrifty desserts and ways to serve soups, meat, fish, shellfish, poultry, cheese, eggs, dried beans, and leftovers.

Time or money, which means more? If a manufacturer does the work, you must pay for it. If you aren't cramped for time, you can save a lot on some food products if you do all the preparation. With others, there's little saving. Check and see.

Serve biscuits, muffins, popovers, homemade rolls, coffeecake. Every family loves them! They dress up economy meals inexpensively.

Let the family have seconds. Don't overload plates; keep servings of average size and let the family ask for more. This eliminates wasting food, may prevent overeating.

Make a daily checkup of leftovers in the refrigerator. Use them as soon as possible.

Know the good-eating chart, p. 676. Using the less expensive foods in each group is a *safe* way to save.

SAVE BY SHOPPING WISELY

Be on the alert. Watch the daily papers for special sales on staples and other foods.

Put it in writing. Make out a written, classified marketing list.

Be flexible. Shop with a list, but don't hesitate to make changes if you run across special buys.

Be an early bird. Shop early for the best selection.

Shop around for the best buys—from store to store, or within the same store.

Shop and compare. Check the cost per serving of fresh, canned, and frozen foods. Prices vary, so you must do your own arithmetic.

How much is edible? Consider food waste in parings. For instance, market fresh green beans are about 93 per cent edible, unshelled green limas only about 45 per cent. Avoid wilt, decay, bruises, soft spots, and other imperfections. (But not all skin flaws mean poor quality.)

Some canned foods may cost less than others and be just as nutritious as the more expensive varieties. Use less-expensive canned fruits and vegetables in dishes like cream-of-corn soup, scalloped tomatoes, mixed vegetables, salads, casseroles, fruit gelatin, fruit cobblers, fruit tapioca, etc.

Canned tuna comes in several styles, differing in price but not in food value. So consider carefully how you plan to use tuna before choosing the style.

Frozen vegetables are often bargains. See p. 244.

Buy foods in the more economical large sizes, and plan to serve them a second or third time. For instance, leftover fruits can be used in salad, vegetables in mixed-vegetable dishes, salads, soups, etc.

But don't buy more food than you'll need. Check ingredient amounts in recipes you'll be using so you'll know exactly what to buy and how much. Replenish staples as needed, of course.

Have you lots of storage space? Buy staples that keep well, and that you use often, in as large a quantity as your storage space and pocketbook permit.

Read labels carefully. When you buy breads, flours, and cereals, be sure "enriched," "restored," or "whole-grain" is printed on the label. You'll get more B vitamins, minerals.

Out of sight, out of mind. If you buy enough for 2 meals, set half aside so you won't nibble. To make a package of frozen vegetables do for 2 days, cut it in two and keep half frozen solid until you're ready to use it.

Buy only graded, cartoned eggs kept under refrigeration in the store. Eggs deteriorate rapidly at room temperature. See What You Should Know About Eggs, p. 223.

Use grade B eggs in puddings, custards, and baking. They furnish just as much food value as grade A eggs. Brown eggs and white eggs are equally fine and nutritious.

Store wisely. At the beginning of several chapters in this book, we give details on best storing methods. Also check Marketing, p. 514.

Good Things To Know

Some foods have practically the same food value but differ in price. For example:

Fresh milk	Evaporated milk and nonfat dry milk
Sharp American cheese	Mild American cheese
Out-of-season fresh vegetables	Canned, frozen, or in-season fresh vegetables
Fresh tomatoes	Canned tomatoes
Calf liver	Beef or pork liver
Porterhouse steak	Chuck steak
Loin chops	Shoulder chops
White eggs	Brown eggs (in some areas)
Ready-to-eat cereal	Hot cereal
Butter	Margarine
Olive oil	Salad oil

These foods give about the same amount of calcium:

1 cup milk (whole, liquefied nonfat, or diluted evaporated)	2 servings ice cream (⅓-pt. servings)
	3 servings cottage cheese (½-cup servings)
1 serving cheese (1¼ oz.)	

These foods give about the same amount of high-quality protein:

½ cup cottage cheese	3 oz. American cheese
2¼ cups milk (whole, liquefied nonfat, or diluted evaporated)	3 oz. cooked lean meat, fish, or poultry
	3 medium eggs

SAVE BY COOKING PROPERLY

Make everything look and taste so good that everyone cleans his plate without urging. Use recipes in this book, and follow them to the letter. Serve food in pretty ways. (A gay garnish takes more imagination than money. See p. 296.)

Know your family's appetite. Take time to look up the amount to cook for your size family so there'll be enough food, with little or nothing left over. Or plan just how you are going to serve the remaining food.

You can afford gourmet touches. Canned tomatoes; onion; garlic; snipped parsley; celery; green peppers in season; herbs such as thyme, basil, orégano; shaker seasonings like monosodium glutamate, seasoned salt, etc. (p. 521) cost little, add much.

Don't cheat your family of flavor and food values by overcooking vegetables. Use vegetable cooking water (or liquids from canned vegetables) to:

1. Add to vegetable or cream soups.
2. Mix with tomato juice for drinking.
3. Serve as liquid in gravies, molded salads.

Be sparing when paring. Cook vegetables with skins on when possible. To pare potatoes, carrots,

apples, pears, etc., use a vegetable parer or sharp knife so you'll lose as little food value as possible.

Don't be ruthless in trimming such vegetables as asparagus, cauliflower, cabbage, lettuce, broccoli. Use outer stalks and leaves of celery in soups, mixed-vegetable dishes, casseroles, gravies, cream sauce, etc.

Make every bit count. Add bits of cooked fish, chicken, or meat, or pieces of cheese, to a tossed salad, casserole, or omelet.

Maybe it's not too old. You can use food that's past its freshest stage. Stale cake and cookies can be crumbled and served over ice cream, used in puddings, etc. A slice of soft bread put in a jar of dried-out cookies softens them.

A penny saved is a penny earned. Use fats from cooking meats or poultry. Chicken fat is grand for gravies; beef fat for browning onions, for casseroles or spaghetti sauce, etc.; ham or bacon fat for frying eggs, seasoning beans or cabbage, or flavoring soups or milk gravy, etc.

Make good use of your oven. See Casserole Dinners, p. 556.

Cook on one burner. All-in-one main dishes are thrifty. Use Dutch oven, deep covered skillet, etc. Or use a pressure cooker (see p. 194).

Thrifty Milk: Both evaporated and nonfat dry milk are important penny savers (just turn to p. 520 for the best use of each milk).

For drinking, try mixing whole milk and liquefied nonfat dry milk, half-and-half.

BREAKFAST FOODS

A good breakfast can save you money. If your family eat well in the morning, they will work better and feel better. Those who lunch away from home won't crave mid-morning snacks or expensive lunches. Our Good Breakfast Chart is on p. 674.

Choose enriched or whole-grain breads and cereals for their extra vitamins and iron.

When choosing cereals, remember, hot cereals such as oatmeal, enriched farina, and dark wheat cereal are somewhat less expensive than the ready-to-eat kind. However, the ready-to-eat cereals are still an inexpensive food and a wonderful timesaver.

Use milk on cereals instead of cream. It's a saving for sure—and has even higher food value.

THE MAIN DISH

Choose fish, cheese, or eggs as the meal's mainstay on occasion.

Quick-frozen fish is delicious, inexpensive eating the year round, as is fresh fish in season. See Fish, p. 168, Shellfish, p. 183.

Cheese-egg-and-milk dishes make inexpensive main dishes too—and they involve no waste.

Eggs rank high in high-quality protein, vitamin A, and iron. Although their price varies, the year-round average makes eggs a budgeter's delight. Try:

Surprise Soufflés, p. 213
Polenta with Tomato Sauce, p. 214
Toasted Cheese Casserole for 1, p. 216
Eggs Divan, p. 229
Western Curried Eggs, p. 231
Eggs Foo Young, p. 230

Serve main dishes made with such dried beans as navy, large lima, kidney, dried peas, lentils, etc. (But if the dish doesn't contain milk, cheese, eggs, fish, meat, or poultry, be sure to include one of these elsewhere in meal.) Try:

Dandy Bean Chowder, p. 42
Old-fashioned Split-Pea Soup, p. 40
Twelve-O'Clock Lentil-Sausages, p. 84
Baked-Bean Casserole, p. 257
Kidney-Lima Casserole, p. 257
Mother's Easy Chili Beans, p. 257

Know how to stretch meat, fish, and poultry. You are being penny-wise and pound-foolish if you stretch any of these dishes without adding cheese, eggs, or milk to insure ample protein. Try:

Baked Chicken Puff, p. 160
(1 cup poultry + ⅓ cup milk + 4 eggs + ⅓ cup cheese = 4 servings)

Ham-and-Noodle Casserole, p. 133
(2 cups ham + 1 cup milk + 1 cup cheese = 4 servings)
Topsy-Turvy Tuna-Lemon Pie, p. 180
(1 cup tuna + ¼ lb. sliced American cheese + 1 egg = 4 or 5 servings)

Or use cheese, eggs, or milk in soup, salad, or dessert. Or serve milk to drink.

Try at least one inexpensive cut of meat each week. Use for savory stews, hash, meat loaf, meat pies, and pot roast. Or try:

Barbecued Short Ribs, p. 61
Braised Oxtails, p. 117
Simmered Beef Heart, p. 113

If your meatman carries commercial and utility grades of meat, remember they are economical and just as nutritious as the more expensive grades.

Choose the best buys in poultry. There are good buys the year round. For instance, large tom turkeys usually sell for less per lb. than small turkeys. Or a stewing chicken takes longer to cook but provides luscious stews, chicken pies, fricassees, etc. (Your pressure cooker can make quick work of it.) Try:

Chicken Fricassee, p. 150
Chicken Chop Suey, p. 149
Different Chicken Curry, p. 148
Susan's Chicken Pie, p. 147

Variety meats are bargains. Liver, kidney, heart, and brains are as rich, or richer, in vitamins and minerals than other more expensive meats. And they are fine sources of high-quality protein. Lamb, beef, and pork liver are cheaper than calf liver. Try:

Lamb Kidneys Piquant, p. 117
Simmered Heart, p. 113 (nice in hash, meat pies, and casseroles)
Creole Beef Liver, p. 112
Columbus Casserole, p. 112

Buy big. The price per pound of a large piece of meat—half a ham, a large round-bone pot roast, or leg of lamb—is often less than that of a small piece or slice. Ask your meatman to cut up the meat; or try cutting it yourself. For instance, a leg of lamb can be cut into chops and a roast.

Serve old reliables new ways. Dishes made from canned luncheon meat or hamburger help keep costs low. (If ready-ground hamburger has lots of fat, it isn't the bargain you think it to be.) Try:

Superb Skillet Burger Loaf, p. 69
Creole-Stuffed Green Peppers, p. 71
Hamburger Upside-down Pie, p. 72
Barbara's Tamale Pie, p. 73

Or you may substitute ground luncheon meat for ground ham in many recipes.

VEGETABLES AND FRUITS

Shop for vegetables and fruits when they're in season.

Carrots are nearly always a food bargain; use them raw or cooked.

Use leafy tops of young beets and turnips. These, like kale, spinach, mustard greens, and collards, are cheap sources of vitamin A.

Know the best buys for vitamin C. Compare prices of fresh, frozen concentrated, and canned citrus juices—all are rich in vitamin C. Also consider canned tomatoes and tomato juice (but use twice as much tomato as orange or grapefruit juice for the same amount of vitamin C). Raw cabbage, turnips, and salad greens, as well as many fruits and berries, are also good sources of vitamin C.

Don't cut down on fruits and vegetables. Your family needs their vitamins, minerals, roughage.

DESSERTS

Dessert adds protein too. For instance, if you're serving cheese and crackers, cheese and fruit, milk to drink, rennet-custard dessert, or packaged pudding, you're serving protein that's as good for you as meat.

Eggs in dessert can also fill out a meal's protein. Try:

Bride's Chocolate Soufflé Cups, p. 384
Kitchenette Caramel Pudding, p. 382
Mousse au Chocolate, p. 390
Snow Custard, p. 394
Baked Marshmallow Custards, p. 395

Desserts aren't extravagant if they contribute important food values and lend a happy ending to a thrifty meal.

1. Try fruit—fresh, canned, and frozen. There are lots of ways to serve fruit on pp. 378 to 382.
2. Try ice cream—see pp. 424 to 436.
3. Try puddings, pies, cakes, and cookies using milk, egg, fruits, and enriched flour. See Index.

THRIFTY DISHES

We all know that food prices vary from month to month and place to place. However, in the lists that follow, we suggest some of the dishes in this book that will help make your food pennies go farther. Look through the book for others that will meet your budget.

Thrifty Meal-in-One Soups

Barnegat Chicken Chowder (for company), p. 42	p. 42 Dinner Chowder, p. 43	Lentil-Burger Soup, p. 41	Bones, p. 36 Susan's Fish Chowder, p. 43
Can-Opener Minestrone, p. 35	Frank-and-Vegetable Soup, p. 41	Old-country Borsch, p. 40	Tangy Chicken Special, p. 41
Corn Chowder, p. 43	Knife-and-Fork Vegetable Soup, p. 39	Old-fashioned Split-Pea Soup, p. 40	Tuna-Corn Chowder, p. 44
Dandy Bean Chowder,		Soup from Leftover	

Thrifty Cheese Dinner and Supper Dishes

Thrifty Beef Dishes

Thrifty Ready-cooked Meat Dishes

Thrifty Pork Dishes

(For thrifty ham dishes, see Thrifty Leftover Dishes, p. 567)

Bacon Chop Suey, p. 93
California Chop Suey, p. 78
Pig's Knuckles with Cabbage, p. 82
Pineapple-Style Baked Beans, p. 94
Rib-and-Bean Barbecue, p. 83
Simmered Smoked Shoulder Butt, p. 89
Spicy Meat Balls en Brochette, p. 77
Sunday Supper
Casserole, p. 84
Sweet-Sour Pork, p. 77
Twelve-O'Clock Lentil Sausages, p. 84

Thrifty Lamb and Veal Dishes

LAMB
Barbecued Breast of Lamb, p. 102
Braised Lamb Shanks de Luxe, p. 102
Individual Lamb Shank Roasts, p. 101
Lamb Stew, p. 98
Lamb Suey, p. 98
Pot Roast of Lamb Shoulder, p. 98
Spanish Lamb-Chop Casserole, p. 101
Yorkshire Hot Pot, p. 101

VEAL
Cold Stuffed Veal-Roll Slices, p. 110
Pot Roast of Veal, p. 104
Sherry Veal Slices (omit sherry and increase lemon to 1 tablesp.), p. 107
Veal Casserole Chow Mein (for a party), p. 110

Delicious Thrifty Variety-Meat Dishes

Beef Kidney Stew, p. 117
Braised Oxtails, p. 117
Braised Pork Liver, p. 112
Braised Stuffed Veal or Lamb Heart,
p. 113
Broiled Kidneys on Toast, p. 116
Columbus Casserole, p. 112
Cooked Tongue, p. 115
Creole Beef Liver,
p. 112
Kidneys en Brochette, p. 117
Lamb Kidneys Piquant, p. 117
Mac's Sautéed Kidneys, p. 116
Oxtail Ragout, p. 118
Sautéed Tripe, p. 116
Simmered Heart (nice in hash, meat pie, casserole), p. 113
Tasty Baked Beef Liver, p. 112

Thrifty Canned Meat Dishes

Celery-Style Corned Beef, p. 125
Chili con Corn, p. 126
Clove Midget, p. 125
Corned-Beef-Hash Puffs, p. 126
Creamed Dried Beef,
p. 127
Deviled Hash, p. 126
Dried Beef Soufflé, p. 127
Dutch Pantry Pie, p. 125
Frizzled Dried Beef, p. 127
Hash Cheeseburgers, p. 126
Hash-Stuffed Tomatoes, p. 126
If It's Canned Luncheon Meat, p. 125
Peach Dinner Loaf, p. 125
Skillet-Boiled Dinner, p. 126
Spicy Baked Luncheon Loaf, p. 125
To Serve (lots of ideas), p. 124

Thrifty Fish and Shellfish Dishes

Baked Salmon Loaf, p. 181
Baked Stuffed Fillets or Steaks, p. 169
Broiled Fillets à la Florentine, p. 174
Clam Burgers, p. 184
Crab-Corn Bake (for
company), p. 185
'Frisco Tuna, p. 179
Golden Scallops, p. 191
Luncheon Clambake, p. 184
Quick-Curried Tuna, p. 179
Sardine-Sandwich
Bake, p. 180
Scallop Broil, p. 191
Scallop Curry, p. 193
Scallop Sauté, p. 191
Superb Fish Scallop, p. 178
Top-Hat Salmon Pie, p. 180
Topsy-Turvy Tuna-Lemon Pie, p. 180
Tuna Supper Casserole, p. 178
Tuna Tomatoes, p. 179

Thrifty Last-of-the-Meat Dishes

Thrifty Poultry Dishes

Thrifty Pressure-Cooker Dinner Dishes

Thrifty Bean, Macaroni, and Rice Main Dishes

Thrifty Egg Dishes for Lunch and Dinner

Deviled-Egg Casserole, p. 231

Dinner Casserole de Luxe, p. 230

Egg-and-Cheese Flapjacks, p. 229

Eggs Divan, p. 229

Eggs Foo Young, p. 230

French Omelet, p. 226 or Puffy Omelet, p. 227 (with cheese, jelly, herbs)

Individual Egg-and-Cheese Casseroles, p. 228

Individual Omelets, p. 227

Lee's Spanish Chili with Eggs, p. 230

Man-Style Baked Eggs, p. 228

New Zealand-Style Eggs, p. 231

Picture-Frame Eggs, p. 229

Shortcake Omelet

(with dried beef), p. 232

Susan's Baked Eggs in Cheese Sauce, p. 231

The Best Creamed Eggs, p. 228

Western Curried Eggs, p. 231

Thrifty Desserts in No Time

Apple Snow, p. 381

Coconut Fingers, p. 381

French-Toasted Slices, p. 381

Ginger Cheese Snaps, p. 382

Hot Apricots, p. 379

Instant Cream Puddings, p. 382

Jiffy Cottage Pudding, p. 400

Just Fruit Desserts (use fresh fruit in season), p. 380

Marmalade Peaches,

p. 379

No-Bake Custards, p. 382

Peach Crumb Dessert (no cream), p. 381

Peanut Marlows, p. 382

Quick Fruit Top-Offs

(use fresh fruit in season), p. 378

Ten Fruit-Cup Desserts (use fresh fruit in season), p. 380

Thrifty Desserts to Do Along with Dinner

Ambrosia, p. 383

Apple Brown Betty, p. 388

Apple Dumplings, p. 386

Baked Applesauce, p. 389

Baked Lemon-Cake Pudding, p. 390

Serve with milk

Bride's Chocolate Soufflé Cups, p. 384

Broiled Grapefruit, p. 389

Camille's Peach Coconut, p. 388

Chilled Grapefruit (13 ways), p. 389

Dutch Plum Cake, p.

387

Fruitful Cobbler, p. 389

Gingerbread Top-Offs (8 of them), p. 384

Hurry-up Apple "Pie," p. 385

Kitchenette Caramel Pudding*, p. 382

Old-fashioned Peach Dumplings, p. 386

Pear-Butterscotch Crisp*, p. 390

Quick Apple Crisp*, p. 388

Thrifty Desserts to Do Ahead

Baked Apples, p. 400

Baked Banana Dessert, p. 401

Buttery Baked Peaches or Pears, p. 401

Creamy Baked Rice Pudding, p. 392

Danish Cream, p. 393

De Luxe Rennet Custard (use all milk), p. 393

Fruited Jelly, p. 402

Fruit Float, p. 392

Ice-Cream-Mix Tricks, p. 433

Red-and-White Sundaes, p. 403

Rhubarb Sauce, p. 402

Rosy Pear Sauce, p. 401

Saucepan Applesauce, p. 400

Spanish Cream, p. 405

Stewed Peaches, p. 401

Stewed Plums or

Fresh Prunes, p. 401

Susan's Baked Custard, p. 394

Susan's Cream Puffs (use packaged pudding mix for filling), p. 395

Susan's Custard Bread Pudding, p. 391

Susan's Rice Custard, p. 391

Susan's Snow-

Pudding Balls, p. 404

Tangerine Delight, p. 401

Tapioca Cream, p. 392

Top-of-Range "Baked" Apples, p. 401

Today's Blancmange (many ideas), p. 393

Quick- and-Easy Meals

There are days in every woman's schedule when the time available for preparing dinner is limited. But that doesn't mean dinner can't be a triumph. Here are suggestions for making preparations in advance and for quick cooking.

MAKE YOURS A SPEEDY KITCHEN

Just as efficiency experts study factories and offices to discover the best ways to handle time and material, you should study your kitchen and your cooking habits.

Take stock of the tools you work with. If they're easy to get at, they can speed your chores. Also read Your Kitchen, p. 691.

Knives: Keep them razor-sharp. Dull knives waste precious time and energy.

Scissors: Have them handy. They're perfect for mincing, dicing, cubing, snipping.

Vegetable Parer: It quickly pares fruits and vegetables paper-thin.

Tool Rack: It keeps knives, forks, spoons, ladles, spatulas, and turners neat, convenient, right at hand.

Minute Timer: It times the cooking, frees you to think of something else.

Modern Pots and Pans: Their tight lids, and bottoms that sit flat on any range, improve your cooking, save fuel and time.

Pressure Cooker: This wonderful cooker cuts cooking time and makes possible quick-and-easy meats, vegetables, and main dishes you couldn't otherwise enjoy. But don't overcook foods.

Electric Mixer: Whether it's full-sized or portable, it makes quick, easy work of beating eggs, mashing potatoes, mixing cakes, etc.

Automatic Coffee Maker: You put coffee and water into the coffee maker; then you plug it into the nearest electric outlet. Coffee brews automatically just the right length of time, then stays hot as long as you wish.

Electric Blender: Makes speedy work of soups, sauces, salad dressings, popovers, etc.

Electric Skillet: It's wonderful. See p. 696.

Freezer. With a freezer, you can shop less often, use more frozen foods. You can freeze leftovers to use later. You can do more cooking ahead too.

PLAN SHORT CUTS

As a starter, read the items and chapters listed below.

Choose two-act dishes like stew; serve it as stew the first day, as meat pie the second.

Plan all-broiled, all-baked, or all-pressure-cooked main courses. They're easy, save time.

Choose dishes that can be made early in the day or night before, or readied in advance.

Serve more of one food so you can cut down on the number of dishes to cook.

Make Saturday's or Sunday's meal an occasion, with all the frills; but eliminate frills Monday through Friday.

On Saturday, cook and bake for the next week.

LOOK FOR SHORT-CUT BUYS

For easy list making, keep pad and pencil in a handy kitchen spot; jot down what you need as you use it up. Review Save by Shopping Wisely, p. 560, and Marketing, p. 514, before you go to market. Here are some of the quick-to-fix foods that make sure-to-please dinners.

If There's to Be a First Course:
1. Canned soups. Vary as on p. 33. Or use frozen soups or packaged soup mixes.
2. Canned and frozen fruits and fruit juices
3. Canned tomato or vegetable juice

For the Main Course:
1. Canned meats—corned beef, corned-beef hash, luncheon meats, etc. They're ready to serve, or to heat and serve. See p. 123.
2. Frozen meats—pan-ready hamburger patties, pork chops, veal cutlets, sliced liver, etc. Look for trusted brands.
3. Frozen meat pies and chicken pies. They just need heating and eating.
4. Ready-cooked meats—franks, ham, sausages, Canadian-style bacon, bologna, tongue, etc. See Meats, p. 46, for delightfully quick-and-easy ways to use them.
5. Fresh meats—hamburgers, sliced liver, veal cutlet, ham slices, kidneys, chops, etc.
6. Fish and shellfish—canned tuna, sardines,

salmon, etc.; frozen fish fillets, fish sticks, etc.; shrimp, oysters, scallops.
7. Chicken and turkey. Buy them fresh or frozen, completely cleaned, all ready to sauté, broil, oven-fry, etc. Or buy chicken and turkey parts by the piece. Or choose canned or frozen cooked chicken, p. 136, or turkey products, p. 152.
8. Cheese. Use packaged slices to save slicing. Use pasteurized process-cheese spread in jars to save making cheese sauce.
9. Canned or frozen chow mein, chop suey, etc. See Chinese foods, p. 514.
10. Spaghetti or macaroni dinners, packaged or canned; pizza mix.
11. Eggs. Scrambled, in omelets, etc. See p. 223.

For Vegetables
1. Fresh vegetables. Sliced or diced, they take less time to cook than those that are whole.

    Shredded cabbage, corn on the cob, sliced summer squash, tomatoes, slivered green beans, okra, all greens, and zucchini are especially quick cooking.

    All fresh vegetables are quick, easy, and tasty cooked in a pressure cooker, p. 195.
2. Canned vegetables. They're more delicious than ever. Just heat and season. See Serve With a Flair, p. 247.
3. Frozen vegetables. They're all ready to cook and take half as much time as fresh vegetables.
4. Packaged precooked rice. It's ready to eat in minutes, needs no watching as it cooks.
5. Canned cooked rice or Spanish rice. Just heat it.
6. Potatoes. Fine cooked sweets or tiny white potatoes come in cans; mashed white ones come frozen or in instant form. Or use frozen French fries, canned shoestring potatoes, etc.
7. Canned stewed tomatoes. They're all seasoned.

For Salads and Relishes
1. Fruit-flavored gelatin. It makes short work of molded fruit salads.
2. Canned tomato aspic. Jells without refrigeration. See p. 315.

3. Ready-to-use salad dressings—several flavors
4. Cranberry sauce. See No-Cook Cranberry Relishes, p. 288, for delightful variations.
5. Relishes. See Quickest-of-All Relishes, p. 292.

For Seasonings, Sauces, Additions:
1. Onion salt, garlic salt, etc. These eliminate the need to mince onion or garlic.
2. Bouillon cubes, canned bouillon. Use to step up meat flavor; or use in In-a-Pinch Gravy, p. 52.
3. Parsley, onion, or mint flakes
4. Canned beef gravy. It's all ready to heat.
5. Canned tomato sauce. It comes already seasoned; or vary it with your own seasonings.
6. Pasteurized process-cheese spread (cheese sauce) in jars. Spoon out, spread, or pour.
7. Canned cream-of-mushroom, cream-of-chicken, tomato soup, etc. make fine, quick sauces. See Extra-Easy Main-Course Sauces, p. 372.
8. Canned mushrooms. They come broiled or plain: whole, sliced, chopped, etc.
9. Nuts—shelled, blanched, chopped. See p. 521.
10. Preserved fruits. They're diced, ready to add.

For Hot Breads, Crackers, etc.:
1. Superb mixes. Take your pick:

Biscuits	Pancakes
Hot rolls	Popovers
Muffins—plain, corn, date, etc.	Waffles, etc.

2. Frozen waffles. Just heat in toaster.
3. Refrigerated pan-ready biscuits. Make them your own, as on p. 325.
4. Canned breads. They're good warm or cold.
5. Bakers' breads, rolls, muffins, brown-and-serves, etc. They needn't be humdrum; see Bread and Rolls You Buy, p. 340.
6. Packaged crackers of all kinds

For Desserts:
1. Wonderful mixes. Take your pick:

Brownies	Ice cream
Cakes	Piecrust
Cookies	Pie fillings
Cupcakes	Puddings—instant
Frostings	or regular,
Fruit-flavored gelatin	tapioca, etc.
Fudge and penuche	Rennet desserts
Gingerbread	Sherbets

2. Bakers' cakes, pies, cream puffs, etc.
3. Cookies—many kinds. They come packaged.
4. Cheese. Buy individual portions, slices.
5. Fruits—fresh, frozen, or canned. All are delicious timesavers. Extra-tender dried fruits cook quickly, are good as is too.
6. Ice creams and sherbets. For glamorous ways to serve them, see When You Buy Ice Cream, p. 424.

For Beverages:
1. Instant coffee, cocoa, tea. They can be made up, hot or cold, in a jiffy.
2. Frozen or canned lemonade, limeade, fruit juices. See Off-the-Shelf Coolers, p. 498.

For the Baby: From breakfast juice to dinner's dessert, baby's foods are ready to use, packed to save Mother time and energy.

SHORT-CUT COOKING

Plan trips to the refrigerator so you can take all the things you'll need out at one time.

Keep a can of your favorite fruit in refrigerator. It will be cold and ready any time.

Grate a large piece of cheese. Refrigerate it, ready to top or add to casseroles, creamed dishes, etc.

If you use buttered bread crumbs often, keep a batch on hand, ready to use, in the refrigerator.

Or instead of buttered bread crumbs, try corn flakes or crisp rice cereal, tossed with melted butter or grated cheese. Nice, quick for casseroles, etc.

Hasten the chilling or setting of sauces, puddings, gelatin desserts, salads, etc., by storing them in an empty ice-cube tray in the freezing compartment a few minutes. Just watch and stir the mixture occasionally; remove when just right.

Mince an extra amount of onions or green peppers; then wrap and freeze for future use.

If a recipe calls for both rind and juice, grate rind first; then squeeze juice.

Stick the garlic clove on a toothpick before dropping it into a mixture. Then you'll find it easily when you want to remove it.

Chop hard-cooked eggs with a pastry blender. It's quick.

Meat

Serve roasts on the weekend. Then you can use leftovers at several weekday meals. (See Let's Have the Last of the Meat, p. 127.)

If canned corned-beef hash is a favorite in your household, keep a can on hand in the refrigerator. To open it, remove both ends from can; push hash out about 1", and cut off a slice. Repeat, cutting off the number of slices needed; refrigerate the rest.

If you're planning to serve hamburger as patties, see To Use Within a Week, p. 64, for a time-saving way to store it.

If dinner calls for meat loaf, bake it in muffin-pan cups as on p. 68. It's quicker.

Deviled ham comes in large and small cans. Keep both on hand, so you won't have to open 2 small cans when 1 large one is just right.

Vegetables

Tightly packed frozen vegetables, such as spinach, chopped broccoli, etc., will cook faster if block is first cut into chunks.

When only 2 servings of a frozen vegetable are needed, use part of package one night (divide block with ice pick if necessary); return what's left, wrapped, to freezer. Use part of another frozen vegetable the next night. Combine the two leftovers for third dinner.

Frozen or canned mixed vegetables make time-saving additions for stews, casseroles, etc.

Scalloped vegetables, etc., will bake in less time if they're arranged in one layer in a 9" or 10" pie plate rather than a deep casserole.

You can season a vegetable quickly, without making a special sauce, by adding a little chili sauce, prepared mustard, Worcestershire, soy sauce, sour cream, canned tomato sauce, or cream-of-mushroom soup.

Try Our Best-Ever Quick-Cooked Asparagus, p. 250, and Chinese Cauliflower, p. 254. They're speedy and superb.

An egg slicer makes quick work of slicing cooked or canned beets.

To cut up celery stalks quickly, hold several together on board; then slice crosswise on a slant, using very sharp knife.

Canned small boiled onions make fine creamed onions in no time. Or they can be rolled in melted butter, seasoned with salt, then sautéed or broiled until golden.

If potatoes are a dinner must, cook a quantity at one time—enough for 2 or 3 days; then promptly refrigerate them. They can reappear fried, creamed, hash-browned, scalloped with cheese, etc.

Canned tiny white potatoes are nice brought to a boil in water to cover, then drained and mashed. Or bring to a boil; drain; roll in melted butter; then brown under broiler. Or slice thin; fry or hash-brown in skillet.

Heat canned shoestring potatoes in butter or margarine in skillet, adding a little cream, then chili sauce if desired.

Use canned sweet potatoes. Glaze, mash, or broil.

Skin tomatoes quickly by first holding them on a fork over flame until skin cracks.

Salads and Salad Dressings

Wash and store salad greens in refrigerator, so they're ready to break into bite-size pieces.

Keep a can of tuna, sardines, tiny white potatoes, or luncheon meat on hand in refrigerator, so it will be already chilled for salad.

See Quick and Easy Dressings, p. 317.

Sauces

Canned tomato sauce is a must for many dishes. Or you can use canned tomato soup diluted with ½ can water and seasoned with minced onion, curry, etc.

For speedy gravies, sauces, etc., blend equal parts of butter or margarine and flour. Refrigerate. Stir 3 tablesp. of this paste into each 1 cup hot mixture you wish to thicken; cook until thickened.

Stir a few tablespoonfuls of sour cream into melted butter or margarine; add seasoned salt, lemon juice. Fine on vegetables.

Canned onion soup or onion-soup mix, thickened a little, makes a speedy sauce for hamburgers, cube steaks, etc.

Use canned beef gravy as base for onion or mushroom gravy.

Freeze or refrigerate a supply of barbecue sauce.

Breads

Wrap party rye bread in aluminum foil; heat at 375°F. about 10 min.

For the crowd, toast split English or corn muffins, bread slices, or chunks of French bread under broiler—you can do a lot at one time.

Don't roll and cut out biscuits. Make dropped ones instead. Sprinkle with grated cheese.

Desserts

Instead of whipped cream, use slightly soft ice cream or sour cream. There's no whipping involved, no egg beater to wash.

Make and refrigerate enough speedy custard sauce, p. 368, to last several days. Luscious on fruit, cake, jellied fruit, etc.

For wonderful speedy cupcakes, use cake mix. You can mix and bake them in about 35 min.

Bake 2 cake layers with cake mix. Freeze one; top the other with ice cream or hot sauce.

For freshly baked cookies on short order, use cookie or brownie mix. Or keep a roll of refrigerator-cookie dough in refrigerator, ready to slice and bake.

As ice-cream topping, keep in refrigerator buffet-size can or package of frozen fruit or berries. One can or package is just enough for 4.

For extra-quick pie or cake fillings, use today's pudding mixes.

Unbaked crusts save time in making chiffon, cream, and ice-cream pies. See p. 410.

For shortcakes and cobblers, let biscuit mix give you a head start.

SHORT CUTS TO SAVE CLEANING

Use pie tape on fruit pies—and you'll have less oven cleaning.

Line muffin and cupcake cups with paper baking cups. Makes dishwashing easier.

Line broiler pan with aluminum foil. Never leave pan in oven after broiling's done; heat cooks fat onto pan more than ever. Rather, before you sit down to dinner, pour off hot fat; wipe out pan and rack well with paper towel; then sprinkle with detergent, and fill with warm water. Steel wool soap pads remove stubborn grease.

Use paper napkins and paper or plastic mats and tablecloths; serve on paper plates. Their quality today makes them socially acceptable for many meals.

Make it a habit to wipe up immediately anything spilled on work surfaces, floor etc.

Wash up cooking utensils as you go along. If you can't wash all pots and pans before dinner, let them soak—in cool water if eggs, starch, or milk have cooked in them, otherwise in hot water. Fill above cooking line.

Pare vegetables and fruit onto a newspaper or paper towel.

Sift flour onto a piece of waxed paper instead of into a bowl.

A dish drainer allows you to rinse a whole batch of dishes at one time instead of piece by piece. Plates and glasses dry by themselves.

DISHES FOR QUICK-AND-EASY MEALS

You'll find quick-and-easy menus in Planning Meals, p. 662; When Company Comes, p. 601; Cooking for One, p. 625; Cooking for Two, p. 631; and Chafing-Dish Cookery, p. 621.

When you're planning your own speedy meals, check through the lists below. They contain some of the dishes in this book that can be made quickly and easily. Most of them can be served on short notice. Others, such as some of the candies, ice-cream desserts, etc., can be made ahead when you've got some spare minutes so they'll be ready later when needed. You'll find lots more quick-and-easy ideas throughout the book.

If You Have a First Course

Cocktails

Cocktails (fruit, fruit juice, tomato juice, sea-food begin-

nings), pp. 17 to 21

Nibblers

Off-the-Shelf Nibblers,

p. 30
Short-Order Nibblers
—Cold, p. 27
Short-Order Nibblers
—Hot, p. 30

Soup

With a Can of Soup,
p. 33
Packaged Soup Mixes,
p. 36

Meal-in-a-Dish Soups

Can-Opener Minestrone, p. 35
Clam Chowder à la
Henry, p. 45
Corn Chowder, p. 43
Dandy Bean
Chowder, p. 42

Dinner Chowder,
p. 43
Oyster Stew, p. 42
Pacific-Coast Clam
Chowder, p. 44
Pantry-Shelf Pea
Soup, p. 35

Shrimp Chowder,
p. 43
Speedy New England
Clam Chowder,
p. 44
Susan's Fish Chowder,
p. 43

Tomato-Cheese Soup,
p. 35
Tomato-Crab Bisque,
p. 35
Tuna-Corn Chowder,
p. 44

Meats

None of the meat dishes listed here requires more than about 1 hr. preparation; many take even less time. A few require advance preparation; they can be finished quickly.

Beef

Bacon-Dill Loaf,
p. 68
Barbecued Hamburgers, p. 66
Beef-and-Eggplant
Casserole, p. 72

Beef-and-Rice Casserole, p. 71
Beef-Bacon Slices,
p. 74
Big Burger, p. 66
Broiled Steak, p. 54
Burgundy Meat Balls,
p. 66

Cheeseburger Loaf,
p. 68
Cube Steaks with
Hasty-Tasty Sauce,
p. 55
E. I.'s Swedish Meat
Balls, p. 67
Hamburger Czarina,

p. 70
Hamburger Go-
Betweens, p. 65
Hamburger Italian,
p. 121
Hamburger on Crisp
Eggplant Slices,
p. 70

Vegetables

Cheese Dishes

Eggs for Lunch or Dinner

Sandwiches—Lunch and Supper Hearties

Rice and Macaroni Dishes

Salads and Salad Dressings

Relishes, Jellies, and Jams

Breads

Beverages

Desserts

Ice Cream

See Ways to Serve Ice Cream You Buy, pp. 424 to 430. Don't miss any of the superb suggestions for sundaes, parfaits, shortcakes, snowballs, flaming desserts, etc., in these pages.

Pies and Piecrusts

Cakes, Fillings, and Frostings

Cookies

Box Lunches

The same food for lunch day after day will make anyone's appetite lag, particularly if he must take his lunch with him to school or work. Here's how to keep him always eager.

WHEN YOU PLAN

Plan ahead—not just for tomorrow but for several days if you can.

Think first of what your lunch toter should have and would like to find in his lunch box, bag, or brief case.

For the sake of his good health, see that each lunch box includes:

1. *Meat, eggs, poultry, cheese, or fish* in sandwiches, salad, or main dish.
2. *Vegetables*—at least one—in sandwiches, salad, or main dish, or as raw relish.
3. *Fruit*—at least one—raw, cooked, frozen, or canned, as is or in salad or dessert.
4. *Breads*—varied from day to day.
5. *Milk*—to fill out the day's quota—as is, as a milk drink, in soup or dessert, etc. To pack in extra nourishment, add a beaten egg or tablespoon of nonfat dry milk or molasses to a milk drink.

Keep a list of box-lunch menus so you can rotate them. Let ours on p. 582 start you off.

Stock up on paper napkins, waxed paper, aluminum foil, saran, sandwich bags, paper or plastic containers, spoons, forks, etc.

Maybe a new bag or lunch box would boost the luncher's morale. Today's jaunty bags—big enough to hold both books and lunch—also boast a vacuum bottle in a hideaway compartment.

Buy one of the new widemouthed and/or regular vacuum bottles. They make it safe to pack soups, salads, baked beans, beverages, etc.

Keep the box lunch in mind when planning dinner the night before. Oftentimes you can prepare enough soup, main dish, bread, or dessert to take care of tomorrow's lunch.

Speed lunch-box packing by doing all you can while cleaning up dinner the night before.

1. Unpack, wash, and scald lunch box and vacuum bottle. Dry thoroughly. Let lunch box air.
2. Wash and refrigerate raw vegetables, salad greens, and fruits.
3. Make up, wrap, and refrigerate or freeze sandwiches the night before. Then pack into lunch box the last possible moment—especially if lunch box cannot be refrigerated.
4. Plan servings as generous as those at home.

WHEN YOU PACK

A Hot Main Dish, Soup, or Beverage: If your box-lunch menu includes a savory stew, chili con carne, chowder, soup, hot drink, or the like, you'll need a widemouthed *and* regular vacuum bottle to carry these *safely* and *hot*.

Fill the vacuum bottle at the last possible

moment. First, let very hot water stand in it a few moments. Then be sure the food or beverage going into it is piping hot too.

P.S. When using canned soups, dilute them with milk instead of water—a nice way to work in some of the day's milk quota.

Bread-and-Butter Sandwiches: Whether they're made from bakers', homemade, or canned bread, bread-and-butter sandwiches always carry well in a lunch box even without refrigeration. The variety is fascinating, includes nut or fruit breads, muffins, rolls, buns, etc. Turn to Sandwich Breads and Crackers, p. 356; Quick Breads, p. 323; and Yeast Breads, p. 339.

Old Reliables: Lunch-box sandwiches made with one or more of the fillings below will keep well even when the lunch can't be refrigerated. Our sandwich chapter gives ways to vary these fillings.

Any cheese spread	Marmalade, apple
Any packaged proc-	butter, jelly, or
ess or natural	jam
cheese	Nuts
Applesauce	Peanut butter
Celery	Pickled tongue
Cream cheese	Thuringer-type dry
Green pepper, car-	sausage
rots, or raisins	

Salad-Type Sandwiches: Sandwiches with salad-type fillings of meat, chicken, fish, egg, etc., should be handled carefully. Include them only when the lunch box can be kept refrigerated. Never let them stand in a lunch box at room temperature longer than 4 hr. before eating.

Such sandwiches are likely to keep better too if they're made from canned meats, fish, chicken, or spreads, or ready-cooked meats, rather than leftovers. Adding chopped olives, lemon juice, catchup, or pickle relish helps too.

Sliced-Meat Sandwiches: Sliced chicken, turkey, or meat sandwiches are a treat. But to be safest and at their best, they should be handled like Salad-Type Sandwiches, above. Mix olives, lemon juice, etc. with the butter or margarine before it's spread on the bread.

Wrap sliced tomatoes and lettuce separately, to add to sandwiches just before eating.

Frozen Sandwiches: Any of the spreads and sandwiches on p. 541 keep well for a couple of weeks. You can pack them into the lunch box frozen, and they will help keep other foods in the box cool, crisp, and fresh.

Egg, Potato, Chicken, Meat, or Fish Salads: These salads are best carried in a widemouthed vacuum bottle. Use only fresh salad ingredients and keep them, as well as the empty vacuum bottle, in refrigerator until needed.

Before filling bottle, let ice cubes or ice water stand in it a while.

If you must use the vacuum bottle for some other food, pack the salad in a covered container. But be sure that the salad is eaten within 4 hr. or that the lunch box will be refrigerated up until lunchtime.

Crisp Vegetable or Fruit Salads: If refrigerated right up until they're packed, these salads keep well in a covered container even if the lunch box cannot be refrigerated. They will be crisper if the salad dressing is carried separately in a small, tightly capped bottle.

Crisp Raw Relishes: Crunchy tuck-ins such as raw carrot or celery sticks, green onions, radishes, cauliflowerets, etc., if thoroughly chilled, carry well even without refrigeration. Wrap them in moisture-vapor-proof paper.

Milk, Lemonade, Fruit Juices, Iced Coffee, etc.: Chill these well; then carry in vacuum bottle.

Fresh, Canned, or Cooked Dried Fruit: These top-offs carry well without refrigeration.

Cakes and Cupcakes: Choose any except custard- and whipped-cream-cakes (these must be kept refrigerated). Wrap each portion well.

Fruit Pies, Deep-Dish Pies, and Turnovers: Any of these are good packers. Never include cream or gelatine pies—they must be refrigerated.

Puddings and Gelatine Desserts: Of course these must go into a widemouthed vacuum bottle.

Make sure both bottle and dessert are refrigerator-cold before packing.

Cookies: They'll travel safely anywhere.

Ice-Cold Fruit, Tomato, or Vegetable Juice (some even come in individual cans): Tuck an unopened can, well wrapped, into lunch box at last minute. It helps keep lunch colder.

Surprise Tuck-Ins: Now and then surprise the luncher with one of these, carefully wrapped:

Cheese-stuffed celery	Potato or corn chips or pretzels
Cracked nuts	Ripe olives
Cutout cookies to suit the season	Salted nuts
Dried apricots, figs, or raisins	Semisweet chocolate Small chunk of fresh coconut
Marshmallows	Small molasses-popcorn ball
Peanut-buttered graham crackers	Stuffed dates, prunes, or nuts
Pineapple chunks on wooden picks	

TWELVE LUNCHES THAT GO PLACES
(to school or to business)

Split-Pea Soup (in vacuum bottle)
Crisp Crackers
Smoked-Tongue Sandwiches
Cabbage Wedge to Dunk in French Dressing
Whole Orange   Brownies

———

Two-Tone Sandwiches (white and rye bread)
Cubes of Susan's Meat Loaf, p. 68
on Wooden Picks (in vacuum bottle)
Celery   Pickles
No-Bake Cookie Balls, p. 480

———

Fried-Egg-and-Thin-Onion Sandwiches
Peas-Cheese-and-Chopped-Pickle Salad
(in vacuum bottle)
Buttered Hard Rolls
Individual Deep-Dish Plum Pie

———

Cream-of-Chicken Soup (in vacuum bottle)
Egg-Salad Sandwiches
Whole Tomato   Seasoned Salt
Grapefruit Salad   Cracked Walnuts

———

Hot Tomato Cocktail, p. 19 (in vacuum bottle)
Sandwiches of Bologna Slices Spread with
Chive Cottage Cheese
Bread-and-Butter Sandwiches
Jim's Applesauce Cake, p. 443
Tangerine

———

Sandwiches of Nut Bread, Cream Cheese, and
Dates
Nut-Bread-and-Butter Sandwiches
Deviled Egg Rolled in Lettuce Leaf
Orange Sections to Dunk in Cinnamon Sugar
Cocoa (in vacuum bottle)

———

Pumpernickel-and-Butter Sandwiches
Dried-Beef Rolls Filled with
Seasoned Cream Cheese
Raw Cauliflowerets   Salt
Buttery Baked Pears, p. 401
or Canned Pears
Crisp Cookies   Milk (in vacuum bottle)

———

Tuna-and-Vegetable Salad
(in vacuum bottle)
Brown-Bread-and-Butter Sandwiches
Apple-Pie Wedge   Cubes of Cheese

———

Cheese Sandwiches on Rye
(grated cheese, chili sauce, and deviled ham)
Lettuce Rolls Filled with Potato Salad
(in vacuum bottle)
Raisin-Stuffed Baked Apple
Sweet Roll or Cookies

———

Breadless Sandwiches with Pickle
(meat-loaf slices with potato-salad filling)
Bread-Butter-and-Onion Sandwiches
Pineapple Chunks Strung on Toothpicks
Sugared Doughnut   Milk (in vacuum bottle)

———

Sandwiches of Chopped Egg, Olives, and
Grated Carrot
Cubes of Cheese on Colored Wooden Picks
Buttered Gingerbread Slices, Sandwich Style
Paper Cup of Applesauce
Milk (in vacuum bottle)

———

Hot Tomato Juice (in vacuum bottle)
Diced-Cheese-and-Vegetable Salad
Corned-Beef Sandwich (use canned meat)
Bunch of Grapes   Ginger Cookies

DISHES FOR BOX LUNCHES

In the lists of recipes below, you'll find many ideas for deliciously varied pack-and-tote lunches. There are lots more ideas throughout the book. Be sure to refrigerate all perishables up to packing time. Follow to the letter the rules in When You Pack, p. 580.

Sandwich-Filling Specials

Pack-and-Carry Sandwiches, p. 362
Baked Canadian-Style Bacon, p. 93

Canned Meats, p. 123
Old-fashioned Ham Loaf, p. 91
Ready-Cooked Meats,

p. 118
Simmered Smoked Shoulder Butt, p. 89

Susan's Meat Loaf, p. 68
Two-Day Caramel Ham Loaf, p. 92

Soups That Make a Meal

Can-Opener Minestrone, p. 35
Corn Chowder, p. 43
Creamy Potato Soup, p. 34
Pacific-Coast Clam

Chowder, p. 44
Pantry-Shelf Pea Soup, p. 35
Speedy New England Clam Chowder, p. 44

Tomato-Crab Bisque, p. 35
Tuna-Corn Chowder, p. 44
Turkey-Corn Chowder, p. 43

With a Can of Soup, Thick and Hearty, p. 34

Salad Hearties

Chicken-Curry Salad, p. 306
"Chilly" con Carne Salad, p. 308
Chunky Egg Salad, p. 307

Cottage-Cheese Salad, p. 307
Crunchy Tuna Salad, p. 309
Curried Vegetable Salad, p. 304

Fruit-Salad Plates, p. 309
Old-fashioned Potato Salad, p. 304
Our Best Chicken Salad, p. 305

Shrimp Salad, p. 308
Shrimp Salad New Orleans, p. 308
Stuffed Tomatoes, p. 303

Other Hearties

Brown-and-Serve Pork Sausage, p. 84
Chicken: Skillet-Fried, p. 139; Sautéed, p.

138; Broiled, p. 139
Roast, p. 143
Chili con Carne (wrap crackers separately),

p. 70
Old-fashioned Boston Baked Beans, p. 256
Quick-Curried Tuna

(omit toast), p. 179
Spareribs, Swedish Style, p. 83

Salads to Accompany Sandwich or Soup

Coleslaw Quartet, p. 303
Dunk-It Salads, p. 303
Floating Island, p. 302
Frosty Half-and-Half, p. 310

Fruit-and-Cheese Dessert Salads (Orange Nut, Stuffed Peaches), p. 311
Green Beans Parmesan, p. 302
Guess-What Salad

(omit lettuce), p. 304
Hearts of Lettuce, p. 300
Lima Supper Salad, p. 302
More Fruit Salads (Banana Roll-Ins, Grape, Strawberry),

p. 311
Some Special Vegetable Salads, p. 305
Winter-Pear Waldorf, p. 310

Relishes and Nibblers

Desserts in No Time

Desserts—For Dinner and Next Day's Box Lunch Too

Drinks—Hot or Cold

You'll find dozens of delicious hot and cold drinks for the box lunch in Drinks—Hot and Cold, pp. 494 to 504.

Treats for Children

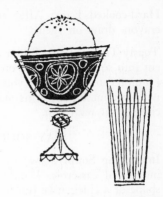

Although most adults prefer to have their food served conventionally, almost every youngster is enchanted by dishes that have some gay twist.

Ways to Be Popular

Appeal of the Miniature: Anything cut down to children's size is twice as much fun—a cupcake frosted all over, an individual meat loaf, a pie just 6″ across.

Color—the More the Better: Be color conscious when selecting vegetables; carrots, beets, squash, cauliflower—all act as foils for green vegetables.

More Color: You can add color with a garnish—a radish, a carrot, a tomato wedge.

The Storybook Approach: Introduce a bit of fun now and then. Make the vegetable plate look like a page out of a storybook as on p. 586.

Personalize It: His name or his initials, or the numerals of his age, are just as precious at six years as at sixty. So "write" them on top of the pudding with raisins or with whipped cream in a cake decorator.

Hidden Treasure: A single raisin in the rice pudding, a green pea in the carrots, and a candy tucked in a cupcake after it's baked are fun whether Junior, Mom, or Dad is the lucky finder.

Foreign Flavor: Whenever you serve a dish that had its origin in a foreign land (see Foreign Flavor, p. 610), be sure to tell Junior. Mashed potatoes become extra-glamorous when you hear about Ireland, shamrocks, and "the wearin' o' the green!"

A Catchy Name: Why not call the white layer cake frosted in pink "princess" cake? And when you're having green beans cut lengthwise, pretend they're Jack and the Beanstalk beans. Point out that cabbage is Peter Rabbit's favorite food.

An Occasion: Ground-hog day, Washington's Birthday, Fourth of July, and all the rest call for family celebrations. Carry out the holiday theme in planning the menu, setting the table.

A Pretty Table: A child loves a pretty table. And with plastic and colorful paper mats available today, it's so easy to set one. He'd be thrilled with place cards for each member of the family. Let him make them.

START THE DAY BRIGHT

Orange Juice: With nail polish, mark rules on glass—a line for babies, one for little boys, one for big boys. Of course "big boys" line is at the bottom.

Cereal Capers: (a good supper dish too): Set baked apple in center of plate; surround with cereal. Or on cereal, in bowl, place raisins for eyes, nose, and mouth. Or put 2 or 3 ready-to-eat cereals in bowl—in separate rows or tossed together.

Eggs: Serve scrambled eggs right in small skillet in which they were cooked. Or serve in Sister's toy skillet.

Hard-cooked Eggs: After cooking eggs, with crayon, draw on shells.

Toasty Tim (below): Butter toast as usual; then cut into squares. Arrange on plate to form doll (Junior can do this). If you wish, spread body with peanut butter, arms and legs with cream cheese, hat with jam.

GAY SOUPS

Interesting Soup: Serve soup in cup, mug, or individual casserole. Wouldn't a bowl in the shape of a chicken be fun for chicken soup?

Two Tone: Simultaneously pour two soups, such as tomato and cream of chicken, into soup plate. Each soup will stay put on its own side.

The House That Jack Built: Make house of cut-up or chopped liver, with mashed-potato windows and doors, plus stalk-of-broccoli tree or any green vegetable for foliage and flowers.

Humpty-Dumpty and His Vegetable Plate: Hold hot unshelled soft- or hard-cooked egg in towel; draw eyes, nose, mouth, with crayon. Set egg in eggcup lined with parsley, set on dinner plate. (Or crackle bottom of egg and stand in nest of parsley on plate.) Surround Humpty with chopped spinach, buttered peas, baked potato, raw-carrot sticks.

SUPER SUPPER DISHES

Pancake Lady (below): Make pancakes from packaged mix as label directs. With tablespoon,

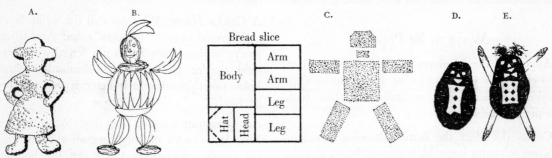

A. PANCAKE LADY, B. CAPTAIN PRUNE-
ABOVE   APPLE ORANGE,
p. 588

C. TOASTY TIM,   D. PADDY POTATO, E. SIR PATRICK,
ABOVE   BELOW   BELOW

Parsley Figures: Sprinkle soup with finely snipped parsley to form child's initial or star, hatchet, or other figure.

Toast Float: Cut toast into animal shapes; float on soup.

Center Star: Set cookie cutter (star or other shape) in center of soup plate. Pour pea soup into cookie cutter, tomato soup around it. Carefully lift out cutter. Serve at once.

STORYBOOK DINNER PLATES

Let some of your dinner plates tell a story. Simply form hot cooked foods into familiar nursery-rhyme figures. It couldn't be easier.

Scarecrow: For body, use baked potato. For head use carrot chunk. Legs and arms are carrots or green beans; buttons and features, peas, carrot bits, or beans.

drop batter onto griddle, to make pancake lady's blouse. Use smaller spoonful of batter for head, dropping it so it joins blouse. Drizzle on batter to form triangle for skirt. Slowly drizzle on arms and legs. Add hat if you like. When pancake is done, add crisp bacon for eyes, nose, mouth. Add creamed spinach for grass.

Other Pancakes: Pancake artistry is so easy you can keep your children guessing what you will create next—snow man, cup and saucer, dog, rabbit, apple, or pussy on the fence? (If you look at pictures of these subjects, you'll find it's a cinch to copy them.)

Paddy Potato (above): Use hot baked potato. Insert sharp knife, twisting it gently, to make eyes, nose, mouth. Cut skin below face in straight line; push back to uncover white inside as vest. Add dabs of butter or margarine for buttons. For Sir Patrick (above), add asparagus for arms and legs; or use broccoli stalks, carrots, or zucchini quartered lengthwise.

Christmas Tree: Make spinach tree growing from chopped-beef earth. Ornaments are diced carrots and peas, or corn and beets.

SIMPLE SALADS

Finger Relishes: Carrot sticks, celery sticks, cauliflowerets, and others in Susan's Raw Relishes, p. 291, are easy to pick up and eat.

Finger Salads: French endive and romaine, as well as water cress, can be good finger foods.

Kabobs: String peeled orange chunks on short lengths of plastic straws.

into quarters to form blocks. With delicately tinted cream cheese in cake decorator, pipe A, B, C, or D on each block.

Cutouts (below): Cutouts have year-round appeal. Santas and stars are good for Christmas, bunnies for Easter, turkeys for Thanksgiving. Cut out one or more shapes from each bread slice. Put together in pairs, with filling.

Rainbow: Make finger sandwiches with cream cheese tinted different shades. Arrange, with cut sides up, in row.

ANIMATED SANDWICHES

Peekaboo: Make sandwich, cutting holes for eyes, nose, and mouth in top slice of bread, so that filling shows through.

A. THE CLOWN, BELOW   B. JUNIOR'S MOSAIC, BELOW   C. EAGLE EYE, BELOW   D. CUTOUTS, ABOVE

Banana-Split Salad: See p. 311.

Cranberry Cutouts: Slice canned jellied cranberry sauce. With cookie cutter, cut into animal shapes (or stars, hearts, and the like). Serve on shredded lettuce.

Gelatin Salads: With cookie cutter, cut set gelatin mixture into shapes; serve on greens. Or serve in sherbet glass lined with shredded lettuce.

JUNIOR SANDWICHES

Junior's Mosaic Sandwich (above): Butter white-bread slice; spread with filling. Top with whole-wheat-bread slice from which star or other design has been cut. Cut star from another slice of white bread; set into star hole in whole-wheat slice.

For the Youngest: Make sandwiches, using canned strained baby foods as fillings. Cut each

The Twins: Cut largest possible round from each of 4 bread slices. Fill pairs. Place on plate. Make face on each pair, using pimento strip for mouth, hard-cooked-egg slices for eyes. Arrange grated carrot salad as hair.

The Clown (above): Make sandwich; trim crusts. Use dried apricots for eyes, pitted date for mouth. For cap, cut second sandwich (with different filling) diagonally in half; use half; trim crusts; dot with raisins. For ears, cut round sandwich in half.

Pussy Cat: Cut largest possible round from each of 2 bread slices. Cut 2 smaller rounds. Fill pairs; set on plate, using larger pair for body, smaller pair for head. Use raisins for eyes and ears, carrot curl for tail.

Eagle Eye (above): Make sandwich; trim crusts; cut diagonally; set on plate as eyes. For eyeballs, use stuffed olive, hard-cooked egg, or raw carrot slices. Add ½ raw tomato for nose; for chin add another small triangular sandwich.

BREAD WITH CHARACTER

Toast Cutouts: With cookie cutter, cut toast into animal, star, and heart shapes. (If you're making many cutouts for a party, first cut out shapes; then toast in broiler.) Butter if desired.

Corral Fence: Cut buttered toast into strips. Pile, one on top of other, to form corral fence.

FRUIT PEOPLE

Perry O'Pear: Choose firm ripe pear. With sharp knife, cut out eyes, nose, mouth. Make arms and legs by stringing grapes on toothpicks; insert in pear. (With aid of 2 extra toothpicks in back, Perry will stand up.)

Don Amigo Banana: For each doll, use 1 long straight unpeeled banana. Trim 1" piece from top; use as hat crown. Make brim of ½ slice unpared red apple and ½ slice unpeeled orange. With ink, draw face and indicate coat and two trouser legs on rest of banana. Make arms and feet of unpared apple pieces, cowboy chaps of unpared apple wedges. (Sprinkle cut apple with orange juice to keep it from darkening.)

Captain Prune-Apple Orange (a pirate, p. 586): Use pitted, cooked whole prunes for head, feet, collar. Peel orange; use ½ orange for body; use orange sections and unpared apple sections for arms, legs. Use bits of apple for eyes, nose, mouth.

OLD FAVORITES

Surprise Custard: Remove spoonful from baked custard. Place bit of jelly or chocolate syrup in hollow. Replace spoonful of custard.

Gelatin Cuts: Gelatin goes down like a charm when it's cut into heart shapes (with cookie cutter) and trimmed with bananas.

Scenic Rice Pudding: Stir pudding into "mountain range," with raisins as birds flying over range or settling in valleys.

Monogram Pudding: With soft cream cheese (tinted if you wish), pipe child's age or initials on top of packaged pudding or applesauce.

Party Applesauce: Sprinkle applesauce with tiny candies, nonpareils, cinnamon hearts.

LITTLE CAKES AND PIES

Clown Cupcake: Frost top of cupcake with Butter Cream Frosting, p. 462. On frosting, make eyes, nose, and mouth of snipped candied cherries. Turn cupcake on side; add colored paper nut cup for hat.

Posy Cupcake: Press tiny rosebud into center of frosted cupcake.

Silhouette Pies: Use Unbaked Crumb Crust, p. 410, to line pie plate, reserving a few crumbs for top garnish (or make extra crumbs). Fill with cream-pie filling; refrigerate. Then, on top of filling, place fancy cookie cutter; partially fill it with crumbs; carefully lift off cutter.

Chocolate Butterflies: See p. 469.

Cookie Crown for Cream and Gelatin Pies: Line pie plate with 2" vanilla or chocolate wafers. Fill with cream- or chiffon-pie filling; top with 3 cookies.

ICE-CREAM TREATS

Recruit help and make these ice-cream treats for a party just before they're served. Or make them ahead and freeze them.

Junior's Alphabet Block: Cut block from firm brick ice cream. Using whipped cream (tinted if desired) and plain tube for writing or star tube in cake decorator (or paper cone), decorate edges and write letters on block.*

Candlelight: Use large ball of pistachio ice cream (No. 8 scoop). Insert tiny green candle, then round green candy as handle. To freeze, wrap ice-cream part only.*

Sweetheart Basket: Fill fluted, colored paper party cup with vanilla ice cream. For posy, insert small lollipop. For leaves, halve long gumdrop stick lengthwise; tuck in at each side of lollipop.

Kitty-Cat (p. 589): Roll small ball of vanilla ice cream (No. 20 scoop) in shredded coconut. Roll larger ball of ice cream (No. 8 scoop) in coconut too. Place small ball atop larger ball. Use corn candy for ears, raisins for eyes, cinna-

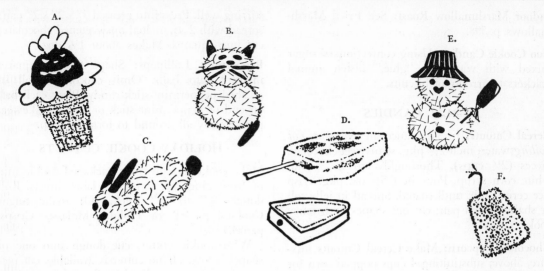

A. MINSTREL MAN, BELOW   B. KITTY-CAT, P. 588   C. FUNNY BUNNY, BELOW
D. CHOCO-MARBLE POPS, BELOW   E. SILLY SNOW MAN, BELOW   F. FIRECRACKER, BELOW

mon candy for nose, slivers of gumdrop sticks for whiskers, long gumdrop strip for tail.*

Silly Snow Man (above): Make Kitty-Cat, using semisweet-chocolate pieces for eyes, cinnamon candy for nose, tiny fluted paper cup for hat, green gumdrops for buttons, lollipop for broom.*

Funny Bunny (above): Make Kitty-Cat, shaping ice cream into ovals. Quickly press in long gumdrop sticks for ears, round gumdrops for eyes and tail, red cinnamon candy for mouth.

Choco-Marble Pops (above): Mix 1 cup milk with 2 tablesp. chocolate syrup and 2 tablesp. heavy cream. Pour into pop forms (sold in housewares departments), filling forms one half to two thirds full. Then press 1 or 2 tablesp. vanilla ice cream into center of each. Freeze. If you don't have enough forms to freeze all mixture at one time, freeze what you can; remove pops; wrap; store in freezer; then start over again.

Firecracker (above): Fill small paper drinking cup with strawberry ice cream, packing well. Insert piece of white string for fuse. Set in freezer until firm. Tear away paper cup; roll firecracker in packaged red sugar. Serve at once; or wrap and freeze.

Minstrel Man (above): Fill flat-bottomed ice-cream cone with chocolate ice cream. Top with round scoop of ice cream. Roll in chocolate sprinkles. With whipped cream and star tube in cake decorator (or paper cone), apply eyes, nose, mouth, hat, and collar.*

Nosegay: From center of 2 or 3 paper doilies laid together, cut out circle large enough to insert ice-cream cone. Secure doilies to top of cone with strip of cellophane tape. Fill cone with ice cream; top with ball of ice cream. Quickly press in gum drops for flowers. Stand each Nosegay in tall glass.*

To store in freezer several days, let firm up in freezer first, before wrapping.

CANDIES JUST FOR CHILDREN

The problem with candy is to get your child to eat the right kind.

Dried-Fruit Animals: With raisins, dates, prunes, and apricots, make animals (prune for body, dates for legs, apricot for head, etc.). Use toothpicks to hold fruits together. (Junior will want to make some of these too.)

Little-Shaver Candies: Dip packaged animal crackers, one by one, into Chocolate Dip, p. 477. With fork, remove to waxed paper to harden.

Mallow Pops: See p. 487.

Indoor Marshmallow Roast: See Fried Marshmallows, p. 598.

Zoo Cookie Candies: Using confectioners' sugar mixed with water for "glue," fasten animal crackers to arrowroot biscuits.

CEREAL CANDIES

Cereal Cutouts: In 3-qt. saucepan over *hot, not boiling* water, melt 2½ pkg. semisweet-chocolate pieces (2½ cups). Thoroughly stir in ⅔ cup white corn syrup. Pour in 1 5½-oz. pkg. crisp rice cereal; mix until coated. Spread in jelly-roll or shallow open pan; cut out shapes with fancy cookie cutter.

Chocolate Popcorn: Make Cereal Cutouts mixture, above, substituting 4 cups popped corn for crisp rice cereal; turn onto waxed paper; separate kernels.

Sugar-Coated Cereal: It comes packaged. Youngsters and grownups eat it by the handful.

Crispy Squares: In double boiler, melt ⅓ cup butter or margarine with ½ lb. marshmallows; add ½ teasp. vanilla extract, beating thoroughly. Place 1 5½-oz. pkg. crisp rice cereal in large buttered bowl; pour on marshmallow mixture,

stirring well. Press into greased 9″ x 9″ x 2″ pan; spread with 2 sq. melted unsweetened chocolate; cut into squares. Makes about 1½ doz.

Peppermint Lollipops: Shape Crispy Squares mixture into balls. Omit chocolate. Roll in crushed peppermint-stick candy. Place each ball on end of peppermint stick or wooden skewer; press gently all around to form lollipop.

HOLIDAY COOKIE CUTOUTS

Make cookie dough from packaged cookie mix or from gingerbread mix as label directs. Roll dough ⅛″ to ¼″ thick. (Or make Sugar Cookies, p. 482, or Holiday Molasses Crisps, p. 484.)

With cookie cutter, cut dough into one of shapes below. (If no cutter is available, cut pattern from cardboard; place floured pattern on cookie dough; with tip of sharp knife, cut around pattern.) Bake as label directs; then decorate. Also see color photo of cookies.

Valentine Hearts: Cut vanilla-cookie dough into 2″ hearts. After cookies are baked, using pink frosting and star tube in cake decorator, make 5 rows of tiny dots, ¼″ apart, on each. Invert each cookie and dip in rainbow-colored nonpareils.

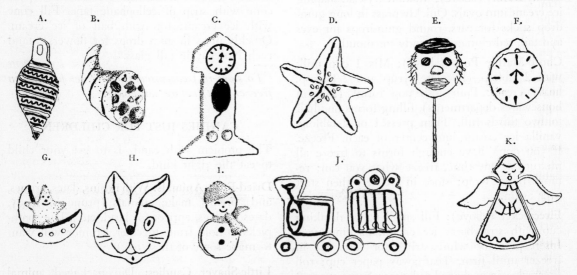

A. TREE-TRIM COOKIES, P. 591   E. LOLLIPOP COOKIES, P. 592   I. THE SNOW MAN, P. 591

B. HORNS OF PLENTY, P. 591   F. NEW YEAR'S CLOCKS, P. 591   J. CIRCUS TRAIN, P. 592

C. HICKORY-DICK, P. 592   G. MAN IN THE MOON, P. 591   K. SINGING ANGEL, P. 591

D. STARFISH, P. 591   H. EASTER BUNNIES, P. 591

Hats for St. Patrick's Day: Cut chocolate-cookie dough into high-crowned 2″ hats. Before baking, into each crown, press shamrock made of 3 slices of green gumdrops.

Easter Bunnies (p. 590): For each bunny's head, cut vanilla-cookie dough into oval. Now cut out 2 ear-shaped pieces of dough. Press "ears" in place on head. After cookies are baked, with Chocolate Glaze, p. 465, outline eyes (make bunny wink), nose, mouth, whiskers.

Liberty Bells: Cut chocolate-cookie dough into 3″ bells. After cookies are baked, using white frosting and plain tube for writing in cake decorator, write "1776" across each and trace crack.

Christmas Bells: Bake Liberty Bells, above. Spread with white frosting. Using green frosting and plain tube for writing in cake decorator, outline holly leaves. To each, add 3 cinnamon drops, for berries, in center of leaves.

Firecrackers: Cut vanilla-cookie dough into 3″ firecrackers with fuse at top end of each. Before baking cookies, sprinkle all but fuses with red sugar. After cookies are baked, frost fuses with white frosting.

Toy Soldiers' Drums: Cut vanilla-cookie dough into 2″ drums. After cookies are baked, frost tops and bottoms with white frosting. Using red frosting and plain tube for writing in cake decorator, make lacings on sides of drums.

Halloween Kitties: Cut chocolate-cookie dough into 2″ cats with arched backs and tails held high. Before baking cookies, press in shredded coconut for whiskers, currants for eyes.

Jack-o'-lantern: Cut vanilla-cookie dough into 2½″ jack-o'-lanterns with stem at top of each. Before baking cookies, sprinkle with orange sugar; press piece of citron into each stem; add currants for eyes, raisin for nose, strip of date for mouth.

Tree-Trim Cookies (p. 590): Cut vanilla- and chocolate-cookie dough into 3″ tree ornaments in shape of toy spinning tops; with a skewer make hole at top of each for ribbon; insert a navy bean. After baking cookies, using red frosting and plain tube for writing in cake decorator, trace diagonal stripes, ¼″ apart, on

each. Fill in every other space with white frosting; fill in rest with wavy lines of green frosting. Or with white frosting, make 2 rows of continuous loops on chocolate cookies; with tweezers, place silver *dragées* in some of loops. Remove beans; insert ribbon.

New Year's Clocks (p. 590). Cut vanilla-cookie dough into 2½″ clock-shaped rounds with piece at top of each for stem. After baking cookies, spread with white frosting, to make clock faces. Using green frosting and plain tube for writing in cake decorator, make hands of clock and 12 short lines for hours.

Starfish (p. 590): Cut chocolate-cookie dough into 3½″ stars; sprinkle centers with chocolate sprinkles. After cookies are baked, make lines with toothpick dipped into Chocolate Glaze, p. 465.

Mr. Rabbit: Cut vanilla-cookie dough into 3½″ tall cookies, showing back view of sitting bunny. After cookies are baked, frost completely with white frosting; sprinkle with snipped shredded coconut. Use Chocolate Glaze, p. 465, for tails.

Horns of Plenty (p. 590): Cut chocolate-cookie dough into cornucopia shapes. Before baking cookies, trace lines with tip of knife; press bits of dried fruits and nuts into place as filling.

The Snow Man (p. 590): For body and head, cut vanilla-cookie dough into 2 circles. For scarf and hat, cut contrasting dough into strips. On cookie sheet, press parts into place. Before baking cookie, press in currants for eyes, red candy for nose, raisin for mouth, dough or raisins for buttons. (Or after cookie is baked, make features with Ornamental Frosting, p. 465.)

Man in the Moon (p. 590): Cut chocolate-cookie dough into stars. Cut vanilla dough into half-moon. On cookie sheet, set star on moon; dot moon with silver *dragées*. After cookie is baked, with frosting, make features on star.

Singing Angel (p. 590): For body, cut gingerbread dough into triangle; for head, cut out circle. For wings, cut vanilla dough into teardrop shapes. On cookie sheet, press parts into place. After cookie is baked, using Ornamental Frosting, p. 465, and plain tube for writing in cake decorator, decorate.

Circus Train (p. 590): Cut gingerbread dough into 3 large squares and 1 smaller square; place on cookie sheet. On each, press little blobs of dough for wheels and fancy tops. After cookies are baked, with Ornamental Frosting, p. 465, "glue" animal cracker to each car. (Smallest car is engine.) Using more frosting and plain tube for writing in cake decorator, decorate.

Hickory-Dick (p. 590): For each clock, cut cookie dough into 1 rectangle, 1 triangle for base, and 1 clock top. On cookie sheet, press parts into place; for mouse, add pitted date. After cookies are baked, using Ornamental Frosting, p. 465, and plain tube for writing in cake decorator, decorate.

LOLLIPOP COOKIES, E. p. 590

1¾ cups sifted all- purpose flour	½ teasp. ground cloves
¾ teasp. baking soda	2 eggs, unbeaten
1 cup soft shortening	¼ cup buttermilk or sour milk
1½ cups brown sugar, packed	1½ cups uncooked rolled oats
1 teasp. salt	1 cup chopped nuts
½ teasp. cinnamon	Packaged plastic straws

Start heating oven to 375°F. Sift flour, soda. Mix shortening with sugar, salt, spices, eggs, and buttermilk until *very light and creamy*. Mix in flour, oats, nuts. Drop by teaspoonfuls, 2″ apart, onto greased cookie sheets. Make face on each cookie—with raisins for eyes, candied cherry for nose, date for mouth, coconut for hair, pitted dried prune for hat. Stick 4″ length of plastic straw into base of each cookie, for necktie. Bake 10 to 15 min. (Let the small fry help make these.) Makes 3½ doz.

DRINKS THEY'LL DRINK

I Like Milk: Gay glasses and mugs make milk more appealing. And don't forget, anything with a straw tastes twice as good!

Jucipher and Juciphine: Choose plump, large, juicy orange or lemon. Just before serving, with knife, make gash in top and insert candy straw down into thick fleshy part of fruit. Children squeeze fruit and suck candy just as they would a straw.

Pink Lemonade: Make Lemonade, p. 501; add drop of food color and a little grape juice or maraschino-cherry juice.

P.S. Also see Planning Meals, p. 662, and Drinks —Hot and Cold, p. 494.

The Bountiful Barbecue

Cook food on the spot or pack it at home and take it along; either way, it will taste all the better in the open.

PLANNING THE BARBECUE

Equip the Outdoor Chef with:

Long-handled fork, spoon, and spatula
Poker to tame fire
Matches
Tongs for turning, lifting
Your biggest skillet, with long handle
Gloves—canvas and asbestos—to save cook's hands. Lots of pot holders
Folding wire broiler
Big wooden board for carving meat
Razor-sharp, sturdy carving knife
Swab to brush on barbecue sauce (tie cheese-cloth onto stick) or pastry brush
Big coffeepot
Rolls of paper towels
Tray of seasonings—monosodium glutamate, seasoned salt, herbs, bottled sauces, etc.

Remember To:

1. *Choose a menu to suit the grill's space.* Plan meal so the first grilling feeds everyone. Try out your menu on the family before inviting guests.
2. *Start the fire about 1 hr. ahead.* You'll need a bed of glowing coals made of charcoal or charcoal briquettes. If you crave a hickory fragrance as you grill, buy some packaged hickory disks. Or use bottled liquid or powdered smoke on meats, etc.

3. *Take meat out of the refrigerator* not more than 1 hr. before grilling. Trim, leaving a minimum of fat, to avoid fat's flaming.
4. *Wrap food* in 2 thicknesses general household foil or 1 thickness heavy-duty foil when grilling food in aluminum foil.
5. *Provide table space near grill* for board on which chef can carve meat.
6. *Time contributions from the kitchen* so they're ready when the grilled food is done.
7. *Serve some help-yourself appetizers* so the chef can carry on unmolested.
8. *Have steel-wool soap pads handy.* They make scouring picnic pots and grills easy.

For Safety's Sake:

1. *Never heat canned food in unopened can.* Can may burst, cause serious burns.
2. *Invest in some kind of insulated container;* fill it with ice if directed to do so. In it, carry all perishables—cream-filled cakes and pies, cream puffs, éclairs, meats, salads, sandwiches, etc.
3. *If sandwiches cannot be refrigerated,* read "A word of warning" and "If sandwiches are for picnic or lunch boxes," p. 357. Eat within 4 hr. after packing them.

MEATS—ALL KINDS

BIG STEAKS

To Buy: Buy steak at least 1″ thick—sirloin, porterhouse, or T-bone if you like 1 large steak, club or rib if you prefer individual steaks. (For details, see p. 53.) Allow ½ to 1 lb. or more per serving.

Preliminaries: Take steak out of refrigerator not more than 1 hr. before grilling. Trim, leaving minimum of fat. Gash edges.

Special Send-offs: Rub with garlic. Or rub with mixture of 1 tablesp. flour, 1 tablesp. prepared mustard, ⅛ teasp. pepper, ¼ teasp. salt. Or spread with prepared mustard.

To Grill: Place on greased grill or in folding wire broiler. Grill 3″ to 5″ from glowing coals (5″ for thick or well-done steak), turning at least once with tongs. To test doneness, cut near bone and note color.

To Serve: See Seasoning Touches, p. 54.

LITTLE STEAKS

Minute Steaks: In a little hot fat in large skillet, sauté minute steaks (¼″ thick) about 1 or 2 min. on each side. Serve with Seasoning Touches, p. 54.

Grilled Cube Steaks: Buy ⅓″ thick top-quality sirloin, round, or chuck steak. Have it scored. Or buy frozen cube steaks. Let stand 15 min. in barbecue sauce or in ½ cup soy sauce mixed with 1 minced clove garlic; or sprinkle with brandy. Grill 15 to 20 min.; or let guests cook their own on long forks or pointed green sticks.

Steak Sandwiches: Serve grilled minute or cube steaks or steak slices in toasted rolls or on toast, with thin onion slices. Or grill frozen sandwich steaks.

London Broil: See p. 57.

CHARCOAL-GRILLED KING STEAK

Buy sirloin steak at least 2½″ thick (9 lb. serves 8). Let stand 1 hr. in ⅓ cup salad oil mixed with 3 minced cloves garlic. Then place steak in folding wire broiler. Sprinkle with salt, pepper; grill over glowing coals 6 to 10 min.—1 min. at a time on each side. Remove from wire broiler; place right on glowing coals till charred —at least 6 min. per side.

Slice steak ¾″ thick (meat will look raw). Meanwhile, in roasting pan, heat 1 or 2 cups water with 1 cup butter or margarine. Place steak slices in pan. Simmer 30 sec. (for rare meat, 15 sec.) per side, not longer. Lift out; serve as is or in buns.

SALT-GRILLED SIRLOIN STEAK

Buy 2″- or 3″-thick sirloin steak. Moisten salt with water to form stiff paste. Spread ½″-thick layer on top of steak. Cover with 2 dampened paper towels. Place in folding wire broiler, with paper side down. Repeat salting, papering, on other side. Grill 5″ from glowing coals, turning at least once. To test doneness, cut near bone and note color. When steak is done, lift off salt, paper.

BARBECUED SPARERIBS

Cut 4 lb. spareribs into 2 or 3 rib portions. Pressure-cook (half at a time) in 1 cup water at 15 lb. pressure 20 min. as manufacturer directs. Then grill over glowing coals, turning and basting with Bert's Superb Barbecue Sauce, p. 374, until deep brown—about 10 min. Makes 5 or 6 servings.

HEAVENLY HAMBURGERS

Place Our Best-Ever Hamburgers, p. 64, in folding wire broiler; grill over glowing coals 4 to 5 min. on each side, or till done as desired.

Or sauté hamburgers in a little hot fat in skillet. (For packaged frozen hamburgers, see label directions.) Serve on toasted, seasoned hamburger buns.

Barbecued Hamburgers: While grilling hamburgers, brush several times with barbecue sauce.

HOT FRANKS

Grilled: Grill franks on green sticks or in frank roaster over glowing coals till brown.

Sautéed: In hot butter or margarine (with a little barbecue sauce or plain, herb, or horseradish-flavored prepared mustard added) in skillet, gently sauté franks till brown.

Wrapped in Foil: Wrap franks in foil; heat over glowing coals 10 min.

In Bacon: Cut lengthwise slit in each frank (don't cut completely through). Smear slit with prepared mustard or chili sauce; stuff with thin sticks of tangy cheese, canned pineapple, or grated sharp cheese with grated onion or pickle relish added. Wrap each frank, spiral-fashion, with bacon strip; secure with toothpick. Grill over glowing coals, turning, till bacon is crisp and franks are hot.

GRILLED HAM

Ham-Banana Roll Ups: Halve peeled bananas lengthwise, then crosswise. Roll each piece in thin slice cooked ham; insert toothpick. Grill in folding wire broiler over glowing coals, turning. Also nice cooked indoors in broiler.

Glazed Ham or Canadian-Style Bacon: Use ¼" slices cooked ham or, smoked boneless shoulder butt, or ready-to-eat or uncooked Canadian-style bacon. Grill over glowing coals, brushing with one of these:

Barbecue sauce
½ cup pineapple juice mixed with ¼ cup garlic vinegar, ½ cup brown sugar, and 1 tablesp. prepared mustard
⅓ cup orange juice mixed with 2 tablesp. peanut butter

Grill-Barbecued Chopped Ham: Cut 1 can chopped ham or luncheon meat into slices. Grill over glowing coals, basting frequently with barbecue sauce. Place in split hamburger buns or between toasted bread slices.

BARBECUED BOLOGNA ROLL

Use 3-lb. piece of bologna, warmed to room temperature. Remove casing; halve crosswise; deeply score surfaces.

Spread with plain or horse-radish-flavored prepared mustard; dot with whole cloves. Put each half on 2 long skewers; grill over glowing coals, turning and basting often with barbecue sauce, until brown and thoroughly heated. Cut into thick or thin slices. Makes 12 servings.

LAMB AND BEEF ALFRESCO

Barbecued Short Ribs: Cut meat from bones of 3 lb. beef shortribs; cut into serving pieces; pound pieces to flatten. Grill over glowing coals, turning and brushing with ½ cup soy sauce mixed with ½ teasp. ground ginger, or with barbecue sauce, till brown. Makes 4 servings.

Barbecued Breast of Lamb: Grill 3 lb. lamb breast over slow fire, turning and basting with barbecue sauce till tender and nicely browned. Makes 4 to 6 servings.

Barbecued Lamb Shanks: Season 4 lamb shanks. Cook in pressure cooker at 15 lb. pressure 30 min. as manufacturer directs. Or simmer, covered, in 2 cups water 1½ hr., or till almost tender. Then grill shanks over glowing coals, turning and brushing often with barbecue sauce, till brown. Makes 4 servings.

KABOBS

To Assemble: String any combination below on 12" to 24" metal skewers. (If you don't have skewers, use medium steel wires. Cut one end of each obliquely, to make sharp point; bend other end to form handle. Or use green branches.) Sprinkle kabobs with salt, pepper.

To Grill: Grill kabobs over glowing coals, turning and brushing with barbecue sauce, or with melted butter or margarine and lemon juice, until done as desired.

To Serve: Rest end of each skewer on plate or in buttered, toasted, split roll; with knife, push food off skewer. Pass barbecue sauce, prepared mustard, chili sauce, Worcestershire, or bottled thick meat sauce, p. 9.

Salami: 1" chunks of lamb steak (from leg), 1½" chunks of salami

Fruit: Canned peach and pineapple and banana chunks

Sea Food: Deveined, shelled raw shrimp; raw scallops; bacon squares

For Company: 1½" chunks of sirloin or veal steak, cooked tiny onions, tomatoes, mushrooms —each on a separate skewer

Teen Rage: Chunks of franks and canned pineapple or apple

Main Dish: Chunks of pickles and franks, spread with prepared mustard; cooked tiny potatoes; tomato wedges

California: Chunks of canned luncheon meat or franks, bacon squares, pitted ripe olives

Brunch: Cubes of calf liver or chicken livers (frozen), bacon squares, mushroom caps

Tropical: Chunks of canned luncheon meat and pineapple, and banana

DONIGIAN'S SHISH KABOB

1 leg of lamb (5 to 7 lb.), boned	1 unpared medium eggplant
½ cup olive oil	14 not-too-ripe tomatoes
1 teasp. salt	14 whole green and red
¼ teasp. pepper	peppers (short, fat)
1 minced clove garlic	14 small white onions

Cut lamb into 1½" chunks. Let stand in oil mixed with salt, pepper, and garlic about 1 hr. Cut eggplant into 2" chunks. On each 24" skewer, string 1 tomato, 1 pepper, 2 chunks eggplant, 1 onion, 5 or 6 chunks lamb, 1 onion, 1 chunk eggplant, 1 pepper, 1 tomato. Grill over glowing coals until tender. Push off onto plates. Serve with Pilaff, p. 235. Makes 5 to 7 servings.

Suren's Shish Kabob: See p. 97.

FISH AND FOWL

CHARCOAL-GRILLED CHICKEN

1. Halve or quarter 2- to 2½-lb. ready-to-cook broiler-fryer. Or if it's quick-frozen, thaw as label directs. Or buy fresh or quick-frozen chicken parts—breasts, thighs, etc.
2. Break hip, knee, and wing joints (some cooks remove wing tips too) to keep bird flat during grilling.
3. Season as in Special Touches, p. 139.
4. When coals are glowing, arrange bird, with cut sides down, on greased grill or in folding wire broiler. Grill slowly, turning with tongs and basting with barbecue sauce, about 25 min., or until tender. When bird is done, knife cuts easily into thick part of leg and no blood shows at bone.

Charcoal-Grilled Turkey: Buy small (3½- to 6-lb.) ready-to-cook turkey, quartered. Grill as above, allowing about 45 min.

CHARCOAL-GRILLED DUCKLING

Remove neck, wings, and backbone from 3½- to 4-lb. ready-to-cook Long Island duckling; then quarter.

Grill as in Charcoal-Grilled Chicken, above, 30 to 40 min., or till tender, brushing occasionally with mixture of ¼ cup honey; 2 teasp. bottled sauce for gravy, p. 9; and ½ teasp. each salt and ground ginger. Or brush with barbecue sauce. Makes about 3 servings.

FISH FRIES AND BARBECUES

Barbecued Swordfish, Salmon, or Halibut Steaks: Cut 3 lb. of fish steaks (¾" thick) into 8 pieces. Place in shallow dish; onto fish, pour combined juice of 1 lemon and ¼ cup salad oil. Refrigerate ½ hr.

Arrange fish in folding wire broiler; brush well with hot barbecue sauce. Grill close to glowing coals (cook fish quickly to prevent drying) about 3 min., or until golden brown. Brush with sauce; turn; grill until easily flaked with fork but still moist. Brush with sauce again; serve. Makes 8 servings.

Bacon-Grilled Trout: Wrap cleaned trout in bacon. Grill in folding wire broiler over glowing coals, turning. When bacon is done, serve.

SHELLFISH ALFRESCO

Roast Clams or Oysters: Scrub 1 doz. raw cherry-stone clams or oysters in shell per person. Place on grill or wire screening laid across glowing coals. Or wrap in foil; place on coals; turn occasionally. When shells open, serve as in Steamed Clams, p. 183.

Steamed Clams: See Steamed Clams, p. 183.

Grilled Live Lobster: Have lobster split, cleaned. Place, with shell side toward heat, on grill 3" from heat. Brush with mixture of melted butter or margarine, salt, pepper, snipped parsley, and minced garlic. Grill over glowing coals about 8 min. Turn flesh side toward heat; brush again; grill about 6 min.; brush. Serve with lemon wedges and melted butter or margarine.

Grilled Rock-Lobster Tails: (See To Buy, p. 188.) Thaw; snip off thin undershell. Grill as in Grilled Live Lobster, above.

VEGETABLES TOO

BEST CORN EVER

Boiled: Husk and boil fresh corn on grill over glowing coals as you would on indoor range (don't boil more than 5 or 6 min.). For easy eating, break ears into thirds.

Grilled: Butter hot boiled ears of corn; quickly toast on grill over glowing coals. Or let each guest grill his own on skewer.

Peanut-Butter-Grilled: Husk fresh corn; spread ears lightly with peanut butter. Wrap each ear with bacon slice; fasten with toothpick. Place on grill; grill over glowing coals, turning, until done—about 10 min. Or grill on long skewers.

Roasted in Husks: About 10 min. before eating, place first round of fresh corn, in husks, on grill over glowing coals. (Some cooks like to plunge corn into salted water first.) Roast, turning often, until husks are steaming hot—about 10 min.; then husk and serve.

That Final Touch: See To Serve Corn, p. 255.

THE POPULAR SPUD

Frozen French Fries or Canned Shoestring Potatoes: Empty potatoes into corn popper; shake over glowing coals till hot; season. Or heat bit of shortening or salad oil in heavy skillet; add potatoes and toss till hot.

Baked in Foil: Scrub baking potatoes; wrap each in foil. Place on glowing coals. Bake, turning occasionally, 1 hr., or till done. Unwrap; cut cross in top of each; season.

Boiled: On grill, boil new potatoes in coffee or shortening can, covered, until fork-tender.

Fried with Bacon: In heavy skillet, fry 4 bacon slices until crisp; remove; crumble. Pare 4 large potatoes; slice very thin; place in bacon drippings. Add 1 teasp. salt, ¼ teasp. pepper. Fry till almost tender and quite brown. Move to edge of grill; add bacon bits; cover; cook till tender. Makes 4 to 6 servings.

SWEET POTATOES

Baked in Foil: Follow directions for baked spuds (above), baking potatoes about 45 min., or till tender.

Grilled: Halve peeled, cooked sweet potatoes lengthwise. Spread with soft butter or margarine. Grill in folding wire broiler over glowing coals, turning often, till bubbly. Top with butter or margarine, salt, pepper.

MIXED-GRILL PARTNERS

Grill or sauté fruits or vegetables in skillet over glowing coals, turning, until brown. (See Mixed Grill, p. 55.)

Mushrooms in Foil: Wash 1 lb. mushrooms. Slice or leave whole. Place on foil. Top with 2 tablesp. butter or margarine, ½ teasp. salt, ⅛ teasp. pepper. Wrap, folding edges of foil under. Place on grill. Cook about 10 to 15 min. Makes 4 generous servings.

VEGETABLES—CANNED AND FROZEN

Canned Baked Beans, Peas, Corn, Mushrooms, etc. Pour one third of contents of 2 cans vegetables into third empty can. Heat all 3 cans on grill over glowing coals, stirring now and then, until piping hot. Add seasonings and a little monosodium glutamate for zest.

Frozen Vegetables—Cooked in Cans: In coffee or shortening cans on grill over glowing coals, cook frozen corn, peas, limas, etc. as label directs. (Break vegetables into chunks if necessary.)

Frozen Vegetables Cooked in Foil: Thaw frozen vegetables until they can be broken into chunks. Place chunks on foil. (Or make individual packets.) Add salt, pepper, butter, or margarine. Shape into long flat package, with edges of foil tucked under. Place on grill; cook over glowing coals about 5 min. longer than label directs. If fire gets too hot, move package to edge of grill. Serve from foil, with edges folded back.

GRILL YOUR BREADS

SAVORY FRENCH OR ITALIAN BREAD

Use yard-long or junior-size loaf of French or Italian bread, or frank rolls. Slash diagonally into thick slices, cutting almost to bottom. Or halve lengthwise; then slash. Between slices and on top, spread one of spreads in Savory French Bread, p. 341. Prop loaf on 2 empty cans on grill or glowing coals; or wrap in foil and place on grill or coals; or use long skewer to hold loaf over coals. Grill, turning often, until toasted.

Chunks: Spread chunks of French bread with one of spreads in Savory French Bread, p. 341. Toast on skewers. Or wrap in foil; place on grill.

GRILL-BAKED BREADS

Camp Biscuits: Use refrigerated pan-ready biscuits; or make ¼″-thick biscuits as in Susan's Hot Baking-Powder Biscuits, p. 323; or use packaged mix. In butter or margarine in skillet, sauté biscuits over low coals, covered, till brown on bottom; turn and brown top. Uncover; stand biscuits on sides till brown.

Waffles: Use frozen waffles. (Or make waffles, p. 334, indoors at your leisure. Refrigerate waffles a day or two; or freeze if storing them for a longer period.) Heat in folding wire broiler over glowing coals. Serve as bread, with butter or margarine.

ROLLS AND MUFFINS

Hot from the Grill: Place rolls and muffins in covered coffee can. Place can on side on grill or glowing coals; roll can occasionally till rolls are heated.

Or place rolls in skillet on grill. Sprinkle with a few drops water. Heat, covered, shaking skillet occasionally.

Toasted: Split rolls or muffins; top with one of spreads in Savory French Bread, p. 341; toast in folding wire broiler or on skewer. Or sauté in butter or margarine in skillet over glowing coals. (English muffins and crumpets are good this way.)

GARLIC-BUTTERED SLICES

Spread white-bread slices with butter or margarine; sprinkle with garlic salt. Put together, sandwich-fashion. Wrap in foil; or place in covered can. Toast on grill over glowing coals, turning often. Use as hamburger rolls.

HOT GRILLED SANDWICHES

Barbecue Sandwiches: Slice cold or hot roast meat or turkey; baked ham, smoked boneless shoulder butt, or meat loaf; tuck into toasted, split buns. Spoon hot barbecue sauce over meat.

Welsh Rabbit in Hand: Brush outside of cheese sandwiches with melted butter or margarine. Toast in skillet or folding wire broiler over glowing coals.

Toasted Peanut Butter: Toast peanut-butter sandwiches (plain or with honey, raisins, or chili sauce) in skillet or folding wire broiler over glowing coals.

Bacon-Cheese Bun: Spread one side of split frankfurter buns with prepared mustard, other side with butter or margarine. Tuck chunk of cheese in each bun. Wrap in bacon; fasten with toothpicks. Grill in folding wire broiler over glowing coals.

Chili Burgers: Let guests make their own sandwiches with hot canned chili con carne, soda crackers or large saltines, plus American-cheese slices, onion rings, or lettuce.

Scrambled-Egg Sandwiches: Provide scrambled-egg mixture in pitcher. Let chef scramble eggs. Let guests toast buns and fill them with eggs, crisp bacon, and catchup or snipped scallions.

Cracker Sandwiches: Make cracker sandwiches (use round scalloped crackers, rye wafers, saltines, or soda crackers) with cheese, peanut butter, etc. Toast in corn popper.

SALADS, see p. 298

NOW FOR DESSERT
THE FRUIT VARIETY

Caramel Roast Apples: Place crisp apples on grill; toast over glowing coals, turning occasionally, till apples' skins burst. Peel; roll in brown sugar. Grill till caramelized.

Walnut Roast (nice with fruit): Roast unshelled walnuts in corn popper over glowing coals.

TEEN-AGE DELIGHTS

Fried Marshmallows: In small skillet over glowing coals, melt butter or margarine. Slowly cook

8 marshmallows until brown on one side. Turn; brown other side. Use to top soda crackers.

Date-Marshmallow Kabobs: Alternate pitted dates and marshmallows on stick; toast over glowing coals.

Shore-Front Baked Bananas: For each serving, slit unpeeled banana lengthwise, part-way through, to within ½″ of ends. Tuck in sweet-chocolate-bar pieces or 1 or 2 snipped marshmallows. Toast bananas, with cut sides up, on green sticks over coals till peel chars and center is soft, hot. Cool slightly; peel.

Marshmallow Treats: Toast 2 marshmallows over coals until gooey and crisp. Place on graham cracker or thin gingerbread slice. Top with piece of sweet-chocolate bar; cover with graham cracker or thin gingerbread slice. Eat sandwich-style.

LET'S HAVE CAKE

Coffeecake: Heat in covered skillet over glowing coals as in Hot from the Grill, p. 598. Serve with butter and jam.

Jelly Roll: Toast sliced bakers' jelly roll on grill or in folding wire broiler over glowing coals.

Cranberry-Coconut Roll Ups: Trim crusts from fresh white-bread slices; lightly roll with rolling pin. Butter each slice; spread with canned jellied cranberry sauce; roll up. Roll in sweetened condensed milk, then in shredded coconut. Secure with toothpicks. Grill over glowing coals, turning often.

Honey Cubes: Drizzle honey on 1″ poundcake cubes. Roll cubes in shredded coconut. Toast on grill over glowing coals, turning often.

CHOOSE A MENU

GALA BARBECUE

Barbecued Spareribs, p. 594
Rosy Fluffy Hot Rice, p. 234
Warm French Bread
Guacamole, p. 303
(serve heaped on thin lettuce slices)
Ice Cream Sprinkled with Coconut
Lime Wedges

COMPANY COMING

Something Cool to Drink
Barbecued Bologna Roll, p. 595
Green Beans with Herbs
Fresh Tomato Relish, p. 290
Rye, Wheat, and White Bread
Lemon-Coconut Cake, p. 398
Tea or Coffee

FAMILY REUNION

Charcoal-Grilled Chicken, p. 596, with
Undercover Flavor, p. 139
Susan's Hashed-Brown Potatoes, p. 268
Frozen Peas Cooked in Foil, p. 597
Cranberry Jelly in Peach Halves
Buttered Bran Muffins
Ginger-Ale Float
(add vanilla ice cream)

TOUCH OF ELEGANCE

Donigian's Shish Kabob, p. 596   Pilaff, p. 235
Huge Green Salad
(use young greens from the garden)
Help-Yourself Melon Tray
(watermelon, honeydew, and cantaloupe wedges)
Iced Tea

BREAKFAST BY THE GRILL

Help-Yourself Pitcher of Fruit Juice
Cereal Buffet
(choice of hot or ready-to-eat cereals, cold milk, brown sugar)
Glazed Ham or Canadian-Style Bacon, p. 595
Grilled Pineapple Slices
Scrambled Eggs   Hot Biscuits
Coffee   Milk

HIKER'S HEAVEN
(a can-opener special)

Juice from Frozen Concentrate
Grill-Barbecued Chopped Ham, p. 595
Canned Peas with Corn Cooked Outdoors, p. 597
Crisp Carrots
Camp Biscuits, p. 598
Caramel Roast Apples, p. 598   Coffee

FRESH-AIR BUFFET

Barbecued Lamb Shanks, p. 595
Casserole of Succotash
Pumpernickel Bread   White Radishes
Platter of 3 kinds of Turnovers
Tall Glassfuls of Milk   Coffee

PROGRESSIVE FOURTH OF JULY

(each course served in a different garden)

Steamed Clams, p. 183
(with butter sauce, clam broth in paper cups,
crisp crackers)
Barbecued Salmon Steaks, p. 596
Grilled Best Corn Ever, p. 597   Olive Coleslaw
Blueberry Pie with Spiced Sour Cream
Hot Coffee (instant)

SATURDAY-NIGHT ROUNDUP

Salametti, p. 241
Rye-Bread-and-Lettuce Sandwiches
Honeydew-Melon Wedges Decked with Tiny
Bunches of Grapes
Chocolate-Chip Cookies   Iced Coffee
Walnut Roast, p. 598

A FISH FRY

Bacon-Grilled Trout, p. 596
(or any fish you wish)
Hush Puppies, p. 176
Sliced Tomatoes, Onions, Cucumbers
Bread and Butter
Watermelon Rounds with Big Blueberries
Coffee

MEN ONLY

Salt-Grilled Sirloin Steak, p. 594
Grilled Corn, p. 597
Floating Salad, p. 302
Toasted, Split Hard Rolls
Green Apple Pie   Camembert Cheese
Coffee

UNDER THE APPLE TREE

Bacon-Cheese Buns, p. 598
Celery Curls
Raspberry Ice-Cream Soda
Fresh Coconut to Nibble

NEIGHBORS' GET-TOGETHER

Roast Beef for a Crowd, p. 644
(hot or cold, carved outdoors)
Bowls of Horse-radish Mustard
Susan's Scalloped Potatoes, p. 270
Toasted Corn Bread, p. 330
Old-fashioned Lettuce, p. 301
Bowl of Fresh Cherries on Ice
Soft Molasses Cookies
Lemonade   Iced Tea

CABIN STYLE

Quick Borsch with Sour Cream
(prepare 1 pkg. chicken-noodle-soup mix as label
directs, adding ½ cup canned diced beets)
Bacon-Cheese Buns, p. 598
Red-Raspberry Cake
(cake layers brought from home, topped with
sugared, hand-picked berries)
Coffee or Tea

ON THE TERRACE

Frosted Pineapple
(berries and pineapple cubes in pineapple halves,
with cottage-cheese topping)
Toasted Peanut-Butter Sandwiches, p. 598
Iced Cocoa

FUN AT THE BEACH

Plenty of Roast Clams or Oysters, p. 596
(for dunking, use tabasco in melted butter)
Lemon Wedges
Savory French or Italian Bread, p. 597
Coconut-Frosted Fruit Cocktail
(tote can of fruit cocktail, package of coconut)
Lots of Coffee

When Company Comes

This chapter is designed to answer the hostess' eternal question, "What shall I serve?" You'll find many helpful menus—all in key with today's gracious informality—for the hostess who, more often than not, manages everything singlehanded.

COMPANY AT ODD HOURS

"Stop by after dinner."
"Come for a few rubbers of bridge."
"There's a committee meeting in the morning."
"Join us for that new TV show."
"The shower's Friday night at eight."

Situations like these call for a drink and a bite to eat. But don't be trite. Serve something that justifies your reputation as a smart hostess.

Serve Punch for a Crowd

Just *which* punch? And *what* do I serve with it? Here are some suggestions to fit the occasion.

Golden-Mint Reception Punch, p. 648, and Ham-and-Chicken Salad, p. 306; hot rolls; bride's cake; thin mints—at a 4 o'clock wedding reception

Tangy Tutti-frutti Punch, p. 649, and bowls of dunks and dips—at an open house

Sherbet-Tea Punch, p. 648, and Susan's Sandwich Party Loaf, p. 363—at a lawn party

Pink-Lemonade Punch, p. 648, and cupcakes with pink candles—for a sweet-sixteen birthday

Mocha Punch, p. 649, and jelly roll, tied diploma-fashion—for a graduation party

Pink-Lady Punch, p. 649, and doughnuts (miniature lifesavers)—for a *bon voyage* party

Lavender Punch, p. 648, and chocolate-filled ladyfingers—at a junior prom

Grandmother Randolph's Eggnog, p. 649, and baking-powder biscuits, filled with ham slices—for an alumnae reunion or open house

Lemon-Strawberry Punch, p. 648, and angelfood cake baked by the ladies' auxiliary—for a strawberry-festival card party

Make It a Cool Drink

A long cool drink and a bit to nibble are almost always a perfect menu at odd hours.

Pineapple-Lime Nectar, p. 500, and nut-stuffed dates—any afternoon or evening

Coffeenog, p. 504, and buttered toast sprinkled with sugar and orange rind—for summer morning coffee

Mocha Float, p. 502, and coconut macaroons—about 10 P.M.

Milk Tinglers, p. 503 (choose one), and peanuts in the shell—while watching TV

Mint Sparkle, p. 500, and bowlful of Bing cherries—on a hot day

Susan's Honey Iced Chocolate, p. 503, and ladyfingers—as an afternoon snack

Tampa Tea, p. 500, and salted peanuts, tossed with puffed cereal and popcorn—whenever good friends meet

Banana Smoothie, p. 502, and spongecake squares—for a lawn party

Caribe Cooler, p. 501, and angel-food cake (from a mix), topped with green candles—for Mother's birthday party

Banana Milk Shake, p. 502, and gingerbread sandwiches—after badminton

Iced Cocoa, p. 498, and marshmallows or nut-bread fingers—sister's sorority's favorite

Let's Have "Mocktails"

Nibblers and a drink are smart to serve when you'd rather not have something sweet

BRIDGE FINALE

Curried-Tuna Toasties, p. 26
Fruit Tray
(dates, canned peach and pineapple chunks, with shredded coconut for dunking)
Iced Tea

TEEN-SET SNACK

Help-Yourself Tray
(one or two dunks, p. 28; heated brown-and-serve sausages; crisp crackers; carrot sticks)
Pitchers of Lemonade (frozen)

A MAJOR PRODUCTION

Hot Baked-Ham Midgets, p. 27
Pickled-Fruit Bowl
Avocado-Cream-Cheese Dunk, p. 28
with Carrot and Celery Sticks
Hot Coffee and Tea

THE CLUB MEETS

Tangy Salmon Dunk, p. 28   Celery Sticks
English Muffinettes—Seeded, p. 30
Hot Tea   Cold Pineapple Juice

A STAG PARTY

Cocktail Pizzas, p. 27
Coffee   Iced Cola Drinks

IN A HURRY

Garlic-Cheese Dunk, p. 28
Potato Chips   Stuffed Olives
Cups of Hot Chicken Bouillon with
Lemon Garnish

KITCHENETTE SIZE

Clam-and-Cheese Dunk, p. 28
Pumpernickel-Bread Fingers   Radishes
Vegetable-Juice Cocktail

Come for Dessert

This is a delightful way to entertain informally with a flair. Suggest that your guests skip dessert at home and stop by right after the dinner hour. Serve dessert and coffee as soon as they arrive. And make a production out of it. For instance, if the choice is pie, try:

French Apple Pie: Serve Crumbly-Crust French Apple Pie, p. 413, slightly warm, topped with coffee whipped cream.

Guests' Choice: Make Fresh Berry Pie, p. 413 (blueberry), and De Luxe Red-Cherry Pie, p. 413. Add spice to sour cream; spoon onto top of pie. Serve coffee of course.

Lunch-Box Turnovers, p. 423: Pile turnovers on platter or in basket; surround with bunchlets of grapes, tangerines (peeled and slightly separated), cheese wedges. Serve milk.

Sundae Tarts, p. 428: Put tarts and toppings on tray; let guests top their own. Serve ginger ale in punch cups with twist of lemon.

Nesselrode Pie, p. 417: Serve demitasse. Let guests nibble on pieces of fresh coconut served in coconut shell.

Rich Walnut Pie, p. 415: Spoon whipped cream (with sherry added) onto each serving. Pass bunches of 3 kinds of grapes.

Fresh Berry Pie, p. 413: Tuck blueberry leaves around pie on chop plate. Serve with ice cream; sprinkle with cinnamon from shaker.

Lemon or Orange Chiffon Pie, p. 416: Place fresh coconut pieces in small basket on tray; place pie wedges around coconut. Between wedges, tuck strawberries with hulls on. Serve tea.

Susan's Fudge-Nut Pie, p. 415: Guests choose topping of unsweetened whipped cream or coffee ice cream, and sprinkle it with shaved chocolate from small bowl. They drink iced coffee.

Year-Round Peach Deep-Dish Pie, p. 414: Serve pie with cottage cheese, fluffed up with cream. Provide coffee and cinnamon-stick muddlers.

Max's Super Cheese Pie, p. 415: Serve with choice of frozen strawberries or crushed pineapple. Provide big pot of coffee.

Royal Chocolate Chiffon Pie, p. 417: Pass candied orange rind, dried apricots.

Susan's Fresh Apple Pie, p. 411: Provide dishes of Brazil nuts, scoops of Cheddar cheese (use teaspoon), orange-hard-sauce balls.

Let's Eat at 10:00 P.M.

Like others, you probably find that an informal after-dinner get-together, with refreshments at 10 P.M., is an easy, pleasant way to entertain.

In planning the food, bear in mind two things: Ten o'clock is not the hour for a full meal, so keep the food light. And have it ready, or serve something that takes only minutes to make. Here are 5 possible ways to do just that.

1. BUFFET SETOUTS

Arrange food and drink on side table or dining table; or wheel them in on a tea wagon, with plates, cups, and silver. Let guests help themselves. Serve:

Burgundy Meat Balls, p. 66
Hard Rolls, Sliced Crosswise and Buttered
Pickles   Coffee

Cook meat balls day before. Reheat; serve from skillet in some of sauce, with toothpicks.

Quick Coffee Ring, p. 351
Cream Cheese   Assorted Jams
Hot Chocolate

Set coffee ring on breadboard, with spreaders, cheese, and jams. Provide hot chocolate in big pitcher, with plate of marshmallows and bowl

of cinnamon-flavored whipped cream for toppings.

Pineapple-Cheese Spread
Crisp Gingersnaps   Plenty of Coffee

Surround small bowl heaped with pineapple-cheese spread (it comes in glasses) with crisp gingersnaps and spreaders.

H.R.M.'s Dessert Salad, p. 310
Salted Crackers or Thin Crisp Cookies
Coffee or Tea

Let hostess serve salad while guests help themselves to coffee and crackers.

2. HELP-YOURSELF REFRESHMENT TRAYS

Everything goes on a big tray (small plates, napkins, silver, cups, saucers, "something good to munch," and a drink); it's easy to transport to the living room. If you're having several tables of bridge, fix one tray for each table.

Piping-Hot Afternoon Tea Scones, p. 326
Dish of Raspberry Jam
Coffee

Plate of Freshly Baked Coffeecake
Coffee

Small Skillet of Halved Brown-and-Serve
Sausages with Toothpicks
Plate of Cheese Cubes and Quick-Pickled
Pineapple, p. 286, with Toothpicks
Crackers   Hot or Cold Drink

Plate of Pitted Dates and Dried Apricot Strips
Interspersed with
Plain and Cheese-Stuffed Celery
Basket of Potato or Corn Chips
Coffee or Tea

Oven-Glass Pie Plate with Little Hot Biscuits
Dish of Honey-Butter Spread   Coffee

3. PARTY PLATES

Each guest's refreshments come from the kitchen, served on an individual plate.

Individual Fruit Plates
Thin Strips of Poundcake
or Peanut-Butter Sandwiches
Salted Nuts   Pitcher of Milk

———

Wedges of Angel, Chiffon, or Spongecake
Heaped with Berry Whipped Cream, p. 369
Spiced Brazil-Nut Chips, p. 492   Coffee

———

Tomato-Cheese Aspic, p. 314, on Lettuce
Topped with Mayonnaise, Crumbled Crisp
Bacon
Celery Curls   Rye or Whole-wheat Wafers
Coffee or Tea

4. KITCHEN COOKUPS

When close friends drop in, invite them to the
kitchen to help prepare these:

Susan's Beanies, p. 361   Gherkins
Coffee

———

French Onion Soup, p. 36   Cheese Toast
Celery   Pickle Slices
Coffee

———

Susan's Cheesy Scramble, p. 225
Heated Chili Sauce   Toast or Hard Rolls
Coffee

5. REFRIGERATOR READIES

Here's party fare all ready for serving when the
game is finished or the program ends.

Bowls of Sandwich Fillings
(see Pack-and-Carry Sandwiches, p. 362)
Salty Rye Bread   Hot Tomato Juice

———

Spread-Your-Owns, p. 29, in Small Bowls
Toast or Crackers   Milk
Basket of Chilled Apples
Mixed Nuts in Shells

———

Smoky Cocktail Spread, p. 29
Crackers   Pumpernickel Bread
Chilled or Hot Cider or Coffee

COMPANY FOR DINNER

If you're cook and hostess too:
1. Limit the menu to no more than 3 courses.
2. Market a day or two ahead.
3. Avoid last-minute hurry and flurry. Do all
you can the night before or early that day.
4. Get linen, silver, china, and glassware ready
early.
5. Set the table and arrange centerpiece ahead.

A Dozen Easy Buffets

A buffet is probably the most popular way to
entertain at dinner or luncheon. Planning and
serving details are on p. 683. Now for the menus.

CO-OP BUFFET

One-Apiece Loaves, p. 68
with Broiled Fruit (use canned or fresh peaches)
Hot Baked-Potato Salad, p. 305
Tossed Salad Bowl   Corn-Meal Crisps, p. 330
Nutted Cheesecake   Coffee

CONNECTICUT WAY

Jane's Company Lobster, p. 189
Tossed Salad with Lemon French Dressing
Toasted French Bread with Poppy Seeds
Coconut Bavarian Tarts
Miniature Chocolates
Coffee

COUNTRY STYLE

Susan's Chicken Pie, p. 147
Spiced Crab Apples and Seckel Pears
Two-Bowl Salad
(large bowl of mixed greens; small
bowl of wine French dressing)
Chocolate Ice Cream
Pecan-Cake Slices, p. 441

MARDI GRAS

Shrimp Creole, p. 193
Oven Dinner Rice, p. 235
Buttered Hot Cheese Biscuits, p. 324
Celery Curls
Lemon-Coconut Cake, p. 398
Coffee

NEW YEAR'S BUFFET

Our Best Chicken Salad, p. 305
Glazed, Simmered Smoked Boneless Shoulder
Butt, p. 89 or Baked Ham
Curried Four-Fruit Bake, p. 287
Custard Corn Pudding, p. 255
Filled Butter-Flake Rolls, p. 342
Chocolate Torte, p. 455   Roasted Walnuts
Coffee (instant)

CARD-TABLE STYLE

Barbecued Fried Chicken, p. 145
Jumbo Baked Potatoes
Tossed Mixed Green Salad
Hot Buttered Rolls
Fruit-Dessert Centerpieces
Coffee—Now and Later

FINGER FOOD

Cold Fried Chicken Superb, p. 140
Southern Corn Pudding, p. 256
Bread-and-Butter Sandwiches
Raw Relishes
Susan's Fudge-Nut Pie Alamode, p. 415
Coffee

COLLEGIATE GET-TOGETHER

E.I.'s Swedish Meat Balls, p. 67
Tomato Ring, p. 314
Filled with Vegetable Salad
Toasted Celery Rolls in Loaf, p. 340
Old English Spiced Cider, p. 501
Walnuts   Cheese Tray

CAREER GIRLS' STAND-BY

Creamed Chicken and Ham, p. 157
Quick-Candied Sweet Potatoes, p. 265
Buttered Split Biscuits   Blackberry Jelly
Dessert Salad
(grapefruit sections, avocado slices, etc.)
Coffee (instant)

EASY TO DO

Corned-Beef Hash and Tomato Bake
Green Beans Parmesan, p. 302
Crisp Rolls
Sherry Fruit Bowl (mixed canned or
frozen fruit with sherry)
Coffee

DONE THE DAY BEFORE

Veal Casserole Chow Mein, p. 110
Cold Artichokes, Asparagus, or Broccoli
with Mustard Hollandaise, p. 374
Buttered Corn Bread   Crisp Celery
Sliced Sweet and Dill Pickles
De Luxe Cheesecake, p. 396
Coffee

KENTUCKY SQUARE DANCE

Can-Opener Minestrone, p. 35
(in soup tureen)
Judy's Salad Tray
(pickled canned peaches, rolled in minced
celery leaves, circled by
Olive Coleslaw, p. 303)
Buttered Pumpernickel
Chocolate Whipped-Cream Cake, p. 398
Coffee

Six Little Dinners

Here, delightful little dinners that even a new
cook can manage gracefully.

SO NICE TO SEE YOU

Oven-Easy Chicken, p. 140
Curried Corn and Peas
Tossed Green Salad with Slivered Swiss Cheese
Crisp French Bread
Berry Deep-Dish Pie, p. 414   Coffee (instant)

A SPRING DINNER

Double Lamb Chops
Broiled Peach Halves with Mint Jelly
Fresh Asparagus   Toasted English Muffins
Chocolate-Coconut Bavarian Pie, p. 421
Demitasse

WHEN THE SHAD RUN

Broiled Shad and Roe, p. 174
Creamed New Potatoes, p. 267
Tossed Green Salad
Heated Rolls
Cherry-Sherry Jubilee, p. 403
Cream-Cheese Smoothies, p. 481
Coffee (instant)

BON VOYAGE

Our Best-Ever Hamburgers, p. 64
Quick Mushroom Sauce, p. 372
Buttered Limas with Chives
Romaine Salad with Parmesan Dressing
Toasted Corn-Bread Squares
Peach Glacé Pie, p. 418   Demitasse

DINNER AT SEVEN

Crab-Corn Bake, p. 185
Tossed Green Salad with Onion and Green-
Pepper Rings
Brown-and-Serve Salt Sticks
Lime-Swirl Chiffon Pie, p. 417
Coffee (instant)

COME SUMMER

Baked Fish Creole, p. 171
Plenty of Corn on the Cob
Hi's Caesar Salad, p. 300
Bread Sticks
Peach Shortcake (see To Vary Fruit, p. 384)
Coffee

The Business Couple Entertains

Entertaining can be fun, but it takes planning
and managing if you both go out to work five
days a week.

SATURDAY-NIGHT CARD-TABLE BUFFET
FOR EIGHT

Barbecued Corned Beef, p. 74
Stuffed-Pepper Twins, p. 260
Lettuce with Cucumber Mayonnaise
Brown-and-Serve Rolls
Fluffy Steamed Fig Pudding, p. 406,
with Whipped Cream or Ice Cream
Coffee (instant)   Milk

Early Saturday: Start simmering corned beef.
To mayonnaise, add minced cucumber, onion,
salt, bit of cream. Stuff peppers. Prepare lettuce;
refrigerate all.
About 2½ hr. before dinner: Make pudding
and start it steaming.
About 30 min. before dinner: Bake corned
beef, peppers.
Last few minutes: Bake rolls; slice meat; toss
salad.

SATURDAY EASY DRESS-UP DINNER
FOR FOUR

Pork-Chop Roast, p. 77
Baked Stuffing Balls, p. 209
Broccoli with Almonds
Coleslaw Soufflé Salad, p. 314
Frosted Spicecake (from mix)
Coffee (instant)   Milk

Day before: Make salad. Prepare stuffing balls.
Prepare roast, ready to cook. Refrigerate all.
Early in day: Bake and frost cake. Sliver
almonds.
About 2¼ hr. before dinner: Start cooking
roast. Bake stuffing balls last 30 min.; cook
frozen broccoli last 20 min.
Last few minutes: Unmold salad. Make gravy.
Add almonds to melted butter; pour over broc-
coli.

WEEKEND GUEST DINNER

Pot Roast of Beef with Wine
(To Cook Pot Roast, p. 59)
Small Whole Carrots
Savory Mashed Potatoes, p. 268
Speedy Pickled Pears, p. 286
Crisp Rolls   Green Salad Bowl
Mallow-Cream Whip, p. 390
Coffee   Milk

Night before: Let your husband sharpen the
carving knife. Prepare pears. Wash salad greens.
Make dessert. Refrigerate all.
About 3½ hr. before dinner: Start pot roast.
About 40 min. before dinner: Cook potatoes
and carrots. Toss salad. Make gravy.

EASYGOING BUFFET FOR FOUR

Spaghetti with Italian Meat Sauce, p. 240
Tossed Green Salad
Junior Loaves, p. 341
with Garlicky Spread, p. 341
Fruit Compote Topped with Lemon Sherbet
Susan's Coconut Refrigerator Cookies, p. 482
Milk

Day before: Make spaghetti sauce and cookie
dough. Combine canned and/or fresh fruit with
sherry. Wash salad greens. Refrigerate all.
Early in day: Buy sherbet; store in freezing
compartment. Bake cookies.
About 1 hr. before dinner: Prepare hard rolls.

Heat spaghetti sauce. Boil spaghetti. Dish out compote; set aside on tray. Bake rolls; toss salad.

THIRTY-MINUTE SUPPER FOR FOUR

Skillet-Barbecued Franks, p. 121
on Parsley Rice
Susan's Coleslaw, p. 303
Toasted Rolls   Jam
Chilled Fresh Apples and Pears
Walnuts in Shell
Milk and Coffee

Early in day: Chill fruit. Shred cabbage; refrigerate.

About 30 min. before dinner: Start barbecued franks; then cook rice. Mix coleslaw. Add snipped parsley and butter or margarine to cooked rice. Serve franks on rice. Toast rolls.

COMPANY FOR LUNCH

Luncheon for guests is usually a light affair. When planning these menus we kept the ladies in mind primarily, however, male preferences weren't entirely forgotten.

Salad Luncheons

EAST-INDIAN INFLUENCE

Curried Sea-Food Salad, p. 309
Curry Accompaniments, p. 193
Tea (hot or iced)
Susan's Pineapple Upside-down Cake, p. 443
Topped with Vanilla Ice Cream

COMPANY COMING

Melon Bowl, p. 311
Thin Slices of Baked Ham in Hot Buttered
Biscuits
Olives   Pickles
De Luxe Pecan Pie, p. 415   Coffee

FOR THE GIRLS

Chicken-Curry Salad, p. 306
with Parsley Tomatoes
Brown-Bread Sandwiches or
Buttered Pumpernickel Slices
Hot Coffee
Peach Halves Topped with Crushed Red
Raspberries

QUICK-MADE LUNCH

Crunchy Tuna Salad, p. 309
in Avocado Halves
Hot Buttered Toast   Little Plum Tomatoes
Hot Bouillon or Consommé

CALIFORNIA STYLE

Fruit Chef Salad, p. 309
Freshly Baked Sugar-and-Spice Buns, p. 347
or Buttered Nut-Bread Slices
Tall Glasses of Milk

COMMITTEE MEETING

Chicken Fruit Buffet, p. 306
Toasted Cheese-Spread English Muffins
Hot Coffee or Tea (instant)

BUFFET STYLE

Tuna-Cucumber Mold, p. 313
Rolled Water-Cress Sandwiches
Susan's Peach Upside-down Cake Alamode,
p. 444
Hot Coffee

Other Luncheons

FOR FOUR OR MORE

Hot Baked Chicken Salad, p. 306
Oven-Cooked Frozen Broccoli, p. 246
Hot Pimento Drop Biscuits, p. 325
Canned Peaches Topped with
Frozen Strawberries

SOUTHERN STYLE

Peppy Tomato Juice, p. 19
Crab Meat Maryland, p. 185
Green Beans with Almonds
Brown-and-Serve Rolls
Fresh Pears   Black Coffee

A SHOWER SUPPER

Oysters in Cream, p. 190
Peas and Mushrooms
Tomato Ring, p. 314   Heated Rolls
Fresh Pineapple with Raspberries and Wine
Ring Cookies (doughnut-shaped)   Tea

A CURRY PARTY

Indian Shrimp Curry, p. 192
or Different Chicken Curry, p. 148
Big Tossed Salad
Susan's 3-Layer Fudge Cake, p. 448

A BRAG PARTY

His Lake Trout, p. 172
Susan's Hashed-Brown Potatoes, p. 268
Olive Coleslaw, p. 303
Blueberry Drop Biscuits, p. 325
Butterscotch Sundaes   Coffee

ON A HOT DAY

Top-Hat Chicken Salad, p. 306
Lots of Hot Biscuits with Currant Jelly
Sparkling Iced Tea with a Glamour Touch,
p. 497

IT'S SPRING

Old-fashioned Tomato Cocktail, p. 18
Welsh Rabbit on Toasted English Muffins
Fresh Asparagus with Poppy Seeds
De Luxe Red-Cherry Pie, p. 413
Tea

LADIES ONLY

Open-face Sandwiches of Broiled Ham,
Pineapple, and Cheese
French Endive Salad
Toasted Coconut Pie, p. 421   Coffee

BRUNCH ON SUNDAY

If you've never considered this kind of entertaining, do. Sunday brunch is a happy solution
for the bachelor, bachelor-girl, or business couple.

WHEN THERE ARE GUESTS

Brunch Appetizer Tray
(chilled pineapple juice and finger fruits—
banana cubes on cocktail picks, etc.)
Chili-Poached Eggs, p. 225
Buttered Toast   Canadian-Style Bacon
Coffee-ettes, p. 325   Coffee

A BIT OF THE SOUTH

Fresh-Fruit Tray
(doubles as centerpiece and fruit course)
Marjie's Fluffy Spoon Bread, p. 330,
with Cranberry Jelly
Crisp Bacon   Chicken Liver Sauté, p. 142
Lots of Coffee (instant)

A LATE ONE

Eye-Opener Small Cups of Coffee
Hash Cheeseburgers, p. 126   Chili Sauce
Toast Strips   Large Cups of Coffee
Cranberry Baked Apples, p. 400
More Toast with Cinnamon-Sugar

COMPANY FOR HOLIDAYS

Holidays call for more or less traditional feast-
ing. Here are menus and detailed directions for
memorable meals.

TRADITION PLUS

Old English Spiced Cider, p. 501
(served in living room)
Roast Turkey with Giblet Gravy
Baked Sweet Potatoes, p. 265
Glazed Small Onions   Buttered Green Beans
Canned Cranberry Sauce
Celery and Carrot Sticks
Mince-Apple Pie, p. 413, with Fluffy Cream
Cheese or
Stuffed Dates (see Stuffed Fruits, p. 492) and
Spiced Brazil-Nut Chips, p. 492
Coffee

Day before: Make dessert. Whip cream cheese
with cream; prepare relishes. Cook and grind
giblets for gravy. Make spiced cider. Refrigerate
all. Prepare crumbs for stuffing.
The day: Make stuffing; stuff turkey. Plan
so turkey is done 20 min. before serving (it will
carve more easily and you will have time to
make gravy). Put potatoes in oven about 1 hr.
before dinner. Prepare onions and beans. Start
cooking onions ½ hr. before dinner, green beans
20 min. before. Reheat cider. Place pie in oven
with heat turned off to warm up during dinner.

YOUNGSTERS-OLDSTERS

Hot Spiced Pineapple Juice, p. 19
(served in living room)
Pair of Roast Chickens
Buttery Moist Giblet-Bread Stuffing, p. 209
Velvety Gravy   Mashed Potatoes, p. 268
Brussels sprouts with Lemon Butter, p. 377
Relishes (mixed pickles, carrot curls)
Jiffy Jellied Fruit (Date-Nut), p. 402
or
Pilgrim Pumpkin or Squash Pie, p. 415
Coffee

Day before: Make dessert; cook and coarsely chop giblets; refrigerate both. Prepare bread for stuffing.
The day: Make stuffing; stuff chickens. Right after breakfast, prepare relishes; clean Brussels sprouts; refrigerate both. Roast chickens so they'll be done 20 min. before serving. Start cooking potatoes 50 min. before dinner, Brussels sprouts about 25 min. before. Then make Lemon Butter, spiced pineapple juice, gravy; complete potatoes.

NEW YEAR'S DAY

Susan's Rib Roast of Beef, p. 50
Horse-radish Sauce I or II, p. 375
Potatoes and Onions (browned with meat)
Lettuce with French Dressing
Brown-and-Serve Rolls
Eggnog Ice Cream
Prickly Butter Balls, p. 479
or Fruitcake
Coffee (instant)   Milk

Several days ahead: Bake cookies or fruitcake. Buy ice cream; store in freezer.
The day: Wash, dry, and refrigerate lettuce. Start roasting beef so it is done 20 min. before serving.
About 1¼ hr. before dinner: Partially cook pared potatoes and onions—about 10 min.; place around meat during last 40 to 60 min. of roasting. Make Horse-radish Sauce. Bake rolls.

EASTER DINNER

Roast Chicken, p. 143
Buttery Fruit-Bread Stuffing, p. 209
New Potatoes with Parsley Butter
Cheesy Asparagus
Tossed Salad with Grated Radishes and Carrots
Assorted Breads and Crackers
Angel Cake with Strawberries   Coffee

Day before: Make angel cake from mix. Get ingredients ready for stuffing, but do not mix.
The day: Make stuffing; stuff chicken. Start roasting chicken so it is done 20 min. before serving. Slice and sugar berries (or use frozen berries). Prepare salad, ready to toss; refrigerate. Start cooking potatoes about 40 min. before dinner, asparagus 15 min. before. Make gravy. Top potatoes with melted butter and snipped parsley; sprinkle seasoned asparagus with grated Parmesan cheese. In basket, arrange crackers, Melba toast, rye wafers, etc. Toss salad.

WITH A HOLIDAY AIR

Peppy Tomato Juice, p. 19, with
Crisp Crackers
(served hot in living room)
Fresh Ham (Roast Pork Leg)
Candied Sweet Potatoes, p. 266
Buttered Peas with Cauliflower
Pickle Relish   Cranberry Sauce
Celery Curls
Lime Milk Sherbet, p. 432
Coffee

Day before: Prepare tomato juice so it's ready to heat. Cook sweet potatoes; prepare celery curls. Refrigerate all.
The day: Make sherbet early. Cook ham and potatoes so they're done 30 min. before serving. Then cook peas and cauliflower; heat tomato juice while you make gravy.

Foreign Flavor

You may think of foreign cookery as an exotic faraway world of splendid spices and simmering sauces. Yet many of our popular everyday foods are adaptations of foreign recipes.

In these pages, we take you on a brief tour of dining tables in homes around the world. And if you'd like to serve dishes with "foreign flavor," we've provided lists of adapted recipes.

Of course, tastes vary not only from country to country, but family to family. So the meals we describe here give you merely a glimpse of the ways our neighbors cook.

FRENCH FINESSE

The French Cuisine: The French achieve wonderfully subtle effects with seasonings, especially with wines and herbs. Everyday dishes such as poached fish, omelets, meats in sauces, and soufflés become gourmet fare in their hands. The French cook almost never considers the additional effort involved; the end justifies the means.

Frogs' legs, snails, eels, mussels (foods we consider gourmet fare) make regular appearances on the tables of most French families. Veal is a favorite meat.

A French cook may serve a wide variety of vegetables, including mushrooms, celery, parsnips, leeks, and artichokes. In fact, she often honors the vegetable by serving it as a separate course, simply seasoned with butter, salt, and pepper.

For dessert, fruit and cheese are universal favorites. Also popular are creations like crepes suzette, *baba au rhum,* a high soufflé, and *meringue glacée.*

Daily Fare: *Petit déjeuner* (breakfast) often consists of *croissants* (sometimes brioche) and *café* *au lait* or *chocolat. Café au lait*—half coffee, half milk—is a popular breakfast beverage.

Déjeuner (lunch), the most important meal of the day, often consists of hors d'oeuvres, a savory meat dish (probably of veal or mutton), vegetable, salad, cheese, fruit, a bottle of wine, and demitasse.

Dîner (dinner) usually means soup, main dish, dessert, and demitasse.

WEEKDAY LUNCH

Pâté   Céleri Rémoulade
Pot-au-feu
Salad   French Bread
Fruit and Cheese   Coffee
Regional Red Wine

SUNDAY LUNCH

Onion Soup or Leek Soup
Roast Duck or Capon
Peas and Scallions
Salad   French Bread
Baba au Rhum   Cheese
Chablis   Demitasse

Dishes with French Flavor

We Americans have incorporated adaptations of French favorites into our everyday and company meals. Here are some of them.

Wonderful Soups

Egg and Cheese Dishes

Meats (Mostly Veal)

Chicken, Duckling, and Game

Wonderful Fish and Shellfish

Salads and Salad Dressing

Breads and Sandwiches

ITALIAN GUSTO

The Italian Way: By and large, Italian food is less complicated than French, but the emphasis on sauces is just as great. Most Italian sauces are the long, slow simmered variety. As for seasonings, tomato paste, garlic, peppers, anchovies, oil, mushrooms, Parmesan, and capers head the list. Herbs are used, with orégano, rosemary, sage, bay leaf, and basil among the favorites. Of course wine is a popular ingredient. And milk-fed veal is often served.

In southern Italy, *pasta* is served in every form. We usually think of it topped with tomato sauce, but often it's served white, tossed with garlic, olive oil, and cheese. In northern Italy, rice and homemade noodles are important dishes.

When it comes to vegetables, eggplant, cauliflower, peas, cabbage, green beans, zucchini, broccoli, asparagus, and mushrooms are among the favorites.

Daily Fare: Italians enjoy eating alfresco (out of doors). Breakfast usually follows the Continental pattern—bread and a hot drink.

The Italians often start the big meal of the day (usually at 1 P.M.) with *antipasto* (an assortment of hors d'oeuvres), then *pasta* or rice instead of soup. Usually the main dish is accompanied by a tossed green salad and a loaf of crisp, crusty Italian bread. Wine is served throughout the meal. Desserts are not important; Italians usually like fresh fruit. (When they do serve a pastry dessert, it's apt to be an elaborate concoction.) Then *espresso* (demitasse made with dark roasted coffee) is served either at the table or in the sitting room.

A light meal at suppertime (8 or 9 P.M.) may consist of soup and meat or eggs or fish with vegetables.

BREAKFAST (PRIMA COLAZIONE)

Bread   Butter   Honey
Coffee with Hot Milk

LUNCH (SECONDA COLAZIONE)

Anchovies and Olives
Spaghetti or *Ravioli*
Chicken Cacciatore
Finocchio or Celery Salad
Crisp Rolls
Fruit and Cheese   Coffee
Water   Chianti Wine (throughout the meal)

DINNER (CENA)

Antipasto
Minestrone
Veal Scaloppine   Zucchini or Artichokes or
Broccoli
Bread Sticks   Romaine Salad
Cassata (like *spumone*) or Zabaglione
Caffé Nero

Dishes with Italian Flavor

We Americans have incorporated adaptations of Italian favorites into our everyday and company meals. Here are some of them.

Soups and Nibblers

Anchovy-Celery Cocktail Dunk, p. 28
Can-Opener Mine-strone, p. 35
Cocktail Pizzas, p. 27

Italian Fish Stew, p. 35

Melon Rolls, p. 24
Minestrone, p. 40

Meats, Chicken, and Squab

Chicken Cacciatore, p. 142
Chicken Tetrazzini, p. 147
Italian Pork-and-Rice

Casserole, p. 77
Italian-Style Flank Steak, p. 58
Roast Squab, p. 155
Salami, p. 119

Scaloppine of Veal Marsala, p. 109
Veal Italian with Carrots, p. 109
Veal Parmigiano,

p. 109
Veal Scaloppine, p. 104

Fish and Shellfish

Leon's Baked Striped-Bass Fillets, p. 170

Mussels Marinière, p. 189

Sautéed Frogs' Legs, p. 177

Shrimp Broil, p. 192

Spaghetti and Rice

Italian Ham and Spaghetti, p. 241
Jane's Buffet Lasagna, p. 242

Mina's Italian Spaghetti, p. 239
Polenta with Tomato Sauce, p. 214

Spaghetti with Clam Sauce, p. 240
Spaghetti with Italian Meat Sauce, p. 240

Spaghetti Parmesan, p. 238

Vegetables

Artichokes—Italian or French, p. 249
Broccoli, p. 251

Eggplant Parmesan, p. 258
Italian Green Peppers,

p. 260
Oven Dinner Rice, Risotto Style, p. 235

Zucchini Casserole au Gratin, p. 276
Zucchini, Italian Style, p. 276

Salads, Breads, Desserts

BRITISH AND IRISH SIMPLICITY

British and Irish Ways: The English, the Scots, and the Irish like simple food with a minimum of seasoning, preferring to add seasonings at the table, along with such condiments as Worcestershire, mustard, and chutney.

The savory is a well-known English tradition at formal dinners. It's a light dish, such as Welsh rabbit or oysters wrapped in bacon, and is served after the sweet (dessert).

In Scotland, haggis is the holiday dish. It's a sheep's stomach, filled with chopped variety meats, herbs, suet, and oatmeal, and is traditionally accompanied by whisky.

When you think of Ireland, you think of potatoes. Colcannon is a famous Irish dish; it's a mountain of potatoes (mashed with onion) and cabbage, and is eaten with lots of butter. Even when it comes to stuffing geese, the Irish use mashed potatoes. The Irish are also noted for their wonderful soda bread, served with tea.

Daily Fare: The English breakfast is famous. It's a hearty one, was formerly served buffet

ENGLISH BREAKFAST

Stewed Fruit or Fruit Juice
Cereal or Porridge
Bacon and Fried Eggs
or
Grilled Kippers
or
Scrambled Eggs on Toast
Toast   Marmalade
Tea or Coffee

style. It's very similar to our American meal, except that fish, particularly finnan haddie and kippered herring, are often served. In Scotland, breakfast can mean porridge with salt and milk.

The English also serve midmorning coffee or tea (elevenses). Lunch follows at midday, and varies with individual appetites.

Everyone knows about the Englishman's afternoon tea (4 P.M.). It's standard procedure even in business offices, where a cup of tea and biscuits (cookies) are usually served. Afternoon tea (at home) may include bread, butter and jam, cake or other sweet, and tea. Or it may be served later as high tea (5 to 6 P.M.), which is a kind of supper and includes meat, salad, possibly sandwiches, fruit, cake. A high tea may be followed at 10 P.M. by a hot drink (tea or cocoa) and cheese and biscuits.

Tea in Scotland is served with scones and shortbread as well as pastry.

The dinner of the British day (at noon or night) usually includes meat, two vegetables, sweet, and possibly soup. Roast beef and Yorkshire pudding are of course an ever-welcome treat.

ENGLISH AFTERNOON TEA

Thin Bread and Butter
Cucumber Sandwiches
Sally Lunn Teacakes
Petit Fours   Poundcake or Fruitcake
Tea with Milk and Sugar

Dishes with English, Scottish, and Irish Flavor

We Americans have incorporated adaptations of English, Scottish, and Irish favorites into our everyday and company meals. Here are some of them.

Meats—Broiled, Boiled, Roasted

Beef Curry Delicious,
p. 62
Beef-Kidney Stew,
p. 117
Boiled Beef with
Horse-radish Sauce,
p. 63

Indian Chicken
Curry, p. 157
Irish Stew, p. 62
Kidneys en Brochette,
p. 117
Let's Have Mutton,
p. 102

Mixed Grill (kidneys,
lamb chops, bacon),
p. 55
Oxtail Ragout, p. 118
Roast Goose, p. 155
Savory Meat Pie,
p. 63

Shepherd's Pie, p. 130
Susan's Rib Roast
of Beef, p. 50
Yorkshire Hot Pot,
p. 101
Yorkshire Pudding,
p. 329

Lots of Game

Braised Partridge
with Cabbage,
p. 201
Braised Pheasant with
Cabbage, p. 200
Bread Sauce, p. 203

Civet of Venison,
p. 203
Roast Grouse, p. 202
Roast Guinea Hen,
p. 201
Roast Partridge,

p. 201
Roast Pheasant,
p. 200
Roast Pigeon
(squab), p. 155
Roast Venison, p. 202

Roast Wild Duck,
p. 201
Roast Woodcock,
p. 202
Salmi of Pheasant,
p. 201

Fish and Eggs

Baked Finnan Haddie,
p. 172
Easy Broiled Fish

(sole), p. 172
Indian Shrimp Curry,
p. 192

Kippered Herring
with Cream, p. 176
New Zealand-Style

Eggs, p. 231
Sautéed Kippered
Herring, p. 176

Vegetables and Relishes

Apple Chutney, p. 295
Asparagus, p. 249
Cauliflower, p. 254
Chipped Potatoes

(see French-Fried
Potatoes, p. 269)
Fried Tomatoes
(Speedy Cream-

Fried Tomatoes, p.
275; omit evaporated
milk)
Susan's Piccalilli,

p. 293
Tomato Sauce, p. 376

Hot Breads

Afternoon Tea Scones,
p. 326
Devonshire Muffins,

p. 365
Irish Soda Bread,
p. 334

Old-time Sally
Lunn, p. 354
Susan's Hot Cross

Buns, p. 353

Shortbread, Fruitcake, Pies, Desserts

Dark Christmas
Fruitcake, p. 444
Edna's Piccadilly
Trifle, p. 398

Grandmother's Plum
Pudding, p. 406
Hard Sauce, p. 370
Holiday White Fruit-

cake, p. 444
Mince Pie, p. 413
Scotch Shortbread,
p. 483

Sherry Christmas
Cupcakes, p. 456
Sterling Sauce, p. 371
Strawberry Dip, p. 379

SCANDINAVIAN VARIETY

Similarities and Differences: The cuisines of Norway, Sweden, and Denmark are similar in many ways. In all three countries favored foods include salt or spiced herring and cheese as appetizers; fish; simple, hearty dishes like meat balls, a stuffed cabbage, and boiled potatoes; dark bread (the Swedes are partial to Limpa, or rye bread); fruit soup as dessert; and beer, aquavit, wine, and coffee as beverages. Dill is a popular seasoning.

Yet in spite of the similarities, each cuisine has a personality of its own. Sweden has a distinctive smorgasbord. Denmark and Norway are famed for *smørrebrød* (artistic open-faced sandwiches). And Denmark is also famous for its pastry.

Daily Fare: Breakfast usually consists· of porridge, bread or rolls and butter, eggs, and coffee.

Lunch is about midday, and in Denmark attractive open-faced sandwiches make the meal. Coffee and cookies are served at 3 or 4 P.M.

Dinner, a hearty meal of meat, potatoes, and vegetables, is served at 5 to 7 P.M. (In the country, the hearty meal is usually served at noon, and a light supper in the evening.)

SWEDISH THURSDAY DINNER

Herring   Cheese   *Knäckebröd*
(crisp rye bread)
Aquavit
Pea Soup with Salt Pork and Mustard
Boiled Potatoes
Plättar (tiny crepes suzette)
with Lingonberries
Coffee

SWEDISH SMORGASBORD

The Swedish smorgasbord, although still a national institution, is not served as often as it used to be. In homes, at dinner, a few plates of appetizers may be set on the table and passed around.

However, those who prefer to be traditional, set out such foods as those below on a buffet table. Guests help themselves to a bit of each—usually fish first, then salads, then hot dishes.

Tiny meat balls in covered casserole
  (see E.I.'s Swedish Meat Balls, p. 67)
Sweet-sour kidney beans in casserole
Strips of Spareribs, Swedish Style, p. 83
Cold cuts: liverwurst, veal loaf, ham
Cold cooked salmon, shrimp
Hard-cooked egg halves with anchovies
Assorted cheeses on a board
Sliced headcheese
Pickled beets
Clamshells filled with liver paste
Herring salad
Crisp bread and rye bread
Raw relishes: celery, radishes, cauliflower, olives
Cucumbers in dressing of vinegar, salad oil, salt, sugar, snipped parsley
Fruit salad

Dishes with Scandinavian Flavor

We Americans have incorporated adaptations of Scandinavian favorites into our every day and company meals. Here are some of them.

Nibblers

Deviled Eggs, p. 229
Quickies—Fish

(sardines, caviar fingers), p. 31

Shrimp Dip (in Sharp Sauce), p. 22

Main Dishes

Boiled Live Lobster, p. 187
Danish Goulash, p. 62
E.I.'s Swedish Meat Balls, p. 67
Inga's Meat Balls,

p. 67
Kippered Herring with Cream, p. 176
Our Best Creamed Fish (halibut, and finnan haddie, served on parsley

potatoes), p. 177
Roast Goose, p. 155
Sautéed Kippered Herring, p. 176
Spareribs, Swedish Style, p. 83

Superb Biff à la Lundstrom, p. 66
Swedish Braised Short Ribs, p. 60

Vegetables and Relishes

Pickled Beets, p. 291
Sharp Sauce, p. 377

Parsnips, p. 264
White Turnips, p. 275

Yellow Turnips, p. 275

Desserts and Coffeecakes

Coffee Kringle, p. 350
Danish Cream, p. 393
Danish Pastry, p. 352

Finnish Butter Strips, p. 479
Fruit Soup, p. 37

Superb Danish Coffee Twist, p. 350
Susan's Rice Cus-

tard, p. 391

CENTRAL EUROPEAN HEARTINESS

Similarities and Differences: The cuisines of Germany, Austria, and Switzerland are, for the most part, substantial. They feature hearty main dishes with rich gravy, sometimes made richer with sour cream. A favorite seasoning is caraway, used in vegetables and meat as well as in bread. Some Central Europeans specialize in sweet-sour flavorings in meats and vegetables.

Desserts are rich too—strudels and layered *dobostorte*. As for beverages, Central Europeans generally like lots of coffee, lots of wine, lots of beer.

Sausages of all kinds are enjoyed, as well as pork and veal dishes, game, cabbage (white or red, or in the form of sauerkraut), kohlrabi, green beans, and lots of good dark bread.

In spite of the similarities, the food, like the people themselves, differs from country to country, and within each country, according to local custom.

Daily Fare: There's usually an early simple breakfast of coffee, rolls, and honey or cherry, berry or apricot jam or jelly. In some areas, a second breakfast may be served around ten o'clock and often includes a meat or cheese.

The noonday meal is generally hearty. Then there's usually an afternoon coffee session and a light supper of cold cuts and cheese.

GERMAN NOONDAY MEAL

Clear Soup with Dumplings
Veal Cutlet
Lyonnaise Potatoes, p. 268   Red Cabbage
Wilted Lettuce
Rye Bread
Dutch Applecake   Coffee with Cream
Beer or Wine

AUSTRIAN NOONDAY MEAL

Clear Beef Soup with Frittaten
(pancakes rolled up and cut into thin strips)
Boiled Beef with Dill Sauce
Hard Rolls (called Emperor Rolls) or Rye Bread
Apple Strudel
Coffee
(served in small cups, so-called "Mocca" cups)
Gespritzter
(light white wine with soda water)

Dishes with Central European Flavor

We Americans have incorporated adaptations of Austrian, German, and Swiss favorites into our everyday and company meals. Here are some of them.

Robust Meat Dishes

Baked Fruit Pork Chops, p. 80
Baked, Stuffed Pork Chops, p. 80
Baked, Stuffed Pork Tenderloin, p. 81
Beef Birds (pressure cooked), p. 196
Bohemian Burgers, p. 65
Bologna or Cervelat (Summer Sausage), p. 118
Braised Oxtails, p. 117
Braised Pork Chops or Steaks with Apple, p. 79

Breaded Pork Tenderloin, p. 81
Breaded Veal Cutlet, p. 107
Cold Stuffed Veal-Roll Slices, p. 110
Cooked Fresh Tripe, p. 116
Double Roll Ups, p. 110
Franks and Sauerkraut—Peasant Style, p. 123
Goulash, Pressure-Cooker Style, p. 196

Hungarian Goulash, p. 63
Liver Cheese (Liver Loaf), p. 118
Liver Sausage (Liverwurst), p. 118
Moravian Beef with Gravy, p. 60
Pigs' Knuckles with Cabbage, p. 82
Pork-Chop Roast, p. 77
Potato Burgers, p. 66
Roast Lamb (use leg), p. 95
Sauerbraten, p. 59

Souse (Headcheese), p. 119
Spareribs and Sauerkraut, p. 83
Stuffed Cabbage, p. 71
Swiss Steak, p. 57
Swiss Steak (pressure cooked), p. 196
Thuringer, p. 119
To Cook Pot Roast, p. 59
Veal Paprika, p. 105
Wiener Schnitzel, p. 108

Hearty Soups and Nibblers

Chicken, Game, and Rabbit

Cheese and Eggs

Tasty Vegetables

Salads and Relishes

Rich Desserts, Frostings, Fillings

CHINESE SUBTLETY

The Far Eastern Way: Most Chinese dishes are created by combining morsels of pork, chicken, duck, or fish with sliced vegetables. These are then cooked for a short time in a little liquid. Each borrows and gives flavor to the others. The result: a subtle blending.

Many condiments are used in Chinese cooking. Soybean sauce supplements the use of salt.

Most of the cooking done in Chinese restaurants in this country is Cantonese.

Daily Fare: There are usually two substantial meals a day—lunch and dinner, with the dinner hour varying from 4 to 7 P.M. Meals are served, as are ours, in courses. Because chopsticks are used, the food is served in small pieces. Rice or steamed bread or noodles appear instead of our bread and potatoes. Tea is almost always served after the meal.

CHINESE DINNER
(Cantonese style, as served in American-Chinese restaurants)

Egg Drop Chicken Soup
Egg Rolls
Sweet-Sour Steamed Fish   Roast Pork
Rice
Preserved Kumquats or Pineapple Chunks
Spongecake   Almond Cakes
Litchi Nuts   Tea

Dishes with Cantonese Flavor

We Americans have incorporated adaptations of Chinese favorites into our everyday and company meals. Here are some of them.

Dishes with Meat and Poultry

California Chop
  Suey, p. 78
Chicken, Chow-Mein
  Style, p. 149

Chicken Chop Suey,
  p. 149
Chinese Sweet-Sour
  Spareribs (pressure

cooked), p. 197
Creamed Chicken,
  Chinese Style,
  p. 158

Lamb Suey, p. 98
Sweet-Sour Pork,
  p. 77

Eggs, Rice, and Fish

Butterfly Shrimp,
  p. 192
Eggs Foo Young,

p. 230
Fried Shrimp (Ju
  Har-Kow), p. 192

Sweet Pungent Fried
  Shrimp, p. 192
Tarantino's Hangtown

Fry, p. 190

Other Dishes

Almond Cookies,
  p. 479

Chinese Cauliflower,
  p. 254

Preserved Kumquats,
  p. 294

MEXICAN PEPPER

As the Mexicans Do It: In Mexico, the food is hot and spicy, and the sauce is important. Corn, frijoles (beans), and rice are mainstays of the meals. *Tortillas* (thin corn-meal pancakes) take the place of bread. These same *tortillas* are the base for making *tacos,* enchiladas, and many other dishes.

You'll find that our native American turkey is a great holiday dish in Mexico. When it comes to salads, avocado—especially in the form of guacamole—takes first place.

Daily Fare: In Mexico, a hearty breakfast starts with native fruits—pineapple, mango, papaya. It may include a thin steak or eggs and beans. Of course, there's strong coffee diluted with a quan-

tity of milk and sweetened with a large amount of sugar. A peasant is likely to have black coffee, *tortillas,* and chili beans.

The main meal is usually served from 2 to 4 P.M. and is often a six-course repast consisting of soup, dry soup (rice), a meat dish, more beans, *tortillas,* and dessert and coffee.

Supper may be a light, late-evening affair.

MEXICAN DINNER
Tequila
Noodle Soup
Dry Soup (rice)
Broiled Beef Steak
Potatoes   Guacamole with Sliced Tomato
Frijoles   *Tortillas* or French Bread
Preserved Fruit   Beer

Dishes with Mexican Flavor

We Americans have incorporated adaptations of Mexican favorites into our everyday and company meals. Here are some of them.

Arroz con Pollo,
    p. 143
Baked Caramel Cus-
    tard, p. 395
Barbara's Tamale

Pie, p. 73
Fluffy Hot Rice, p.
    233
Fresh Tomato Relish,
    p. 290

Guacamole, p. 303
Mexican Wedding
    Cakes, p. 479
Papayas, p. 528
Sautéed Bananas,

p. 289
Susan's Rice Custard,
    p. 391

DISHES WITH BALTIC OR NEAR EASTERN FLAVOR

We Americans have incorporated adaptations of Baltic or Near Eastern favorites into our every-day and company meals. Here are some of them.

Baked Beets with
    Onions, p. 251
Beef-and-Eggplant
    Casserole, p. 72
Beef Stroganoff, p. 56

Delight Squares, p. 486
Donigian's Shish
    Kabob, p. 596
Hamburger Stro-
    ganoff, p. 70

Old-Country Borsch,
    p. 40
Pilaff, p. 235
Suren's Shish Kabob,
    p. 97

Tangy Chicken
    Special, p. 41

Chafing-Dish Cookery

Almost anything that can be made in a skillet or double boiler can also be made in many chafing dishes. It's that simple!

The upper pan, called the blazer, usually has a long handle and can be used over direct heat, alone, without the lower (hot-water) pan, just as you use a skillet.

Put water in the hot-water pan, set the blazer in it, and you have a double boiler!

CHAFING-DISH TECHNIQUE

With a chafing dish, you can cook and serve right before your guests' very eyes. But, like an actor who is going to perform, you must set the scene and do a bit of rehearsing.

1. *Know your recipe thoroughly.* Have a dress rehearsal if you're new at it.
2. *Collect pretty bowls and pitchers of different sizes* for spices and condiments.
3. *Have your props ready beforehand.* Arrange all ingredients and utensils on one tray. Set up the chafing dish on another tray.
4. *Plan on a first course* to keep your guests busy while you play chef.
5. *Cook noiselessly.* Use a long wooden spoon.

COOK AS IN A SKILLET

There's nothing complicated about chafing-dish cookery. Of course you'll study the manufacturer's directions on how to use and regulate the heat. And you'll reread the hints above on technique.

To cook, place blazer (skillet) of chafing dish over direct heat—and pretend it's just an ordinary skillet on the kitchen range. If you can cook any of the following dishes in the kitchen, you can cook it in a chafing dish.

MEAL-IN-ONE CLASSICS

Served with something hot to drink, these make delightful "little suppers" at midnight. For a luncheon or supper at a more conventional hour, add a tossed green salad and dessert.

Scrambled Eggs, and All Its Variations: See p. 224. If you're serving eggs on, or with, toast, let a guest man the toaster while you preside at the chafing dish.

Old-time Welsh Rabbit and Welsh Rabbit with Beer: Both are on p. 214. These are always included in a chafing-dish repertoire. Serve them on crisp crackers; buttered hot biscuits; toasted, split corn bread or English muffins; buttered rusks; or canned baked beans.

Swiss Fondue: See p. 214. This luscious cheese dish is a treat any time, especially at New Year's.

French Omelet: See p. 226. Choose one of the 10 fine fillings.

Oyster Stew: See p. 42. Try clam and lobster too!

Lobster Newburg: See p. 188. This is an aristocratic chafing-dish specialty. (Beginners may wish to make it over the hot-water pan.)

Creamed Dried Beef: See p. 127.

NEW MEAL-IN-ONE SPECIALTIES

Guests will expect scrambled eggs, Welsh rabbit, Swiss fondue, omelets, oyster stew, or lobster Newburg, etc., but you can surprise them with any of the dishes below. Serve them with a salad, bread, and dessert—for a gay luncheon or supper.

These dishes can be made in the blazer (skillet) over direct heat.

Bacon Chop Suey: See p. 93; or heat canned chow mein in chafing dish. Pass crisp chow-mein noodles.

Sardines Portuguese: Heat sardines in butter or margarine in chafing dish; sprinkle with snipped parsley. Serve on toast, with lemon wedges.

Indian Chicken Curry: See p. 157. Serve with rice.

Turkey and Peas Thermidor: See p. 159. Cook peas ahead.

Grilled Mushrooms: Sauté small whole mushrooms in butter or margarine in chafing dish until tender. Add a little sherry. Serve on toast.

Other Favorites:
Skillet-Barbecued Franks, p. 121
Hamburger Stroganoff, p. 70
Lamb Suey, p. 98
Easygoing Supper, p. 112
Shrimp Creole, p. 193
Rice with Shrimp, p. 236
Ellen's Turkey-Olive Curry, p. 156
Very Quick Creamed Chicken, p. 157
French-Toasted Sandwiches, p. 362
Easy Poached Eggs, p. 225

MEAT HEARTIES

Make the following in blazer (skillet) of chafing dish over direct heat.
Mac's Sautéed Kidneys, p. 116
Lamb Kidneys Piquant, p. 117
Franks, Country Style, p. 120
Chef's Lamb and Mushrooms, p. 131
Lamb Barbecue, p. 131
Barbecued Hamburgers, p. 66
Noodle Stroganoff, p. 70
Savory Baked Beans and Hamburger, p. 257
Frank Suey, p. 121
Ham Gala, p. 135

SOUP SPECIALS

Make the following in blazer (skillet) of chafing dish over direct heat.
Creamy Potato Soup, p. 34
French Onion Soup, p. 36
Tuna-Corn Chowder, p. 44

CHICKEN OR TURKEY

Make the following in blazer (skillet) of chafing dish over direct heat.
Ellen's Turkey-Olive Curry, p. 156
Creamed Chicken, Chinese Style, p. 158
Chicken Liver Sauté, p. 142
Luscious Turkey Hash, p. 158

FISH SPECIALS

Make the following in blazer (skillet) of chafing dish over direct heat.
Quick-Curried Tuna, p. 179
Panned Oysters, p. 190
Sautéed Kippered Herring, p. 176
Golden Scallops, p. 191
Scallop Sauté, p. 191
Sautéed Scallops with Scallions, p. 191
Shrimp Sauté, p. 192
Sherry Tuna, p. 180

CHEESE-AND-EGG DISHES

Make the following in blazer (skillet) of chafing dish over direct heat.
Corn Fritters—Northern Style, p. 255
Grilled Cheese Sandwiches, p. 361
Country Poached Eggs, p. 226
Western Curried Eggs, p. 231
Eggs Foo Young, p. 230

NIBBLERS—BUFFET STYLE

The chafing dish is the love of the five-o'clock hostess both for making and serving nibblers. Make the following in blazer (skillet) over direct heat. Then keep warm in blazer over hot-water pan.

Barbecuettes: Heat bottled barbecue sauce or Jiffy Barbecue Sauce, p. 622, in blazer of chafing dish. Spear cocktail-size franks or Vienna sausage on toothpicks; arrange in sauce.

Curried Shrimp: In blazer of chafing dish, mix and heat 1 can undiluted condensed mushroom soup, ⅓ cup milk, 2 teasp. curry powder. Stick cooked, cleaned shrimp on toothpicks for guests to dunk into sauce.

Rabbit Toasties: Heat Old-time Welsh Rabbit (p. 214 or from a jar) in blazer of chafing dish. Let guests dunk crisp crackers in rabbit.

Swiss Fondue: See p. 214.

NIBBLERS—OFF THE PANTRY SHELF

Heat one of these off-the-shelf nibblers in blazer (skillet) of chafing dish. Then keep warm in blazer over hot-water pan.

Canned Chili con Carne: Guests spoon hot chili onto crisp crackers or 1″ pieces of corn sticks.

Cheese Dip: Guests dunk crisp crackers or tomato wedges into hot Old-time Welsh Rabbit, p. 214, or hot pasteurized process-cheese spread (cheese sauce) from jar.

Baked Beans: Heat canned baked beans with chili sauce and prepared mustard to taste. Guests dunk small pieces of canned brown bread into beans.

Cocktail Franks or Brown-and-Serve Sausages: Heat franks or sausages in ½ cup catchup thinned with beer. Serve with toothpicks.

GLAMOUR DESSERTS

Make the following in blazer (skillet) of chafing dish over direct heat.

Sautéed Bananas: See p. 289. Before serving, sprinkle bananas with sugar, nutmeg, and rum.

Cherries Flambé: See p. 427. This is a festive way to serve ice cream.

Mincemeat Aflame: See p. 427. Spoon, blazing, over vanilla ice cream.

Crepes Suzette: See p. 387. It's a most famous dessert!

Dessert Crepes: Soften cream cheese with a very little milk. Spread on Crepes, p. 387; roll. Serve with currant jelly, beaten with fork.

Choco-Nut Crepes: Add chopped nuts to batter for Crepes, p. 387. Roll crepes; sprinkle generously with grated sweet chocolate.

Crepe Pie: Soften 3-oz. pkg. cream cheese with 1 tablesp. orange juice. Add 1 teasp. sugar and 1 tablesp. grated orange rind. Spread mixture on Crepes, p. 387, made about 7″ in diameter. Stack 4 crepes together with filling. Cut into wedges; dust with fruit sugar.

Popcorn: Place a little salad oil in blazer (skillet) of chafing dish. Pour in enough popcorn to cover bottom of pan 1-kernel deep; add salt. Shake or stir until corn starts to pop. Then immediately cover; continue shaking until all corn pops.

Caramel Puffs: This is a wonderful brunch bread. Melt ¼ cup butter or margarine in blazer (skillet) of chafing dish. In it, sauté 4 corn muffins on all sides. When muffins are golden, add ⅓ cup pecans or walnut halves. Now, over each muffin, squeeze juice of ¼ orange (cut into wedge) or 1 tablesp. sherry. Pour 1 cup dark corn syrup and 1 teasp. vanilla extract around muffins; stir; baste until syrup is hot, muffins well coated. Serve hot, topped with ice cream or whipped cream. Makes 4 servings.

Broiled Grapefruit, Skillet Style, for 2: See p. 390.

Top-of-Range "Baked" Apples: See p. 401. Just before serving, spoon a little bourbon over apples; heat. Serve alamode.

Old English Spiced Cider: See p. 501. Halve each ingredient; make in hot-water pan over direct heat.

COOK AS IN A DOUBLE BOILER

Set the hot-water pan of your chafing dish in place. Top with the blazer, and you have a double boiler. Proceed as if you were at the kitchen range. Anything you can cook in a double boiler you can cook here. (Practice, of course, develops showmanship.)

Cheese Ditty: See p. 214.

Chicken à la Queen: See p. 158.

Oysters in Cream: See p. 190.

Rabbit Scramble: See p. 232.

Scrambled Eggs: See p. 224. Use "In Double Boiler" variation.

USE AS A SERVING DISH TOO

The chafing dish is not only a cooking utensil but a handsome serving dish. Food can be cooked in the kitchen in advance, transferred to the chafing dish, and taken to the table.

Besides being glamorous, a chafing dish keeps food hot and appetizing even unto the second helpings. To keep food hot for short periods of time, use just the blazer (skillet). For longer periods, keep it warm over hot-water pan.

INFORMAL BUFFET

Mina's Italian Spaghetti, p. 239
(sauce goes in chafing dish, spaghetti in bowl)
Green Olives   Celery Sticks
Toasted French Bread
Ice-Cream Tarts (bought)
Black Coffee

A LITTLE SUPPER

Hamburger Stroganoff, p. 70, on
Parsley Noodles
Dill-Pickle Sticks
Rye-Bread-and-Butter Fingers
Baked Apples with Mincemeat Aflame
(See pp. 401 and 427)
Salted Nuts   Coffee (instant)

SOMETHING FOR THE GIRLS

Quick-Curried Crab, p. 186
Broccoli Platter (hot or cold)
Toasted Corn-Muffin Slices
Peach Melba, p. 427   Coffee   Macaroons

CHAFING-DISH PARTIES

The chafing dish fits into almost any type of party. Just remember to feature the dish you are cooking before an audience by planning a simple menu around it. For instance:

DROP IN FOR A BITE

French-Toasted Sandwiches, p. 362
Currant Jelly   Hot Coffee

A DUNKING PARTY

Swiss Fondue, p. 214   Hot Coffee
Grapes
(The biggest bunch you can find)
Salted Almonds

COME AT FIVE

Spicy Meat Balls, p. 26
Cocktails or "Mocktails"

BRUNCH WITH US

Tomato-and-Clam Juice
Susan's Cheesy Scramble, p. 225
Deviled-Ham-Spread Toast
Strips of Coffeecake   Currant Jelly
Hot Coffee

DINNER FOR FOUR

Lamb Kidneys Piquant, p. 117, on Fluffy Rice
Sliced Tomatoes Marinated in French Dressing
Frozen Fruit Sauté, p. 379
Crisp Cookies   Coffee

Cooking for One

To be successful, cooking for just one person requires careful planning, smart shopping, and skillful food preparation. But it can be fun.

PLAN CAREFULLY

Plan menus ahead of time, to provide variety and to use leftovers in interesting ways.

Plan easy-to-fix dishes. If the dish can be made quickly, there's less temptation to skip it. See also Quick and Easy Meals, p. 569, and Cooking for Two, p. 631.

Plan streamlined menus. Serve just a few items, but have plenty of each.

Plan a roast for the weekend. The leftovers will be a wonderful help the next week.

Plan your buying. Buy:
1. Small quantities to avoid waste.
2. Eight-ounce cans of fruits and vegetables. They're just right for a family of one.
3. Frozen and canned foods. They're ready to use, involve no waste, and you can use just part of a package if you wish.
4. Packaged mixes. They save time and work, with fine results assured. See Mixes in Index.

Cook for the next day while you're out in the kitchen doing dishes, etc.

Use a pressure cooker. It makes short order of so many dishes. See Pressure Cooking, p. 194.

When food is left over, see Leftovers, p. 550, for wonderful ways to use it up.

SHOP AND USE FOOD WISELY

So many foods are made to order for you! They come as single portions, or in small quantities. Or you can use part of a food and save the rest for later.

Breads and Crackers:
1. Packaged biscuit, muffin, or popover mix
2. Brown-and-serve rolls. Heat what you need; store rest for next day as label directs.
3. Canned breads. Use for sandwiches.
4. Refrigerated pan-ready biscuits. Reheat leftovers as in Leftover Biscuits, p. 326
5. Small packages of crisp crackers

Cheese: Keep several kinds on hand, to add heartiness to salads, sandwiches, etc. Also see Cheese as Dessert, p. 216.

Chicken:
1. Chicken parts. Fry, broil, or simmer.
2. Frozen chicken pie, à la king, etc.
3. Canned chicken fricassee, etc. See p. 136. Chicken chow mein, etc. See p. 514.
4. Broiler-fryers. Sauté as on p. 138. Or cook half a chicken as in Oven-Easy Chicken, p. 140, and broil the rest next day, p. 138. Or broil it all!

Desserts:
1. Cookies. Keep the cookie jar filled. Use packaged cookies or cookie or brownie mix. Or make dough for Susan's Vanilla Refrigerator Cookies, p. 481; refrigerate it; slice off and bake as many cookies as you wish.
2. Cake, cupcakes, or gingerbread. With today's fine cake and gingerbread mixes, you can

have cake when you like. You can freeze part of a cake for later use as on p. 539. There are frosting mixes too.

3. Ice cream. Buy it or make it from a mix. See Ice Creams and Sherbets, p. 424.
4. Cheese and fruit. This is gourmet fare! Try dates, cheese, and crackers. See Cheese as Dessert, p. 216.
5. Canned fruit (including purple plums). Use as dessert or breakfast fruit.
6. Fresh fruit. Keep a variety on hand—berries, grapefruit, cantaloupe, oranges, bananas, watermelon wedges, etc.
7. Fruit-flavored gelatins, rennet custards
8. Packaged puddings. See Today's Blancmange, p. 393, for ways to serve them.

Eggs: Serve them scrambled, poached, hard-cooked, creamed, in omelets, etc. See Eggs, p. 223.

Fish and Shellfish:
1. Frozen fish sticks, fish fillets, rock-lobster tails, etc.
2. Canned tuna, salmon, crab meat, minced clams
3. Fresh fillets, small whole fish, oysters, shrimp, scallops, etc.

Meats:
1. Canned meats. See p. 123 for ways to serve them.
2. Ready-cooked meats. See p. 118 for ways to serve them.
3. Chops, small steaks. See Meats, p. 46.
4. Franks. Broil, simmer, or pan-broil. Or use right from the package in sandwiches, etc.
5. Frozen beef pie. It's ready to heat and eat.
6. Frozen meats—packaged hamburger patties, veal cutlets, grill steaks, liver, etc.
7. Ham slice. Pan-fry, broil, or bake.
8. Hamburger. Buy just enough for one meal. Or buy enough for two meals; use part for patties, rest in some other favorite way. See p. 63.
9. Lamb and veal kidneys
10. Pork sausage. Buy fresh or brown-and-serve kind.
11. Pork tenderloin. Stuff, for a special treat.
12. Smoked boneless butt (a fine small ham). Simmer; then finish as you like it.

Salad Makings: Keep salad makings on hand.
1. Greens. See Salad Greens, p. 298.
2. Tomatoes, etc. See Salad Extras, p. 299.

3. Fruit-flavored gelatin. Use it to make molded fruit salads quickly; serve as salad today, dessert tomorrow.
4. Canned tomato aspic. See p. 315. Slice as needed; refrigerate between times.

Salad Dressings: Personalize ready-to-use salad dressings as on pp. 317 to 318.

Sauces:
1. Pasteurized process-cheese spread. This makes a wonderful cheese sauce for vegetables, meats, sandwiches.
2. Canned beef gravy. This is a fine top-off for chops, hamburgers, etc., and can be added to stew, meat pie, and the like.
3. Canned tomato sauce
4. Canned condensed cream soups. Use as sauce. See Quick Cream Sauce, p. 374.

Seasonings:
1. Monosodium glutamate; seasoned, garlic, celery, and onion salt. They step up flavors.
2. Herbs and spices. These give new flavor to old favorites.
3. A little wine. Does wonders for a soup, main dish, or dessert. See Cook with Wine, p. 506.

Soups:
1. Canned and frozen soups and soup mixes
2. Canned and frozen chowders
3. Chowders. They're so easy to make from canned minced clams, corn, or tuna or frozen fish fillets.
4. Oyster stew—it comes frozen, too.

Vegetables:
1. Frozen vegetables. Cook ½ pkg. at a time.
2. Canned vegetables. Serve part hot, the rest in salad the next day.
3. Potatoes. Frozen French fries or canned white or sweet potatoes eliminate paring and short-cut the cooking process.
4. Canned macaroni and spaghetti dishes, baked beans, etc. They pinch-hit for potatoes.
5. Rice. It's easy to cook in a small quantity.
6. Canned rice

MAKE COOKING EASY

For an Unhurried Breakfast

1. Set the table the night before.
2. Keep these breakfast work savers on hand:

Canned or frozen fruit juices
Frozen waffles; pancake, biscuit, muffin, or popover mix
Individual packages of ready-to-eat cereal
Quick-cooking hot cereals
Brown-and-serve pork sausages
Instant coffee, instant cocoa mix, etc.
Powdered cream, etc.
3. Don't dry breakfast dishes except glasses and silver. Cover rest with clean towel; let drain until dinner. Remember to use paper cups and plates (some are plastic-coated).

Dinner Menus for One

I'LL HAVE SOUP

Cream-of-Mushroom Soup
Club Sandwich of Deviled Ham, Tomato, and Lettuce on Toast
Hot Apricots, p. 379   Gingersnaps   Coffee

———

Oyster Stew, p. 42
Chopped Raw-Vegetable Sandwich
Coffee Jelly   Chocolate Cookies   Tea

———

Black-Bean Soup
Tuna-and-Celery Sandwich on Toast
Melon Wedge Alamode
Ladyfingers   Milk

———

Tomato Soup
Chopped-Chicken-Liver-and-Bacon Sandwich on Toast
Orange Gelatin with Cut-up Orange and Dates
Milk

I'LL HAVE CHICKEN OR HAM

Frozen Chicken Pie
Frozen Cranberry-Orange Relish
Buttered Canned Blue Lake Green Beans
Fresh Pear with Cream Cheese
Crackers or Cookies   Coffee

———

Ham-Banana Roll Ups, p. 133   Buttered Rice
Tossed Romaine Salad
Coffee Ice Cream with Grated Chocolate
Coffee

———

Mixed Grill, p. 55
(chicken, cooked sweet potatoes and zucchini)
Stuffed Celery   Rhubarb Sauce
Cookies   Coffee

———

Pan-broiled Ham or Picnic Slice, p. 90
Sautéed Pineapple or Peaches
Peas   Coleslaw
Marshmallow Chocolate Pudding
(put marshmallow in dish; pour hot packaged chocolate pudding over it)
Coffee

I'LL HAVE FISH

Broiled Rock-Lobster Tail, p. 188
Hot Buttered Peas   Lettuce Sandwich
Sliced Fresh Peaches with Currant Sauce
(melt currant jelly)

———

Easy Broiled Fish, p. 172, or Scallop Broil, p. 191
Frozen French Fries
Old-fashioned Tomatoes
(chill seasoned canned tomatoes)
Sliced Bananas   Milk

I'LL HAVE EGGS

Tomato Juice
Individual Omelets, p. 227
(spread with chili sauce or cheese)
Canned Shoestring Potatoes
Raw-Carrot Salad
Canned Prunes   Cinnamon Toast   Milk

———

Scrambled Eggs, p. 224, on Toast Spread with Deviled Ham
Frozen Limas   Tossed Lettuce Salad
Canned Pineapple   Cream Cheese, Crackers
Coffee

———

Easy Poached Eggs, p. 225, on Toasted, Split English Muffins Spread with Cheese Spread
Tossed Green Salad
Instant Vanilla Pudding with Currant Jelly
Chocolate Cookies   Tea

I'LL HAVE FRANKS OR HAMBURGERS

Franks with Heated Chili Sauce
Buttered Green Limas
Pear-and-Cream-Cheese Salad
Pretzel Sticks   Coffee

———

Sautéed, Sliced Franks
Baked Acorn Squash, p. 272, with Peas
Lettuce Wedges
Packaged Tapioca Pudding with Chocolate
Sauce

———

Hot Tomato Juice
Our Best-Ever Hamburgers, p. 64
Parsley Canned Potatoes   Green Beans
Pineapple-and-Date Salad
Toasted Crackers   Cocoa

———

Sausage-Stuffed Squash, p. 123
Sautéed Apple Slices
Celery Stalks   Whole-wheat Bread
De Luxe Rennet Custard, p. 393, with
Chopped Nuts

I'LL HAVE SPAGHETTI

Chili con Carne on Spaghetti or Rice
Coleslaw
Broiled Grapefruit   Milk or Tea

———

Canned Spaghetti with Meat Sauce,
Parmesan Cheese
Spinach-and-Radish Salad Bowl
Crisp Crackers and Smoky Cheese
Tangerines   Hot Coffee

I'LL HAVE LIVER OR SAUSAGE

Liverwurst and Bacon, p. 112
Buttered Carrots
Celery Sticks   Rye-Bread Toast
Fresh Berries with Sweet or Sour Cream

———

Brown-and-Serve Sausage, p. 84
Packaged Macaroni-and-Cheese Dinner
Frozen Broccoli   Romaine Salad
Chocolate-Almond Rennet Custard, p. 393

I'LL TAKE IT EASY COME SUMMER

Creamed Eggs on Deviled-Ham Toast
More Buttered Toast   Jam or Jelly
Pear Salad with French Dressing   Tea

———

Toasted Peanut-Butter Sandwiches
Bowl of Tossed Green Salad, Plus Bits of
Grated Process Cheese and Crisp Bacon
No-Bake Custards, p. 382   Oatmeal Cookies
Iced Coffee

———

Curried Cream-of-Tomato Soup
(add pinch of curry powder to soup)
Toasted Raisin-Bread-and-Cottage-Cheese
Sandwiches
Fruit Jelly Alamode   Iced Tea

———

Easygoing Supper, p. 112
(halve recipe for a guest and you)
Crusty Rolls
Canned Pears (sprinkled with nutmeg)   Tea

DISHES FOR ONE

Soup

With a Can of Soup, p. 33 (serve in cup; sip with main course)

Eggs and Cheese for Lunch or Dinner

Baked (Shirred) Eggs (3 variations), p. 226
Cheese Fondue (for 2), p. 214

Cheese Toast with Bacon (halve ingredients)*, p. 215
Individual Omelets

(choose one of Ten Omelet Fillings), p. 227
Scrambled Eggs, p. 224

Toasted Cheese Casserole for 1, p. 216

Meats and Poultry

Braised **Pork Chops** or Steaks (6 ways), p. 79

Broiled **Chicken** (with 5 variations), p. 138

Broiled **Kidneys** on Toast, p. 116

Broiled **Lamb Chops** and Steaks, p. 99

Broiled **Liver**, p. 112

Broiled **Steak** (filet mignon or club), p. 54

Chef's **Lamb** and Mushrooms*, p. 131

Fully Cooked Brown-and-Serve **Pork Sausage**, p. 84

Hamburger Mixed Grill, p. 66

If Meat Can Be Sliced (leftovers), p. 127

If Meat Is in Small Pieces (leftovers), p. 128

Kabobs, p. 595

Kidneys en Brochette, p. 117

Lamb Barbecue*, p. 131

Little **Steaks**, p. 594

Liverwurst and Bacon (use ¼ recipe), p. 112

Mac's Sautéed **Kidneys**, p. 116

Mixed **Grill** (many ideas), p. 55

Our Best-Ever **Hamburgers**, plus dozens of ideas for Hamburger Spoon-Ons, Spread-Ons, Go-Betweens, Toss-Ins, pp. 64 to 66

Oven-Easy **Chicken**, p. 140

Pan-broiled **Minute** or Cube Steaks, p. 55

Pan-Fried **Sweetbreads**, p. 114

Quick **Beef Stew**, p. 62

Sautéed **Chicken** (with seasonings or variations), p. 138

Sautéed **Squab**, p. 155

Skillet-Fried **Chicken**, p. 139

To Cook **Fresh-Pork Sausage**, p. 84

To Serve **Ready-Cooked Meats** (15 wonderful ways), p. 119

Veal Italian with Carrots, p. 109

Virginia Franks, p. 122

* *Makes a dinner-in-a-dish for one, with salad.*

Fish and Shellfish

Baked **Fish** Rolls or Baked, Stuffed Fillets or Steaks (use 1 tablesp. butter, 1 teasp. lemon juice, onion salt, for butter mixture), p. 169

Broiled **Live Lobster**, p. 187

Broiled **Rock-Lobster** Tails, p. 188

Broiled, Stuffed **Lobster**, p. 188

Deviled **Crabs** (for 2)*, p. 186

Easy Baked **Fillets** or Steaks, p. 168

Lobster-Tail Feast, p. 189

Mixed **Fish** Grill, p. 174

Oven-Fried **Fish**, p. 177

Panned **Oysters**, p. 190

Poached **Fish**, U.S.A., p. 175

Scallop Broil, p. 191

Scallop Sauté, p. 191

Skillet-Fried **Oysters**, p. 190

Soft-shell **Crabs** (boiled or broiled), p. 185

Susan's Sautéed **Fish**, p. 175

* *Makes a dinner-in-a-dish for one, with salad.*

Sauces

Extra-Easy **Dessert Sauces**, p. 367

Jiffy **Barbecue**, p. 372

Quick **Tartar**, p. 373

Zippy **Cheese Sauce**, p. 374

Hearty Sandwiches and Breads

Sandwiches

Broiled Open-Face **Sandwiches**, p. 357

Clubs or Double Deckers, p. 359

Frank Burgers, p. 358

Frank Rolls, p. 359

French-Toasted **Sandwiches**, p. 362

Grilled **Cheese** Sandwiches, p. 361

Hamburgers, p. 361

Hot or Cold Meat

Sandwiches (tongue, bacon, cube steaks, ham), p. 360

Junior **Clubs**, p. 360

Salad Burgers, p. 357

Salad Rolls, p. 358

Breads

Easy **Bread Sticks**, p. 342

Junior **Loaves**, p. 341

Slicettes, p. 342

Speedy **Waffles**, p. 337

Toast (5 ways), p. 344

Cooking for Two

Twosomes include young couples, and older couples whose children are away, and pairs of career men or women. They go to their jobs, hurry home at day's end, then work together to get a good dinner in double-quick time. If you count yourself among these twosomes, read on.

PLAN TO SAVE TIME AND MONEY

Plan future meals soon after you've eaten. If you plan when you aren't ravenously hungry, you'll do a better job of balancing nutritional values and keeping within the budget.

Plan to have leftovers. You can prepare part of tomorrow's dinner as you cook tonight's. For instance:

Serve tonight	*Serve tomorrow*
Mashed potatoes	Potato cakes
Boiled rice	Rice custard
Stewed apricots	Upside-down cake

Refer to Quick-and-Easy Meals, p. 569, for dishes especially nice to make after a day's work.

Plan the next day's lunch ahead when feasible.

Plan to have plenty of each item, but serve fewer items. Get variety from day to day rather than by serving a number of dishes in any one menu. For example, a double helping of any green or yellow vegetable is just as nutritious as one serving of each of two, and is less trouble to buy and prepare.

Plan to serve plates from the kitchen, dividing food proportionately. This cuts down dishwashing, eliminates unmanageable leftovers.

Plan on an occasional luxury item—a stuffed squab, a soupçon of caviar.

MARKETING FOR TWO

Read Shop and Use Food Wisely, p. 625. The many marketing tips for the solo cook apply to you too.

Read Look for Short-cut Buys, p. 570, for foods that save time and effort.

How much to buy? That all-important question is answered in the Amount to Buy paragraphs in Meats, p. 46; Poultry, p. 136; Fish, p. 168, and Vegetable Chart, p. 278. Also see recipes throughout book for "For 2" directions.

If you both go to business, market for staples on weekends. Divide daily shopping chores.

Look for ready-made wares. Some specialty items can give a lift to everyday meals—chocolate leaves, brioche, special relishes, etc.

WHEN TWO COOK

Use tools that fit. In cooking, it's important to have the right equipment in the right sizes. You'll want regular-size equipment when you cook for company. So use list in Pots and Pans, p. 692. Also choose a few items especially suitable for your small-scale cooking, such as:

Small skillet, with cover
1-qt. casserole, plus cover that doubles as 6″ pie plate
2-cup saucepans
Small mixing bowls
2- or 4-cup coffee maker
Individual baking dishes that can serve as salad bowls too

If you both work, let the first one home start the cooking. Agree ahead of time on who will start what.

See To Vary and To Serve hints at the ends of our recipes. With a few changes, a dish can seem brand-new when you make it again.

Leftovers can be a problem, but if you know what to do with them, they're really a plus! For lots of ideas, see Leftovers, p. 550.

HOW TO TAILOR RECIPES FOR TWO

Recipes for Two: Many recipes in this book may be made as directed; then they'll provide second helpings for two. Many others can be halved and directions followed without change. Where changes are necessary, special directions have been given in a "For 2" paragraph.

To Halve Recipes: Use Equivalent Measures, p. 16, as a guide in halving ingredients. Jot down reduced amounts in margin of each recipe, so you won't have to look up these amounts again.

Meats, Fish, Poultry, Vegetables for Two: In the chapters on these subjects, the basic cooking methods given apply to "For 2" amounts as well as to larger quantities. Be sure to check Amount to Buy paragraphs. (See How Much To Buy, p. 631.)

If You Make Full Recipe For:

1. *Soups and Chowders:* Refrigerate leftovers, covered; reheat next day in double boiler.
2. *Molded Salads and Desserts:* Leftovers keep beautifully till a day or so later.

3. *Salad Dressings:* Most dressings keep well in refrigerator. (For those that don't—sour-cream, cream-cheese, and cottage-cheese dressings, etc.—halve ingredients.)
4. *Quick Breads:* Serve part fresh and hot; next day, serve rest warmed or toasted. See Leftover Biscuits, p. 326; Leftover Muffins, p. 327; Leftover Corn Bread or Muffins, p. 329; Toasted Afternoon Tea Scones, p. 326; Leftover Coffeecake, p. 330.
5. *Yeast Breads:* Refrigerator rolls are especially nice for two. See Susan's Refrigerator Rolls, p. 348.

   Bakers' breads and rolls need not always be the same; see Bread and Rolls You Buy, p. 340, for wonderful things to do with them.
6. *Desserts:* Serve leftovers a different way the second time; check through Desserts, p. 378, and Sauces, p. 367, for ideas. Most frozen desserts keep handsomely in a freezer or freezing compartment.

To Freeze Leftovers: See Freezing, p. 533.

To Use Leftovers: See Leftovers, p. 550.

SERVING TWO NICELY

First impressions often sell a meal. How do your dinners rate aesthetically?

Make the scene glamorous. Light candles and play low music on the radio. Use a fresh posy, a bit of ivy, for a centerpiece.

If you're serving a roast, let your partner carve it at the table for practice.

Serve individual casseroles; they look festive. Garnish food (a bit of green does wonders).

Occasionally serve in the living room—juice or a nibbler before the meal, coffee after the meal.

Celebrate every holiday and birthday with a special dish or special table setting.

Cut down on the number of courses, to avoid jumping-jack tactics.

DINNERS THAT TWO CAN COOK

EASY SUNDAY DINNER
(the newlyweds)

Broiled Chicken, p. 138
or Sautéed Chicken, p. 138
Fluffy Hot Rice, p. 233, with
Quick Mushroom Sauce, p. 372
Buttered Peas
Cranberry-Celery Salad
Butterscotch-Nut Biscuits, p. 325
Milk   Coffee or Tea

Start cooking chicken first, then rice; then heat canned, or cook frozen, peas. Prepare sauce. Get biscuits ready for baking (they're dessert). For each salad, place slice of canned jellied cranberry sauce on greens; garnish with cut celery; top with French dressing.

P.S. Ask Mr. Newlywed if he'd like to try his hand at broiling the chicken.

CHICKEN FEAST
(two career girls)

Barbecue-Broiled Chicken, p. 139
Broiled Sweet Potatoes
Canned-Green-Bean-and-Onion Salad
Broiler-Toasted Cheese Rolls
Coffee Quick Pudding
Milk   Coffee or Tea

In morning, Mary puts can of green beans (such as Blue Lake variety) in refrigerator. At dinnertime, she makes instant vanilla pudding, adding 1 tablesp. instant coffee; then she puts salad together.

Edna barbecues chicken and broils canned sweet potatoes and cheese-sprinkled rolls.

TOP-STOVE DINNER
(Mother and Dad)

Skillet Corned Beef with Sauerkraut
Mashed Potatoes   Crisp Celery
Peaches or Pears in Burgundy
or Chilled Fruit Cocktail Supreme
Milk   Tea or Coffee

Mother starts cooking potatoes in pressure cooker while Dad opens 1 can each corned beef and sauerkraut. He slices about two thirds of beef, refrigerates rest for next day's lunch. Mother heats 1 tablesp. bacon fat in skillet, spreads drained sauerkraut in skillet, adds 2 tablesp. water, tops it with corned-beef slices, and simmers mixture, covered, 10 min. She pours ¼ cup light cream over kraut and heats it 2 or 3 min.

When potatoes are done, Dad whips them with electric mixer or potato masher while Mother prepares celery.

For dessert, Mother places peach halves in dessert dishes and pours on wine. (Or she adds unpared red-apple cubes and sliced bananas to canned fruit cocktail.)

FOR THE NOVICE COOK

TWO-BURNER DINNER FOR FOUR

Superb Skillet Burger Loaf, p. 69
Boiled New Potatoes   Buttered Canned Corn
Radish Coleslaw
Mousse au Chocolat, p. 390   Coffee

As soon as you get home, make dessert. (Or serve packaged instant chocolate pudding, topped with chocolate sauce.) After turning dessert into sherbet glasses, set in coldest part of refrigerator.

Next, boil unpared small new potatoes (or heat canned potatoes) in bottom of double boiler. Then put canned corn in top of double boiler, over potatoes; add lump of butter, salt, pepper; cover; heat. Make burger loaf in skillet over another burner. While this cooks, make coleslaw, adding radish slices.

STARRING CORNED-BEEF HASH

Baked Corned-Beef Hash with Poached Eggs
Speedy Cream-Fried Tomatoes, p. 275
Cucumber-and-Radish Salad   Hard Rolls
Fruit-Shortcake Tarts   Tea

Slice ½ can corned-beef hash into 2 patties. Sauté with tomatoes till golden on both sides. Meanwhile, make salad. Remove hash. Finish tomatoes. Poach 2 eggs; serve on hash.

At desserttime, fill packaged dessert shells with sliced bananas, peaches, or seedless grapes; spoon melted currant jelly or apricot jam over fruit.

P.S. Heat leftover hash and use with pickle relish as filling for toasted sandwiches.

CHOP SUEY TONIGHT

Hot Tomato Juice
Bacon Chop Suey, p. 93
Buttered Frozen Broccoli
Tossed Green Salad with Grated Carrots
Crisp Crackers   Margarine or Butter
Canned Crushed Pineapple
Packaged Chocolate Cookies
Milk   Coffee or Tea

Place pineapple in sherbet glasses; refrigerate. Start chop suey. Cook broccoli as label directs. Make salad. Heat tomato juice; serve in cups with main course.

WE LOVE VEAL

Scaloppine of Veal Marsala, p. 109,
on Parsley Rice
Buttered Canned Beets
Iceberg-Lettuce Chunks with Salad Dressing
Rye Bread   Butter or Margarine
Banana Fingers in Chilled Cranberry Juice or
Broiled Grapefruit, Skillet Style, for 2, p. 390

Chill cranberry juice in coldest part of refrigerator. Start veal. Prepare packaged precooked rice as label directs. Heat beets.

Tear crisp iceberg lettuce into small chunks. Before serving, toss with dressing. Add butter to rice; fluff with fork; sprinkle with snipped parsley. Season beets to taste with butter, onion salt, pepper.

At desserttime, quarter bananas lengthwise; then halve crosswise; pour cranberry juice over them; sprinkle with cinnamon.

FOR COMPANY

Cream-of-Tomato Soup Parmesan
'Frisco Tuna, p. 179
Buttered Peas   Crisp Celery
Canned Jellied Cranberry Sauce
Bananas on the Half Shell, p. 378
Milk   Tea or Coffee

Prepare, bake, tuna. Prepare, refrigerate, celery. Cook frozen, or heat canned, peas; season.

Meanwhile, heat canned soup with milk as label directs. Sprinkle each serving of hot soup with grated Parmesan cheese.

Arrange food on dinner plates in kitchen. At desserttime, prepare bananas.

IN NO TIME AT ALL

Old-fashioned Tomato Cocktail, p. 18
Deviled Hamburger Toast, p. 358
Parsley Corn
Lettuce with Cheese Dressing
Spiced Applesauce   Packaged Cupcakes
Milk   Coffee or Tea

Prepare tomatoes; chill quickly in ice-cube tray. Season canned applesauce with a little nutmeg, cinnamon, grated lemon rind, and lemon juice; chill quickly.

Make Deviled Hamburger Toast; broil. Meanwhile, cook frozen, or heat canned, corn; season; add snipped parsley. Prepare lettuce, adding Parmesan to dressing.

SOUTH OF THE BORDER

Chilled Pineapple Juice
Chili con Carne on Spaghetti
Big Bowl of Tossed Green Salad
French Bread   Margarine or Butter
Peach-Almond Shortcake
Milk   Coffee or Tea

Chill small glassfuls of pineapple juice. Cook spaghetti. Heat canned chili con carne. Whip cream for shortcake; add bit of almond extract. Prepare salad (add a little crumbled blue cheese). Drain, season, spaghetti; top with chili.

At desserttime, assemble shortcake. Top bakers' spongecake with drained canned or thawed frozen peaches, then with whipped cream.

SO GOOD

Veal Italian with Carrots, p. 109
Buttered Hominy or Noodles
Hard Rolls   Butter or Margarine
Fruit-and-Cheese Dessert Salad
Milk   Coffee or Tea

Start veal dish. Meanwhile, prepare a combination of fruits in season for salad; refrigerate.

Slowly heat ½ No. 2½ can hominy (or cook noodles as label directs); season; sprinkle with snipped parsley. (Use rest of hominy with green beans or corn for supper next day.)

Crumble a bit of blue cheese into French dressing; serve with salad.

FISH TONIGHT

Savory Tuna on Toast, p. 179
or Shrimp Creole, p. 193
Tossed Green-and-Mixed-Vegetable Salad
Buttered Toast
Sweet Pickles or Salted Peanuts
Canned Peach Halves Almondine
Butterscotch Squares, p. 485
Milk   Coffee or Tea

Cook frozen mixed vegetables (or use leftover or drained canned mixed vegetables); chill quickly in ice-cube tray.

Place peaches in serving dishes; add a little almond extract to syrup; chill. Now prepare tuna on toast or Shrimp Creole. Toss salad. Prepare as many Butterscotch Squares as you'll need.

BUILDING UP TO DESSERT

Platter of Ready-Cooked Meats
and Sliced Tomatoes
Jiffy Macaroni-and-Cheese Casserole
Rye Bread   Butter or Margarine   Pickles
Strawberry Drop Shortcakes
Tea or Coffee (hot or iced)   Milk

About 30 min. before dinner: Prepare fresh, or thaw frozen, berries. Heat oven to 450°F. Place canned macaroni in cheese sauce in casserole; top with buttered crumbs; bake 15 min., or until crumbs are browned.

Arrange meat platter: Overlap tomato slices down center; circle with parsley; border with sliced meats.

Mix drop-biscuit or shortcake dough, using packaged biscuit mix. Remove macaroni from oven. Bake shortcakes; then split; butter; fill and top with strawberries.

SOUTHERN STYLE

Hickory Corn Fritters, p. 255
(sauté 2 or 3 extra franks)
Canned Stewed Tomatoes
Lettuce Sandwiches on Rye Bread
Cookies from Cookie Jar
Cocoa

Make cocoa; let stand to mellow. Then make sandwiches; refrigerate.

Heat tomatoes. (Save leftover canned stewed tomatoes—they come seasoned—for first course next day; serve cold in sherbet glasses.) Make corn fritters.

SO EASY

Skillet-Barbecued Franks, p. 121
Raw Cauliflowerets and Raw-Carrot Sticks
Easy Bread Sticks from Frankfurter Rolls, p. 342
Hot Blended Maple Syrup on Ice Cream
Coffee

Cook franks. Prepare cauliflowerets and carrots, then bread sticks. Heat syrup.

NEW ENGLAND DINNER

Skillet-Boiled Dinner, p. 126
(corned beef, potatoes, and carrots)
Cheese-Stuffed Celery
Hard Rolls
So-Easy Chocolate Refrigerator Cake
Tea

In ice-cube tray, stack poundcake slices, spreading Chocolate Whipped Cream, p. 369, between them; place in freezing compartment of refrigerator till chilled.

Start cooking boiled dinner. Stuff celery.

SEPTEMBER, OCTOBER, NOVEMBER

Harvest Twosome, p. 121
Potato Chips   Susan's Coleslaw, p. 303
Rye Bread
Coconut-Ice-Cream Balls Topped
with Crushed Pineapple or Sliced Peaches
Coffee (instant)

Make Harvest Twosome. While it bakes, scoop out ice-cream balls; roll in coconut; freeze. Make coleslaw. Open canned pineapple; chill.

AND POPOVERS FOR TWO

Easygoing Supper, p. 112
Romaine Salad Bowl
Hot Popovers (from a mix) or
Toasted English Muffins
Marshmallow-Topped Coffee Ice Cream
Tea

Make and bake popovers (reheat leftovers for breakfast next day). Start main dish cooking. Then prepare romaine; refrigerate. (If serving English muffins, split; butter; top with grated cheese or sprinkling of caraway or poppy seeds before toasting.) Toss salad. Use marshmallow cream (it comes in jars) on coffee ice cream.

SPAGHETTI FEED

Salametti, p. 241
Tossed Green Salad
with Sliced Stuffed Olives
Bread Sticks
Lemon Sherbet   Warm Fudge Cuts, p. 476
Coffee

Make and bake fudge cuts—they take 12 min. Start cooking Salametti. Prepare salad.

TWO'S COMPANY

Individual Chicken or Beef Pies
Frozen Cranberry Relish
Buttered Green Beans
Tossed Green Salad
Tray of Fresh Pears and Grapes
Cheese and Crackers   Coffee

Early in day: Place frozen cranberry relish in food compartment of refrigerator to thaw. As soon as you get home from work, start heating frozen chicken or beef pies in oven. Cook beans. Arrange dish of relish and tray of fruit, cheese, and crackers. Toss salad.

BACHELOR GIRLS

Tomato Bouillon
Chicken à la King
on Toasted English or Corn Muffins
Buttered Peas
Raw-Vegetable Relish Tray
Baked Apples or Applesauce Alamode
Coffee

Heat 1 pkg. frozen (or 1 can) chicken à la king as label directs, adding 2 tablesp. heavy cream and ¼ teasp. dried thyme.

For tomato bouillon, heat ½ bouillon cube with 1¼ cups tomato juice. Heat canned, or cook frozen, peas. For relish tray, prepare celery, onions, pickles, cottage cheese. Toast buttered, split muffins.

Serve canned baked apples; or top chilled canned applesauce with ice cream and bit of cinnamon.

DISHES FOR TWO

Below are listed some of the recipes in this book that are especially nice for two. See also suggestions in Cooking for One, p. 625; many of them can be useful to you too. Check through the book for the many other recipes with their special "For 2" directions, and look over Quick-and-Easy Meals, p. 569.

Eggs (lunch or dinner)

Baked (Shirred) Eggs, p. 226
Country Poached Eggs, p. 226
Dinner Casserole de

Luxe (with second servings), p. 230
Eggs Foo Young, p. 230
French Omelet, p. 226
Individual Omelets, p. 227

Man-Style Baked Eggs, p. 228
New Zealand-Style Eggs (a meal with salad), p. 231
Puffy Omelet, p. 227
Rabbit Scramble,

p. 232
Scrambled Eggs, p. 224
Zippy Hot Egg Salad, p. 307

Hearty Cheese Dishes

Baked Cheese Pudding, p. 215
Cheese Fondue, p. 214
Cheese Souffle for 3,

p. 213
Cheese Strata, p. 215
Cheese Toast with Bacon (a meal with salad), p. 215

Susan's Swiss Pie (a meal with salad), p. 212
Toasted Cheese Casserole for 1, p. 216

Wonder Cheese Custard, p. 216

Hearty Soups (a meal with salad)

Blender Vichyssoise, p. 37

Can-Opener Mine-strone, p. 35

Clam Chowder à la Henry, p. 45

Creamy Potato Soup (nice with cheese sandwich), p. 34

Oyster Stew, p. 42

Pantry-Shelf Pea Soup, p. 35

Swiss Cream-of-Potato Soup, p. 38

Tomato-Cheese Soup, p. 35

Meats

Barbecued Spareribs (a feast), p. 82

Braised Veal Chops, Steaks, and Cutlets (use small skillet), p. 107

Breaded Veal Cutlet, p. 107

Broiled Kidneys on Toast, p. 116

Broiled Liver, p. 112

Canned Luncheon Meat, p. 125

Cooked Tongue, p. 115

Creamed Dried Beef, p. 127

Cube Steaks with Hasty-Tasty Sauce, p. 55

Deviled Tongue Mold, p. 131

Easy Beef-Noodle Casserole (pressure cooked), p. 197

Frank Curry Bake, p. 123

French Veal Cutlets, p. 108

Fully Cooked Brown-and-Serve Sausages, p. 84

Harvest Twosome, p. 121

Mac's Sautéed Kidneys, p. 116

Mixed Grill, p. 55

One-Apiece Loaves (halve ingredients), p. 68

Our Best-Ever Hamburgers, p. 64

Pan-broiled Steak, p. 55

Planked Broiled Steak, p. 55

Ready-to-Eat Beef Tongue, p. 115

Sausage-Stuffed Squash, p. 123

Sautéed Tripe, p. 116

Scaloppine of Veal Marsala, p. 109

Sherry Veal Slices (if appetites are hearty), p. 107

Simmered Smoked

Boneless Shoulder Butt, p. 89

Superb Skillet Burger Loaf, p. 69

Susan's Meat Loaf, p. 68

To Serve Canned Meats, p. 124

To Serve Franks, p. 120

Veal Italian with Carrots, p. 109

Veal Scaloppine, p. 104

Virginia Franks, p. 122

Poultry

A Man's Barbecued Chicken, p. 145

Barbecued Fried Chicken, p. 145

Broiled Chicken, p. 138

Broiled Duckling, p. 155

Chicken Cacciatore, p. 142

Chicken Chasseurs, p. 141

Chicken Chop Suey, p. 149

Chicken Marengo, p. 143

Chicken Paprika, p. 141

Dumplings for Stew, p. 151

Easy Chicken Divan, p. 156

Ellen's Turkey-Olive Curry, p. 156

Minute Chicken Pie (a meal with salad), p. 156

Roast Duckling, p. 154

Roast Guinea Hen, p. 155

Roast Squab, p. 155

Sautéed Chicken, p. 138

Skillet-Fried Chicken, p. 139

Turkey Pie, Broiler Style, p. 160

Fish

Baked Fillets Parmesan, p. 170

Baked Split Whole Fish (second servings), p. 172

Clam Burgers (second servings), p. 184

Crab Meat Maryland, p. 185

Creamed Tuna Supreme, p. 180

Deviled Crabs, p. 186

Easy Broiled Fish, p. 172

Fried Oysters, p. 190

'Frisco Tuna, p. 179

His Lake Trout (second servings), p. 172

Lobster-Tail Feast, p. 189

Oven-Fried Fish, p. 177

Savory Tuna on Toast, p. 179

Scallop Broil, p. 191

Scallop Sauté, p. 191

Shrimp Creole, p. 193

Shrimp Sauté (halve recipe), p. 192

Skillet-Fried Oysters, p. 190

Susan's Scalloped Oysters, p. 190

Top-Hat Salmon Pie, p. 180

Tuna Supper Casserole (a meal with salad), p. 178

Tuna Tomatoes, p. 179

Desserts

Apple Brown Betty, p. 388

Banana-Coconut Rolls, p. 385

Broiled Grapefruit (skillet version), p. 390

Camille's Peach Coconut, p. 388

Chocolate Almond Cream (plan on leftovers), p. 393

Chocolate Fluff (make ½ recipe), p. 464

Chocolate Whipped-Cream Cake, p. 398

Coffee Jelly (left-overs perhaps), p. 405

Cottage Pudding (plan on left-overs), p. 400

De Luxe Rennet Custard (plan on left-overs), p. 393

Desserts in No Time (dozens of ideas), pp. 378 to 382

Dutch Plum Cake, p. 387

Favorite Fruit Desserts (11 recipes plus variations), p. 400

Gingerbread Top-Offs (plan on left-overs), p. 384

Hurry-Up Apple "Pie" (leftovers perhaps), p. 385

Little Orange Chiffon Cake, p. 451

Luscious Cream Filling (use half as filling for 1 cake layer, halved crosswise; use rest as dessert), p. 461

Miracle Cake, p. 440

Quick Apple Crisp (leftovers perhaps), p. 388

Simplicity 1-Egg Cake, p. 446

Spanish Cream, p. 405

Susan's Custard Bread Pudding, p. 391

Susan's Rice Custard, p. 391

Susan's Snow-Pudding Balls, p. 404

Susan's Strawberry Shortcake, p. 383

Tapioca Cream (plan on leftovers), p. 392

Today's Blancmange (plan on leftovers), p. 393

Zabaglione (serve it hot or cold), p. 388

Frozen Desserts

See Ways to Serve Ice Cream You Buy, p. 424. Keep some ice cream on hand to use in these wonderful desserts.

Cooking for a Crowd

Most of you occasionally serve refreshments, tea, luncheon, or dinner at home to a crowd of twenty-five or more guests. Or you may find yourself chairman of the food committee of your club or church group, serving a hundred or so persons. Either event may seem like a large undertaking. Actually they're only a matter of enlarging the same plans you would make to entertain a small group.

Line Up Your Helpers

If you're food chairman of a club or church affair, it will be up to you to organize the work and spread responsibility. Remember that "many hands make light work" only when each pair of hands knows exactly what to do. Before starting to make plans, do call on two or three other club members to work with you.

Decide Where and How to Serve

Before you do much else, decide how and where you can best handle the serving. If plenty of room is available, you may choose to serve the guests at tables. If space is limited, it may be simpler to serve buffet style, as on p. 683, or to serve plates in the kitchen and pass them to guests, who stand or sit, depending upon available facilities.

Next Choose Your Menu

After deciding on the manner of serving, choose the menu. To help you decide on what to serve, see our quantity recipes and quantity chart for serving 50, pp. 642 to 651. Also consider these points:

If you're serving an expensive main dish, such as a roast, serve a low-cost vegetable and salad.

If a low-cost casserole is to be your main course, a more expensive vegetable and salad may be featured. One high spot in the meal—whether it's the main course, salad, or dessert—makes for success.

Figure What You'll Charge

1. Estimate the total cost of the food.
2. To this total, add 4 to 6 per cent more, to cover any unpreventable loss in handling. This will help keep you on the safe side of the ledger.
3. Now compute the cost per person by dividing the total cost by the actual number of paying guests. Add to that figure if you wish to make a profit.
4. If you're aiming for a profit, check these:

What will all the donated food cost?
What will labor—serving and cooking help—cost?

Will you be charged overhead—fuel, light, rent?

Will you have laundry charges?

How much will paper napkins cost?

Will flowers be furnished, or will you buy them?

What extras will be classified "miscellaneous"?

Will you have a guaranteed number of paying guests to depend on, whether they come or not? Or must you allow for possible losses from canceled reservations?

How many nonpaying persons must be fed?

When You Make Up Your Marketing List

When deciding total amount of food you'll need, refer to Quantities to Serve 50 Persons, p. 650. For 25 persons, divide amounts called for by 2. For 100 persons, multiply by 2.

Order all staples well in advance, buying them in wholesale lots, if possible, from school lunchrooms, wholesale dealers, or retail stores willing to quote special prices on large-quantity purchases.

Once you have figured out how large each portion should be, make sure those who serve are not overgenerous. Otherwise your profits will disappear.

Check These Items Too

What about china, silver, etc.? Be sure to check on table linen, silver, china, glass, and other table appointments, to make sure you'll have enough of everything. List all needed items in a little notebook, checking each off as you get it lined up. If the occasion is an anniversary, wedding reception, or the like at your own home, friends and neighbors will usually be happy to lend their best appointments.

You can mix china patterns, so don't worry if, to accommodate all guests, you have to use two china patterns and two glass patterns on your tables. Just alternate the patterns at each cover, and your table will have an attractive orderliness.

If you're using flowers, discuss your table centerpiece with the florist ahead of time so he will be sure to have just what you want.

List cooking utensils you'll need. Plan to buy or borrow any extra utensils needed to take care of the large amounts of food.

Clear the decks. Look around your kitchen and pantry; temporarily put away any unnecessaries so you'll have more work space.

Make refrigerator space: You will need every bit of storage space your refrigerator affords. So remove any foods that can be safely left out for this period. Have plenty of refrigerator bags, bowl covers, waxed paper, aluminum foil, saran, etc. on hand for wrapping and storing foods.

Don't Forget These Points

Do as much as possible the day before. For instance, if you're preparing hot breads, mix together the dry ingredients the day before. Make gelatin desserts and salad dressing the day before too; refrigerate.

If you're roasting meat, don't crowd pans. Leave 2″ to 3″ between roasts. Plan roasting time so roasts can be taken from oven 30 to 40 min. before serving time; then make gravy. Start carving about 20 min. before serving; stack 10 to 12 portions in pile in heated shallow pan; place in warm oven with heat turned off. See Roasts for a Crowd, p. 644.

Keep soups, vegetables, etc., warm. If you do not have a steam table to hold food a few min. before serving, fill large roasting pans with hot water; set over low heat. Set kettles of soup, vegetables, etc., in these pans.

If you're serving salads on individual plates, arrange about half of them just before serving time; arrange the rest while first guests are being served.

When you're serving dessert, cut pie or cake 1 hr. before serving; refrigerate it if it has a cream or custard filling or frosting. Whip cream 1 hr. before serving; refrigerate.

If you're serving cafeteria or buffet style, on serving table, arrange foods (in serving dishes), with proper serving silver, in this order: meat, gravy, potatoes, vegetable, rolls, butter (if not placed on tables in advance), salads, desserts, coffee (optional).

If you're serving a sit-down meal, let kitchen assistants form kitchen assembly line: Each person serves one item and passes plate to next person. When plates are filled, they are placed on tray, which waitress carries to dining room. For very large crowds, arrange two assembly lines, ending both at table where waitresses pick up trays. A waitress with a little experience can handle 18 to 20 guests.

Beware of Food Poisoning

Tragic cases of food poisoning at picnics, community suppers, and institutions have been traced to failure to keep refrigerated perishable food mixtures of meat, fish, or chicken, etc. (for sandwich fillings and salads), as well as fillings for cream puffs, layer cakes, etc. Cool such mixtures quickly by setting container for a short time in sink with cold water running; or set in bowl of crushed ice. Then store mixture *immediately,* while warm, in refrigerator. Keep refrigerated until served.

POPULAR MAIN DISHES

MELLOW HAM LOAVES

7 eggs
1½ teasp. salt
¼ teasp. pepper
4½ lb. uncooked (cook-before-eating) ham, ground
1½ lb. veal shoulder, ground
1½ lb. pork shoulder, ground
5 cups 2-day-old ½" bread squares
2¼ cups nonfat dry milk
2¼ cups water
1½ cups brown sugar, packed
¼ cup vinegar
1 tablesp. dry mustard

About 2 hr. before serving: Start heating oven to 325°F. Lightly beat eggs, salt, pepper. Gently mix in ham, veal, pork. Add bread squares, dry milk, water. Mix lightly but well. Pack into 3 10" x 6" x 3" loaf pans. Bake 30 min. Then mix brown sugar, vinegar, mustard; boil 1 min.; spoon over loaves. Bake loaves 40 to 45 min. longer, or until firm. Pour off excess juice; let stand 15 min. before slicing. When serving, pass juice. Makes 25 servings.

CALICO HAM CASSEROLE

4 pkg. frozen mixed vegetables
¼ cup butter or margarine
3 cups ½" fresh bread squares
1 cup flour
1 teasp. salt
¼ teasp. pepper
2 teasp. dry mustard
2 teasp. Worcestershire
6 cups milk
¾ cup butter or margarine
1 grated medium onion
2 to 3 cups grated process sharp American cheese (½ to ¾ lb.)
2 lb. fully cooked or ready-to-eat ham, cut into strips about 1½" long and ¼" wide

Day ahead: Cook vegetables as label directs. Meanwhile, in large kettle, melt ¼ cup butter; add bread squares; toss well. Remove buttered crumbs; set aside.

In bowl, mix flour with salt, pepper, mustard, Worcestershire; slowly stir in about 2 cups milk. Heat rest of milk in same large kettle used for crumbs; then stir in flour mixture and ¾ cup butter. Cook over low heat, stirring often, until smooth and thickened; add onion and cheese. Cook, stirring often, until cheese is melted. Add drained vegetables and ham. Pour into 2 12" x 8" x 2" baking dishes. Refrigerate along with crumbs.

About 1 hr. before serving: Start heating oven to 350°F. Sprinkle top of each baking dish with buttered crumbs. Bake, uncovered, 40 min., or until hot. Makes 25 servings.

BARBECUED FRANKS

¼ cup butter or margarine
1 cup minced onions
½ teasp. salt
⅛ teasp. pepper
2 teasp. dry mustard
3 tablesp. brown sugar
1½ cups catchup
1½ cups water
¼ cup vinegar
1½ tablesp. Worcestershire
⅛ teasp. tabasco
About 50 franks (6 lb.)

About 1¼ hr. before serving: In saucepan, melt butter; add onions; cook slowly until tender. Add salt and rest of ingredients except franks.

Cook slowly, uncovered, 30 min. Start heating oven to 350°F. Arrange franks in 1 layer in shallow open pans; pour on sauce. Bake, uncovered, 25 min., turning franks occasionally. Serve from pans. Makes 25 servings.

SPAGHETTI WITH MEAT SAUCE

1 cup salad or olive oil	4 No. 2 cans tomatoes
2 cups minced onions	(10 cups)
4 lb. chuck, ground	2 tablesp. salt
8 minced cloves garlic	2 teasp. pepper
8 3-oz. cans sliced	1 teasp. sugar
mushrooms	6 lb. spaghetti
1 cup snipped parsley	1 lb. diced sharp
2 cups sliced stuffed	American cheese
olives	2 2-oz. jars grated Parmesan cheese
4 8-oz. cans tomato	
sauce	

Day before: In hot oil in large kettle, simmer onions 5 min. Add beef, garlic; cook, stirring, until beef is slightly browned. Add undrained mushrooms, parsley, olives, tomato sauce. Force tomatoes through sieve; add to beef, with salt, pepper, sugar. Simmer, covered, 1 hr. Uncover; simmer 2 hr. longer, stirring occasionally. Cool; then refrigerate.

About ½ hr. before serving: Cook spaghetti as label directs; drain. Meanwhile, heat sauce; add diced cheese; heat, stirring occasionally, till cheese is melted.

To serve: Arrange spaghetti on individual plates, or platters; pour on sauce; top with grated Parmesan cheese; or pass grated cheese in small bowls. Makes 25 to 30 servings.

MACARONI AND CHEESE, FRANK STYLE

2 lb. elbow macaroni	sharp American
2 qt. milk	cheese (2 lb.)
¾ cup butter or	¼ cup minced onion
margarine	2 teasp. Worcestershire
1 cup all-purpose flour	25 tomato slices, sliced
1 tablesp. salt	¼″ thick
1½ teasp. dry mustard	About 25 franks, halved
8 cups grated natural	lengthwise (3 lb.)

About 1½ hr. before serving: Cook macaroni as label directs; drain. Meanwhile, in double boiler, heat milk. In large kettle, melt butter; stir in flour, salt, mustard; cook, stirring often, 10 min. Stir in heated milk; cook, stirring con-

stantly, until thickened. Add cheese, onion, Worcestershire; stir gently until cheese is melted. Remove from heat; stir in macaroni.

Start heating oven to 400°F. Pour macaroni mixture into 2 shallow open pans, about 15″ x 11″. Bake, uncovered, 20 min. On top of macaroni in each pan, arrange tomato slices, then franks. Bake 15 to 20 min. longer, or until franks are golden brown. Let stand about 5 min. before serving. Makes 25 servings.

Macaroni and Cheese: Just omit franks.

CHICKEN TETRAZZINI

18 to 20 cups cooked	3 lb. sliced mushrooms
chicken or turkey,	Chicken broth
in large pieces *	2 tablesp. salt
½ cup butter or	3 8-oz. pkg. fine
margarine	noodles
¾ cup all-purpose flour	½ cup melted butter
5 teasp. salt	or margarine (optional)
¼ teasp. pepper	tional)
½ teasp. nutmeg	2 tablesp. fresh, frozen,
2 qt. chicken broth	or canned lemon
1 cup heavy cream	juice
¾ cup butter or	⅔ cup grated Parmesan cheese
margarine	

Day before: To cook chicken and prepare broth, follow directions in Simmered Chicken, p. 644, then refrigerate.

About 1¼ hr. before serving: In large double-boiler top over direct heat, or in kettle, melt ½ cup butter; stir in flour, 5 teasp. salt, pepper, nutmeg. Now stir in 2 qt. chicken broth, cream. Cook over boiling water, stirring occasionally, until thickened.

In ¾ cup butter, sauté mushrooms, about 1 lb. at a time until brown. Bring to boil any remaining chicken broth plus 2 tablesp. salt and enough water to make 8 qt. liquid. Add noodles; cook until tender—10 to 15 min.; drain; if desired, add ½ cup melted butter; season with more salt and pepper if needed. To sauce, add chicken and mushrooms; heat.

To serve: Add lemon juice to chicken mixture. Arrange noodles on dinner plates; top with chicken; sprinkle with cheese. Makes 25 servings.

* You may substitute canned chicken or turkey for cooked chicken.

CHICKEN CURRY ON PARSLEY RICE

18 to 20 cups cooked chicken or turkey, in large pieces *	¾ cup all-purpose flour
	4 teasp. salt
	⅛ teasp. pepper
¾ cup butter or margarine	2 tablesp. curry powder
	3 cups milk
4 lb. mushrooms, sliced ¼″ thick	3 cups chicken broth
	3 cups raw regular or processed white rice (12 cups cooked)
¾ cup butter or margarine	
1⅓ cups minced onions	2 tablesp. salt
4 cups diced, pared, cored cooking apples	¾ cup snipped parsley

Day before: To cook chicken and prepare broth, follow directions in Simmered Chicken, below, then refrigerate.

About 1½ hr. before serving: In ¾ cup butter in large double-boiler top over direct heat, or in kettle, sauté mushrooms, about 1 lb. at a time, until browned; remove mushrooms; set aside. In another ¾ cup butter in same double-boiler top, sauté onions and apples until tender.

Now place 2 large kettles of water over heat to boil. Remove double-boiler top from heat; stir in flour, 4 teasp. salt, pepper, curry. Slowly stir in milk and chicken broth. Cook over boiling water, stirring, until thickened. Cook, covered, 20 min. longer.

Meanwhile, add half of rice and 1 tablesp. salt to each kettle of boiling water. Cook, uncovered, 20 min., or until tender; drain; toss with parsley. Then add mushrooms and chicken to curry mixture; heat thoroughly.

To serve: Spoon chicken over rice. Makes 25 servings.

* You may substitute canned chicken or turkey for cooked chicken.

SIMMERED CHICKEN

(for creamed chicken, à la king, salad, etc.)

How Much to Buy: One 3½- to 4-lb. ready-to-cook stewing chicken yields about 3 cups cooked meat. One 20-lb. ready-to-cook turkey, quartered, yields about 18 cups (4½ qt.) cooked meat.

The Simmering:

1. Cook whole chicken or quartered turkey in covered kettle or Dutch oven. For each 3½- to 4-lb. ready-to-cook stewing chicken or 20-lb.

turkey, add warm water to just cover, plus 1 clove-studded onion, 1 carrot, 3 celery tops, 3 teasp. salt, and 1 bay leaf. Simmer chicken, covered, as label directs. Or simmer about 3 to 4 hr., or until fork-tender. Simmer turkey, covered, about 2 to 4 hr., or until fork-tender.

2. When chicken or turkey is cooked, cool quickly. Lift bird from broth to wire rack to cool. Cool kettle of broth in cold water in sink, changing water and stirring broth often.

3. Now remove meat from bones in as large pieces as possible; leave meat as is, or cut into pieces as recipe directs. Wrap meat. Refrigerate meat and broth at once until ready to use.

LEMON-BARBECUED CHICKEN

The Sauce:

3 medium cloves garlic	(use 15 lemons, or use frozen or canned juice)
3 teasp. salt	
1¾ cups salad oil	
¾ cup minced onions	1 tablesp. pepper
3 cups lemon juice	1 tablesp. dried thyme

The Chickens:

6 to 7 2- to 2½-lb. ready-to-cook broiler-fryers, quartered	Fat or salad oil for frying

Day before: Combine all ingredients for sauce. Refrigerate along with chickens.

About 3 hr. before serving: In medium saucepan, heat 1½″ fat to 350°F. on deep-fat frying thermometer as on p. 7. Fry chicken, 3 pieces at a time, until golden—about 5 min. Drain on paper towels. Place in layers, with skin sides up, in 1 large, or 2 medium, baking pans. Start heating oven to 325°F. Pour sauce over chicken pieces. Bake, uncovered, 1½ to 1¾ hr., or until tender, basting 3 times with sauce.

To serve: Arrange chicken on individual plates or platter. Pass extra sauce. Makes 25 servings.

ROASTS FOR A CROWD

If you're serving roast lamb, pork, veal, or turkey, or baked ham, be sure all roasts are approximately the same weight so they'll be done at the same time. Follow our roasting directions and times. (See Index.)

If you're roasting extra-large standing or rolled ribs of beef, follow roasting directions on p. 50, but use roasting schedule below. Use shallow open pans; add no water; do not baste.

Because roasting time periods can only be approximate, always use a roast-meat thermometer; insert thermometer into largest roast being cooked.

ROASTING SCHEDULE FOR BEEF
(beef refrigerated until roasting time)

Weight	Oven Temperature	Approximate Roasting Time	Meat-Thermometer Reading
Standing Ribs			
4 ribs			
(10 to 11 lb.)	325° F.	4½ hr.	140° F. (rare)
		5 hr.	150° F. (medium)
5 ribs			
(13 to 14 lb.)	325° F.	5 hr.	140° F. (rare)
		5½ hr.	150° F. (medium)
7 ribs			
(20 to 22 lb.)	300° F.	4¼ hr.	130° F. (rare)
		5 hr.	140° F. (medium)
Rolled Ribs			
11½ lb.	300° F.	5¼ hr.	130° F. (rare)
		6 hr.	140° F. (medium)
		6½ hr.	150° F. (well done)

LIKABLE SALADS

CHICKEN SALAD DE LUXE

13 to 15 cups cooked chicken or turkey, in large pieces *
1 cup snipped scallions (1 bunch); or 1 cup finely minced onions
6 cups sliced celery with tops (about 2 bunches)
1 doz. eggs
1½ cups coarsely chopped walnuts

2 tablesp. butter or margarine
3 cups cooked salad dressing or mayonnaise
½ cup wine vinegar
1½ cups milk or chicken broth
2 teasp. salt
¼ teasp. pepper
2 heads lettuce
½ bunch water cress

Day before: To cook chicken, follow directions in Simmered Chicken, p. 644; then refrigerate.

Prepare scallions. Prepare celery (slice through bunch on angle, crosswise, without separating stalks; then wash in strainer). Simmer eggs in water to cover 20 min.; cool in running cold water; shell; chop. Refrigerate all.

At least 2½ hr. before serving: Sauté nuts in butter until crisp and golden—5 min. Drain on paper towels; cool. Combine salad dressing, vinegar, milk, salt, pepper. Toss with chicken meat, eggs, nuts, scallions, celery. Refrigerate until serving time.

To serve: Arrange salad on beds of lettuce; garnish with water cress. Makes 25 servings.

* You may substitute canned chicken or turkey for cooked chicken.

ELLEN KERN'S POTATO SALAD

7 lb. unpared potatoes
3 cups snipped parsley (1 big bunch)
½ cup snipped chives
4 cups sliced celery (1 big bunch)

1 qt. cooked salad dressing
½ cup vinegar
2 tablesp. salt
1 teasp. pepper

About 8 hr. before serving: Start boiling potatoes. Prepare parsley and chives (snip onto separate sheets of waxed paper). Prepare celery; set aside in bowl. Mix salad dressing with vinegar. When potatoes are just tender, peel.

Now slice layer of hot potatoes into large bowl or kettle (about 8 qt.); sprinkle with some of salt and pepper; then add, in order, thin layers of parsley, chives, celery, and salad-dressing mixture. Repeat all layers, starting with potatoes, salt, and pepper; continue until all are used. Then, with clean hands, quickly and lightly turn salad upside down in bowl (about 2 turns). Refrigerate 5 to 6 hr. Makes 20 servings.

SUMMERTIME TUNA SALAD

9 cans chunk-style or solid-pack tuna (9 cups)
6 cups raw spinach leaves
1½ cups snipped scallions (tops and all) or diced celery
1½ teasp. salt
¾ teasp. pepper
2 cups French dressing
6 heads lettuce

Early in day: If using solid-pack tuna, drain well; then break into pieces. Wash spinach; remove stems; drain well; reserve about 1 cup tiny crisp leaves to use as garnish. Toss tuna with 5 cups spinach, rest of ingredients except lettuce. Refrigerate. Clean lettuce and separate leaves; drain. Refrigerate till needed.

About ½ hr. before serving: Arrange salad in lettuce cups on large platters. Garnish with reserved spinach leaves. Makes 25 servings.

GREEN-PEPPER COLESLAW

12 lb. trimmed crisp cabbage (4½ medium, or 4 large, heads)	3 tablesp. salt
	1½ teasp. pepper
	1½ teasp. paprika
	3 cups cooked salad dressing or mayonnaise
12 green peppers	
3 cups vinegar	
3 cups granulated sugar	

Several hours before serving: Chop or shred cabbage very fine. Cut green peppers into fine strips. Refrigerate both.

About ½ hr. before serving: Mix vinegar, sugar, salt, pepper, paprika; add to cabbage; let stand 15 min.; then drain. Mix green peppers with cabbage; then add salad dressing, tossing lightly.

Serve as relish in large bowl; or garnish with lettuce and serve as individual salads. Makes 50 servings.

TOMATO-OLIVE ASPIC

1 46-oz. can tomato juice (5¾ cups)	gelatin
	2¼ cups sliced stuffed olives
Dash pepper	
2 bay leaves	2 heads lettuce
1 minced small onion	1 pt. cooked salad dressing
3 pkg. lemon-flavored	

At least 6 hr. ahead: Simmer 2 cups tomato juice with pepper, bay leaves, onion; strain. Pour over gelatin, stirring until dissolved. Add rest of tomato juice. Refrigerate till slightly thickened. Add olives. Pour into 2 9″ x 5″ x 3″ loaf pans. Refrigerate till set.

To serve: Unmold salads; cut each into 7 slices; then halve each slice crosswise. Serve each slice in lettuce cup, garnished with 1 tablesp. dressing. Makes about 25 servings.

SANDWICHES FOR 50
(see Production-Line Techniques, p. 356)

Choose a Bread and Spread:

Thin sliced (about 1 lb.)	4 to 5 loaves
Regular sliced (about 1 lb.)	6 to 7 loaves
Butter or margarine	1½ lb.
Mayonnaise (as spread for bread)	1 qt.

Choose a Filling:

Pineapple-Ham: Mix 2 lb. coarsely ground, cooked ham; 2 lb. soft cream cheese; 2 No. 2 cans crushed pineapple, drained.

Ham Salad: Mix 3 lb. coarsely ground, cooked ham; 2 cups minced celery; 1 cup minced green peppers; 1½ cups pickle relish; 2 cups mayonnaise; 2 tablesp. Worcestershire.

Ham and Cheese: Mix 1½ lb. coarsely ground, cooked ham; 1½ lb. coarsely grated process American cheese; 1 cup undiluted evaporated milk; 1½ cups pickle relish; 2 teasp. dry mustard; 1 teasp. salt; ¼ teasp. pepper.

Chicken Salad: Mix about 8 cups diced, cooked chicken (3 4-lb. ready-to-cook stewing chickens; or 2 32-oz. cans boned chicken); 3 cups diced celery; 2 to 3 cups mayonnaise.

Tuna Salad: Substitute 8 cans (8 cups) chunk-style tuna for chicken in Chicken Salad, above.

Egg Salad: Substitute 40 chopped, hard-cooked eggs for chicken in Chicken Salad, above.

Turkey or Ham, Tomato, and Bacon: Use 1 30-lb., or 2 18-lb., ready-to-cook turkeys or 6 to 8 lb. canned ham, sliced; 3 heads lettuce; 6 to 7 lb. sliced tomatoes; 5 to 6 lb. crisp cooked bacon. Arrange, in layers, between 2 bread slices.

Cream Cheese: Mix 4 lb. soft cream cheese with one of these:

2 lb. crumbled crisp bacon
3½ cups chopped stuffed olives
2 cups chopped nuts

Peanut Butter: Mix 3 lb. peanut butter with 2 lb. crumbled crisp bacon or 1 qt. minced, cooked ham.

Cream Cheese or Peanut Butter and Jelly: Use 4 lb. soft cream cheese or 3 lb. peanut butter and 1 qt. jelly or preserves.

Sliced Meat—Cold or Hot: To serve cold sandwiches, use 3 heads lettuce and one of the following meats. To serve hot sandwiches, substitute 7 qt. gravy for lettuce:

Ready-cooked meats (salami, liverwurst, etc.)	7 to 9 lb.
Roast beef, rolled rib (weight, bone in)	20 to 25 lb.
Roast leg of lamb	25 lb.
Roast veal	20 to 25 lb.
Smoked tongue	20 lb.
Roast turkey (ready-to-cook weight)	1 30-lb. bird; or 2 18-lb. birds

BEVERAGES, OF COURSE

STEEPED COFFEE

½ lb. drip-grind coffee (2 cups plus	6 tablesp.)
	4¼ qt. boiling water

Tie coffee loosely, bag-fashion, in fine cheesecloth or light muslin. Drop into boiling water in kettle. Cover; turn heat very low; let steep (stand) 15 min., moving bag around in kettle often. Then remove bag. Serve as much coffee as is needed. Keep remaining coffee hot, *but not boiling,* over very low heat. Makes 25 average coffee-cup-size servings.

P.S. Coffee for a crowd can be made easily and quickly with instant coffee. Follow label directions.

ICED TEA

4 qt. plus 2¾ cups boiling water	¾ cup plus 1½ teasp. tea
	Ice

Pour boiling water over tea. Let steep (stand) 5 min. Strain; cool 3 hr. at room temperature. Then add ice and serve. Makes 25 glassfuls.

HOT COCOA FOR A CROWD

1 to 1¼ cups cocoa	4 qt. milk
1 cup granulated sugar	1 tablesp. vanilla
¾ teasp. salt	extract
1½ qt. water	

In saucepan, blend cocoa, sugar, salt; stir in water slowly until smooth. Boil 10 min. Meanwhile, scald milk in large double boiler. Stir in cocoa mixture. Let stand, covered, over low heat ½ hr. to "mellow." Add vanilla. Serve with dash of cinnamon or whipped cream. Makes 25 servings.

▶ **For 50:** Double ingredients.

PARTY PUNCH POINTERS

Concocting the Punch:

Ginger Ale or Soda: Chill well; always add just before serving.

For Quick Service: Fill cups in kitchen; pass filled cups on trays; serve refills from punch bowl.

For Extra-Quick Service: If punch does not contain sparkling water, you can fill cups ahead and refrigerate them on trays. Chill rest of punch in bottles.

Ice: Use small block rather than cubes; remember, ice dilutes flavor.

Leftover Punch: Freeze in ice-cube tray. Use to chill fruit juices or iced tea. Or when making favorite fruit gelatine, use unflavored gelatine; omit sugar; substitute leftover punch for liquid.

The Punch Bowl: Circle bowl with ring of smilax, ivy, blueberry, or laurel leaves. Or cover sides of bowl with wire; tuck roses, ferns, into holes. If you have no punch bowl, use big wooden salad bowl or gay mixing bowl, with soup ladle and paper cups.

Gay Garnishes (to top punch):

Melon balls or strawberries
Lemon, orange, or lime slices
Twists of orange or lemon peel
Thick banana slices
Summer blossoms, ivy leaves
Small scoops of sherbet or ice cream

Ice Float: Half fill large loaf pan (not glass) with water; freeze. Arrange washed unhulled strawberries on top of ice; cover well with water; finish freezing. Use special pan for this purpose, because freezing water may force pan out of shape.

Or freeze water or canned fruit cocktail or pineapple chunks (fruit plus juice) in 8" x 8" x 2" pan, heart-shaped pan, or ring mold.

To unmold ice block, just dip pan in hot water until block slips out easily. Float in punch bowl. Top with tiny bouquet for bride; roses for sweet sixteener; or lemon, orange, or lime wedges. Or make Christmas wreath of mint leaves and maraschino cherries.

GOLDEN-MINT RECEPTION PUNCH

30 to 35 mint sprigs	1 No. 2 can pineapple
2 cups granulated sugar	juice
2 qt. boiling water	1 qt. ginger ale
2⅓ cups fresh, frozen,	1 qt. sparkling water
or canned lemon	12 mint sprigs
juice	1 cup thinly slivered
2 qt. orange juice	lemon rind

Wash mint. In 4-qt. saucepan, place 30 to 35 mint sprigs, sugar, water. Simmer, uncovered, 10 min. Chill, along with rest of ingredients.

Just before serving: Strain mint syrup. Add lemon, orange, and pineapple juices; ginger ale; sparkling water. Top with 12 mint sprigs and rind. Serve at once. Makes 50 punch-cup servings.

PINK-LEMONADE PUNCH

4 cans frozen lemonade	1 qt. chilled ginger ale
concentrate	Block of ice
8 cups cranberry-juice	1 pt. lemon sherbet
cocktail	

Just before serving: Reconstitute lemonade. Pour into punch bowl. Add cranberry juice, ginger ale; mix well. Add ice. Float scoops of sherbet on top. Makes 56 punch-cup servings.

LAVENDER PUNCH

1 cup water	½ cup lime juice
2 cinnamon sticks	Block of ice
¼ teasp. whole cloves	2 qt. chilled ginger ale
3 cans frozen grape-	Seedless grapes
juice concentrate	

In saucepan, combine water, cinnamon, cloves; bring to boil. Remove from heat; let stand 5 min. Chill; strain.

Just before serving: Combine chilled mixture with grape and lime juices; mix well. Pour over ice in punch bowl; add ginger ale. Garnish with grapes. Makes 30 punch-cup servings.

SHERBET-TEA PUNCH

2 cups strong hot tea	or canned lemon
1 cup granulated sugar	juice
1 cup orange juice	1 pt. chilled ginger ale
½ cup fresh, frozen,	1 pt. orange sherbet

Pour hot tea over sugar; stir until sugar dissolves; add juices. Chill. Then pour into punch bowl. Add ginger ale. Spoon on sherbet. Makes 16 punch-cup servings.

LEMON-STRAWBERRY PUNCH

1½ cups strawberries	concentrate
½ cup granulated sugar	1 qt. chilled ginger ale
3 cans frozen lemonade	Block of ice

Wash and hull berries; crush. Add sugar; let stand ½ hr. Reconstitute lemonade; blend with berries.

Just before serving: In punch bowl, place berry mixture, ginger ale; mix well. Add ice. Makes 32 punch-cup servings.

CRANBERRY PUNCH, SWEDISH STYLE

½ cup unblanched	1 stick cinnamon
almonds	1 qt. water
1 cup light or dark	4 1-pt. bottles cran-
raisins	berry-juice cocktail
Peel from 2 oranges	2 No. 2 cans pineapple
1 teasp. whole cloves	juice
½ teasp. whole allspice	

In saucepan, place almonds, raisins, peel. Tie cloves, allspice, and cinnamon in cheesecloth; add with water to almonds. Simmer, uncovered, 15 min.; cool; discard spice bag and peel.

Just before serving: Combine cooled mixture with cranberry and pineapple juices.

Serve cold, over ice in punch bowl. Or serve hot, adding claret or port to taste, if desired. Spoon a few raisins and 1 almond into each serving. Makes about 24 punch-cup servings.

TANGY TUTTI-FRUTTI PUNCH

½ cup fresh, frozen, or canned lemon juice
1 cup pineapple juice
2 cans frozen orange-juice concentrate

¼ cup maraschino-cherry juice
Block of ice
2 qt. chilled ginger ale
Maraschino cherries

Combine lemon, pineapple, orange, and maraschino juices; mix well. Pour over ice in punch bowl; add ginger ale. Garnish with cherries. Makes 25 punch-cup servings.

PINK-LADY PUNCH

4 cups cranberry-juice cocktail
1½ cups granulated sugar

4 cups pineapple or grapefruit juice
2 qt. chilled ginger ale

Slowly add cranberry juice to sugar; stir until sugar dissolves. Add pineapple juice; chill. Pour into punch bowl; add ginger ale. Makes 32 punch-cup servings.

WINE CHAMPAGNE

Combine equal parts of chilled sauterne and sparkling lemon-flavored beverage or sparkling water. Serve at once in cold glasses.

GRANDMOTHER RANDOLPH'S EGGNOG

12 eggs, separated
1 cup granulated sugar
½ cup brandy
1½ cups whisky

¼ cup peach brandy
1½ qt. milk
1¼ teasp. nutmeg

Day before: In large bowl, beat egg yolks until thick; gradually add sugar, beating until thick and lemon-colored. Add ½ cup brandy, drop by drop, beating. Then add whisky and peach brandy same way. Refrigerate overnight, along with egg whites.

Next day: Stir in milk, nutmeg. At serving time, beat egg whites in large bowl until peaks form when beater is raised; fold into milk mixture. Nice with shortbread. Makes 16 punch-cup servings.

MOCHA PUNCH

1 cup heavy cream
½ teasp. almond extract
Few grains salt
1 qt. chilled coffee (instant, regular,

or decaffeinated)
1 qt. chocolate ice cream
¼ teasp. nutmeg

Whip cream; add extract, salt. In cold punch bowl, blend coffee and half of ice cream until smooth. Fold in whipped cream, rest of ice cream. Top with nutmeg. Makes 16 punch-cup servings.

ORANGE EGGNOG

6 eggs
¼ cup granulated sugar
¼ teasp. cinnamon
¼ teasp. ginger
¼ teasp. ground cloves
2 qt. chilled orange juice

½ cup fresh, frozen, or canned lemon juice
1 qt. vanilla ice cream
1 qt. chilled ginger ale
Nutmeg

Beat eggs until light-colored; add sugar, cinnamon, ginger, cloves. Stir in orange and lemon juices. Into punch bowl, cut ice cream into small cubes; pour in orange-juice mixture and ginger ale. Sprinkle with nutmeg. Makes 20 to 25 punch-cup servings.

QUANTITIES TO SERVE 50 PERSONS

Food as Purchased	Approximate Amount for 50 Servings	Size of Each Serving
Beverages and Drinks		
Coffee, instant	1½ small jars	¾ cup
Coffee, regular	1 to 1¼ lb.	¾ cup
Cream for coffee	1¼ qt.	1½ tablesp.
Fruit-juice concentrates, frozen	9 6-oz. cans	½ cup
Fruit or tomato juice, canned	4 46-oz. cans	½ cup
Lemon for tea	5 large	1 thin slice
Lemonade concentrate, frozen	13 6-oz. cans	8 oz.
Punch	2 gal.	⅔ cup
Sugar, lump	1⅛ lb.	2 lumps
Tea	¼ lb.	¾ cup
Meat, Poultry, Fish		
Bacon	6 lb.	2 slices
Beef, rolled rib roast	25 lb. before boning	½ lb.
Beef, standing rib roast	35 lb.	¾ lb.
Chicken, to roast	35 to 40 lb. (ready-to-cook weight)	¾ lb.
Chicken, stewing, for dishes using cut-up, cooked chicken	20 to 25 lb. (ready-to-cook weight)	
Fish fillets, frozen	13 1-lb. pkg.	¼ lb.
Ham, canned, boned	1 14-lb. can	¼ lb.
Ham, bone in, to bake	22 to 25 lb.	⅓ lb.
Hamburgers	12½ to 15 lb.	4- to 5-oz. patty
Lamb, leg to roast	25 lb.	½ lb.
Meat, chopped, for meat loaf	12 lb.	¼ lb. meat
Oysters, for scalloped oysters	6 qt.	½ cup scalloped oysters
Oysters, for stew	6 qt.	2 cups stew
Pork, chops (3 to 1 lb.)	17 lb.	1 chop, ¾″ thick
Pork, loin to roast	25 lb.	½ lb.
Sausage, bulk or links	12½ lb.	4 oz.
Turkey, for dishes using cut-up, cooked turkey	16 lb. (ready-to-cook weight)	
Turkey, to roast	35 to 40 lb. (ready-to-cook weight)	½ to ⅔ lb.
Vegetables		
Any canned vegetable	14 No. 303 cans; or 11 No. 2 cans	½ cup
Asparagus spears, canned (medium-sized)	11 No. 2 cans	4 to 6 spears
Asparagus, market fresh	20 lb.	4 or 5 stalks
Cabbage (in eighths)	15 lb.	

Food as Purchased	Approximate Amount for 50 Servings	Size of Each Serving
Vegetables—Continued		
Carrots	16 lb. (tops off)	⅓ lb.
Cauliflower	15 lb. (flowerets only)	¼ lb.
Corn on the cob	50 ears	1 ear
Frozen vegetables	13 to 17 pkg. (10 to 12 oz. each)	About ½ cup
Green beans (or wax), market fresh	12½ lb.	¼ lb.
Onions, for creaming	15 lb.	½ cup (3 or 4)
Potatoes, for creaming	12½ to 15 lb.	½ cup
Potatoes, frozen French fries	16 9-oz. pkg.	
Potatoes, mashed	25 lb.	½ cup
Potatoes, to scallop	12½ lb.	½ cup
Potatoes, sweet, glazed	25 lb.	1 potato
Relishes and Salads		
Cabbage, for slaw	12 to 15 lb.	⅓ cup
Chicken salad	6¼ qt.	½ cup
Cranberry sauce, jellied	6 1-lb. cans	½" slice
French dressing	1 to 1½ qt.	1½ to 2 tablesp.
Fruit salad	9 qt.	¾ cup
Lettuce, for lettuce hearts	12 medium heads	⅕ head
Lettuce, leaf, for salad	6 heads	2 or 3 leaves
Mayonnaise or salad dressing	1 qt.	1 tablesp.
Olives	2 qt.	2 olives
Pears, for salad	7 No. 2½ cans	1 pear half
Pickles	2 qt.	2 small pickles
Potato salad	6¼ qt.	½ cup
Salmon, for salad	8 No. 1 tall cans	⅓ cup salad
Tuna, for salad	16 cans solid pack or chunk style	⅓ cup salad
Tomatoes, for salad	30 medium	3 slices
Miscellaneous		
Apples, cooking, for sauce	25 lb.	½ cup
Applesauce, canned	14 No. 2 cans	½ cup
Bread (about 1-lb. loaf)	5 loaves	1½ slices
Butter or margarine	1 to 1¼ lb.	1 pat, ½" thick
Crackers	1 lb.	2 crackers
Cream, heavy, to top desserts	1 qt.	1 rounded tablesp. whipped
Fruits, frozen, to top ice cream	13 to 17 pkg. (10 to 12 oz.)	¼ to ⅓ cup
Ice cream, brick or bulk	2 to 2½ gal.	About ⅙ qt.
Jelly	8 8-oz. glasses	About 1 tablesp.
Rolls or Biscuits	6½ doz.	1½
Soup, canned, condensed	20 cans	1 cup

Note: For 25 persons, divide indicated amount by 2. For 100 persons, multiply by 2.

Your Weight

WHAT SHOULD IT BE?

During childhood and youth, it's desirable to weigh somewhat more than the average for your height and age.

By middle age, it is better to maintain the ideal weight for a twenty-five-year-old of your height and sex. After twenty-five, you tend to slow down your activities, yet your appetite may remain as hearty and you may eat more than you should. Unless you are among those few who stay thin no matter what, you gain.

As you grow older, you should not exceed this ideal weight. (Excellent tables, giving correct ideal weights according to build, weight, and sex are available. Consult them.)

WHEN YOU WANT TO LOSE WEIGHT

1. If you are considerably overweight and wish to reduce, consult a physician and get his permission to go on a low-calorie diet.
2. Our Five-Meal-a-Day Reducing Plan, p. 653, is a low-calorie diet that provides adequate protein, vitamins, and minerals; lots of bulk; interesting flavors; variety. Have your physician check it.
3. When following this diet, roast, broil, or pan-broil meat; do not use fat left in pan. Do not eat any fat on meat.
4. Choose soft- or hard-cooked, or poached, eggs, which do not require fat for cooking.
5. Use skim milk (see When It's Nonfat Dry Milk, p. 520) or buttermilk; avoid cream or whole milk.
6. Use salt lightly in cooking, none at table.
7. Follow diet strictly, except for vegetables and fruits, for which you may wish to choose substitutes. See Vegetables and Fruits in Your Calorie Count, p. 658. Also see There Are Dietetic Packs Too, p. 516.
8. On salads, use only Low-Calorie Dressings, p. 321.
9. If you are constipated, drink plenty of water, including 2 glasses of warm water on arising. Drink buttermilk for its laxative effect; take plenty of exercise. If this is not entirely effective, consult your doctor.

OVERWEIGHT IN THE TEENS

To Lose or Not to Lose: In many families, there is a boy or girl who is definitely overweight. Some extra pounds during adolescence are not harmful and are often lost naturally as the child matures. But an excessively overweight child presents a real problem.

The First Step: First, be sure the child has a thorough physical examination to determine the cause of overweight. The doctor should have the thorough co-operation of the parents. Discuss the problem with your child, to arouse his interest and to explain why certain measures are necessary. While he's reducing, the child should be under the doctor's care.

A Reducing Diet for Teen-agers

A teen-ager's reducing diet should restrict high-calorie foods such as fats (butter, margarine, cream, chocolate, fat meat, fried foods, etc.), sugars (including sugar on fruit, rich desserts, candy), and starches (potatoes, cereals, bread).

Be sure the child has a quart of skim milk daily. Its proteins, minerals, and B vitamins are essential for growth and health. (See When It's Nonfat Dry Milk, p. 520.)

Serve low-calorie vegetables often (see Vegetables in Your Calorie Count, p. 661), both raw and cooked. Celery makes an excellent between-meal snack.

Keep your child from nibbling between meals if possible, but don't make him suffer. After school, serve hot bouillon or tomato juice.

Avoid rich desserts. Serve fresh fruit or canned dietetic-pack fruits. Or serve frozen or sweetened canned fruits, allowing your child a smaller quantity than usual.

Use lean meat only. Remove fat from child's meat before serving. Lamb, veal, and lean beef are better than pork, ham, and bacon.

Give him generous servings of lean meat, fish, poultry, or eggs for lunch and dinner. Include at least one egg a day—soft-cooked, coddled, or poached—served without butter.

Ask your doctor about supplementing the child's diet with vitamin D or other vitamins.

Help your child by making the foods he may eat attractive and flavorful and by encouraging him. Keep forbidden foods out of sight as much as possible.

Keep a weight chart to show a steady weekly loss. If there is no loss one week, discuss this with your child. Don't scold. Reducing simply means consuming fewer calories than are used by the body. Needed extra calories must be supplied by using body fat.

FIVE MEAL-A-DAY REDUCING PLAN
MEAL 1—BREAKFAST

Choose	How Much to Eat
Juice	1 4-oz. glass orange, grapefruit, blend of grapefruit and orange, *or* pineapple juice (fresh, frozen, or canned, unsweetened) 1 8-oz. glass tomato juice
or Fruit	½ cup blueberries, strawberries, *or* raspberries (fresh or canned dietetic pack) ½ melon *or* 1 peach *or* 2 plums
and Cereal and Toast	½ cup hot cereal *or* ¾ cup ready-to-eat cereal (any kind) *with* ½ cup skim milk, *plus* 1 slice enriched-white or whole-wheat toast, spread with 1 tablesp. cottage cheese
or Egg and Toast	1 soft-cooked *or* poached egg *with* 2 slices enriched-white or whole-wheat toast, spread with 1 tablesp. cottage cheese
or French Toast	1 slice French toast *with* 1 tablesp. table syrup and 1 crisp bacon slice
or Toast and a Spread	2 slices enriched-white or whole-wheat toast *with* either 2 tablesp. cottage cheese *or* 1 teasp. butter *or* margarine, *plus* 1 teasp. jam, jelly, *or* marmalade
and Tea *or* Coffee	No cream, milk, or sugar

(cont'd.)

FIVE MEAL-A-DAY REDUCING PLAN — (continued)

MEALS 2 AND 4—MIDMORNING AND MIDAFTERNOON SNACK

Choose	How Much to Eat
Milk and Crackers	1 8-oz. glass skim milk *with* 1 graham cracker *or* 2 saltines *or* 4 thin wheat crackers *or* 2 small gingersnaps *or* 1 plain cookie
or Crackers and a Spread	2 graham crackers *or* 4 saltines *or* 8 thin wheat crackers *with* 1 teasp. jam, jelly, *or* marmalade, *or* 2 tablesp. cottage cheese

or
Sandwich
	1 sandwich made with 1 bread slice (enriched-white, whole-wheat, or rye) spread with *one* of the following:
	    2 teasp. jam, jelly, or marmalade
	    2 teasp. honey
	    1 thin slice canned tongue or luncheon meat
	    ½ cup chopped raw vegetables, mixed with 1 tablesp. Low-Calorie French Dressing, p. 321
	    2 tablesp. cottage cheese
	    ½ chopped, hard-cooked egg, mixed with 1 teasp. mayonnaise

or Fresh Fruit and Cookies	1 medium banana *or* 1 large orange *or* ½ grapefruit *or* 4 dates *or* 2 figs *or* 1 large apple *or* 1 bunch grapes (about 30) *with* 2 small gingersnaps *or* 1 plain cookie
or Juice and Crackers	1 8-oz. glass tomato juice *or* vegetable-juice cocktail *with* 1 graham cracker *or* 2 saltines *or* 4 thin wheat crackers *with* 1 tablesp. cottage cheese
or Fruit and Crackers	1 cup unsweetened applesauce *or* ½ cup canned fruit cocktail *with* 2 small gingersnaps *or* 1 plain cookie
or Dessert and Cookies	½ cup fruit-flavored gelatin *with* 2 small gingersnaps *or* 1 plain cookie
P.S.	If you *must* eat a little more, take another snack at bedtime. This will add about 125 calories per day, but will slow down your weight loss only slightly. Coffee or tea (no cream, milk, or sugar) can be added to any meal.

MEAL 3—LUNCH

Choose a Menu	How Much to Eat
Soup	½ cup (4-oz.) cream-of-asparagus, -celery, *or* -mushroom soup (if canned condensed, dilute with water)
Fruit or Vegetable Salad	Fruit salad (orange and grapefruit sections, grapes, apple, 1 tablesp. Low-Calorie Fruit-Salad Dressing, p. 321) *Or* raw-vegetable salad (cabbage, carrots, green pepper, cucumber, and 1 tablesp. Low-Calorie French Dressing, p. 321)
Melba Toast Milk	2 slices Melba toast, lightly buttered 1 8-oz. glass buttermilk *or* skim milk

Choose a Menu	How Much to Eat
Shrimp, Crab, *or* Lobster Salad	Shrimp, crab, *or* lobster salad (10 to 12 cooked, cleaned medium shrimp *or* ½ cup flaked crab meat *or* lobster, *plus* 2 lettuce leaves, ½ cup diced celery, 1 medium tomato, 1 tablesp. Low-Calorie Tomato-Juice Dressing, p. 321)
Bread *or* Crackers	1 thin slice enriched-white bread *or* 2 saltines *or* 6 thin wheat crackers *with* 1 tablesp. cottage cheese
Fruit Gelatin	½ cup fruit gelatin
Tea *or* Coffee	No cream, milk, or sugar
Broiled *or* Steamed Fish	1 serving broiled or steamed fish (haddock, halibut, perch, or flounder) *with* lemon juice
Vegetable	1 large serving asparagus, broccoli, cauliflower, spinach, *or* green beans *with* 1 teasp. butter *or* margarine
Coleslaw, Tomatoes, *or* Cucumbers	½ cup coleslaw *or* 1 sliced medium tomato *or* 1 sliced small cucumber with 1 tablesp. Low-Calorie French Dressing, p. 321
Fruit and Cookies	½ cup unsweetened applesauce *or* ½ grapefruit (no sugar) *or* 2 canned dietetic-pack pear halves *or* ½ melon *with* 2 small gingersnaps *or* 1 plain cookie
Hamburger Patty *or* Eggs	1 hamburger patty on toasted roll (no butter or margarine) *Or* plain omelet (2 eggs) *or* 2 scrambled eggs *or* 2 poached eggs on 1 slice enriched-white toast
Lettuce-and-Tomato Salad	2 lettuce leaves, 1 medium tomato, 1 tablesp. Low-Calorie Buttermilk Dressing, p. 322
Fresh Fruit	1 apple *or* 1 peach *or* 1 pear *or* 2 plums *or* 1 bunch grapes (about 30)
Tea *or* Coffee	No cream, milk, or sugar
Hot or Cold Sandwich	1 slice American cheese, melted, on 1 slice enriched-white toast (no butter or margarine) *with* 1 crisp bacon slice *Or* 1 tomato-lettuce-and-bacon sandwich (2 enriched-white bread slices, 2 tomato slices, 2 crisp bacon slices, 1 teasp. butter or margarine) *Or* 1 egg-and-olive sandwich (2 enriched-white bread slices; 1 chopped, hard-cooked egg; 3 chopped olives; 1 tablesp. Low-Calorie French Dressing, p. 321)
Applesauce *or* Fruit Gelatin	½ cup unsweetened applesauce *Or* ½ cup fruit gelatin
Tea *or* Coffee	No cream, milk, or sugar
Vegetable Soup	¾ cup (6-oz.) vegetable soup
Frank *or* Tongue Sandwich	1 frank on 1 roll *with* mustard *and* 2 small sweet pickles *Or* 2 slices cooked tongue on 1 enriched-white-bread slice, spread with mustard *and* 1 teasp. pickle relish
Celery and Carrot Sticks	Raw celery *and* carrot sticks
Tea *or* Coffee	No cream, milk, or sugar

(cont'd.)

FIVE MEAL-A-DAY REDUCING PLAN — (continued)
MEAL 5—DINNER

Choose a Menu	How Much to Eat
Soup *or* Fruit	¾ cup (6-oz.) canned tomato soup (made with water) *or* ¾ cup (6-oz.) canned clam chowder *or* ½ grapefruit *or* ½ melon *or* ½ cup canned dietetic-pack fruit cocktail
Broiled or Roast Meat	2 lean lamb chops *or* 2 slices beef *or* calf liver *or* 1 serving broiled or roast chicken, *or* 1 slice roast veal
Green Leafy Vegetables	1 large serving any green leafy vegetable *with* lemon juice
Celery and Carrot Sticks	Raw celery *and* carrot sticks
Sherbet *or* Pie	½ cup sherbet *Or* 1 small slice (½ regular serving) any pie
Tea *or* Coffee	No cream, milk, or sugar
Juice *or* Fruit (first course *or* dessert)	1 4-oz. glass apple, grapefruit, *or* pineapple juice *Or* 1 8-oz. glass tomato, vegetable, *or* clam juice *Or* ½ melon
Roast, Broiled, or "Boiled" Meat *or* Fish	1 serving lean roast, broiled, or "boiled" (simmered) meat (beef, lamb, or veal) *Or* 1 serving broiled or "boiled" (steamed) fish (bass, haddock, halibut, flounder, perch, or whitefish)
Baked or Boiled Potato	1 medium baked or boiled potato *with* 1 teasp. butter *or* margarine
Tomato Salad *or* Fruit Salad *or* Vegetables	1 tomato stuffed with 2 tablesp. cottage cheese and diced celery, 2 lettuce leaves, 1 tablesp. Low-Calorie French Dressing, p. 321 *Or* fruit salad (grapefruit and orange sections, apple, grapes, lettuce, 1 tablesp. Low-Calorie Fruit-Salad Dressing, p. 321) *Or* 1 serving peas, green limas, *or* parsnips *with* 1 serving stewed tomatoes
Tea *or* Coffee	No cream, milk, or sugar
Stuffed Pepper *or* Welsh Rabbit *or* Croquettes	1 green pepper stuffed with chopped beef and rice *with* ¼ cup tomato sauce *Or* ¾ cup Welsh Rabbit on ½ toasted English muffin *Or* 1 croquette (meat or fish) *with* 1 tablesp. medium white sauce
Mixed-Green Salad *or* Green Leafy Vegetable	1 large serving mixed-green salad *with* 1 tablesp. Low-Calorie French Dressing, p. 321 *Or* 1 serving any green leafy vegetable *with* lemon juice
Spongecake and Fruit *or* Fruit and Cookies *or* Tapioca Pudding	1 slice spongecake *with* fresh fruit (1 sliced peach, ½ cup berries) *Or* sliced fresh fruit (orange or grapefruit sections, or peach slices) *with* 2 plain cookies *or* 4 small gingersnaps *Or* ½ cup tapioca pudding
Tea *or* Coffee	No cream, milk, or sugar

WHEN YOU WANT TO GAIN WEIGHT

To put on weight often seems more difficult than to take it off. Very often underweight is caused by some physical disturbance. Therefore, the first step should be a complete physical examination.

Sometimes loss of weight is due to lack of proper food, which results in poor appetite. A poor appetite may come from poor tone of the digestive tract induced by inadequate amounts of certain vitamins in the diet. Also excessive smoking often affects appetite. Confine smoking, if any, to end of meal.

To add weight, eat generously of foods that are low in bulk but high in calories, such as whole milk, cream, butter or margarine, cereals, breads, root vegetables, desserts, gravies, mayonnaise. Eat extra meals when possible.

Be sure to get enough sleep. Allow yourself at least 8 hours in bed. More is better. Try not to take your worries to bed with you. Many people find that a warm milk drink at bedtime is soothing.

Suggestions for Gaining Weight

Drink at least a quart of whole milk a day. Part of this can be consumed in between-meal snacks at 10:30 A.M., 4:00 P.M., and bedtime.

To increase the calorie value of milk:
  Add cream to increase fat content.
  Add 1 beaten egg, 1 tablesp. sugar, speck salt, ¼ teasp. vanilla, and dash of nutmeg to make eggnog.
  Add chocolate syrup or a packaged chocolate-flavored milk-drink powder.
  Add malted milk, or 1 egg and malted milk.
  Eat crackers with these drinks, to add food value.

Immediately after arising in the morning drink a glass of cold unsweetened fruit juice. It washes off mouth surfaces, often stimulates the appetite.

Allow time for a hearty breakfast. Have fruit or fruit juice; cereal with cream and sugar; eggs; at least 2 buttered toast slices with jam; and milk, coffee, or tea with cream and sugar.

At each meal, eat at least one extra slice of bread, and use generous amounts of butter or margarine on vegetables, breads, etc.

Eat high-calorie vegetables twice a day—white and sweet potatoes, beets, carrots, peas, green limas, etc.

Eat dessert at lunch and dinner. Enjoy the ice cream, puddings, cakes, and pies your overweight sister cannot have.

Eat gravies, sauces, and extra cream.

Use mayonnaise on salads rather than other dressings.

Eat cheese. It is another concentrated food that's high in calories. Eat some kind each day, with salad or dessert.

Vitamin B_1 stimulates the appetite, so include some food that furnishes it in large quantities. For instance:

  Eat 1 to 2 tablesp. dried brewer's yeast daily. Mix it with milk or tomato juice; sprinkle it on cereal; or use it in recipes.
  Sprinkle 2 tablesp. wheat germ on cereal. Consult your doctor about a vitamin supplement.

Remember, you will not accomplish wonders overnight. So don't watch those scales too closely. Once a month is sufficient. And don't worry. Just map out a campaign, form good eating and sleeping habits, and see if each month doesn't register a steady gain.

VEGETABLES FOR DIETERS

(reducers, gainers, or diabetics)

For those of your family who are reducing, trying to gain weight, or are diabetic, the following chart will be helpful.

The vegetables in the 6 per cent group contain twice as much carbohydrate as those in the 3 per cent group, the 9 per cent group three times as much, etc. So if you are reducing or are diabetic, you will probably choose many of your vegetables from the low-carbohydrate groups. If you wish to gain weight, you will be especially interested in the high-carbohydrate groups.

CARBOHYDRATE CONTENT OF VEGETABLES

3%

Asparagus
Broccoli
Cabbage, green,
  Chinese, or red
Cauliflower
Celery
Cucumbers
Endive
Escarole
Green beans, canned
Lettuce
Mushrooms
Parsley
Radishes
Spinach
Squash, summer
Swiss chard
Tomatoes
Water cress
Zucchini

6%

Avocados
Dandelion greens
Eggplant
Green beans, fresh
Green peppers
Kale
Kohlrabi

Pumpkin
Squash, winter
Turnips, white

9%

Artichokes
Beets
Brussels sprouts
Carrots
Onions
Peas, canned
Turnips, yellow

15%

Corn, white or
  yellow (fresh,
young)
Green limas, canned
Parsnips
Peas, fresh

18%

Corn, white or
  yellow, canned
Potatoes, white

21%

Corn, white or
  yellow (fresh,
  medium old)
Green limas, fresh
Potatoes, sweet

YOUR CALORIE COUNT

Beverages:

APPROXIMATE CALORIES

Ale or beer (1 8-oz. glass)	100
Cider, sweet (1 8-oz. glass)	70
Cocktails—1 dry Martini or Manhattan	90
Cocoa, made with milk (1 cup)	180
Coffee or tea, without sugar and cream	0
Cola drinks (1 6-oz. glass)	75
Distilled liquors:	
Brandy (1 1-oz. brandy glass)	75
Rum (1 jigger)	150
Ginger ale (1 8-oz. glass)	80
Soft drinks or carbonated beverages (1 8-oz. glass)	90
Whiskies:	
Bourbon, gin, rye (1 jigger)	120
Scotch (1 jigger)	110
Wines:	
Dry (1 2-oz. wineglass)	90
Sweet (1 2-oz. wineglass)	160

Breads and Cereals

Breads:	
Boston brown or white raisin (1 slice)	100
Melba toast (1 slice)	20
Rye or whole-wheat (1 slice)	75
White, enriched (1 slice)	60
Cereals, hot—corn meal, farina, rolled oats (¾ cup cooked)	100
Cereals, ready-to-eat:	
Corn, rice, or wheat flakes (1 cup)	105
Puffed corn, rice, or wheat (1 cup)	50
Shredded wheat (1 biscuit)	100
Wheat germ (1 tablesp.)	30

Crackers:

Graham (1 2¾″ square)	40
Round scalloped or saltine (1)	15
Thin wheat (1)	9
Doughnuts, plain (1)	120
French toast (1 slice)	105
Macaroni, noodles, spaghetti (¾ cup cooked plain)	200
Muffins:	
Bran (1 2¾″ diameter)	100
Corn meal (1 2¾″ diameter)	140
English (1 3½″ diameter)	130
Plain (1 2¾″ diameter)	130
Pretzels (5 2″ long sticks)	7
Rice—brown, processed, packaged precooked, or regular (¾ cup cooked plain)	105
Rolls, plain (1 4″ x 2½″ x 2″)	100
Waffles (1 6″ diameter or 4½″ x 5⅝″ x ½″)	225

Dairy Products and Eggs

Butter or margarine (1 tablesp.)	100
Cheeses:	
American (1 slice)	110
Cottage, plain (1/3 cup)	75
Cream (1 oz.)	95
Chocolate-milk drink (1 8-oz. glass)	180
Cream, heavy (1 tablesp.)	60
Eggnog (1 8-oz. glass)	230
Eggs:	
Fried (1 medium)	105
Hard- or soft-cooked, or poached (1 medium)	70
Omelet (2 eggs with butter or margarine)	215
Scrambled (2 eggs with 2 tablesp. milk, 1 tablesp. butter or margarine)	245

Milk:
- Buttermilk, cultured (1 8-oz. glass) 85
- Evaporated (½ cup undiluted) 170
- Liquid, skim (1 8-oz. glass) 85
- Liquid, whole (1 8-oz. glass) 165
- Nonfat-dry-milk powder (¼ cup, or 1 oz.) 85
- Sweetened condensed (1 tablesp.) 60

Yoghurt made from skim milk (1 8-oz. cup) 80

Desserts and Sweets

Brownie (1 piece, 2″ x 2″ x ¾″) 145
Cakes:
- Angel or sponge (1 2″ wedge) 115
- Cheese (1 2½″ wedge) 275
- Chocolate cupcake with icing
  (1 2¾″ diameter) 200
- Chocolate layer cake with icing
  (2-layer piece, 2″ wedge) 400
- Fruit or pound (1 piece, 1⅞″ x 1⅞″ x ⅜″) ... 115
- White layer cake with icing (2-layer piece, 2″
  wedge) 325

Candy:
- Bar (1) 295
- Chocolate cream or mint (1 medium) 50

Cookies:
- Iced sandwich (1 small) 70
- Macaroon (1 large) 110
- Sugar (1 medium, 2½″ diameter) 50

Corn syrup, honey, maple syrup (1 tablesp.) 60
Custard, baked (½ cup) 130
Eclair, iced, with 1/3 cup custard or ice-cream
  filling 200
Fruit gelatin (½ cup) 65
Ice cream (1/6 qt.) 200
Marmalade, jam, jelly (1 tablesp.) 100
Pies (3½″ wedge, or ⅛ 9″ pie)
- Apple, blueberry, or strawberry 250
- Cherry, lemon meringue, or mince 350

Puddings:
- Bread, with raisins (½ cup) 250
- Chocolate (½ cup) 200
- Cornstarch (½ cup) 140
- Tapioca (½ cup) 125

Sauces:
- Butterscotch (2 tablesp.) 210
- Chocolate (2 tablesp.) 130

Sherbet, orange (1/6 qt.) 150
Sugars:
- Brown (1 tablesp.) 35
- Confectioners' (1 tablesp.) 45
- Granulated (1 tablesp.) 50

Sundaes:
- Chocolate nut (1/6 qt. chocolate ice cream, 2
  tablesp. chocolate sauce, 2 pecans, chopped) 425

Fish and Sea Food
(Cooked unless otherwise noted)

Bass (1 piece, 3″ x 2¼″ x 1″) 100
Bluefish (1 piece, 3½″ x 3″ x ½″) 190
Clams, raw (6) 100
Crabs, deviled (1 medium) 200
Crab meat, canned or fresh (½ cup) 70
Halibut (1 steak, 4″ x 3″ x ½″) 225
Lobster, canned or fresh (½ cup) 80
Mackerel (1 piece, 3″ x 3″ x 1″) 160
Oysters, raw (8) 100
Salmon (1 steak, 4″ x 3″ x ½″, or 1 cup canned) 200
Sardines, canned in oil (4, 3″ long) 75
Scallops, fried (6 medium) 225
Shrimp (10 to 12 medium) 75
Tuna, canned (½ cup drained) 155
Whitefish (1 piece, 3¾″ x 2¼″ x ¾″) 100

Fruits

Apples (1 medium, 2½″ diameter) 75
Applesauce:
- Sweetened, canned (½ cup) 85
- Unsweetened, canned (½ cup) 45

Apricots:
- Canned halves (6 medium, plus 3 tablesp.
  syrup) 200
- Dried (4 to 6 halves) 90
- Fresh (2 to 3 medium) 60
- Stewed, sweetened dried (½ cup) 200

Avocado (½ medium) 250
Banana (1 medium, 6″ long) 100
Blackberries (½ cup) 50
Blueberries (½ cup) 45
Cantaloupe (½, 5″ diameter) 40
Cherries, sweet, canned (½ cup plus 3 tablesp.
  syrup) or fresh (20 ⅞″ diameter) 100
Cranberry sauce, sweetened, canned, or cooked
  fresh (1 tablesp.) 35
Dates, dried (4) 100
Figs, dried (2 medium) 100
Fruit cocktail, canned (½ cup fruit plus syrup) 80
Grapefruit (½ medium or ½ cup fresh sections) 85
Grapes:
- Concord or green (15) 45
- Malaga (15) 75

Honeydew melon (1 2″ x 7″ wedge) 50
Loganberries (½ cup) 50
Orange (1 medium, 3″ diameter) 70
Peach (½ canned or 1 medium fresh) 50
Pear (2 canned halves plus 2 tablesp. syrup or 1
  medium fresh) 45

YOUR CALORIE COUNT — (continued)

Pineapple, fresh (1 slice, ¾″ thick) 50

Pineapple, canned (1 slice, ¾″ thick plus 1 tablesp. syrup) 85

Plum (1 2″ diameter) 30

Prunes dried (4 medium) 100

Prunes, stewed, sweetened (4 plus ¼ cup syrup) 150

Raisins, light or dark (¼ cup) 85

Raspberries (½ cup) 50

Rhubarb, stewed and sweetened (½ cup) 175

Strawberries (½ cup, or 10 large) 40

Tangerine (1 2½″ diameter) 40

Watermelon (1 slice, 6″ diameter, 1½″ thick) ... 190

Juices (Fresh, Canned, and Frozen)

Apple, canned (½ cup) 60

Cranberry, canned (½ cup) 45

Grape, canned or frozen (½ cup) 90

Grapefruit:

    Sweetened, canned or frozen (½ cup) 65

    Unsweetened, canned or frozen (½ cup) 50

Lemon, fresh, canned, or frozen (¼ cup) 20

Orange, fresh, canned, or frozen (½ cup) 70

Pineapple, unsweetened, canned or frozen (½ cup) 60

Prune, canned (½ cup) 85

Tomato or vegetable cocktail, canned (½ cup) .. 25

Whole-fruit nectars, canned—apricot, peach, pear, or plum (½ cup) 55

Meats and Poultry (Cooked)

Bacon, lean, crisp (1 thin slice, 5″ long) 30

Beef:

    Corned, canned (2 slices, 3″ x 2″ x ¼″) 100

    Dried or chipped (½ cup, or 2 oz.) 115

    Hamburger (1 patty, 2¾″ diameter, 1″ thick) 150

    Roast or steak (1 serving 4½″ x 3″ x ½″) 275

Franks, (1) 100

Lamb:

    Chops (1 lean rib, 2″ x 1½″ x ¾″) 100

    Roast (1 slice, 3½″ x 4½″ x ⅛″) 100

Liver—beef, calf, pork (1 slice 2¾″ x 2″ x ¼″) 85

Liverwurst or other ready-to-eat or canned meat (1 slice, 3¼″ diameter, ¼″ thick) 70

Pork—ham, fresh or smoked (1 slice, 4½″ x 4½″ x ¼″) 330

Poultry:

    Chicken (3 slices, 3½″ x 2½″ x ¼″) 200

    Duckling or turkey (3 slices, 3½″ x 2½″ x ¼″) 315

Sausage (1 link, 3″ long, ½″ diameter) 95

Sweetbreads (¾ cup) 175

Tongue (4 slices, 3″ x 2″ x ⅛″) 100

Veal:

    Cutlet, breaded (1 chop, 4″ x 2¼″ x ½″) 280

    Roast (1 slice, 4″ x 2½″ x ½″) 190

Salad Dressings

Cooked (1 tablesp.) 85

French (1 tablesp.) 50

Mayonnaise (1 tablesp.) 100

Russian (1 tablesp.) 80

Salads

(Each salad includes 2 lettuce leaves and 1 tablesp. dressing)

Cabbage, shredded (½ cup) with French dressing 65

Chicken and celery (½ cup) with mayonnaise ... 250

Crab meat and celery (2 heaping tablesp. crab meat, 2 teasp. celery) with mayonnaise ... 160

Cream cheese and pineapple (1 pineapple slice, 2 tablesp. cheese) with French dressing 200

Mixed greens (½ cup) with French dressing ... 50

Orange and grapefruit (2 orange slices, 3 grapefruit sections) with salad dressing 150

Perfection—jellied vegetables (½ cup), no dressing 40

Potato (½ cup) with mayonnaise 200

Salmon and celery (½ cup) with mayonnaise ... 195

Shrimp (½ cup) with mayonnaise 170

Tomato and lettuce (1 small tomato) with no dressing 30

Tuna and celery (½ cup) with mayonnaise 220

Waldorf (½ cup) with mayonnaise 185

Sandwiches

(Each sandwich includes 2 bread slices—rye, enriched-white, or whole-wheat. Includes light buttering)

Bacon, lettuce, and tomato (4 slices crisp bacon, 2 slices tomato) 300

Chicken salad with lettuce (2 tablesp. chicken, 2 teasp. mayonnaise) 245

Cream cheese and jelly (2 tablesp. cream cheese, 1 tablesp. jelly) 340

Egg salad with lettuce (½ egg, 1 tablesp. mayonnaise) 290

Frank on roll (1 frank) 180

Ham with lettuce (1 slice ham) 270
Hamburger on roll (1 hamburger patty) 250
Peanut butter (1½ tablesp. peanut butter) 300
Swiss cheese (1 slice cheese) 270

Soups (Canned)

Asparagus, cream of (¾ cup) 115
Bouillon or consommé (¾ cup) 15
Chicken noodle (¾ cup) 95
Clam chowder (¾ cup) 75
Mushroom, cream of (¾ cup) 200
Pea, cream of (¾ cup) 115
Tomato:
   Clear (¾ cup) 80
   Cream of (¾ cup) 160
Vegetable (¾ cup) 85

Vegetables

(Cooked unless otherwise noted. No butter or margarine used)

Asparagus, fresh (12 stalks, 5" long) 25
Beans:
   Baked, canned, with pork and tomato sauce
     (1 cup) 295
   Green (½ cup, 1" pieces) 30
   Limas, dried or green (½ cup) 100
Beet greens (½ cup) 20
Beets (2, or ½ cup diced) 50
Broccoli (½ cup) 20
Brussels sprouts (7) 60
Cabbage (½ cup) 20

Carrots, cooked or raw (½ cup diced) 25
Cauliflower (¼ small head, 4½" diameter) 25
Celery, raw (½ cup, or 4 7" long pieces) 10
Corn, sweet, fresh (1 ear, 5" long, 1¾" diameter) 85
Cucumbers, raw (6 slices, ⅛" thick) 5
Eggplant, fried (1 slice, 4" diameter, ⅜" thick) .. 135
Endive, French, raw (2 stalks, 5¾" long) 25
Kale, kohlrabi, dandelion greens, Swiss chard (½
   cup) 30
Lettuce, raw (3 large leaves) 10
Limas, green (½ cup) 100
Mushrooms (4 large) 8
Onion, raw (1 medium) 50
Parsley, raw (1 tablesp. snipped, or 8 sprigs) 4
Peas, green (½ cup) 65
Peppers, raw green (1, 3½" long) 20
Potatoes:
   French fried (8 pieces, 2" x ½" x ½") 160
   Sweet, baked (1 medium, 5" x 2") 185
   Sweet, candied (3½" x 2¼") 315
   White, baked or boiled (1 medium) 100
   White, mashed with milk, butter added (½
     cup) 120
Pumpkin (½ cup) 35
Radishes, raw (5 medium) 10
Sauerkraut, canned (½ cup) 15
Spinach (½ cup) 20
Succotash (½ cup) 115
Summer squash (½ cup) 20
Tomatoes, canned (½ cup) or fresh (1 medium) 25
Turnips, white (½ cup) 25
Water cress, raw (1 bunch 3" long, 3" diameter) 20

Planning Meals

Cooking the meal is just half the job. The other half is planning it.

MEALS CAN BE FUN TO PLAN

Make meal planning a real adventure instead of a gruesome chore. Here are some hints that make the job more fun:

Collect recipes.

Index them. Clip and paste favorites on 3″ x 5″ cards or in a loose-leaf notebook. Or if they're in a cook book or magazine, jot down the page number and title on a card.

Classify your favorites. Print headings on index tabs—cheese dishes, stews, casseroles, quick-dinner dishes, one-dish meals, skillet dishes, left-over main dishes, etc. Attach tabs to cards or pages of loose-leaf notebook.

Make holidays special. To keep family dinners exciting, play up holidays—cherry pie for Washington's Birthday, corned beef and cabbage for St. Patrick's day.

Serve at least one brand-new dish each week. Check the recipes in this book as you try them. See if you can eventually check almost all.

Change the pattern. Don't serve meat-and-potato dinners every day. Everyone enjoys a change—the cook most of all. So try all-in-one casserole, Dutch-oven, or skillet meals; hearty soups; the main-dish salads. Choose a luscious hot bread and dessert to go with them, and the most militant male will be pleased.

Look for new inspiration. No matter how easy it is for you to plan menus, you always need new ideas. Send for manufacturers' booklets; look over a magazine or two each month.

THE EASY WAY TO PLAN

Here's how to plan meals in the easiest, pleasantest way.

You're off to a flying start when you plan a meal two or more days ahead. Don't wait till you're at the grocer's or till you open the refrigerator door.

The same dinner again! You don't want to repeat dishes too conspicuously. But do consult the refrigerator for leftovers. There are lots of ideas on how to vary the repeat performance in Leftovers, p. 550.

Now consider the day's three meals as a unit—breakfast, lunch, and dinner—and they'll be better both esthetically *and* nutritionally.

Make these meals healthy. Turn to These Pyramids Show You What to Eat and Why, p. 676. It's a guide to help you make certain your family has enough of the foods they need every day.

Choose the main dish first. What will it be? A casserole, stew, main-dish salad, hearty soup?

Vegetables come next. Usually it's potatoes and a nonstarchy vegetable, or two nonstarchy ones.

Or instead of potatoes, serve buttered macaroni, spaghetti, noodles, or rice. (Never serve both at the same meal.)

But if you'd like a starchy dessert, such as rice, cornstarch, or tapioca pudding, it's wiser to serve only nonstarchy vegetables.

Vary the seasonings as in Serve with a Flair, p. 247.

Then select a dessert. If the main course is to be salad or soup, you'll want a hearty dessert—pie alamode, a cobbler with rich sauce, or chocolate-frosted layer cake, etc.

But if you're having goulash with noodles or mashed potatoes, you'll want something light, such as fruit gelatin and cookies.

Also ask yourself, would a cold or hot dessert taste better?

Now which salad will you choose? The tossed green salad is the perfect answer almost anytime. But for variety's sake, consider raw relishes, a jellied salad, fruit or vegetable salad, etc.

What about bread? Does your meal need a *hot* bread or will a *cold* one do? Often the choice is plain bread and butter or margarine; now and then it's no bread at all.

Other times you may crave the crispness of toast or French bread, or the glamour of hot muffins, biscuits, or rolls.

Take another look at your menu, for the job isn't done. Consider color, texture, flavor. The dishes of a well-planned meal do not clash in color, flavor, or texture, but do include contrasts.

How much time and effort is involved in getting the meal on the table? Will the cooking be on top of the stove or in the oven? Can you manage it all?

ABOUT CHILDREN'S MEALS

You'll be surprised how soon your children will graduate to eating with the family. They will get everything a growing child needs if in planning your meals you follow These Pyramids Show You What to Eat and Why, p. 676.

A GOOD DINNER

Here are family dinners (or suppers) especially planned for the four seasons of the year.

They incorporate the principles of good meal planning. And with them you'll find notes on how to get dinner on time without fuss.

Thirteen Spring Dinners

In spring the family appetite picks up. Never is there so much interest in "What's for dinner?"

SATURDAY—PORK TONIGHT

Sweet-Sour Pork, p. 77,
with Sweet Potatoes
Guess-What Salad, p. 304   French Bread
Fruit-Gelatin Cubes with Banana Fluff
Coffee or Tea   Milk

Early in day: Start cooking pork as recipe directs. Make fruit-flavored gelatin in shallow pan; refrigerate.

About 30 min. before dinner: Start cooking sweet potatoes. Complete pork dish. Make, chill, salad. (No one will guess it's parsnips!) Cut gelatin into cubes; heap in sherbet glasses. Mash 1 or 2 ripe bananas; add lemon juice, confectioners' sugar to taste; spoon over gelatin.

SUNDAY—CALIFORNIA STYLE

Creamy Lamb Stew, p. 197
Fluffy Hot Rice, p. 234
Diced-Beet-and-Pineapple Salad
with Blue-Cheese French Dressing
Hot Toast (optional)
Strawberry-Ice-Cream Cake
Coffee (instant)   Milk

About 50 min. before dinner: Start stew in pressure cooker. Meanwhile, make and chill salad, dressing. Cook rice. Serve stew, New Orleans gumbo style, in soup plates; then pass rice, to spoon onto stew. Make toast at table.

At desserttime: Place strawberry ice cream between thin slices of unfrosted cake, sandwich style; top with strawberry jam.

MONDAY—OVEN HELPS OUT

Tomato Sauerkraut, p. 271, with Wieners
Creamed New Potatoes
Radishes   Crisp Celery
Rye Bread   Milk
Hurry-Up Apple "Pie," p. 385
Coffee (instant)

About 45 min. before dinner: Start heating oven. Prepare apple "pie"; put in oven to bake.
Dice cooked or canned potatoes; spread in baking dish. Make Thin White Sauce, p. 376; add some grated cheese; pour over potatoes; heat in oven. Cook kraut with wieners on top of stove. Prepare radishes and celery. If desired, butter several slices of rye bread; put back together; wrap in foil; heat in oven last few minutes.

TUESDAY—INDOOR PICNIC

Barbecued Hamburgers, p. 66
Old-fashioned Potato Salad, p. 304
Buttered Peas   Sliced Bread
Spiced Pineapple   Packaged Fig Bars
Cold Milk

Early in day: Make potato salad; refrigerate it and canned crushed pineapple.
About 45 min. before dinner: Start cooking hamburgers. Cook peas.
Just before dinner: Add dash of nutmeg to pineapple.

WEDNESDAY—SPAGHETTI SUPPER FOR FOUR

Sausage-and-Spaghetti Special
Buttered Spinach with Lemon Wedges
Crisp Red Radishes   Hard Rolls
Rhubarb Sauce, p. 402   Fudge Cuts, p. 476
Tea or Coffee   Milk

Early in day: Make Fudge Cuts—they're quick and easy. While they bake, cook rhubarb; prepare radishes; refrigerate both.
About 15 min. before supper: In skillet, heat ½ lb. fully cooked brown-and-serve sausages. Add 2 cans spaghetti in tomato sauce with cheese; heat; if desired, serve with grated cheese. Meanwhile, cook spinach.

THURSDAY—OLD-FASHIONED GOODNESS

Kidney-Lima Casserole, p. 257
Buttered Swiss Chard   Crisp Rolls
Dill-Pickle Slices
Chilled Canned Peach Halves
Topped with Cottage Cheese
Coffee or Tea   Milk

About 45 min. before dinner: Prepare casserole. Wash chard (or spinach or other greens). While vegetable cooks, handle remaining details.

FRIDAY—SECONDS REQUESTED

Susan's Meat Loaf—Cold, p. 68
or Oven-Fried Fish, p. 177
Creamy Carrots and Corn, p. 253
Vinegar Slaw   Packaged Rolls
Canned Purple Plums
Peanut Puffs, p. 485   Milk

Early in day: Bake meat loaf; refrigerate, along with canned plums.
About ½ hr. before dinner: Cook carrots and corn as directed. (If you're having fish, start it now.) Finely shred cabbage; season to taste with vinegar, salt, pepper. Heat rolls in oven. Get puffs ready to broil at desserttime.

SATURDAY—FAMILY FAVORITE

Slices of Cold Canned Corned Beef or
Browned Canned Corned-Beef Hash
Mustard or Catchup
Swedish Kidney Beans
Tossed Green Salad   Buttered Toast
Peach Dessert Cake, p. 387
Tea or Coffee   Milk

Day before: For beans, in saucepan, combine 2 tablesp. sugar, 2 teasp. cornstarch; then stir in 2 tablesp. each water and vinegar. Add 1 No. 2 can kidney beans, undrained. Cook, stirring occasionally, 10 min. Refrigerate.
About 1 hr. before dinner: Bake cake. Prepare salad so it's ready to toss; chill. If you're having hash, slice into patties; dip into flour; sauté in small amount of fat until golden. Heat beans. Make toast at table.

SUNDAY—DAD'S FAVORITE

Pan-Fried Smoked Boneless Shoulder Butt,
p. 89
Golden Cauliflower
Green-Lima-and-Apple Salad
Whole-wheat or White Bread
Fresh Strawberry Tapioca, p. 392
Gingersnaps   Milk

Early in day or day before: Make tapioca. Simmer butt as directed. Refrigerate all.

About 30 min. before dinner: Break cauliflower into flowerets; cook as on p. 280. For salad, toss together 1 drained 10½-oz. can green limas (or 1¼ cups cooked limas), 1 or 2 cubed unpared red apples, and ¼ cup French dressing; chill. Fold cream into tapioca. Sauté sliced butt; remove to heated platter; keep warm. Drain cauliflower; place in same skillet; toss gently over heat until lightly browned.

MONDAY—A QUICKIE

Broiled Hamburgers and Potato Halves
with Sautéed Onions, p. 263
Marinated Raw-Carrot Sticks
Bread Slices
Walnut-Butterscotch Pudding
with Light Cream
Coffee or Tea (instant)

Early in day: Cook potatoes in jackets. Prepare carrot sticks; let stand in French dressing. Make packaged pudding; add chopped nuts. Shape hamburgers. Slice onions. Refrigerate all.

About 30 min. before dinner: Sauté onions. Halve potatoes; brush with bacon fat; broil with meat. Beat pudding with fork.

TUESDAY—A LITTLE SPECIAL

Susan's Pan-Fried Liver and Bacon
with a French Touch, p. 111
Old-fashioned Creamed Vegetables, p. 247
Spring Salad   French Dressing
Cheese-Toasted Rolls
Ambrosia, de Luxe Style, p. 383
Packaged Cookies
Milk

Early in afternoon: Prepare ambrosia; refrigerate.

About 30 min. before dinner: Cook frozen mixed vegetables, and make sauce for them. Mix lettuce, radish slices, and green onions so they're ready to toss with French dressing; chill. Split rolls; spread with cheese. Sauté liver, bacon. Broil rolls. Toss salad.

WEDNESDAY—EGGS FOR SUPPER

French Omelet, p. 226, or Scrambled Eggs, p. 224
Bacon-Tossed Carrots
Buttered Frozen Broccoli
Sliced Head of Lettuce with French Dressing
Toast   Apple Jelly
Tea   Milk

About 30 min. before dinner: Clean carrots; start cooking them, then broccoli. Season cooked carrots with bacon fat. Cook omelet. Prepare salad. Make toast at table. No dessert is needed.

THURSDAY—COUNTRY FARE

Fried Sausages and Canadian-Style Bacon
Creamed New Potatoes and Peas, p. 268
Hard Rolls   Dill-Pickle Strips
Susan's Baked Custard, p. 394
Cookies (from the cookie jar)
Tea   Milk

Early in day: Make custard, adding a generous sprinkling of coconut before baking; refrigerate.

About 40 min. before dinner: Cook new potatoes, peas; meanwhile, make sauce. Pan-fry sausages; when they're almost done, add and pan-fry Canadian-style-bacon slices. Quarter pickles lengthwise.

Fourteen Cool Summer Dinners

Too hot to cook? Almost too hot to eat? Why not make the whole operation as simple and cool as possible?

SUNDAY—PRESSURE SPECIAL

Veal Paprika, p. 105, on Noodles with
Poppy Seeds
Buttered Zucchini   Sliced Head of Lettuce
Peach Ice Cream Topped with Peach Preserves
Crisp Cookies   Coffee or Tea

About 25 min. before dinner: Cook veal. Halve zucchini lengthwise; cook as on p. 285 12 min.

Cook noodles; add poppy seeds. Slice head of lettuce; drizzle on French dressing. For dessert, top ice cream with peach preserves.

MONDAY—PORCH BUFFET FOR THE FAMILY

Sliced Tongue with Water Cress and
Deviled Eggs
Double-Boiler-Scalloped Cabbage, p. 252
Icicle Relish Bowl   Savory Toasted Rolls
Chilled Fruit Cocktail   Oatmeal Cookies
Coffee (instant)

Early in day: Refrigerate canned, cooked, or ready-to-eat beef tongue (p. 115). Cook cabbage briefly, then "scallop" so it's ready for final cooking. Prepare deviled eggs and carrot, celery, and green-pepper sticks. Add grated orange rind to fruit cocktail. Refrigerate all.

About 35 min. before dinner: Start cooking cabbage. Stand relishes in bowl of crushed ice. Then prepare tongue platter. Spread split rolls with butter or margarine mixed with prepared mustard; broil till golden.

TUESDAY—FOR A COOLER DAY

Big Salads of Tuna, Cucumber, and
Tomatoes in Lettuce Cups
Cheese Drop Biscuits   Butter or Margarine
Camille's Peach Coconut, p. 388
Milk   Tea (hot or iced)

Early in day: Clean lettuce. Refrigerate, along with canned tuna, cucumber, tomatoes.

About 30 min. before dinner: Prepare dessert so it's ready to bake; make sauce. Meanwhile, make drop biscuits from packaged mix, adding some grated cheese. Bake biscuits and dessert. Arrange salads.

WEDNESDAY—NICE TO COME HOME TO

Broiled Onion-Cheese Sandwiches, p. 357
Broiled Liverwurst Slices   Raw Carrot Sticks
Fresh Berry Pie, p. 413
(blueberry or blackberry)
or Berries with Susan's Coconut Refrigerator
Cookies, p. 482
Milk   Hot Coffee

Early in day: Make pie or cookies before day warms up. Prepare carrot sticks; refrigerate.

About 30 min. before dinner: Prepare sandwiches; broil, along with thick liverwurst slices. Put pie in oven to warm up.

THURSDAY—EASY TO SHOP

Pan-broiled Minute or Cube Steaks, p. 55
Fluffy Hot Rice, p. 234
Spinach or Chard   Buttered Hard Rolls
Tomato Wedges in Lettuce Cups
Grape Cooler, p. 403
Milk   Tea or Coffee (iced)

Early in day: Make dessert. Dip tomatoes into boiling water; then plunge immediately into cold water; store, unpeeled, in refrigerator. If you're using fresh greens, wash; refrigerate.

About 15 min. before dinner: Start cooking rice, using packaged precooked rice. Cook spinach. Peel and quarter tomatoes; arrange in lettuce cups; top with mayonnaise, thinned with milk and seasoned with bit of curry powder. Prepare cooler. Cook steaks at last minute.

FRIDAY—A SNAP

Broiled Tomato Slices with
Canadian-Style Bacon
Hashed-Brown Potatoes
Buttered Rye Bread
Lettuce Slices with Egg-Salad Dressing
Crackers   Cheese   Fresh Plums
Milk   Tea with Lemon (hot or iced)

Early in day: Cook potatoes. Hard-cook eggs; chop; add to French dressing. Refrigerate all.

About 20 min. before dinner: Dice potatoes. Heat fat in skillet; add potatoes; cook slowly, turning often, until crisp and brown. Meanwhile, prepare, then broil, tomatoes and bacon. Cut lettuce into slices; top with dressing. Arrange cheese, crackers, and fruit on tray.

SATURDAY—COLD SUPPER, HOT DRINK

"Chilly" con Carne Salad, p. 308
Buttered French Bread   Pickles   Radishes
Cups of Hot Tomato Bouillon
Sliced Fresh Pears with Sugared Raspberries
or Orange Marshmallow Jelly

Early in day: Mix "Chilly" con Carne. Mash berries; sweeten; refrigerate with pears. Or make, then chill, orange-flavored gelatin till consistency of unbeaten egg white; beat with egg beater; fold in few snipped marshmallows; chill.

About 10 min. before supper: Heat canned tomato juice with bouillon cube (use 1 cube for 2 cups juice): serve, cup style, with main course. Prepare radishes, pickles. If the menu seems light, add milk and cookies.

SUNDAY—COMPANY SUPPER

Gladys' Chicken Salad, p. 306
Grilled Cheese Sandwiches
Pickled Peaches   Canned Cranberry Sauce
Vanilla Ice Cream with Grated Chocolate
Packaged Macaroons   Coffee

Day before: Prepare Simmered Chicken, p. 150. Remove meat from bones; refrigerate.

Early in day: Make dressing for salad; refrigerate. Sauté walnuts for salad. Make sandwiches, ready to be toasted on griddle. Chill canned peach halves.

Just before supper: Toss salad with dressing; refrigerate. Start grilling sandwiches. Spoon some pickle relish into each peach half; arrange with cranberry sauce in serving dish. Before serving dessert, grate unsweetened chocolate onto ice cream.

MONDAY—FEW DISHES TO WASH

Corned Beef with Horse-radish and Mustard
Parsley Green Limas   Hard Rolls
Banana-Split Salad, p. 311
Cookies or Jelly Roll (bought or homemade)
Cocoa (hot or iced)

Early in day: Cook corned beef in pressure cooker. (Or buy canned corned beef.) Make cocoa, ready to add milk. Refrigerate all.

About ½ hr. before dinner: Cook frozen limas; season; add snipped parsley or chives. Slice corned beef. Put prepared mustard and horse-radish in relish dishes. Make salad.

TUESDAY—NEW WAY WITH HAMBURGER

Potato Burgers, p. 66
Creamed Carrots
Bread   Butter or Margarine
Cucumbers and Onions in Celery-Seed Vinegar
Sugared Red Raspberries with Cinnamon Toast
Milk   Coffee (hot or iced)

Early in day: Cover thinly sliced cucumbers and onions with slightly diluted vinegar; add salt, pepper, a few celery seeds. Refrigerate all.

About 20 to 25 min. before dinner: Cook carrots; make and add Vegetable Sauce, p. 376. Cook burgers. Prepare raspberries. Make toast.

WEDNESDAY—AFTER-WORK PICNIC

Big Pot of Baked Beans with Franks
Cabbage Salad with Tomato Mayonnaise
Brown-Bread-and-Cream-Cheese Sandwiches
Milk   Chilled Watermelon
Soft Drinks

When you get home: Place canned baked beans and franks in easy-to-carry kettle; heat till bubbling hot. Meanwhile, shred cabbage; refrigerate. Make sandwiches.

At last minute: Mix diced tomatoes with mayonnaise; toss with cabbage; season. Wrap heated kettle of beans in several thicknesses of newspaper. (For safety's sake, plan to eat within 4 hr.) Don't forget watermelon and a big knife.

THURSDAY—COUNTRY SUPPER

Frizzled Ham   Wilted Lettuce, p. 301
Old-fashioned Potato Salad, p. 304
Bread   Milk
Saucepan Applesauce, p. 400, Alamode
Soft Molasses Cookies, p. 478
Coffee or Tea (hot or iced)

Early in day: Hard-cook eggs for salad. Make potato salad. Make applesauce; or use canned. Refrigerate all. Make (or buy) cookies.

About 20 min. before supper: To potato salad, add extra mayonnaise, if needed, and snipped parsley. Heat fully-cooked or ready-to-eat ham slices in skillet; remove to hot platter. Prepare wilted lettuce in drippings left in skillet, adding enough salad oil to make ¼ cup fat and omitting bacon. Top applesauce with ice cream; sprinkle with nutmeg.

FRIDAY—NO ADVANCE PREPARATION

Old-time Welsh Rabbit, p. 214
Fluffy Hot Rice, p. 234
Buttered Peas   Radishes and Scallions
Crisp Rye or Whole-wheat Wafers
Two-Fruit Dessert Salad
with Currant Salad Dressing
Favorite Cold Drink

About 25 min. before dinner: Get cold drink ready. Cook rice. Meanwhile, make Welsh rabbit. Cook or heat peas. Arrange peach and pear quarters (or apricot, melon, or other fruit) on salad plates with greens; add currants to French dressing. Prepare radishes and scallions.

SATURDAY—LITTLE DINNER
(or Big Lunch)

Chilled Vegetable-Juice Cocktail
Eggs Scrambled with Corn   Bacon Garnish
Big Tossed Green Salad
Toast   Apricot or Strawberry Jam
Gingerbread Squares   Milk or Buttermilk

About 1 hr. before dinner: Pour juice into glasses; refrigerate. Bake gingerbread (use mix). Prepare salad so it's ready to toss.

About 20 min. before dinner: Fry bacon; remove from skillet; pour off most of drippings. For 4 people, beat 6 eggs with fork; add ½ to 1 cup cooked frozen or canned vacuum-packed whole-kernel corn, ¼ cup milk, salt, and pepper; scramble in skillet. Toss salad. Make toast at table.

Fourteen Early-Autumn Dinners

SUNDAY FEASTING

Fried Chicken Superb, Crunchy Style, p. 140
Old-fashioned Creamed Vegetables, p. 247
Celery and Cucumber Sticks
Susan's Blueberry Muffins, p. 327
Sliced Peaches Topped with Tapioca Cream
Coffee (instant)

Early in day: Get chicken ready to fry. Make tapioca cream and sauce for vegetables. Prepare celery and cucumber sticks. Refrigerate.

About 50 min. before dinner: Make muffins (or use packaged corn-muffin mix and blueberries); bake while chicken fries. Slice peaches; toss with lemon juice. Cook frozen, or heat canned, mixed vegetables with seasoned salt; add to reheated sauce.

MONDAY—GOOD, EASY EATING

Superb Skillet Burger Loaf, p. 69
Lazy-daisy Corn in Frankfurter Rolls
Lettuce with Relish French Dressing
Fruit-Nut Gelatin Bowl
Iced Tea

Early in day: Make Fruited Jelly, p. 402, adding some chopped nuts. Clean lettuce; add pickle relish to French dressing. Refrigerate all.

About 25 min. before dinner: Cook meat and ears of corn. Split frankfurter rolls; spread generously with butter or margarine; put ear of corn in each. Each person rolls corn around in bun, then eats corn as usual.

TUESDAY—PLANNED AROUND A BIG
DESSERT

Tomato Soup
Susan's Skillet Potato Salad, p. 304
Sliced-Bologna-and-Cheese Platter
Brown-and-Serve Rolls
Sweet-and-Sour Pickles
Old-fashioned Peach Dumplings, p. 386
with Cream
Coffee (hot or iced)

Early in day: Prepare dumplings so they're ready to bake; refrigerate, along with pickles.

About 1 hr. before dinner: Bake dumplings. Prepare salad. Heat rolls and canned soup. Arrange pickles in dish. Prepare meat platter.

WEDNESDAY—GRIDDLE SPECIAL

French-Toasted Sandwiches, p. 362
Jellied Cranberry Sauce
Green Beans and Carrots in Cream
Lettuce Slices with Lemon French Dressing,
p. 319
Cantaloupe Rings with Sliced Peaches
Hot Coffee (instant)

Early in day: Make Lemon French Dressing. Put sandwiches together, using deviled ham as filling. Clean lettuce. Refrigerate all, along with melon rings and can of cranberry sauce.

About 20 min. before dinner: Cook beans and carrots. Dip and sauté sandwiches. Add cream to vegetables. Slice peaches at last moment.

THURSDAY—BACK-YARD SUPPER

Steak Sandwiches, p. 361
with Jiffy Barbecue Sauce, p. 372
Skillet Spaghetti or Frozen French Fries
Salad Kabobs
(tomato wedges, gherkin pickles, ripe olives)
Cheese-and-Cherry Tray   Tea

Early in day: Wash cherries, leaving stems on; refrigerate, along with makings of kabobs. Make barbecue sauce.

About 15 min. before dinner: Arrange cherries and cheese on glossy leaves on tray. String kabobs on toothpicks. Grill steaks. Heat canned spaghetti in tomato sauce with cheese; or heat French fries in ¼″ hot oil in skillet.

FRIDAY—SEA FOOD PLUS

Tomato Juice
Lobster Tails à la Barber, p. 188
New Potatoes and Peas
Crisp Radishes
Fruit Sherbet with Grated Chocolate
Coffee

Early in day: Boil lobster tails; remove meat. Clean radishes. Buy sherbet. Refrigerate all, along with canned tomato juice.

About 40 min. before dinner: Cook potatoes. Complete lobster dish. Cook frozen, or heat canned peas; toss with potatoes; season.

SATURDAY—COOL OVEN COOKING

Two-Day Caramel Ham Loaf, p. 92
Karen's Green Limas, p. 260
Stuff-Your-Own Celery
Hard Rolls
Saucepan Applesauce, p. 400
Peanut Whirligigs, p. 483   Iced Tea or Coffee

Early in day: Make whirligigs. Make applesauce; clean celery; refrigerate both.

About 1¼ hr. before dinner: Make ham loaf; bake with limas. On dish, arrange celery and cheese wedges (each person stuffs his own.)

SUNDAY—REALLY DIFFERENT

Chicken-with-Rice Soup
Cold Sliced Ham Loaf
(from yesterday)
Frosted Green-Bean Salad, p. 302
Thin Pumpernickel Slices
Angel or Chiffon Cake with Strawberries
Iced Tea

Early in day: Make bean salad, and egg topping; refrigerate. Make or buy cake. Clean berries.

About 10 min. before dinner: Heat canned soup; serve in cups, with lemon slices. Meanwhile, surround cake with berries. On large platter, arrange salad and ham loaf.

MONDAY—FIFTEEN MINUTES DOES IT

Corned-Beef-Hash Puffs, p. 126, Island Style
Broiled Canned Sweet Potatoes and
Peach Halves
Radishes to Munch
Chocolate-Rennet-Custard Dessert
So-Easy Jam Cake   Tea

Early in day: Make rennet custard, using light cream; clean radishes; refrigerate both.

About 20 min. before dinner: Broil hash puffs, substituting canned pineapple slices for tomato. Broil sweet potatoes and peach halves, brushed with melted butter or margarine, along with puffs. Slice leftover angel-food or chiffon cake; toast in broiler; spread with raspberry jam.

TUESDAY—MEAL-IN-A-LOAF

Susan's Party Sandwich Loaf, p. 363
Raw-Carrot and Dill-Pickle Strips
Cups of Cream-of-Mushroom Soup
(to sip with sandwich loaf)
Honeydew Melon with Orange and Lemon
Sherbets
Coffee (instant)

Early in day: Assemble sandwich loaf; refrigerate, along with melon, carrot sticks, and dill pickles, cut into strips.

About 10 min. before dinner: Garnish loaf while canned soup heats. Serving is easy.

WEDNESDAY—VERY SPECIAL

Veal Inverness on Green Rice, p. 108
Chinese Cabbage Slaw with
Tarragon Sour-Cream Dressing, p. 318
Hard Rolls
Basket of Plums and Dried Apricots
Fresh Coconut for Nibbling
Iced Tea with
Pitcherful of Lemon Juice

Early in day: Let veal stand in sauce. Make salad dressing. Refrigerate both, plus fruits. Prepare coconut (p. 517).

About 35 min. before dinner: Cook veal and rice. Prepare slaw. Prepare dessert basket.

THURSDAY—OUTDOORS-INDOORS

Chicken-Liver Kabobs
Lots of Corn
Canned Brown Bread, Heated and Sliced
Big Fruit Salad Plates, p. 309
Cool Buttermilk or Hot Coffee

Early in day: String chicken livers, bacon squares, and tomato wedges on skewers. Refrigerate, along with fruits for salad.

About 25 min. before dinner: Heat bread in double boiler. Broil kabobs as in Kitchen Kabobs, p. 97. Cook halved ears of corn. Prepare salad, omitting sandwiches called for. Sprinkle buttermilk with paprika, salt.

VEGETABLE DINNER, MAN STYLE

Tomatoes Stuffed with Macaroni and Cheese, p. 274
Sliced Zucchini   Dill Baby Carrots
Toasted Rolls in Loaf, p. 340
Tossed Green Salad
Lemon Chiffon Pie, p. 416
with Baked Crumb Crust, p. 410
Iced Coffee

Early in day: Make pie, using gingersnaps for crust. (Or make pie several weeks ahead; freeze as on p. 539.) Get salad greens ready. Prepare vegetables, rolls. Refrigerate all.

About 45 min. before dinner: Make, then bake, macaroni dish. Bake rolls at same time. Meanwhile, cook carrots 20 to 30 min., zucchini 15 min.; season. On large platter, arrange, in rows, tomatoes, zucchini, carrots, rolls. Snip dill over carrots. Toss salad.

SATURDAY—ALL-ON-ONE PLATE

Chili con Carne (pressure cooked), p. 196, on Corn Chips
Lettuce-Avocado Salad
Gala Dessert Fruit Plate, p. 382
Iced Coffee (instant)

Early in day: Make chili con carne (or use canned). Refrigerate, along with lettuce, avocado, dessert ingredients. Buy packaged corn chips.

At last minute: Heat chili con carne. Make salad. Prepare fruit plate.

Fourteen Winter Dinners

SUNDAY—COULDN'T BE SIMPLER

Susan's Rib Roast of Beef, p. 50
or Pot Roast (see To Cook Pot Roast, p. 59)
Franconia, or Pan-Roasted, Potatoes, p. 267
Toasted Rolls
Lettuce with French Dressing
Strawberry Ice Cream
Frosted Chocolate Cookies   Coffee

Several hours before dinner: Start roasting or pot-roasting beef. Bake potatoes with meat last 40 to 60 minutes. (Plan to cook plenty of meat and vegetables, for hash tomorrow.) Clean and slice lettuce; refrigerate.

About 15 min. before dinner: Prepare lettuce. Split rolls; butter; toast in broiler while making gravy. (Buy ice cream, cookies.)

MONDAY—A HALF HOUR DOES IT

Wonderful Hash, p. 129
Stewed Celery and Tomatoes
Sliced Sweet Pickles
White Bread
Canned Peach Halves
Topped with Cottage Cheese
Milk   Tea or Coffee

About 45 min. before dinner: Make hash. (If you're short of meat for hash, make 4 depressions in top; plan to add eggs later.)

About 20 min. before dinner: Cook diced celery as on p. 280; add to canned stewed tomatoes. Last 10 min., break egg into each depression in hash; cover; finish cooking. Slice pickles. Top peach halves with cheese.

TUESDAY—DOUBLE DUTY

Skillet Custard Corn Bread, p. 329
Baked Sausage Links, p. 84
Creamed or Buttered Green Beans
Crisp Cold Apples
Packaged Gingersnaps or Fig Bars

About 45 min. before dinner: Put corn bread in oven.

About 10 min. later: Start baking sausages.

Cook green beans. Meanwhile, make white sauce for beans. Apples serve as salad and dessert.

WEDNESDAY—ON A COLD DAY

Little Sherry-Barbecued Loaves, p. 69
Mashed Turnips   Buttered Peas
Peach or Watermelon Pickles
White Bread
Tapioca Cream, p. 392, with Grated Chocolate
Peanut Cookies   Coffee

Early in day or day before: Make tapioca cream; make, shape, meat loaves; refrigerate.
About 1¼ hr. before dinner: Bake meat loaves. Start cooking turnips. Heat canned, or cook frozen, peas. Grate chocolate over tapioca.

THURSDAY—SIMPLE BUT SATISFYING

Savory Lima-Bean Pot, p. 256
Rye Bread
Peanut-Butter-Stuffed Celery
Doughnuts (warmed and rolled in sugar)
Milk   Coffee (instant)

Day before or 3½ hr. before dinner: Start cooking beans.
About 1½ hr. before dinner: Bake beans.
At last minute: Mix peanut butter with pickle relish; use to stuff celery. When beans are baked, remove from oven; turn off heat. Put doughnuts in oven to warm up.

FRIDAY—OVEN DINNER

Chip-Tuna Casserole, p. 179
Buttery Shredded Beets, p. 250
Spinach with Onion
Hard Rolls
Cinnamon Peaches or Apricots, p. 401
Milk   Coffee (instant)

About 1 to 1½ hr. before dinner: Bake peaches. Meanwhile, make tuna casserole.
About 40 min. before dinner: Bake tuna. Cook beets. Sauté a little minced onion; cook spinach; add onion.

SATURDAY—BARBECUE SPECIAL

Rib-and-Bean Barbecue, p. 83
Chopped Coleslaw, p. 303   White Bread
Winter Fruit Medley
(apples, grapefruit, oranges, bananas)
Packaged Raisin Cookies   Tea or Coffee

About 2½ hr. before dinner: Start cooking ribs. Make coleslaw; refrigerate. Prepare fruit.

SUNDAY—UNEXPECTED COMPANY

Baked Ham or Picnic Slice, p. 89
Oven-Cooked Frozen Squash, p. 246
Succotash, p. 256
Canned Cranberry Sauce in Lettuce Cups
Heated Rolls
Coconut Layer Cake Alamode

About 1¼ hr. before dinner: Remove cake layer from freezer (or use bakers'). Cook squash and ham in oven together. Cook succotash. Heat rolls last few minutes.
Just before dinner: Prepare salad. Frost cake with whipped cream; sprinkle with coconut.
At desserttime: Serve cake with ice cream.

MONDAY—FOR HEARTY APPETITES

Braised Pork Chops with Herbs, p. 79
Hot Butter Beans
Rye Bread   Waldorf Coleslaw, p. 303
Warm Gingerbread
Milk

About 1½ hr. before dinner: Start cooking chops. Make gingerbread. Prepare slaw and dressing; refrigerate; toss at last minute. Heat canned butter beans.

TUESDAY—FOR FOUR

Cube Steaks with Hasty-Tasty Sauce, p. 55
Fluffy Hot Rice, p. 234
Parsley Carrots
Sliced Onions in Vinegar
Cranberry Baked Apples, p. 400
Coffee (instant)   Milk

About 1 hr. before dinner: Bake apples.
About 25 min. before dinner: Cook rice and carrots. Slice onions; add a little sugar, salt, black pepper, vinegar. Cook steak and sauce. Add snipped parsley to carrots.

WEDNESDAY—HOT BREAD TONIGHT

Quick-Fried Liver and Franks
Quick Scalloped Potatoes, p. 270
Popovers, p. 328
Lettuce with French Dressing
Orange Gelatin Topped with
Diced Oranges and Chopped Walnuts
Tea   Milk

Early in day: Make gelatin. Prepare fruit and nuts for topping.

About 1 hr. before dinner: Make your own popovers, or use packaged mix. Scallop potatoes. Prepare lettuce. Quickly pan-fry liver and franks in same skillet.

THURSDAY—BUSY AFTERNOON AHEAD

Tomato Juice (to sip with meal)
Susan's Brown Beef Stew, p. 61
Buttered Toast   Pickles
Layer Cake with Penuche Frosting, p. 467
Coffee or Tea   Milk

Early in day: Simmer meat for stew; refrigerate. Make layer cake, using packaged mix; cool; frost.

About 35 min. before dinner: Heat stew meat; add vegetables; finish cooking. Serve in soup plates, reserving about one third of stew for Saturday's pie. Make toast at table.

FRIDAY—BUSINESSWOMAN'S SUPPER

Easy Broiled Fish, p. 172
Golden Noodles
Broccoli with Mustard Sauce
Hard Rolls
Spiced Canned Purple Plums
Coffee or Tea   Milk

About 30 min. before dinner: Start cooking broccoli, noodles, then fish. Serve broccoli with mayonnaise seasoned to taste with prepared mustard and lemon juice or vinegar. Spoon plums into bowl; add bit of nutmeg and grated orange rind. Heat rolls in broiler with heat turned off. Add some grated cheese to drained, seasoned noodles.

SATURDAY—NEW LOOK

Meat Pie with Drop-Biscuit Crust
Lettuce with French Dressing
Tropical Cocktail
Cookies (from cookie jar)
Coffee (instant)   Milk

About 45 min. before dinner: Does the leftover stew look meager? Add 1 can meat balls and gravy, plus 1 small can undrained green beans. Heat in casserole at 400° F. 15 min. Drop biscuit dough, made from packaged mix, over hot stew;

bake 25 min. Prepare lettuce. To canned fruit cocktail, add banana and shredded coconut.

A GOOD LUNCH

What to serve at lunch depends on where it's eaten. If the noonday meal is served at home, the leftovers that won't stretch to make a family dinner can be the start of this meal.

Or you may pack a lunch box (see p. 580).

If any of the family eats out, be sure he chooses foods that round out the rest of the day's meals.

Salad-and-Sandwich Lunches

Crunchy Tuna Salad, p. 309
Peanut-Butter-and-Jelly Sandwiches
Kitchen Milk Shake

———

Grilled Cheese Sandwiches Garnished with Bacon
Citrus-Fruit Salad
Iced Cocoa

———

Junior Clubs, p. 360
Golden Dessert Salad
(top cottage cheese with stewed or canned apricots and dash of cinnamon)
Chocolate Milk

———

Mac's Spinach-Bacon Salad Bowl, p. 301
Spread-Your-Owns
(cheese spread, crackers)
Spiced Fruit Cocktail
(add lemon juice, grated lemon rind, and pinch of mace to canned fruit cocktail)

———

Salad Plate
(tomato-tuna salad, potato chips)
Bread-and-Butter Sandwiches
Peanut-Butter Cookies   Pitcherful of Milk

———

Baked-Ham Sandwiches with
Quick Mushroom Sauce, p. 372
Fruit Slaw
(cabbage, pineapple, dates)
Coffee (hot or iced)

Kidney-Bean-and-Vegetable Salad Bowl
Hot Toasted Luncheon-Meat Sandwiches
Chilled Watermelon Slices
Milk

———

Tossed Mixed-Vegetable Salad
Toasted Cheese or Liver *Pâté* Roll Ups
(Make Roll-Ups, p. 23, using cheese spread
or liver *pâté* as filling)
Cake (from day before) or Packaged Cookies
Tall Glasses of Orange Juice

———

Dunk Salad
(tomato and lettuce wedges, plus cucumber
sticks, to dunk in salad dressing)
Meat-Loaf Sandwiches
Banana Milk Shake   Fig Bars to Munch

———

Barbecued Franks, p. 121, in Toasted Buns
Raw-Relish Plate
(radishes, celery and carrot sticks, green-pepper
strips)
Cream-Filled Chocolate Cookies
Mugs of Milk

Soup-and-Sandwich Lunches

Creamy Potato Soup, p. 34
Toasted Peanut-Butter-and-Chili-Sauce
Sandwiches
Canned Crushed Pineapple

———

Canned Clam Chowder
Cottage Cheese and Chopped Dill Pickle
on Toast
Tangerines   Chocolate Candy Bar

———

Corn Soup, p. 36
Tuna on Rye
Rhubarb Sauce   Tea or Coffee (instant)

———

Oyster or Clam Stew
Toasted Cheese-and-Lettuce Sandwiches
Gingerbread   Tea

———

Chilled Asparagus Soup
(heat canned cream-of-asparagus soup; then
chill)
Crisp Bacon on Toasted Cheese Bread
Spiced Applesauce   Coffee

———

Canned Green-Pea Soup
French Frankwiches, p. 359
Pineapple Chunks on Toothpicks
Coffee (hot or iced)

———

Canned Bean Soup
Thin Burgers with Tomato Slices on Toasted
Buns
Red Sundae
(raspberry gelatin topped with vanilla ice cream)

———

Tomato-Mushroom Bisque
(combine canned tomato and cream-of-mush-
room soups)
Scrambled Eggs on Toast
Canned Peaches (add squeeze of lemon)
Chocolate-Chip Cookies

———

Canned Chicken-Noodle Soup
(add lemon slice)
Egg-and-Green-Pepper Sandwiches
Vanilla Pudding with Sour-Cherry Sauce

———

Canned Vegetable Soup
Double-Decker Sandwiches
(crisp bacon, cream cheese, lettuce, horse-radish)
Chilled Grapes or Salted Peanuts
Cocoa (hot or iced, instant or mix)

———

Tomato Soup with Chopped-Pickle Garnish
Baked Beans and Bologna on Boston Brown
Bread
Melon Wedges

———

Consommé or Hot Tomato Juice
Club Sandwiches
(sliced tongue with cabbage-and-raisin slaw)
Cut-Up Oranges and Coconut

A GOOD BREAKFAST

There's no substitute for a good breakfast. The most nutrition-packed lunch in the world won't compensate for a skipped morning meal. And the best-balanced dinner won't carry you through in peak form till the following noon. It's been proved: People who eat a good breakfast work better, think better, react faster, and are altogether pleasanter, happier people.

Good Breakfast Patterns

Choose one of these patterns, and your breakfast will be a good nutritious one.

Pattern No. 1
Fruit or fruit juice
Ready-to-eat or hot cereal with milk
Enriched white or whole-grain bread, rolls, or toast; butter or margarine
Coffee; milk for children

Pattern No. 2
Fruit or fruit juice
Eggs and bacon
Enriched white or whole-grain bread, rolls, or toast; butter or margarine
Coffee; milk for children

Pattern No. 3
Your growing son or daughter and your husband (if his work is heavy) needs:

Fruit or fruit juice
Ready-to-eat or hot cereal with milk
Eggs (and breakfast meat, if budget allows)
Enriched white or whole-grain bread, rolls, or toast; butter or margarine
Coffee; milk for children

How to Break Bad Breakfast Habits

Develop an appetite! It's possible. Our eating patterns are very much a matter of habit, and with just a little self-discipline, we can adjust and improve them.

If you are eating 50, 60, or even 70 per cent of the day's food at dinnertime, then try this experiment: Eat a little more at lunch, a little less at dinner. Go easy on high-calorie desserts, etc.; then make yourself eat your "good breakfast," hungry or not. Keep this up for a week or 10 days, and you'll find you are looking forward to breakfast and are automatically eating less for dinner.

Take Time for Breakfast. Aren't several hours of feeling happily energetic worth getting up 15 min. earlier?

Or Plan Ahead. When dinner's out of the way (or even later), set the breakfast table.

Good Breakfast Chart

(Suggestions based on These Pyramids Show You What to Eat and Why, p. 676)

JUICE OR FRUIT RICH IN VITAMIN C

Juices—fresh, frozen, or canned: Use orange, grapefruit (or blend of these), or tomato juice.

Grapefruit: Serve halves or sections (canned or fresh), as is or with grape juice, cut-up oranges, or seedless grapes.

Oranges: Sprinkle sections, slices, or halves with cloves or cinnamon. Or use tangerines.

Strawberries or Melons

OR ONE OF THESE FRUITS

(if a vitamin-C-rich fruit appears at another meal)

Apple, Baked: Stuff with cut-up prunes, pitted dates, a few raisins, or teaspoonful of orange marmalade.

Applesauce: Flavor with grated orange or lemon rind, a few raisins, a bit of canned crushed pineapple, or cranberry sauce. Also add sprinkling of cinnamon, mace, or cloves.

Apricots, Dried: Eat right from package. Or stew with raisins, prunes, grated orange or lemon rind, and a clove or two.

Bananas: Serve sprinkled with cinnamon or nutmeg. Or serve in orange or pineapple juice.

Juices, Fruit Nectars: Try pineapple, prune, or vegetable juice; or try apricot, peach, or pear nectar.

Prunes, Dried: Simmer with a clove or two, or grated orange or lemon rind. Or serve with orange or grapefruit sections. Nice right from package too.

BREAKFAST CEREAL AND MILK

Hot Cereal: Try any of these—oatmeal, farina, whole-grain wheat, rice, hominy, etc.—as suggested below:

1. Add cut-up, pitted dates, raisins, or stewed apricots or prunes a few minutes before serving.
2. Top with canned, frozen, fresh, or cooked fruits, such as peaches, apples, prunes, apricots, bananas, figs.
3. Top with molasses, table syrup, brown sugar, shaved or soft maple sugar, preserves, jelly, or butter.
4. Sprinkle with a little ready-to-eat cereal.
5. Instead of water, use half or all milk in cooking. (Or add some nonfat dry milk while cooking.)

Ready-to-Eat Cereal: Take your pick of corn, wheat, rice, or oat cereals in many enticing forms to serve, as below:

1. Serve 2 or 3 kinds, side by side, in each cereal bowl.
2. Top with sliced bananas or peaches, crushed pineapple, or baked apple.
3. Mix 2 kinds of cereal in each bowl.

BREAD WITH BUTTER OR MARGARINE

Bread as Is or Toasted: Use enriched white, raisin, rye, cracked-wheat, whole-wheat, fruit, or nut bread, etc. If you're making cinnamon toast, vary it by adding grated orange rind, brown sugar, or a sprinkling of nuts.

Biscuits (homemade or from a mix): Cut out or drop. Or make brown-sugar-and-nut pin wheels. Or split, butter, and toast biscuits left over from dinner.

Coffeecakes and Doughnuts: Warm in oven. Or split; butter; toast.

French Toast: Serve with bacon or ham; butter or margarine and table syrup, honey, or applesauce; or lemon wedge and sprinkling of confectioners' sugar.

Muffins (homemade or from a mix): Make plain, bran, corn, fruit, or nut muffins.

Pancakes or Waffles (from packaged mixes): Serve plain, buckwheat, corn-meal, or sour-milk pancakes or waffles, with butter or margarine, table syrup, honey, apple butter, or molasses.

Rolls (bought, your own, or from a mix): Serve plain, fruit, nut, or sweet rolls.

BEVERAGE

Milk, Milk Drinks, Cocoa (hot or cold): Each adult should get 3 8-oz. cups of milk every day (use skim milk if you're reducing).

Coffee or Tea: Serve to adults—provided they are getting enough milk.

PROTEIN-RICH ADDITIONS

Breakfast Meats: Try Canadian-style bacon, ham, canned luncheon meat, sausages, scrapple, etc.

Eggs: Serve them creamed, fried, in omelets (fluffy or French), poached, scrambled, shirred, soft-cooked.

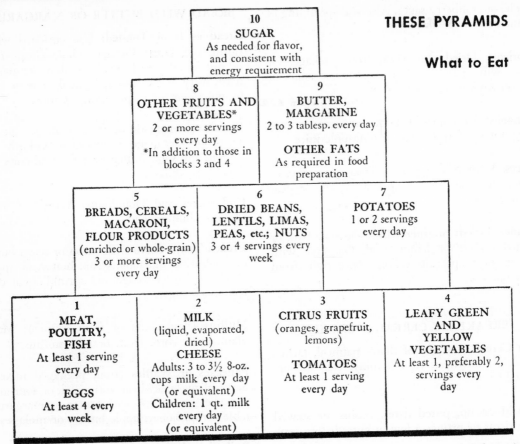

THESE PYRAMIDS

What to Eat

HOW TO USE THESE PYRAMIDS

1. MEAT, POULTRY, FISH, EGGS

• Less expensive cuts and grades of meat are just as nutritious as costlier ones.

• Utilize poultry giblets; they're a wonderful source of protein, vitamins, and minerals.

• Serve fat with meat (unless you are watching calories); it adds flavor, energy.

• Salt-water fish and shellfish are our richest, most dependable source of iodine.

• For protein, 2 eggs can take the place of a serving of meat, fish, or poultry.

2. MILK (liquid, evaporated, dried), CHEESE

• Milk need not always be drunk; it's as nourishing in soups, sauces, puddings, ice cream, etc.

• Cheese can take the place of meat, poultry, fish, and eggs in main dishes.

3. CITRUS FRUITS (oranges, grapefruit, lemons), TOMATOES

• Your daily vitamin-C needs can be met if breakfast includes orange or grapefruit juice, tomato juice, a whole orange, or ½ grapefruit.

4. LEAFY GREEN AND YELLOW VEGETABLES

• Make use of the wonderful variety of these vegetables. Study the chapter in this book on vegetables. You'll find the entire family will eat their share if vegetables are cooked till tender-crisp in a minimum amount of water—to preserve food value and flavor.

5. BREADS, CEREALS, MACARONI, etc.

• Don't underestimate the value of the fine supplementary protein in this group—a value that is further enhanced when these foods are used in combination with even small amounts of complete protein. (That's why cereal and milk are a wonderful combination.)

• Macaroni and noodles are fine "stretchers."

• Sandwiches made with enriched-white or whole-grain breads have fine food value, particu-

SHOW YOU

and Why

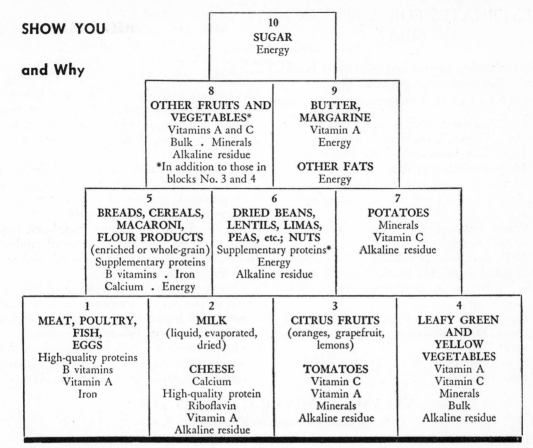

	10 **SUGAR** Energy	

8 **OTHER FRUITS AND** **VEGETABLES*** Vitamins A and C Bulk . Minerals Alkaline residue *In addition to those in blocks No. 3 and 4	**9** **BUTTER,** **MARGARINE** Vitamin A Energy **OTHER FATS** Energy

5 **BREADS, CEREALS,** **MACARONI,** **FLOUR PRODUCTS** (enriched or whole-grain) Supplementary proteins B vitamins . Iron Calcium . Energy	**6** **DRIED BEANS,** **LENTILS, LIMAS,** **PEAS, etc.; NUTS** Supplementary proteins* Energy Alkaline residue	**7** **POTATOES** Minerals Vitamin C Alkaline residue

1 **MEAT, POULTRY,** **FISH,** **EGGS** High-quality proteins B vitamins Vitamin A Iron	**2** **MILK** (liquid, evaporated, dried) **CHEESE** Calcium High-quality protein Riboflavin Vitamin A Alkaline residue	**3** **CITRUS FRUITS** (oranges, grapefruit, lemons) **TOMATOES** Vitamin C Vitamin A Minerals Alkaline residue	**4** **LEAFY GREEN** **AND** **YELLOW** **VEGETABLES** Vitamin A Vitamin C Minerals Bulk Alkaline residue

* Complete proteins in many nuts

larly when the filling rounds out the nutritional contribution of the bread.

6. DRIED BEANS, LENTILS, LIMAS, PEAS, NUTS
• These foods are thrifty and give variety to your main dishes as well as hearty nourishment.
• Give your family the delightful taste and texture of nuts added to crisp green salads.

7. POTATOES
• Potatoes contribute important vitamins and minerals, and are an energy food as well.
• Because they leave an alkaline residue after digestion, they help maintain the body's normal acid-alkaline balance.

8. OTHER FRUITS AND VEGETABLES
• There's no easier way to add flavor and color to menus—along with fine food value—than with fresh, canned, or frozen fruits and vegetables.

9. BUTTER, MARGARINE, OTHER FATS
• Fats greatly enhance the flavor, appetite appeal, and staying quality of many foods.
• Properly fried foods are just as digestible as any other kind.
• Every well-planned diet should contain fat, even reducing diets.

10. SUGAR
• Keep the rest of meal in mind when planning dessert—a substantial one to end a light meal, a lighter one after a heavy meal.
• Use dessert to round out the total food value of a meal. Serve one made with eggs or milk with a vegetable main dish, a fruit dessert to complete the day's requirements of vitamin C, and so on.
• Candy is good food and can be dessert or a high-energy between-meal snack for active children.

ALTERNATES FOR A SERVING OF MEAT

When planning menus, keep this table beside you. It lists foods—and amounts—that may alternate for a serving of meat.

1. *Fish, shellfish, poultry, game, or variety meat* (liver, kidney, heart, etc.)—a serving
2. *Eggs*—2 medium, cooked any way
3. *Milk*—1 pt. whole or skim
4. *Cottage cheese*—6 tablesp. (about 3 oz.)
5. *American cheese*—½ cup grated (about 2 oz.)
6. *Peanut butter*—4 tablesp., plus a milk dessert or milk to drink
7. *Dried peas, beans, lentils, or soybeans* (such as baked beans, chili beans, cooked limas, or red kidney beans, or split-pea soup)—about ¾ to 1 cup*
8. *Cereal main dish*—1 cup macaroni and cheese, or cheese fondue, or 2 slices French toast*
9. *A vegetable plate,* plus a dessert made with milk, such as:

Rennet custard dessert
Milk and eggs (baked custard or jellied fruit with custard sauce)
Milk and cereal (Indian pudding)
Milk and cereal (bread or rice pudding)

10. *A hearty soup*—generous bowls of it, with a salad of tossed greens, vegetables, or fruit, plus a dessert to step up protein (such as Spanish cream, cream pie, ice cream, or desserts in 9)
11. *A main-dish salad* (meats, eggs, cheese, or poultry combined with macaroni or rice and vegetables), plus one of desserts in 9 and 10 to round out the meal's protein

* *A Reminder:* When serving dried beans (soybeans, dried peas, or lentils) or cereal products (bread, breakfast cereals, or macaroni, etc.) as a main dish, be sure to:

a. Choose a recipe in which the dried beans or cereal product is combined with a small amount of high-quality protein food, such as milk, cheese, eggs, fish, meat, or poultry.
b. Or serve with it a milk or milk-and-egg dessert, or milk beverage, or a salad containing cheese, or a dessert of cheese and crackers.

VITAMINS, MINERALS, AND YOU
(why we need them and foods that supply them)

WHY YOU NEED THEM	THEIR RICHEST NATURAL SOURCES	
Vitamin A		
Helps resist nose and throat infections (colds)	Liver	Cream
	Fish-liver oils	Milk (whole, evaporated)
Helps prevent night blindness and other eye diseases	Yellow vegetables (carrots, sweet potatoes)	Whole-milk cheese
Promotes children's growth	Butter or margarine	Egg yolk
		Dried apricots
Vitamin B₁ (Thiamine)		
Necessary for functioning of nerve tissues	Lean pork	sweetbreads)
Affects body's utilization of carbohydrates, fats	Whole-grain or enriched breads, cereals, and flours	Lean meats
	Peanuts	Fish
Promotes children's growth	Dried peas	Chicken
Stimulates appetite and good muscle tone	Dried beans	Milk (whole, skim, evaporated, nonfat dry)
	Lentils	Brewer's yeast
	Variety meats (liver, kidneys,	Wheat germ
Vitamin B₂ (Riboflavin)		
Necessary for healthy skin and hair, good digestion, sound nerves	Liver	Green and leafy vegetables (turnip greens, beet greens, kale, green limas, collards, mustard greens, etc.)
	Kidney	
	Lean meats	
Increases resistance to infection, general weakness, and poor eye conditions	Fish	
	Chicken	Dried peas
	Eggs	Brewer's yeast
	Milk (whole, skim, evaporated, nonfat dry)	Wheat germ

WHY YOU NEED THEM	THEIR RICHEST NATURAL SOURCES	
Vitamin C (Ascorbic Acid)		
Prevents and cures scurvy	Citrus Fruits	Tomatoes
Increases strength of capillary walls, lessening the possibility of hemorrhages	(oranges, grapefruit, lemons, tangerines)	Raw cabbage
		Potatoes
Increases resistance to infection	Strawberries	Green and leafy vegetables (green
Necessary for sound teeth and gums	Cantaloupe	peppers, mustard greens, Brussels sprouts, kale, parsley, etc.)
	Pineapple	
Vitamin D		
Aids in utilizing calcium and phosphorus in building bones, teeth	Sunshine	evaporated milk
	Fish-liver oils	Vitamin-D enriched cereals
	Liver	Fresh and canned oily fish
Prevents rickets in children	Vitamin-D enriched milk and	Egg yolk
Niacin		
Is chief factor in cure and prevention of pellagra	Liver	Brewer's yeast
	Kidney	Wheat germ
Helps maintain a healthy skin condition	Heart	Green peas
	Lean meat	Milk (whole, skim, evaporated, nonfat dry)
	Fish	
	Green and leafy vegetables (green beans, broccoli, kale, cabbage, etc.)	Whole-grain or enriched breads, cereals, and flours
*Calcium		
Builds strong bones and teeth	Milk (whole, skim, evaporated, nonfat dry)	Sardines
Necessary for lactation; coagulation of blood; heart, nerve, and muscle functions		Green and leafy vegetables (green beans, broccoli, kale, cabbage, etc.)
	Cream	
	Cheese	
Helps maintain alkalinity of the blood		
*Phosphorus		
Builds bones and teeth	Green and leafy vegetables (green beans, broccoli, kale, cabbage, etc.)	Wheat germ
Necessary for utilization of fats and carbohydrates by the body		Eggs
		Fish
	Milk (whole, skim, evaporated, nonfat dry)	Shellfish
		Liver
	Cheese	Meats
	Cereals	Brewer's yeast
Iron		
Helps form red blood corpuscles	Liver	beans, broccoli, kale, cabbage, etc.)
	Oysters	
Helps carry oxygen in blood	Molasses	Egg yolk
Aids in tissue respiration	Dried apricots	Potatoes
Prevents nutritional anemia	Green and leafy vegetables (green	Whole-grain or enriched breads, cereals, and flours

* *The correct functioning of both calcium and phosphorus depends on sufficient amounts of* both, *as well as of vitamin D.*

Serving the Meals

WHEN YOU'RE COOK AND HOSTESS TOO

No one—least of all the hostess—enjoys a dinner when the hostess is constantly jumping up from the table to replenish this dish or bring on that. Yet many of us must be cook, waitress, and hostess too. Below we suggest numerous ways to handle a dinner *and* at the same time cut down on steps, dishes, time.

Choose the Right Dinner Menu

1. Plan dinners with not more than two or three easy-to-serve courses. It's correct, smart.
2. Eliminate last-minute chores. Choose dishes that can be completely cooked in advance or can be made ready for cooking early in day and kept in refrigerator.
3. Choose dishes that can wait if dinner is delayed or that can be cooked at last minute.

Meats that don't mind waiting are:

Chicken Cacciatore, p. 142
Coq au Vin, p. 146
Hamburger Stroganoff (add cream at last minute), p. 70
Inga's Meat Balls, p. 67
Pineapple Sparerib Barbecue, p. 82

Vegetables that will cook quickly are:

Any packaged	Corn on the cob
frozen or canned	Greens
vegetable	Summer squash
Asparagus	

Potato, macaroni, and rice dishes that don't mind waiting are:

Potatoes in Cream, p. 270
Susan's Scalloped Potatoes, p. 270
Orange Rice, p. 236
Nancy's Curried Spaghetti, p. 238

Desserts that are easy to make:

Do-Aheads, p. 390
In No Time at All, p. 378

4. Instead of serving the first course at the table, serve it in the living room—fruit, tomato, clam, or vegetable juice; or a hot soup served in mugs or punch glasses. While guests sip, you can slip out of the room and put main course on table. (See Cocktails, p. 17; Soups and Chowders, p. 33.)
5. Or serve first course with main course: Place glass of fruit, tomato, clam or vegetable juice to right of each water glass.
6. If you're serving hors d'oeuvres, choose Spread-Your-Owns, p. 29, or Dunks, p. 28.
7. Serve course-in-one main dishes, such as casseroles, stews, hearty soups, hearty salads, etc.
8. Choose foods that can be cooked and served in the same dish—casserole main dishes, bread puddings, brown Bettys, biscuits baked in oven-glass pie plates or baking dishes, etc.
9. Choose a salad that can be tossed in salad bowl and served at table rather than one that must be arranged on individual plates. Or if you prefer individual salads, serve them with

main course, placing salad plate to left of each dinner plate just before guests sit down.

10. Or instead of salad, serve crisp raw relishes —celery, radishes, raw carrot sticks, coleslaw, etc.—with main course.

Have a Pretty Centerpiece

The way your table looks is just as important as the way the meal tastes. So set a pretty table, have a pretty centerpiece. It's worth the extra minute or two. Try one of these:

OF FRUIT

Row on Row: Down 2 long sides of table, about 15″ in from edge, arrange long narrow rows of green or autumn leaves. Top with tangerines, green grapes, nuts, etc.

Frosted Fruits: Dip fruits into egg whites beaten until frothy; then dip into granulated sugar. Set on cake rack to dry. Arrange in compote or silver bowl; tuck in laurel leaves.

Grapes and Wheat: Top sheaths of wheat with bunches of purple grapes and nuts.

Philodendron: Set plant on brass tray. Group oranges and green grapes around it.

Basket: Set basket on its side, with apples, cranberries, or other fruit tumbling out.

Pineapple Plus: With corer, make 3 holes in top of 1 pineapple. Insert long taper candles.

Red and Blue: Fill wire egg basket with red cherries and blue and red plums.

OF FLOWERS

Springtime: In bowl, arrange tall curve of pussy willows, with short daffodils nestled at base.

Saucy: Flank flowers with candlesticks tied with bows that have long streamers.

Informal: Set 3 pots of ivy, African violets, or geraniums along center of table.

Figurines: Set figurines on either side of bowl of delicate greenery and sweet peas.

Pansies: Arrange pansies in several individual casseroles.

Garnet Roses: Arrange roses in champagne or other goblets.

Morning or Afternoon: Arrange tiny bunches of violets in Victorian teacups, or in eggcups for breakfast.

China Dog: Put collar of flowers on china dog.

OF VEGETABLES

Green Peppers: In wire lettuce basket, arrange green peppers, green grapes, red apples.

Wooden Bowl: In wooden bowl, heap onions, tiny zucchini, green peppers, tomatoes.

Bread and Wheat: Arrange, right on table, 3 loaves of bread (French, round, Italian) and sheaths of wheat.

Lemons and Limes: Use magnolia or croton leaves with lemons and limes.

Leafy: Use purple cabbage, rhubarb, and/or Swiss chard, with eggplant, purple and white onions.

TO EAT

For Small Fry: Fill basket with green leaves; insert large lollipops.

Pie in Center: Surround pie on tray with green or autumn leaves. Nestle cheese wedges or cheese pumpkins among leaves.

Relish: Use new pinpoint flower holder in low dish to hold scallions, celery hearts, carrot sticks, radish roses, and olives, in flowerlike display.

Choose Candles

Use silver, glass, brass, or pewter candlesticks, with white, ivory, or colored candles. Be sure candle flame is above eye level.

To Set the Dinner Table According to Hoyle

The Table Linen: Use easy-to-wipe-off or cloth place mats. Or choose a simple, attractive, easy-to-launder linen cloth.

Fold dinner napkins into oblongs. Lay on dinner plate. Or if you are serving a first course, place napkin to left of fork.

Placing Silver, China, etc.:

1. Place dinner plate in center of each place, 1″ in from edge of place mat or table.
2. Set each place with flat silver, 1″ in from edge of place mat or table, as in diagram below. Notice dessertspoon is to right of knife. If dessert requires a fork, place to right of dinner fork. Or if preferred, place spoon or fork on each dessert plate and serve dessert from kitchen. (Spoons for coffee or tea belong on saucers, never on table.) Arrange plates and glasses as shown.
3. If you prefer a fruit cup or soup as the first course, place teaspoon or soupspoon to right of dessertspoon.
4. Just before family and guests sit down, place butter pat on each bread-and-butter plate.
5. Place salad plates as in diagram.

   If you're serving fruit cup, place filled sherbet glass on small plate on dinner plate. If you're having soup, arrange filled cream-soup cup on saucer, or attractive soup bowl on small plate, on dinner plate.

GUEST DINNER SETTING:

a. dinner fork to be used for both main dish and salad (or place salad fork to right of dinner fork)
b. dinner knife
c. dessertspoon
d. dinner plate
e. bread-and-butter plate, with butter spreader
   across it
f. salad on 7″ or 8″ plate
g. water glass
h. glass of fruit juice to be enjoyed during main course
i. dinner napkin, folded into oblong, on dinner plate

P. S. On Setting the Table

Simplicity, not convention, makes the rules today. Don't be afraid to adopt compromises like these when you're cook and hostess too.

1. Place carving set, if any, before host, with fork to left and knife and serving spoon to right of space reserved for platter.
2. Place serving silver near serving dishes.
3. Use tray or tea wagon for setting and clearing table, etc.
4. Set tea wagon or small table at hostess' right, for serving salad, dessert, and tea or coffee, or for making waffles.
5. If table is narrow, at host's right, place small table from which he can serve vegetables.
6. Let individual salad plates double as bread-and-butter plates.

To Seat the Guests

As family and guests come into the dining room, the hostess tells each one where he or she is to sit. (Plan your seating arrangement beforehand.)

Usually the host sits at one end of table, the hostess at the other. To host's immediate right is lady guest of honor and to his left next lady to whom special honor is due.

To hostess' immediate right sits gentleman guest of honor, with male guest of next importance to her left. Remaining places are filled as hostess suggests.

To Serve the Guests

1. Serve hot food hot. Check cooking time for each food on your menu; start food cooking so all is done at same time. This way, you will avoid having to keep part of dinner warm while waiting for rest to cook.
2. A double boiler is useful for keeping food hot. But if you have more than one food to keep warm, pour boiling water into large shallow pan over low heat; set covered utensils of food in pan.

3. An automatic coffee maker can keep coffee hot indefinitely.

4. Dovetail meat and vegetables. If meat is sliced or already in individual portions, arrange one or more vegetables around it on platter. Or put vegetables in center, meat around them. This saves table space.

5. Or if possible, arrange vegetables on one platter. For example, place peas in center and broiled tomatoes around them. Or use a compartmented vegetable dish that holds 2 vegetables.

6. Plan to let host serve the main course—meat, vegetables, gravy. You, as hostess, may serve salad, dessert, and beverage.

7. Host arranges a main-course serving on plate in front of him. This is passed to hostess. She exchanges it for her empty dinner plate, which is returned to host for next serving. Person to her right is served next, and so on around the table (see The ABCs of Serving, 1, p. 688).

8. Let the children help take dishes to and from the table.

9. If you want to eliminate all at-table serving, in kitchen, arrange entire main course on heated individual dinner plates.

10. Hot breads—popovers, muffins, corn bread, biscuits, hot rolls, gingerbread—seem all the more tempting if served right from pan in which they were baked. But don't forget a table pad under the hot dish!

11. The beverage may be poured by hostess at table—at desserttime or immediately after dessert has been cleared. Bring in tray with coffeepot or coffee maker (or teapot), sugar bowl, creamer (or plate of lemon), etc., as well as cups and saucers with spoons in place (each spoon is placed at back of saucer, with handle parallel to cup handle).

12. Or fill coffee cups in kitchen; place cup, with spoon in place on saucer, to right of each guest.

13. Or serve coffee in living room after dessert. Carry coffee tray to living room; place on low table where beverage can be poured comfortably. Or pass tray with filled demi-

tasse or regular coffee cups, sugar bowl, and creamer.

14. Or omit dessert at table and, with coffee in living room, pass cookies, special candy, or finger fruit.

15. You and the host will put on an A 1 performance if you have also read Maid for the Occasion, p. 688.

BUFFET-STYLE SUPPERS

You may want to serve from a sideboard, dining table, living-room table (pulled out from, or pushed against, a wall), or top of a low bookcase or chest of drawers.

It's Easy If. . . .

1. All dishes are completely or partly made ahead.

2. A light first course is served in living room while you handle last-minute details.

3. The food is all fork food—no large pieces that require knife cutting, nothing unmanageable on plates.

4. Whole main course fits on one large dinner plate.

5. Bread is buttered, ready to eat.

6. Casseroles are part of the menu. (You can cook and serve in same dish—and keep food hot longer as well.)

7. You replenish food when necessary and invite guests to come again for seconds.

8. Water and glasses, coffee and cups, spoons, etc., wait on a side table, where guests may help themselves at any time during meal.

9. A friend removes main-course dishes while you clear buffet table for dessert.

How to Route Traffic

At a buffet supper, guests should be able to move easily around the serving table and to serve themselves in logical order. To set the buffet table you may want to use one of the arrangements diagrammed on p. 684.

Arrange plates and food (each dish with its

own serving silver), etc., so they can be picked up in this order: napkins, dinner plates, hot dishes, cold dishes (or cold dishes, hot dishes), salad, bread, relishes, forks.

If you can, leave enough room between serving dishes so guests can put down their plates while serving themselves.

What to Do About Dessert

When the main course is over, ask a friend to remove dinner plates to kitchen while you clear buffet table and reset it with dessert, dessert plates, silver, and coffee service.

Or use a combination centerpiece-dessert—a

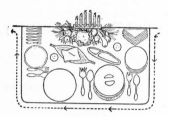

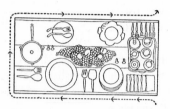

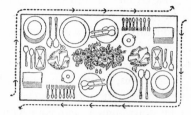

A. WHEN THE BUFFET TABLE IS AGAINST A WALL

B. FOR A BUFFET TABLE IN THE CENTER OF THE ROOM

C. IF THE CROWD IS LARGE, A DUPLICATE SERVICE

If the Crowd Is Large

If you have invited quite a large group, you will expedite proceedings if you arrange duplicate services and let guests form two lines instead of one. (See diagram C, above.) Guests help themselves; or for extra-speedy service, let two friends serve main dishes and let guests help themselves to salad, bread, relishes.

Who'll Sit Where

Set up bridge or folding tables in dining or living room. (If space is short, have someone do this while guests serve themselves.)

Or serve, buffet style, from sideboard, and seat guests at dining table just as you would for a sit-down supper.

Or provide trays already set with silver, napkins, etc. Let guests eat from trays on their laps.

Or let guests use end tables, coffee table, desktop, nest of tables, etc.—any surface they can find —to accommodate their coffee, glasses, etc.

Or (especially for a young crowd) let guests sit on stairs, floor, or anywhere they like.

basket of fruit or a decorated cake—and let guests help themselves whenever they're ready.

Or serve a dessert of nuts and candy, fruit salad, or crackers and cheese—to go on dinner plate with main course.

Or serve dessert yourself in kitchen and simply pass filled dessert plates.

Or set up dessert on side table.

If coffee accompanies the main course but the buffet table won't accommodate it, put it on a side table, with cups, cream, sugar, etc., plus water pitcher and glasses if you like. If it's to be served only with dessert, put it on the buffet table or a side table.

Centerpieces for Buffets
(see Have a Pretty Centerpiece, p. 681)

Old-fashioned: Fill teapot with evergreens. Tie bows to branches. Flank with candles.

Winter: Scatter large paper snowflakes on table. At back of table, along wall, line evergreens, white candles.

Easter: Paint small, medium, and large eggs silver and gold. Arrange in silver bowl. (Eggs are for decoration only. Do not eat.)

Informal: Use large head of green cabbage, 3 bunches of radishes.

Springtime: Put ivy in bird cage. Attach paper butterflies.

Sophisticate: Set magnolia branch in low bowl. Coat with spray-on silver hair powder.

IF YOU GO FORMAL

The Table Linen: For formal use, it's still linen, lace, organdy, a fine synthetic in white or pastel, or an embroidered cloth. Use linen or fine rayon damask over a table pad (for protection); or use a lace, embroidered, or organdy cloth on a bare table. (Cloth overhang should be about 15″ to 18″.) Or use fine lace or embroidered organdy place mats.

Fold each napkin into oblong. Place on service plate. Or if you are serving a first course, place to left of fork.

FORMAL DINNER SETTING

a. dinner fork
b. salad fork
c. dinner knife
d. cream-soup spoon or dessertspoon for soup
e. oyster fork for sea-

food cocktail
f. dinner napkin, folded into oblong
g. service plate
h. water goblet
i. wineglasses

Placing Silver, China, etc.:

1. Place service plate in center of each place, 1″ in from edge of place mat or table. Bread-and-butter plates are not used.
2. Set up each place with flat silver, 1″ in from edge of place mat or table, as in diagram, above. Arrange plate, goblet, and wineglasses

as shown. Dessert silver is placed just before dessert course as in Serving Dessert, p. 690.

If you're serving soup, use bouillon cups or rimmed soup plates; place on table as in Dinner Is Served, 5, p. 689.

Centerpiece: Place flowers in center of table, alone or flanked by 2 smaller units of flowers; by fruits; or by silver, china, or glass ornaments. Also see Have a Pretty Centerpiece, p. 681.

Candles: See Choose Candles, p. 681.

Seating Guests: See To Seat the Guests, p. 682.

Serving Dinner: See Maid for the Occasion, p. 688.

LUNCHEON IS SERVED

Simplicity, not convention, should determine the rules if you want a serene but maidless luncheon. Don't be afraid to adopt the several compromises suggested below.

The Table Linen: Use an attractive cloth or place mats of rayon, linen, organdy, cotton, a blend of fibres, or lace. Or use easy-to-wipe-off plastic, straw, reed, or paper mats.

Fold each napkin into oblong. Lay on luncheon plate. Or if you are serving a first course, place napkin to left of fork.

Placing Silver, China, etc.:

1. Place 9″ luncheon plate in center of each place, 1″ in from edge of table or mat.
2. Set each place with flat silver, 1″ in from edge of table or mat, as in diagram, p. 686. Place dessert silver as in Serving Dessert, 2, p. 690. Also arrange plates, glasses, etc., as shown.

To Save Yourself Energy:

1. Instead of serving a first course at table, serve it in the living room or with the main course as in Choose the Right Dinner Menu, 4 or 5, p. 680.
2. Dispense with bread-and-butter plates. Set 7″ or 8″ plate to left of each napkin, to hold both salad and bread. Serve bread-and-butter sand-

wiches, or buttered hot breads, to eliminate need for butter.

3. Dispense with salad forks and let guests use luncheon forks for both main course and salad.
4. Serve coffee, tea, or cocoa as in To Serve the Guests, 11, 12, 13, or 14, p. 682.

Centerpiece: See Have a Pretty Centerpiece, p. 681.

Candles: Candles are not used at a luncheon unless the room is dark.

Seating Guests: See To Seat the Guests, p. 682.

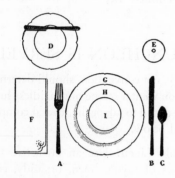

LUNCHEON SETTING WITH FIRST COURSE IN PLACE:

a. luncheon fork to be used for both main dish and salad
b. luncheon knife
c. teaspoon for fruit cocktail (substitute soupspoon if first course is soup)
d. bread-and-butter plate

with butter spreader across it
e. water glass
f. luncheon napkin, folded into oblong
g. 9" luncheon plate for main course
h. 7" or 8" plate
i. fruit-cocktail glass

AFTERNOON TEA FOR A FEW

Allow half an hour to enjoy tea and clear it away if you're busy, an hour or longer if you're having a few friends in.

The Tea Tray

Place tray—before or after guests arrive—on table at which you can sit comfortably and located so you can answer doorbell easily. On nearby table, place dessert plates and tea napkins —plus tea snacks if there's room. Or put tea snacks on another table. On tray, place:

Pot of hot tea (p. 496)
Jug or pitcher of hot water
Bowl of lump sugar
Pitcher of milk or light cream
Plate of lemon or orange slices, with fork
Rosebud in tiny pitcher or vase, if desired
Teacups (no saucers), teaspoons (if preferred, use saucers as well as dessert plates)

Place teapot and jug of hot water, with handles toward you, on right side of tray. Place sugar, creamer, lemon, cups (in piles of two each), and spoons on tray so they can be reached easily.

The Tea Snack

Make it something that's easy to eat. Choose one or two of the following foods. (Don't plan on hot food unless someone is helping in the kitchen or unless everyone can be served at once.)

Thin bread and butter
Doughnut "holes"
Toasted English muffins with jam
Candied fruit
Tiny squares of gingerbread or cake
Tiny cheese-topped baking-powder biscuits
Fruitcake slices filled with butter frosting
Chocolate cookies filled with cream cheese
Bite-size turnovers or tarts
Nut-bread slices and jelly, jam, or cream cheese
Strawberries dipped into melted jelly
Frosted Grapes, p. 290
Orange, cinnamon, or honey toast
Lettuce or cucumber sandwiches
Layer cake, to eat with fork

Tea, Properly Poured

To serve each guest, set teacup on dessert plate. Pour tea, adding lemon, milk or cream, and sugar as guest prefers. Place spoon on plate at back of cup, with its handle parallel to handle of cup; pass to guest, with napkin beneath plate. Let guests help themselves to the tea snack; or have a guest pass it; or pass it yourself after all have been served tea.

In Summer: In warm weather, you may wish to serve a choice of hot or iced tea. If so, arrange a tray near tea table. On it, place iced-tea glasses, iced-tea spoons, plate of mint sprigs, bowl of ice cubes, tongs, plate of lemon wedges, and bowl of fruit sugar. Pour hot tea from pot into ice-filled glasses.

A LARGE TEA
The Table

1. The dining table (or large table set in living room) is spread with your prettiest cloth—lace, organdy, or even chintz in a tiny floral design.
2. At one end of table, place tea tray with pot of hot tea, jug of hot water, bowl of lump sugar, creamer (have all handles pointing toward pourer), and plate of lemon slices. At back and sides of tray, or beside tray, arrange cups on saucers, with spoons in place. (You can put extra cups and saucers on sideboard or side table.) If possible, set up one cup and saucer ready for tea.
3. At other end of table, set up a similar tray for coffee. (In warm weather, punch, sherbet, or ice cream may replace tea or coffee.)
4. On table, attractively arrange dessert plates, napkins, and 2 or 3 kinds of tea snack (see below).

Tea Snacks
(bite size is the right size)

Nothing sticky or moist should be served at a large tea. Everything should be easily eaten with fingers. Choose from these:

Cookies of all kinds
Tiny cupcakes or *petits fours*
Miniature Danish pastries or tarts
Dainty sandwiches
Petit cream puffs, filled, frosted if desired
Mints or nuts, or both

The Pourers

The hostess asks two friends to pour for her, and two or more friends to be "relief pourers." (Hostess, with guest of honor nearby, greets guests.) Guests pick up dessert plates and napkins, are passed cups of tea, then help themselves to snacks.

JUST FAMILY FOR BREAKFAST

The Table Linen: Use easy-to-wipe-off place mats of plastic, straw, reed, or novelty fabric, or use paper place mats. Or use attractive cotton, cotton-and-rayon, or linen table cloth or place mats.

Fold each breakfast napkin into oblong. Place to left of luncheon fork.

Placing Silver, China, etc.:

1. Place 9″ luncheon plate in center of each place, 1″ in from edge of place mat or table.
2. Set up each place with flat silver, 1″ in from edge of place mat or table, as in diagram, below. Arrange plates and glasses as shown.
3. Just before family sits down, place butter pat on each bread-and-butter plate. Or place plate of butter pats on table, to be passed.

BREAKFAST SETTING WITH CEREAL IN PLACE

a. luncheon fork
b. luncheon knife
c. dessertspoon or tea-spoon for cereal
d. bread-and-butter plate, with butter spreader across it
e. water glass
f. breakfast napkin
g. glass of fruit juice
h. 9″ luncheon plate
i. bowl of cereal
j. cup of coffee, tea, or cocoa, with teaspoon in place

Setting the Rest of the Table:

1. To avoid delay in getting the family off on time, let Mother make toast and serve coffee. Place toaster to left of Mother's place, with tray of bread slices nearby.
2. Place tile for coffee maker at Mother's right. Near coffee maker, group coffee cups, each on a saucer, with teaspoon at back of cup and handle of spoon parallel to handle of cup.
3. Place sugar bowl and creamer just above Mother's plate, with handles pointing toward her.
4. If dining table is too small to accommodate toaster and coffee maker, set them on a small table or tea wagon at Mother's right.
5. When fruit juice and cereal have been finished, remove juice glasses and cereal bowls, with spoons in them. Luncheon plates are now ready for main dish.

Note: If you prefer grapefruit or melon to fruit juice, set fruit on 7″ or 8″ salad or dessert plate on top of luncheon plate at each place. When fruit has been eaten, remove salad plates and replace with cereal.

JUST FAMILY FOR LUNCH OR DINNER

Today's methods of setting the table and serving meals to guests are so simple and practical, there needn't be a double standard. Treat the family just like company. See Luncheon Is Served, p. 685, and When You're Cook and Hostess Too, p. 680.

MAID FOR THE OCCASION

(basic information every hostess should have)

Smooth service at the table is the ambition of every hostess. Whether you have employed a full-time or part-time maid, she can make a dinner or luncheon party a real joy or a complete nightmare. Everything depends on the training and instructions the maid gets.

Until your maid is letter-perfect, it's helpful to write out for her the menu plus a set of de-

tailed directions. Plan to practice beforehand so she knows exactly what is expected of her. Here are the directions to give her.

The ABCs of Serving

1. Serve hostess first, unless otherwise directed, then person to her right, and so on around table to her right. Exception: When serving 4 persons, skip host; then step back and serve him last, so guest at hostess' left will not be last.
2. Stand at left of each person to place, remove, and offer dishes. Exceptions: To place beverages and dessert silver, stand at right, to avoid reaching in front of guest.
3. To exchange plates, remove used plate with left hand; place new one with right hand, standing at left side of each person as above.
4. To offer food, hold platter or serving dish flat on palm of left hand. If platter or dish is especially heavy, it may be steadied with right hand. Always offer side of platter or serving dish. See that handles of serving fork (at left) and spoon or knife (at right) are pointed toward person being served. (Rearrange, if necessary, after each guest has helped himself.) Offer dish low enough and close enough to guest to make serving easy.
5. What about service napkin and tray? Fold service napkin (like table napkin if possible) into square. Place on left hand; use, like a tray, under all serving dishes; do not use when exchanging plates, removing salad or bread-and-butter plates, or carrying two plates. Napkin protects hand from warm and cold dishes, hides hand under glass dishes. For small dishes, use small tray (with napkin under it).
6. Refill water goblets when they're empty, but do not lift them from table. Keep napkin in left hand to catch stray drops.
7. Before starting to serve, have everything for that course ready.
8. Serve hot food on heated plates; serve cold food on chilled dishes.
9. Move quietly and unobtrusively. In emer-

gencies, or if you are uncertain, do the thing that disturbs a guest least.

10. Do not touch guests when serving.
11. Handle lower part of goblets, never top.
12. Do not let thumb extend over rim of plates.
13. Do not start to remove a course until all persons have finished eating.
14. To remove dishes, remove all serving dishes and platters first; then used plates, glasses, silver, etc.; then unused silver, salts and peppers, etc.

Dinner Is Served

1. Fill goblets three quarters full of water.
2. If you're using bread-and-butter plates, place individual butter pat or ball on each plate.
3. Set chair at each place, with front of seat flush with table edge.
4. Light candles.
5. If fruit, fruit or sea-food cocktails, or oysters are being served as the first course, place service on service plates on table before dinner is announced.

    If soup is the first course, place service on table just before or after guests are seated.
6. Announce dinner: Stand in doorway; catch hostess' eye; say softly, "Dinner is served."
7. During first course, pass crackers, etc.

Serving the Main Course

1. Bring heated dinner plates from kitchen, one at a time; exchange for first-course service and service plates. Or bring two dinner plates from kitchen at a time; leave one on serving table while exchanging other for first-course service. Take out 2 first-course services and service plates together.
2. Offer platter of meat, then vegetables, gravy, bread, and relishes.
3. Take meat platter and vegetable serving dishes back to kitchen; rearrange for second servings, ready to pass.
4. Or if host carves or serves meat, after exchanging first course for heated dinner plates as above, bring in carving set on tray or nap-

kin. Place carving fork (at left) and knife and serving spoon (at right) in front of host. Then place meat platter before host.

5. Stand at host's left, with extra heated dinner plate in right hand. When he has arranged meat on dinner plate in front of him, pick it up with left hand and replace it with extra dinner plate in right hand. Take filled plate to hostess, removing her heated plate with right hand and placing filled dinner plate with left hand. Take this heated plate back to host, and proceed as before. Repeat until everyone is served. Then pass vegetables, gravy, bread, relishes.
6. Serve additional butter; refill water goblets when empty.

Serving Salad

1. Remove meat platter and carving set or serving silver if used at table.
2. Bring in individual salads (one or two at a time) as in Serving the Main Course, 1, above, exchanging them for dinner plates.
3. Or replace dinner plates with empty individual salad plates; then pass salad bowl.
4. Or place salad fork and spoon, then salad bowl and pile of salad plates, in front of, or a little to left of, hostess. As hostess fills each salad plate, place it.
5. Sometimes a simple salad of tossed greens is served with the main course. In this case, when setting table, place salad plate to left of service plate at each place. Then after meat, vegetables, and gravy have been served, pass salad bowl.

Clearing the Table for Dessert

1. Remove salad bowl. From each place, remove salad plate with right hand and bread-and-butter plate with left hand. Or if salad was served with main course, remove dinner plate with right hand and salad plate with left. Then remove bread-and-butter plates, two at a time.

2. Remove salts, peppers, and unused silver onto small tray.
3. Crumb table if necessary, using small napkin and plate.
4. Refill water goblets.

Serving Dessert

1. At each place, place dessert plate, with dessert fork on left side of plate and dessertspoon on right side, parallel to each other. (Guest removes fork and spoon to table, placing fork to left and spoon to right of dessert plate.) Pass dessert, then sauce or cakes.
2. Or put dessert silver on small tray—1 dessert fork and dessertspoon or teaspoon for each person—and place to right of each place. Then place dessert, which has been arranged on individual dessert plates in kitchen.
3. Or for a very simple meal, arrange dessert on individual serving dishes in kitchen, with necessary silver—fork or spoon—in place on each plate. Then place.

If Finger Bowls Are Used

1. If finger bowls are used, fill one third full with lukewarm water. Place bowl, with small doily under it, on each dessert plate, with dessert fork to left and dessertspoon to right of finger bowl on plate. Place before each guest from left.
2. Then pass dessert. (Guest removes fork and spoon to table, placing fork to left and spoon to right of dessert plate. He places finger bowl with doily a little to left, just above, dessert plate.)

If a Fruit Course Follows Dessert

1. If fruit is to be served after dessert, do not serve finger bowls on dessert plates. Instead, place dessert plate, with silver in place, at each cover; then pass dessert.
2. When dessert has been completed, exchange each dessert plate for fruit plate, with finger bowl and doily in center and fruit fork to left and fruit knife to right of bowl on plate. (Guest removes silver and finger bowl as in If Finger Bowls Are Used, 2, above.) Pass bowl of fruit.

Serving Coffee

Serve at table, as in To Serve the Guests, 11, 13 or 14, p. 683.

Your Kitchen

KITCHEN ARRANGEMENT

This chapter is devoted to the selection, use, and care of kitchen equipment. However, even if you have the best of equipment and give it the best of care, your energies can be wasted to a great extent if your kitchen is inconveniently arranged.

Many manufacturers of kitchen cabinets and some appliance manufacturers offer booklets and other types of help on kitchen arrangement. These can give you ideas not only for building or remodeling a kitchen but also for rearranging your present kitchen.

In addition to grouping equipment and utensils according to their use, at work areas, there are a number of ways you can simplify your kitchen work:

1. Provide yourself with adequate counter work space. In small kitchens, this is often difficult to do. Perhaps a new table is the answer, or an extension to your present one. A hinged tabletop or shelf, which can rest flat against the wall when not in use, can be used if floor space is inadequate.
2. Store food and equipment *conveniently;* this is as important as having plenty of storage space.
   Use racks or shelves with hooks for hanging utensils near the range. Keep staple groceries arranged in single rows on step-back shelves in a cabinet above your work space.
3. A cutlery rack is more convenient than a drawer for storing kitchen cutlery. Magnetic racks for holding knives are available in a variety of sizes.
4. Only a tour of the housewares' department of your favorite store can tell you how many really practical ideas are available for kitchen efficiency. Drawer dividers, rubber-coated dish drainers, spice shelves, new developments in canister sets are just a few of the countless items you will see. Many times a small expenditure of money will save many hours and much energy in the kitchen.

DISHCLOTHS AND DISH TOWELS FOR THE KITCHEN

6 pot holders
6 dishcloths
6 cloths for clean-up work in kitchen
12 dish towels
Dress-up and work aprons, plastic and cloth

For dish towels, the old stand-bys, cotton and linen, or a combination of fibers such as linen, cotton, and spun rayon are available. When you finish dishwashing, hang dish towels and dishcloth to dry; use another time or two, but remember to replace them frequently with fresh, clean ones.

Black streaks on dish towels (from improperly cleaned utensils) require prelaundering treatment. Rub soap directly into stains; then wash as usual.

Remember, a chlorine bleach in wash water helps keep the colors of dish towels and cloths fresh.

POTS AND PANS

If you are checking your supply of pots and pans or if you are equipping your first kitchen, use the following list as a guide. Buy enough good utensils to start with; then add others as you need them. We have starred those items we suggest for your first purchases.

AT OR NEAR KITCHEN CABINET

* 2 or 3 standard measuring cups (see p. 11)
* 2 sets of measuring spoons
1 set of storage jars
* 1 set of mixing bowls, in graduated sizes
* 6 custard cups or ramekins
* 1 set of graters
* 1 pastry blender
1 fruit-juice extractor
* 1 coffee maker
* 3 stirring spoons (1 wooden)

1 narrow metal spatula
* 1 bottle opener
* 1 can opener
* 1 jar opener
* Flour sifter
* 1 cake turner (if you have no broad spatula)
* 1 bread or cutting board
1 utility tray (on which to set measuring cups, spoons, etc., when in use)
* 1 rolling pin with stockinet cover
* 2 sets of muffin pans

(6 to 8 in a set)
1 utility baking dish
* 1 square cake pan, 8" x 8" x 2"
* 1 loaf pan, 10" x 5" x 3"
* 2 layer-cake pans, 8" or 9"
* 1 cake tester
* 1 cookie sheet, 14" x 10"
* 1 open roasting pan, 15" x 10", and wire rack
* 2 wire cake racks
* 2 casseroles
1 vegetable parer

* 1 egg beater
* 1 pair kitchen shears
* 1 knife sharpener
* 1 kitchen-cutlery set
* 1 cutlery rack
1 set biscuit cutters
1 breadbox (if not part of cabinet)
* 2 pie plates, 8" or 9"
* 1 potato masher
1 electric mixer
1 set of refrigerator dishes
1 cakebox (if not part of cabinet)

AT OR NEAR RANGE

* 1 pressure cooker (4-qt. size is most useful)

* 1 small skillet, 5" or 7"
* 1 covered kettle, 10"

* 1 teakettle
* 1 double boiler, 1½ to 2 qt.

* 3 covered saucepans, 2 to 4 qt.

AT OR NEAR SINK

* Vegetable and bottle brushes
1 colander
* 1 dish-draining rack

* 2 medium wire strainers, coarse and fine
* 1 garbage can

* 1 wastebasket
1 paper-towel holder and paper towels
* 1 towel rack

1 bottle hand lotion
* 1 small fruit-juice strainer
* Plate scraper

IN STORAGE CABINET

1 automatic electric frying pan or regular griddle, 10"
1 food chopper

1 large covered pan, 6 to 10 qt. (this may be a kettle, sauce-

pan, Dutch oven, or electric casserole)
1 roll each waxed

paper, aluminum foil, saran
* 1 toaster

OPTIONAL EQUIPMENT

Household scales
1-quart measure
1 or more molds
1 candy thermometer
1 roast-meat thermometer
1 waffle iron
1 egg poacher

Paper baking cups
1 tube cake pan
1 ice-cream freezer
1 vegetable bin
1 electric fryer or deep-frying kettle with basket
1 deep-fat frying

thermometer
2 butter-ball paddles
1 funnel
1 ice crusher
1 apple corer
1 pastry board or cloth
1 dishpan, 12-qt.

capacity
1 doughnut cutter
Refrigerator bags and bowl covers (for conventional or dry-cold refrigerator. See p. 694)
Cheesecloth

Choosing Wares in Pots and Pans

When you embark on a shopping trip for pots and pans, you may find a matched set that's exactly what you want. But if you don't, we suggest you collect your own sets, buying various kinds of ware to suit your needs.

The ware you select is of major importance. You'll be wise to keep comparative advantages in mind.

Aluminum is practically unbeatable for all-round use. It requires a bit more than average care to keep it clean and shiny but will more than compensate by giving even heat distribution no matter what kind of range you have.

Stainless steel falls in a somewhat more expensive category, but it is easy to clean and practically indestructible. If you select stainless-steel pans, be sure they have copper, aluminum, or laminated-steel bottoms, to give an equal distribution of heat and to keep pans from acquiring dark heat spots.

Copper alone is handsome for seldom used or decorative pieces. Although it is an excellent heat conductor, it is hard to keep bright. Copper plated with tin on the inside is easier to clean, but eventually the tin wears through and the pan must be replated.

Glass is wonderful for the oven, but it must be used with care on top of the stove.

Enamelware is not used as much today as it once was, but you may want a few pieces of it. Actually, enamelware is glass fused onto metal, so it must be handled carefully to prevent cracking, chipping, or discoloring.

Cast iron is sturdy ware for skillet or Dutch-oven use, but it must be kept seasoned to prevent rust. To retain the seasoning, it should be washed with soap rather than a detergent. *To season cast iron,* spread melted shortening or salad oil on inside of utensil and on its cover. (Glass cover need not be treated.) *Do not use any fat that contains salt.* Place in warm oven or over low heat for several hours, swabbing sides and cover occasionally with more fat. Wipe off excess fat or oil with paper towels. The utensil is then ready to use. Cast iron with porcelain-enamel finish needs no seasoning.

Use and Care of Pots and Pans

1. *Keep food boiling gently* (it cooks just as fast as when it's boiling hard) so it won't boil over and leave burned food to be scoured off later. Gentle boiling also reduces chances of the pan's boiling dry and getting scorched.
2. *Do not leave griddles and skillets over the heat,* waiting for food, and do not let them get hotter than necessary.
3. *Reduce the heat under all utensils* after cooking has started.
4. *To soak pans* after emptying them, fill with warm sudsy water.
5. *Wash utensils in hot sudsy water;* rinse; dry.
6. *Use a fine abrasive powder to remove all stains.* To remove baked- or burned-on food particles from utensils, or to scour aluminum and cast iron, use scourers such as steel-wool soap pads, copper or bronze sponges, and plastic balls.
7. *If you keep your utensils in good condition,* you need not hesitate to use any of them— skillet, Dutch oven, or attractively designed saucepan, as well as casseroles—for both cooking and serving. This makes it easy to serve food deliciously hot, saves dishwashing too.
8. *We are still asked whether aluminum utensils are safe.* Foods cooked in aluminum utensils may absorb very minute quantities of aluminum, but minute quantities also occur naturally in many foods. Authorities agree that these small amounts have no harmful effect. And good aluminum utensils do not destroy the flavor or nutritive value of the foods cooked in them.

APPLIANCES

The best possible suggestion for the most satisfactory use and care of kitchen appliances is to follow the manufacturer's instructions. A leaflet or book is shipped with every appliance, large or small, when it leaves the factory. A careful reading of this material will answer your questions and eliminate confusion.

If for any reason the instruction booklet is not in your hands, a post card mailed to the manufacturer will bring it to you. Give the model number of the appliance, and the manufacturer will be able to serve you more quickly.

Here are a few general suggestions:

Ranges

The Oven:

1. Complete oven meals are convenient and economical. See Oven Dinners, p. 556.
2. When cooking pot roasts or other less tender cuts of meat in the oven, brown meat first on top of range. Then cover and cook in oven.
3. Tender cuts of meat, such as rib roasts, are best roasted on a rack in a shallow pan, uncovered, with no moisture added.
4. Vegetables cooked with an oven meal should be placed in covered containers so their steam will not affect the crispness of the roast or the browning of the pie or other dessert.
5. Remove broiler pan from oven before baking.
6. When the oven has cooled off after being used, clean off at once any greasy or burned-on food. Use one of the new chemical oven cleaners that soften and loosen grease. Follow label precautions carefully. Or use a steel-wool soap pad, copper, or plastic cleaner with household cleanser. Clean lining, racks, rack glides. Keeping oven walls and bottom clean helps to eliminate excess smoking when oven is being used.
7. In some electric ranges, the elements can be taken out to facilitate cleaning the oven. When putting them back, push securely into outlets.

The Broiler: Many people neglect to use the range's boiler, in the belief that broiling is a difficult and/or expensive cooking process. This is not true. Meat, to be broiled successfully, must be a tender cut (sirloin, T-bone, and porterhouse steaks are good examples) or a quick-cooking variety (ground meat and frankfurters). It need not be expensive.

If you follow the manufacturer's instructions for using the broiler, you should have no trouble. Many appetizing food combinations can be broiled. Remember, most vegetables to be broiled must be precooked. See p. 55 for fruits and vegetables for broiler meals. A few general suggestions are:

1. For rare meat, place broiler pan close to heating element or burner (1″ to 2″). For medium or well-done meat, place broiler pan farther away. Again, follow manufacturer's instructions.
2. In practically all electric ranges, the oven door is left partially open during the broiling process. Usually the oven door is balanced so that it will stay at a definite broiling position. When broiling food in a gas range, keep broiler door closed.
3. *To clean broiler pan:* A sheet of aluminum foil placed in the bottom of the broiler pan will make cleaning easier. In any event, pour off fat before it congeals; then allow pan to cool before cleaning it. With paper towels, wipe off excess fat from bottom of pan and from rack. Wash both pan and rack in hot sudsy water, using a steel-wool soap pad if necessary.

REFRIGERATORS

Because refrigerators have changed extensively in recent years, both in appearance and mechanically, it is particularly important that you follow the manufacturer's instructions carefully. Only by doing this can you be assured of the most satisfactory use of your refrigerator.

STORING FOOD

There was a time when in all mechanical refrigerators, food was stored covered, to prevent its drying out and to keep odors and flavors from mingling. This is still true in the conventional (or dry-cold) models. However, if your refrigerator is one of the moist-cold models, most foods can be stored uncovered for several days. (Certain foods, such as fruit juices, milk, and butter are usually covered in any kind of refrigerator.) Again, check your instruction booklet for the best methods of using your refrigerator.

Food stored in the freezing section of any refrigerator should be well wrapped in moisture-vapor-proof material to keep it from losing moisture, color, flavor, and food value. See Home Freezing, p. 533.

KEEPING YOUR REFRIGERATOR CLEAN

Automatic Defrosting: This is another recent development in refrigerators. Systems vary, so see your instruction book to learn exactly what care your particular model requires. Remember, even automatic defrosting does not eliminate the need to give the refrigerator's freezer section an occasional thorough cleaning.

Cleaning Methods: Regardless of the type of refrigerator you have, keeping it clean is of paramount importance. A weekly, thorough cleaning from top to bottom, inside and out, will be good life insurance.

And that weekly cleaning will be simpler and easier if, between times, you observe a few rules:

1. Wipe up at once any food spilled in refrigerator.
2. Check leftovers often so they will not accumulate and be left too long.
3. Keep the rubber gasket around the refrigerator door clean and free of grease.
4. To prevent finger marks on refrigerator finish, use handle when opening and closing door.

Plastic Parts: Most refrigerators today are trimmed in plastic, or have accessories made of plastic.

Plastic is used because it has certain advantageous qualities. For example, plastic has excellent insulating properties and, in its use in crispers, is lightweight and easy to handle.

When cleaning any plastic parts, use warm sudsy water; rinse in clear water; dry thoroughly. Do not use harsh cleansing agents or abrasives.

PLUS VALUES

A refrigerator can be a major help in meal planning and preparation.

Plan your meals several days in advance, shop less frequently, and store perishable supplies in the refrigerator. Most meals can be at least partially prepared in advance, either the night before or in the morning, then stored in the refrigerator until time to be cooked or served.

Small Electric Appliances

The many practical small appliances available now can add immeasurably to your kitchen's convenience. The whole list is far too long to be given here, but an exploratory shopping tour is well worth your time if your present appliances are not adequate.

Electric roasters, broilers, rotisseries, deep-fat fryers, casserole cookers, skillets, waffle irons, and sandwich grills are useful appliances in any kitchen, particularly in country cottages or small-apartment kitchenettes. Since they are portable, they can be used outside the kitchen—at the dining-room table, in the living room, on the porch.

Electric Roasters: Despite their large size, these portable ovens plug into a 110-volt outlet, which means no special wiring is required. As with all appliances, however, it is important that they be used on a circuit that is *not* overloaded.

The electric roaster successfully takes care of any cooking process that an oven handles—roasting, baking, steaming, complete meal cooking, even broiling (with a broiling attachment) —with, of course, some space limitations.

Roasters may also be used for cooking large quantities of food such as corn on the cob or stews for parties; for simmering a large ham, tongue, etc.; or for blanching food for freezing. To cook large amounts of food, remove racks and small pans and cook directly in the cooking well.

Cleaning Note: Never immerse roaster or broiling unit in water. To do so will ruin the heating elements. Wipe off roaster with damp cloth. Wash large inset pan and smaller pans as you would other kitchen utensils.

Rotisseries: A comparatively new addition to the small-appliance list is the rotisserie-broiler. In top or de luxe models, you can broil, roast, barbecue, fry, toast, and grill foods. Follow the manufacturer's directions but, in general, preheat 5 to 10 minutes for broiling. When using the rotisserie, be sure to balance food evenly on the spit. It is very important to clean these appliances after each use. Such parts as shelf glides are usually removable and all but the elements can be washed in, or wiped off with, hot sudsy water.

Electric Fryers: These appliances are not limited to deep-fat frying. They can be used for boiling, stewing, braising, pot roasting, cooking casserole dishes, and even popping corn. Fat should not be left in a fryer indefinitely. As often as is practical, remove all fat; strain it; refrigerate. At the same time, clean the fryer thoroughly, with hot sudsy water and steel-wool soap pads. To remove stubborn grease, fill the well with hot water; add soap or detergent; then turn on the heat until the water boils. Place the basket in the fryer for thorough cleaning too. Drain; rinse; dry.

Electric Skillets: These appliances can be used for frying, sautéeing, pan-broiling, grilling, stewing, and braising. Thermostatic controls provide the correct heat, making these skillets wonderfully convenient for cooking procedures that require careful heat control.

Follow the manufacturer's instructions for cleaning, since methods vary.

Electric Mixers: Electric mixers are available in either countertop or junior-size models (to be held in the hand). They bring accuracy to mixing processes, take most of the labor out of making cakes and icings, mashing potatoes, etc. Give an electric mixer space near an appliance outlet so it will be ready for use. Junior-size models often come with wall brackets for mounting.

Time beating periods closely. Electric mixing is a much faster process than hand mixing; a few minutes' overbeating, particularly of cakes, may spoil the mixture. To mix cakes with an electric mixer, see p. 446.

Investigate the many attachments available for countertop mixers (such as slicer, shredder, grater, and meat chopper) and decide which ones you need. Follow the manufacturer's instructions for cleaning and periodic oiling.

Electric Blenders: The blender mixes, grinds, chops, purées, and pulverizes both liquid and solid foods. Its care is simple. Merely rinse the container and wash it as you would any other plastic or glass container. Wipe the base with a damp cloth, and dry it thoroughly. *Never* introduce a spoon, knife, or spatula into the blender container when the blades are in action.

Repair Service

Usually the quickest source of repair service on an appliance is the store from which it was purchased. Sometimes the local distributor of the product handles service. If not, he can tell you how to proceed. It may be necessary to write the manufacturer.

In any case, whether you telephone or write, matters will be expedited if you can give the appliance's model number. This will be found on a small plate, usually bearing the manufacturer's name and the model and serial numbers. The instruction booklet usually tells you where this plate can be found.

Index